Cases and Materials on

Civil Terrorism

David J. Strachman
James P. Steck

 **Lawyers & Judges**
Publishing Company, Inc.
Tucson, Arizona

This publication is designed to provide accurate and authoritative information in regard to the subject matter covered. It is sold with the understanding that the publisher is not engaged in rendering legal, accounting, or other professional service. If legal advice or other expert assistance is required, the services of a competent professional person should be sought.

—From a Declaration of Principles jointly adopted by
a Committee of the American Bar Association
and a Committee of Publishers and Associations.

The publisher, editors and authors must disclaim any liability, in whole or in part, arising from the information in this volume. The reader is urged to verify the reference material prior to any detrimental reliance thereupon. Since this material deals with legal, medical and engineering information, the reader is urged to consult with an appropriate licensed professional prior to taking any action that might involve any interpretation or application of information within the realm of a licensed professional practice.

 **Lawyers & Judges
Publishing Company, Inc.**

P.O. Box 30040 • Tucson, AZ 85751-0040
(800) 209-7109 • FAX (800) 330-8795
e-mail: sales@lawyersandjudges.com
www.lawyersandjudges.com

Library of Congress Cataloging-in-Publication Data

Strachman, David J.
  Case and materials on civil terrorism law / David J. Strachman, James P. Steck.
    p. cm.
  Includes index.
  ISBN-13: 978-1-933264-46-2 (softcover)
  ISBN-10: 1-933264-46-2 (softcover)
  1. Terrorism--United States--Digests. 2. Victims of terrorism--United States--Digests. I. Steck, James P. II.
Title.
  KF9430.A53S78 2008
  345.73'02--dc22

                    2008010595

ISBN 13: 978-1-933264-46-2
ISBN 10: 1-933264-46-2
Printed in the United States of America
10 9 8 7 6 5 4 3 2 1

Contents

Chapter 1

Introduction to Civil Terrorism Law

In 1789, when Congress enacted the Alien Tort Claims Act, the United States was an isolated nation far removed from the international arena. As the nation's prominence slowly grew, Congress sought to provide a forum for the adjudication of citizens' claims arising in the international context. Among the first types of claims were those of American citizens traveling abroad and involving the Barbary States.

The statute was rarely used for approximately 200 years. Thus, by the 1970s Judge Edwards, in the *Tel Oren* case, called the act an "obscure" and "an aged but little-noticed provision of the First Judiciary Act of 1789, which gives federal courts jurisdiction over a minute class of cases implicating the law of nations."

In recent decades the internationalization of law paralleled the growth of international commerce and foreign travel by U.S. citizens. Accordingly, the Alien Tort Claims Act became the starting point for victims of international terrorism seeking justice against terrorists and their patrons. However, because it applies only to the claims of aliens, its usefulness in this context is extremely limited.

Increasing incidents of international terrorism in which Americans were injured and killed along with the inability of the legal system to adjudicate victims' claims, suggested the need for a new legal paradigm. For instance, in 1985 the wheelchair bound Leon Klinghoffer found himself on a Libyan cruise boat traveling in the Mediterranean, after purchasing his tickets from a travel agency in New Jersey, departing from New York and boarding the boat in Egypt. The cruise liner was attacked by Palestinian terrorists who allegedly received instructions from handlers in Tunisia. After Klinghoffer was brutally pushed overboard by Palestinian terrorists while still in his wheelchair, his family returned to the U.S. and vowed to fight back in the uniquely American manner – litigation.

Barely two months later, the Klinghoffer family filed suit against a variety of entities, including the owner of the vessel and two travel agencies. Interestingly, they did not sue the terrorists or the organization responsible for the attack. This was left to the defendants, American businesses who impleaded the Palestine Liberation Organization, led by the notorious terrorist Yasser Arafat. This third party proceeding ignited the field of civil terrorism law.

At the outset, the case was plagued by numerous incongruities of the law. The Klinghoffer suit was a classic first year law school torts exam fiasco — which law applied, how could jurisdiction be obtained over a foreign defendant, what was the proper venue, what was the role of "international law," and which causes of action applied. Also, questions concerning the legal nature of the PLO (i.e. a corporation, an unincorporated association, or partnership) pointed up the anachronistic categories that the law used to adjudicate the modern plague of terrorism. And these were only some of the many fundamental preliminary issues to address before even reaching the merits of the case.

After wandering through the court system for several years and receiving no redress, the victims proceeded to Washington to seek a legislative remedy. Their lobbying produced the Anti-Terrorism Act of 1990, also known as "The Klinghoffer Act," which, for the first time, provided a federal cause of action specifically for acts of international terrorism. The act was designed to address the procedural problem that plagued the Klinghoffer litigation. As Senator Charles Grassley noted, "[u]nfortunately, victims who turn to the common law of tort or Federal statutes, find it virtually impossible to pursue their claims because of reluctant courts and numerous jurisdictional hurdles." 136 Cong. Rec. 7592 (1990). It was expected that 18 U.S.C. §2333 would provide a method by which victims could "join the fight against the terrorists." Thus, Senator Grassley proclaimed, it was important to hit terrorists "where it hurts them most: at their lifeline, their funds," and that §2333 would put terrorists on notice "to keep their hands off Americans and their eyes on their assets." 136 Cong. Rec. S14279-01. He specifically urged "victims to pursue renegade terrorist organizations, their leaders, and the resources that keep them in business, their money." 138 Cong. Rec. S17252 (1992).

Alas, it was not until a decade later when the statute was effectively used for the first time. The orphaned children of

Yaron Ungar, an American citizen who was murdered near Jerusalem, brought suit in Rhode Island against the PLO, Yasser Arafat, Palestinian Authority, and other Palestinian terrorists.

In the interim, significant developments occurred with respect to litigation against terror sponsoring nations. Following the murder of 260 Americans aboard Pam Am flight 103 over Lockerbie, Scotland, the families of the victims sued those responsible for the attack. However, they too sought a legislative solution after being stymied by inadequacies of the Foreign Sovereign Immunities Act and the Alien Tort Claims Act in their suit against Libya. Around the same time, the Flatow family sought justice for the senseless murder of their daughter by Palestinian terrorists. After finding legal avenues closed, they also sought the assistance of Congress. Ultimately, the solutions to the barrier of sovereign immunity were the enactment of the terrorism exception to the Foreign Sovereign Immunities Act, 18 U.S.C. §1605(a)(7), and the Flatow Amendment, §1605 note.

These statutes were intended to be powerful tools to assist victims of terrorism in asserting their claims. Indeed, they have generated dozens of cases over the last decade against state sponsors of terrorism, their non-state partners, several terrorist organizations and financial institutions. The efficiency of these suits in stopping terrorism, or even slowing it down, is not in dispute. To date, most would agree that terrorism suits have not had their intended effect. Plaintiffs have been unable to satisfy their judgments and terrorist incidents have multiplied in parallel with the growth in civil terrorism suits.

The universe of civil terrorism law is narrow, both legally and factually. It involves events that typically occur in only a small section of the world. Civil terrorism litigation takes place almost exclusively in the federal courts in Washington and New York. There are now only five state sponsors of terrorism amenable to suit and only a slightly larger group of terrorist organizations and financial institutions that are realistic targets of litigation.

In large measure, the law of civil terrorism is built upon an unusual playing field. Unlike criminal jurisprudence, virtually all targets of the plaintiffs' claims, with the exception of financial institutions, have been previously determined by the U.S. government to be either state sponsors of terrorism or designated terrorist organizations, or proudly admit and acknowledge their terrorist activities. Thus this field is unlike many other areas of the law where the underlying policy considerations are balanced against conflicting claims of interested parties, i.e. the accused and the state, borrowers and lenders, landlords and tenants, suppliers and purchasers, regulators and regulated industries. In traditional areas of law, it is axiomatic that both sides to a dispute

have legitimate, rational, and honorable intentions, that all sides are assumed to be guilt free upon the commencement of the proceeding and that the courts, the law and society have a shared interest in balancing conflicting but assuredly legitimate rights.

These premises, however, are not operative in the field of terrorism law. This is largely due to the fact that the defendants in virtually all F.S.I.A. and Klinghoffer Act cases (with the exception of banks and other financial institutions) have been previously determined by the U.S. government to be either terrorists or their sponsors and typically boast about the acts they commit. However, it still remains for the plaintiffs in each case to prove that the defendant sovereign or terrorist organization is responsible for the terrorist attack at issue.

The cases in the chapters that follow demonstrate the efforts of terrorism victims to obtain justice in the American judicial system. They also catalogue the attempts by foreign sovereigns, avowed terrorist organizations, and the U.S. government to block, delay, and undermine the adjudication of these claims.

This book exclusively addresses cases and materials dealing with civil terrorism litigation. Although terrorism has become a topic of widespread interest in both the political arena and the courts, our focus is limited and does not encompass the entire legal spectrum in which issues related to terrorism are adjudicated. Thus, criminal matters, the government's policy response to terrorism, intelligence and security issues, foreign surveillance, military action and detentions are beyond the modest scope of this work.

This book is an outgrowth of courses taught at Southern New England School of Law and Roger Williams University. When preparing to teach courses on civil terrorism law, no course books were available. We hope that this book will fill that gap and provide a structure for law school and undergraduate courses on civil terrorism law.

Additionally, we hope that this book will contribute to the scholarship of this intriguing subject. Terrorism law is a rapidly developing area that has attracted significant attention from the scholarly community, politicians, as well as the media. We would be pleased if this book makes it easier for law schools and universities to offer courses in this field and encourage the development of terrorism law as a distinct area of the law.

David J. Strachman
James Steck

Providence, Rhode Island
December 2007

Chapter 2

Historical Attempts to Bring Terrorists to Justice

2.1 Alien Tort Claims Act, 28 U.S.C. §1350
A. Text of Act
The district courts shall have original jurisdiction of any civil action by an alien for a tort only, committed in violation of the law of nations or a treaty of the United States.

Notes:

1. In order for a court to obtain jurisdiction under the Act, a plaintiff must establish that: 1) he is an alien, 2) the action must be for a tort only, and 3) the tort was committed in violation of the law of nations. How, if at all, does this statute assist a citizen of the United States in bringing suit against non-citizens? In 1991, Congress enacted 28 U.S.C. §1350 note, the Torture Victim Protection Act, extending "a civil remedy to U.S. citizens who may have been tortured abroad." See H.R.Rep. No. 102-367 at 4; see also *Sarei v. Rio Tinto, PLC*, 487 F.3d 1193, 1215-1216 (9th Cir. 2007).

2. The history of the Alien Tort Claims Act has been described as "murky." One commentator stated "[t]he legislative history of the Judiciary Act neither mentions the ATCA nor provides conclusive evidence as to Congress's intent in enacting it." Helen C. Lucas, *The Adjudication of Violations of International Law Under the Alien Tort Claims Act: Allowing Alient Plaintiffs Their Day in Court*, 36 DePaul L. Rev. 231, 236 (1987). Another stated that "For almost 200 years, the ATCA lay dormant. Occasional references in the case law failed to generate interest in the act." William J. Aceves, *Affirming the Law of the Nations in U.S. Courts*, 49-JUN Fed. Law. 33 (2002).

In 1975, almost 200 years after its adoption, the Court of Appeals for the Second Circuit described the statute's history,

> This old but little used section is a kind of legal Lohengrin; although it has been with us since the first Judiciary Act, s 9, 1 Stat. 73, 77 (1789), no one seems to know whence it came. We dealt with it some years ago in *Khedivial Line, S.A.E. v. Seafarers' Union*, 278 F.2d 49, 52 (2d Cir. 1960) (per curiam). At that time we could find only one case where jurisdiction under it had been sustained, in that instance violation of a treaty, *Bolchos v. Darrell*, 3 Fed.Cas.No.1,607, p. 810 (D.S.C.1795).

IIT v. Vencap, Ltd., 519 F.2d 1001, 1015 (2nd Cir. 1975).

B. *Filartiga v. Pena-Irala*, 630 F.2d 876 (2d Cir. 1980)
Before FEINBERG, Chief Judge, KAUFMAN and KEARS, Circuit Judges.

IRVING R. KAUFMAN, Circuit Judge:

Upon ratification of the Constitution, the thirteen former colonies were fused into a single nation, one which, in its relations with foreign states, is bound both to observe and construe the accepted norms of international law, formerly known as the law of nations. Under the Articles of Confederation, the several states had interpreted and applied this body of doctrine as a part of their common law, but with the founding of the "more perfect Union" of 1789, the law of nations became preeminently a federal concern.

Implementing the constitutional mandate for national control over foreign relations, the First Congress established original district court jurisdiction over "all causes where an alien sues for a tort only (committed) in violation of the law of nations." Judiciary Act of 1789, ch. 20, s 9(b), 1 Stat. 73, 77 (1789), codified at 28 U.S.C. s 1350. Construing this rarely-invoked provision, we hold that deliberate torture perpetrated under color of official authority violates universally accepted norms of the international law of human rights, regardless of the nationality of the parties. Thus, whenever an alleged torturer is found and served with process by an alien within our borders, s 1350 provides federal jurisdiction. Accordingly, we reverse the judgment of the district court dismissing the complaint for want of federal jurisdiction.

I

The appellants, plaintiffs below, are citizens of the Republic of Paraguay. Dr. Joel Filartiga, a physician, describes himself as a longstanding opponent of the government of President Alfredo Stroessner, which has held power in Paraguay since 1954. His daughter, Dolly Filartiga, arrived in the United States in 1978 under a visitor's visa, and has since applied for permanent political asylum. The Filartigas brought this action in the Eastern District of New York against Americo Norberto Pena-Irala (Pena), also a citizen of Paraguay, for wrongfully causing the death of Dr. Filartiga's seventeen-year old son, Joelito. Because the district court dismissed the action for want of subject matter jurisdiction, we must accept as true the allegations contained in the Filartigas' complaint and affidavits for purposes of this appeal.

The appellants contend that on March 29, 1976, Joelito Filartiga was kidnapped and tortured to death by Pena, who was then Inspector General of Police in Asuncion, Paraguay. Later that day, the police brought Dolly Filartiga to Pena's home where she was confronted with the body of her brother, which evidenced marks of severe torture. As she fled, horrified, from the house, Pena followed after her shouting, "Here you have what you have been looking for for so long and what you deserve. Now shut up." The Filartigas claim that Joelito was tortured and killed in retaliation for his father's political activities and beliefs.

Shortly thereafter, Dr. Filartiga commenced a criminal action in the Paraguayan courts against Pena and the police for the murder of his son. As a result, Dr. Filartiga's attorney was arrested and brought to police headquarters where, shackled to a wall, Pena threatened him with death. This attorney, it is alleged, has since been disbarred without just cause.

During the course of the Paraguayan criminal proceeding, which is apparently still pending after four years, another man, Hugo Duarte, confessed to the murder. Duarte, who was a member of the Pena household, [FN1] claimed that he had discovered his wife and Joelito in flagrante delicto, and that the crime was one of passion. The Filartigas have submitted a photograph of Joelito's corpse showing injuries they believe refute this claim. Dolly Filartiga, moreover, has stated that she will offer evidence of three independent autopsies demonstrating that her brother's death "was the result of professional methods of torture." Despite his con-

fession, Duarte, we are told, has never been convicted or sentenced in connection with the crime.

FN1. Duarte is the son of Pena's companion, Juana Bautista Fernandez Villalba, who later accompanied Pena to the United States.

In July of 1978, Pena sold his house in Paraguay and entered the United States under a visitor's visa. He was accompanied by Juana Bautista Fernandez Villalba, who had lived with him in Paraguay. The couple remained in the United States beyond the term of their visas, and were living in Brooklyn, New York, when Dolly Filartiga, who was then living in Washington, D. C., learned of their presence. Acting on information provided by Dolly the Immigration and Naturalization Service arrested Pena and his companion, both of whom were subsequently ordered deported on April 5, 1979 following a hearing. They had then resided in the United States for more than nine months.

Almost immediately, Dolly caused Pena to be served with a summons and civil complaint at the Brooklyn Navy Yard, where he was being held pending deportation. The complaint alleged that Pena had wrongfully caused Joelito's death by torture and sought compensatory and punitive damages of $10,000,000. The Filartigas also sought to enjoin Pena's deportation to ensure his availability for testimony at trial. [FN2] The cause of action is stated as arising under "wrongful death statutes; the U. N. Charter; the Universal Declaration on Human Rights; the U. N. Declaration Against Torture; the American Declaration of the Rights and Duties of Man; and other pertinent declarations, documents and practices constituting the customary international law of human rights and the law of nations," as well as 28 U.S.C. s 1350, Article II, sec. 2 and the Supremacy Clause of the U. S. Constitution. Jurisdiction is claimed under the general federal question provision, 28 U.S.C. s 1331 and, principally on this appeal, under the Alien Tort Statute, 28 U.S.C. s 1350. [FN3]

FN2. Several officials of the Immigration and Naturalization Service were named as defendants in connection with this portion of the action. Because Pena has now been deported, the federal defendants are no longer parties to this suit, and the claims against them are not before us on this appeal.
FN3. Jurisdiction was also invoked pursuant to 28 U.S.C. ss 1651, 2201 & 2202, presumably in connection with appellants' attempt to delay Pena's return to Paraguay.

Judge Nickerson stayed the order of deportation, and Pena immediately moved to dismiss the complaint on the grounds that subject matter jurisdiction was absent and for forum non conveniens. On the jurisdictional issue, there has been no suggestion that Pena claims diplomatic immunity from suit. The Filartigas submitted the affidavits of a number of distinguished international legal scholars, who stated unanimously that the law of nations prohibits absolutely the use of torture as alleged in the complaint. [FN4] Pena, in support of his motion to dismiss on the ground of forum non conveniens, submitted the affidavit of his Paraguayan counsel, Jose Emilio Gorostiaga, who averred that Paraguayan law provides a full and adequate civil remedy for the wrong alleged. [FN5] Dr. Filartiga has not commenced such an action, however, believing that further resort to the courts of his own country would be futile.

FN4. Richard Falk, the Albert G. Milbank Professor of International Law and Practice at Princeton University, and a former Vice President of the American Society of International Law, avers that, in his judgment, "it is now beyond reasonable doubt that torture of a person held in detention that results in severe harm or death is a violation of the law of nations." Thomas Franck, professor of international law at New York University and Director of the New York University Center for International Studies offers his opinion that torture has now been rejected by virtually all nations, although it was once commonly used to extract confessions. Richard Lillich, the Howard W. Smith Professor of Law at the University of Virginia School of Law, concludes, after a lengthy review of the authorities, that officially perpetrated torture is "a violation of international law (formerly called the law of nations)." Finally, Myres MacDougal, a former Sterling Professor of Law at the Yale Law School, and a past President of the American Society of International Law, states that torture is an offense against the law of nations, and that "it has long been recognized that such offenses vitally affect relations between states."

FN5. The Gorostiaga affidavit states that a father whose son has been wrongfully killed may in addition to commencing a criminal proceeding bring a civil action for damages against the person responsible. Accordingly, Mr. Filartiga has the right to commence a civil action against Mr. Duarte and Mr. Pena-Irala since he accuses them both of responsibility for his son's death. He may commence such a civil action either simultaneously with the commencement of the criminal proceeding, during the time that the criminal proceeding lasts, or within a year after the criminal proceeding has terminated. In either event, however, the civil action may not proceed to judgment until the criminal proceeding has been disposed of. If the defendant is found not guilty because he was not the author of the case under investiga-

tion in the criminal proceeding, no civil action for indemnity for damages based upon the same deed investigated in the criminal proceeding, can prosper or succeed.

Judge Nickerson heard argument on the motion to dismiss on May 14, 1979, and on May 15 dismissed the complaint on jurisdictional grounds. [FN6] The district judge recognized the strength of appellants' argument that official torture violates an emerging norm of customary international law. Nonetheless, he felt constrained by dicta contained in two recent opinions of this Court, *Dreyfus v. von Finck*, 534 F.2d 24 (2d Cir.), *cert. denied*, 429 U.S. 835, 97 S.Ct. 102, 50 L.Ed.2d 101 (1976); *IIT v. Vencap, Ltd.*, 519 F.2d 1001 (2d Cir. 1975), to construe narrowly "the law of nations," as employed in s 1350, as excluding that law which governs a state's treatment of its own citizens.

FN6. The court below accordingly did not consider the motion to dismiss on forum non conveniens grounds, which is not before us on this appeal.

The district court continued the stay of deportation for forty-eight hours while appellants applied for further stays. These applications were denied by a panel of this Court on May 22, 1979, and by the Supreme Court two days later. Shortly thereafter, Pena and his companion returned to Paraguay.

II

Appellants rest their principal argument in support of federal jurisdiction upon the Alien Tort Statute, 28 U.S.C. s 1350, which provides: "The district courts shall have original jurisdiction of any civil action by an alien for a tort only, committed in violation of the law of nations or a treaty of the United States." Since appellants do not contend that their action arises directly under a treaty of the United States, [FN7] a threshold question on the jurisdictional issue is whether the conduct alleged violates the law of nations. In light of the universal condemnation of torture in numerous international agreements, and the renunciation of torture as an instrument of official policy by virtually all of the nations of the world (in principle if not in practice), we find that an act of torture committed by a state official against one held in detention violates established norms of the international law of human rights, and hence the law of nations.

FN7. Appellants "associate themselves with" the argument of some of the amici curiae that their claim arises directly under a treaty of the United States, Brief for Appellants at 23 n.*, but nonetheless primarily rely upon treaties and other international instruments as evidence of an emerging norm of customary international law, rather then independent sources of law.

The Supreme Court has enumerated the appropriate sources of international law. The law of nations "may be ascertained by consulting the works of jurists, writing professedly on public law; or by the general usage and practice of nations; or by judicial decisions recognizing and enforcing that law." *United States v. Smith*, 18 U.S. (5 Wheat.) 153, 160-61, 5 L.Ed. 57 (1820); *Lopes v. Reederei Richard Schroder*, 225 F.Supp. 292, 295 (E.D.Pa.1963). In Smith, a statute proscribing "the crime of piracy (on the high seas) as defined by the law of nations," 3 Stat. 510(a) (1819), was held sufficiently determinate in meaning to afford the basis for a death sentence. The Smith Court discovered among the works of Lord Bacon, Grotius, Bochard and other commentators a genuine consensus that rendered the crime "sufficiently and constitutionally defined." Smith, *supra*, 18 U.S. (5 Wheat.) at 162, 5 L.Ed. 57.

The Paquete Habana, 175 U.S. 677, 20 S.Ct. 290, 44 L.Ed. 320 (1900), reaffirmed that where there is no treaty, and no controlling executive or legislative act or judicial decision, resort must be had to the customs and usages of civilized nations; and, as evidence of these, to the works of jurists and commentators, who by years of labor, research and experience, have made themselves peculiarly well acquainted with the subjects of which they treat. Such works are resorted to by judicial tribunals, not for the speculations of their authors concerning what the law ought to be, but for trustworthy evidence of what the law really is. *Id.* at 700, 20 S.Ct. at 299. Modern international sources confirm the propriety of this approach. [FN8]

FN8. The Statute of the International Court of Justice, Arts. 38 & 59, June 26, 1945, 59 Stat. 1055, 1060 (1945) provides:
Art. 38
1. The Court, whose function is to decide in accordance with international law such disputes as are submitted to it, shall apply:
(a) international conventions, whether general or particular, establishing rules expressly recognized by the contesting states;
(b) international custom, as evidence of a general practice accepted as law;
(c) the general principles of law recognized by civilized nations;
(d) subject to the provisions of Article 59, judicial decisions and the teachings of the most highly qualified publicists of

the various nations, as subsidiary means for the determination of the rules of law.
2. This provision shall not prejudice the power of the Court to decide a case ex aequo et bono, if the parties agree thereto.
Art. 59
The decision of the Court has no binding force except between the parties and in respect of that particular case.

Habana is particularly instructive for present purposes, for it held that the traditional prohibition against seizure of an enemy's coastal fishing vessels during wartime, a standard that began as one of comity only, had ripened over the preceding century into "a settled rule of international law" by "the general assent of civilized nations." *Id.* at 694, 20 S.Ct. at 297; accord, *Id.* at 686, 20 S.Ct. at 297. Thus it is clear that courts must interpret international law not as it was in 1789, but as it has evolved and exists among the nations of the world today. See *Ware v. Hylton*, 3 U.S. (3 Dall.) 198, 1 L.Ed. 568 (1796) (distinguishing between "ancient" and "modern" law of nations).

The requirement that a rule command the "general assent of civilized nations" to become binding upon them all is a stringent one. Were this not so, the courts of one nation might feel free to impose idiosyncratic legal rules upon others, in the name of applying international law. Thus, in *Banco Nacional de Cuba v. Sabbatino*, 376 U.S. 398, 84 S.Ct. 923, 11 L.Ed.2d 804 (1964), the Court declined to pass on the validity of the Cuban government's expropriation of a foreign-owned corporation's assets, noting the sharply conflicting views on the issue propounded by the capital-exporting, capital-importing, socialist and capitalist nations. *Id.* at 428-30, 84 S.Ct. at 940-41.

The case at bar presents us with a situation diametrically opposed to the conflicted state of law that confronted the Sabbatino Court. Indeed, to paraphrase that Court's statement, *Id.* at 428, 84 S.Ct. at 940, there are few, if any, issues in international law today on which opinion seems to be so united as the limitations on a state's power to torture persons held in its custody.

The United Nations Charter (a treaty of the United States, see 59 Stat. 1033 (1945)) makes it clear that in this modern age a state's treatment of its own citizens is a matter of international concern. It provides:

With a view to the creation of conditions of stability and well-being which are necessary for peaceful and friendly relations among nations...the United Nations shall promote... universal respect for, and observance of, human rights and fundamental freedoms for all without distinctions as to race, sex, language or religion.

Id. Art. 55. And further:

All members pledge themselves to take joint and separate action in cooperation with the Organization for the achievement of the purposes set forth in Article 55.

Id. Art. 56.

While this broad mandate has been held not to be wholly self-executing, *Hitai v. Immigration and Naturalization Service*, 343 F.2d 466, 468 (2d Cir. 1965), this observation alone does not end our inquiry. [FN9] For although there is no universal agreement as to the precise extent of the "human rights and fundamental freedoms" guaranteed to all by the Charter, there is at present no dissent from the view that the guaranties include, at a bare minimum, the right to be free from torture. This prohibition has become part of customary international law, as evidenced and defined by the Universal Declaration of Human Rights, General Assembly Resolution 217 (III)(A) (Dec. 10, 1948) which states, in the plainest of terms, "no one shall be subjected to torture." [FN10] The General Assembly has declared that the Charter precepts embodied in this Universal Declaration "constitute basic principles of international law." G.A.Res. 2625 (XXV) (Oct. 24, 1970).

FN9. We observe that this Court has previously utilized the U.N. Charter and the Charter of the Organization of American States, another non-self-executing agreement, as evidence of binding principles of international law. *United States v. Toscanino*, 500 F.2d 267 (2d Cir. 1974). In that case, our government's duty under international law to refrain from kidnapping a criminal defendant from within the borders of another nation, where formal extradition procedures existed, infringed the personal rights of the defendant, whose international law claims were thereupon remanded for a hearing in the district court.

FN10. Eighteen nations have incorporated the Universal Declaration into their own constitutions. 48 Revue Internationale de Droit Penal Nos. 3 & 4, at 211 (1977). Particularly relevant is the Declaration on the Protection of All Persons from Being Subjected to Torture, General Assembly Resolution 3452, 30 U.N. GAOR Supp. (No. 34) 91, U.N.Doc. A/1034 (1975), which is set out in full in the margin. [FN11] The Declaration expressly prohibits any state from permitting the dastardly and totally inhuman act of torture. Torture, in turn, is defined as "any act by which severe

pain and suffering, whether physical or mental, is intentionally inflicted by or at the instigation of a public official on a person for such purposes as…intimidating him or other persons." The Declaration goes on to provide that "(w)here it is proved that an act of torture or other cruel, inhuman or degrading treatment or punishment has been committed by or at the instigation of a public official, the victim shall be afforded redress and compensation, in accordance with national law." This Declaration, like the Declaration of Human Rights before it, was adopted without dissent by the General Assembly. Nayar, "Human Rights: The United Nations and United States Foreign Policy," 19 Harv.Int'l L.J. 813, 816 n.18 (1978).

FN11. Article 1
1. For the purpose of this Declaration, torture means any act by which severe pain or suffering, whether physical or mental, is intentionally inflicted by or at the instigation of a public official on a person for such purposes as obtaining from him or a third person information or confession, punishing him for an act he has committed or is suspected of having committed, or intimidating him or other persons. It does not include pain or suffering arising only from, inherent or incidental to lawful sanctions to the extent consistent with the Standard Minimum Rules for the Treatment of Prisoners.
2. Torture constitutes an aggravated and deliberate form of cruel, inhuman or degrading treatment or punishment.
Article 2
Any act of torture or other cruel, inhuman or degrading treatment or punishment is an offense to human dignity and shall be condemned as a denial of the purposes of the Charter of the United Nations and as a violation of human rights and fundamental freedoms proclaimed in the Universal Declaration of Human Rights.
Article 3
No state may permit or tolerate torture or other cruel, inhuman or degrading treatment or punishment. Exceptional circumstances such as a state of war or a threat of war, internal political instability or any other public emergency may not be invoked as a justification of torture or other cruel, inhuman or degrading treatment or punishment.
Article 4
Each state shall, in accordance with the provisions of this Declaration, take effective measures to prevent torture and other cruel, inhuman or degrading treatment or punishment from being practiced within its jurisdiction.
Article 5
The training of law enforcement personnel and of other public officials who may be responsible for persons deprived of their liberty shall ensure that full account is taken of the pro-

hibition against torture and other cruel, inhuman or degrading treatment or punishment. This prohibition shall also, where appropriate, be included in such general rules or instructions as are issued in regard to the duties and functions of anyone who may be involved in the custody or treatment of such persons.

Article 6

Each state shall keep under systematic review interrogation methods and practices as well as arrangements for the custody and treatment of persons deprived of their liberty in its territory, with a view to preventing any cases of torture or other cruel, inhuman or degrading treatment or punishment.

Article 7

Each state shall ensure that all acts of torture as defined in Article I are offenses under its criminal law. The same shall apply in regard to acts which constitute participation in, complicity in, incitement to or an attempt to commit torture.

Article 8

Any person who alleges he has been subjected to torture or other cruel, inhuman or degrading treatment or punishment by or at the instigation of a public official shall have the right to complain to, and to have his case impartially examined by, the competent authorities of the state concerned.

Article 9

Wherever there is reasonable ground to believe that an act of torture as defined in Article I has been committed, the competent authorities of the state concerned shall promptly proceed to an impartial investigation even if there has been no formal complaint.

Article 10

If an investigation under Article 8 or Article 9 establishes that an act of torture as defined in Article I appears to have been committed, criminal proceedings shall be instituted against the alleged offender or offenders in accordance with national law. If an allegation of other forms of cruel, inhuman or degrading treatment or punishment is considered to be well founded, the alleged offender or offenders shall be subject to criminal, disciplinary or other appropriate proceedings.

Article 11

Where it is proved that an act of torture or other cruel, inhuman or degrading treatment or punishment has been committed by or at the instigation of a public official, the victim shall be afforded redress and compensation, in accordance with national law.

Article 12

Any statement which is established to have been made as a result of torture or other cruel, inhuman or degrading treat-

ment or punishment may not be invoked as evidence against the person concerned or against any other person in any proceeding.

These U.N. declarations are significant because they specify with great precision the obligations of member nations under the Charter. Since their adoption, "(m)embers can no longer contend that they do not know what human rights they promised in the Charter to promote." Sohn, "A Short History of United Nations Documents on Human Rights," in The United Nations and Human Rights, 18th Report of the Commission (Commission to Study the Organization of Peace ed. 1968). Moreover, a U.N. Declaration is, according to one authoritative definition, "a formal and solemn instrument, suitable for rare occasions when principles of great and lasting importance are being enunciated." 34 U.N. ESCOR, Supp. (No. 8) 15, U.N. Doc. E/cn.4/1/610 (1962) (memorandum of Office of Legal Affairs, U.N. Secretariat). Accordingly, it has been observed that the Universal Declaration of Human Rights "no longer fits into the dichotomy of 'binding treaty' against 'non-binding pronouncement,' but is rather an authoritative statement of the international community." E. Schwelb, Human Rights and the International Community 70 (1964). Thus, a Declaration creates an expectation of adherence, and "insofar as the expectation is gradually justified by State practice, a declaration may by custom become recognized as laying down rules binding upon the States." 34 U.N. ESCOR, *supra*. Indeed, several commentators have concluded that the Universal Declaration has become, in toto, a part of binding, customary international law. Nayar, *supra*, at 816-17; Waldlock, "Human Rights in Contemporary International Law and the Significance of the European Convention," Int'l & Comp. L.Q., Supp. Publ. No. 11 at 15 (1965).

Turning to the act of torture, we have little difficulty discerning its universal renunciation in the modern usage and practice of nations. Smith, *supra*, 18 U.S. (5 Wheat.) at 160-61, 5 L.Ed. 57. The international consensus surrounding torture has found expression in numerous international treaties and accords. E. g., American Convention on Human Rights, Art. 5, OAS Treaty Series No. 36 at 1, OAS Off. Rec. OEA/Ser 4 v/II 23, doc. 21, rev. 2 (English ed., 1975) ("No one shall be subjected to torture or to cruel, inhuman or degrading punishment or treatment"); International Covenant on Civil and Political Rights, U.N. General Assembly Res. 2200 (XXI)A, U.N. Doc. A/6316 (Dec. 16, 1966) (identical language); European Convention for the Protection of Human Rights and Fundamental Freedoms, Art. 3, Council of Europe, European Treaty Series No. 5 (1968), 213 U.N.T.S. 211 (semble). The substance of these international agreements is reflected in modern municipal i. e. national law as well. Although torture was once a routine concomitant of criminal interrogations in many nations, during the modern and hopefully more enlightened era it has been universally renounced. According to one survey, torture is prohibited, expressly or implicitly, by the constitutions of over fifty-five nations, [FN12] including both the United States [FN13] and Paraguay. [FN14] Our State Department reports a general recognition of this principle:

There now exists an international consensus that recognizes basic human rights and obligations owed by all governments to their citizens…There is no doubt that these rights are often violated; but virtually all governments acknowledge their validity.

FN12. 48 Revue Internationale de Droit Penal Nos. 3 & 4 at 208 (1977).
FN13. U.S.Const., Amend. VIII ("cruel and unusual punishments" prohibited); *Id*. Amend. XIV.
FN14. Constitution of Paraguay, Art. 45 (prohibiting torture and other cruel treatment).

Department of State, Country Reports on Human Rights for 1979, published as Joint Comm. Print, House Comm. on Foreign Affairs, and Senate Comm. on Foreign Relations, 96th Cong. 2d Sess. (Feb. 4, 1980), Introduction at 1. We have been directed to no assertion by any contemporary state of a right to torture its own or another nation's citizens. Indeed, United States diplomatic contacts confirm the universal abhorrence with which torture is viewed:

In exchanges between United States embassies and all foreign states with which the United States maintains relations, it has been the Department of State's general experience that no government has asserted a right to torture its own nationals. Where reports of torture elicit some credence, a state usually responds by denial or, less frequently, by asserting that the conduct was unauthorized or constituted rough treatment short of torture. [FN15]

FN15. The fact that the prohibition of torture is often honored in the breach does not diminish its binding effect as a norm of international law. As one commentator has put it, "The best evidence for the existence of international law is that every actual State recognizes that it does exist and that it is itself under an obligation to observe it. States often violate international law, just as individuals often violate municipal law; but no more than individuals do States defend their vio-

lations by claiming that they are above the law." J. Brierly, The Outlook for International Law 4-5 (Oxford 1944).

Having examined the sources from which customary international law is derived the usage of nations, judicial opinions and the works of jurists [FN16] we conclude that official torture is now prohibited by the law of nations. The prohibition is clear and unambiguous, and admits of no distinction between treatment of aliens and citizens. Accordingly, we must conclude that the dictum in *Dreyfus v. von Finck, supra*, 534 F.2d at 31, to the effect that "violations of international law do not occur when the aggrieved parties are nationals of the acting state," is clearly out of tune with the current usage and practice of international law. The treaties and accords cited above, as well as the express foreign policy of our own government, [FN17] all make it clear that international law confers fundamental rights upon all people vis-a-vis their own governments. While the ultimate scope of those rights will be a subject for continuing refinement and elaboration, we hold that the right to be free from torture is now among them. We therefore turn to the question whether the other requirements for jurisdiction are met.

FN16. See note 4, *supra*: see also *Ireland v. United Kingdom*, Judgment of Jan. 18, 1978 (European Court of Human Rights), summarized in (1978) Yearbook, European Convention on Human Rights 602 (Council of Europe) (holding that Britain's subjection of prisoners to sleep deprivation, hooding, exposure to hissing noise, reduced diet and standing against a wall for hours was "inhuman and degrading," but not "torture" within meaning of European Convention on Human Rights).
FN17. E. g., 22 U.S.C. s 2304(a)(2) ("Except under circumstances specified in this section, no security assistance may be provided to any country the government of which engages in a consistent pattern of gross violations of internationally recognized human rights."); 22 U.S.C. s 2151(a) ("The Congress finds that fundamental political, economic, and technological changes have resulted in the interdependence of nations. The Congress declares that the individual liberties, economic prosperity, and security of the people of the United States are best sustained and enhanced in a community of nations which respect individual civil and economic rights and freedoms").

III

Appellee submits that even if the tort alleged is a violation of modern international law, federal jurisdiction may not be exercised consistent with the dictates of Article III of the Constitution. The claim is without merit. Common law courts of general jurisdiction regularly adjudicate transitory tort claims between individuals over whom they exercise personal jurisdiction, wherever the tort occurred. Moreover, as part of an articulated scheme of federal control over external affairs, Congress provided, in the first Judiciary Act, s 9(b), 1 Stat. 73, 77 (1789), for federal jurisdiction over suits by aliens where principles of international law are in issue. The constitutional basis for the Alien Tort Statute is the law of nations, which has always been part of the federal common law.

It is not extraordinary for a court to adjudicate a tort claim arising outside of its territorial jurisdiction. A state or nation has a legitimate interest in the orderly resolution of disputes among those within its borders, and where the lex loci delicti commissi is applied, it is an expression of comity to give effect to the laws of the state where the wrong occurred. Thus, Lord Mansfield in *Mostyn v. Fabrigas*, 1 Cowp. 161 (1774), quoted in *McKenna v. Fisk*, 42 U.S. (1 How.) 241, 248, 11 L.Ed. 117 (1843) said:

(I)f A becomes indebted to B, or commits a tort upon his person or upon his personal property in Paris, an action in either case may be maintained against A in England, if he is there found…(A)s to transitory actions, there is not a colour of doubt but that any action which is transitory may be laid in any county in England, though the matter arises beyond the seas.

Mostyn came into our law as the original basis for state court jurisdiction over out-of-state torts, *McKenna v. Fisk*, *supra*, 42 U.S. (1 How.) 241, 11 L.Ed. 117 (personal injury suits held transitory); *Dennick v. Railroad Co.*, 103 U.S. 11, 26 L.Ed. 439 (1880) (wrongful death action held transitory), and it has not lost its force in suits to recover for a wrongful death occurring upon foreign soil, *Slater v. Mexican National Railroad Co.*, 194 U.S. 120, 24 S.Ct. 581, 48 L.Ed. 900 (1904), as long as the conduct complained of was unlawful where performed. Restatement (Second) of Foreign Relations Law of the United States s 19 (1965). Here, where in personam jurisdiction has been obtained over the defendant, the parties agree that the acts alleged would violate Paraguayan law, and the policies of the forum are consistent with the foreign law, [FN18] state court jurisdiction would be proper. Indeed, appellees conceded as much at oral argument.

FN18. Conduct of the type alleged here would be actionable under 42 U.S.C. s 1983 or, undoubtedly, the Constitution, if performed by a government official.

Recalling that Mostyn was freshly decided at the time the Constitution was ratified, we proceed to consider whether the First Congress acted constitutionally in vesting jurisdiction over "foreign suits," Slater, *supra*, 194 U.S. at 124, 24 S.Ct. at 582, alleging torts committed in violation of the law of nations. A case properly "aris(es) under the…laws of the United States" for Article III purposes if grounded upon statutes enacted by Congress or upon the common law of the United States. See *Illinois v. City of Milwaukee*, 406 U.S. 91, 99-100, 92 S.Ct. 1385, 1390-91, 31 L.Ed.2d 712 (1972); *Ivy Broadcasting Co., Inc. v. American Tel. & Tel. Co.*, 391 F.2d 486, 492 (2d Cir. 1968). The law of nations forms an integral part of the common law, and a review of the history surrounding the adoption of the Constitution demonstrates that it became a part of the common law of the United States upon the adoption of the Constitution. Therefore, the enactment of the Alien Tort Statute was authorized by Article III.

During the eighteenth century, it was taken for granted on both sides of the Atlantic that the law of nations forms a part of the common law. 1 Blackstone, Commentaries 263-64 (1st Ed. 1765-69); 4 *Id.* at 67. [FN19] Under the Articles of Confederation, the Pennsylvania Court of Oyer and Terminer at Philadelphia, per McKean, Chief Justice, applied the law of nations to the criminal prosecution of the Chevalier de Longchamps for his assault upon the person of the French Consul-General to the United States, noting that "(t)his law, in its full extent, is a part of the law of this state…" *Respublica v. DeLongchamps*, 1 U.S. (1 Dall.) 113, 119, 1 L.Ed. 59 (1784). Thus, a leading commentator has written:

FN19. As Lord Stowell said in *The Maria*, 165 Eng.Rep. 955, 958 (Adm.1807): "In the first place it is to be recollected, that this is a Court of the Law of Nations, though sitting here under the authority of the King of Great Britain. It belongs to other nations as well as to our own; and what foreigners have a right to demand from it, is the administration of the law of nations, simply, and exclusively of the introduction of principles borrowed from our own municipal jurisprudence, to which it is well known, they have at all times expressed no inconsiderable repugnance."

It is an ancient and a salutary feature of the Anglo-American legal tradition that the Law of Nations is a part of the law of the land to be ascertained and administered, like any other, in the appropriate case. This doctrine was originally conceived and formulated in England in response to the demands of an expanding commerce and under the influence of theories widely accepted in the late sixteenth, the seventeenth and the eighteenth centuries. It was brought to America in the colonial years as part of the legal heritage from England. It was well understood by men of legal learning in America in the eighteenth century when the United Colonies broke away from England to unite effectively, a little later, in the United States of America. Dickenson, "The Law of Nations as Part of the National Law of the United States," 101 U.Pa.L.Rev. 26, 27 (1952).

Indeed, Dickenson goes on to demonstrate, *Id.* at 34-41, that one of the principal defects of the Confederation that our Constitution was intended to remedy was the central government's inability to "cause infractions of treaties or of the law of nations, to be punished." 1 Farrand, Records of the Federal Convention 19 (Rev. ed. 1937) (Notes of James Madison). And, in Jefferson's words, the very purpose of the proposed Union was "(t)o make us one nation as to foreign concerns, and keep us distinct in domestic ones." Dickenson, *supra*, at 36 n. 28.

As ratified, the judiciary article contained no express reference to cases arising under the law of nations. Indeed, the only express reference to that body of law is contained in Article I, sec. 8, cl. 10, which grants to the Congress the power to "define and punish...offenses against the law of nations." Appellees seize upon this circumstance and advance the proposition that the law of nations forms a part of the laws of the United States only to the extent that Congress has acted to define it. This extravagant claim is amply refuted by the numerous decisions applying rules of international law uncodified in any act of Congress. E.g., *Ware v. Hylton*, 3 U.S. (3 Dall.) 198, 1 L.Ed. 568 (1796); *The Paquete Habana, supra*, 175 U.S. 677, 20 S.Ct. 290, 44 L.Ed. 320; *Sabbatino, supra*, 376 U.S. 398, 84 S.Ct. 923, 11 L.Ed.2d 804 (1964). A similar argument was offered to and rejected by the Supreme Court in *United States v. Smith, supra*, 18 U.S. (5 Wheat.) 153, 158-60, 5 L.Ed. 57 and we reject it today. As John Jay wrote in The Federalist No. 3, at 22 (1 Bourne ed. 1901), "Under the national government, treaties and articles of treaties, as well as the laws of nations, will always be expounded in one sense and executed in the same manner, whereas adjudications on the same points and questions in the thirteen states will not always accord or be consistent." Federal jurisdiction over cases involving international law is clear.

Thus, it was hardly a radical initiative for Chief Justice Marshall to state in *The Nereide*, 13 U.S. (9 Cranch) 388, 422, 3 L.Ed. 769 (1815), that in the absence of a congressional enactment, [FN20] United States courts are "bound by the law of nations, which is a part of the law of the land." These words were echoed in *The Paquete Habana, supra*, 175 U.S. at 700, 20 S.Ct. at 299: "[i]nternational law is part

of our law, and must be ascertained and administered by the courts of justice of appropriate jurisdiction, as often as questions of right depending upon it are duly presented for their determination."

FN20. The plainest evidence that international law has an existence in the federal courts independent of acts of Congress is the long-standing rule of construction first enunciated by Chief Justice Marshall: "an act of congress ought never to be construed to violate the law of nations, if any other possible construction remains..." *The Charming Betsy*, 6 U.S. (2 Cranch), 34, 67, 2 L.Ed. 208 (1804), quoted in *Lauritzen v. Larsen*, 345 U.S. 571, 578, 73 S.Ct. 921, 926, 97 L.Ed. 1254 (1953).

The Filartigas urge that 28 U.S.C. s 1350 be treated as an exercise of Congress's power to define offenses against the law of nations. While such a reading is possible, see *Lincoln Mills v. Textile Workers*, 353 U.S. 488, 77 S.Ct. 912, 1 L.Ed.2d 972 (1957) (jurisdictional statute authorizes judicial explication of federal common law), we believe it is sufficient here to construe the Alien Tort Statute, not as granting new rights to aliens, but simply as opening the federal courts for adjudication of the rights already recognized by international law. The statute nonetheless does inform our analysis of Article III, for we recognize that questions of jurisdiction "must be considered part of an organic growth part of an evolutionary process," and that the history of the judiciary article gives meaning to its pithy phrases. *Romero v. International Terminal Operating Co.*, 358 U.S. 354, 360, 79 S.Ct. 468, 473, 3 L.Ed.2d 368 (1959). The Framers' overarching concern that control over international affairs be vested in the new national government to safeguard the standing of the United States among the nations of the world therefore reinforces the result we reach today.

Although the Alien Tort Statute has rarely been the basis for jurisdiction during its long history, [FN21] in light of the foregoing discussion, there can be little doubt that this action is properly brought in federal court. [FN22] This is undeniably an action by an alien, for a tort only, committed in violation of the law of nations. The paucity of suits successfully maintained under the section is readily attributable to the statute's requirement of alleging a "violation of the law of nations" (emphasis supplied) at the jurisdictional threshold. Courts have, accordingly, engaged in a more searching preliminary review of the merits than is required, for example, under the more flexible "arising under" formulation. Compare *O'Reilly de Camara v. Brooke*, 209 U.S. 45, 52, 28 S.Ct. 439, 441, 52 L.Ed. 676 (1907) (question of Alien Tort Statute jurisdiction disposed of "on the merits") (Holmes, J.), with *Bell v. Hood*, 327 U.S. 678, 66 S.Ct. 773, 90 L.Ed. 939 (1946) (general federal question jurisdiction not defeated by the possibility that the averments in the complaint may fail to state a cause of action). Thus, the narrowing construction that the Alien Tort Statute has previously received reflects the fact that earlier cases did not involve such well-established, universally recognized norms of international law that are here at issue.

FN21. Section 1350 afforded the basis for jurisdiction over a child custody suit between aliens in *Adra v. Clift*, 195 F.Supp. 857 (D.Md.1961), with a falsified passport supplying the requisite international law violation. In *Bolchos v. Darrell*, 3 Fed.Cas. 810 (D.S.C.1795), the Alien Tort Statute provided an alternative basis of jurisdiction over a suit to determine title to slaves on board an enemy vessel taken on the high seas.

FN22. We recognize that our reasoning might also sustain jurisdiction under the general federal question provision, 28 U.S.C. s 1331. We prefer, however, to rest our decision upon the Alien Tort Statute, in light of that provision's close coincidence with the jurisdictional facts presented in this case. See *Romero v. International Terminal Operating Co.*, 358 U.S. 354, 79 S.Ct. 468, 3 L.Ed.2d 368 (1959).

For example, the statute does not confer jurisdiction over an action by a Luxembourgeois international investment trust's suit for fraud, conversion and corporate waste. *IIT v. Vencap*, 519 F.2d 1001, 1015 (1975). In IIT, Judge Friendly astutely noted that the mere fact that every nation's municipal law may prohibit theft does not incorporate "the Eighth Commandment, 'Thou Shalt not steal'...(into) the law of nations." It is only where the nations of the world have demonstrated that the wrong is of mutual, and not merely several, concern, by means of express international accords, that a wrong generally recognized becomes an international law violation within the meaning of the statute. Other recent s 1350 cases are similarly distinguishable. [FN23]

FN23. *Dreyfus v. von Finck*, 534 F.2d 24 (2d Cir.), *cert. denied*, 429 U.S. 835, 97 S.Ct. 102, 50 L.Ed.2d 101 (1976), concerned a forced sale of property, and thus sought to invoke international law in an area in which no consensus view existed. See *Sabbatino, supra*, 376 U.S. at 428, 84 S.Ct. at 940. Similarly, *Benjamins v. British European Airways*, 572 F.2d 913 (2d Cir. 1978), *cert. denied*, 439 U.S. 1114, 99 S.Ct. 1016, 59 L.Ed.2d 72 (1979), held only that an air disaster, even if caused by "wilful" negligence, does not constitute a law of nations violation. *Id*. at 916. In *Khedivial Line, S.A.E. v. Seafarers' International Union*, 278 F.2d 49 (2d Cir. 1960), we found that the "right" to free access to the ports of a foreign nation was at best a rule of comity, and not a binding rule of international law.

The cases from other circuits are distinguishable in like manner. The court in *Huynh Thi Anh v. Levi*, 586 F.2d 625 (6th Cir. 1978), was unable to discern from the traditional sources of the law of nations "a universal or generally accepted substantive rule or principle" governing child custody, *Id*. at 629, and therefore held jurisdiction to be lacking. Cf. *Nguyen Da Yen v. Kissinger*, 528 F.2d 1194, 1201 n.13 (9th Cir. 1975) ("the illegal seizure, removal and detention of an alien against his will in a foreign country would appear to be a tort...and it may well be a tort in violation of the 'law of nations' ") (s 1350 question not reached due to inadequate briefing). Finally, the district court in *Lopes v. Reederei Richard Schroder*, 225 F.Supp. 292 (E.D.Pa.1963) simply found that the doctrine of seaworthiness, upon which the plaintiff relied, was a uniquely American concept, and therefore not a part of the law of nations.

IIT adopted a dictum from *Lopes v. Reederei Richard Schroder*, 225 F.Supp. 292 (E.D.Pa.1963) to the effect that "a violation of the law of nations arises only when there has been 'a violation by one or more individuals of those standards, rules or customs (a) affecting the relationship between states or between an individual and a foreign state and (b) used by those states for their common good and/or in dealings inter se.' " *IIT, supra*, 519 F.2d at 1015, quoting *Lopes, supra*, 225 F.Supp. at 297. We have no quarrel with this formulation so long as it be understood that the courts are not to prejudge the scope of the issues that the nations of the world may deem important to their interrelationships, and thus to their common good. As one commentator has noted:

the sphere of domestic jurisdiction is not an irreducible sphere of rights which are somehow inherent, natural, or fundamental. It does not create an impenetrable barrier to the development of international law. Matters of domestic jurisdiction are not those which are unregulated by international law, but those which are left by international law for regulation by States. There are, therefore, no matters which are domestic by their 'nature.' All are susceptible of international legal regulation and may become the subjects of new rules of customary law of treaty obligations.

Preuss, "Article 2, Paragraph 7 of the Charter of the United Nations and Matters of Domestic Jurisdiction," Hague Receuil (Extract, 149) at 8, reprinted in H. Briggs, The Law of Nations 24 (1952). Here, the nations have made it their business, both through international accords and unilateral action, [FN24] to be concerned with domestic human rights violations of this magnitude. The case before us therefore falls within the Lopes/IIT rule.

FN24. As President Carter stated in his address to the United Nations on March 17, 1977:

All the signatories of the United Nations Charter have pledged themselves to observe and to respect basic human rights. Thus, no member of the United Nations can claim that mistreatment of the citizens is solely its own business. Equally, no member can avoid its responsibilities to review and to speak when torture or unwarranted deprivation occurs in any part of the world.

Reprinted in 78 Department of State Bull. 322 (1977); see note 17, *supra*. Since federal jurisdiction may properly be exercised over the Filartigas' claim, the action must be remanded for further proceedings. Appellee Pena, however, advances several additional points that lie beyond the scope of our holding on jurisdiction. Both to emphasize the boundaries of our holding, and to clarify some of the issues reserved for the district court on remand, we will address these contentions briefly.

IV

Pena argues that the customary law of nations, as reflected in treaties and declarations that are not self-executing, should not be applied as rules of decision in this case. In doing so, he confuses the question of federal jurisdiction under the Alien Tort Statute, which requires consideration of the law of nations, with the issue of the choice of law to be applied, which will be addressed at a later stage in the proceedings. The two issues are distinct. Our holding on subject matter jurisdiction decides only whether Congress intended to confer judicial power, and whether it is authorized to do so by Article III. The choice of law inquiry is a much broader one, primarily concerned with fairness, see *Home Insurance Co. v. Dick*, 281 U.S. 397, 50 S.Ct. 338, 74 L.Ed. 926 (1930); consequently, it looks to wholly different considerations. See *Lauritzen v. Larsen*, 345 U.S. 571, 73 S.Ct. 921, 97 L.Ed. 1254 (1954). Should the district court decide that the Lauritzen analysis requires it to apply Paraguayan law, our courts will not have occasion to consider what law would govern a suit under the Alien Tort Statute where the challenged conduct is actionable under the law of the forum and the law of nations, but not the law of the jurisdiction in which the tort occurred. [FN25]

FN25. In taking that broad range of factors into account, the district court may well decide that fairness requires it to apply Paraguayan law to the instant case. See *Slater v. Mexican National Railway Co.*, 194 U.S. 120, 24 S.Ct. 581, 48 L.Ed. 900 (1904). Such a decision would not retroactively oust the federal court of subject matter jurisdiction, even though plaintiff's cause of action would no longer properly be "created" by a law of the United States. See *American Well Works Co. v. Layne & Bowler Co.*, 241 U.S. 257, 260, 36 S.Ct. 585, 586, 60 L.Ed. 987 (1916) (Holmes, J.). Once federal jurisdiction is established by a colorable claim under federal law at a preliminary stage of the proceeding, subsequent dismissal of that claim (here, the claim under the general international proscription of torture) does not deprive the court of jurisdiction previously established. See *Hagans v. Lavine*, 415 U.S. 528, 94 S.Ct. 1372, 39 L.Ed.2d 577 (1974); *Romero v. International Terminal Operating Co.*, 358 U.S. 354, 79 S.Ct. 468, 3 L.Ed.2d 368 (1959); *Bell v. Hood*, 327 U.S. 678, 66 S.Ct. 773, 90 L.Ed. 939 (1946). Cf. *Huynh Thi Ahn, supra*, 586 F.2d at 633 (choice of municipal law ousts s 1350 jurisdiction when no international norms exist).

Pena also argues that "(i)f the conduct complained of is alleged to be the act of the Paraguayan government, the suit is barred by the Act of State doctrine." This argument was not advanced below, and is therefore not before us on this appeal. We note in passing, however, that we doubt whether action by a state official in violation of the Constitution and laws of the Republic of Paraguay, and wholly unratified by that nation's government, could properly be characterized as an act of state. See *Banco Nacionale de Cuba v. Sabbatino, supra*, 376 U.S. 398, 84 S.Ct. 923, 11 L.Ed.2d 804; *Underhill v. Hernandez*, 168 U.S. 250, 18 S.Ct. 83, 42 L.Ed. 456 (1897). Paraguay's renunciation of torture as a legitimate instrument of state policy, however, does not strip the tort of its character as an international law violation, if it in fact occurred under color of government authority. See Declaration on the Protection of All Persons from Being Subjected to Torture, *supra* note 11; cf. *Ex parte Young*, 209 U.S. 123, 28 S.Ct. 441, 52 L.Ed. 714 (1908) (state official subject to suit for constitutional violations despite immunity of state).

Finally, we have already stated that we do not reach the critical question of forum non conveniens, since it was not considered below. In closing, however, we note that the foreign relations implications of this and other issues the district court will be required to adjudicate on remand underscores the wisdom of the First Congress in vesting jurisdiction over such claims in the federal district courts through the Alien Tort Statute. Questions of this nature are fraught with implications for the nation as a whole, and therefore should not be left to the potentially varying adjudications of the courts of the fifty states.

In the twentieth century the international community has come to recognize the common danger posed by the flagrant disregard of basic human rights and particularly the right to be free of torture. Spurred first by the Great War, and then the Second, civilized nations have banded together to prescribe acceptable norms of international behavior. From the ashes of the Second World War arose the United Nations Organization, amid hopes that an era of peace and cooperation had at last begun. Though many of these aspirations have remained elusive goals, that circumstance cannot diminish the true progress that has been made. In the modern age, humanitarian and practical considerations have combined to lead the nations of the world to recognize that respect for fundamental human rights is in their individual and collective interest. Among the rights universally proclaimed by all nations, as we have noted, is the right to be free of physical torture. Indeed, for purposes of civil liability, the torturer has become like the pirate and slave trader before him hostis humani generis, an enemy of all mankind. Our holding today, giving effect to a jurisdictional provision enacted by our First Congress, is a small but important step in the fulfillment of the ageless dream to free all people from brutal violence.

Notes:

1.   Despite the apparent usefulness of the Alien Tort Claims Act for cases against terrorist states, jurisdiction over those states cannot be obtained by virtue of this act alone. In *Argentine Republic v. Amerada Hess Shipping Corp.*, 488 U.S. 428 (1989), the Supreme Court ruled that the Alien Tort Claims Act does not grant jurisdiction over foreign sovereigns independently of the Foreign Sovereign Immunities Act of 1976, 28 U.S.C. §1601 et seq., (FSIA), discussed *infra*, Chapter 3. In that case, the Hercules, an oil tanker owned by a Liberian corporation and chartered by Amerada Hess Corp., another Liberian corporation, was attacked by Argentine military during the Falkland Islands War between Great Britain and Argentina. At the time of the attack, the Hercules was sailing in international waters, outside of the designated "war zones." Following unsuccessful attempts to obtain relief in Argentina, the Liberian corporations resorted to suit in the United States. They sought to obtain jurisdiction under the Alien Tort Claims Act. After the District Court for the Southern District of New York dismissed the claims for lack of subject-matter jurisdiction, ruling that their actions were barred by the FSIA, the corporations appealed to

the United States Court of Appeals for the Second Circuit. The Second Circuit reversed the District Court, finding that the action fell under the purview of the Alien Tort Claims Act because the parties were aliens (Liberian corporations), the action sounded in tort (the bombing of a ship), and it asserted a violation of international law. See *Argentine Republic v. Amerada Hess Shipping Corp.*, 488 U.S. 428, 433 (1989).

The Supreme Court reversed the Second Circuit, holding that the "text and structure of the FSIA demonstrate Congress' intention that the FSIA be the sole basis for obtaining jurisdiction over a foreign state in our courts." *Id.* at 434. The Court reasoned that "Congress' decision to deal comprehensively with the subject of foreign sovereign immunity in the FSIA, and the express provision in §1604 that 'a foreign state shall be immune from the jurisdiction of the courts of the United States and of the States except as provided in sections 1605-1607,' preclude a construction of the Alien Tort Statute that permits the instant suit. See *Red Rock v. Henry*, 106 U.S. 596, 601-602, 1 S.Ct. 434, 438-439, 27 L.Ed. 251 (1883); *United States v. Tynen*, 78 U.S. (11 Wall.) 88, 92, 20 L.Ed. 153 (1871). The Alien Tort Statute by its terms does not distinguish among classes of defendants, and it of course has the same effect after the passage of the FSIA as before with respect to defendants other than foreign states." *Id.* at 438. The court distinguished *Filartiga* by pointing out that in that case, the Paraguayan government was not joined as a defendant.

2.   The Supreme Court had occasion to consider the Alien Tort Claims Act in *Sosa v. Alvarez-Machain*, 542 U.S. 692 (2004), where the Court ruled that the ATCA was solely a jurisdictional statute, and did not give rise to new causes of action. In *Sosa*, a Mexican physician filed suit in the Central District of California against another Mexican national under the Federal Tort Claims Act, 28 U.S.C. §2674, and the ATCA. The case originated out of the capture in Mexico of a Drug Enforcement Administration agent who was tortured over the course of a 2-day interrogation and then murdered. DEA officials believed that Alvarez-Machain, the Mexican physician, was involved in the interrogation and torture. The DEA hired Mexican nationals, including Sosa, to bring Alvarez to the United States from Mexico. Sosa and the others abducted Alvarez, held him overnight in a motel, and brought him to El Paso, Texas, where he was arrested by federal officers. Alvarez went to trial, but the district court granted his motion for a judgment of acquittal. After returning to Mexico, Alvarez filed suit.

Sosa argued that the action under the ATCA should be dismissed because the statute merely provided the court with jurisdiction but did not authorize the courts to recognize any particular right of action without further congressional action. The Supreme Court agreed, holding:

> As enacted in 1789, the ATS gave the district courts "cognizance" of certain causes of action, and the term bespoke a grant of jurisdiction, not power to mold substantive law. See, e.g., The Federalist No. 81, pp. 447, 451 (J. Cooke ed. 1961) (A.Hamilton) (using "jurisdiction" interchangeably with "cognizance"). The fact that the ATS was placed in §9 of the Judiciary Act, a statute otherwise exclusively concerned with federal-court jurisdiction, is itself support for its strictly jurisdictional nature. * * * In sum, we think the statute was intended as jurisdictional in the sense of addressing the power of the courts to entertain cases concerned with a certain subject.

Id. at 713. For a case which followed the holding in *Sosa* on different facts, see *Enahoro v. Abubakar*, 408 F.3d 877 (7th Cir. 2005).

C. Tel-Oren v. Libyan Arab Republic, 726 F.2d 774 (D.C. Cir. 1984)

Before EDWARDS and BORK, Circuit Judges, and ROBB, Senior Circuit Judge.

Concurring opinions filed by Circuit Judge HARRY T. EDWARDS, Circuit Judge BORK, and Senior Circuit Judge ROBB.

EDWARDS, Circuit Judge, concurring:

Plaintiffs in this action, mostly Israeli citizens, are survivors and representatives of persons murdered in an armed attack on a civilian bus in Israel in March 1978. They filed suit for compensatory and punitive damages in the District Court, naming as defendants the Libyan Arab Republic, the Palestine Liberation Organization, the Palestine Information Office, the National Association of Arab Americans, and the Palestine Congress of North America.
* * *

In their complaint, plaintiffs alleged that defendants were responsible for multiple tortious acts in violation of the law of nations, treaties of the United States, and criminal laws of the United States, as well as the common law. Jurisdiction was claimed under four separate statutes: 28 U.S.C. §1331 (federal question jurisdiction); 28 U.S.C. §1332 (diversity jurisdiction); 28 U.S.C. §1350 (providing jurisdiction over actions by an alien alleging a tort commit-

ted in violation of the law of nations or a treaty of the United States); and the Foreign Sovereign Immunities Act of 1976, 28 U.S.C. §§1330, 1602-1611. For purposes of our jurisdictional analysis, we assume plaintiffs' allegations to be true.

The District Court dismissed the action both for lack of subject matter jurisdiction and as barred by the applicable statute of limitations. *Hanoch Tel-Oren v. Libyan Arab Republic*, 517 F.Supp. 542 (D.D.C.1981). Plaintiffs appeal the District Court's rulings on two of their claimed jurisdictional bases, 28 U.S.C. §§1331, 1350, and on the statute of limitations issue.

We affirm the dismissal of this action. Set out below are separate concurring statements of Judge Edwards, Judge Bork, and Senior Judge Robb, indicating different reasons for affirming the result reached by the District Court.

HARRY T. EDWARDS, Circuit Judge, concurring:

This case deals with an area of the law that cries out for clarification by the Supreme Court. We confront at every turn broad and novel questions about the definition and application of the "law of nations." As is obvious from the laborious efforts of opinion writing, the questions posed defy easy answers.

At issue in this case is an aged but little-noticed provision of the First Judiciary Act of 1789, which gives federal courts jurisdiction over a minute class of cases implicating the law of nations. Thus, it is not startling that the central controversy of this action has now produced divided opinions between and within the circuits. The opinions of Judge Bork and Judge Robb are fundamentally at odds with the decision of the Second Circuit in *Filartiga v. Pena-Irala*, 630 F.2d 876 (2d Cir.1980), which, to my mind, is more faithful to the pertinent statutory language and to existing precedent. Although I cannot concur in the opinions of my colleagues, I do agree with them that the decision of the District Court should be affirmed. I write separately to underscore the rationale for my decision; I do this because, as will be apparent, there are sharp differences of viewpoint among the judges who have grappled with these cases over the meaning and application of 28 U.S.C. §1350 (1976).
* * *

My analysis also is limited to the allegations against the Palestine Liberation Organization. I agree with the District Court that the complainants' allegations against the Palestine Information Office and the National Association of Arab Americans are too insubstantial to satisfy the §1350 requirement that a violation of the law of nations be stated. *Hanoch Tel-Oren v. Libyan Arab Republic*, 517 F.Supp. 542, 549 (D.D.C.1981). Jurisdiction over Libya is barred by the Foreign Sovereign Immunities Act, 28 U.S.C. §§1330, 1602-

1611 (1976), which preserves immunity for tort claims unless injury or death occurs in the United States. 28 U.S.C. §§1604, 1605(a)(5) (1976).

I. BACKGROUND

On March 11, 1978, thirteen heavily armed members of the Palestine Liberation Organization (hereinafter "the PLO") turned a day trip into a nightmare for 121 civilian men, women and children. The PLO terrorists landed by boat in Israel and set out on a barbaric rampage along the main highway between Haifa and Tel Aviv. They seized a civilian bus, a taxi, a passing car, and later a second civilian bus. They took the passengers hostage. They tortured them, shot them, wounded them and murdered them. Before the Israeli police could stop the massacre, 22 adults and 12 children were killed, and 73 adults and 14 children were seriously wounded. Most of the victims were Israeli citizens; a few were American and Dutch citizens. They turned to our courts for legal redress and brought this action for damages asserting jurisdiction under 28 U.S.C. §§1331 and 1350 (1976). The District Court dismissed the action for lack of subject matter jurisdiction. The critical issue on appeal is whether plaintiffs alleged sufficient facts to meet the jurisdictional elements of those sections.

II. THE FILARTIGA DECISION

My inquiry into the sufficiency of plaintiffs' allegations is guided by the Second Circuit's decision in *Filartiga*. For reasons set out below, I adhere to the legal principles established in *Filartiga* but find that factual distinctions preclude reliance on that case to find subject matter jurisdiction in the matter now before us. Specifically, I do not believe the law of nations imposes the same responsibility or liability on non-state actors, such as the PLO, as it does on states and persons acting under color of state law. Absent direction from the Supreme Court on the proper scope of the obscure section 1350, I am therefore not prepared to extend *Filartiga's* construction of section 1350 to encompass this case.

The pertinent allegations in *Filartiga* are as follows. Dr. Joel Filartiga, a Paraguayan known to oppose the Paraguayan Stroessner regime, and his daughter, Dolly, alleged that, in 1976, the defendant Pena-Irala, a Paraguayan police official, had kidnapped and tortured to death Dr. Filartiga's 17-year-old son, Joelito. They claimed he was killed in retaliation for his father's political activities. On the day of the murder, Dolly Filartiga was taken to Pena's home and confronted with her brother's body, which bore marks of severe torture. Thereafter, Filartiga commenced a murder ac-

tion against Pena in a Paraguayan court. The action was still pending at the time of the Second Circuit opinion.

Pena entered the United States in 1978 on a visitor's visa and remained beyond the term of the visa, living in Brooklyn, New York. Dolly Filartiga, living in Washington, D.C., learned of his presence and notified the Immigration and Naturalization Service. She also filed a civil complaint against him, alleging that he had wrongfully caused her brother's death by torture and seeking compensatory and punitive damages of ten million dollars. Jurisdiction was claimed under the general federal question provision, 28 U.S.C. §1331 (1976), and under the Alien Tort Statute, 28 U.S.C. §1350 (1976). The District Court dismissed the complaint on jurisdictional grounds. In so doing, the trial court relied on prior cases in which the Second Circuit had defined the "law of nations" to encompass only relationships between states, or an individual and a foreign state, and not a state's treatment of its own citizens. E.g., *Dreyfus v. von Finck*, 534 F.2d 24, 30-31 (2d Cir.), *cert. denied*, 429 U.S. 835, 97 S.Ct. 102, 50 L.Ed.2d 101 (1976); *IIT v. Vencap, Ltd.*, 519 F.2d 1001, 1015 (2d Cir.1975). It concluded that a Paraguayan plaintiff's suit against a Paraguayan defendant did not implicate the law of nations and, therefore, did not fit within the jurisdictional limits of section 1350. The Second Circuit reversed the district court and remanded for further proceedings.

* * *

In the absence of an allegation of a treaty violation, the critical issue in *Filartiga* was whether torture constitutes a violation of the law of nations. In determining that it does, Judge Kaufman reviewed the accepted sources of international law-the usage of nations, judicial opinions and the works of jurists-and concluded that *official torture* of both aliens and citizens is prohibited by the law of nations. 630 F.2d at 884. That section 1350 was enacted in the Judiciary Act of 1789, ch. 20, §9, 1 Stat. 73, 77, when world perceptions both of the role of international law and its substantive provisions differed considerably from perceptions of today, did not preclude this result. Judge Kaufman took guidance from *The Paquete Habana*, 175 U.S. 677, 20 S.Ct. 290, 44 L.Ed. 320 (1900) (holding that the traditional prohibition against seizure of an enemy's coastal fishing vessels had ripened from a standard of comity into a settled rule of international law), and observed that "courts must interpret international law not as it was in 1789, but as it has evolved and exists among the nations of the world today." 630 F.2d at 881.

The opinion thus established several propositions. First, the "law of nations" is not stagnant and should be construed as it exists today among the nations of the world. *Id.* Second, one source of that law is the customs and usages of civilized nations, as articulated by jurists and commentators. *Id.* at 884. Third, international law today places limits on a state's power to torture persons held in custody, and confers "fundamental rights upon all people" to be free from torture. *Id.* at 885. Fourth, section 1350 opens the federal courts for adjudication of the rights already recognized by international law. *Id.* at 887.

Because I am substantially in accord with these four propositions, and Judge Bork and Judge Robb apparently are not, I am unable to join in their opinions.

III. SECTION 1350 AS THE SOURCE OF THE "RIGHT TO SUE"

First, and most fundamentally, I diverge from the views of my colleague Judge Bork regarding the necessary elements of this court's jurisdiction. The Second Circuit did not require plaintiffs to point to a specific right to sue under the law of nations in order to establish jurisdiction under section 1350; rather, the Second Circuit required only a showing that the defendant's actions violated the substantive law of nations. In contrast, Judge Bork would deny jurisdiction to any plaintiff-presumably including those in *Filartiga*-who could not allege a specific right to sue apart from the language of section 1350 itself.

* * *

A. Section 1350 Provides a Right of Action and a Forum: The Filartiga *Formulation*

Judge Bork's suggestion that section 1350 requires plaintiffs to allege a right to sue granted by the law of nations is seriously flawed. Initially, it assumes that the "law of nations" could provide a specific, articulated right to sue in a form other than a treaty or executive agreement. Yet no evidence is offered to indicate that jurists or commentators have ever looked to the law of nations to determine when a wrongful deed is *actionable*. This absence of evidence is not surprising, because it is clear that "[i]nternational law itself, finally, does not require any particular reaction to violations of law…Whether and how the United States wished to react to such violations are domestic questions…" L. HENKIN, FOREIGN AFFAIRS AND THE CONSTITUTION 224 (1972) (footnote omitted).

The law of nations thus permits countries to meet their international duties as they will, see L. HENKIN, R. PUGH, O. SCHACHTER & H. SMIT, INTERNATIONAL LAW 116 (1980); cf. 1 C. HYDE, INTERNATIONAL LAW 729 n. 5 (2d rev. ed. 1945). In some cases, states have undertaken to carry out their obligations in agreed-upon ways, as in a United Nations Genocide Convention, which commits states to make genocide a crime, L. HENKIN, R. PUGH, O. SCHACHTER & H. SMIT, *supra*, or in bilateral or multilateral treaties. Otherwise, states may make available their municipal laws in the manner they consider appropriate. See RESTATEMENT (SECOND) OF FOREIGN RELATIONS LAWW §3 comment h & illustration 5 (1965) (domestic law of a state may provide a remedy to a person injured by a violation of a rule of international law). As a result, the law of nations never has been perceived to create or define the civil actions to be made available by each member of the community of nations; by consensus, the states leave that determination to their respective municipal laws. Indeed, given the existing array of legal systems within the world, a consensus would be virtually impossible to reach-particularly on the technical accoutrements to an action-and it is hard even to imagine that harmony ever would characterize this issue.

In consequence, to require international accord on a right to sue, when in fact the law of nations relegates decisions on such questions to the states themselves, would be to effectively nullify the "law of nations" portion of section 1350. There is a fundamental principle of statutory construction that a statute should not be construed so as to render any part of it "inoperative or superfluous, void or insignificant," 2A C. SANDS, STATUTES AND STATUTORY CONSTRUCTION §46.06 (4th ed. 1973), and there exists a presumption against a construction yielding that result. See *Federal Trade Commission v. Manager, Retail Credit Co., Miami Branch Office*, 515 F.2d 988, 994 (D.C.Cir.1975). Yet, the construction offered by Judge Bork would have the effect of voiding a significant segment of section 1350. [FN2]

FN2. In obvious contrast is a treaty, which may create judicially enforceable obligations when that is the will of the parties to it. See *People of Saipan v. Department of Interior*, 502 F.2d 90, 97 (9th Cir.1974) (elaborating criteria to be used to determine whether international agreement establishes affirmative and judicially enforceable obligations without implementing legislation), *cert. denied*, 420 U.S. 1003, 95 S.Ct. 1445, 43 L.Ed.2d 761 (1975). Unlike the law of nations, which enables each state to make an independent judgment as to the extent and method of enforcing internationally recognized norms, treaties establish both obligations and the extent to which they shall be enforceable.

We therefore must interpret section 1350 in keeping with the fact, well-known to the framers of section 1350, that a treaty and the law of nations are entirely different animals. As Judge Bork states, for two hundred years it has been established that treaties by their terms and context may create enforceable obligations. Similarly, for two hundred years, it has been established that the law of nations leaves up to municipal law whether to provide a right of action to enforce obligations created by the law of nations. Section 1350 opened federal courts to aliens to challenge violations of treaties insofar as treaty terms expressly or impliedly established affirmative and judicially enforceable obligations. Congress also opened courts to aliens to challenge violations of the law of nations, to the extent that the law of nations established a binding obligation. Section 1350 thus provides a forum for actions brought to enforce obligations binding on parties, whether as a result of treaties or the law of nations. To argue that §1350, under any formulation, could create a right to sue or somehow make all treaties self-executing, when parties to the treaties intend otherwise, is to thoroughly misconstrue the nature of treaty law.

Judge Bork argues that the statute retains meaning under his interpretation because he recognizes that the drafters of section 1350 perceived of certain offenses against the law of nations. He enumerates three offenses recognized by Blackstone-violation of safe-conducts, infringement of the rights of ambassadors, and piracy-and insists that these were the offenses that the drafters of section 1350 had in mind. This explanation is specious, not responsive. Judge Bork does nothing more than concede that, in 1789, the law of nations clause covered three substantive offenses. However, under his construction of section 1350, this concession is meaningless unless it is also shown that the law of nations created a private right of action to avenge the three law of nations violations to which Blackstone averted-a showing that would require considerable skill since the law of nations simply does not create rights to sue. Indeed, in the very passage quoted by Judge Bork, Blackstone makes clear that it was the municipal laws of England, not the law of nations, that made the cited crimes offenses: "The principal offenses against the law of nations, *animadverted on as such by the municipal laws of England*, are of three kinds: 1. Violation of safeconducts; 2. Infringement of the rights of embassadors; and, 3. Piracy." 4 BLACKSTONE'S COMMENTARIES 67 (Welsby ed. 1854) (emphasis added). In short, under Judge Bork's construction of the statute, section 1350 would lose virtually all meaning.

Equally basic, to require an express right to sue is directly at odds with the language of the statute, which grants jurisdiction over civil actions for a tort "committed in violation of the law of nations." Unlike section 1331, which requires that an action "arise under" the laws of the United States, section 1350 does not require that the action "arise under" the law of nations, but only mandates a "violation of the law of nations" in order to create a cause of action. * * *

However, for several reasons I believe plaintiffs' claim under §1331 fails as well. My analysis on that issue proceeds on two paths, depending on whether the plaintiff is a citizen or an alien.

As to aliens, most of the plaintiffs here, jurisdiction under §1331 is available at least to the extent that §1350 applies. If it does, their action "arises under" §1350 and, therefore, under a law of the United States, as required by §1331.

Citizens of the United States, in this action the Tel-Oren plaintiffs, do not meet the alienage requirement of §1350 and must seek other law under which their action might arise. The only plausible candidate is the law of nations itself.

Assuming, without deciding, that the law of nations constitutes a law of the United States for §1331 jurisdictional purposes, see Moore, *Federalism and Foreign Relations*, 1965 DUKE L.J. 248, 291-97 (arguing that §1331 includes cases arising under a federal decisional law of foreign relations); cf. L. HENKIN, FOREIGN AFFAIRS AND THE CONSTITUTION 222-23 (1972) (federal courts determine international law and apply it as though it were federal law), the language of §1331, unlike §1350, suggests that plaintiffs must identify a remedy granted by the law of nations or argue successfully for one to be implied. Plaintiffs here are not able to point to a right to sue in international law and I decline to imply one, given my belief, set out *supra*, that the law of nations consciously leaves the provision of rights of action up to the states.

As an alternative basis for declining §1331 jurisdiction, I note that the law of nations quite tenably does not provide these plaintiffs with any substantive right that has been violated. * * * I do not believe that the law of nations, as currently developed and construed, holds individuals responsible for most private acts; it follows logically that the law of nations provides no substantive right to be free from the private acts of individuals, and persons harmed by such acts have no right, under the law of nations, to assert in federal court. Thus, even if the law of nations constitutes a law of the United States, and even if §1331 did not require that a right to sue be granted by the relevant law of the United States, plaintiffs still would have no §1331 jurisdiction because no legal right has been violated.

Indeed, a 1907 opinion of the United States Attorney General suggests just the opposite. It asserts that section 1350 provides both a right to sue and a forum. Responding to an inquiry about the remedies available to Mexican citizens harmed by the actions of an American irrigation company along the Rio Grande River, the Attorney General wrote,

As to indemnity for injuries which may have been caused to citizens of Mexico, I am of opinion that existing statutes *provide a right of action and a forum.* Section 563, Revised Statutes, clause 16, gives to district courts of the United States jurisdiction "of all suits brought by any alien for a tort only in violation of the law of nations or of a treaty of the United States."...*I repeat that the statutes thus provide a forum and a right of action.* I can not, of course, undertake to say whether or not a suit under either of the foregoing statutes would be successful. That would depend upon whether the diversion of the water was an injury to substantial rights of citizens of Mexico under the principles of international law or by treaty, and could only be determined by judicial decision. 26 Op. Att'y Gen. 250, 252-53 (1907) (emphasis added). The opinion bolsters the view of the Second Circuit, [FN5] which I endorse, that section 1350 itself provides a right to sue for alleged violations of the law of nations. * * *

FN5. The Second Circuit read §1350 "not as granting new rights to aliens, but simply as opening the federal courts for adjudication of the rights already recognized by international law." *Filartiga,* 630 F.2d at 887. I construe this phrase to mean that aliens granted substantive rights under international law may assert them under §1350. This conclusion as to the meaning of this crucial yet obscure phrase results in part from the noticeable absence of any discussion in *Filartiga* on the question whether international law granted a right of action.

Judge Bork, in his rejection of *Filartiga,* reasons as follows: (a) international law grants plaintiffs no express right to sue in a municipal court; (b) for numerous reasons, primarily related to separation of powers, it would be inappropriate to imply one; (c) since section 1350 requires that international law give plaintiffs a cause of action, and it does not, we cannot find jurisdiction. In my view, the first two steps in the analysis are irrelevant and the third step is erroneous. The decision in *Filartiga* did not hold that, under section 1350, the law of nations must provide a cause of action-that is, a right to sue-in order to find jurisdiction. The existence of an express or implied cause of action was immaterial to the jurisdictional analysis of the Second Circuit. By focusing on this issue, Judge Bork has skirted the threshold question whether the statute even requires that the law of nations grant a cause of action. I do not believe that the statute requires such a finding, or that the decision in *Filartiga* may be lightly ignored.

At this point, it is appropriate to pause to emphasize the extremely narrow scope of section 1350 jurisdiction un-

der the *Filartiga* formulation. Judge Kaufman characterized the torturer in *Filartiga* as follows: "Indeed, for purposes of civil liability, the torturer has become-like the pirate and slave trader before him- *hostis humani generis,* an enemy of all mankind." *Filartiga,* 630 F.2d at 890. The reference to piracy and slave-trading is not fortuitous. Historically these offenses held a special place in the law of nations: their perpetrators, dubbed enemies of all mankind, were susceptible to prosecution by any nation capturing them. As one writer has explained,

Before International Law in the modern sense of the term was in existence, a pirate was already considered an outlaw, a '*hostis humani generis.*' According to the Law of Nations the act of piracy makes the pirate lose the protection of his home State, and thereby his national character...Piracy is a so-called 'international crime'; the pirate is considered the enemy of every State, and can be brought to justice anywhere.

1 L. OPPENHEIM, INTERNATIONAL LAW §272, at 609 (H. Lauterpacht 8th ed. 1955) (footnote omitted); see also *Id.* §151, at 339 (every state can punish crimes like piracy or slave trade on capture of the criminal, whatever his nationality); Dickinson, *Is the Crime of Piracy Obsolete?,* 38 HARV.L.REV. 334, 335 (1925). Judge Kaufman did not argue that the torturer is like a pirate for criminal prosecution purposes, but only for civil actions. The inference is that persons may be susceptible to civil liability if they commit *either* a crime traditionally warranting universal jurisdiction *or* an offense that comparably violates current norms of international law. To identify such crimes, I look for guidance to the RESTATEMENT OF THE LAW OF FOREIGN RELATIONS (REVISED)))))) §702 (Tent.Draft No. 3, 1982), which enumerates as violations of international law state-practiced, -encouraged or - condoned (a) genocide; (b) slavery or slave trade; (c) the murder or causing the disappearance of individuals; (d) torture or other cruel, inhuman or degrading treatment or punishment; (e) prolonged arbitrary detention; (f) systematic racial discrimination; (g) consistent patterns of gross violations of internationally recognized human rights. See also Blum & Steinhardt, *Federal Jurisdiction over International Human Rights Claims: The Alien Tort Claims Act after Filartiga v. Pena-Irala,* 22 HARV.INT'L L.J. 53, 90 (1981) (focusing on genocide, summary execution, torture and slavery as core human rights violations). I, of course, need not determine whether each of these offenses in fact amounts to a law of nations violation for section 1350 purposes. The point is simply that commentators have begun to identify a handful of heinous actions-each of

which violates definable, universal and obligatory norms, see Blum & Steinhardt, *supra*, at 87-90-and in the process are defining the limits of section 1350's reach. [FN7]

FN7. Indeed, international law itself imposes limits on the extraterritorial jurisdiction that a domestic court may exercise. It generally recognizes five theories of jurisdiction, the objective territorial, national, passive, protective and universal. See RESTATEMENT OF THE LAW OF FOREIGN RELATIONS (REVISED) §402 (Tent.Draft No. 2, 1981); see also *United States v. James-Robinson*, 515 F.Supp. 1340, 1344 n. 6 (S.D.Fla.1981). The premise of universal jurisdiction is that a state "may exercise jurisdiction to define and punish certain offenses recognized by the community of nations as of universal concern," RESTATEMENT OF THE LAW OF FOREIGN RELATIONS (REVISED) , *supra*, §404, even where no other recognized basis of jurisdiction is present.

The *Filartiga* formulation is not flawless, however. While its approach is consistent with the language of section 1350, it places an awesome duty on federal district courts to derive from an amorphous entity- i.e., the "law of nations"- standards of liability applicable in concrete situations. The difficult law of nations questions animating this particular case suggest the burden that would attach to each case of this kind. In the 18th century this pursuit was no doubt facilitated both by a more clearly defined and limited body of "international crimes" than exists today, and by the working familiarity of jurists with that body of law. Although I am convinced that it is possible to discover governing standards of liability, the formidable research task involved gives pause, and suggests consideration of a quite plausible alternative construction of section 1350.

* * *

IV. MEANING OF THE "LAW OF NATIONS"

In addition to our disagreement over the "right to sue" issue, I also have great difficulty in understanding Judge Bork's effort to restrict the scope of section 1350 to the principal offenses against the law of nations recognized centuries ago by Blackstone, see text at notes 2-3, *supra*, instead of construing it in accord with the current definition of the law of nations. While conceding that the legislative history offers no hint of congressional intent in passing the statute, my colleague infers Congress' intent from the law of nations at the time of the passage of section 1350. The result of this analytical approach is to avoid the dictates of *The Paquete Habana* and to limit the "law of nations" language to its

18th century definition. In *The Paquete Habana*, the Supreme Court noted that, in construing the "law of nations,"

where there is no treaty, and no controlling executive or legislative act or judicial decision, resort must be had to the customs and usages of civilized nations, and, as evidence of these, to the works of jurists and commentators, who by years of labor, research and experience, have made themselves peculiarly well acquainted with the subjects of which they treat. Such works are resorted to by judicial tribunals, not for the speculations of their authors concerning what the law ought to be, but for trustworthy evidence of what the law really is.

175 U.S. at 700, 20 S.Ct. at 299. As was pointed out in *Filartiga*,

Habana is particularly instructive for present purposes, for it held that the traditional prohibition against seizure of an enemy's coastal fishing vessels during wartime, a standard that began as one of comity only, had ripened over the preceding century into "a settled rule of international law" by "the general assent of civilized nations." *Id*. at 694, 20 S.Ct. at 297; accord, *Id*. at 686, 20 S.Ct. at 297. Thus it is clear that courts must interpret international law not as it was in 1789, but as it has evolved and exists among the nations of the world today. See *Ware v. Hylton*, 3 U.S. (3 Dall.) 198, 1 L.Ed. 568 (1796) (distinguishing between "ancient" and "modern" law of nations).

630 F.2d at 881.

In light of the evidence at hand, it seems clear beyond cavil that violations of the "law of nations" under section 1350 are not limited to Blackstone's enumerated offenses. Indeed, the Supreme Court stated as much almost a century ago, when it announced that counterfeiting of foreign securities constitutes an offense against the law of nations. See *United States v. Arjona*, 120 U.S. 479, 7 S.Ct. 628, 30 L.Ed. 728 (1887).

V. THE DUTY TO EXERCISE JURISDICTION

To the extent that Judge Bork rejects the *Filartiga* construction of section 1350 because it is contrary to his perception of the appropriate role of courts, I believe he is making a determination better left to Congress. It simply is not the role of a judge to construe a statutory clause out of existence merely on the belief that Congress was ill-advised in passing the statute. If Congress determined that aliens should be permitted to bring actions in federal courts, only Congress is authorized to decide that those actions "exacerbate tensions" and should not be heard.

To be sure, certain judge-made abstention rules, such as the Act of State Doctrine, require courts to decline to reach certain issues in certain instances, notwithstanding a statutory grant of jurisdiction. Where the Act of State Doctrine applies, the Supreme Court has directed the courts not to inquire into the validity of the public acts of a *recognized* foreign sovereign committed *within its own territory. Banco Nacional de Cuba v. Sabbatino*, 376 U.S. 398, 401, 84 S.Ct. 923, 926, 11 L.Ed.2d 804 (1964). The doctrine does *not* require courts to decline jurisdiction, as does the Foreign Sovereign Immunities Act, but only not to reach the merits of certain issues. As Judge Bork admits, the doctrine is not controlling here. Indeed, to apply it at this stage of the case would be to grossly distort the doctrine, first by considering it as a jurisdictional issue, and second, by extending it beyond its carefully limited confines. Unless and until the Supreme Court reconsiders the Act of State Doctrine and applies it as a jurisdictional matter to acts by non-recognized entities committed in the territory of a recognized state, it simply is not relevant to this case.

While not claiming that the Act of State Doctrine controls, Judge Bork looks for guidance toward the concerns that he believes animate it. To ignore the Supreme Court's cautious delineation of the doctrine in *Banco Nacional de Cuba v. Sabbatino* and its progeny, and to cite the doctrine's rationale as broad justification for effectively nullifying a statutory grant of jurisdiction, is, to my view, an inappropriate exercise of lower federal court power. It is particularly so in this case, given the considerable disagreement among the Justices regarding the rationale, scope, and flexibility of the doctrine, see *First National City Bank v. Banco Nacional de Cuba*, 406 U.S. 759, 773-76, 92 S.Ct. 1808, 1816-17, 32 L.Ed.2d 466 (1972) (Powell, J., concurring in judgment), and congressional efforts to override judicial abdication of the kind directed by the Act of State Doctrine. See 22 U.S.C. §2370(e) (1976) (barring judicial invocation of Act of State Doctrine in certain expropriation actions).

My troubles with Judge Bork's efforts to limit the reach of section 1350 go even deeper. Contrary to my colleague's intimations, I do recognize that there are separate branches of Government. In fact, that is precisely my point. I am the first to admit that section 1350 presents difficulties in implementation, but to construe it out of existence on that ground is to usurp Congress' role and contravene its will.

Judge Bork virtually concedes that he is interposing a requirement that the law of nations provide a right to sue simply to void a statute of which he does not approve-and to avoid having to extend and distort existing doctrine on non-

justiciability to reach the same result. As a first step, he sets forth an interpretation of the statute that completely writes out of the statute the clause at issue. The law of nations provides no private right to sue for the only offenses against the law of nations that he recognizes. Under his view, therefore, the clause in the statute had no meaning when passed by Congress and none today. To enforce a construction that yields that result is not only to insult Congress, but inappropriately to place judicial power substantially above that of the legislature.

Logically, of course, under Judge Bork's formulation, were the law of nations ever to provide a right to sue, federal courts would have to hear the cases. To avoid this contingency, Judge Bork adds yet another obstacle, stating that "considerations of justiciability" would, necessarily, come into play in that event. With this remark, Judge Bork virtually concedes that he would keep these cases out of court under any circumstance, and he places himself squarely beside Judge Robb, who advocates dismissal of this action on political question grounds. Vigorously waving in one hand a separation of powers banner, ironically, with the other he rewrites Congress' words and renounces the task that Congress has placed before him.

Most surprisingly, Judge Bork's analysis-and his critique of my own- *completely* overlooks the existence of state courts. Subject to the same constraints that face federal courts, such as personal jurisdiction, and perhaps in some instances to other limitations, such as preemption, state courts could hear many of the common law civil cases, brought by aliens, that Judge Bork believes should not be heard at all. As best we can tell, the aim of section 1350 was to place in federal court actions potentially implicating foreign affairs. The intent was not to provide a forum that otherwise would not exist-as Judge Bork assumes-but to provide an *alternative* forum to state courts. Indeed, the Supreme Court has at least twice cited section 1350 as a statutory example of congressional intent to make questions likely to affect foreign relations originally cognizable in federal courts. See *Banco Nacional de Cuba v. Sabbatino*, 376 U.S. 398, 427 & n. 25, 84 S.Ct. 923, 939 & n. 25, 11 L.Ed.2d 804 (1964); *Ex Parte Quirin*, 317 U.S. 1, 27-30 & n. 6, 63 S.Ct. 1, 10-12 & n. 6, 87 L.Ed. 3 (1942). Not only is it patently indefensible to ignore this mandate. It is also erroneous to assume that the troublesome cases will disappear altogether from state courts, as well as federal, if section 1350 becomes mere historical trivia. In that event, no doubt, my colleagues would either assert nonjusticiability generally or turn the issue on its head and argue, precisely as the section 1350 drafters recognized, that state courts are inappropriate fora for resolution of issues implicating foreign affairs.

VI. LIABILITY OF THE NON-STATE ACTOR UNDER THE LAW OF NATIONS

While I endorse the legal principles set forth in *Filartiga*, I also believe the factual distinctions between this case and the one faced by the Second Circuit mitigate its precedential value in this case. To be sure, the parallels between the two cases are compelling. Here, as in *Filartiga*, plaintiffs and defendants are both aliens. Plaintiffs here allege torture in their complaint, as did plaintiffs in *Filartiga*. [FN20] Here, as in *Filartiga*, the action at issue undoubtedly violated the law of the nation in which it occurred (in this case, the law of Israel). See *Filartiga*, 630 F.2d at 889.

FN20. On the basis of international covenants, agreements and declarations, commentators have identified at least four acts that are now subject to unequivocal international condemnation: torture, summary execution, genocide and slavery. See Blum & Steinhardt, *Federal Jurisdiction over International Human Rights Claims: The Alien Tort Claims Act after Filartiga v. Pena-Irala*, 22 HARV.INT'L L.J. 53, 90 (1981); see also P. SIEGHART, THE INTERNATIONAL LAW OF HUMAN RIGHTS 48 (1983) (cataloguing as recognized international crimes certain war crimes, crimes against humanity, genocide, apartheid and, increasingly, torture). Plaintiffs in this action allege both torture and murder that amounts to summary execution. *Filartiga* accepted the view that official torture in fact amounts to a law of nations violation. Analysis along the same lines would likely yield the conclusion that state-sponsored summary executions are violations as well. However, by definition, summary execution is "murder conducted in uniform," as opposed to lawful, state-imposed violence, Blum & Steinhardt, *supra*, at 95, and would be inapplicable here. See *Id.* at 95-96. Therefore, for purposes of this concurrence, I focus on torture and assume, *arguendo*, that torture amounts to a violation of the law of nations when perpetrated by a state officer. I consider only whether non-state actors may be held to the same behavioral norms as states.

The two fact patterns diverge, however, on the issue of *official torture*. The Palestine Liberation Organization is not a recognized state, and it does not act under color of any recognized state's law. In contrast, the Paraguayan official in *Filartiga* acted under color of state law, although in violation of it. The Second Circuit surveyed the law of nations and concluded that *official torture* constituted a violation. Plaintiffs in the case before us do not allege facts to show that official or state-initiated torture is implicated in this ac-

tion. Nor do I think they could, so long as the PLO is not a recognized member of the community of nations. * * *

I note, however, that it is conceivable that a state not recognized by the United States is a state as defined by international law and therefore bound by international law responsibilities. To qualify as a state under international law, there must be a people, a territory, a government and a capacity to enter into relations with other states. See 3 U.N. SCOR (383d Mtg.) at 9-12, U.N. Doc. S/P.V. 383, pp. 21-35 (1948) (remarks of Professor Philip C. Jessup advocating Israeli membership in the United Nations), quoted in Liang, *Notes on Legal Questions Concerning the United Nations*, 43 AM.J.INT'L L. 288, 300 (1949). Jurisdiction over the territory must be exclusive. G. VON GLAHN, LAW AMONG NATIONS 62 (4th ed. 1981). Even assuming, *arguendo*, that the law of nations obligates unrecognized states that meet this standard, and that §1350's intent was to hold liable even those states the U.S. does not recognize, there is no allegation here that the PLO does or could meet this standard.

A. The Lack of Consensus on Individual Responsibility

The question therefore arises whether to stretch *Filartiga's* reasoning to incorporate torture perpetrated by a party other than a recognized state or one of its officials acting under color of state law. The extension would require this court to venture out of the comfortable realm of established international law-within which *Filartiga* firmly sat-in which states are the actors. [FN22] It would require an assessment of the extent to which international law imposes not only rights but also obligations on individuals. It would require a determination of where to draw a line between persons or groups who are or are not bound by dictates of international law, and what the groups look like. Would terrorists be liable, because numerous international documents recognize their existence and proscribe their acts? See generally R. LILLICH, TRANSNATIONAL TERRORISM: CONVENTIONS AND COMMENTARY (1982) (reprinting numerous international anti-terrorism accords); see also Lauterpacht, *The Subjects of the Law of Nations* (pt. 1), 63 L.Q. REV. 438, 444-45 (discussing international obligations of insurgents). Would all organized political entities be obliged to abide by the law of nations? Would *everybody* be liable? As firmly established as is the core principle binding states to customary international obligations, these fringe areas are only gradually emerging and offer, as of now, no obvious stopping point. Therefore, heeding the warning of the Supreme Court in *Sabbatino*, to wit, "the greater the degree of codification or consensus concerning a particular area of international law, the more appropriate it is for the judiciary to render decisions regarding it," 376 U.S. at 428, 84 S.Ct. at 940. I am not prepared to extend the definition of the "law of nations" absent direction from the Supreme Court. The degree of "codification or consensus" is simply too slight.

FN22. Classical international law was predominantly statist. The law of nations traditionally was defined as "the body of rules and principles of action which are binding *upon civilized states* in their relations with one another." J. BRIERLY, *supra* note 11, at 1 (emphasis added); see also G. VON GLAHN, *supra* note 21, at 61-62; 1 C. HYDE, INTERNATIONAL LAW CHIEFLY AS INTERPRETED AND APPLIED BY THE UNITED STATES §2A, at 4 (2d ed. rev. 1945). Non-state actors could assert their rights against another state only to the extent that their own state adopted their claims, and as a rule they had no recourse against their own government for failure to assist or to turn over any proceeds. 1 C. HYDE, *supra*, §11B, at 36. See also Sohn, *The New International Law: Protection of the Rights of Individuals Rather than States*, 32 AM.U.L.REV. 1, 9 (1982). That the International Court of Justice permits only party-states to appear in cases before the court highlights this outlook. Article 34(1), Statute of the International Court of Justice, *done* June 26, 1945, 59 Stat. 1055, T.S. No. 993, 3 Bevans 1153 (entered into force for United States October 24, 1945).

* * *

Numerous other §1350 actions have been dismissed on jurisdictional grounds for failure to allege a violation of the law of nations, see generally Annot., 34 A.L.R. FED. 388 (1977) (reviewing cases). The most common shortcoming of these actions is in the allegation of a municipally recognized tort, such as fraud, *Trans-Continental Inv. Corp., S.A. v. Bank of Commonwealth*, 500 F.Supp. 565 (C.D.Cal.1980), or libel, *Akbar v. New York Magazine Co.*, 490 F.Supp. 60 (D.D.C.1980), that does not have the stature of a law of nations violation.

B. Historical Evolution of the Role of the Individual in International Law

That the individual's status in international law has been in flux since section 1350 was drafted explains in part the current mix of views about private party liability. Through the 18th century and into the 19th, writers and jurists believed that rules of international law bound individuals as well as states. * * * In the 19th century, the view emerged that states alone were subjects of international law, and they alone were able to assert rights and be held to duties devolved from the law of nations. Under that view-which became firmly en-

trenched both in doctrine and in practice, see Korowicz, *supra*, 50 AM.J.INT'L L. at 535, 541-individual rights existed only as rights of the state, see Lauterpacht, *The Subjects of the Law of Nations (pt. 1)*, 63 L.Q.REV. 438, 439-40 (1947), and could be asserted, defended or withdrawn by the state. *See* P. REMEC, THE POSITION OF THE INDIVIDUAL IN INTERNATIONAL LAW ACCORDING TO GROTIUS AND VATTEL 38 (1960); see also note 22, *supra*.

In this century, once again writers have argued that both the rights and duties of international law should be applied to private parties. See P. REMEC, *supra*, at 8-18; Hill, *International Affairs: The Individual in International Organization*, 28 AM.POL.SCI.REV. 276, 282 & nn. 20-23 (1934) (describing shift from statism and emergence of view that individual is subject of international law); Korowicz, *supra*, 50 AM.J.INT'L L. at 537-39 (observing trend toward recognition of international personality of individuals, especially in their assertion of rights). However, their discussions are more prescriptive than descriptive; they recognize shifts in firmly entrenched doctrine but are unable to define a clear new consensus. And for each article sounding the arrival of individual rights and duties under the law of nations, another surveys the terrain and concludes that there is a long distance to go. See, e.g., Brownlie, *The Place of the Individual in International Law*, 50 VA.L.REV. 435 (1964).

C. Whether Torture, Like Piracy, Is an Exception to the Rule

One strand of individual liability apparently survived the 19th century swing toward statism-private responsibility for piracy. It remained, with only a handful of other private acts, such as slave trading, as a confutation of the general principle of statism. * * *

It is worthwhile to consider, therefore, whether torture today is among the handful of crimes to which the law of nations attributes individual responsibility. Definitions of torture set out in international documents suggest it is not. For example, torture is defined in the Draft Convention on the Elimination of Torture in part as any act "by which severe pain or suffering" is inflicted, "when such pain or suffering is inflicted by or at the instigation of or with the consent or acquiescence of a public official or other person acting in an official capacity." Report of the Working Group on a Draft Convention against Torture and Other Cruel, Inhuman or Degrading Treatment or Punishment (E/CN.4/L 1576) of 6 March 1981, reprinted in P. SIEGHART, *supra* note 20, §14.3.5, at 162. Similarly, the United Nations General Assembly definition requires that the actor be "a public official." See Declaration on the Protection of All Persons from Being Subjected to Torture and Other Cruel, Inhuman or Degrading Treatment or Punishment, G.A.Res. 3452, 30 U.N.GAOR Supp. (No. 34) at 91-92, U.N.Doc. A/10034 (1975), reprinted in P. SIEGHART, *supra* note 20, §14.3.5, at 162. See also Blum & Steinhardt, *supra* note 20, at 93, 95-96. Against this background, I do not believe the consensus on non-official torture warrants an extension of *Filartiga*. While I have little doubt that the trend in international law is toward a more expansive allocation of rights and obligations to entities other than states, I decline to read section 1350 to cover torture by non-state actors, absent guidance from the Supreme Court on the statute's usage of the term "law of nations."

VII. TERRORISM AS A LAW OF NATIONS VIOLATION

I turn next to consider whether terrorism is itself a law of nations violation. [FN25] While this nation unequivocally condemns all terrorist attacks, that sentiment is not universal. Indeed, the nations of the world are so divisively split on the legitimacy of such aggression as to make it impossible to pinpoint an area of harmony or consensus. Unlike the issue of individual responsibility, which much of the world has never even reached, terrorism has evoked strident reactions and sparked strong alliances among numerous states. Given this division, I do not believe that under current law terrorist attacks amount to law of nations violations.

FN25. At least one law review note has suggested that we decide this case in favor of plaintiffs by identifying terrorism as a law of nations violation. See Note, *Terrorism as a Tort in Violation of the Law of Nations*, 6 FORDHAM INT'L L.J. 236 (1982).

To witness the split one need only look at documents of the United Nations. They demonstrate that to some states acts of terrorism, in particular those with political motives, are legitimate acts of aggression and therefore immune from condemnation. For example, a resolution entitled "Basic principles of the legal status of the combatants struggling against colonial and alien domination and racist regimes," G.A.Res. 3103, 28 U.N. GAOR at 512, U.N.Doc. A/9102 (1973), declared:

The struggle of peoples under colonial and alien domination and racist regimes for the implementation of their right to self-determination and independence is legitimate and in full accordance with the principles of international law.

It continued that armed conflicts involving such struggles have the full legal status of international armed conflicts, and that violation of that status "entails full responsibility in accordance with norms of international law." *Id.* at 513. See also Definition of Aggression, G.A.Res. 3314, 29 GAOR Supp. (No. 31) at 142-44, U.N.Doc. A/9631 (1974) (nothing in definition of term "aggression" should prejudice right of self-determination or struggle, particularly of peoples under "colonial and racist regimes or other forms of alien domination"). In contrast, there is of course authority in various documents and international conventions for the view that terrorism is an international crime. Many Western nations condemn terrorist acts, either generally, as in the Convention to Prevent and Punish the Acts of Terrorism Taking the Forms of Crime Against Persons and Related Extortion That Are of International Significance, * * * or with reference to particular terrorist acts, as in the International Convention Against the Taking of Hostages, * * * or the Hague Convention on the Suppression of Unlawful Seizure of Aircraft. * * * See also R. FRIEDLANDER, TERROR-VIOLENCE: ASPECTS OF SOCIAL CONTROL 38 (1983) (describing the international division on the legitimacy of terrorist acts); see generally R. LILLICH, TRANSNATIONAL TERRORISM: CONVENTIONS AND COMMENTARY (1982).

The divergence as to basic norms of course reflects a basic disagreement as to legitimate political goals and the proper method of attainment. Given such disharmony, I cannot conclude that the law of nations-which, we must recall, is defined as the principles and rules that states feel themselves bound to observe, and do commonly observe * * * -outlaws politically motivated terrorism, no matter how repugnant it might be to our own legal system.

VIII. MY COLLEAGUES' OPINIONS

My colleague Judge Robb argues that this case is a nonjusticiable "political question" and that it therefore was properly dismissed. With all due respect, I disagree with this approach to appellate adjudication. A judge should not retreat under facile labels of abstention or nonjusticiability, such as the "political question doctrine," merely because a statute is ambiguous. In the words of one eminent jurist, "*[o]bscurity of statute* or of precedent or of customs or of morals, or collision between some or all of them, may leave the law unsettled, and *cast a duty upon the courts to declare it* retrospectively in the exercise of a power frankly legislative in function." B. CARDOZO, THE NATURE OF THE JUDICIAL PROCESS 128 (1921) (emphasis added). Or, as another jurist framed the issue, "The intrinsic difficulties of language and the emergence after enactment of situations not anticipated by the most gifted legislative imagination, reveal doubts and ambiguities in statutes that compel judicial construction." Frankfurter, *Some Reflections on the Reading of Statutes*, 47 COLUM.L.REV. 527, 529 (1947).

Nonjusticiability based upon "political question" is *at best a limited* doctrine, and it is wholly inapposite to this case. In *Baker v. Carr*, 369 U.S. 186, 82 S.Ct. 691, 7 L.Ed.2d 663 (1962), the Supreme Court held that the question whether a state legislative district apportionment plan violates the Constitution is not a political question and therefore not nonjusticiable. In so doing, the Court rejected the notion that the doctrine rendered nonjusticiable all "political cases"-a doctrine advanced by Justice Frankfurter writing for a plurality of the Court in *Colegrove v. Green*, 328 U.S. 549, 66 S.Ct. 1198, 90 L.Ed. 1432 (1946). Instead, it observed, the nonjusticiability of a question is "essentially a function of the separation of powers." 369 U.S. at 217, 82 S.Ct. at 710. * * * The opinion also observed that the doctrine in no respect requires that all questions implicating foreign affairs be ruled political questions. *Id.* at 211, 82 S.Ct. at 706.

* * *

Initially, the action before us does not implicate separation of powers principles, and therefore is not even related to the central concern of the political question doctrine. See *Baker v. Carr*, 369 U.S. at 210, 217, 82 S.Ct. at 706, 710. We have here no clash between two branches of government that requires us to resolve the apportionment of power between them. Nor do we potentially transgress by reviewing any exercise of authority by another branch of government, much less one committed to another branch by the Constitution. Far from it, in fact; in implementing section 1350, courts merely carry out the existing view of the legislature that federal courts should entertain certain actions that implicate the law of nations. * * * Moreover, none of the categories identified in *Baker* is applicable here. We do not lack judicially discoverable and manageable standards. The parties do not invoke constitutional or statutory provisions that resist judicial application. The Supreme Court, in *The Paquete Habana*, explicitly acceded to the task of applying the law of nations and instructed lower courts on how to approach the task of discovering it. I therefore can hardly conclude that courts *lack* the means of determining what standards to apply. That the task might be difficult should in no way lead to the conclusion that it should not be accomplished. Nor do I believe either that any of the other concerns in *Baker* arise here. * * *

The doctrine applies only to judicial review of the acts of *recognized* foreign governments committed *within their own territory*. See *Banco Nacional de Cuba v. Sabbatino*, 376 U.S. 398, 428, 84 S.Ct. 923, 940, 11 L.Ed.2d 804 (1964). It is, in effect, a doctrine of deference, requiring that courts not second-guess the judgments of such sovereigns in a category of contexts. When a §1350 action implicates such action by a recognized sovereign, the Act of State Doctrine might bar further inquiry. Such is not the case here. Similarly, the Foreign Sovereign Immunities Act restrains courts from asserting jurisdiction, but, again, only to the extent Congress has deemed appropriate. Considering that the Supreme Court-in the Act of State Doctrine-and the Congress-in the Foreign Sovereign Immunities Act-have each delimited the scope of necessary judicial restraint in cases involving foreign affairs, I am not inclined to fashion yet another doctrine of nonjusticiability simply because this case, and the intricacies of the law of nations, are not of easy resolution or implicate foreign affairs generally.

* * *

It is therefore clear that the political question doctrine is a very limited basis for nonjusticiability. It certainly does not provide the judiciary with a carte blanche license to block the adjudication of difficult or controversial cases. And the doctrine surely may not be employed here to vitiate section 1350.

I decline to address further Judge Bork's critique of my opinion. He has completely misread my opinion to say that the primary purpose of section 1350 was to authorize courts to "regulate the conduct of other nations and individuals abroad, conduct without an effect upon the interests of the United States." I only wish the issues posed were so simple. Judge Bork seriously distorts my basic premises and ignores my expressed reservations. Accordingly, I prefer to let this opinion speak for itself, in the belief that it belies my colleague's mischaracterizations, and that any further exposition would be redundant.

IX. CONCLUSION

In light of the foregoing, I conclude that the appellants have not, and could not, allege facts sufficient to remain in court under existing precedent. I therefore vote to affirm the District Court's dismissal for lack of subject matter jurisdiction.

BORK, Circuit Judge, concurring:
* * *

We agree that the complaint must be dismissed, although our reasons for agreement differ. I believe, as did the district court, that, in the circumstances presented here, appellants have failed to state a cause of action sufficient to support jurisdiction under either of the statutes on which they rely. 28 U.S.C. §§1331, 1350 (1976 & Supp. V 1981).

* * * Neither the law of nations nor any of the relevant treaties provides a cause of action that appellants may assert in courts of the United States. Furthermore, we should not, in an area such as this, infer a cause of action not explicitly given. In reaching this latter conclusion, I am guided chiefly by separation of powers principles, which caution courts to avoid potential interference with the political branches' conduct of foreign relations.

I.

* * *

In this appeal, appellants agree with the district court that, for purposes of the issues raised in this case, the jurisdictional requirements of sections 1331 and 1350 are the same. See Brief for Appellants at 35-36; 517 F.Supp. at 549 n. 2 ("[P]laintiffs themselves recognize that the jurisdictional bases of §1331 and §1350 are identical as to the role of the law of nations."). Contrary to the holding of the district court, however, they contend that at least some of the treaties they cite in their complaint impliedly provide private rights of action for the claims in Count III and that federal common law provides private rights of action for the claims in Count II. Thus, appellants argue, section 1350 gives jurisdiction over the claims of the alien plaintiffs and section 1331 gives jurisdiction over the claims of all the plaintiffs, including those who are United States citizens. [FN6]

FN6. The Tel-Oren plaintiffs are citizens of the United States, and the Drory plaintiffs are citizens of the Netherlands. The other plaintiffs are citizens of Israel. All the plaintiffs reside in Israel.

For the reasons given below, appellants' contentions must be rejected. I first consider separation of powers principles that counsel courts, in a case like this, not to infer any cause of action not expressly granted. I then show that the treaties on which appellants rely create no private causes of action. Turning next to appellants' claim under general principles of international law, I conclude that federal common law does not automatically accord appellants a cause of action and that appellants have not been granted a cause of action by federal statute or by international law itself. Finally, in order to clarify what I believe we should and should not have decided, I discuss the recent decision of the Second Circuit in *Filartiga v. Pena-Irala*, 630 F.2d 876 (2d Cir.1980), a case having some similarities to this one.

II.

The question in this case is whether appellants have a cause of action in courts of the United States for injuries they suffered in Israel. Judge Edwards contends, and the Second Circuit in *Filartiga* assumed, that Congress' grant of jurisdiction also created a cause of action. That seems to me fundamentally wrong and certain to produce pernicious results. For reasons I will develop, it is essential that there be an explicit grant of a cause of action before a private plaintiff be allowed to enforce principles of international law in a federal tribunal. It will be seen below, however, that no body of law expressly grants appellants a cause of action; the relevant inquiry, therefore, is whether a cause of action is to be inferred. That inquiry is guided by general principles that apply whenever a court of the United States is asked to act in a field in which its judgment would necessarily affect the foreign policy interests of the nation.

The Supreme Court explained in *Davis v. Passman*, 442 U.S. 228, 99 S.Ct. 2264, 60 L.Ed.2d 846 (1979), that to ask whether a particular plaintiff has a cause of action is to ask whether he "is a member of the class of litigants that may, as a matter of law, appropriately invoke the power of the court." *Id.* at 240 n. 18, 99 S.Ct. at 2274 n. 18. The Court said that the "question of who may enforce a *statutory* right is fundamentally different from the question of who may enforce a right that is protected by the Constitution." *Id.* at 241, 99 S.Ct. at 2275 (emphasis in original). * * *

This case presents a question not covered by the analyses described by the *Davis* Court for statutory and constitutional causes of action. An analysis of the appropriateness of providing appellants with a cause of action must take into account the concerns that are inherent in and peculiar to the field of international relations. My assessment of those concerns leads me to a conclusion different from that reached in *Davis*, for here there appear to be "special factors counselling hesitation in the absence of affirmative action by Congress." *Bivens v. Six Unknown Named Agents of Federal Bureau of Narcotics*, 403 U.S. 388, 396, 91 S.Ct. 1999, 2004, 29 L.Ed.2d 619 (1971). The factors counselling hesitation are constitutional; they derive from principles of separation of powers.

The crucial element of the doctrine of separation of powers in this case is the principle that "[t]he conduct of the foreign relations of our Government is committed by the Constitution to the Executive and Legislative-'the political'-Departments." *Oetjen v. Central Leather Co.*, 246 U.S. 297,

302, 38 S.Ct. 309, 311, 62 L.Ed. 726 (1918). That principle has been translated into a limitation on judicial power in the international law area principally through the act of state and political question doctrines. Whether or not this case falls within one of these categories, the concerns that underlie them are present and demand recognition here.

"The act of state doctrine in its traditional formulation precludes the courts from inquiring into the validity of the public acts a recognized foreign sovereign power committed within its own territory." *Banco Nacional de Cuba v. Sabbatino*, 376 U.S. 398, 401, 84 S.Ct. 923, 926, 11 L.Ed.2d 804 (1964). Originally, the doctrine rested primarily on notions of sovereignty and comity. See *Underhill v. Hernandez*, 168 U.S. 250, 252, 18 S.Ct. 83, 84, 42 L.Ed. 456 (1897). In more recent formulations, there has been "a shift in focus from the notions of sovereignty and the dignity of independent nations...to concerns for preserving the 'basic relationships between branches of government in a system of separation of powers,' and not hindering the executive's conduct of foreign policy by judicial review or oversight of foreign acts." *Mannington Mills, Inc. v. Congoleum Corp.*, 595 F.2d 1287, 1292 (3d Cir.1979) (quoting *Sabbatino*, 376 U.S. at 423, 84 S.Ct. at 937).

* * *

Prominent on the surface of any case held to involve a political question is found a textually demonstrable constitutional commitment of the issue to a coordinate political department; or a lack of judicially discoverable and manageable standards for resolving it; or the impossibility of deciding without an initial policy determination of a kind clearly for nonjudicial discretion; or the impossibility of a court's undertaking independent resolution without expressing lack of the respect due coordinate branches of government; or an unusual need for unquestioning adherence to a political decision already made; or the potentiality of embarrassment from multifarious pronouncements by various departments on one question.

Questions touching on the foreign relations of the United States make up what is likely the largest class of questions to which the political question doctrine has been applied. * * * If it were necessary, I might well hold that the political question doctrine bars this lawsuit, since it is arguable, as much of the remainder of this opinion will show, that this case fits several of the categories listed in *Baker v. Carr*. Such a determination is not necessary, however, because many of the same considerations that govern application of the political question doctrine also govern the question of the appropriateness of providing appellants with a cause of action. * * *

I do not conceive that, in a case like this, the political question doctrine must be considered first because it is juris-dictional. The jurisdictional aspect of that doctrine extends no further than its rationale: to prevent courts from reaching the merits of issues that, for a variety of reasons, are not theirs to decide. *Baker v. Carr*, 369 U.S. at 217, 82 S.Ct. at 710. By deciding that there is no private cause of action here we do not reach substantive issues that are best decided by the political branches. It may be, moreover, that while the existence of a cause of action is not a jurisdictional issue in the ordinary case, it is, or is closely akin, to a jurisdictional issue when its decision implicates, as here, considerations linked to the proper exercise of the judicial power granted by Article III of the Constitution. It is probably better not to invoke the political question doctrine in this case. That the contours of the doctrine are murky and unsettled is shown by the lack of consensus about its meaning among the members of the Supreme Court, see *Goldwater v. Carter*, 444 U.S. 996, 100 S.Ct. 533, 62 L.Ed.2d 428 (1979), and among scholars, see, e.g., Henkin, *Is There A "Political Question" Doctrine?*, 85 Yale L.J. 597, 622-23 (1976). Given this situation, I would rather not decide whether a political question is involved in a case where that issue has not been briefed and argued. By contrast, the grounds upon which I do decide were thoroughly explored through vigorous adversarial presentations.

Neither is there a need to consider whether the act of state doctrine applies to bar this case from going forward. Although the act of state doctrine might well apply to Libya's alleged role in the 1978 bus attack, it would seem not to apply, in its current formulation, to the alleged acts of the PLO, the PIO, and the NAAA, none of which would seem to be a state under international law.

* * *

There is no need to decide here under what circumstances considerations such as these might deprive an individual of a cause of action clearly given by a state, by Congress, by a treaty, or by international law. In the absence of such a cause of action, they lead to the conclusion that adjudication of appellants' claims would present grave separation of powers problems. It is therefore inappropriate to recognize a cause of action allowing appellants to bring this suit.

* * *

The potential for interference with foreign relations is not diminished by the PLO's apparent lack of international law status as a state. Nor does it matter whether the Executive Branch officially recognizes, or has direct dealings with, the PLO. The fact remains that the PLO bears significantly upon the foreign relations of the United States. If any indication of that role is needed, it is provided by the official "observer" status that the PLO has been accorded at the United Nations, G.A.Res. 3237, 29 U.N.GAOR Supp. (No. 31) at

4, U.N.Doc. A/9631 (1974), as well as by the diplomatic relations that the PLO is reported to have with some one hundred countries around the world, see Kassim, *supra*, 9 Den.J.Int'l L. & Pol'y at 19; Friedlander, *The PLO and the Rule of Law: A Reply to Dr. Anis Kassim*, 10 Den.J.Int'l L. & Pol'y 221, 232 (1981).

The nature of appellants' international law claims provides a further reason for reluctance to recognize a cause of action for appellants. Adjudication of those claims would require the analysis of international legal principles that are anything but clearly defined and that are the subject of controversy touching "sharply on national nerves." *Banco Nacional de Cuba v. Sabbatino*, 376 U.S. at 428, 84 S.Ct. at 940. The *Sabbatino* Court warned against adjudication of such international law issues. *Id.* Because I believe that judicial pronouncements on the merits of this case should be avoided, I mention only briefly some of the difficulties raised by some of the claims in appellants' complaint.

Appellants would have to argue, if their case were adjudicated, for an exception to the general rule that international law imposes duties only on states and on their agents or officials. See L. Henkin, R. Pugh, O. Schachter & H. Smit, *International Law*, 246-47 (1980); *Restatement of the Foreign Relations Law of the United States (Revised)* §101, at 21 (Tent.Draft No. 1, 1980) (" 'International law'…deals with the conduct of states and international organizations, and with their relations inter se, as well as some of their relations with persons, whether natural or juridical."); *Id.* §§701-722, at 137-257 (Tent.Draft No. 3, 1982) (stating international law protections of persons solely in terms of state obligations).

* * *

Another difficulty presented by appellants' complaint is that some of the documents on which they rely as statements of customary principles of international law expressly make the purposes of an action relevant to its unlawfulness. For example, appellants allege that appellees violated the proscription, in article 51 of the Protocol I of the Geneva Conventions of 12 August 1949, on "[a]cts or threats of violence the primary purpose of which is to spread terror among the civilian population." They also allege that appellees violated the proscription on genocide, defined in the Convention on the Prevention and Punishment of the Crime of Genocide, Dec. 9, 1948, 78 U.N.T.S. 277, to mean acts calculated to bring about the physical destruction, in whole or in part, of a national, ethnic, racial, or religious group. Adjudication of these claims would require inquiry into the PLO's intention in planning the 1978 bus attack (assuming the PLO's involvement) and into the organizational goals of the PLO. The dangers of such inquiry into the intentions of the PLO

are similar to those attending an inquiry into the intentions of a state. See *Hunt v. Mobil Oil Corp.*, 550 F.2d at 77 (act of state doctrine bars inquiry into Libya's motivation for actions: "Inquiry could only be fissiparous, hindering or embarrassing the conduct of foreign relations which is the very reason underlying the policy of judicial abstention…").

In addition, appellants' principal claim, that appellees violated customary principles of international law against terrorism, concerns an area of international law in which there is little or no consensus and in which the disagreements concern politically sensitive issues that are especially prominent in the foreign relations problems of the Middle East. * * [N]o consensus has developed on how properly to define "terrorism" generally. G. von Glahn, *Law Among Nations* 303 (4th ed. 1981). As a consequence, " '[i]nternational law and the rules of warfare as they now exist are inadequate to cope with this new mode of conflict.' " *Transnational Terrorism: Conventions and Commentary* xv (R. Lillich ed. 1982) (quoting Jenkins, International Terrorism: A New Mode of Conflict 16 (California Seminar on Arms Control and Foreign Policy, Research Paper No. 48, 1975)). "The dismal truth is that the international community has dealt with terrorism ambivalently and ineffectually." Shestack, *Of Private and State Terror-Some Preliminary Observations*, 13 Rutgers L.J. 453, 463 (1982).

Customary international law may well forbid states from aiding terrorist attacks on neighboring states. See Lillich & Paxman, *State Responsibility for Injuries to Aliens Occasioned by Terrorist Activities*, 26 Am.U.L.Rev. 217, 251-76 (1977). Although that principle might apply in a case like this to a state such as Libya (which is not a proper party here, see *supra* note 13), it does not, at least on its face, apply to a nonstate like the PLO. More important, there is less than universal consensus about whether PLO-sponsored attacks on Israel are lawful. * * *

There is, of course, no occasion here to state what international law should be. Nor is there a need to consider whether an extended and discriminating analysis might plausibly maintain that customary international law prohibits the actions alleged in the complaint. It is enough to observe that there is sufficient controversy of a politically sensitive nature about the content of any relevant international legal principles that litigation of appellants' claims would present, in acute form, many of the problems that the separation of powers principles inherent in the act of state and political question doctrines caution courts to avoid. The lack of clarity in, and absence of consensus about, the legal principles invoked by appellants, together with the political context of the challenged actions and the PLO's impingement upon American foreign relations, lead to the conclusion that appellants' case is not the sort that is appropriate for federal-court adjudication, at least not without an express grant of a cause of action.

I turn next to examine treaties, common law, congressional enactments, and customary international law to determine whether any of these sources of law provides a cause of action for appellants. In light of what has been said, it would require a very clear showing that these other bodies of law grant appellants a cause of action before my concerns about the principles of separation of powers could be overcome. But, as will be seen, there is no clear grant of a cause of action to be found. In truth, the law concerning treaties and customary international law of its own force appears actually to deny appellants any cause of action.

III.

Treaties of the United States, though the law of the land, do not generally create rights that are privately enforceable in courts. *Foster v. Neilson*, 27 U.S. (2 Pet.) 253, 314, 7 L.Ed. 415 (1829), *overruled on other grounds*, *United States v. Percheman*, 32 U.S. (7 Pet.) 51, 8 L.Ed. 604 (1883); *Canadian Transport Co. v. United States*, 663 F.2d 1081, 1092 (D.C.Cir.1980); *Dreyfus v. Von Finck*, 534 F.2d 24, 29-30 (2d Cir.), *cert. denied*, 429 U.S. 835, 97 S.Ct. 102, 50 L.Ed.2d 101 (1976). Absent authorizing legislation, an individual has access to courts for enforcement of a treaty's provisions only when the treaty is self-executing, that is, when it expressly or impliedly provides a private right of action. *Head Money Cases*, 112 U.S. 580, 598-99, 5 S.Ct. 247, 253-54, 28 L.Ed. 798 (1884); *Z&F Assets Realization Corp. v. Hull*, 114 F.2d 464, 470-71 (D.C.Cir.1940), *aff'd on other grounds*, 311 U.S. 470, 489, 61 S.Ct. 351, 355, 85 L.Ed. 288 (1941); *Mannington Mills, Inc. v. Congoleum Corp.*, 595 F.2d at 1298. When no right is explicitly stated, courts look to the treaty as a whole to determine whether it evidences an intent to provide a private right of action. See *Diggs v. Richardson*, 555 F.2d 848, 851 (D.C.Cir.1976).

In Count III of the complaint, appellants alleged that defendants violated the following "treaties of the United States":

-Geneva Convention Relative to the Protection of Civilian Persons in Time of War, Aug. 12, 1949, 6 U.S.T. 3516, T.I.A.S. No. 3365, 75 U.N.T.S. 287;

-Articles 1 and 2 of the Charter of the United Nations, June 26, 1945, 59 Stat. 1031, T.S. No. 993;

-Convention With Respect to the Laws and Customs of War on Land, July 29, 1899, 32 Stat. 1803, T.S. No. 403; Convention Respecting the Laws and Customs of War on Land, Oct. 18, 1907, 36 Stat. 2277, T.S. No. 539 (Hague Conventions);

-Geneva Convention Relative to the Treatment of Prisoners of War, Aug. 12, 1949, 6 U.S.T. 3316, T.I.A.S. 3364, 75 U.N.T.S. 135;

-Convention to Prevent and Punish the Acts of Terrorism Taking the Forms of Crime Against Persons and Related Extortion That Are of International Significance, Feb. 2, 1971, 27 U.S.T. 3949, T.I.A.S. No. 8413 (Organization of American States (OAS) Convention);

-Protocols I and II to the Geneva Conventions of 12 August 1949, June 7, 1977, Diplomatic Conference on Reaffirmation and Development of International Humanitarian Law Applicable in Armed Conflict, reprinted in 16 I.L.M. 1391, 1442 (1977);

-Declaration on Principles of International Law Concerning Friendly Relations and Co-operation Among States in Accordance with the Charter of the United Nations, G.A.Res. 2625, 25 U.N.GAOR Supp. (No. 28) at 121, U.N.Doc. A/8028 (1970);

-Universal Declaration of Human Rights, G.A.Res. 217, U.N. 3 GAOR, U.N.Doc. 1/777 (1948);

-International Covenant on Civil and Political Rights, Annex to G.A.Res. 2200, 21 U.N.GAOR Supp. (No. 16) at 52, U.N.Doc. A/6316 (1966);

-Basic Principles for the Protection of Civilian Populations in Armed Conflicts, G.A.Res. 2675, 25 U.N.GAOR Supp. (No. 28) at 76, U.N.Doc A/8028 (1970);

-Convention on the Prevention and Punishment of the Crime and Genocide, Dec. 9, 1948, 78 U.N.T.S. 277;

-Declaration of the Rights of the Child, G.A.Res. 1386, 14 U.N.GAOR Supp. (No. 16) at 19, U.N. Doc. A/4354 (1959); and

-American Convention on Human Rights, Nov. 22, 1969, O.A.S. Official Records OEA/Ser. K/XVI/1.1, Doc. 65, Rev. 1, Corr. 1, reprinted in 9 I.L.M. 101 (1970), 65 Am.J.Int'l L. 679 (1971).

Only the first five of these alleged treaties are treaties currently binding on the United States. See Treaties Affairs Staff, Office of the Legal Adviser, Department of State, *Treaties in Force* (1983). Even if the remaining eight are relevant to Count II of the complaint as evidence of principles of international law, they are not treaties of the United States. Since Count III (tortious actions in violation of the treaties of the United States) purports to state a cause of action distinct from that stated in Count II (tortious actions in violation of the law of nations), the last eight of the thirteen alleged treaties of the United States can provide no basis for jurisdiction over the claims in Count III under the treaty components of sections 1331 and 1350.

Of the five treaties in force, none provides a private right of action. Three of them-the Geneva Convention for the Protection of Civilian Persons in Time of War, the Geneva Convention Relative to the Treatment of Prisoners of War, and the OAS Convention to Prevent and Punish Acts of Terrorism-expressly call for implementing legislation. A treaty that provides that party states will take measures through their own laws to enforce its proscriptions evidences its intent not to be self-executing. See *Foster v. Neilson*, 27 U.S. (2 Pet.) at 311-14, 7 L.Ed. 415; *United States v. Postal*, 589 F.2d 862, 876-77 (5th Cir.), *cert. denied*, 444 U.S. 832, 100 S.Ct. 61, 62 L.Ed.2d 40 (1979). These three treaties are therefore not self-executing. Indeed, with respect to the first Geneva Convention, one court has already so held. *Huynh Thi Anh v. Levi*, 586 F.2d 625, 629 (6th Cir.1978).

Articles 1 and 2 of the United Nations Charter are likewise not self-executing. They do not speak in terms of individual rights but impose obligations on nations and on the United Nations itself. They address states, calling on them to fulfill in good faith their obligations as members of the United Nations. Sanctions under article 41, the penultimate bulwark of the Charter, are to be taken by states against other states. Articles 1 and 2, moreover, contain general "purposes and principles," some of which state mere aspirations and none of which can sensibly be thought to have been intended to be judicially enforceable at the behest of individuals. * * * These considerations compel the conclusion that articles 1 and 2 of the U.N. Charter were not intended to give individuals the right to enforce them in municipal courts, particularly since appellants have provided no evidence of a contrary intent. * * *

The Hague Conventions similarly cannot be construed to afford individuals the right to judicial enforcement. Although the Conventions contain no language calling for implementing legislation, they have never been regarded as law private parties could enforce. * * *

None of the five treaties relied on by appellants thus even impliedly grants individuals the right to seek damages for violation of their provisions. Appellants have, therefore, failed to state a cause of action for violation of any treaties of the United States. Count III of their complaint, consequently, does not come within the arising-under jurisdiction of section 1331. Nor does it come within section 1350, because this provision, like section 1331, is merely a jurisdiction-granting statute and not the implementing legislation required by non-self-executing treaties to enable individuals to enforce their provisions. See *Dreyfus v. Von Finck*, 534 F.2d at 28 (affirming dismissal for lack of cause of action under treaties in suit by alien where jurisdiction expressly based on sections 1331 and 1350). * * *

IV.

Appellants' argument that they may recover damages for violations of international law is simple. International law, they point out, is part of the common law of the United States. This proposition is unexceptionable. See, e.g., *The Paquete Habana*, 175 U.S. 677, 20 S.Ct. 290, 44 L.Ed. 320 (1900); *United States v. Smith*, 18 U.S. (5 Wheat.) 153, 5 L.Ed. 57 (1820). But appellants then contend that federal common law automatically provides a cause of action for international law violations, as it would for violations of other federal common law rights. I cannot accept this conclusion. * * *

Thus, the step appellants would have us take-from the phrase "common law" to the implication of a cause of action-is not a simple and automatic one. Neither is it advisable. The considerations of separation of powers rehearsed above provide ample reason for refusing to take a step that would plunge federal courts into the foreign affairs of the United States.
* * *

First, appellants' broad reading would have to apply equally to actions brought to recover damages for torts committed in violation of treaties, since treaties stand in exactly the same position in section 1350 as principles of customary international law (the law of nations). Such an application would render meaningless, for alien plaintiffs, the well-established rule that treaties that provide no cause of action cannot be sued on without (express or implied) federal law authorization. See *supra* p. 784.

Judge Edwards' approach, as well as the analysis of the Second Circuit in *Filartiga*, would also make all United States treaties effectively self-executing. As appellants here seek evidence of a cause of action to vindicate an asserted international law right that they do not assert itself affords them a private right of action, their claim is indistinguishable, under the language of section 1350, from a claim brought to vindicate rights set forth in a non-self-executing treaty.

In addition, appellants' construction of section 1350 is too sweeping. It would authorize tort suits for the vindication of any international legal right. * * * [T]hat result would be inconsistent with the severe limitations on individually initiated enforcement inherent in international law itself, and would run counter to constitutional limits on the role of federal courts. Those reasons demand rejection of appellants' construction of section 1350 unless a narrow reading of the provision is incompatible with congressional intent. There is no evidence, however, that Congress intended the result appellants suggest.
* * *

A broad reading of section 1350 runs directly contrary to that desire. It is also relevant to a construction of this provision that until quite recently nobody understood it to empower courts to entertain cases like this one or like *Filartiga*. [FN21] * * *

FN21. In nearly two hundred years, jurisdiction has been predicated successfully under section 1350 only three times. *Filartiga v. Pena-Irala*, 630 F.2d 876 (2d Cir.1980) (jurisdiction over allegation of official torture not ratified by official's state); *Adra v. Clift*, 195 F.Supp. 857 (D.Md.1961) (child custody dispute between two aliens; wrongful withholding of custody is a tort, and defendant's falsification of child's passport to procure custody violated law of nations); *Bolchos v. Darrel*, 3 F.Cas. 810 (D.S.C.1795) (No. 1607) (suit for restitution of three slaves who were on board a Spanish ship seized as a prize of war; treaty with France superseded law of nations; 1350 alternative basis of jurisdiction).

* * * What kinds of alien tort actions, then, might the Congress of 1789 have meant to bring into federal courts? According to Blackstone, a writer certainly familiar to colonial lawyers, "the principal offences against the law of nations, animadverted on as such by the municipal laws of England, [were] of three kinds; 1. Violation of safe-conducts; 2. Infringement of the rights of ambassadors; and 3. Piracy." 4 W. Blackstone, *Commentaries* 68, 72, quoted in 1 W.W. Crosskey, *Politics and Constitution in the History of the United States* 459 (1953) ("Crosskey"). One might suppose that these were the kinds of offenses for which Congress wished to provide tort jurisdiction for suits by aliens in order to avoid conflicts with other nations. * * *

The Constitution, of course, gave particular attention to piracy and to the rights of ambassadors. Article I, section 8, links piracy and the law of nations by granting Congress power "to define and punish Piracies and Felonies committed on the high Seas, and Offences against the Law of Nations." And Article III, section 2, gives the Supreme Court original jurisdiction over "all Cases affecting Ambassadors, other Public Ministers and Consuls." Section 9 of the Judiciary Act of 1789 (now section 1350) gave jurisdiction to district courts, concurrent with that of state courts and circuit courts, over tort suits by aliens for violations of the law of nations. Judiciary Act of 1789, ch. 20, §9, 1 Stat. 73, 76-77. This may well have envisaged a tort like piracy (a citizen could use diversity jurisdiction). * * *

Opening federal courts to tort suits based on piracy would not, apparently, have involved courts in foreign relations since piracy was, as stated in *United States v. Smith*, merely robbery on the high seas. It could not be committed by nations, or by anyone acting for reasons other than for plunder. According to Hackworth, "when the acts in question are committed from purely political motive, it is hardly possible to regard them as acts of piracy involving all the important consequences which follow upon the commission of that crime." G. Hackworth, *Digest of International Law* §203, at 681 (1941).

The idea that section 9 of the original Judiciary Act, now section 1350, was concerned with the rights of ambassadors (and other foreign representatives) is suggested by another provision of the statutes. Section 13 gave the Supreme Court such original and exclusive jurisdiction over all suits *against* ambassadors "as a court of law can have or exercise consistently with the law of nations" (emphasis added). Judiciary Act of 1789, ch. 20, §13, 1 Stat. 73, 80-81. That section, however, gave the Court original but not exclusive jurisdiction of "all suits brought *by* ambassadors, or other public ministers, or in which a consul, or vice consul, shall be a party" (emphasis added). This appears to tie in to the grant of tort jurisdiction for suits by aliens in what is now section 1350. (Section 1350's use of the broader term "aliens" may merely indicate that the torts of piracy and violations of safe-conduct, which would involve plaintiffs other than ambassadors, were included.)

An intent to protect the rights of ambassadors is also plausible historically. * * *

These thoughts as to the possible original intention underlying section 1350 are admittedly speculative, and those who enacted the law may well have had additional torts in mind. I offer these possibilities merely to show that the statute could have served a useful purpose even if the larger tasks assigned it by *Filartiga* and Judge Edwards are rejected. Moreover, if the offenses against the law of nations listed by Blackstone constituted the torts the framers of section 1350 had in mind, then the creation of federal jurisdiction for the redress of aliens' grievances would tend to ease rather than inflame relations with foreign nations. That result comports with Hamilton's expressed desire. Whether evidence so slim as to the intended office of the statute provides materials from which courts today may properly make substantive law is a jurisprudential issue with which, given the grounds upon which I would place our decision, I need not grapple today. But when courts go beyond the area in which there is any historical evidence, when they create the substantive rules for topics such as that taken up in *Filartiga* or in Judge Edwards' formulations, then law is made with no legislative guidance whatever. When that is so, it will not do to insist that the judge's duty is to construe the statute in order not to flout the will of Congress. On these topics, we have, at the moment, no evidence what the intention of Congress was. When courts lack such evidence, to "construe" is to legislate, to act in the dark, and hence to do many things that, it is virtually certain, Congress did not intend. Any correspondence between the will of Congress in 1789 and the decisions of the courts in 1984 can then be only accidental. Section 1350 can probably be adequately understood only in the context of the premises and assumptions of a legal culture that no longer exists. Perhaps historical research that is beyond the capacities of appellate judges will lift the darkness that now envelops this topic, but that has not yet occurred, and we should not attempt to anticipate what may or may not become visible.

Congress' understanding of the "law of nations" in 1789 is relevant to a consideration of whether Congress, by enacting section 1350, intended to open the federal courts to the vindication of the violation of any right recognized by international law. Examining the meaning of the "law of nations" at the time does not, contrary to my colleague's charges, "avoid the dictates of *The Paquete Habana*" and "limit the 'law of nations' to its 18th Century definition." Edwards' op. at 29. The substantive rules of international law may evolve and perhaps courts may apply those new rules, but that does not solve the problem of the existence of a cause of action. If plaintiffs were explicitly provided with a cause of action by the law of nations, as it is currently understood, this court might-subject to considerations of justiciability-be required by section 1350 to entertain their claims. But, as discussed below, see *infra* pp. 816 - 819, international law today does not provide plaintiffs with a cause of action. * * *

Recognition of suits presenting serious problems of interference with foreign relations would conflict with the primary purpose of the adoption of the law of nations by federal law-to promote America's peaceful relations with other nations. See *The Federalist* No. 80 (A. Hamilton); *The Federalist* No. 83 (A. Hamilton). Judge Edwards cites this rationale as a reason for reading section 1350 as creating a cause of action for private parties. The inference from that rationale seems to me, however, to run in precisely the opposite direction. Adjudication of international disputes of this sort in federal courts, disputes over international violence occurring abroad, would be far more likely to exacerbate tensions with other nations than to promote peaceful relations.

* * *

V.

Whether current international law itself gives appellants a cause of action requires more extended discussion. Appellants' claim, in Count II of their complaint, is that appellees have committed the "torts of terror, torture, hostage-taking and genocide," Brief for Appellants at 29, in violation of various customary principles of international law. Such principles become law by virtue of the "general assent of civilized nations." *The Paquete Habana*, 175 U.S. at 694, 20 S.Ct. at 297. Unlike treaties and statutes, such law is not authoritatively pronounced by promulgation in a written document but must be found in the "customs and usages of civilized nations" as evidenced by the works of "jurists and commentators." *Id.* at 700, 20 S.Ct. at 299; see Statute of the International Court of Justice, art. 38, 59 Stat. 1055 (1945), T.S. No. 993; *Restatement of the Foreign Relations Law of the United States (Revised)* §§102-103, at 24-38 (Tent. Draft No. 1, 1980). Consequently, any cause of action that might exist, like the precise meaning of the customary principles themselves, must be inferred from the sources that are evidence of and attempt to formulate the legal rules. The district court found, and appellants have not argued to the contrary, that none of the documents appellants have put forth as stating the international legal principles on which they rely expressly state that individuals can bring suit in municipal courts to enforce the specified rights. See 517 F.Supp. at 548-49. Moreover, we have been pointed to nothing in their language, structure, or circumstances of promulgation that suggests that any of those documents should be read as implicitly declaring that an individual should be able to sue in municipal courts to enforce the specified rights. In any event, there is no need to review those documents and their origins in further detail, for, as a general rule, international law does not provide a private right of action, and an exception to that rule would have to be demonstrated by clear evidence that civilized nations had generally given their assent to the exception. Hassan, *supra*, 4 Hous.J.Int'l L. at 26-27.

International law typically does not authorize individuals to vindicate rights by bringing actions in either international or municipal tribunals. " 'Like a general treaty, the law of nations has been held not to be self-executing so as to vest a plaintiff with individual legal rights.'" *Dreyfus v. Von Finck*, 534 F.2d at 31 (quoting *Pauling v. McElroy*, 164 F.Supp. at 393). "[T]he usual method for an individual to seek relief is to exhaust local remedies and then repair to the executive authorities of his own state to persuade them to champion his claim in diplomacy or before an international tribunal." *Banco Nacional de Cuba v. Sabbatino*, 376 U.S. at 422-23, 84 S.Ct. at 937-38.

This general relegation of individuals to a derivative role in the vindication of their legal rights stems from "[t]he traditional view of international law…that it establishes substantive principles for determining whether one country has wronged another." 376 U.S. at 422, 84 S.Ct. at 937. One scholar explained the primary role of states in international law as follows:

Since the Law of Nations is based on the common consent of individual States, States are the principal subjects of International Law. This means that the Law of Nations is primarily a law for the international conduct of States, and not of their citizens. As a rule, the subjects of the rights and duties arising from the Law of Nations are States solely and exclusively.

1 L. Oppenheim, *International Law: A Treatise* 19 (H. Lauterpacht 8th ed. 1955).

* * *

Appellants, therefore, are not granted a private right of action to bring this lawsuit either by a specific international legal right or impliedly by the whole or parts of international law.

VI.

In *Filartiga v. Pena-Irala*, 630 F.2d 876 (2d Cir.1980), the Second Circuit, which did not address the issue of the existence of a cause of action, held that section 1350 afforded jurisdiction over a claim brought by Paraguayan citizens against a former Paraguayan official. The plaintiffs, a father and daughter, alleged that the defendant had tortured his son, her brother, in violation of international law's proscription of official torture. To highlight what I believe should be the basis for our holding, it is worth pointing out several significant differences between this case and *Filartiga*.

First, unlike the defendants in this case, the defendant in *Filartiga* was a state official acting in his official capac-

ity. Second, the actions of the defendant in *Filartiga* were in violation of the constitution and laws of his state and were "wholly unratified by that nation's government." 630 F.2d at 889. Third, the international law rule invoked in *Filartiga* was the proscription of official torture, a principle that is embodied in numerous international conventions and declarations, that is "clear and unambiguous" in its application to the facts in *Filartiga*, *Id.* at 884, and about which there is universal agreement "in the modern usage and practice of nations." *Id.* at 883.

Thus, in *Filartiga* the defendant was clearly the subject of international-law duties, the challenged actions were not attributed to a participant in American foreign relations, and the relevant international law principle was one whose definition was neither disputed nor politically sensitive. None of that can be said about this case. For these reasons, not all of the analysis employed here would apply to deny a cause of action to the plaintiffs in *Filartiga*.

I differ with the *Filartiga* decision, however, because the court there did not address the question whether international law created a cause of action that the private parties before it could enforce in municipal courts. For the reasons given, that inquiry is essential.

* * *

ROBB, Senior Circuit Judge:

I concur in the result, but must withhold approval of the reasoning of my colleagues. Both have written well-researched and scholarly opinions that stand as testaments to the difficulty which this case presents. Both agree that this case must be dismissed though their reasons vary greatly. Both look backward to *Filartiga v. Pena-Irala*, 630 F.2d 876 (2d Cir.1980), and forward to the future efforts of others maimed or murdered at the hands of thugs clothed with power who are unfortunately present in great numbers in the international order. But both Judges Bork and Edwards fail to reflect on the inherent inability of federal courts to deal with cases such as this one. It seems to me that the political question doctrine controls. This case is nonjusticiable.

A. This case involves standards that defy judicial application.

Tort law requires both agreement on the action which constitutes the tort and the means by which it can be determined who bears responsibility for the unlawful injury. Federal courts are not in a position to determine the international status of terrorist acts. Judge Edwards, for example, notes that "the nations of the world are so divisively split on the legitimacy of such aggression as to make it impossible to pinpoint an area of harmony or consensus." Edwards Opinion at 795. This nation has no difficulty with the question in the context of this case, of course, nor do I doubt for a moment that the attack on the Haifa highway amounts to barbarity in naked and unforgivable form. No diplomatic posturing as represented in sheaves of United Nations documents-no matter how high the pile might reach-could convince me otherwise. But international "law", or the absence thereof, renders even the search for the least common denominators of civilized conduct in this area an impossible-to-accomplish judicial task. Courts ought not to engage in it when that search takes us towards a consideration of terrorism's place in the international order. Indeed, when such a review forces us to dignify by judicial notice the most outrageous of the diplomatic charades that attempt to dignify the violence of terrorist atrocities, we corrupt our own understanding of evil.

Even more problematic would be the single court's search for individual responsibility for any given terrorist outrage. International terrorism consists of a web that the courts are not positioned to unweave. To attempt to discover the reach of its network and the origins of its design may result in unintended disclosures imperiling sensitive diplomacy. This case attempts to focus on the so-called P.L.O. But which P.L.O.? Arafat's, Habash's, or Syria's? And can we conceive of a successful attempt to sort out ultimate responsibility for these crimes? Many believe that most roads run East in this area. [FN1] Are courts prepared to travel these highways? Are they equipped to do so? It is one thing for a student note-writer to urge that courts accept the challenges involved. [FN2] It is an entirely different matter for a court to be asked to conduct such a hearing successfully. The dangers are obvious. To grant the initial access in the face of an overwhelming probability of frustration of the trial process as we know it is an unwise step. As courts could never compel the allegedly responsible parties to attend proceedings much less to engage in a meaningful judicial process, they ought to avoid such imbroglios from the beginning.

FN1. See, e.g. *Implementation of the Helsinki Accords, Hearing Before the Commission on Security and Cooperation in Europe, The Assassination Attempt on Pope John Paul II*, 97th Cong., 2d Sess. 20 (Statement of Michael A. Ledeen) ("[M]any terrorist organizations get support from the Soviet Union and its many surrogates around the world. I do not think there should be much doubt about the matter. The Russians train PLO terrorists in the Soviet Union, supervise the training of terrorists from all over the world in Czechoslovakia-or at least they did until recently, according to a leading

defector, General Jan Sejna-and work hand in glove with countries like Libya, Cuba, and South Yemen in the training of terrorists.") See also Adams, *Lessons and Links of Anti-Turk Terrorism*, Wall St.J., Aug. 16, 1983, at 32, col. 6 (The Armenian Secret Army for the Liberation of Armenia "remains a prime suspect for the charge of KGB manipulation of international terror. But in this area, one researcher in the field advises, 'You will never find the smoking gun'."); Barron, *KGB* 151, 255-257 (1974); Barron, *KGB Today: The Hidden Hand*, 21-22, 255-256 (1983).
FN2. Note, *Terrorism as a Tort in Violation of the Law of Nations*, 6 Fordham Int'l L.J. (1982).

B. This case involves questions that touch on sensitive matters of diplomacy that uniquely demand a singlevoiced statement of policy by the Government.

Judge Bork's opinion finds it necessary to treat the international status of the P.L.O., and to suggest that that organization "bears significantly on the foreign relations of the United States." Bork Opinion at 805. This is considerably more in the way of official recognition than this organization has ever before gained from any institution of the national government. I am not in a position to comment with authority on any of these matters. There has been no executive recognition of this group, and for all our purposes it ought to remain an organization "of whose existence we know nothing…" *United States v. Klintock*, 18 U.S. 144, 149 (5 Wheat.) 5 L.Ed. 55 (1820). As John Jay noted: "It seldom happens in the negotiations of treaties, of whatever nature, but that perfect *secrecy* and immediate *dispatch* are sometimes requisite." *The Federalist*, # 64, Jay (Paul L. Ford, ed.). What was then true about treaties remains true for all manner of modern diplomatic contacts. It may be necessary for our government to deal on occasion with terrorists. It is not, however, for courts to wonder aloud as to whether these negotiations have, are, or will be taking place. Western governments have displayed a near uniform reluctance to engage in much discussion on the organization and operation of terrorist groups, much less on any hidden contacts with them. [FN3] When a genre of cases threatens to lead courts repeatedly into the area of such speculations, then that is a signal to the courts that they have taken a wrong turn. The President may be compelled by urgent matters to deal with the most undesirable of men. The courts must be careful to preserve his flexibility and must hesitate to publicize and perhaps legitimize that which ought to remain hidden and those who deserve the brand of absolute illegitimacy. By jumping the political question threshold here, my colleagues appear to be leading us in just the opposite direction.

FN3. C. Sterling, *The Terror Network* (1981). Sterling repeatedly points out, and often criticizes, the reluctance of Western governments to openly detail the international cooperation that girds most terrorist activities. She writes:

No single motive could explain the iron restraint shown by Italy, West German, and all other threatened Western governments in the face of inexorably accumulating evidence… Both, and all their democratic allies, also had compelling reasons of state to avoid a showdown with the Soviet Union…All were certainly appalled at the thought of tangling with Arab rulers…

[P]olitical considerations were almost certainly paramount for government leaders under seige who…wouldn't talk.

Id. at 291, 294. Whatever the merits of Sterling's criticisms of this near uniform silence, the fact remains that our government, like those of its closest allies, is extremely wary of publicity in this area. Commenting on the refusal of Western governments to openly discuss the possibility of Soviet complicity in the attempt to assassinate Pope John Paul II, Congressman Ritter, a member of the bipartisan commission drawn from both the executive and legislative branches which is charged with monitoring compliance with the Helsinki Accords, commented that "[t]he involved governments have stayed away from this hot potato for a variety of reasons." *Implementation of the Helsinki Accord s, Hearing Before the Commission on Security and Cooperation in Europe, The Assassination Attempt on Pope John Paul II, supra,* at 16. Both Sterling's book and the hearings in which Congressman Ritter participated are indispensable background reading for a court confronted with a question such as the one before us. These and other texts bring home the hopelessness of any attempt by an American court to trace a reliable path of responsibility for almost every terrorist outrage. These labyrinths of international intrigue will admit no judicial Theseus.

C. Questions connected to the activities of terrorists have historically been within the exclusive domain of the executive and legislative branches.

The conduct of foreign affairs has never been accepted as a general area of judicial competence. Particular exceptions have, of course, arisen. When the question is precisely defined, when the facts are appropriately clear, the judiciary has not hesitated to decide cases connected with American foreign policy. [FN4]

FN4. See, e.g., *Haig v. Agee*, 453 U.S. 280, 292, 101 S.Ct. 2766, 2774, 69 L.Ed.2d 640 (1981) ("Matters intimately related to foreign policy are rarely proper subjects for judicial intervention.); *Dames & Moore v. Regan*, 453 U.S. 654, 101 S.Ct. 2972, 69 L.Ed.2d 918 (1981).

But cases which would demand close scrutiny of terrorist acts are far beyond these limited exceptions to the traditional judicial reticence displayed in the face of foreign affairs cases. That traditional deference to the other branches has stemmed, in large part, from a fear of undue interference in the affairs of state, not only of this nation but of all nations. Judge Mulligan, writing in *Hunt v. Mobil Oil Corp.*, 550 F.2d 68 (2d Cir.), *cert. denied* 434 U.S. 984, 98 S.Ct. 608, 54 L.Ed.2d 477 (1977), warned that a "Serbian Bog" awaits courts that inquire into the policies of foreign sovereigns. *Id.* at 77. A model of judicial deference, appropriately invoked, is *Diggs v. Richardson*, 555 F.2d 848 (D.C.Cir.1976). In that case this court was asked to enforce a United Nations Security Council Resolution. This court ruled in effect that the matter was nonjusticiable, and a part of the reasoning supporting that conclusion was that the Resolution did not provide specific standards suitable to "conventional adjudication". *Id.* at 851. The court added that the standards that were supplied were "foreign to the general experience and function of American courts". *Id.* In refusing to allow the case to be jimmied into our judicial process, the court was fully aware that its deference did not abdicate all American participation in the issues raised by the Resolution. Our nation's involvement in the diplomatic arena was in no way circumscribed by judicial circumspection.

Similarly, the issues raised by this case are treated regularly by the other branches of the national government. One need only review the work of the Subcommittee on Security and Terrorism of the Senate Committee on the Judiciary to recognize that the whole dangerous dilemma of terrorism and the United States response to it are subjects of repeated and thorough inquiry. See, e.g., *Historical Antecedents of Soviet Terrorism Before the Subcomm. on Security and Terrorism of the Senate Comm. on Judiciary*, 97th Cong., 1st Sess. 1 (1981). See also, *Extradition Reform Act of 1981: Hearings on H.R. 5227 Before the Subcomm. on Crime of the House Comm. on the Judiciary*, 97th Cong., 2d Sess. 1 (1982). The executive branch is also deeply involved in the monitoring and attempted control of terrorist activities. See, e.g., *The Role of Cuba in International Terrorism and Subversion, Intelligence Activities of the DGI, Before the Subcomm. on Security and Terrorism of the Senate Comm. on Judiciary*, 97th Cong., 2d Sess. 85 (1982) (statement of

Fred C. Ikle, Undersecretary of Defense for Policy). The President has repeatedly demonstrated his concern that terrorism be combated, both in his statements at home, and in the declarations that have accompanied his meetings with our allies. See 18 *Weekly Compilation of Presidential Documents*, 35, 575, 763, 783, 1352 (1982). It is thus obvious that even with this declaration of nonjusticiability by the court, the work of tracing and assessing responsibility for terrorist acts will continue by those parts of the government which by tradition and accumulated expertise are far better positioned than the courts to conduct such inquiries.

D. Cases such as this one are not susceptible to judicial handling.

As noted above in section A, the pragmatic problems associated with proceedings designed to bring terrorists to the bar are numerous and intractable. One other note must be added. Courts have found it extremely difficult to apply the "political exception" doctrine in extradition proceedings when those proceedings have concerned prisoners who are accused of terrorist activities. See *Abu Eain v. Adams*, 529 F.Supp. 685 (N.D.Ill.1980) and *McMullen v. Immigration and Naturalization Service*, 658 F.2d 1312 (9th Cir.1981). This difficulty is so pronounced that one member of the executive branch has testified to Congress that there is simply "no justiciable standard to the political offense," and that when courts have been confronted with such situations, "there has been a tendency for a breakdown in the ability of our courts to process extradition questions," with the result that courts "tend to beg the question…" *Extradition Reform Act of 1981, Hearings on H.R. 5227 Before Subcomm. on Crime of the House Comm. on the Judiciary*, 97th Cong., 2d Sess. 24-25 (Testimony of Roger Olson, Deputy Asst. Attorney General, Criminal Division, U.S. Dept. of Justice). If courts are vexed by these questions within the limited context of extradition proceedings-an area in which there is considerable judicial experience-it is easy to anticipate the breakdowns that would accompany proceedings under 28 U.S.C. §1350 if they are allowed to go forward. Sound consideration of the limits of judicial ability demands invocation of the political question doctrine here. This is only common sense and a realistic measure of roles that courts are simply not equipped to play.

E. The possible consequences of judicial action in this area are injurious to the national interest.

The certain results of judicial recognition of jurisdiction over cases such as this one are embarrassment to the nation,

the transformation of trials into forums for the exposition of political propaganda, and debasement of commonly accepted notions of civilized conduct.

We are here confronted with the easiest case and thus the most difficult to resist. It was a similar magnet that drew the Second Circuit into its unfortunate position in *Filartiga*. [FN5] But not all cases of this type will be so easy. Indeed, most would be far less attractive. The victims of international violence perpetrated by terrorists are spread across the globe. It is not implausible that every alleged victim of violence of the counter-revolutionaries in such places as Nicaraugua and Afghanistan could argue just as compellingly as the plaintiffs here do, that they are entitled to their day in the courts of the United States. The victims of the recent massacres in Lebanon could also mount such claims. Indeed, there is no obvious or subtle limiting principle in sight. Even recognized dissidents who have escaped from the Soviet Union could conceivably bring suit for violations of international law having to do with the conditions of their earlier confinements. Each supposed scenario carries with it an incredibly complex calculus of actors, circumstances, and geopolitical considerations. The courts must steer resolutely away from involvement in this manner of case. It is too glib to assert simply that courts are used to dealing with difficult questions. They are not used to this kind of question.

FN5. I do not doubt for a moment the good intentions behind Judge Kauffman's opinion in *Filartiga*. But the case appears to me to be fundamentally at odds with the reality of the international structure and with the role of United States courts within that structure. The refusal to separate rhetoric from reality is most obvious in the passage which states that "for the purposes of civil liability, the torturer has become-like the pirate and slave trader before him- *hostis humani generis*, an enemy of all mankind." 630 F.2d at 890. This conclusion ignores the crucial distinction that the pirate and slave trader were men without nations, while the torturer (and terrorist) are frequently pawns, and well controlled ones, in international politics. When Judge Kauffman concluded that "[o]ur holding today, giving effect to a jurisdictional provision enacted by our First Congress, is a small but important step in the fulfillment of the ageless dream to free all people from brutal violence," *Id.*, he failed to consider the possibility that *ad hoc* intervention by courts into international affairs may very well rebound to the decisive disadvantage of the nation. A plaintiff's individual victory, if it entails embarrassing disclosures of this country's approach to the control of the terrorist phenomenon, may in fact be the collective's defeat. The political question doctrine is designed to prevent just this sort of judicial gambling, however apparently noble it may appear at first reading.

The more arcane aspects of international law connected to this case are dealt with by my colleagues. Their reviews of the subject are quite exhaustive and their speculations on the riddle of §1350 are innovative. But it is all quite unnecessary. Especially inappropriate is their apparent reliance for guidance on the distinguished commentators in this field. I agree with the sentiment expressed by Chief Justice Fuller in his dissent to *The Paquete Habana*, 175 U.S. 677, 20 S.Ct. 290, 44 L.Ed. 320 (1900), where he wrote that it was "needless to review the speculations and repetitions of writers on international law…Their lucubrations may be persuasive, but are not authoritative." *Id.* at 720, 20 S.Ct. at 307 (Fuller, J. dissenting). Courts ought not to serve as debating clubs for professors willing to argue over what is or what is not an accepted violation of the law of nations. Yet this appears to be the clear result if we allow plaintiffs the opportunity to proceed under §1350. Plaintiffs would troop to court marshalling their "experts" behind them. Defendants would quickly organize their own platoons of authorities. The typical judge or jury would be swamped in citations to various distinguished journals of international legal studies, but would be left with little more than a numbing sense of how varied is the world of public international "law".

Judge Edwards writes that "[t]his case deals with an area of law that cries out for clarification by the Supreme Court. We confront at every turn broad and novel questions about the definition and application of the 'law of nations'." Edwards Opinion at 775. I must disagree. When a case presents broad and novel questions of this sort, courts ought not to appeal for guidance to the Supreme Court, but should instead look to Congress and the President. Should these branches of the Government decide that questions of this sort are proper subjects for judicial inquiry, they can then provide the courts with the guidelines by which such inquiries should proceed. We ought not to parlay a two hundred years-old statute into an entree into so sensitive an area of foreign policy. We have no reliable evidence whatsoever as to what purpose this "legal Lohengrin", as Judge Friendly put it, was intended to serve. *ITT v. Vencap, Ltd.*, 519 F.2d 1001, 1015 (2d Cir.1975). We ought not to cobble together for it a modern mission on the vague idea that international law develops over the years. Law may evolve, but statutes ought not to mutate. To allow §1350 the opportunity to support future actions of the sort both countenanced in *Filartiga* and put forward here is to judicially will that statute a new life. Every consideration that informs the sound application of the political question doctrine militates against this result.

My colleagues concede that the origins and purposes of this statute are obscure, but it is certainly obvious that it was never intended by its drafters to reach this kind of case. Accordingly, I concur in the decision to affirm the dismissal of this case.

Notes:

1. A significant part of the discussion in both *Filartiga* and *Tel-Oren* centered on the courts' interpretation of "the law of nations." In applying the "law of nations," the *Filartiga* court looked to "the works of jurists, writing professedly on public law; or by the general usage and practice of nations; or by judicial decisions recognizing and enforcing that law." *Filartiga v. Pena-Irala*, 630 F.2d 876 (2d Cir. 1980). The case involved allegations of torture committed by a state official. Can the rationale of *Filartiga* be extended to application of the law of nations to non-state actors?

In *Kadic v. Karadzic*, 70 F.3d 232, 239 (2d Cir. 1995), the court held:

We do not agree that the law of nations, as understood in the modern era, confines its reach to state action. Instead, we hold that certain forms of conduct violate the law of nations whether undertaken by those acting under the auspices of a state or only as private individuals. An early example of the application of the law of nations to the acts of private individuals is the prohibition against piracy. See *United States v. Smith*, 18 U.S. (5 Wheat.) 153, 161, 5 L.Ed. 57 (1820); *United States v. Furlong*, 18 U.S. (5 Wheat.) 184, 196-97, 5 L.Ed. 64 (1820). In *The Brig Malek Adhel*, 43 U.S. (2 How.) 210, 232, 11 L.Ed. 239 (1844), the Supreme Court observed that pirates were "*hostis humani generis*" (an enemy of all mankind) in part because they acted "without…any pretense of public authority." See generally 4 William Blackstone, *Commentaries on the Laws of England* 68 (facsimile of 1st ed. 1765-1769, Univ. of Chi. ed., 1979). Later examples are prohibitions against the slave trade and certain war crimes. See M. Cherif Bassiouni, *Crimes Against Humanity in International Criminal Law* 193 (1992); Jordan Paust, *The Other Side of Right: Private Duties Under Human Rights* Law, 5 Harv.Hum.Rts.J. 51 (1992).

In *Kadic*, the plaintiffs sued Radovan Karadzic, the President of the self-proclaimed Bosnian-Serb Republic of "Srpska." They asserted causes of action for genocide, rape, forced prostitution and impregnation, torture and other cruel, inhuman, and degrading treatment, assault and battery, sex and ethnic inequality, summary execution, and wrongful death. The court extended the application of the international prohibition against genocide, war crimes, torture, and summary execution, holding that it applied to individuals as well. How does this holding impact the opinion of Judge Edwards in *Tel-Oren*?

2.   Since its classic enunciation in the *Barcelona Traction Case* in 1970, *Barcelona Traction (Belg. v. Spain)*, 1970 I.C.J. 2, 33 (Feb. 5), the concept of international obligations *erga omnes* has spawned robust scholarly debate about the scope and meaning of the doctrine. While there have been some vigorous dissents to the plausibility and usefulness of its existence, see, e.g. Prosper Weil, *Towards Relative Normativity in International Law?*, 77 A.J.I.L. 413, 431 (1983), it has become generally accepted in the international community, as evidenced by the many references to the concept in several decisions of the International Court and scholarly literature. Until recently, the concept has only been identified by the rights that qualify as *erga omnes* themselves, not by the general characteristics of those rights. This has created much confusion as to the limits of the doctrine, and its applicability to emerging rights, with authors advocating the inclusion of rights spanning from torture, American Law Institute, Restatement of the Law (Third), The Foreign Relations Law of the United States (1987), §702, to protection of the environment, Rene Provost, *International Criminal Environmental Law*, in The Reality of International Law: Essays in Honor of Ian Brownlie 439, 443 (Goodwin-Gell & Talmon eds., 1999), to property rights. Robert L. Muse, *International Symposium on the Cuban Liberty and Democratic Solidarity (LIBERTAD) Act of 1996: A Public International Law Critique of the Extraterritorial Jurisdiction of the Helms-Burton Act*, 30 GW J. Int'l L. & Econ. 207, 255-256 (1996). The American Law Institute, in its Restatement (Third) of the Foreign Relations Law of the United States, also included genocide; slavery or slave trade; the murder or causing the disappearance of individuals; cruel, inhuman, or degrading treatment or punishment; prolonged arbitrary detention; systematic racial discrimination; or a consistent pattern of gross violations of internationally recognized human rights in the list.

The International Court itself has expressly mentioned only five rights it considers *erga omnes*, four of them in dictum of the *Barcelona Traction Case*:

33. ...In particular, an essential distinction should be drawn between the obligations of a State to-

wards the international community as a whole, and those arising vis-à-vis another State in the field of diplomatic protection. By their very nature the former are the concern of all States. In view of the importance of the rights involved, all States can be held to have a legal interest in their protection; they are obligations *erga omnes*.

34. Such obligations derive, for example, in contemporary international law, from outlawing of acts of aggression, and of genocide, as also from the principles and rules concerning the basic rights of the human person, including protection from slavery and racial discrimination. Some of the corresponding rights of protection have entered into the body of general international law...; others are conferred by international instruments of a universal or quasi-universal character.

Barcelona Traction, *supra*, at para. 33-34. As the above excerpt indicates, the International Court expressly mentioned acts of aggression, genocide, slavery, and racial discrimination. The International Law Commission has interpreted these statements to mean that there is "a number, albeit a small one, of international obligations which, by reason of the importance of their subject-matter for the international community as a whole, are - unlike the others - obligations in whose fulfillment all States have a legal interest." Documents of the Twenty-eighth Session, 2 Y.B. Int'l. L. Comm'n, pt. 2 at 99, (1976), UN Doc. A/CN.4/SER.A/1976/Add.1. The fifth right that the International Court has endorsed is the right of self-determination, first in the *East Timor Case*, and more recently in the Advisory Opinion on the *Legal Consequences of the Construction of a Wall in the Occupied Palestinian Territory*.

Does international terrorism fit into this category of rights?

3.   Is Judge Bork accurate in describing the U.N. charter as containing "mere aspirations"? Are members of the U.N., as opposed to citizens of those member states, and U.N. agencies likely to share this view?

4.   Why would the obscure and ephemeral "law of nations" prohibit only state sponsored terrorism and not terrorism committed by non-states purporting to act on behalf of a national entity? What does the hesitancy to apply the "law of nations" show about the state of American law prior to the enactment of the Flatow Amendment and the Klinghoffer Act?

5. Why did the plaintiffs have to resort to employing the Alien Tort Claims Act? How could a one-sentence statute created in 1789 and barely used in 200 years of American jurisprudence be the main legal vehicle for victims of terrorism seeking redress? Why weren't modern statutes and legal doctrines sufficient to assist victims?

6. Why does the legal framework existing at the time of *Tel-Oren* create so many conceptual impediments to adjudication of the victims' claims?

7. What is the source of the "Law of Nations" and "International Law"? Where is it found or codified?

8. In summing up the law prior to enactment of civil terrorism statutes, one commentator noted,

> Because the decisions of the Supreme Court were unfavorable to human rights claims brought under the Foreign Sovereign Immunities Act, such claims, on the whole, have had very little success in U.S. domestic courts. Even suits based on the Nazi holocaust against the Jews or terrorist murders of American citizens were dismissed out of hand.

Joseph W. Dellapenna, *Civil Remedies For International Terrorism*, 12 DePaul Bus. L.J. 169, 252 (1999/2000).

9. Despite this inhospitable legal terrain, one scholar noted that ironically public international law was a burgeoning field,

> Several years ago, I called attention to the burgeoning of "transnational public law litigation": suits brought in United States courts by individual and governmental litigants challenging violations of international law. As recent examples of this phenomenon, I included international human rights suits brought by aliens against foreign and United States governments and officials under the Alien Tort Statute, as well as actions by foreign governments against individual, American government, and corporate defendants.

> Like its domestic counterpart (christened fifteen years ago by Abram Chayes), transnational public law litigation seeks to vindicate public rights and values through judicial remedies. In both settings, parties bring "public actions," asking courts to declare and explicate public norms, often with the goal of provoking institutional reform. Much as

domestic public law litigants have pursued Bivens and Section 1983 litigation in federal courts seeking redress, deterrence, and reform of state and federal institutions through judicial enunciation of constitutional norms, transnational public law litigants have sought redress, deterrence, and reform of national governmental policies through clarification of rules of international conduct.

What makes transnational public law litigation unique, however, is its melding of two conventional modes of litigation that have traditionally been considered distinct. In traditional domestic litigation, private individuals bring private claims against one another based on national law before competent domestic judicial fora, seeking both enunciation of norms and damages relief in the form of a retrospective judgment. In traditional international litigation, nation-states bring public claims against one another based on treaty or customary international law before international tribunals of limited competence. Although state litigants ostensibly seek judgments from such tribunals, their primary goal is usually the enunciation of a public international norm that will stimulate "relief" in the form of a negotiated political settlement.

Transnational public law litigation merges these two classical modes of litigation. Private individuals, government officials, and nations sue one another directly, and are sued directly, in a variety of judicial fora, most prominently, domestic courts. In these fora, these actors invoke claims of right based not solely on domestic or international law, but rather, on a body of "transnational" law that blends the two. Moreover, contrary to "dualist" views of international jurisprudence, which see international law as binding only upon nations in their relations with one another, individual plaintiffs engaged in this mode of litigation usually claim rights arising directly from this body of transnational law.

As in traditional domestic litigation, transnational public lawsuits focus retrospectively upon achieving compensation and redress for individual victims. But as in traditional international law litigation, the transnational public law plaintiff pursues a prospective aim as well: to provoke judicial articulation of a norm of transnational law, with an eye toward using that declaration to promote a political settlement in which both governmental and nongovernmental entities will participate. Thus, although transnational public law plaintiffs routinely request retrospective damages or even prospective injunctive relief, their broader strategic goals are often served by a declaratory or default judgment announcing that a transnational norm has been violated. Even a judgment that the plaintiff cannot enforce against the defendant in the rendering forum empowers the plaintiff by creating a bargaining chip for use in other political fora.

Harold Hongju Koh, *Transnational Public Law Litigation*, 100 Yale L.J. 2347, 2347-2349 (1991).

2.2 Charter of the United Nations
Smith v. Socialist People's Libyan Arab Jamahiriya, 886 F.Supp. 306 (E.D.N.Y. 1995)

MEMORANDUM & ORDER

PLATT, District Judge.

Plaintiffs Bruce Smith and Paul Hudson, as personal representatives of victims who died in the bombing of Pan American Airways, Inc. (Pan Am) Flight 103 over Lockerbie, Scotland, on December 21, 1988, seek to recover civil damages. [FN1] Smith sues the Socialist People's Libyan Arab Jamahiriya, the Libyan Arab Airlines, The Libyan External Security Organization, Abdel Basset Ali Al-Megrahi and Lamen Khalifa Fhimah as agents and instrumentalities of Libya. Hudson sues the Socialist People's Libyan Arab Jamahiriya (heretofore defendants for both cases are referred to as "Libya"). [FN2] For the purposes of this motion, the claims of Mr. Smith and Mr. Hudson will be considered in tandem. Pursuant to Federal Rule Civil Procedure 12(b), Libya moves this Court to dismiss plaintiffs' claims. Defendants' motion to dismiss both actions is granted as the Federal Sovereign Immunities Act precludes the plaintiffs from bringing this action in the United States courts against the State of Libya and its agents.

FN1. Bruce Smith represents the estate of his deceased wife Ingrid Smith. Paul Hudson represents the estate of his deceased wife Melina K. Hudson.
FN2. Since the filing of this Motion to Dismiss, plaintiff Hudson has filed an Amended Complaint in which he sues additional parties. This Court will consider the Motion to Dismiss as to the defendants named in the original complaint, as that was the complaint at issue at the time of the filing of the Motion.

BACKGROUND

On December 31, 1988, Pan Am Flight 103 left Frankfurt, Germany bound for Detroit with stops in London and New York. At about 7:00 p.m., Flight 103 exploded over Lockerbie, Scotland killing all 270 persons aboard, including passengers Mrs. Smith and Mrs. Hudson.

Plaintiff Smith alleges that Pan Am Flight 103 was destroyed by a bomb and that "[t]he actions of Libya in encouraging and sustaining these private acts [of terrorism] led to the deliberate and willful destruction of [the plane]." (Smith Complaint ¶ 11). Smith asserts tort claims for wrongful death, battery, infliction of emotional distress, loss of consortium and violation of international law. Plaintiff Hudson claims the alleged bomb "was placed on board the aircraft and detonated by and at the direction of Libya…" (Hudson Complaint ¶ 11). Hudson seeks to recover for the intentional torts of wrongful death and personal injury. (H.Complt. ¶¶ 15-20).

Mr. Smith and Mr. Hudson have sued previously to recover for the injuries alleged in this matter. In June, 1993, Smith filed a wrongful death action against Libya in Scotland. Hudson joined in the multidistrict tort action (MDL 799) against Pan Am before this Court in which the jury held Pan Am responsible for the destruction of the airplane.

DISCUSSION

Pursuant to FRCP Rule 12(b) the defendants move this Court to dismiss plaintiffs' claims for (i) lack of subject matter jurisdiction under the Foreign Sovereign Immunities Act (FSIA); (ii) lack of subject matter jurisdiction under principles of International Law; (iii) lack of personal jurisdiction on the grounds of Constitutional due process; (iv) pendency of prior parallel actions; and (v) as time barred.

Plaintiffs contend the FSIA sovereign immunity defense does not foreclose their claims because (i) the United States is party to certain international agreements within the United Nations system which authorize United States Courts to exercise subject matter jurisdiction over Libya; (ii) the injuries tortiously inflicted by Libya occurred in the United States for the purposes of applying the FSIA; and (iii) Libya impliedly waived sovereign immunity under FSIA when it provided a guaranty to pay certain compensation and/or when it violated the *jus cogens* norm.

As the FSIA controls whether a foreign sovereign is to be denied sovereign immunity, this Court only considers the issues raised here in the context of the FSIA. See, *Argentine Republic v. Amerada Hess Shipping Corp.*, 488 U.S. 428,

439, 109 S.Ct. 683, 690, 102 L.Ed.2d 818 (1989) (the FSIA is the "sole basis for obtaining jurisdiction over a foreign state in federal court").

Foreign Sovereign Immunities Act

The Foreign Sovereign Immunities Act, 28 U.S.C. §§1602-11, provides that "[s]ubject to existing international agreements to which the United States is a party at the time of enactment of this Act a foreign state shall be immune from the jurisdiction of the courts of the United States and of the States except as provided in sections 1605 and 1607 of this chapter." 28 U.S.C. §1604 (1988). The excepted categories which preclude foreign nations from using the sovereign immunity defense are:

§1605 General exceptions to the jurisdictional immunity of a foreign state. 28 U.S.C. §1605 (1988).

(a) A foreign state shall not be immune from the jurisdiction of the courts of the United States...in any case-

(1) in which the foreign state has waived its immunity either explicitly or by implication, notwithstanding any withdrawal of the waiver which the foreign state may purport to effect in accordance with the terms of the waiver.

(2) in which the action is based upon a commercial activity carried on in the United States by the foreign state; or upon an act outside the territory of the United States in connection with a commercial activity of the foreign state elsewhere and that act causes a direct effect in the United States

(3) in which rights in property taken in violation of international law are in issue...

(4) in which rights in property in the United States acquired by succession...

(5) not otherwise encompassed in paragraph (2) above, in which money damages are sought against a foreign state for personal injury or death...occurring in the United States and caused by the tortious act or omission of that foreign state or of any official or employee of that foreign state while acting within the scope of his office or employment; except this paragraph shall not apply to-

(A) any claim based upon the exercise or performance...[of] a discretionary function regardless of whether the discretion be abused, or

(B) any claim arising out of malicious prosecution, abuse of process, libel, slander, misrepresentation, deceit, or interference with contract rights...

§1607. Counterclaims...

1. Subject Matter Jurisdiction Based on the 28 U.S.C. §1604 Existing Agreement Exception.

As noted, FSIA preserves jurisdiction over a foreign state to the extent such jurisdiction exists under any international agreement to which the United States was a party at the time the statute was enacted. 28 U.S.C. §1604. This "existing agreement" exception "applies when international agreements 'expressly conflic[t] with the immunity provisions of the FSIA.'" *Amerada Hess*, 488 U.S. at 442, 109 S.Ct. at 692 (citing and quoting H.R.Rep. No. 94-1487, p. 17 (1976) (H.R.Rep.); S.Rep. No. 94-1310, p. 17 (1976) (S.Rep.), U.S.Code Cong. & Admin.News 1976, p. 6604).

a. Time Limit

Plaintiffs assert that the United Nations ("UN") Charter of 1945 (Charter), entered into by the United States prior to the passage of the FSIA in 1976, is an agreement which could preserve jurisdiction over a foreign nation pursuant to §1604. [FN3] Plaintiffs seek to expand the jurisdiction provided by §1604 to include resolutions passed by the UN Security Counsil, pursuant to Article VII, regardless of the date of passage, on the theory that such resolutions are "elaborations" of the terms of the Charter and therefore should be accorded the same status as the Charter. [FN4] U.N. CHARTER art. VII. Specifically, plaintiffs request that Security Council Resolutions 731 and 748, which call on Libya to accept responsibility for the bombing of Pan Am 103, be deemed international agreements which confer jurisdiction under §1604. S.Res. 731, U.N. SCOR, 3033rd Mtg. (1992); S.Res. 748, U.N. SCOR, 3063rd Mtg. (1992).

FN3. The United Nations Charter "is part of the supreme law of the land." *United States v. Steinberg*, 478 F.Supp. 29, 33 (N.D.Ill.1979).
FN4. Article VII of the Charter specifies the U.N.'s Police Power.

Article 25 of the Charter provides "[t]he members of the United Nations agree to accept and carry out the decisions of the Security Council in accordance with the present Charter."
Security Counsil Resolutions 731 and 748 do not confer ju-

risdiction upon this Court as they do not meet the criteria set forth in the "existing agreement" exception in §1604. The plain language of §1604 requires that the international agreement at issue be in existence in 1976 when the FSIA was passed. Security Council Resolutions 731 and 748 were passed in 1992. This Court does not adopt plaintiffs' broad view that because the Resolutions were passed pursuant to powers created by the UN Charter that they are an "elaboration" of the Charter so that this Court should treat them as being passed on the same date as the Charter.

b. Conflict with FSIA Immunity Provisions

Even if the plaintiffs convinced this Court that the Security Council Resolutions related back to the Charter so as to meet the time requirement, plaintiffs claims would fail as Article VII of the UN Charter and Resolutions 731 and 748 do not conflict expressly with the FSIA immunity provisions. See, *Id.* Article VII addresses the UN's police powers in the face of actual or threatened armed aggression and makes no mention of how victims of such armed aggression can seek civil relief. The Resolutions at issue condemn terrorism and seek to impose diplomatic and economic sanctions against Libya. As neither Article VII nor the Resolutions address the FSIA immunity provisions, there is no conflict between the provisions at issue which could provide the basis for jurisdiction.

c. Private Right of Action

If jurisdiction was granted on the basis of the U.N. Resolutions plaintiffs' claims would not survive because the "agreement" at issue creates no private right of action. Plaintiffs argue that the incorporation of S/23308 [FN5] into Resolution 748, which calls on Libya to accept responsibility for the actions of Libyan officials and pay appropriate compensation, provides the basis for a private right of action against Libya for the victims of Pan Am # 103.

FN5. S/23308: JOINT DECLARATION OF THE UNITED STATES AND UNITED KINGDOM

The British and American Governments today declare that the Government of Libya must:

-surrender for trial purposes all those charged with the crime; and accept responsibility for the actions of Libyan officials:

-disclose all it knows of this crime...

-pay appropriate compensation.

We expect Libya to comply promptly and in full. G.A. S/23308, U.N. GAOR, 46th Sess., U.N.Doc. A/46/827 (1991).

"Treaties of the United States, though the law of the land do not generally create rights that are privately enforceable in courts." *Tel-Oren v. Libyan Arab Republic*, 726 F.2d 774, 808 (D.C.Cir.1984) (Bork, J. concurring) (citations omitted), *cert. denied*, 470 U.S. 1003, 105 S.Ct. 1354, 84 L.Ed.2d 377 (1985). If there is no legislation providing an individual right of action, the Court may entertain a private claim only if the treaty is self-executing. [FN6] *Id.* (citations omitted). To determine if a treaty is self-executing the court examines "the intent of the signatory parties as manifested by the language of the instrument, and, if the instrument is uncertain, recourse must [be determined by examining] the circumstances surrounding its execution." *Diggs v. Richardson*, 555 F.2d 848, 851 (D.C.Cir.1976) (citing *Sei Fujii v. State*, 38 Cal.2d 718, 721-22, 242 P.2d 617, 620 (1952)). [FN7] The *Diggs* action was not viable because the provisions of the Resolution "were not addressed to the judicial branch of our government...[and did not] by their terms confer rights upon individual citizens." *Id.* Rather, "they call[ed] upon governments to take certain action." *Id.*

FN6. A treaty is self-executing when it expressly or impliedly provides a private right of action.

FN7. *Diggs v. Richardson* considered whether a Security Council Resolution is self-executing. The Court found individual plaintiffs could not maintain a suit against the United States when the U.S. allegedly violated Security Council Resolution 301, which prohibited certain relations with South Africa.

Upon a careful reading of Article VII of the UN Charter and Security Counsel Resolutions 731 and 748, this Court holds that the Resolutions are not self-executing. As noted above, the Resolutions at issue condemn terrorism and impose economic and diplomatic sanctions against Libya. This Court finds that the primary purpose of S/23308 is to demand Libya participate in the criminal investigation of the Lockerbie disaster. The vague directive that Libya must "pay appropriate compensation" does not refer to our judiciary system or confer upon an individual the right to sue Libya to recover "appropriate compensation." Cf., *Amerada Hess*, 488 U.S. at 442, 109 S.Ct. at 692 (The fact the Geneva Convention on the High Seas and the Pan American Maritime Neutrality Convention set forth substantive rules of conduct and state that compensation shall be paid for certain wrongs does not create private rights of action.)

2. Subject Matter Jurisdiction Based on the 28 U.S.C. §1605(a)(2) Commercial Activity Exception.

FSIA §1605(a)(2) grants an exception from sovereign immunity for claims based on commercial activity by the foreign nation that has a sufficient connection to the United States. As the plaintiffs' seek recovery for solely tortious injury, the commercial activity exception is not applicable in this case. [FN8]

FN8. The plaintiffs included this claim in their complaint but did not argue it in the Plaintiffs' Memorandum of Points and Authorities in Opposition to Defendants' Motion to Dismiss. This Court interprets the plaintiffs' decision not to include this matter in their motion papers as an indication of the weakness of this claim.

3. Subject Matter Jurisdiction Based on the 28 U.S.C. §1605(a)(5) Non Commercial Tort Exception.

As noted above, §1605(a)(5) denies foreign sovereign immunity in any case "in which money damages are sought against a foreign state for personal injury occurring in the United States and caused by the tortious act or omission of that foreign state…" Defendants contend that the plaintiffs' case does not meet the requirement that the injury occur in the United States because Pan Am Flight 103 exploded in Scottish airspace and crashed on Scottish soil. Plaintiffs response is that the strict locality test should not be used in aviation cases and that as Pan Am was an American airline the plane was actually part of the United States.

a. Strict Locality Test

Plaintiffs claim that airplanes are "geographically unrestrained" so that the locality rule should be replaced with a flexible analysis, analogous to either maritime law principles or the modern approach for deciding conflicts of laws issues, [FN9] to determine where an aviation disaster occurred for the purpose of assigning jurisdiction. *Executive Jet Aviation, Inc. v. City of Cleveland, Ohio*, 409 U.S. 249, 266-68, 93 S.Ct. 493, 503-04, 34 L.Ed.2d 454 (1972) (In both death and injury cases…it is evident that while distinctions based on locality often are…relevant where water vessels are concerned, they entirely lose their significance where aircraft…are concerned." (quoting 7A J. Moore, *Federal Practice, Admiralty* ¶.330(5), at 3772-3 (2d ed. 1972)).

FN9. §145 of the Restatement of Conflicts of Law, Second provides the basis for the modern approach to conflicts law.

(1) The rights and liabilities of the parties with respect to an issue in tort are determined by the local law of the state which, with respect to that issue, has the most significant relationship to the occurrence and the parties under the principles stated in §6.

(2) Contacts to be taken into account in applying the principles of §6 to determine the law applicable to an issue include:

(a) the place where the injury occurred.

(b) the place where the conduct causing the injury occurred.

(c) the domicil, residence, nationality, place of incorporation and place of business of the parties,

(d) and the place where the relationship, if any, between the parties is centered.

These contacts are to be evaluated according to their relative importance with respect to the particular issue.

Plaintiffs' reliance on the reasoning employed in *Executive Jet* to come to the conclusion that the locality rule should not be applied in aviation tort cases is unfounded. The *Executive Jet* case wrestled with the issue of whether maritime tort law should apply when a domestic flight crashes into navigable waters within state territorial limits and in determining that issue the Court discussed the random nature of the location of aviation accidents. 409 U.S. at 261-65, 93 S.Ct. at 501-03. That case does not reach the issue of how to determine jurisdiction if the plane crashes over land and it does not touch upon the issue of foreign sovereign immunity. Furthermore, the admiralty jurisdiction of the federal courts in relation to foreign governments in now ruled by the FSIA, which was not in effect in 1972 when the *Executive Jet* decision was rendered. 28 U.S.C. §1605(b); *Amerada Hess*, 488 U.S. at 438, 109 S.Ct. at 690.

The remainder of the cases relied upon by the plaintiffs relate to issues of conflicts of law which arise from domestic aviation disasters. See, *In re Air Crash at Washington, D.C.*, 559 F.Supp. 333, 340-42 (D.C.Cir.1983) (which state's law should apply when residents of various states are involved in the same disaster); *O'Keefe v. Boeing Company*, 335 F.Supp. 1104, 1110-11 (S.D.N.Y.1971) (which state's conflicts law should apply when an Air Force plane stationed in Massachusetts crashed in Maine and the wrongful death action was brought in New York). In accordance with plaintiffs' use of conflicts of law principles they claim that because the plane was destined for the United States, Pan Am was an American airline and the majority of passengers were citizens of the United States the situs of the tort was actually the United States.

This Court finds plaintiffs' call for a flexible approach for determining the location of an international aviation tort for the purposes of determining jurisdiction unpersuasive as the law to be applied in this action is the FSIA, not federal maritime law or conflicts law. The plain language of §1605(a)(5) states that foreign immunity is excepted only when the tort occurs in the United States. The Supreme Court restricts the definition the "United States" for the purposes of this statute to "the continental United States and those islands that are part of the United States or its possessions..." *Amerada Hess*, 488 U.S. at 440, 109 S.Ct. at 691. As this flight exploded above Lockerbie, Scotland and crashed into Scottish soil, and there is no authority which stands for the proposition that the locality test should not be used, this Court finds this tortious injury was inflicted in Scotland, not the United States.

b. Pan Am Flight 103 as "Territory" of the United States

Plaintiffs seek to expand the maritime law principle that ships are the territory of their flag nation to include commercial airplanes. See, e.g., *United States v. Flores*, 289 U.S. 137, 155, 53 S.Ct. 580, 585, 77 L.Ed. 1086 (1933) ("a merchant vessel...is deemed to be a part of the territory" of "the sovereignty whose flag it flies."); *United States v. Cordova*, 89 F.Supp. 298, 302 (E.D.N.Y.1950) ("American flag vessel is itself territory of the United States"). Applying this territorial approach, the plaintiffs argue that Pan Am Flight 103 was American territory so that the tortious activity injury inflicted on Mrs. Hudson and Mrs. Smith "occurred in the United States."

Adopting plaintiffs' approach would require this Court to expand Supreme Court precedent and overstep the bounds of judicial authority. As noted above, for the purpose of enforcing the FSIA the Supreme Court has defined the United States as "the continental United States and those islands that are part of the United States or its possessions..." *Amerada Hess*, 488 U.S. at 440, 109 S.Ct. at 691. This Court has no authority to broaden that clear definition to include American commercial aircraft. If this Court were to rule in plaintiffs' favor it would be interfering with foreign relations as each nation has the right to regulate the land on which a distressed plane might crash and its own air space. See,

e.g., 49 U.S.C.App. §1348 (1988) (authorizing Secretary of Transportation to regulate use of navigable air space). This Court reiterates that the tortious injury suffered in this case occurred on foreign soil and therefore does not fall within the non-commercial tort exception to the FSIA.

4. Subject Matter Jurisdiction Based on an Implied Waiver Pursuant to 28 U.S.C. §1605(a)(1).

According to §1605(a)(1), a foreign state can waive immunity "either explicitly or by implication..." In interpreting the FSIA "[f]ederal courts have been virtually unanimous in holding that the implied waiver provision of Section 1605(a)(1)...is to be construed narrowly." *Shapiro v. Republic of Bolivia*, 930 F.2d 1013, 1017 (2nd Cir.1991). Plaintiffs claim that Libya impliedly waived immunity when (1) Libya agreed to guaranty satisfaction of any civil damage awards against its operatives as a result of the bombing of Pan Am Flight 103 and (2) when Libya acted in a "non-sovereign" manner.

a. The Guaranty

On February 27, 1992, Ibrahim M. Bishari, Secretary of the Libyan government's "People's Committee for Foreign Liaison and International Cooperation", sent a letter to the Secretary of the United Nations which stated:

Despite the fact that discussion of the question of compensation is premature, since it would only follow from a civil judgment based on a criminal judgment, Libya guarantees the payment of any compensation that might be incurred by the responsibility of the two suspects who are its nationals in the event that they are unable to pay. S/23672, Report of Secretary-General (1992).

The plaintiffs contend this guaranty necessarily means that Libya contemplated the possibility of being haled into an United States court and therefore impliedly waived its right to sovereign immunity.

This Court disagrees with plaintiffs' self-serving interpretation of Mr. Bishari's letter. The above quoted clause indicates the Libyan government only agrees to guaranty civil damages which the Libyan criminal suspects cannot afford to pay when and if those suspects are convicted of criminal activity. The letter, read in totality, makes it clear that Libya does not intend to activate the provisions of that letter unless and until certain conditions are met. Specifically, the correspondence states "[t]he proposals contained in this draft shall be binding [when]...State terrorism against Libya shall end, there shall be a halt to threats and provocations against it…the economic boycott shall be ended…and its name shall finally be removed from the roster of terrorism." S/23672. As those conditions have not been met, this letter does not represent a true "international agreement" and therefore no provision therein can create an implied waiver of sovereign immunity.

Even if the Libyan government had guaranteed civil damages it does not necessarily follow that this Court would find Libya had impliedly waived its right to sovereign immunity pursuant to FSIA. "[B]y signing an international agreement that contains no mention of a waiver of immunity to suit in United States courts or even the availability of a cause of action in the United States" a foreign nation may not waive its immunity pursuant to §1605(a)(1). *Amerada Hess*, 488 U.S. at 442-43, 109 S.Ct. at 693. As the letter makes no reference to our judicial system or the creation of a private right of action to be adjudicated in the United States, it does not necessarily impliedly waive Libya's right to immunity.

b. Violations of the *Jus Cogens* Norm

To interpret the language of §1605(a)(1) plaintiffs argue that the implied waiver of immunity provision codified pre-FSIA case law which held a state is divested of its sovereign character, including immunity, when it participates in non-sovereign acts. See, *United States v. Deutsches Kalisyndikat Gesellschaft*, 31 F.2d 199, 203 (S.D.N.Y.1929) (The Government of France's role as a shareholder in a private French corporation was not sovereign activity so that the corporation was not immune from suit in the United States). To define those acts which amount to an implied waiver plaintiffs look to "standards recognized under international law." H.R.Rep. No. 1487, 94th Cong., 2d Sec. 18, reprinted in 1976 U.S.Code Cong. & Admin.News 6604, 6617. Particularly, plaintiffs assert that Libya's alleged involvement in this bombing impliedly waived immunity as it was a non-sovereign action in the form of a violation of the *jus cogens* norm.

Jus cogens norm is an international law principle which is "accepted by the international community of States as a whole as a norm from which no derogation is permitted…" *Committee of U.S. Citizens in Nicaragua v. Reagan*, 859 F.2d 929, 940 (D.C.Cir.1988) (quoting Vienna Convention on the Law of Treaties, May 23, 1969, art. 53, U.N.Doc. A/ Conf. 39/27, 8 I.L.M. 679). *Jus cogens* violations include "a handful of heinous activities-each of which violates defin-

able, universal and obligatory norms." *Tel-Oren*, 726 F.2d at 781 (Edwards, J., concurring).

There is no authority which provides federal courts with the discretion to determine whether a nation has impliedly waived immunity by examining if that nation was acting in a "sovereign" or "non-sovereign" manner. The legislative history indicates that to decide whether immunity is impliedly waived courts are to inquire as to the foreign government's subjective intent to avail itself to American jurisdiction. *Shapiro*, 930 F.2d at 1017. Congress provided three examples of activity which would warrant the finding of an implied waiver: (1) an agreement to arbitrate in another country, (2) an agreement that the laws of another nation will govern a contract, and (3) the filing of a responsive pleading without raising the sovereign immunity defense. *Id.* (citing H.R.Rep. No. 1487, 94th Cong., 2d Sec. 18, reprinted in 1976 U.S.Code Cong. & Admin.News 6604, 6617). As the instant case is not analogous to these three examples and because participating in "terrorist" activity does not indicate a foreign sovereign's amenability to suit, Libya has not impliedly waive its immunity pursuant to §1605(a)(1).

The District of Colombia Circuit recently determined that the violation of the *jus cogens* norm is not an implied waiver of sovereign immunity. *Princz v. Federal Republic of Germany*, 26 F.3d 1166, 1174 (D.C.Cir.1994), *cert. denied*, 513 U.S. 1121, 115 S.Ct. 923, 130 L.Ed.2d 803 (1995). That case concerned an American Jewish Holocaust survivor who was seeking to sue Germany for war reparations. *Id.* at 1168. The Circuit Court found the atrocities inflicted in the Nazi concentration camps were definitely horrendous violations of the *jus cogens* norm, but that such actions did not create an implied waiver of sovereign immunity as neither the Third Reich nor the modern German government ever indicated "its amenability to suit." *Id.* at 1168-69, 1174. This Court adopts the reasoning in *Princz*. Libya's alleged behavior was inhumane and violative of the *jus cogens* principle, but such actions do not demonstrate that Libya purposefully availed itself to our courts.

CONCLUSION

Although Libya's alleged participation, if true, in this tragedy is outrageous and reprehensible and the human suffering involved is heartbreaking, this Court may not rightly obtain jurisdiction over Libya for the purposes of these private rights of action. Libya's alleged terrorist actions do not fall within the enumerated exceptions to the Foreign Sovereign Immunities Act and therefore Libya must be accorded sovereign immunity from suit.

Notes:

1. In order for a treaty to provide the basis for a cause of action in the courts of the United States, it must be self-executing or there must be legislation providing for a cause of action. Judge Bork, in *Tel-Oren, infra*, Chapter 2.1.C., discussed this principle in relation to the U.N. Charter, finding that Articles 1 and 2 are not self-executing:

> Treaties of the United States, though the law of the land, do not generally create rights that are privately enforceable in courts. *Foster v. Neilson*, 27 U.S. (2 Pet.) 253, 314, 7 L.Ed. 415 (1829), *overruled on other grounds*, *United States v. Percheman*, 32 U.S. (7 Pet.) 51, 8 L.Ed. 604 (1883); *Canadian Transport Co. v. United States*, 663 F.2d 1081, 1092 (D.C.Cir.1980); *Dreyfus v. Von Finck*, 534 F.2d 24, 29-30 (2d Cir.), *cert. denied*, 429 U.S. 835, 97 S.Ct. 102, 50 L.Ed.2d 101 (1976). Absent authorizing legislation, an individual has access to courts for enforcement of a treaty's provisions only when the treaty is self-executing, that is, when it expressly or impliedly provides a private right of action. *Head Money Cases*, 112 U.S. 580, 598-99, 5 S.Ct. 247, 253-54, 28 L.Ed. 798 (1884); *Z & F Assets Realization Corp. v. Hull*, 114 F.2d 464, 470-71 (D.C.Cir.1940), *aff'd on other grounds*, 311 U.S. 470, 489, 61 S.Ct. 351, 355, 85 L.Ed. 288 (1941); *Mannington Mills, Inc. v. Congoleum Corp.*, 595 F.2d at 1298. When no right is explicitly stated, courts look to the treaty as a whole to determine whether it evidences an intent to provide a private right of action. See *Diggs v. Richardson*, 555 F.2d 848, 851 (D.C.Cir.1976).

***

> Articles 1 and 2 of the United Nations Charter are * * * not self-executing. They do not speak in terms of individual rights but impose obligations on nations and on the United Nations itself. They address states, calling on them to fulfill in good faith their obligations as members of the United Nations. Sanctions under article 41, the penultimate bulwark of the Charter, are to be taken by states against other states. Articles 1 and 2, moreover, contain general "purposes and principles," some of which state mere aspirations and none of which can sensibly be thought to have been intended to be judicially enforceable at the behest of individuals....These considerations compel the conclusion that articles 1 and 2 of the U.N. Charter were not intended to give individuals the right to enforce them in municipal courts, particularly since appellants have provided no evidence of a contrary intent. See *Pauling v. McElroy*, 164 F.Supp. 390, 393 (D.D.C.1958), *aff'd*, 278 F.2d 252 (D.C.Cir.), *cert. denied*, *810 **420 364 U.S. 835, 81 S.Ct. 61, 5 L.Ed.2d 60 (1960); *Dreyfus v. Von Finck*, 534 F.2d at 30; *People of Saipan v. Department of Interior*, 502 F.2d 90, 100-03 (9th Cir.1974) (Trask, J., concurring), *cert. denied*, 420 U.S. 1003, 95 S.Ct. 1445, 43 L.Ed.2d 761 (1975); *Sei Fujii v. State*, 38 Cal.2d 718, 242 P.2d 617 (1952).

Tel-Oren v. Libyan Arab Republic, 726 F.2d 774, 808-809 (D.C. Cir. 1984). If this is true, then how did the plaintiffs in *Smith* try to use the U.N. Charter in a different manner?

2.   Does terrorism differ from other forms of human activity that are easily adjudicated by the law? Is terrorism sufficiently unique to suggest that a new legal and conceptual framework was needed to provide adequate remedies for victims? From an organizational perspective, is terrorism very different from global, or even local, commercial and criminal enterprises?

3.   Is it true that the "tort was inflicted in Scotland?" What does the court's use of this fiction suggest about the state of the law?

4.   The plaintiffs sought to invoke the United Nations Charter and Security Council Resolutions to create a cause of action. Why did the plaintiffs resort to alleging that causes of action could be found in these sources? Was this an argument they would have preferred not to make? What alternative legal avenues were available to them?

5.   They also tried to convince the court to apply maritime law to airplanes. What does this demonstrate about the state of U.S. law in 1995? What legal desideratum would have helped the plaintiffs?

6.   For an excellent and detailed account of the history, politics and jurisprudence of the *Smith* case written by the plaintiffs' lead counsel, see Allan Gerson and Jerry Adler, *The Price of Terror*.

2.3 Maritime Jurisdiction

Klinghoffer v. SNC Achille Lauro, 937 F.2d 44 (2d Cir. 1991)

Before OAKES, Chief Judge, TIMBERS and KEARSE, Circuit Judges.

OAKES, Chief Judge:

The Palestine Liberation Organization (the "PLO") appeals from a judgment of the United States District Court for the Southern District of New York, Louis L. Stanton, *Judge*, reported at 739 F.Supp. 854, denying its motion to dismiss various complaints brought against it in connection with the October 1985 seizure of the Italian passenger liner Achille Lauro and the killing of passenger Leon Klinghoffer. The district court rejected the PLO's claims that it is immune from suit in United States courts, that the complaints against it raise non-justiciable political questions, that service of process on its Permanent Observer to the United Nations (the "UN") was insufficient under Rule 4 of the Federal Rules of Civil Procedure, and that personal jurisdiction could not be asserted over it in the state of New York. For the reasons set forth below, we agree with the district court that the PLO is not immune from suit and that this case does not present a non-justiciable political question. However, because we conclude that the remaining questions cannot be resolved on the record before us, we vacate the judgment of the district court and remand the case for further findings.

BACKGROUND

1. The PLO and its Activities in New York

The PLO, which is headquartered in Tunis, Tunisia, describes itself as

the internationally recognized representative of a sovereign people who are seeking to exercise their rights to self-determination, national independence, and territorial integrity. The PLO is the internationally recognized embodiment of the nationhood and sovereignty of the Palestinian people while they await the restoration of their rights through the establishment of a coomprehensive [sic], just and lasting peace in the Middle East.

739 F.Supp. at 857 (quoting affidavit of Ramsey Clark). On November 15, 1988, the Palestine National Council issued a Declaration of Statehood, proclaiming the existence of the State of Palestine and vesting the powers of the provisional government in the executive committee of the PLO. The United States does not give diplomatic recognition to Palestine, although several other nations do.

Since 1974, the PLO, through its representative Zuhdi Labib Terzi, has participated at the UN as a permanent observer. To support its activities at the UN, the PLO purchased a building in Manhattan, which it uses as its UN Mission (the "Mission"). Mr. Terzi and his family reside at the Mission, and eight other employees work there as well. From time to time, other high-ranking officers of the PLO, including its Chairman, Yassar Arafat, use the Mission. In addition to owning a building, the PLO owns an automobile and maintains a bank account in New York, and has a telephone listing in the NYNEX white pages. From time to time, the PLO has engaged in various fundraising and propaganda efforts in New York and elsewhere.

In 1987, Congress enacted the Anti-Terrorism Act (the "ATA"), 22 U.S.C. §§5201-5203 (1988), which makes it unlawful "to receive anything of value except informational material from the PLO" or "to expend funds from the PLO" if the purpose is to further the PLO's interests. *Id.* §5202(1)-(2). The ATA also forbids the establishment or maintenance of "an office, headquarters, premises, or other facilities or establishments within the jurisdiction of the United States at the behest or direction of, or with funds provided by the Palestine Liberation Organization or any of its constituent groups, any successor to any of those, or any agents thereof." *Id.* §5202(3). The ATA does not apply, however, to the PLO's Mission in New York. See *United States v. Palestine Liberation Organization*, 695 F.Supp. 1456, 1464-71 (S.D.N.Y.1988).

2. The Achille Lauro Hijacking

On October 7, 1985, four persons seized the Italian cruise liner Achille Lauro in the Eastern Mediterranean Sea. During the course of the incident, the hijackers murdered an elderly Jewish-American passenger, Leon Klinghoffer, by throwing him and the wheelchair in which he was confined overboard. Shortly after the incident, the hijackers surrendered in Egypt. They were then extradited to Italy, where they were charged and convicted of crimes related to the seizure.

At this point, it remains unclear what role, if any, the PLO played in the events described above. According to some reports, the seizure was undertaken at the behest of Abdul Abbas, who is reportedly a member of the PLO. The PLO, however, denies any responsibility for the hijacking, and maintains that its involvement in the affair was limited to helping to secure the surrender of the hijackers and to ensure the safety of the ship and its passengers.

On November 27, 1985, Marilyn Klinghoffer [FN1] and the estate of Leon Klinghoffer filed suit in the Southern District of New York against the owner of the Achille Lauro, the charterer of the vessel, two travel agencies, and various other defendants. Other passengers who were aboard the Achille Lauro during the hijacking also commenced actions in the Southern District against the ship's owner and charterer, as well as against the travel agencies. The defendants in these actions then impleaded the PLO, seeking indemnification or contribution, as well as compensatory and punitive damages for tortious interference with their businesses. On October 7, 1988, two other passengers on the Achille Lauro brought separate actions in the Southern District against the PLO directly.

FN1. After Marilyn Klinghoffer's death, Ilsa Klinghoffer and Lisa Klinghoffer Arbitter, as co-executors of both Marilyn and Leon's estates, were substituted for Marilyn Klinghoffer as plaintiffs.

On April 27, 1987, the PLO moved to dismiss the third party complaints against it. This motion was later extended to encompass the two direct suits as well. In an opinion and order dated June 7, 1990, the court denied the PLO's motion. The PLO then moved for reargument, as well as for certification of the case for interlocutory appeal. The court denied the PLO's motion for reargument, but granted the motion for certification. Thereafter, in an opinion dated December 7, 1990, we granted the PLO's petition for permission to appeal, see 921 F.2d 21, and this appeal followed.

DISCUSSION

1. Immunity from Suit

The PLO first argues that it is a sovereign state and therefore immune from suit under the Foreign Sovereign Immunities Act (the "FSIA"), 28 U.S.C. §1602 et seq. (1988). As support for this argument, it relies on its "political and governmental character and structure, its commitment to and practice of its own statehood, and its unlisted and indeterminable membership." Brief for Appellant at 7. However, this Court has limited the definition of "state" to " 'entit[ies] that ha[ve] a defined territory and a permanent population, [that are] under the control of [their] own government, and that engage[ ] in, or ha[ve] the capacity to engage in, formal relations with other such entities.' " *National Petrochemical Co. v. M/T Stolt Sheaf*, 860 F.2d 551, 553 (2d Cir.1988)

(quoting *Restatement (Third) of the Foreign Relations Law of the United States* §201 (1987)), *cert. denied*, 489 U.S. 1081, 109 S.Ct. 1535, 103 L.Ed.2d 840 (1989). It is quite clear that the PLO meets none of those requirements.

First, the PLO has no defined territory. To be sure, the PLO's November 15, 1988 Declaration of Statehood "contemplates" that the state's territory will consist of the West Bank, the Gaza Strip, and East Jerusalem. The fact that the PLO hopes to have a defined territory at some future date, however, does not establish that it has a defined territory now. Indeed, the Declaration's assertion that "[t]he State of Palestine is the state of Palestinians wherever they may be" underscores the PLO's current lack of a territorial structure. In addition, because the PLO does not have a defined territory, it cannot have a permanent population.

The PLO is also unable to demonstrate that the State of Palestine is under the control of its own government. After all, without a defined territory, what, we ask, could the PLO possibly control? Moreover, even accepting the PLO's contention that the State of Palestine incorporates the West Bank, the Gaza Strip, and East Jerusalem, these areas are all under the control of the State of Israel, not the PLO.

Finally, despite the fact that some countries have "recognized" the PLO, the PLO does not have the capacity to enter into genuine formal relations with other nations. This is true primarily because, without a defined territory under unified governmental control, the PLO lacks the ability actually to implement the obligations that normally accompany formal participation in the international community. See Note, *The International Legal Implications of the November 1988 Palestinian Declaration of Statehood*, 25 Stan.J.Int'l L. 681, 696 (1989).

Contrary to the PLO's assertions, *Tel-Oren v. Libyan Arab Republic*, 726 F.2d 774 (D.C.Cir.1984), *cert. denied*, 470 U.S. 1003, 105 S.Ct. 1354, 84 L.Ed.2d 377 (1985), does not establish that the PLO is a sovereign nation entitled to immunity under the FSIA. In *Tel-Oren*, the D.C. Circuit affirmed the dismissal on jurisdictional grounds of a suit brought by Israeli citizens against persons allegedly responsible for an armed attack on a civilian bus in Israel. [FN2] Although each of the three judges in *Tel-Oren* agreed that the suit should be dismissed, they did so in three separate opinions, each with its own distinct reasoning. The PLO suggests that at least two of these opinions support the theory that the PLO is a state entitled to sovereign immunity. Nothing could be further from the truth. Judge Edwards, in his opinion, wrote that "the PLO is not a recognized member of the community of nations," *Id.* at 791, Judge Bork noted that the PLO "apparent [ly] lack[ed]…international law status as a state," *Id.* at 805, and Judge Robb concluded simply that the PLO "ought to remain an organization 'of whose existence we know nothing...' " *Id.* at 824 (quoting *United States v. Klintock*, 18 U.S. (5 Wheat.) 144, 149, 5 L.Ed. 55 (1820)). How the PLO reads these statements to support its claim to statehood we do not see.

FN2. Because the incident in *Tel-Oren* did not occur on the high seas, as did the hijacking here, admiralty was not an available basis of jurisdiction. Thus, the court had to decide whether the incident presented a federal question, or, in the alternative, whether jurisdiction could be asserted under 28 U.S.C. §1350, which provides for jurisdiction over civil actions "by an alien for a tort only, committed in violation of the law of nations or a treaty of the United States."
The PLO also maintains that it is immune from suit as a result of its status as a permanent observer at the UN. It relies for this argument on the Agreement Between the United Nations and the United States of America Regarding the Headquarters of the United Nations (the "Headquarters Agreement"), reprinted at 22 U.S.C.A. §287 Note. By its terms, however, the Headquarters Agreement extends immunity only to representatives of members of the UN, not to observers such as the PLO. See *Id.* §15. We see no reason to extend the immunities provided by the Headquarters Agreement beyond those explicitly stated.

Finally, the PLO claims that, because the United States has not extended it formal diplomatic recognition, it lacks the capacity to be sued in United States courts. This claim is without merit. While unrecognized regimes are generally precluded from appearing as plaintiffs in an official capacity without the Executive Branch's consent, see *Banco Nacional v. Sabbatino*, 376 U.S. 398, 410-11, 84 S.Ct. 923, 931, 11 L.Ed.2d 804 (1964); *National Petrochemical Co.*, 860 F.2d at 554-55, there is no bar to suit where an unrecognized regime is brought into court as a defendant. Cf. *United States v. Lumumba*, 741 F.2d 12, 15 (2d Cir.1984) (contempt proceeding against attorney claiming to be representative of the "Republic of New Afrika," an unrecognized nation), *cert. denied*, 479 U.S. 855, 107 S.Ct. 192, 93 L.Ed.2d 125 (1986). Accordingly, the fact that the United States has not recognized the PLO does not provide a basis for immunity.

2. Political Question

The PLO next argues that this case constitutes a non-justiciable political question because it "raises foreign policy questions and political questions in a volatile context lacking satisfactory criteria for judicial determination." Brief for Appellant at 27. This claim, it appears, rests on the

concededly correct observation that the PLO is a political organization that engenders strong feelings of both support and opposition, and that any decision the district court enters will surely exacerbate the controversy surrounding the PLO's activities. However, the doctrine "is one of 'political questions,' not one of 'political cases.' " *Baker v. Carr*, 369 U.S. 186, 217, 82 S.Ct. 691, 710, 7 L.Ed.2d 663 (1962). The fact that the issues before us arise in a politically charged context does not convert what is essentially an ordinary tort suit into a non-justiciable political question.

In *Baker*, the Court wrote that:

[p]rominent on the surface of any case held to involve a political question is found [1] a textually demonstrable constitutional commitment of the issue to a coordinate political department; or [2] a lack of judicially discoverable and manageable standards for resolving it; or [3] the impossibility of deciding without an initial policy determination of a kind clearly for nonjudicial discretion; or [4] the impossibility of a court's undertaking independent resolution without expressing lack of the respect due coordinate branches of government; or [5] an unusual need for unquestioning adherence to a political decision already made; or [6] the potentiality of embarrassment from multifarious pronouncements by various departments on one question.

Id. Although no one factor is dispositive, Justice Brennan, the author of *Baker*, has suggested that the first question-whether there is a "textually demonstrable constitutional commitment of the issue to a coordinate political department"-is of particular importance. See *Goldwater v. Carter*, 444 U.S. 996, 1006, 100 S.Ct. 533, 538, 62 L.Ed.2d 428 (1979) (Brennan, J., dissenting) ("Properly understood, the political-question doctrine restrains courts from reviewing an exercise of foreign policy judgment by the coordinate political branch to which authority to make that judgment has been 'constitutional[ly] commit[ted].' "). Here, we are faced with an ordinary tort suit, alleging that the defendants breached a duty of care owed to the plaintiffs or their decedents. The department to whom this issue has been "constitutionally committed" is none other than our own-the Judiciary. This factor alone, then, strongly suggests that the political question doctrine does not apply.

All of the other factors identified in *Baker*, moreover, also militate against applying the political question doctrine here. First, because the common law of tort provides clear and well-settled rules on which the district court can easily rely, this case does not require the court to render a decision in the absence of "judicially discoverable and manageable standards." Second, because the PLO has maintained throughout this litigation that the hijacking was an act of piracy, rather than a terrorist act, a finding for or against the PLO does not depend on a prior political assessment about the value of terrorism, and thus no "initial policy decision of a kind clearly for nonjudicial discretion" need be made. [FN3] Third, given the fact that both the Executive and Legislative Branches have expressly endorsed the concept of suing terrorist organizations in federal court, see Letter from Abraham D. Sofaer, United States Department of State, Office of the Legal Adviser, to Justice Carmen B. Ciparick, (Sept. 4, 1986); 18 U.S.C.A. §2333(a) (West Supp.1990) (providing a civil remedy in federal court for United States nationals injured by acts of international terrorism), resolution of this matter will not exhibit "a lack of the respect due coordinate branches of government." Fourth, this case does not require us to display "unquestioning adherence to a political decision already made," because no prior political decisions are questioned-or even implicated-by the matter before us. Finally, because this lawsuit is consistent with both the Executive and Legislative Branch's attitude toward terrorists, resolution of this case does not have the potential for "embarrassment from multifarious pronouncements by various departments on one question."

FN3. For this reason, the opinions of Judges Bork and Robb in *Tel-Oren, supra*, which suggested that judgments about the role of terrorism in international struggles are best entrusted to the Executive Branch, see 726 F.2d at 805 (Bork, J.); *Id.* at 825-26 (Robb, J.), are inapplicable here. In any event, given the Executive Branch's repeated condemnations of international terrorism, we believe that any initial policy decision that might conceivably be required has already been made.

Accordingly, we agree with the district court that the political question doctrine does not bar the claims presented here.

3. Personal Jurisdiction

The PLO next contends that its contacts with New York are insufficient to support an assertion of personal jurisdiction over it in the Southern District of New York. [FN4] For the reasons set forth below, we believe this claim cannot be resolved on the record before us, and we therefore remand to the district court for further findings of fact.

FN4. At the outset, we disagree with appellee Chandris that the PLO waived its right to contest personal jurisdiction by

participating in discovery in these proceedings. First, we have no way of knowing whether Chandris is correct that the PLO participated in the depositions of plaintiffs Seymour and Viola Meskin on August 5 and 6, 1987, as Chandris has not included any documentary support for this claim-such as, for example, a deposition transcript-in the appellate record. In any event, even if the PLO did participate in those hearings, it did so before any complaints were filed against it. Thus, no assertion of jurisdiction had yet been made over it, and there was accordingly no jurisdictional defense that it could have waived.

Based on the principles discussed by Judge Leisure in *Andros Compania Maritima S.A. v. Intertanker Ltd.*, 714 F.Supp. 669, 673-74 (S.D.N.Y.1989), as well as the natural implications of our opinion in *Arrowsmith v. United Press Int'l*, 320 F.2d 219, 223 (2d Cir.1963) (en banc), the law of the forum state-here, New York-governs the issue of personal jurisdiction in admiralty cases. Under the New York long-arm statute, the only plausible basis for jurisdiction over the PLO is section 301 of the New York Civil Practice Law and Rules ("CPLR"), which provides for general jurisdiction over defendant corporations that are "doing business" in New York. [FN5] See *Laufer v. Ostrow*, 55 N.Y.2d 305, 310-11, 449 N.Y.S.2d 456, 458, 434 N.E.2d 692, 694 (1982). The New York Court of Appeals has not yet decided whether the "doing business" rule applies to unincorporated associations. However, because "the form of organization by which a defendant does business is irrelevant to any policy governing acquisition of jurisdiction," 1 J. Weinstein, H. Korn & A. Miller, *New York Civil Practice*, ¶ 301.15, at 3-31, we see no reason to distinguish between corporate and non-corporate organizations in this regard. Cf. *Forgash v. Paley*, 659 F.Supp. 728, 730 (S.D.N.Y.1987) (Weinfeld, J.) (applying the "doing business" test to non-corporate, individual defendants). Accordingly, if the PLO meets the doing business standard, jurisdiction under section 301 would be appropriate. [FN6]

FN5. Appellee Chandris suggests an alternative basis for jurisdiction-namely, that the PLO consented to jurisdiction in this case by participating in an unrelated lawsuit in state court. A party's consent to jurisdiction in one case, however, extends to that case alone. It in no way opens that party up to other lawsuits in the same jurisdiction in which consent was given, where the party does not consent and no other jurisdictional basis is available.

FN6. In addressing this question ourselves, we reject appellee Chandris's claim that the decision in *United States v. PLO*, 695 F.Supp. 1456 (S.D.N.Y.1988), resolved the question whether the PLO meets the doing business standard of section 301. In *United States v. PLO*, the statute at issue created a federal, rather than a state, jurisdictional standard. See *Id.* at 1461. Because the jurisdictional bases of New York law are more limited than those allowed under federal standards, see CPLR §302, McLaughlin Practice Commentary, the fact that jurisdiction may have been appropriate under federal law does not establish that jurisdiction is now appropriate under CPLR §301.

An organization is "doing business" under section 301 when it is engaged in " 'such a continuous and systematic course' " of activity that it can be deemed to be "present" in the state of New York. *Laufer*, 55 N.Y.2d at 310-11, 449 N.Y.S.2d at 458, 434 N.E.2d at 694 (citations omitted). Whether this test is met depends on the aggregate of the organization's activities; the key question is whether "the quality and nature" of the defendant's contacts with New York "make it reasonable and just according to ' "traditional notions of fair play and substantial justice" ' that it be required to defend the action" in New York. 55 N.Y.2d at 311, 449 N.Y.S.2d at 458, 434 N.E.2d at 694 (citations omitted).

Here, the PLO has a number of contacts with the state of New York. It owns a building in Manhattan, which it uses as an office and residence for its employees, and it owns an automobile, maintains a bank account, and has a telephone listing in New York as well. In terms of its activities, it participates actively at the United Nations headquarters in Manhattan as a Permanent Observer, and its representatives have at times engaged in speaking tours and fundraising activities throughout the State. The question, then, is whether these activities amount to "doing business" within the meaning of section 301.

The district court concluded that all of the above activities, when viewed as a whole, indicate that the PLO is engaged in business in New York State. See 739 F.Supp. at 863. This analysis, however, fails to distinguish those activities the PLO conducts as an observer at the UN from those activities it conducts for other purposes. In our view, only those activities not conducted in furtherance of the PLO's observer status may properly be considered as a basis of jurisdiction.

We reach this conclusion for two reasons. First, were the PLO not a permanent observer at the UN, it would not be entitled to enter New York at all. See *United States v. PLO*, 695 F.Supp. 1456, 1471 (S.D.N.Y.1988) (finding that, pursuant to the ATA, the PLO is prohibited from engaging in any activities in this country other than the maintenance of a mission to the UN). It is allowed to come to New York only because the Headquarters Agreement effectively removes control over the UN Headquarters and related areas from the jurisdiction of the United States. In other words, the PLO's participation in the UN is dependent on the legal fiction that the UN Headquarters is not really United States territory at all, but is rather neutral ground over which the United States has ceded control. For a federal court then to turn around and conclude that the PLO has been doing business in New York as a result of its UN activities would, we believe, be rather duplicitous.

Second, and more importantly, basing jurisdiction on the PLO's participation in UN-related activities would put an undue burden on the ability of foreign organizations to participate in the UN's affairs. In an analogous context, courts have held that jurisdiction in the District of Columbia may not be grounded on a non-resident's "getting information from or giving information to the government, or getting the government's permission to do something." *Investment Co. Inst. v. United States*, 550 F.Supp. 1213, 1216-17 (D.D.C.1982). Although this "government contacts" rule is based in part on the constitutional right "to petition the Government for redress of grievances," see *Naartex Consulting Corp. v. Watt*, 722 F.2d 779, 786-87 (D.C.Cir.1983), *cert. denied*, 467 U.S. 1210, 104 S.Ct. 2399, 81 L.Ed.2d 355 (1984)-a right not implicated here-it also appears to be based on non-constitutional policy considerations, such as the Judiciary's reluctance to interfere with the smooth functioning of other governmental entities. [FN7] As appellees conceded at oral argument, these same concerns militate against basing jurisdiction over the PLO on its UN-related activities. Accordingly, we conclude that jurisdiction may be asserted over the PLO only if its non-UN related activities rise to the level of doing business under section 301.

FN7. The use of jurisdictional immunities to further non-constitutional policy goals is not limited to the context of government lobbying. See, e.g., *Stewart v. Ramsay*, 242 U.S. 128, 37 S.Ct. 44, 61 L.Ed. 192 (1916) (holding that service of process may not be executed on a non-resident who comes into the jurisdiction to participate in litigation as a plaintiff, defendant, or witness); *Shapiro & Son Curtain Corp. v. Glass*, 348 F.2d 460 (2d Cir.) (exempting witnesses who appear in judicial proceedings from service of process), *cert. denied*, 382 U.S. 942, 86 S.Ct. 397, 15 L.Ed.2d 351 (1965).

With regard to the PLO's non-UN activities, Judge Stanton noted that "[e]very month or two, Mr. Terzi speaks in public and to the media in New York in support of the PLO's cause," 739 F.Supp. at 863, and appellees have pointed to a number of other proselytizing and fundraising activities the PLO has undertaken. Taken together, we believe these activities would suffice to meet the doing business standard. However, the evidence in the record concerning the PLO's non-UN activities is limited to deposition testimony taken before the end of 1987, [FN8] when Congress passed the ATA. In light of the ATA, it is quite possible that the PLO was forced to cease its non-UN activities in New York some time after 1987. Thus, because personal jurisdiction depends on the defendant's contacts with the forum state at the time the lawsuit was filed, see 4 C. Wright & A. Miller, *Federal Practice and Procedure*, §1051, at 160-62 (1987), personal jurisdiction over the PLO may be lacking with respect to those complaints that were filed after 1987. [FN9]

FN8. The only indication in the record that the PLO has engaged in fundraising and propaganda activities comes from the depositions of Mr. Terzi, taken on March 31, 1986, and Hasan Abdul-Rahman, taken on October 6, 1987.

FN9. This conclusion is not affected by the Supreme Court's recent decision in *Freeport-McMoRan, Inc. v. K N Energy, Inc.*, 498 U.S. 426, 111 S.Ct. 858, 112 L.Ed.2d 951 (1991) (per curiam), which held that diversity jurisdiction, once established, is not defeated by the addition of a non-diverse party to the action. In *Freeport*, the Court concluded that the addition of a non-diverse party to the *original complaint* does not destroy diversity, on the theory that, "if jurisdiction exists at the time an action is commenced, such jurisdiction may not be divested by subsequent events." 111 S.Ct. at 860. This holding is inapplicable to the present case for two reasons. First, it relates only to the question of subject matter jurisdiction, and says nothing about the question of personal jurisdiction with which the present controversy is concerned. Second, the third-party complaints and the two direct suits filed against the PLO were not simply additions to the original complaint, as was the amendment to the complaint in *Freeport*, but were new actions entirely. As such, defects in personal jurisdiction as to those new complaints cannot be overcome by the fact that personal jurisdiction over the PLO may have existed at the time the first complaint was filed.

Accordingly, on remand, the court should determine whether the PLO's non-UN-related contacts with New York provided a sufficient basis for jurisdiction at the time each of the complaints was filed. In conducting this analysis, it should pay careful attention to those complaints filed after 1987, and determine whether the PLO continued in its fundraising and proselytizing activities after the ATA was passed.

4. Service of Process

Even if the court concludes on remand that personal jurisdiction may be asserted over the PLO with respect to some or all of the complaints, the question remains as to whether service of process on the PLO's Permanent Observer to the UN was sufficient. For the reasons set forth below, we believe further findings are required before the district court can resolve this question conclusively.

Although its arguments on this point are somewhat muddled, it appears that the PLO's service of process argument essentially breaks down to two distinct claims. The first claim is that the law of the forum state determines the procedure for suing an unincorporated association such as the PLO, and that, because New York law provides that unincorporated associations can be sued only by naming (and accordingly serving) the president or treasurer personally, service on the PLO's Permanent Observer was insufficient. [FN10] See N.Y.Gen.Ass'ns Law §13 (McKinney Supp.1991). The second claim is that, even if New York law does not apply, and suing the PLO in its common name is sufficient, service of process on the Permanent Observer was deficient under federal standards.

FN10. We state that the PLO's arguments are muddled because, at times, it appears that its claim is simply that the parties failed to comply with New York's requirement of *naming* the President and Treasurer, rather than the requirement of *serving* the President and Treasurer personally. To the extent the claim is, in fact, that the requirement of naming the President and Treasurer was not met, however, it is undermined by the complaints' reference to "John Doe as President and Richard Roe as Treasurer."

Our first task is to determine whether New York law is controlling on this issue, or whether a federal standard is to govern. Under Rule 17(b) of the Federal Rules of Civil Procedure, the law of the forum state determines the manner in which an unincorporated association must be sued, except where the complaint alleges violations of "substantive right[s] existing under the Constitution or laws of the United States," in which case federal law governs. Thus, if the claims asserted here are non-federal causes of action, the complaints would have to comport with the law of New York, which, as noted above, would require naming and serving the PLO's president or treasurer. See N.Y.Gen.Ass'ns Law §13. If they are federal claims, however, naming the PLO in its common name and delivering service of process to its managing or general agent would suffice. See *Oyler v. National Guard Ass'n*, 743 F.2d 545, 550 (7th Cir.1984). At the outset, then, we must determine whether the complaints raise federal or non-federal law claims.

The district court concluded that the claims in this case are federal, because "federal maritime law applies." See 739 F.Supp. at 865-66. However, the court did not engage in a choice of law analysis, and itself noted that, "at this point[,] it is not clear which [jurisdiction's] law will apply." *Id.* at 866. As such, although it stated that federal maritime *law* applies, what it probably meant to say was that the case was brought under the admiralty and maritime *jurisdiction* of the federal courts. An assertion of admiralty jurisdiction, however, does not mean that the underlying claims raise "substantive right[s] existing under the Constitution or laws of the United States" within the meaning of Rule 17(b). Cf. *Romero v. International Terminal Operating Co.*, 358 U.S. 354, 368, 79 S.Ct. 468, 478, 3 L.Ed.2d 368 (1959) (holding that maritime cases not involving federal statutes do not arise under the laws of the United States for purposes of federal question jurisdiction). Rather, under *Lauritzen v. Larsen*, 345 U.S. 571, 73 S.Ct. 921, 97 L.Ed. 1254 (1953), another nation's contacts with a particular event may be so great as to warrant the application of the law of that nation, even if jurisdiction has properly been asserted in federal court on the basis of admiralty. See *Bilyk v. Vessel Nair*, 754 F.2d 1541, 1543-45 (9th Cir.1985) (applying *Lauritzen*).

Indeed, the district court was fully aware that, under *Lauritzen*, Italian law might ultimately be found to apply on the facts of this case. See 739 F.Supp. at 866. However, it concluded that "[i]f...foreign law applies, it will be because federal law requires its use," *Id.*, and that, as a result, the complaints would remain federal for purposes of Rule 17(b). This analysis, we believe, confuses federal *choice* of foreign law with federal *incorporation* of state and foreign law rules. In the latter situation, a federal court that has the power to create a federal rule of decision may choose to exercise that power by incorporating legal principles derived from state or foreign law. See, e.g., *United States v. Kimbell Foods, Inc.*, 440 U.S. 715, 728, 99 S.Ct. 1448, 1458, 59 L.Ed.2d 711 (1979); *Barkanic v. General Admin. of Civil Aviation*, 923 F.2d 957, 961 (2d Cir.1991). When state or foreign law is used in this sense, it becomes a federal rule for all practical purposes; for example, it is binding on state courts under the Supremacy Clause. See Field, *Sources of Law: The Scope of Federal Common Law*, 99 Harv.L.Rev. 881, 963-64 (1986). By contrast, where a federal court concludes that another jurisdiction has the greatest interest in regulating a particular situation, it applies that law outright-indeed, it may be constitutionally prohibited from applying another jurisdiction's law to the case. See *Allstate Ins. Co. v. Hague*, 449 U.S. 302, 310-13, 101 S.Ct. 633, 638-40, 66

L.Ed.2d 521 (1981) (concluding that courts may not apply the law of jurisdictions that lack significant contacts with the case); P. Bator, D. Meltzer, P. Mishkin & D. Shapiro, Hart & Wechsler's *The Federal Courts and the Federal System* 798-99 (3d ed. 1988) (noting that *Hague* applies to federal courts). Under these circumstances, the foreign rule does not simply give content to what is essentially a federal substantive right, but rather applies of its own force. Thus, it does not assume the status of federal law.

Accordingly, if the district court concludes that *Lauritzen* requires it to apply Italian law to this case, no federal right would be involved, and Rule 17(b) would require the application of New York law with respect to the method of bringing suit against an unincorporated association. Thus, because New York law mandates serving the PLO's president or treasurer, service of process on the Permanent Observer would be inadequate, and the complaints would have to be dismissed. [FN11]

FN11. Such a dismissal, of course, would be without prejudice. See 5A C. Wright & A. Miller, *Federal Practice and Procedure* §1353, at 285-86 (1990).

If, however, the court determines that United States maritime law governs, naming the PLO in its common name would be sufficient, and service could then be made on the PLO's "managing or general agent." Fed.R.Civ.P. 4(d)(3). Under those circumstances, the only issue would be whether the PLO's Permanent Observer to the UN constitutes a managing or general agent within the meaning of Rule 4(d)(3). In our view, the evidence in the record indicates that the Permanent Observer's functions in New York are comparable to those of a general agent. Accordingly, in the event the district court concludes that United States law governs, a dismissal on service of process grounds would be unwarranted.

Vacated and remanded, with instructions to determine whether personal jurisdiction can be asserted over the PLO with respect to some or all of the complaints at issue here, and, if so, whether service of process on the PLO's Permanent Observer to the UN was sufficient.

Notes:

1. Interestingly, *Klinghoffer* was not originally a terrorism case at all. The plaintiffs in the case, Marilyn Klinghoffer and the estate of Leon Klinghoffer, filed suit against the owner of the Achille Lauro, the charterer of the vessel, two travel agencies, and various other defendants. They did not file suit directly against the PLO. The PLO was impleaded

by the defendants, who filed a third party claim for indemnification or contribution. What accounts for the plaintiffs' apparent reluctance to sue the PLO, which was suspected of involvement in the attack?

2. Why were fundamental, basic, threshold procedural issues, such as service of process and personal jurisdiction, so hotly contested in *Klinghoffer*?

3. Certainly, this was not the first case against a foreign non-state entity in U.S courts concerning acts that occurred on the high seas. Accordingly, why was it unclear whether U.S. maritime law applied?

4. If a statute could be enacted to remedy the procedural obstacles confronted by the Klinghoffers, what would it look like? What elements would it contain? What language would be helpful to overcome the numerous threshold issues confronted by the parties in this case?

2.4 Foreign Sovereign Immunities Act— Commercial Exception

Cicippio v. Islamic Republic of Iran, **30 F.3d 164 (D.C. Cir. 1994)**

SILBERMAN, Circuit Judge:

Appellants appeal from the district court's order dismissing their action against the Islamic Republic of Iran for lack of subject matter jurisdiction. Concluding that kidnapping is not, by its nature, a commercial act, that dealings directly between two sovereign states do not constitute "commercial activity" within the meaning of the Foreign Sovereign Immunities Act, and that the "noncommercial tort" exception does not apply, we affirm.

I.

This case arises out of the well-publicized abductions of appellants Joseph Cicippio and David Jacobson in Lebanon. [FN1] Appellants' complaint alleges that while working in Lebanon, Cicippio and Jacobson were abducted by Islamic fundamentalists hired by the State of Iran and held by those agents for an extended period of time, during which they were tortured. [FN2] Iran conditioned the release of Cicippio and Jacobson on the return of Iranian assets frozen in this country by the United States government. That abduction, it is also alleged, caused direct effects in the United States through the emotional harm suffered by the victims' families, the payment of monies to the captors by Mrs. Cicippio, and the unfreezing of Iranian assets. Jacobson and

Cicippio, on the basis of these factual allegations, sought damages for a number of intentional torts and for violations of international law. They invoked the "commercial activity" and the "noncommercial tort" exceptions to the Foreign Sovereign Immunities Act (FSIA) as bases for federal court jurisdiction.

FN1. Appellants include Cicippio's wife, Elham Cicippio, as well.

FN2. In reviewing an order dismissing for lack of jurisdiction under FED.R.CIV.P. 12(b)(1) we take all well-pleaded facts as true.

Appellee, the Islamic Republic of Iran, moved to dismiss the suit on grounds that the court lacked subject matter jurisdiction under the FSIA as well as personal jurisdiction over the defendant. The district court granted the motion to dismiss on lack of subject matter jurisdiction. It concluded that although Iran's alleged actions did appear to constitute "commercial activity" within the meaning of the FSIA-at least under the Supreme Court's analysis-"state-supported kidnapping, hostage-taking, and similar universally criminal ventures were simply not the sorts of proprietary enterprises within the contemplation of Congress when it enacted the 'commercial activity' exception to [the] FSIA." This appeal followed.

II.

The Foreign Sovereign Immunities Act of 1976, 28 U.S.C. §1602 *et seq.* (1988), provides that a "foreign state shall be immune from the jurisdiction of the courts of the United States and of the States." 28 U.S.C. §1604 (1988). The Act does create, however, a number of exceptions to this immunity. Two are invoked here: the "commercial activity" and the "noncommercial tort" exceptions. See 28 U.S.C. §§1605(a)(2), 1605(a)(5) (1988). We consider them in turn.

A.

The Act permits a suit against a foreign government to proceed in any case in which the action is based upon a commercial activity carried on in the United States by a foreign state; or upon an act performed in the United States in connection with a commercial activity of the foreign state elsewhere; or *upon an act outside the United States in connection with a commercial activity of the foreign state elsewhere and that act causes a direct effect in the United States.* 28 U.S.C. §1605(a)(2) (1988) (emphasis added).

Appellants rely on the third clause of this subsection; i.e., they claim that the government of Iran committed an act in connection with commercial activity elsewhere. The FSIA defines "commercial activity" as "either a regular course of commercial conduct or a particular commercial transaction or act." 28 U.S.C. §1603(d) (1988). The subsection further directs that the "commercial character of an activity shall be determined by reference to the nature of the course of conduct or particular transaction or act, rather than by reference to its purpose." *Id.* We have not a little difficulty in understanding appellants' precise theory of the case because they do not clearly identify which of the allegations is the "act" and which makes up the "commercial activity". As best we can determine, appellants treat "hostage taking for profit" as both the act and the commercial activity. In other words, appellants do not specifically claim that the freezing or prospective unfreezing of Iranian assets (or the payments made by Cicippio's relatives) to gain his release constitute commercial activity, and that the kidnapping is an act in connection with that transaction. Instead, appellants present the situation as one integrated activity of a commercial nature which suggests that they should be suing under the first clause. We assume, however, that appellants are implicitly claiming that one of the acts relating to the abduction takes place "elsewhere" from the commercial activity. We therefore consider whether a foreign sovereign's alleged use of non-official agents to conduct alleged hostage takings to gain economic advantages can be considered a commercial activity.

The Supreme Court first had occasion to apply the FSIA's phrase "commercial activity" in *Republic of Argentina v. Weltover, Inc.*, 504 U.S. 607, 112 S.Ct. 2160, 119 L.Ed.2d 394 (1992). There the government of Argentina had issued bonds payable in dollars to support its guarantee of payments of loans its domestic borrowers took from foreign creditors. When the Argentine government unilaterally extended the time of payment it was sued in New York (where payment was to be made) by foreign creditors. Drawing on the legislative history of the FSIA, as well as on the pre-Act practice of the State Department, the Court conclude[d] that when a foreign government acts, not as regulator of a market, but in the *manner* of a private player within it, the foreign sovereign's actions are "commercial" within the meaning of the FSIA…[T]he issue is whether the particular actions that the foreign state performs (whatever the motive behind them) are the *type* of actions by which a private party engages in "trade and traffic or commerce." Thus, a foreign government's issuance of regulations limiting foreign currency exchange is a sovereign activity, because such authoritative control of commerce cannot be exercised by a

private party; whereas a contract to buy army boots or even bullets is a "commercial" activity, because private parties can similarly use sales contracts to acquire goods. *Weltover*, 504 U.S. at ___, 112 S.Ct. at 2166 (citations omitted) (emphasis added). The government of Argentina, recognizing that the statute made its purpose irrelevant, nevertheless argued that one could not ignore the context in which it issued the bonds-which was in order to enhance the ability of its citizens to borrow foreign capital, not like the ordinary commercial issuance of debt to raise capital or refinance debt. The court assumed *arguendo* that the notions of context and purpose might be different but rejected Argentina's argument because the bonds had been issued, just as might be done by a private actor, to restructure the government's existing obligations. Putting aside for now the relationship between purpose and context, we take from *Weltover* the key proposition that in determining whether a given government activity is commercial under the act, we must ask whether the activity is one in which commercial actors typically engage.

Appellants insist that this formulation does not mean that when a sovereign is alleged to have engaged in *illegal* activities such activities should be thought not commercial *per se*. The Second Circuit had earlier determined that kidnapping (and assassination) could not be considered commercial activities under FSIA because a private person could not engage in such activity *lawfully*. See *Letelier v. Republic of Chile*, 748 F.2d 790, 797 (2d Cir.1984). Appellants point out, however, that all causes of action can be thought, in some sense, to accuse a defendant of acting unlawfully, and the distinction between tortious and criminal acts is not always clear.

The most recent FSIA Supreme Court decision, *Saudi Arabia v. Nelson*, 507 U.S. 349, 113 S.Ct. 1471, 123 L.Ed.2d 47 (1993), may well undermine the Second Circuit's categorical approach. There an American plaintiff hired in the United States to work in a Saudi hospital claimed that he had been wrongly imprisoned and tortured by Saudi police in retaliation "for his whistle blowing" directed at certain hospital practices. Although the Second Circuit's approach offered the most obvious line of analysis, the Court did not take it. Instead, the Court concluded that since the basis of the claim was the alleged tortious-perhaps criminal-actions of the Saudi police (not the arguably commercial activity in recruiting Nelson), and private parties cannot exercise that "*sort*" of power while engaging in commerce, the activity could not be thought "commercial." [FN3]

FN3. The claim was brought under Clause 1 of the Act so the Court did not consider whether the torture could be regarded as an act in connection with the commercial activity of operating the hospital.

The Court dismissed the contention that the Saudi government typically uses such techniques to resolve commercial disputes by emphasizing that the "powers allegedly abused were those of police and penal officers" and noting that "[i]n any event the argument is off the point, for it goes to purpose." 507 U.S. at ___, 113 S.Ct. at 1480. The last observation, it seems to us, makes abundantly clear, on top of the statute and *Weltover*, that in this case we cannot consider the alleged motive of the Iranian government in determining whether appellants' claim if true would involve commercial activity. It is to the character and type of activity to which we should look; purpose must be disregarded and a plaintiff cannot, by describing the act in question as intertwined with its purpose, avoid the statutory preclusion. That leaves the issue whether the hostage taking itself can be described as a commercial activity-without regard to its purpose.

Appellants, relying on *Nelson*, assert that it can and should be so regarded. Because the Supreme Court in *Nelson* rested on the governmental status of the police alleged to have tortured the plaintiff, rather than the character of the act, one might believe that if those very acts had been conducted on behalf of the Saudi government by contract thugs the Saudi government would not have enjoyed immunity under the statute. Justice White, concurring, made exactly that point. 507 U.S. at ___, ___, 113 S.Ct. at 1481, 1482.

We do not think, however, that appellants (or Justice White) correctly read the Court's opinion-which, admittedly, is somewhat puzzling. [FN4] The Court never conceded the validity of Justice White's supposition. By focusing on the status of the perpetrators, the Court avoided the hypothetical Justice White posed: "we do not address the case where a claim [based on commercial activity] consists of both commercial and sovereign elements [such as where private individuals had been employed to torture the plaintiffs]. We do conclude, however, that where a claim rests entirely upon activities sovereign in character-as here-jurisdiction will not exist under the clause regardless of any connection the sovereign acts may have with commercial activity." *Id.* at ___, 113 S.Ct. at 1478 n. 4 (internal citation omitted).

FN4. Justice White accused the majority of a "single minded focus on the exercise of police power, [which] while simplifying the case hardly does it justice." 507 U.S. at ___ - ___, 113 S.Ct. at 1482-83. The majority's focus does seem a bit artificial.

In our case, since we cannot say that the alleged tortious conduct rests entirely upon activities sovereign *in character*, because the kidnappers are not alleged to have been officials of the Iranian government, we cannot dismiss appellants' claim on that basis. On the other hand, to accept appellants' claim would be to declare that all such acts, regardless of context, sponsored openly or covertly by a sovereign power are outside the immunity granted by the FSIA unless conducted directly by acknowledged government officials. We think that cannot be what Congress intended. Although the purpose and perhaps the illegal character of the alleged acts are irrelevant in judging their commercial character, to return to the notion assumed *arguendo* in *Weltover*, the context in which the acts take place must be germane. Even Justice White, who thought the allegations in *Nelson* did make out a claim of commercial activity, rested his view on the commercial character of the hospital where Nelson was employed. 507 U.S. at ___ - ___, 113 S.Ct. at 1481-82. Unless an act takes place in a commercial context it would be impossible to determine whether it is conducted in the manner of a private player in the market. Otherwise, any act directed by a foreign government and carried out by irregular operatives in whatever circumstances could be thought commercial including isolated acts of assassination, extortion, blackmail, and kidnapping (for, perhaps, the sexual pleasure of a depraved monarch). That can hardly be what Congress meant by commercial activity nor what the *Weltover* Court thought were typical acts of market participants.

Insisting that a given act be judged in context before concluding whether it is commercial activity is not inconsistent with eschewing consideration of purpose. The provision of the statute which requires us to ignore purpose was obviously designed to prevent the foreign sovereign from casting a governmental purpose, which always can be found, as a cloak of protection over typical commercial activities, not to reach out to cover all sorts of alleged nefarious acts that are grist for John Le Carre novels. Here the kidnapping *by itself* cannot possibly be described as an act typically performed by participants in the market (unless one distorts the notion of a marketplace to include a hostage bazaar). That money was allegedly sought from relatives of the hostages could not make an ordinary kidnapping a commercial act any more than murder by itself would be treated as a commercial activity merely because the killer is paid. Perhaps a kidnapping of a commercial rival could be thought to be a commercial activity. If so, it would not be because the kidnappers demanded a ransom, but because the kidnapping took place in a commercial context.

There remains the question whether the kidnapping can be thought as an act, not itself a commercial activity, but taken in connection with commercial activity elsewhere. The commercial activity under that reading would be presumably, the Iranian government's continued effort to gain the unfreezing of its assets in the United States. [FN5] We do not think, however, that those efforts are properly regarded under the Act as commercial. The United States government was acting purely as a sovereign regulator when it froze the assets of Iran and its citizens, and the government of Iran's alleged efforts to release the freeze were likewise peculiarly sovereign. When two governments deal directly with each other *as governments*, even when the subject matter may relate to the commercial activities of its citizens or governmental entities, or even the commercial activity conducted by government subsidiaries, those dealings are not akin to that of participants in a marketplace. Governments negotiating with each other invariably take into account non-marketplace considerations-most obviously political relations- and so they cannot be thought to be behaving, in that setting, as businessmen. [FN6]

FN5. As we have already noted ordinary kidnapping for ransom is not a commercial activity so the alleged request that Cicippio's wife pay money for his return adds nothing.
FN6. We, therefore, need not decide whether there were "direct effects" in the United States.

B.

Appellants alternatively invoke the "noncommercial tort" exception to the FSIA. That exception, codified at 28 U.S.C. §1605(a)(5), provides that a foreign state shall not be immune in any case "in which money damages are sought against a foreign state for personal injury…occurring in the United States and caused by the tortious act or omission of that foreign state…" We have held that this exception requires that both the tortious act as well as the injury occur in the United States. See *Persinger v. Islamic Republic of Iran*, 729 F.2d 835, 842 (D.C.Cir.1984). [FN7] Appellants criticize that opinion, but we are of course bound by it. There is no dispute that the tortious actions of which appellants complain occurred in Lebanon. Accordingly, the noncommercial tort exception to the FSIA's grant of immunity is inapplicable.

FN7. The Supreme Court apparently reached the same result in *Argentine Republic v. Amerada Hess Shipping Corp.*, 488 U.S. 428, 109 S.Ct. 683, 102 L.Ed.2d 818 (1989), although the matter is not entirely free from doubt and its statements on this point were in *dicta*. In the course of concluding that

"[b]ecause respondents' *injury* unquestionably occurred well outside the 3-mile limit then in effect for the territorial waters of the United States, the exception for noncommercial torts cannot apply," *Id.* at 441, 109 S.Ct. at 692 (emphasis added), the Court noted that the "tortious *attack*" on respondent's ship occurred outside the United States, *Id.* at 440, 109 S.Ct. at 691 (emphasis added), a statement that might imply that the tortious conduct, as well as the injury, must occur within the United States. The Court, however, might simply have relied on the location of the attack as grounds for concluding that the "injury" occurred outside the United States. At any rate, having concluded that Amerada Hess' injury did not occur in the United States-a requirement explicitly imposed by the FSIA-any statements about where the *tortious conduct* occurred were *dicta*. It is therefore still unclear what position the Supreme Court would take if faced with a suit alleging tortious conduct occurring abroad that caused injury in the United States.

* * * * * *

For the foregoing reasons, the judgment of the district court is affirmed.

Notes:

1.   Plaintiffs have had significant difficulty attempting to establish jurisdiction under the commercial exception contained in §1605(a)(2). In *Saudi Arabia v. Nelson*, 507 U.S. 349 (1993), the plaintiff was a United States citizen, who responded to an ad in a trade periodical for a monitoring systems engineer at a hospital in Saudi Arabia. He signed an employment contract with the hospital and moved to Saudi Arabia. During the course of his work, he discovered safety defects in the hospital which he brought to the attention of hospital officials, but was instructed to ignore the problems. His "reward" for recognizing the defects was arrest by the Saudi Arabian government, and 39 days of beatings, torture, and imprisonment.

The plaintiff sued Saudi Arabia, alleging jurisdiction under the commercial exception to the Foreign Sovereign Immunities Act. He claimed that because he was recruited for work by the hospital, signed an employment agreement, and was subsequently employed, the actions of Saudi Arabia were commercial in nature. The court disagreed, finding that in order for an action to qualify under the commercial exception, that action must be "based upon" a commercial activity, and the tortuous conduct that the plaintiff alleged failed to meet that test:

[T]he intentional conduct alleged here (the Saudi Government's wrongful arrest, imprisonment, and torture of Nelson) could not qualify as commercial under the restrictive theory. The conduct boils down to abuse of the power of its police by the Saudi Government, and however monstrous such abuse undoubtedly may be, a foreign state's exercise of the power of its police has long been understood for purposes of the restrictive theory as peculiarly sovereign in nature. * * * Exercise of the powers of police and penal officers is not the sort of action by which private parties can engage in commerce. "[S]uch acts as legislation, or the expulsion of an alien, or a denial of justice, cannot be performed by an individual acting in his own name. They can be performed only by the state acting as such." Lauterpacht, The Problem of Jurisdictional Immunities of Foreign States, 28 Brit.Y.B.Int'l L. 220, 225 (1952); see also *Id.*, at 237.

Saudi Arabia v. Nelson, 507 U.S. 349, 361-62 (1993).

2.   The history of sovereign immunity doctrine was succinctly described in *Price v. Socialist People's Libyan Arab Jamahiriya*, 274 F.Supp.2d 20, 26 (D.D.C. 2003), a civil terrorism case:

Prior to the twentieth century: as a matter of common law, foreign nations were absolutely immune from suit in the federal courts. See, e.g., The *Schooner Exchange v. M'Faddon*, 11 U.S. (7 Cranch) 116, 3 L.Ed. 287 (1812); *Berizzi Bros. Co. v. Pesaro*, 271 U.S. 562, 46 S.Ct. 611, 70 L.Ed. 1088 (1926). However, with the growth of international trade and shipping, the United States began to recognize the restrictive theory of foreign sovereign immunity, which allowed suits that arose from a foreign nation's commercial dealings. See S. Sucharitkul, *State Immunities And Trading Activities In International Law* (1959); Friedmann, *Changing Social Arrangements in State-Trading States and Their Effect on International Law*, 24 Law & Contemp. Probss. 350 (1959). The passage of the FSIA in 1976 codified this theory. It provided that suits against foreign nations were barred by sovereign immunity unless they fell within one or more of a series of enumerated exceptions, all involving commercial dealings with the United States.

3.   The enactment of the Foreign Sovereign Immunities Act was a historic event and of widespread interest:

The unavailability of judicial remedies in the United States and the resulting dissatisfaction among traders quickly generated demands for legal adjustments to reflect the shifted role of the state in the new command economies. In response, U.S. courts commenced a series of experiments designed to accommodate, on the one hand, the interests of commercial actors who demanded restricted immunity for state commercial entities, and, on the other hand, the interests of the executive branch in maintaining sovereign immunity and avoiding the acute politicization of international commercial disputes, which could be initiated by private parties at a moment convenient to them but quite inconvenient to the government. However, none of the experiments, whether initiated by the courts or by the executive, was particularly successful.

Finally, after over ten years of negotiation between representatives from the three branches of government, from the private bar, from the commercial sector, and, indirectly, from foreign governments, the legislature arrived at a solution. In 1976, Congress enacted the Foreign Sovereign Immunities Act (FSIA). The FSIA was a complex legal instrument that subjected foreign states to the jurisdiction of U.S. courts in a variety of commercial matters, as interpreted and understood by the United States. Moreover, it gave courts, rather than the executive, the power to determine whether, in a particular instance, the foreign state was immune. The FSIA thus effectively restored the playing field that existed before the development of command economies, again enabling judicial relief for international commercial disputes regardless of whether one party to the dispute was a government entity.

The FSIA was expected to be, and in fact was, a major event in international commercial law. However, the impact that the FSIA had on the protection of human rights by national courts was not anticipated. Until the FSIA's enactment in 1976, the human rights bar had, rather unsuccessfully, sought to enforce and implement human rights before intergovernmental bodies, because those bodies were, in effect, "the only game in town." With passage of the FSIA, American human rights lawyers shifted their efforts for enforcement of human rights from various international fora to the national judiciary. By combining the new FSIA with the Alien Tort Claims Act (ATCA), an obscure instrument dating from the earliest days of the Republic, human rights lawyers discovered a venue for suits in U.S. courts against foreign governments that allegedly had violated the human rights of their own nationals.

W. Michael Reisman and Monica Hakimi, *Illusion And Reality In The Compensation Of Victims Of International Terrorism*, 54 Ala. L. Rev. 561, 563-564 (2003).

4.   The district court described the plaintiffs' attempt to navigate around the "commercial exception" rule of the FSIA:

> Plaintiffs allege, and insist that they can prove, that Iran embarked upon a particularly grisly form of commercial activity that they describe as "commercial terrorism." Cicippio and Jacobson assert that Iran regards hostages as articles of commerce, and that it offers (and in their case did offer) to trade captives seized by Iranian agents in Lebanon for more conventional commodities, i.e., military supplies; for money, i.e., sums paid by Mrs. Cicippio to her husband's captors; and for financial concessions, i.e., the release of frozen Iranian assets in the United States. They allege that the United States government did, however reluctantly, finally accept the offers-in their own cases it returned assets located in the United States to Iran in exchange for their freedom-and thus the United States became a party to a somewhat sordid but nevertheless "commercial" transaction, and one indisputably having a "direct effect in the United States." The consequence, they say, is that Iran is amenable to suit in a United States district court under 28 U.S.C. §1330(a), and that it possesses no immunity to suit. Having caused Cicippio and Jacobson, and others, to be seized and held for barter, Iran was engaged in a "commercial activity" within the ambit of 28 U.S.C. §1605(a)(2).
>
> Although trafficking in persons and property captured by sovereign entities solely for profit is certainly not unknown within the international community, this Court is of the opinion that state-supported kidnapping, hostage-taking, and similar universally criminal ventures were simply not the sorts of proprietary enterprises within the contemplation of Congress when it enacted the "commercial activity" exception to FSIA in conferring jurisdiction upon federal courts to entertain cases against foreign sovereigns. It will, therefore, dismiss the complaint. The implications of a contrary ruling would extend far beyond the circumstances of this case.

Cicippio v. Islamic Republic of Iran, 1993 WL 730748 at 2 (D.D.C. 1993).

5.   It is interesting to note that Iran appeared in both the district and appellate courts to proffer procedural defenses to the plaintiffs' claims. However, after the FSIA was amended in 1996 to specifically allow claims against state sponsors of terrorism, and as evidenced in several of the cases in the following chapters, Iran subsequently refused to respond to complaints or appear in virtually every case brought by victims under the terrorism exceptions to the FSIA. What might account for this change in policy?

6.   How does the following statement by the court indicate that the law had not caught up to the realities of international terrorism, even while some states openly acknowledged (and bragged about) their terrorist activities?

> Here the kidnapping *by itself* cannot possibly be described as an act typically performed by participants in the market (unless one distorts the notion of a marketplace to include a hostage bazaar).

For a revolutionary regime like Iran, isn't terrorism admittedly its stock and trade? Later cases typically discuss Iran's "exporting of terrorism" as a national policy and the training centers it operates for foreign terrorists. See *Higgins v. The Islamic Republic of Iran*, 2000 WL 33674311 at 5 (D.D.C. 2000).

7.   What do the types of arguments plaintiffs utilize suggest about the relationship between law and the then current political environment?

Chapter 3

Statutory Remedies for Victims of Terrorism

3.1 The Antiterrorism and Effective Death Penalty Act of 1996, 28 U.S.C. §1605(a)(7)

(a) A foreign state shall not be immune from the jurisdiction of courts of the United States or of the States in any case...

(1) in which the foreign state has waived its immunity either explicitly or by implication, notwithstanding any withdrawal of the waiver which the foreign state may purport to effect except in accordance with the terms of the waiver;

(2) in which the action is based upon a commercial activity carried on in the United States by the foreign state; or upon an act performed in the United States in connection with a commercial activity of the foreign state elsewhere; or upon an act outside the territory of the United States in connection with a commercial activity of the foreign state elsewhere and that act causes a direct effect in the United States;

(3) in which rights in property taken in violation of international law are in issue and that property or any property exchanged for such property is present in the United States in connection with a commercial activity carried on in the United States by the foreign state; or that property or any property exchanged for such property is owned or operated by an agency or instrumentality of the foreign state and that agency or instrumentality is engaged in a commercial activity in the United States;

(4) in which rights in property in the United States acquired by succession or gift or rights in immovable property situated in the United States are in issue;

(5) not otherwise encompassed in paragraph (2) above, in which money damages are sought against a foreign state for personal injury or death, or damage to or loss of property, occurring in the United States and caused by the tortious act or omission of that foreign state or of any official or employee of that foreign state while acting within the scope of his office or employment; except this paragraph shall not apply to--

(A) any claim based upon the exercise or performance or the failure to exercise or perform a discretionary function regardless of whether the discretion be abused, or

(B) any claim arising out of malicious prosecution, abuse of process, libel, slander, misrepresentation, deceit, or interference with contract rights;

(6) in which the action is brought, either to enforce an agreement made by the foreign state with or for the benefit of a private party to submit to arbitration all or any differences which have arisen or which may arise between the parties with respect to a defined legal relationship, whether contractual or not, concerning a subject matter capable of settlement by arbitration under the laws of the United States, or to confirm an award made pursuant to such an agreement to arbitrate, if (A) the arbitration takes place or is intended to take place in the United States, (B) the agreement or award is or may be governed by a treaty or other international agreement in force for the United States calling for the recognition and enforcement of arbitral awards, (C) the underlying claim, save for the agreement to arbitrate, could have been brought in a United States court under this section or section 1607, or (D) paragraph (1) of this subsection is otherwise applicable; or

(7) not otherwise covered by paragraph (2), in which money damages are sought against a foreign state for personal injury or death that was caused by an act of torture, extrajudicial killing, aircraft sabotage, hostage taking, or the provision of material support or resources (as defined in section 2339A of title 18) for such an act if such act or provision of material support is engaged in by an official, employee, or agent of such foreign state while acting within the scope of his or her office, employment, or agency, except that the court shall decline to hear a claim under this paragraph--

(A) if the foreign state was not designated as a state sponsor of terrorism under section 6(j) of the Export Administration Act of 1979 (50 U.S.C. App. 2405(j)) or section 620A of the Foreign Assistance

Act of 1961 (22 U.S.C. 2371) at the time the act occurred, unless later so designated as a result of such act or the act is related to Case Number 1:00CV03110(EGS) in the United States District Court for the District of Columbia; and

(B) even if the foreign state is or was so designated, if--

> (i) the act occurred in the foreign state against which the claim has been brought and the claimant has not afforded the foreign state a reasonable opportunity to arbitrate the claim in accordance with accepted international rules of arbitration; or
>
> (ii) neither the claimant nor the victim was a national of the United States (as that term is defined in section 101(a)(22) of the Immigration and Nationality Act) when the act upon which the claim is based occurred.

Notes:

1.   Why was the Executive Branch given the right to designate state sponsors of terrorism and lift the immunity of such states? How does the history of sovereign immunity in the United States suggest an answer to this question?

2.   Following the murder of 270 Americans aboard Pam Am flight 103 over Lockerbie, Scotland, by a bomb allegedly placed by Libyan sponsored terrorists, attempts were made to amend the exceptions to foreign sovereign immunity contained §1605(a) to include acts of terrorism. As a result of State Department pressure, the proposals failed. Ironically, an act of *domestic* terrorism, the bombing of a federal office building in Oklahoma City by Timothy McVeigh, provided the impetus for Congress to finally act and pass the "terrorism exception" contained in §1605(a)(7). At the time, President Clinton stated, "I am gratified that the Senate has passed a sweeping, bipartisan antiterrorism bill, as I called for in the wake of the bombing in Oklahoma City. This legislation will give law enforcement the tools it needs to do everything possible to prevent this kind of tragedy from happening again." 31 Weekly Comp. Pres. Doc. 993 (June 7, 1995).

3.   What is the constitutional basis for creating "extraterritorial jurisdiction" for civil claims? One law review article notes that this issue was barely considered by the drafters or debated by Congress when enacting the terrorism exceptions to the FSIA:

A diligent search of the background documents revealed *virtually no reference* to any constitutional due process problem in extending federal jurisdiction to such cases. Jamison Borek, Deputy Legal Adviser to the State Department, perhaps came closest to raising the territorial jurisdiction issue in her testimony on an earlier version of the bill. Her testimony-in opposition to the bill-expressed concern with the expansive assertion of jurisdiction in the bill "over such tortuous conduct of a sovereign state without territorial limitations." However, Ms. Borek's reasons lacked even a suggestion of constitutional grounding. Instead, she argued that expansive assertions of jurisdiction under the amendment would lead foreign states to "apply our standards against us as a matter of reciprocity," would be unprecedented in international practice, would "tend to erode the credibility of the FSIA," and "would tend to inject a new unpredictable element in these very delicate relationships with foreign states."

Other witnesses raised similar concerns about the consequences such broad jurisdiction would have on international relations. For example, Abraham Sofaer, former Legal Adviser to the State Department, noted that the FSIA generally limits tort actions to claims arising in the United States, and that in most cases broader jurisdiction is not "warranted by international law." Mr. Sofaer supported the bill, however, as "a limited exception" to the general requirement that claims under the FSIA have a "substantial nexus" with the United States. His testimony, like Ms. Borek's, did not raise any concerns about the possible infringement of foreign states' due process rights under *International Shoe*. Furthermore, his support of the bill indicates that he perceived no constitutional problem with the "limited exception" he advocated.

Even members of the House Judiciary Committee who dissented from the 1994 House version of the amendment based their objections on foreign policy concerns, not constitutional due process objections. The dissent from the report concluded that the bill would be "poor public policy," could lead to reciprocal *687* extensions of jurisdiction by other countries, and would be a "fundamental departure from the international legal theory upon which the Foreign Sovereign Immunities Act is based."

Thus, the legislative history of §1605(a)(7) reveals that the debate over this provision centered on the foreign policy ramifications of exerting such jurisdiction, not the constitutionality of such action. It is puzzling that the debate over §1605(a)(7)-which reflects "a sea change in the United States' approach to foreign sovereign immunity" -includes no discussion of the constitutional constraints on territorial jurisdiction so consistently belabored by the federal courts.

Joseph W. Glannon and Jeffery Atik, *Politics And Personal Jurisdiction: Suing State Sponsors Of Terrorism Under The 1996 Amendments To The Foreign Sovereign Immunities Act,* 87 Geo. L.J. 675, 685-687 (1999) (citations omitted).

4. The amendments to the FSIA were contained in the Antiterrorism and Effective Death Penalty Act of 1996 ("AEDPA"), which one commentator has alleged is discriminatory against Arabs. What is the significance of the fact that in virtually all civil terrorism cases, the defendants are Arabs, Arab states, and Iran (which the author (mis)describes as an Arab country)?

Arabs in America have been particularly burdened by AEDPA. Of the approximately two dozen immigrants currently detained on secret evidence, almost all are either Arab or Muslim. Of the twenty-eight "foreign terrorist organizations" designated by the Secretary of State in 1999, half are either Muslim or Arab. These burdens have been imposed despite the fact that Arabs have been responsible for very few terrorist attacks on American soil. This Note places the Arab experience in the context of American history, where society has repeatedly targeted and stigmatized immigrant groups and ethnic minorities, and contends AEDPA is a modern example of such discrimination. Specifically, AEDPA violates the principle of "equal justice" by unjustly stigmatizing Arab people in America. "Equal justice," as derived from ancient philosophy and American constitutional principles, demands equal treatment of the law to prevent stigmatization of certain groups and guarantee their optimal contribution to society.

Michael J. Whidden, *Unequal Justice: Arabs In America And United States Antiterrorism Legislation,* 69 Fordham L. Rev. 2825, 2828-2829 (May 2001) (footnotes omitted). Is this a fair critique? Do the terrorism amendments to the FSIA target Arabs?

5. One court described the terrorism exception to the FSIA as follows:

Section 1605(a)(7) has some notable features which reveal the delicate legislative compromise out of which it was born. First, not all foreign states may be sued. Instead, only a defendant that has been specifically designated by the State Department as a "state sponsor of terrorism" is subject to the loss of its sovereign immunity. §1605(a)(7)(A). Second, even a foreign state listed as a sponsor of terrorism retains its immunity unless (a) it is afforded a reasonable opportunity to arbitrate any claim based on acts that occurred in that state, and (b) either the victim or the claimant was a U.S. national at the time that those acts took place. §1605(a)(7)(B).

Bettis v. Islamic Republic of Iran, 315 F.3d 325, 329 (D.C. Cir. 2003). What other issues were addressed in this "delicate compromise?" How likely is a rogue, state sponsor of terrorism to submit a victim's claim to arbitration?

3.2 The Flatow Amendment, 28 U.S.C. §1605 note
Civil Liability for Acts of State Sponsored Terrorism

(a) An official, employee, or agent of a foreign state designated as a state sponsor of terrorism designated under section 6(j) of the Export Administration Act of 1979 [section 2405(j) of the Appendix to Title 50, War and National Defense] while acting within the scope of his or her office, employment, or agency shall be liable to a United States national or the national's legal representative for personal injury or death caused by acts of that official, employee, or agent for which the courts of the United States may maintain jurisdiction under section 1605(a)(7) of title 28, United States Code [subsec. (a)(7) of this section] for money damages which may include economic damages, solatium, pain, and suffering, and punitive damages if the acts were among those described in section 1605(a)(7) [subsec. (a)(7) of this section].

(b) Provisions related to statute of limitations and limitations on discovery that would apply to an action brought under 28 U.S.C. 1605(f) and (g) [subsecs. (f) and (g) of this section] shall also apply to actions brought under this section.

No action shall be maintained under this action [SIC] if an official, employee, or agent of the United States, while acting within the scope of his or her office, employment, or agency would not be liable for such acts if carried out within the United States.

Notes:

1.   Why was legislation like the Flatow Amendment needed by terrorism victims in order to clear a legal path for their
claims against state sponsors of terrorism? What hole does
it plug in the list of exceptions to sovereign immunity contained in the Foreign Sovereign Immunities Act, 28 U.S.C.
§1605, thus enabling victims to bring suit against state sponsors of terrorism?

2.   The Flatow Amendment is named after Alisa Flatow, a
Brandeis University student murdered in a Gaza bus bombing. As in the past, following her murder her family lobbied
Congress to create a legal mechanism for victims to bring
suits against foreign states responsible for sponsoring such attacks and the individuals and organizations directly involved.
One of the first attempts to create a legal terrain hospitable
to claims by victims was initiated by the Klinghoffer family,
which resulted in the Klinghoffer Act, 18 U.S.C. §2333 (see
infra Chapter 3.3). Subsequently, the family members of the
victims of Pan Am 103 and the Brothers to the Rescue pilots
shot down by the Cuban Air Force over the Straits of Florida
joined the Flatow family and others to successfully lobby
for the enactment of the terrorism amendments to the FSIA.
See *Rein v. Socialist People's Libyan Arab Jamahiriya*, 995
F.Supp. 325 (E.D.N.Y. 1998), *Alejandre v. The Republic of
Cuba*, 996 F.Supp. 1239 (S.D. Fla. 1997).

3.   Why was this "note" needed to amend the §1605(a)(7)?
What added element does it provide? What is its relationship to §1605(a)(7)?

4.   What role do statutory "notes" play in the law of terrorism? Why are important legislative initiatives codified in
"notes" as opposed to the statute itself?

5.   The codification of the Flatow Amendment as a "note"
has itself created confusion as to its exact status. Thus, Judge
Lamberth, in *Flatow v. Islamic Republic of Iran*, 999 F.Supp.
1, 12 (D.D.C. 1998), stated that "The Flatow Amendment is
apparently an independent pronouncement of law, yet it has
been published as a note to 28 U.S.C. §1605, and requires
several references to 28 U.S.C. §1605(a)(7) *et seq.* to reach
even a preliminary interpretation."

6.   Some academics have questioned the terrorism amendments to the FSIA from a "human rights" perspective:

> From a human rights perspective, a judgment
> [under the §1605(a)(7) and the Flatow Amend-

ment] contributes to the implementation of the human rights program only if it is enforced against
those held responsible for the damages they cause.
If state sponsors of terrorism are not the ones actually paying damages for their evil, then the courts
are not enforcing human rights so much as they
are pronouncing and implementing a policy statement concerning our national community's duty to
provide compensation to victims of human rights
violations. Thus, for the human rights advocate, the
decision of whether to applaud the congressional
and judicial action surrounding the 1996 legislation turns, in considerable measure, on whether
the terrorist states actually pay the awards issued
against them.

W. Michael Reisman and Monica Hakimi, *Illusion And Reality In The Compensation Of Victims Of International Terrorism*, 54 Ala. L. Rev. 561, 578 (2003).

7.   In questioning the efficacy of the terrorism exception,
one commentator suggested that civil lawsuits hinder the
fight against terrorism:

> By passing the "State Sponsors of Terrorism" ex-
> ception to sovereign immunity, Congress sought
> to achieve two primary purposes: ending terrorism
> and compensating American victims. However,
> by placing the burden on U.S. courts to decide the
> proper compensation for terrorist victims, Congress
> failed to sufficiently meet either goal. Ironically, it
> appears now that attempts by U.S. courts to pro-
> vide compensation for terrorist victims are actually
> undermining the executive branch's ability to fight
> terrorism through its foreign policy measures.

Jeewon Kim, *Making State Sponsors Of Terrorism Pay: A
Separation Of Power discourse Under the Foreign Sovereign Immunities Act*, 22 Berkeley J. Int'l L. 513, 514-515
(2004).

8.   However, another commentator has compared the potential for terrorism lawsuits with attempts to bankrupt racist
groups. In describing the prospect of civil terrorism suits to
impact the "war on terrorism," a leading terrorism scholar
has stated:

> Although it is tempting to downplay the role of
> civil lawsuits in light of the extensive action of the
> past decade in criminal law enforcement, bear in

mind that some of the most severe blows struck at the Ku Klux Klan was a series of lawsuits by which the Klan and its supporters lost most of their assets and thus much of their ability to function.

Wayne McCormack, *Understanding the Law of Terrorism*, p 75.

9.   Why is a particularly generous statute of limitations necessary in terrorism cases?

10.   What is the relationship between the "restrictive theory" of sovereign immunity and the Flatow Amendment? What role does the State Department continue to play in determining the sovereign immunity of foreign states with respect to acts of terrorism? What other tools are available to the State Department to inject itself in terrorism lawsuits?

11.   What are the main differences between the pre- and post-statutory eras of civil terrorism law with respect to the type of plaintiffs and defendants, jurisdiction, venue, damages, and causes of action available?

3.3 The Klinghoffer Act, 18 U.S.C. §2331 et seq.

§2331. Definitions

As used in this chapter--

(1) the term "international terrorism" means activities that--

(A) involve violent acts or acts dangerous to human life that are a violation of the criminal laws of the United States or of any State, or that would be a criminal violation if committed within the jurisdiction of the United States or of any State;

(B) appear to be intended--

(i) to intimidate or coerce a civilian population;

(ii) to influence the policy of a government by intimidation or coercion; or

(iii) to affect the conduct of a government by mass destruction, assassination, or kidnapping; and

(C) occur primarily outside the territorial jurisdiction of the United States, or transcend national boundaries in terms of the means by which they are accomplished, the persons they appear intended to intimidate or coerce, or the locale in which their perpetrators operate or seek asylum;

(2) the term "national of the United States" has the meaning given such term in section 101(a)(22) of the Immigration and Nationality Act;

(3) the term "person" means any individual or entity capable of holding a legal or beneficial interest in property;

(4) the term "act of war" means any act occurring in the course of--

(A) declared war;

(B) armed conflict, whether or not war has been declared, between two or more nations; or

(C) armed conflict between military forces of any origin; and

(5) the term "domestic terrorism" means activities that--

(A) involve acts dangerous to human life that are a violation of the criminal laws of the United States or of any State;

(B) appear to be intended--

(i) to intimidate or coerce a civilian population;

(ii) to influence the policy of a government by intimidation or coercion; or

(iii) to affect the conduct of a government by mass destruction, assassination, or kidnapping; and

(C) occur primarily within the territorial jurisdiction of the United States.

§2333. Civil remedies

(a) Action and jurisdiction.--Any national of the United States injured in his or her person, property, or business by reason of an act of international terrorism, or his or her estate, survivors, or heirs, may sue therefor in any appropriate district court of the United States and shall recover threefold the damages he or she sustains and the cost of the suit, including attorney's fees.

(b) Estoppel under United States law.--A final judgment or decree rendered in favor of the United States in any criminal proceeding under section 1116, 1201, 1203, or 2332 of this title or section 46314, 46502, 46505, or 46506 of title 49 shall estop the defendant from denying the essential allegations of the criminal offense in any subsequent civil proceeding under this section.

(c) Estoppel under foreign law.--A final judgment or decree rendered in favor of any foreign state in any criminal proceeding shall, to the extent that such judgment or decree may be accorded full faith and credit under the law of the United States, estop the defendant from denying the essential allegations of the criminal offense in any subsequent civil proceeding under this section.

§2334. Jurisdiction and venue

(a) General venue.--Any civil action under section 2333 of this title against any person may be instituted in the district court of the United States for any district where any plaintiff resides or where any defendant resides or is served, or has an agent. Process in such a civil action may be served in any district where the defendant resides, is found, or has an agent.

(b) Special maritime or territorial jurisdiction.--If the actions giving rise to the claim occurred within the special maritime and territorial jurisdiction of the United States, as defined in section 7 of this title, then any civil action under section 2333 of this title against any person may be instituted in the district court of the United States for any district in which any plaintiff resides or the defendant resides, is served, or has an agent.

(c) Service on witnesses.--A witness in a civil action brought under section 2333 of this title may be served in any other district where the defendant resides, is found, or has an agent.

(d) Convenience of the forum.--The district court shall not dismiss any action brought under section 2333 of this title on the grounds of the inconvenience or inappropriateness of the forum chosen, unless--

(1) the action may be maintained in a foreign court that has jurisdiction over the subject matter and over all the defendants;
(2) that foreign court is significantly more convenient and appropriate; and
(3) that foreign court offers a remedy which is substantially the same as the one available in the courts of the United States.

§2335. Limitation of actions

(a) In general.--Subject to subsection (b), a suit for recovery of damages under section 2333 of this title shall not be maintained unless commenced within 4 years after the date the cause of action accrued.

(b) Calculation of period.--The time of the absence of the defendant from the United States or from any jurisdiction in which the same or a similar action arising from the same facts may be maintained by the plaintiff, or of any concealment of the defendant's whereabouts, shall not be included in the 4-year period set forth in subsection (a).

§2336. Other limitations

(a) Acts of war.--No action shall be maintained under section 2333 of this title for injury or loss by reason of an act of war.

(b) Limitation on discovery.--If a party to an action under section 2333 seeks to discover the investigative files of the Department of Justice, the Assistant Attorney General, Deputy Attorney General, or Attorney General may object on the ground that compliance will interfere with a criminal investigation or prosecution of the incident, or a national security operation related to the incident, which is the subject of the civil litigation. The court shall evaluate any such objections in camera and shall stay the discovery if the court finds that granting the discovery request will substantially interfere with a criminal investigation or prosecution of the incident or a national security operation related to the incident. The court shall consider the likelihood of criminal prosecution by the Government and other factors it deems to be appropriate. A stay of discovery under this subsection shall constitute a bar to the granting of a motion to dismiss under rules 12(b)(6) and 56 of the Federal Rules of Civil Procedure. If the court grants a stay of discovery under this subsection, it may stay the action in the interests of justice.

(c) Stay of action for civil remedies.-
(1) The Attorney General may intervene in any civil action brought under section 2333 for the purpose of seeking a stay of the civil action. A stay shall be granted if the court finds that the continuation of the civil action will substantially interfere with a criminal prosecution which involves the same subject matter and in which an indictment has been returned, or interfere with national security operations related to the terrorist incident that is the subject of the civil action. A stay may be granted for up to 6 months. The Attorney General may petition the court for an extension of the stay for additional 6-month periods until the criminal prosecution is completed or dismissed.

(2) In a proceeding under this subsection, the Attorney General may request that any order issued by the court for release to the parties and the public omit any reference to the basis on which the stay was sought.

§2337. Suits against Government officials

No action shall be maintained under section 2333 of this title against--

(1) the United States, an agency of the United States, or an officer or employee of the United States or any agency thereof acting within his or her official capacity or under color of legal authority; or

(2) a foreign state, an agency of a foreign state, or an officer or employee of a foreign state or an agency thereof acting within his or her official capacity or under color of legal authority.

§2338. Exclusive Federal jurisdiction

The district courts of the United States shall have exclusive jurisdiction over an action brought under this chapter.

Notes:

1.   The civil provisions of the Antiterrorism Act of 1990 are sometimes referred to as the "Klinghoffer Act" because the family of Leon Klinghoffer, the wheelchair bound American, who was thrown overboard in the Mediterranean by Palestinian terrorists while aboard the Achille Lauro, was instrumental in lobbying for its passage. Having been stymied in their efforts at obtaining justice in federal court for several years, Klinghoffer's family sought passage of a law that would help cure the procedural and substantive legal difficulties they faced in their case.

2.   The Report of the House of Representatives recognized explicitly that existing laws were inadequate for private citizens to sue terrorists,

> The recent case of the Klinghoffer family is an example of this gap in our efforts to develop a comprehensive legal response to international terrorism. Leon Klinghoffer, a passenger on the Achille Lauro cruise liner, was executed and thrown overboard in a 1985 terrorist attack. His widow, Marilyn Klinghoffer, and family took their case to the courts in their home state of New York. Only by virtue of the fact that the attack violated certain Admiralty laws and that the organization involved-the Palestine Liberation Organization-had assets and carried on activities in New York, was the court able to establish jurisdiction over the case. A similar attack occurring on an airplane or in some other locale might not have been subject to civil action in the U.S. In order to facilitate civil actions against such terrorists the Committee recommends H.R. 2222.

H.R. Rep. 102-1040, at 5 (1992).

3.   The legislative history makes clear that the Klinghoffer Act was intended to be construed broadly in order to maximize its effectiveness in compensating victims of terrorism. Senator Grassley, the bill's co-sponsor, indicated that "it empowers victims with all the weapons available in civil litigation." *Antiterrorism Act of 1991*, Hearing Before the Subcommittee on Intellectual Property and Judicial Administration of the Committee on the Judiciary, House of Representatives, 102nd Congress, September 18, 1992 at 10. Thus, Congress intended that the full gamut of legal tools available in civil litigation would be harnessed to the task of providing remedies to victims of terrorism.

4.   Indeed, the legislative history is replete with statements by the congressional sponsors and supporters, as well as representatives of the executive branch, who testified in support of the bill, praising the wide scope and broad effect of its provisions. Nothing in the history or purpose of the ATA suggests that it should be interpreted narrowly. The first circuit court to discuss the purpose of §2333 noted that,

> [Its] history, in combination with the language of the statute itself, evidences an intent by Congress to codify general common law tort principles and to extend civil liability for acts of international terrorism to the full reaches of traditional tort law.

Boim v. Quranic Literacy Institute, 291 F.3d 1000, 1010 (7th Cir. 2002).

5. The ATA is intended to protect important national interests:

> The legislative history of the ATA...reveal[s] this country's profound and compelling interest in combating terrorism at every level, including disrupting the financial underpinnings of terrorist networks.
>
> Therefore, Congress has explicitly granted private parties the right to pursue common tort claims against terrorist organizations and those that provide material support or financing to terrorist organizations...Certainly, private tort actions directed at compensating victims of terrorism and thwarting the financing of terrorism vindicate the national and international public interest.

Weiss v. Nat'l Westminster Bank, PLC, 242 F.R.D. 33, 46 (E.D.N.Y. 2007) (citations omitted).

6.   The class of plaintiffs who may bring a civil action under §2333 is purposely extensive. The original language of §2333 "was intended to be broad enough to allow indirect victims, such as common carriers, to sue for damage to property, for indemnity and lost profits." *Antiterrorism Act of 1990*, Hearing Before the Subcommittee on Courts and Administrative Practice of Committee on the Judiciary, United States Senate, 101st Congress, Second Session July 25 1990 at 86 ("Senate Hearing"). Yet, because the original language allowed compensation only for "any national of the United States" (possibly excluding family members of terrorism victims), the Justice Department urged Congress to modify the text of the bill to explicitly allow suits by the family members of victims (as "survivors" and "heirs" of the victim). Senate Hearing at 8, 38. Thus,

> The Department supports legislation to provide a new civil remedy against terrorists and a federal forum for the families and relatives of victims to pursue claims for compensatory damages.

Id. at 34.

7.   One scholar noted that the statute is a "potent civil remedy tool [and] should be a powerful tool in cases where terrorists act outside of the United States and kill or injure United States citizens in foreign countries." Georgene Vairo, *Remedies for Victims of Terrorism*, 35 Loy. L.A. L. Rev. 1265, 1271-1272 (2002).

8.   Another described the inadequacy of the legal environment prior to enactment of 18 U.S.C. §2333,

> The civil litigation that international terrorist acts had instigated prior to 1990 raised many fundamental legal questions. In the absence of comprehensive civil legislation, federal courts were given the opportunity to articulate legal standards regarding international terrorism. The courts, however, diverged on the questions of whether terrorists should be required to compensate victims seeking civil redress and to what extent terrorists should be required to pay civil damages for their criminal acts. The courts also differed upon the fundamental policy question of judicial interference in foreign affairs. Thus, the goal of creating civil antiterrorist remedies seemed more attainable in the legislative forum.

Jennifer A. Rosenfeld, *The Antiterrorism Act of 1990: Bringing Terrorists to Justice the American Way*, 15 Suffolk Transnat'l L.J., 726, 729 -731 (1992)

9.   How are the problems confronted by the Klinghoffers addressed in the statute? What specific remedies are created by the Klinghoffer Act? What issues are not addressed in the act? What ambiguities exist in the statute? Why would Congress expand the statute of limitations provisions contained in 18 U.S.C. §2335(b) with respect to the concealment of the defendant's whereabouts? Why is this especially important with respect to terrorism suits?

10. Why is it significant that the sections of the Klinghoffer Act which create a cause of action are contained in a much larger criminal statute? How do the criminal provisions assist plaintiffs in bringing cases against terrorists? How are the definitional sections helpful?

11. What role does the United States government have in cases brought under this statute? How likely is it that the United States government would pursue terrorists who murdered American citizens?

12. To what common law theories of liability can the Klinghoffer Act, 18 U.S.C. §2333 be compared? How does it compare to state and federal RICO statutes?

13. What features of terrorism suggest that prior legal doctrines did not "fit" the terrorism context?

14. Tal Becker notes that the "definition of terrorism has acquired a special reputation for controversy and elusiveness." *Terrorism and the State: Rethinking the Rules of State Responsibility*, p. 84. Another problem is the over abundance of definitions,

> In the United States, the difficulties in definition are not related to a reluctance to use the term terrorism, but rather rest in the sheer number of different government instrumentalities that have offered independent interpretations of terrorism which, while similar, are not identical.

Jeffrey F. Addicott, *Terrorism Law: the Rule of Law and the War on Terror Second Edition*, 2004 p.3. Despite this widely acknowledged *academic* topic, why has it not generated equal controversy in the jurisprudence of civil terrorism cases?

15. A definition of terrorism is found in 28 C.F.R. §0.85(l),

> Terrorism includes the unlawful use of force and violence against persons or property to intimidate or coerce a government, the civilian population, or any segment thereof, in furtherance of political or social objectives.

3.4 The Torture Victim Protection Act, 28 U.S.C. §1350 note

Section 1. Short Title.

This Act may be cited as the 'Torture Victim Protection Act of 1991'.

Sec. 2. Establishment of civil action.

(a) Liability.--An individual who, under actual or apparent authority, or color of law, of any foreign nation--
(1) subjects an individual to torture shall, in a civil action, be liable for damages to that individual; or
(2) subjects an individual to extrajudicial killing shall, in a civil action, be liable for damages to the individual's legal representative, or to any person who may be a claimant in an action for wrongful death.

(b) Exhaustion of remedies.--A court shall decline to hear a claim under this section if the claimant has not exhausted adequate and available remedies in the place in which the conduct giving rise to the claim occurred.

(c) Statute of limitations.--No action shall be maintained under this section unless it is commenced within 10 years after the cause of action arose.

Sec. 3. Definitions.

(a) Extrajudicial killing.--For the purposes of this Act, the term 'extrajudicial killing' means a deliberated killing not authorized by a previous judgment pronounced by a regularly constituted court affording all the judicial guarantees which are recognized as indispensable by civilized peoples. Such term, however, does not include any such killing that, under international law, is lawfully carried out under the authority of a foreign nation.

(b) Torture.--For the purposes of this Act--
(1) the term 'torture' means any act, directed against an individual in the offender's custody or physical control, by which severe pain or suffering (other than pain or suffering arising only from or inherent in, or incidental to, lawful sanctions), whether physical or mental, is intentionally inflicted on that individual for such purposes as obtaining from that individual or a third person information or a confession, punishing that individual for an act that individual or a third person has committed or is suspected of having committed, intimidating or coercing that individual or a third person, or for any reason based on discrimination of any kind; and
(2) mental pain or suffering refers to prolonged mental harm caused by or resulting from--
(A) the intentional infliction or threatened infliction of severe physical pain or suffering;
(B) the administration or application, or threatened administration or application, of mind altering substances or other procedures calculated to disrupt profoundly the senses or the personality;
(C) the threat of imminent death; or
(D) the threat that another individual will imminently be subjected to death, severe physical pain or suffering, or the administration or application of mind altering substances or other procedures calculated to disrupt profoundly the senses or personality.

Notes:

1. What does the codification of the TVPA as a "note" to the Alien Tort Claims Act indicate about its intended purpose?

2. This statute explicitly creates a cause of action. How does it differ from the terrorism amendment to the Foreign Sovereign Immunities Act, 28 U.S.C. §1605(a)(7) and the Flatow Amendment, 28 U.S.C. §1605 note.

3. Does the TVPA only apply to victims of torture and those actually murdered by an "extrajudicial killing?" What about a victim who was injured in an attack involving an extrajudicial killing or hostage taking of another individual? Could a victim who was neither taken hostage nor killed in an attack bring suit under the TVPA?

4. In *Wyatt v. Syrian Arab Republic*, 362 F.Supp.2d 103, 112 (D.D.C. 2005) the court dismissed a claim filed by hostages alleging an "extrajudicial killing" against Syria. The murders of soldiers were found to be incidental to the kidnapping:

> The deaths of two Turkish soldiers are events separate from the events that caused the injuries the plaintiffs allegedly suffered. Nevertheless, the

plaintiffs attempt to lump together their own injuries and the death of the soldiers into an overall terrorist operation of extrajudicial killing-as if to say, but for the hostage taking, the deaths of the Turkish soldiers would not have occurred...here, the death of Turkish soldiers caused no injury to the plaintiffs, other than perhaps diminishing their hopes of a rescue.

5.   Recently, the Alien Tort Claims Act has been revived as a tool by plaintiffs. When combined with the claims of American citizens under 18 U.S.C. §2333, it has been particularly helpful with bank financing cases. Hence one court found that:

Here, in contrast, the conduct alleged falls precisely within the norm evidenced by the sources discussed. As already explained, plaintiffs' allegations essentially track the conduct specifically condemned in the Financing and Bombing Conventions, as well as in the ATA sections which implement those Conventions. Thus, the norm is of sufficiently definite content and acceptance among nations of the world as the historical paradigms familiar when §1350 was enacted.

Almog v. Arab Bank, PLC, 471 F.Supp.2d 257, 284 -285 (E.D.N.Y. 2007).

Chapter 4

Subject Matter Jurisdiction

4.1 Tate Letter, 24 Dep't of State Bull. 984-985 (1952)

Letter from Jack B. Tate, Acting Legal Adviser, U.S. Dept. of State, to Acting U.S. Attorney General Philip B. Perlman (May 19, 1952), reprinted in 26 Dept. State Bull. 984-985 (1952)

May 19, 1952.

My Dear Mr. Attorney General:

The Department of State has for some time had under consideration the question whether the practice of the Government in granting immunity from suit to foreign governments made parties defendant in the courts of the United States without their consent should not be changed. The Department has now reached the conclusion that such immunity should no longer be granted in certain types of cases. In view of the obvious interest of your Department in this matter I should like to point out briefly some of the facts which influenced the Department's decision.

A study of the law of sovereign immunity reveals the existence of two conflicting concepts of sovereign immunity, each widely held and firmly established. According to the classical or absolute theory of sovereign immunity, a sovereign cannot, without his consent, be made a respondent in the courts of another sovereign. According to the newer or restrictive theory of sovereign immunity, the immunity of the sovereign is recognized with regard to sovereign or public acts (jure imperii) or a state, but not with respect to private acts (jure gestionis). There is agreement by proponents of both theories, supported by practice, that sovereign immunity should not be claimed or granted in actions with respect to real property (diplomatic and perhaps consular property excepted) or with respect to the disposition of the property of a deceased person even though a foreign sovereign is the beneficiary.

The classical or virtually absolute theory of sovereign immunity has generally been followed by the courts of the United States, the British Commonwealth, Czechoslovakia, Estonia, and probably Poland.

The decisions of the courts of Brazil, Chile, China, Hungary, Japan, Luxembourg, Norway, and Portugal may be deemed to support the classical theory of immunity if one or at most two old decisions anterior to the development of the restrictive theory may be considered sufficient on which to base a conclusion.

The position of the Netherlands, Sweden, and Argentina is less clear since although immunity has been granted in recent cases coming before the courts of those countries, the facts were such that immunity would have been granted under either the absolute or restrictive theory. However, constant references by the courts of these three countries to the distinction between public and private acts of the state, even though the distinction was not involved in the result of the case, may indicate an intention to leave the way open for a possible application of the restrictive theory of immunity if and when the occasion presents itself.

A trend to the restrictive theory is already evident in the Netherlands where the lower courts have started to apply that theory following a Supreme Court decision to the effect that immunity would have been applicable in the case under consideration under either theory.

The German courts, after a period of hesitation at the end of the nineteenth century have held to the classical theory, but it should be noted that the refusal of the Supreme Court in 1921 to yield to pressure by the lower courts for the newer theory was based on the view that that theory had not yet developed sufficiently to justify a change. In view of the growth of the restrictive theory since that time the German courts might take a different view today.

The newer or restrictive theory of sovereign immunity has always been supported by the courts of Belgium and Italy. It was adopted in turn by the courts of Egypt and of Switzerland. In addition, the courts of France, Austria, and Greece, which were traditionally supporters of the classical theory, reversed their position in the 20's to embrace the restrictive theory. Rumania, Peru, and possibly Denmark also appear to follow this theory.

Furthermore, it should be observed that in most of the countries still following the classical theory there is a school of influential writers favoring the restrictive theory and the views of writers, at least in civil law countries, are a major factor in the development of the law. Moreover, the leanings of the lower courts in civil law countries are more significant in shaping the law than they are in common law countries where the rule of precedent prevails and the trend in these lower courts is to the restrictive theory.

Of related interest to this question is the fact that ten of the thirteen countries which have been classified above as supporters of the classical theory have ratified the Brussels Convention of 1926 under which immunity for government owned merchant vessels is waived. In addition the United States, which is not a party to the Convention, some years ago announced and has since followed, a policy of not claiming immunity for its public owned or operated merchant vessels. Keeping in mind the importance played by cases involving public vessels in the field of sovereign immunity, it is thus noteworthy that these ten countries (Brazil, Chile, Estonia, Germany, Hungary, Netherlands, Norway, Poland, Portugal, Sweden) and the United States have already relinquished by treaty or in practice an important part of the immunity which they claim under the classical theory.

It is thus evident that with the possible exception of the United Kingdom little support has been found except on the part of the Soviet Union and its satellites for continued full acceptance of the absolute theory of sovereign immunity. There are evidences that British authorities are aware of its deficiencies and ready for a change. The reasons which obviously motivate state trading countries in adhering to the theory with perhaps increasing rigidity are most persuasive that the United States should change its policy. Furthermore, the granting of sovereign immunity to foreign governments in the courts of the United States is most inconsistent with the action of the Government of the United States in subjecting itself to suit *in* these same courts *in* both contract and tort and with its long established policy of not claiming immunity in foreign jurisdictions for its merchant vessels. Finally, the Department feels that the widespread and increasing practice on the part of governments of engaging in commercial activities makes necessary a practice which will enable persons doing business with them to have their rights determined in the courts. For these reasons it will hereafter be the Department's policy to follow the restrictive theory of sovereign immunity in the consideration of requests of foreign governments for a grant of sovereign immunity.

It is realized that a shift in policy by the executive cannot control the courts but it is felt that the courts are less likely to allow a plea of sovereign immunity where the executive has declined to do so. There have been indications that at least some Justices of the Supreme Court feel that in this matter courts should follow the branch of the Government charged with responsibility for the conduct of foreign relations.

In order that your Department, which is charged with representing the interests of the Government before the courts, may be adequately informed it will be the Department's practice to advise you of all requests by foreign governments for the grant of immunity from suit and of the Department's action thereon.

Sincerely yours,
For the Secretary of State:
Jack B. Tate
Acting Legal Adviser

Note:

1.   The Tate Letter represents a drastic change in American foreign policy regarding the application of sovereign immunity in U.S. courts. This was the first instance in which the United States adopted the restrictive theory of immunity as opposed to the absolute theory. Prior practice involved obtaining opinions from the State Department as to whether a suit could go forward. See *Verlinden B.V. v. Central Bank of Nigeria*, 461 U.S. 480 (1983). How does the Tate Letter depart from previous practice? What is the significance of the Tate Letter? Describe the attempt to balance between diplomacy and justice in the Tate Letter.

4.2 State Department Designation of State Sponsors of Terrorism
http://www.state.gov/s/ct/c14151.htm

Countries determined by the Secretary of State to have repeatedly provided support for acts of international terrorism are designated pursuant to three laws: section 6(j) of the Export Administration Act, section 40 of the Arms Export Control Act, and section 620A of the Foreign Assistance Act. Taken together, the four main categories of sanctions resulting from designation under these authorities include restrictions on U.S. foreign assistance; a ban on defense exports and sales; certain controls over exports of dual use items; and miscellaneous financial and other restrictions.

Designation under the above-referenced authorities also implicates other sanctions laws that penalize persons and countries engaging in certain trade with state sponsors. Currently there are five countries designated under these authorities: Cuba, Iran, North Korea, Sudan and Syria.

Country	Designation Date
Cuba	March 1, 1982
Iran	January 19, 1984
North Korea	January 20, 1988
Sudan	August 12, 1993
Syria	December 29, 1979

Notes:

1.   What are the Due Process implications of designation as a state-sponsor of terrorism? In *Wyatt v. Syrian Arab Republic*, 362 F.Supp.2d 103 (D.D.C. 2005), Syria challenged it's designation as a violation of the Due Process Clause of the United States Constitution. The court, relying on *Price v. Socialist People's Libyan Arab Jamahiriya*, 294 F.3d 82 (D.C. Cir. 2002) (*Price I*), denied their challenge. "Indeed, as the court stated in *Price I*, 'the Constitution imposes no limitation on the exercise of personal jurisdiction by the federal courts over [foreign sovereigns.]'" 294 F.3d at 86.

2.   "As a result of the historic decision taken by Libya's leadership in 2003 to renounce terrorism and to abandon its WMD programs, the United States rescinded Libya's designation as a state sponsors of terrorism on June 30. Since pledging to renounce terrorism in 2003, Libya has cooperated closely with the United States and the international community on counterterrorism efforts." http://www.state.gov/s/ct/rls/crt/2006/82736.htm. More details on each of the listed state sponsors of terrorism may be found on the State Department's website at: http://www.state.gov/s/ct/rls/crt/2005/64337.htm.

3.   What happens when a state is delisted as a state sponsor of terrorism? In *Acree v. Republic of Iraq*, 370 F.3d 41, 56 (D.C.Cir. 2004) the court stated "when a country, once designated as a state sponsor of terrorism, is subsequently restored to good standing, that country is still amenable to suit for acts that took place prior to the restoration of its sovereign immunity."

4.   Are civil terrorism statutes a substitute for diplomacy? Are civil suits and diplomacy mutually exclusive activities? Does the legislative history of both the Klinghoffer Act and the FSIA terrorism amendments suggest that their drafters intended the statutes to be a panacea for victims? Some com-

mentators have indicated that terrorism lawsuits are an inappropriate mechanism to provide even a modicum of redress to victims and that they will not deter future terrorism.

The solutions to the problems posed by international terrorism lie in federal funds for the victims and their families and in multilateral global diplomacy. Putting the matter in the hands of litigators and haling foreign sovereigns into U.S. courts based on an expansive notion of the passive personality principle and politically motivated notions of whether a given nation is a "State Sponsor of Terrorism" or an "ally" is not the solution. But we seem bent on moving backward into unilateralism. Are we entering the age of the Pax Americana, or, alternatively, Imperial America? "America will lead the world to peace," according to President Bush. But can it do so unilaterally? Look at the state sponsors of terrorism exception to sovereign immunity in the context of other recent events. The United States has refused to sign the Kyoto Protocols on global warming, already signed by some 150 countries; unilaterally withdrawn from the 1972 Anti-Ballistic Missile Treaty; made a blockbuster eleventh hour announcement that scuttled the antibioterrorism meeting; delivered an ill-conceived "axis of evil" speech that has disturbed allies; opened up a discussion of developing nuclear weapons for use against sponsors of terrorism; refused to participate in the creation of a permanent war crimes tribunal; and planned military tribunals that have troubled Spain and other European allies. The victims of prior terror and those at risk in the future will both be better served by a little more diplomacy and a little less unilateralism.

Keith Sealing, "*State Sponsors Of Terrorism*" *Is A Question, Not An Answer: The Terrorism Amendment To The FSIA Makes Less Sense Now Than It Did Before 9/11*, 38 Tex. Int'l L.J. 119, 143-144 (2003).

A. Export Administration Act, 50 U.S.C. §2405(j)

(j) Countries supporting international terrorism

(1) A validated license shall be required for the export of goods or technology to a country if the Secretary of State has made the following determinations:

(A) The government of such country has repeatedly provided support for acts of international terrorism.

(B) The export of such goods or technology could make a significant contribution to the military potential of such country, including its military logistics capability, or could enhance the ability of such country to support acts of international terrorism.

(2) The Secretary and the Secretary of State shall notify the Committee on Foreign Affairs of the House of Representatives and the Committee on Banking, Housing, and Urban Affairs and the Committee on Foreign Relations of the Senate at least 30 days before issuing any validated license required by paragraph (1).

(3) Each determination of the Secretary of State under paragraph (1)(A), including each determination in effect on December 12, 1989, shall be published in the Federal Register.

(4) A determination made by the Secretary of State under paragraph (1)(A) may not be rescinded unless the President submits to the Speaker of the House of Representatives and the chairman of the Committee on Banking, Housing, and Urban Affairs and the chairman of the Committee on Foreign Relations of the Senate--

(A) before the proposed rescission would take effect, a report certifying that--

(i) there has been a fundamental change in the leadership and policies of the government of the country concerned;

(ii) that government is not supporting acts of international terrorism; and

(iii) that government has provided assurances that it will not support acts of international terrorism in the future; or

(B) at least 45 days before the proposed rescission would take effect, a report justifying the rescission and certifying that--

(i) the government concerned has not provided any support for international terrorism during the preceding 6-month period; and

(ii) the government concerned has provided assurances that it will not support acts of international terrorism in the future.

(5)(A) As used in paragraph (1), the term "repeatedly provided support for acts of international terrorism" shall include the recurring use of any part of the territory of the country as a sanctuary for terrorists or terrorist organizations.

(B) In this paragraph--

(i) the term "territory of a country" means the land, waters, and airspace of the country; and

(ii) the term "sanctuary" means an area in the territory of a country--

(I) that is used by a terrorist or terrorist organization--

(aa) to carry out terrorist activities, including training, financing, and recruitment; or

(bb) as a transit point; and

(II) the government of which expressly consents to, or with knowledge, allows, tolerates, or disregards such use of its territory.

(6) The Secretary and the Secretary of State shall include in the notification required by paragraph (2)--

(A) a detailed description of the goods or services to be offered, including a brief description of the capabilities of any article for which a license to export is sought;

(B) the reasons why the foreign country or international organization to which the export or transfer is proposed to be made needs the goods or services which are the subject of such export or transfer and a description of the manner in which such country or organization intends to use such articles, services, or design and construction services;

(C) the reasons why the proposed export or transfer is in the national interest of the United States;

(D) an analysis of the impact of the proposed export or transfer on the military capabilities of the foreign country or international organization to which such export or transfer would be made;

(E) an analysis of the manner in which the proposed export would affect the relative military strengths of countries in the region to which the goods or services which are the subject of such export would be delivered and whether other countries in the region have comparable kinds and amounts of articles, services, or design and construction services; and

(F) an analysis of the impact of the proposed export or transfer on the United States relations with the countries in the region to which the goods or services which are the subject of such export would be delivered.

B. Foreign Assistance Act of 1961, 22 U.S.C. §2371

(a) Prohibition

The United States shall not provide any assistance under this chapter, the Agricultural Trade Development and Assistance Act of 1954 [U.S.C.A. §1691 et seq.], the Peace Corps Act [22 U.S.C.A. §2501 et seq.], or the Export-Import Bank Act of 1945 [12 U.S.C.A. §635 et seq.] to any country if the Secretary of State determines that the government of that country has repeatedly provided support for acts of international terrorism.

(b) Publication of determinations

Each determination of the Secretary of State under subsection (a) of this section, including each determination in effect on December 12, 1989, shall be published in the Federal Register.

(c) Rescission

A determination made by the Secretary of State under subsection (a) of this section may not be rescinded unless the President submits to the Speaker of the House of Representatives and the chairman of the Committee on Foreign Relations of the Senate--
(1) before the proposed rescission would take effect, a report certifying that--
(A) there has been a fundamental change in the leadership and policies of the government of the country concerned;
(B) that government is not supporting acts of international terrorism; and
(C) that government has provided assurances that it will not support acts of international terrorism in the future; or
(2) at least 45 days before the proposed rescission would take effect, a report justifying the rescission and certifying that--
(A) the government concerned has not provided any support for international terrorism during the preceding 6-month period; and
(B) the government concerned has provided assurances that it will not support acts of international terrorism in the future.
(d) Waiver

Assistance prohibited by subsection (a) of this section may be provided to a country described in that subsection if--
(1) the President determines that national security interests or humanitarian reasons justify a waiver of subsection (a) of this section, except that humanitarian reasons may not be used to justify assistance under subchapter II of this chapter (including part IV, part VI, and part VIII), or the Export-Import Bank Act of 1945 [12 U.S.C.A. §635 et seq.]; and
(2) at least 15 days before the waiver takes effect, the President consults with the Committee on Foreign Affairs of the House of Representatives and the Committee on Foreign Relations of the Senate regarding the proposed waiver and submits a report to the Speaker of the House of Representatives and the chairman of the Committee on Foreign Relations of the Senate containing--
(A) the name of the recipient country;

(B) a description of the national security interests or humanitarian reasons which require the waiver;
(C) the type and amount of and the justification for the assistance to be provided pursuant to the waiver; and
(D) the period of time during which such waiver will be effective.
The waiver authority granted in this subsection may not be used to provide any assistance under this chapter which is also prohibited by section 2780 of this title.

C. *Daliberti v. Republic of Iraq*, 97 F.Supp.2d 38 (D. D.C. 2000)

PAUL L. FRIEDMAN, District Judge.

Plaintiffs have brought suit seeking damages for claims arising out of various instances of alleged torture suffered at the hands of the defendant, the Republic of Iraq, a sovereign nation. Defendant has moved to dismiss for lack of personal and subject matter jurisdiction and for failure to state a claim under Rule 12(b)(1), (2) and (6) of the Federal Rules of Civil Procedure. Iraq asserts that the Foreign Sovereign Immunities Act ("FSIA"), 28 U.S.C. §§1602 *et seq.*, gives it immunity from suit in the courts of this country and that none of the exceptions to the FSIA applies in this instance. It also argues that because Iraq has insufficient contacts with the United States, no U.S. court has personal jurisdiction over Iraq. Finally, defendant asserts that the case should be dismissed under the act of state doctrine.

The Court concludes that defendant's alleged actions fall within a category of conduct that Congress specifically intended to exempt from FSIA protection when it amended the FSIA to include an exception for state sponsored acts of terrorism. The Court also concludes that defendant's alleged conduct does not fall under any of the other exceptions to the FSIA, and that claims brought exclusively under those exceptions, including claims brought by the spouses of those asserting they were victims of terrorism, must be dismissed for lack of subject matter jurisdiction and for failure to state a claim. With regard to the surviving claims, the Court concludes both that it has personal jurisdiction and that plaintiffs have adequately stated claims upon which relief can be granted. The act of state doctrine does not bar this suit.

I. BACKGROUND

Plaintiffs' claims arise out of three separate but similar incidents in which the defendant arrested and detained the male plaintiffs, all of whom are United States citizens who were doing business in Kuwait. The four male plaintiffs seek damages for acts of kidnapping, false imprisonment and torture; the spouses of the four men seek damages for pain and suffering and loss of consortium.

Plaintiff Chad Hall was removing land mines within the borders of Kuwait in October 1992 when he allegedly was kidnapped at gunpoint and removed from Kuwait to Baghdad, Iraq. Compl. ¶ 15. Hall was held as a prisoner by the government of Iraq, although it is not clear from the pleadings for how long, and he claims that Iraq tortured him while he was a prisoner. *See id.* Hall's claims arise out of acts both within defendant's territorial jurisdiction (the imprisonment and torture), and outside its territorial jurisdiction (the kidnapping in Kuwait). Hall brought suit on these same claims prior to enactment of the state sponsored terrorism exception to the FSIA, and his claims initially were dismissed for lack of subject matter jurisdiction. See *Hall v. Socialist People's Republic of Iraq*, Civil Action No. 92-2842, Memorandum and Order (D.D.C. Dec. 9, 1994), *aff'd without opinion*, 80 F.3d 558 (D.C.Cir.1996).

Plaintiff Kenneth Beaty was traveling within the borders of Kuwait in April 1993 when he approached a border checkpoint between Kuwait and Iraq. Compl. ¶ 10. Beaty asked an Iraqi border guard for directions to an oil well on the Kuwaiti side of the border without entering Iraq. *Id.* Beaty was arrested by agents of Iraq and taken to Baghdad where he was allegedly held under inhumane circumstances and subjected to torture. *Id.* Beaty was tried in an Iraqi court on charges of "illegal entry" and espionage and found not guilty. Compl. ¶ 11. Beaty was told that he was free to leave the Republic of Iraq, but before he could actually leave he was informed that "notwithstanding the [acquittal], [ ] he was sentenced to eight years…in prison." Compl. ¶¶ 11, 12. Beaty was held for a period of 205 days, at which point his release was secured with the assistance of former Senator David Boren who traveled to Iraq at the behest of the President of the United States for the express purpose of negotiating Beaty's release. Compl. ¶¶ 12, 14. In addition to the efforts of Senator Boren, Beaty's wife, Robin Beaty (also a plaintiff in this action), arranged for the delivery of "several million dollars" in humanitarian aid to Iraq. Compl. ¶ 14. Beaty's claims, like Hall's, arise out of acts committed both within Iraq (the imprisonment and torture) and in Kuwait or international "no-man's-land" (the "arrest" at the border checkpoint).

Plaintiffs David Daliberti and William Barloon were traveling within the borders of Kuwait in March 1995 when they approached a border checkpoint between that nation and Iraq. Compl. ¶ 4. An agent of the defendant examined the identification papers of the two plaintiffs which identified them as American citizens. *Id.* The agent then "raised the barricade blocking the path…and gave permission to Plain-

tiffs…to enter the territory of Defendant." *Id.* After entering defendant's territory, Daliberti and Barloon determined that they "had not arrived at their intended lawful destination." Compl. ¶ 5. They then returned to the border checkpoint and requested passage back into Kuwait. *Id.* They were arrested by the defendant's agents, threatened at gunpoint, and taken to prison, where they allegedly were tortured and held under inhumane conditions. Compl. ¶¶ 5, 6. Daliberti and Barloon were tried in an Iraqi court and found guilty of "illegal entry," without being afforded an opportunity to defend themselves. Compl. ¶ 7. They were held for 126 days before their release was secured by negotiations between the government of Iraq and Congressman Bill Richardson who had been dispatched by President Clinton to secure their release. Compl. ¶ 9. Daliberti and Barloon's complaints arise out of acts that occurred entirely within the borders of Iraq.

Plaintiffs Kathy Daliberti, Robin Beaty, Elizabeth Hall and Linda Barloon (the "spouse plaintiffs") seek recovery for claims of intentional infliction of emotional distress and loss of consortium as a result of the acts committed against their husbands. Compl. ¶¶ 17, 20, 21, 25. None of the spouse plaintiffs was in the territory of Iraq at any time relevant to these proceedings. The spouse plaintiffs therefore allege harm based on conduct committed only in Kuwait and Iraq, but affecting them in the United States.

Each of the male plaintiffs is seeking compensatory damages of $20 million, and each of the spouse plaintiffs is seeking compensatory damages of $5 million. Compl. at 13-14. Plaintiffs ask that any judgment in their favor be enforced through the seizure of Iraqi assets in this country. Compl. ¶ 32.

Plaintiffs filed their complaint in May 1996. As part of the process to secure jurisdiction under the FSIA, they afforded the defendant an opportunity to arbitrate these claims pursuant to international rules of arbitration. Compl. ¶ 1; *see also* 28 U.S.C. §1605(a)(7)(B)(i) (claim will be dismissed unless there is an offer to arbitrate). Summonses were served on the defendant via the United States Interests Section of the Polish Embassy in Baghdad. *See* Notice of Service of Summons & Complaint, Sept. 12, 1996. On October 25, 1996, plaintiffs moved for, and subsequently were granted, an entry of default against the defendant for its failure to file a response. *See* Default, Nov. 27, 1996. Plaintiffs were directed by the Court to file a motion for default judgment accompanied by factual evidence of their claims, *see* 28 U.S.C. §1608(e); Order of Jan. 13, 1997, which plaintiffs did on January 29, 1997. On February 23, 1998, the parties jointly filed a stipulation asking that the default entered by the Clerk be vacated. The Court approved the stipulation, set aside the entry of default and denied plaintiffs' motion for default judgment as moot. *See* Order of Mar. 6, 1998; Order of Mar. 9, 1998.

II. THE FOREIGN SOVEREIGN IMMUNITIES ACT

The Foreign Sovereign Immunities Act is "the sole basis for obtaining jurisdiction over a foreign state in our courts." *Argentine Republic v. Amerada Hess Shipping Corp.*, 488 U.S. 428, 434, 109 S.Ct. 683, 102 L.Ed.2d 818 (1989). Federal district courts have exclusive jurisdiction over civil actions against a foreign state, regardless of the amount in controversy, provided that the foreign state is not entitled to immunity under the FSIA. *See* 28 U.S.C. §§1330, 1604; *Argentine Republic v. Amerada Hess Shipping Corp.*, 488 U.S. at 434-35, 109 S.Ct. 683. Under the FSIA, a foreign state is presumed to be immune from suit, 28 U.S.C. §1604, and is in fact immune unless one or more of the exceptions to immunity enumerated in the FSIA apply. See 28 U.S.C. §§1605-1607; *Saudi Arabia v. Nelson*, 507 U.S. 349, 355, 113 S.Ct. 1471, 123 L.Ed.2d 47 (1993). Once a defendant presents a prima facie case that it is a foreign sovereign, plaintiffs bear the burden of producing evidence to show that there is no immunity and that the court therefore has jurisdiction over the claims. See *Drexel Burnham Lambert Group Inc. v. Committee of Receivers for Galadari*, 12 F.3d 317, 325 (2d Cir.1993), *cert. denied*, 511 U.S. 1069, 114 S.Ct. 1644, 128 L.Ed.2d 365 (1994); *Cargill Int'l S.A. v. M/T Pavel Dybenko*, 991 F.2d 1012, 1016 (2nd Cir.1993).

A court may dismiss a complaint brought under the FSIA only if it appears beyond doubt that plaintiffs can prove no set of facts in support of their claims that would entitle them to relief. See *Neitzke v. Williams*, 490 U.S. 319, 326-27, 109 S.Ct. 1827, 104 L.Ed.2d 338 (1989) (quoting *Hishon v. King & Spalding*, 467 U.S. 69, 73, 104 S.Ct. 2229, 81 L.Ed.2d 59 (1984)); *Kowal v. MCI Communications Corp.*, 16 F.3d 1271, 1276 (D.C.Cir.1994); cf. *Saudi Arabia v. Nelson*, 507 U.S. at 351, 113 S.Ct. 1471 (in reviewing dismissal under FSIA, court accepts all factual allegations as true). Once plaintiff has produced evidence that an exception applies, defendant must produce evidence of its entitlement to immunity; "[i]f any of the exceptions appears in the pleadings or is not refuted by the foreign state asserting the defense, the motion to dismiss the complaint must be denied." *Baglab Ltd. v. Johnson Matthey Bankers Ltd.*, 665 F.Supp. 289, 294 (S.D.N.Y.1987). Since at this stage the Court must accept as true all facts alleged by the plaintiffs, the question is whether the facts alleged are sufficient to establish the jurisdiction of this Court under an exception to immunity under the FSIA and sufficient to state a claim upon which relief may be granted.

A. *State Sponsored Terrorism Exception*

The state sponsored terrorism exception was enacted by Congress as part of the Antiterrorism and Effective Death Penalty Act of 1996 ("AEDPA"), for the purpose of holding rogue states accountable for acts of terrorism perpetrated on United States citizens. *See* Antiterrorism and Effective Death Penalty Act of 1996, Pub.L. No. 104-132, §221(a), 110 Stat. 1214 (codified at 28 U.S.C. §1605(a)(7)). It provides a cause of action against a foreign state for anyone who alleges that he or she has suffered injury "caused by an act of torture, extrajudicial killing, aircraft sabotage, hostage taking, or the provision of material support or resources…for such an act." 28 U.S.C. §1605(a)(7). [FN1] The legislation was motivated, at least in part, by the ordeal that plaintiff Chad Hall alleges in this suit. *See Foreign Terrorism and U.S. Courts: Hearings Before the Subcomm. on Courts and Admin. Practice of the Senate Comm. on the Judiciary, Regarding S.825, the Foreign Sovereign Immunities Act*, 103d Cong. (June 21, 1994), *available in* 1994 WL 274204 (F.D.C.H.) (statement of Chad Hall). While the AEDPA was enacted well after the events alleged by Hall and all of the other claimants in this case occurred, Congress clearly intended the Act to apply to "any cause of action arising before, on, or after the date of enactment." Pub.L. No. 104-132, §221(c), 110 Stat. 1214 (codified at 28 U.S.C. §1605 note). Retroactivity principles therefore are no bar to the application of the state sponsored terrorism exception to this action. See *Cicippio v. Islamic Republic of Iran*, 18 F.Supp.2d 62, 68-69 (D.D.C.1998); *Flatow v. Islamic Republic of Iran*, 999 F.Supp. 1, 13-14 (D.D.C.1998); *Alejandre v. Republic of Cuba*, 996 F.Supp. 1239, 1247 n. 4 (S.D.Fla.1997).

FN1. Because the AEDPA did not provide a specific cause of action for victims of state sponsored terrorism, a separate piece of legislation was enacted to fill the void. Civil Liability for Acts of State Sponsored Terrorism, Pub.L. No. 104-208, §589, 110 Stat. 3009 (1996) (codified at 28 U.S.C. §1605 note). Also known as the "Flatow Amendment," the legislation provides a cause of action against a foreign state and its agents for any act which would give a court jurisdiction under 28 U.S.C. §1605(a)(7). *See* 28 U.S.C. §1605 note; *Flatow v. Islamic Republic of Iran*, 999 F.Supp. 1, 12-13 (D.D.C.1998). Plaintiffs may seek recovery under this enactment for pain and suffering, economic damages, solatium and punitive damages. 28 U.S.C. §1605 note.

Several suits have been brought under the state sponsored terrorism exception to the FSIA since it has been enacted and codified at 28 U.S.C. §1605(a)(7). See *Anderson v. Islamic Republic of Iran*, 90 F.Supp.2d 107 (D.D.C.2000) (suit arising out of hostage taking in Lebanon); *Cicippio v. Islamic Republic of Iran*, 18 F.Supp.2d 62 (D.D.C.1998) (suit arising out of hostage taking in Lebanon); *Flatow v. Islamic Republic of Iran*, 999 F.Supp. 1 (D.D.C.1998) (suit arising out of bombing in Israel which killed American student); *Alejandre v. Republic of Cuba*, 996 F.Supp. 1239 (S.D.Fla.1997) (suit arising out of downing of civilian planes by Cuban Air Force); *Rein v. Socialist People's Libyan Arab Jamahiriya*, 995 F.Supp. 325 (E.D.N.Y.), *aff'd in relevant part*, 162 F.3d 748 (2d Cir.1998), *cert. denied*, 525 U.S. 1003, 119 S.Ct. 2337, 144 L.Ed.2d 235 (1999) (suit by survivors of victims of bombing of Pan Am flight 103 over Lockerbie, Scotland). [FN2]

FN2. In only one of these cases other than this one, *Rein v. Socialist People's Libyan Arab Jamahiriya*, did the defendant respond to the complaint. The decisions in *Anderson, Cicippio, Flatow* and *Alejandre* all resulted in default judgments. As in suits against the United States, however, the FSIA requires that the court make findings of fact sufficient to support the entry of a default judgment. *See* 28 U.S.C. §1608(e); *Flatow v. Islamic Republic of Iran*, 999 F.Supp. at 6. In *Anderson, Cicippio, Flatow*, and *Alejandre*, therefore, the courts heard evidence-albeit only from the plaintiffs-and entered findings of fact.

Section 1605(a)(7) provides an exception to a foreign sovereign's immunity from suit for actions where money damages are sought against a foreign sovereign for:

personal injury or death that was caused by an act of torture, extrajudicial killing, aircraft sabotage, hostage taking, or the provision of material support or resources (as defined in section 2339A of title 18) for such an act if such an act or provision of material support is engaged in by an official, employee, or agent of such foreign state while acting within the scope of his or her office, employment, or agency.

28 U.S.C. §1605(a)(7). Three conditions must be met in order to bring suit under this section: (1) the foreign state must have been designated as a state sponsor of terrorism pursuant to either Section 6(j) of the Export Administration Act of 1979 (50 U.S.C.App. §2405(j)) or Section 620A of the Foreign Assistance Act of 1961 (22 U.S.C. §2371); (2) if the actionable conduct of the foreign state occurred within that state's territory, then the state must be offered an opportunity to arbitrate the claims; and (3) the plaintiff or the victim must be a United States national. 28 U.S.C. §1605(a)(7)(A), (B).

The Export Administration Act calls upon the Secretary of State to make a determination that a foreign state has "repeatedly provided support for acts of international terrorism," to notify the relevant committees of both houses of Congress, and to publish the determination in the Federal Register. *See* 50 U.S.C.App. §2405(j). Once the Secretary's determination has been promulgated, the foreign state must be considered a state sponsor of terrorism until the country in question has provided assurances that it will no longer support acts of international terrorism. *Id.*

On September 12, 1990, Acting Secretary of State Lawrence Eagleburger caused to be published in the Federal Register his determination that Iraq was a state sponsor of terrorism. Determination Iraq, 55 Fed.Reg. 37,793 (1990) (codified at 31 C.F.R. §596.201). No rescission of this designation has been published pursuant to statute, and Iraq remains so designated. *See* 31 C.F.R. §596.201. [FN3] The plaintiffs, being United States nationals, and having offered to arbitrate, therefore need only show that Iraq committed one of the predicate acts under 28 U.S.C. §1605(a)(7) in order for the state sponsored terrorism exception to the FSIA to apply. [FN4] Defendant argues that the actions complained of did not constitute "torture" or "hostage taking" under the FSIA and therefore do not provide subject matter jurisdiction and do not give rise to a claim upon which relief may be granted. *See* Def. Motion at 27-28.

FN3. The other states so designated are Cuba, Iran, Libya, North Korea, Sudan and Syria. 31 C.F.R. §596.201.

FN4. Plaintiffs filed their Offer to Arbitrate the same day that they filed the complaint initiating this action. *See* Offer to Arbitrate, May 17, 1996; Compl. ¶ 1. Defendant has not claimed that there was an inadequate opportunity to arbitrate these claims.

The FSIA adopts the following definition of "torture" from the Torture Victim Protection Act of 1991 ("TVPA"):

any act, directed against an individual in the offender's custody or physical control, by which severe pain or suffering (other than pain or suffering arising only from or inherent in, or incidental to, lawful sanctions), whether physical or mental, is intentionally inflicted on that individual for such purposes as obtaining from that individual or a third person information or a confession, punishing that individual for an act that individual or a third person has committed or is suspected of having committed, intimidating or coercing that individual or a third person, or for any reason based on discrimination of any kind.

Pub.L. No. 102-256, 106 Stat. 73, §3(b)(1) (1992) (codified at 28 U.S.C. §1350 note §3(b)); *see* 28 U.S.C. §1605(e)(1) ("[T]he terms 'torture' and 'extrajudicial killing' have the meaning given those terms in section 3 of the Torture Victim Protection Act of 1991."). Similarly, the FSIA adopts by reference the following definition for "hostage taking" from the International Convention Against the Taking of Hostages:

Any person who seizes or detains and threatens to kill, to injure or to continue to detain another person (hereinafter referred to as the "hostage") in order to compel a third party, namely, a State, an international intergovernmental organization, a natural or juridical person, or a group of persons, to do or abstain from doing any act as an explicit or implicit condition for the release of the hostage commits the offense of taking of hostages ("hostage-taking") within the meaning of this Convention.

International Convention Against the Taking of Hostages, Dec. 17, 1979, art. 1, T.I.A.S. No. 11,081; *see* 28 U.S.C. §1605(e)(2) ("[T]he term 'hostage taking' has the meaning given that term in Article 1 of the International Convention Against the Taking of Hostages.").

The complaint alleges that Iraq tortured each of the four male plaintiffs and held plaintiffs David Daliberti, William Barloon and Kenneth Beaty as hostages. Compl. ¶¶ 6-16. David Daliberti and William Barloon allege that they were "blindfolded, interrogated and subjected to physical, mental and verbal abuse" while in captivity. Compl. ¶ 6. They allege that during their arrests one of the agents of the defendant threatened them with a gun, allegedly causing David Daliberti "serious mental anguish, pain and suffering." Compl. ¶ 5. During their imprisonment in Abu Ghraib prison, Daliberti and Barloon were "not provided adequate or proper medical treatment for serious medical conditions which became life threatening." Compl. ¶ 8. The alleged torture of Kenneth Beaty involved holding him in confinement for eleven days "with no water, no toilet and no bed." Compl. ¶ 10. Similarly, Chad Hall allegedly was held for a period of at least four days "with no lights, no window, no water, no toilet and no proper bed." Compl. ¶ 15. Plaintiffs further proffer that Hall was "stripped naked, blindfolded and threatened with electrocution by placing wires on his testicles…in an effort to coerce a confession from him." Brief in Opp. at 2.

Such direct attacks on a person and the described deprivation of basic human necessities are more than enough to meet the definition of "torture" in the Torture Victim Protection Act and thus to give rise to a claim under the state sponsored terrorism exception to foreign sovereign immunity. *See* 28 U.S.C. §1605(e)(1). Plaintiffs have alleged sufficient facts to allow a fact-finder to conclude that the pain they suffered did not arise from and was not incident to or inherent in lawful sanctions, but was in fact "torture" under the FSIA. Should this case reach trial, the question of whether plaintiff can prove by a preponderance of the evidence that the defen-

dant committed acts of torture as defined by the statute will be one for the finder of fact. Cf. *Hilao v. Estate of Marcos*, 103 F.3d 789, 792-93 (9th Cir.1996) (jury instructed with TVPA definition of torture in liability phase of trial against former dictator).

The Court also finds that plaintiffs have alleged sufficient facts to allow a reasonable inference that Daliberti, Barloon and Beaty were subjected to "hostage taking" as defined by the International Convention Against the Taking of Hostages. *See* 28 U.S.C. §1605(e)(2). Plaintiffs allege that David Daliberti and William Barloon were held in prison in an effort to coerce the United States and the United Nations to lift the economic sanctions imposed on Iraq at the end of the Gulf War. Compl. ¶ 9. This purpose was communicated personally by Saddam Hussein to Congressman Bill Richardson, who had traveled to Iraq seeking the release of Daliberti and Barloon. *Id.* Kenneth Beaty was held until the delivery of several million dollars worth of humanitarian aid was arranged by Robin Beaty. Compl. ¶ 14. This aid has been described as "ransom." *Id.*

In sum, the male plaintiffs have met their burden of showing that the actions they complain of fall under the state sponsored terrorism exception to foreign sovereign immunity in 28 U.S.C. §1605(a)(7). This Court therefore has jurisdiction over the subject matter of this suit. In addition, it is apparent that the male plaintiffs have adequately stated claims under this statute. Accepting the factual allegations in the complaint as true, as it must on a motion to dismiss, the Court therefore must deny defendant's motion to dismiss for want of subject matter jurisdiction and for failure to state a claim under Rule 12(b)(1) and (b)(6) of the Federal Rules of Civil Procedure.

Arguably, the claims of the spouse plaintiffs could also have been brought under the state sponsored terrorism exception to the FSIA. *See* 28 U.S.C. §§1605(a)(7), 1605 note; *Flatow v. Islamic Republic of Iran*, 999 F.Supp. at 12-13. Since the spouse plaintiffs bring their claims under the commercial activity exception to the FSIA rather than under the state sponsored terrorism exception, however, the Court will consider only whether it has jurisdiction and whether the spouse plaintiffs have stated claims under the exception they have pleaded in the complaint. It would be inappropriate for this Court, *sua sponte*, to consider the claims of the spouse plaintiffs under exceptions not pleaded. *Compare Anderson v. Islamic Republic of Iran*, 90 F.Supp.2d at 113 (spouse permitted to proceed under state sponsored terrorism exception); *Cicippio v. Islamic Republic of Iran*, 18 F.Supp.2d at 68 n. 7 (same).

B. Commercial Activity Exception

Plaintiffs also assert jurisdiction under the commercial activity exception to the FSIA for the wrongs allegedly committed against Chad Hall and as a basis for the claims of the spouse plaintiffs. Compl. ¶¶ 15, 17, 18. The commercial activity exception, 28 U.S.C. §1605(a)(2), provides that a foreign state is not immune from suit where the claim is based on (1) a commercial activity carried on by the foreign state in the United States, (2) an act performed in the United States in connection with a commercial activity of the foreign state elsewhere, or (3) "an act outside the territory of the United States in connection with a commercial activity of the foreign state elsewhere and that act causes a direct effect in the United States." 28 U.S.C. §1605(a)(2). Quite clearly, plaintiffs rely only on the third category of commercial activity exception. The term "commercial activity" is defined under the Act as a "regular course of commercial conduct or a particular commercial transaction or act." 28 U.S.C. §1603(d). "The commercial character of an activity shall be determined by reference to the nature of the course of conduct or particular transaction or act, rather than by reference to its purpose." *Id.*

In examining this statutory language, the Supreme Court has concluded that "the issue is whether the particular actions that the foreign state performs...are the type of actions by which a private party engages in trade and traffic or commerce" *Republic of Argentina v. Weltover, Inc.*, 504 U.S. 607, 614, 112 S.Ct. 2160, 119 L.Ed.2d 394 (1992) (internal quotation omitted) (finding commercial activity exception to immunity applied where Argentina had sold bonds in the United States and then unilaterally extended time of repayment). "[A] state engages in commercial activity...where it exercises only those powers that can also be exercised by private citizens, rather than those powers peculiar to sovereigns." *Saudi Arabia v. Nelson*, 507 U.S. at 349-50, 113 S.Ct. 1471 (holding commercial activity exception did not apply where Saudi Arabia arrested and imprisoned U.S. citizen hired in the United States to work in Saudi Arabia).

The Supreme Court's decision in *Nelson* is controlling here. In *Nelson*, the plaintiff was a United States national hired to work in a hospital in Saudi Arabia. After he became a whistleblower as to certain practices of the hospital, he was arrested and imprisoned by the Saudi government. The Supreme Court concluded that only a government has the power to arrest and imprison someone in its territory, even if the arrest was unjustified or motivated by an aspect of a commercial relationship. The arrest and imprisonment therefore could not be considered "commercial" in nature. *Saudi Arabia v. Nelson*, 507 U.S. at 362-63, 113 S.Ct. 1471.

In this case, the actions complained of arise out of the arrest and imprisonment of the plaintiff Hall (and the other male plaintiffs). Under the reasoning of the Supreme Court in *Nelson*, Iraq cannot be sued under the commercial activity exception, regardless of Iraq's motivation or justification, because Iraq was exercising its sovereign powers and not the kind of powers exercised by private citizens.

With respect to the spouses of the victims of torture, plaintiffs argue (1) that, through its "torture of plaintiff Hall and the holding as hostages of plaintiffs Beaty, Daliberti and Barloon, [Iraq] caused a direct effect in the United States on [the spouse plaintiffs]," Compl. ¶ 17; and (2) that Iraq, through its agents, "promoted, financed, directed, controlled, supported, supplied and developed terrorism in order to further its activities pursuant to 28 U.S.C. §1605(a)(2)." Compl. ¶ 18. Neither of these allegations is sufficient to provide jurisdiction or to state a claim under the commercial activity exception.

While plaintiffs identify acts outside the United States-torture and hostage-taking and the promotion, support and development of terrorism-and allege that at least some of these activities had a "direct effect" on the spouse plaintiffs who were in the United States, plaintiffs do not identify any "commercial activity" of the defendant besides the funding of terrorism. With respect to that activity, they fail sufficiently to allege that any of the noncommercial acts that had a direct effect on the spouses in the United States were taken "in connection with a commercial activity," an essential predicate for application of the commercial activity exception. While Iraq might have engaged in arguably commercial activity by funding terrorism outside its borders, the acts complained of inside its borders that arguably had a direct effect on the spouses in the United States had no connection with a commercial activity. See *Saudi Arabia v. Nelson*, 507 U.S. at 356-58, 113 S.Ct. 1471 (in order for claim to lie under commercial activity exception the commercial activity itself must give rise to the cause of action). Because the torture and hostage-taking at issue were not done in connection with a commercial activity, there is no jurisdiction under the commercial activity exception. The claims of the spouse plaintiffs and the claim of Chad Hall based on the commercial activity exception therefore must be dismissed for lack of subject matter jurisdiction and for failure to state a claim. [FN5]

FN5. Plaintiffs also allege, without explanation, that the Court has jurisdiction over Iraq pursuant to 28 U.S.C. §1605(a)(1) (the so-called "waiver" exception). Compl. ¶ 15. This exception provides that a foreign state shall not be immune from suit where it has waived its immunity "either explicitly or by implication." 28 U.S.C. §1605(a)(1). Because there is no explicit waiver here, the question is whether Iraq has implicitly waived its sovereign immunity in this case. "[A]n implied waiver depends upon the foreign government's having at some point indicated its amenability to suit." *Princz v. Federal Republic of Germany*, 26 F.3d 1166, 1174 (D.C.Cir.1994); *cert. denied*, 513 U.S. 1121, 115 S.Ct. 923, 130 L.Ed.2d 803 (1995). In keeping with the restrictive theory of foreign sovereign immunity embodied in the FSIA, see *Verlinden B.V. v. Central Bank of Nigeria*, 461 U.S. 480, 486-87, 103 S.Ct. 1962, 76 L.Ed.2d 81 (1983), the courts are "virtually unanimous" in construing the implied waiver provision very narrowly. *Creighton Ltd. v. Government of State of Qatar*, 181 F.3d 118, 122 (D.C.Cir.1999); see *Shapiro v. Republic of Bolivia*, 930 F.2d 1013, 1017 (2d Cir.1991); *Foremost-McKesson, Inc. v. Islamic Republic of Iran*, 905 F.2d 438, 444 (D.C.Cir.1990); *Joseph v. Office of the Consulate General of Nigeria*, 830 F.2d 1018, 1022 (9th Cir.1987); *Frolova v. Union of Soviet Socialist Republics*, 761 F.2d 370, 377 (7th Cir.1985). Because plaintiffs have failed to allege even a single fact that would support a finding of waiver, the Court concludes that the defendant has not, either explicitly or implicitly, waived its immunity from suit in this matter.

III. CONSTITUTIONAL CHALLENGES TO THE FSIA

Iraq argues that even if the state sponsored terrorism exception might otherwise apply to the facts of this case, it cannot destroy Iraq's immunity from suit because the exception is unconstitutional. *See* Def. Motion at 5. There are three bases for this contention: (1) that the requirement that a state be designated by the Secretary of State as a state sponsor of terrorism as a precondition for the filing of a lawsuit constitutes an impermissible legislative delegation of power to the Executive Branch to determine the courts' jurisdiction; (2) that the statutory exception to foreign sovereign immunity set out in 28 U.S.C. §1605(a)(7) violates Iraq's due process right to equal protection by discriminating against those sovereigns designated as state sponsors of terrorism; and (3) that the FSIA as a whole, or at least the state sponsored terrorism exception, violates due process by abrogating the minimum contacts requirement that is always necessary for the exercise of personal jurisdiction. *See* Def. Motion at 5-13.

Preliminarily, the Court notes that there is a serious question whether Iraq has standing to assert these constitutional challenges. "[T]he issue of whether a foreign state is a 'person' for the purposes of Constitutional Due Process analysis has rarely, if ever, been squarely presented for con-

sideration," *Flatow v. Islamic Republic of Iran*, 999 F.Supp. at 19 (citing *Republic of Argentina v. Weltover*, 504 U.S. at 619-20, 112 S.Ct. 2160). When the issue has arisen, courts have applied different reasoning in different contexts. The most direct statement on the issue is found in *South Carolina v. Katzenbach*, 383 U.S. 301, 86 S.Ct. 803, 15 L.Ed.2d 769 (1966), in which South Carolina complained that several aspects of the Voting Rights Act violated its due process rights by impermissibly delegating power, limiting judicial access and acting as a bill of attainder. The Supreme Court quickly disposed of these claims:

[T]hese contentions may be dismissed at the outset. The word "person" in the context of the Due Process Clause of the Fifth Amendment cannot, by any reasonable mode of interpretation, be expanded to encompass the States of the Union, and to our knowledge this has never been done by any court. Likewise, courts have consistently regarded the Bill of Attainder Clause of Article I and the principle of the separation of powers only as protections for individual persons and private groups, those who are peculiarly vulnerable to non-judicial determinations of guilt.

State of South Carolina v. Katzenbach, 383 U.S. at 323-24, 86 S.Ct. 803 (citations omitted).

It would seem that a foreign sovereign should enjoy no greater due process rights than the sovereign States of the Union. As Judge Richey noted: "If the States of the Union have no due process rights, then a 'foreign mission' *qua* 'foreign mission' surely can have none." Palestine Information *Office v. Shultz*, 674 F.Supp. 910, 919 (D.D.C.1987). And Judge Lamberth concluded in *Flatow* that "[g]iven the parallels in the procedural deference granted to both the United States and foreign states…foreign states should hold comparable status to States of the Union and the federal government for the purposes of Constitutional Due Process analysis." *Flatow v. Islamic Republic*, 999 F.Supp. at 21.

This reasoning has not held, however, in situations where personal jurisdiction under the FSIA has been the subject of challenge. In *Weltover*, the Supreme Court decided simply to "assum[e], without deciding, that a foreign state is a 'person' for purposes of the Due Process Clause," and thus for the required minimum contacts analysis necessary to determine personal jurisdiction. *Republic of Argentina v. Weltover, Inc.*, 504 U.S. at 619-20, 112 S.Ct. 2160 (finding minimum contacts existed where "direct effects" prong of commercial activity exception was met). See *Creighton Ltd. v. Government of State of Qatar*, 181 F.3d at 124-25 (recognizing dispute in dicta, but not deciding whether foreign state is "person" for purpose of due process analysis), *El-Hadad v. Embassy of the United Arab Emirates*, 69 F.Supp.2d 69, 77 n. 7 (D.D.C.1999) ("because the D.C. Circuit has not yet resolved whether the due process clause applies to foreign states, the Court considers the [foreign state] a 'person' and conducts the constitutional due process analysis" in commercial activity exception case). Judge Lamberth noted in *Flatow*:

Most courts have simply assumed that foreign states were entitled to Constitutional Due Process protections, just as courts have assumed that foreign corporations are entitled to Constitutional Due Process protections, at least with respect to the assertion of personal jurisdiction. Once these trends were initiated, on the basis of an assumption, courts have been reluctant to reexamine this issue…The merger of subject matter and personal jurisdictional inquiries under the FSIA has contributed to the confusion in the jurisprudence of personal jurisdiction over foreign states. The majority of cases brought under the FSIA involve commercial activity, which requires an evaluation of the activity's effects in the United States. "Direct effects" language closely resembles that of Constitutional Due Process "minimum contacts." Tandem consideration of these overlapping yet fundamentally discrete analyses as a matter of practice in several Circuits has exacerbated the situation.

Flatow v. Islamic Republic of Iran, 999 F.Supp. at 19-20. Indulging the same assumptions as have other courts that a foreign sovereign may enjoy at least certain constitutional protections, the Court will address Iraq's constitutional challenges on their merits.

A. Separation of Powers

Iraq argues that the state sponsored terrorism exception, by requiring a finding by the Secretary of State, impermissibly delegates to an Executive Branch official the power that properly resides in Congress to set the limits of the jurisdiction of the federal courts. *See* Def. Motion at 6-7. This is not so. Prior to the enactment of the FSIA, the State Department always played a substantial and appropriate role in effecting when a foreign sovereign state would enjoy immunity in the courts of the United States. See *National City Bank of New York v. Republic of China*, 348 U.S. 356, 360-61, 75 S.Ct. 423, 99 L.Ed. 389 (1955) ("As the responsible agency for the conduct of foreign affairs, the State Department is the normal means of suggesting to the courts that a sovereign be granted immunity from a particular suit. Its failure or refusal to suggest such immunity has been accorded significant weight by this Court.") (citations omitted). In enacting the FSIA, Congress codified the standards for the recognition of foreign sovereign immunity, as well as the exceptions to such immunity. See *Verlinden B.V. v. Central Bank of Nigeria*, 461 U.S. at 496-97, 103 S.Ct. 1962. With the state spon-

sored terrorism exception, Congress continued this process by providing that terrorist states are subject to suit in the federal courts. Congress simply chose to define the members of the class of "terrorist states" by reference to a separate determination made by the Secretary of State, an Executive Branch official uniquely situated to make such judgments.

The delegation by Congress of this decision to the Secretary of State does not violate separation of powers. Indeed, the Supreme Court has long recognized the "value of congressional delegation," and has upheld its constitutionality. See *Milk Industry Foundation v. Glickman*, 949 F.Supp. 882, 890 (D.D.C.1996). The principle that Congress may delegate to the Executive Branch the duty to find facts upon which certain enactments are made conditional is firmly established:

The Constitution…does not require that Congress find for itself every fact upon which it desires to base legislative action or that it make for itself detailed determinations which it has declared to be prerequisite to the application of the legislative policy to particular facts and circumstances impossible for Congress itself properly to investigate. The essentials of the legislative function are the determination of the legislative policy and its formulation and promulgation as a defined and binding rule of conduct…These essentials are preserved when Congress has specified the basic conditions of fact upon whose existence or occurrence, ascertained from relevant data by a designated administrative agency, it directs that its statutory command shall be effective. It is no objection that the determination of facts and the inferences to be drawn from them in the light of the statutory standards and declaration of policy call for the exercise of judgment, and for the formulation of subsidiary administrative policy within the prescribed statutory framework…[T]he doctrine of separation of powers [does not] deny to Congress power to direct that an administrative officer properly designated for that purpose have ample latitude within which he is to ascertain the conditions which Congress has made prerequisite to the operation of its legislative command.

Yakus v. United States, 321 U.S. 414, 424-25, 64 S.Ct. 660, 88 L.Ed. 834 (1944). The Supreme Court has upheld such delegations of power in scores of cases, see *Milk Industry Foundation v. Glickman*, 949 F.Supp. at 889-90, and in fact has declared such delegations of power unconstitutional only twice in its history, "both in the same year and both involving delegations under the same statute, the National Industrial Recovery Act." *Id.* at 889 (citing *Panama Refining Co. v. Ryan*, 293 U.S. 388, 55 S.Ct. 241, 79 L.Ed. 446 (1935); *A.L.A. Schechter Poultry Corp. v. United States*, 295 U.S. 495, 55 S.Ct. 837, 79 L.Ed. 1570 (1935)); see also *Clinton v. City of New York*, 524 U.S. 417, 485-86, 118 S.Ct. 2091, 141 L.Ed.2d 393 (1998) (Breyer, J., dissenting).

By enacting the state sponsored terrorism exception to the FSIA, Congress has manifested its intent that United States victims of terrorist states be given a United States judicial forum in which to seek redress. See *Flatow v. Islamic Republic of Iran*, 999 F.Supp. at 12-13, 15. [FN6] It has separately directed the Executive branch to determine which foreign nations are "terrorist states" for the purpose of controlling the export of certain goods, a determination to be made in accordance with standards established by Congress in the Export Administration Act. *See* 50 U.S.C.App. §2405(j). The FSIA simply references the factual question of whether that designation has been made. The decision of Congress to vest jurisdiction in the federal courts over the class of sovereigns identified as terrorist states and to delegate to the Secretary of State the decision, based on the facts then at her disposal, to determine which sovereign states fall within the class, fully conforms to the requirements of the Constitution. See *Milk Industry Foundation v. Glickman*, 949 F.Supp. at 891 ("[b]y conditioning [its legislative actions] on the making of [an Executive] finding, Congress did not run afoul of the nondelegation doctrine"); cf. *Weidner v. International Telecommunications Satellite Organization*, 392 A.2d 508 (D.C.App.1978) (where International Organizations Immunities Act gave immunity to organizations designated by executive order, such designation was within Presidential authority).

FN6. The inclusion of plaintiff Chad Hall's testimony in the legislative history of the Act leads the Court to the further conclusion that Congress in fact intended that *this very suit* proceed in the courts of the United States. *See Foreign Terrorism and U.S. Courts: Hearings Before the Subcomm. on Courts and Admin. Practice of the Senate Comm. on the Judiciary, Regarding S.825, the Foreign Sovereign Immunities Act*, 103d Cong. (June 21, 1994)., *available in* 1994 WL 274204 (F.D.C.H.) (statement of Chad Hall).
The Second Circuit considered this very issue in *Rein v. Socialist People's Libyan Arab Jamahiriya*, 162 F.3d at 762-64, and concluded that there was no violation of separation of powers. It relied for its conclusion on a century-old Supreme Court case and on one of its own recent precedents. In *Jones v. United States*, 137 U.S. 202, 11 S.Ct. 80, 34 L.Ed. 691 (1890), jurisdiction over the defendant in a murder trial turned on whether the scene of the crime, the Caribbean island of Navassa, was United States Territory. The Supreme Court agreed with the government that the island was U.S. Territory on the basis of a factual determination delegated to and made by the Secretary of State under the Guano Islands Act of 1856 that the island "appertained to the United States." In *Matimak Trading Co. v. Khalily*, 118 F.3d 76

(2d Cir.1997), jurisdiction turned on whether Hong Kong was a "foreign state" under the alienage statute, 28 U.S.C. §1332(a). The Second Circuit acknowledged that recognition of foreign states was a prerogative of the Executive Branch, and noted that the court's alienage jurisdiction over a party depended on whether the party's place of citizenship had been recognized by the Executive as a foreign state. The court found that the district court lacked jurisdiction because Hong Kong had not been recognized as a foreign state by the Executive. *Matimak Trading Co. v. Khalily*, 118 F.3d at 79-84. On the basis of these precedents, the court in *Rein* found no violation of separation of powers in Congress delegating to the Secretary of State the decision whether a particular sovereign nation is a terrorist state. See *Rein v. Socialist People's Libyan Arab Jamahiriya*, 162 F.3d at 764.
Furthermore, like the situation presented to the court in *Rein*, Iraq was already on the list of states designated as state sponsors of terrorism at the time the AEDPA was enacted. Thus, Congress, not the Executive, actually made the determination that Iraq would be subject to suit under the new FSIA exception, since Congress in enacting the statute knew that, regardless of what the Secretary of State might do in the future, the state sponsored terrorism exception would apply to an identifiable group of sovereign states of which Iraq was already a member. "No decision whatsoever of the Secretary of State was needed to create jurisdiction over [Iraq]…That jurisdiction existed the moment that the AEDPA amendment became law." *Rein v. Socialist People's Libyan Arab Jamahiriya*, 162 F.3d at 764; *see* H.R.Rep. No. 104-383, at 181-83 (1995), *available in* 1995 WL 731698.

B. Equal Protection

Defendant next argues that the state sponsored terrorism exception violates the equal protection guarantees of the Due Process Clause by discriminating between sovereign nations on the basis of their status as "sponsors of terrorism." *See* Def. Motion at 9. In order to demonstrate a violation of equal protection, Iraq must show not only that the statute makes distinctions, but that it makes distinctions on constitutionally impermissible grounds. While certain types of classifications, such as those based on race, are given strict scrutiny, see, e.g., *Hunt v. Cromartie*, 526 U.S. 541, 546, 119 S.Ct. 1545, 143 L.Ed.2d 731 (1999); *Regents of University of California v. Bakke*, 438 U.S. 265, 290-91, 98 S.Ct. 2733, 57 L.Ed.2d 750 (1978), a court will review other legislative classifications only to determine if they bear a rational relationship to the stated goal of the legislation. See, e.g., *F.C.C. v. Beach Communications, Inc.*, 508 U.S. 307, 313-14, 113 S.Ct. 2096, 124 L.Ed.2d 211 (1993); *Pennell v. City of San*

Jose, 485 U.S. 1, 14, 108 S.Ct. 849, 99 L.Ed.2d 1 (1988). The court simply examines the statute to see "if there is a rational relationship between the disparity of treatment and some legitimate governmental purpose." *Heller v. Doe by Doe*, 509 U.S. 312, 320, 113 S.Ct. 2637, 125 L.Ed.2d 257 (1993) (citing *Nordlinger v. Hahn*, 505 U.S. 1, 11, 112 S.Ct. 2326, 120 L.Ed.2d 1 (1992)). "Because no fundamental right is implicated by the [Secretary of State's] classification, the appropriate test is whether the statute is rationally related to a legitimate governmental purpose." *Rein v. Socialist People's Libyan Arab Jamahiriya*, 995 F.Supp. at 331-31.

Here, the intent of Congress is abundantly clear. Concerned with acts of terrorism perpetrated against United States citizens abroad, Congress sought to provide a method whereby victims of such acts could seek redress in United States courts against such nations. *See* H.R.Rep. No. 104-383, at 181-83. The nations that Congress singled out are those that consistently operate outside the bounds of the international community by sponsoring and encouraging acts generally condemned by civilized nations. As Congress has noted:

These outlaw states consider terrorism a legitimate instrument of achieving their foreign policy goals. They have become better at hiding their material support for their surrogates, which includes the provision of safe havens, funding, training, supplying weaponry, medical assistance, false travel documentation, and the like. For this reason, the Committee has determined that allowing suits in the federal courts against countries responsible for terrorist acts where Americans and/or their loved ones suffer injury or death at the hands of the terrorist states is warranted. [The state sponsored terrorism exception] will give American citizens an important economic and financial weapon against these outlaw states.

H.R.Rep. No. 104-383, at 182-83.

Those nations that operate in a manner inconsistent with international norms should not expect to be granted the privilege of immunity from suit that is within the prerogative of Congress to grant or withhold. The distinction made by Congress between those states that have been designated as sponsors of terrorism and those that have not is rationally related to its purpose of protecting U.S. citizens by deterring international terrorism and providing compensation for victims of terrorist acts. 28 U.S.C. §1605(a)(7) does not violate the equal protection guarantees of the Due Process Clause.

C. Personal Jurisdiction

Defendant's final constitutional argument is that the state sponsored terrorism exception to the FSIA abrogates the minimum contacts requirement of due process necessary for the assertion of personal jurisdiction. *See* Def. Motion at 10-11. Because all of the conduct alleged in the complaint occurred outside the borders of the United States, defendant argues that it had no "fair warning that a particular activity [would] subject [it] to the jurisdiction of a foreign sovereign," *Burger King Corp. v. Rudzewicz*, 471 U.S. 462, 472, 105 S.Ct. 2174, 85 L.Ed.2d 528 (1985) (quoting *Shaffer v. Heitner*, 433 U.S. 186, 218, 97 S.Ct. 2569, 53 L.Ed.2d 683 (1977)), and that "maintenance of the suit [would] offend 'traditional notions of fair play and substantial justice.' " *International Shoe Co. v. State of Washington*, 326 U.S. 310, 316, 66 S.Ct. 154, 90 L.Ed. 95 (1945) (quoting *Milliken v. Meyer*, 311 U.S. 457, 463, 61 S.Ct. 339, 85 L.Ed. 278 (1940)). The Court disagrees.

Congress expressly addressed the minimum contacts requirement in enacting the FSIA by providing that "[p]ersonal jurisdiction over a foreign state shall exist as to every claim for relief over which the district courts have jurisdiction" pursuant to the exceptions of the FSIA, and where service has been made. 28 U.S.C. §1330(b); see *Shapiro v. Republic of Bolivia*, 930 F.2d 1013, 1020 (2d Cir.1991) ("Under the FSIA, therefore, personal jurisdiction equals subject matter jurisdiction plus valid service of process."). Indeed, Congress explicitly considered *International Shoe* before passing the original FSIA:

[28 U.S.C. §] 1330(b) provides, in effect, a Federal long-arm statute over foreign states (including political subdivisions, agencies, and instrumentalities of foreign states). It is patterned after the long-arm statute Congress enacted for the District of Columbia. Public Law 91-358, sec. 132(a), title I, 84 Stat. 549. The requirements of minimum jurisdictional contacts and adequate notice are embodied in the provision. Cf. *International Shoe Co. v. Washington*, 326 U.S. 310, 66 S.Ct. 154, 90 L.Ed. 95 (1945), and *McGee v. International Life Ins. Co.*, 355 U.S. 220, 223, 78 S.Ct. 199, 2 L.Ed.2d 223 (1957). For personal jurisdiction to exist under section 1330(b), the claim must first of all be one over which the district courts have original jurisdiction under section 1330(a), meaning a claim for which the foreign state is not entitled to immunity. Significantly, each of the immunity provisions in the bill, sections 1605-1607, requires some connection between the lawsuit and the United States, or an express or implied waiver by the foreign state of its immunity from jurisdiction. These immunity provisions, therefore, prescribe the necessary contacts which must exist before our courts can exercise personal jurisdiction. Besides incorporating these jurisdictional contacts by reference, section 1330(b) also satisfies the due process requirement of adequate notice by prescribing that proper service be made under section 1608 of the bill. Thus, sections 1330(b), 1608, and 1605-1607 are all carefully interconnected.

H.R.Rep. No. 94-1487, at 13-14 (1976) (footnotes omitted), *reprinted in* 1976 U.S.C.C.A.N. 6604, 6612, quoted in *Thos. P. Gonzalez Corp. v. Consejo Nacional de Produccion de Costa Rica*, 614 F.2d 1247, 1255 n. 5 (9th Cir.1980).

When it enacted the state sponsored terrorism exception in the AEDPA, however, Congress arguably changed the topology of the FSIA. Unlike other FSIA exceptions, the connection between the lawsuit and the United States may seem less obvious under 28 U.S.C. §1605(a)(7). Yet the analytic inquiry remains the same: Have states that sponsor terrorism been given adequate warning that terrorist acts against United States citizens, no matter where they occur, may subject them to suit in a United States court? Have they been provided with that "degree of predictability…that allows potential defendants to structure their primary conduct with some minimum assurance as to where that conduct will and will not render them liable to suit?' " *Burger King Corp. v. Rudzewicz*, 471 U.S. at 472, 105 S.Ct. 2174 (quoting *World-Wide Volkswagen Corp. v. Woodson*, 444 U.S. 286, 297, 100 S.Ct. 559, 62 L.Ed.2d 490 (1980)). In the context of this statute, the purpose for which it was enacted, and the nature of the activity toward which it is directed, the Court concludes that it is reasonable that foreign states be held accountable in the courts of the United States for terrorist actions perpetrated against U.S. citizens anywhere.

As Judge Lamberth has noted, "terrorism is…the modern era's *hosti humani generis*-an enemy of all mankind." *Flatow v. Islamic Republic of Iran*, 999 F.Supp. at 23. It has become the insidious method by which certain rogue states operate to influence the international community, outside the normal bounds of international communication. No nation openly professes to support the use of terrorist methods, though several clandestinely do. Although there are traditional methods of effecting change on the world stage-including diplomacy, trade and economic sanctions, and even the use of organized armed conflict under established international rules of war-certain states instead choose to conduct their policy through naked violence directed at individuals. In such circumstances, "traditional notions of fair play and substantial justice" are stretched to the limits. Yet, as Judge Lamberth has correctly concluded:

All states are on notice that state sponsorship of terrorism is condemned by the international community. United States policy towards state sponsors of terrorists, has been made abundantly clear since the 1979-1981 hostage crisis in Tehran and the ensuing suspension of diplomatic relations with and establishment of international boycotts against foreign state sponsors of terrorism. Foreign state sponsors

of terrorism could not reasonably have expected that the United States would not respond to attacks on its citizens, and not undertake measures to prevent similar attacks in the future. In light of the mounting Congressional frustration at the inability of United States victims of foreign state abuses to obtain relief from any forum, it is manifest that Congress enacted 28 U.S.C. §1605(a)(7) to ensure fair play and substantial justice for American victims of state sponsored terrorism.

Flatow v. Islamic Republic of Iran, 999 F.Supp. at 23. The state sponsored terrorism exception "provides an express jurisdictional nexus based upon the victim's United States nationality." *Id*. at 22.

Plaintiffs allege that the purpose behind detaining Kenneth Beaty, David Daliberti and William Barloon was to prompt certain actions by the United States, particularly the lifting of economic sanctions against Iraq and the delivery of millions of dollars worth of humanitarian goods. Compl. ¶¶ 9, 14. Kenneth Beaty was released only after such goods were delivered from the United States. The detention of these three plaintiffs had a direct effect in the United States and was consciously designed to affect United States policy. Under the circumstances, Iraq cannot now claim surprise at the assertion of jurisdiction by this Court over claims brought in response to its actions. It is reasonable that Iraq be held to answer in a United States court for acts of terrorism against United States citizens. [FN7]

FN7. In a related argument, defendant moves to dismiss this action on grounds of *forum non conveniens*, suggesting that it would present an undue burden on Iraq to force it to defend itself in this forum. *See* Def. Motion at 28-29. Defendant's request must fail because Congress has explicitly authorized this action, and in doing so has already balanced the interests of the United States in hearing such a suit in the federal courts of this country against the interests of Iraq in not being forced to defend here. It would be inappropriate for this Court to second-guess Congress and apply its own balancing test where none is called for by the statute or manifest principles of constitutional law. See *Flatow v. Islamic Republic of Iran*, 999 F.Supp. at 25.

IV. ACT OF STATE DOCTRINE

Finally, Iraq moves to dismiss this action for failure to state a claim on the grounds that adjudication of its conduct would violate the act of state doctrine. *See* Def. Motion at 25-27. This doctrine "directs United States courts to refrain from deciding a case when the outcome turns upon the legality or illegality…of official action by a foreign sovereign performed within its own territory." *Riggs Nat'l Corp. & Subsidiaries v. Commissioner of IRS*, 163 F.3d 1363, 1367 (D.C.Cir.1999) (citing *W.S. Kirkpatrick & Co., Inc. v. Environmental Tectonics Corp.*, 493 U.S. 400, 406, 110 S.Ct. 701, 107 L.Ed.2d 816 (1990)). It is rooted in the "domestic separation of powers, reflecting 'the strong sense of the Judicial Branch that its engagement in the task of passing on the validity of foreign acts of state may hinder' the conduct of foreign affairs." *W.S. Kirkpatrick & Co., Inc. v. Environmental Tectonics*, 493 U.S. at 404 (quoting *Banco Nacional de Cuba v. Sabbatino*, 376 U.S. 398, 423, 84 S.Ct. 923, 11 L.Ed.2d 804 (1964)). The act of state doctrine is designed, at least in part, to avoid having the Judiciary "embarrass" the Executive and Legislative Branches, which are the branches constitutionally empowered to decide matters relating to foreign policy. See *Banco Nacional de Cuba v. Sabbatino*, 376 U.S. at 421-24, 84 S.Ct. 923 (act of state derives from judicial concern with possible interference with the political branches' conduct of foreign affairs).

While the act of state doctrine seeks to prevent courts from interfering in the foreign affairs powers of the President and the Congress, it does not prohibit Congress and the Executive from using the threat of legal action in the courts as an instrument of foreign policy. The designation of Iraq as a terrorist state was made by the Secretary of State on behalf of the Executive Branch under an express grant of authority by Congress. For this Court to grant defendant's motion to dismiss on act of state grounds would constitute more of a judicial interference in the announced foreign policy of the political branches of government than to allow the suit to proceed under the explicit authorization of Congress.

V. CONCLUSION

The four male plaintiffs have established sufficient grounds to allow their claims to proceed under the state sponsored terrorism exception to the FSIA, 28 U.S.C. §1605(a)(7). The claims of the spouse plaintiffs and all other claims brought under the commercial activity exception, 28 U.S.C. §1605(a)(2), will be dismissed for lack of subject matter jurisdiction. The Court has personal jurisdiction under the FSIA. The state sponsored terrorism exception is not unconstitutional as applied to the defendant. Finally, the act of state doctrine is no bar to this suit. Defendant's motion to dismiss therefore will be denied. Iraq must file an answer and the case will proceed to discovery and trial.

An appropriate Order will issue this same day.

Notes:

1. On a practical level, why would Congress pass a statute which allows the State Department to determine which foreign states are amenable to suit as state sponsors of terrorism?

2. What does Congress' delegation to the State Department "of the duty to find facts upon which certain enactments are made conditional" suggest about the nature of the issues at stake in terrorism litigation? Does this "duty to find facts" suggest that an administrative record will be made by the State Department before designating a foreign state a "state sponsor of terrorism?"

3. Of the almost 200 states in the world, only seven have ever been on the list of state sponsors of terrorism and now only five remain. What does this suggest about the efficacy and scope of the terrorism amendments? Or about the politics of terrorism?

4. If a state boasts of providing material support and assistance to terrorist organizations but is not designated by the State Department, do the terrorism amendments apply to permit victims to sue? What standing do victims have to add states to the list of state sponsors of terrorism?

5. The issue of whether foreign states should be afforded Due Process rights under the Fifth Amendment had been a longstanding controversy in the federal courts. For instance, the Supreme Court decided a case shortly before the enactment of the FSIA terrorism amendments by "assume[ing] without deciding, that a foreign state is a 'person' for purposes of the Due Process Clause." *Republic of Argentina v. Weltover, Inc.*, 504 U.S. 607, 619 (1992). Interestingly, the issue was finally addressed in the context of a terrorism suit where the issue was front and center. In *Price v. Socialist People's Libyan Arab Jamahiriya*, 294 F.3d 82, 96-97 (D.C. 2002) the court fully addressed the issue,

> And, with the issue directly before us, we hold that foreign states are not "persons" protected by the Fifth Amendment.
>
> Our conclusion is based on a number of considerations. First, as the Supreme Court noted in *Will v. Michigan Department of State Police*, there is an "often-expressed understanding that 'in com-

mon usage, the term "person" does not include the sovereign, and statutes employing the word are ordinarily construed to exclude it.'"…In this case, however, what is at issue is the meaning of the Due Process Clause, not a statutory provision. And, on this score, it is highly significant that in *South Carolina v. Katzenbach*, 383 U.S. 301, 323-24, 86 S.Ct. 803, 815-16, 15 L.Ed.2d 769 (1966), the Court was unequivocal in holding that "the word 'person' in the context of the Due Process Clause of the Fifth Amendment cannot, by any reasonable mode of interpretation, be expanded to encompass the States of the Union." Therefore, absent some compelling reason to treat foreign sovereigns more favorably than "States of the Union," it would make no sense to view foreign states as "persons" under the Due Process Clause.

Indeed, we think it would be highly incongruous to afford greater Fifth Amendment rights to foreign nations, who are entirely alien to our constitutional system, than are afforded to the states, which help make up the very fabric of that system. The States are integral and active participants in the Constitution's infrastructure, and they both derive important benefits and must abide by significant limitations as a consequence of their participation. *Compare* U.S. CONST. art. IV §4 ("The United States shall guarantee to every State in this Union a Republican form of Government, and shall protect each of them against Invasion;"), *with id.* at art. VI, cl. 2 ("This Constitution…shall be the supreme Law of the Land; and the Judges in every State shall be bound thereby, any Thing in the Constitution or Law of the State to the Contrary notwithstanding."), *and id.* at art. 1 §10 (listing specific acts prohibited to the States). However, a "foreign State lies outside the structure of the Union." *Principality of Monaco v. Mississippi*, 292 U.S. 313, 330, 54 S.Ct. 745, 751, 78 L.Ed. 1282 (1934). Given this fundamental dichotomy between the constitutional status of foreign states and States within the United States, we cannot perceive why the former should be permitted to avail themselves of the fundamental safeguards of the Due Process Clause if the latter may not.

It is especially significant that the Constitution does not limit foreign states, as it does the States of the Union, in the power they can exert against the United States or its government. Indeed, the federal government cannot invoke the Constitution,

save possibly to declare war, to prevent a foreign nation from taking action adverse to the interest of the United States or to compel it to take action favorable to the United States. It would therefore be quite strange to interpret the Due Process Clause as conferring upon Libya rights and protections *against* the power of federal government.

In addition to text and structure, history and tradition support our conclusion. Never has the Supreme Court suggested that foreign nations enjoy rights derived from the Constitution, or that they can use such rights to shield themselves from adverse actions taken by the United States. This is not surprising. Relations between nations in the international community are seldom governed by the domestic law of one state or the other…

Rather, the federal judiciary has relied on principles of comity and international law to protect foreign governments in the American legal system. This approach recognizes the reality that foreign nations are external to the constitutional compact, and it preserves the flexibility and discretion of the political branches in conducting this country's relations with other nations…

6.   However, even after *Price* rejected Libya's due process claim, the former Attorney General of the United States, Ramsey Clark, representing Syria, continued to allege that the designation of a foreign state as a state sponsor of terrorism violates the Due Process Clause of the Constitution and that application of extra territorial jurisdiction violates international law:

Syria argues that jurisdiction in this court would violate Syria's due process rights because Syria lacks minimum contacts with the United States and is unable to challenge the Executive Branch's designation of Syria as a terrorist state. Defs.' Mot. at 7. The court need not linger long on these arguments, for as the defendant concedes, binding law in this circuit is not in its favor. *Id.* at 8 (citing *Price I*, 294 F.3d at 99). Indeed, as the court stated in *Price I*, "the Constitution imposes no limitation on the exercise of personal jurisdiction by the federal courts over [foreign sovereigns.]" 294 F.3d at 86.

In addition to their due process claims under American law, the defendant generally claims that this court's exercise of jurisdiction over Syria "is unreasonable and impermissible under applicable principles of international law." Def.'s Mot. at 9 (citing RESTATEMENT (THIRD) FOREIGN RELATIONS LAW OF THE UNITED STATES (1986) at §403). In *Flatow v. Islamic Republic of Iran*, a case involving Iran's provision of material support to a terrorist group that engaged in homicide bombings, Iran raised a similar argument. 999 F.Supp. 1, 15 n. 7 (D.D.C.1998). The court in that case limited its analysis to a determination that Congress intended extraterritorial application of §1605(a)(7), but also noted that jurisdiction over Iran would be consistent with international law. *Id.* As the court stated, "extraterritorial application of the state sponsored terrorism exceptions is consistent with international law; three of the five bases for the exercise of extraterritorial jurisdiction are implicated in actions by United States victims of foreign state sponsored terrorism: passive personality (nationality of victim), protective (national security interests), and universal (subject to jurisdiction wherever the offender may be found)." *Id.* (citing RESTATEMENT (THIRD) FOREIGN RELATIONS LAW OF THE UNITED STATES (1986) at §§402(2)-(3), 403, 423). This court sees no reason to depart from the analysis in *Flatow*. Accordingly, assuming *arguendo* that the defendant may raise principles of international law as a defense to personal jurisdiction, the court determines that it can maintain jurisdiction over Syria consistent with the principles of international law governing extraterritorial jurisdiction. *Id.*

Wyatt v. Syrian Arab Republic, 362 F.Supp.2d 103, 115-116 (D.D.C. 2005).

7. Concerning "international norms," the *Dalberti* court ruled,

Those nations that operate in a manner inconsistent with international norms should not expect to be granted the privilege of immunity from suit that is within the prerogative of Congress to grant or withhold. The distinction made by Congress between those states that have been designated as sponsors of terrorism and those that have not is rationally related to its purpose of protecting U.S. citizens by deterring international terrorism and providing compensation for victims of terrorist acts. 28 U.S.C. §1605(a)(7) does not violate the equal protection guarantees of the Due Process Clause.

Is this reasoning circular? Would a similar process be permitted with respect to non-states?

8. Is there a mechanism for foreign governments to challenge the State Department's designation? If so, in what forum does that occur and what, if any, role do victims have in the process?

9. The designation of the state sponsors of terrorism is contained in 22 C.F.R. §126.1(d):

Terrorism. Exports to countries which the Secretary of State has determined to have repeatedly provided support for acts of international terrorism are contrary to the foreign policy of the United States and are thus subject to the policy specified in paragraph (a) of this section and the requirements of section 40 of the Arms Export Control Act (22 U.S.C. 2780) and the Omnibus Diplomatic Security and Anti-Terrorism Act of 1986 (22 U.S.C. 4801, note). The countries in this category are: Cuba, Iran, North Korea, Sudan and Syria.

4.3 *Flatow v. Islamic Republic of Iran*, 999 F.Supp. 1 (D. D.C. 1998)
LAMBERTH, District Judge.

FINDINGS OF FACT AND CONCLUSIONS OF LAW

This is an action for wrongful death resulting from an act of state-sponsored terrorism. Defendants have not entered an appearance in this matter. This Court entered Defendants' default on September 4, 1997, pursuant to 28 U.S.C. §1608(e) and Fed.R.Civ.P. 55(a). Notwithstanding indicia of Defendants' willful default, [FN1] however, this Court is compelled to make further inquiry prior to entering a judgment by default against Defendants. As with actions against the federal government, the Foreign Sovereign Immunities Act ("FSIA") requires that a default judgment against a foreign state be entered only after plaintiff "establishes his claim or right to relief by evidence that is satisfactory to the Court." 28 U.S.C. §1608(e); see *Compania Interamericana Export-Import, S.A. v. Compania Dominicana de Aviacion*, 88 F.3d 948, 951 (11th Cir.1996).

FN1. Service of process was accomplished with the assistance of the Swiss Embassy in Tehran, the United States' protecting power in the Islamic Republic of Iran, on June 8, 1997. This Court has yet to receive any response from Defendants, either through counsel's entry of appearance, or through a diplomatic note. The Islamic Republic of Iran is an experienced litigant in the United States federal court system generally and in this Circuit. See, e.g., *Cicippio v. Islamic Republic of Iran*, 30 F.3d 164 (D.C.Cir.1994), *cert. denied* 513 U.S. 1078, 115 S.Ct. 726, 130 L.Ed.2d 631 (1995); *Foremost-McKesson v. Islamic Republic of Iran*, 905 F.2d 438 (D.C.Cir.1990); *Persinger v. Islamic Republic of Iran*, 729 F.2d 835 (D.C.Cir.1984); *Berkovitz v. Islamic Republic of Iran*, 735 F.2d 329 (9th Cir.1984), *McKeel v. Islamic Republic of Iran*, 722 F.2d 582 (9th Cir.1983). The Islamic Republic of Iran also apparently attempted to evade service of process by international registered mail, pursuant to 28 U.S.C. §1608(a)(3). When the service package was returned to counsel in June 1997, the package had been opened, the return receipt, which counsel had not received, had been completely removed, and the message "DO NOT USA" was written in English across the back of the envelope. This contumacious conduct bolsters the entry of a default judgment. See *Commercial Bank of Kuwait v. Rafidain Bank*, 15 F.3d 238 (2d Cir.1994).

Plaintiff brings this action pursuant to two recently enacted amendments to the FSIA, which grant jurisdiction over foreign states and their officials, agents and employees, and create federal causes of action related to personal injury or death resulting from state-sponsored terrorist attacks. Given these novel enactments, and this Court's special role in the development of foreign sovereign immunity jurisprudence, *see* 28 U.S.C. §1391(f)(4), this Court has engaged in a systematic review of dispositive legal issues prior to making its determination that Plaintiff has established his claim and right to relief to the satisfaction of this Court. [FN2]

FN2. This Court knows of only one other Court which has interpreted these new provisions, the United States District Court for the Southern District of Florida, in an action brought by the families of the Brothers to the Rescue pilots shot down by the Cuban Air Force over the Straits of Florida on February 24, 1996. *Alejandre, et al. v. The Republic of Cuba*, et al., 996 F.Supp. 1239 (1997). Cases resulting from the bombing of Pan Am Flight 103 have been re-filed under these provisions, and are currently pending before the United States District Court for the Eastern District of New York. See, e.g., *Rein v. Socialist People's Libyan Arab Jamahiriya*, 995 F.Supp. 325 (E.D.N.Y.1998).

FINDINGS OF FACT

This matter came before the Court for an evidentiary hearing on March 2-3, 1998. The Plaintiff proceeded in the manner of a nonjury trial before the Court and the following

findings of fact are based upon the sworn testimony and documents entered into evidence in accordance with the Federal Rules of Evidence. Plaintiff has "establishe[d] his claim or right to relief by evidence that is satisfactory to the Court" as required by 28 U.S.C. §1608(e). This Court finds the following facts to be established by clear and convincing evidence, which would have been sufficient to establish a *prima facie* case in a contested proceeding:

1 Plaintiff Stephen M. Flatow, a domiciliary of the State of New Jersey, is the father of Alisa Michelle Flatow, decedent, and is also the Administrator of the Estate of Alisa Michelle Flatow. He brings this action in his own right, as Administrator of the Estate of Alisa Michelle Flatow, and on behalf of decedent's heirs-at-law, including Rosalyn Flatow, decedent's mother, and decedent's siblings, Gail, age 21, Francine, age 18, Ilana, age 16, and Etan, age 14, all decedent's siblings. Affidavit (Exhibit 2) (Exhibit 2) and testimony of Stephen M. Flatow.

2 Alisa Michelle Flatow was born on October 5, 1974 in the United States. She maintained her United States citizenship throughout her life, and was a United States citizen at the time of her death. Affidavit (Exhibit 2) and testimony of Stephen M. Flatow; Report of the Death Of An American Citizen Abroad (Exhibit 9).

3 At the time of her death, Alisa Michelle Flatow was a twenty-year-old Brandeis University student. For the 1995 spring semester, her junior year at Brandeis University, Alisa Michelle Flatow arranged for and participated in an independent foreign study program in Israel. Affidavit (Exhibit 2) and testimony of Stephen M. Flatow; testimony of Dr. Jonathan Sarna; testimony of Alan Mitrani; testimony of Lauren Sloane; testimony of Gail Flatow; testimony of Francine Flatow; decedent's academic records from Brandeis University.

4 While in Israel, she communicated with her father, Plaintiff Stephen M. Flatow, to ask whether she could travel to a community on the Mediterranean Sea with friends. He reviewed their itinerary with her, and as he believed that the Israeli government would not provide civilian passenger bus service unless it were safe to do so and he gave her permission to travel in Gaza. Affidavit (Exhibit 2) and testimony of Stephen M. Flatow.

5 On April 9, 1995, decedent Alisa Michelle Flatow was a passenger on the number 36 Egged bus, which was traveling

from Ashkelon, Israel to a Mediterranean resort in the Gush Katif community. Testimony of Kesari Rusa.

6 At or about 12:05 p.m. local time, near Kfar Darom in the Gaza Strip, a suicide bomber drove a van loaded with explosives into the number 36 Egged bus, causing an explosion that destroyed the bus. Testimony of Kesari Rusa; testimony of Orit Taft; testimony of Ezra Mordecai testimony of and videotape by David Shaenbaum; U.S. DEP'T OF STATE, PATTERNS OF GLOBAL TERRORISM 1995 (April 1996).

7 As a result of the explosion, a piece of shrapnel pierced Alisa Michelle Flatow's skull casing and lodged in her brain, causing a severe head injury. Testimony of Dr. Allen Fisher; decedent's medical records from the Soroka Medical Center, with translation from Hebrew (Exhibit 3).

8 Immediately after the explosion, Alisa Michelle Flatow slumped over onto her traveling companion, Kesari Rusa. Her eyes were open and her hands clutched. She received emergency medical treatment on the scene. Because her injuries were so severe, she was among the first of the injured which the Israeli Defense Forces medivac'ed by helicopter to the Soroka Medical Center in B'er Sheva for immediate medical attention. Testimony of Kesari Rusa; testimony of and videotape by David Shaenbaum; testimony of Orit Taft.

9 Upon her arrival at the Soroka Medical Center approximately one hour after the bombing, Alisa Michelle Flatow's pulse and respiration were good without medical assistance. Her pupils reacted to light and she responded to deep pain stimuli. She was assessed as a 5 of a possible 15 on the Glasgow coma scale. She had sustained a depressed skull fracture and intracerebral lacerations. Testimony of Dr. Allen Fisher; decedent's medical records from the Soroka Medical Center, with translation from Hebrew (Exhibit 3).

10 From approximately 3 to 5 pm local time, Alisa Michelle Flatow was in emergency surgery; the entrance wound was debrided and a partial craniotomy was performed in order to alleviate pressure from the intracerebral hemorrhaging and concomitant swelling of brain tissue within the skull. Testimony of Dr. Allen Fisher; decedent's medical records from the Soroka Medical Center, with translation from Hebrew (Exhibit 3).

11 To a reasonable degree of medical certainty, Alisa Michelle Flatow suffered extreme bodily pain and suffering for at least three to five hours as a result of the injuries she sustained in the bombing. Testimony of Dr. Gregory Threatte.

12 Plaintiff Stephen M. Flatow first heard of the attack on the radio on April 9, 1995 at approximately 7:45 am EST; he immediately began attempts to contact his daughter. That decedent had been on the number 36 Egged bus was confirmed when one of her traveling companions telephoned her family in the United States. Plaintiff made extraordinary efforts to locate his daughter; after several hours, the Medical Center confirmed that she was being treated there and that she was in grave condition. Plaintiff immediately flew to Israel to be with his daughter. Affidavit (Exhibit 2) and testimony of Stephen M. Flatow; testimony of Rosalyn Flatow; testimony of Alan Mitrani.

13 Shortly after his arrival at the Soroka Medical Center the morning of April 10, 1995, the hospital director and Dr. Allen Fisher, the attending physician, informed Stephen M. Flatow that Alisa Michelle Flatow showed no brain activity, that all physical functions relied upon artificial life support, and that there was no hope for her recovery. Affidavit (Exhibit 2) and testimony of Stephen M. Flatow; testimony of Dr. Allan Fisher; decedent's medical records from the Soroka Medical Center, with translation from Hebrew (exhibit 3).

14 The Flatow family is Jewish and observes Orthodox Jewish practice. Orthodox doctrine reveres the sanctity of life and of the body; the traditional view is that all means should be exerted to prolong life, and that the body must be buried intact. However, Orthodox doctrine also considers the saving of one life to be the saving of an entire universe. Alisa Michelle Flatow's condition presented an opportunity to save lives through organ donation, which is extremely rare in Israel precisely because it is incompatible with the sanctity of life and of the body. After consulting with several Rabbis, Stephen M. Flatow requested that no further extraordinary efforts be exerted on behalf of his daughter, that life support be terminated, and that his daughter's organs be harvested for transplant. Alisa Michelle Flatow died at approximately 10:00 a.m. local time on April 10, 1995. Her organs saved three lives and significantly improved the quality of life for several other persons. Affidavit (Exhibit 2) and testimony of Stephen M. Flatow, testimony of Dr. Allan Fisher decedent's medical records from the Soroka Medical Center, with translation from Hebrew (Exhibit 3); testimony of Ari Mendelson (organ recipient).

15 Alisa Michelle Flatow had been accompanied on the bus by two companions who were also United States nationals and were injured as a result of the explosion. United States nationals often rode this bus line. The attack on the bus caused seven other deaths and many injuries, all involving non-United States nationals. Testimony of Kesari Rusa; testimony of Orit Taft; U.S. DEP'T OF STATE, PATTERNS OF GLOBAL TERRORISM 1995 (April 1996).

16 The Shaqaqi faction of Palestine Islamic Jihad claimed responsibility for and in fact perpetrated the terrorist act which caused the death of Alisa Michelle Flatow. Palestine Islamic Jihad is series of loosely affiliated factions rather than a cohesive group. The Shaqaqi faction is a terrorist cell with a small core membership. Its sole purpose is to conduct terrorist activities in the Gaza region, and its sole source of funding is the Islamic Republic of Iran. Testimony of Dr. Reuven Paz; testimony of Dr. Patrick Clawson; testimony of former FBI Deputy Assistant Director for Counterterrorism Harry Brandon; U.S. DEP'T OF STATE, PATTERNS OF GLOBAL TERRORISM 1995 (April 1996).

17 The Israeli government informed Stephen M. Flatow that the Shaqaqi faction of Palestine Islamic Jihad had claimed responsibility for the bombing, and that their investigation had confirmed that claim. Affidavit of Stephen M. Flatow (Exhibit 2).

18 In July 1996, Plaintiff Stephen M. Flatow and his counsel met with Ambassador Philip Wilcox, who then served as the Department of State's Coordinator for Counterterrorism. During that meeting, he informed Mr. Flatow that the Department of State was satisfied that the group which had claimed responsibility for the bombing, the Shaqaqi faction of Palestine Islamic Jihad, had in fact perpetrated the bombing, and that the Islamic Republic of Iran provided approximately two million dollars to Palestine Islamic Jihad annually in support of its terrorist activities. Affidavit of Stephen M. Flatow (Exhibit 2).

19 Defendant the Islamic Republic of Iran is a foreign state and has been designated a state sponsor of terrorism pursuant to section 6(j) of the Export Administration Act of 1979 (50 U.S.C.App. §2405(j)) continuously since January 19, 1984. Defendant provides material support and resources to Palestine Islamic Jihad by supplying funds and training for the Shaqaqi faction's terrorist activities in the Gaza Strip region. Testimony of Dr. Reuven Paz, testimony of Dr. Patrick Clawson, testimony of former FBI Deputy Assistant Director for Counterterrorism Harry Brandon.

20 Defendant the Islamic Republic of Iran sponsors the Shaqaqi faction's terrorist activities within the meaning of 28 U.S.C. §1605(a)(7) and 28 U.S.C. §1605 note by providing it with all of its funding. Testimony of Dr. Reuven Paz; testimony of Dr. Patrick Clawson; testimony of former FBI Deputy Assistant Director for Counterterrorism Harry Brandon.

21 Defendant the Iranian Ministry of Information and Security is the Iranian intelligence service, functioning both within and beyond Iranian territory. Acting as an agent of the Islamic Republic of Iran, the Iranian Ministry of Information and Security performed acts within the scope of its agency, within the meaning of 28 U.S.C. §1605(a)(7) and 28 U.S.C.A. §1605 note, which caused the death of Alisa Michelle Flatow. Specifically, the Iranian Ministry of Information and Security acted as a conduit for the Islamic Republic of Iran's provision of funds and training to the Shaqaqi faction for its terrorist activities in the Gaza Strip region. Testimony of Dr. Reuven Paz; testimony of Dr. Patrick Clawson; testimony of former FBI Deputy Assistant Director for Counterterrorism Harry Brandon.

22 Defendant Ayatollah Ali Hoseini Khamenei is the Supreme Leader of the Islamic Republic of Iran. Acting as an official of the Islamic Republic of Iran, Defendant Ayatollah Ali Hoseini Khamenei performed acts within the scope of his office, within the meaning of 28 U.S.C. §1605(a)(7) and 28 U.S.C.A. §1605 note, which caused the death of Alisa Michelle Flatow. Specifically, Defendant Khamenei approved the provision of material support and resources to the Shaqaqi faction of Palestine Islamic Jihad. Testimony of Dr. Reuven Paz; testimony of Dr. Patrick Clawson; testimony of former FBI Deputy Assistant Director for Counterterrorism Harry Brandon.

23 Defendant Ali Akbar Hashemi-Rafsanjani is the former President of the Islamic Republic of Iran. Acting as an official of the Islamic Republic of Iran, Defendant Ali Akbar Hashemi-Rafsanjani performed acts within the scope of his office, within the meaning of 28 U.S.C. §1605(a)(7) and 28 U.S.C.A. §1605 note, which caused the death of Alisa Michelle Flatow. Specifically, Defendant approved the provision of material support and resources to the Shaqaqi faction of Palestine Islamic Jihad. Testimony of Dr. Reuven Paz; testimony of Dr. Patrick Clawson; testimony of former FBI Deputy Assistant Director for Counterterrorism Harry Brandon.

24 Defendant Ali Fallahian-Khuzestani is the former head of the Iranian Ministry of Information and Security. Acting as an official of the Islamic Republic of Iran, Defendant Ali Fallahian-Khuzestani performed acts within the scope of his office, within the meaning of 28 U.S.C. §1605(a)(7) and 28 U.S.C.A. §1605 note, which caused the death of Alisa Michelle Flatow. Specifically, Defendant Fallahian approved the provision of material support and resources by the Islamic Republic of Iran to the Shaqaqi faction. Testimony of Dr. Reuven Paz; testimony of Dr. Patrick Clawson; testimony of former FBI Deputy Assistant Director for Counterterrorism Harry Brandon.

25 Defendants the Islamic Republic of Iran, the Iranian Ministry of Information and Security, while acting as an agent of the Islamic Republic of Iran, and Iranian officials Ayatollah Ali Hoseini Khamenei, former President Ali Akbar Hashemi-Rafsanjani, and former Minister Ali Fallahian-Khuzestani, each acting in his official capacity, conspired to provide material support and resources to the Shaqaqi faction of Palestine Islamic Jihad, a terrorist organization, within the meaning of 28 U.S.C. §1605(a)(7) and 28 U.S.C.A. §1605 note, which caused the death of Alisa Michelle Flatow. Testimony of Dr. Reuven Paz; testimony of Dr. Patrick Clawson; testimony of former FBI Deputy Assistant Director for Counterterrorism Harry Brandon.

26 Alisa Michelle Flatow's death was caused by a willful and deliberate act of extrajudicial killing because the explosion was caused by a bomb that was deliberately driven into the bus by a member of the Shaqaqi faction of the Palestine Islamic Jihad acting under the direction of Defendants the Islamic Republic of Iran, the Iranian Ministry of Information and Security, Ayatollah Ali Hoseini Khamenei, Ali Akbar Hashemi-Rafsanjani and Ali Fallahian-Khuzestani.

27 As a result of Alisa Michelle Flatow's death, her Estate suffered a loss of accretions which could have been expected to occur during the course of her anticipated life expectancy in the amount of $1,508,750.00. Report (Exhibit 6) and testimony of Dr. Jerome S. Paige.

28 As a result of Alisa Michelle Flatow's death, her heirs-at-law have suffered an economic loss for the expenses associated with her funeral and final services in the amount of $4,470.00. Funeral Home Invoice (Exhibit 4).

29 As the result of Alisa Michelle Flatow's death, her parents and her surviving sisters and brother have suffered and will continue to suffer severe mental anguish and the loss

of her society. Testimony of Stephen M. Flatow; testimony of Rosalyn Flatow; testimony of Gail Flatow; testimony of Francine Flatow, testimony of Ilana Flatow, testimony of Etan Flatow, testimony of Alan Mitrani, testimony of Lauren Sloane, testimony of Kesari Rusa.

I. CONCLUSIONS OF LAW WITH RESPECT TO JURISDICTION

A. THE FOREIGN SOVEREIGN IMMUNITIES ACT CONTROLS THIS ACTION.

As this action is brought against a foreign state, its intelligence service acting as its agent, and three of its officials, acting in their official capacity, [FN3] the Foreign Sovereign Immunities Act of 1976, 28 U.S.C. §§1602- 1611 *et seq.* ["FSIA"], as amended, controls this action. The FSIA must be applied in every action involving a foreign state defendant. *Verlinden B.V. v. Central Bank of Nigeria*, 461 U.S. 480, 489, 103 S.Ct. 1962, 76 L.Ed.2d 81 (1983); 28 U.S.C. §1330. The sole bases for subject matter jurisdiction in an action against a foreign state defendant are the FSIA's enumerated exceptions to immunity. *Argentine Republic v. Amerada Hess Shipping Corp.*, 488 U.S. 428, 434, 109 S.Ct. 683, 102 L.Ed.2d 818 (1989). This Court lacks jurisdiction over this matter unless it falls within one of the FSIA's enumerated exceptions to foreign sovereign immunity. See *Saudi Arabia v. Nelson*, 507 U.S. 349, 355, 113 S.Ct. 1471, 123 L.Ed.2d 47 (1993).

FN3. This Circuit has previously recognized that although the FSIA neither prohibits nor provides for its application to defendants who are natural persons, maintenance of a coherent practice regarding foreign sovereign immunity weighs heavily in favor of applying the FSIA to individuals. *First American Corp. v. Al Nahyan*, 948 F.Supp. 1107, 1120 (D.D.C.1996) citing *Herbage v. Meese*, 747 F.Supp. 60, 66 (D.D.C.1990). The FSIA has thus been construed to apply to individuals for acts performed in their official capacity on behalf of either a foreign state or its agency or instrumentality. *El-Fadl v. Central Bank of Jordan*, 75 F.3d 668, 671 (D.C.Cir.1996), citing *Chuidian v. Philippine Nat. Bank,* 912 F.2d 1095, 1099-1103 (9 Cir.1990); *In re Estate of Ferdinand E. Marcos Human Rights Litigation*, 978 F.2d 493, 496-97 (9th Cir.1992); *Kline v. Kaneko*, 685 F.Supp. 386 (S.D.N.Y.1988); *Rios v. Marshall*, 530 F.Supp. 351, 371-72 (S.D.N.Y.1981).

Until the beginning of this century, the United States afforded foreign states absolute immunity from suit in courts of the United States as a matter of common law. See, e.g.,

The Schooner Exchange v. M'Faddon, 11 U.S. (7 Cranch) 116, 3 L.Ed. 287 (1812); *Berizzi Bros. Co. v. S.S. Pesaro*, 271 U.S. 562, 46 S.Ct. 611, 70 L.Ed. 1088 (1926). With the rise of Communism and the consequent outgrowth of state trading and shipping companies, however, the United States began to recognize the restrictive theory of foreign sovereign immunity, which permitted suits arising from a foreign state's commercial activities. *See* S. SUCHARITKUL, STATE IMMUNITIES AND TRADING ACTIVITIES IN INTERNATIONAL LAW (1959); Friedmann, *Changing Social Arrangements in State-Trading States and their Effect on International Law*, 24 LAW & CONTEMP. PROBS. 350 (1959).

The issuance of the Tate Letter, on May 19, 1952, officially marked this transition for United States practice. *See* Letter from Jack B. Tate, Acting Legal Advisor, to Acting Attorney General (May 19, 1952), *reprinted at* 26 DEP'T OF STATE BULL. 984-985 *and reprinted at* Appendix 2 to *Alfred Dunhill of London v. Republic of Cuba*, 425 U.S. 682, 711, 96 S.Ct. 1854, 48 L.Ed.2d 301 (1976) [hereinafter "Tate Letter"]. The Tate Letter announced that the United States would henceforth follow the restrictive theory in making foreign sovereign immunity determinations. In 1976, in order to promote uniform and apolitical determinations, Congress transferred immunity determinations from the Department of State to the judiciary and otherwise essentially codified the Tate Letter's restrictive theory of foreign sovereign immunity in the FSIA. *See* H.R. REP. NO. 1487, 94th CONG., 2D SESS. at 12, *reprinted in* 1976 U.S.C.C.A.N. 6604, 6610-11; GARY B. BORN AND DAVID WESTIN, INTERNATIONAL CIVIL LITIGATION IN UNITED STATES COURTS at 452-453 (2d ed.1992); *see also* M. Sandler, D. Vagts & B. Ristau, eds., *Sovereign Immunity Decisions of the Department of State*, DIGEST OF UNITED STATES PRACTICE IN INTERNATIONAL LAW 1977 at 1017.

Courts steadfastly refused to extend the FSIA as originally enacted beyond commercial activities, *jure gestionis*, to reach public acts, *jure imperii*, outside the United States. This judicial restraint permitted foreign states to use the FSIA as a shield against civil liability for violations of the law of nations committed against United States nationals overseas. See, e.g., *Nelson*, 507 U.S. 349, 113 S.Ct. 1471, 123 L.Ed.2d 47; *Smith v. Socialist People's Libyan Arab Jamahiriya*, 101 F.3d 239 (2d Cir.1996), *cert. denied* 520 U.S. 1204, 117 S.Ct. 1569, 137 L.Ed.2d 714, *reh'g denied* 520 U.S. 1259, 117 S.Ct. 2427, 138 L.Ed.2d 189 (1997) [hereinafter *"Pan Am 103"*]; *Cicippio v. Islamic Republic of Iran*, 30 F.3d 164

(D.C.Cir.1994), *cert. denied* 513 U.S. 1078, 115 S.Ct. 726, 130 L.Ed.2d 631 (1995); *Princz v. Federal Republic of Germany*, 26 F.3d 1166 (D.C.Cir.1994), *cert. denied*, 513 U.S. 1121, 115 S.Ct. 923, 130 L.Ed.2d 803 (1995).

1. RECENT AMENDMENTS TO THE FOREIGN SOVEREIGN IMMUNITIES ACT CREATE SUBJECT MATTER JURISDICTION AND FEDERAL CAUSES OF ACTION FOR CERTAIN ACTS OF STATE SPONSORED TERRORISM.

In 1996 Congress took action which effectuated an even greater change than that represented by the Tate Letter. In the Antiterrorism and Effective Death Penalty Act of 1996, Congress lifted the immunity of foreign states for a certain category of sovereign acts which are repugnant to the United States and the international community-terrorism. Pub.L. 104-132, Title II, §221(a), (April 24, 1996), 110 Stat. 1241 *codified at* 28 U.S.C.A. §1605 (West 1997 Supp.) [hereinafter "state sponsored terrorism exception"]. That Act created an exception to the immunity of those foreign states officially designated by the Department of State as terrorist states [FN4] if the foreign state commits a terrorist act, or provides material support and resources to an individual or entity which commits such an act, which results in the death or personal injury of a United States citizen. *See* 28 U.S.C. §1605(a)(7) [FN5]; *see also* H.R.REP. NO. 383, 104TH CONG., 1ST SESS.1995 at 137-38, *available at* 1995 WL 731698.

FN4. In addition to the Islamic Republic of Iran, the foreign states currently designated as sponsors of terrorism pursuant to 50 U.S.C.App. §2405(j) are: Cuba, Syria, Iraq, Libya, Sudan and North Korea. *See* 22 C.F.R. §126.1(d) (current through October 31, 1997).
FN5. Pub.L. 105-11 (April 25, 1997), 111 Stat. 22, §1 amended 28 U.S . C. §1605(a)(7)(B)(ii) to substitute "neither the claimant nor the victim was" for "the claimant or victim was not"; *see also* H.R.Rep. No. 48, 105TH CONG ., 1ST SESS. (April 10, 1997), *available at* 1997 WL 177368.
Although the Antiterrorism Act created a forum competent to adjudicate claims arising from offenses of this nature, serious issues remained, in particular, the causes of action available to plaintiffs. Congressman Jim Saxton sponsored an amendment to 28 U.S.C. §1605(a)(7) with the intent to clarify this and other issues. In Congressman Saxton's experience as Chairman of the House Task Force on Counterterrorism and Unconventional Warfare and member of the House National Security Committee, in order for the exception for immunity to have the desired deterrent effect, the

potential civil liability for foreign states which commit and sponsor acts of terrorism would have to be substantial. *See* Congressman Jim Saxton, News Release: *Saxton to the Flatow Family: "Be Strong, America Is Behind You"* (February 26, 1997); *see also* NORMAN J. SINGER, 2 SUTHERLAND ON STATUTORY CONSTRUCTION t §48.16 (5th ed.1992, 1997 Supp.) citing *Brock v. Pierce County*, 476 U.S. 253, 106 S.Ct. 1834, 90 L.Ed.2d 248 (1986). Therefore, the amendment to 28 U.S.C. §1605(a)(7) expressly provided, *inter alia*, that punitive damages were available in actions brought under the state sponsored terrorism exception to immunity. *See* H.R. CONF. REP. 863, 104TH CONG, 2ND SESS. 1996 *reprinted at* 1996 U.S.C.C.A.N. 924; Senator Frank Lautenberg, News Release: *Flatow Family's Unprecedented Lawsuit Against Iran Will Help Deter Future Acts of Terrorism* (February 26, 1997). The amendment, *Civil Liability for Acts of State Sponsored Terrorism*, was enacted on September 30, 1996 as part of the 1997 Omnibus Consolidated Appropriations Act, Pub.L. 104-208, Div. A, Title I §101(c) [Title V, §589] (September 30, 1996), 110 Stat. 3009-172 *reprinted at* 28 U.S.C.A. §1605 note (West 1997 Supp.). This provision of law is commonly referred to as the "Flatow Amendment."

The Flatow Amendment is apparently an independent pronouncement of law, yet it has been published as a note to 28 U.S.C. §1605, and requires several references to 28 U.S.C. §1605(a)(7) *et seq.* to reach even a preliminary interpretation. As it also effects a substantial change to 28 U.S.C. §1605(a)(7), it appears to be an implied amendment. *See* 1A SUTHERLAND ON STATUTORY CONSTRUCTION at §22.13 ("An implied amendment is an act which purports to be independent, but which in substance alters, modifies, or adds to a prior act."); *see also id.* at §22.20-21. The brief explanation of the Flatow Amendment's purpose in the House Conference Report explicitly states that it was intended to increase the measure of damages available in suits under 28 U.S.C. §1605(a)(7). *See* H.R. CONF. REP. 863, 104TH CONG, 2ND SESS.1996, *reprinted at* 1996 U.S.C.C.A.N. 924. Both the Flatow Amendment and 28 U.S.C. §1605(a)(7) address the same subject matter, and were enacted during the same session of Congress, only five months apart. Interpretation *in pari materia* is therefore the most appropriate approach to the construction of both provisions, 1A SUTHERLAND ON STATUTORY CONSTRUCTION at §22.32. The amendment should be considered to relate back to the enactment of 28 U.S.C. §1605(a)(7) as if they had been enacted as one provision, *id.* at §§22.29-31, 34-36, and the two provisions should be construed together and in reference to one another. *Id.* at §22.29 n. 16 citing

United States v. Dickerson, 310 U.S. 554, 60 S.Ct. 1034, 84 L.Ed. 1356 (1940). Interpretation of 28 U.S.C. §1605(a)(7) and the Flatow Amendment *in pari materia* demonstrates the coherent legislative intent behind the two enactments.

2. 28 U.S.C. §1605(a)(7) AND 28 U.S.C.A. §1605 note APPLY RETROACTIVELY FOR THE PURPOSES OF ESTABLISHING SUBJECT MATTER AND PERSONAL JURISDICTION.

Although the events complained of herein occurred more than a year prior to the enactment of the Antiterrorism and Effective Death Penalty Act of 1996, 28 U.S.C. §1605(a)(7) provides a basis for subject matter jurisdiction. Congress has expressly directed the retroactive application of 28 U.S.C. §1605(a)(7) in order to further a comprehensive counterterrorism initiative by the legislative branch of government:

The amendments made by this subtitle shall apply to any cause of action arising before, on or after the date of the enactment of this Act [April 24, 1996].

§221(c) of Pub.L. 104-132. As the Supreme Court has stated with respect to the application of legislation to pre-enactment conduct, "[w]here congressional intent is clear, it governs." *Kaiser Aluminum & Chemical Corp. v. Bonjorno*, 494 U.S. 827, 837, 110 S.Ct. 1570, 108 L.Ed.2d 842 (1990). Although the application of statutes to pre-enactment conduct is traditionally disfavored, see *Bowen v. Georgetown University Hospital*, 488 U.S. 204, 109 S.Ct. 468, 102 L.Ed.2d 493 (1988), where "Congress has expressly prescribed the statute's proper reach[,] there is no need to resort to judicial default rules." *Landgraf v. USI Film Products*, 511 U.S. 244, 271, 114 S.Ct. 1483, 128 L.Ed.2d 229 (1994).

Furthermore, the state sponsored terrorism exception to foreign sovereign immunity is a remedial statute. It creates no new responsibilities or obligations; it only creates a forum for the enforcement of pre-existing universally recognized rights under federal common law and international law. See, e.g., *Alvarez-Machain v. United States*, 107 F.3d 696, 702 (9th Cir.1996), *cert. denied*, 522 U.S. 814, 118 S.Ct. 60, 139 L.Ed.2d 23 (1997) (discussing Torture Victim Protection Act). As with all other civil jurisdiction statutes, 28 U.S.C. §1605(a)(7) " 'speak[s] to the power of the courts rather than to the rights or obligations of the parties.' " *Landgraf*, 511 U.S. at 274 (discussing Civil Rights Act of 1991) (citation omitted). Almost all courts have upheld the retroactive application of long-arm statutes. *See* 2 SUTHERLAND ON STATUTORY CONSTRUCTION at §41.09 citing *McGee v. International Life Ins. Co.*, 355 U.S. 220, 78 S.Ct. 199, 2 L.Ed.2d 223 (1957).

At the time of the act complained of herein, the terrorist acts enumerated in 28 U.S.C. §1605(a)(7) were federal criminal offenses, *see* 18 U.S.C. §2331. Given mounting Congressional frustration at the refusal of the federal courts to find jurisdiction in cases such as *Princz, Pan Am 103, Cicippio*, and *Nelson*, and the progressive development of United States legislation and jurisprudence on the subject of *jus cogens* violations, see, e.g., *Hilao v. Estate of Marcos*, 103 F.3d 767; *Kadic v. Karadzic*, 70 F.3d 232; *Abebe-Jira v. Negewo*, 72 F.3d 844 (11th Cir.1996), *cert. denied*, 519 U.S. 830, 117 S.Ct. 96, 136 L.Ed.2d 51 (1996); *Cabiri v. Assasie-Gyimah*, 921 F.Supp. 1189 (S.D.N.Y.1996); *Filartiga v. Pena-Irala*, 630 F.2d 876 (2d Cir.1980); *Xuncax v. Gramajo*, 886 F.Supp. 162 (D.Mass.1995). See also *Princz*, 26 F.3d at 1176 (D.C.Cir.1994) (Wald, J., dissenting), the creation of an exception to foreign sovereign immunity which provides jurisdiction over foreign state perpetrators of the acts enumerated in 28 U.S.C. §1605(a)(7) should not have been unanticipated. "[A]ny expectation…[to the contrary]…is rightly disturbed." *Cabiri*, 921 F.Supp. at 1195-96 (S.D.N.Y.1996) (discussing Torture Victim Protection Act), citing *Landgraf*, 511 U.S. at 273-275.

The Islamic Republic of Iran in particular has been aware of United States policy condemning international terrorism at least since the 1979-1981 hostage crisis in Tehran. It has been continuously designated a state sponsor of terrorism since January 19, 1984. Its continued support of terrorist groups has prompted the United States to suspend diplomatic relations and participate in the international embargo, including extraordinary enforcement measures such as trade restrictions. *See* U.S. DEP'T OF STATE, PATTERNS OF GLOBAL TERRORISM at 23; Iran and Libya Sanctions Act of 1996, Pub.L. 104-72, 104TH CONG., 2D SESS. (August 5, 1996), 110 Stat. 1541. As international terrorism is subject to universal jurisdiction, Defendants had adequate notice that their actions were wrongful and susceptible to adjudication in the United States. Eric S. Kobrick, *The Ex Post Facto Prohibition and the Exercise of Universal Jurisdiction over International Crimes*, 87 COLUM. L. REVV. 1515, 1528-30 (1987) (concluding that criminal statutes apply retroactively to international terrorist acts).

Therefore, the state sponsored terrorism provision implicates no Constitutionally protected interest which would prohibit the application of 28 U.S.C. §1605(a)(7) to pre-enactment conduct.

3. FEDERAL COMMON LAW PROVIDES THE RULES OF DECISION IN CASE BROUGHT PURSUANT TO 28 U.S.C. §1605(a)(7) AND 28 U.S.C.A. §1605 note.

This action is brought pursuant to a new exception to the FSIA which was created as part of a federal initiative to combat international terrorism, the Antiterrorism and Effective Death Penalty Act of 1996. The state sponsored terrorism provisions represent a sea change in the United States' approach to foreign sovereign immunity. For the first time, Congress has expressly created an exception to immunity designed to influence the sovereign conduct of foreign states and affect the substantive law of liability for non-immune acts. *Cf.* H.R. Rep. 94 1487 at 12, *reprinted at* 1976 U.S.C.C.A.N. at 6610; *First National City Bank v. Banco para el Comercio Exterior de Cuba*, 462 U.S. 611, 619-20, 103 S.Ct. 2591, 77 L.Ed.2d 46 (1983).

Cases under the FSIA have considered choice of law issues almost exclusively within the commercial context, and have applied state rules of decision. See, e.g. *First National City Bank*, 462 U.S. at 620; *Joseph v. Office of the Consulate General of Nigeria*, 830 F.2d 1018, 1025 (9th Cir.1987); *Guzel v. State of Kuwait*, 818 F.Supp. 6, 10 (D.D.C.1993); *Skeen v. Federative Republic of Brazil*, 566 F.Supp. 1414, 1417 (D.D.C.1983); *see also* Joel Mendal Overton, II, *Will the Real FSIA Choice-of-Law Rule Please Stand Up?*, 49 WASH. & LEE L. REV. 1591 (1992). The notable exception is *Liu v. Republic of China*; however in that case, as the political assassination occurred in California, there was no true conflict for choice of law purposes. 892 F.2d 1419, 1425-26 (9th Cir.).

The federal choice of law rule follows that of the RESTATEMENT (SECOND) OF CONFLICTS, which provides that the law of the place of the tort is to apply. *See Liu*, 892 F.2d at 1425 *citing* RESTATEMENT (SECOND) OF CONFLICTS §175 (1969). The Gaza legal code derives from an amalgamation of British mandate law, Egyptian law and Palestinian Authority directives and laws. *See* 1 996 COUNTRY REPORTS ON HUMAN RIGHTS: ISRAEL AND THE OCCUPIED TERRITORIES at §1(e); *available at* http://www.state.gov./www/global/-human_rights/1996_hrp_report/occterr.html; in addition to the administrative difficulties associated with interpreting this unfamiliar foreign law, the United States has a much stronger interest than the Palestinian Authority in Gaza in adjudicating this action arising from a United States citizen's wrongful death. When another jurisdiction has a stronger interest and closer connections to the case, it is appropriate to apply that jurisdiction's law. RESTATEMENT (SECOND) OF CONFLICTS §175 (1969).

The Supreme Court has recognized that the FSIA "codifies the standards governing foreign sovereign immunity as an aspect of substantive federal law" and that its application will "generally require interpretation of numerous points of federal law." *Verlinden*, 461 U.S. at 497. Subsequently, Congress created jurisdiction and federal causes of action for personal injury or death resulting from state-sponsored terrorism, including its own statute of limitations. These actions indicate Congressional intent that the federal courts create coherent national standards to support this initiative of national significance. In the interest of promoting uniformity of determinations with respect to the liability of foreign states for the terrorist acts of its officials, agents, and employees, this Court will employ interstitial federal common law to determine whether the terrorist acts were within the scope of their office, agency, or employment, as well as any other conclusions of law which typically rely upon state law. [FN6] See *United States v. Belmont*, 301 U.S. 324, 57 S.Ct. 758, 81 L.Ed. 1134 (1937); In re *Air Crash Disaster Near Saigon, South Vietnam, on April 4, 1975*, 476 F.Supp. 521, 527 (D.D.C.1979); see also Sandra Engle, *Note, Choosing the Law for Attributing Liability Under the Foreign Sovereign Immunities Act; A Proposal for Uniformity*, 15 FORDHAM INT'L L.J. 1060 (1991/1992).

FN6. As the dedicated venue for actions against foreign states, *see* 28 U.S.C. §1391(f)(4), the law of District of Columbia provides an appropriate model in developing a federal standard for this determination. See also *Stanford v. Kuwait Airways Corp.*, 89 F.3d 117 (2d Cir.1996).

4. THE EXTRATERRITORIAL APPLICATION OF THE FSIA'S RECENT AMENDMENTS IS PROPER.

Article I of the Constitution establishes that Congress has "authority to enact laws applicable to conduct beyond the territorial boundaries of the United States." *Aramco*, 499 U.S. at 260-61 (1991). This Court's only duty is to determine "whether Congress chose to attach liability to the conduct outside the United States…[A]s a court of the United States, we cannot look beyond our own law." [FN7] *United States v. Alcoa*, 148 F.2d 416, 443 (2d Cir.1945). Congressional intent and legislative purpose demonstrate that 28 U.S.C. §1605(a)(7) not only applies to extraterritorial conduct, but that one of its express purposes is to affect the conduct of terrorist states outside the United States, in order to promote the safety of United States citizens traveling overseas.

See 142 C.R. S3454-1 (April 17, 1996) (remarks of Senator Hank Brown on consideration of the conference report); 142 C.R. H2129-05, H2132 (March 13, 1996) (remarks of Representative Ileana Ros-Lehtinen on the proposed Antiterrorism Act); *see* 2A SUTHERLAND ON STATUTORY CONSTRUCTION §45.05, §45.09.

FN7. Nevertheless, the extraterritorial application of the state sponsored terrorism exceptions is consistent with international law; three of the five bases for the exercise of extraterritorial jurisdiction are implicated in actions by United States victims of foreign state sponsored terrorism: passive personality (nationality of victim), protective (national security interests), and universal (subject to jurisdiction wherever the offender may be found). *See* RESTATEMENT (THIRD) FOREIGN RELATIONS LAW OF THE UNITED STATES (1986) at §402(2)-(3), §403, §423.

Indicia of Congressional intent are readily apparent. See, e.g., *EEOC v. Aramco*, 499 U.S. 244, 260, 111 S.Ct. 1227, 113 L.Ed.2d 274 (1991) (superseded by statute) (Marshall, J., dissenting) *citing Foley Brothers*, 336 U.S. at 285 (1949) (extraterritorial application may be discerned from the entire range of conventional sources). As 28 U.S.C. §1605(a)(5) already provides jurisdiction over state-sponsored terrorist acts in the United States, *see Liu*, 892 F.2d 1419; *Letelier v. Republic of Chile*, 488 F.Supp. 665 (D.D.C.1980), the state sponsored terrorism exception would be redundant if it were held to apply only within the United States. The provision's arbitration requirement indicates that Congress intended 28 U.S.C. §1605(a)(7) to create subject matter jurisdiction for claims arising from conduct which occurred within a foreign state. If Congress did not intend for 28 U.S.C. §1605(a)(7) to apply to extraterritorial conduct, the arbitration requirement, which only applies in cases arising from acts which occur within a defendant foreign state's territory, would be superfluous. *See* 28 U.S.C. §1605(a)(7)(B)(i). Therefore Congress inherently expressed its understanding that this provision would necessarily apply to extraterritorial conduct.

The general presumption against extraterritorial application exists to prevent inadvertent interference with foreign relations. See *NLRB v. Catholic Bishop of Chicago*, 440 U.S. 490, 500, 99 S.Ct. 1313, 59 L.Ed.2d 533 (1979); *McCulloch v. Sociedad Nacional de Marineros de Honduras*, 372 U.S. 10, 21-22, 83 S.Ct. 671, 9 L.Ed.2d 547 (1963); *Foley Brothers v. Filardo*, 336 U.S. 281, 69 S.Ct. 575, 93 L.Ed. 680 (1949). In actions pursuant to the state sponsored terrorism provisions, however, there is no danger of inadvertent interference with foreign relations; Congress specifically restricted its application to foreign state defendants which the State Department has determined are foreign state sponsors of terrorism. *See* 28 U .S.C. §1605(a)(7)(A). There is nothing inadvertent about these two new amendments. Indeed, Justice Blackmun has opined that the presumption against extraterritorial application is inherently inapposite to statutes which on their face involve foreign relations, as Congress necessarily considered "distinctively international subject matter." *Sale v. Haitian Centers Council*, 509 U.S. 155, 206-07, 113 S.Ct. 2549, 125 L.Ed.2d 128 (1993) (Blackmun, J., dissenting) (distinguishing *United States v. Curtiss-Wright Export Corp.*, 299 U.S. 304, 57 S.Ct. 216, 81 L.Ed. 255 (1936)).

This Court concludes that the application of the state sponsored terrorism provisions to extraterritorial conduct is proper.

B. SUBJECT MATTER JURISDICTION

In order to establish subject matter jurisdiction pursuant to 28 U.S.C. §1605(a)(7), a claim must contain the following statutory elements:

(1) that personal injury or death resulted from an act of torture, extrajudicial killing, aircraft sabotage, or hostage taking; and

(2) the act was either perpetrated by the foreign state directly or by a non-state actor which receives material support or resources from the foreign state defendant; and

(3) the act or the provision of material support or resources is engaged in by an agent, official or employee of the foreign state while acting within the scope of his or her office, agency or employment; and

(4) that the foreign state be designated as a state sponsor of terrorism either at the time the incident complained of occurred or was later so designated as a result of such act; and

(5) if the incident complained of occurred with the foreign state defendant's territory, plaintiff has offered the defendants a reasonable opportunity to arbitrate the matter; and

(6) either the plaintiff or the victim was a United States national at the time of the incident; and

(7) similar conduct by United States agents, officials, or employees within the United States would be actionable.

28 U.S.C. §1605(a)(7) and 28 U.S.C.A. §1605 note. While elements (4)-(6) are pure questions of fact, elements (1)-(3) and (7) are mixed questions of law and fact, and, in the absence of settled precedent, require interpretation.

1. A SUICIDE BOMBING IS AN ACT OF EXTRAJUDICIAL KILLING.

Plaintiff describes the cause of his daughter's death as an "extrajudicial killing" within the meaning of 28 U.S.C. §1605(a)(7). The state-sponsored terrorism exception to immunity expressly adopts the definition of extrajudicial killing set forth in the Torture Victim Protection Act of 1991. *See* 28 U.S.C. §1605(e)(1). That Act defines an "extrajudicial killing" as

a *deliberated killing* not authorized by a previous judgment pronounced by a regularly constituted court affording all judicial guarantees which are recognized as indispensable by civilized peoples. Such term, however, does not include any such killing that, under international law, is lawfully carried out under the authority of a foreign nation.

Pub.L. 102-256 at §3(a), 106 Stat. 73 (March 12, 1992), *reprinted at* 28 U.S.C.A. §1350 note. (emphasis added). Deliberate is defined as:

…Carried on coolly and steadily, especially according to a preconceived design; given to weighing facts and arguments with a view to a choice or decision; careful in considering the consequences of a step;…

BLACK'S LAW DICTIONARY 426-27 (6th ed.1990); *see also* H.REP. 102-367(I), 1992 U.S.C.C.A.N. 84. Other courts have found that summary executions, for example, would be considered "extrajudicial killings" within the meaning of 28 U.S.C.A. §1350 note. See *Lafontant v. Aristide*, 844 F.Supp. 128 (E.D.N.Y.1994) (dicta). In actions brought under the Alien Tort Statute, 28 U.S.C. §1350, and the Torture Victim Protection Act, courts have suggested, in the context of command responsibility, that a course of indiscriminate brutality, known to result in deaths, rises to the level of "extrajudicial killings." *See Hilao*, 103 F.3d at 776-77; *Kadic*, 70 F.3d at 242; *Paul v. Avril*, 901 F.Supp. 330, 335 (S.D.Fla.1994); *Xuncax v. Gramajo*, 886 F.Supp. 162, 170 (D.Mass.1995); *Forti v. Suarez-Mason*, 672 F.Supp. 1531, 1537-38 (N.D.Cal.1987). *See also In re Yamashita*, 327 U.S.

1, 14, 66 S.Ct. 340, 90 L.Ed. 499 (1946) ("…a deliberate plan and purpose to massacre and exterminate…unarmed noncombatant civilians…*without cause or trial*…and without military necessity.") (emphasis added).

The state sponsored terrorism exception to immunity was enacted as part of a comprehensive legislative initiative to squelch international terrorism-the Antiterrorism and Effective Death Penalty Act of 1996. *See* 2A SUTHERLAND ON STATUTORY CONSTRUCTION at §47.03. Previous treatments of international terrorism by Congress therefore appropriately inform the interpretation of "deliberated killing". *Id.* at §22.32. One statute *in pari materia* defines terrorism as

…mean[ing] premeditated, politically motivated violence perpetrated against noncombatant targets by subnational groups or clandestine agents.

22 U.S.C. §2656f(d)(2). As the state sponsored terrorism exception expressly incorporates a definition from the United States criminal code chapter on international terrorism, another definition from that chapter is also apropos:

(1) the term "international terrorism" means activities that-

A. involve violent acts or acts dangerous to human life that are a violation of the criminal laws of the United States or of any State, or that would be a criminal violation if committed within the jurisdiction of the United States or of any State;

B. appear to be intended-

i) to intimidate or coerce a civilian population;

ii) to influence the policy of a government by intimidation or coercion;

iii) to affect the conduct of a government by assassination or kidnapping; and

(C) occur primarily outside the territorial jurisdiction of the United States, or transcend national boundaries in terms of the means by which they are accomplished, the persons they appear intended to intimidate or coerce, or the locale in which their perpetrators operate or seek asylum;…

18 U.S.C. §2331. Attempts to reach a fixed, universally accepted definition of international terrorism have been frustrated both by changes in terrorist methodology and the lack

of any precise definition of the term "terrorism." *See, e.g.,* U.S. DEP'T OF STATE, PATTERNS OF GLOBAL TERRORISM at vi, 1, 17; Louis Rene Beres, *The Meaning of Terrorism-Jurisprudential and Definitional Clarifications,* 28 VAND. J. TRANSNAT'L L. 239 (1995). Therefore, the United States characterizes rather than enumerates acts for the purposes of designating foreign state sponsors of terrorism and defining criminal terrorist offenses under federal law. Each of the acts listed in 28 U.S.C. §1605(a)(7) fully conform with the foregoing definitions and provisions.

This Court concludes that a suicide bombing conforms with each of the foregoing provisions and definitions, and therefore is an act of "extrajudicial killing" within the meaning of 28 U.S.C. §1605(a)(7).

2. THE ROUTINE PROVISION OF FINANCIAL ASSISTANCE TO A TERRORIST GROUP IN SUPPORT OF ITS TERRORIST ACTIVITIES CONSTITUTES THE PROVISION OF MATERIAL SUPPORT OR RESOURCES WITHIN THE MEANING OF 28 U.S.C. §1605(a)(7).

The state-sponsored terrorism provision adopts the definition of "provid[ing] material support or resources" set forth in the federal criminal code. 28 U.S.C. §1605(a)(7) incorporates 18 U.S.C. §2339A(a) by reference, which provides that:

…"material support or resources" means currency or other financial securities, financial services, lodging, training, safehouses, false documentation or identification, communications equipment, facilities, weapons, lethal substances, explosives, personnel, transportation, and other physical assets, but does not include humanitarian assistance to persons not directly involved in such violations.

This Court concludes that the routine provision of financial assistance to a terrorist group in support of its terrorist activities constitutes "providing material support or resources" for a terrorist act within the meaning of 28 U.S.C. §1605(a)(7). Furthermore, as nothing in 18 U.S.C. §2339A or 28 U.S.C. §1605(a)(7) indicates otherwise, this Court also concludes that a plaintiff need not establish that the material support or resources provided by a foreign state for a terrorist act contributed directly to the act from which his claim arises in order to satisfy 28 U.S.C. §1605(a)(7)'s statutory requirements for subject matter jurisdiction. Sponsorship of a terrorist group which causes the personal injury or death of a United States national alone is sufficient to invoke jurisdiction.

3. THE PROVISION OF MATERIAL SUPPORT AND RESOURCES TO A TERRORIST GROUP IS AN ACT WITHIN THE SCOPE OF A FOREIGN STATE'S AGENT'S AND HIGH OFFICIALS' AGENCY AND OFFICES.

The law of *respondeat superior* demonstrates that if a foreign state's agent, official or employee provides material support and resources to a terrorist organization, such provision will be considered an act within the scope of his or her agency, office or employment. See, e.g., *Guzel*, 818 F.Supp. at 10; *Skeen*, 566 F.Supp. at 1417.

In the District of Columbia, whether an employer is liable for the torts of its employee depends on whether the tort was at least in part "actuated" by an intent to advance the employer's business, and the tort must be foreseeable given the employee's duties. *Weinberg v. Johnson*, 518 A.2d 985, 990 (D.C.1986); *Guzel*, 818 F.Supp. at 10. The acts of an employee under these circumstances, whether lawful or not, and whether expressly prohibited by the employer or not, can be imputed to the employer.

In order for an agent, official, or employee's unlawful conduct to be imputed to a government, however, the government must share a degree of responsibility for the wrongful conduct. The government must have engaged in the wrongful conduct, either deliberately or permissively, as a matter of policy or custom. See, e.g., *Monell v. N.Y. Dep't of Social Services*, 436 U.S. 658, 694-95, 98 S.Ct. 2018, 56 L.Ed.2d 611 (1978) (discussing municipal liability under 42 U.S.C. §1983). This Court concludes that if a foreign state's heads of state, intelligence service, and minister of intelligence routinely provide material support or resources to a terrorist group, whose activities are consistent with the foreign state's customs or policies, then that agent and those officials have acted squarely within the scope of their agency and offices within the meaning of 28 U.S.C. §1605(a)(7) and 28 U.S.C.A. §1605 note.

4. UNITED STATES OFFICIALS WOULD BE LIABLE FOR PROVIDING MATERIAL SUPPORT OR RESOURCES TO A TERRORIST GROUP WITHIN THE UNITED STATES.

The Flatow Amendment, 28 U.S.C.A. §1605 note, clarifies that the liability of foreign states and their officials must be comparable to that of the United States and its agents, officials, and employees officials. This Court concludes that if officials of the United States, while acting in their official capacities, provide material support and resources to a ter-

rorist group which executed a suicide bombing within the United States, those officials would not be immune from civil suits for wrongful death and personal injury. *See* U.S. CONST. AMEND. 5; 42 U.S.C. §1983.

* * *

CONCLUSION

This Court possess subject matter jurisdiction over this action and personal jurisdiction over Defendants. Plaintiff has established to this Court's satisfaction, pursuant to 28 U.S.C. §1608(e), and by clear and convincing evidence, that Defendants, the Islamic Republic of Iran, the Iranian Ministry of Information and Security, Ayatollah Ali Hoseini Khamenei, former President Ali Akbar Hashemi-Rafsanjani, and former Minister Ali Fallahian-Khuzestani, are jointly and severally liable for all damages awarded by this Court to Plaintiff Stephen M. Flatow, in his own right, as Administrator of the Estate of Alisa Michelle Flatow, and on behalf of decedent's heirs-at-law, for their provision of material support and resources to a terrorist group which caused the extrajudicial killing of Alisa Michelle Flatow.

Notes:

1.   What is "federal common law" and why did the Flatow court resort to employing it?

2.   Did Congress usurp at least a measure of the Executive's foreign policy prerogative in enacting legislation (28 U.S.C. §1605(a) (7) and §1605 note) "designed to influence the sovereign conduct of foreign states?" Or the Judiciary's role when it was told "to support this initiative of national significance"?

3.   How are traditional notions of jurisdiction impacted by enactment of a statute specifically designed to provide a forum for American victims against foreign states that may have no ties to the U.S. and concerning attacks that typically occur outside of the defendant foreign state's borders?

4.   In a recent proceeding, Syria argued to the Court of Appeal for the District of Columbia Circuit that provisions of the United Nations Charter conflict with the Foreign Sovereign Immunities Act and therefore foreign states that have been designated "state sponsors of terrorism" are not amenable to suit in the US:

The principles of the United Nations are set forth in Chapter I, Article 2, which provides "The Organization and its Members, in pursuit of the Purposes stated in Article 1, shall act in accordance with the following Principles." The first principle is mandated in paragraph

"1: The Organization is based on the principle of the sovereign equality of all its Members."

The second paragraph of Article 2 requires "2: All Members, in order to ensure to all of them the rights and benefits resulting from membership, shall fulfill in good faith the obligations assumed by them in accordance with the present Charter".

Paragraphs 3 and 4 of Chapter I, Article 2 of the U.N. Charter impose further duties on its Members:

"3: All Members shall settle their international disputes by peaceful means in such a manner that international peace and security, and justice, are not endangered."

"4: All Members shall refrain in their international relations from the threat or use of force against the territorial integrity or political independence of any state, or in any other manner inconsistent with the Purposes of the United Nations."

The United States and Syria have both ratified the Charter and been accepted as Members of the United Nations. Both the U.S. and Syria are bound by the Charter of the United Nations, the most universally accepted and important treaty among nations, which embodies humanity's best chance for peace. Both the United States and Syria have committed themselves to faithfully observe the principle of the sovereign equality of all its Members on which the United Nations is based.

The unilateral, arbitrary act of the United States seeking to strip Syria of its equal sovereignty by denying it immunity from claims brought against it in Courts of the United States, by arbitrary, unilateral, and secret executive action of the U.S. Secretary of State based on unknown charges and evidence violates the duties of the United states under the United Nations Charter, a treaty that is a part the "supreme Law of the Land", Article VI, second paragraph, Constitution of the United States.

...

§1604 of the FSIA makes the provisions of the FSIA "Subject to existing international agreements to which the United States is a party at the time of the enactment of this Act..." which would include the United Nations Charter. This appears to affirmatively make the provisions of the Charter controlling. At the very least it demonstrates that Congress was aware that international agreements were applicable and it did not seek to revoke any international agreements in part, or whole.

Further, in the proceedings leading to the enactment of Section 1605(a)(7) Congress did not reveal any consideration of U.S. obligations under the Charter of the United Nations, or its first principle set forth in Chapter I, Article 2, paragraph 1. Nor did Congress express a purpose to alter the obligation of the United States to abide by the provisions of the Charter. The FSIA cannot therefore be construed to revoke the treaty agreement by the United States in the Charter of the United Nations to respect the sovereign equality of all U.N. Members.

Nothing in the words of the FSIA, its Section 1605(a) (7), or the legislative history of their enactment implies that Congress intended to violate the first principle of the Charter of the United Nations: "...the sovereign equality of all its Members." It is unlikely that the Congress of the United States would ever do so.

Wyatt v. Syrian Arab Republic, 2007 WL 552111 (Appellate Brief) (D.C.Cir. Feb 16, 2007). What is the fallacy in this argument and why was it easily rejected by the appellate court?

5.   In §1605(a)(7) actions where default enters against a non-appearing foreign state sponsor of terrorism, subject matter jurisdiction and the merits of the case are melded into one analysis:

To date, the vast majority of cases decided under this section are default judgments, which put all of the issues, including subject-matter jurisdiction and liability, squarely before the court at the same time. Given this circumstance, courts will generally conflate subject-matter jurisdiction and liability, as the plaintiff must make some showing of liability for the court to assert subject-matter jurisdiction under section 1605 (a)(7). See, e.g., *Peterson v. Islamic Republic of Iran*, 264 F.Supp.2d 46 (D.D.C.2003)

(Lamberth, J.). This case, however, is distinguishable from the default cases because defendants Libya and LESO have appeared and made a motion to dismiss for lack of subject-matter jurisdiction. Therefore, the issue of liability is not before the court at this time. Nonetheless, the plaintiff must advance evidence to support his allegations through jurisdictional discovery. Once the plaintiff meets this burden, the defendant must be given a chance to contest this evidence and challenge the plaintiff's allegations before the court can rule on the issue of liability. A defendant's challenge to the plaintiff's evidence, therefore, is proper at the trial, not on a motion to dismiss. If the court decided otherwise, it would be forcing a mini-trial of the case's substantive issues on a motion to dismiss.

Kilburn v. Republic of Iran, 277 F.Supp.2d 24, 28 fn.2 (D.D.C. 2003). What are the ramifications of combining the determination of subject matter with liability in a contested case?

6. In *Smith v. Islamic Emirate of Afghanistan*, 262 F.Supp.2d 217 (S.D.N.Y. 2003), victims of the 9/11 attacks sued various foreign entities including states, individuals and terrorist organizations. Were the attacks on the World Trade Center acts of "international terrorism?" Judge Baer analyzed the issue as follows:

> As an initial matter, it is not self-evident that the events of September 11 fall within the statute's definition of "international terrorism." Specifically, the statute defines "international terrorism" in con-

tradistinction to "domestic terrorism." The main difference is that domestic terrorism involves acts that "occur primarily within the territorial jurisdiction of the United States," while international terrorism involves acts that "occur primarily outside the territorial jurisdiction of the United States, or transcend[s] national boundaries in terms of the means by which they are accomplished, the persons they appear intended to intimidate or coerce, or the locale in which their perpetrators operate or seek asylum." The acts of September 11 clearly "occurred primarily" in the United States-indeed, they occurred entirely in the United States: airplanes owned and operated by U.S. carriers took off from U.S. airports and were in route to U.S. destinations when they were hijacked and crashed into U.S. landmarks. However, acts of international terrorism also encompass acts that "transcend national boundaries in terms of the means by which they are accomplished...or the locale in which their perpetrators operate." Arguably, this broad provision includes the case at bar, which was carried out by foreign nationals who apparently received their orders and funding and some training from foreign sources. Although mindful that an expansive interpretation of "international terrorism" might render "domestic terrorism" superfluous, I conclude that these facts fall within the statute's definition of "international terrorism" and thus plaintiffs have pled a valid cause of action against the al Qaeda defendants.

Id. at 221.

Chapter 5

Defenses

5.1 Justiciability

Baker v. Carr, **369 U.S. 186, 82 S.Ct. 691, 7 L.Ed.2d 663 (1962).**

We have said that 'In determining whether a question falls within (the political question) category, the appropriateness under our system of government of attributing finality to the action of the political departments and also the lack of satisfactory criteria for a judicial determination are dominant considerations.' *Coleman v. Miller*, 307 U.S. 433, 454-455, 59 S.Ct. 972, 982, 83 L.Ed. 1385. The nonjusticiability of a political question is primarily a function of the separation of powers. Much confusion results from the capacity of the 'political question' label to obscure the need for case-by-case inquiry. Deciding whether a matter has in any measure been committed by the Constitution to another branch of government, or whether the action of that branch exceeds whatever authority has been committed, is itself a delicate exercise in constitutional interpretation, and is a responsibility of this Court as ultimate interpreter of the Constitution. To demonstrate this requires no less than to analyze representative cases and to infer from them the analytical threads that make up the political question doctrine. We shall then show that none of those threads catches this case.

Foreign relations: There are sweeping statements to the effect that all questions touching foreign relations are political questions. [FN31] Not only does resolution of such issues frequently turn on standards that defy judicial application, or involve the exercise of a discretion demonstrably committed to the executive or legislature;[FN32] but many such questions uniquely demand single-voiced statement of the Government's views. [FN33] Yet it is error to suppose that every case or controversy which touches foreign relations lies beyond judicial cognizance. Our cases in this field seem invariably to show a discriminating analysis of the particular question posed, in terms of the history of its management by the political branches, of its susceptibility to judicial handling in the light of its nature and posture in the specific case, and of the possible consequences of judi-cial action. For example, though a court will not ordinarily inquire whether a treaty has been terminated, since on that question 'governmental action * * * must be regarded as of controlling importance,' if there has been no conclusive 'governmental action' then a court can construe a treaty and may find it provides the answer. Compare *Terlinden v. Ames*, 184 U.S. 270, 285, 22 S.Ct. 484, 490, 46 L.Ed. 534, with *Society for the Propagation of the Gospel in Foreign Parts v. New Haven*, 8 Wheat. 464, 492-495, 5 L.Ed. 662. [FN34] Though a court will not undertake to construe a treaty in a manner inconsistent with a subsequent federal statute, no similar hesitancy obtains if the asserted clash is with state law. Compare *Whitney v. Robertson*, 124 U.S. 190, 8 S.Ct. 456, 31 L.Ed. 386, with *Kolovrat v. Oregon*, 366 U.S. 187, 81 S.Ct. 922, 6 L.Ed.2d 218.

FN31. E.g., 'The conduct of the foreign relations of our government is committed by the Constitution to the executive and legislative-'the political'-departments of the government, and the propriety of what may be done in the exercise of this political power is not subject to judicial inquiry or decision.' *Oetjen v. Central Leather Co.*, 246 U.S. 297, 302, 38 S.Ct. 309, 311, 62 L.Ed. 726.

FN32. See *Doe ex dem. Clark v. Braden*, 16 How. 635, 657, 14 L.Ed. 1090; *Taylor v. Morton*, 23 Fed.Cas. page 733, No. 13,799 (C.C.D.Mass.) (Mr. Justice Curtis), affirmed, 2 Black 481, 17 L.Ed. 277.

FN33. See *Doe v. Braden*, 16 How. 635, 657, 14 L.Ed. 1090.

FN34. And see *Clark v. Allen*, 331 U.S. 503, 67 S.Ct. 1431, 91 L.Ed. 1633.

While recognition of foreign governments so strongly defies judicial treatment that without executive recognition a foreign state has been called 'a republic of whose existence we know nothing,'[FN35] and the judiciary ordinarily follows the executive as to which nation has sovereignty over disputed territory, [FN36] once sovereignty over an area is politically determined and declared, courts may examine the resulting status and decide independently whether a statute

applies to that area. [FN37] Similarly, recognition of bel-
ligerency abroad is an executive responsibility, but if the
executive proclamations fall short of an explicit answer, a
court may construe them seeking, for example, to determine
whether the situation is such that statutes designed to assure American neutrality have become operative. The Three
Friends, 166 U.S. 1, 63, 66, 17 S.Ct. 495, 502, 503, 41 L.Ed.
497. Still again, though it is the executive that determines a
person's status as representative of a foreign government,
Ex parte Hitz, 111 U.S. 766, 4 S.Ct. 698, 28 L.Ed. 592, the
executive's statements will be construed where necessary to
determine the court's jurisdiction, In re Baiz, 135 U.S. 403,
10 S.Ct. 854, 34 L.Ed. 222. Similar judicial action in the
absence of a recognizedly authoritative executive declaration occurs in cases involving the immunity from seizure of
vessels owned by friendly foreign governments. Compare
Ex parte Republic of Peru, 318 U.S. 578, 63 S.Ct. 793, 87
L.Ed. 1014, with *Mexico v. Hoffman*, 324 U.S. 30, 34-35, 65
S.Ct. 530, 532, 89 L.Ed. 729.

FN35. *United States v. Klintock*, 5 Wheat. 144, 149, 5 L.Ed.
55; see also *United States v. Palmer*, 3 Wheat. 610, 634-635,
4 L.Ed. 471.
FN36. *Foster & Elam v. Neilson*, 2 Pet. 253, 307, 7 L.Ed.
415, and see *Williams v. Suffolk Insurance Co.*, 13 Pet. 415,
420, 10 L.Ed. 226.
FN37. *Vermilya-Brown Co. v. Connell*, 335 U.S. 377, 380,
69 S.Ct. 140, 142, 93 L.Ed. 76; *De Lima v. Bidwell*, 182 U.S.
1, 180-200, 21 S.Ct. 743, 746-754, 45 L.Ed. 1041.

It is apparent that several formulations which vary
slightly according to the settings in which the questions
arise may describe a political question, although each has
one or more elements which identify it as essentially a function of the separation of powers. Prominent on the surface of
any case held to involve a political question is found a textually demonstrable constitutional commitment of the issue
to a coordinate political department; or a lack of judicially
discoverable and manageable standards for resolving it; or
the impossibility of deciding without an initial policy determination of a kind clearly for nonjudicial discretion; or the
impossibility of a court's undertaking independent resolution without expressing lack of the respect due coordinate
branches of government; or an unusual need for unquestioning adherence to a political decision already made; or the
potentiality of embarrassment from multifarious pronouncements by various departments on one question.

Unless one of these formulations is inextricable from the
case at bar, there should be no dismissal for non-justiciability
on the ground of a political question's presence. The doctrine

of which we treat is one of 'political questions,' not one of
'political cases.' The courts cannot reject as 'no law suit' a
bona fide controversy as to whether some action denominat-
ed 'political' exceeds constitutional authority. The cases we
have reviewed show the necessity for discriminating inquiry
into the precise facts and posture of the particular case, and
the impossibility of resolution by any semantic cataloguing.

Notes:

1.   By creating a statute providing for recovery against
terrorist states, has not Congress removed the difficulty of
determining whether an action against one of those states
implicates the political question doctrine? Has Congress
determined that actions within the ambit of the statute are
properly adjudicated by the judicial branch?

***Klinghoffer v. S.N.C. Achille Lauro*, 937 F.2d 44 (2d Cir.
1991).**

Before OAKES, Chief Judge, TIMBERS and KEARSE,
Circuit Judges.

OAKES, Chief Judge:

The Palestine Liberation Organization (the "PLO") appeals from a judgment of the United States District Court for
the Southern District of New York, Louis L. Stanton, *Judge*,
reported at 739 F.Supp. 854, denying its motion to dismiss
various complaints brought against it in connection with the
October 1985 seizure of the Italian passenger liner Achille
Lauro and the killing of passenger Leon Klinghoffer. The
district court rejected the PLO's claims that it is immune
from suit in United States courts, that the complaints against
it raise non-justiciable political questions, that service of process on its Permanent Observer to the United Nations (the
"UN") was insufficient under Rule 4 of the Federal Rules
of Civil Procedure, and that personal jurisdiction could not
be asserted over it in the state of New York. For the reasons
set forth below, we agree with the district court that the PLO
is not immune from suit and that this case does not present
a non-justiciable political question. However, because we
conclude that the remaining questions cannot be resolved on
the record before us, we vacate the judgment of the district
court and remand the case for further findings.

BACKGROUND

1. The PLO and its Activities in New York

The PLO, which is headquartered in Tunis, Tunisia, describes itself as

the internationally recognized representative of a sovereign people who are seeking to exercise their rights to self-determination, national independence, and territorial integrity. The PLO is the internationally recognized embodiment of the nationhood and sovereignty of the Palestinian people while they await the restoration of their rights through the establishment of a coomprehensive [sic], just and lasting peace in the Middle East.

739 F.Supp. at 857 (quoting affidavit of Ramsey Clark). On November 15, 1988, the Palestine National Council issued a Declaration of Statehood, proclaiming the existence of the State of Palestine and vesting the powers of the provisional government in the executive committee of the PLO. The United States does not give diplomatic recognition to Palestine, although several other nations do.

Since 1974, the PLO, through its representative Zuhdi Labib Terzi, has participated at the UN as a permanent observer. To support its activities at the UN, the PLO purchased a building in Manhattan, which it uses as its UN Mission (the "Mission"). Mr. Terzi and his family reside at the Mission, and eight other employees work there as well. From time to time, other high-ranking officers of the PLO, including its Chairman, Yassar Arafat, use the Mission. In addition to owning a building, the PLO owns an automobile and maintains a bank account in New York, and has a telephone listing in the NYNEX white pages. From time to time, the PLO has engaged in various fundraising and propaganda efforts in New York and elsewhere.

In 1987, Congress enacted the Anti-Terrorism Act (the "ATA"), 22 U.S.C. §§5201-5203 (1988), which makes it unlawful "to receive anything of value except informational material from the PLO" or "to expend funds from the PLO" if the purpose is to further the PLO's interests. Id. §5202(1)-(2). The ATA also forbids the establishment or maintenance of "an office, headquarters, premises, or other facilities or establishments within the jurisdiction of the United States at the behest or direction of, or with funds provided by the Palestine Liberation Organization or any of its constituent groups, any successor to any of those, or any agents thereof." Id. §5202(3). The ATA does not apply, however, to the PLO's Mission in New York. See *United States v. Palestine Liberation Organization*, 695 F.Supp. 1456, 1464-71 (S.D.N.Y.1988).

2. The Achille Lauro Hijacking

On October 7, 1985, four persons seized the Italian cruise liner Achille Lauro in the Eastern Mediterranean Sea. During the course of the incident, the hijackers murdered an elderly Jewish-American passenger, Leon Klinghoffer, by throwing him and the wheelchair in which he was confined overboard. Shortly after the incident, the hijackers surrendered in Egypt. They were then extradited to Italy, where they were charged and convicted of crimes related to the seizure.

At this point, it remains unclear what role, if any, the PLO played in the events described above. According to some reports, the seizure was undertaken at the behest of Abdul Abbas, who is reportedly a member of the PLO. The PLO, however, denies any responsibility for the hijacking, and maintains that its involvement in the affair was limited to helping to secure the surrender of the hijackers and to ensure the safety of the ship and its passengers.

On November 27, 1985, Marilyn Klinghoffer [FN1] and the estate of Leon Klinghoffer filed suit in the Southern District of New York against the owner of the Achille Lauro, the charterer of the vessel, two travel agencies, and various other defendants. Other passengers who were aboard the Achille Lauro during the hijacking also commenced actions in the Southern District against the ship's owner and charterer, as well as against the travel agencies. The defendants in these actions then impleaded the PLO, seeking indemnification or contribution, as well as compensatory and punitive damages for tortious interference with their businesses. On October 7, 1988, two other passengers on the Achille Lauro brought separate actions in the Southern District against the PLO directly.

FN1. After Marilyn Klinghoffer's death, Ilsa Klinghoffer and Lisa Klinghoffer Arbitter, as co-executors of both Marilyn and Leon's estates, were substituted for Marilyn Klinghoffer as plaintiffs.

On April 27, 1987, the PLO moved to dismiss the third party complaints against it. This motion was later extended to encompass the two direct suits as well. In an opinion and order dated June 7, 1990, the court denied the PLO's motion. The PLO then moved for reargument, as well as for certification of the case for interlocutory appeal. The court denied the PLO's motion for reargument, but granted the motion for certification. Thereafter, in an opinion dated December 7, 1990, we granted the PLO's petition for permission to appeal, *see* 921 F.2d 21, and this appeal followed.

DISCUSSION

1. Immunity from Suit

The PLO first argues that it is a sovereign state and therefore immune from suit under the Foreign Sovereign Immunities

Act (the "FSIA"), 28 U.S.C. §1602 *et seq.* (1988). As support for this argument, it relies on its "political and governmental character and structure, its commitment to and practice of its own statehood, and its unlisted and indeterminable membership." Brief for Appellant at 7. However, this Court has limited the definition of "state" to " 'entit[ies] that ha[ve] a defined territory and a permanent population, [that are] under the control of [their] own government, and that engage[ ] in, or ha[ve] the capacity to engage in, formal relations with other such entities.' " *National Petrochemical Co. v. M/T Stolt Sheaf*, 860 F.2d 551, 553 (2d Cir.1988) (quoting *Restatement (Third) of the Foreign Relations Law of the United States* §201 (1987)), *cert. denied*, 489 U.S. 1081, 109 S.Ct. 1535, 103 L.Ed.2d 840 (1989). It is quite clear that the PLO meets none of those requirements.

First, the PLO has no defined territory. To be sure, the PLO's November 15, 1988 Declaration of Statehood "contemplates" that the state's territory will consist of the West Bank, the Gaza Strip, and East Jerusalem. The fact that the PLO hopes to have a defined territory at some future date, however, does not establish that it has a defined territory now. Indeed, the Declaration's assertion that "[t]he State of Palestine is the state of Palestinians wherever they may be" underscores the PLO's current lack of a territorial structure. In addition, because the PLO does not have a defined territory, it cannot have a permanent population.

The PLO is also unable to demonstrate that the State of Palestine is under the control of its own government. After all, without a defined territory, what, we ask, could the PLO possibly control? Moreover, even accepting the PLO's contention that the State of Palestine incorporates the West Bank, the Gaza Strip, and East Jerusalem, these areas are all under the control of the State of Israel, not the PLO.

Finally, despite the fact that some countries have "recognized" the PLO, the PLO does not have the capacity to enter into genuine formal relations with other nations. This is true primarily because, without a defined territory under unified governmental control, the PLO lacks the ability actually to implement the obligations that normally accompany formal participation in the international community. *See* Note, *The International Legal Implications of the November 1988 Palestinian Declaration of Statehood*, 25 Stan.J.Int'l L. 681, 696 (1989).

Contrary to the PLO's assertions, *Tel-Oren v. Libyan Arab Republic*, 726 F.2d 774 (D.C.Cir.1984), *cert. denied*, 470 U.S. 1003, 105 S.Ct. 1354, 84 L.Ed.2d 377 (1985), does not

establish that the PLO is a sovereign nation entitled to immunity under the FSIA. In *Tel-Oren*, the D.C. Circuit affirmed the dismissal on jurisdictional grounds of a suit brought by Israeli citizens against persons allegedly responsible for an armed attack on a civilian bus in Israel. [FN2] Although each of the three judges in *Tel-Oren* agreed that the suit should be dismissed, they did so in three separate opinions, each with its own distinct reasoning. The PLO suggests that at least two of these opinions support the theory that the PLO is a state entitled to sovereign immunity. Nothing could be further from the truth. Judge Edwards, in his opinion, wrote that "the PLO is not a recognized member of the community of nations," *id.* at 791, Judge Bork noted that the PLO "apparent [ly] lack[ed]…international law status as a state," *id.* at 805, and Judge Robb concluded simply that the PLO "ought to remain an organization 'of whose existence we know nothing…,' " *id.* at 824 (quoting *United States v. Klintock*, 18 U.S. (5 Wheat.) 144, 149, 5 L.Ed. 55 (1820)). How the PLO reads these statements to support its claim to statehood we do not see.

FN2. Because the incident in *Tel-Oren* did not occur on the high seas, as did the hijacking here, admiralty was not an available basis of jurisdiction. Thus, the court had to decide whether the incident presented a federal question, or, in the alternative, whether jurisdiction could be asserted under 28 U.S.C. §1350, which provides for jurisdiction over civil actions "by an alien for a tort only, committed in violation of the law of nations or a treaty of the United States."

The PLO also maintains that it is immune from suit as a result of its status as a permanent observer at the UN. It relies for this argument on the Agreement Between the United Nations and the United States of America Regarding the Headquarters of the United Nations (the "Headquarters Agreement"), *reprinted at* 22 U.S.C.A. §287 Note. By its terms, however, the Headquarters Agreement extends immunity only to representatives of members of the UN, not to observers such as the PLO. See *id.* §15. We see no reason to extend the immunities provided by the Headquarters Agreement beyond those explicitly stated.

Finally, the PLO claims that, because the United States has not extended it formal diplomatic recognition, it lacks the capacity to be sued in United States courts. This claim is without merit. While unrecognized regimes are generally precluded from appearing as plaintiffs in an official capacity without the Executive Branch's consent, see *Banco Nacional v. Sabbatino*, 376 U.S. 398, 410-11, 84 S.Ct. 923, 931, 11 L.Ed.2d 804 (1964); *National Petrochemical Co.*, 860 F.2d at 554-55, there is no bar to suit where an unrecognized regime is brought into court as a defendant. Cf. *United States v. Lumumba*, 741 F.2d 12, 15 (2d Cir.1984) (contempt proceeding against attorney claiming to be representative of the "Republic of New Afrika," an unrecognized nation), *cert. denied*, 479 U.S. 855, 107 S.Ct. 192, 93 L.Ed.2d 125 (1986). Accordingly, the fact that the United States has not recognized the PLO does not provide a basis for immunity.

2. Political Question

The PLO next argues that this case constitutes a non-justiciable political question because it "raises foreign policy questions and political questions in a volatile context lacking satisfactory criteria for judicial determination." Brief for Appellant at 27. This claim, it appears, rests on the concededly correct observation that the PLO is a political organization that engenders strong feelings of both support and opposition, and that any decision the district court enters will surely exacerbate the controversy surrounding the PLO's activities. However, the doctrine "is one of 'political questions,' not one of 'political cases.' " *Baker v. Carr*, 369 U.S. 186, 217, 82 S.Ct. 691, 710, 7 L.Ed.2d 663 (1962). The fact that the issues before us arise in a politically charged context does not convert what is essentially an ordinary tort suit into a non-justiciable political question.

In *Baker*, the Court wrote that:

[p]rominent on the surface of any case held to involve a political question is found [1] a textually demonstrable constitutional commitment of the issue to a coordinate political department; or [2] a lack of judicially discoverable and manageable standards for resolving it; or [3] the impossibility of deciding without an initial policy determination of a kind clearly for nonjudicial discretion; or [4] the impossibility of a court's undertaking independent resolution without expressing lack of the respect due coordinate branches of government; or [5] an unusual need for unquestioning adherence to a political decision already made; or [6] the potentiality of embarrassment from multifarious pronouncements by various departments on one question.

Id. Although no one factor is dispositive, Justice Brennan, the author of *Baker*, has suggested that the first question-whether there is a "textually demonstrable constitutional commitment of the issue to a coordinate political department"-is of particular importance. See *Goldwater v. Carter*, 444 U.S. 996, 1006, 100 S.Ct. 533, 538, 62 L.Ed.2d 428 (1979) (Brennan, J., dissenting) ("Properly understood, the political-question doctrine restrains courts from reviewing an exercise of foreign policy judgment by the coordinate political branch to which authority to make that judgment has been 'constitutional[ly] commit[ted].' "). Here, we are faced with an ordinary tort suit, alleging that the defendants breached a duty of care owed to the plaintiffs or their decedents. The department to whom this issue has been "constitutionally committed" is none other than our own-the Judiciary. This factor alone, then, strongly suggests that the political question doctrine does not apply.

All of the other factors identified in *Baker*, moreover, also militate against applying the political question doctrine here. First, because the common law of tort provides clear and well-settled rules on which the district court can easily rely, this case does not require the court to render a decision in the absence of "judicially discoverable and manageable standards." Second, because the PLO has maintained throughout this litigation that the hijacking was an act of piracy, rather than a terrorist act, a finding for or against the PLO does not depend on a prior political assessment about the value of terrorism, and thus no "initial policy decision of a kind clearly for nonjudicial discretion" need be made. [FN3] Third, given the fact that both the Executive and Legislative Branches have expressly endorsed the concept of suing terrorist organizations in federal court, *see* Letter from Abraham D. Sofaer, United States Department of State, Office of the Legal Adviser, to Justice Carmen B. Ciparick, (Sept. 4, 1986); 18 U.S.C.A. §2333(a) (West Supp.1990) (providing a civil remedy in federal court for United States nationals injured by acts of international terrorism), resolution of this matter will not exhibit "a lack of the respect due coordinate branches of government." Fourth, this case does not require us to display "unquestioning adherence to a political decision already made," because no prior political decisions are questioned-or even implicated-by the matter before us. Finally, because this lawsuit is consistent with both the Executive and Legislative Branch's attitude toward terrorists, resolution of this case does not have the potential for "embarrassment from multifarious pronouncements by various departments on one question."

FN3. For this reason, the opinions of Judges Bork and Robb in *Tel-Oren, supra*, which suggested that judgments about the role of terrorism in international struggles are best entrusted to the Executive Branch, *see* 726 F.2d at 805 (Bork, J.); *id*. at 825-26 (Robb, J.), are inapplicable here. In any event, given the Executive Branch's repeated condemnations of international terrorism, we believe that any initial policy decision that might conceivably be required has already been made.

Accordingly, we agree with the district court that the political question doctrine does not bar the claims presented here.

* * *

Vacated and remanded, with instructions to determine whether personal jurisdiction can be asserted over the PLO with respect to some or all of the complaints at issue here, and, if so, whether service of process on the PLO's Permanent Observer to the UN was sufficient.

Notes:

1. Terrorism has played such a large role in American political discourse over the last three decades that many political scientists and politicians have called it the defining national security issue of the post Cold War era. By definition, acts of terrorism are designed to influence public opinion and to achieve political goals. Those who conduct terrorism are typically politically astute and see themselves as ideological actors performing on a world stage. The federal statutes designed to provide remedies for American citizens are created by politicians responding to political pressure and intended to "send a message" to terrorists and their sponsors. Accordingly, can terrorism cases be adjudicated in a non-political context? Is it intellectually sound to argue that politics is merely the "context" for civil terrorism litigation but that victims' cases can be adjudicated without resort to political standards? Are terrorism suits really just "ordinary tort suits"? *Ungar v. Palestinian Authority*, 228 F.Supp.2d 40, 45 (D.R.I. 2002).

2. How could the court determine whether in fact the defendants "breached a duty of care owed to the plaintiffs" without first identifying the source of law?

3. What assumptions are contained in the court's statement "because this lawsuit is consistent with both the Executive and Legislative Branch's attitude toward terrorists"? Why are their assumptions relevant? What importance would the "attitudes" of the President and Congress have in other cases such as securities or anti-trust litigation? What if the President and Congress had conflicting positions concerning a specific terrorist organization, with one branch of government calling them "freedom fighters" while another passes resolutions or takes administrative action to designate the group a "specially designated terrorist group"?

4. Does the court's use of the word "terrorists" and "terrorism" assume a political value judgment? If the activity on the Achille Lauro that gave rise to this suit had been committed by Samuel Adams against a loyalist just prior the American Revolution would the conduct be considered terrorism? Would the answer impact the adjudication of the victim's claim?

5. In virtually every contested terrorism case, the defendants move for dismissal under the political question doctrine. Courts routinely reject such requests. A typical response is found in *Knox v. Palestine Liberation Organization*, 306 F.Supp.2d 424, 449 (S.D.N.Y. 2004),

> Defendants urge the Court to dismiss the case on the ground that it raises non-justiciable political questions. Specifically, Defendants assert that this case will require the Court to "assess[ ] the Palestinian-Israeli conflict over the years" and to "adjudicate history in progress." (Def. Mem. at 26-27.) The Court disagrees. As explained more fully above, the Court will not, and need not, endeavor to answer or otherwise lend its views towards these broader and intractable political questions which form the backdrop to this lawsuit. This lawsuit will simply adjudicate whether and to what extent the Plaintiffs may recover against Defendants under certain causes of action for the violence that occurred in Hadera, Israel on the night of January 17, 2002.
>
> In this connection, the Court cannot ignore the incongruity and conflict with statutory intent that the Defendants' argument would countenance. Plaintiffs' claims allege unprovoked savagery that encompasses even murder. Defendants' view essentially would ask the Court to hold that, even if the facts were to verify the accusations here, a wanton massacre of innocents would still be "non-justiciable." This proposition cuts against the grain of what compels the business of the courts. It would rub every syllable of justice out of the concept of justiciability and do equal violence to the ATA.
>
> In American jurisprudence, the instances in which atrocities committed against United States nationals are deemed beyond the justiciable reach of the law, and in which our courts are thus utterly unable to perform their ordained functions, are rare indeed. Ordinarily only the intervention of superseding political or juridical constraints would take such grievous wrongs outside the bounds of the courts' remedial arm. The jurisdictional force actuating the ATA aims precisely to further narrow the scant exceptions, so as to extend the law to the vindication of rights and reparation of international

injuries that otherwise would not be rectifiable in our courts. In fact, at its core, the statute embodies a precept that goes to the heart of its design, a principle of survival. It manifests that for American victims of international terrorism, finality comes to rest not in violence, but in justice, and that, when all is said and done, the larger and more enduring end lies in the judicial remedy the law uniquely prescribes to survive and redress the terrorist's assault.

6.   The Klinghoffer case was filed prior to the enactment of 18 U.S.C. §2333 and the court made only brief mention of the statute in passing. However, 15 years later, this provision has been the basis for several lawsuits (including several against the Palestine Liberation Organization and the newly created Palestinian Authority).

7.   In *Klieman v. Palestinian Authority*, 424 F.Supp.2d 153, 162 (D.D.C. 2006)(citations omitted), the Court noted:

> …the Court has access to "judicially manageable standards for resolving the issue[s] before it," *id.*, from both existing ATA case law and traditional tort case law. The "initial policy determination" involved here has already been made by the U.S. Congress: Americans injured by terrorist acts can sue their attackers in U.S. courts and the Court can manage this case to resolution of Defendants' alleged liability without "expressing lack of the respect due coordinate branches of government."

How does this compare with the ruling in *Klinghoffer*?

5.2 Act of War

Biton v. Palestinian Interim Self-Government Authority, **412 F.Supp.2d 1 (D. D.C. 2005).**

COLLYER, District Judge.

Avigail Lewis Biton, individually and on behalf of her children, and Rachel Asraf bring suit under the Antiterrorism Act of 1991 ("ATA"), 18 U.S.C. §2333, and various tort theories against the Palestinian Interim Self-Government Authority, also known as the Palestinian Authority or the Palestinian National Authority ("PA") and the Palestine Liberation Organization ("PLO"). [FN1] Pending before the Court are Defendants' Supplemental Motion to Dismiss pursuant to Rules 12(b)(1) and 12(b)(6) of the Federal Rules of Civil Procedure and Plaintiffs' Motion for Partial Summary Judgment. [FN2] By Order entered on April 18, 2005, the Court deemed the record closed.

FN1. In an earlier decision, this Court dismissed claims against Yasser Arafat, former president of the PA and chairman of the PLO; two senior members of the Palestinian Preventive Security Service ("PPSS"); two members of the Palestinian Police Service ("PPS"); and 99 John Does. See *Biton v. Palestinian Interim Self-Government Authority*, 310 F.Supp.2d 172 (D.D.C.2004).

FN2. On May 24, 2004, the Court granted Defendants' Motion for Limited Reconsideration Upon a Supplemented Record of the Court's Conclusions on Palestinian Statehood, Sovereignty and Immunity In Its Memorandum Opinion and Order of March 18, 2004. Pursuant to the Court's grant of Defendants' Motion for Limited Reconsideration, Defendants submitted a Supplemental Motion to Dismiss on August 18, 2004. It is that motion upon which the Court will render its decision.

I. BACKGROUND

The underlying facts of this case may be simply stated: at approximately 7:30 a.m. on November 20, 2000, a roadside device exploded near a bus that was transporting elementary school children and their teachers from Kfar Darom, a former Israeli settlement in the southern Gaza Strip, toward Gush Katif. The bombing took the life of Plaintiff Biton's husband, Gabriel Biton, and injured Plaintiff Rachel Asraf. Plaintiffs contend that Defendants are responsible for this bombing and the resulting deaths and injuries. The bombing is believed by the Defendants to have been part of the "al-Aqsa Intifada," a series of violent demonstrations and clashes between Palestinians and Israeli Defense Forces that ensued following (now-Israeli Prime Minister) Ariel Sharon's controversial visit to the Temple Mount/Haram al-Sharif in Jerusalem in September 2000. *See* Defendants' First Motion to Dismiss ("Defs.' Mem."), Ex. 1.

The Defendants' Supplemental Motion to Dismiss seeks dismissal on grounds of sovereign and governmental immunity based on Palestine's asserted statehood and Defendants' roles as "essential core elements of Palestine." Defendants' PA and PLO Supporting Memorandum of Points and Authorities in Support of Their Supplemental Rule 12(b) Motion ("Defs.' Supp. Mem.") at 1-2. They also argue that this action raises nonjusticiable questions and that the school bus bombing was an "act of war" as defined in 18 U.S.C. §2331 and therefore the suit is barred by 18 U.S.C. §2336(a). Although the Plaintiffs styled their pleading a "Motion for Partial Summary Judgment," it directly addresses each of the points raised in Defendants' Supplemental Motion to Dismiss and will be treated as a formal response to which the Defendants have filed no reply.

C. *"Act of War"*

The more complex question is whether the alleged actions of Defendants are not subject to litigation in a U.S. court because they were "acts of war" over which the ATA does not extend jurisdiction. 18 U.S.C. §2336(a) provides that "[n]o action shall be maintained under section 2333 of this title for injury or loss by reason of an act of war." "Act of war" is defined in §2331 as "any act occurring in the course of- (A) declared war; (B) armed conflict, whether or not war has been declared, between two or more nations; or (C) armed conflict between military forces of any origin." Defendants limit their arguments to (C), asserting that the bombing of the school bus was an act of war occurring in the course of armed conflict between military forces of any origin. [FN5] Plaintiffs contend that attacks against civilians are not countenanced in U.S. law as "acts of war" that would allow terrorists to escape the judgment for which the ATA was adopted. Plaintiffs urge the Court to decide, as a matter of law, that bombing civilian targets is not an action that occurs "in the course of" war, as that term is construed by U.S. courts.

FN5. *See* Defs.' Supp. Mem. at 12. This limitation is sensible. Subsections (A) and (B) do not apply. There is no "declared war" between Israel and Palestine and, as found earlier, since Palestine is not a state, the armed conflict between the two entities does not constitute a conflict "between two or more nations." 18 U.S.C. §2336(a). Defendants previously took the position that the bombing of a school bus full of children and teachers "may well be" an act of war but that the "facts cannot be determined." Defs.' Mem. at 22-24. For that reason, the Court declined to reach the issue. See *Biton*, 310 F.Supp.2d at 185. Defendants now appear to argue that the precise facts are irrelevant and that modern warfare properly includes attacks on civilian targets, for which the aggressors cannot be tried as terrorists.

The parties do not dispute that there was an "armed conflict" in the southern Gaza Strip in November 2000, as the nightly news also demonstrated to Americans during that time. There was armed conflict between military forces in Gaza and other occupied Palestinian [areas] at all relevant times.

The armed conflict is shown on this motion by numerous newspaper articles reporting on day-to-day fighting and violence as it occurred, often characterizing the conflict as war or reporting remarks to this effect by Israelis or Palestinians. Many such articles are included in defendants' exhibits on this motion…

Israel has repeatedly and consistently reported the fighting between the IDF and Palestinians to be armed conflict, and,

at times, armed conflict short of war. The latter would of course be within the statutory definition of 'act of war.'

Defs.' Supp. Mem. at 20. However, while Plaintiffs do not dispute that there was an "armed conflict" as a matter of fact, they disagree as to whether an "armed conflict" existed as a matter of law for purposes of the ATA. Memorandum in Support of Plaintiffs' Motion for Partial Summary Judgment Against Defendants Palestinian Authority and Palestine Liberation Organization ("Pls.' Mem.") at 24 ("[A]ttacks on civilians are excluded as a matter of law from being considered part of an armed conflict even when they are a part of such conflict as a matter of fact.").

1. *Applying the Phrase "In the Course of"*

Plaintiffs' argument begins with the accurate statement that "[u]nder §2331(4), 'acts of war' include only acts 'occurring in the course of' declared war or armed conflict." Pls.' Mem. at 16. While there appears to be no precedent interpreting §2331(4), Plaintiffs argue

[I]n numerous other contexts, the courts have consistently interpreted the phrase "in the course of" as a "gatekeeper" phrase that is intended to exclude as a *matter of law* a subset of conduct which-because of its nature and substance-deviates from and/or is insufficiently related to the general set of conduct governed by the provision in question.

Id. at 17 (emphasis in original). The Controlled Substances Act prohibits the distribution of narcotics, 21 U.S.C. §829, except, *inter alia*, by a licensed "practitioner" as defined, including doctors who dispense "a controlled substance in the course of professional practice…" 21 U.S.C. §802(21). "Manifestly the language 'in the course of professional practice' is intended to limit the immunity of a licensed practitioner…[who] is expected to prescribe or dispense drugs within the bounds of his professional practice of medicine." *United States v. Collier*, 478 F.2d 268, 272 (5th Cir.1973). "[T]he phrase 'in the course of professional practice'…has been in the statute books since 1914…The language clearly means that a doctor is not exempt from the statute when he takes actions that he does not in good faith believe are for legitimate medical purposes." *United States v. Rosenberg*, 515 F.2d 190, 197-198 (9th Cir.1975) (citing *Jim Fuey Moy v. United States*, 254 U.S. 189, 194, 41 S.Ct. 98, 65 L.Ed. 214 (1920) (doctor must act "strictly within the appropriate bounds of a physician's professional practice"); *United States v. Behrman*, 258 U.S. 280, 287, 42 S.Ct. 303, 66 L.Ed. 619 (1922) (immunity confined to dispensing narcotics in "the regular and lawful course of professional practice"); *Boyd v. United States*, 271 U.S. 104, 105, 46 S.Ct. 442, 70 L.Ed. 857 (1926) ("good faith in the course of his professional practice")).

Similarly, the protections afforded a seaman under the Jones Act, 46 App. U.S.C.A. §688, are limited to recovery for injury or death suffered "in the course of his employment." This phrase refers to "the nature of the service and its relationship to the operation of the vessel plying in navigable waters" that led to injury or death, not the physical location of the seaman when injured. *O'Donnell v. Great Lakes Dredge & Dock Co.*, 318 U.S. 36, 63 S.Ct. 488, 87 L.Ed. 596 (1943); see also *Vincent v. Harvey Well Service*, 441 F.2d 146, 147 (5th Cir.1971); *Magnolia Towing Co. v. Pace*, 378 F.2d 12 (5th Cir.1967). As a result, the question of whether a given injury occurred "in the course of" a seaman's employment is primarily a question of law, not fact. *Colon v. Apex Marine Corp.*, 832 F.Supp. 508, 515 (D.R.I.1993), *aff'd*, 35 F.3d 16 (1st Cir.1994), *cert. denied*, 514 U.S. 1018, 115 S.Ct. 1363, 131 L.Ed.2d 220 (1995). The Warsaw Convention (reprinted following 49 U.S.C. §40105), an international treaty governing air carrier liability, also contains the phrase "in the course of" which has been interpreted by U.S. courts in a limiting fashion. Specifically, Article 17 of the Convention provides that an air carrier:

[S]hall be liable for damages sustained in the event of the death or wounding of a passenger or any other bodily injury suffered by a passenger if the accident which caused the damage so sustained took place on board the aircraft or *in the course of* any of the operations of embarking or disembarking.

Id. (emphasis added). As with the interpretations of the same phrase in the Jones Act, courts look to the nature of the passenger's activity, under whose control or direction the passenger was acting, and the location of the passenger's activity to determine whether the damage or injury occurred "in the course of" embarking or disembarking. *Day v. Trans World Airlines, Inc.*, 528 F.2d 31 (2d Cir.1975); see also *Dazo v. Globe Airport Security Services*, 268 F.3d 671, 677 (9th Cir.2001); *Kalantar v. Lufthansa German Airlines*, 276 F.Supp.2d 5 (D.D.C.2003). "Location should not be considered alone... when determining if plaintiff was in the course of embarking upon defendant's flight. In addition to the location of the accident, the nature of the activity in which the plaintiff was engaged must be examined to determine if that activity can fairly be considered part of 'the operations of embarking.' " *Abu Hamdeh v. American Airlines, Inc.*, 862 F.Supp. 243, 248 (E.D.Mo.1994) (quoting *Evangelinos v. Trans World Airlines, Inc.*, 550 F.2d 152, 155 (3rd Cir.1977)).

From these precedents, Plaintiffs argue that the phrase "in the course of" armed combat excludes from its scope an attack on a civilian bus because such an attack on civilians violates the rules of war and cannot occur "in the course of" war as a matter of law.

2. Rules of War

Although Rules of War and the carnage of battle appear to be incongruous, attacks on civilian noncombatants have been reviled for centuries. In *Henry II*, Shakespeare will not let us forget the French attack on the English baggage boys at Agincourt. Many still remember the American revulsion to the My Lai massacre during the Vietnam War, even as we sympathized with the soldiers facing a hidden enemy. Plaintiffs build on this tradition to argue that the November 20, 2000, attack on the school bus from Kfar Darom violated the Rules of War and could not, as a matter of law, come within the exception to the ATA.

Plaintiffs turn to the "political offense exception" to extradition to make their point. "Most [extradition] treaties list categories of crimes or specific offense[s] for which extradition may be requested. There usually are, however, exceptions...Many treaties include 'political crimes' among those exceptions," without further defining the term. *Eain v. Wilkes*, 641 F.2d 504, 512 (7th Cir.1981), *cert. denied*, 454 U.S. 894, 102 S.Ct. 390, 70 L.Ed.2d 208 (1981). In developing a definition, U.S. courts have limited "political crimes" to "acts committed *in the course of* and incidental to a violent political disturbance such as a war, revolution or rebellion." *Id.* at 518 (emphasis added). See also *Garcia-Guillern v. United States*, 450 F.2d 1189, 1192 (5th Cir.1971), *cert. denied*, 405 U.S. 989, 92 S.Ct. 1251, 31 L.Ed.2d 455 (1972) (offense must occur "in the course of or incidental to" hostilities). Even more to the point, the question for extradition purposes is not just whether there was a war in fact, but whether the offense occurred "in the course of and incidental to" that war, depending upon the nature and circumstances of the violent act and the identity of the victims.

In determining whether the "incidental to" prong has been met, federal courts have examined the circumstances of the attack and the victims targeted. See *Ornelas v. Ruiz*, 161 U.S. 502, 511, 16 S.Ct. 689, 40 L.Ed. 787 (1896) (focusing on status of victim, "mode of attack," and "the character of the foray"); *Ahmad v. Wigen*, 910 F.2d at 1066 (attack on civilian passenger bus was not a political offense); *Artukovic v. Rison*, 628 F.Supp. 1370, 1376 (C.D.Cal.1986) ("[T]he focus of the inquiry is on the circumstances, and on the status of those harmed." [*aff'd* 784 F.2d 1354 (9th Cir.1986)]).

Marzook v. Christopher, 1996 WL 583378, at *2 (S.D.N.Y. Oct.10, 1996). "A rational nexus between the alleged crimes and the prevailing turmoil must be demonstrated. In searching for such a connection, the focus of the inquiry is on the circumstances, and on the status of those harmed, and not on whether the acts merely were committed during the disorder." *Artukovic*, 628 F.Supp. at 1376.

3. *Application to Bombing at Kfar Darom*

Kfar Darom-now evacuated by the Israelis-was an Israeli settlement in the southern Gaza Strip, an area originally partitioned by the United Nations in 1947 to be under Palestinian control. The U.N. "formulated a plan that involved the creation of two independent states within the [former United Kingdom] mandate territory: one Jewish, the other Arab." *Ungar*, 402 F.3d at 285. The Palestinians, representing two-thirds of the population, refused to accept the idea of partition. *Id.* at 285. When the British withdrew, Jewish leaders announced the establishment of the State of Israel within the borders set by the United Nations; Arab forces immediately invaded. *Id.* (citing United Nations Dep't of Pub. Info., The Question of Palestine & The United Nations at 11, U.N. Doc. DPI/2276, U.N. Sales No. 04,I.15 (2003)). When this first Arab-Israeli war ended, "Egypt had taken control of the Gaza Strip, Jordan was in control of the West Bank (including East Jerusalem), and Israel had taken command of the remainder of the former mandate territory." *Id.* By the end of the war, nearly three-quarters of a million Palestinian refugees had fled from the areas controlled by Israel. *Id.* Egypt, Jordan and Syria went to war against Israel again in 1967. This conflict lasted six days, at the end of which Israel occupied "the Gaza Strip and the West Bank, as well as the Sinai peninsula (previously under Egyptian rule) and the Golan Heights region of Syria." *Id.* Strenuous efforts to establish a stable peace between Palestine and Israel within separate national borders have progressed and retreated in the years since 1967 without resolution.

This history is important because Kfar Darom was an Israeli settlement in an area that was intended by the United Nations to be under Palestinian control. The entire Gaza Strip is about twice the size of Washington, D.C., yet its population in 2002 was approximately 1,300,000 Palestinians and 7,000 Israelis. The phenomena of small Israeli towns established in occupied but presumptively Palestinian territory has enormously complicated the peace efforts. Encouraged by their government, Israeli settlers in the Gaza Strip knowingly ventured into lands that the Palestinians claim and that the United Nations partitioned in Palestinian favor. It is not immediately obvious that an attack on a settler, who intentionally went into Palestinian territory to

claim it for Israel, would automatically and necessarily be a "terrorist" attack against a "civilian."

The Court does not have to venture a decision on this point. Israel is withdrawing from the Gaza Strip and Kfar Darom is evacuated. Nonetheless, it is clear that children are not the proper targets of war. War should be fought between combatants and not between combatants and children. Defendants do not dispute that the bus from Kfar Darom contained only children and teachers. The *fact* of the settlement at Kfar Darom might be the cause of Palestinian anger; the *settlement itself* might even be an object for attack by Palestinians and defense by Israeli military, during which children might be hurt. But the *children of the settlement* cannot be direct targets of Palestinian force without liability as terrorists. The circumstances of the alleged attack-on a recognized school bus full of students and teachers-and the status of those noncombatants lead the Court to conclude that the attack did not occur "during the course of" an armed conflict as a matter of law. Accordingly, Defendants' Supplemental Motion to Dismiss will be DENIED. A memorializing order accompanies this memorandum opinion.

Notes:

1. What was the assumption underlying the Palestinian Authority's position in *Biton*? Why did the PA attempt to frame the argument in terms of the historic Arab-Israeli conflict?

2. How did the defendants attempt to use this case as a sword in its long-standing fight against Israel? What rulings did they seek to extract from the court? If defendants were successful, how would the court's ruling help their political cause? Which side is truly injecting politics into the case? How did the court avoid this potential trap?

3. In *Klieman v. Palestinian Authority*, 424 F.Supp.2d 153, 163 (D.D.C. 2006) the court remarked that,

> ...defendants contend that the "ATA encompasses acts of war against civilians" and that as a "general proposition violent acts on civilians and their property are readily considered acts of war." *Id.* at 37 (noting that the events of September 11, 2001 have been treated as an act of war by President Bush, the United Nations and U.S. courts).

4. How does President Bush's description of the 9/11 attacks support defendants' position that an attack on a public bus is an "act of war"? Is there merit to this argument?

Chapter 6

Personal Jurisdiction

6.1 States

Mwani v. bin Laden, **417 F.3d 1 (D.C. Cir. 2005).**

GARLAND, Circuit Judge.
On August 7, 1998, a devastating truck bomb exploded outside the American embassy in Nairobi, Kenya. The blast killed more than 200 people, including 12 Americans, and wounded more than 4000 others. Most of the casualties were Kenyan. The plaintiffs in this case are all Kenyan: victims, relatives of victims, and businesses harmed in the attack. They sued defendants Osama bin Laden and al Qaeda for orchestrating the bombing, and defendant Afghanistan for providing logistical support to bin Laden and al Qaeda. The district court dismissed the claims against Afghanistan for lack of subject matter jurisdiction, and those against bin Laden and al Qaeda for lack of personal jurisdiction.

Although we agree that the Foreign Sovereign Immunities Act bars the plaintiffs' claims against Afghanistan, we reverse the dismissal of their actions against bin Laden and al Qaeda. Those defendants "engaged in unabashedly malignant actions directed at [and] felt" in this country. *GTE New Media Servs., Inc. v. BellSouth Corp.*, 199 F.3d 1343, 1349 (D.C.Cir.2000). Bin Laden and al Qaeda should therefore "reasonably anticipate being haled into court" here by those injured as a result of those actions, *Burger King Corp. v. Rudzewicz*, 471 U.S. 462, 473-74, 105 S.Ct. 2174, 85 L.Ed.2d 528 (1985), regardless of the plaintiffs' nationality.

I

In early 1999, Odilla Mutaka Mwani and his fellow plaintiffs filed this action in the United States District Court for the District of Columbia. They sought compensatory damages and other relief from Osama bin Laden, the terrorist organization known as al Qaeda, and the nation of Afghanistan for the injuries they sustained in the embassy bombing. [FN1] The plaintiffs predicated subject matter jurisdiction for their claims against Afghanistan on the Foreign Sovereign Immu-

nities Act (FSIA), 28 U.S.C. §§1602 *et seq.*, and for those against bin Laden and al Qaeda on the Alien Tort Claims Act (ATCA), 28 U.S.C. §1350. The latter provides that "[t]he district courts shall have original jurisdiction of any civil action by an alien for a tort only, committed in violation of the law of nations or a treaty of the United States." *Id.*

FN1. The plaintiffs also named the United States and Sudan as defendants. The district court dismissed those claims, and the plaintiffs have not appealed.

On February 12, 1999, the plaintiffs moved to serve defendants bin Laden and al Qaeda by publication. On August 2, 1999, the district court granted the plaintiffs leave to serve those defendants by "publishing...notice for six weeks in the Daily Washington Law Reporter, the International Herald Tribune, and Al-Quds Al-Arabi (in Arabic)." *Mwani v. United States*, No. 99-125, Order at 4 (D.D.C. Aug. 2, 1999) ("August 1999 Order"). The plaintiffs later advised the court that the notice had run in all three newspapers, as well as in two additional East African publications.

To no one's surprise, neither bin Laden nor al Qaeda responded. On August 11, 2000, the plaintiffs moved for entry of default against them. Because the district court was not satisfied that it had personal jurisdiction over bin Laden and al Qaeda, it denied the motion without prejudice, granting plaintiffs additional time to pursue the issue. See *Mwani v. United States*, No. 99-125, Mem. Op. at 2-3, 5 (D.D.C. Mar. 15, 2001) ("March 2001 Opinion"). The plaintiffs responded with a renewed motion for entry of default in July 2001, and with supplemental memoranda in August, September, and October of that year. In these papers, the plaintiffs argued that bin Laden and al Qaeda had sufficient nationwide contacts with the United States to satisfy constitutional limits on the court's exercise of jurisdiction. [FN2]

FN2. The plaintiffs offered two additional bases for personal jurisdiction, one grounded in the concept of "universal jurisdiction" and the other in the "effects doctrine." Pls.' Renewed Mot. for Entry of Default at 19, 21 (July 16, 2001). The district court rejected both, as well as the contention that the defendants' nationwide contacts were sufficient to permit the exercise of jurisdiction. Because we conclude that the nationwide contacts were in fact sufficient, we do not address the plaintiffs' additional bases.

On September 30, 2002, the district court held that, to enter a default, it "must have jurisdiction over the party against whom the judgment is sought," and the plaintiffs must demonstrate such jurisdiction by a preponderance of the evidence. *Mwani v. United States*, No. 99-125, Mem. Op. at 2 (D.D.C. Sept. 30, 2002) ("September 2002 Opinion") (internal quotation marks omitted). Applying those principles, the court concluded that the plaintiffs had "failed to sustain their burden of proving that this Court can exercise personal jurisdiction over" bin Laden and al Qaeda. *Id.* That was so, the court said, both because of the quality of the plaintiffs' evidence, and because of its failure to establish sufficient contacts between the defendants and the forum to permit the exercise of jurisdiction under the District of Columbia's long-arm statute and the U.S. Constitution. See *id.* at 9-11.

The dismissal of the plaintiffs' claims against bin Laden and al Qaeda left Afghanistan as the only remaining defendant. The plaintiffs effected service of process by certified mail on Afghanistan's Ministry of Foreign Affairs, through that country's embassy in the District of Columbia. An appearance was entered by the Transitional Islamic State of Afghanistan (hereinafter Afghanistan)-"the interim government for Afghanistan established by the Bonn Accords of December 2002, which were implemented under the United Nations' auspices after the Taliban's armed forces were defeated by an international coalition and the Northern Alliance." Appellees Br. at 4. Afghanistan then moved to dismiss the plaintiffs' claims for lack of personal and subject matter jurisdiction, citing the FSIA.

In June 2004, the district court granted Afghanistan's motion to dismiss, rejecting the plaintiffs' contention that the case fell within two exceptions to the FSIA-for implicit waiver and commercial activities. *Mwani v. United States*, No. 99-125, Mem. Op. at 12 (D.D.C. June 22, 2004) ("June 2004 Opinion"). At the same time, it denied the plaintiffs' request for jurisdictional discovery because it did " 'not see what facts additional discovery could produce that would affect [its] jurisdictional analysis.' " *Id.* at 11 (quoting *Goodman Holdings v. Rafidain Bank*, 26 F.3d 1143, 1147 (D.C.Cir.1994)).

The plaintiffs filed a timely appeal. In Part II, we consider their contention that the district court erred in dismissing the claims against bin Laden and al Qaeda. In Part III, we address their challenge to the dismissal of the claims against Afghanistan.

II

We review the dismissal of a claim for lack of jurisdiction de novo. See, e.g., *Gorman v. Ameritrade Holding Corp.*, 293 F.3d 506, 509 (D.C.Cir.2002). In evaluating the district court's dismissal of the claims against bin Laden and al Qaeda, we must consider two distinct determinations made by the court. The first is the appropriate burden and standard of proof for establishing personal jurisdiction over an absent defendant at this stage of the litigation. The second is whether the plaintiffs satisfied those requirements.

A

The district court correctly noted that the entry of a default judgment [FN3] is not automatic, and that a court should satisfy itself that it has personal jurisdiction before entering judgment against an absent defendant. March 2001 Opinion at 2. [FN4] The court acknowledged that when ruling upon personal jurisdiction without an evidentiary hearing, a court ordinarily demands only a prima facie showing of jurisdiction by the plaintiffs. September 2002 Opinion at 6. [FN5] It is only if the court takes evidence on the issue or rules on the personal jurisdiction question in the context of a trial that a heightened, preponderance of the evidence standard applies. *Id.* [FN6] Nonetheless, the district court concluded that in this case it should require the plaintiffs to establish jurisdiction by a preponderance of the evidence, because it was "on the cusp of a default judgment proceeding…and… Defendants are not presently before the Court." September 2002 Opinion at 6. And it further determined that, to satisfy that burden, the plaintiffs would have to proffer evidence meeting the standards of admissibility ordinarily reserved for the summary judgment and trial stages of litigation. See *id.* at 12-14.

FN3. The district court intentionally collapsed the two stages of default, treating the plaintiffs' motion for entry of default by the clerk, *see* FED. R. CIV. P. 55(a), as a motion for entry of a default judgment by the court, see *id.* 55(b)(2). *See* 10A CHARLES ALAN WRIGHT, ARTHUR R. MILLER & MARY KAY KANE, FEDERAL PRACTICE AND PROCEDURE §§2682, 2685 (3d ed.1998) (hereinafter WRIGHT & MILLER).

FN4. See *Dennis Garberg & Assocs. v. Pack-Tech Int'l Corp.*, 115 F.3d 767, 772 (10th Cir.1997) ("[A] district court must determine whether it has jurisdiction over the defendant before entering judgment by default against a party who has not appeared in the case."); 10A WRIGHT & MILLER §2682, at 14.

FN5. See *Edmond v. United States Postal Serv. Gen. Counsel*, 949 F.2d 415, 424 (D.C.Cir.1991); *First Chi. Int'l v. United Exch. Co.*, 836 F.2d 1375, 1378-79 (D.C.Cir.1988); *Dennis Garberg & Assocs.*, 115 F.3d at 773; 2 JAMES W. MOORE, MOORE'S FEDERAL PRACTICE §12.31[5] (3d ed.2002) (hereinafter MOORE'S).

FN6. See *Dennis Garberg & Assocs.*, 115 F.3d at 773; MOORE'S §12.31[5].

We reject this approach. The absence of the defendant is precisely the reason the Federal Rules of Civil Procedure provide for default judgments, which safeguard plaintiffs "when the adversary process has been halted because of an essentially unresponsive party. In that instance, the diligent party must be protected lest he be faced with interminable delay and continued uncertainty as to his rights." *Jackson v. Beech*, 636 F.2d 831, 836 (D.C.Cir.1980) (internal quotation marks omitted). Far from constituting a rationale for increasing the plaintiffs' burden of proof, if anything the absence of the defendants counsels greater flexibility toward the plaintiffs because it impedes their ability to obtain jurisdictional discovery. There is thus no reason for the district court to insist upon an evidentiary hearing, and it did not do so in this case.

In the absence of an evidentiary hearing, although the plaintiffs retain "the burden of proving personal jurisdiction, [they] can satisfy that burden with a *prima facie* showing." *Edmond v. United States Postal Serv. Gen. Counsel*, 949 F.2d 415, 424 (D.C.Cir.1991) (citation omitted). Moreover, to establish a prima facie case, plaintiffs are not limited to evidence that meets the standards of admissibility required by the district court. Rather, they may rest their argument on their pleadings, bolstered by such affidavits and other written materials as they can otherwise obtain. [FN7]

FN7. See, e.g., *Naartex Consulting Corp. v. Watt*, 722 F.2d 779, 787-88 (D.C.Cir.1983); *Glencore Grain Rotterdam B.V. v. Shivnath Rai Harnarain Co.*, 284 F.3d 1114, 1119 (9th Cir.2002); *Ball v. Metallurgie Hoboken-Overpelt, S.A.*, 902 F.2d 194, 197 (2d Cir.1990).

Adherence to these principles does not unduly disadvantage those absent defendants who truly are beyond the power of the court. Entry of a default judgment is not the court's final

say on a matter. Rule 55(c) provides that "[f]or good cause shown the court may set aside...a judgment by default...in accordance with Rule 60(b)." FED. R. CIV. P. 55(c). Under the rule, a defendant can successfully challenge a default judgment in the rendering court on the ground of lack of personal jurisdiction. See, e.g., *Combs v. Nick Garin Trucking*, 825 F.2d 437, 438 (D.C.Cir.1987). And a defendant is "always free to ignore the judicial proceedings, risk a default judgment, and then challenge that judgment on jurisdictional grounds in a collateral proceeding." *Insurance Corp. of Ireland, Ltd. v. Compagnie des Bauxites de Guinee*, 456 U.S. 694, 706, 102 S.Ct. 2099, 72 L.Ed.2d 492 (1982); *see* 10 JAMES W. MOORE, MOORE'S FEDERAL PRACTICE §55.50[2][b][i] (3d ed.2005).

B

Having set forth the appropriate burden and standard of proof, we now consider whether the plaintiffs have satisfactorily shown that the district court may exercise personal jurisdiction over bin Laden and al Qaeda. In the first section below, we address the sources of authority for such an exercise. In the second section, we consider whether the exercise of that jurisdiction would contravene constitutional due process.

1

"Before a federal court may exercise personal jurisdiction over a defendant, the procedural requirement of service of summons must be satisfied." *Omni Capital Int'l, Ltd. v. Rudolf Wolff & Co.*, 484 U.S. 97, 104, 108 S.Ct. 404, 98 L.Ed.2d 415 (1987). The district court did not dispute that the plaintiffs had accomplished service by an acceptable method. Rule 4 of the Federal Rules sets forth the various methods by which a summons may be served in federal court proceedings, and Rule 4(f) specifically addresses "[s]ervice upon individuals in a foreign country." It provides, in relevant part:

Unless otherwise provided by federal law, service upon an individual from whom a waiver has not been obtained and filed...may be effected in a place not within any judicial district of the United States...by...means not prohibited by international agreement *as may be directed by the court.*

FED. R. CIV. P. 4(f)(3) (emphasis added).

Here, the district court authorized the plaintiffs to serve bin Laden and al Qaeda by publication. The court observed that their "address is not known, nor is it easily ascertainable," August 1999 Order at 3, and that bin Laden had published at least one *fatwa* in *Al-Quds Al-Arabi*, *id.* at 4. It concluded that publication was "reasonably calculated to apprise [bin Laden and al Qaeda] of the lawsuit and afford them an opportunity to present their objections." *Id.* In *Mullane v. Central Hanover Bank & Trust Co.*, the Supreme Court sanctioned service by publication "where it is not reasonably possible or practicable to give more adequate warning," holding that, "in the case of persons missing or unknown, employment of an indirect and even a probably futile means of notification is all that the situation permits and creates no constitutional bar to a final decree foreclosing their rights." 339 U.S. 306, 317, 70 S.Ct. 652, 94 L.Ed. 865 (1950).

The district court correctly recognized, however, that service of process does not alone establish personal jurisdiction. As the Supreme Court said in *Omni Capital*, "[b]efore a court may exercise personal jurisdiction over a defendant, there must be more than notice to the defendant." 484 U.S. at 104, 108 S.Ct. 404. There also must be "authorization for service of summons on the defendant," and a "constitutionally sufficient relationship between the defendant and the forum." *Id.*; see *id.* at 103 n. 6, 108 S.Ct. 404 (noting the distinction between an "objection to the method of service" and an objection "to amenability to service"). To determine whether these requirements were satisfied here, the district court undertook a traditional inquiry. It asked first whether there was an applicable long-arm statute that would authorize service on the defendants, and then whether the application of such a statute would comply with the demands of due process. See, e.g., *GTE*, 199 F.3d at 1347; *Jungquist v. Sheikh Sultan Bin Khalifa Al Nahyan*, 115 F.3d 1020, 1030-31 (D.C.Cir.1997).

With respect to the availability of a long-arm statute, the district court said that, "[b]ecause there is no federal equivalent, District of Columbia law provides the long-arm statute applicable in this case." September 2002 Order at 3-4. Citing one of our precedents, the court declared that the District's long-arm statute "is as far-reaching as due process allows, meaning that only minimum contacts with the District are necessary to sustain jurisdiction here." *Id.* at 4 (quoting *Caribbean Broadcasting System, Ltd. v. Cable & Wireless PLC*, 148 F.3d 1080, 1089 (D.C.Cir.1998)). While it is true that some provisions of the District's long-arm statute reach as far as due process permits, [FN8] the only provision applicable here does not. That provision is D.C.Code §13-423(a)(4), which provides that

FN8. The plaintiffs in *Caribbean Broadcasting* sought to predicate jurisdiction on the sale of advertising, which falls under the "transacting any business" provision of the statute, D.C. CODE §13-423(a)(1). That provision states that a District of Columbia "court may exercise personal jurisdiction over a person...as to a claim for relief arising from the person's...transacting any business in the District of Columbia." *Id.* The District courts have, in fact, concluded that "the transacting any business provision is coextensive with the due process clause." *Hummel v. Koehler*, 458 A.2d 1187, 1190 (D.C.1983) (internal quotation marks omitted).

[a] District of Columbia court may exercise personal jurisdiction over a person...as to a claim for relief arising from the person's...causing tortious injury in the District of Columbia by an act or omission outside the District of Columbia *if he regularly does or solicits business, engages in any other persistent course of conduct, or derives substantial revenue from goods used or consumed, or services rendered, in the District of Columbia.*

D.C. CODE §13-423(a)(4) (emphasis added). It is unlikely that the defendants would be susceptible to jurisdiction under that provision, as no evidence was proffered that meets the italicized prerequisites. But it is also clear that the Due Process Clause does not demand the level of contacts required by that provision, and hence that the provision does not extend as far as the Clause. Indeed, as the District of Columbia Court of Appeals has said, in "contrast to §13-423(a)(1), which we have held to be coextensive with the Constitution's due process limit, 'the drafters of [§13-423(a)(4)] apparently intended that [this] subsection would not occupy all of the constitutionally available space.'" *Parsons v. Mains*, 580 A.2d 1329, 1331 (D.C.1990) (quoting *Crane v. Carr*, 814 F.2d 758, 762 (D.C.Cir.1987)) (alterations in original).

Prior to 1993, the absence of a state long-arm statute reaching the defendants' activity would have denied the district court personal jurisdiction, since the federal cause of action at issue here-the ATCA-contains no long-arm provision of its own. As the Supreme Court explained in its 1987 decision in *Omni Capital*, at that time the Federal Rules generally authorized service beyond the territorial limits of the state in which the district court was situated only when service was authorized by "a federal statute or...the long-arm statute of [that] State." *Omni Capital*, 484 U.S. at 105, 108 S.Ct. 404 (citing then-FED. R. CIV. P. 4(e)). Indeed, the problem the plaintiffs faced in *Omni Capital* was identical to that faced by the plaintiffs here. Like the ATCA, the statute providing their federal cause of action (a provision of the Commodity Exchange Act) did not authorize service on the foreign defendants. And like the District of Columbia's long-arm statute, the applicable state long-arm did not reach the *Omni Capital* defendants because it was limited to a defendant who "regularly does or solicits business, or engages in any other persistent course of conduct, or derives substantial revenue from goods used or consumed or services rendered" in the state. *Id.* at 108, 108 S.Ct. 404 (quoting LA. REV. STAT. ANN. §13:3201(d)). Thus, the Federal Rules did not authorize service of process on the defendants. See *id.*

In *Omni Capital*, the Supreme Court rejected a suggestion by the dissenters in the court below that it should "remed[y] this 'bizarre hiatus in the Rules' with an ad hoc authorization of service of process on [the defendants] based on their contacts with the United States as a whole." *Id.* at 102, 108 S.Ct. 404 (quoting *Point Landing, Inc. v. Omni Capital International, Ltd.*, 795 F.2d 415, 428 (5th Cir.1986) (en banc) (Wisdom, J., concurring in part and dissenting in part)). Nonetheless, the Court was "not blind to the consequences of the inability to serve process on" the foreign defendants, *id.* at 111, 108 S.Ct. 404, and it offered the following suggestion:

A narrowly tailored service of process provision, authorizing service on an alien in a federal-question case when the alien is not amenable to service under the applicable state long-arm statute, might well serve the ends of [certain] federal statutes. It is not for the federal courts, however, to create such a rule as a matter of common law. That responsibility, in our view, better rests with those who propose the Federal Rules of Civil Procedure and with Congress.

Id.

Those "who propose the Federal Rules of Civil Procedure" took notice of the Court's suggestion, and a revision was enacted in 1993. Although no case in this Circuit has yet cited that revision, the Rules now contain their *own* long-arm provision which, in some circumstances, eliminates the need to employ the forum state's long-arm statute. Rule 4(k)(2) now provides:

If the exercise of jurisdiction is consistent with the Constitution and laws of the United States, serving a summons...is also effective, with respect to claims arising under federal law, to establish personal jurisdiction over the person of any defendant who is not subject to the jurisdiction of the courts of general jurisdiction of any state.

FED. R. CIV. P. 4(k)(2). [FN9] Rule 4(k)(2) thus permits a federal court to exercise personal jurisdiction over a defendant (1) for a claim arising under federal law, (2) where a summons has been served, (3) if the defendant is not subject to the jurisdiction of any single state court, (4) provided that the exercise of federal jurisdiction is consistent with the Constitution (and laws) of the United States.

FN9. The Advisory Committee's Notes for the 1993 amendments to Rule 4 provide the following background regarding paragraph (k)(2):
This paragraph corrects a gap in the enforcement of federal law. Under the former rule, a problem was presented when the defendant was a non-resident of the United States having contacts with the United States sufficient to justify the application of United States law..., but having insufficient contact with any single state to support jurisdiction under state long-arm legislation or meet the requirements of the Fourteenth Amendment limitation on state court territorial jurisdiction...In this respect, the revision responds to the suggestion of the Supreme Court made in *Omni Capital*... FED. R. CIV. P. 4(k) advisory committee's notes to 1993 amendments.
In the instant case, the claims arise under federal law (the ATCA), and the summons was served by publication pursuant to Rule 4(f). Whether the exercise of jurisdiction is consistent with the Constitution turns on whether a defendant has sufficient contacts with the nation as a whole to satisfy due process. *See* FED. R. CIV. P. 4(k) advisory committee's notes to 1993 amendments. We address that question in Part II.B.2. The remaining question here is whether bin Laden and al Qaeda are "subject to the jurisdiction of the courts of general jurisdiction of any state." FED. R. CIV. P. 4(k)(2).

Determining whether a defendant is subject to the jurisdiction of a court "of any state" presents no small problem. One could, of course, ponderously "traipse through the 50 states, asking whether each could entertain the suit." *ISI Int'l, Inc. v. Borden Ladner Gervais LLP*, 256 F.3d 548, 552 (7th Cir.2001). To avoid that daunting task, the Seventh Circuit has adopted the following burden-shifting framework:

A defendant who wants to preclude use of Rule 4(k)(2) has only to name some other state in which the suit could proceed. Naming a more appropriate state would amount to a consent to personal jurisdiction there (personal jurisdiction, unlike federal subject-matter jurisdiction, is waivable). If, however, the defendant contends that he cannot be sued in the forum state and refuses to identify any other where suit is possible, then the federal court is entitled to use Rule 4(k)(2).

Id. We find this resolution eminently sensible, and, like the Fifth Circuit, we adopt the Seventh Circuit's view that "so long as a defendant does not concede to jurisdiction in another state, a court may use 4(k)(2) to confer jurisdiction." *Adams v. Unione Mediterranea Di Sicurta*, 364 F.3d 646, 651 (5th Cir.2004).

Needless to say, defendants bin Laden and al Qaeda have not conceded to the jurisdiction of any state. Accordingly, we now move to the final issue under Rule 4(k)(2). [FN10]

FN10. Although the plaintiffs did not expressly rely on Rule 4(k)(2), we agree with the Seventh Circuit that "it is best to excuse the forfeiture." *ISI Int'l*, 256 F.3d at 551. "Federal courts are entitled to apply the right body of law, whether the parties name it or not." *Id.* While the plaintiffs did not name Rule 4(k)(2) specifically, they certainly identified the correct body of law, asserting "the availability of national contacts personal jurisdiction...under F.R. Civ. P. 4," and citing the section of a treatise discussing paragraph (k)(2). Appellants Br. at 21 (citing 4 WRIGHT & MILLER §1068.1); Pls.' Mot. for Recons. at 3 & n. 4 (Oct. 11, 2002) (same).

2

Whether the exercise of jurisdiction is "consistent with the Constitution" for purposes of Rule 4(k)(2) depends on whether a defendant has sufficient contacts with the United States as a whole to justify the exercise of personal jurisdiction under the Due Process Clause of the Fifth Amendment. *See* FED. R. CIV. P. 4(k) advisory committee's notes to 1993 amendments; see also *Adams*, 364 F.3d at 651; *ISI Int'l*, 256 F.3d at 551. The Clause "protects an individual's liberty interest in not being subject to the binding judgments of a forum with which he has established no meaningful 'contacts, ties, or relations,'" *Burger King*, 471 U.S. at 472, 105 S.Ct. 2174 (quoting *International Shoe Co. v. Washington*, 326 U.S. 310, 319, 66 S.Ct. 154, 90 L.Ed. 95 (1945)), and "requir[es] that individuals have 'fair warning that a particular activity may subject [them] to the jurisdiction of a foreign sovereign,'" *id.* (quoting *Shaffer v. Heitner*, 433 U.S. 186, 218, 97 S.Ct. 2569, 53 L.Ed.2d 683 (1977)) (second alteration in original). "Where a forum seeks to assert specific jurisdiction over an out-of-state defendant who has not consented to suit there, this 'fair warning' requirement is satisfied if the defendant has 'purposefully directed' his activities at residents of the forum," *id.* (quoting *Keeton v.*

Hustler Magazine, Inc., 465 U.S. 770, 774, 104 S.Ct. 1473, 79 L.Ed.2d 790 (1984)), "and the litigation results from alleged injuries that 'arise out of or relate to' those activities," *id.* (quoting *Helicopteros Nacionales de Colombia, S.A. v. Hall*, 466 U.S. 408, 414, 104 S.Ct. 1868, 80 L.Ed.2d 404 (1984)).

In reaching the conclusion that it lacked personal jurisdiction over bin Laden and al Qaeda, the district court focused on a list of specific, physical contacts that the plaintiffs alleged the defendants had made with the District of Columbia and its environs. Those contacts included: the publication of *fatwas* in a newspaper distributed in the United States; the shipment to Virginia of the power supply for a cell phone that bin Laden used in Afghanistan; the scheduling of a bin Laden interview in Afghanistan through an agent in Washington, D.C.; and the transmission of bin Laden's views to the District via interviews on CNN and ABC. *See* September 2002 Opinion at 28-29. Much of this evidence came from the indictment and closing argument in *United States v. Bin Laden*, No. 98-CR-1023 (S.D.N.Y.), as well as from government speeches, press releases, and other reports. "All of Plaintiffs' submissions to the Court have various evidentiary problems," the district court said. September 2002 Opinion at 14; see *id.* at 13-14 (concluding that several submissions constituted "inadmissible hearsay"). And those problems aside, the court thought the evidence did not demonstrate "that [bin Laden] and al Qaeda 'purposefully directed' [their] activities at the United States" and "that this litigation *results* from alleged injuries that arise out of or relate to those activities." *Id.* (quoting *Burger King*, 471 U.S. at 472, 105 S.Ct. 2174). [FN11]

FN11. The district court rejected the plaintiffs' subsequent offers of additional evidence in motions for reconsideration, in part because the proffered evidence, even if newly discovered, "would not change the Court's...ruling on personal jurisdiction." *Mwani v. United States*, No. 99-125, Mem. Op. at 4 (D.D.C. Sept. 30, 2003) (denying motion for reconsideration).

As we noted in Part II.A, the district court's emphasis on satisfying strict evidentiary standards at this stage of the litigation was incorrect. While understandable given the absence of Circuit precedent regarding Rule 4(k)(2), so, too, was its exclusive focus on contacts with the District of Columbia, rather than with the nation as a whole. *See supra* Part II.B.1. But the fundamental problem with the court's analysis was its focus on specific, *physical* contacts between the defendants and the forum. Although "the constitutional touchstone remains whether the defendant purposefully established 'minimum contacts' in the forum," *Burger King*, 471 at 474, 105 S.Ct. 2174 (quoting *International Shoe*, 326 U.S. at 316, 66 S.Ct. 154), the "foreseeability" of causing injury in the forum can establish such contacts where "the defendant's conduct and connection with the forum…are such that he should reasonably anticipate being haled into court there." *Id.* (quoting *World-Wide Volkswagen Corp. v. Woodson*, 444 U.S. 286, 295, 100 S.Ct. 559, 62 L.Ed.2d 490 (1980)). "Jurisdiction in these circumstances may not be avoided merely because the defendant did not *physically* enter the forum." *Id.* at 477, 105 S.Ct. 2174. Rather, "[s]o long as [an] actor's efforts are 'purposefully directed' toward residents of another [forum]," the Supreme Court has "consistently rejected the notion that an absence of physical contacts can defeat personal jurisdiction there." *Id.* at 476, 105 S.Ct. 2174 (quoting *Keeton*, 465 U.S. at 774, 104 S.Ct. 1473); see *GTE*, 199 F.3d at 1349 (noting that "jurisdiction may attach if the defendant's conduct is aimed at or has an effect in the forum state" (quoting *Panavision International, LP v. Toeppen*, 141 F.3d 1316, 1321 (9th Cir.1998))).

In this case, there is no doubt that the defendants "engaged in unabashedly malignant actions directed at [and] felt in this forum." *Id.* The plaintiffs' allegations and evidence were that bin Laden and al Qaeda orchestrated the bombing of the American embassy in Nairobi, not only to kill both American and Kenyan employees inside the building, but to cause pain and sow terror in the embassy's home country, the United States. Nor were the plaintiffs' allegations and evidence of contacts with the United States limited to the Nairobi bombing. The plaintiffs described an ongoing conspiracy to attack the United States, with overt acts occurring within this country's borders. Putting to one side the acts that took place after the embassy bombing (including the attacks on the World Trade Center and the Pentagon on September 11, 2001), the plaintiffs pointed to the 1993 World Trade Center bombing, as well as to the plot to bomb the United Nations, Federal Plaza, and the Lincoln and Holland Tunnels in New York. [FN12]

FN12. In addition to the allegations of their complaint and pleadings, the plaintiffs supported their contentions with, inter alia: a February 1998 *fatwa* issued by bin Laden and al Qaeda, calling upon Muslims to kill Americans, military and civilian, "in any country in which it is possible to do it," Pls.' Renewed Mot. for Entry of Default at 5; a similar August 1996 *fatwa*, see *id.* at 3; two television interviews, broadcast in the U.S. in 1997 and 1998, in which bin Laden exhorted his followers to "take the fighting to America,"

Third Supplemental Filing in Supp. of Pls.' Mot. for Entry of a Default at 2 (Oct. 10, 2001); the indictment and argument in a criminal case brought by the United States regarding the Nairobi attack and the simultaneous bombing of the American embassy in Tanzania, see *United States v. bin Laden*, 98-CR-1023 (S.D.N.Y); President Bush's address to Congress, attributing the September 11, 2001 attacks and the embassy bombings to the same group, *see* Second Supplemental Filing in Supp. of Pls.' Mot. for Entry of Default at Pls.' Ex. 4 (Sept. 27, 2001); and a British government report to the same effect, Third Supplemental Filing at 2. *The 9/11 Commission Report*, cited by the plaintiffs before this court, but issued after the district court's decisions in this case, provides substantial further support for the plaintiffs' allegations. *See* THE 9/11 COMMISSION REPORT: FINAL REPORT OF THE NATIONAL COMMISSION ON TERRORIST ATTACKS UPON THE UNITED STATES at 47-71 (2004).

The plaintiffs thus amply made a prima facie showing that bin Laden and al Qaeda " 'purposefully directed' [their] activities at residents" of the United States, *Burger King*, 471 U.S. at 472, 105 S.Ct. 2174 (quoting *Keeton*, 465 U.S. at 774, 104 S.Ct. 1473), and that this litigation results from injuries to the plaintiffs "that 'arise out of or relate to' those activities," *id.* (quoting *Helicopteros Nacionales*, 466 U.S. at 414, 104 S.Ct. 1868). Bin Laden and al Qaeda therefore had "fair warning" that their activities would "subject [them] to the jurisdiction" of the United States. *Id.* (quoting *Shaffer*, 433 U.S. at 218, 97 S.Ct. 2569).

The fact that injured Kenyans, not injured Americans, are the plaintiffs in this case does not deny the court personal jurisdiction over the defendants. See *Calder v. Jones*, 465 U.S. 783, 788, 104 S.Ct. 1482, 79 L.Ed.2d 804 (1984) ("The plaintiff's lack of 'contacts' [with the forum] will not defeat otherwise proper jurisdiction."); *Keeton*, 465 U.S. at 780, 104 S.Ct. 1473 ("[The] plaintiff's residence in the forum State is not a separate requirement, and lack of residence will not defeat jurisdiction established on the basis of the defendant's contacts."). [FN13] The defendants' decision to purposefully direct their terror at the United States, and the fact that the plaintiffs' injuries arose out of one of those terrorist activities, should suffice to cause the defendants to "reasonably anticipate being haled into" an American court. *Burger King*, 471 U.S. at 474, 105 S.Ct. 2174 (quoting *World-Wide Volkswagen*, 444 U.S. at 297, 100 S.Ct. 559). Of course, a plaintiff's citizenship may affect whether the court has subject matter jurisdiction or the plaintiff has a cause of action. Here, however, the plaintiffs have sued under the Alien Tort Claims Act, which the Supreme Court has held to supply both subject matter jurisdiction and a cause of action for a narrow set of claims brought by aliens and involving violation of the law of nations. See *Sosa v. Alvarez-Machain*, 542 U.S. 692, 124 S.Ct. 2739, 2754, 2761-62, 159 L.Ed.2d 718 (2004). The *Mwani* plaintiffs certainly have more than a colorable argument that their claims fall within that narrow set. [FN14]

FN13. *Cf. Keeton*, 465 U.S. at 776, 104 S.Ct. 1473 (holding that a state had a significant interest in redressing a libel action brought by nonresident plaintiffs because, inter alia, "[f]alse statements of fact harm both the subject of the falsehood *and* the readers of the statement," and a state "may rightly employ its libel laws to discourage the deception of its citizens").

FN14. In *Sosa*, the Court determined that the First Congress understood the ATCA to "recognize private causes of action for certain torts in violation of the law of nations," including "violation of safe conducts, infringement of the rights of ambassadors, and piracy." 124 S.Ct. at 2761. It concluded that "courts should require any claim based on the present-day law of nations to rest on a norm of international character accepted by the civilized world and defined with a specificity comparable to the features of [those] 18th-century paradigms." *Id.* at 2761-62. The plaintiffs' contention that bin Laden and al Qaeda attacked the American embassy intending, among other things, to kill American diplomatic personnel inside, would appear to fall well within those paradigms. See *id.* at 2756 (noting that the 18th-century paradigm included "assault against an ambassador").

It is true that even after "it has been decided that a defendant purposefully established minimum contacts within the forum...., these contacts may be considered in light of other factors to determine whether the assertion of personal jurisdiction would comport with 'fair play and substantial justice.' " *Burger King*, 471 U.S. at 476, 105 S.Ct. 2174 (quoting *International Shoe*, 326 U.S. at 320, 66 S.Ct. 154). But "where a defendant who purposefully has directed his activities at forum residents seeks to defeat jurisdiction, he must present a compelling case that the presence of some other considerations would render jurisdiction unreasonable." *Id.* at 477, 105 S.Ct. 2174. Here, the defendants purposefully directed their activities at forum residents, and the fact that the plaintiffs are Kenyans who were injured in the process is not a consideration that would render the assertion of American jurisdiction incompatible with substantial justice.

In sum, we conclude that there is "authorization for service of summons on the defendant[s]" and a "constitutionally sufficient relationship between the defendant[s] and the forum." *Omni Capital*, 484 U.S. at 104, 108 S.Ct. 404. As a consequence, the district court "may exercise personal jurisdiction over" them. *Id.*

III

We now turn to the plaintiffs' appeal from the dismissal of their claims against the remaining defendant, Afghanistan. The Foreign Sovereign Immunities Act "provides the sole basis for obtaining jurisdiction over a foreign state in the courts of this country." *Saudi Arabia v. Nelson*, 507 U.S. 349, 355, 113 S.Ct. 1471, 123 L.Ed.2d 47 (1993) (internal quotation marks omitted). Under the FSIA, a foreign state is immune from the jurisdiction of American courts unless the case falls within a statutory exception. 28 U.S.C. §1604; see *id.* §§1605-1607. If no exception applies, the district court lacks subject matter jurisdiction. *Id.* §1604. If an exception does apply, the district court has jurisdiction. *Id.* §1330(a); see *Kilburn v. Socialist People's Libyan Arab Jamahiriya*, 376 F.3d 1123, 1126 (D.C.Cir.2004); *World Wide Minerals, Ltd. v. Republic of Kazakhstan*, 296 F.3d 1154, 1161 (D.C.Cir.2002).

In the district court, the plaintiffs relied on two statutory exceptions-for implicit waiver, 28 U.S.C. §1605(a)(1), and for commercial activity, 28 U.S.C. §1605(a)(2). [FN15] The plaintiffs have abandoned the former on appeal and now rely solely on the latter, the third clause of which provides:

FN15. The plaintiffs concede that another exception, 28 U.S.C. §1605(a)(7), is inapplicable to this case. That provision "vitiates immunity in cases 'in which money damages are sought against a foreign state for personal injury or death that was caused' " by specified acts of terrorism " 'or the provision of material support or resources...for such an act if such act or provision of material support is engaged in by an official, employee, or agent of such foreign state while acting within the scope of his or her office, employment, or agency.' " *Price v. Socialist People's Libyan Arab Jamahiriya*, 294 F.3d 82, 88 (D.C.Cir.2002) (quoting 28 U.S.C. §1605(a)(7)); see *Cicippio-Puleo v. Islamic Republic of Iran*, 353 F.3d 1024, 1032 (D.C.Cir.2004). The provision does not apply, however, unless the defendant foreign state "has been specifically designated by the State Department as a 'state sponsor of terrorism.' " *Price*, 294 F.3d at 89 (quoting 28 U.S.C. §1605(a)(7)(A)). The plaintiffs acknowledge that the United States has never so designated Afghanistan, thus rendering §1605(a)(7) inapplicable here and depriving the district court of jurisdiction even to consider a claim against Afghanistan absent some other exception to sovereign immunity.

A foreign state shall not be immune from the jurisdiction of courts of the United States...in any case...in which the action is based...upon an act outside the territory of the United States in connection with a commercial activity of the foreign state elsewhere and that act causes a direct effect in the United States.

28 U.S.C. §1605(a)(2). The FSIA defines "commercial activity" as "either a regular course of commercial conduct or a particular commercial transaction or act," and states that "the commercial character of an activity shall be determined by reference to the nature of the course of conduct or particular transaction or act, rather than by reference to its purpose." *Id.* §1603(d).

It is the defendant's burden to prove that a plaintiff's allegations do not fall within the bounds of an FSIA exception. See *Kilburn*, 376 F.3d at 1131. " 'If the defendant challenges only the legal sufficiency of the plaintiff's jurisdictional allegations, then the district court should take the plaintiff's factual allegations as true and determine whether they bring the case within any of the exceptions to immunity invoked by the plaintiff.' " *Id.* at 1127 (quoting *Phoenix Consulting, Inc. v. Republic of Angola*, 216 F.3d 36, 40 (D.C.Cir.2000)). Although Afghanistan does not expressly concede the truth of the plaintiffs' factual allegations, it argues that even if taken as true, the allegations are insufficient to come within the commercial activity exception. This amounts to a challenge to the legal sufficiency of the allegations, and we must thus "decide *de novo* whether [the alleged jurisdictional] facts are sufficient to divest the foreign sovereign of its immunity." *Price v. Socialist People's Libyan Arab Jamahiriya*, 389 F.3d 192, 197 (D.C.Cir.2004).

The gravamen of the plaintiffs' claim to the commercial activity exception is well-described in their appellate brief:

Afghanistan had served as a place of refuge for international terrorists since the 1980's. The Taliban actively aided Bin Laden by assigning him guards for security, permitting him to build and maintain terrorist camps, and refusing to cooperate with efforts by the international community to extradite him. Bin Laden provided approximately $10-$20 million per year to the Taliban in return for safe haven.

Appellants Br. at 27 (citations and internal quotation marks omitted). But the plaintiffs' contention that "[t]his conduct constitutes commercial activity as defined by the FSIA and the case law interpreting it," *id.* at 34, cannot stand in the face of the Supreme Court's precedents, or those of this court.

In *Nelson*, the Supreme Court observed that the FSIA largely codifies the "restrictive" theory of foreign sovereign immunity, and that under that theory a state engages in commercial activity

where it exercises "only those powers that can also be exercised by private citizens," as distinct from those "powers peculiar to sovereigns." Put differently, a foreign state engages in commercial activity for purposes of the restrictive theory only where it acts "in the manner of a private player within" the market.

507 U.S. at 360 (quoting *Republic of Argentina v. Weltover, Inc.*, 504 U.S. 607, 614, 112 S.Ct. 2160, 119 L.Ed.2d 394 (1992)). Moreover, the Court emphasized that "whether a state acts 'in the manner of' a private party is a question of behavior and not motivation." *Id.* (quoting *Weltover*, 504 U.S. at 614, 112 S.Ct. 2160). As the Court elaborated:

[B]ecause the Act provides that the commercial character of an act is to be determined by reference to its "nature" rather than its "purpose," the question is not whether the foreign government is acting with a profit motive or instead with the aim of fulfilling uniquely sovereign objectives. Rather, the issue is whether the particular actions that the foreign state performs (whatever the motive behind them) are the *type* of actions by which a private party engages in "trade and traffic or commerce."

Id. at 360-61, 113 S.Ct. 1471 (quoting *Weltover*, 504 U.S. at 614, 112 S.Ct. 2160) (citations omitted). In accordance with this standard, the *Nelson* Court rejected an argument that Saudi Arabia's wrongful arrest, imprisonment, and torture of the plaintiff, assertedly used by the government to resolve a commercial dispute with the plaintiff, could qualify a claim for the commercial activity exception. As it explained:

Exercise of the powers of police and penal officers is not the sort of action by which private parties can engage in commerce. Such acts as legislation, or the expulsion of an alien, or a denial of justice, cannot be performed by an individual acting in his own name. They can be performed only by the state acting as such.

Id. at 362, 113 S.Ct. 1471 (internal quotation marks and alterations omitted).

This court has reached a similar conclusion in a different setting. In *Cicippio v. Islamic Republic of Iran*, we held that hostage-taking for profit did not fall within the commercial activity exception. *See* 30 F.3d 164, 168 (D.C.Cir.1994). This was so, we said, because the act giving rise to jurisdiction must itself take place in a commercial context. And kidnapping, we concluded,

cannot possibly be described as an act typically performed by participants in the market (unless one distorts the notion of a marketplace to include a hostage bazaar). That money was allegedly sought from relatives of the hostages could not make an ordinary kidnapping a commercial act any more than murder by itself would be treated as a commercial activity merely because the killer is paid.

Id.

Nelson and *Cicippio* foreclose the plaintiffs' argument that the transactions between the Taliban, Afghanistan's former rulers, and al Qaeda, a terrorist organization, qualify as commercial activity. The plaintiffs attempt to characterize Afghanistan's harboring of terrorist camps as the "paradigmatically mercantile" provision of land for money, Appellants Reply Br. at 4, but such reductive logic would transform the retaliatory torture in *Nelson* into "commercial dispute resolution," and the kidnapping in *Cicippio* into an "exchange of goods for cash." The key inquiry in determining whether particular conduct constitutes commercial activity is not to ask whether its purpose is to obtain money, but rather whether it is "the sort of action by which private parties can engage in commerce." *Nelson*, 507 U.S. at 362, 113 S.Ct. 1471. Granting refuge to terrorist training camps is a uniquely sovereign act; it is not the sort of benefit that a commercial landlord can bestow upon a commercial tenant. As the plaintiffs themselves describe, refuge involved both the "assigning [of] guards for security" and the "refus[al] to...extradite" bin Laden. Appellants Br. at 27. But the Court made clear in *Nelson* that this "[e]xercise of the powers of police" and of authority over "the expulsion of an alien" cannot "be performed by an individual acting in his own name. They can be performed only by the state acting as such." 507 U.S. at 362, 113 S.Ct. 1471 (internal quotation marks omitted).

Finally, we also reject the plaintiffs' contention that the district court abused its discretion by denying them jurisdic-

tional discovery against Afghanistan. Although the plaintiffs are correct that the "Federal Rules of Civil Procedure generally provide for liberal discovery to establish jurisdictional facts," *Goodman Holdings*, 26 F.3d at 1147, "[n]evertheless, the scope of discovery lies within the district court's discretion." *Id.* And when we "do not see what facts additional discovery could produce that would affect our jurisdictional analysis," we must "conclude the district court did not abuse its discretion in dismissing the action when it did." *Id.* That is the situation here, because even assuming that the Taliban engaged in all of the conduct alleged in the complaint, the commercial activity exception would not apply.

IV

We affirm the district court's dismissal of the plaintiffs' claims against Afghanistan for lack of subject matter jurisdiction under the Foreign Sovereign Immunities Act. We reverse the dismissal of their claims against bin Laden and al Qaeda, however, because the plaintiffs have satisfied their burden of showing that the district court can properly exercise personal jurisdiction over those defendants.

Notes:

1.   What is the motivation behind a suit against Osama Bin Laden, an underground terrorist that the United States government has been unable to locate in 6 years despite a worldwide search and the invasion of several countries?

2.   What is revolutionary about the jurisdictional analysis in this case? Is it true that terrorists expect to be haled into U.S. courts in the same manner as other foreign commercial defendants?

3.   Why did the plaintiffs invoke the "commercial exception" of the FSIA in suing Afghanistan?

4.   The distinction between the types of sovereign actions was succinctly described in *Republic of Argentina v. Weltover, Inc.*, 502 U.S. 607, 617 (1992), "When a foreign government acts, not as a regulator of a market, but in the manner of a private player within it, the foreign sovereign's actions are 'commercial' within the meaning of the FSIA."

5.   Does the "private player" vs. "regulator of markets" distinction hinder or help jurisdictional analysis in terrorism cases? Does this dichotomy break down in the context of multinational, ideological conspiracies (i.e. HAMAS, Hezbollah) intent on affecting the policies of a world power

and influencing the international community to achieve religious and political goals?

6.   If the defendants refuse to participate in jurisdictional discovery, how will the plaintiffs be able to prove their case?

7.   What practical problems do plaintiffs confront in establishing personal jurisdiction, even by the low prima facie standard?

8.   Why do plaintiffs routinely name in their complaints terrorists and organizations that cannot even be served?

9.   How does traditional due process analysis square with the court's acknowledgment that the defendants sought to "cause pain and sow terror in the embassy's home country, the United States"? What does this analysis suggest about the application of traditional principles of jurisprudence in the modern era? Has the law caught up to our technologically based era in which emails, satellites, faxes, the internet, inexpensive air travel and computerization are the norm?

6.2 Non-states

Biton v. Palestinian Authority, **310 F.Supp.2d 172 (D. D.C. 2004).**

COLLYER, District Judge.

Avigail Lewis Biton, individually and on behalf of her husband's estate and her children, and Rachel Asraf bring suit under the Antiterrorism Act of 1991 ("ATA"), 18 U.S.C. §2333, and various tort theories against the Palestinian Interim Self-Government Authority, also known as the Palestinian Authority or the Palestinian National Authority ("PA"); the Palestine Liberation Organization ("PLO"); Yasser Arafat, president of the PA and chairman of the PLO; two senior members of the Palestinian Preventive Security Service ("PPSS"); two members of the Palestinian Police Service ("PPS"); and 99 "John Does" for their alleged involvement in the bombing of a school bus in the Gaza Strip on November 20, 2000, that killed two passengers (including Gabriel Biton, husband to Ms. Biton and the father of her children) and wounded nine others (including Ms. Asraf). Pending before the Court is the defendants' motion to dismiss pursuant to Rules 12(b)(1), (b)(2), and (b)(6) of the Federal Rules of Civil Procedure. The defendants assert a lack of personal jurisdiction over the five named individual defendants and the PA; immunity as a sovereign state and a lack of subject matter jurisdiction under the ATA; a lack of subject matter jurisdiction for the Biton family's claims

under the ATA and state law; and non-justiciability. The defendants also remark that the conduct in question might be deemed an "act of war" not subject to the ATA, and that Palestinian resistance and self-defense against Israel do not constitute terrorism. The plaintiffs, not surprisingly, oppose dismissal on these grounds.

After a full consideration of the parties' briefs, the entire record, and applicable law, the Court finds that it lacks personal jurisdiction over the named individual defendants but that it may exercise jurisdiction over the PA and PLO. The named individual defendants therefore will be dismissed. The remainder of the motion to dismiss will be denied.

I. BACKGROUND

For purposes of ruling on the instant motion to dismiss, the underlying facts of this case may be simply stated: at approximately 7:30 a.m. on November 20, 2000, a roadside device exploded near a bus that was transporting elementary school children and their teachers from Kfar Darom, an Israeli settlement in the southern Gaza Strip, towards Gush Katif. [FN1] The plaintiffs contend that the defendants are responsible for this bombing and the resulting deaths and injuries. [FN2] At issue now is the jurisdiction of the Court to hear and decide this case. On this preliminary issue, the plaintiffs' respective causes of action and the parties' relationships to the United States are critical.

FN1. These facts are not in genuine dispute at this stage of the litigation, although the defendants point to a lack of evidence that U.S. citizens were the target of the bombing.
FN2. The roadside bombing of the school bus that took Mr. Biton's life and injured Ms. Asraf is believed by some to have been part of the "al-Aqsa Intifada," a series of violent demonstrations and clashes between Palestinians and Israeli Defense Forces that ensued following (now Israeli Prime Minister) Ariel Sharon's controversial visit to the Temple Mount/Haram al-Sharif in Jerusalem in September 2000. *See* Defs.' Mot. to Dismiss Exh. 1.
Plaintiff Avigail Lewis Biton is an American citizen, the widow of Gabriel Biton, and the mother of the Biton children. She sues in her individual capacity under the ATA, which established a federal cause of action for damages resulting from terrorist attacks in foreign countries. Specifically, that statute provides:

Any national of the United States injured in his or her person, property, or business by reason of an act of international terrorism, or his or her estate, survivors, or heirs, may sue therefor in any appropriate district court of the United States and shall recover threefold the damages he or she sustains and the cost of the suit, including attorney's fees. [FN3]

FN3. The ATA defines "international terrorism" as:
activities that-(A) involve violent acts or acts dangerous to human life that are a violation of the criminal laws of the United States or of any State, or that would be a criminal violation if committed within the jurisdiction of the United States or of any State; (B) appear to be intended-(i) to intimidate or coerce a civilian population; (ii) to influence the policy of a government by intimidation or coercion; or (iii) to affect the conduct of a government by mass destruction, assassination, or kidnapping; and (C) occur primarily outside the territorial jurisdiction of the United States, or transcend national boundaries in terms of the means by which they are accomplished, the persons they appear intended to intimidate or coerce, or the locale in which their perpetrators operate or seek asylum[.]
18 U.S.C. §2331(1).
18 U.S.C. §2333(a). Ms. Biton and her children sue for wrongful death, negligence, intentional and negligent infliction of emotional distress, and battery under federal common law. The amended complaint does not allege that any Biton family member, save for Ms. Biton, is or was an American citizen. Plaintiff Rachel Asraf is an American citizen who sues for herself under the ATA and for negligence, intentional and negligent infliction of emotional distress, battery, and assault.

The defendants are the PA, the PLO, and Yasser Arafat (collectively "the Palestinian leadership"); three senior Palestinian officials, Muhammed Dahlan, allegedly the commander in charge of the PPSS, Rashid Abu Shabak, allegedly the deputy commander of the PPSS, and Ghazi Jabali, allegedly the regional commander in the Gaza Strip of the PPS; Muhammed Eid Abdel Kadar Issa, allegedly a member of the PPS and an agent of the "Fatah" faction of the PLO, as well as the "Tanzim" terrorist unit; and John Does 1-99, who allegedly planned and carried out the bombing with the other defendants. None of the named individual defendants is alleged to have any presence, asset, or activity in the United States, except for President Arafat's occasional visits to the United Nations in New York City. The defendants assert that the PA also "is not present in the U.S." Defs.' Mot. to Dismiss at 7.

II. LEGAL STANDARDS

Under Rule 12(b)(1) of the Federal Rules of Civil Procedure, the plaintiffs bear the burden of proving by a preponderance of the evidence that the Court has subject matter jurisdiction to hear this case. *Jones v. Exec. Office of the President*, 167 F.Supp.2d 10, 13 (D.D.C.2001). In deciding such a motion, the Court must accept as true all of the factual allegations set forth in the amended complaint; however, such allegations " 'will bear closer scrutiny in resolving a 12(b)(1) motion' than in resolving a 12(b)(6) motion for failure to state a claim." *Grand Lodge of the Fraternal Order of Police v. Ashcroft*, 185 F.Supp.2d 9, 13-14 (D.D.C.2001) (quoting 5A CHARLES ALAN WRIGHT & ARTHUR R. MILLER, FEDERAL PRACTICE & PROCEDURE §1350). The Court may consider matters outside the pleadings. *Lipsman v. Sec'y of the Army*, 257 F.Supp.2d 3, 6 (D.D.C.2003).

To thwart dismissal under Rule 12(b)(2) of the Federal Rules of Civil Procedure, the plaintiffs must establish personal jurisdiction over each defendant. To this end, the Court may look outside the allegations of the amended complaint. *Helmer v. Doletskaya*, 290 F.Supp.2d 61, 65 (D.D.C.2003). "[T]he Court must accept Plaintiff[s'] claims as true in ruling on a Rule 12(b)(2) motion, unless they are directly contradicted by an affidavit..." *Novak-Canzeri v. Turki Bin Abdul Aziz Al Saud*, 864 F.Supp. 203, 206 (D.D.C.1994).

A motion to dismiss for failure to state a claim under Rule 12(b)(6) of the Federal Rules of Civil Procedure tests the legal sufficiency of the amended complaint. The Court must accept as true all of the plaintiffs' well-pled factual allegations and draw all reasonable inferences in favor of the plaintiff; however, the Court does not need to accept as true any of the plaintiffs' legal conclusions. *Alexis v. District of Columbia*, 44 F.Supp.2d 331, 336-37 (D.D.C.1999). "[An amended] complaint should not be dismissed for failure to state a claim unless it appears beyond doubt that the plaintiff[s] can prove no set of facts in support of [their] claim which would entitle [them] to relief." *Conley v. Gibson*, 355 U.S. 41, 45-46, 78 S.Ct. 99, 2 L.Ed.2d 80 (1957).

III. ANALYSIS

A. Personal Jurisdiction Over the Named Individual Defendants

The defendants begin their motion to dismiss by arguing that the Court may not exercise personal jurisdiction over the five named individual defendants, President Arafat and Messrs. Dahlan, Abu Shabak, Jabali, and Issa. As far as the record reveals, these defendants have no personal connection with the United States. Indeed, the plaintiffs acknowledge that "none of the individual defendants is a resident of the United States or has any commercial or other activities within the United States." Pls.' Opp. to Mot. to Dismiss at 49. The plaintiffs nonetheless assert that the named individual defendants have sufficient contacts with the United States for purposes of establishing personal jurisdiction, in conjunction with proper service of process, under Rule 4(k)(2) of the Federal Rules of Civil Procedure.

Rule 4(k)(2) states:

If the exercise of jurisdiction is consistent with the Constitution and laws of the United States, serving a summons or filing a waiver of service is also effective, with respect to claims arising under federal law, to establish personal jurisdiction over the person of any defendant who is not subject to the jurisdiction of the courts of general jurisdiction of any state.

FED. R. CIV. P. 4(k)(2). The Rule therefore "allows a district court to acquire jurisdiction over a foreign defendant which has insufficient contacts with any single state but has 'contacts with the United States as a whole...' " *In re Vitamins Antitrust Litig.*, 94 F.Supp.2d 26, 31 (D.D.C.2000) (citing Advisory Comm. Note to 1993 Amendment). In *United States v. Swiss American Bank, Ltd.*, 191 F.3d 30 (1st Cir.1999), the First Circuit discussed the parameters of this procedural device.

The rule's fabric contains three strands: (1) the plaintiff's claim must be one arising under federal law; (2) the putative defendant must be beyond the jurisdictional reach of any state court of general jurisdiction; and (3) the federal courts' exercise of personal jurisdiction over the defendant must not offend the Constitution or other federal law.

Id. at 38. In applying this tripartite test here, the question is whether the named individual defendants have sufficient contacts with the United States to satisfy the Due Process Clause of the Fifth Amendment to the U.S. Constitution. [FN4]

FN4. The plaintiffs state that they "have initiated service of process on the defendants pursuant to Fed.R.Civ.P. 4(f)(1) and 4(h)(2) and the provisions of the Hague Convention, and expect that it will be completed during the pendency of this motion." Pls.' Opp. to Mot. to Dismiss at 47.
The plaintiffs urge the Court to adopt "a due process analysis specifically fitted to the unique circumstances of civil actions against foreign terrorists and their sponsors" that has been applied by a fellow district judge of this Court,

as well as a district judge on the United States District Court for the Eastern District of New York. Pl.'s Opp. to Mot. to Dismiss at 49. In a case involving the Antiterrorism and Effective Death Penalty Act of 1996 ("AEDPA"), 28 U.S.C. §1605(a)(7)-which amended the Foreign Sovereign Immunities Act ("FSIA"), 28 U.S.C. §1602, to permit lawsuits against state sponsors of terrorism-Judge Royce C. Lamberth of this Court concluded that "a foreign state that causes the death of a United States national through an act of state-sponsored terrorism has the requisite 'minimum contacts' with the United States so as not to offend 'traditional notions of fair play and substantial justice.' " *Eisenfeld v. Islamic Republic of Iran*, 172 F.Supp.2d 1, 7 (D.D.C.2000) (quoting *International Shoe Co. v. Washington*, 326 U.S. 310, 326, 66 S.Ct. 154, 90 L.Ed. 95 (1945)); see also *Flatow v. Islamic Republic of Iran*, 999 F.Supp. 1, 22 (D.D.C.1998) (same). Judge Thomas C. Platt made a similar ruling in *Rein v. Socialist People's Libyan Arab Jamahiriya*, 995 F.Supp. 325 (E.D.N.Y.1998), *aff'd in part and appeal dismissed in part*, 162 F.3d 748 (2d Cir.1998), which also dealt with the 1996 amendment to the FSIA. Judge Platt stated that "the relevant inquiry with respect to the minimum contacts analysis is whether the effects of a foreign state's actions upon the United States are sufficient to provide 'fair warning' such that the foreign state may be subject to the jurisdiction of the courts of the United States." *Id.* at 330. In finding that Libya could stand trial for the 1988 bombing of Pan Am Flight 103 in Lockerbie, Scotland, Judge Platt held:

Any foreign state would know that the United States has substantial interests in protecting its flag carriers and its nationals from terrorist activities and should reasonably expect that if these interests were harmed, it would be subject to a variety of potential responses, including civil actions in United States courts.

Id.

There is some merit, in early 2004, to the plaintiffs' argument that no foreign terrorist today can fairly assert a lack of "fair warning" that it could be "haled into court" in the United States, *Burger King Corp. v. Rudzewicz*, 471 U.S. 462, 472, 105 S.Ct. 2174, 85 L.Ed.2d 528 (1985); *World-Wide Volkswagen Corp. v. Woodson*, 444 U.S. 286, 297, 100 S.Ct. 559, 62 L.Ed.2d 490 (1980), particularly given the exhaustive antiterrorism policies and other measures implemented by the United States Government following the terrorist attacks on September 11, 2001. However, the differences between the ATA and the FSIA are too great for their common focus on antiterrorism to allow cross-pollination on this issue. The Court consequently declines to extend the due process analysis set forth in *Eisenfeld/Flatow* and *Rein* to ATA claims filed against individual (non-state) defendants. [FN5]

FN5. This Court is not alone in employing a traditional due process analysis to determine whether it may exercise personal jurisdiction over individual defendants in a lawsuit brought under the ATA. In *Ungar v. Palestinian Authority*, 153 F.Supp.2d 76 (D.R.I.2001), a district judge on the United States District Court for the District of Rhode Island considered this same issue-with similar arguments in support and in opposition-and dismissed ATA claims against individual officers of various PA/PLO law enforcement and intelligence agencies.

There is one very simple reason why a district court may exercise personal jurisdiction over a foreign state defendant under the FSIA but not a similarly-situated individual defendant under the ATA. Section 1330(b) of the FSIA provides that "personal jurisdiction over a foreign state shall exist as to every claim for relief over which the district courts have jurisdiction...where service has been made under section 1608 of this title." 28 U.S.C. §1330(b); see also *Practical Concepts, Inc. v. Republic of Bolivia*, 811 F.2d 1543, 1548 n. 11 (D.C.Cir.1987) ("[U]nder the FSIA, 'subject matter jurisdiction plus service of process equals personal jurisdiction.'") (quoting *Texas Trading & Milling Corp. v. Fed. Republic of Nigeria*, 647 F.2d 300, 308 (2d Cir.1981)). The ATA, in contrast, does not contain such an explicit grant of personal jurisdiction. See *Ungar v. Palestinian Auth.*, 153 F.Supp.2d 76, 95 (D.R.I.2001) (noting that §2334(a) provides for venue and nationwide service of process). Of course, a statute cannot confer personal jurisdiction when the U.S. Constitution forbids it. *Gilson v. Republic of Ireland*, 682 F.2d 1022, 1028 (D.C.Cir.1982). The D.C. Circuit held in *Price v. Socialist People's Libyan Arab Jamahiriya* that "foreign states are not 'persons' protected by the Fifth Amendment[.]" 294 F.3d 82, 96 (D.C.Cir.2002). Therefore, so long as subject matter jurisdiction exists under the FSIA and service was proper, there is no "need to examine whether [a foreign state defendant] has the minimum contacts that would otherwise be a prerequisite for personal jurisdiction under the Due Process Clause of the Fifth Amendment." *I.T. Consultants, Inc. v. Islamic Republic of Pakistan*, 351 F.3d 1184, 1191 (D.C.Cir.2003).

Unless the named individual defendants have minimum contacts with the United States that square with the Due Process Clause, which they admittedly do not, the Court may not exercise personal jurisdiction over them under Rule 4(k)(2)

of the Federal Rules of Civil Procedure. Accordingly, the named individual defendants will be dismissed from this case.

B. Personal Jurisdiction Over the Palestinian Authority

The defendants also move to dismiss the amended complaint against the PA for lack of personal jurisdiction. [FN6] Unlike the named individual defendants, the PA appears to have sufficient contacts with the United States to satisfy due process concerns. See *Ungar*, 153 F.Supp.2d at 88 (holding that the plaintiffs in that case had "made a prima facie showing that defendants PA and PLO have minimum contacts with the United States as a whole."). The plaintiffs assert that the PA maintains offices and agents, including Hasan Abdel Rahman, in the United States. [FN7] In support, they submit an article from the National News stating that Mr. Abdel Rahman "has been the Washington representative of the Palestine Liberation Organization and Palestinian National Authority since 1994"; a transcript from an online discussion forum hosted by the Washington Post introducing Mr. Abdel Rahman as "chief representative of the Palestinian National Authority and Palestine Liberation Organization, [*sic*] in the United States"; and a biography purportedly received from the PA/PLO describing Mr. Abdel Rahman as "Chief Representative of the P.L.O. and the P.N.A. in the United States [.]" Pls.' Opp. to Mot. to Dismiss Exhs. 6, 7, 4. The plaintiffs further argue that the PA conducts extensive activities in the United States. For example, the PA has employed the lobbying firm of Bannerman & Associates to provide advocacy training and assistance with developing a public relations campaign in the United States. See *id.* Exhs. 5, 9, 10. The PA (and PLO) also entered into a commercial telecommunications contract with International Technologies Integration, Inc. ("ITI"), a Virginia corporation. See *Int'l Techs. Integration, Inc. v. Palestine Liberation Org.*, 66 F.Supp.2d 3 (D.D.C.1999). A lawsuit brought by ITI to confirm an arbitration award "revealed that the PA and the PLO maintain several bank accounts in New York with deposits totaling approximately $18 million [ ]." *Ungar*, 153 F.Supp.2d at 88; see also Pls.' Opp. to Mot. to Dismiss Exh. 11.

FN6. The defendants do not challenge the Court's exercise of personal jurisdiction over the PLO.

FN7. The plaintiffs filed a "return of service" affidavit indicating that Mr. Abdel Rahman was served on March 14, 2001, in Washington, D.C. With no evidence or argument to the contrary-the defendants merely state that "[s]ervice on the PA which is not present in the United States is challenged" without explaining why, Defs.' Mot. to Dismiss at

7-the Court finds that Mr. Abdel Rahman is a "managing or general agent" of the PA for purposes of Rule 4(h) of the Federal Rules of Civil Procedure. *See infra* pp. 179-80.

For these reasons, the Court concludes that it may exercise personal jurisdiction over the PA. The plaintiffs have adequately shown that the PA has minimum contacts with the United States under the Fifth Amendment and, in any event, that Mr. Abdel Rahman was personally served with process in Washington, D.C. The motion to dismiss the PA for lack of personal jurisdiction therefore will be denied.

C. Palestinian Statehood

Citing §2337(2) of the ATA and §1604 of the FSIA, the defendants move to dismiss this action on the grounds that Palestine is a sovereign entity. Section 2337(2) prohibits the maintenance of a civil ATA lawsuit against "a foreign state, an agency of a foreign state, or an officer or employee of a foreign state or an agency thereof acting within his or her official capacity or under color of legal authority." 18 U.S.C. §23r37(2). The FSIA directs that, with exceptions, "a foreign state shall be immune from the jurisdiction of the courts of the United States and of the States..." 28 U.S.C. §1604; see also *Argentine Republic v. Amerada Hess Shipping Corp.*, 488 U.S. 428, 443, 109 S.Ct. 683, 102 L.Ed.2d 818 (1989) ("[T]he FSIA provides the sole basis for obtaining jurisdiction over a foreign state in the courts of this country[.]").

The defendants contend that Palestine is a "foreign state" under the definition set forth in the Restatement (Third) of the Foreign Relations Law of the United States ("Restatement"). [FN8] Section 201 of the Restatement provides: "Under international law, a state is an entity that has a defined territory and a permanent population, under the control of its own government, and that engages in, or has the capacity to engage in, formal relations with other such entities." Despite the obvious magnitude and controversial nature of this issue, the defendants do not offer or cite any evidence in support of their bid for recognition of Palestinian statehood. *See* Pls.' Opp. to Mot. to Dismiss at 17-18. They simply argue:

FN8. The Second Circuit employs the Restatement's definition of the term "state" when interpreting the FSIA. See *Klinghoffer v. S.N.C. Achille Lauro*, 937 F.2d 44, 47 (2d Cir.1991) (holding that the PLO is not a "state" with immunity).

The State of Palestine has a defined territory in the West Bank, and the Gaza Strip and East Jerusalem, a permanent population numbering in the millions under the control of

its own government and engages in and has the capacity to engage in foreign relations with other states.

Palestine issued a declaration of its independence on November 15, 1988 that has at all times thereafter been extant. November 15 is annually celebrated by Palestinians throughout the state and world as independence day.

Statehood is not dependent on recognition.

The mid-east peace process carried forward by the Oslo Accord and other diplomatic measures and means envisions full recognition of Palestinian statehood...The recently expressed willingness of the United States to recognize Palestinian statehood confirms that the definition's criteria are satisfied. The reasons recently given by President Bush and other U.S. Executive Branch officers for delay in expressing recognition signify no doubt that Palestine meets the definitional criteria for statehood, but rather seek to induce adherence to U.S. foreign policies unrelated to the criteria.

Defs.' Mot. to Dismiss at 9-10.

The long-running conflict between the Israelis and the Palestinians has its very origins in the question of statehood between them. The current record does not permit the Court to overlook this reality or to declare that Palestine is now a sovereign state among nations. As a result, the Court must conclude that neither §2337(2) of the ATA nor §1604 of the FSIA bars this lawsuit. See *Tel-Oren v. Libyan Arab Republic*, 726 F.2d 774, 804 (D.C.Cir.1984) (Bork, C.J., concurring) (expressing the view that neither the PLO, the Palestine Information Office, nor the National Association of Arab Americans "seem[s] to be a state under international law"); *Knox v. Palestine Liberation Org.*, No. 03-4466, 306 F.Supp.2d 424, ___, 2004 WL 385024, *5, 2004 U.S. Dist. LEXIS 3128, at *16 (S.D.N.Y. Mar. 2, 2004) (holding that "there does not exist a state of Palestine which meets the legal criteria for statehood...").

D. Stating a Claim under the ATA and Supplemental Jurisdiction

The defendants assert that Avigail Lewis Biton "has no claim under Sec. 2333(a)...because she was not on the bus and was not injured in her 'person, property or business by an act of international terrorism.'" [FN9] Defs.' Mot. to Dismiss at 14. The plaintiffs respond that Ms. Biton's injury is the death of Gabriel Biton, her spouse. This allegedly has caused her to suffer emotional distress, a loss of consortium, and a loss of solatium.

FN9. As the plaintiffs' note, §2333(a) actually states that "[a]ny national of the United States injured in his or her person, property, or business *by reason of* an act of international terrorism, *or his or her estate, survivors, or heirs*, may sue therefor..." 18 U.S.C. §2333(a) (emphasis added).
It is clear that Ms. Biton cannot recover under the ATA as a representative of Mr. Biton's estate or as his survivor, because he was not a U.S. national. If Ms. Biton sues as the principal victim herself, however, she may be able to state a claim if she can allege a cognizable injury that arose by reason of an act of international terrorism. 18 U.S.C. §2333(a). The amended complaint avers that Ms. Biton is "an American citizen" and that her husband's death resulted from "a bombing attack on an Israeli civilian vehicle traveling in the Gaza Strip." [FN10] 2nd Am. Compl. ¶¶ 4, 22. Accordingly, the pertinent issues here are (1) whether emotional distress, a loss of consortium, and a loss of solatium constitute injuries in Ms. Biton's "person, property, or business" and, if so, (2) whether the bombing reasonably could be considered the "cause" of her injuries. 18 U.S.C. §2333(a).

FN10. The Court accepts these facts as true when deciding this Rule 12(b)(6) motion.
The Court concludes that Ms. Biton has properly alleged an "injur[y] in...her person" for purposes of the ATA. *Id.* The statute does not specifically require that a plaintiff suffer *physical* harm prior to filing suit. Moreover, the term "personal injury" means "[a]ny invasion of a personal right, including mental suffering and false imprisonment." [FN11] BLACK'S LAW DICTIONARY (7th ed.1999). Ms. Biton's alleged injuries fall within this widely-accepted definition. The forced loss of "material services[,]...affection, companionship, sexual relations, and the customary amenities of married life" is ordinarily deleterious. *Curry v. Giant Food Co. of the District of Columbia*, 522 A.2d 1283, 1294 (D.C.1987) (defining consortium). Similarly, "mental anguish, emotional pain and suffering, [and] loss of society, companionship, comfort, protection, marital care, attention, advice or counsel" are harmful. *Brooks v. Bienkowski*, 150 Md.App. 87, 818 A.2d 1198, 1200 (2003) (defining solatium). These injuries are cognizable under the plain language, as well as a common-sense interpretation, of the ATA. Consider the following hypothetical scenario: during a terrorist attack in a foreign country, the perpetrators throw a grenade at a car that is owned by a U.S. national and being driven by her (foreign) husband. The car explodes and the driver is killed. It seems unlikely that Congress would have consid-

ered damage to a car to constitute an "injury" for purposes of the ATA but not emotional trauma and a loss of companionship from the death of a spouse occurring in the same attack. [FN12] Which would you rather lose, a car or a spouse?

FN11. The ATA "contains all of the elements of a traditional tort...and we must therefore look to tort law and the legislative history to determine [its scope]." *Boim v. Quranic Literary Inst.*, 291 F.3d 1000, 1010 (7th Cir.2002).
FN12. Under the defendants' interpretation of §2333(a), "Mrs. Biton could sue for the value of the cash in her husband['s] pockets that was incinerated by the bombing, but not for the harm caused to her by the actual death of her husband." Pls.' Opp. to Mot. to Dismiss at 64 n.54.

Ms. Biton also has properly alleged that the bus bombing was the legal cause of her injuries. The Seventh Circuit has interpreted the clause "by reason of" to require a showing of proximate cause. *Boim v. Quranic Literacy Inst.*, 291 F.3d 1000, 1011-12 (7th Cir.2002). "Foreseeability is the cornerstone of proximate cause, and in tort law, a defendant will be held liable only for those injuries that might have reasonably been anticipated as a natural consequence of the defendant's actions." *Id.* at 1012. In most instances, "the existence of proximate cause is a question of fact for the jury." *District of Columbia v. Freeman*, 477 A.2d 713, 716 (D.C.1984). Based on the allegations of the amended complaint, a reasonable jury could find that Ms. Biton's (non-physical) injuries were the foreseeable and natural result of the bombing that killed her husband.

Therefore, the Court finds that Ms. Biton, suing in her individual capacity, has properly stated a claim against the defendants under the ATA.

The defendants next assert that the Court lacks subject matter jurisdiction to hear the Biton family's tort claims. The Bitons predicate jurisdiction of these claims on "the rules of supplemental jurisdiction." 2nd Am. Compl. ¶ 2. The defendants contend that "[t]he Biton plaintiffs have no colorable claim whatsoever under sec. 2333(a) or any other provision of law within this Court's original jurisdiction that could serve as the basis for this Court's exercise of supplemental jurisdiction over the *Biton* pendent claims and the *Biton* children as pendent parties." Defs.' Mot. to Dismiss at 14. Given the defendants' incorrect assumption that none of the plaintiffs has a "colorable claim" under the ATA, *see supra* pp. 13-15, this argument fails.

Section 1367(a) of Title 28 of the United States Code extends to federal district courts supplemental jurisdiction over "claims that are so related to claims in the action within… original jurisdiction that they form part of the same case or controversy under Article III of the United States Constitution. Such supplemental jurisdiction shall include claims that involve the joinder or intervention of additional parties." 28 U.S.C. §1367(a). This provision embodies "the practice of 'pendent party' jurisdiction, allowing the joinder of a party even though there is no independent federal question jurisdiction over that party's claims." *Burnett v. Al Baraka Inv. & Dev. Corp.*, 274 F.Supp.2d 86, 98 (D.D.C.2003). In this case, Ms. Biton has advanced a federal cause of action under the ATA over which this Court has original jurisdiction. All of the plaintiffs' claims "derive from a common nucleus of operative fact"- *i.e.*, the bus bombing in the Gaza Strip. *United Mine Workers of Am. v. Gibbs*, 383 U.S. 715, 725, 86 S.Ct. 1130, 16 L.Ed.2d 218 (1966). The Court chooses to exercise its discretion to hear these related claims in the interests of "economy, convenience, fairness, and comity [.]" *Carnegie-Mellon Univ. v. Cohill*, 484 U.S. 343, 357, 108 S.Ct. 614, 98 L.Ed.2d 720 (1988). Thus, this portion of the motion to dismiss will be denied.

* * *

IV. CONCLUSION

The motion to dismiss will be granted in part and denied in part. The Court concludes that it may exercise personal jurisdiction over the PA and the PLO; that Palestine is not a "state" for purposes of the FSIA based on the current record; that Avigail Lewis Biton has properly stated a claim under the ATA; that supplemental jurisdiction exists over the Biton family's tort claims; and that this case does not present a non-justiciable political question. The Court also finds that it may not exercise personal jurisdiction over the named individual defendants; the amended complaint allegations against these defendants will be dismissed. Finally, the Court takes under advisement the defendants' act of war/ self-defense arguments. A separate order accompanies this memorandum opinion.

Notes:

1.   Compare the ruling in *Mwani* and this opinion with respect to personal jurisdiction over individuals and organizations that in all likelihood never set foot in the United States. What accounts for the different rulings?

2.   Why did Judge Garland find:

> The plaintiffs thus amply made a prima facie showing that bin Laden and al Qaeda "'purposefully directed' [their] activities at residents" of the United States, and that this litigation results from injuries to the plaintiffs "that 'arise out of or relate to' those activities. Bin Laden and al Qaeda therefore had "fair warning" that their activities would "subject [them] to the jurisdiction" of the United States.

While Judge Collyer found,

> This Court is not alone in employing a traditional due process analysis to determine whether it may exercise personal jurisdiction over individual defendants in a lawsuit brought under the ATA. In *Ungar v. Palestinian Authority*, 153 F.Supp.2d 76 (D.R.I. 2001), a district judge on the United States District Court for the District of Rhode Island considered this same issue-with similar arguments in support and in opposition-and dismissed ATA claims against individual officers of various PA/ PLO law enforcement and intelligence agencies.

***Ungar v. Palestinian Authority*, 153 F.Supp.2d 76 (D. R.I. 2001).**

LAGUEUX, District Judge.

Plaintiffs filed the instant action pursuant to 18 U.S.C. §2333 *et seq.* after Yaron Ungar, a United States citizen, and his wife, Efrat Ungar, were killed in Israel by the terrorist group Hamas. Enacted as part of the Antiterrorism Act of 1991 ("ATA"), 18 U.S.C. §2333 provides a cause of action for American nationals injured in their person, property, or business by reason of an act of international terrorism. The complaint names the Palestinian Authority ("PA"), the Palestine Liberation Organization ("PLO"), Yasser Arafat ("Arafat"), and the officers of various law enforcement and intelligence agencies operating within the territories controlled by the PA and the PLO as defendants (hereinafter "the PA defendants"), as well as Hamas and the individual Hamas members responsible for the Ungars' deaths.

This matter is before the Court on the PA defendants' motion to dismiss the complaint for lack of subject matter jurisdiction, lack of personal jurisdiction, improper venue, insufficient service of process, failure to state a claim upon which relief can be granted, and inconvenience of the forum. However, the most significant issue this Court must address is whether the Court's exercise of personal jurisdiction over the PA defendants is consistent with the constitutional requirements of minimum contacts and due process. For the reasons that follow, this Court concludes that it may exercise personal jurisdiction over defendant PA and defendant PLO, but cannot exercise jurisdiction over the remaining PA defendants. Because the Court concludes that it has jurisdiction over defendants PA and PLO, it also addresses the additional 12(b) motions filed by the PA defendants.

I. Background

On June 9, 1996, United States citizen Yaron Ungar, his wife Efrat Ungar, and their nine month old son, plaintiff Yishai Ungar, were traveling home from a wedding. Near Beit Shemesh, Israel, a vehicle driven by defendant Raed Fakhri Abu Hamdiya ("Abu Hamdiya") approached the Ungars' vehicle. Defendants Abdel Rahman Ismail Abdel Rahman Ghanimat ("Rahman Ghanimat") and Jamal Abdel Fatah Tzabich Al Hor ("Hor"), opened fire on the Ungars' car with two Kalashnikov machine guns. Yaron and Efrat Ungar were killed in the shooting attack. Yishai Ungar survived the attack unscathed. Plaintiff Dvir Ungar, the Ungars' older son, was not in the car at the time of the shooting.

Abu Hamdiya, Rahman Ghanimat, and Hor were arrested following the shooting attack. A fourth man, defendant Iman Mahmud Hassan Fuad Kafishe ("Kafishe") was also arrested in connection with the shooting. In addition, a warrant was issued for the arrest of Ibrahim Ghanimat on charges relating to the murders of Yaron and Efrat Ungar. Ibrahim Ghanimat remains at large and is believed to be residing within territory controlled by defendant PA.

All five men involved in the shooting are members of Hamas Islamic Resistance Movement, also known as "Harakat Al-Muqawama Al-Islamiyya" ("Hamas"). A terrorist group dedicated to murdering Israeli and Jewish individuals through bombings, shootings, and other violent acts, Hamas is based in and operates from territories controlled by defendants PA, PLO, and Yasser Arafat. Terrorist attacks are staged by small groups of Hamas members organized as a cell for the purpose of carrying out terrorist activities. Abu Hamdiya, Rahman Ghanimat, Hor, Kafishe, and Ibrahim Ghanimat comprised the terrorist cell that murdered the Ungars.

On May 3, 1998, Abu Hamdiya was convicted by an Israeli court of membership in Hamas and of abetting the shooting murders of Yaron Ungar and Efrat Ungar. On October 21, 1998, an Israeli court convicted Rahman Ghanimat and Hor of membership in defendant Hamas and of the murders of Yaron Ungar and Efrat Ungar. On November 3, 1998, Kafishe was convicted by an Israeli court of membership in Hamas and of being an accessory to the murders of Yaron and Efrat Ungar.

Thereafter, on October 25, 1999, an Israeli court appointed attorney David Strachman ("Strachman") as administrator of the Estates of Yaron and Efrat Ungar. Strachman was appointed as the administrator of the Ungars' estates for the express purpose of administering and realizing assets, rights, and causes of action that could be pursued on behalf of the Ungars' estates within the United States.

On March 13, 2000, plaintiffs filed an action pursuant to 18 U.S.C. §2333 *et seq.* and related torts in the United States District Court for the District of Rhode Island. The following parties are listed as plaintiffs: the Estate of Yaron Ungar and the Estate of Efrat Ungar, represented by Strachman; Dvir Ungar and Yishai Ungar, the minor children and heirs-at-law of Yaron Ungar and Efrat Ungar; Professor Meyer Ungar and Judith Ungar, the parents of Yaron Ungar and the legal guardians of plaintiffs Dvir and Yishai Ungar; Rabbi Uri Dasberg and Judith Dasberg, the parents of Efrat Ungar and the legal guardians of plaintiffs Dvir and Yishai Ungar; and Amichai Ungar, Dafna Ungar, and Michal Cohen, the siblings of Yaron Ungar. Plaintiffs Professor Meyer Ungar and Judith Ungar bring this action both as the legal guardians of plaintiffs Dvir and Yishai Ungar and in their individual capacities. Similarly, plaintiffs Rabbi Uri Dasberg and Judith Dasberg bring this action both as the legal guardians of plaintiffs Dvir and Yishai Ungar and in their individual capacities.

The defendants named in this lawsuit can be divided into two groups. The first group is comprised of the PA defendants. Included in this group are: the PA; the PLO; Arafat, President of defendant PA and Chairman of defendant PLO; Jibril Rajoub ("Rajoub") and Muhammed Dahlan ("Dahlan"), who commanded and controlled the Palestinian Preventive Security Services; Amin Al-Hindi ("Al-Hindi") and Tawfik Tirawi ("Tirawi"), who commanded and controlled the Palestinian General Intelligence Services; and Razi Jabali ("Jabali"), who commanded and controlled the Palestinian Police. The Palestinian Preventive Security Services, Palestinian General Intelligence Services, and Palestinian Police are all official law enforcement agencies of defendant PA responsible for law enforcement, maintaining public order and the prevention of violence and terrorism in the territories controlled by the PA and PLO.

The second group of defendants is comprised of the Hamas defendants ("Hamas defendants"). This group includes Hamas, as well as the individual operatives of Hamas responsible for the shooting attack that killed Yaron and

Efrat Ungar: Rahman Ghanimat, Hor, Abu Hamdiya, Kafishe, and Ibrahim Ghanimat.

Plaintiffs' complaint states five causes of action. With the exception of Count III, all claims are brought on behalf of all plaintiffs as against all defendants. Count I alleges that defendants engaged in acts of international terrorism as defined by 18 U.S.C. §§2331 and 2333. Count II of the complaint alleges death by wrongful act. Count III of the complaint, which is brought against the PA defendants only, is for negligence. Count IV alleges intentional infliction of emotional distress, and Count V alleges negligent infliction of emotional distress.

The factual basis for each claim is the same. Essentially, plaintiffs' allege that the PA defendants failed to maintain public order and security in the territories under their control, and instead "provided defendant Hamas and its members with safe haven, a base of operations, shelter, financial support and other material support and resources." Pls.' Compl. ¶ 41. Plaintiffs further allege that the Hamas defendants planned and executed acts of violence against civilians in Israel, Gaza and the West Bank, including the murders of Yaron and Efrat Ungar. Plaintiffs contend that defendants' actions constitute acts of international terrorism because their actions: (1) were dangerous to human life and are a violation of the criminal laws of the United States, [FN1] (2) appear to be intended to intimidate or coerce a civilian population, or to influence the policy of a government by means of intimidation or coercion, and (3) occurred outside the territorial jurisdiction of the United States.

FN1. Specifically, plaintiffs allege that the actions of the Hamas defendants constitute violations of 18 U.S.C. §2332 (homicide of a United States national outside of the United States), and that the actions of the PA defendants constitute, *inter alia*, violations of 18 U.S.C. §3 (Accessory After the Fact) and of 18 U.S.C. §2339A (Providing Material Support to Terrorists).

On June 15, 2000, the PA defendants filed a motion pursuant to Fed.R.Civ.P. 12(b) to dismiss the complaint against them on the grounds of lack of jurisdiction over the subject matter, lack of jurisdiction over the person, insufficiency of service of process, improper venue, failure to state a claim upon which relief can be granted, and inconvenience of the forum. Plaintiffs objected to the PA defendants' motion, and a hearing was scheduled on the matter.

Thereafter, this Court held a hearing on the PA defendants' motion to dismiss. [FN2] At the conclusion of the hearing, the Court took the matter under advisement and granted the parties additional time to prepare supplemen-

tal briefs on the issue of personal jurisdiction. Those briefs have been received and considered, and the matter is now in order for decision.

FN2. Prior to the hearing on the PA defendants' motion to dismiss, plaintiffs filed a motion for entry of default as to the Hamas defendants. A default was entered as to the Hamas defendants on September 7, 2000. It is questionable whether this Court has personal jurisdiction over any of the Hamas defendants, but that issue is not presently before the Court.

II. Discussion

The PA defendants' motion to dismiss the complaint is made on several grounds. First, the PA defendants challenge the Court's authority to hear this lawsuit on three bases: lack of subject matter jurisdiction, lack of personal jurisdiction over the PA defendants, and insufficient service of process. Second, the PA defendants assert that the District of Rhode Island is an improper venue for this lawsuit, or in the alternative, move to dismiss based on inconvenience of the forum. Finally, the PA defendants attack the sufficiency of the pleadings, arguing that plaintiffs have failed to state a claim upon which relief can be granted. This Court will deal with each of the PA defendants' arguments in turn.

A. Subject Matter Jurisdiction

The PA defendants request dismissal of the complaint under 12(b)(1) for lack of jurisdiction over the subject matter. Because federal courts are courts of limited jurisdiction, plaintiffs bear the burden of proving the existence of subject matter jurisdiction. *Viqueira v. First Bank*, 140 F.3d 12, 16 (1st Cir.1998). In determining whether subject matter jurisdiction exists, "the district court must construe the complaint liberally, treating all well-pleaded facts as true and indulging all reasonable inferences in favor of the plaintiff." *Aversa v. United States*, 99 F.3d 1200, 1210 (1st Cir.1996). If any evidence has been submitted in the case, such as depositions or exhibits, the court may consider the motion to dismiss in light of that evidence. *Id.* at 1210.

Count I of plaintiffs' complaint pleads a federal cause of action pursuant to 18 U.S.C. §2333. 18 U.S.C. §2333 provides that:

[a]ny national of the United States injured in his or her person, property, or business by reason of an act of international terrorism, or his or her estate, survivors, or heirs, may sue therefor in any appropriate district court of the United States

and shall recover threefold the damages he or she sustains and the cost of the suit, including attorney's fees.

18 U.S.C. §2333(a). In addition, 18 U.S.C. §2338 provides that "[t]he district courts of the United States shall have exclusive jurisdiction over an action brought under this chapter." 18 U.S.C. §2338 (1994). Therefore, this Court has subject matter jurisdiction over Count I of plaintiffs' complaint if plaintiffs have alleged sufficient facts to invoke §2333.

Plaintiffs' complaint alleges that Yaron Ungar is a United States citizen. Pls.' Compl. ¶ 1. It further alleges that Yaron Ungar was murdered by an act of international terrorism as defined by 18 U.S.C. §2331. *Id.* at ¶¶ 1, 21-23. The Estate of Yaron Ungar is represented by a court-appointed administrator, plaintiff Strachman, a resident and domiciliary of the State of Rhode Island. *Id.* at ¶ 4. Although the complaint alleges additional facts demonstrating the existence of subject matter jurisdiction as to Count I of the complaint, the Court need not go any further. Viewing the complaint in the light most favorable to plaintiffs, they have alleged sufficient facts to demonstrate that this Court has subject matter jurisdiction over Count I of the complaint.

The remaining counts in plaintiffs' complaint are state law claims. Accordingly, this Court can only have subject matter jurisdiction over the state law claims under the doctrine of supplemental jurisdiction. 28 U.S.C. §1367 provides that "in any civil action of which the district courts have original jurisdiction, the district courts shall have supplemental jurisdiction over all other claims that are so related to claims in the action…that they form part of the same case or controversy." 28 U.S.C. §1367 (1994). Thus, this Court has the power to hear both state and federal claims if they would ordinarily be expected to be tried in one judicial proceeding. See *Penobscot Indian Nation v. Key Bank of Maine,* 112 F.3d 538, 563-64 (1st Cir.1997). In particular, "[t]he state and federal claims must derive from a common nucleus of operative fact." *United Mine Workers v. Gibbs,* 383 U.S. 715, 725, 86 S.Ct. 1130, 16 L.Ed.2d 218 (1966).

In the case at bar, plaintiffs allege that Yaron and Efrat Ungar were murdered in a terrorist attack perpetrated by the Hamas defendants. Plaintiffs also allege the PA defendants knew that Hamas was based in and operated out of territories controlled by the PA and the PLO, that the PA defendants failed to apprehend the Hamas defendant or curtail Hamas' terrorist activities, and that the PA defendants provided material support to Hamas. Thus, the federal claim and the state law claims derive from a common nucleus of operative fact, and this Court has subject matter jurisdiction over the state law claims under the doctrine of supplemental jurisdiction.

B. Personal Jurisdiction

The PA defendants also request dismissal of the complaint under Fed.R.Civ.P. 12(b)(2) for lack of personal jurisdiction. The PA defendants argue that they do not have minimum contacts with the State of Rhode Island; therefore, this Court could not exercise personal jurisdiction over them without running afoul of the constitutional requirements of minimum contacts and due process.

Plaintiffs contend that the Court may exercise personal jurisdiction over the PA defendants consistent with the Due Process Clause of the Fifth Amendment. As to defendants PA and PLO, plaintiffs argue that this Court has personal jurisdiction through nationwide service of process pursuant to 18 U.S.C. §2334(a) and Federal Rule of Civil Procedure 4(k)(1)(D), or, in the alternative, pursuant to Federal Rule of Civil Procedure 4(k)(2). As to defendants Arafat, Rajoub, Dahlan, Al-Hindi, Tirawi, and Jibali (hereinafter "the individual defendants"), plaintiffs argue that this Court has personal jurisdiction pursuant to Federal Rule of Civil Procedure 4(k)(2).

In order to survive a motion to dismiss for lack of personal jurisdiction, a plaintiff must provide competent evidence to establish a prima facie showing of personal jurisdiction. Under the most common approach, referred to simply as the prima facie standard, the district court must "restrict its inquiry to whether the plaintiff has proffered evidence which, if credited, suffices to support a finding of personal jurisdiction." *Barrett v. Lombardi,* 239 F.3d 23, 26 (1st Cir.2001). The court need not "credit conclusory allegations or draw farfetched inferences," *Ticketmaster-New York, Inc. v. Alioto,* 26 F.3d 201, 203 (1st Cir.1994), but must credit specific facts set forth in the record and supported by competent evidence, see *Barrett,* 239 F.3d at 26. The role of the district court in this regard is not to act as a fact finder, but rather to accept properly supported evidence proffered by the plaintiff as true. See *Microfibres, Inc. v. McDevitt-Askew,* 20 F.Supp.2d 316, 319 (D.R.I.1998). In addition, the court considers all uncontradicted facts put forward by the defendant. *Massachusetts Sch. of Law at Andover, Inc. v. Am. Bar Assoc.,* 142 F.3d 26, 34 (1st Cir.1998)(citing *Topp v. CompAir, Inc.,* 814 F.2d 830, 836-37 (1st Cir.1987)).

In a federal question case, the starting point of this Court's minimum contacts analysis is the Due Process Clause of the Fifth Amendment. U.S. Const. amend. V. "When the district court's *subject-matter* jurisdiction rests wholly or in part on the existence of a federal question, the constitutional limits of the court's *personal* jurisdiction are drawn in the first instance with reference to the due process clause of the fifth amendment." *Lorelei Corp. v. County of*

Guadalupe, 940 F.2d 717, 719 (1st Cir.1991). The relevant inquiry under such circumstances is whether the defendant has minimum contacts with the United States as a whole, rather than whether the defendant has minimum contacts with the particular state in which the federal court sits. See *id.* at 719-20.

The reasoning behind this rule of law was aptly explained by Judge Selya in *United Elec., Radio and Mach. Workers v. 163 Pleasant St. Corp.*, 960 F.2d 1080 (1st Cir.1992).

Inasmuch as the federalism concerns which hover over the jurisdictional equation in a diversity case are absent in a federal question case, a federal court's power to assert personal jurisdiction is geographically expanded. In such circumstances, the Constitution requires only that the defendant have the requisite "minimum contacts" with the United States, rather than with the particular forum state (as would be required in a diversity case).

Id. at 1085 (citing *Lorelei*, 940 F.2d at 719; *Trans-Asiatic Oil Ltd. v. Apex Oil Co.*, 743 F.2d 956, 959 (1st Cir.1984)).

Despite the fact that "the physical scope of the court's constitutional power is broad," *Lorelei*, 940 F.2d at 719, this Court's inquiry is not yet complete. Before a district court can exercise personal jurisdiction over a defendant in a federal question case, plaintiff must also establish that service of process is authorized by a federal statute or rule. See *id.* This statutory limitation on the district court's exercise of personal jurisdiction must be satisfied, for although service of process and personal jurisdiction are distinct concepts, they are also closely related, and a court cannot obtain personal jurisdiction without effective service of process. *Lorelei*, 940 F.2d at 719-20 n. 1 (citing *Driver v. Helms*, 577 F.2d 147, 155 (1st Cir.1978)).

Defendants PA and PLO

Plaintiffs argue that jurisdiction over defendants PA and PLO is established through the nationwide service of process provision found at 18 U.S.C. §2334(a) and Federal Rule of Civil Procedure 4(k)(1)(D). Rule 4(k)(1)(D) provides that "[s]ervice of a summons…is effective to establish jurisdiction over the person of a defendant when authorized by a statute of the United States." Fed.R.Civ.P. 4(k)(1)(D). 18 U.S.C. §2334(a) states that "[p]rocess in [a civil action under section 2333 of this title] may be served in any district where the defendant resides, is found, or has an agent." 18 U.S.C. §2334(a). Therefore, plaintiffs have made a prima facie showing of personal jurisdiction as to defendants PA

and PLO if: (1) defendants PA and PLO have minimum contacts with the United States as a whole, and (2) defendants PA and PLO were served in any district where they reside, are found, or have an agent.

Plaintiffs' Memorandum in Opposition to Defendants' Motion to Dismiss ("Pls.' Mem.") and Memorandum in Further Opposition to Defendants' Motion to Dismiss ("Pls.' Supp. Mem.") provide this Court with sufficient evidence to conclude that defendants PA and PLO have minimum contacts with the United States. First, the PLO maintains an office in Washington, D.C. The office is headed by Hasan Abdel Rahman, the Chief Representative of both the PLO and the PA in the United States, and employs nine staff members. Pls.' Supp. Mem., Exs. A and B. For the six month period ending March 31, 1999, the office expended $200,132.74 on activities ranging from conducting interviews, giving lectures, and contacting the media. *See* Report of the Attorney General to the Congress of the United States on the Administration of the Foreign Agents Registration Act of 1938, as amended, for the Six Months Ending June 30, 1999, *available at* http://www.doj.gov/ criminal/fara/fara1st99/COUNTRY /PALESTIN.HTM. Because Rahman represents himself as the Chief Representative of both the PA and PLO, plaintiffs contend that these activities constitute contacts on behalf of the PA and the PLO with the United States.

Defendant PLO also maintains an Observer Mission to the United Nations in New York. The Permanent Observer and Deputy Permanent Observer employed by the Observer Mission represent the views of Palestine to the U.N., but also participate in public speaking engagements outside of the U.N. The PLO's activities in New York were examined by the Second Circuit on appeal in *Klinghoffer v. S.N.C. Achille Lauro*, 937 F.2d 44 (2d Cir.1991). Although the appeals court ruled that the PLO's U.N. activities could not be considered for purposes of establishing personal jurisdiction, it also held that all of the PLO's activities unrelated to its observer status could be considered. See *id.* at 51. On remand, the district court concluded that the PLO's fundraising activities and other public speaking engagements were sufficient for purposes of New York's long-arm statute. *Klinghoffer v. S.N.C. Achille Lauro*, 795 F.Supp. 112, 114 (S.D.N.Y.1992).

In addition to the above activities, defendant PA employs the lobbying firm of Bannerman & Associates to assist the PA with advocacy training and developing a public relations campaign in the United States. *See* Pls.' Supp. Mem., Exs. E and F. Furthermore, plaintiffs allege that the PLO and the PA have significant commercial contacts with the United States, citing a recent case arising from a dispute over a telecommunications contract that the PLO and the

PA entered into with International Technologies Integration, Inc. See *Int'l Techs. Integration, Inc. v. Palestine Liberation Organization*, 66 F.Supp.2d 3 (D.D.C.1999). The proceedings in that case revealed that the PA and the PLO maintain several bank accounts in New York with deposits totaling approximately $18 million dollars. *See* Pls.' Supp. Mem., Ex. G.

On the basis of this evidence, the Court concludes that plaintiffs' have made a prima facie showing that defendants PA and PLO have minimum contacts with the United States as a whole. Plaintiffs' evidence goes beyond the allegations in the complaint, providing competent evidence of defendant PA's and defendant PLO's contacts with the United States as a whole. However, before this Court can conclude that it may constitutionally exercise personal jurisdiction over the PA defendants, plaintiffs must also demonstrate that the PA defendants were served in a district where they reside, are found, or have an agent.

Plaintiffs contend that defendants PA and PLO were served with process in this action pursuant to Federal Rule of Civil Procedure 4(h)(1), which pertains to service upon corporations and associations. "An unincorporated association is defined as a body of persons acting together and using certain methods for prosecuting a special purpose or common enterprise." *Motta v. Samuel Weiser, Inc.*, 768 F.2d 481, 485 (1st Cir.1985)(citing Black's Law Dictionary 111 (5th ed.1979)), *cert. denied*, 474 U.S. 1033, 106 S.Ct. 596, 88 L.Ed.2d 575 (1985).

It has previously been determined that the PLO qualifies as an unincorporated association because "[i]t is composed of individuals, without a legal identity apart from its membership, formed for specific objectives." *Klinghoffer v. S.N.C. Achille Lauro Ed*, 739 F.Supp. 854, 858 (S.D.N.Y.1990). Defendant PA also qualifies as an unincorporated association for purposes of service of process. The PA is not presently recognized as a foreign state by the United States. Therefore, it may also be categorized as an organization composed of individuals seeking to achieve specific objectives, and which has no legal identity in the United States apart from its membership.

Under Rule 4(h)(1), service of process on an unincorporated association shall be effected "by delivering a copy of the summons and of the complaint to an officer, [or] a managing or general agent." Fed.R.Civ.P. 4(h)(1). Plaintiffs allege that service of process was delivered to Hasan Abdel Rahman (the Chief Representative of the PA and the PLO in the United States) on April 13, 2000, in Washington, D.C., and to Marwan Jilani (the PLO's Deputy Permanent Observer to the United Nations) on March 23, 2000 in Massachusetts. Plaintiffs provided affidavits of service of process as

exhibits to their Memorandum in Opposition to Defendants' Motion to Dismiss.

Delivery of a copy of the summons and complaint to Jilani and Rahman is effective to confer jurisdiction over defendant PA and defendant PLO only if Jilani and Rahman are officers and/or managing or general agents of the PA and the PLO. Defendant PA and defendant PLO claim that Jilani and Rahman do not qualify as managing or general agents because they are not authorized to accept service of process on behalf of the PA or the PLO. In addition, they claim that Jilani is immune from service pursuant to the Headquarters Agreement treaty between the U.N. and the United States, 22 U.S.C. §287 Note (1994)("the Headquarters Agreement"), and that Rahman is immune from service under the Foreign Missions Act ("FMA"), 22 U.S.C. §4301 *et seq.*

In a federal question case, federal law determines whether a person is an agent for purposes of service under Rule 4. See *Nat'l Equip. Rental, Ltd. v. Szukhent*, 375 U.S. 311, 316, 84 S.Ct. 411, 11 L.Ed.2d 354 (1964); *Dodco, Inc. v. Am. Bonding Co.*, 7 F.3d 1387, 1388 (8th Cir.1993). In *Klinghoffer*, the district court addressed the question of whether the PLO's Permanent Observer to the U.N. qualified as a managing or general agent where he was not specifically designated as such by the PLO. See *Klinghoffer*, 739 F.Supp. 854. The district court stated that service "is not limited to titled officials of the association or those expressly authorized to accept service," and held that a general or managing agent is an individual with the authority to exercise independent judgment and discretion in the performance of his or her duties. *Id.* at 867 (citing *Grammenos v. Lemos*, 457 F.2d 1067, 1073 (2d Cir.1972)). Thus, "service is sufficient when made upon an individual who stands in such a position as to render it fair, reasonable and just to imply the authority on his part to receive service." *Id.* (citations omitted).

In the present case, plaintiffs contend that Jilani and Rahman are *both* managing or general agents of defendant PA and defendant PLO. The PLO is not a member of the United Nations, but does maintain a Permanent Observer Mission to the U.N. In 1988, the U.N. adopted a resolution to use the designation "Palestine" instead of the designation "PLO" in the United Nations system. Pls.' Mem., Ex. C. Significantly, the PA also identifies the Observer Mission as its official representative to the U.N. *Id.*, Ex. J. Mr. Jilani is the Deputy Permanent Observer of the Permanent Observer Mission of Palestine to the United Nations, and has served in the Mission since 1996. Decl. of Marwan Jilani, ¶ 1. In his declaration, Mr. Jilani stated that he acts at the direction of the Permanent Observer, but also stated that he acts for the Permanent Observer in his absence. *Id.* at ¶ 2. As Mr. Jilani indicated, the purpose of the Permanent Observer is to present the views of Palestine, not only before the U.N., but "in all activities, discussion, dialogues and debates...to the people of the world who are concerned with those issues." *Id.*

At the time he was served, Mr. Jilani was participating as a guest speaker in a program on the Middle East peace process held in Brookline, Massachusetts. See *id.* Mr. Jilani attended the program to present the views of Palestine to the interested public. Under these circumstances, it is reasonable to conclude that Jilani is a managing or general agent of the PLO and the PA. Mr. Jilani's presence as the representative of the Observer Mission renders it "fair, reasonable and just" to imply his authority to receive service on behalf of the PLO and the PA because both entities have designated the Observer Mission as their official representative to the U.N. Given the fact that Jilani attended the panel discussion as the sole representative of the Observer Mission to present the views of Palestine, it also reasonable to conclude that he was not "under direct superior control," but instead exercised some degree of discretion and judgment in the fulfillment of his duties.

The declaration of Mr. Rahman establishes that he is the Chief Representative of the PLO in the United States. Decl. of Hasan Abdel Rahman, ¶ 1. He is also registered with the U.S. Department of Justice as an agent for the PLO. Pls.' Mem., Ex. F ("Short Form Listing of Registrant's Foreign Agents", *available at* http:// www.usdoj.gov /criminal/fara/ fara1st99 /SHRTFORM/ SHRTFORM.HTM). Mr. Rahman states that defendant PA has no representatives in the United States. Decl. of Hasan Abdel Rahman, ¶ 3. However, plaintiffs have submitted the biography of Mr. Rahman, allegedly distributed by Rahman's office in Washington D.C., which describes Rahman as the Chief Representative of the Palestine Liberation Organization and the Palestinian National Authority. Pls.' Supp. Mem., Ex. A. In addition, plaintiffs point out that Mr. Rahman has spoken on behalf of both the PLO and the PA on more than one occasion. See *id.* at Exs. B and C.

This evidence is sufficient to establish that Rahman qualifies as a general or managing agent of the PLO and the PA. As the Chief Representative of both entities in the United States, it is reasonable to conclude that he exercises independent judgment and discretion in the performance of his duties. It is also fair, reasonable and just to imply his authority to accept service on behalf of the PLO and the PA, notwithstanding his assertions to the contrary.

In *Klinghoffer*, the district court also rejected the PLO's argument that the PLO's Permanent Observer to the United Nations is immune from service of process under the Headquarters Agreement, concluding that the Headquarters Agreement only confers diplomatic immunity on Members of the United Nations. *Klinghoffer*, 739 F.Supp. at 864; *aff'd*, 937 F.2d at 48. Because the PLO is not a Member of the U.N., but only an Observer, the PLO has no claim to diplomatic immunity. *Klinghoffer*, 739 F.Supp. at 864-65. In the case at bar, defendants offer nothing new in support of this claim, but merely reiterate the same arguments made in *Klinghoffer*. Therefore, the argument must fail here as well.

This Court also rejects the PA defendants' claim that the FMA confers immunity from service of process on Rahman. As noted by plaintiffs, the PA defendants have not cited any specific provision or interpretation of the FMA to support this position. The sole provision in the Act related to immunities is 22 U.S.C. §4310, which provides in pertinent part that "[n]o act or omission by any foreign mission...in compliance with this chapter shall be deemed to be an implied waiver of any immunity otherwise provided for by law." 22 U.S.C. §4310 (1994). This provision does not render representatives of foreign missions immune from service; it simply preserves immunities that may be provided for by law. The PA defendants have not identified any such immunity. Therefore, the FMA does not render Mr. Rahman immune from service of process.

Accordingly, it is the determination of this Court that it has personal jurisdiction over defendant PA and defendant PLO pursuant to the nationwide service of process provision of 18 U.S.C. §2334(a) and Rule 4(k)(1)(D). [FN3] Defendant PA and defendant PLO have minimum contacts with the United States as a whole, and each defendant was served through the delivery of a copy of the summons and complaint to a managing or general agent of each defendant. Therefore, this Court may exercise personal jurisdiction over defendant PA and defendant PLO consistent with the Due Process Clause of the Fifth Amendment.

FN3. Because the Court concludes that it has personal jurisdiction over defendants PA and PLO on these grounds, it does not reach the question of whether it could exercise personal jurisdiction over defendants PA and PLO pursuant to Rule 4(k)(2).

Individual PA Defendants

This Court must now determine whether it has personal jurisdiction over the individual PA defendants. Plaintiffs argue that personal jurisdiction has been established pursuant to Federal Rule of Civil Procedure 4(k)(2). Rule 4(k)(2) states:

If the exercise of jurisdiction is consistent with the Constitution and laws of the United States, serving a summons or filing a waiver of service is also effective, with respect to claims arising under federal law, to establish personal jurisdiction over the person of any defendant who is not subject to the jurisdiction of the courts of general jurisdiction of any state.

Fed.R.Civ.P. 4(k)(2).

The PA defendants strenuously argue that plaintiffs cannot establish personal jurisdiction pursuant to Rule 4(k)(2) because plaintiffs cannot show that this Court's exercise of personal jurisdiction over the individual PA defendants would be consistent with the United States Constitution.

The PA defendants' argument is based in large part on *United States v. Swiss Am. Bank, Ltd.*, 191 F.3d 30 (1st Cir.1999), wherein the First Circuit delineated the circumstances under which a plaintiff may utilize Rule 4(k)(2) to establish personal jurisdiction over a defendant. By its terms, Rule 4(k)(2) requires that the following factors be present: (1) the plaintiff's claim must arise under federal law, (2) no state court of general jurisdiction can have personal jurisdiction over the putative defendant, and (3) the federal court's exercise of personal jurisdiction over the defendant must be consistent with the Constitution or other federal law. *Id.* at 38; Fed.R.Civ.P. 4(k)(2).

However, the First Circuit recognized that requiring a plaintiff to prove the so-called "negation prong" (that the defendant is beyond the reach of any state court of general jurisdiction), "in effect requires a plaintiff to prove a negative fifty times over-an epistemological quandary which is compounded by the fact that the defendant typically controls much of the information needed to determine the existence and/or magnitude of its contacts with any given jurisdiction." *Swiss American*, 191 F.3d at 40. Accordingly, the court of appeals devised the following burden-shifting framework.

As a initial matter, a plaintiff seeking to invoke Rule 4(k)(2) must make out a prima facie case for applicability of the rule. Plaintiff's prima facie case consists of three elements: (1) the claim arises under federal law, (2) no situation-specific federal statute confers personal jurisdiction over the defendant, and (3) the defendant's contacts with the nation as a whole are sufficient to comply with the constitutional requirements of due process and minimum contacts. *Id.* at 41. In addition, plaintiff must certify that "based on the information that is readily available to the plaintiff and his counsel, the defendant is not subject to suit in the courts of general jurisdiction of any state." *Id.*

At this point, the burden of production shifts to the defendant to produce evidence which, if credited, demonstrates either that the defendant's contacts with the United States are constitutionally insufficient, or that it is subject to suit in a state court of general jurisdiction. *Id.* If the defendant chooses the latter course, the plaintiff may either move for transfer to a district within that state, discontinue the action, or contest the defendant's evidence on this score. *Id.* at 42. If the defendant instead contends that it does not have sufficient contacts with the United States to justify the exercise of personal jurisdiction, the negation requirement is conceded, and the plaintiff "need only prove that his claim arises under federal law and that the defendant has contacts with the United States as a whole sufficient to permit a federal court constitutionally to exercise personal jurisdiction over it." *Id.*

In the instant case, the PA defendants argue that plaintiffs failed to make out their prima facie case because they cannot demonstrate that the individual defendants' contacts with the nation as a whole meet the constitutional requirements of due process and minimum contacts. Because plaintiffs argue that the individual defendants' contacts with the United States as a whole are sufficient to confer general personal jurisdiction, plaintiffs must demonstrate that the individual defendants have engaged in "continuous and systematic activity, unrelated to the suit" in the forum. *Noonan v. Winston*, 135 F.3d 85, 89 (1st Cir.1998).

It is patently obvious to this Court that plaintiffs cannot meet this burden. Plaintiffs have not offered any evidence that demonstrates that the individual defendants have any contact with the United States whatsoever. Instead, plaintiffs seek to persuade this Court to adopt the due process analysis applied by the district courts in the District of Columbia and the Eastern District of New York in several recent decisions interpreting and applying the state-sponsored terrorism exception of the Federal Sovereign Immunities Act ("FSIA"), 28 U.S.C. §1605(a)(7) and §1605 Note (Supp.2001).

The state-sponsored terrorism exception was enacted as an amendment to the FSIA by the Anti-Terrorism and Effective Death Penalty Act of 1996 ("AEDPA"). It provides that a foreign state which has been officially designated as a state sponsor of terrorism by the Department of State [FN4] shall not be immune from suit where the foreign state, or an official, employee, or agent of the foreign state causes personal injury or death to a United States citizen as a result of an act of terrorism, or through the provision of material support and resources to an individual or entity that commits such an act. 28 U.S.C. §1605(a)(7).

FN4. Currently, Cuba, Iran, Iraq, North Korea, Sudan, and Syria are designated as sponsors of terrorism pursuant to 50 U.S.C.App. §2405(j). *See* 22 C.F.R. §126.1(d) (current through June 5, 2001).

Confronted with the question of whether the federal courts could exercise personal jurisdiction over foreign state defendants, the district courts in the District of Columbia and the Eastern District of New York concluded that the due process analysis applicable to foreign state defendants that are sued pursuant to §1605(a)(7) differs from the traditional due process analysis. E.g., *Flatow v. Islamic Republic of Iran,* 999 F.Supp. 1 (D.D.C.1998); *Rein v. Socialist People's Libyan Arab Jamahiriya,* 995 F.Supp. 325 (E.D.N.Y.1998).

The primary reason behind the analysis of those courts is that 28 U.S.C. §1330(b) provides that "[p]ersonal jurisdiction over a foreign state shall exist as to every claim for relief over which the district courts have jurisdiction…where service has been made under section 1608 of this title." 28 U.S.C. §1330(b); *see also* 28 U.S.C. §1608 (providing for the manner of service upon a foreign state or political subdivision of a foreign state). Relying on this statutory provision, the courts have determined that "subject-matter jurisdiction together with proper service of process gives the court personal jurisdiction." *Rein,* 995 F.Supp. at 330.

However, the *Flatow* Court also looked beyond §1330(b), grounding its conclusion that the exercise of personal jurisdiction over foreign state defendants in accordance with §§1605(a)(7) and 1330(b) is consistent with the due process clause on several additional bases. In particular, the court found that the exceptions to sovereign immunity contained in the FSIA encompass conduct that, by definition, goes beyond what is necessary to establish minimum contacts. See *Flatow,* 999 F.Supp. at 20. Thus, "an inquiry into personal jurisdiction over a foreign state need not consider the rubric of 'minimum contacts'; the concept of 'minimum contacts' is inherently subsumed within the exceptions to immunity defined by the statute." *Id.*

For example, a foreign state subject to suit under the "commercial activities" exception to the FSIA necessarily has minimum contacts with the United States because §1605(a)(2) requires that the action be based on a commercial activity carried on in the United States, an act performed in the United States, or on act that causes a "direct effect" in the United States. 28 U.S.C. §1605(a)(2). This conduct "requires something more substantial than 'minimum contacts' with the United States," rendering an independent minimum contacts analysis unnecessary. *Flatow,* 999 F.Supp. at 20.

Whether or not the minimum contacts analysis is subsumed by the state-sponsored terrorism exception of §1605(a)(7) appears to be somewhat of an open question. The district courts have stated that it is, noting that minimum contacts with the United States are established through the victim's nationality. See *Rein,* 995 F.Supp. at 330. However, the Second Circuit, hearing *Rein* on appeal, stated that "[t]he elements of §1605(a)(7), unlike those of the commercial activities exception…do not entail any finding of minimum contacts." *Rein v. Socialist People's Libyan Arab Jamahiriya,* 162 F.3d 748, 761 (2d Cir.1998). This statement seriously undermines the idea that the due process clause is satisfied merely by alleging a cause of action under the state-sponsored terrorism exception to the FSIA.

A third justification for the approach used by these district courts focuses on the extent of contacts that must be present in the context of a case brought pursuant to §1605(a)(7). As stated in *Flatow,* "a foreign state that sponsors terrorist activities which causes the death or personal injury of a United States national will invariably have sufficient contacts with the United States to satisfy Due Process." 999 F.Supp. at 23. The contacts likely to be present in such a case are the sovereign contacts between the foreign state defendant and the United States, as well as the nationality of the victim. In light of the policy decisions inherent in Congress' enactment of the state-sponsored terrorist exception to the FSIA, the *Flatow* Court concluded that such contacts, seemingly inadequate under a traditional due process analysis, are nonetheless reasonable in the context of the FSIA. See *id.* at 22.

Finally, the *Flatow* Court held that a foreign state is not a "person" for purposes of constitutional due process analysis. *Id.* at 19-21. Accordingly, the Court found that no minimum contacts analysis is required.

Plaintiffs suggest that the due process analysis applied by the courts in *Flatow* and *Rein* should also be applied in cases brought pursuant to §2333. To support their argument, plaintiffs cite to the legislative history of the ATA, under which 18 U.S.C. §2333 was enacted, and compare it with the legislative purpose behind the AEDPA. The purpose of the ATA is to "provide for Federal civil remedies for American victims of international terrorism…The ATA removes the jurisdictional hurdles in the courts confronting victims and it empowers victims with all the weapons available in civil litigation." 137 Cong. Rec. 8143 (1991). Likewise, the AEDPA "was created as part of a federal initiative to combat international terrorism." *Flatow,* 999 F.Supp. at 14. Plaintiffs also point out that the provision of material support and resources to terrorists "is actionable under both the AEDPA (against a foreign state) and the ATA (against a non-state defendant), clearly indicating the common purpose and Congressional intent which produced both statutes." Pls.' Supp. Mem., p. 20.

Despite the apparent similarity in legislative purpose, there are several important differences between the ATA and the AEDPA. First and foremost, there is no express provision for the district court's exercise of personal jurisdiction over the defendant in an action brought pursuant to 18 U.S.C. §2333. While §2334(a) provides for venue and nationwide service of process, it does not contain a statutory basis for the exercise of personal jurisdiction similar to the one provided for by 28 U.S.C. §1330(b) in FSIA actions. Second, unlike the exceptions to sovereign immunity contained in 18 U.S.C. §1605(a), the elements of a §2333 claim do not, by definition, subsume a minimum contacts analysis. Third, non-state defendants, such as the individual defendants in this case, do not have sovereign contacts with the United States sufficient to confer general personal jurisdiction. Finally, there is no question as to whether an individual defendant, as opposed to a foreign state defendant, is entitled to the constitutional protections afforded by the Due Process Clause.

In light of these differences, this Court declines plaintiffs' invitation to extend the due process analysis applied by the district courts under the state-sponsored terrorist exception to the FSIA to the case currently before the Court. In reaching this decision, the Court notes that it does not decide whether the approach to personal jurisdiction used by the district courts of the District of Columbia and the Eastern District of New York in FSIA cases is consistent with the Due Process Clause. Rather, this Court holds that, in cases brought pursuant to 18 U.S.C. §2333, a plaintiff must demonstrate that the defendant has sufficient minimum contacts to satisfy a traditional due process analysis. In the instant case, the Court cannot conclude that the individual defendants engaged in the kind of systematic and continuous activity necessary to support the exercise of general personal jurisdiction over the individual PA defendants. Accordingly, the claims against the individual defendants must be dismissed for lack of personal jurisdiction.

C. Improper Venue

The PA defendants also move to dismiss the complaint under Rule 12(b)(3) on the grounds that the District of Rhode Island is not the proper venue for this lawsuit. Defendants argue that venue is improper in the instant case because no plaintiff is authorized to bring an action pursuant to §2333. This argument can be disposed of quickly.

18 U.S.C. §2334(a) provides that "[a]ny civil action under section 2333 of this title against any person may be insti-

tuted in the district court of the United States for any district where any plaintiff resides or where any defendant resides or is served, or has an agent." 18 U.S.C. §2334(a). Thus, venue is proper in this case as long as at least one plaintiff is a resident of the State of Rhode Island. Plaintiffs allege that plaintiff David Strachman is a resident and domiciliary of the State of Rhode Island. He was appointed as the administrator of the Estate of Yaron Ungar and the Estate of Efrat Ungar, for the limited purpose of realizing and handling assets, rights, and causes of action in the United States, by the Jerusalem District Rabbinical Court of the State of Israel. Pls.' Mem., Ex. A. Therefore, venue is proper because plaintiff Strachman is a resident of the State of Rhode Island.

D. Insufficient Service of Process

A motion to dismiss for insufficient service of process pursuant to Rule 12(b)(5) challenges the mode of delivery or the lack of delivery of the summons and complaint. 5A Charles Alan Wright & Arthur R. Miller, *Federal Practice and Procedure* §1353 (2d ed.1987). Plaintiffs bear the burden of proving proper service. *Rivera-Lopez v. Municipality of Dorado*, 979 F.2d 885, 887 (1st Cir.1992).

In the instant case, the PA defendants have not articulated any objection to the mode of delivery of the summonses and complaints to Jilani, nor have they argued that the summonses and complaints were not delivered to Jilani. [FN5] However, they allege a defect in service on Rahman. In his declaration, Mr. Rahman states that "a bundle of papers was found in the front room of the Mission office containing separate Summonses and Complaints." Decl. of Hasan Abdel Rahman, ¶ 2. Thus, the objection raised by the PA defendants is directed at the delivery of the summonses and complaints.

FN5. To the extent that the PA defendants challenge service of process on the grounds of a lack of agency relationship between Jilani or Rahman and the PA defendants, that argument has been addressed in the preceding section discussing this Court's exercise of personal jurisdiction.

However, plaintiffs provided proof of service on Rahman through the affidavit of Freeman R. Woodbury, the process server who delivered the summonses and complaints to Rahman at the PLO office in Washington, D.C. In his affidavit, Mr. Woodbury states that on April 13, 2000, he identified Mr. Rahman from a picture he was carrying, and rode alongside Mr. Rahman in the elevator of the building where the PLO's Washington, D.C. office is located. Aff. of Freeman R. Woodbury, ¶ 1. In the elevator, Mr. Woodbury identified himself and notified Rahman that he was being served with summonses and complaints. *Id.* at ¶ 3. Mr. Woodbury followed Rahman to his office, and repeated that he was serving summonses and complaints on Rahman. *Id.* at ¶ 4. Mr. Woodbury states that Mr. Rahman "refused to accept the documentation so I placed the summonses and complaints on the desk beside him." *Id.* at ¶ 5.

The purpose of Rule 4 is to provide notice to the party to be served. With this objective in mind, Mr. Woodbury twice informed Rahman that he was being served, and left the papers on the desk in Rahman's office only after Rahman refused to accept the summonses and complaints. An agent of a defendant cannot successfully thwart service of process by simply refusing hand delivery of the summons and complaint. In fact, it has been stated that:

[i]f defendant attempts to evade service or *refuses to accept delivery after being informed by the process server of the nature of the papers*, it usually is sufficient for the process server to touch the party to be served with the papers and leave them in defendant's presence or, if a touching is impossible, simply to leave them in defendant's physical proximity.

4A Charles Alan Wright and Arthur R. Miller, *Federal Practice and Procedure* §1095 (2d ed.1987)(emphasis added). Therefore, under the circumstances of the delivery as attested to by Mr. Woodbury, it is the determination of this Court that the delivery of the summonses and complaints to Rahman was sufficient.

E. Failure to State a Claim Upon Which Relief Can Be Granted

The PA defendants also move to dismiss the complaint pursuant to Rule 12(b)(6) for failure to state a claim upon which relief can be granted. In ruling on a motion to dismiss for failure to state a claim, the court construes the complaint in the light most favorable to the plaintiff, taking all well-pleaded allegations as true and giving plaintiff the benefit of all reasonable inferences. *Figueroa v. Rivera,* 147 F.3d 77, 80 (1st Cir.1998). Dismissal under Rule 12(b)(6) is appropriate only if there is no set of facts under which the plaintiff could prevail on his or her claim. *Conley v. Gibson*, 355 U.S. 41, 45-46, 78 S.Ct. 99, 2 L.Ed.2d 80 (1957).

The Federal Claim

As an initial matter, the PA defendants contend that the §2333 claim filed by the Estate of Efrat Ungar must be dis-

missed because there is no allegation that Efrat Ungar was a national of the United States. This Court is in agreement. Section 2333 authorizes civil actions only on behalf on United States nationals, or their estates, survivors, or heirs. There is no allegation in the complaint that Efrat Ungar was a national of the United States. Therefore, the §2333 claim on behalf of the Estate of Efrat Ungar must be dismissed for failure to state a claim upon which relief can be granted.

In addition, the §2333 claims filed by the survivors and/or heirs of Efrat Ungar must also be dismissed for failure to state a claim, as these claims are dependent on Efrat Ungar's status as a United States national. Accordingly, the §2333 claims filed by plaintiffs Rabbi Uri Dasberg and Judith Dasberg in their individual capacities must be dismissed for failure to state a claim. The Court also notes that, insofar as the §2333 claims filed on behalf of plaintiffs Dvir and Yishai Ungar seek damages for losses suffered as a result of the death of Efrat Ungar, those claims cannot be maintained under this statute.

The PA defendants argue that the remaining §2333 claims must be dismissed because the activity attributed to the PA defendants in plaintiffs' complaint, the alleged facilitation, condonation, and failure to prevent terrorist activities in general, does not amount to acts of "international terrorism" as defined by 18 U.S.C. §2331, and is therefore not actionable under 18 U.S.C. §2333.

Section 2331(1) defines "international terrorism" as activities that:

(A) involve violent acts or acts dangerous to human life that are a violation of the criminal laws of the United States or of any State, or that would be a criminal violation if committed within the jurisdiction of the United States or of any State;

(B) appear to be intended-

(i) to intimidate or coerce a civilian population;

(ii) to influence the policy of a government by intimidation or coercion; or

(iii)to affect the conduct of a government by assassination or kidnapping; and

(C) occur primarily outside the territorial jurisdiction of the United States, or transcend national boundaries in terms of the means by which they are accomplished, the persons they appear intended to intimidate or coerce, or the locale in which their perpetrators operate or seek asylum.

18 U.S.C. §2331(1).

Plaintiffs allege that the PA defendants provided defendant Hamas "with safe haven and a base of operations, by permitting and/or encouraging defendant HAMAS to operate freely and conduct activities in the territory in their control or in which they maintained a police presence." Pls.' Compl., ¶ 35. Plaintiffs further allege that the PA defendants granted material and financial support to the families of Hamas members who had been captured or killed while carrying out terrorist attacks, employed member of Hamas as policemen or security officials, repeatedly praised and lauded defendant Hamas and its members who engaged in acts of terrorism against Israeli targets and Jewish civilians, and repeatedly refused the requests of Israeli officials to surrender for prosecution suspected terrorists. See id. at ¶¶ 37-39, 46.

Plaintiffs allege that these activities involve violent acts or acts dangerous to human life, which, if committed within the jurisdiction of the United States, would constitute violations of 18 U.S.C. §3 ("Accessory After the Fact"), and of 18 U.S.C. §2339A ("Providing Material Support to Terrorists"). Id. at ¶ 44. Plaintiffs also allege that the PA defendants' activities appear to be intended to intimidate or coerce a civilian population, and to influence the policy of a government by intimidation or coercion. Id. at ¶ 46. Finally, plaintiffs allege that these activities occurred outside the territorial jurisdiction of the United States. See id. at ¶¶ 27-48.

Viewing the allegations in the complaint in the light most favorable to plaintiffs and giving plaintiffs the benefit of all reasonable inferences, it is the determination of this Court that the complaint sufficiently states a cause of action under 18 U.S.C. §2333.

The State Law Claims

The remaining counts in the complaint are state law claims for death by wrongful act (Count II), negligence (Count III), intentional infliction of emotional distress (Count IV), and negligent infliction of emotional distress (Count V). Because the state law claims arise from the same set of facts as the §2333 claim, the complaint incorporates the allegations made in support of the federal claim. In short, plaintiffs allege that the PA defendants failed to prevent terrorist activities in the territories under their control, and instead actively encouraged and incited terrorist activities. Plaintiffs further allege that those acts and/or omissions resulted in the murders of Yaron and Efrat Ungar. The PA defendants contend that these allegations are legally insuf-

ficient to sustain the causes of action alleged, and ask that the state law claims be dismissed.

In order to determine whether the allegations in a complaint are sufficient to state a claim upon which relief can be granted, a court must necessarily refer to the law on which the complaint is grounded. In the present case, the complaint does not identify the law that is to be applied by this Court in measuring the sufficiency of the state law claims. This Court applies Rhode Island law to issues of state law that arise in federal court because the *Erie* doctrine extends to actions in which federal jurisdiction is premised on supplemental jurisdiction over state law claims. *Doty v. Sewall*, 908 F.2d 1053, 1063 (1st Cir.1990)(citing *United Mine Workers v. Gibbs*, 383 U.S. 715, 722, 86 S.Ct. 1130, 16 L.Ed.2d 218 (1966)). This includes the application of Rhode Island's conflict-of-laws provisions. See *Dykes v. Depuy, Inc.*, 140 F.3d 31, 39 (1st Cir.1998). Therefore, this Court must determine what law a Rhode Island court would apply.

All four of the state law claims sound in tort. "Rhode Island employs an 'interest-weighing' approach to choice of law in tort matters." *Fashion House, Inc. v. K mart Corp.*, 892 F.2d 1076, 1092 (1st Cir.1989)(citing *Berardi, U.S.A., Ltd. v. Employers Mut. Cas. Co.*, 526 A.2d 515 (R.I.1987)). The "interest weighing" approach requires a court to consider "numerous factors which include the place of injury; the place where the tortious conduct occurred; the domicile, residence, and place of business of the parties; and the place where the relationship, if any, between the parties was centered." *Berardi*, 526 A.2d at 516-17.

Applying these factors to the case at bar, this Court finds that the injuries occurred in Israel; the tortious conduct occurred in Israel or in territories controlled by the PA defendants; and that all parties, with the exception of plaintiff Strachman, appear to be domiciled in either Israel or in territories controlled by the PA defendants. Accordingly, it is the determination of this Court that Rhode Island law requires the application of Israeli law to the state law claims contained in plaintiffs' complaint.

It is the obligation of the plaintiff to plead and prove foreign law. See R.I. Gen. Laws §9-19-7. Plaintiffs here did not plead Israeli law in their complaint. The Court has no way of knowing whether Israeli law recognizes these four causes of action based on the facts pleaded in this case. Therefore, Counts II, III, IV, and V must be dismissed for failure to state a cause of action. However, plaintiffs will be given 30 days from the date hereof to file an amended complaint against defendants PA and PLO under Israeli law making the necessary allegations.

F. Inconvenience of the Forum

As a final matter, the PA defendants contend that the complaint against them should be dismissed under the doctrine of forum non conveniens. This doctrine permits a district court "to dismiss a case where an alternative forum is available in another country that is fair to the parties and substantially more convenient for them or the courts." *Nowak v. Tak How Invs., Ltd.*, 94 F.3d 708, 719 (1st Cir.1996).

There is a strong presumption in favor of the plaintiff's choice of forum. See *Mercier v. Sheraton Int'l, Inc.*, 935 F.2d 419, 423-24 (1st Cir.1991). As a result, the defendant bears the burden of demonstrating both that: (1) an adequate alternative forum exists, and (2) considerations of convenience and judicial efficiency strongly favor litigating the claim in the alternative forum. *Iragorri v. Int'l Elevator, Inc.*, 203 F.3d 8, 12 (1st Cir.2000).

In general, the first requirement is usually satisfied if the defendant shows that an alternative forum provides redress for the type of claims alleged in the plaintiff's complaint and that the defendant is amenable to suit in the alternative forum. *Id.* (citing *Piper Aircraft Co. v. Reyno*, 454 U.S. 235, 254 n. 22, 102 S.Ct. 252, 70 L.Ed.2d 419 (1981)). To satisfy the second requirement, the defendant must demonstrate that the balance of factors "relevant to the private and public interests implicated by the case strongly favors dismissal." *Id.* (citing *Gulf Oil Corp. v. Gilbert*, 330 U.S. 501, 508-509, 67 S.Ct. 839, 91 L.Ed. 1055 (1947)).

An illustrative list of considerations relevant to the private interest includes: "the relative ease of access to sources of proof; availability of compulsory process for attendance of unwilling, and the cost of obtaining attendance of willing, witnesses; possibility of view of premises, if view would be appropriate to the action; and all other practical problems that make trial of a case easy, expeditious, and inexpensive." *Gulf Oil Corp. v. Gilbert*, 330 U.S. at 508, 67 S.Ct. 839. Factors of public interest include administrative difficulties for courts with overloaded dockets, the imposition of jury duty on a community with no connection to the underlying dispute, the "local interest in having localized controversies decided at home," and the court's familiarity with the law to be applied in the case. *Id.* at 508-509, 67 S.Ct. 839.

In the usual case, the court has the discretion to grant or deny a motion to dismiss based on the doctrine of forum non conveniens after consideration of the relevant factors. The case at bar presents a different situation. 18 U.S.C. §2334(d) limits the circumstances under which a court can entertain a motion to dismiss on the grounds of the inconvenience of the forum. Specifically, §2334(d) provides:

The district court shall not dismiss any action brought under section 2333 of this title on the grounds of the inconvenience or inappropriateness of the forum chosen, unless—

(1) the action may be maintained in a foreign court that has jurisdiction over the subject matter and over all the defendants;

(2) that foreign court is significantly more convenient and appropriate; and

(3) that foreign court offers a remedy which is substantially the same as the one available in the courts of the United States.

18 U.S.C. §2334(d).

The PA defendants argue that this case should be dismissed because all defendants, potential witnesses, physical evidence related to the Ungars' murders, and all plaintiffs, with the exception of plaintiff Strachman, are located in Israel or elsewhere in the Middle East. The PA defendants also contend that courts "functioning and available in the immediate area" are significantly more convenient, offer remedies substantially the same as those available in the United States, and are familiar with the law that will govern most issues in the case. Defs.' Mem. Supp. Mot. Dismiss Compl., p. 6-7.

Notably absent from the PA defendants' argument is the naming of a *specific* adequate alternative forum. The First Circuit has stated that "[i]n considering a forum non conveniens claim, an inquiring court should begin by determining the existence *vel non* of an adequate alternative forum for the prosecution of the action." *Iragorri*, 203 F.3d at 13. This Court cannot begin to evaluate whether an alternative forum is adequate where the PA defendants have failed to designate such a forum and without some degree of proof as to whether the alternative forum has jurisdiction over the subject matter and all defendants, and offers a remedy which is substantially the same as the one available in this Court. For these reasons, the PA defendants' motion to dismiss under the doctrine of forum non conveniens is denied.

III. Conclusion

For the preceding reasons, the PA defendants' motion to dismiss for lack of subject matter jurisdiction is denied; the motion to dismiss for lack of jurisdiction over the person is granted as to the individual PA defendants: Arafat, Rajoub, Dahlan, Al-Hindi, Tirawi, and Jabali, but denied as to defendants PA and PLO; the motion to dismiss for improper venue is denied; the motion to dismiss for insufficient service of process is denied; the motion to dismiss for failure to state a claim with respect to Count I is granted as to plaintiff Estate of Efrat Ungar and plaintiffs Rabbi Uri Dasberg and Judith Dasberg, in their individual capacities, but denied as to the remaining plaintiffs; the motion to dismiss for failure to state a claim with respect to Counts II, III, IV, and V is granted with leave to amend; and the motion to dismiss for inconvenience of the forum is denied.

It is so ordered:

Notes:

1.   What are the factual and legal difficulties confronted by plaintiffs in proving personal jurisdiction in terrorism cases? How effective is the Klinghoffer Act in assisting plaintiffs in obtaining personal jurisdiction over foreign terrorists? How are these problems different in FSIA cases brought against foreign state sponsors of terrorism?

2.   There have been many cases brought against the Palestinian Authority and the Palestine Liberation Organization under the Klinghoffer Act. What impact will have prior rulings with respect to personal jurisdiction on later cases?

Chapter 7

Causes of Action

Price v. Socialist People's Libyan Arab Jamahiriya, 294 F.3d 82 (D.C. Cir. 2002).

HARRY T. EDWARDS, Circuit Judge:
This case involves a lawsuit brought under the Foreign Sovereign Immunities Act ("FSIA"), 28 U.S.C. §§1330, 1602-1611 (1999), by two American citizens who sued the Socialist People's Libyan Arab Jamahiriya ("Libya") for torture and hostage taking. Plaintiffs' lawsuit seeks cover under a recent amendment to the FSIA which strips certain foreign states -including Libya - of their sovereign immunity in American courts when they engage in such conduct. *See* 28 U.S.C. §1605(a)(7).

In response to plaintiffs' suit, Libya moved to dismiss, claiming sovereign immunity and a lack of personal jurisdiction. The District Court denied the motion to dismiss and Libya now seeks review in this interlocutory appeal. Two central questions have been raised on appeal: first, whether plaintiffs have alleged facts that are legally sufficient to revoke Libya's immunity under the FSIA; and, second, whether the assertion of personal jurisdiction over Libya in the manner specifically authorized by the FSIA violates the Due Process Clause.

We hold, first, that plaintiffs have failed to state a claim for hostage taking adequate to abrogate sovereign immunity and establish subject matter jurisdiction. The allegations set forth in the complaint do not come close to satisfying the definition of "hostage taking" prescribed by the FSIA. We hold further that the allegations supporting plaintiffs' torture claim are not adequate to bring the case within the statutory exceptions to foreign sovereign immunity. The complaint in its present form is simply too conclusory to satisfy §1605(a)(7). In contrast to the hostage-taking claim, however, plaintiffs have at least intimated that they can allege facts that might state a proper claim for torture under the FSIA. Accordingly, we will remand the case to allow plaintiffs to attempt to amend their complaint in an effort to satisfy the statute's rigorous definition of torture. As a word of caution, we note that there is a question as to whether the complaint states a claim for relief upon which plaintiffs can recover; although this matter is not properly before us on interlocutory review, we are not foreclosing review of the issue in the District Court.

Finally, we hold that Libya, as a foreign state, is not a "person" within the meaning of the Due Process Clause. We therefore conclude that the Constitution imposes no limitation on the exercise of personal jurisdiction by the federal courts over Libya.

I. BACKGROUND

The facts and procedural history of this case are relatively straightforward. Plaintiffs Michael Price and Roger Frey, Americans who had been living in Libya in the employ of a Libyan company, were arrested in March of 1980 after taking pictures of various places in and around Tripoli. Libyan government officials apparently believed that these photographs constituted anti-revolutionary propaganda, because they would portray unfavorable images of life in Libya.

Price and Frey allege that, following their arrest, they were denied bail and kept in a "political prison" for 105 days pending the outcome of their trial. In their complaint, plaintiffs assert that they endured deplorable conditions while incarcerated, including urine-soaked mattresses, a cramped cell with substandard plumbing that they were forced to share with seven other inmates, a lack of medical care, and inadequate food. The complaint also asserts that the plaintiffs were "kicked, clubbed and beaten" by prison guards, and "interrogated and subjected to physical, mental and verbal abuse." Compl. at ¶ 4. The complaint contends that this incarceration was "for the purpose of demonstrating Defendant's support of the government of Iran which held hostages in the U.S. Embassy in Tehran, Iran." *Id.* at ¶ 7.

Ultimately, plaintiffs were tried and acquitted of the crimes with which they had been charged. After the verdict was announced, however, the Libyan government retained their passports for another 60 days while the prosecution pursued an appeal, which is permitted under the Libyan Code of Criminal Procedure. When this appeal was eventually rejected, plaintiffs were permitted to leave Libya.

On May 7, 1997, Price and Frey commenced a civil action against Libya in federal court. Their complaint asserted claims for hostage taking and torture and sought $20 million in damages for each man. Following receipt of process, Libya filed a motion to dismiss, arguing that (1) the grant of subject matter jurisdiction over plaintiffs' action was unconstitutional, (2) the court's exercise of personal jurisdiction was unconstitutional, and (3) plaintiffs had failed to state a claim on which relief could be granted. The District Court rejected each of these arguments, thus vitiating Libya's sovereign immunity defense and allowing the court to assert both subject matter jurisdiction over plaintiffs' claims and personal jurisdiction over the defendant. Libya now pursues an interlocutory appeal.

II. DISCUSSION

On appeal, Libya has not renewed its constitutional attack on the court's subject matter jurisdiction. Instead, it claims that the District Court erred in not resolving certain disputed issues of fact, proceeding instead as if plaintiffs' factual allegations had already been established. Libya also argues that, even assuming that these facts were true, the plaintiffs have failed to make out a valid claim either for torture or hostage taking under the FSIA. Finally, Libya asserts that the Due Process Clause does not permit an American court to take jurisdiction over a foreign sovereign based on conduct that has no connection to the United States save for the nationality of the plaintiff.

A. Plaintiffs' Cause of Action

Before we address the issues arising under the FSIA and the Due Process Clause, we first want to make it clear that our decision today does not address or decide whether the plaintiffs have stated a *cause of action* against Libya. The parties appear to assume that a substantive claim against Libya arises under the FSIA, but this is far from clear. The FSIA is undoubtedly a jurisdictional statute which, in specified cases, eliminates foreign sovereign immunity and opens the door to subject matter jurisdiction in the federal courts. See *First Nat'l City Bank v. Banco Para El Comercio Exterior*

de Cuba, 462 U.S. 611, 620, 103 S.Ct. 2591, 2596-97, 77 L.Ed.2d 46 (1983). There is a question, however, whether the FSIA creates a federal cause of action for torture and hostage taking *against foreign states*. See *Roeder v. Islamic Republic of Iran*, 195 F.Supp.2d 140, 171-73 (D.D.C.2002).

The "Flatow Amendment" to the FSIA confers a right of action for torture and hostage taking against an "official, employee, or agent of a foreign state," Pub. L. No. 104-208, Div. A, Title I, §101(c) (Sept. 30, 1996), *codified at* 28 U.S.C. §1605 (note); see *Flatow v. Islamic Republic of Iran*, 999 F.Supp. 1, 12-13 (D.D.C.1998), but the amendment does not list "foreign states" among the parties against whom such an action may be brought. While it is possible that such an action could be brought under the "international terrorism" statute, 18 U.S.C. §2333(a), cf. *Boim v. Quranic Literacy Inst.*, 291 F.3d 1000 (7th Cir.2002), no such claim has been raised in this case.

The question relating to plaintiffs' cause of action has yet to be raised or addressed in the District Court, and it was neither briefed nor argued by the parties during this appeal. Therefore, although we flag the issue, we will leave its disposition to the District Court in the first instance following remand of this case. We will turn our attention now to the matters before us, *i.e.*, the issues arising under the FSIA and the Due Process Clause.

B. The 1996 Amendments to the Foreign Sovereign Immunities Act

The FSIA provides a basis for asserting jurisdiction over foreign nations in the United States. *Argentine Republic v. Amerada Hess Shipping Corp.*, 488 U.S. 428, 443, 109 S.Ct. 683, 693, 102 L.Ed.2d 818 (1989). The statute, which was originally enacted in 1976, confers immunity on foreign states in all cases that do not fall into one of its specifically enumerated exceptions. See 28 U.S.C. §§1605, 1607; *McKesson HBOC, Inc. v. Islamic Republic of Iran*, 271 F.3d 1101, 1105 (D.C.Cir.2001). These exceptions were crafted in order to codify the "restrictive theory" of sovereign immunity, under which immunity is generally limited to a foreign state's public or governmental acts (*jure imperii*) but withheld from its private or commercial acts (*jure gestionis*). See H.R. REP. NO. 94-1487, at 7 (1976); *Jackson v. People's Republic of China*, 794 F.2d 1490, 1493 (11th Cir.1986).

The FSIA thus begins with a presumption of foreign sovereign immunity, 28 U.S.C. §1604, qualified by a list of specific circumstances in which that immunity is unavailable.

These include cases in which the state has waived its immunity, *id.* at §1605(a)(1), cases based upon various forms of commercial activity, *id.* at §1605(a)(2), takings of property in violation of international law, *id.* at §1605(a)(3), and torts committed in the United States, *id.* at §1605(a)(5). The original FSIA was not intended as human rights legislation. *See* Jennifer A. Gergen, *Human Rights and the Foreign Sovereign Immunities Act*, 36 VA. J. INT'L L. 765, 771 (1996). Thus, no matter how allegedly egregious a foreign state's conduct, suits that did not fit into one of the statute's discrete and limited exceptions invariably were rejected. See, e.g., *Saudi Arabia v. Nelson*, 507 U.S. 349, 113 S.Ct. 1471, 123 L.Ed.2d 47 (1993) (holding that a claim arising from the detention and torture of an American citizen in Saudi Arabia was not "based upon a commercial activity carried on in the United States"); *Smith v. Socialist People's Libyan Arab Jamahiriya*, 101 F.3d 239 (2d Cir.1996) (holding that Libya retained its sovereign immunity for the bombing of Pam Am 103 over Lockerbie, Scotland); *Princz v. Fed. Republic of Germany*, 26 F.3d 1166 (D.C.Cir.1994) (holding that plaintiff could not recover for slave labor performed at Nazi concentration camps, because Germany's conduct was not commercial activity causing a "direct effect in the United States" and did not constitute an implied waiver of sovereign immunity); *Siderman de Blake v. Republic of Argentina*, 965 F.2d 699 (9th Cir.1992) (holding that Argentina was immune from liability for acts of torture committed by the ruling junta); *Tel-Oren v. Libyan Arab Republic*, 726 F.2d 774, 775 n. 1 (D.C.Cir.1984) (Edwards J., concurring) (FSIA precludes jurisdiction over Libya for armed attack on civilian bus in Israel); cf. *Amerada Hess*, 488 U.S. at 436, 109 S.Ct. at 689 ("[I]mmunity is granted in those cases involving violations of international law that do not come within one of the FSIA's exceptions.").

Under the original FSIA, therefore, terrorism, torture, and hostage taking committed abroad were immunized forms of state activity. *See* H.R. REP. NO. 103-702, at 4 (1994) ("[T]he FSIA does not currently allow U.S. citizens to sue for gross human rights violations committed by a foreign sovereign on its own soil."). Indeed, in *Nelson*, the Supreme Court recognized that conduct of the sort alleged in the present case - "wrongful arrest, imprisonment, and torture" - amounted to abuses of police power, and "however monstrous such abuse undoubtedly may be, a foreign's state's exercise of the power of its police has long been understood for purpose of the restrictive theory as peculiarly sovereign in nature." 507 U.S. at 361, 113 S.Ct. at 1479; *see also* Mathias Reimann, *A Human Rights Exception to Sovereign Immunity: Some Thoughts on* Princz v. Federal Republic of Germany, 16 MICH. J. INT'L L. 403, 417-18 (1995) (observing that under the unamended FSIA "efforts to persuade the courts to recognize a human rights exception to sovereign immunity" had failed).

The mounting concern over decisions such as these eventually spurred the political branches into action. *See* John F. Murphy, *Civil Liability for the Commission of International Crimes as an Alternative to Criminal Prosecution*, 12 HARV. HUM. RTS. J. 1, 34 (1999). In 1996, as part of the comprehensive Antiterrorism and Effective Death Penalty Act("AEDPA"), Pub. L. No. 104-132, §221(a), 110 Stat. 1214 (Apr. 24, 1996), Congress amended the FSIA to add a new class of claims for which certain foreign states would be precluded from asserting sovereign immunity. Specifically, the amendment vitiates immunity in cases

in which money damages are sought against a foreign state for personal injury or death that was caused by an act of torture, extrajudicial killing, aircraft sabotage, hostage taking, or the provision of material support or resources...for such an act if such act or provision of material support is engaged in by an official, employee, or agent of such foreign state while acting within the scope of his or her office, employment, or agency[.]

28 U.S.C. §1605(a)(7). In enacting this provision, Congress sought to create a judicial forum for compensating the victims of terrorism, and in so doing to punish foreign states who have committed or sponsored such acts and deter them from doing so in the future. See *Daliberti v. Republic of Iraq*, 97 F.Supp.2d 38, 50 (D.D.C.2000); Molora Vadnais, *The Terrorism Exception to the Foreign Sovereign Immunities Act*, 5 UCLA J. INT'L L. & FOREIGN AFF. 199, 216 (2000).

While such legislation had long been sought by victims' groups, it had been consistently resisted by the executive branch. *See* ALAN GERSON & JERRY ADLER, THE PRICE OF TERROR 212-26 (2001); H.R. REP. NO. 102-900, at 3-4, 11 (1992). Executive branch officials feared that the proposed amendment to FSIA might cause other nations to respond in kind, thus potentially subjecting the American government to suits in foreign countries for actions taken in the United States. *See* Murphy, *supra*, at 35-37; H.R. REP. NO. 103-702, at 12 (1994). Although these reservations did not prevent the amendment from passing, they nevertheless left their mark in the final version of the bill.

Section 1605(a)(7) has some notable features which reveal the delicate legislative compromise out of which it was born. First, not all foreign states may be sued. Instead, only a defendant that has been specifically designated by the State Department as a "state sponsor of terrorism" is subject to the loss of its sovereign immunity. §1605(a)(7)(A). Second, even a foreign state listed as a sponsor of terrorism retains its immunity unless (a) it is afforded a reasonable opportunity to arbitrate any claim based on acts that occurred in that state, and (b) either the victim or the claimant was a U.S. national at the time that those acts took place. §1605(a)(7)(B). In the present case, Libya has been designated as a sponsor of terrorism. See 31 C.F.R. §596.201 (2001); Rein v. Socialist People's Libyan Arab Jamahiriya, 162 F.3d 748, 764 (2d Cir.1998). Moreover, both plaintiffs are American citizens, and Libya does not contend that it has been denied a chance to arbitrate their claims.

If service of process has been made under §1608, personal jurisdiction over a foreign state exists for every claim over which the court has subject matter jurisdiction. See 28 U.S.C. §1330(b). In turn, the statute automatically confers subject matter jurisdiction whenever the state loses its immunity pursuant to §1605(a)(7). See id. at §1330(a). Personal jurisdiction determinations always have been made in this way under the FSIA. See JOSEPH W. DELLAPENNA, SUING FOREIGN GOVERNMENTS AND THEIR CORPORATIONS 9 (1988) (commenting on this "significant compression," whereby both "competence [subject matter jurisdiction] and personal jurisdiction depend upon whether the foreign state is immune under the substantive rules in the act"); see also Harris v. VAO Intourist, Moscow, 481 F.Supp. 1056, 1065 (E.D.N.Y.1979) (Weinstein, J.) (noting the way in which the FSIA collapses subject matter jurisdiction, in personam jurisdiction, and sovereign immunity into a single inquiry).

Under the original FSIA, however, it was generally understood that in order for immunity to be lost, there had to be some tangible connection between the conduct of the foreign defendant and the territory of the United States. See Verlinden B.V. v. Cent. Bank of Nigeria, 461 U.S. 480, 490 & n. 15, 103 S.Ct. 1962, 1969 & n. 15, 76 L.Ed.2d 81 (1983); Lee M. Caplan, The Constitution and Jurisdiction over Foreign States: The 1996 Amendments to the Foreign Sovereign Immunities Act in Perspective, 41 VA. J. INT'L L. 369, 406-08 (2001); cf. McKeel v. Islamic Republic of Iran, 722 F.2d 582, 588 (9th Cir.1983) ("[N]othing in the legislative history [of the 1976 Act] suggests that Congress intended to assert jurisdiction over foreign states for events occurring wholly within their own territory. Such an intent would not be consistent with the prevailing practice in international law."). In this way, the original statute's immunity exceptions "prescribe[d] the necessary contacts which must exist before our courts can exercise personal jurisdiction." H.R. REP. NO. 94-1487, at 13 (describing the Act's personal jurisdiction provisions as a kind of federal long-arm statute, one patterned after the District of Columbia's own long-arm law); see also Jurisdiction of U.S. Courts in Suits against Foreign States: Hearings Before the Subcommittee on Administrative Law and Governmental Relations of the House Committee on the Judiciary on H.R. 11315, 94th Cong., 2d Sess. 31 (1976) (statement of Bruno A. Ristau) (noting that this feature of the bill "will insure that only those disputes which have a relation to the United States are litigated in the courts of the United States").

When Congress passed the original FSIA, it was assumed that the exercise of personal jurisdiction over foreign states under the statute always would satisfy the demands of the Constitution. See Joseph W. Glannon & Jeffery Atik, Politics and Personal Jurisdiction: Suing State Sponsors of Terrorism under the 1996 Amendments to the Foreign Sovereign Immunities Act, 87 GEO. L.J. , 681-82 (1999). This assumption proved accurate. See, e.g., Shapiro v. Republic of Bolivia, 930 F.2d 1013, 1020 (2d Cir.1991); Callejo v. Bancomer, S.A., 764 F.2d 1101, 1107 n. 5 (5th Cir.1985); cf. S & Davis Int'l, Inc. v. Republic of Yemen, 218 F.3d 1292, 1304 (11th Cir.2000) (noting that "the 'direct effects' language of §1605(a)(2) closely resembles the 'minimum contacts' language of constitutional due process and these two analyses have overlapped"). Indeed, as some courts have noted, the nexus requirements imposed by the original FSIA sometimes exceeded the constitutional standard. See In re Papandreou, 139 F.3d 247, 253 (D.C.Cir.1998) ("substantial contact" required by §1603(e) requires more than the "minimum contacts" necessary to ensure due process).

The antiterrorism amendments changed this statutory framework. Under §1605(a)(7), the only required link between the defendant nation and the territory of the United States is the nationality of the claimant. Thus, §1605(a)(7) now allows personal jurisdiction to be maintained over defendants in circumstances that do not appear to satisfy the "minimum contacts" requirement of the Due Process Clause. See Caplan, supra, at 408 ("Under its plain terms, the new law extends extraterritoriality much further than the traditional reach of the International Shoe [Co. v. Washington, 326 U.S. 310, 66 S.Ct. 154, 90 L.Ed. 95 (1945)] standard.").

C. Challenges to the Factual Underpinnings of an FSIA Complaint

Before we turn to the due process issue, as well as to the antecedent question of whether plaintiffs have stated valid claims under §1605(a) for hostage taking and torture, we must first address a separate argument that Libya has advanced on appeal. Libya contends that the District Court erred in assuming the truth of the factual allegations in plaintiffs' complaint for purposes of determining whether it had subject matter jurisdiction. Appellant correctly points out that in *Phoenix Consulting, Inc. v. Republic of Angola*, 216 F.3d 36, 40 (D.C.Cir.2000), we held that when a foreign state defendant raises "a dispute over the factual basis of the court's subject matter jurisdiction under the FSIA," the trial court is required to "go beyond the pleadings and resolve any disputed issues of fact the resolution of which is necessary to a ruling upon the motion to dismiss."

Libya now claims that it did not engage in the actions described in plaintiffs' complaint. Thus, it contends that we must reverse the District Court's finding of subject matter jurisdiction and remand for further fact-finding on that issue. See *Foremost-McKesson, Inc. v. Islamic Republic of Iran*, 905 F.2d 438, 448-49 (D.C.Cir.1990) (holding that where the "conclusory allegations" in a plaintiff's complaint are challenged by a sovereign defendant, "the district court must do more than just look to the pleadings to ascertain whether to grant the motion to dismiss"). We reject this argument.

In its original motion to dismiss, Libya specifically stated that, for purposes of that pleading, it was not challenging "the well-pleaded facts in the complaint." *Def.'s Mot. to Dismiss*, at 2 (Jan. 21, 1998). When it renewed this motion, Libya still did not challenge the factual basis of plaintiffs' allegations. Instead, it wrote that, "[e]ven viewed in the light most favorable to the plaintiffs, the facts alleged in the complaint do not establish 'acts of torture' by Libya." *Def.'s Mot. to Dismiss*, at 26 (Feb. 9, 2000). The District Court then properly "[took] the plaintiff's factual allegations as true and determine[d] whether they [brought] the case within any of the exceptions to immunity invoked by the plaintiff." *Phoenix Consulting*, 216 F.3d at 40. It now falls to this court to review this determination, which we do *de novo*. See *McKesson HBOC*, 271 F.3d at 1105.

D. Appellate Jurisdiction

Price and Frey claim that we lack jurisdiction over Libya's appeal, because the denial of a motion to dismiss for failure to state a claim is neither a "final decision," *see* 28 U.S.C. §1291, nor the proper subject of an immediate appeal under the "collateral order" doctrine, see *Cohen v. Beneficial Indus. Loan Corp.*, 337 U.S. 541, 546, 69 S.Ct. 1221, 1225-26, 93 L.Ed. 1528 (1949); *Coopers & Lybrand v. Livesay*, 437 U.S. 463, 98 S.Ct. 2454, 57 L.Ed.2d 351 (1978). These propositions are generally correct; however, insofar as the instant appeal addresses the denial of Libya's motion to dismiss on grounds of foreign sovereign immunity, that question is immediately appealable. See *Princz v. Federal Republic of Germany*, 998 F.2d 1, 1 (D.C.Cir.1993); *Foremost-McKesson*, 905 F.2d at 443 (observing that sovereign immunity confers not merely a defense against liability but a right not to be tried). Thus, an FSIA defendant can take an immediate appeal if the District Court rejects its argument that the facts alleged in the plaintiff's complaint do not bring the case within one of the statute's immunity exceptions.

This is in substance what Libya argued below, and what it now asserts on appeal. *See* Br. for Appellant 24 ("The fact that Price & Frey received a trial and were acquitted and subsequently released, must *deprive the district court of subject matter jurisdiction* as their confinement cannot be considered an act of hostage taking under §1605(a)(7).") (emphasis added). In other words, the basis for Libya's motion to dismiss and for this appeal was that plaintiffs had not set forth an adequate factual basis for applying the FSIA's torture and hostage taking exceptions. It follows therefore that we have jurisdiction to review this challenge at this time.

E. Torture

The FSIA's definition of torture derives from the meaning given that term in section 3 of the Torture Victim Protection Act of 1991 ("TVPA"), Pub. L. No. 102-256, 106 Stat. 73 (Mar. 12, 1992), *codified at* 28 U.S.C. §1350 (note). *See* 28 U.S.C. §1605(e)(1). Section 3(b)(1) of the TVPA defines "torture" to include

any act, directed against an individual in the offender's custody or physical control, by which *severe* pain or suffering (other than pain or suffering arising only from or inherent in, or incidental to, lawful sanctions), whether physical or mental, is intentionally inflicted on that individual *for such purposes* as obtaining from that individual or a third person information or a confession, punishing that individual for an act that individual or a third person has committed or is suspected of having committed, intimidating or coercing that individual or a third person, or for any reason based on discrimination of any kind.

(Emphases added). This definition, in turn, borrows extensively from the 1984 United Nations Convention Against Torture and Other Cruel, Inhuman or Degrading Treatment or Punishment, G.A. Res. 39/46, U.N. GAOR, 39th Sess., Supp. No. 51, at 197, U.N. Doc. A/39/51 (1984) ("Torture Convention"), which the United States signed in 1988 and ratified two years later. *See* H.R. REP. NO. 102-367, Part 1, at 4-5 (1991). Indeed, the TVPA was passed in part to fulfill the Convention's mandate that ratifying nations take action to ensure that torturers are held legally accountable for their actions. *See* S. REP. NO. 02-249, at 3 (1991).

While the legislative history of AEDPA gives no indication as to how broadly the definition of torture was intended to sweep, Congress considered this question both in ratifying the Torture Convention and in enacting the TVPA. *See* BETH STEPHENS & MICHAEL RATNER, INTERNATIONAL HUMAN RIGHTS LITIGATION IN U.S. COURTS 64 & n.4 (1996). Specifically, the drafting histories of both the Convention and the statute address two ambiguities lurking in that definition that must be confronted as we consider whether Price and Frey have alleged facts sufficient to bring this case within the FSIA's definition of torture. The first concerns the meaning of "severe": how much actual pain or suffering must defendants inflict before their conduct rises to the level of torture? The second involves the "for such purposes" language: what must plaintiffs prove about the motivation for the alleged torture if they hope to deprive foreign states of their immunity?

The severity requirement is crucial to ensuring that the conduct proscribed by the Convention and the TVPA is sufficiently extreme and outrageous to warrant the universal condemnation that the term "torture" both connotes and invokes. *See* David P. Stewart, *The Torture Convention and the Reception of International Criminal Law Within the United States*, 15 NOVA L. REV. 449, 455 (1991) (noting that what the Convention forbade was likely already illegal under most domestic legal systems); *Filartiga v. Pena-Irala*, 630 F.2d 876, 890 (2d Cir.1980) ("Among the rights universally proclaimed by all nations...is the right to be free of physical torture."); S. REP. NO. 102-249, at 3 ("Official torture...violate[s] standards accepted by virtually every nation."). The drafters of the Convention, as well as the Reagan Administration that signed it, the Bush Administration that submitted it to Congress, and the Senate that ultimately ratified it, therefore all sought to ensure that "only acts of a

certain gravity shall be considered to constitute torture." J. HERMAN BURGERS & HANS DANELIUS, THE UNITED NATIONS CONVENTION AGAINST TORTURE 117 (1988); *see also* S. EXEC. REP. NO. 101-30, at 14 (1990) ("The term 'torture,' in the United States and international usage, is usually reserved for extreme, deliberate and unusually cruel practices, for example, sustained systematic beating, application of electric currents to sensitive parts of the body, and tying up or hanging in positions that cause extreme pain.").

The critical issue is the degree of pain and suffering that the alleged torturer intended to, and actually did, inflict upon the victim. The more intense, lasting, or heinous the agony, the more likely it is to be torture. *See* S. EXEC. REP. NO. 101-30, at 15 ("The United States understands that, in order to constitute torture, an act must be a deliberate and calculated act of an extremely cruel and inhuman nature, specifically intended to inflict excruciating and agonizing physical or mental pain or suffering.") (internal quotation marks omitted). This understanding thus makes clear that torture does not automatically result whenever individuals in official custody are subjected even to direct physical assault. Not *all* police brutality, not *every* instance of excessive force used against prisoners, is torture under the FSIA.

As to the purposes for which abuse must be inflicted, it is clear from the text of the TVPA that the list of purposes provided was not meant to be exhaustive. *See* Murphy, *supra*, at 27. Instead, this list was included in order to reinforce that torture requires acts both intentional and malicious, and to illustrate the common motivations that cause individuals to engage in torture. *See* S. EXEC. REP. NO. 101-30, at 14. The "for such purposes" language thus suggests that any non-enumerated purpose would have to be similar in nature to those mentioned in order to elevate an act of violence into an act of torture. *See* BURGERS & DANELIUS 118-19 (suggesting that there must be some, even if remote, connection with the interests or policies of the State). Moreover, this requirement ensures that, whatever its specific goal, torture can occur under the FSIA only when the production of pain is purposive, and not merely haphazard. In order to lose its sovereign immunity, a foreign state must impose suffering cruelly and deliberately, rather than as the unforeseen or unavoidable incident of some legitimate end.

When reviewing a plaintiff's unchallenged factual allegations to determine whether they are sufficient to deprive a foreign state defendant of sovereign immunity, we assume those allegations to be true. *Foremost-McKesson*, 905 F.2d at 440 n. 3. Thus, where the defendant contests only the legal sufficiency of plaintiff's jurisdictional claims, the standard is similar to that of Rule 12(b)(6), under which dismissal is warranted if no plausible inferences can be drawn from the facts alleged that, if proven, would provide grounds for relief. See *Browning v. Clinton*, 292 F.3d 235, 241-42 (D.C.Cir.2002). A claimant need not set out all of the precise facts on which the claim is based in order to survive a motion to dismiss. *Sinclair v. Kleindienst*, 711 F.2d 291, 293 (D.C.Cir.1983). However, in light of the serious and far-reaching implications of the 1996 FSIA amendments, it is especially important for the courts to ensure that foreign states are not stripped of their sovereign immunity unless they have been charged with actual torture, and not mere police brutality.

In this case, plaintiffs' complaint offers no useful details about the nature of the kicking, clubbing, and beatings that plaintiffs allegedly suffered. As a result, there is no way to determine from the present complaint the severity of plaintiffs' alleged beatings - including their frequency, duration, the parts of the body at which they were aimed, and the weapons used to carry them out - in order to ensure that they satisfy the TVPA's rigorous definition of torture. In short, there is no way to discern whether plaintiffs' complaint merely alleges police brutality that falls short of torture. Thus, the facts pleaded do not reasonably support a finding that the physical abuse allegedly inflicted by Libya evinced the degree of cruelty necessary to reach a level of torture.

Furthermore, the present complaint says virtually nothing about the purpose of the alleged torture. Plaintiffs seemingly have left it for the courts to conjure some illicit purpose to fill in this pleading gap. Obviously this will not do.

In sum, plaintiffs' allegations of torture as presently stated are insufficient to survive defendant's motion to dismiss. Plaintiffs must allege more than that they were abused. They must demonstrate in their pleadings that Libya's conduct rose to such a level of depravity and caused them such intense pain and suffering as to be properly classified as torture. Although it is far from certain, their complaint hints that they might be able to state a proper claim for torture under the FSIA. Accordingly, we will remand the case to the District Court to allow plaintiffs to attempt to amend their complaint in an effort to satisfy TVPA's stringent definition of torture.

F. Hostage Taking

As with torture, the FSIA draws its definition of "hostage taking" from an exogenous legal source, here article 1 of the International Convention Against the Taking of Hostages. *See* 28 U.S.C. §1605(e)(2). This provision reads as follows:

Any person who seizes or detains and threatens to kill, to injure or to continue to detain another person *in order to compel a third party*, namely, a State, an international governmental organization, a natural or judicial person or a group of persons, *to do or abstain from doing any act as an explicit or implicit condition for the release of the hostage* commits the offense of taking hostages within the meaning of the Convention.

(Emphases added). Under no reasonable reading of the plaintiffs' complaint does their admittedly unpleasant imprisonment qualify as hostage taking so defined.

The Convention does not proscribe all detentions, but instead focuses on the intended purpose of the detention. In this case, the complaint asserts only that Libya incarcerated Price and Frey "for the purpose of demonstrating Defendant's support of the government of Iran which held hostages in the U.S. Embassy in Tehran, Iran." Compl., at ¶ 7. Such motivation does not satisfy the Convention's intentionality requirement. The definition speaks in terms of conditions of release; the defendant must have detained the victim in order to compel some particular result, specifically to force a third party either to perform an act otherwise unplanned or to abstain from one otherwise contemplated so as to ensure the freedom of the detainee. Accordingly, detention for the goal of expressing support for illegal behavior - even for behavior that would itself qualify as "hostage taking" -does not constitute the taking of hostages within the meaning of the FSIA.

In this case, the plaintiffs have suggested no demand for *quid pro quo* terms between the government of Libya and a third party whereby Price and Frey would have been released upon the performance or non-performance of any action by that third party. Indeed, even when read most favorably to them, their complaint points to no nexus between what happened to them in Libya and any concrete concession that Libya may have hoped to extract from the outside world. The one purpose that plaintiffs have alleged is plainly inadequate, and they have advanced no others. Their allegation thus falls short of the standard for hostage taking under §1605(a)(7).

For these reasons, Libya cannot be stripped of its sovereign immunity based on plaintiffs' allegation of hostage taking. The District Court thus erred in refusing to dismiss this count. Accordingly, we reverse on this point.

G. Personal Jurisdiction

The last question that we face is whether the Due Process Clause is offended by the District Court's assertion of personal jurisdiction over Libya. If, on remand, plaintiffs can state a claim of torture under §1605(a)(7) sufficient to survive a motion to dismiss, and if they have properly served process on the defendant, personal jurisdiction will be established under the FSIA. *See* 28 U.S.C. §1330(b); *Practical Concepts, Inc. v. Republic of Bolivia*, 811 F.2d 1543, 1548 n. 11 (D.C.Cir.1987) (noting that under the FSIA, "subject matter jurisdiction plus service of process equals personal jurisdiction"). However, it is well-settled that "a statute cannot grant personal jurisdiction where the Constitution forbids it." *Gilson v. Republic of Ireland*, 682 F.2d 1022, 1028 (D.C.Cir.1982).

The Due Process Clause requires that if the defendant "be not present within the territory of the forum, he have certain minimum contacts with it such that the maintenance of the suit does not offend 'traditional notions of fair play and substantial justice.' " *Int'l Shoe*, 326 U.S. at 316, 66 S.Ct. at 158 (quoting *Milliken v. Meyer*, 311 U.S. 457, 463, 61 S.Ct. 339, 343, 85 L.Ed. 278 (1940)). In the absence of such contacts, the liberty interest protected by the Due Process Clause shields the defendant from the burden of litigating in that forum. See *Burger King Corp. v. Rudzewicz*, 471 U.S. 462, 471-72, 105 S.Ct. 2174, 2181-82, 85 L.Ed.2d 528 (1985). Libya argues that foreign states, no less than private individuals and corporations, are protected by these constitutional strictures.

In the present case, it is undisputed that Libya has no connection with the District of Columbia or with the United States, except for the alleged fact that it tortured two American citizens in Libya. This would be insufficient to satisfy the usual "minimum contacts" requirement. See, e.g., *IMO Indus., Inc. v. Kiekert AG*, 155 F.3d 254, 265-66 (3d Cir.1998) (holding that minimum contacts do not exist in an intentional tort case unless the defendant "*expressly aimed* its tortious conduct at the forum"; the mere fact that the harm

caused by the defendant was primarily felt in the forum because the plaintiff resided there is not enough); *Wallace v. Herron*, 778 F.2d 391, 394-95 (7th Cir.1985) (rejecting the suggestion that "any plaintiff may hale any defendant into court in the plaintiff's home state, where the defendant has no contacts, merely by asserting that the defendant has committed an intentional tort against the plaintiff"). Therefore, Libya argues, the Fifth Amendment precludes the exercise of personal jurisdiction in this case.

Implicit in Libya's argument is the claim that a foreign state is a "person" within the meaning of the Due Process Clause. *See* U.S. CONST. amend. V ("nor shall any person…be deprived of life, liberty, or property, without due process of law"). In previous cases, we have proceeded *as if* this proposition were true, but we have never so held. *See, e.g., Gilson*, 682 F.2d at 1028 (finding that Ireland had sufficient contacts with the United States to allow for personal jurisdiction without specifically addressing whether it was a person protected by the Fifth Amendment); *Foremost-McKesson*, 905 F.2d at 442 n. 10 (noting, in a case against Iran, the Fifth Amendment's minimum contacts requirements, but ultimately finding that the defendant had waived any such constitutional defense to personal jurisdiction).

Moreover, both the Supreme Court and this court have expressly indicated that the constitutional issue remains an open one. See *Republic of Argentina v. Weltover, Inc.*, 504 U.S. 607, 619, 112 S.Ct. 2160, 2168-69, 119 L.Ed.2d 394 (1992) (assuming without deciding that a foreign state is a person for purposes of the Due Process Clause); *Creighton Ltd. v. Gov't of Qatar*, 181 F.3d 118, 124-25 (D.C.Cir.1999) (noting that the view that foreign states are entitled to constitutional due process is merely an "unchallenged assumption"). Now, however, this assumption has been challenged. And, with the issue directly before us, we hold that foreign states are not "persons" protected by the Fifth Amendment.

Our conclusion is based on a number of considerations. First, as the Supreme Court noted in *Will v. Michigan Department of State Police*, there is an "often-expressed understanding that 'in common usage, the term "person" does not include the sovereign, and statutes employing the word are ordinarily construed to exclude it.' " 491 U.S. 58, 64, 109 S.Ct. 2304, 2308, 105 L.Ed.2d 45 (1989) (quoting *Wilson v. Omaha Indian Tribe*, 442 U.S. 653, 667, 99 S.Ct. 2529, 2537-38, 61 L.Ed.2d 153 (1979)). In the context of a specific statute, "person" may be given a broader meaning. *Compare Will*, 491 U.S. at 71, 109 S.Ct. at 2312 (holding that a State is not a "person" within the meaning of 42 U.S.C. §1983), and *Breard v. Greene*, 523 U.S. 371, 378, 118 S.Ct. 1352, 1356, 140 L.Ed.2d 529 (1998) (holding that a foreign state is not a "person" entitled to bring suit under §1983), with *Pfizer v. Government of India*, 434 U.S. 308, 320, 98 S.Ct. 584, 591-92, 54 L.Ed.2d 563 (1978) (holding that a foreign state is a "person" entitled to sue under the federal antitrust laws). In this case, however, what is at issue is the meaning of the Due Process Clause, not a statutory provision. And, on this score, it is highly significant that in *South Carolina v. Katzenbach*, 383 U.S. 301, 323-24, 86 S.Ct. 803, 815-16, 15 L.Ed.2d 769 (1966), the Court was unequivocal in holding that "the word 'person' in the context of the Due Process Clause of the Fifth Amendment cannot, by any reasonable mode of interpretation, be expanded to encompass the States of the Union." Therefore, absent some compelling reason to treat foreign sovereigns more favorably than "States of the Union," it would make no sense to view foreign states as "persons" under the Due Process Clause.

Indeed, we think it would be highly incongruous to afford greater Fifth Amendment rights to foreign nations, who are entirely alien to our constitutional system, than are afforded to the states, who help make up the very fabric of that system. The States are integral and active participants in the Constitution's infrastructure, and they both derive important benefits and must abide by significant limitations as a consequence of their participation. *Compare* U.S. CONST. art. IV §4 ("The United States shall guarantee to every State in this Union a Republican form of Government, and shall protect each of them against Invasion;"), *with id.* at art. VI, cl. 2 ("This Constitution…shall be the supreme Law of the Land; and the Judges in every State shall be bound thereby, any Thing in the Constitution or Law of the State to the Contrary notwithstanding."), and *id.* at art. 1 §10 (listing specific acts prohibited to the States). However, a "foreign State lies outside the structure of the Union." *Principality of Monaco v. Mississippi*, 292 U.S. 313, 330, 54 S.Ct. 745, 751, 78 L.Ed. 1282 (1934). Given this fundamental dichotomy between the constitutional status of foreign states and States within the United States, we cannot perceive why the former should be permitted to avail themselves of the fundamental safeguards of the Due Process Clause if the latter may not.

It is especially significant that the Constitution does not limit foreign states, as it does the States of the Union, in the power they can exert against the United States or its government. Indeed, the federal government cannot invoke the Constitution, save possibly to declare war, to prevent a foreign nation from taking action adverse to the interest of the United States or to compel it to take action favorable to the

United States. It would therefore be quite strange to interpret the Due Process Clause as conferring upon Libya rights and protections *against* the power of federal government.

In addition to text and structure, history and tradition support our conclusion. Never has the Supreme Court suggested that foreign nations enjoy rights derived from the Constitution, or that they can use such rights to shield themselves from adverse actions taken by the United States. This is not surprising. Relations between nations in the international community are seldom governed by the domestic law of one state or the other. *See* Lori Fisler Damrosch, *Foreign States and the Constitution*, 73 VA. L. REV. 483, 520 (1987) ("The most a foreign state can demand is that other states observe *international* law, not that they enforce provisions of domestic law."). And legal disputes between the United States and foreign governments are not mediated through the Constitution. See *Nat'l Council of Resistance of Iran v. Dep't of State*, 251 F.3d 192, 202 (D.C.Cir.2001) (recognizing that "sovereign states interact with each other through diplomacy and even coercion in ways not affected by constitutional protections such as the Due Process Clause").

Rather, the federal judiciary has relied on principles of comity and international law to protect foreign governments in the American legal system. This approach recognizes the reality that foreign nations are external to the constitutional compact, and it preserves the flexibility and discretion of the political branches in conducting this country's relations with other nations. *See* Damrosch, *supra*, at 521 (describing the ways in which "the recognition that foreign states and the United States interact as juridical equals on the level of international law and diplomacy outside the constitutional system, with rights and duties on the international plane not deriving from the Constitution, has shaped the Supreme Court's approach to various problems of domestic law"); *Harisiades v. Shaughnessy*, 342 U.S. 580, 588-89, 72 S.Ct. 512, 518-19, 96 L.Ed. 586 (1952) (matters such as the conduct of foreign relations are "so exclusively entrusted to the political branches of government as to be largely immune from judicial inquiry or interference").

An example of this approach is seen with respect to the right of access to the courts. Private individuals have "a constitutional right of access to the courts," *Bounds v. Smith*, 430 U.S. 817, 821, 97 S.Ct. 1491, 1494, 52 L.Ed.2d 72 (1977), that is, the "right to sue and defend in the courts," *Chambers v. Baltimore & Ohio R.R.*, 207 U.S. 142, 148, 28 S.Ct. 34, 35, 52 L.Ed. 143 (1907). See also *Wolff v. McDonnell*, 418 U.S. 539, 579, 94 S.Ct. 2963, 2986, 41 L.Ed.2d 935

(1974) (holding that this right derives from the Due Process Clause). Foreign states also have been afforded the right to use the courts of the United States to prosecute civil claims "upon the same basis as a domestic corporation or individual might do." *Pfizer*, 434 U.S. at 318-19, 98 S.Ct. at 591; see also *Principality of Monaco*, 292 U.S. at 323 n. 2, 54 S.Ct. at 748 n. 2 ("There is no question but that foreign States may sue private parties in the federal courts."). But the right of access enjoyed by foreign nations derives from "principles of comity," and it is "neither a matter of absolute obligation, on the one hand, nor of mere courtesy and good will, upon the other." *Banco Nacional de Cuba v. Sabbatino*, 376 U.S. 398, 408-09, 84 S.Ct. 923, 930, 11 L.Ed.2d 804 (1964) (quoting *Hilton v. Guyot*, 159 U.S. 113, 164-65, 16 S.Ct. 139, 143-44, 40 L.Ed. 95 (1895)). This privilege is not to be denied lightly, because to do so "would manifest a want of comity and friendly feeling." *The Sapphire*, 78 U.S. (11 Wall.) 164, 167, 20 L.Ed. 127 (1870). Nonetheless, foreign nations do not have a *constitutional* right of access to the courts of the United States. Indeed, only nations recognized by and at peace with the United States may avail themselves of our courts, and "it is within the exclusive power of the Executive Branch to determine which nations are entitled to sue." *Pfizer*, 434 U.S. at 319-20, 98 S.Ct. at 591 (noting that the rule is one of "complete judicial deference to the Executive Branch").

While we recognize that the present case implicates not the right of affirmative access to the courts, but rather its reverse - the right not to be haled into court - this does not change the analysis under the Due Process Clause. The personal jurisdiction requirement is not a structural limitation on the power of courts. Rather, "[t]he personal jurisdiction requirement recognizes and protects an individual liberty interest. It represents a restriction on judicial power not as a matter of sovereignty, but as a matter of individual liberty." *Ins. Corp. of Ire. v. Compagnie des Bauxites de Guinee*, 456 U.S. 694, 702, 102 S.Ct. 2099, 2104, 72 L.Ed.2d 492 (1982). This makes sense, because "[t]he requirement that a court have personal jurisdiction flows not from Art. III, but from the Due Process Clause." *Id.* And the "core of the concept" of due process is "to secure the individual from the arbitrary exercise of the powers of government, unrestrained by the established principles of private right and distributive justice." *County of Sacramento v. Lewis*, 523 U.S. 833, 845-46, 118 S.Ct. 1708, 1716, 140 L.Ed.2d 1043 (1998). It is thus quite clear that the constitutional law of personal jurisdiction secures interests quite different from those at stake when a sovereign nation such as Libya seeks to defend itself against the prerogatives of a rival government. It therefore

follows that foreign states stand on a fundamentally different footing than do private litigants who are compelled to defend themselves in American courts.

Unlike private entities, foreign nations are the juridical equals of the government that seeks to assert jurisdiction over them. *See* Damrosch, *supra*, at 519-20 & n. 150 ("Foreign states exist within the United States as coequal sovereigns on the international plane. International law recognizes the juridical equality of each member of the international community, and establishes for all states a series of rights and duties flowing from this principle."). If they believe that they have suffered harm by virtue of being haled into court in the United States, foreign states have available to them a panoply of mechanisms in the international arena through which to seek vindication or redress. *Id.* at 525 . These mechanisms, not the Constitution, set the terms by which sovereigns relate to one another. We would break with the norms of international law and the structure of domestic law were we to extend a constitutional rule meant to protect individual liberty so as to frustrate the United States government's clear statutory command that Libya be subject to the jurisdiction of the federal courts in the circumstances of this case. The constitutional limits that have been placed on the exercise of personal jurisdiction do not limit the prerogative of our nation to authorize legal action against another sovereign. Conferring on Libya the due process trump that it seeks against the authority of the United States is thus not only textually and structurally unsound, but it would distort the very notion of "liberty" that underlies the Due Process Clause.

The distinction between *privileges* conferred on foreign states without reference to the Constitution and corresponding *rights* enjoyed by other entities because of the Constitution extends to sovereign immunity itself. The Supreme Court has made clear that Congress lacks the power under Article I to abrogate the sovereign immunity of the *States of the Union. Alden v. Maine*, 527 U.S. 706, 712, 119 S.Ct. 2240, 2246, 144 L.Ed.2d 636 (1999); *Seminole Tribe of Fl. v. Florida*, 517 U.S. 44, 72-73, 116 S.Ct. 1114, 1131-32, 134 L.Ed.2d 252 (1996). Such immunity from suit, if not *created* by the Constitution, see *Blatchford v. Native Village of Noatak*, 501 U.S. 775, 779, 111 S.Ct. 2578, 2581, 115 L.Ed.2d 686 (1991), is at least *protected* by it. Thus, the national government is prevented from undoing this immunity except under limited and unusual circumstances. See, e.g., *Bd. of Trustees of Univ. of Ala. v. Garrett*, 531 U.S. 356, 121 S.Ct. 955, 148 L.Ed.2d 866 (2001). In contrast, however, nothing in the Constitution limits congressional authority to modify or remove the sovereign immunity that foreign states otherwise enjoy. Instead, like the right of access to courts, such immunity is "a matter of grace and comity on the part of the United States, and not a restriction imposed by the Constitution." *Verlinden*, 461 U.S. at 486, 103 S.Ct. at 1967.

In short, we are unwilling to interpret the Due Process Clause as conferring rights on foreign nations that States of the Union do not possess. Neither the text of the Constitution, Supreme Court decisions construing the Due Process Clause, nor long standing tradition provide a basis for extending the reach of this constitutional provision for the benefit of foreign states.

Finally, it is worth noting that serious practical problems might arise were we to hold that foreign states may cloak themselves in the protections of the Due Process Clause. For example, the power of Congress and the President to freeze the assets of foreign nations, or to impose economic sanctions on them, could be challenged as deprivations of property without due process of law. The courts would be called upon to adjudicate these sensitive questions, which in turn could tie the hands of the other branches as they sought to respond to foreign policy crises. The Constitution does not command this. See *Regan v. Wald*, 468 U.S. 222, 242, 104 S.Ct. 3026, 3037-38, 82 L.Ed.2d 171 (1984); *DKT Mem'l Fund Ltd. v. Agency for Int'l Dev.*, 887 F.2d 275, 291 (D.C.Cir.1989) (describing the need for the nation to speak with "a single voice" in foreign affairs); *People's Mojahedin Org. of Iran v. Dep't of State*, 182 F.3d 17, 22 (D.C.Cir.1999) ("No one would suppose that a foreign nation had a due process right to notice and a hearing before the Executive imposed an embargo on it for the purpose of coercing a change in policy.").

In sum, we hold that the Fifth Amendment poses no obstacle to the decision of the United States government to subject Libya to personal jurisdiction in the federal courts. Our decision on this point reaches only an actual foreign government; we express no view as to whether other entities that fall within the FSIA's definition of "foreign state" -including corporations in which a foreign state owns a majority interest, *see* 28 U.S.C. §1603(b) - could yet be considered persons under the Due Process Clause. We also note that the unavailability of constitutional due process protections will not render foreign states helpless when sued in the United States, for the doctrine of *forum non conveniens* remains fully applicable in FSIA cases. See *Verlinden*, 461 U.S. at 490 n. 15, 103 S.Ct. at 1970 n. 15; *Proyecfin de Venezuela,*

S.A. v. Banco Industrial de Venezuela, S.A., 760 F.2d 390, 394 (2d Cir.1985) (suggesting that the *forum non conveniens* doctrine helps mitigate the concern that "United States courts will become the courts of choice for local disputes between foreign plaintiffs and foreign sovereign defendants and thus be reduced to international courts of claims") (internal quotation marks omitted).

III. CONCLUSION

For the reasons given above, we reverse in part and remand the case to the District Court for further proceedings consistent with this opinion.

Notes:

1. The first case brought under the 1996 amendments to the Foreign Sovereign Immunities Act was *Alejandre v. The Republic of Cuba*, 996 F.Supp. 1239, 1249 (S.D. Fla. 1997) which addressed the claims of the plaintiffs as follows,

> Having established an exception to foreign sovereign immunity, Plaintiffs base their substantive cause of action on a different statute, also enacted in 1996, entitled Civil Liability for Acts of State Sponsored Terrorism, Pub.L. 104-208, §589, 110 Stat. 3009 (codified at 28 U.S.C.A. §1605 note (West.Supp.1997)) ("Civil Liability Act"). The Civil Liability Act creates a cause of action against agents of a foreign state that act under the conditions specified in FSIA section 1605(a)(7). It thus serves as an enforcement provision for acts described in section 1605(a)(7). If Plaintiffs prove an agent's liability under this Act, the foreign state employing the agent would also incur liability under the theory of respondeat superior. See *Skeen v. Federative Republic of Brazil*, 566 F.Supp. 1414, 1417 (D.D.C.1983) (explaining that section 1605(a)(5) "is essentially a respondeat superior statute, providing an employer (the foreign state) with liability for certain tortious acts of its employees").

2. From 1997 to 2002, when *Price* was decided by the Court of Appeals for the District of Columbia Circuit, virtually all of the dozens of FSIA terrorism decisions assumed that a cause of action was specified in the Flatow Amendment.

3. In *Roeder v. Islamic Republic of Iran*, 195 F.Supp.2d 140, 171-173 (D.D.C. 2002) the court raised the issue as

to whether the terrorism amendments to the FSIA, itself merely a jurisdictional statute, were intended by Congress to create a new cause of action,

> However, even if this Court ultimately agrees with these courts that the purpose and history of this legislation could support reading into this statute a cause of action against a foreign government, these cases in no way support plaintiffs' claim that the language of these statutes *unambiguously* requires such a conclusion. Indeed, the previous opinions by this Court demonstrate Congress' lack of clarity and the lengths to which this Court had to go to interpret these provisions consistently... The Court agrees that it is *possible* to read these statutory provisions, in the context of legislative history and intent, to provide for a cause of action against Iran. While all these pieces of legislation are less than the epitome of clarity, and their enactment via appropriations rider leaves this Court with scant legislative history to consider, the history that does exist does indicate an intent to allow plaintiffs to proceed with their claims against Iran. This Court will not go so far as to conclude that the text of the Flatow Amendment and Subsection 626(c), separated from any legislative history or intent, unambiguously precludes the cause of action here. However, the fact that an interpretation of these statutory provisions, when considered in the context of legislative intent and purpose, allowing plaintiffs to proceed against Iran is possible, does not end this Court's inquiry. Because these statutory provisions are at best ambiguous with respect to whether plaintiffs can sue Iran, if Congress has not expressed a sufficiently clear intent to abrogate the Algiers Accords, this Court *must* construe the statutes at issue to preclude such a suit.

4.   What language of the Flatow Amendment, 28 U.S.C. §1605 note, suggests ambiguity as to whether it contains or creates a cause of action against a state sponsor of terrorism? Why was the "cause of action" issue the subject of so much litigation?

5.   As the *Cicippeo* court notes, even after *Price*,

> some district court opinions in this circuit have held or assumed that the Flatow Amendment creates a cause of action against foreign states. See *Cronin v. Islamic Republic of Iran*, 238 F.Supp.2d

222, 231 (D.D.C. 2002) (holding that the Flatow Amendment provides a cause of action against a foreign state). See also *Regier v. Islamic Republic of Iran*, 281 F.Supp.2d 87, 98-99 (D.D.C. 2003) (adopting *Cronin's* reasoning that there is a cause of action against foreign states under the Flatow Amendment); *Kilburn v. Republic of Iran*, 277 F.Supp.2d 24, 36-37 (D.D.C. 2003) (same).

> This court, however, has never affirmed a judgment that the Flatow Amendment, either alone or in conjunction with section 1605(a)(7), provides a cause of action against a foreign state. The issue was raised in *Bettis v. Islamic Republic of Iran*, 315 F.3d 325, 333 (D.C.Cir. 2003), but the appeal was resolved on other grounds.

Cicippio-Puleo v. Islamic Republic of Iran, 353 F.3d 1024, 1032 (D.C.Cir. 2004).

6.   Until the Court of Appeals clarified this issue, the ambiguity continued to lead to awkward results. For example in *Campuzao v. Islamic Republic of Iran*, 281 F.Supp.2d 258 (D.D.C. 2003) two separate cases involving the victims of a single attack bombing were consolidated for trial and decision. The "Campuzanos" alleged that the Flatow Amendment created a cause action while the "Rubins" argued alternately for relief alleging common law claims as well. The court found,

> One final point regarding liability merits attention. In addition to their claim for liability pursuant to the FSIA, specifically, the Flatow Amendment, the *Rubin* plaintiffs also claim liability pursuant to common law for the torts of assault, battery, and intentional infliction of emotional distress and present proposed conclusions of law for these claims. [FN5] *Rubin* Pls.' Prop. Findings of Fact and Conclusions of Law at 22-46. However, the *Rubin* plaintiffs' proposed findings of fact and conclusions of law leave unclear whether they included their common law causes of action as an alternative or additional theory of liability. *Id.* Because the court has concluded that the defendants are liable for the personal injuries caused to the plaintiffs by the defendants' actions, the analysis of these claims is redundant with the FSIA liability analysis. Nevertheless, out of an abundance of caution, the court will briefly address the common law claims, which are valid claims that the plaintiffs have proven.

FN5. In contrast, the *Campuzano* plaintiffs limit their proposed conclusions of law to liability pursuant to the FSIA and the Flatow amendment. *Campuzano* Pls.' Prop. Findings of Fact and Conclusions of Law at 22-29. While many FSIA judgments have founded liability on the FSIA and the Flatow Amendment alone, some have instead founded liability on common law causes of action including assault, battery, and intentional infliction of emotional distress. Compare, e.g., *Elahi*, 124 F.Supp.2d at 106-08 (basing liability on the FSIA and the Flatow amendment) and *Mousa v. Islamic Republic of Iran*, 238 F.Supp.2d 1, 10-11 (D.D.C. 2001) (same) with, e.g., *Bettis v. Islamic Republic of Iran*, 315 F.3d 325, 332 (D.C.Cir. 2003) (affirming district court's application of common law to the plaintiffs' claims for intentional infliction of emotional distress) and *Jenco v. Islamic Republic of Iran*, 154 F.Supp.2d 27, 38 (D.D.C. 2001) (determining that the defendants were liable pursuant to the plaintiff's common law claims for battery, assault, and intentional infliction of emotional distress).

Id. 270-271. What does this holding demonstrate about the evolving legal terrain of terrorism law and the concerns plaintiffs must have in drafting pleadings?

7.   Was the Court of Appeals' statement that the plaintiffs "may have been misled in assuming that the Flatow Amendment afforded a cause of action against state sponsors of terrorism" accurate? If so, how were they misled? How could they have avoided this concern?

8.   Why was it so important to define the exact cause of action that could be pled against Iran, when the court acknowledges that several common law claims were applicable if the amendments to the FSIA did not create a separate cause of action?

9.   What were the policy concerns of the United States? Why would the government take a position in opposition to American victims and, effectively, in favor and support of a "rogue nation" that the administration considered part of the "axis of evil"? How did the government's position conflict with the purpose of the terrorism amendments to the FSIA?

***Acree v. Republic of Iraq*, 370 F.3d 41 (D.C. Cir. 2004).**

HARRY T. EDWARDS, Circuit Judge:

Appellees in this case are 17 American soldiers, joined by their close family members, who were captured and held as prisoners of war by the Iraqi Government while serving in the Gulf War in early 1991. Appellees brought suit in the District Court under the terrorism exception to the Foreign Sovereign Immunities Act ("FSIA"), 28 U.S.C. §1605(a)(7) (2000), against the Republic of Iraq, the Iraqi Intelligence Service, and Saddam Hussein, in his official capacity as President of Iraq (collectively "Iraq"), seeking compensatory and punitive damages for the horrific acts of torture they suffered during their captivity. After Iraq failed to appear, the District Court examined appellees' evidentiary submissions and entered judgment in their favor. The District Court awarded damages against Iraq totaling over $959 million. See *Acree v. Republic of Iraq*, 271 F.Supp.2d 179 (D.D.C.2003) ("*Acree I*").

Two weeks after the District Court entered its judgment for appellees, the United States filed a motion to intervene for the purpose of contesting the District Court's subject matter jurisdiction. The United States argued that recently enacted provisions of the Emergency Wartime Supplemental Appropriations Act, Pub. L. No. 108-11, §1503, 117 Stat. 559, 579 (2003), made the terrorism exception to the FSIA inapplicable to Iraq and thereby stripped the District Court of its jurisdiction over appellees' lawsuit. The District Court denied the United States' motion to intervene as untimely, see *Acree v. Republic of Iraq*, 276 F.Supp.2d 95 (D.D.C.2003) ("*Acree II*"), and the United States now appeals.

We hold that the District Court abused its discretion in finding the United States' motion to intervene to be untimely and erred in denying that motion. The United States possesses weighty foreign policy interests that are clearly threatened by the entry of judgment for appellees in this case. Although the United States filed its motion after the District Court had entered its judgment, appellees have asserted no prejudice arising from the intervention. On the merits of the United States' jurisdictional challenge, we hold that the District Court properly exercised jurisdiction in appellees' lawsuit. Although it presents a close question of statutory interpretation, we conclude that the disputed language in the emergency supplemental appropriations act does not encompass the terrorism exception to the FSIA.

We nevertheless conclude that the District Court's judgment in favor of appellees must be vacated and their lawsuit dismissed for failure to state a cause of action. The District Court's judgment against Iraq rests solely on causes of action purportedly arising under the terrorism exception and the Flatow Amendment to the FSIA. Neither appellees' complaint, nor their submissions to this court, nor the District Court's decision in their favor offers any other coherent alternative causes of action in support of appellees' claims against Iraq. Our recent decision in *Cicippio-Puleo v. Islamic Republic of Iran*, 353 F.3d 1024 (D.C.Cir.2004) ("*Cicippio*"), makes it plain that the terrorism exception to the FSIA is merely a jurisdictional provision and does not provide a cause of action against foreign states. *Cicippio* also holds that the Flatow Amendment to the FSIA, which provides a cause of action against an "official, employee, or agent of a foreign state," 28 U.S.C. §1605 note (2000), does not afford a cause of action against a foreign state itself. We are therefore constrained to vacate the judgment of the District Court and dismiss appellees' suit for failure to state a cause of action.

I. BACKGROUND

A. The POW Lawsuit

The facts in this case are undisputed. While serving in the Gulf War following the Iraqi invasion of Kuwait, Colonel Clifford Acree and 16 other American soldiers who are appellees in this case were captured and held as prisoners of war in Kuwait and the Republic of Iraq between January and March 1991. On April 4, 2002, these POWs and their close family members filed a complaint in the District Court against the Republic of Iraq, the Iraqi Intelligence Service, and Saddam Hussein, in his official capacity as President of Iraq, for personal injuries caused to them and their family members as a result of their treatment by Iraq. In their complaint, the POW plaintiffs described brutal and inhumane acts of physical and psychological torture suffered during their captivity, including severe beatings, starvation, mock executions, dark and unsanitary living conditions, and other violent and shocking acts. By these alleged atrocities, the plaintiffs' captors created a "climate [of] humiliation and degradation," in which the POWs "liv[ed] in constant fear of death and torture." Compl. ¶ 5, *reprinted in* Joint Appendix ("J.A.") 35.

Jurisdiction in the plaintiffs' lawsuit was based on the terrorism exception to the Foreign Sovereign Immunities Act, 28 U.S.C. §1605(a)(7). Under the FSIA, foreign states enjoy immunity from suit in American courts, unless that immunity has been waived or abrogated pursuant to an exception enumerated in the FSIA. *See* 28 U.S.C. §1604; *see also* 28 U.S.C. §1330(a) (limiting the district courts' jurisdiction over suits against foreign states to cases in which the foreign state is not entitled to immunity under the FSIA). Section 1605(a)(7), added to the FSIA in 1996, creates an exception to foreign sovereign immunity in civil suits "in which money damages are sought against a foreign state for personal injury or death that was caused by an act of torture" or other terrorist acts. 28 U.S.C. §1605(a)(7). This exception applies only if the defendant foreign state was designated as a state sponsor of terrorism at the time the alleged acts of torture occurred. *See* 28 U.S.C. §1605(a)(7)(A). Pursuant to §6(j) of the Export Administration Act, 50 U.S.C.App. §2405(j) (1988 & Supp. I 1989), the Republic of Iraq was designated as a state sponsor of terrorism on September 13, 1990, shortly after the Iraqi invasion of Kuwait and before the events took place that formed the basis of the plaintiffs' claims. *See* 55 Fed. Reg. 37,793 (Sep. 13, 1990). Iraq was therefore amenable to suit in federal court under the FSIA at the time the plaintiffs commenced their lawsuit.

Citing several decisions of the District Court, the plaintiffs - appellees herein - premised their cause of action on §1605(a)(7), as amended by the so-called "Flatow Amendment," which was adopted shortly after §1605(a)(7) was added to the FSIA in 1996. *See* Compl. ¶ 596, J.A. 143. The Flatow Amendment provides that:

[A]n official, employee, or agent of a foreign state designated as a state sponsor of terrorism…while acting within the scope of his or her office, employment, or agency shall be liable to a United States national or the national's legal representative for personal injury or death caused by acts of that official, employee, or agent for which the courts of the United States may maintain jurisdiction under [§1605(a)(7)] for money damages which may include economic damages, solatium, pain, and suffering, and punitive damages if the acts were among those described in [§1605(a)(7)].

28 U.S.C. §1605 note. Appellees alleged that the acts of torture set forth in their complaint constituted "traditional torts of assault, battery and intentional infliction of emotional distress," Compl. ¶ 597, J.A. 143, and requested compensatory and punitive damages for each of the POW plaintiffs and their family members.

Appellees effected proper service of process through diplomatic channels, pursuant to 28 U.S.C. §1608. The Iraqi defendants failed to appear, and the Clerk of the District Court accordingly entered default against the defendants on September 25, 2002. On March 31, 2003, appellees submitted evidence to support their assertion of liability and claim for damages. These submissions provided further details regarding the factual basis of appellees' claims and again asserted the existence of a cause of action based on §1605(a)(7), as amended by the Flatow Amendment, for assault, battery, and intentional infliction of emotional distress. *See* Pls.' Proposed Findings of Fact and Conclusions of Law at 80-90.

On July 7, 2003, the District Court entered final judgment in favor of appellees. *See Acree I*, 271 F.Supp.2d 179. The District Court held that "[s]uits brought under §1605(a)(7) may be based on conventional common law torts." *Id.* at 215. Based on extensive findings of fact regarding the specific injuries suffered by each plaintiff, the District Court awarded compensatory and punitive damages to all of the POW plaintiffs and their family members totaling over $959 million. *Id.* at 224-25.

B. Legal and Military Developments in Iraq

As the proceedings in the District Court were running their course, the legal and military situation in Iraq was changing rapidly. In connection with Iraq's designation as a state sponsor of terrorism in September 1990, Congress had passed various statutes imposing sanctions on Iraq and prohibiting the United States Government and private parties from sending assistance to Iraq or conducting business or trade with Iraq. Most notably, Congress enacted the Iraq Sanctions Act of 1990, which condemned the Iraqi invasion of Kuwait and provided for the maintenance of a trade embargo and economic sanctions against Iraq. *See* Pub. L. No. 101-513, §§586-586J, 104 Stat. 1979, 2047-55 (1990) (codified at 50 U.S.C. §1701 note (2000)) ("ISA"). These provisions required that all assistance, exports, loans, credits, insurance, or other guarantees be denied to Iraq, with exceptions for limited humanitarian relief. Section 586F(c) of the ISA also required full enforcement against Iraq of §620A of the Foreign Assistance Act of 1961, which prohibits the grant of any assistance to any country determined by the Secretary of State to have "repeatedly provided support for acts of international terrorism," Pub. L. No. 87-195, §620A, *as added* Pub. L. No. 94-329, §303, 90 Stat. 729, 753 (1976) (codified as amended at 22 U.S.C. §2371) ("FAA"). Along with the FAA, the ISA required that several other enumerated provisions of law be fully enforced against Iraq, as well as "all other provisions of law that impose sanctions against a country which has repeatedly provided support for acts of international terrorism." ISA §586F(c), 104 Stat. 1979, 2051.

Both the Iraq Sanctions Act and the Foreign Assistance Act provide for rescission of the prohibitions they impose on aid to Iraq and other designated states, but only after the President certifies to Congress that there has been a fundamental change in the government or policies of the designated state and that the leadership is no longer supporting acts of terrorism. *See* ISA §586H, 104 Stat. 1979, 2052-53; FAA, 22 U.S.C. §2371(c) (2000). A similar certification is required to rescind the Secretary of State's determination under the Export Administration Act that Iraq is a country that has repeatedly provided support for acts of international terrorism. *See* 50 U.S.C.App. §2405(j)(4) (2000).

Shortly after the commencement of the most recent military action against Iraq in 2003, which resulted in the ouster of Saddam Hussein's regime, the United States' policy toward Iraq changed to reconstructing Iraq's government and rebuilding the country's infrastructure. In furtherance of these new objectives, Congress took several steps to eliminate restrictions on the ability of the United States Government and private parties to provide assistance to or conduct business with Iraq. In April 2003, Congress enacted the Emergency Wartime Supplemental Appropriations Act ("EWSAA" or "Act"), which appropriated additional funding for military operations in Iraq, homeland security efforts in the United States, and bilateral economic assistance to America's allies in the war in Iraq. *See* Pub. L. No. 108-11, 117 Stat. 559 (2003). The bulk of the $78.5 billion appropriated in this Act was allocated to national defense activities. In addition, the Act appropriated nearly $2.5 billion for a new Iraq Relief and Reconstruction Fund, to be used for the development of physical and government infrastructure and humanitarian activities in Iraq. *See* H.R. CONF. REP. No. 108-76, at 70-72 (2003). The Act provided that assistance to Iraq under the Iraq Relief and Reconstruction Fund and other aid programs could be provided "notwithstanding any other provision of law." *See* EWSAA §1502, 117 Stat. 559, 578.

Of particular relevance to this appeal, §1503 of the EWSAA authorized the President to "suspend the application of any provision of the Iraq Sanctions Act of 1990." EWSAA §1503, 117 Stat. 559, 579. Section 1503 "[p]rovided further, [t]hat the President may make inapplicable with respect to Iraq section 620A of the Foreign Assistance Act of 1961 or any other provision of law that applies to countries that have supported terrorism." *Id.* The suspension of these provisions would permit American assistance to Iraq to proceed without awaiting completion of the lengthy certification process required to rescind the Secretary of State's previous determination as to Iraq's status as a sponsor of terrorism.

On May 7, 2003, President Bush carried out the authority granted in §1503 of the EWSAA by issuing Presidential Determination No. 2003-23, which "ma[d]e inapplicable with respect to Iraq section 620A of the Foreign Assistance Act of 1961…and any other provision of law that applies to countries that have supported terrorism." Presidential Determination No. 2003-23 of May 7, 2003, 68 Fed. Reg. 26,459 (May 16, 2003). In a message to Congress delivered on May 22, 2003, President Bush explained the need to protect Iraqi assets from attachment, judgment, or other judicial process, and stated his view that the May 7 Determination applied to, *inter alia*, the terrorism exception to the FSIA, 28 U.S.C. §1605(a)(7). *See* Message to the Congress Reporting the Declaration of a National Emergency With Respect to the Development Fund for Iraq, 39 WEEKLY COMP. PRES. DOC. 647, 647-48 (May 22, 2003).

C. The United States' Motion to Intervene

On July 21, 2003, two weeks after the District Court entered judgment for appellees, the United States moved to intervene for the sole purpose of contesting the subject matter jurisdiction of the District Court. This challenge rested on legal developments that had occurred in the wake of the United States' invasion of Iraq in March 2003. The United States argued that §1605(a)(7) is a "provision of law that applies to countries that have supported terrorism" within the meaning of §1503 of the EWSAA, as implemented by the May 7 Presidential Determination, and was therefore made inapplicable to Iraq by operation of those provisions. The District Court, the Government argued, was therefore divested of jurisdiction over appellees' lawsuit as of May 7, 2003, two months prior to the entry of judgment against the Iraqi defendants.

On August 6, 2003, the District Court denied the Government's motion to intervene as untimely. *See Acree II*, 276 F.Supp.2d at 98-99. The District Court noted that the United States had waited 75 days after the Presidential Determination to file its motion, and the court was particularly reluctant to permit the Government to intervene after appellees' case had proceeded to final judgment. See *id.* The District Court further held that, even if the United States' motion was not untimely, appellees' lawsuit did not threaten to impair any cognizable interest of the United States and that allowing the Government to intervene at that late stage would cause undue delay and prejudice to the parties. See *id.* at 99-102. Finally, the District Court considered its own subject matter jurisdiction and concluded that it retained jurisdiction under the FSIA, despite the EWSAA and the Presidential Deter-

mination. See *id.* at 100-01. On August 22, 2003, the United States filed this appeal of the District Court's decision.

D. Related Developments

Just before the United States moved to intervene, appellees filed a second suit in the District Court against the Secretary of the Treasury, seeking to satisfy their newly won judgment against Iraq by attaching funds from seized Iraqi bank accounts, pursuant to the Terrorism Risk Insurance Act of 2002 ("TRIA"). *See Acree v. Snow*, 276 F.Supp.2d 31 (D.D.C.2003). Section 201(a) of the TRIA provides that a person who has obtained a judgment against a foreign state designated as a state sponsor of terrorism may seek to attach the blocked assets of that state in satisfaction of an award of compensatory damages based on an act of terrorism. *See* Pub. L. No. 107-297, §201, 116 Stat. 2322, 2337 (2002) (codified at 28 U.S.C. §1610 note). Although appellees initially prevailed in obtaining a temporary restraining order, precluding the Secretary of the Treasury from spending down the United States' seized Iraqi assets, the District Court ultimately awarded summary judgment to the United States. See *Acree v. Snow*, 276 F.Supp.2d at 33. The District Court held that §1503 of the EWSAA, as implemented by the May 7 Determination, made the TRIA inapplicable to Iraq and therefore unavailable to appellees as a mechanism for satisfying their judgment. See *id.* at 32-33.

This court affirmed the decision of the District Court by judgment. See *Acree v. Snow*, 78 Fed.Appx. 133 (D.C.Cir.2003). The court did not address the applicability or effect of the EWSAA and the Presidential Determination, however. Rather, the court adopted the reasoning of the Second Circuit's decision in *Smith v. Federal Reserve Bank of New York*, 346 F.3d 264 (2d Cir.2003). In that case, the Second Circuit held that plaintiffs proceeding under the TRIA to attach seized Iraqi assets in satisfaction of a judgment were precluded from doing so because the President had previously confiscated the blocked assets and vested title in them in the United States Department of the Treasury, thereby rendering those funds insusceptible to execution or attachment. See *id.* at 272 (discussing Exec. Order No. 13,290 of Mar. 20, 2003, 68 Fed. Reg. 14,307 (Mar. 24, 2003)). The Second Circuit - and by extension this court - therefore did not reach the issue of whether §1503 or the Presidential Determination made the TRIA inapplicable to Iraq and expressed no views on the scope or validity of those provisions. See *id.*

In another important development, this court issued its decision in *Cicippio*, 353 F.3d 1024, three months before oral argument in this case. That case presented the question whether 28 U.S.C. §1605(a)(7) or the Flatow Amendment, 28 U.S.C. §1605 note, created a cause of action against a foreign state. Several decisions in the District Court had held or assumed that these provisions did create a cause of action against foreign states. See *Cicippio*, 353 F.3d at 1032 (citing cases). The court of appeals had not previously affirmed any of these judgments, however, or otherwise squarely confronted the issue. See *Roeder v. Islamic Republic of Iran*, 333 F.3d 228, 234 n. 3 (D.C.Cir.2003) (noting that it is "far from clear" whether a plaintiff has a cause of action against a foreign state under the FSIA, but resolving the appeal on other grounds); *Bettis v. Islamic Republic of Iran*, 315 F.3d 325, 333 (D.C.Cir.2003) (raising but not resolving the question of whether the FSIA creates a cause of action against foreign states); *Price v. Socialist People's Libyan Arab Jamahiriya*, 294 F.3d 82, 87 (D.C.Cir.2002) ("There is a question…whether the FSIA creates a federal cause of action for torture and hostage taking *against foreign states*.") (emphasis in original).

In *Cicippio*, this court definitively ruled that "neither 28 U.S.C. §1605(a)(7) nor the Flatow Amendment, nor the two considered in tandem, creates a private right of action against a foreign government." 353 F.3d at 1033. We held that §1605(a)(7) merely waived the immunity of foreign states, without creating a cause of action against them, and that the Flatow Amendment provides a cause of action only against officials, employees, and agents of a foreign state, not against the foreign state itself. See *id*. We further held that "insofar as the Flatow Amendment creates a private right of action against officials, employees, and agents of foreign states, the cause of action is limited to claims against those officials in their *individual*, as opposed to their official, capacities." *Id*. at 1034. Because of its clear relevance to the instant case, in which the only named defendants are the Republic of Iraq, the Iraqi Intelligence Service, and Saddam Hussein in his official capacity as President of Iraq, we ordered the parties here to consider the implications of our ruling in *Cicippio* for appellees' suit and to be prepared to discuss the issue at oral argument. See *Acree v. Republic of Iraq*, No. 03-5232 (D.C.Cir. Apr. 5, 2004).

II. ANALYSIS

This case requires us to consider whether §1503 of the EWSAA, as implemented by the May 7 Presidential Determination, makes the terrorism exception to the FSIA inapplicable with respect to Iraq. While it is a close question,

we agree with appellees that 28 U.S.C. §1605(a)(7) is not a provision of law that falls within the scope of §1503. The District Court therefore properly exercised jurisdiction over appellees' lawsuit under the FSIA. Having reached this conclusion, we need not address the additional issues debated by the parties concerning the retroactive scope and constitutional validity of §1503 and the Presidential Determination.

Although we find that the District Court had jurisdiction in this matter, the judgment for appellees must nonetheless be vacated. This court's recent decision in *Cicippio* makes it clear that plaintiffs cannot state a cause of action against a foreign state under §1605(a)(7) or the Flatow Amendment, the sole bases for appellees" action in this case. Although *Cicippio* was decided after the District Court's judgment in this case, it is nonetheless the controlling precedent to which we must look in determining whether appellees have stated a cause of action. Because appellees' action fails under *Cicippio*, we conclude that the District Court's judgment in favor of appellees must be vacated and their suit dismissed for failure to state a cause of action.

Before reaching any of these merits issues, however, we must consider the propriety of the District Court's order denying the United States' motion to intervene. For, in any appeal, " 'the first and fundamental question is that of jurisdiction, first, of [the appellate] court, and then of the court from which the record comes.' " *Steel Co. v. Citizens for a Better Env't*, 523 U.S. 83, 94, 118 S.Ct. 1003, 1012, 140 L.Ed.2d 210 (1998) (quoting *Great S. Fire Proof Hotel Co. v. Jones*, 177 U.S. 449, 453, 20 S.Ct. 690, 691-92, 44 L.Ed. 842 (1900)). If the United States were not properly a party to this case, then it would have no right to appeal the District Court's judgment, see *Marino v. Ortiz*, 484 U.S. 301, 304, 108 S.Ct. 586, 587-88, 98 L.Ed.2d 629 (1988), and we would be required to dismiss this case without passing upon its merits for lack of a proper appellant.

A. The Motion to Intervene

The District Court's denial of a motion to intervene is an appealable final order. See *Fund for Animals, Inc. v. Norton*, 322 F.3d 728, 732 (D.C.Cir.2003). Our standard of review in such an appeal is mixed. We review pure questions of law *de novo*, findings of fact for clear error, and discretionary issues such as timeliness for abuse of discretion. See *id*. In this case, we find that the District Court abused its discretion in finding the United States' motion to be untimely and erred in denying the motion.

Under Rule 24 of the Federal Rules of Civil Procedure, a prospective intervenor must be permitted to intervene as of right if the applicant claims an interest relating to the subject matter of the case, if the disposition of the case stands to impair that interest, and if the applicant's interest is not adequately represented by the existing parties. *See* FED. R. CIV. P. 24(a). Alternatively, an applicant may be permitted to intervene if his claim shares a question of law or fact in common with the underlying action and if the intervention will not unduly delay or prejudice the rights of the original parties. *See* FED.R.CIV.P. 24(b). Under either test, the prospective intervenor's motion must be "timely." *See* FED. R.CIV.P. 24(a), (b). Evaluation of the timeliness of a motion to intervene lies within the sound discretion of the District Court. See *Fund for Animals*, 322 F.3d at 732 (citing *Mass. Sch. of Law at Andover, Inc. v. United States*, 118 F.3d 776, 779 (D.C.Cir.1997) ("*MSL*")).

Courts are generally reluctant to permit intervention after a suit has proceeded to final judgment, particularly where the applicant had the opportunity to intervene prior to judgment. See *Associated Builders & Contractors, Inc. v. Herman*, 166 F.3d 1248, 1257 (D.C.Cir.1999); *MSL*, 118 F.3d at 783 n. 5; *see also* 7C CHARLES ALAN WRIGHT, ARTHUR R. MILLER, AND MARY KAY KANE, FEDERAL PRACTICE AND PROCEDURE §1916 (2d ed. 1986) ("WRIGHT & MILLER"). The timeliness of a motion to intervene must be considered in light of all the circumstances of the case, however, *see* WRIGHT & MILLER §1916, including the purpose for which intervention is sought, the need for intervention as a means of preserving the applicant's rights, and the possibility of prejudice to the existing parties, see *Smoke v. Norton*, 252 F.3d 468, 471 (D.C.Cir.2001) (quoting *United States v. AT&T*, 642 F.2d 1285, 1295 (D.C.Cir.1980)). Post-judgment intervention is often permitted, therefore, where the prospective intervenor's interest did not arise until the appellate stage or where intervention would not unduly prejudice the existing parties. *See* WRIGHT & MILLER §1916. In particular, courts often grant post-judgment motions to intervene where no existing party chooses to appeal the judgment of the trial court. See *id*.

In *Smoke*, we reversed the District Court's denial of a post-judgment motion to intervene where the existing party indicated it might not bring an appeal. *See* 252 F.3d at 470-71. In doing so, we noted that the would-be intervenor's interests, which had been consonant with those of the existing party, were no longer adequately represented by that party's litigation of the case. See *id*. at 471. In those circumstances, we found the post-judgment motion to intervene for the pur-

pose of prosecuting an appeal to be timely, because " 'the potential inadequacy of representation came into existence only at the appellate stage.' " *Id*. (quoting *Dimond v. District of Columbia*, 792 F.2d 179, 193 (D.C.Cir.1986)); see also *United Airlines, Inc. v. McDonald*, 432 U.S. 385, 395, 97 S.Ct. 2464, 2470, 53 L.Ed.2d 423 (1977) (holding that the trial court erred in denying as untimely a post-judgment motion to intervene filed promptly after judgment and noting that this holding was "consistent with several decisions of the federal courts permitting post-judgment intervention for the purpose of appeal"); *Dimond*, 792 F.2d at 193-94 (reversing the District Court's denial of post-judgment intervention where the intervenor sought to participate only at the appellate stage).

In this case, the District Court denied the United States' motion to intervene largely because it came after the court had already entered judgment in the case. *See Acree II*, 276 F.Supp.2d at 98-99. The District Court noted that approximately two months had intervened between the May 7 Presidential Determination and the entry of final judgment for appellees, during which time the United States could have filed its motion. See *id*. However, in reaching this judgment, the District Court failed to consider adequately the unique circumstances of this case.

In particular, the District Court failed to weigh the importance of this case to the United States' foreign policy interests and the purposes for which the Government sought to intervene. This is not a case in which the United States was simply seeking to weigh in on the merits. Rather, the Government's sole purpose in intervening was to raise a highly tenable challenge to the District Court's subject matter jurisdiction in a case with undeniable impact on the Government's conduct of foreign policy and to preserve that issue for appellate review.

In the face of these weighty interests, appellees assert no prejudice arising from the United States' intervention. Nor could they, given the District Court's independent obligation to assure itself of its own jurisdiction. The only result achieved by denial of the motion to intervene in this case is the effective insulation of the District Court's exercise of jurisdiction from all appellate review. In these circumstances, we find that the District Court abused its discretion in denying the United States' motion as untimely. See *United Airlines*, 432 U.S. at 395-96, 97 S.Ct. at 2470-71; *Smoke*, 252 F.3d at 470-71. In light of its clear foreign policy interests, the United States was entitled to intervene as of right pursuant to Rule 24. See *Roeder*, 333 F.3d at 233 (permitting the United States to intervene in a case implicating foreign policy concerns). We therefore reverse the decision of the District Court denying the United States' motion to intervene and turn to the merits of the Government's jurisdictional challenge.

B. Subject Matter Jurisdiction Under the FSIA

It is uncontested that at the time appellees commenced their lawsuit in April 2002, the District Court had jurisdiction over the case under §1605(a)(7), because appellees sought damages for injuries arising from alleged acts of torture that occurred while Iraq was designated as a state sponsor of terrorism. The United States now argues that §1503 of the EWSAA, as implemented by the May 7 Presidential Determination, made §1605(a)(7) inapplicable to Iraq and thereby divested the District Court of its jurisdiction in appellees' case. Appellees respond that §1605(a)(7) is not a provision of law that falls within the scope of §1503 of the EWSAA. Appellees alternatively contend that §1503 and the Presidential Determination cannot be applied against them in this case without resulting in impermissible retroactive effects or violating constitutional principles of separation of powers. We review the District Court's exercise of jurisdiction *de novo*. See *Empagran S.A. v. F. Hoffman-LaRoche, Ltd.*, 315 F.3d 338, 343 (D.C.Cir.2003).

In our view, while it is an exceedingly close question, the language of §1503 of the EWSAA does not embrace the terrorism exception to the FSIA. We conclude that §1503, read in the context of the EWSAA as a whole and its legislative history, is aimed at legal provisions that present obstacles to assistance and funding for the new Iraqi Government and was not intended to alter the jurisdiction of the federal courts under the FSIA.

This issue presents us with a basic question of statutory interpretation. We therefore begin with the language of the EWSAA. See *Holloway v. United States*, 526 U.S. 1, 6, 119 S.Ct. 966, 969, 143 L.Ed.2d 1 (1999). Section 1503 provides, in its entirety:

The President may suspend the application of any provision of the Iraq Sanctions Act of 1990: *Provided*, That nothing in this section shall affect the applicability of the Iran-Iraq Arms Non-Proliferation Act of 1992, except that such Act shall not apply to humanitarian assistance and supplies: *Provided further, That the President may make inapplicable with respect to Iraq section 620A of the Foreign Assistance Act of 1961 or any other provision of law that applies to*

countries that have supported terrorism: Provided further, That military equipment, as defined by title XVI, section 1608(1)(A) of Public Law 102-484, shall not be exported under the authority of this section: *Provided further*, That section 307 of the Foreign Assistance Act of 1961 shall not apply with respect to programs of international organizations for Iraq: *Provided further*, That provisions of law that direct the United States Government to vote against or oppose loans or other uses of funds, including for financial or technical assistance, in international financial institutions for Iraq shall not be construed as applying to Iraq: *Provided further*, That the President shall submit a notification 5 days prior to exercising any of the authorities described in this section to the Committee on Appropriations of each House of the Congress, the Committee on Foreign Relations of the Senate, and the Committee on International Relations of the House of Representatives: *Provided further*, That not more than 60 days after enactment of this Act and every 90 days thereafter the President shall submit a report to the Committee on Appropriations of each House of the Congress, the Committee on Foreign Relations of the Senate, and the Committee on International Relations of the House of Representatives containing a summary of all licenses approved for export to Iraq of any item on the Commerce Control List contained in the Export Administration Regulations, including identification of end users of such items: *Provided further*, That the authorities contained in this section shall expire on September 30, 2004, or on the date of enactment of a subsequent Act authorizing assistance for Iraq and that specifically amends, repeals or otherwise makes inapplicable the authorities of this section, whichever occurs first.

EWSAA §1503, 117 Stat. 559, 579 (citations omitted) (emphasis added). The controversy in this case concerns the second proviso of §1503, authorizing the President to "make inapplicable with respect to Iraq section 620A of the Foreign Assistance Act of 1961 *or any other provision of law that applies to countries that have supported terrorism.*" *Id.* (emphasis added). The United States argues that this language embraces the authority to make §1605(a)(7) inapplicable to Iraq, and that the President carried out that authority in the May 7 Presidential Determination.

The logic of this interpretation is straightforward: Section 1605(a)(7) creates an exception to the sovereign immunity normally enjoyed by foreign states in American courts for suits based on acts of torture or other terrorist acts. This exception applies only if the defendant foreign state was designated as a sponsor of terrorism at the time the acts took place. Section 1605(a)(7) is thus a "provision of law that applies to countries that have supported terrorism." The EWSAA authorizes the President to make such provisions inapplicable to Iraq, which authority the President exercised in the May 7 Determination. Section 1605(a)(7) therefore no longer applies to Iraq and cannot provide a basis for jurisdiction in appellees' case. *Quod erat demonstrandum.*

The difficulty with this view is that it focuses exclusively on the meaning of one clause of §1503, divorced from all that surrounds it. This approach violates "the cardinal rule that a statute is to be read as a whole, since the meaning of statutory language, plain or not, depends on context." *King v. St. Vincent's Hosp.*, 502 U.S. 215, 221, 112 S.Ct. 570, 574, 116 L.Ed.2d 578 (1991) (citations omitted). In interpreting any statute, we must " 'consider not only the bare meaning' of the critical word or phrase 'but also its placement and purpose in the statutory scheme.' " *Holloway*, 526 U.S. at 6, 119 S.Ct. at 969 (quoting *Bailey v. United States*, 516 U.S. 137, 145, 116 S.Ct. 501, 506-07, 133 L.Ed.2d 472 (1995)).

Traditional interpretive canons likewise counsel against a reading of the second proviso of §1503 that ignores the context of §1503 and the EWSAA as a whole. In particular, the canons of *noscitur a sociis* and *ejusdem generis* remind us that "[w]here general words follow specific words in a statutory enumeration, the general words are construed to embrace only objects similar in nature to those objects enumerated by the preceding specific words." *Wash. State Dep't of Soc. & Health Servs. v. Guardianship Estate of Keffeler*, 537 U.S. 371, 384, 123 S.Ct. 1017, 1025, 154 L.Ed.2d 972 (2003) (internal quotation marks and citations omitted). In addition, where statutory language is phrased as a proviso, the presumption is that its scope is confined to that of the principal clause to which it is attached. See *United States v. Morrow*, 266 U.S. 531, 534-35, 45 S.Ct. 173, 174-73, 69 L.Ed. 425 (1925).

Applying the foregoing principles, we conclude that the scope of §1503 is narrower than the Government suggests. The primary function of the EWSAA was to provide emergency appropriations in support of the United States' military operations in Iraq. The Act also provided additional funding for homeland security activities in the United States. Chapter 5 of the Act, entitled "Bilateral Economic Assistance," appropriated funds for a variety of assistance programs to Iraq and other American allies. See EWSAA, ch. 5, 117 Stat. 559, 572-81. In addition to the Iraq Relief and Reconstruction Fund, these programs included the Child Survival and Health Programs Fund, International Disaster Assistance, the Economic Support Fund (providing assistance to the

governments of Jordan, Egypt, Turkey, the Philippines, and Afghanistan), Loan Guarantees to Israel, the Emergency Refugee and Migration Assistance Fund, peacekeeping operations, and similar activities. Thus, each program funded in Chapter 5 of the EWSAA addresses matters of bilateral economic assistance to Iraq and other countries. The United States points to nothing in this portion of the Act - or elsewhere in the EWSAA, for that matter - that addresses the jurisdiction of the federal courts.

Section 1503 is one of several "general provisions" within Chapter 5 of the EWSAA. *See* EWSAA §§1501-1506, 117 Stat. 559, 578-81. These "general provisions" all supply specific instructions or impose conditions upon the outlays of money appropriated throughout the Chapter. For example, §1501 provides that the President has authority to transfer money between the several programs funded in the Chapter, upon proper notification to Congress. Section 1502 provides that "[a]ssistance or other financing under this chapter may be provided for Iraq notwithstanding any other provision of law," subject to certain provisos. Section 1504 authorizes the President to export certain nonlethal military equipment to Iraq, notwithstanding any other provision of law, subject to certain conditions and reporting requirements. Section 1503 thus finds itself situated among several other provisions that govern the distribution of assistance to Iraq within the context of ongoing military operations and against a backdrop of legal obstacles that would otherwise prohibit such assistance.

Section 1503 itself authorizes the President to suspend the application of any provision of the Iraq Sanctions Act of 1990, subject to eight provisos. *See* EWSAA §1503, 117 Stat. 559, 579. Three of the provisos impose notification or reporting requirements and provide for expiration of the suspension authority granted in §1503. The remaining provisos are each responsive to a specific aspect of the ISA or other statutes that are implicated by the suspension authority granted in §1503, thereby resolving potential ambiguities that may arise in the statutory landscape as a result of the suspension of the ISA. Thus, the first proviso, stating that nothing in §1503 shall affect the applicability of the Iran-Iraq Arms Non-Proliferation Act of 1992, reflects the fact that portions of the Non-Proliferation Act incorporate the ISA by reference and are to remain in effect despite suspension of the ISA. *See* Iran-Iraq Arms Non-Proliferation Act of 1992, Pub. L. No. 102-484, §§1601-1608, 106 Stat. 2315, 2571-75 (codified at 50 U.S.C. §1701 note (2000)). Similarly, the fifth proviso states that "provisions of law that direct the United States Government to vote against or oppose loans or other uses of funds, including for financial or technical assistance, in international financial institutions for Iraq shall not be construed as applying to Iraq." This language responds in part to §586G(a)(5) of the ISA, which requires the United States to oppose any loan or financial or technical assistance to Iraq by international financial institutions, pursuant to other provisions of law incorporated into the ISA. *See* ISA §586G(a)(5), 104 Stat.1979, 2052. This fifth proviso thus makes clear that the President may suspend not only the ISA, but also those provisions of law that are incorporated by reference into the ISA's prohibition on American support for assistance to Iraq from international financial institutions. The remaining provisos are similarly tied to specific features of the ISA and the other statutes with which the ISA interacts.

The second proviso of §1503 - which lies at the heart of the controversy in the instant case - provides that "the President may make inapplicable with respect to Iraq section 620A of the Foreign Assistance Act of 1961 or any other provision of law that applies to countries that have supported terrorism." Just like the other provisos in §1503, this language is responsive to a particular section of the ISA. As we have seen, the ISA required that certain enumerated provisions of law, including §620A of the Foreign Assistance Act of 1961, and "all other provisions of law that impose sanctions against a country which has repeatedly provided support for acts of international terrorism" be fully enforced against Iraq. *See* ISA §586F(c), 104 Stat.1979, 2051. The second proviso in §1503 thus makes clear that the authority in §1503 to suspend the ISA includes the authority to make inapplicable to Iraq §620A of the FAA and those additional provisions of law incorporated into §586F(c) of the ISA.

As previously noted, §620A of the FAA prohibits the grant of assistance to any country determined by the Secretary of State to have "repeatedly provided support for acts of international terrorism." 22 U.S.C. §2371(a). A survey of the other provisions enumerated in §586F(c) of the ISA indicates that all of those provisions deal with restrictions on assistance to state sponsors of terrorism. These provisions include §40 of the Arms Export Control Act, 22 U.S.C. §2780 (2000); §§555 and 556 of the Foreign Operations, Export Financing, and Related Programs Appropriations Act of 1991, Pub. L. No. 101-513, §§555-556, 104 Stat. 1979, 2021-22 (1990); and §555 of the International Security and Development Cooperation Act of 1985, Pub. L. No. 99-83, §555, 99 Stat. 190, 227. Each of these provisions calls for the imposition of economic sanctions on countries that are determined to have supported international terrorism, including

restrictions on exports, aviation boycotts, and prohibitions on loans, credits, or other financial assistance. Read within this context, the reference in the ISA to "all other provisions of law that impose sanctions against a country which has repeatedly provided support for acts of international terrorism" is best read to denote provisions of law that call for economic sanctions and prohibit grants of assistance to state sponsors of terrorism.

To recapitulate, the meaning of the disputed language in §1503, like each of the other substantive provisos in that section, is thus illuminated by consideration of the corresponding provisions of the ISA. See *Morrow*, 266 U.S. at 534-35, 45 S.Ct. at 174-75 ("The general office of a proviso is to except something from the enacting clause, or to qualify and restrain its generality and prevent misinterpretation. Its grammatical and logical scope is confined to the subject-matter of the principal clause.") (citations omitted). The reference in §586F(c) of the ISA to §620A of the FAA and "all other provisions of law" that impose sanctions on state sponsors of terrorism appears clearly to encompass laws which, like the FAA and the other enumerated provisions, impose obstacles to assistance to designated countries. None of these provisions remotely suggests any relation to the jurisdiction of the federal courts. Thus, when read in juxtaposition with this portion of the ISA, the second proviso of §1503 is more persuasively interpreted as sharing a similar scope. That is, it authorizes the President to make inapplicable with respect to Iraq those provisions of law that impose economic sanctions on Iraq or that present legal obstacles to the provision of assistance to the Iraqi Government. This interpretation reflects a central function of Chapter 5 of the EWSAA, which is to provide for relief and reconstruction in post-war Iraq.

Although sparse, the legislative history of §1503 of the EWSAA likewise supports our interpretation of the disputed language in §1503. The EWSAA began as a request from the President to Congress for emergency supplemental appropriations to support Department of Defense operations in Iraq and for other purposes. *See* Letter from President George W. Bush to Rep. Dennis Hastert, Speaker of the House of Representatives (Mar. 25, 2003), *reprinted in* H.R. DOC. No. 108-55, at 1 (2003). The portion of the President's request dealing with bilateral economic assistance included language repealing the Iraq Sanctions Act of 1990, subject to the proviso "[t]hat the President may make inapplicable with respect to Iraq section 620A of the Foreign Assistance Act of 1961, as amended, or other provision of law that applies to countries that have supported terrorism." H.R. DOC.

No. 108-55, at 24. The request explained that this language would "authorize the President to make inapplicable with respect to Iraq section 620A, and section 620G, and section 307 of the Foreign Assistance Act." *Id.*

One week after the President issued this request for supplemental appropriations, the Committees on Appropriations of the Senate and House reported bills that each contained language similar to that proposed by the President. The Senate version, reported on April 1, 2003, repeated exactly the language of the President's request, repealing the ISA and authorizing the President to "make inapplicable with respect to Iraq section 620A of the Foreign Assistance Act of 1961, as amended, or other provision of law that applies to countries that have supported terrorism." S. 762, 108th Cong. §503 (2003). The accompanying committee report explained that this section of the Senate bill "provide[d] the request for the repeal of the Iraqi Sanctions Act of 1990 [sic], and *other limitations on assistance for Iraq.*" S. REP. No. 108-33, at 21 (2003) (emphasis added). The House version, reported on April 2, 2003, included the same language that became §1503 of the EWSAA. *See* H.R. 1559, 108th Cong. §1402 (2003). The committee report accompanying the House bill explained that this language was "similar to the authority requested by the President that would repeal the Iraq Sanctions Act of 1990 and authorize the President to make inapplicable with respect to Iraq section 620A and section 307 of the Foreign Assistance Act." H.R. REP. No. 108-55, at 30 (2003).

The Conference Committee agreed to the language proposed in the House version of the supplemental appropriation. *See* H.R. CONF. REP. No. 108-76, at 21 (2003). The conferees reported that §1503 of the conference agreement "would make inapplicable the Iraq Sanctions Act of 1990 and authorize the President to make inapplicable with respect to Iraq section 620A and section 307 of the Foreign Assistance Act." *Id.* at 76. The language of the conference agreement was passed by both houses on April 12, 2003, without further amendment to §1503, and signed by the President on April 16, 2003.

While not conclusive, this legislative history bolsters our conclusion as to the scope of §1503. There is no reference in the legislative history to the FSIA in particular or to federal court jurisdiction in general. Rather, the legislative history of the EWSAA reflects an underlying legislative concern with eliminating statutory restrictions on aid and exports needed for the reconstruction of Iraq. This concern is easily

understood. Any effort by the United States Government or private businesses in the United States to provide assistance or conduct business with the new Iraqi regime, in the absence of §1503, would be barred by numerous provisions of law until such time as the President and the Secretary of State could make the necessary certifications to Congress to remove Iraq's designation as a state sponsor of terrorism. *See, e.g.,* 22 U.S.C. §2371(c) (rescission provisions of the Foreign Assistance Act of 1961); 50 U.S.C.App. §2405(j)(4) (rescission provisions of the Export Administration Act). Section 1503 permits assistance and reconstruction efforts to proceed without waiting for this lengthy and complex certification process to run its course by setting aside the ISA and "other limitations on assistance for Iraq," S. REP. No. 108-33, at 21 (2003). This legislative history, along with the other provisions in §1503, the EWSAA as a whole, and the complex web of economic sanctions and prohibitions on assistance that previously applied to Iraq thus supports our interpretation that the general reference in §1503 to "other provision[s] of law that appl[y] to countries that have supported terrorism" embraces only those provisions of law that constitute legal restrictions on assistance to and trade with Iraq.

Because we find, as a matter of statutory interpretation, that §1503 does not make the terrorism exception to the FSIA inapplicable to Iraq, we need not consider whether §1503 operates retroactively to appellees' pending lawsuit. Nevertheless, comparison of the temporal scope of 28 U.S.C. §1605(a)(7) with that of §1503 lends further support to our resolution of the statutory interpretation issue. The language of §1503 is broad, general, and unclear. Yet, the United States seeks to employ it to supersede the much more precise language of §1605(a)(7), which already provides in quite specific terms for the prospective restoration of sovereign immunity once a country is decertified as a sponsor of terrorism. Specifically, §1605(a)(7) provides that the terrorism exception to foreign sovereign immunity arises only when a defendant country is designated as a sponsor of terrorism "at the time the act occurred, unless later so designated as a result of such act." 28 U.S.C. §1605(a)(7)(A). Thus, the FSIA specifically provides that when a country, once designated as a state sponsor of terrorism, is subsequently restored to good standing, that country is still amenable to suit for acts that took place prior to the restoration of its sovereign immunity. As the United States would have it, however, waiver of §1605(a)(7) in the case of Iraq pursuant to §1503 would restore Iraq's immunity even for acts that occurred while Iraq was still considered a sponsor of terrorism.

This perplexing result appears even more bizarre when the sunset provisions of §1503 are taken into account. The final proviso in §1503 states that "the authorities contained in this section shall expire on September 30, 2004, or on the date of enactment of a subsequent Act authorizing assistance for Iraq and that specifically amends, repeals or otherwise makes inapplicable the authorities of this section, whichever occurs first." EWSAA §1503, 117 Stat. 559, 579. If the United States were correct in its interpretation of §1503, then this sunset provision would mean that, absent intervening events, §1605(a)(7) would once again be available as a basis of jurisdiction after September 30, 2004. At such time, the District Court would properly have jurisdiction over a suit against Iraq based on events that occurred while Iraq was designated as a state sponsor of terrorism. It makes little sense to say that between the date of the May 7 Presidential Determination and the date of expiration of the authorities conferred in §1503, there is no federal court jurisdiction for suits against Iraq, but that after that period elapses, such suits will again be available. Yet, this is precisely the result that follows if one imposes the unwieldy language of §1503 upon the otherwise careful and precise scheme established under the FSIA. Thus, considerations of temporal scope weigh in favor of an interpretation of §1503 that avoids this conflict.

The United States contends that, even if the disputed clause in §1503 must be construed to reach only those provisions of law that are similar in nature to the legal restrictions on assistance to Iraq that are enumerated elsewhere in §1503, the terrorism exception to the FSIA still falls within the scope of provisions the President is authorized to make inapplicable to Iraq. Specifically, the United States points out that §1605(a)(7) shares a "criterion of similarity" with the other provisions mentioned in §1503, Reply Br. at 17, namely, that it is a provision of law that imposes penalties on foreign nations as a result of their designation as sponsors of terrorism. This contention has some attraction, because §1605(a)(7) arguably poses a threat of a sort to American reconstruction efforts in Iraq by providing jurisdiction in American courts for cases seeking huge liability judgments against the Iraqi Government. Under this view, it is plausible to suggest that §1503 encompasses the terrorism exception to the FSIA.

It is true that section 1605(a)(7) is not totally dissimilar to laws imposing economic sanctions or prohibitions on assistance and trade, in that it penalizes countries designated as supporters of terrorism. However, even if the FAA and the other economic penalties discussed above could be said to share this single common attribute with §1605(a)(7), the FSIA's rules of federal court jurisdiction would still be several steps removed from those other provisions, which are all much more closely analogous to one another. Because §1503, the EWSAA as a whole, and the relevant legislative history all reflect an overriding concern for economic assistance, trade, and reconstruction in Iraq, we find that this context counsels against a reading of §1503 that stretches so far as to reach a law, like the FSIA, that is largely dissimilar to all of the "look-alike" provisions affected by §1503.

We conclude that when §1503 is read in the context of the other provisions of the EWSAA and its legislative history, as it must be, that provision is best understood as applying only to legal restrictions on assistance and funding for the new Iraqi Government. There is nothing in the language of §1503, the EWSAA as a whole, or its legislative history to suggest that Congress intended by this statute to alter the jurisdiction of the federal courts under the FSIA. We acknowledge that this is a close question. We nevertheless conclude that §1503 was not intended to apply to §1605(a)(7). The scope of the May 7 Presidential Determination is immaterial, because it cannot exceed the authority granted in §1503. We therefore affirm the District Court's exercise of jurisdiction over appellees' claims under 28 U.S.C. §1605(a)(7).

C. Cause of Action

Having concluded that jurisdiction in this case properly lies in the District Court, we arrive at the clear conflict between the District Court's judgment in favor of appellees and this court's recent holding in *Cicippio-Puleo v. Islamic Republic of Iran*, 353 F.3d 1024. In *Cicippio*, we held that neither §1605(a)(7) nor the Flatow Amendment, nor the two considered together, supplies a cause of action against foreign states. *See* 353 F.3d at 1033. In the instant case, the District Court predicated its finding of liability on precisely those provisions, and appellees point to no alternative cause of action. We therefore conclude that appellees have failed to state a cause of action.

Because of the default of the Iraqi defendants, no party questioned the existence of appellees' cause of action during the proceedings in the District Court. Nor did the United States raise this issue in its motion to intervene. Nevertheless, no party contests this court's discretion to reach this issue on our own motion in light of the intervening change in law.

Appellees rightly contend that non-jurisdictional defenses such as the failure to state a cause of action are waivable and that courts generally do not permit parties to raise such issues for the first time on appeal. The right of a party to *advance* this objection is not coextensive with the discretion of the court to *consider* the issue, however. As we have held, "[c]ourts of appeals are not rigidly limited to issues raised in the tribunal of first instance; they have a fair measure of discretion to determine what questions to consider and resolve for the first time on appeal." *Roosevelt v. E.I. Du Pont de Nemours & Co.*, 958 F.2d 416, 419 n. 5 (D.C.Cir.1992) (addressing the existence of a cause of action for the first time on appeal in light of a relevant intervening Supreme Court decision). Thus, while we will ordinarily refrain from reaching non-jurisdictional questions that have not been raised by the parties or passed on by the District Court, we may do so on our own motion in "exceptional circumstances." *Id.* ("Qualifying circumstances include…an intervening change in the law…").

Our intervening decision in *Cicippio*, which definitively resolved a previously open question of law that we find to be dispositive in appellees' case, surely qualifies as the type of exceptional circumstance that justifies our exercise of discretion. See *id.* at 419. The issue before us is "purely one of law important in the administration of federal justice, and resolution of the issue does not depend on any additional facts not considered by the district court." *Id.* at 419 n.5. The circumstances of this case are even more extraordinary when one considers the stakes: Appellees have obtained a nearly-billion dollar default judgment against a foreign government whose present and future stability has become a central preoccupation of the United States' foreign policy. In these circumstances, it would be utterly unseemly for this court to ignore the clear implications of our holding in *Cicippio*. We therefore find it appropriate to exercise our discretion to determine whether appellees' case must be dismissed for failure to state a cause of action.

In their complaint, appellees premised their claim of liability on §1605(a)(7), as amended, asserting that this provision "creates a federal cause of action for torture…of American nationals, or for the benefit of American national claimants, when such acts are committed by a foreign state designated as a state sponsor of terrorism." Compl. ¶ 596, J.A. 143. The complaint pointed to several decisions of the District Court that proceeded on the assumption that §1605(a)(7), as amended by the Flatow Amendment, "not only waives sovereign immunity and provides jurisdiction but also creates a cause of action within its scope of applicability." *Id.* While appellees also alluded to the "traditional torts of assault, battery and intentional infliction of emotional distress" in their generic form, Compl. ¶ 597, J.A. 143, they did not point to

any other specific source in state, federal, or foreign law for their cause of action.

The District Court similarly relied on §1605(a)(7) and the Flatow Amendment, finding that those provisions "create[] a federal cause of action against officials, employees and agents of a foreign state, as well as the state and its agencies and instrumentalities themselves." *Acree I*, 271 F.Supp.2d at 215. In company with appellees, the District Court reasoned that "[s]uits brought under §1605(a)(7) may be based on conventional common law torts such as assault, battery, and intentional infliction of emotional distress," *id.*, and found that the facts appellees alleged satisfied the elements of several such torts, see *id.* at 215-17. The District Court cited no alternative cause of action.

In *Cicippio*, we held that neither §1605(a)(7) nor the Flatow Amendment, nor the two together, creates a cause of action against foreign states themselves. See *Cicippio*, 353 F.3d at 1033. This holding applies also to suits against "agenc[ies] or instrumentalit[ies]" of a foreign state, which are included in the FSIA's definition of "foreign state," see 28 U.S.C. §1603(a), (b); see also *Roeder*, 333 F.3d at 234 (explaining that an official state entity whose core functions are governmental is treated as the foreign state itself for purposes of the FSIA); Compl. ¶ 3, J.A. 33 (stating that the Iraqi Intelligence Service is an agency or instrumentality of Iraq and therefore also a "foreign state" within the meaning of the FSIA). *Cicippio* also made clear that any suit against an official of a foreign state must be a suit in that official's *personal* capacity. See 353 F.3d at 1034; *cf.* Com pl. ¶¶ 2-3, J.A. 31-33 (naming as a defendant Saddam Hussein "in his official capacity as President of the Republic of Iraq."). The causes of action advanced by appellees before the District Court therefore do not suffice to state claims for which relief may be granted.

In response to our order to consider this issue in preparation for oral argument, appellees did not advance any alternative causes of action. At oral argument, counsel for appellees gestured again toward generic common law torts, see Oral Argument Tr. at 23-29, but generic common law cannot be the *source* of a federal cause of action. The shared common law of the states may afford useful guidance as to the rules of decision in a FSIA case where a cause of action arises from some specific and concrete source of law. See *Bettis*, 315 F.3d at 333 (assuming, *arguendo*, that plaintiffs stated a cause of action under the Flatow Amendment and then turning to generic common law to flesh out the controlling substantive law). But there is no support for the proposition that generic common law itself may furnish the cause of action. Rather, as in any case, a plaintiff proceeding under the FSIA must identify a particular cause of action arising out of a specific source of law. Appellees failed to do so in this case.

Here, appellees pointed to no source of liability other than §1605(a)(7) and the Flatow Amendment. When pressed repeatedly at oral argument, appellees offered no coherent alternative. We therefore find no cause to remand this case to the District Court in order to allow appellees to amend their complaint to state a cause of action under some other source of law. See *Cicippio*, 353 F.3d at 1036. In *Cicippio*, we permitted such a remand because the state of the law at the time of that appeal "may have…misled" the plaintiffs in that case into assuming that the Flatow Amendment afforded a cause of action against the foreign state defendant. See *id.* In addition, we noted that *amici* in that case had advanced the possibility that an alternative source of law might supply a viable cause of action. See *id.* In this case, by contrast, our decision in *Cicippio* and our order to the parties prior to oral argument put appellees on notice of this issue. Despite this notice, appellees offered no alternative cause of action when asked to do so at oral argument. Accordingly, appellees' suit must be dismissed for failure to state a cause of action.

III. CONCLUSION

We are mindful of the gravity of appellees' allegations in this case. That appellees endured this suffering while acting in service to their country is all the more sobering. Nevertheless, we cannot ignore the magnitude of their default judgment or its impact on the United States' conduct of foreign policy where the law is indisputably clear that appellees were not legally entitled to this judgment. We reverse the order of the District Court denying the United States' motion to intervene, *Acree II*, 276 F.Supp.2d. 95. We vacate the District Court's judgment for appellees, *Acree I*, 271 F.Supp.2d 179, and dismiss appellees' suit against the Republic of Iraq, the Iraqi Intelligence Service, and Saddam Hussein in his official capacity as President of Iraq on the grounds that appellees have failed to state a cause of action.

So ordered.

ROBERTS, Circuit Judge, concurring in part and concurring in the judgment:
I agree with the majority that the district court erred in denying the United States' motion to intervene. I also concur in the court's judgment of dismissal, but I reach that result by a different path than the majority has taken. In my view, Section 1503 of the EWSAA includes the authority to make Section 1605(a)(7) of the FSIA-on its face a "provision of law that applies to countries that have supported terrorism"-inapplicable to Iraq, and the Presidential Determination of May 7, 2003 therefore ousted the federal courts of jurisdiction in cases that relied on that exception to Iraq's sovereign immunity. I also conclude that this ouster of jurisdiction is properly applied to pending cases, and that the district court's judgment should thus be vacated and the case dismissed for want of jurisdiction.

A. The Scope of Section 1503 of the EWSAA

1. The pertinent language of Section 1503 is straightforward, authorizing the President to make inapplicable to Iraq Section 620A of the Foreign Assistance Act of 1961 and "*any* other provision of law that applies to countries that have supported terrorism" (emphasis added). As this court recently observed, "the Supreme Court has consistently instructed that statutes written in broad, sweeping language should be given broad, sweeping application." *Consumer Elecs. Ass'n v. FCC*, 347 F.3d 291, 298 (D.C.Cir.2003). "Any other provision" should be read to mean "any other provision," not, as the majority would have it, "provisions that present obstacles to assistance and funding for the new Iraqi Government." *Ante* at 51.

This is particularly true given that Congress knows how to use more limited language along the lines of the majority's construction when it wants to. Congress did just that in another appropriations statute enacted just two months prior to the EWSAA. In that statute, Congress declared that certain restrictions on funding to foreign countries should not be construed to restrict assistance to nongovernmental organizations in those countries, but provided that this easing of restrictions would not apply "with respect to section 620A of the Foreign Assistance Act of 1961 or any *comparable* provision of law *prohibiting assistance* to countries that support international terrorism." Consolidated Appropriations Resolution, 2003, Pub. L. No. 108-7, Div. E, §537(c)(1), 117 Stat. 11, 196 (Feb. 20, 2003) (emphases added). The EWSAA, of course, refers to the very same section of the Foreign Assistance Act but includes substantially broader language in its subsequent catchall phrase. This use of different language in two statutes so analogous in their form and content, enacted so close in time, suggests that the statutes differ in their meaning, and that the facially broader language was in fact intended to have the broader scope.

2. The majority notes that Section 1605(a)(7) of the FSIA already "specifically provides that when a country, once designated as a state sponsor of terrorism, is subsequently restored to good standing, that country is still amenable to suit for acts that took place prior to the restoration of its sovereign immunity." *Ante* at 56. The majority then concludes that the general power conferred by Section 1503 of the EWSAA should not be read to authorize the President to restrike this previously-fixed balance between the interests of a newly non-terrorist state and those of victims of terrorism.

I respectfully disagree. The majority's reading simply assumes that the balance Congress struck in 1996 was left untouched by the EWSAA. In 2003, however, Congress *for the first time* confronted the prospect that a friendly successor government would, in its infancy, be vulnerable under Section 1605(a)(7) to crushing liability for the actions of its renounced predecessor. *See* U.S. DEP'T OF STATE, PATTERNS OF GLOBAL TERRORISM 1999, at 2 (April 2000) (noting that the list of state sponsors of terrorism had been unchanged since 1993); U.S. DEP'T OF STATE, PATTERNS OF GLOBAL TERRORISM 2001, at 63 (May 2002) (listing the same states). Certainly there is no evidence indicating that, when it enacted Section 1605(a)(7), Congress contemplated that a successor government's cessation of support for terrorism would come about under circumstances like those in Iraq. Given the broad language of the EWSAA and the circumstances surrounding its enactment, it is entirely possible-and surely not "perplexing," *ante* at 56-that Congress in 2003 made an *ad hoc* decision to strike a different balance in favor of the new government of Iraq. The whole point of Section 1503 was to change existing rules to respond to new realities; it is not a compelling argument against a construction of the section to object that it would do just that.

3. The majority further finds that construing the EWSAA to authorize an ouster of jurisdiction over Iraq in Section 1605(a)(7) cases would be "bizarre" in light of the sunset provisions of Section 1503. *Ante* at 56. "[A]bsent intervening events," the majority states, "[Section] 1605(a)(7) would once again be available as a basis of jurisdiction after September 30, 2004." *Id.* at 57. Given the range of possibilities contained in the majority's careful caveat, the prediction itself is overwrought. As one member of Congress has explained, in relation to a different statute, "[s]unsetting laws does not mean repealing them. Laws would only expire if Congress failed to meet its responsibility to reexamine and renew these statutes within a specified period of

time." S.REP. NO. 104-85, at 64 (1995) (statement of Sen. Grams).

One need look no further than the title of the EWSAA to discern its emergency nature; a sunset provision in such a statute is intended to buy time for fuller consideration of the issues, rather than to establish an immutable date for the statute's presumed extinction. And it hardly needs saying that the sunset provision in Section 1503 applies not only to the proviso at issue in this case, but to all of that section. If the majority's prediction of abject congressional lassitude is accurate, the Iraq Sanctions Act of 1990 will itself return to full strength on September 30, 2004. Nothing in the ISA requires that Iraq be included on the State Department's list of state sponsors of terrorism, so even an orderly de-listing of Iraq by the executive branch under the procedures of 22 U.S.C. §2371(c) would not alter the ISA's restrictions on assistance. In short, the occurrence of "intervening events" is far more likely than their absence.

4. I agree with the majority that this question of statutory interpretation is close, and I do not suggest that the EWSAA is entirely unambiguous. But the plaintiffs err in their assumption that the government must somehow prove that Congress intended the statute's broad terms to be construed broadly. *See* Appellees' Br. at 25 ("There is no indication that the proviso [in Section 1503] was intended to be a broad tool of foreign policy involving a retroactive restoration of sovereign immunity"); *cf. ante* at 56 ("There is no reference in the legislative history [of Section 1503] to the FSIA in particular or to federal court jurisdiction in general."). The burden is precisely the opposite: the party seeking to narrow the application of the statute must demonstrate that Congress intended something less than what the law on its face says. See, e.g., *Harrison v. PPG Industries*, 446 U.S. 578, 589, 100 S.Ct. 1889, 1896, 64 L.Ed.2d 525 (1980) ("[T]he phrase, 'any other final action,' in the absence of legislative history to the contrary, must be construed to mean exactly what it says"). And as this court has stated, "the plainer the language, the more convincing contrary legislative history must be." *Cole v. Harris*, 571 F.2d 590, 597 (D.C.Cir.1977) (internal quotation marks and citation omitted).

Harrison in fact resembles this case in significant respects: the Court was interpreting an amendment to the Clean Air Act that provided for review, in the appropriate federal court of appeals, of "locally and regionally applicable actions" taken by the Environmental Protection Agency "under specifically enumerated provisions of the Act, and of ' *any other final action* of the [EPA under the Act]...which is locally or regionally applicable.' " 446 U.S. at 579, 100 S.Ct. at 1891 (quoting 42 U.S.C. §7607(b)(1) (1976 & Supp. II)) (emphasis and ellipsis in original). The respondents, citing the *ejusdem generis* canon of interpretation (the corollary *noscitur a sociis* was not then in vogue), urged the court to construe the phrase "any other final action" to mean only final actions similar to those specifically identified in the statute. *Id.* at 587, 100 S.Ct. at 1895. The Court refused, noting that the *ejusdem generis* canon should be applied only when the meaning of the text is uncertain and finding "no uncertainty in the meaning of the phrase, 'any other final action.' " *Id.* at 588, 100 S.Ct. at 1895.

Significantly, the Court also rejected the respondents' argument-based on the "scant" legislative history of the amendment-that it was "unlikely...that Congress would have expanded so radically the jurisdiction of the courts of appeals, and divested the district courts of jurisdiction, without some consideration and discussion of the matter." *Id.* at 591, 592, 100 S.Ct. at 1897-98. "In ascertaining the meaning of a statute," the Court stated, "a court cannot, in the manner of Sherlock Holmes, pursue the theory of the dog that did not bark." *Id.* at 592, 100 S.Ct. at 1897-98. The Court concluded that the statutory language meant "exactly what it sa[id], namely, *any other* final action." *Id.* at 589, 100 S.Ct. at 1896 (emphasis in original).

More recently, the Court unanimously rejected the suggestion that certain broad terms of the Federal Power Act (FPA) should be construed narrowly in light of Congress's focused intent to overrule one of the Court's prior cases: "[E]ven if [the prior case] catalyzed the enactment of the FPA, [it] does not define the outer limits of the statute's coverage." *New York v. FERC*, 535 U.S. 1, 21, 122 S.Ct. 1012, 1025, 152 L.Ed.2d 47 (2002). In my view, *Harrison* and *New York* illustrate the appropriate approach to a broadly worded statute such as Section 1503 of the EWSAA. The absence of any reference to the FSIA in the legislative history does not compel the conclusion that Section 1503 does not reach it, and the fact that Congress may have been focused primarily on removing barriers to the flow of aid to Iraq does not mean that the statute refers exclusively to such barriers. See *PGA Tour, Inc. v. Martin*, 532 U.S. 661, 689, 121 S.Ct. 1879, 1896-97, 149 L.Ed.2d 904 (2001) ("the fact that a statute can be applied in situations not expressly anticipated by Congress does not demonstrate ambiguity. It demonstrates breadth.") (quoting *Pennsylvania Dep't of Corr. v. Yeskey*, 524 U.S. 206, 212, 118 S.Ct. 1952, 1955-56, 141 L.Ed.2d 215 (1998)). [FN1] Because the legislative history contains no "convincing" indication, *Cole*, 571 F.2d at 597, that Con-

gress did *not* intend to include Section 1605(a)(7) of the FSIA among the "any other" provisions that the President could render inapplicable to Iraq, I conclude that the President was authorized to-and did, with the Presidential Determination-oust the federal courts of jurisdiction over Iraq in Section 1605(a)(7) cases.

FN1. Application of the *ejusdem generis* canon seems particularly inappropriate in this case because the statute provides only one point of reference (Section 620A of the Foreign Assistance Act) from which to extrapolate.

5. I do not mean to suggest that the contrast between the language of the Consolidated Appropriations Resolution and that of the EWSAA is conclusive proof of Congress's intent-but then neither is the majority's invocation of the pre-existing balance struck in Section 1605(a)(7). I appreciate that my view of Congress's purpose in restriking that balance is necessarily speculative-but then so is the majority's more limited view of Congress's purpose to reach only aid statutes. The majority can cite *United States v. Morrow*, 266 U.S. 531, 45 S.Ct. 173, 69 L.Ed. 425 (1925), for a presumption that supports its construction of the pertinent proviso, *see ante* at 52-53, 54-but I can respond with a case of similar vintage for the opposite proposition that "a frequent use of the proviso in Federal legislation [is] to introduce...new matter extending rather than limiting or explaining that which has gone before." *Interstate Commerce Comm'n v. Baird*, 194 U.S. 25, 37, 24 S.Ct. 563, 566, 48 L.Ed. 860 (1904). And both I and the majority (and everyone else, for that matter) are on tenuous ground when it comes to predicting whether Congress will act prior to the sunset date in Section 1503. [FN2]

FN2. There is of course an established framework that governs judicial review of statutory interpretations by agencies in the executive branch. See *Chevron USA Inc. v. Natural Res. Def. Council*, 467 U.S. 837, 104 S.Ct. 2778, 81 L.Ed.2d 694 (1984). In such circumstances, we defer to any reasonable construction adopted by the entity Congress has entrusted with administering the statute. *Id.* at 843-45, 104 S.Ct. at 2781-83. There is no doubt that the President's interpretation of Section 1503 to cover Section 1605(a)(7) is at least a reasonable one. The applicability of *Chevron* to presidential interpretations is apparently unsettled, see *Chamber of Commerce of the United States v. Reich*, 74 F.3d 1322, 1325 (D.C.Cir.1996); Note, *Extending* Chevron *Deference to Presidential Interpretations of Ambiguities in Foreign Affairs and National Security Statutes Delegating Lawmaking Power to the President*, 86 CORNELL L. REV. 411 (2001), but it is interesting to note that this would be an easy case had the EWSAA provided that, say, the Secretary of State may exercise the authority conferred under Section 1503. It is puzzling why the case should be so much harder when the authority is given to the Secretary's boss.

In such circumstances I prefer to rest on the firmer foundation of the statutory language itself. Give me English words over Latin maxims. The words here-"any other provision of law that applies to countries that have supported terrorism"-are, even if not entirely unambiguous, plain enough to impose a heavy burden on those who would rely on canons, or structure, or assumed purposes to conclude the words do not reach a law that applies, by its terms, to a foreign state "designated as a state sponsor of terrorism." 28 U.S.C. §1605(a)(7)(A). The majority ably marshals the arguments on the other side, but at the end of the day I find greater solace in the words themselves. See *Connecticut Nat'l Bank v. Germain*, 503 U.S. 249, 253-54, 112 S.Ct. 1146, 1149-50, 117 L.Ed.2d 391 (1992) ("canons of construction are no more than rules of thumb that help courts determine the meaning of legislation, and in interpreting a statute a court should always turn first to one, cardinal canon before all others. We have stated time and again that courts must presume that a legislature says in a statute what it means and means in a statute what it says there."). [FN3]

FN3. The plaintiffs argue that the grant of such authority to the President is unconstitutional in light of *Clinton v. New York*, 524 U.S. 417, 118 S.Ct. 2091, 141 L.Ed.2d 393 (1998), because such a grant would empower the President "to change the text of §1605(a)(7) so that Iraq's immunity no longer turns on its status at the time the act occurred" or to "repeal[ ] §1605(a)(7) solely as it relates to Iraq." Appellees' Br. at 50. The actions authorized by the EWSAA are a far cry from the line-item veto at issue in *Clinton*, and are instead akin to the waivers that the President is routinely empowered to make in other areas, particularly in the realm of foreign affairs. *See, e.g.*, 22 U.S.C. §7207(a)(3) (authorizing the President to waive a statutory prohibition on assistance to certain countries if he determines that a waiver is in the national security interest).

B. Application to Pending Cases

The plaintiffs argue that even if Section 1503 is properly read to include an ouster of jurisdiction under the FSIA, applying the statute to pending cases such as this one would be impermissibly retroactive under *Landgraf v. USI Film Products*, 511 U.S. 244, 114 S.Ct. 1483, 128 L.Ed.2d 229 (1994). This court reviewed the applicability of the *Landgraf* framework to jurisdictional statutes in *LaFontant v.*

INS, 135 F.3d 158 (D.C.Cir.1998), and concluded that the pertinent question-assuming Congress had not explicitly addressed retroactivity-was whether the statute spoke to the power of the court or instead to the substantive rights of the parties. Retroactive application is permissible in the former case, but not the latter. *Id.* at 163.

We recently held that Section 1605(a)(7) of the FSIA is solely a jurisdictional provision that creates no cause of action and does not affect the substantive law determining the liability of a foreign state. *Cicippio-Puleo v. Islamic Republic of Iran*, 353 F.3d 1024, 1033-34 (D.C.Cir.2004). Rendering Section 1605(a)(7) inapplicable, therefore, can only affect the power of the court and not the substantive rights of the parties. Application of the EWSAA to Section 1605(a)(7) is accordingly not impermissibly retroactive with respect to pending cases.

Moreover, the concern animating the Supreme Court's retroactivity jurisprudence is that "settled expectations should not be lightly disrupted." *Landgraf*, 511 U.S. at 265, 114 S.Ct. at 1497 (footnote omitted). At the time of the primary conduct at issue here, the jurisdictional grant of Section 1605(a)(7) did not even exist. We now know that the cause of action plaintiffs invoke did not exist then or now. *Cicippio*, 353 F.3d at 1033-34; *see ante* at 58-60. Any claim plaintiffs could have brought was in any event always subject to compromise or abrogation by the Executive. See *American Ins. Ass'n v. Garamendi*, 539 U.S. 396, 123 S.Ct. 2374, 2386-87, 156 L.Ed.2d 376 (2003); *Dames & Moore v. Regan*, 453 U.S. 654, 686, 101 S.Ct. 2972, 2990, 69 L.Ed.2d 918 (1981). Under these circumstances, there is no impediment to application of the normal rule that provisions addressing the power of a court be given retroactive effect.

* * *

For the foregoing reasons, I would hold that Section 1503 of the EWSAA and the Presidential Determination deprived the courts of jurisdiction over suits against Iraq under Section 1605(a)(7), and that the new jurisdictional rule applies to pending cases, including this one. I therefore agree that the judgment of the district court should be vacated and the case dismissed.

Notes:

1. What does the timing of the United States' motion to intervene demonstrate about the role of the government in terrorism cases?

2.   The *Acree* court considered political and legal events occurring both within the U.S. and Iraq during the pendency of the litigation. What does this say about the fluidity of the legal and factual terrain of civil terrorism law? What steps can plaintiffs take to avoid having a judgment entered only to be overturned in this manner?

3.   In an address to Congress weeks before the District Court entered judgment for the plaintiffs, President Bush stated:

> . . . I hereby report that I have exercised my authority to declare a national emergency to deal with the unusual and extraordinary threat posed to the national security and foreign policy of the United States by the threat of attachment or other judicial process against the Development Fund for Iraq, Iraqi petroleum and petroleum products, and interests therein, and proceeds, obligations, or any financial instruments of any nature whatsoever arising from or related to the sale or marketing thereof, and interests therein.
>
> A major national security and foreign policy goal of the United States is to ensure that the newly established Development Fund for Iraq and other Iraqi resources, including Iraqi petroleum and petroleum products, are dedicated for the well-being of the Iraqi people, for the orderly reconstruction and repair of Iraq's infrastructure, for the continued disarmament of Iraq, for the costs of indigenous civilian administration, and for other purposes benefiting the people of Iraq. The Development Fund for Iraq and other property in which Iraq has an interest may be subject to attachment, judgment, decree, lien, execution, garnishment, or other judicial process, thereby jeopardizing the full dedication of such assets to purposes benefiting the people of Iraq. To protect these assets, I have ordered that, unless licensed or otherwise authorized pursuant to my order, any attachment, judgment, decree, lien, execution, garnishment, or other judicial process is prohibited, and shall be deemed null and void . . .

Message to the Congress Reporting the Declaration of a National Emergency With Respect to the Development Fund for Iraq, 39 WEEKLY COMP. PRES. DOC. 647, 647-48 (May 22, 2003). This message creates the anomalous result that plaintiffs' judgment, legally obtained, approved by the judiciary and encouraged by Congress is determined to be contrary to U.S. interests and an "unusual and extraordinary threat posed to the national security and foreign policy of the United States." How could a lawsuit by U.S. citizens, prodded and approved by two branches of their own government, have become threatening and violative of American interests?

4.   As a result of the government's actions in *Acree*, will any judgment creditor of a foreign state sponsor of terrorism feel secure in knowing that his judgment will stand?

5.   The court noted that the plaintiffs' counsel did not identify a source of law which would supply a cause of action,

> In response to our order to consider this issue in preparation for oral argument, appellees did not advance any alternative causes of action. At oral argument, counsel for appellees gestured again toward generic common law torts, *see* Oral Argument Tr. at 23-29, but generic common law cannot be the *source* of a federal cause of action. The shared common law of the states may afford useful guidance as to the rules of decision in a FSIA case where a cause of action arises from some specific and concrete source of law. See *Bettis*, 315 F.3d at 333 (assuming, *arguendo*, that plaintiffs stated a cause of action under the Flatow Amendment and then turning to generic common law to flesh out the controlling substantive law). But there is no support for the proposition that generic common law itself may furnish the cause of action. Rather, as in any case, a plaintiff proceeding under the FSIA must identify a particular cause of action arising out of a specific source of law. Appellees failed to do so in this case.
>
> Here, appellees pointed to no source of liability other than §1605(a)(7) and the Flatow Amendment. When pressed repeatedly at oral argument, appellees offered no coherent alternative. We therefore find no cause to remand this case to the District Court in order to allow appellees to amend their complaint to state a cause of action under some other source of law.

Could a cause of action under state law have been easily identified?

6.   Previously, in adjudicating terrorism claims, the court relied on "federal common law." For instance in *Stethem v. Islamic Republic of Iran*, 201 F.Supp.2d 78, 89 (D.D.C.

2002), the court discussed several causes of action under federal common law,

> Pursuant to their claim for wrongful death under federal common law, the Estate of Robert Stethem is entitled to monetary damages for funeral expenses and loss of prospective income if Robert's premature death was wrongful and proximately caused by an act of terrorism...this Court has recognized this cause of action under the federal common law

by relying upon the Second Restatement of Torts: " '[O]ne who by extreme and outrageous conduct intentionally or recklessly causes severe emotional distress to another is subject to liability for such emotional distress.' "

Id. at 87- 89. After *Acree,* what if anything remains of "federal common law" in the context of civil terrorism jurisprudence? Does our understanding of the nature of "federal common law" in other contexts suggest why the court so resoundingly rejected its use in FSIA cases?

Chapter 8

Causation

Boim v. Quranic Literacy Institute and Holy Land Foundation, 291 F.3d 1000 (7th Cir. 2002).

ROVNER, Circuit Judge.

In this case of first impression, the parents of a young United States citizen murdered in Israel by Hamas terrorists have sued several individuals and organizations for the loss of their son. Two of the organizational defendants moved to dismiss the complaint, and the district court denied the motion. In this interlocutory appeal, we are asked to consider the viability of a claim brought under the never-tested 18 U.S.C. §2333, which allows U.S. nationals who have been injured "by reason of an act of international terrorism" to sue therefor and recover treble damages. We affirm the district court's denial of the defendants' motion to dismiss.

I.

We derive the facts from the allegations of the complaint. At this stage of the proceedings, we must accept these allegations as true, extending to the plaintiffs the benefit of every reasonable inference that may be drawn from the complaint. *Leatherman v. Tarrant County Narcotics Intelligence and Coordination Unit*, 507 U.S. 163, 164, 113 S.Ct. 1160, 122 L.Ed.2d 517 (1993); *Slaney v. The International Amateur Athletic Federation*, 244 F.3d 580, 597 (7th Cir.2001), *cert. denied*, 534 U.S. 828, 122 S.Ct. 69, 151 L.Ed.2d 35 (2001); *Camp v. Gregory*, 67 F.3d 1286, 1290 (7th Cir.1995), *cert. denied*, 517 U.S. 1244, 116 S.Ct. 2498, 135 L.Ed.2d 190 (1996). We may affirm the dismissal of that complaint only if it appears beyond doubt that the plaintiffs can prove no set of facts in support of their claim that would entitle them to relief. *Slaney*, 244 F.3d at 597.

David Boim was the son of Joyce and Stanley Boim, who are United States citizens. David held dual citizenship in the United States and Israel. In 1996, the Boims were living in Israel, where seventeen-year-old David was studying at a yeshiva. On May 13, 1996, David was murdered as he wait-

ed with other students at a bus stop near Beit El in the West Bank. He was struck by bullets fired from a passing car, and was pronounced dead within an hour of the shooting. His two attackers were later identified as Amjad Hinawi and Khalil Tawfiq Al-Sharif. The Palestinian Authority apprehended Hinawi and Al-Sharif, and temporarily imprisoned them in early 1997. They were released shortly thereafter, apparently pending trial. Al-Sharif subsequently killed himself and five civilians and injured 192 other people in a suicide bombing in Jerusalem on September 4, 1997. Two other suicide bombers joined him in this action. Hinawi, who confessed to participating in the shooting of David Boim, was eventually tried for David's murder by a Palestinian Authority court and was sentenced to ten years' imprisonment on February 17, 1998.

Both Hinawi and Al-Sharif were known members of the military wing of Hamas. The Boims describe Hamas as an extremist, Palestinian militant organization that seeks to establish a fundamentalist Palestinian state. The group is divided into two branches, one political and one military. The military branch receives orders and material support from the political branch. Hamas seeks to advance its political objectives through acts of terrorism and works to undermine the Middle East peace process through violent attacks on civilians. Hamas has a global presence, and terrorist operatives in Gaza and the West Bank receive their instructions, funds, weapons and practical support for their missions from Hamas organizers throughout the world. The Boims believe that Hamas has command and control centers in the United States, Britain and several Western European countries. The leaders of these control centers coordinate fund-raising efforts from sympathetic parties in these various countries and then launder and channel the money to Hamas operatives in Gaza and the West Bank. They also arrange for the purchase of weapons and for the recruitment and training of military personnel. They work with local commanders in the West Bank and Gaza to plan terrorist attacks. Hamas was designated a terrorist organization by President William Jefferson

Clinton in 1995 by Executive Order. [FN1] In 1997, Hamas was designated a foreign terrorist organization pursuant to 8 U.S.C. §1189. [FN2]

FN1. Exec. Order No. 12947, 60 Fed.Reg. 5079 (January 23, 1995). President Clinton invoked 50 U.S.C. §1701, et seq. (the International Emergency Economic Powers Act), 50 U.S.C. 211601 et seq. (the National Emergencies Act), and 3 U.S.C. §301 (authorizing the President to delegate certain functions) to label Hamas and eleven other groups as "terrorist organizations which threaten to disrupt the Middle East peace process."

FN2. Section 1189 provides a procedure by which the Secretary of State, in consultation with the Secretary of the Treasury and the Attorney General, may designate certain organizations as "foreign terrorist organizations." In order to be so designated, a foreign organization must "engage in terrorist activity" as defined in 8 U.S.C. §1182(a)(3)(B). "Terrorist activities" include a number of illegal acts such as sabotaging or highjacking a vessel, aircraft or vehicle; detaining a person and threatening to kill, injure or further detain that person in order to compel a third person to do something; violently attacking an internationally protected person; assassinating any person; using a biological agent, chemical agent, nuclear device, explosive or firearm with intent to endanger the safety or one or more persons or to cause substantial damage to property; or threatening, attempting or conspiring to do any of these things. 8 U.S.C. §1882(a)(3)(B)(ii). "Engage in terrorist activity" is further defined to include providing material support to anyone conducting a terrorist act, where material support includes: preparation and planning of a terrorist activity; gathering of information on potential targets for terrorist activity; providing a safe house, transportation, communications, funds, false documentation or identification, weapons, explosives, or training to any individual the actor knows or has reason to believe has committed or plans to commit a terrorist activity; soliciting funds or other things of value for any terrorist organization; or soliciting any individual for membership in a terrorist organization or to engage in terrorist activity. 8 U.S.C. §1182(a)(3)(B)(iii). After notifying Congress of the designation, the Secretary of the Treasury may require United States financial institutions to freeze the assets of a foreign terrorist organization. The statute provides that Congress may revoke the designation in certain circumstances and also provides that any foreign terrorist organization may seek judicial review of the designation. 8 U.S.C. §1189. The Boims allege that Hamas' military wing depends on foreign contributions, with approximately one-third of its multi-million dollar annual budget coming from fund-raising in

North America and Western Europe. The Boims believe that the Quranic Literacy Institute ("QLI") and the Holy Land Foundation for Relief and Development ("HLF"), along with other defendants not involved in this appeal, are the main fronts for Hamas in the United States. They allege that these organizations' allegedly humanitarian functions mask their core mission of raising and funneling money and other resources to Hamas operatives in support of terrorist activities.

QLI is an Illinois not-for-profit corporation that purports to translate and publish sacred Islamic texts, but the Boims believe it is also engaged in raising and laundering money for Hamas. QLI also employed another defendant, Mohammed Abdul Hamid Khalil Salah, nominally as a computer analyst. The FBI has seized $1.4 million in cash and property from Salah, who is the admitted United States based leader of the military branch of Hamas. He has been prosecuted for channeling money to Hamas and for recruiting, organizing and training terrorist operatives in Israel. Salah is named on a list of Specially Designated Terrorists compiled by the United States Treasury Department's Office of Foreign Assets Control. [FN3]

FN3. The United States has proceeded against Salah and Mousa Mohammed Abu Marzook in an unrelated action to seize funds used in terrorism. See *United States v. One 1997 E35 Ford Van VIN 1FBJS31L3VHB70844*, 50 F.Supp.2d 789 (N.D.Ill.1999). In that action, the United States has alleged that Salah and Marzook employed a number of charitable organizations in the United States to raise and launder money for Hamas. The FBI presented evidence in that action that Salah actively recruited Hamas terrorists, arranged for and financed their training, served as a financial conduit for Hamas operations directed from the U.S., paid for plane tickets to transport terrorists from the U.S. to the Middle East, and gave approximately $100,000 to another Hamas operative for the express purpose of procuring weapons.

HLF is also a not-for-profit corporation, whose ostensible mission is to fund humanitarian relief and development efforts. HLF's director has acknowledged providing money to Hamas, and the Boims allege that, although HLF purports to have a charitable purpose, its true function is to raise and channel money to Hamas for terrorist activities. The U.S. base of HLF's operations is in Texas. HLF also has offices in Jerusalem and in Illinois. HLF, QLI and the other organizational defendants are linked by interlocking directorates and by ties to Salah and Mousa Mohammed Abu Marzook, another individual defendant (not involved in this appeal) who has a leadership role in the military branch of Hamas. [FN4]

FN4. According to the Boims, Marzook has admitted in an extradition proceeding filed against him that he is the leader of the political wing of Hamas and he has raised money for Hamas. Evidence presented in his extradition proceeding established that he transferred funds to Salah, recruited Salah to raise funds for the Hamas military activities, knew that Hamas operatives were carrying out terrorist activities in Israel, and gave one of the organizers of these terrorist activities a book of blank, signed checks to fund Hamas operations. The United States has also proceeded against Marzook in the *Ford Van* forfeiture action referenced in note 3, *supra*.

According to the Boims, money flows from American contributors to Hamas in a three-step process: first, the front organizations solicit contributions; second, the leaders arrange for the money to be laundered and wired overseas; and third, Hamas operatives in Gaza and the West Bank use the money to finance terrorist activities. Because it is illegal to provide financial support to recognized terrorist groups, the money flows through a series of complicated transactions, changing hands a number of times, and being commingled with funds from the front organizations' legitimate charitable and business dealings. The funds are laundered in a variety of ways, including through real estate deals and through Swiss bank accounts. The Boims allege that money raised by HLF and QLI was transferred to Hamas terrorists using these various methods in order to finance terrorist activities. Hamas used the money raised in this way to purchase weapons to carry out terrorist attacks, including the attack on David Boim. Hamas regularly drew money from a pool of laundered funds in order to finance training, weapons purchases, lodging, false identification, communications equipment, lethal substances, explosives, personnel, transportation and other material support for terrorist operations. The Boims believe that expenditures from this pool of funds paid for the vehicle, machine guns and ammunition used to kill David Boim, and also paid for the training of Hinawi, Al-Sharif and other Hamas operatives involved in the attack on David Boim. The funds were also used to provide a stipend for Al-Sharif's family, as it is a common practice to pay the families of suicide bombers in order to encourage others to volunteer for these activities.

The Boims bring their suit against HLF, QLI and other organizational and individual defendants pursuant to 18 U.S.C. §2333. They charge that all of the defendants are civilly liable for David's murder. They name Hinawi and Al-Sharif as the persons who actually killed David, but allege that the other defendants aided, abetted and financed Hinawi and Al-Sharif. They assert that the organizational defendants provided material support or resources to Hamas as those terms are defined in 18 U.S.C. §§2339A and 2339B. The Boims seek compensation for the extreme physical pain David suffered before his death, and for the cost of his funeral and the loss of accretion to his estate due to his death at age seventeen. They also seek damages for their own extreme mental anguish and loss of the society of their son. They ask for $100,000,000 compensatory damages, $100,000,000 punitive damages, plus costs and attorney's fees, and request the trebling of damages pursuant to the statute.

In the district court, QLI and HLF moved to dismiss the complaint for failure to state a claim upon which relief may be granted. In particular, the defendants argued that section 2333 does not support a cause of action for aiding and abetting acts of international terrorism, and that the suit is foreclosed by the Supreme Court's ruling in *Central Bank of Denver, N.A. v. First Interstate Bank of Denver, N.A.*, 511 U.S. 164, 114 S.Ct. 1439, 128 L.Ed.2d 119 (1994). Because the defendants believed that aiding and abetting was the sole basis for the Boims' cause of action, they maintained that the complaint should be dismissed. The Boims argued to the district court that their section 2333 complaint could be sustained under any one of three different theories of liability. First, they maintained that providing material support to a terrorist organization was itself an act of international terrorism as defined in section 2331. Second, they argued that the defendants could be held civilly liable under section 2333 because they violated sections 2339A and 2339B, the criminal statutes prohibiting the provision of material support to terrorists. [FN5] Third, they contended that the defendants could be held liable under section 2333 on an aiding and abetting theory, and that the Supreme Court's holding in *Central Bank*, which addressed civil liability for aiding and abetting in the context of securities fraud claims, was distinguishable.

FN5. The Boims also argued in the district court that Congress clarified section 2331(1) in its later passage of sections 2339A and 2339B. According to the Boims, Congress demonstrated in sections 2339A and 2339B that the provision of material support or resources to terrorists is an activity that *involves* violent acts or acts dangerous to human life. The Boims' argument on this point is thus two-fold: first, they claim that violations of sections 2339A and 2339B give rise to civil liability under section 2333. Second, they maintain that sections 2339A and 2339B clarify the meaning of "involve" in section 2331(1). In particular, sections 2339A and 2339B demonstrate that providing material support or resources is an activity that "involves" violent acts. We will address both prongs of the Boims' argument *infra*.

The district court denied the motion to dismiss. *Boim v. Quranic Literacy Institute*, 127 F.Supp.2d 1002, 1021 (N.D.Ill.2001). Addressing the Boims' first theory, the court found that funding, without more, does not "involve violent acts or acts dangerous to human life." The court began with the statutory language, which sweepingly defines acts of international terrorism to include "activities involving violent acts or acts dangerous to human life," and found that this phrase was so broad that it provided little guidance concerning where to draw limits on the conduct Congress sought to curb. 127 F.Supp.2d at 1013-14. Instead, "[c]ontributions to a foreign organization...without a further allegation of participation by the contributor, appear too far removed to constitute direct acts of international terrorism." *Id.* The district court concluded that Congress meant to reach beyond the persons directly involved in the violent act, but that liability should be limited to persons or organizations that knew about the violent act and participated in the preparation of the plan to commit the violent act. 127 F.Supp.2d at 1014-15. Thus, as a matter of statutory interpretation, the Boims' allegations of funding terrorist organizations, without more direct dealing with the group, did not constitute activity involving violent acts or acts dangerous to human life. 127 F.Supp.2d at 1015. Relying on a Fourth Circuit case, the court noted that where funding a terrorist group was the main allegation, the plaintiffs must also be able to show that the defendants providing the funds knew about the violent act and participated in the preparation of the plan to commit the violent act. See *United States v. Wells*, 163 F.3d 889 (4th Cir.1998), *cert. denied*, 528 U.S. 841, 120 S.Ct. 109, 145 L.Ed.2d 92 (1999). Because Salah was alleged to have participated in recruiting and training terrorists as well as channeling money to Hamas for terrorist activities, the court found that the claim against him could stand. 127 F.Supp.2d at 1015. The court found the allegations of funding alone against the organizational defendants inadequate on a straight reading of the statute because, although the Boims alleged that HLF and QLI knew about Hamas' plans for terrorist activities, they did not allege that these groups participated in the preparation of the planning for the violent acts. *Id.*

The court then considered whether the action could be sustained under the Boims' second theory, that violations of 18 U.S.C. §§2339A and 2339B sufficed to create civil liability under section 2333. Sections 2339A and 2339B created criminal liability for persons providing material support to

terrorists. The court agreed that conduct prohibited by sections 2339A and 2339B constituted "international terrorism" as that term was defined in section 2333. 127 F.Supp.2d at 1016. The court noted that sections 2339A and 2339B require that support provided to terrorists be both knowing and material, but that civil liability for violations of sections 2339A or 2339B was limited to the period of time after sections 2339A and 2339B became law (1994 for section 2339A and 1996 for section 2339B). 127 F.Supp.2d at 1016-17.

The court also addressed the Boims' closely related theory that Congress clarified the meaning of "acts of international terrorism" when it passed sections 2339A and 2339B. According to the district court, these criminal provisions demonstrated Congress' intent to include the provision of material support to terrorists in its definition of conduct involving violent acts under section 2331. If Congress imposed criminal liability for the provision of material support to terrorists, the district court reasoned, it surely meant for civil liability to reach at least that far. The court found further support for the proposition that Congress viewed the provision of material support to terrorists as an act of international terrorism in the repeal of jurisdictional immunity of a foreign state that has been designated a state sponsor of terrorism when the state is sued for personal injury or death caused by the state's provision of material support or resources to terrorists as defined in section 2339A. *See* 28 U.S.C. §1605(a)(7). "Considering Congress has permitted foreign states that have been designated state-sponsors of terrorism to be sued in United States courts for violating §2339A, it is hard to argue that Congress did not intend to include such violations in its definition of 'terrorism' under the statutory scheme." 127 F.Supp.2d at 1016.

Because section 2339A was enacted in 1994 and section 2339B was enacted in 1996, the court found that the plaintiffs would have to rely on their third theory of liability, aiding and abetting in order to reach conduct that occurred before 1994. 127 F.Supp.2d at 1017. The court rejected the defendants' contention that the Supreme Court generally precluded aiding and abetting liability in federal civil causes of action in the *Central Bank* decision. *Id.* Rather, the district court found that aiding and abetting liability was available when a statute provided for it. Section 2333 relies on section 2331(1) for its definition of "international terrorism," and the court found that any action that falls under the definition of section 2331(1) may be the basis for a civil action under section 2333. Noting that aiding and abetting an act of international terrorism is itself a criminal violation, the court concluded that aiding and abetting terrorism is an activity that involves violent acts or acts dangerous to human life. The court sustained the Boims' cause of action on the theory that they had sufficiently alleged that the defendants aided and abetted international terrorism. 127 F.Supp.2d at 1017-18. The court relied on the liberal standards of pleading under Federal Rule of Civil Procedure 8 to find that the Boims had alleged their claim sufficiently, reasoning that the complaint provided the defendants with adequate notice of the charges against them. 127 F.Supp.2d at 1018.

The district court also rejected the defendants' claim that the Boims had inadequately alleged causation. HLF and QLI argued that the Boims had shown no connection between the defendants' provision of money to Hamas and the murder of David Boim. The defendants characterized the Boims' complaint as alleging funding only through 1993, and maintained the funding was too remote in time to have proximately caused David's murder in 1996. The court first noted that the Boims alleged the defendants' funding extended beyond 1993, contrary to the defendants' characterization. The court also found that Congress indicated by its passage of sections 2339A and 2339B its belief that funding terrorism causes the harm of the terrorists' subsequent actions. 127 F.Supp.2d at 1019. According to the court, sections 2339A and 2339B required that the aid to the terrorists be "material," a term that provides the causal link between the provision of funds and the injury from the terrorist action. The court found the complaint sufficient and stated that the plaintiffs would have to prove the funding at issue here was material to David Boim's murder. 127 F.Supp.2d at 1019-20.

Finally, the court rejected the defendants' First Amendment challenge, finding that the complaint was not seeking to impose liability for mere political association or belief but rather for knowing and intentional support of the illegal aims of the defendant organizations. 127 F.Supp.2d at 1020-21. Because the Boims are required to prove that HLF and QLI intended to further Hamas' illegal activities, either by aiding and abetting the terrorist action or by violating sections 2339A or 2339B, the district court found that the claim survived First Amendment scrutiny. *Id.* HLF and QLI appeal.

II.

The district court granted HLF and QLI's motion for a certificate of appealability, and we subsequently granted them leave to file an interlocutory appeal. *See* 28 U.S.C. §1292(b). Interlocutory appeal is appropriate when (1) the appeal presents a question of law; (2) it is controlling; (3) it

is contestable; (4) its resolution will expedite the resolution of the litigation, and (5) the petition to appeal is filed in the district court within a reasonable amount of time after entry of the order sought to be appealed. *Ahrenholz v. Board of Trustees of the University of Illinois*, 219 F.3d 674, 675 (7th Cir.2000). We have interpreted "question of law" to refer to a question regarding the meaning of a statutory or constitutional provision, regulation or common law doctrine. *Id.*, 219 F.3d at 676. In this case, the district court correctly certified three issues for appeal:

(1) Does funding, *simpliciter*, of an international terrorist organization constitute an act of terrorism under 18 U.S.C. §2331?

(2) Does 18 U.S.C. §2333 incorporate the definitions of international terrorism found in 18 U.S.C. §§2339A and 2339B?

(3) Does a civil cause of action lie under 18 U.S.C. §§2331 and 2333 for aiding and abetting international terrorism?

See *Boim v. Quranic Literacy Institute, et al.*, Case No. 00-C-2905, Order (N.D.Ill. February 22, 2001). The interpretation of sections 2331 and 2333 presents questions of law which will control the outcome of this case. As these are questions of first impression, the application of these statutes to the facts alleged here is certainly contestable, and the resolution of these issues will facilitate the conclusion of the litigation. The defendants filed their motions for certificates of appealability in the district court within a reasonable amount of time after entry of the district court's order denying their motion to dismiss (the district court's order was docketed January 10, 2001, QLI filed its motion on February 14, 2001 and HLF filed its motion on February 15, 2001). A panel of this Court granted the defendants' subsequent petitions for interlocutory appeal on April 6, 2001, and we now consider the issues certified by the district court.

We review *de novo* a district court's ruling on a 12(b)(6) motion to dismiss a complaint for failure to state a claim on which relief may be granted. *Slaney*, 244 F.3d at 597. At this stage of the proceedings, we accept all factual allegations in the complaint and draw all reasonable inferences from those facts in favor of the Boims, the plaintiffs here. *Id.* We examine the complaint as a whole, and we will allow the case to proceed unless it appears beyond doubt that the Boims can prove no set of facts in support of their claim which would entitle them to relief. *Id.*; *Pokuta v. Trans World Airlines, Inc.*, 191 F.3d 834, 839 (7th Cir.1999). Federal Rule 8(a)(2) requires only that a complaint include a "short and plain statement of the claim showing that the pleader is entitled to relief." Fed.R.Civ.P. 8(a)(2); *Leatherman*, 507 U.S. at 168, 113 S.Ct. 1160. The Boims thus need not set out in detail all of the facts upon which they base their claim. Rule 8(a) requires only that the complaint give the defendants fair notice of what their claim is and the grounds upon which it rests. *Leatherman*, 507 U.S. at 168, 113 S.Ct. 1160. With these standards in mind, we turn to the statutes at issue here.

The Boims seek to recover against HLF and QLI pursuant to 18 U.S.C. §2333, which provides, in relevant part:

Any national of the United States injured in his or her person, property, or business by reason of an act of international terrorism, or his or her estate, survivors, or heirs, may sue therefor in any appropriate district court of the United States and shall recover threefold the damages he or she sustains and the cost of the suit, including attorney's fees.

18 U.S.C. §2333(a). "International terrorism," in turn, is a defined term:

[T]he term "international terrorism" means activities that-

(A) involve violent acts or acts dangerous to human life that are a violation of the criminal laws of the United States or of any State, or that would be a criminal violation if committed within the jurisdiction of the United States or of any State;

(B) appear to be intended-

(i) to intimidate or coerce a civilian population;

(ii) to influence the policy of a government by intimidation or coercion; or

(iii) to affect the conduct of a government by assassination or kidnapping; and

(C) occur primarily outside the territorial jurisdiction of the United States, or transcend national boundaries in terms of the means by which they are accomplished, the persons they appear intended to intimidate or coerce, or the locale in which their perpetrators operate or seek asylum.

18 U.S.C. §2331(1). These provisions became law in 1992. [FN6] We turn now to the Boims' three theories of liability under section 2333:(1) that funding Hamas, without more, is an act of international terrorism because it is conduct that in-

volves violent acts or acts dangerous to human life; (2) that funding Hamas constitutes the provision of material support or resources to a terrorist organization in violation of the criminal provisions set forth in sections 2339A and 2339B, and that violations of these criminal provisions give rise to civil liability under section 2333; and (3) that aiding and abetting an act of terrorism gives rise to civil liability under section 2333. [FN7]

FN6. Sections 2331 and 2333 were initially enacted in 1990 as the Anti-Terrorism Act of 1990, Pub.L. No. 101-519, §132, 104 Stat. 2250 (1990), but were repealed as the result of a technical deficiency. They were subsequently re-enacted as part of the Federal Courts Administration Act of 1992, Pub.L. No. 102-572, 106 Stat. 4506 (1992).

FN7. Because the questions presented in the appeal implicate, at least in part, the relation between section 2333 and two criminal statutes, sections 2339A and 2339B, we asked the United States to file a brief *amicus curiae*. The United States accepted our invitation and the plaintiffs and defendants were afforded an opportunity to respond to the views presented by the United States.

A.

The plaintiffs' first theory is that the simple provision of funds to Hamas by QLI and HLF constitutes an act of international terrorism because it "involve[s] violent acts or acts dangerous to human life." The Boims liken payments to Hamas to murder for hire: the person who pays for the murder does not himself commit a violent act, but the payment "involves" violent acts in the sense that it brings about the violent act and provides an incentive for someone else to commit it. The Boims urge us to adopt a very broad definition of "involves" that would include any activity that touches on and supports a violent act. They argue that David's murder was indisputably a violent act, and we have no quarrel with that premise. But they further argue that the provision of money or in-kind services to persons outside the country who set up the infrastructure used to recruit and train David's murderers, buy their weapons, and compensate their families also "involves" violent acts. The defendants, in turn, urge us to read the statute to hold liable only those who actually commit a violent act.

No court has yet considered the meaning or scope of sections 2331 and 2333, and so we write upon a tabula rasa. The starting point in all statutory analysis is the plain language of the statute itself. *United States v. Wagner*, 29 F.3d 264, 266 (7th Cir.1994). We look to the language in order to determine what Congress intended, and we also look to the statute's structure, subject matter, context and history for this same purpose. *Almendarez-Torres v. United States*, 523 U.S. 224, 228, 118 S.Ct. 1219, 140 L.Ed.2d 350 (1998) ("We therefore look to the statute before us and ask what Congress intended...In answering this question, we look to the statute's language, structure, subject matter, context, and history-factors that typically help courts determine a statute's objectives and thereby illuminate its text."). The controversy here centers on the definition of international terrorism, and in particular on the definition of the word "involve," which is susceptible to many meanings. The statutory definition of international terrorism in section 2331(1) is drawn *verbatim* from the Foreign Intelligence Surveillance Act, 50 U.S.C. §1801(c) ("FISA"). No court has yet expounded on the meaning or scope of "international terrorism" as it is used in FISA either, so we are not aided by that origin. [FN8] A dictionary definition of "involve" demonstrates the many levels of participation that could constitute involvement. To involve is: to enfold or envelop so as to encumber; to engage as a participant; to oblige to take part; to occupy (as oneself) absorbingly; to commit emotionally; to relate closely; to have within or as part of itself; to require as a necessary accompaniment; to have an effect on. WEBSTER'S NINTH NEW COLLEGIATE DICTIONARY (1983). Because of these many possibilities, we agree with the district court that we must look to the structure, context and legislative history of the statute to determine what Congress intended.

FN8. A few courts, however, have touched on the application of the term "international terrorism" in the context of FISA. See *United States v. Sarkissian*, 841 F.2d 959, 965 (9th Cir.1988) (investigation of "international terrorism" by definition requires investigation of activities that constitute crimes); *United States v. Duggan*, 743 F.2d 59 (2d Cir.1984) (asking a court to apply the definition of "international terrorism" does not embroil the court in a political question and thereby violate the separation of powers doctrine).
The government, in its very helpful *amicus curiae* brief, delineates some of the legislative history of sections 2331 and 2333. That history, in combination with the language of the statute itself, evidences an intent by Congress to codify general common law tort principles and to extend civil liability for acts of international terrorism to the full reaches of traditional tort law. *See* 137 Cong. Rec. S4511-04 (April 16, 1991) ("The [antiterrorism act] accords victims of terrorism the remedies of American tort law, including treble damages and attorney's fees."); *Antiterrorism Act of 1990*, Hearing Before the Subcommittee on Courts and Administrative Practice of Committee on the Judiciary, United States

Senate, 101st Congress, Second Session, July 25, 1990 (hereafter "Senate Hearing"), Testimony of *Joseph Morris*, at 136 ("[T]he bill as drafted is powerfully broad, and its intention...is to...bring [in] all of the substantive law of the American tort law system."). In particular, the statute itself contains all of the elements of a traditional tort: breach of a duty (i.e., committing an act of international terrorism); injury to the person, property or business of another; and causation (injured "by reason of"). Although the statute defines the class of plaintiffs who may sue, it does not limit the class of defendants, and we must therefore look to tort law and the legislative history to determine who may be held liable for injuries covered by the statute.

The legislative record is replete with references to the then-recent decision in *Klinghoffer v. Palestine Liberation Organization*, 739 F.Supp. 854 (S.D.N.Y.1990), *vacated*, 937 F.2d 44 (2d Cir.1991). *See* Senate Hearing at 1, 12, 17, 79, 83, 122, 133; H.R. Rep. 102-1040, at 5 (1992); 137 Cong. Rec. S4511-04 (April 16, 1991); 136 Cong. Rec. S4568-01 (1990). [FN9] Leon Klinghoffer was a U.S. citizen who was murdered in a terrorist attack on a cruise ship in the Mediterranean Sea. The district court found that his survivors' claims were cognizable in federal court under federal admiralty jurisdiction and the Death on the High Seas Act because the tort occurred in navigable waters. 739 F.Supp. at 858-59. The repeated favorable references to *Klinghoffer* indicate a desire on the part of Congress to extend this liability to land-based terrorism that occurred in a foreign country. See Senate Hearing at 12, Testimony of Alan Kreczko, Deputy Legal Advisor, Department of State ("This bill...expands the *Klinghoffer* opinion."); H.R. Rep. 102-1040, at 5 (1992) ("Only by virtue of the fact that the [Klinghoffer] attack violated certain Admiralty laws and the organization involved-the Palestinian Liberation Organization-had assets and carried on activities in New York, was the court able to establish jurisdiction over the case. A similar attack occurring on an airplane or in some other locale might not have been subject to civil action in the U.S. In order to facilitate civil actions against such terrorists the Committee [on the Judiciary] recommends [this bill]."); 137 Cong. Rec. S4511-04 (April 16, 1991), Statement of Senator Grassley (section 2333 would "codify [the *Klinghoffer*] ruling and makes the right of American victims definitive"); 136 Cong. Rec. S4568-01 (1990).

FN9. One of Mr. Klinghoffer's surviving daughters testified before both the House and the Senate in favor of the passage of the Antiterrorism Act of 1990. *See* Senate Hearing; H.R. Rep. 102-1040 at 4.

The statute clearly is meant to reach beyond those persons who themselves commit the violent act that directly causes the injury. The Senate report on the bill notes that "[t]he substance of [an action under section 2333] is not de fined by the statute, because the fact patterns giving rise to such suits will be as varied and numerous as those found in the law of torts. This bill opens the courthouse door to victims of international terrorism." S. Rep. 102-342, at 45 (1992). This same report also remarks that the legislation, with "its provisions for compensatory damages, treble damages, and the imposition of liability *at any point along the causal chain of terrorism*," would "interrupt, or at least imperil, the flow of money." *Id.* at 22 (emphasis added). *See also* Statement of Senator Grassley, 136 Cong. Rec. S4568-01 at S4593 ("With the enactment of this legislation, we set an example to the world of how the United States legal system deals with terrorists. If terrorists have assets within our jurisdictional reach, American citizens will have the power to seize them."); Senate Hearing at 17, Statement of Alan Kreczko ("[F]ew terrorist organizations are likely to have cash assets or property located in the United States that could be attached and used to fulfill a civil judgment. The existence of such a cause of action, however, may deter terrorist groups from maintaining assets in the United States, from benefitting from investments in the U.S. and from soliciting funds within the U.S."); Senate Hearing at 79, Statement of Joseph Morris ("[A]nything that could be done to deter money-raising in the United States, money laundering in the United States, the repose of assets in the United States, and so on, would not only help benefit victims, but would also help deter terrorism."). All of this history indicates an intent by Congress to allow a plaintiff to recover from anyone along the causal chain of terrorism.

But to the extent that the Boims urge a reading of the statute that would lead to liability for merely giving money to Hamas, a group which then sponsored a terrorist act in the manner the Boims have alleged, we agree with the district court, the defendants and the government that those allegations would be inadequate. To say that funding *simpliciter* constitutes an act of terrorism is to give the statute an almost unlimited reach. Any act which turns out to facilitate terrorism, however remote that act may be from actual violence and regardless of the actor's intent, could be construed to "involve" terrorism. Without also requiring the plaintiffs to show knowledge of and intent to further the payee's violent criminal acts, such a broad definition might also lead to constitutional infirmities by punishing mere association with groups that engage in terrorism, as we shall discuss later in addressing the First Amendment concerns raised here.

Additionally, the statute itself requires that in order to recover, a plaintiff must be injured "by reason of" an act of international terrorism. The Supreme Court has interpreted identical language to require a showing of proximate cause. See *Holmes v. Securities Investor Protection Corp.*, 503 U.S. 258, 265-68, 112 S.Ct. 1311, 117 L.Ed.2d 532 (1992) (interpreting "by reason of" language in civil RICO provision to require a showing that the defendant's conduct proximately caused the plaintiff's injury). Foreseeability is the cornerstone of proximate cause, and in tort law, a defendant will be held liable only for those injuries that might have reasonably been anticipated as a natural consequence of the defendant's actions. *Suzik v. Sea-Land Corp.*, 89 F.3d 345, 348 (7th Cir.1996); Restatement (2d) of Torts, §§440-447. In the circumstances of this case, the Boims cannot show that David Boim was injured "by reason of" the defendants' payments to Hamas in the traditional tort sense of causation unless they can also show that murder was the reasonably foreseeable result of making the donation. To hold the defendants liable for donating money without knowledge of the donee's intended criminal use of the funds would impose strict liability. Nothing in the language of the statute or its structure or history supports that formulation. The government, in its amicus brief, maintains that funding may be enough to establish liability if the plaintiff can show that the provider of funds was generally aware of the donee's terrorist activity, and if the provision of funds substantially assisted the terrorist act in question. See *Halberstam v. Welch*, 705 F.2d 472, 477 (D.C.Cir.1983) (describing the standards for joint liability for tortious acts). We will consider the government's proposed standard separately in our discussion of aiding and abetting liability. For now we note only that the complaint cannot be sustained on the theory that the defendants themselves committed an act of international terrorism when they donated unspecified amounts of money to Hamas, neither knowing nor suspecting that Hamas would in turn financially support the persons who murdered David Boim. In the very least, the plaintiffs must be able to show that murder was a reasonably foreseeable result of making a donation. [FN10] Thus, the Boims' first theory of liability under section 2333, funding *simpliciter* of a terrorist organization, is insufficient because it sets too vague a standard, and because it does not require a showing of proximate cause.

FN10. The defendants have also argued that Congress listed exhaustively in section 2333(b) all of the offenses which could give rise to liability under section 2333(a). We reject this contention because "international terrorism" is a defined term that includes conduct much broader than the offenses listed in section 2333(b). *See* 18 U.S.C. §2331. Reading the statute as the defendants urge would require us to disregard Congress' express definition of the term "international terrorism."

B.

The Boims' second theory of liability is that the defendants' violation of sections 2339A and 2339B, the criminal counterparts to section 2333, gives rise to civil liability under section 2333. The Boims further contend that sections 2339A and 2339B demonstrate Congress' intent to include the provision of material support to terrorist organizations in the definition of international terrorism for the purposes of section 2333. The district court concluded that Congress viewed violations of sections 2339A and 2339B as "activities involving violent acts or acts dangerous to human life," and therefore found that violations of sections 2339A and 2339B gave rise to civil liability under section 2333. Because much of the conduct the Boims alleged occurred before the passage of sections 2339A and 2339B, however, the district court ruled that the Boims would have to rely primarily on their aiding and abetting theory.

In 1994, Congress passed 18 U.S.C. §2339A, which criminalizes the provision of material support to terrorists:

Whoever, within the United States, provides material support or resources or conceals or disguises the nature, location, source, or ownership of material support or resources, knowing or intending that they are to be used in preparation for, or in carrying out, a violation of section 32, 37, 81, 175, 351, 831, 842(m) or (n), 844(f) or (i), 930(c), 956, 1114, 1116, 1203, 1361, 1362, 1363, 1366, 1751, 1992, 2155, 2156, 2280, 2281, 2332, 2332a, 2332b, 2332c, or 2340A of this title or section 46502 of title 49, or in preparation for, or in carrying out, the concealment or an escape from the commission of any such violation, shall be fined under this title, imprisoned not more than 10 years, or both.

18 U.S.C. §2339A(a). [FN11] "Material support or resources" is a defined term:

FN11. The crimes covered by this diverse and extensive list include, in Title 18: §32, destruction of aircraft or aircraft facilities; §37, violence at international airports; §81, arson within special maritime and territorial jurisdiction; §175, prohibitions with respect to biological weapons; §351, Congressional, Cabinet, and Supreme Court assassination, kidnapping, and assault; §831, prohibited transactions involv-

ing nuclear materials; §842(m), importing and exporting certain plastic explosives; §842(n), shipping, transporting, transferring, receiving or possessing certain plastic explosives; §844(f), maliciously damaging or destroying personal or real property belonging to the United States; §844(i), maliciously damaging or destroying personal or real property used in interstate or foreign commerce; §930(c), killing or attempting to kill a person in a federal facility while illegally possessing a firearm or other dangerous weapon in that facility; §956, conspiracy to kill, kidnap, maim, or injure persons or damage property in a foreign country; §1114, protection of officers and employees of the United States; §1116, murder or manslaughter of foreign officials, official guests or internationally protected persons; §1203, hostage taking; §1361, injuries to government property or contracts; §1362, injury to communication lines, stations or systems; §1363, damaging buildings or property within the special maritime and territorial jurisdiction; §1366, destruction of an energy facility; §1751, Presidential and Presidential staff assassination, kidnapping, and assault; §1992, wrecking trains; §2155, destruction of national defense materials, premises or utilities; §2156, production of defective national defense material, premises or utilities; §2280, violence against maritime navigation; §2281, violence against maritime fixed platforms; §2332, killing of a United States national outside the United States; §2332a, use of certain weapons of mass destruction; §2332b, acts of terrorism transcending national boundaries; or §2340A, torture outside the United States. Section 2332c has been repealed. Title 49, §46502 prohibits aircraft piracy.

In this section, the term "material support or resources" means currency or other financial securities, financial services, lodging, training, safehouses, false documentation or identification, communications equipment, facilities, weapons, lethal substances, explosives, personnel, transportation, and other physical assets, except medicine or religious materials.

18 U.S.C. §2339A(b). Two years later, Congress extended criminal liability to those providing material support to foreign terrorist organizations:

Whoever, within the United States or subject to the jurisdiction of the United States, knowingly provides material support or resources to a foreign terrorist organization, or attempts or conspires to do so, shall be fined under this title or imprisoned not more than 10 years, or both.

18 U.S.C. §2339B(a)(1). Section 2339B adopts the definition of "material support or resources" provided in section

2339A, and looks to 8 U.S.C. §1189 for the definition of "terrorist organization."[FN12]

FN12. *See* note 2, *supra*.

HLF and QLI, of course, protest the district court's conclusion that funding may form the basis for a section 2333 civil action if the funding meets the standards for criminal liability under sections 2339A or 2339B. The defendants also fault the district court for relying on Congress' repeal of the jurisdictional immunity of a foreign state that has been designated a state sponsor of terrorism as evidence of Congressional intent to allow a section 2333 civil action against persons who violate sections 2339A and 2339B. *See* 28 U.S.C. §1605(a)(7). HLF and QLI present a number of puzzling arguments against the Boims' theory of civil liability through violations of these criminal statutes. According to HLF and QLI, Congress neither expressly nor impliedly amended the definition of "international terrorism" when it enacted section 2339A and 2339B because (1) these sections set forth criminal offenses separate from the statute making violent acts of international terrorism illegal under U.S. law;[FN13] (2) these sections provide for relatively minor criminal penalties compared to the penalties for violent terrorist acts; (3) nothing in the text of either sections 2339A or 2339B suggests that violations of these provisions are acts of international terrorism remediable under section 2333; (4) the inclusion of sections 2339A and 2339B in the terrorism section of Title 18 alone does not mean that Congress intended for violations of these provisions to constitute acts of international terrorism for the purposes of section 2333; and (6) section 2339B contains a separate remedial scheme that does not include a private right of action but instead provides for civil enforcement by the United States. The defendants also argue that even if violations of sections 2339A and 2339B create civil liability under section 2333, the Boims have insufficiently alleged violations of those criminal statutes.

FN13. Presumably, they are referring to 18 U.S.C. §§332, 2332a, 2332b and 2332d. These sections proscribe murder, physical violence, the use of weapons of mass destruction, acts of terrorism transcending national boundaries, and engaging in financial transactions with designated terrorist countries. These provisions apply to the person directly engaged in the prohibited activity, as opposed to persons providing material support to those directly engaged in the prohibited activity.

Most of these arguments are tautologous. For example, sections 2339A and 2339B certainly do proscribe different conduct than sections 2332, 2332a, 2332b and 2332d. These latter provisions address the primary perpetrators of violent acts of terrorism, while sections 2339A and 2339B apply to those persons who provide material support to the primary perpetrators of violent acts of terrorism. When it passed sections 2339A and 2339B, Congress undoubtedly intended that the persons providing financial support to terrorists should also be held criminally liable for those violent acts. Indeed, as we have already noted, the Congressional record for section 2333 indicates an intention to cut off the flow of money in support of terrorism generally. S. Rep. 102-342 at 22 (1992). Sections 2339A and 2339B further this goal by imposing criminal liability for financial support of terrorist activities and organizations. The fact that Congress imposed lesser criminal penalties for the financial supporters indicates perhaps that they found the financiers less dangerous or less culpable than the terrorists they finance, but it does not in any way indicate that Congress meant to limit civil liability to those who personally committed acts of terrorism. On the contrary, it would be counterintuitive to conclude that Congress imposed criminal liability in sections 2339A and 2339B on those who financed terrorism, but did not intend to impose civil liability on those same persons through section 2333.

Section 2339A prohibits the provision of material support for an extensive list of violent crimes associated with terrorism-assassination, kidnapping, arson, destruction of aircraft-that make clear what types of conduct Congress had in mind when it defined "international terrorism" in section 2331(1) as not just the violent acts themselves, but also "activities that *involve* violent acts or acts dangerous to human life." There is no textual, structural or logical justification for construing the civil liability imposed by section 2333 more narrowly than the corresponding criminal provisions. Because Congress intended to impose criminal liability for funding violent terrorism, we find that it also intended through sections 2333 and 2331(1) to impose civil liability for funding at least as broad a class of violent terrorist acts. If the plaintiffs could show that HLF and QLI violated either section 2339A or section 2339B, that conduct would certainly be sufficient to meet the definition of "international terrorism" under sections 2333 and 2331. Such acts would give rise to civil liability under section 2333 so long as knowledge and intent are also shown, as we shall discuss shortly in the context of aiding and abetting.

We hasten to add that, although proof of a criminal violation under sections 2339A or 2339B might satisfy the definition of international terrorism under section 2333, such proof is not necessary to sustain a section 2333 claim. As we discuss in the context of aiding and abetting, we believe Congress intended for civil liability for financing terrorism to sweep more broadly than the conduct described in sections 2339A and 2339B. We also note that the district court seems to have inadvertently redefined the term "material" in the context of sections 2339A and 2339B as meaning substantial or considerable. The statute itself defines "material support or resources" as "currency or other financial securities, financial services, lodging, training, safehouses, false documentation or identification, communications equipment, facilities, weapons, lethal substances, explosives, personnel, transportation, and other physical assets, except medicine or religious materials." 18 U.S.C. §2339A(b). Thus, the term relates to the type of aid provided rather than whether it is substantial or considerable. For civil liability, section 2333 requires that the plaintiff be injured "by reason of" the act of international terrorism. Because we believe Congress intended to import standard tort law into section 2333, causation may be demonstrated as it would be in traditional tort law. Congress has made clear, though, through the criminal liability imposed in sections 2339A and 2339B, that even small donations made knowingly and intentionally in support of terrorism may meet the standard for civil liability in section 2333. Congress' goal of cutting off funding for terrorism would be seriously compromised if terrorist organizations could avoid liability by simply pooling together small donations to fund a terrorist act.

We turn finally to 28 U.S.C. §1605(a)(7). In relevant part, the statute provides:

A foreign state shall not be immune from the jurisdiction of courts of the United States or of the States in any case…in which money damages are sought against a foreign state for personal injury or death that was caused by an act of torture, extrajudicial killing, aircraft sabotage, hostage taking, or the provision of material support or resources (as defined in section 2339A of title 18) for such an act if such act or provision of material support is engaged in by an official, employee, or agent of such foreign state while acting within the scope of his or her office, employment, agency[.]

Contrary to the defendants' characterization, the district court did not rely solely on the passage of section 1605(a)(7) in finding that Congress viewed the provision of material support and resources as an act of international terrorism. After finding support in both the text and the structure of sections 2333 and 2331 for this proposition, the court found further reasons in section 1605(a)(7). As the district court noted, "Considering that Congress has permitted foreign

states that have been designated state sponsors of terrorism to be sued in United States courts for violating §2339A, it is hard to argue that Congress did not intend to include such violations in its definition of 'terrorism' under the statutory scheme." *Boim*, 127 F.Supp.2d at 1016. We take the district court to mean that section 1605(a)(7) implies a foreign state may be sued in the United States for acts that would give rise to criminal liability under section 2339A, not that section 2339A itself has a civil provision. The mechanism for suing a foreign state for these acts that would give rise to criminal liability under section 2339A is section 2333. The defendants complain that Congress did not specifically mention section 2333 as the device by which plaintiffs might sue foreign governments for violations of section 2339A, but they fail to point to any other source of civil liability. We agree that Congress made clear in section 1605(a)(7) its intent to characterize violations of section 2339A as acts of international terrorism under section 2333.

The district court believed there was a timing problem for the Boims in making their case under these criminal provisions because much of the funding conduct allegedly committed by HLF and QLI occurred prior to the passage of sections 2339A and 2339B. Indeed, Hamas was not designated a terrorist organization under section 1189 until 1997, after David's murder. Certainly HLF and QLI could not be held criminally liable for conduct that occurred before the statutes were enacted, but that argument misses the point. We are using sections 2339A and 2339B not as independent sources of liability under section 2333, but to amplify what Congress meant by "international terrorism." Sections 2339A and 2339B merely lend further support to our finding that Congress considered the provision of material support to terrorists an act of international terrorism. This reading simply amplifies the conclusion we have already reached by examining the language and legislative history of section 2333. Sections 2339A and 2339B provide criminal liability for the provision of material support, and section 2333 provides civil liability. The Boims may thus show that QLI and HLF committed an act of international terrorism subject to civil liability under section 2333 by proving that QLI and HLF provided material support to terrorist organizations. No timing problem arises because sections 2339A and 2339B merely elucidate conduct that was already prohibited by section 2333.

C.

We turn next to the Boims' theory that HLF and QLI may be held civilly liable under section 2333 for aiding and abetting an act of international terrorism. Under this theory, the Boims urge us to find that aiding and abetting a violent act is conduct that "involves" a violent act as that word is used in section 2331(1). HLF and QLI contend that section 2333 does not provide for aiding and abetting liability, and that the Supreme Court in *Central Bank* held that aiding and abetting liability is available only when a statute expressly provides for it. See *Central Bank of Denver N.A. v. First Interstate Bank of Denver, N.A.*, 511 U.S. 164, 114 S.Ct. 1439, 128 L.Ed.2d 119 (1994); *Alexander v. Sandoval*, 532 U.S. 275, 121 S.Ct. 1511, 149 L.Ed.2d 517 (2001). The Boims counter that neither *Central Bank* nor *Sandoval* apply to *malum in se* torts such as the murder alleged here. The Boims also contend that section 2333 explicitly extends liability to aiders and abettors because it extends civil liability to "activities that involve violent acts...that are a violation of the criminal laws of the United States." Because 18 U.S.C. §2 criminalizes aiding and abetting the commission of a felony, the Boims maintain there is no doubt Congress intended to include liability for aiding and abetting in section 2333. The government, in its *amicus* brief, adds that the language and legislative history of section 2333 indicate an intent by Congress to import into section 2333 civil tort law principles as expressed in the Restatement Second of Torts, and as applied in the cases. Under that jurisprudence, according to the government, aiding and abetting liability should be applied under section 2333, and that result is in no way inconsistent with *Central Bank* and *Sandoval*. Because of *Central Bank's* pivotal importance to our analysis, we will begin by reviewing the Court's reasoning there.

In *Central Bank*, the Supreme Court held that a private plaintiff may not maintain an aiding and abetting suit under section 10(b) of the Securities Exchange Act of 1934. 511 U.S. at 177-78, 114 S.Ct. 1439. As the Court has interpreted it, section 10(b) imposes private civil liability on those who commit a manipulative or deceptive act in connection with the purchase or sale of securities. 511 U.S. at 167, 114 S.Ct. 1439. Yet, that section contains no express cause of action giving private plaintiffs a right to sue. Nonetheless, through judicial interpretation of the securities laws, an implied right of action was created allowing private parties to sue for damages for violations of section 10(b). Prior to *Central Bank*, some lower courts had interpreted the statute to create a private right of action not only against those who violate section 10(b), but also against those who aid and abet a violation of section 10(b); other courts had found that there was no private right of action for aiding and abetting liability. The Court granted certiorari to resolve the continuing confusion in the circuit courts over the existence and scope of an

aiding and abetting action under section 10(b). 511 U.S. at 170, 114 S.Ct. 1439.

The securities laws contain a number of provisions creating an extensive scheme of civil liability. The 1933 and 1934 Acts contain express private rights of action, and the courts have also found private rights of actions to be implied by the terms of sections 10(b) and 14(a) of the 1934 Act. 511 U.S. at 171, 114 S.Ct. 1439. The SEC adopted Rule 10b-5 to further describe the conduct prohibited, and it is under this rule that plaintiffs often brought their actions. The Court noted that determining the elements of rule 10b-5 private action claims had posed difficulty because Congress had not expressly provided for a private 10(b) action and thus had no occasion to offer guidance about the elements of a private liability scheme. 511 U.S. at 172, 114 S.Ct. 1439. The courts thus had to infer how the 1934 Congress would have addressed the issue had the 10b-5 action been included as an express provision of the 1934 Act. 511 U.S. at 173, 114 S.Ct. 1439. Because adherence to the statutory language is the starting point of any case involving construction of a statute, the Supreme Court refused to allow 10b-5 liability for conduct not prohibited by the text of section 10(b). 511 U.S. at 174, 114 S.Ct. 1439. In view of the fact that section 10(b) made no mention of aiding and abetting liability, the Court found that there could be no private right of action for aiding and abetting a 10(b) violation.

The Court rejected a claim that language in the statute imposing liability on any person who "directly or indirectly" employs a deceptive practice meant that Congress intended to cover aiding and abetting:

The problem, of course, is that aiding and abetting liability extends beyond persons who engage, even indirectly, in a proscribed activity; aiding and abetting liability reaches persons who do not engage in the proscribed activities at all, but who give a degree of aid to those who do.

511 U.S. at 175-76, 114 S.Ct. 1439. Citing section 876(b) of the Restatement (Second) of Torts, the Court acknowledged that aiding and abetting a wrongdoer ought to be actionable in certain other circumstances, but the issue here was whether aiding and abetting was covered by the statute. The Court stated that it was inconsistent with settled methodology in section 10(b) cases to extend liability beyond the scope of conduct prohibited by the statutory text. The Court found that the statute prohibited only the making of a material misstatement (or omission) or the commission of a manipulative act. Because the statute did not proscribe giving aid to

a person who commits a manipulation or deceptive act, the Court declined to extend liability to aiders and abettors. 511 U.S. at 177-78, 114 S.Ct. 1439.

The Court further noted that it could reach the same result by examining the express causes of action identified in the 1933 and 1934 Acts as models for implied rights of action under those same sections. None of the express causes of actions in the 1934 Act imposed liability on aiders and abettors, and the Court found it would be "anomalous to impute to Congress an intention in effect to expand the defendant class for 10b-5 actions beyond the bounds delineated for comparable express causes of action." 511 U.S. at 180, 114 S.Ct. 1439. This analysis was bolstered by the conclusion that an action against aiders and abettors would allow liability when at least one element critical for recovery under rule 10b-5 is absent: reliance. *Id.* An aiding and abetting action would allow a defendant to be held liable without the usual requisite showing that the plaintiff relied on the defendant's statements or actions, in contravention of the careful limits on 10b-5 recovery mandated by earlier cases. *Id.*

The Court also examined the history of aiding and abetting liability, noting first that Congress enacted 18 U.S.C. §2, a general aiding and abetting statute applicable to all federal crimes, in 1909. The statute provides that persons who provide knowing aid to those committing federal crimes, with the intent to facilitate the crime, are themselves committing a crime. 511 U.S. at 181, 114 S.Ct. 1439. The Restatement (Second) of Torts similarly provides for civil liability for aiders and abettors by holding an actor liable for harm resulting to a third person from the tortious conduct of another if the actor knows the other's conduct constitutes a breach of duty and the actor gives substantial assistance or encouragement to the other. Restatement (Second) of Torts, §876(b). But Congress did not enact a general aiding and abetting statute covering civil actions, either for suits by the government or suits by private parties.

Thus, when Congress enacts a statute under which a person may sue and recover damages from a private defendant for the defendant's violation of some statutory norm, there is no general presumption that the plaintiff may also sue aiders and abettors.

Central Bank, 511 U.S. at 182, 114 S.Ct. 1439.

Instead, the Court found, Congress had taken a statute-by-statute approach to civil aiding and abetting liability. In sum, the Court found that there was no reason to attach aiding

and abetting liability in all federal civil statutes, that Congress had not expressed any intent to extend aiding and abetting liability in this particular statute, and that none of the express causes of action in the 1934 Act extended aiding and abetting liability. Even considering the history of aiding and abetting liability in the criminal and the civil context, the Court found no reason to extend that liability to private causes of action in the securities statutes. Indeed, Congress had expressly provided for another type of secondary liability in the 1934 Act-"controlling person" liability-and thus the absence of aiding and abetting liability appeared to have been a deliberate choice. 511 U.S. at 183-84, 114 S.Ct. 1439.

The *Central Bank* analysis provides guidance but is not determinative here for a number of reasons. First, *Central Bank* addressed extending aiding and abetting liability to an implied right of action, not an express right of action as we have here in section 2333. Second, Congress expressed an intent in the terms and history of section 2333 to import general tort law principles, and those principles include aiding and abetting liability. Third, Congress expressed an intent in section 2333 to render civil liability at least as extensive as criminal liability in the context of the terrorism cases, and criminal liability attaches to aiders and abettors of terrorism. *See* 18 U.S.C. §2. Fourth, failing to extend section 2333 liability to aiders and abettors is contrary to Congress' stated purpose of cutting off the flow of money to terrorists at every point along the chain of causation.

Although we have found no support in the cases for the Boims' argument that *Central Bank* does not apply to *malum in se* torts, we also have found no support for the defendants' claim that *Central Bank* eliminates all aiding and abetting liability in federal civil cases except when the words "aid and abet" appear in a statute. [FN14] The Court carefully crafted *Central Bank*'s holding to clarify that aiding and abetting liability would be appropriate in certain cases, albeit not under 10(b). *Central Bank*, 511 U.S. at 177, 114 S.Ct. 1439. The first significant factor distinguishing section 2333 from section 10(b) is that section 2333 provides for an express civil right of action by private parties whereas the courts have created an implied right of action under section 10(b). Thus, the courts were already inferring an intent by Congress to create a private civil cause of action with section 10(b), and they would have been stacking another inference on top of that one in extending liability to aiders and abettors in rule 10b-5 actions. The Court was understandably reluctant to pile inference upon inference in determining Congressional intent. But no such stacking is required in section 2333, which expressly creates a private right of action for plaintiffs who are injured by reason of an act of international terrorism. *Sandoval* is distinguishable for the very same reason; it addressed an implied right of action founded on a regulation promulgated under Title VI. Here we have an express private right of action, where Congress' intent is clear from the language and structure of the statute itself as well as from the legislative history. As we will discuss below, although the words "aid and abet" do not appear in the statute, Congress purposely drafted the statute to extend liability to all points along the causal chain of terrorism. It is not much of a leap to conclude that Congress intended to extend section 2333 liability beyond those persons directly perpetrating acts of violence. Indeed, the statute itself defines international terrorism so broadly-to include activities that "involve" violent acts-that we must construe it carefully to meet the constitutional standards regarding vagueness and First Amendment rights of association.

FN14. The Fourth Circuit, in *Rice v. Paladin Enterprises, Inc.*, 128 F.3d 233, 252-53 (4th Cir.1997), considered the First Amendment implications of a civil suit seeking to hold liable the publishers of a book for a murder committed by a reader. The book, entitled "*Hit Man: A Technical Manual for Independent Contractors*," detailed how to commit murder-for-hire, and the publisher stipulated that it both knew and intended that its readers would use the book to commit murder. Under those circumstances, the court held that liability for aiding and abetting a *malum in se* crime such as murder via speech intended to assist and encourage others in that crime would not run afoul of the First Amendment. Although the *Rice* court did not expressly reference *Central Bank*, its holding is consistent with the Boims' reading of that case.

The next distinguishing factor is that the language and legislative history of section 2333 evidence an intent to import general tort law principles into the statute, a factor glaringly absent from section 10(b). *See* 137 Cong. Rec. S4511-04 (April 16, 1991); Senate Hearing at 136. Nothing in section 10(b) reflects an intent to incorporate general tort law principles, and a careful review of that statute demonstrates to the contrary that Congress intended to limit liability in certain instances. As the Supreme Court noted, Congress imposed some forms of secondary liability in section 10(b) (such as controlling person liability), but not others, manifesting a deliberate choice to exclude aiding and abetting liability. In contrast, the language of section 2333 tracks the traditional elements of tort law as expressed in the Restatement, and the legislative history expressly references tort principles in setting out the perimeters of Congress' intent.

Unlike section 10(b), Congress also expressed an intent in section 2333 to make civil liability at least as extensive as criminal liability. The statute defining "international terrorism" includes activities that "involve violent acts or acts dangerous to human life that are a violation of the criminal laws of the United States or of any State, or that would be a criminal violation if committed within the jurisdiction of the United States or of any State." 18 U.S.C. §2331(1). This language, embracing activities that "involve" violent acts, taken at face value would certainly cover aiding and abetting violent acts. Remember, too, the criminal laws include 18 U.S.C. §2, which creates liability for aiding and abetting violations of any other criminal provisions. By incorporating violations of any criminal laws that involve violent acts or acts dangerous to human life, Congress was expressly including aiding and abetting to the extent that aiding and abetting "involves" violence. As we discussed earlier, "involve" is a rather broad word. If we were to interpret "involve" literally, we would be attributing almost unlimited liability to any act that had some link to a terrorist act. Congress could not have meant to attach unlimited liability to even remote acts; it must have meant something else. As we have seen from the language and legislative history of section 2333, that something else is traditional tort and criminal liability. Aiding and abetting, which is surely subsumed in the definition of acts that "involve" certain criminal violations, is a well known and well defined doctrine. See *Damato v. Hermanson*, 153 F.3d 464, 472 n. 10 (7th Cir.1998) (in the criminal context, the aider and abettor knowingly assists the principal in the attainment of the illegal objective and therefore is sanctioned as the principal); *United States v. Zafiro*, 945 F.2d 881, 887 (7th Cir.1991), *aff'd*, 506 U.S. 534, 113 S.Ct. 933, 122 L.Ed.2d 317 (1993) (the crime of aiding and abetting requires knowledge of the illegal activity that is being aided and abetted, a desire to help that activity succeed, and some act of helping). See also *Halberstam v. Welch*, 705 F.2d 472, 477 and 481-84 (D.C.Cir.1983) (setting forth the elements for civil liability for aiding and abetting). That Congress did not use the words "aid and abet" in the statute is not determinative when it did use words broad enough to include all kinds of secondary liability. See *Harris Trust*, 530 U.S. at 246, 120 S.Ct. 2180 (holding that ERISA reaches farther than the immediate wrongdoer because the statute focuses not on the class of possible defendants but rather on redressing a particular act or practice which violates the statute). Indeed, limiting the term "involve" to the familiar definitions of aiding and abetting (or even conspiracy, for that matter) provides the necessary clarification that saves the statute from vagueness. *Central Bank* is thus distinguishable on this ground as well.

Finally, if we failed to impose liability on aiders and abettors who knowingly and intentionally funded acts of terrorism, we would be thwarting Congress' clearly expressed intent to cut off the flow of money to terrorists at every point along the causal chain of violence. S. Rep. 102-342, at 22 (by imposing "liability at any point along the causal chain of terrorism, it would interrupt, or at least imperil, the flow of money."). Unlike section 10(b) where Congress' intent could be met without imposing liability on aiders and abettors, Congress' purpose here could not be met unless liability attached beyond the persons directly involved in acts of violence. The statute would have little effect if liability were limited to the persons who pull the trigger or plant the bomb because such persons are unlikely to have assets, much less assets in the United States, and would not be deterred by the statute. See *Central Bank*, 511 U.S. at 188, 114 S.Ct. 1439 (policy considerations may be used to interpret the text and structure of a statute when a literal reading would lead to a result so bizarre that Congress could not have intended it). Also, and perhaps more importantly, there would not be a trigger to pull or a bomb to blow up without the resources to acquire such tools of terrorism and to bankroll the persons who actually commit the violence. Moreover, the organizations, businesses and nations that support and encourage terrorist acts are likely to have reachable assets that they wish to protect. The only way to imperil the flow of money and discourage the financing of terrorist acts is to impose liability on those who knowingly and intentionally supply the funds to the persons who commit the violent acts. For all of these distinguishing reasons, we do not think *Central Bank* controls the result here, but that aiding and abetting liability is both appropriate and called for by the language, structure and legislative history of section 2333.

D.

The defendants raise two First Amendment objections to this section 2333 action against them. First, they argue that the Boims seek to hold them liable for their mere association with Hamas. Harking back to a line of cases involving the Communist party, HLF and QLI contend that, when an organization has both legal and illegal aims, a person may not be punished for mere membership in or association with that organization, but may be held civilly liable only if he or she possesses the specific intent to further the organizations' illegal purposes. Second, they contend that, to the extent the Boims' claim is founded on a violation of section 2339B, it cannot withstand First Amendment scrutiny because section 2339B fails to account for the intent and the associational rights of the contributors who donate money for humani-

tarian purposes. The National Coalition to Protect Political Freedom and the Center for Constitutional Rights have jointly filed an *amicus* brief in support of the defendants' First Amendment arguments, and we will consider their contentions as well.

1.

HLF and QLI begin their argument with the well-established proposition that the Constitution protects against the imposition of liability based solely upon association with a group. See *NAACP v. Claiborne Hardware Co.*, 458 U.S. 886, 920, 102 S.Ct. 3409, 73 L.Ed.2d 1215 (1982) ("[c]ivil liability may not be imposed merely because an individual belonged to a group, some members of which committed acts of violence."); *Healy v. James*, 408 U.S. 169, 185-86, 92 S.Ct. 2338, 33 L.Ed.2d 266 (1972) ("the Court has consistently disapproved governmental action imposing criminal sanctions or denying rights and privileges solely because of a citizen's association with an unpopular organization."); *United States v. Robel*, 389 U.S. 258, 265, 88 S.Ct. 419, 19 L.Ed.2d 508 (1967) (where a statute establishes guilt by association alone, the inhibiting effect on First Amendment rights is clear); *Scales v. United States*, 367 U.S. 203, 229, 81 S.Ct. 1469, 6 L.Ed.2d 782 (1961) (a blanket prohibition of association with a group having both legal and illegal aims presents a real danger that legitimate political expression or association would be impaired). We have no quarrel with that general proposition or with its corollary, that in order to impose liability on an individual for association with a group, it is necessary to establish that the group possessed unlawful goals and that the individual held a specific intent to further those illegal aims. *Claiborne Hardware*, 458 U.S. at 920-21, 102 S.Ct. 3409; *National Organization for Women, Inc. v. Scheidler*, 267 F.3d 687, 703 (7th Cir.2001), *cert. granted*, 535 U.S. 1016, 122 S.Ct. 1604, 152 L.Ed.2d 619 and 535 U.S. 1016, 122 S.Ct. 1605, 152 L.Ed.2d 619 (2002).

HLF and QLI protest that the Boims have not alleged their specific intent to further the illegal activities of Hamas, and that the claim does not, therefore, survive First Amendment scrutiny. Rather, HLF complains, the Boims have simply alleged that HLF has admitted providing funds to Hamas, that HLF functions as a front organization for Hamas, that HLF raises and channels funds to Hamas to finance terrorist activities in Israel, and that HLF solicits donations over the internet. HLF protests that even if these allegations suffice to show a present intent to further terrorist acts, they do not show that HLF had that intent prior to David Boim's murder. Rather, HLF believes the Boims are lumping their organization in with other groups that may have had an intent to commit illegal acts, and that the Boims are seeking to hold them liable for their mere association with these other organizations. QLI similarly argues that the Boims have not alleged a specific intent on the part of QLI to further the illegal goals of Hamas, and that they may not be held liable for merely associating with organizations that might have intended to aid the illegal operations of Hamas.

Amici also emphasize that individuals may not be penalized for their association with a political organization that engages in both lawful and unlawful ends, absent a showing of specific intent to further the organization's illegal goals. *Claiborne Hardware*, 458 U.S. at 919-20, 102 S.Ct. 3409. The arguments of the defendants and *amici* beg the question, though, because section 2333 does not seek to impose liability for association alone but rather for involvement in acts of international terrorism. The defendants nonetheless object that the definition of acts of international terrorism is so broad that they might be held liable for involvement in terrorist activity when all they intended was to supply money to fund the legitimate, humanitarian mission of Hamas or other organizations. To resolve the tension that arises when a group engages in both protected advocacy and unprotected criminal acts, we look to *Claiborne Hardware* and to earlier cases that arose out of the McCarthy era, when the government sought to impose liability on persons for their association with the Communist Party.

In *Claiborne Hardware*, a group of white merchants and business owners sued the National Association for the Advancement of Colored People ("NAACP") for engaging in a boycott of white-owned businesses. The merchants alleged that, in enforcing the boycott, some of the members of the defendant NAACP had engaged in acts of physical force and violence, and that the NAACP should therefore be held liable for the merchants' losses. The Court first held that speeches and nonviolent picketing in support of the boycott were activities normally entitled to protection under the First Amendment. 458 U.S. at 907, 102 S.Ct. 3409. The Court noted that the right of association, the right to join many voices together to strengthen a message and make certain it is heard, is an important constitutional guarantee. 458 U.S. at 908, 102 S.Ct. 3409. That right "to associate does not lose all constitutional protection merely because some members of the group may have participated in conduct or advanced doctrine that is itself not protected." 458 U.S. at 908, 102 S.Ct. 3409. At the same time, "[t]he First Amendment does not protect violence." 458 U.S. at 916, 102 S.Ct. 3409.

Certainly violence has no sanctuary in the First Amendment, and the use of weapons, gunpowder, and gasoline may not constitutionally masquerade under the guise of "advocacy."

Claiborne Hardware, 458 U.S. at 916, 102 S.Ct. 3409 (quoting *Samuels v. Mackell*, 401 U.S. 66, 75, 91 S.Ct. 764, 27 L.Ed.2d 688 (1971) (Douglas, J., concurring)). The Court concluded that no federal rule of law restricts a state from imposing tort liability for business losses caused by violence or the threat of violence, but that when such conduct occurs in the context of constitutionally protected activity, precision of regulation is required. *Claiborne Hardware*, 458 U.S. at 916, 102 S.Ct. 3409. When activity protected by the First Amendment is present, damages are restricted to the direct consequences of the illegal violent conduct and may not include the consequences resulting from associated peaceful picketing or other protected First Amendment activity. 458 U.S. at 918, 102 S.Ct. 3409 (citing *United Mine Workers of America v. Gibbs*, 383 U.S. 715, 729, 86 S.Ct. 1130, 16 L.Ed.2d 218 (1966)). Citing *Scales*, *Healy* and *Noto*, the Court summarized the rule to be applied:

Civil liability may not be imposed merely because an individual belonged to a group, some members of which committed acts of violence. For liability to be imposed by reason of association alone, it is necessary to establish that the group itself possessed unlawful goals and that the individual held a specific intent to further those illegal aims.

Claiborne Hardware, 458 U.S. at 920, 102 S.Ct. 3409.

We have already held that the Boims may prevail on their claim by showing, among other things, that the defendants aided and abetted David's murder. This requires them to prove that the defendants knew of Hamas' illegal activities, that they desired to help those activities succeed, and they engaged in some act of helping the illegal activities. See *Zafiro*, 945 F.2d at 887. If the Boims are able to prove the defendants aided and abetted terrorist acts, liability would not offend the principles announced in *Claiborne Hardware*. The Boims have alleged that HLF and QLI supplied money to Hamas to fund terrorist operations, that they are "front" organizations with ostensibly legitimate purposes which are actually engaged in fund-raising and money laundering in support of terrorist activities. They have alleged that HLF and QLI provided the money to purchase the weapons and train the men who killed David Boim. HLF and QLI, of course, deny these allegations and argue that as a factual matter, Hamas is primarily a humanitarian organization, and that any money supplied to Hamas by QLI and HLF was intended to fund humanitarian efforts, not terrorism. This is a classic factual dispute, not suitable for resolution on a motion to dismiss for failure to state a claim. If the Boims are able to prove their allegations, that HLF and QLI provided legitimate-looking fronts for raising money to support the terrorist operation that resulted in David Boim's murder, their claim will not run afoul of the First Amendment. The Boims are not seeking to hold HLF and QLI liable for their mere association with Hamas, nor are they seeking to hold the defendants liable for contributing money for humanitarian efforts. Rather, they are seeking to hold them liable for aiding and abetting murder by supplying the money to buy the weapons, train the shooters, and compensate the families of the murderers. That Hamas may also engage in legitimate advocacy or humanitarian efforts is irrelevant for First Amendment purposes if HLF and QLI knew about Hamas' illegal operations, and intended to help Hamas accomplish those illegal goals when they contributed money to the organization. *Claiborne Hardware*, 458 U.S. at 932, 102 S.Ct. 3409; *Scales*, 367 U.S. at 229, 81 S.Ct. 1469; *Noto*, 367 U.S. at 298, 81 S.Ct. 1517; *Healy*, 408 U.S. at 186, 92 S.Ct. 2338; *Scheidler*, 267 F.3d at 703.

Moreover, we believe the Boims' allegations lend adequate support to their claims against QLI and HLF. Rule 8(a) requires only a short and plain statement of the claim showing that the Boims are entitled to relief. The defendants repeatedly confuse what must be alleged with what must be proved. The plaintiffs need not set out in detail all of the facts upon which they base their claim. They need only give QLI and HLF fair notice of what their claim is and the grounds upon which it rests. *Leatherman*, 507 U.S. at 168, 113 S.Ct. 1160. This they have done.

They allege that QLI and HLF violated section 2333 by aiding and abetting Hinawi and Al-Sharif in committing the murder of David Boim. An aiding and abetting claim will require the Boims to prove that QLI and HLF knew about Hamas' illegal operations and provided aid to Hamas with the intent to facilitate those illegal activities. In support of the claim that HLF and QLI aided and abetted the terrorists who murdered David, the Boims allege that HLF and QLI were engaged in raising and laundering money for Hamas; that HLF and QLI functioned as fronts for Hamas in the United States; that HLF raised and channeled funds to Hamas to finance terrorist activities in Israel; that David's attackers were Hamas terrorists; that Hamas' central purpose is to advance its political goals through terrorism; that HLF and QLI's purportedly humanitarian functions masked their core mission of raising and funneling money and other resources to Hamas in support of its terrorist campaigns; that HLF and QLI commingled money destined for terrorist causes with funds from their legitimate charitable and business dealings in order to avoid laws against providing financial support to terrorists; that money gathered in this way was sent by the front organizations (including HLF and QLI) from the United States to Hamas to buy weapons and carry out terrorist attacks, including the murder of David Boim; and that money provided by the front organizations to finance terrorist activities was in fact used for that purpose and in particular was used to purchase the vehicle, machine guns, and ammunition used to kill David, as well as to train his killers and to provide a stipend for the family of one of his murderers. That is more than sufficient to notify the defendants of the nature of the claims against them. These allegations also implicitly assert that the defendants had the intent to further the illegal aims of Hamas prior to David's murder, contrary to the defendants' characterization. The Boims' theory of the case, that QLI and HLF aided and abetted Hamas in murdering David Boims, does not offend the First Amendment because they seek to hold QLI and HLF liable not for their associations or speech but for their knowing and intentional financial support of illegal activities. We also note that discovery will certainly clarify the Boims' theory of the case, and we will not dismiss a complaint before discovery unless it appears beyond doubt that the Boims can prove no set of facts in support of their claim which would entitle them to relief. *Slaney*, 244 F.3d at 597. Although the defendants claim to have been supporting only the humanitarian mission of Hamas, that is a fact question that cannot be resolved at this early stage of the litigation.

2.

We turn next to the defendants' contention that any section 2333 claim founded on a violation of section 2339B must fail because section 2339B violates the First Amendment. As we noted above, section 2339B subjects to criminal liability anyone who, within the United States or subject to the jurisdiction of the United States, knowingly provides material support or resources to a foreign terrorist organization, or attempts or conspires to do so. 18 U.S.C. §2339B(a)(1). The defendants complain that, because section 2339B imposes liability without regard to the intent of the donor, it violates the First Amendment. They maintain that section 2339B unnecessarily interferes with the associational rights of contributors who donate money solely for humanitarian purposes by failing to limit liability to those who intend to support the illegal goals of an organization. They contend that section 2339B will chill legitimate fund-raising for humanitarian purposes if a charitable organization could be prosecuted for providing food for the needy in the Middle East that happens to make its way into the mouths of the families of terrorists. They urge us to reject the reasoning of the Ninth Circuit in *Humanitarian Law Project v. Reno*, 205 F.3d 1130 (9th Cir.2000), *cert. denied*, 532 U.S. 904, 121 S.Ct. 1226, 149 L.Ed.2d 136 (2001), in upholding the constitutionality of section 2339B against a First Amendment challenge. They argue that *Humanitarian Law Project* is inconsistent with *Claiborne Hardware*, and that even if it is not, it is factually distinguishable from the instant case.

These arguments miss the mark because the constitutionality of section 2339B is not before us. The defendants have not been charged with a criminal violation of section 2339B. As we discussed above, section 2339B is relevant to the Boims' claim only to the extent that it helps define what conduct Congress intended to include in its definition of "international terrorism." Section 2339B provides further support to the Boims' theory that Congress meant to include funding terrorism as an act "involving" violence. It is the constitutionality of section 2333 that concerns us today, and as we have just found, funding that meets the standard for aiding and abetting terrorist acts does not offend the First Amendment. We take the defendants' argument to be that a section 2333 claim founded solely on conduct that would render a person criminally liable under section 2339B would violate the First Amendment. With this refinement to the question, we turn to the Ninth Circuit's analysis of section 2339B.

The plaintiffs in *Humanitarian Law Project* were organizations and individuals who wished to provide money to two groups that had been designated as foreign terrorist organizations under 8 U.S.C. §1189. They sought a preliminary injunction barring enforcement of section 2339B against them, and maintained that they intended only to support the nonviolent humanitarian and political activities of the designated groups. They argued, as HLF and QLI do here, that 2339B violates the First Amendment because it imposes liability on persons who provide material support to terrorist organizations regardless of whether the donor intends to further the unlawful goals of the organization. The plaintiffs relied on *Claiborne Hardware* for the proposition that "[f]or liability to be imposed by reason of association alone, it is necessary to establish that the group itself possessed unlawful goals and that the individual held a specific intent to further those illegal aims." *Humanitarian Law Project*, 205 F.3d at 1133 (quoting *Claiborne Hardware*, 458 U.S. at 920, 102 S.Ct. 3409).

Claiborne Hardware and the similar cases we have discussed *supra* apply to situations where the government seeks to impose liability on the basis of association alone, *i.e.*, on the basis of membership alone or because a person espouses the views of an organization that engages in illegal activities. Conduct giving rise to liability under section 2339B, of course, does not implicate associational or speech rights. *Humanitarian Law Project*, 205 F.3d at 1133. Under section 2339B, and indeed under section 2333, HLF and QLI may, with impunity, become members of Hamas, praise Hamas for its use of terrorism, and vigorously advocate the goals and philosophies of Hamas. Section 2339B prohibits only the provision of material support (as that term is defined) to a terrorist organization. There is no constitutional right to provide weapons and explosives to terrorists, nor is there any right to provide the resources with which the terrorists can purchase weapons and explosives. 205 F.3d at 1133.

Advocacy is always subject to the highest levels of scrutiny under the First Amendment, but donations are not always equivalent to advocacy and are subject to greater government regulation. In *Buckley v. Valeo*, 424 U.S. 1, 96 S.Ct. 612, 46 L.Ed.2d 659 (1976), the Supreme Court upheld the $1000 limit on political contributions to candidates for federal offices by individual donors. The Court acknowledged the expressive element of a contribution to a political campaign, noting that a contribution serves as a general expression of support for a candidate and the candidate's views, but does not communicate the underlying basis for the support. 424 U.S. at 21, 96 S.Ct. 612. Because the expression involved in donating money "rests solely on the undifferentiated, symbolic act of contributing," the size of the donation provides only a very rough estimate of the intensity of the contributor's support for the candidate. 424 U.S. at 21, 96 S.Ct. 612. The Court concluded that a limitation on the amount of money a person may contribute thus involved little direct restraint on the donor's political communication. Any size contribution will permit a symbolic expression of support, but a limitation on the size does not infringe the contributor's freedom to discuss issues. The Court acknowledged that the funds might be used by the candidate to present views to voters, but "the transformation of contributions into political debate involves speech by someone other than the contributor." 424 U.S. at 21, 96 S.Ct. 612. The Court found that associational interests were also implicated because making a contribution affiliates a person with a candidate, and enables like-minded people to pool their resources to further political goals. 424 U.S. at 22, 96 S.Ct. 612. Setting the standard for reviewing governmental regulation in this context, the Court held that "[e]ven a significant interference with protected rights of political association may be sustained if the State demonstrates a sufficiently important interest and employs means closely drawn to avoid unnecessary abridgement of associational freedoms." 424 U.S. at 25, 96 S.Ct. 612 (internal quote marks omitted).

Applying the *Buckley* standard to section 2333 claims founded on conduct that would give rise to criminal liability under section 2339B, we conclude that the government's interest in preventing terrorism is not only important but paramount. *Humanitarian Law Project*, 205 F.3d at 1135. Although that interest has been made all the more imperative by the events of September 11, 2001, the terrorist threat to national security was substantial in 1992 when Congress passed section 2333 and in 1996 when Congress passed section 2339B. That interest is unrelated to suppressing free expression. A section 2333 suit founded on conduct violating section 2339B does not punish membership in a designated terrorist organization, or penalize the expression of views held by these organizations. Rather, such a suit is aimed at prohibiting the funding of violent acts that these organizations wish to carry out. 205 F.3d at 1135.

The only remaining question is whether a section 2333 action based on conduct that violates section 2339B employs means closely drawn to avoid unnecessary abridgement of associational freedoms. Section 2339B forbids the provision of any amount of "material support or resources" to a foreign terrorist organization. "Material support or resources" includes, among other things, money, training, weapons, lethal substances, explosives and personnel. Congress determined that "foreign organizations that engage in terrorist activity are so tainted by their criminal conduct that any contribution to such an organization facilitates that conduct." Pub.L. 104-132, Section 301. Terrorist organizations use funds for illegal activities regardless of the intent of the donor, and Congress thus was compelled to attach liability to all donations to foreign terrorist organizations. In order to be designated a terrorist organization, a group must engage in terrorist activity that threatens the security of United States nationals or the national security of the United States. 8 U.S.C. §1189(a). "Terrorist activity" is defined, in relevant part, as unlawful activity which involves any of the following: the hijacking or sabotage of any aircraft, vessel or vehicle; the seizing, detaining or threatening to kill, injure or continue detaining an individual in order to compel a third person to do or abstain from doing any act as a condition for the release of the individual detained; a violent act upon an internationally protected person; an assassination; the use of any biological agent, chemical agent, nuclear weapon or

device, or explosive or firearm, with intent to endanger the safety of one or more individuals or cause substantial damage to property. 8 U.S.C. §1182(a)(3)(B)(ii). Given the stringent requirements that must be met before a group is designated a foreign terrorist organization, Congress carefully limited its prohibition on funding as narrowly as possible in order to achieve the government's interest in preventing terrorism. We note that Congress did not attach liability for simply joining a terrorist organization or zealously espousing its views. By prohibiting funding alone, Congress employed means closely drawn to avoid unnecessary abridgement of associational freedoms. A section 2333 action founded on conduct violating section 2339B is sufficiently tailored to achieve an important government interest and does not run afoul of the First Amendment. *Humanitarian Law Project*, 205 F.3d at 1136.

III.

In short, we answer the three questions certified by the district court as follows: funding, *simpliciter*, of a foreign terrorist organization is not sufficient to constitute an act of terrorism under 18 U.S.C. §2331. However, funding that meets the definition of aiding and abetting an act of terrorism does create liability under sections 2331 and 2333. Conduct that would give rise to criminal liability under section 2339B is conduct that "involves" violent acts or acts dangerous to human life, and therefore may meet the definition of international terrorism as that term is used in section 2333. Finally, as we have set forth the elements of an action under section 2333, civil liability for funding a foreign terrorist organization does not offend the First Amendment so long as the plaintiffs are able to prove that the defendants knew about the organization's illegal activity, desired to help that activity succeed and engaged in some act of helping. The plaintiffs have not yet had an opportunity to develop the facts of their case. Today we hold that dismissal would be premature at this stage of the litigation because we can envision a set of facts in support of the claim they have alleged that would entitle them to relief.

AFFIRMED.

Notes:

1.   What was the alleged relationship between the defendants and the purported murderers of David Boim? What fairly obvious alternative targets were available to the plaintiffs to sue? What were the advantages of suing Holy Land Foundation and the Quranic Literacy Institute as opposed

to foreign state sponsors or the terrorists themselves? What issues must be considered when determining whether potential defendants will be included in a civil terrorism lawsuit?

2.   A premise of the plaintiffs' case was the unity of HAMAS as an organization and that the actions of the dawa (its so called "charitable wing") and the Battalions of Izz A-din Al-Qassam (its so called "political wing") are in fact symbiotic. In large measure, the court's opinion rests on the notion that even though HAMAS may have several divisions and conducts some humanitarian work, its terrorism activity is the heart and soul of the organization. *Matter of Extradition of Marzook*, 924 F.Supp. 565 (S.D.N.Y. 1996) is a primer on the inner working and activities of HAMAS. For details about HAMAS financial operations in the United States, see *U.S. v. One 1997 E35 Ford Van, VIN 1FBJS31L3VHB70844*, 50 F.Supp.2d 789 (N.D.Ill. 1999).

3.   In *Boim*, the court found that:

> [T]o the extent that the Boims urge a reading of the statute that would lead to liability for merely giving money to Hamas, a group which then sponsored a terrorist act in the manner the Boims have alleged, we agree with the district court, the defendants and the government that those allegations would be inadequate. To say that funding *simpliciter* constitutes an act of terrorism is to give the statute an almost unlimited reach. Any act which turns out to facilitate terrorism, however remote that act may be from actual violence and regardless of the actor's intent, could be construed to "involve" terrorism. Without also requiring the plaintiffs to show knowledge of and intent to further the payee's violent criminal acts, such a broad definition might also lead to constitutional infirmities by punishing mere association with groups that engage in terrorism, as we shall discuss later in addressing the First Amendment concerns raised here.

What were the competing policy arguments that the court was grappling with? Why did the appellate court reject the "funding simpliciter" argument? How does this type of argument hold up in other contexts, such as common law conspiracy cases and RICO suits? How would the acceptance of the "funding simpliciter" argument impact traditional legitimate domestic charities and fundraising organizations?

4.   What was the U.S. government's position with respect to whether the defendants' funding of HAMAS was sufficient to create liability?

5.   In *Boim*, why did the U.S. government defend the positions asserted by the Holy Land Foundation? Why did the government become involved with the case?

6.   The U.S. government has taken seemingly inconsistent positions with respect to the Holy Land Foundation in several venues. For example, in December 2001, the Treasury Department's Office of Foreign Asset Control ("OFAC") designated the Holy Land Foundation as a "specially designated terrorist" and a "specially designated global terrorist," and blocked all of its assets pursuant to the International Emergency Economic Powers Act, 50 U.S.C. §1701 *et seq.* and Executive Orders 13224 and 12947. In the Holy Land Foundation's challenge to the government's designation and administrative action, the district court found,

> The seven volume, 3130 page administrative record in this case provides substantial support for OFAC's determination that HLF acts for or on behalf of Hamas. Specifically, as the following analysis demonstrates, the administrative record contains ample evidence that (1) HLF has had financial connections to Hamas since its creation in 1989; (2) HLF leaders have been actively involved in various meetings with Hamas leaders; (3) HLF funds Hamas-controlled charitable organizations; (4) HLF provides financial support to the orphans and families of Hamas martyrs and prisoners; (5) HLF's Jerusalem office acted on behalf of Hamas; and (6) FBI informants reliably reported that HLF funds Hamas.

Holy Land Foundation for Relief and Development v. Ashcroft, 219 F.Supp.2d 57, 69 (D.D.C. 2002).

7.   On the other hand, in *U.S. v. Holy Land Foundation for Relief and Development*, 493 F.3d 469 (5th Cir. 2007), an unusual 16 judge en banc panel upheld the government's actions preventing the orphaned judgment creditors of an American citizen murdered by HAMAS from attaching and levying approximately $5 million of the Holy Land Foundation's blocked assets to satisfy a judgment entered pursuant to 18 U.S.C. §2333.

8. The government is also prosecuting the Holy Land Foundation in Dallas, Texas,

> Meanwhile, on July 26, 2004, the United States filed a forty-two count indictment against HLF in federal district court for the Northern District of Texas. The indictment charged HLF with material support of a terrorist organization, tax evasion, and money laundering and the Government sought forfeiture of HLF property.

Id. at 472.

9. How do the government's actions in *U.S. v. Holy Land Foundation* and its prosecution of the organization conflict with the position taken by the United States in *Boim*?

10. How does the court's decision in *Boim* square with the explicit legislative intent that enactment of §2333,

> [The act] would allow the law to catch up with contemporary reality by providing victims of terrorism with a remedy for a wrong that, by its nature, falls outside the usual jurisdictional categories of wrongs that national legal systems have traditionally addressed. By its provisions for compensatory damages, tremble damages, and the imposition of liability at any point along the causal chain of terrorism, it would interrupt, or at least imperil, the flow of money.

H.R. Rep. 102-1040 at 22.

11. Is it likely that plaintiffs in terrorism suits will be able to obtain, either from their own investigation or in pre-trial discovery from the defendants or other sources, sufficient evidence to satisfy the standards in *Boim*?

12. For a further analysis of the provisions of 18 U.S.C. §2333 et seq. (and especially §2339A-C) see *Linde v. Arab Bank, PLC*, 384 F.Supp.2d 571 (E.D.N.Y. 2005).

Kilburn v. Socialist People's Libyan Arab Jamahiriya, 376 F.3d 1123 (D.C. Cir. 2004)

Before: GINSBURG, Chief Judge, and GARLAND and ROBERTS, Circuit Judges.

GARLAND, Circuit Judge:

This case arises out of the kidnapping and murder of an American citizen in Lebanon between November 1984 and April 1986. Libya appeals from the denial of its motion to dismiss the case, arguing that sovereign immunity protects it from suit and that the plaintiff lacks a viable cause of action. We reject the first contention, concluding that the "terrorism exception" of the Foreign Sovereign Immunities Act (FSIA), 28 U.S.C. §1605(a)(7), strips Libya of the shield of sovereign immunity. We decline to exercise appellate jurisdiction over the second.

I

Blake Kilburn brought suit against the Socialist People's Libyan Arab Jamahiriya (Libya), the Libyan External Security Organization (LESO), the Islamic Republic of Iran, and the Iranian Ministry of Information and Security, seeking damages on his own behalf and as executor of the estate of his brother, Peter Kilburn (together, the plaintiff), for Peter's kidnapping, sale, torture, and death. The allegations of the complaint, as further detailed in district court pleadings and a declaration, are as follows.

Peter Kilburn was an American citizen who lived in Lebanon and worked as an instructor and librarian at the American University of Beirut. On November 30, 1984, he was abducted from his apartment; Hizbollah, a terrorist organization funded by Iran, claimed responsibility. In late 1985, the American government was approached by an intermediary who claimed to be acting on behalf of Kilburn's captors and who sought a ransom for his return. For the next several months, the United States negotiated for Kilburn's release.

On April 14, 1986, while Kilburn was still in captivity, the United States conducted airstrikes on Tripoli, Libya, in retaliation for Libya's involvement in the bombing of a Berlin nightclub that killed two American soldiers. Thereafter, Libya made it known that it wanted to purchase an American hostage to murder in revenge for the airstrikes. Sometime between April 14 and 17, the Arab Revolutionary Cells (ARC), a terrorist organization sponsored by Libya, bought Kilburn from Hizbollah for approximately $3 million and subsequently tortured him. On or about April 17, 1986, ARC murdered Kilburn and left his body by the side of a road near Beirut, alongside the bodies of two British hostages. In a note found nearby, ARC claimed responsibility.

Blake Kilburn's complaint, filed on June 12, 2001, alleged that his brother was the victim of hostage taking, torture, and extrajudicial killing, for which the defendants were responsible. The complaint sought recovery through multiple causes of action, including the Flatow Amendment, 28 U.S.C. §1605 (note), and theories of wrongful death, battery, assault, false imprisonment, slave trafficking, torture, and intentional infliction of emotional distress. Although the complaint did not specify the legal sources of the latter causes of action, later pleadings asserted that they arose under state common law, foreign law, and international law, and that additional federal statutory causes of action might also be available.

The Iranian defendants did not appear, and the plaintiff sought a default judgment against them. That motion remains pending in the district court. The Libyan defendants did appear, and the parties agreed to a limited course of jurisdictional discovery. Thereafter, the Libyan defendants filed a motion to dismiss the complaint pursuant to Federal Rule of Civil Procedure 12(b)(1), contending that their sovereign immunity deprived the court of subject-matter jurisdiction, and pursuant to Rule 12(b)(6), contending that the plaintiff had failed to state a claim upon which relief could be granted. The district court denied both requests. Sua sponte, the court also considered a question not raised by the parties - whether the plaintiff could assert a claim for punitive damages against defendant LESO - and answered in the affirmative. This appeal followed. [FN1]

FN1. The defendants also sought, and the district court denied, dismissal on the ground that the court's exercise of personal jurisdiction over them violated the due process clause of the Fifth Amendment. Although the defendants recognize that this circuit has held that "foreign states are not 'persons' protected by the Fifth Amendment," *Price v. Socialist People's Libyan Arab Jamahiriya*, 294 F.3d 82, 96 (D.C.Cir.2002), they raise the issue solely to preserve the possibility of further appellate review.

II

We begin with the question of the Libyan defendants' sovereign immunity. The district court's decision to deny their motion to dismiss plainly did not end the case; to the contrary, it permitted the case to go forward. Ordinarily, that would preclude our hearing this interlocutory appeal, because our jurisdiction is generally confined to "final decisions of the district court." 28 U.S.C. §1291; see *id.* §1292 (permitting interlocutory appeals in certain circumstances not present here). Under the collateral order doctrine, however, an order qualifies as "final" under §1291 if it: "(1) conclusively determine[s] the disputed question, (2) resolve [s] an impor-

tant issue completely separate from the merits of the action, and (3) is effectively unreviewable on appeal from a final judgment." *Puerto Rico Aqueduct & Sewer Auth. v. Metcalf & Eddy, Inc.*, 506 U.S. 139, 144, 113 S.Ct. 684, 687-88, 121 L.Ed.2d 605 (1993) (internal quotation marks omitted); see *Cohen v. Beneficial Indus. Loan Corp.*, 337 U.S. 541, 546, 69 S.Ct. 1221, 1225-26, 93 L.Ed. 1528 (1949). The denial of a motion to dismiss on the ground of sovereign immunity satisfies all three criteria, and is therefore subject to interlocutory review. See, e.g., *Price v. Socialist People's Libyan Arab Jamahiriya*, 294 F.3d 82, 92 (D.C.Cir.2002); *Jungquist v. Sheikh Sultan Bin Khalifa Al Nahyan*, 115 F.3d 1020, 1025-26 (D.C.Cir.1997); *Foremost-McKesson, Inc. v. Islamic Republic of Iran*, 905 F.2d 438, 443 (D.C.Cir.1990). In particular, with respect to the last criterion, an "order denying dismissal for immunity is effectively unreviewable on appeal because 'sovereign immunity is an immunity from trial and the attendant burdens of litigation, and not just a defense to liability on the merits.' " *Jungquist*, 115 F.3d at 1026 (quoting *Foremost-McKesson*, 905 F.2d at 443).

Under the FSIA, a foreign state is immune from the jurisdiction of American courts unless the case falls within one of a list of statutory exceptions (or as provided by international agreements). 28 U.S.C. §1604; see *id.* §§1605-1607. If no exception applies, the district court lacks subject matter jurisdiction. *Id.* §1604. If an exception does apply, the district court has jurisdiction. *Id.* §1330(a); see *World Wide Minerals, Ltd. v. Republic of Kazakhstan*, 296 F.3d 1154, 1161 (D.C.Cir.2002); *Phoenix Consulting, Inc. v. Republic of Angola*, 216 F.3d 36, 39 (D.C.Cir.2000).

Congress amended the FSIA in the Antiterrorism and Effective Death Penalty Act of 1996, adding an additional exception colloquially known as the "terrorism exception." That exception denies sovereign immunity in any case:

in which money damages are sought against a foreign state for personal injury or death that was caused by an act of torture, extrajudicial killing, aircraft sabotage, hostage taking, or the provision of material support or resources (as defined in section 2339A of title 18) for such an act if such act or provision of material support is engaged in by an official, employee, or agent of such foreign state while acting within the scope of his or her office, employment, or agency...

28 U.S.C. §1605(a)(7). This exception applies only if three additional criteria are also satisfied: the foreign state was designated a "state sponsor of terrorism" at the time the act occurred; the foreign state was given a reasonable opportu-

nity to arbitrate a claim regarding an act that occurred within the state's borders; and the claimant or victim was a national of the United States. *Id.* §1605(a)(7)(A), (B). There is no dispute that these criteria are satisfied here. The only question is whether the plaintiff's claims fall within the main body of the exception, upon which the jurisdiction of the district court depends.

"In order to preserve the full scope of sovereign immunity, the district court must make the 'critical preliminary determination' of its own jurisdiction as early in the litigation as possible." *Phoenix Consulting*, 216 F.3d at 39 (quoting *Foremost-McKesson*, 905 F.2d at 449). In making that determination, the nature of the court's inquiry depends on the nature of the defendant's challenge. "If the defendant challenges only the legal sufficiency of the plaintiff's jurisdictional allegations, then the district court should take the plaintiff's factual allegations as true and determine whether they bring the case within any of the [FSIA] exceptions to immunity invoked by the plaintiff." *Id.* at 40. But if the defendant challenges "the factual basis of the court's jurisdiction, the court may not deny the motion to dismiss merely by assuming the truth of the facts alleged by the plaintiff and disputed by the defendant. Instead, the court must go beyond the pleadings and resolve any disputed issues of fact the resolution of which is necessary to a ruling upon the motion to dismiss." *Id.*

In their motion to dismiss, the Libyan defendants challenged both the legal and factual sufficiency of the plaintiff's claims. For the sake of clarity, we address these challenges separately in Parts III and IV. Our standard of review is de novo. See *Price*, 294 F.3d at 91.

III

The Libyan defendants maintain that, even if the allegations of the complaint are true, they fail to bring this case within the compass of the terrorism exception. That contention is founded on two legal arguments regarding the scope of the exception.

A

The defendants' first argument is that §1605(a)(7) requires, as a matter of jurisdiction, a causal connection between the foreign state's alleged acts and the victim's alleged injuries. Stated at that level of generality, the defendants are plainly right. The section provides an exception to sovereign im-

munity in any case in which money damages are sought for injury or death "that was *caused by* an act of torture, extrajudicial killing, aircraft sabotage, hostage taking, or the provision of material support or resources...for such an act." 28 U.S.C. §1605(a)(7) (emphasis added). As we are generally required to give effect to every statutory term, *Duncan v. Walker*, 533 U.S. 167, 174, 121 S.Ct. 2120, 2125, 150 L.Ed.2d 251 (2001), we cannot ignore the phrase "caused by." Moreover, because §1605(a)(7) is a jurisdictional provision, see *Cicippio-Puleo v. Islamic Republic of Iran*, 353 F.3d 1024, 1032 (D.C.Cir.2004), causation is indeed a jurisdictional requirement.

It is here, however, that we part company with the defendants. They contend not merely that §1605(a)(7) requires a causal connection, but that it specifically requires "but for" causation: that is, an allegation (and, ultimately, evidence) that "but for" Libya's actions, Peter Kilburn would not have been purchased, tortured, or killed. The defendants apparently regard "but for" as a particularly restrictive standard of causation, and insist that nothing less will do. [FN2]

FN2. "But for" causation may be restrictive in some circumstances, such as the multiple actors example discussed in the text below. See PROSSER & KEETON ON THE LAW OF TORTS 66-67 (5th ed. 1984). Often, however, it is viewed as an expansive theory. See, e.g., *Pryor v. American President Lines*, 520 F.2d 974, 978 n. 4 (4th Cir.1975) (describing "but for" causation as a potentially "limitless" standard under which "Eve's trespass caused all our woe" (citing 2 HARPER & JAMES, THE LAW OF TORTS 1108 (1956))); *see generally* PROSSER & KEETON, at 266 (noting that the breadth of "but for" causation may depend on whether it is employed as a rule of inclusion or exclusion).
As a moment's inspection of §1605(a)(7) makes clear, there is no textual warrant for this claim: the words "but for" simply do not appear; only "caused by" do. Cf. *Republic of Argentina v. Weltover, Inc.*, 504 U.S. 607, 618, 112 S.Ct. 2160, 2168, 119 L.Ed.2d 394 (1992) (rejecting the suggestion that the FSIA's commercial activity exception, 28 U.S.C. §1605(a)(2), which requires a "direct effect" in the United States for acts performed elsewhere, "contains any unexpressed requirement of 'substantiality' or 'foreseeability'"). In *Jerome B. Grubart, Inc. v. Great Lakes Dredge & Dock Co.*, 513 U.S. 527, 536-38, 115 S.Ct. 1043, 1049-51, 130 L.Ed.2d 1024 (1995), the Supreme Court interpreted "caused by" in another jurisdictional statute to require only a showing of "proximate cause." We follow the Court's example here.

In *Grubart*, jurisdiction turned on the meaning of the Extension of Admiralty Jurisdiction Act, which provides that the admiralty jurisdiction of the United States "shall extend to...all cases of damage or injury...*caused by* a vessel on navigable water." 46 U.S.C. app. §740 (emphasis added). Rejecting the contention that "caused by" means that the damage must be close in time and space to the activity that caused it, the Court held that the phrase means only "what tort law has traditionally called 'proximate causation.' " *Grubart*, 513 U.S. at 536, 115 S.Ct. at 1049-50. As the Court explained, "this classic tort notion normally eliminates the bizarre." *Id.*; *see generally* PROSSER & KEETON ON THE LAW OF TORTS 263 (5th ed. 1984) (noting that an "essential element of the plaintiff's cause of action" for any tort "is that there be some reasonable connection between the act or omission of the defendant and the damage which the plaintiff has suffered," a "connection usually...dealt with by the courts in terms of what is called 'proximate cause' "). "There is no need or justification," the Supreme Court said, "for imposing an additional nonremoteness hurdle in the name of jurisdiction." *Grubart*, 513 U.S. at 538, 115 S.Ct. at 1050-51.

The essence of the Libyan defendants' argument is that here there is a "need or justification" for imposing an additional hurdle beyond proximate cause, and that "but for" cause is the appropriate hurdle. They offer the following hypothetical:

A terrorist organization is supported by two foreign states. One specifically instructs the organization to carry out an attack against a U.S. citizen. Can the state which only provides general support, but was not involved with the act giving rise to the suit, also be stripped of its immunity?

Reply Br. at 13. "The answer" to this hypothetical, the defendants assert, "clearly must be no." *Id.* Libya's argument fails to persuade for several reasons.

First, we are not moved by the plight of Libya's hypothetical foreign state. We see no reason why there would be a greater justification for - or why Congress would have a greater interest in - protecting a party haled into court under §1605(a)(7) than one trying to resist admiralty jurisdiction. After all, the only defendants that are subject to §1605(a)(7) in the first place are those that the State Department has designated as "state sponsor(s) of terrorism." 28 U.S.C. §1605 (a)(7)(A).

Second, §1605(a)(7) permits actions for injuries caused by "material support" of terrorist acts by such state sponsors, and, as Congress recognized, such support is difficult to trace. As the House Report on the terrorism exception stated:

[S]tate sponsors of terrorism include Libya, Iraq, Iran, Syria, North Korea, Cuba, and Sudan. These outlaw states consider terrorism a legitimate instrument of achieving their foreign policy goals. *They have become better at hiding their material support for their surrogates*, which includes the provision of safe havens, funding, training, supplying weaponry, medical assistance, false travel documentation, and the like. *For this reason, the Committee has determined that allowing suits in the federal courts against countries responsible for terrorist acts...is warranted.*

H.R. Rep. No. 104-383, at 62 (1995) (emphasis added). Accordingly, the more likely situation is not Libya's hypothetical, involving one direct and one general state sponsor, but rather the case in which multiple foreign states claim to be providing only "general support." Such a case, in which application of a "but for" standard to joint tortfeasors could absolve them all, is precisely the one for which courts generally regard "but for" causation as inappropriate. *See* PROSSER & KEETON, at 266-67.

Third, Libya's hypothetical (and its argument) deals solely with a claim based on a state's general "material support" for a terrorist organization. But "the provision of material support" for a terrorist act is only one of the predicates for the §1605(a)(7) exception. Foreign states also lose immunity for acts (of torture, extrajudicial killing, or hostage taking) "engaged in by an official, employee, or agent" of the state itself. 28 U.S.C. §1605(a)(7). Libya makes no argument at all as to why a restrictive standard of causation should be imposed in direct action cases, yet the statutory phrase "caused by" applies equally to every §1605(a)(7) case. [FN3]

FN3. Prosser suggests that a standard like "but for" is particularly ill-suited to direct action cases. *See* PROSSER & KEETON, at 266 (stating that the "but for" rule fails in the following case: "A stabs C with a knife, and B fractures C's skull with a rock; either wound would be fatal, and C dies from the effects of both").

Finally, we underline that the only issue before us here is *jurisdictional* causation, because §1605(a)(7) is solely a jurisdictional provision. *Cicippio-Puleo*, 353 F.3d at 1032. To succeed in the end, the plaintiff must go beyond jurisdiction and provide proof satisfying a substantive cause of action. *Id.* The plaintiff has alleged a number of sources that could provide a cause of action, including state, federal, foreign, and international law. Whatever the ultimate source may be, it will no doubt carry with it - as a matter of substantive law - its own rules of causation. Of these, there are a large variety. *See* PROSSER & KEETON, at 266-68, 273. Any concerns about reaching too far to charge foreign states with the attenuated impact of their financial activities are better addressed as questions of substantive law. Indeed, to go further as a matter of jurisdiction - to accept Libya's contention that §1605(a)(7) requires a single causation standard that is more restrictive than the base-line standard of proximate cause - runs afoul of the FSIA's injunction that a non-immune "foreign state shall be liable in the same manner and to the same extent as a private individual under like circumstances." 28 U.S.C. §1606.

In this case, there is no doubt that the plaintiff's allegations satisfy the proximate cause standard. The complaint alleges that, after the United States bombed Tripoli, "Libyan agents in Lebanon made it known that they wanted to purchase an American hostage to murder in retaliation." Compl. ¶ 13. It specifically asserts that Peter Kilburn "was purchased and killed by members of the Arab Revolutionary Cells," *id.* ¶ 21, "whose acts were funded *and directed* by Libya," *id.* ¶ 26 (emphasis added). A subsequent declaration makes clear that the plaintiff's allegation is not just that ARC was "supported" and "funded" by the Libyan government, but that it was "directed" by that government "and acted as its agent in Lebanon to carry out terrorist activities, including the purchase and assassination of Peter Kilburn." Decl. of Ambassador Robert Oakley (Ret.) ¶ 14 (hereinafter "Oakley Decl."). If proven, these allegations are more than sufficient to establish that the acts of the Libyan defendants were the proximate cause of Peter Kilburn's injury and death.

B

The Libyan defendants also advance a second argument in favor of a restrictive view of §1605(a)(7). Noting that the statute denies sovereign immunity for claims involving injury caused by "an act of torture, extrajudicial killing, aircraft sabotage, hostage taking, or the provision of material support or resources...*for such an act*," 28 U.S.C. §1605(a)(7) (emphasis added), they insist that to come within this provision, a state's material support must go directly for the specific act (e.g., torture) that gives rise to the claim. In the instant case, the defendants contend that §1605(a)(7) re-

quires the plaintiff to allege (and, ultimately, to prove) that Libya *directly* funded ARC's purchase, torture, and murder of Peter Kilburn - not just that Libya provided material support to ARC.

Although the defendants pose this as an independent restriction on the scope of §1605(a)(7), it is closely tied to their causation argument and suffers from some of the same defects. On the one hand, imposing a jurisdictional requirement that a state sponsor's financial assistance to a terrorist organization must be *directly* traceable to a particular terrorist act would likely render §1605(a)(7)'s material support provision ineffectual. Money, after all, is fungible, and terrorist organizations can hardly be counted on to keep careful bookkeeping records. On the other hand, the requirement that the plaintiff's injury be "caused by" the provision of material support - in the sense of proximate causation, see *supra* Part III.A - should ameliorate most concerns about remoteness. Any further concerns will likely be addressed by the substantive law that governs the applicable cause of action. See generally *Doe v. Dominion Bank of Washington, N.A.,* 963 F.2d 1552, 1560 (D.C.Cir.1992) (noting that it "is axiomatic that under a negligence regime, one has a duty to guard only against foreseeable risks"); *Boim v. Quranic Literacy Inst. & Holy Land Found. for Relief & Dev.,* 291 F.3d 1000, 1012 (7th Cir.2002) (holding that, to establish a private cause of action for material support of terrorism under 18 U.S.C. §§2333, 2339A, "the plaintiffs must be able to show that [the murder of their son by Hamas] was a reasonably foreseeable result of [defendants'] making a donation" to Hamas).

In any event, Libya's textual argument has no application here. The plaintiff does not allege that Libya merely provided material support to ARC, but rather that it specifically funded and directed Peter Kilburn's purchase and murder. *See* Oakley Decl. ¶ 16; see also *id.* ¶¶ 6, 11-14; Compl. ¶ 23. Indeed, the plaintiff's claims rest not only on a theory of material support, but also on a theory of agency. The plaintiff asserts that ARC was not just some independent organization that Libya provided with funds, but rather an "agent" of Libya. *See* Oakley Decl. ¶ 14. In statutory terms, plaintiff's allegation is that Peter Kilburn's injuries and death were caused by terrorist acts "engaged in by an...*agent* of [a] foreign state" - and not merely by "provision of material support...for such an act." 28 U.S.C. §1605(a)(7) (emphasis added). The "for such an act" language that Libya highlights plays no textual role with respect to those kinds of allegations. To the contrary, Libya is responsible for the acts of its agent "within the scope of...[its] agency," *id.,* regardless of whether Libya financed those acts - provided, of course, that the elements of agency are established. See *Foremost-McKesson*, 905 F.2d at 445 (holding that a foreign state is responsible for the actions of a commercial entity if it "exercise[s] the necessary degree of control over [it] to create a principal/agent relationship"); see also *Transamerica Leasing, Inc. v. La Republica de Venezuela*, 200 F.3d 843, 848-49 (D.C.Cir.2000) (same); *Gilson v. Republic of Ireland*, 682 F.2d 1022, 1026 n. 16 (D.C.Cir.1982) (same).

IV

We turn next to defendants' challenge to the factual basis for the district court's jurisdiction. As explained above, if a defendant invoking sovereign immunity challenges "the factual basis of the court's jurisdiction," the court "must go beyond the pleadings and resolve any disputed issues of fact the resolution of which is necessary to a ruling upon the motion to dismiss." *Phoenix Consulting*, 216 F.3d at 40. To resolve such a factual dispute, however, the court "retains 'considerable latitude in devising the procedures it will follow to ferret out the facts pertinent to jurisdiction.' " *Id.* (quoting *Prakash v. American Univ.*, 727 F.2d 1174, 1179-80 (D.C.Cir.1984)); see *Grubart*, 513 U.S. at 537, 115 S.Ct. at 1050-51 (noting that "any litigation of a contested subject-matter jurisdictional fact issue occurs in comparatively summary procedure").

Contrary to defendants' assertion, the district court understood its responsibilities in this regard. See *Kilburn v. Republic of Iran*, 277 F.Supp.2d. 24, 29-30, 33 (D.D.C.2003) (citing *Phoenix Consulting*, 216 F.3d at 40). In this case, the parties agreed to limited jurisdictional discovery, pursuant to which the plaintiff provided the defendants with supporting documents from the CIA and State Department, and with a declaration by retired Ambassador Robert Oakley. Oakley was the State Department's Coordinator for Counterterrorism during the period of Peter Kilburn's kidnapping and murder. Plaintiff also produced a list of witnesses who would testify to Libya's responsibility. No depositions were conducted or sought. After reviewing these materials, the district court concluded that denial of the motion to dismiss was warranted. We agree.

" 'In accordance with the restrictive view of sovereign immunity reflected in the FSIA,' the defendant bears the burden of proving that the plaintiff's allegations do not bring its case within a statutory exception to immunity." *Phoenix Consulting*, 216 F.3d at 40 (quoting *Transamerican S.S. Corp. v. Somali Democratic Republic*, 767 F.2d 998, 1002

(D.C.Cir.1985)); see *Princz v. Federal Republic of Germany*, 26 F.3d 1166, 1171 (D.C.Cir.1994). We have never decided whether, in addition to the ultimate burden of persuasion, the defendant also bears the initial burden of production. [FN4] But even if the plaintiff has the burden of production, he has satisfied it. Ambassador Oakley's declaration states that he would testify - both as an expert and based on first-hand knowledge of some of the events in question - that ARC was an agent of Libya, that it purchased, tortured, and killed Peter Kilburn, and that the Libyan government expressly provided the funds for the purchase and directed the killing. *See* Oakley Decl. ¶¶ 11-17. Given that the only discovery to date has been that which the plaintiff has voluntarily accorded the defendants, and that the plaintiff has not yet had an opportunity to conduct any, that is more than sufficient to satisfy any possible burden of production at this stage of the litigation. [FN5]

FN4. Compare *Gould, Inc. v. Pechiney Ugine Kuhlmann & Trefimetaux*, 853 F.2d 445, 451 & n. 5 (6th Cir.1988) (indicating that the foreign state defendant bears the burden of going forward with evidence that the alleged act does not come within an exception to sovereign immunity), *and* H.R.Rep. No. 94-1487, at 6616 (1976) (same), with *Virtual Countries, Inc. v. Republic of South Africa*, 300 F.3d 230, 241 (2d Cir.2002) (holding that the burden of production shifts to the plaintiff if the defendant presents a prima facie case that it is a foreign sovereign).

FN5. See *Phoenix Consulting*, 216 F.3d at 40 (holding that the district court "must give the plaintiff ample opportunity to secure and present evidence relevant to the existence of jurisdiction") (citation and internal quotation marks omitted); see also *Grubart*, 513 U.S. at 537-38, 115 S.Ct. at 1050-51 ("Normal practice permits a party to establish jurisdiction at the outset of a case by means of a nonfrivolous assertion of jurisdictional elements...and any litigation of a contested subject-matter jurisdictional fact issue occurs in comparatively summary procedure before a judge alone (as distinct from litigation of the same fact issue as an element of the cause of action, if the claim survives the jurisdictional objection).") (citations omitted).

It is equally plain that the Libyan defendants have so far satisfied neither a burden of production nor their required burden of persuasion. They submitted no affirmative evidence whatsoever to show that they fall outside the terrorism exception. They did not, for example, file an affidavit denying that their agents purchased or killed Peter Kilburn. Cf. *Phoenix Consulting*, 216 F.3d at 39 (noting that, by filing a sworn declaration that an alleged written contract was a forgery, the foreign state defendant disputed the plaintiff's claim that it had waived sovereign immunity through the contract). They did not proffer testimony denying that they had provided material support for those acts. They did not even deny that ARC was their agent.

What the defendants did do, instead, was to point out what they see as "contradictions" between the plaintiff's claims and some passages in the CIA and State Department documents. These asserted contradictions primarily involve reports that multiple terrorist organizations had claimed responsibility for hostage taking in Lebanon during the relevant period. Although the defendants do not explain the significance of these reports or what they contradicted, presumably the defendants believe the reports suggest that a Libyan-sponsored organization did not carry out the acts in question. But the reports do not deny that a Libyan-sponsored organization purchased or killed Peter Kilburn; nor do they suggest that such an organization was not a proximate cause of those acts, even if not the sole cause. In fact, it is not apparent that the asserted "contradictions" have any relevance at all to this case. [FN6]

FN6. Some of those asserted contradictions do not appear to relate to Peter Kilburn. For example, although the defendants point to a CIA report that five terrorist organizations had claimed responsibility for hostages taken in Lebanon in March of 1984, *see* CIA, Terrorism Review 735 (Apr. 8, 1985) (attached to Defs.' Mot. to Dismiss, App. D), Kilburn was not kidnapped until November of that year. Others do not appear to relate to the Libyan defendants. For example, although the defendants stress a State Department document stating that Kilburn was originally kidnapped by Islamic Jihad (presumably in contradiction to the allegation that the original kidnapping was by Hizbollah), *see* Department of State, Unclassified Documents 3 (attached to Defs.' Mot. to Dismiss, App. F), the complaint does not allege that Libya played a role in the original kidnapping. Nor does the document address the complaint's contention that Islamic Jihad and Hizbollah are one and the same. *See* Compl. ¶ 4.

In short, the defendants have failed to satisfy their "burden of proving that the plaintiff's allegations do not bring its case within a statutory exception to immunity." *Phoenix Consulting*, 216 F.3d at 40. The district court was therefore right to deny their motion to dismiss for lack of jurisdiction under Rule 12(b)(1).

V

In addition to challenging the district court's jurisdiction, the Libyan defendants also sought dismissal pursuant to

Rule 12(b)(6), contending that the plaintiff had failed to state a claim upon which relief could be granted. The district court denied that motion and, at the same time and sua sponte, held that defendant LESO could be subject to punitive damages if it were ultimately found liable. The Libyan defendants seek review of both decisions. In particular, they note that this circuit has recently held that one of the causes of action plaintiff asserted, the Flatow Amendment, 28 U.S.C. §1350 (note), does not "creat[e] a private right of action against a foreign government." *Cicippio-Puleo*, 353 F.3d at 1033. The Libyan defendants further argue that *no* other cause of action is available to plaintiffs who bring suit under §1605(a)(7). But cf. *id.* at 1035 (declining to decide whether terrorism victims invoking §1605(a)(7) have other causes of action).

Denial of a motion to dismiss for failure to state a claim under Rule 12(b)(6) is not ordinarily subject to interlocutory appeal. It is neither a final decision nor a proper subject for appeal under the "collateral order" doctrine. *Price*, 294 F.3d at 91. Whether conclusive or not, it plainly is not separate from the merits. And it is eminently reviewable on appeal from the final judgment; indeed, that is the usual way in which Rule 12(b)(6) decisions are appealed. See generally *Cohen*, 337 U.S. at 541, 69 S.Ct. at 1221. The defendants do not disagree. Instead, they urge us to assume jurisdiction over the non-immunity issues as "pendent" to the sovereign immunity decision over which we have interlocutory jurisdiction.

The leading case on pendent appellate jurisdiction is *Swint v. Chambers County Commission*, 514 U.S. 35, 115 S.Ct. 1203, 131 L.Ed.2d 60 (1995). In *Swint*, the Supreme Court expressed some skepticism about the existence of pendent appellate jurisdiction altogether, and particularly about a "'liberal' or 'flexible' approach" to the issue. 514 U.S. at 47 n. 5, 115 S.Ct. at 1210 n. 5. The Court ultimately concluded that it "need not definitively or preemptively settle here whether or when it may be proper for a court of appeals, with jurisdiction over one ruling, to review, conjunctively, related rulings that are not themselves independently appealable." *Id.* at 50-51, 115 S.Ct. at 1211-12. But it held that there was no such jurisdiction in that case, because the proposed pendent issue and the properly appealable issue were not "inextricably intertwined," and because review of the former decision was not "necessary to ensure meaningful review" of the latter. *Id.* at 51, 115 S.Ct. at 1211-12. Subsequently, in *Clinton v. Jones*, 520 U.S. 681, 707 n. 41, 117 S.Ct. 1636, 1651 n. 41, 137 L.Ed.2d 945 (1997), the Court held that pendent jurisdiction was proper where both the "inextricably intertwined" and "necessary to ensure meaningful review" conditions were satisfied.

In *Gilda Marx, Inc. v. Wildwood Exercise, Inc.*, 85 F.3d 675 (D.C.Cir.1996), we declined to exercise pendent jurisdiction over the appeal of an order holding a party liable for attorney's fees. We said that we would "exercis[e] pendent appellate jurisdiction sparingly," and "only when substantial considerations of fairness or efficiency demand it." 85 F.3d at 678-79. We also said, however, that while "[s]ome courts read *Swint* to permit pendent appellate jurisdiction *only* when the [two *Swint* conditions] obtain," we did "not think [*Swint*] meant to prescribe a definitive or exhaustive list of conditions." *Id.* at 679 n. 4.

The other circuits have taken a different path, saying that they will take pendent appellate jurisdiction *only* when one or both of the *Swint* conditions appear, [FN7] and criticizing our more permissive reading of *Swint*. [FN8] But despite using more expansive language, we have so far largely confined the doctrine to cases that come within one or the other of the *Swint* conditions, [FN9] or that involve questions like personal jurisdiction [FN10] or the statute of limitations [FN11] - which we have described as "logically antecedent" or "threshold" issues. See *Barbour v. WMATA*, 2003 WL 22095655, at *1 (D.C.Cir.2003).

FN7. See *Limone v. Condon*, 372 F.3d 39, 50-52 (1st Cir.2004); *Rein v. Socialist People's Libyan Arab Jamahiriya*, 162 F.3d 748, 758 (2d Cir.1998) ; *E.I. DuPont de Nemours & Co. v. Rhone Poulenc Fiber & Resin*, 269 F.3d 187, 203 (3d Cir.2001) ; *Taylor v. Waters*, 81 F.3d 429, 437 (4th Cir.1996); *Thornton v. General Motors Corp.*, 136 F.3d 450, 453-54 (5th Cir.1998); *Chambers v. Ohio Dep't of Human Servs.*, 145 F.3d 793, 797 (6th Cir.1998); *Jones v. InfoCure Corp.*, 310 F.3d 529, 536 (7th Cir.2002); *Woolfolk v. Smith*, 81 F.3d 741, 743 (8th Cir.1996); *Watkins v. Oakland*, 145 F.3d 1087, 1091 (9th Cir.1998); *Sevier v. Lawrence*, 60 F.3d 695, 701 (10th Cir.1995); *Hudson v. Hall*, 231 F.3d 1289, 1294 (11th Cir.2000).
FN8. See *Rein*, 162 F.3d at 758; see also *Limone*, 372 F.3d at 50-52.
FN9. See, e.g., *National R.R. Passenger Corp. v. ExpressTrak, L.L.C.*, 330 F.3d 523, 528 (D.C.Cir.2003) (exercising pendent jurisdiction where both *Swint* conditions existed); *United States ex rel. Long v. SCS Bus. & Tech Inst., Inc.*, 173 F.3d 870, 873-86 (D.C.Cir.1999) (same where the issues were "inextricably intertwined"); *Twelve John Does v. District of Columbia*, 117 F.3d 571, 574-75 (D.C.Cir.1997) (same).

FN10. See *Jungquist*, 115 F.3d 1020.
FN11. See *Griggs v. WMATA*, 232 F.3d 917, 919 & n. 2 (D.C.Cir.2000); *Rendall-Speranza v. Nassim*, 107 F.3d 913, 916-17 (D.C.Cir.1997).

This case does not fit any of those rubrics. Whether state tort law properly provides the plaintiff with a cause of action, for example, is not inextricably linked with, or necessary for meaningful review of, the proper scope of jurisdictional causation under §1605(a)(7). To the contrary, as we noted in Part III, these are analytically distinct questions. Nor can the cause of action question fairly be characterized as an antecedent or threshold issue. The question of whether the plaintiff has a cognizable cause of action (and what that cause of action might be) is not a question separate from the merits; it *is* the merits. See *Steel Co. v. Citizens for a Better Env't*, 523 U.S. 83, 89, 118 S.Ct. 1003, 1009-10, 140 L.Ed.2d 210 (1998). And all of this is, of course, a fortiori regarding the question of whether LESO, if liable, can be assessed punitive damages.

It is true that we did, in one case, decide to take pendent jurisdiction over a merits question (whether the Washington Metropolitan Area Transit Authority was subject to the District of Columbia's Freedom of Information Act), in order to avoid what we described as a "difficult" state sovereign immunity question. See *KiSKA Constr. Corp.-U.S.A. v. WMATA*, 167 F.3d 608, 611 (D.C.Cir.1999). [FN12] But that decision is not precedent for taking pendent appellate jurisdiction here. As we have already decided that Libya lacks immunity, there is nothing for us to avoid in this case. [FN13] Nor would it be fair to characterize the immunity questions discussed in Parts III and IV as particularly "difficult." Although we have discussed the legal aspects of causation in some detail, the allegations that the Libyan defendants were directly involved in Peter Kilburn's ordeal make the bottom-line conclusion that the defendants lack immunity quite easy. And, as we said in *Gilda Marx*, "parties should not be encouraged to bring insignificant, but final, matters before this court as mere vehicles for pendent review of numerous or complex orders that are not independently appealable." 85 F.3d at 679; see also *Swint*, 514 U.S. at 49-50, 115 S.Ct. at 1211-12 (warning that "a rule loosely allowing pendent appellate jurisdiction would encourage parties to parlay *Cohen*-type collateral orders into multi-issue interlocutory appeal tickets").

FN12. In another interlocutory appeal, *Simpson v. Socialist People's Libyan Arab Jamahiriya*, 326 F.3d 230, 234 (D.C.Cir.2003), we decided a merits question after deciding an immunity question. We did not, however, discuss our authority to do so, and "the existence of unaddressed jurisdictional" questions deprives a decision of "precedential effect" on those questions. *Lewis v. Casey*, 518 U.S. 343, 353 n. 2, 116 S.Ct. 2174, 2181 n. 2, 135 L.Ed.2d 606 (1996); see *Steel Co.*, 523 U.S. at 91, 118 S.Ct. at 1010-11.

FN13. Compare also *Long*, 173 F.3d at 893, 895 (distinguishing *Steel Co.* and holding that the availability of a statutory cause of action may be determined before deciding the "quasi-jurisdictional" question of Eleventh Amendment immunity), with *Steel Co.*, 523 U.S. at 93, 118 S.Ct. at 1011-12 (holding that a merits issue may not be determined before a jurisdictional question), *and* 28 U.S.C. §1604 (providing that "a foreign state shall be immune from the *jurisdiction* of the courts" unless the FSIA provides an exception) (emphasis added).

The Libyan defendants complain that, if we decline to take pendent jurisdiction over the non-immunity rulings, they may be required to go through an entire trial on a complaint that may eventually be determined to have no cognizable cause of action. This possibility would concern us, of course, had we not already concluded that the defendants lack immunity from this litigation. In light of that conclusion, however, the Libyan defendants are in the same position as any others. To permit an appeal of the denial of a Rule 12(b)(6) motion merely because it might spare the defendants the pain of trial would greatly expand the "small category of decisions" subject to the collateral order doctrine, *Swint*, 514 U.S. at 42, 115 S.Ct. at 1207-08, and undermine our promise to exercise pendent appellate jurisdiction "sparingly," *Gilda Marx*, 85 F.3d at 679. As the court said in *Swint* with respect to the collateral order doctrine: " '§1291 requires courts of appeals to view claims of a right not to be tried with skepticism, if not a jaundiced eye,' for 'virtually every right that could be enforced appropriately by pretrial dismissal might loosely be described as conferring a right not to stand trial.' " 514 U.S. at 43, 115 S.Ct. at 1208 (quoting *Digital Equip. Corp. v. Desktop Direct, Inc.*, 511 U.S. 863, 873, 114 S.Ct. 1992, 1998-99, 128 L.Ed.2d 842 (1994)).

We do not dispute that both the district court and the parties would benefit from advance knowledge of this circuit's view as to whether the plaintiff has a cause of action against the defendants. But the Supreme Court has rejected that as a sufficient reason to permit appeal on a theory of pendent jurisdiction. [FN14] And Congress has expressly provided another route for just such a situation. Section 1292(b) of Title 28 authorizes a district court to certify in writing that an "order involves a controlling question of law as to which there is substantial ground for difference of opinion and

that an immediate appeal from the order may materially advance the ultimate termination of the litigation." 28 U.S.C. §1292(b). When the district court so certifies, the court of appeals "may thereupon, in its discretion, permit an appeal to be taken from such order." *Id.* Indeed, the *Swint* court pointed to §1292(b) as a reason for caution regarding pendent appellate jurisdiction:

FN14. See *Swint*, 514 U.S. at 43-44, 115 S.Ct. at 1208-09 (rejecting an argument that judicial economy warranted the exercise of pendent jurisdiction in that case, notwithstanding that if the defendant were correct, "reviewing the district court's order would put an end to the entire case" against it) (internal quotation marks omitted).

Congress thus chose to confer on district courts first line discretion to allow interlocutory appeals. If courts of appeals had discretion to append to a *Cohen*-authorized appeal from a collateral order further rulings of a kind neither independently appealable nor certified by the district court, then the two-tiered arrangement §1292(b) mandates would be severely undermined.

Swint, 514 U.S. at 47, 115 S.Ct. at 1210. The district court has not issued a §1292(b) certification here.

In the final balance, whether or not we have authority to exercise pendent appellate jurisdiction in this case, there is no question that we have discretion to decline to do so. See *Sparrow v. United Air Lines, Inc.*, 216 F.3d 1111, 1118 (D.C.Cir.2000); *Gilda Marx*, 85 F.3d at 679-80. For the foregoing reasons, and because taking pendent jurisdiction here would mean straying far from *Swint*, we decline to pass on the rulings of the district court that are not related to the question of the defendants' immunity.

VI

We affirm the district court's determination that it had subject-matter jurisdiction to adjudicate the plaintiff's claims against the Libyan defendants. We decline to exercise appellate jurisdiction over defendants' other challenges.

Notes:

1.   Commentators and pundits have noted that most terrorism cases involve defaulting defendants which results in skewed decisions, "As a result, a very unusual and lopsided body of case law has developed under the Act, comprised almost entirely of unrefuted and unchallenged evidence presented by plaintiffs in the cases." William P. Hoye, *Fight-

ing Fire With…Mire? Civil Remedies And The New War On State-Sponsored Terrorism, 12 Duke J. Comp. & Int'l L. 105, 136 (2002). Is this an accurate depiction of the level of proof and evidence provided to the Court in *Kilburn*? What does this analysis suggest about the federal judges who have heard and decided terrorism cases? Are federal judges being duped in terrorism cases? Would the level of evidence be lower if the defaulting defendants had appeared to challenge the evidence presented by the plaintiffs? What types of evidence would be available to plaintiffs if the defaulting states appeared and responded to discovery requests?

2.   Are there evidentiary reasons why foreign states (and other defendants in civil terrorism suits) choose not to appear? What is the strategic reason for not appearing? What, if anything, is gained politically or legally by purposely not contesting the merits of a civil terrorism suit?

3.   How do the facts of *Kilburn* point up the issue of causation? What is unique about Libya that places the causation argument in a rarified context?

4.   What is unique about "jurisdictional causation" in the context of civil terrorism litigation?

5.   Will evidence of "jurisdictional causation" be sufficient to prove "substantive causation"? Are the standards identical?

6.   What is the interplay between Fed.R.Civ.P. 12(b)(6) and "jurisdictional causation" in setting a standard of proof?

7.   Following *Kilburn*, when faced with Sudan's challenge to "jurisdictional causation" and its attempt to have the court adopt a "but for" standard, the Fourth Circuit stated,

> …we agree that proximate cause is the appropriate standard to apply at this juncture. It serves simultaneously to weed out the most insubstantial cases without posing too high a hurdle to surmount at a threshold stage of the litigation. We find nothing in the relevant authority nor in the text of §1605(a)(7) to support Sudan's call for a more stringent standard. See *Kilburn*, 376 F.3d at 1128. Instead, Plaintiffs must establish jurisdictional causation by alleging facts sufficient to establish a reasonable connection between a country's provision of material support to a terrorist organization and the damage arising out of a terrorist attack.

Rux v. Republic of Sudan, 461 F.3d 461, 473 (4th Cir. 2006).

8.   In another case involving Libya the court stated, "the court rejects the defendants' argument that the material support provided by a nation to a terrorist organization must fund the specific acts that caused the alleged injury." *Collette v. Socialist Peoples' Libyan Arab Jamahiriya*, 362 F.Supp.2d 230, 236 (D.D.C. 2005). What accounts for this ruling?

Heiser v. Islamic Republic of Iran, 466 F.Supp.2d 229 (D. D.C. 2006).

LAMBERTH, District Judge.

BACKGROUND

These actions arise from the June 25, 1996 bombing at Khobar Towers, a residence on a United States military base in Dhahran, Saudi Arabia. The plaintiffs in this consolidated action are the family members and estates of 17 of the 19 servicemen killed in the attack. Plaintiffs allege that the Islamic Republic of Iran ("Iran"), the Iranian Ministry of Information and Security ("MOIS"), the Iranian Islamic Revolutionary Guard Corp ("IRGC" or "the Pasdaran"), and "John Does 1-99" are liable for damages from the attack because they provided material support and assistance to Hezbollah, [FN1] the terrorist organization that orchestrated and carried out the bombing. [FN2] Plaintiffs have relied upon causes of action founded upon provisions of the Foreign Sovereign Immunities Act ("FSIA"), *inter alia*, 28 U.S.C. §1605(a)(7).

FN1. According to the Oxford English Dictionary, the term "Hezbollah" is synonymous with the terms "Hizbollah" and "Hizbullah," all of which are English transliterations of the Arabic term referring to the extremist Shiite Muslim group also known as the "Party of God." *See* Oxford English Dictionary (2d ed.1989). Accordingly, to the extent that any of these terms are used within this opinion, they shall be used interchangeably.
FN2. At other points during the case, plaintiffs sought redress for their losses from various other defendants who have since been dismissed from the case, namely Hezbollah and Osama Bin Laden.

PROCEDURAL HISTORY

In their second amended complaints, plaintiffs named as defendants (1) the Islamic Republic of Iran; (2) the Iranian

Ministry of Information and Security ("MOIS"); (3) the Iranian Islamic Revolutionary Guard Corps ("IRGC" or "the Pasdaran"); (4) and "John Does 1-99[.]" Second Amended Complaints, ¶ 1; see also id., ¶¶ 24, 25, 27, 29. Plaintiffs sought damages for wrongful death (Count I); survival action (Count II); "economic damages" (Count III); intentional infliction of emotional distress (Count IV); for plaintiffs Ibis S. Haun, Marie R. Campbell, Shyrl L. Johnson, Katie L. Marthaler and Dawn Woody, loss of consortium (Count V); solatium (Count VI); and "punitive damages" (Count VII).

Plaintiffs requested judgment in their favor against all of the defendants. In addition, the plaintiffs in Civil Action No. 00-2329 sought compensatory damages against all defendants in the amount of $890,000,000, "plus economic damages in an amount to be determined at trial for each of Decedents' Estates"; punitive damages against defendants MOIS, the IRGC and John Does 1-99 in the amount of $500,000,000; and reasonable costs, expenses and attorneys' fees. The plaintiffs in Civil Action No. 01-2104 sought compensatory damages against all defendants in the amount of $3,660,000,000 "plus economic damages in an amount to be determined at trial for each of Decedents' Estates"; punitive damages against defendants MOIS, the IRGC and John Does 1-99 in the amount of $500,000,000; and reasonable costs, expenses and attorneys' fees.

On February 1, 2002, the court (Jackson, J.) consolidated the two civil actions, and in Civil Action No. 00-2329, granted the plaintiffs' motion for entry of default as to defendants Islamic Republic of Iran, MOIS and the IRGC. February 1, 2002 Order (Docket No. 9, Civil Action No. 00-2329) at 1. On February 6, 2002, the Clerk entered a default in Civil Action No. 00-2329 against defendants Islamic Republic of Iran, MOIS and the IRGC. Default (Docket No. 10, Civil Action No. 00-2329). On July 30, 2002, both actions were referred to Magistrate Judge Robinson for all purposes. (July 30, 2002 Order (Docket No. 11) at 1.) On October 4, 2002, Magistrate Judge Robinson granted plaintiffs' motion in Civil Action No. 01-2104 for entry of default as to defendants Islamic Republic of Iran, MOIS and the IRGC. (October 4, 2002 Order (Docket No. 11, Civil Action No. 01-2104) at 1.) On October 8, 2002, the Clerk entered a default in Civil Action No. 01-2104 against defendants Islamic Republic of Iran, MOIS and the IRGC. Default (Docket No. 12, Civil Action No. 01-2104) at 1. On March 14, 2003, plaintiffs moved for a continuance of the hearing on liability and damages. Plaintiffs' counsel represented that counsel "has learned that certain immediate family members of the soldiers killed in the Khobar Towers terrorist attack-family members who have cognizable claims under the Foreign Sovereign Immunities Act ('FSIA')-are not current-

ly named as parties in these consolidated actions." (Motion for Continuance of Trial Date and Request for Scheduling Conference (Docket No. 16) at 2.) Counsel further represented that the firm "is in the process of identifying all such family members and anticipates filing amended complaints within the next several weeks." Id. Magistrate Judge Robinson granted plaintiffs' motion, and, in accordance with the request of plaintiffs' counsel, "tentatively" scheduled the hearing for "the period of December 1, 2003 to December 18, 2003[.]" (March 17, 2003 Order (Docket No. 17) at 1.) Plaintiffs filed their second amended complaints on May 6, 2003.

Upon consideration of plaintiffs' motions to vacate their consent to proceed before a magistrate judge for all purposes and to clarify the purpose of the referral to a magistrate judge, the court re-referred the consolidated civil actions to Magistrate Judge Robinson "to hear and determine pretrial matters as permitted thereby, and pursuant to 28 U.S.C. §636(b)(1)(B), to conduct hearings, and to submit proposed findings and recommendations for the disposition by the Court of any motion for judgment by default upon the evidence submitted in accordance with 28 U.S.C. §1608(e)." (Docket No. [20] at 1-2.) The Court denied plaintiffs' motion for clarification of the referral. (August 22, 2003 Order (Docket No. 25) at 1.) On September 3, 2003, Magistrate Judge Robinson scheduled the hearing on liability and damages for December 1 through December 18, 2003. (September 3, 2003 Order (Docket No. 26) at 1.)

Plaintiffs filed their pretrial statement on October 31, 2003 ((Docket No. 30).) In accordance with Magistrate Judge Robinson's Final Pretrial Order (Docket No. 32), plaintiffs filed a memorandum regarding issues relevant to liability. See Supplemental Bench Memorandum on Liability Issues ("Memorandum on Liability") (Docket No. 33). In the memorandum, plaintiffs stated that they "do not expect to identify [Defendants] John Does 1-99 before the commencement of the trial[,]" and that "[a]ccordingly, Plaintiffs will not seek a finding of liability against the co-conspirators John Does 1-99, who were named as defendants when the complaints in this consolidated action were filed." (Memorandum on Liability at 9.) On November 19, 2003, plaintiffs moved for entry of default against the Islamic Republic of Iran, MOIS and the IRGC. (Plaintiffs' Motion for Entry of Default (Docket No. 38) at 1.) The Court granted the motion. November 26, 2003 Order. (Docket No. 39, Civil Action No. 00-2329; Docket No. 32, Civil Action No. 01-2104.)

Plaintiffs examined witnesses and offered other evidence with respect to liability and damages on December 1, 2, 3, 4, 5, 8, 9, 10, 11, 12, 16, 18 and 19, 2003. On December 19, 2003, plaintiffs moved to voluntarily dismiss Defendants "John Does 1-99," and Magistrate Judge Robinson granted the motion. (December 19, 2003 Tr. (Docket No. 128) at 69-70.) The magistrate judge recessed the hearing until February 5, 2004, the earliest date that plaintiffs' counsel, plaintiffs' witnesses and the court were be available to continue. Magistrate Judge Robinson received further evidence on February 5, 6, 9 and 10, 2004.

During the recess in the evidentiary hearing a panel of the *District of Columbia Circuit decided Cicippio-Puleo v. Islamic Republic of Iran*, 353 F.3d 1024 (D.C.Cir.2004). Plaintiffs asked that the hearing resume on February 5, 2004 as scheduled. On February 6, 2004, when the schedule for the conclusion of the evidentiary hearing and for closing argument was addressed by Magistrate Judge Robinson, counsel for plaintiffs asked that counsel's closing argument be deferred until counsel filed Plaintiffs' proposed findings of fact and conclusions of law. Magistrate Judge Robinson ordered that plaintiffs file their proposed findings and conclusions on April 1, 2004, the date proposed by plaintiffs' counsel. Magistrate Judge Robinson scheduled plaintiffs' closing argument for April 15, 2004, the date proposed by Plaintiffs' counsel. On April 9, 2004, Magistrate Judge Robinson postponed the April 15 closing argument, intending to order supplemental briefing of issues relevant to the liability of the remaining defendants.

In light of the D.C. Circuit's opinions in *Cicippio-Puleo* and *Acree v. Republic of Iraq*, [FN3] plaintiffs moved to modify the magistrate judge's Final Pretrial Order, or in the alternative to file third amended complaints so as to incorporate claims based in state law. On August 4, 2004, Magistrate Judge Robinson denied plaintiffs' Motion for Reconsideration; granted plaintiffs' motion for leave to file third amended complaints; and ordered that plaintiffs file the third amended complaints by August 9, 2004. (Aug. 4, 2004 Order (Docket No. 103) at 2-3.)

FN3. 370 F.3d 41 (D.C.Cir.2004).

Plaintiffs filed the third amended complaints on August 4, 2004. Plaintiffs named as defendants in the third amended complaints the Islamic Republic of Iran, the "Iranian Ministry of Information and Security[,]" and the "Iranian Islamic Revolutionary Guard Corps[.]" Plaintiffs again alleged that "[t]he Hizbollah terrorist organization is a creation and agent of the Islamic Republic of Iran"; that "[i]n 1995, Hizbollah began plotting a terrorist attack against United States interests in Saudi Arabia"; and that "[Hizbollah] ultimately detonated a bomb outside Khobar Towers." (Third Amended Complaints at 2.) Plaintiffs allege that "[u]nder United States law, the Islamic Republic of Iran-which funds, trains, and directs Hizbollah through the Iranian Ministry of Infor-

mation and Security and the Iranian Revolutionary Guard Corps-is responsible for this terrorist attack and for the murder of [Plaintiffs' decedents]." *Id.*

FINDINGS OF FACT [FN4]

FN4. A detailed discussion of the facts and circumstances associated with each individual plaintiff will not be addressed in this section, but rather in the respective portions of this opinion relating to the merits of each individual plaintiff's cause of action against the defendants. See *infra* Conclusions of Law, Part VI.

1. In June 1996, Master Sergeant Michael Heiser, Captain Leland Timothy Haun, Airman First-Class Justin R. Wood, Senior Airman Earl F. Cartrette, Jr., Airman First-Class Brian McVeigh, Sergeant Millard D. Campbell, Staff-Sergeant Kevin J. Johnson, Airman First-Class Joseph E. Rimkus, Airman First-Class Brent E. Marthaler, Technical Sergeant Tranh ("Gus") Nguyen, Airman First-Class Joshua E. Woody, Airman First-Class Peter J. Morgera, Master Sergeant Kendall Kitson, Jr., Captain Christopher Adams, Airman First-Class Christopher Lester, Senior Airman Jeremy A. Taylor, and Technical Sergeant Patrick P. Fennig were citizens of the United States and members of the United States Air Force. They were stationed in Dhahran, Saudi Arabia, and resided in the Khobar Towers.

2. The United States military presence in Saudi Arabia was with the consent of that host country. *Blais v. Islamic Republic of Iran*, 2006 WL 2827372, *2 (D.D.C. Sept.29, 2006) (Lamberth, J.). It was part of a coalition of forces, primarily from the United States, Great Britain, and France, that was charged with monitoring Iraq's compliance with United Nations Security Council resolutions enforcing the cease-fire that had brought an end to the 1991 "Desert Storm" ejection of Iraqi occupying forces from Kuwait. *Id.*

3. The deployment of U.S. troops to the region was considered a peacetime deployment within a friendly host country. *Id.*

4. The seventeen decedents represented in this action were engaged in routine peace time operations while stationed in Saudi Arabia, and were charged with enforcing the "no fly zone" in southern Iraq.

5. Defendant Iran "is a foreign state and has been designated a state sponsor of terrorism pursuant to section 69(j) of the Export Administration Act of 1979 (50 U.S.C.A. §2405(j)) continuously since January 19, 1984." *Flatow v. Islamic Republic of Iran*, 999 F.Supp. 1, 11, (D.D.C.1998) (Lamberth, J.).

6. Defendant the IRGC is a non-traditional instrumentality of Iran. It is the military arm of a kind of shadow gov-

ernment answering directly to the Ayatollah and the mullahs who hold power in Iran. It is similar to the Nazi party's SA organization prior to World War II. The IRGC actively supports terrorism as a means of protecting the Islamic revolution that brought the Ayatollah to power in Iran in 1979. It has its own separate funding sources, derived from confiscation of the assets of the former Shah of Iran in 1979, when the Shah was deposed. *Blais*, 459 F.Supp.2d at 46-47.

7. The Khobar Towers was a residential complex in Dhahran, Saudi Arabia, which housed the coalition forces charged with monitoring compliance with U.N. security council resolutions. *Id.* at 47-48.

The Attack on the Khobar Towers

8. At approximately 10 minutes before 10 pm on June 25, 1996, a large gasoline tanker truck pulled up alongside the perimeter wall of the Khobar Towers complex. The driver jumped out, ran into a waiting car that had pulled up near the truck, and sped off. *Id.*

9. Although security guards near the top of Building 131 started to give warnings about the unusual vehicle location, the truck exploded with great force within about 15 minutes. The investigation determined that the force of the explosion was the equivalent of 20,000 pounds of TNT. The Defense Department said that it was the largest non-nuclear explosion ever up to that time. *Id.*

10. The explosion sheared off the face of Building 131, where Paul Blais and his crewmates were housed, and reduced most of it to rubble. Nineteen United States Air Force personnel were killed in the explosion, and hundreds of others were injured. *Id.*

Iranian Support and Sponsorship of the Attack

11. The attack was carried out by individuals recruited principally by a senior official of the IRGC, Brigadier General Ahmed Sharifi. Sharifi, who was the operational commander, planned the operation and recruited individuals for the operation at the Iranian embassy in Damascus, Syria. He provided the passports, the paperwork, and the funds for the individuals who carried out the attack. *Id.*

12. The truck bomb was assembled at a terrorist base in the Bekaa Valley which was jointly operated by the IRGC and by the terrorist organization known as Hezbollah. The individuals recruited to carry out the bombing referred to themselves as "Saudi Hezbollah," and they drove the truck bomb from its assembly point in the Bekaa Valley to Dhahran, Saudi Arabia. *Id.*

13. The terrorist attack on the Khobar Towers was approved by Ayatollah Khameini, the Supreme leader of Iran at the time. It was also approved and supported by the Iranian

Minister of Intelligence and Security ("MOIS") at the time, Ali Fallahian, who was involved in providing intelligence security support for the operation. Fallahian's representative in Damascus, a man named Nurani, also provided support for the operation. *Id.*

14. Under Louis Freeh, the FBI conducted a massive and thorough investigation of the attack, using over 250 agents. *Id.*

15. Based on that investigation, an Alexandria, Virginia, grand jury returned an indictment on June 21, 2001, against 13 identified members of the pro-Iran Saudi Hezbollah organization. The indictment's description of the plot to bomb the Khobar Towers complex frequently refers to direction and assistance from Iranian government officials. *Id.*

16. In addition, as a result of this investigation, the FBI also obtained a great deal of information linking the defendants to the bombing from interviews with six admitted members of the Saudi Hezbollah organization, who were arrested by the Saudis shortly after the bombing. *Id.* at 11-30. These six individuals admitted to the FBI their complicity in the attack on the Khobar Towers, and admitted that senior officials in the Iranian government provided them with funding, planning, training, sponsorship, and travel necessary to carry out the attack on the Khobar Towers. (Exh. 7 at 11, 13-14, 27; *see also* Dec. 18, 2003 Tr. at 24-30.) The six individuals also indicated that the selection of the target and the authorization to proceed was done collectively by Iran, MOIS, and IRGC, though the actual preparation and carrying out of the attack was done by the IRGC. (Dec. 18, 2003 Tr. at 25.)

17. According to Director Freeh. the FBI obtained specific information from the six about how each was recruited and trained by the Iranian government *in Iran* and Lebanon, and how weapons were smuggled into Saudi Arabia from Iran through Syria and Jordan. One individual described in detail a meeting about the attack at which senior Iranian officials, including members of the MOIS and IRGC, were present. (Dec. 18, 2003 Tr. at 23.) Several stated that IRGC directed, assisted, and oversaw the surveillance of the Khobar Towers site, and that these surveillance reports were sent to IRGC officials for their review. Another told the FBI that IRGC gave the six individuals a large amount of money for the specific purpose of planning and executing the Khobar Towers bombing.

18. Louis Freeh has publicly and unequivocally stated his firm conclusion, based on evidence gathered by the FBI during their five-year investigation, that Iran was responsible for planning and supporting the Khobar Towers attack. *Blais* at 48-49.

19. Dale Watson was formerly the deputy counterterrorism chief of the FBI in 1996, and subsequently became the section chief for all international terrorism in 1997. Mr. Watson was responsible for day to day oversight of the FBI investigation of the Khobar Towers attack. Mr. Watson has given sworn testimony that information uncovered in the investigation, "clearly pointed to the fact that there was Iran MOIS and IRGC involvement in the bombing." *Id.*

20. Dr. Patrick Clawson testified as an expert in three areas: (1) the government of Iran; (2) Iran's sponsorship of terrorism; and (3) the Iranian economy. Dr. Clawson's expert opinion regarding the perpetrators of the Khobar Towers bombing is based on his involvement on a Commission investigating the bombing, his top-secret security clearance, his discussions with Saudi officials, as well as his academic research on the subject. Exh. 9 at 62-63.

21. Dr. Clawson testified that the government of Iran formed the Saudi Hezbollah organization. *Id.* at 56. He testified that the IRGC was responsible for providing military training to Hezbollah terrorists as to how to carry out a terrorist attack. *Id.* at 28. He also testified as to the defendants' state-sponsorship of terrorism, noting that at the time of the Khobar Towers bombing, Iran spent an estimated amount of between $50 million and $150 million on terrorist activities. Exh. 10 at 46.

22. In light of all these facts, Dr. Clawson stated conclusively his opinion that the government of Iran, MOIS, and IRGC were responsible for the Khobar Towers bombing, and that Saudi Hezbollah carried out the attack under their direction. Exh. 9 at 67-68.

23. Dr. Clawson's expert opinion is supported by Dr. Bruce Tefft, whose expert opinion this Court adopted in *Blais*. Dr. Tefft was one of the founding members of the CIA's counterterrorism bureau in 1985. He served in the CIA until 1995, and has continued to work as a consultant on terrorism since that time, including work as an unofficial adviser to the New York Police Department's counterterrorism and intelligence divisions. He retains a top-secret security clearance in connection with his work. He has been qualified as an expert witness in numerous other cases involving Iranian sponsorship of terrorism. He was qualified as an expert witness on terrorism in this case. *Id.*

24. Dr. Tefft expressed the opinion that defendants the Islamic Republic of Iran and the Iranian Revolutionary Guards Corp were responsible for planning and supporting the attack on the Khobar Towers, including providing operational and financial support. He stated that there was "no question about it. It wouldn't have happened without Iranian support." *Id.*

25. Dr. Tefft based his conclusion on publicly available sources that were not inconsistent with classified information known to him from his time at the CIA and from his security clearances since that time. He relied on the public sources described above, as well as several others, which he described as authoritative and reliable, including congressional testimony by Matthew Levitt, senior fellow and director of the Washington Institute's Terrorism Studies Program, and articles published by the Federation of American Scientists as well as the Free Muslims Coalition. *Id.*

CONCLUSIONS OF LAW

I. Jurisdiction

In the United States, the Foreign Sovereign Immunities Act provides the sole basis for asserting jurisdiction over foreign sovereigns. *Argentine Republic v. Amerada Hess Shipping Corp.*, 488 U.S. 428, 434-34, 109 S.Ct. 683, 102 L.Ed.2d 818 (1989). Normally, a party may not bring an action for money damages in U.S. courts against a foreign state. 28 U.S.C. §1604. The "state-sponsored terrorism" exception, however, removes a foreign state's immunity to suits for money damages brought in U.S. courts where plaintiffs are seeking damages against the foreign state for personal injury or death caused by "an act of torture, extrajudicial killing, aircraft sabotage, hostage taking, or the provision of material support or resources (as defined in section 2339A of title 18) for such an act if such act or provision of material support is engaged by an official, employee, or agent of such foreign state while acting within the scope of his or her office, employment or agency." 28 U.S.C. §1605(a)(7).

In order to subject a foreign sovereign to suit under section 1605(a)(7), plaintiffs must show that: (1) the foreign sovereign was designated by the State Department as a "state sponsor of terrorism"; (2) the victim or plaintiff was a U.S. national at the time the acts took place; and (3) the foreign sovereign engaged in conduct that falls within the ambit of the statute. *Prevatt v. Islamic Republic of Iran*, 421 F.Supp.2d 152, 158 (D.D.C. Mar.28, 2006).

Each of the requirements is met in this case. First, defendant Iran has been designated a state sponsor of terrorism continuously since January 19, 1984, and was so designated at the time of the attack. *See* 31 C.F.R. §596.201 (2001); *Flatow*, 999 F.Supp. at 11, ¶ 19. Second, the plaintiffs have described themselves as "the Estates and family members" of 17 of the 19 servicemen who were killed on June 25, 1996, after "Hizbollah terrorists detonated a 5,000 pound truck bomb outside of Khobar Towers, a United States military complex in Dhahran, Saudi Arabia." Second Amended Complaint, at 3. Both the plaintiffs and the victims to which they are related were United States nationals at the time the bombing occurred. Finally, defendant Iran's support of an entity that committed an extrajudicial killing squarely falls within the ambit of the statute. Defendants MOIS and the IRGC are considered to be a division of state of Iran, and thus the same determinations apply to their conduct. *Roeder*, 333 F.3d at 234; see also *Salazar v. Islamic Republic of Iran*, 370 F.Supp.2d 105, 116 (D.D.C.2005) (Bates, J.) (analogizing the IRGC to the MOIS for purposes of liability, and concluding that both must be treated as the state of Iran itself).

Personal jurisdiction exists over a non-immune sovereign so long as service of process has been made under section 1608 of the FSIA. See *Stern v. Islamic Republic of Iran*, 271 F.Supp.2d 286, 298 (D.D.C.2003) (Lamberth, J.). In this case, service of process has been made. Accordingly, this Court has *in personam* jurisdiction over defendants Iran, MOIS, and IRGC.

II. Legal Standard for FSIA Default Judgment

Under the Foreign Sovereign Immunities Act, "[n]o judgement by default shall be entered by a court of the United States or of a state against a foreign state...unless the claimant establishes his claim or right to relief by evidence satisfactory to the court." 28 U.S.C. §1608(e); *Roeder v. Islamic Republic of Iran*, 333 F.3d 228, 232-33 (D.C.Cir.2003), *cert. denied*, 542 U.S. 915, 124 S.Ct. 2836, 159 L.Ed.2d 287 (2004). In default judgment cases, plaintiffs may present evidence in the form of affidavits. *Bodoff v. Islamic Republic of Iran*, 424 F.Supp.2d 74, 82 (D.D.C. Mar.29, 2006) (quoting *Campuzano v. Islamic Republic of Iran*, 281 F.Supp.2d 258, 268 (D.D.C.2003)). Upon evaluation, the court may accept plaintiffs' uncontroverted evidence as true. *Campuzano*, 281 F.Supp.2d at 268. This Court accepts the uncontested evidence and testimony submitted by plaintiffs as true in light of the fact that the defendants in this action have not objected to it or even appeared in this action to contest it.

III. Magistrate Judge's Report and Recommendation of Proposed Findings of Fact and Conclusions of Law

A. Standard of Review of a Magistrate Judge's Proposed Findings and Recommendation

Under the Federal Magistrate's Act, "a judge may...designate a magistrate judge to conduct hearings, including evidentiary hearings, and to submit to a judge of the court proposed findings of fact and recommendations for the disposition." 28 U.S.C. §636(b)(1)(B). Once the magistrate judge's proposed findings and recommendation are submitted to the court and copies have been served on the parties, the parties may serve and file within ten days from receipt

of service written objections to any proposed finding or recommendations made within the magistrate judge's report and recommendation. 28 U.S.C. §636(b). In reviewing the objections made to the magistrate judge's report and recommendation, the district court judge shall make a *de novo* review of the portions of the report and recommendation objected to by the parties. *Id.* Upon review, "[a] judge of the court may accept, reject, or modify, in whole or in part, the findings or recommendations made by the magistrate judge." *Id.*; see also *Roell v. Withrow*, 538 U.S. 580, 585, 123 S.Ct. 1696, 155 L.Ed.2d 775 (2003) (noting that a district court is "free to do as it sees fit with [a] magistrate judge's recommendations" made under authority of 28 U.S.C. §636(b)(1)). [FN5] The district court "must not be a rubber stamp" of the magistrate judge's recommendations. *Reese v. Meritor Automotive, Inc.*, 113 F.Supp.2d 822, 824 (W.D.N.C.2000) (quoting 12 CHARLES ALAN WRIGHT, ARTHUR R. MILLER & RICHARD L. MARCUS, FEDERAL PRACTICE AND PROCEDURE §3070.2 (2006)).

FN5. Plaintiffs have requested pursuant to LCvR 72.3(c) and LCvR 78.1 that the Court hold a hearing on plaintiffs' objections to the magistrate judge's Report and Recommendation. Pl. Obj. to Report and Recommendation, at 1. Though the district court must consider any objections that have been made regarding the magistrate judge's proposed findings, the language of 28 U.S.C. §636(b)(1) does not obligate the court to hold a hearing on those objections. See *United States v. Raddatz*, 447 U.S. 667, 674-76, 100 S.Ct. 2406, 65 L.Ed.2d 424 (1980). Rather, by "providing for a '*de novo* determination' rather than *de novo* hearing [in the statutory language], Congress intended to permit whatever reliance a district judge, in the exercise of sound judicial discretion, chose to place on a magistrate's proposed findings and recommendations." *Id.* at 676, 100 S.Ct. 2406. Accordingly, to the extent that plaintiffs have objected to Magistrate Judge Robinson's Report and Recommendation to this Court, those objections have been considered and will be addressed within the purview of this written opinion, and not at a hearing before this Court.

B. Magistrate Judge Robinson's Proposed Findings of Fact and Recommendation

In her Report and Recommendation, Magistrate Judge Robinson recommended that plaintiffs' motion for default judgment be denied on the basis that plaintiffs had not presented evidence satisfactory to the Court of defendants' liability. (Rep. and Reco. [129] 30.) The magistrate judge proposed that "Plaintiffs failed to establish a nexus between the June 25, 1996 bombing and any action or decision of any of the

Defendants in these consolidated actions." *Id.* As a result, Magistrate Judge Robinson recommended that this Court find that plaintiffs failed to "[establish] [their] claim or right to relief by evidence that is satisfactory to the Court[.]" *Id.* (quoting *Haim v. Islamic Republic of Iran*, 425 F.Supp.2d 56, 60 (D.D.C.2006)) (internal citation omitted). The magistrate judge also discussed generally, but made no specific findings or recommendations concerning, two additional issues, namely: (1) whether plaintiffs, as members of the United States Air Force operating under peacetime rules of engagement, may qualify for recovery under the FSIA; and (2) whether an apparent conflict of interest existed with respect to plaintiffs' representation by DLA Piper Rudnick Gray Cary U.S. LLP. [FN6] (Rep. and Reco. [129] 15-17, 25-26.)

FN6. Previously, Piper Rudnick LLP.

Plaintiffs objected to the magistrate judge's finding as to the insufficiency of the evidence, [FN7] as well as to other portions of the report and recommendation. (*See* Pl.'s Obj. to Report and Recommendation [130] 4-5.) In addition to the objection as to the sufficiency of their evidence, plaintiffs objected to: (1) whether Magistrate Judge Robinson had jurisdiction to preside over an evidentiary hearing or to make a report and recommendation regarding default judgment; (2) the magistrate judge's discussion of whether plaintiffs, as members of the United States Air Force, could recover as noncombatants under peacetime rules of engagement at the time of their deaths; and (3) her discussion of an apparent conflict of interest with respect to plaintiffs' counsel. (Pl.'s Obj. to Report and Recommendation [130] 5.)

FN7. As to the magistrate judge's finding and recommendation regarding the sufficiency of the evidence plaintiffs submitted, plaintiffs object on the grounds that the evidence presented is sufficient to find the defendants liable, that such evidence is "consistent with and virtually identical to-and even more direct than-liability evidence found to be sufficient as a matter of law in 23 other [FSIA] cases," and that this Court may take judicial notice of evidence, findings and conclusions entered by this *Court in Blais v. Islamic Republic of Iran*, 2006 WL 2827372, at *3-4 (D.D.C. Sept.29, 2006) (Lamberth, J.). (Pl.'s Obj. to Report and Recommendation [130] 4-5.)

Having reviewed *de novo* the objected-to portions of Magistrate Judge Robinson's report and recommendation to this Court, and for the reasons set forth in this opinion, this Court makes the following determinations. First, the Court finds that Magistrate Judge Robinson had proper jurisdiction to hear evidence and render a report and recommendation

in this matter. Second, the Court finds that plaintiffs may properly recover under the FSIA as noncombatants under peacetime rules of engagement. Third, this Court finds that no conflict of interest presently exists arising out of plaintiffs' representation by DLA Piper Rudnick Gray Cary U.S. LLP. Finally, the Court finds that plaintiffs have provided evidence satisfactory to this Court to establish their claim or right to relief. In light of the foregoing findings, judgment shall be entered in favor of the plaintiffs and against the defendants.

IV. Analysis and Review of Objections to Magistrate Judge Robinson's Report and Recommendation

A. Plaintiff's Objection that Magistrate Judge Robinson Lacked Jurisdiction to Hear Evidence and Render an Opinion in this Matter

Plaintiffs objected to the magistrate judge's report and recommendation in its entirety on the grounds that she lacked jurisdiction to conduct an evidentiary hearing or issue a recommendation on plaintiffs' motion for default judgment against the defendants. At the heart of their objections is the notion that appointment of a magistrate judge in lieu of an Article III Judge is unauthorized by the Magistrates Act and might run afoul of the parties' due process and Article III rights under the U.S. Constitution. [FN8]

FN8. Plaintiffs chief concern is that any final judgment might be collaterally attacked by defendants on these grounds.

Plaintiffs' objection is unfounded. As noted above, [FN9] such an appointment is clearly authorized by the Magistrates Act. The plain language of 28 U.S.C. §636(b)(1)(B) clearly states that a district court "may...designate a magistrate judge to conduct hearings, including evidentiary hearings, and to submit to a judge of the court proposed findings of fact and recommendations for the disposition." 28 U.S.C. §636(b)(1)(B). Additionally, the Supreme Court held that this statute "strikes the proper balance between the demands of due process and the constraints of Article III." *Raddatz*, 447 U.S. at 683-84, 100 S.Ct. 2406. Delegation under this provision does not run afoul of Article III "so long as the ultimate decision is made by the district court." *Raddatz*, 447 U.S. at 683, 100 S.Ct. 2406. Moreover, the parties' due process rights are protected by the fact that "the district court judge alone acts as the ultimate decisionmaker, [and] the statute grants the judge the broad discretion to accept, reject, or modify the magistrate's proposed findings." *Id.* at 680, 100 S.Ct. 2406. Here, Magistrate Judge Robinson heard evidence from the parties, and rendered a report and recommendation to this Court, pursuant to 28 U.S.C. §636(b), and this Court alone is responsible for rendering the ultimate decision as to the merits of this case. Accordingly, this Court finds that neither of the parties' due process or Article III rights were violated by appointing Magistrate Judge Robinson to conduct an evidentiary hearing. This Court finds that Magistrate Judge Robinson had proper jurisdiction under 28 U.S.C. §636(b) to conduct an evidentiary hearing and submit a report and recommendation thereon.

FN9. See *supra* Part III.A.

B. Plaintiffs' Ability to Recover Under State-Sponsored Terrorism Exception to the FSIA

Magistrate Judge Robinson raised in her report and recommendation the issue of whether plaintiffs, as relatives of active servicemen on duty at the time of their deaths, were able to recover for damages arising from those servicemen's deaths. Plaintiffs argued that they are not excluded under the state-sponsored terrorism exception to the FSIA from recovering.

Previously, this Court has awarded damages to United States service members who were injured or killed as a result of state-sponsored terrorist attacks and their families. [FN10] In *Peterson*, this Court held that a service member and his or her family may recover under the state-sponsored terrorism exception to the FSIA only if the service member was a non-combatant not engaged in military hostilities. There, the Court established a two-prong test to determine whether a military service member was a non-combatant. Under this test, a service member is deemed a non-combatant if he or she was: (1) engaged in a peacekeeping mission; and (2) operating under peacetime rules of engagement. *Peterson*, 264 F.Supp.2d at 60.

FN10. See, e.g., *Blais*, 459 F.Supp.2d 40 (D.D.C.2006) (Lamberth, J.); *Prevatt v. Islamic Republic of Iran*, 421 F.Supp.2d 152 (D.D.C. Mar.27, 2006) (Lamberth, J.); *Dammarell v. Islamic Republic of Iran*, 404 F.Supp.2d 261 (D.D.C.2005) (Bates, J.); *Salazar v. Islamic Republic of Iran*, 370 F.Supp.2d 105 (D.D.C.2005) (Bates, J.); *Peterson v. Islamic Republic of Iran*, 264 F.Supp.2d 46 (D.D.C.2003) (Lamberth, J.).

Here, plaintiffs have conclusively demonstrated that the servicemen who died at the Khobar Towers satisfy the two-prong test under *Peterson*. Colonel Douglas Cochran testified on December 2, 2003, that the service members who died at the Khobar Towers were deployed as a part of a peacekeeping mission sanctioned by United Nations Resolutions. (Dec. 12, 2003 Tr. at 12.) He also stated that the decedents were operating under standing rules of engage-

ment, [FN11] under which the decedents did not have the right to participate directly in hostilities. *Id.* at 10-12, 15. The decedents were not allowed to attack unless attacked or in peril of immediate attack resulting in death or serious bodily harm. *Id.* at 15. Moreover, as noted by the Reports of Casualty and personnel records for each of the decedents in this case, the cause of the service members' deaths was indisputably the result of a terrorist bombing, and not a result of combat hostilities. (Dec. 1, 2003 Tr. at 29; *see also* Dec. 2, 2003 Tr. at 35-38.) In light of the above-mentioned evidence, this Court finds that plaintiffs have satisfied the two-prong test under *Peterson*. Therefore, this Court finds that plaintiffs are not excluded from recovering under the state-sponsored terrorism exception to the FSIA.

FN11. According to Col. Cochran, the term "standing rules of engagement" is synonymous with the term "peacetime rules of engagement." (Dec. 2, 2003 Tr. at 15.)

C. Apparent Conflict of Interest

Next, in her discussion of the procedural history of the case, the magistrate judge discussed an apparent conflict of interest resulting from plaintiffs' representation in this matter by DLA Piper Rudnick Gray Cary U.S. LLP (the "Firm"), and the Firm's representation of the Government of Sudan ("Sudan"), the defendant in the separate matter of *Owens v. Republic of Sudan* (Civ. Action No. 01-2244(JDB)). [FN12] The magistrate judge was concerned that the Firm's representation in the *Owens* matter created a conflict of interest because defendants Iran, IRGC, and MOIS were co-defendants with Sudan in *Owens*, and because the Firm's representation of Sudan would cause the Firm to make an argument in *Owens* that was directly contrary to the arguments it made on behalf of plaintiffs in this matter. Plaintiffs raise an objection and allege that no conflict of interest (apparent or otherwise) exists in this matter.

FN12. The magistrate judge had the parties brief the issue of whether a conflict of interest existed.

Under District of Columbia Rules of Professional Conduct 1.7, unless a lawyer obtains informed consent from both clients, a lawyer shall not represent one client in a matter if the position taken by that client is adverse to the position taken by another client. D.C. Rule of Prof. Conduct 1.7. As the District of Columbia Bar Legal Ethics Committee has noted, "the lawyer may not, without informed consent of all parties, accept simultaneous representation of both clients where such representation creates a substantial risk that representation of one client will adversely effect the representation of the other." District of Columbia Bar Legal Ethics Committee Formal Op. 265 (1996).

Upon a review of the pleadings and evidence in this matter, the Court finds that no conflict of interest exists. First, the Firm's prior representation in another matter of a codefendant to the defendants in this matter does not create a conflict of interest. Though the defendants in this matter were co-defendants along with Sudan in the *Owens* matter, the Firm has stated that it never represented Iran, MOIS, or IRGC in the *Owens* matter or any other matter. (Pl.'s Resp. to Apr. 16, 2004 Court Order 1.) Moreover, the Firm has withdrawn completely from representing Sudan in *Owens* as Rule 1.7 states it must in such situations.

Next, the Court is satisfied that no apparent conflict exists that would preclude the Firm from continuing to represent plaintiffs' interests in this matter. As the Firm's pleadings to the magistrate judge plainly show, upon discovering that an apparent conflict had arisen, the Firm took immediate steps to eliminate it. The Co-Chair of the Firm's Professional Responsibility function instructed the partners representing the Government of Sudan that they were not to continue to represent Sudan in light of the fact that such representation would force the Firm to argue conflicting positions in both matters. Unbeknownst to the heads of the Firm, however, the specific attorneys responsible for representing Sudan disregarded the partners' instruction, and continued to represent Sudan, entering filings on their behalf. Still, when the Firm's management discovered the actions of events, it promptly sought withdrawal as counsel for Sudan in the *Owens* matter, notified the D.C. Bar Counsel and this Court's Committee on Grievances of the sequence of events, and wrote off fees and expenses otherwise due from Sudan as a former client. In addition, the attorneys who disregarded the Firm's instructions to cease representation have left the Firm. [FN13]

FN13. Of additional import is the fact that the former attorneys at the Firm who represented Sudan-and who thereby placed the Firm in the position of a potential conflict of interest-did not take part in the Firm's work related to the present matter before the Court.

Finally, this Court is persuaded that no conflict of interest exists by considering the manner in which the magistrate judge ultimately dealt with the issue. After the Firm issued its responses on the conflict issue to Magistrate Judge Robinson's Orders dated April 13 and April 16, 2004, [FN14] the magistrate judge proceeded forth with the remaining portions of the trial, and never issued a ruling on whether a conflict existed as a result of the Firm's representation of plaintiffs in this matter, and their representation of Sudan in

Owens. Moreover, in her report and recommendation to this Court, the magistrate judge included the "apparent conflict of interest" issue solely within her discussion of the case's procedural history. She neither issued nor recommended within her report and recommendation any finding that a conflict existed. Surely, were the magistrate judge of the opinion that a conflict of interest did exist, she would have taken more substantive steps to ensure that such a representation would not continue.

FN14. *See* Docket Nos. [77] and [79], respectively (ordering plaintiffs to file memoranda addressing the conflict of interest issue).

In light of these facts, the Court finds that no conflict of interest exists arising from the Firm's representation of plaintiffs in this matter and Sudan in the *Owens* case.

D. Sufficiency of Liability Evidence Provided by Plaintiffs
Magistrate Judge Robinson recommended that plaintiffs' motion for default judgment be denied on the grounds that she found plaintiffs had not submitted evidence satisfactory to the Court of defendants' liability. She found Director Freeh and Mr. Watson's respective testimony to be unsatisfactory on the grounds that each witness' testimony was largely conclusory, and that each was testifying in his personal capacity and not as a representative of the FBI. She also found that the testimony given by Doctor Clawson was conclusory as to defendants' liability, and failed to provide evidence of the link between Saudi Hezbollah, Hezbollah, and Iran.

Plaintiffs objected to these findings on three grounds. They argued that the evidence submitted is legally sufficient to sustain a finding of liability against defendants. They also argue that the evidence presented is consistent with, nearly identical to and-in some instances-more direct than liability evidence found by this Court to be sufficient as a matter of law in prior cases arising under the state-sponsor of terrorism exception to the FSIA. Finally, plaintiffs argue that the Court may take judicial notice of the facts and findings in *Blais v. Islamic Republic of Iran* 2006 WL 2827372 (D.D.C. Sept.29, 2006) (Lamberth, J.), a case arising out of the same attack on the Khobar Towers. They argue that the facts from *Blais*, combined with the evidence submitted by plaintiffs in this matter, support a finding that defendants are liable in this matter.

1. Testimony of Director Louis J. Freeh and Dale L. Watson
To establish the defendant's liability for the bombing, plaintiffs offered the testimony of Louis J. Freeh, a former Director at the FBI, and Dale L. Watson, an agent and investigator

at the FBI and CIA with over 20 years experience in the counterterrorism and counterintelligence fields. Over the course of the approximately four year investigation into the Khobar Towers bombing, both Freeh and Watson "reviewed all reports prepared by the FBI investigators, and spoke directly with FBI agents and Saudi officials" all of which established a link between the defendants and the bombing. All of the information conveyed to both Freeh and Watson was communicated by FBI agents who were on the scene.

Based on this knowledge of the investigation, Mr. Freeh testified at the evidentiary hearing before the magistrate judge as to the defendants' involvement in the Khobar Towers attack. [FN15] In his testimony, Director Freeh testified that, during the course of the investigation into the explosion, it was concluded that the Khobar Towers explosion was the cause of a fertilizer-based explosive device. (Dec. 18, 2003 Tr. at 10.) It was also concluded, Director Freeh testified, that the bombing was an act of terrorism. *Id.*

FN15. Mr. Freeh's testimony mirrors the testimony he provided at a Joint Hearing before the United States House of Representatives Permanent Select Committee on Intelligence and the United States Senate Select Committee on Intelligence, in which he testified under oath as to the defendants' involvement in sanctioning, funding and directing the Khobar Towers attack. A transcript of this testimony was admitted into evidence as Plaintiffs' Exhibit 24. *See also* Pl.'s Exh. 25 (May 20, 2003, *Wall Street Journal* article written by Mr. Freeh in which Mr. Freeh indicated that the FBI's investigation indicated Iran, IRGC, and MOIS's involvement in funding and coordinating the attack on the Khobar Towers).

According to Director Freeh, the FBI also obtained a great deal of information linking the defendants to the bombing from interviews with six individuals arrested by the Saudis shortly after the bombing. *Id.* at 11-30. These six individuals, who were members of the Saudi Hezbollah organization, admitted to the FBI their complicity in the attack on the Khobar Towers. Exh. 7 at 11, 13-14, 27. The six individuals admitted that senior officials in the Iranian government provided them with funding, planning, training, sponsorship, and travel necessary to carry out the attack on the Khobar Towers. (*Id.* at 13-14; *see also* Dec. 18, 2003 Tr. at 24-30.) The six individuals also indicated that the selection of the target and the authorization to proceed was done collectively by Iran, MOIS, and IRGC, though the actual preparation and carrying out of the attack was done by the IRGC. (Dec. 18, 2003 Tr. at 25.)

More specifically, Mr. Freeh testified, the FBI obtained specific information from the six about how each was recruited and trained by the Iranian government *in Iran* and Lebanon, and how weapons were smuggled into Saudi Arabia from Iran through Syria and Jordan. One individual described in detail a meeting about the attack at which senior Iranian officials, including members of the MOIS and IRGC, were present. (Dec. 18, 2003 Tr. at 23.) Several stated that IRGC directed, assisted, and oversaw the surveillance of the Khobar Towers site, and that these surveillance reports were sent to IRGC officials for their review. Another told the FBI that IRGC gave the six individuals a large amount of money for the specific purpose of planning and executing the Khobar Towers bombing.

Adding credence to Mr. Freeh's testimony is the reliability of the information he relied on in linking the defendants with the attack. First, Director Freeh testified that the information obtained from the six individuals was communicated to the FBI on more than one occasion. Second, there was a great deal of cross-corroboration among the individuals' stories, even when each was interviewed by the FBI separately. Third, he testified that the material portions of each of the individuals' accounts of the bombing did not contradict. Fourth, and perhaps most importantly, in many instances the FBI was able to corroborate independently the statements made by the six individuals.

As a result of this information and his direct participation in the four year investigation into the bombing, Director Freeh testified that it was his ultimate opinion that the bombing was the result of a terrorist attack by Saudi Hezbollah, organized and sponsored by the defendants in this case: Iran, MOIS, and IRGC.

Mr. Watson, who was also an active member in the investigation into the Khobar Towers bombing, testified similarly to Director Freeh. According to Mr. Watson, the bases for his opinion were the direct conversations with the six Saudi Hezbollah members, the corroborating facts discovered from their confessions, his historical knowledge and public record of the Hezbollah organization and statements proffered in an indictment filed in the Eastern District of Virginia. (Dec. 18, 2003 Tr. at 52, 63.) All of this information was information Mr. Watson gleaned as a result either of his own personal research or his involvement in the Khobar Towers bombing investigation. Most importantly, Mr. Watson reached the same conclusion as Director Freeh that the bombing was the result of a terrorist attack by Saudi Hezbollah members, organized and sponsored by the defendants.

2. Dr. Clawson's Expert Testimony as to Involvement by Iran, IRGC, and MOIS

Plaintiffs also relied upon the testimony of Dr. Patrick Clawson to establish a more complete picture as to the involvement of Iran, MOIS, and IRGC in helping carry out the attack on the Khobar Towers. At trial, Dr. Clawson testified as an expert in three areas: (1) the government of Iran; (2) Iran's sponsorship of terrorism; and (3) the Iranian economy. Dr. Clawson's expert opinion regarding the perpetrators of the Khobar Towers bombing is based on his involvement on a Commission investigating the bombing, his top-secret security clearance, his discussions with Saudi officials, as well as his academic research on the subject. Exh. 9 at 62-63.

Dr. Clawson testified that the government of Iran formed the Saudi Hezbollah organization. *Id.* at 56. He testified that the IRGC was responsible for providing military training to Hezbollah terrorists as to how to carry out a terrorist attack. *Id.* at 28. He also testified as to the defendants' state-sponsorship of terrorism, noting that at the time of the Khobar Towers bombing, Iran spent an estimated amount of between $50 million and $150 million on terrorist activities. Exh. 10 at 46. In light of all these facts, Dr. Clawson stated conclusively his opinion that the government of Iran, MOIS, and IRGC were responsible for the Khobar Towers bombing, and that Saudi Hezbollah carried out the attack under their direction. Exh. 9 at 67-68.

3. Judicial Notice of Findings and Conclusions in Blais v. Islamic Republic of Iran [FN16]

FN16. *Blais v. Islamic Republic of Iran*, 2006 WL 2827372 (D.D.C. Sept.29, 2006) (Lamberth, J.).

Plaintiffs argue that the Court should take judicial notice of the facts and conclusions made by this Court in its recent consideration of the matter of *Blais v. Islamic Republic of Iran*, an action brought against the same defendants for damages resulting from the same 1996 attack on the Khobar Towers. As has recently been noted in a FSIA case within this Circuit, "[a] court may take judicial notice of related proceedings and records in cases before the same court." *Salazar v. Islamic Republic of Iran*, 370 F.Supp.2d 105, 109 n. 6 (D.D.C.2005) (Bates, J.). As Judge Bates noted in *Salazar*, under Federal Rules of Evidence 201(e), a "party opposing judicial notice of a given fact must be afforded an opportunity to be heard...and may certainly make recognized objections to the admissibility of such judicially noticed facts as evidence in the case..." *Id.* (internal citations omitted). Defendants in this case have failed to make such objections, or even make an appearance at all before this Court. Accordingly, in addition to the unopposed trial

submissions made by plaintiffs in this matter, this Court will take judicial notice of the findings made in *Blais* as to the defendants involvement in and liability for the Khobar Towers bombing.

In *Blais*, this Court found as fact that the Khobar Towers attack was carried out by individuals who referred to themselves as the group "Saudi Hezbollah." *Blais*, 459 F.Supp.2d at 47-48. The Court found that these individuals were recruited by Brigadier General Ahmed Sharifi, a senior official of the IRGC. *Id.* Brigadier General Sharifi planned the operation, and recruited the individual members of Saudi Hezbollah at the Iranian Embassy in Damascus, Syria. *Id.* He was also responsible for providing the funds, passports, and paperwork for the individuals who carried out the attack. *Id.* In addition to acknowledging General Sharifi's involvement in the attack, this Court found that the attack was approved by the Ayatollah Khameini, Iran's Supreme Leader at the time, and was approved and supported by Ali Fallahian, the head of MOIS at the time. *Id.* [FN17]

FN17. This Court also found that Mr. Fallahian's representative in Damascus, Syria, a man by the name of Nurani, provided additional direct support for the operation. *Id.*

This Court heard testimony from and accepted documentary evidence considered by Dr. Bruce Tefft. [FN18] Dr. Tefft expressed his opinion "that defendants the Islamic Republic of Iran and the Iranian Revolutionary Guards Corp were responsible for planning and supporting the attack on the Khobar Towers, including providing operational and financial support." *Blais*, 459 F.Supp.2d at 48-49. Dr. Tefft's testimony and the evidence accompanying his testimony are consistent with the testimony and evidence from *Blais*, including testimony made by Mr. Freeh. In fact, Dr. Tefft not only relied upon the conclusions put forth by Messrs. Freeh and Watson in forming his own opinion in this matter, but Dr. Tefft stated that he agreed with their conclusions regarding the connection between Iran and Saudi Hezbollah in bringing about the bombing on the Khobar Towers. When asked as to the defendants' involvement in the attack, Dr. Tefft stated that there was " 'no question about it. It wouldn't have happened without Iranian support.' " *Id.*

FN18. As noted in Finding of Fact # 23 in the *Blais* opinion:

Dr. Bruce Tefft was one of the founding members of the CIA's counterterrorism bureau in 1985. He served in the CIA until 1995, and has continued to work as a consultant on terrorism since that time, including work as an unofficial adviser to the New York Police Department's counterterrorism and intelligence divisions. *Id.* He retains a top-secret security clearance in connection with his work. *Id.* He has been qualified as an expert witness in numerous other cases involving Iranian sponsorship of terrorism. Ex. 1 at 3. He was qualified as an expert witness on terrorism in this case. *Blais*, 459 F.Supp.2d at 48-49.

Finally, this Court considered written testimony from both former FBI Director Louis Freeh and former Deputy Counterterrorism Chief Dale Watson. In his written statement, Director Freeh stated that, based upon his involvement in the FBI's five year investigation into the attack on the Khobar Towers, Iran was responsible for supporting and funding the attack. *Id.* Mr. Watson likewise stated unequivocally that, based upon information uncovered in the investigation into the attack, [FN19] there was Iranian, MOIS, and IRGC involvement in the bombing. *Id.* As here, the Court found the conclusions of Messrs. Freeh and Watson in *Blais* to be amply reliable and probative as to the question of the defendants' involvement in the Khobar Towers bombing.

FN19. An investigation for which Watson was responsible for day-to-day oversight. *Id.*

4. Conclusion

Upon *de novo* review of the evidence, the Court is convinced that the evidence is sufficiently satisfactory to establish liability. First, contrary to the magistrate judge's recommendation, the testimony by Freeh and Watson is not conclusory because the asserted statements made by Freeh and Watson do not lack supporting evidence. Director Freeh and Mr. Watson based their testimony upon their four year direct involvement in the investigation into the bombing, and their extensive years of experience in the counterintelligence and counterterrorism fields. Throughout this time, Messrs. Freeh and Watson, and the FBI agents they directly supervised, uncovered and synthesized a great deal of information about the attack on Khobar Towers and its perpetrators. The facts unearthed by this investigation led them to the six captured participants in the bombing, each of whom implicated the defendants as having organized, funded, and supported the attack. Accordingly, the Court finds that the facts testified to by Freeh and Watson were supported by more than a sufficient basis for the witnesses' conclusions that Iran, MOIS, and IRGC were responsible for the Khobar Towers bombing carried out by Saudi Hezbollah.

The Court also fails to see the rationale behind Magistrate Judge Robinson's conclusion that the testimony offered by Freeh and Watson was somehow less credible because it was made in their individual capacities, and not on behalf of the FBI for whom they were no longer employed. The

reliability of a witness' testimony should not and indeed does not hinge solely upon that person's employment with a particular organization. Rather, the reliability and credibility of a witness' testimony is determined by considering a myriad of factors including, *inter alia*, the witness' demeanor, the ability of the witness to observe the information about which he is testifying, whether the testimony is corroborated by other facts introduced into evidence, as well as the witness' prior experience.

Applying these factors to the testimony of Messrs. Freeh and Watson, this Court finds their testimony to be undeniably credible and reliable. Each was directly involved in the investigation into the Khobar Towers bombing, and was personally familiar with the results from that investigation. This is bolstered by the fact that Freeh and Watson occupied leadership positions in overseeing the entirety of the investigation into the bombing. Such positions would undoubtedly place Freeh and Watson in the best possible position to assess *all* the information about the attack and make a logical conclusion as to the cause and perpetrators of the attack. In addition, their testimony was consistent with each other, with the testimony by Dr. Clawson, and with information available in the public record. Moreover, this Court has previously relied upon Freeh and Watson's conclusions as to the involvement of Iran, IRGC, and MOIS in the Khobar Towers attack, and sees no reason to discount the credence of their testimony as conclusive on the grounds that they are not currently employed by the FBI. See *Blais v. Islamic Republic of Iran*, 459 F.Supp.2d 40, 47-49 (D.D.C.2006) (Lamberth, J.) (finding as fact both Mr. Freeh and Mr. Watson's conclusion as to the involvement of Iran, IRGC, and MOIS in the Khobar Towers bombing).

The fact that neither testified about the attack as agents of the FBI does not nullify the credibility of their statements. Messrs. Freeh and Watson's intricate involvement with the investigation into the Khobar Towers bombing while they were with the FBI provides more than an adequate basis for their testimony and the conclusions each drew therein as to the perpetrators of the attack.

The Court also disagrees with the magistrate judge's recommendation that Dr. Clawson's testimony, whether evaluated alone or in conjunction with the testimony by Freeh and Watson, was unsatisfactory to establish liability. To the contrary-Dr. Clawson is a renowned scholar of Middle Eastern politics, who has studied and written about Iran for years. In over 20 cases, Dr. Clawson has repeatedly provided this Court with reliable and credible testimony regarding the involvement of Iran, MOIS, and IRGC in sponsoring and organizing acts of terrorism carried out against citizens of the United States. [FN20] The Court sees no reason to deviate from the judges in prior cases who found Dr. Clawson's testimony to be satisfactorily reliable.

FN20. See, e.g., *Greenbaum v. Islamic Republic of Iran*, 2006 WL 2374241 (D.D.C. Aug.10, 2006) (Lamberth, J.); *Prevatt v. Islamic Republic of Iran*, 421 F.Supp.2d 152 (D.D.C. Mar.27, 2006) (Lamberth, J.); *Haim v. Islamic Republic of Iran*, 425 F.Supp.2d 56 (D.D.C. Mar.24, 2006) (Lamberth, J.); *Stern v. Islamic Republic of Iran*, 271 F.Supp.2d 286 (D.D.C.2003) (Lamberth, J.); *Weinstein v. Islamic Republic of Iran*, 184 F.Supp.2d 13 (D.D.C.2002) (Lamberth, J.).

Accordingly, having considered the evidence and testimony admitted at trial in the present case, this Court finds that plaintiffs have met their burden under the state-sponsored terrorism exception of the FSIA by establishing their right to relief "by evidence that is satisfactory to the Court[.]" The totality of the evidence at trial, combined with the findings and conclusions entered by this Court in *Blais*, firmly establishes that "the Khobar Towers bombing was planned, funded, and sponsored by senior leadership in the government of the Islamic Republic of Iran; the IRGC had the responsibility and worked with Saudi Hizbollah to execute the plan, and the MOIS participated in the planning and funding of the attack." Proposed Findings and Conclusions at 9, ¶ 28.

V. Liability

A. Proper Causes of Action Under the FSIA

Once a foreign state's immunity has been lifted under Section 1605 and jurisdiction is found to be proper, Section 1606 provides that "the foreign state shall be liable in the same manner and to the same extent as a private individual under like circumstances." 28 U.S.C. §1606. Section 1606 acts as a "pass-through" to substantive causes of action against private individuals that may exist in federal, state or international law. *Dammarell v. Islamic Republic of Iran*, Civ. A. No. 01-2224, 2005 WL 756090, at *8-10, 2005 U.S. Dist. LEXIS 5343, at *27-32 (D.D.C. Mar. 29, 2005) (Bates, J.) [hereinafter *Dammarell II*].

In this case, state law provides a basis for liability. First, the law of the United States applies rather than the law of the place of the tort or any other foreign law because the United States has a "unique interest" in having its domestic law apply in cases involving terrorist attacks on United States citizens. See *Dammarell II*, 2005 WL 756090, at *20, 2005 U.S. Dist. LEXIS 5343, at *63.

B. Applicable State Law Governing Causes of Action

Having established that the laws of the United States apply in this action, the Court must determine the applicable state law to govern the action. As the forum state, District of Columbia choice of law rules apply to determine which state's law shall apply. Under District of Columbia choice of law rules, courts employ a modified government interest analysis under which they "evaluate the governmental policies underlying the applicable laws and determine which jurisdiction's policy would be most advanced by having its law applied to the facts of the case under review." *Hercules & Co. v. Shama Rest. Corp.*, 566 A.2d 31, 41 (D.C.1989) (citations and internal quotations omitted). Generally, application of this governmental interest test points to the law of *each* plaintiff's domicile at the time of the attack as having the greatest interest in providing redress to its citizens. See *Dammarell II*, 2005 WL 756090, at *20-21, 2005 U.S. Dist. LEXIS 5343, at *66-67 (citing RESTATEMENT (THIRD) FOREIGN RELATIONS LAW §402(3) (1987)).

Plaintiffs' claims involve consideration of the law of thirteen different states. The estates and surviving family members of persons killed in the bombing have asserted wrongful death claims and intentional infliction of emotional distress claims. In order to avoid repetition, the discussion will be organized by state, with an initial overview of each state's law followed by a discussion of each plaintiff's asserted claims under those laws.

C. Vicarious Liability

The basis of defendants' liability is that they provided material support and resources to Saudi Hezbollah, which personally completed the attack. One may be liable for the acts of another under theories of vicarious liability, such as conspiracy, aiding and abetting and inducement. This Court finds that civil conspiracy provides a basis of liability for Iran, MOIS, and IRGC, and accordingly declines to reach the issue of whether they might also be liable on the basis of aiding and abetting and/or inducement.

The doctrine of civil conspiracy is recognized under the laws of each of the states each claimant has brought an action. [FN21] Though each state has its own particular means of describing civil conspiracy, upon inspection of each state's laws the elements of civil conspiracy are met in each state if it can be demonstrated that: (1) there is an agreement between two or more persons or entities; (2) to do an unlawful act, or an otherwise lawful act by unlawful means; (3) there was an overt act committed in furtherance of this unlawful agreement; and (4) damages were incurred by the plaintiff as a proximate result of the actions taken pursuant to the conspiracy. [FN22]

FN21. *Rusheen v. Cohen*, 37 Cal.4th 1048, 39 Cal.Rptr.3d 516, 128 P.3d 713, 722 (2006) ("The elements of an action for civil conspiracy are (1) formation and operation of the conspiracy and (2) damage resulting to plaintiff (3) from a wrongful act done in furtherance of the common design."); *Walters v. Blankenship*, 931 So.2d 137 (Fla.Dist.Ct.App. Apr.28, 2006) (finding that a civil conspiracy exists under Florida law where there is "(a) a conspiracy between two or more parties, (b) to do an unlawful act or to do a lawful act by unlawful means, (c) the doing of some overt act in pursuance of the conspiracy, and (d) damage to plaintiff as a result of the acts performed pursuant to the conspiracy"); *Sims v. Beamer*, 757 N.E.2d 1021 (Ind.Ct.App.2001) (" 'Civil conspiracy' consists of a combination of two or more persons, by concerted action, to accomplish an unlawful purpose or to accomplish some purpose, not in itself unlawful, by unlawful means."); *Sullivan v. Wallace*, 859 So.2d 245, 248 (La.App.2003) ("To recover under a civil conspiracy theory of liability, the plaintiff must prove that an agreement existed to commit an illegal or tortious act which resulted in plaintiff's injury."); *Harding v. Ohio Cas. Ins. Co. of Hamilton, Ohio*, 230 Minn. 327, 41 N.W.2d 818, 824 (Minn.1950) ("A conspiracy is a combination of persons to accomplish an unlawful purpose or a lawful purpose by unlawful means.") (quoting *Dairy Region Land Co. v. Paulson*, 160 Minn. 42, 199 N.W. 398 (1924)); *In re Appeal of Armaganian*, 147 N.H. 158, 784 A.2d 1185, 1189 (2001) ("[U]nder New Hampshire law, the elements of a civil conspiracy are: (1) two or more persons...; (2) an object to be accomplished (i.e., an unlawful object to be achieved by lawful or unlawful means or a lawful object to be achieved by unlawful means); (3) an agreement on the object or course of action; (4) one or more unlawful overt acts; and (5) damages as the proximate result thereof.") (quoting *Jay Edwards, Inc. v. Baker*, 130 N.H. 41, 534 A.2d 706, 709 (1987)); *Piccoli A/S v. Calvin Klein Jeanswear Co.*, 19 F.Supp.2d 157 (S.D.N.Y.1998) ("Elements of a civil conspiracy under New York law are (1) the corrupt agreement between two or more persons, (2) an overt act, (3) their intentional participation in the furtherance of a plan or purpose, and (4) the resulting damage."); *Boyd v. Drum*, 129 N.C.App. 586, 501 S.E.2d 91, 96 (1998) ("A civil conspiracy claim consists of: (1) an agreement between two or more persons; (2) to do an unlawful act or to do a lawful act in an unlawful way; (3) which agreement resulted in injury to the plaintiff."); *Matthews v. New Century Mortg. Corp.*, 185 F.Supp.2d 874 (S.D.Ohio 2002) ("Under Ohio law, the tort of civil conspiracy is a malicious combination of two or more persons to injure another in person or property, in a way not competent for one alone, resulting in actual damages."); *Jenkins v. Entergy Corp.*, 187 S.W.3d 785, 2006 WL 488580 (Tex.App.Corpus Christi 2006), reh'g overruled, (Apr. 7, 2006) ("Elements of a civil conspiracy claim include: (1) two or more persons; (2) an object to be accomplished; (3) a meeting of the minds on the object or course of action; (4) one or more unlawful, overt acts; and (5) damages as a proximate result."); *Onderdonk v. Lamb*, 79 Wis.2d 241, 255 N.W.2d 507, 510 (1977) ("To state a cause of action for civil conspiracy, the complaint must allege: (1) The formation and operation of the conspiracy; (2) the wrongful act or acts done pursuant thereto; and (3) the damage resulting from such act or acts.").

FN22. See *supra* note 21.

In this case, the elements of civil conspiracy between Iran, MOIS, the IRGC and Saudi Hezbollah have been satisfied. As this Court has previously held, "sponsorship of terrorist activities inherently involves a conspiracy to commit terrorist attacks." *Flatow*, 999 F.Supp. at 27. It is undisputed that Saudi Hezbollah committed the attack on the Khobar Towers. It has been established by evidence satisfactory to this Court that Saudi Hezbollah and defendants Iran, MOIS and the IRGC conspired to commit the terrorist attack on the Khobar Towers. [FN23] The evidence elicited from the FBI's investigation and interview of the six detained members of Saudi Hezbollah shows that senior Iranian, MOIS and IRGC officials participated in the planning of, and provided material support and resources to Saudi Hezbollah for the attack on the Khobar Towers. The evidence also shows that the defendants also provided money, training and travel documents to Saudi Hezbollah members in order to facilitate the attacks. Moreover, the sheer gravity and nature of the attack demonstrate the defendants' unlawful intent to inflict severe emotional distress upon the American servicemen as well as their close relatives. The defendants' acts of financing, training and providing travel documents ably satisfy the overt act requirement for civil conspiracy. Finally, as will be discussed below, the plaintiffs in this action incurred damages resulting from the deaths caused by the conspiracy. Accordingly, the elements of civil conspiracy are established between Saudi Hezbollah and the defendants Iran, MOIS and the IRGC.

FN23. This Court also found in *Blais* that "Saudi Hezbollah, Iran, MOIS and the IRGC reached an understanding to do an unlawful act, namely the murder and maiming of American servicemen."

D. Cause of Death

Thomas R. Parsons, M.D., an associate medical examiner, was received by the Court as an expert in the field of forensic pathology. (Feb. 9, 2004 A.M. Tr. at 82-83; Ex. 232.) On June 25, 1996, Dr. Parsons was on active duty as a major in the United States Air Force. He was a medical examiner with the Armed Forces Institute of Pathology ("AFIP"). Dr. Parsons first learned of the June 25, 1996 bombing at Khobar Towers in Dharan, Saudi Arabia on June 26, 1996. Dr. Parsons and three other medical examiners performed the autopsies of the 19 officers and airman killed in the Khobar Towers bombing at Dover AFB on June 27 and 28, 1996. *Id.* at 83-84.

Based on his performance of several of the autopsies in June of 1996, his review of the complete autopsy files and photographs from the AFIP, and his training and experience as a forensic pathologist, Dr. Parsons testified that the cause of death of each of the 17 decedents represented in the present litigation "was the explosion that occurred near their barracks [in Dharan, Saudi Arabia]." *Id.* at 105-106. This conclusion, Dr. Parsons noted, was corroborated by the types of severe blast injuries sustained by each of the deceased plaintiffs. Dr. Parsons testified that the injuries of these 17 decedents were "very severe. As a matter of fact. This is about as bad as you can get until you get to body fragmentation." *Id.* at 110.

Based on his performance of several of the autopsies in June of 1996, his review of the complete autopsy files and photographs from the AFIP, and his training and experience as a forensic pathologist, Dr. Parsons testified as to his opinion to a reasonable degree of certainty that 16 of the 17 individuals were rendered immediately unconscious and died immediately or shortly after the explosion. *Id.* at 110-111. According to Dr. Parsons, Airman Christopher Lester, the single plaintiff who did not die immediately after the explosion, died after a significant post-injury survival period. *Id.* at 111.

E. Damages

Before assessing the merits of the individual claims, this Court must briefly discuss damages in actions against foreign states arising under the FSIA. To obtain damages against defendants under the FSIA, the plaintiffs must prove that the consequences of the defendants' conduct were " 'reasonably certain' (i.e., more likely than not) to occur, and must prove the amount of damages by a 'reasonable estimate' consistent with this [Circuit's] application of the American rule on damages." *Salazar*, 370 F.Supp.2d at 115-16 (quoting *Hill v. Republic of Iraq*, 328 F.3d 680, 681 (D.C.Cir.2003)) (internal quotations omitted).

1. Compensatory Damages

As a result of the wrongful conduct of defendants Iran, MOIS, and the IRGC, plaintiffs have suffered and will continue to suffer pain and mental anguish. Under the FSIA, if a foreign state may be held liable, it "shall be liable in the same manner and to the same extent as a private individual under like circumstances." 28 U.S.C. §1606. Accordingly, plaintiffs are entitled to the typical bases of damages that may be awarded against tortfeasors under the laws under which each claim is brought.

In determining the appropriate amount of compensatory damages, the Court may look to prior decisions awarding damages for pain and suffering, and to those awarding damages for solatium. *Prevatt*, 421 F.Supp.2d at 160. "While intervening changes in law have ruled many cases' reliance on federal common law improper, such findings need not disturb the accuracy of the analogy between solatium and intentional infliction of emotional distress." *Haim*, 425 F.Supp.2d at 71.

In determining the amount of compensatory damages awards to family members of a surviving victim, this Court has held that these awards are determined by the "nature of the relationship" between the family member and victim, and "the severity of the pain suffered by the family member." *Haim*, 425 F.Supp.2d at 75. Spouses typically receive greater damage awards than parents, who, in turn, receive greater awards than siblings. Compare, e.g., *Anderson v. Islamic Republic of Iran*, 90 F.Supp.2d 107, 113 (D.D.C.2000) (Jackson, J.) (awarding $10 million to the wife of a hostage and torture victim); *Cicippio*, 18 F.Supp.2d at 70 (same), with *Eisenfeld*, 172 F.Supp.2d at 8 (awarding $5 million each to the parents and $2.5 million each to the siblings of victims of a suicide bombing on a passenger bus); see also *Flatow*, 999 F.Supp. at 31 (awarding parents each $5 million and siblings each $2.5 million of victim who was killed in the same passenger bus bombing in which Seth was injured). Moreover, "families of victims who have died are typically awarded greater damages than families of victims who remain alive." *Id.* While the loss suffered by the plaintiffs in these cases is undeniably difficult to quantify, courts typically award between $8 million and $12 million for pain and suffering resulting from the death of a spouse [FN24] approximately $5 million to a parent whose child was killed [FN25] and approximately $2.5 million to a plaintiff whose sibling was killed. [FN26]

FN24. See, e.g., *Anderson v. Islamic Republic of Iran*, 90 F.Supp.2d 107, 113 (D.D.C.2000) (Jackson, J.) (awarding $10 million to the wife of a hostage and torture victim); *Weinstein* (granting $8 million to the widow of a bus bombing victim); *Kerr v. Islamic Republic of Iran*, 245 F.Supp.2d 59, 64 (D.D.C.2003) (awarding $10 million to the widow of a murder victim); *Salazar*, 370 F.Supp.2d at 116 (awarding $10 million to the widow of a bombing victim). As this Court noted in *Greenbaum*, however, "larger awards are typically reserved for cases with aggravating circumstances that appreciably worsen the surviving spouse's pain and suffering, such as cases involving torture or kidnaping of a spouse, or in which the victim survives with severe physical and emotional conditions that continue to cause severe suffering by the spouse." *Greenbaum v. Islamic Republic of Iran*, 451 F.Supp.2d 90, 108 (D.D.C. August 10, 2006) (Lamberth, J.) (citing *Cicippio*, 18 F.Supp.2d at 70; *Acree*, 271 F.Supp.2d at 222.)

FN25. *Eisenfeld*, 172 F.Supp.2d at 8.

FN26. *Prevatt v. Islamic Republic of Iran*, 421 F.Supp.2d 152, 161 (D.D.C.2006) (Lamberth, J.).

2. Pain and Suffering Damages

Dr. Dana Cable testified as an expert for the plaintiffs concerning the grief process and the factors which cause it to be more extensive and intensive. (Feb. 10, 2004 Tr. at 9-28; Ex. 267.) Dr. Cable testified concerning the impact of each decedent's death on his particular family. (Feb. 10, 2004 Tr. at 28-214.) Dr. Cable is a licensed psychologist, a certified death educator, and a certified grief therapist. (*Id.* at 5; Ex. 267.)

Dr. Cable described the grief process and the seven stages of grief: (1) shock; (2) disorganization; (3) volatile emotions; (4) guilt; (5) loss & loneliness (usually lasting 1-2 years); (6) relief (can go on with life, but experience some guilt for going on); and (7) reestablishment. (Feb. 10, 2004 Tr. at 9-11.) Dr. Cable stated that each of the surviving family members were still in the "loss and loneliness" stage of the grief process. *Id.* at 11. Dr. Cable described this stage of the grief process as "the most intense part of the grief process." *Id.* at 10.

Though a person who loses someone to death is only in the "loss and loneliness" stage for a year or two, Dr. Cable explained that a number of issues present in this case complicate the grieving process and cause the "loss and loneliness" stage to last much longer for family members of terrorism victims. *Id.* at 11-12; 19-23. According to Dr. Cable, the grief process is made worse for the family members because none of them were present at the time the terrorist act took place at Khobar Towers. *Id.* at 26.

The Court's review of the testimony and the demeanor of the plaintiffs, as well as the testimony accepted via affi-davit, leads the Court to agree with Dr. Cable's opinion that all of the plaintiffs are still in the "loss and loneliness" stage of the grief process, even seven and one-half years after the death of their loved ones.

3. Punitive Damages

In addition to seeking compensatory damages against the defendants, plaintiffs have also sought punitive damages against the defendants. Punitive damages, however, are not available against foreign states. 28 U.S.C. §1606; *Blais*, 459 F.Supp.2d at 60-61. Accordingly, plaintiffs' claim for punitive damages against defendant Islamic Republic of Iran cannot be maintained, and is denied.

Moreover, "punitive damages are not recognized against divisions of a foreign state that are considered to be the state itself, instead of an agent or instrumentality thereof."[FN27] In order to determine whether the entity is sufficiently linked to the foreign state for punitive damages purposes, the court must assess the core functions of the entity. See *Roeder*, 333 F.3d at 234. Entities that are governmental are considered a part of the foreign state itself, while commercial entities are deemed agencies or instrumentalities of the foreign state, and thereby subject to punitive damages. *Id.* Plaintiff has an affirmative burden of producing evidence that the entity is commercial. *Blais*, 459 F.Supp.2d at 60-61.

FN27. *Prevatt*, 421 F.Supp.2d at 161(citing *Roeder v. Islamic Republic of Iran*, 333 F.3d 228, 234 (D.C.Cir.2003)). Here, there is inadequate evidence for this Court to determine that either MOIS or IRGC is sufficiently commercial as to justify the imposition of punitive damages against them. Therefore, this Court lacks authority to grant plaintiffs' request for punitive damages against MOIS and IRGC because both MOIS and IRGC are governmental entities, and parts of the state of Iran itself. Accordingly, plaintiffs' claim for punitive damages as to the remaining two defendants is denied.

VI. Specific Findings and Conclusions, By State

Plaintiffs' claims in this action involve the consideration of the laws of eleven different states. The estates and family members of the seventeen servicemen killed in the attack on the Khobar Towers have asserted wrongful death claims and intentional infliction of emotional distress claims. The following discussion is organized by state, first providing an overview of the causes of action under that state's law, and then discussing each plaintiff's individual claims as applied under those laws.

A. Florida

1. Causes of Action

a. Wrongful Death

Under Florida law, a right of action exists for wrongful death in favor of the personal representative of the decedent's estate for the benefit of certain designated beneficiaries. Fla. Stat. Ann. §§768.16-768.25 (2005). Under the Florida Wrongful Death Act,

When the death of a person is caused by the wrongful act...of any person [or entity]...and the event would have entitled the person injured to maintain an action and recover damages if death had not ensued, the person [or entity]...that would have been liable in damages if death had not ensued shall be liable for damages as specified in this act notwithstanding the death of the person injured, although death was caused under circumstances constituting a felony. [FN28]

FN28. Fla. Stat. Ann. §§768.19 (2005).

Moreover, the Florida Wrongful Death Act allows the decedent's personal representative to bring an action for the benefit of the decedent's estate *and* the decedent's "survivors." Fla. Stat. Ann. §768.20-768.21. Under the Act, "survivors" who may be entitled to recovery include the decedent's: (1) spouse, (2) children, (3) parents, and (4) blood relatives, provided these blood relatives can demonstrate they are partly or wholly dependent on the decedent for support. Fla. Stat. Ann. §768.18. [FN29]

FN29. Accordingly, siblings of a decedent are not considered "survivors" unless evidence is presented demonstrating that sibling's dependence upon the decedent. Fla. Stat. Ann. §768.18. As the Florida Supreme Court has held, a plaintiff's dependency upon the decedent must be proven irrespective of any relationship or legal right to support. *Benoit v. Miami Beach Electric Co.*, 85 Fla. 396, 96 So. 158, 159 (1923). Moreover, in cases where adults-siblings or otherwise-claim dependency upon the deceased, the plaintiff must show "an actual inability to support themselves and an actual dependence upon some one for support, coupled with a reasonable expectation of support, or with some reasonable claim for support from the deceased." *Id.*

If the decedent has a surviving spouse or lineal descendants or the decedent is an adult with a surviving parent but no dependents, then the decedent's personal representative may recover the present value of the "loss of the prospective net accumulations" of the decedent that might reasonably have been expected but for the wrongful death. Fla. Stat. Ann. §768.21(6). [FN30] A personal representative may re-

cover on behalf of minor children the value of lost support and services, the loss of parental companionship, instruction and guidance, and for mental pain and suffering from the date of injury. Fla. Stat. Ann. §§768.21(1), (3). A decedent's surviving spouse and children may recover for mental pain and suffering from the date of the injury. Fla. Stat. Ann. 768.21(2), (3). [FN31] A decedent's surviving parents may also recover for mental pain and suffering if the decedent is under 25 years old. Fla. Stat. Ann. §768.21(4). If the decedent is 25 years old or older, then the decedent's surviving parents may only recover for mental pain and suffering if there are no other survivors. Fla Stat. Ann. §768.21(4).

FN30. The Act defines "net accumulations" as the portion of the decedent's expected net business or salary income that the decedent would have retained if the decedent had lived her or his normal life expectancy. Fla. Stat. Ann. §786.18(5). "Net business or salary income" means the part of decedent's probable gross income after taxes and after the decedent's costs of maintenance. *Id.*

FN31. Each parent of an adult child may recover for mental pain and suffering if there are no other survivors. *Id.*

b. Intentional Infliction of Emotional Distress

Florida courts have adopted Section 46 of the RESTATEMENT (SECOND) OF TORTS (1965) as the definition of the tort of intentional infliction of emotional distress. *Metropolitan Life Ins. Co. v. McCarson*, 467 So.2d 277, 278-79 (Fla.1985). Specifically, under Florida law, a defendant is liable for intentional infliction of emotional distress if the defendant's "extreme and outrageous conduct intentionally or recklessly causes severe emotional distress to another..." *Id.* (quoting RESTATEMENT (SECOND) OF TORTS §46(1) (1965)).

In evaluating the degree of severity of the defendant's conduct, Florida courts have held that liability for intentional infliction of emotional distress is found "only where the conduct has been so outrageous in character, and so extreme in degree, as to go beyond all possible bounds of decency, and to be regarded as atrocious, and utterly intolerable in a civilized community." *McCarson*, 467 So.2d at 279 (quoting RESTATEMENT (SECOND) OF TORTS §46 cmt. d (1965)). A defendant's conduct is deemed intentional where the defendant "knows that such distress is certain, or substantially certain, to result from his conduct..." *McCarson*, 467 So.2d at 279 (quoting RESTATEMENT (SECOND) OF TORTS §46 cmt. i (1965)). Plaintiffs who are the spouse, child, sibling, or parent of a decedent have standing to recover for intentional infliction of emotional distress even though plaintiffs were not present at the scene. *Williams v. City of Minneola*, 575 So.2d 683, 690 (Fla.App.1991).

2. Plaintiffs

a. Estate and Surviving Family Members of Brent Marthaler [FN32]

FN32. As will be discussed further below, plaintiffs Matthew and Kirk Marthaler, Brent's brothers, cannot recover under Florida's wrongful death statute because no evidence was put forth that they were dependent upon the decedent, their brother. Accordingly, each must demonstrate that he may recover under a valid cause of action under the laws of Minnesota, the state in which each was domiciled at the time of the attack. A more detailed discussion of both Matthew and Kirk's claims will be provided later in this opinion. See *infra* Part VI.G.2.a.

i. Estate of Brent Marthaler

Airman First-Class Brent Marthaler was born in 1976, and was raised in Minnesota. He is survived by his wife, plaintiff Katie Lee Marthaler, his parents plaintiffs Herman C. Marthaler III and Sharon Marthaler, as well as his brothers, plaintiffs Kirk and Matthew Marthaler.

Brent graduated from high school in June of 1994 and joined the U.S. Air Force. Brent graduated from boot camp in September 1994, and Katie drove to Texas with Brent's parents to attend his graduation. (Dec. 2, 2003 Tr. at 62-63.) Brent went to technical school in Texas after his graduation from basic training. After graduation, Brent was then assigned to Shepherd AFB for his advanced technical training. (Dec. 3, 2003 Tr. at 21.) After advanced training, Brent was permanently assigned to Eglin AFB in Florida. (Dec. 2, 2003 Tr. at 62-63.)

Brent was scheduled to be deployed to Saudi Arabia in April 1996. Two days prior to his deployment, however, Brent and Katie Lee Marthaler, his high school sweetheart of five years, were married to each other. According to Katie, Brent "just felt better going to Saudi Arabia and knowing that we were married and that we were taking on the world together then." *Id.* at 73-74.

While he was away, Brent stayed in regular contact with Katie and his family, talking with Katie on the phone once a week, and writing letters to her four or five times a week. Brent clearly had high hopes for his life ahead with Katie. In one letter to Katie, Brent told her that "I think of you and all the fun that we have had and all the fun that will come in the next 50 years or so. I can truly say that you are the person that keeps a smile on my face 24-7 and for that I

can never repay you, but I'm going to try my hardest." *Id.* at 78-79. Brent was scheduled to return home from Saudi Arabia on June 27, 1996, a mere two days after the attack on the Khobar Towers.

Brent Marthaler's estate is represented by his wife, Katie Lee Marthaler. Brent's estate has asserted claims under Florida's wrongful death statute because he was last domiciled in Florida. As the personal representative of Brent's estate, Katie Lee Marthaler is the proper plaintiff to bring a wrongful death action under Florida law. *See* Fla. Stat. Ann. §768.20-768.21. Because Brent had no children, and no evidence was put forth at trial that his siblings were dependent upon him, any recovery under this wrongful death action is for the benefit of Brent's wife Katie, and his parents, Herman C. Marthaler and Sharon Marthaler. *See* Fla. Stat. Ann. §768.18.

Based upon the pleadings and evidence presented to the Court, the estate of Brent Marthaler has made out a valid claim for wrongful death under Florida law, and the beneficiaries of this estate are entitled to recover the present value of any "loss of the prospective net accumulations" of the decedent that might reasonably have been expected but for the wrongful death. Fla. Stat. Ann. §768.21(6). Additionally, as Brent's widow, Katie Lee Marthaler is entitled to recover personally for the loss of Brent's companionship and protection, as well as for her mental pain and suffering she sustained as a result of her husband's death. Fla. Stat. Ann. §768.21(2). Moreover, Brent's parents are entitled to recover for their own mental pain and suffering due to the fact that Brent was under 25 years of age. *See* Fla. Stat. Ann. §768.21(4).

Dr. Herman Miller, an economic consultant testified as an expert that, were it not for Brent's untimely death, he experienced a net economic loss of $1,598,688.00. The Court should therefore award the Estate of Brent Marthaler, by Katie Lee Marthaler as personal representative, $1,598,688.00 in economic damages for the benefit of Katie Lee Marthaler, Herman C. Marthaler, and Sharon Marthaler, to be distributed in a manner consistent with the statute governing intestate distribution of property under Florida law. As for the intangible economic damages of the wrongful death recovery, the Court will address those awards below, in an individualized discussion of the claims of Katie Lee Marthaler, and Herman and Sharon Marthaler.

ii. Katie Lee Marthaler

Plaintiff Katie Lee Marthaler is the widow of Brent Marthaler. Katie is participating in this lawsuit both as the personal representative to her husband's estate, and on her own behalf.

Ms. Marthaler is a United States citizen. She is 25 years old and was born on March 15, 1978 in Robbinsdale, Minnesota. (Dec. 2, 2003 Tr. at 52.) Her parents are Dennis and Jennifer Barthel who have been married for 30 years. She has one sister, Sarah, who is 22 years old. Katie grew up in Rogers, Minnesota. When Katie was 17, her family moved to nearby St. Michael, Minnesota. She attended elementary school in Rogers and junior and senior high school in Oak River, Minnesota. *Id.* at 53-54.

Katie met Brent Marthaler in 1991 when she was in the eighth grade and had just turned 14. Brent had just turned 16, and was in the tenth grade. Brent lived in Cambridge, Minnesota. Soon after Katie and Brent met each other, they began dating. Katie dated no one other than Brent from the time she met him when she was 14 years old until his death at Khobar Towers in June 1996. *Id.* at 55-56. Katie described Brent as a thoughtful and caring person. Brent was also close to Katie's parents. Katie's family treated Brent as if he were part of their family for many years. *Id.* at 56-57.

Brent graduated from high school in June of 1994 and joined the U.S. Air Force. Katie kept in touch with him, but it was not easy to keep in touch during boot camp because the young airmen do not have much time to write or call. Once he was out of boot camp, they kept in regular touch. Even during boot camp Brent would write letters once or twice a week and would call Katie when he would get his "morale call." Brent graduated from boot camp in September 1994, and Katie drove to Texas with Brent's parents to attend his graduation. *Id.* at 62-63.

Upon graduation, Brent was permanently assigned to Eglin AFB in Florida. Brent and Katie spoke almost every night; some nights it was for a half hour, and other nights it was for hours. Brent came home for Katie's junior prom in May 1995. Brent came home to Minnesota in October of 1995 and asked Katie to marry him. Katie was only a junior in high school so they had much to do to convince their parents. Brent had prepared a strategic plan which he had written down. Katie remembers that her mother was crying and her father did not say a whole lot. Brent had brought home a registration form for Katie to go to college. Katie's father requested that they visit Father McLaughlin at St. Michael's Church. After they met with him, Father McLaughlin announced that Brent and Katie were the perfect couple and he did not see any reason why they should not get married, no matter what their ages were. As a result, by the end of the weekend, everyone was excited. As Katie explained, Brent's "plan worked, so he had it all figured out." *Id.* at 71-72.

Katie visited Brent in Florida during her Spring vacation, which was in the first week of April 1996. Brent was scheduled to deploy with his squadron to Saudi Arabia two days after the end of Katie's vacation. Katie had just turned 18. Two days before Katie was scheduled to leave, Brent explained that he was worried about going to Saudi Arabia. He knew that it was an unfriendly place and he wanted to make sure that they had gotten married before he went there. Katie explained that Brent "just felt better going to Saudi Arabia and knowing that we were married and that we were taking on the world together then." *Id.* at 73-74.

So Brent and Katie went to the Courthouse and got married. They agreed not to tell anybody because they knew their parents would be upset. Invitations, a wedding dress, and a wedding cake for a September 1996 wedding had already been ordered. They agreed not to tell anybody until after Brent returned from Saudi Arabia. Brent did not want Katie to have to tell everyone by herself. *Id.* at 74-75.

In the weeks after Brent was killed, Katie was very angry. She did not want to eat. Her mother would make her eat by placing a plate of food in front of her and refusing to allow her to leave the table until she ate. Katie could not sleep but she still wanted to be in bed all the time. Her family would have to drag her out of bed. *Id.* at 90-91.

In the years since Brent's death, Katie has had many bad days. After September 11, 2001, Katie relived her experience and was very angry. She could not go to work for a couple of days because she felt so badly for the families. She was scared that terrorism was occurring in our country. *Id.* at 91. Katie has a recurring dream about Brent. She dreams that she is sleeping with him, and she knows that he is behind her. She wakes up and rolls over and puts her arm around him, and he is laying in bed like he was in the coffin with his head wrapped in gauze and a plastic device in place of his chin. *Id.* at 91.

Katie still keeps mementos of Brent in her home. She displays her wedding picture and also a picture of Brent in his jet with a big smile and his arms stretched out. She has a hope chest with the gifts that Brent had given her, her wedding dress, and all the letters that he sent her. *Id.* at 91-92.

As Dr. Cable testified, Katie "is in loss and loneliness…She has tried to rebuild her life. She has tried to go on…She still thinks about Brent all the time, and that will never change…When someone so close to you dies at 18, your new husband…you worry about everybody else close to you. What if something happened to them, too?…She has had to grow up very fast, and that's been difficult…And there will always be those questions of: the life we should have had together; all the plans we had and all the promise. That will never fade. That will always stay present." (Feb. 10, 2004 Tr. at 69-71.)

Based on the evidence presented to the Court, it is clear that Katie Lee Marthaler has experienced and continues to experience extreme mental anguish and suffering resulting from the loss of her husband. Accordingly, the Court shall award the Estate of Brent Marthaler, by Katie Lee Marthaler as Personal Representative, $8 million for the benefit of his surviving wife, Katie Lee Marthaler, to compensate her for the loss of Brent's companionship and protection, as well as for her mental pain and suffering she sustained as a result of her husband's death.

iii. Herman C. Marthaler & Sharon Marthaler

Sharon A. Marthaler, Brent Marthaler's mother and a United States citizen, was born in Ortona, Minnesota on January 11, 1946. She was raised on a dairy farm where she lived with her mother, father and two brothers. After graduating from high school, Sharon took a one year course at the University of Minnesota to train as a medical technician. She then began working as a medical technician at Riverview Memorial Hospital in West St. Paul. On February 26, 1971, she married Herm Marthaler. (Dec. 3, 2003 Tr. at 2-5.)

Herman Charles Marthaler III, Brent Marthaler's father and a United States citizen, was born in St. Paul, Minnesota on January 12, 1947. He was raised on the Marthaler homestead in West St. Paul, Minnesota. Herm's parents were Donna Ann Merit and Herman Charles Marthaler, Jr. Herm's father served in the United States Air Corps as a navigator on a B-29 during World War II, flew 22 combat missions out of Guam and "was in the air with 400 planes when they dropped the atom bomb." After his discharge from the military, Herm's father owned Marthaler Calf and Cattle where he bought and sold feeder cattle. After graduating from high school in 1965, Herm went to the University of Minnesota for one year and then he enlisted in the Air Force in the Fall of 1966. Herm served in five campaigns in Vietnam. On February 26, 1971, he married Sharon Marthaler. (Dec. 3, 2003 Tr. at 41-44.)

Sharon and Herman Marthaler initially lived in West St. Paul and then moved to Emery Grove, Minnesota where they had three sons within 30 months. The oldest, Kirk, was born in 1974. Matt was born in 1975 and Brent was born 1976. After Brent was born, the Marthaler family moved to Cambridge, Minnesota. *Id.* at 5-7.

In the first years after Brent's death, it was extremely difficult for Sharon to go to work and get through each day. She testified that as time goes on, it gets a little easier, "but it is always still there. You finally come to realize things will never be the same." Every once in a while, Sharon has dreams about Brent, and he tells her that "things aren't as bad as you think." *Id.* at 36-37.

Sharon has visited Eglin AFB twice since Brent's death. The first time was for a bricklaying ceremony in September of 1996. She went with Katie and Katie's mother. The second time was January of 1998. She and Herm went there to take pictures of a memorial that had been erected to honor the victims of the Khobar Towers bombing and to meet some of Brent's friends again. By that time, however, most of the young airmen that Brent had served with had left Eglin AFB. Sharon recalled "[t]here weren't a lot of the old crew there anymore." *Id.* at 37. Sharon and Herm visit Brent's grave two or three times a year. They usually go on Memorial Day, Columbus Day and Veteran's Day. They leave a wreath by his grave on Veteran's Day because in Minnesota, the cemetery will leave the wreath in place until March when they do their Spring cleanup. Herman and Sharon also have a flag garden and a flag in their yard where they plant flowers. *Id.* at 37.

Sharon and Herman keep numerous mementos of Brent around their house. They have two tall cabinets in his old bedroom full of notes and cards that Brent wrote to them. They have also kept his baseball and football cards. Sharon also had a flag flown over the United States Capitol for Brent and the other 18 airmen killed at the Khobar Towers. *Id.* at 38. The Marthalers put a poster on their mailbox every June 25th with a picture of Brent taken just before he left for Saudi Arabia and the words "Remember the 19." Sharon contributes money in Brent's name to an organization called The Little Farm which is a nursery for disadvantaged children. Sharon makes the contribution in Brent's name periodically because it makes her feel good to write his name. *Id.* at 40-41.

Herman testified about the impact of Brent's death on his wife, Sharon, "[s]he'll never be the same. Absolutely never." Herm thinks of Brent "every second of every day." He testified "[w]hen I don't perform well enough is the day I wear [Brent's] T-shirt. When I am not going fast enough [Brent]'s right here and he says, you can do this, pop, just bend with the knees and lift harder. So it's every second of every day…This is why Sharon and I sit down every day for two and a half hours from the moment she gets home." The holidays are difficult for the Marthaler family. Herman testified "Christmas is tough because we know [Brent] really loved Christmas. Veteran's Day…is the one that we get to put the wreath down and they'll leave…it until Spring." Herman believes that "the holidays that [Brent] liked the best is when it hurts us the most." *Id.* at 77-80.

According to Dr. Cable, Herman "is still in loss and loneliness. Brent was a very important part of his life…His grief will continue in the future…[and] there will be for him a very strong void that will never be filled [t]hat will continue to cause pain and just is never going to go away." (Feb. 10, 2004 Tr. at 72-73.) Similarly, Dr. Cable testified that Sharon "is still in loss and loneliness. She thinks of [Brent] all the time, so very much a part of her life…She, too, has grief that will continue in the future. I see her as one who slowly will recover, but who will experience what we sometimes refer to as waves of grief; that is, where it comes back and sort of hits us again and when we perhaps are least prepared and least expect it…[S]he is going to be contending with that in the years ahead." *Id.* at 75.

Based upon the evidence presented at trial, both Herman and Sharon Marthaler have experienced severe mental anguish and suffering as a result of their son's untimely death. Therefore, this Court shall award to the estate of Brent Marthaler, by Katie Lee Marthaler as Personal Representative, $5 million for the benefit of his father Herman Marthaler, and $5 million for the benefit of his mother Sharon Marthaler to compensate both for the mental pain and suffering both have sustained as a result of their son's death.

b. Estate and Surviving Family Member of Justin Wood [FN33]

FN33. As will be discussed further below, plaintiff Shawn Wood, Justin Wood's brother, cannot recover under Florida's wrongful death statute because no evidence was put forth that he was dependent upon the decedent. Accordingly, he must demonstrate that he may recover under a valid cause of action under the laws of California, the state in which he was domiciled at the time of the attack. A more detailed discussion of his claim will be provided later in this opinion. See *infra* Part VI.B.2.c.

i. Estate of Justin Wood
Airman First-Class Justin R. Wood was killed in the Khobar Towers bombing on June 25, 1996. Pl.Ex. 2. Justin was born on July 16, 1975 and was 20 years old when he died. (Dec. 4, 2003 P.M. Tr. at 11.) Justin is survived by his father Richard Wood, his mother Kathleen Wood, and his older brother Shawn Wood.

From a very young age, Justin was always interested in sports. He particularly loved soccer and basketball. But as Justin got older, he played less soccer and devoted more and more time to basketball. "Basketball was his love." Justin was also a trivia whiz when it came to basketball and could recite the names and statistics of college basketball players, particularly players from his favorite teams. (*Id.* at 107-108; Dec. 4, 2003 P.M. Tr. at 15.) In addition to playing basketball and soccer, Justin also took karate and participated in karate tournaments. (Dec. 4, 2003 A.M. Tr. at 107-108.)

Soon after graduating from high school, Justin joined the Air Force. Rich and Kathy were surprised by this deci-

sion. Growing up, Justin always said he would not join the military because "when you go in the service you die." Rich and Kathy do not know where Justin got this idea from, but he never wanted to join the service. Then one day, after Justin graduated from high school, he came home and told his parents that he had enlisted in the Air Force along with his friend Travis Hudson. (*Id.* at 113-114; Dec. 4, 2003 P.M. Tr. at 19.)

One of the reasons Justin joined the service was because he wanted to attend college. Justin knew that Rich and Kathy could not afford to send him to college and he knew that he could get that college money by joining the Air Force. He told Kathy that in the Air Force, " 'I can build up a college fund, save money for college, and I can take college classes while I'm there.' " (Dec. 4, 2003 A.M. Tr. at 113; Dec. 4, 2003 P.M. Tr. at 20.)

After joining the Air Force, Justin attended basic training at Lackland AFB, then went to Albuquerque, New Mexico for specialized training. He ultimately became a loadmaster with a search and rescue squad that was based at Patrick AFB in Florida. Justin was the first airman to go straight from boot camp to a loadmaster position with search and rescue. (Dec. 4, 2003 A.M. Tr. at 114.) Justin loved his job, particularly the crew of guys he was working with in the search and rescue squad. *Id.* at 117.

Justin Wood's estate is represented by his father, plaintiff Richard Wood. Justin's estate has asserted claims under Florida's wrongful death statute because he was last domiciled in Florida. As the personal representative of Justin's estate, Richard Wood is the proper plaintiff to bring a wrongful death action under Florida law. *See* Fla. Stat. Ann. §768.20-768.21. In light of the fact that Justin had no spouse, or children, and that no evidence was submitted demonstrating that his brother Shawn was financially dependent upon Justin, any recovery under this wrongful death action is for the benefit of Justin's parents, Richard and Kathleen Wood. *See* Fla. Stat. Ann. §768.18.

Based upon the pleadings and evidence presented to the Court, the estate of Justin Wood has made out a valid claim for wrongful death under Florida law. The beneficiaries of this estate, however, are not entitled to recover the present value of any "loss of the prospective net accumulations" of the decedent that might reasonably have been expected but for the wrongful death because Justin was under 25 years old when he died, and did not have either a surviving spouse or any surviving lineal descendants. Fla. Stat. Ann. §768.21(6)(a)(1). Still, Justin's parents are entitled to recover for their own mental pain and suffering arising out of this wrongful death action due to the fact that Justin was under 25 years of age when he died. *See* Fla. Stat. Ann.

§768.21(4). A discussion of these intangible economic damages of the wrongful death recovery will be addressed below in an individualized discussion of the claims of Richard and Kathleen Wood.

ii. Richard Wood & Kathleen Wood

Richard ("Rich") Wood is the father of Justin Wood. He was born in Hillsboro, Wisconsin on November 12, 1945. He is an American citizen. (Dec. 4, 2003 A.M. Tr. at 99.) Kathy Wood is the mother of Justin Wood. She was born in Los Banos, California on October 7, 1949. She is an American citizen. (Dec. 4, 2003 P.M. Tr. at 2.)

When Rich moved to Modesto to work at the Gallo's warehouse, he met his wife, Kathy Wood. Rich worked at Ernest and Julio Gallo's winery in Modesto, California for 34 years before retiring. (Dec. 4, 2003 A.M. Tr. at 103, 135.) After Rich and Kathy married, they had two children: Shawn, who was born in March of 1971, and Justin, who was born in July of 1975. (Dec. 4, 2003 P.M. Tr. at 11.)

Rich does not remember what he and Kathy did after they learned about their son's death, other than hold each other and cry. He felt numb. (Dec. 4, 2003 A.M. Tr. at 122-24.) Kathy was in shock. "All I could do is just sit and pray for it not to be true." (Dec. 4, 2003 P.M. Tr. at 31.)

The day Kathy learned of Justin's death, her doctor prescribed Xanax to help her deal with everything. She did not want the drug, but she did take it and it helped her sleep. Days after Justin's death, Rich, Kathy, and Shawn attended a memorial service at Patrick AFB. Upon arriving at Patrick AFB, they were met by Justin's flight squad, who whisked them away and took care of them for the next few days. "They did not want us to be anxious about anything. They went overboard to make sure that we were comfortable and well taken care of." The squad took Rich and Kathy to the hotel, to the base, to their squad room, and to a squad member's home, where they had a huge gathering and met the squad members' families. (*Id.* at 36; Dec. 4, 2003 A.M. Tr. at 125-26.)

Since the Modesto ceremony and the burial service, Rich and Kathy have attended numerous Khobar Towers memorials and dedications. They attended the opening of the Khobar Towers display at Heritage Hall, which is the museum for enlisted men in Montgomery, Alabama. (Dec. 4, 2003 A.M. Tr. at 118-19, 130.) They attended the dedication ceremony for the monument to the victims of Khobar Towers at Patrick AFB. They also attended the FBI briefing held in Quantico, Virginia, where certain family members were briefed about the status of the Khobar Towers criminal investigation. *Id.* at 130.

After Justin's death, Rich "just shut down." He shut himself up in a room in his house and spent time on the computer and away from everyone else. "I couldn't talk to my wife because if I talked to my wife, she'd cry or if she talked to me I'd cry. I just had a real difficult time." Rich became reclusive and did not want to have anything to do with anyone. *Id.* at 130-31. Rich even began showing physical manifestations of his problems and began breaking out in welts. (Dec. 4, 2003 P.M. Tr. at 41.)

Rich began seeing a psychiatrist two to three times a week after Justin died and continued seeing her throughout the year following Justin's death. (Dec. 4, 2003 A.M. Tr. at 130, 132.) The psychiatrist prescribed Rich a medication that helped with his emotional suffering. Rich stayed on this medication for three to four years. After Rich started taking the drug, he began to feel better and thought he could stop taking the drug. But shortly after he went off the medication, Rich "went bananas" and shut down again. The psychiatrist was so concerned that she placed him in a medical facility called Crossroads, where he stayed for a week. *Id.* at 132-33.

It has been difficult for Rich to get rid of any of Justin's possessions since he died and Rich's home is now full of them. He has Justin's Persian rug, aquarium, lamps, furniture, and all of his military uniforms. Moreover, Rich has encountered a hard time coping with life since Justin died. Rich finds it difficult to make decisions, he gets confused, and gets lost. He also cries at the drop of a hat. It is difficult for him to watch the news and see soldiers being killed because he knows what the parents are going through. September 11, 2001 was particularly difficult. Rich's relationship with his family has also been dramatically altered since Justin was killed. Today, Rich cannot talk about things with his family the way he used to. *Id.* at 140. Holidays are no longer enjoyable for Rich. *Id.* at 138.

Rich and Kathy have created a number of lasting memorials in Justin's honor. "I have his flag box on his coffee table. I have eagles all over the place. I put up a flag pole out in the front [of the house]. Together with the PTA at Rose Avenue School where he went to grade school, we put in a rose garden…And then we have a plaque and planted a tree at the high school he attended." *Id.* at 141.

Today, Rich still has moments where he just falls apart. *Id.* at 131-132. The biggest problem is that the hurt never goes away. *Id.* at 136. "I think about Justin every single day. There's no particular thing that sets it off. It's just always there." *Id.* at 139.

According to Dr. Cable, Rich

is in extreme loss and loneliness. He is also having volatile emotions. I think the real difficulty for him, in terms of his loss and loneliness, he doesn't want to get better…He is very lonely. He is very bitter. He is withdrawn from all of those people who could support him, all of those people who love him…[His prognosis is] really very poor…His grief will last a lifetime. He doesn't want to forget. He doesn't want to let go of the pain, and I fear will permanently damage any family relationships. [FN34]

FN34. (Feb. 10, 2004 Tr. at 204-05.)

After Justin's death, Kathy was coping with her own profound grief but also was dealing with her husband, who "was very angry, very upset, very distraught." Rich's reaction to Justin's death caused a great deal of friction between Kathy and Rich, resulting in nearly constant arguments between Kathy and Rich. *Id*. at 39-40. To help Kathy forced herself to go back to work and this was helpful, because there was a support system in place for her there. "If someone's having problems, we do what we can to make them feel good and strengthen them up as well, and I needed my friends." Going back to work prevented Kathy from going into a deeper depression. *Id*. at 41-42. But Kathy felt bad about going back to work because Rich could not bring himself to do the same thing and because she began shutting him out more, in the hope that doing so would prevent further anxiety for him. *Id*. at 41.

As a result of the rift between Kathy and Rich, Kathy began doing more things by herself. She regularly attends church-related events and has girls' night out with her friends. She still does not go out with Rich like she used to before Justin died. *Id*. at 45. To this day, Kathy and Rich's relationship has not returned to normal. *Id*. at 40. Kathy and Rich's physical relationship has also not returned to normal.

Kathy still thinks about Justin all of the time and likes to keeps things around that remind her of him. She put together a scrapbook of pictures from Justin's childhood that she carries with her often.

As to her emotional state, Dr. Cable testified that Kathy is in loss and loneliness. "She has tried to move on and I think really wants to, but there is a lot of personal grief still present. Then, of course, it's complicated by how her husband has dealt with all of this and then the anger and intense grief he has got…[H]er grief will continue for a long period of time. I believe her marriage will suffer…may full break down." (Feb. 10, 2004 Tr. at 207.)

Based upon the evidence presented at trial, both Richard and Kathleen Wood have experienced severe mental anguish and suffering as a result of their son's untimely death. Therefore, this Court shall award to the estate of Justin Wood, by Richard Wood as Personal Representative, $5 million for the

benefit of his father Richard Wood, and $5 million for the benefit of his mother Kathleen Wood to compensate both for the mental pain and suffering both have sustained as a result of their son's death.

c. Estate and Surviving Family Members of Michael Heiser

i. Estate of Michael Heiser

Michael ("Mike") Heiser was killed in the Khobar Towers bombing on June 25, 1996. (Dec. 5, 2003 A.M. Tr. at 29; Ex. 2.) Mike was born on September 20, 1960 and was 35 years old when he died. (*Id*. at 5, Ex. 67.) Mike was unmarried and had no siblings. Mike is survived by his parents, Francis ("Fran") and Gary Heiser. Though Gary is not Mike's biological father, he legally adopted Mike. *Id*. at 8, 53-54. Mike had a special and rewarding childhood in Germany. On weekends and holidays, he would travel with Fran and Gary to see the German countryside and became involved in collecting antiques and other items. Mike was a natural businessman and even at a young age, helped Fran and Gary purchase antiques, refurbish them, and sell them for a profit. *Id*. at 7.

As a child, Mike was smart, funny, and considerate. He also had a passion for learning. Reading many books and participating in school activities. Through his travels, he had many friends all over the world. Mike was also a hard worker, both during his years as a student and after he joined the military. *Id*. at 8-11.

Mike enlisted in the Air Force on June 25, 1979. Because Gary had served in the Army for 22 years, Mike initially talked to a recruiter about joining the Army. Gary testified that he knew the benefits of being in the Air Force and persuaded Mike look at the Air Force. Mike ultimately decided that the Air Force was a better career choice, so he enlisted soon after graduating from high school. *Id*. at 14, 55.

After attending boot camp and advanced training, Mike developed a specialty in the communications field and was sent to Mildenhall AFB in England. After spending three years at Mildenhall, Mike was promoted and reassigned to Ramstein AFB in Germany, where he was responsible for communications operations on the Air Force's fleet of Gulfstream planes. During Mike's three years at Ramstein, he took part in several exciting missions. For example, he was assigned to the first airplane escorted into the new, free Russia; he was assigned to General Schwarzkopf's personal plane during the Gulf War; and he was assigned to coordinate communications when President Clinton visited Ramstein. Mike loved working and flying on the Gulfstreams. After spending three years in England and three years in Germany,

Mike transferred back to the United States and was assigned to Patrick AFB in Florida, and was later assigned to Saudi Arabia.

Michael Heiser's estate is represented by his parents, Fran and Gary Heiser. Michael's estate has asserted claims under Florida's wrongful death statute because he was last domiciled in Florida. As the personal representatives of Michael's estate, Fran and Gary Heiser are the proper plaintiffs to bring a wrongful death action under Florida law. *See* Fla. Stat. Ann. §768.20-768.21. In light of the fact that Michael had no spouse or dependents, any recovery under this wrongful death action is for the benefit of Michael's parents, Fran and Gary Heiser. *See* Fla. Stat. Ann. §768.18.

Based upon the pleadings and evidence presented to the Court, the estate of Michael Heiser has made out a valid claim for wrongful death under Florida law. Accordingly, the beneficiaries of this estate are entitled to recover the present value of any "loss of the prospective net accumulations" of the decedent that might reasonably have been expected but for the wrongful death. *See* Fla. Stat. Ann. §768.21(6). Additionally, though Michael was over 25 years of age at the time of his death, Michael's parents are nonetheless entitled to recover for their own mental pain and suffering arising out of this wrongful death action due to the fact that Michael died without any other survivors. *See* Fla. Stat. Ann. §768.21(4).

Dr. Herman Miller, an economic consultant testified as an expert that, due to Michael's untimely death, he experienced a net economic loss of $3,720,019.00. The Court should therefore award the Estate of Michael Heiser, by Fran and Gary Heiser as personal representatives, $3,720,019.00 in economic damages for the benefit of Michael's parents, Fran and Gary Heiser. As for the intangible economic damages of the wrongful death recovery, the Court will address those awards below, in an individualized discussion of the claims of Fran and Gary Heiser.

ii. Francis and Gary Heiser

Francis ("Fran") and Gary Heiser were Mike's parents. Fran was born in New Jersey on December 23, 1941 and was 54 years old when Mike was killed. (Dec. 5, 2003 A.M. Tr. at 4.) Gary was born in Pennsylvania on March 22, 1937 and was 59 years old when Mike was killed. *Id.* at 52. Gary was Mike's adoptive father. *Id.* at 53-54.

Shortly after graduating from high school, Fran married and gave birth to Mike who was her only child. After six years of marriage, Fran and her husband divorced. Fran's ex-husband, who was Mike's biological father, did not play a role in Mike's life after the divorce. In Fran's words, her ex-husband "divorced both of us." *Id.* at 5-6, 8. Later, Fran

met Gary, and they were eventually married on February 14, 1970. *Id.* at 6, 53.

When Fran and Gary married, Mike was only nine years old. *Id.* at 6, 53. Gary could see that Mike needed a male influence in his life, and Gary filled that role. In addition to raising Mike as his own son, Gary formally adopted Mike. *Id.* at 8, 53-54, Ex. 67.

Since burying Mike, Fran and Gary have dedicated themselves to attending numerous memorials all around the country. "[W]e've been to any that we know about." Fran and Gary have also kept scrapbooks memorializing these events and have created a book called "The Story of a Lifetime," to preserve Mike's memory. By posting it on a website, they have shared this book with other victims of terrorism, including the other families of the victims of the Khobar Towers bombing. *Id.* at 33, 43, 68.

Fran has been deeply affected by the loss of her only child. After Mike's death, she did not want to see or speak with anyone. *Id.* at 34. It has been particularly difficult for her to see other people's children and grandchildren without becoming emotional. Mike's death dramatically impacted Fran's family life. She is upset how her already small family broke-down even further when Mike was killed. *Id.* at 36, 38. Fran does not even like holidays anymore.

Fran has experienced severe sleep problems ever since Mike died. This still occurs today. After Mike's death, Fran and Gary decided to sell the family business. There was no longer a reason to keep the business. The business had been growing fast, Gary was considering retiring, and with Mike gone, there was nobody to take over the business. So after Fran and Gary received an offer, they sold the company. *Id.* at 37.

Fran attended counseling for a short period of time after Mike died, but did not find it helpful. She then attended a support group meeting for the Tragedy Assistance Program for Survivors ("TAPS") in Washington, D.C., which was a support group for family members of deceased servicemen. Fran found several of the TAPS support groups helpful, and has made TAPS a beneficiary of her will. Fran also involved herself with an organization called Alive Alone, an organization for parents whose children have died at a young age. *Id.* at 34-35.

Since Mike's death, Fran has dedicated much of her life to being an advocate for victims of terrorism. She has contacted congressmen about terrorism issues, has attempted to change the laws to protect United States servicemembers, and has tried to place terrorism on the agendas of politicians. She has also spent a great deal of time reading and educating herself about terrorism. Some people think Fran is obsessed with it. *Id.* at 39-40.

To this day, much of Fran and Gary's home is decorated with mementos from Mike's life. Fran and Gary have also set up the Michael G. Heiser Foundation, in remembrance of all victims of terrorism. Money donated to the Foundation is used for ROTC scholarships and to assist victims of terrorism, through TAPS, Alive Alone, and another support organization called No Greater Love. *Id.* at 41-42.

As Dr. Cable stated, Fran

is very much in loss and loneliness, and that's complicated or enhanced by the lack of family for her future. So it's not just present loneliness, but it's future loneliness as well; the family that can never be there...She will continue in grief the rest of her life, because there is nothing besides her husband to put herself into. There is no one to love. There is an emptiness there that's not going to go away for her. There will never be grandchildren. So that real emptiness is long term.

(Feb. 10, 2004 Tr. at 139.)

Gary's entire life has been affected by the death of his son. He and Fran always had a small family, but now they are left without their only child, and their lives have been shattered. "[O]ur future goes only to the point when I go and my wife goes. That's it. The family ceases to exist." This has caused great emotional pain for Gary. It forced Gary and Fran to sell their family business, which they had planned on passing down to their son. (Dec. 5, 2003 A.M. Tr. at 69-71.)

Like Fran, Gary does not celebrate holidays anymore. Until Mike died, Gary enjoyed Christmas. But he cannot enjoy the holiday anymore. Additionally, birthdays and other holidays are equally tough for Gary to handle. As Dr. Cable testified, Gary

is in loss and loneliness. As with his wife, there is no future. There was a very strong relationship because of the adoptive choice that was made between [Gary and Mike]... His grief will continue for a great deal of time. Again, the future is gone. He will move on with his life, but the grief will always be there. Part of that will always be also seeing the pain his wife is going through.

(Feb. 10, 2004 Tr. at 141-42.)

Based upon the evidence presented at trial, both Fran and Gary Heiser have experienced severe mental anguish and suffering as a result of their son's untimely death. Therefore, this Court shall award to the estate of Michael Heiser, by Fran and Gary Heiser as Personal Representatives, $5 million for the benefit of his mother Fran Heiser, and $5 million for the benefit of his father Gary Heiser to compensate both for the mental pain and suffering both have sustained as a result of their son's death.

d. Estate and Surviving Family Members of Earl Cartrette, Jr. [FN35]

FN35. As will be discussed further below, plaintiff Lewis Cartrette, Earl Cartrette, Jr.'s brother, cannot recover under Florida's wrongful death statute because no evidence was put forth that he was dependent upon the decedent. Accordingly, he must demonstrate that he may recover under a valid cause of action under the laws of Indiana, the state in which he was domiciled at the time of the attack. A more detailed discussion of his claim will be provided later in this opinion. See *infra* Part VI.K.2.a.

i. Estate of Earl Cartrette, Jr.

Senior Airman Earl Cartrette, Jr. ("J.R.") was born March 2, 1974, and was the eldest of three sons; J.R.'s two younger brothers are Lewis, born on November 1, 1976; and Anthony ("Tony"), born on March 15, 1978. He was killed on June 25, 1996 while stationed at Khobar Towers. (Dec. 5, 2003 P.M. Tr. at 2-3; Ex. 9.) J.R. attended grade and middle school at St. Anthony's Catholic School in Sellersburg, Indiana, where his grandmother worked. His grandmother was in charge of the school cafeteria. After St. Anthony's, J.R. attended Providence High School, a catholic high school in Clarksville, Indiana. J.R. played football from the third grade through his junior year in high school. He also ran track all through grade school, middle school and his junior year of high school. When he was younger he played soccer and basketball and wrestled. *Id.* at 7-8.

J.R. decided to join the U.S. Air Force after high school. J.R. underwent basic training at Lackland AFB and advanced technical school at Shepherd AFB, both in Texas. He was then assigned to Eglin AFB in Florida. *Id.* at 20-21. He was deployed with the 58th Fighter Squadron to Saudi Arabia in March 1996, and was scheduled to return on June 27, 1996, two days after the bombing.

J.R.'s estate is represented by his mother, Denise Eichstaedt. J.R.'s estate has asserted claims under Florida's wrongful death statute because he was last domiciled in Florida. As the personal representative of J.R.'s estate, Denise Eichstaedt is the proper plaintiff to bring a wrongful death action under Florida law. *See* Fla. Stat. Ann. §768.20-768.21. In light of the fact that J.R. had no spouse or lineal descendants, and because no evidence was presented as to his siblings' financial dependence upon J.R., any recovery under this wrongful death action is for the benefit of J.R.'s mother, Denise Eichstaedt. *See* Fla. Stat. Ann. §768.18.

Based upon the pleadings and evidence presented to the Court, the estate of Earl Cartrette, Jr. has made out a valid claim for wrongful death under Florida law. The beneficiaries of this estate, however, are not entitled to recover the present value of any "loss of the prospective net accumulations" of the decedent that might reasonably have been expected but for the wrongful death because J.R. was under 25 years old when he died, and did not have either a surviving spouse or any surviving lineal descendants. Fla. Stat. Ann. §768.21(6)(a)(1). Still, J.R.'s mother is entitled to recover for her own mental pain and suffering arising out of this wrongful death action due to the fact that J.R. left no other survivors. *See* Fla. Stat. Ann. §768.21(4). [FN36] A discussion of these intangible economic damages of the wrongful death recovery, will be addressed below in an individualized discussion of the claim of Denise Eichstaedt.

FN36. In addition to being survived by his mother, J.R. was survived by his two brothers. J.R.'s brothers, however, are not considered "survivors" under the Florida wrongful death statute because they have not put forth evidence of any dependence upon J.R. See *supra* note 29. Therefore, any potential recovery under the wrongful death claim brought be J.R.'s estate shall be solely for the benefit of his mother, Denise Eichstaedt. To the extent that J.R.'s brothers can recover, they must make a valid intentional infliction of emotional distress claim under the laws of the states in which each was domiciled at the time of the attack.

ii. Denise Eichstaedt
Denise Eichstaedt, a United States citizen, was Senior Airman Earl Cartrette, Jr.'s mother. Denise was born on March 8, 1953 in Jeffersonville, Indiana. She had three brothers and a sister and grew up in the Jeffersonville area. Denise is married to James Eichstaedt. She is a nurse. Her first husband was Earl Cartrette, Sr. who died on February 18, 1992, the year that J.R. graduated from high school. Denise had three sons with Earl Cartrette, Sr.: J.R. who was born March 2, 1974; Lewis who was born on November 1, 1976; and Anthony ("Tony") who was born on March 15, 1978. Denise raised the three boys in Sellersburg, Indiana, a small town approximately 6 miles north of Jeffersonville where Denise's parents still live. *Id.* at 4-5.

Denise did not attempt to return to work for two and one-half months after J.R. was killed. When she did return to work, she was unable to perform her duties because she worked on a floor with terminally ill patients, where it was difficult to work without crying. As a result, the hospital gave her more time off, and she stayed home for six months. At that point, however, she decided that it was in everyone's best interest for her to resign because she felt as though she could not do that type of work anymore. In mid-February 1997, she went to work in a pediatrician's office. In the days

and weeks following J.R.'s death, Denise did not want to sleep. That period of time is essentially "a blur" for her. *Id.* at 36-37.

Denise has attempted to obtain professional counseling over the years. She went to see a civilian psychiatrist and did not continue because he wanted to put her on medication for depression. Denise explained that she did not want to take drugs. Denise believes that she is better off sitting at home contemplating in her own mind, talking to herself, rather than taking medication. Denise also attempted to go to a couple of meetings of an organization called Compassionate Friends which includes the parents of children who have been killed. She concluded, however, that she did not fit in because they did not understand what happens to a parent when her child is killed by a terrorist. *Id.* at 36-38. When Denise looks at a picture of J.R., she begins to cry. Sometimes she cries for a short period of time and sometimes she cries off and on for a couple of days.

As Dr. Cable testified, Denise

is still certainly in the loss and loneliness [stage]. She is still having a very difficult time. The things that keep her going are her work and her faith...[S]he has still got a room almost as a museum [which] shows that she is frozen in time at a point back where this happened...Her pain will continue for quite a period of time. She is trying to do better. She works at it. She makes her own effort, but she is still have a difficult time and will.

(Feb. 10, 2004 Tr. at 121-22.)

Based upon the evidence presented at trial, Denise Eichstaedt has experienced severe mental anguish and suffering as a result of her son's untimely death. Therefore, this Court shall award to the estate of Earl Cartrette, Jr., by Denise Eichstaedt as Personal Representative, $5 million for the benefit of his mother Denise Eichstaedt to compensate her for the mental pain and suffering she sustained as a result of her son's death.

iii. Anthony Cartrette
Anthony W. Cartrette ("Tony") is a United States citizen, and is one of the two brothers of Earl Cartrette, Jr. Ex. 280 ¶¶ 1-3. J.R. and Tony lived together in the same home for 14 years while both were growing up, and still in school. J.R. was a very supportive big brother to Tony, and always took care of him. Tony was always able to confide in J.R. and ask for his guidance. "J.R. was the glue that held everyone together." Ex. 280, ¶ 6.

After the memorial services, Tony had a "melt down." He was unable to sleep for days and did not eat very much. Tony was only 17 years old when J.R. died. It is very difficult for Tony to accept that J.R. is gone. Tony has not been able to talk to anyone else about J.R.'s death. Ex. 280, ¶ 13.

Tony misses J.R. the most when he goes home to visit their family and realizes that J.R. will not be joining them. Birthdays and holidays are also difficult for Tony. There are still times when Tony is alone that he wants to pick up the phone and call J.R. and realizes that Tony can't. J.R. is on Tony's mind every second of every day and Tony misses him more each day. J.R.'s death was a shock. There is no closure because Tony didn't get to say good-bye. Ex. 280, ¶¶ 14-16.

According to Dr. Cable, Tony

is in loss and loneliness certainly…[H]e also has some unresolved issues with his brother, kind of unfinished business issues that probably evoke some earlier stages of grief as well. It's very intense grief and problems…He will have continuing difficulties for quite a period of time…He need to be able to talk about all of his feeling, including guilt feelings, unfinished business, and all. So it's a long road ahead for him.

(Feb. 10, 2004 Tr. at 125-26.)

As the brother of Earl Cartrette, Jr., Anthony Cartrette has brought an intentional infliction of emotional distress claim against the defendants for pain and suffering caused by the death of his brother. Based on the evidence presented to the Court, Anthony Cartrette has satisfied the elements to establish a valid claim for intentional infliction of emotional distress under Florida law. First, defendants Iran, MOIS, and the IRGC provided material support to Saudi Hezbollah with the intent that Saudi Hezbollah would carry out attacks that would cause severe emotional distress. Second, the tragic bombing of the Khobar Towers by means of material support and civil conspiracy is an act that is nothing short of extreme, outrageous, and beyond all bounds of civil decency. As is the nature of terrorism, terrorists seek to perform acts that are deliberately outrageous and bring about extreme suffering in order to achieve political ends. Third, defendants' actions in facilitating and supporting the Khobar Towers bombing proximately caused Tony's emotional distress because the material support and direction given to Saudi Hezbollah ensured the event would occur. Finally, the evidence shows that Tony suffered emotional distress, and that his emotional distress was severe. Accordingly, the Court finds that Anthony Cartrette is entitled to recover from defendants $2.5 million in compensatory damages for the mental anguish and suffering associated with the loss of his brother.

e. Estate and Surviving Family Members of Patrick Fennig [FN37]

FN37. As will be discussed further below, plaintiffs Paul and Mark Fennig, Patrick's brothers, cannot recover under Florida's wrongful death statute because no evidence was put forth that either was dependent upon the decedent. Accordingly, each must demonstrate that he may recover under a valid cause of action under the laws of Wisconsin, the state in which each was domiciled at the time of the attack. A more detailed discussion of their claims will be provided later in this opinion. See *infra* Part VI.H.2.a, b.

i. Estate of Patrick Fennig

Patrick Fennig ("Pat") is a United States citizen, who was born on April 17, 1962 in Wisconsin. Pat had two older brothers, Mark who was born on March 24, 1959, and Paul who was born on January 17, 1961. As a child, Pat loved airlines and reading. Cassie testified that Pat "liked being a little boy. He was a fun child, always busy." Pat had a very good relationship with his two brothers. They played together and like each other. Ted testified that as a child Pat "enjoyed doing everything." (Dec. 9, 2003 Tr. at 8-9, 48-50.)

Ted testified that "[w]hen Pat was about six or seven years old, somehow-well, his interest in airplanes kind of came together. And he said, 'Dad, when I graduate from high school, I'm going to join the Air Force.'…And he graduated from high school and he lived up to his convictions and joined the Air Force." *Id.* at 50. Pat attended basic training at Lackland AFB and corresponded with his parents during this period of time. Pat had a great interest in maintaining jets in the Air Force, developed a high level of professional acuity and was selected maintenance maintainer of the year. Pat's first permanent assignment was Malmstrom AFB in Montana. Pat's second permanent duty assignment was Ramstein AFB in Germany. Pat received the Airman of the Year Award from the Air Force in 1990. Pat was "very proud that he won it, and happy that he came to that point in his life; that he did something that he was proud of." After completing his assignment in Germany, Pat came home on leave for three weeks around Christmas. (Dec. 9, 2003 Tr. at 18-21, 52.)

Next, Pat was assigned to Hill AFB in Utah, and then reassigned to England. Pat was later deployed to Kunsan AFB in Korea. While stationed in Korea, Pat was selected with a few other mechanics and officers to retrieve and fix a plane that was forced to make an emergency landing on an island. Pat's next permanent assignment was Edwards AFB in California. Ted testified that while he was stationed at Edwards AFB, Pat was recruited to work in the private sector by aircraft manufacturing companies. Pat loved the Air Force and decided to wait to seek employment in the private sector until after he retired from the Air Force. (Dec. 9, 2003 Tr. at 21-24, 53-54.) In July of 1993, Pat was reassigned to Eglin AFB in Florida. *Id.* at 24-27. From Florida, Pat was assigned to Saudi Arabia. Pat was scheduled to return from Saudi Arabia on June 27, 1996. *Id.* at 30-31.

Pat's estate is represented by his parents, Thaddeus C. Fennig and Catherine Fennig. Pat's estate has asserted claims under Florida's wrongful death statute because he was last domiciled in Florida. As the personal representatives of Pat's estate, Thaddeus C. Fennig and Catherine Fennig are the proper plaintiffs to bring a wrongful death action under Florida law. *See* Fla. Stat. Ann. §768.20-768.21. In light of the fact that Pat had no spouse or other survivors as defined by Fla. Stat. Ann. §768.18, any recovery under this wrongful death action is for the benefit of Pat's parents, Thaddeus and Catherine Fennig. *See* Fla. Stat. Ann. §768.18.

Based upon the pleadings and evidence presented to the Court, the estate of Patrick Fennig has made out a valid claim for wrongful death under Florida law. The beneficiaries of this estate are entitled to recover the present value of any "loss of the prospective net accumulations" of the decedent that might reasonably have been expected but for the wrongful death because Pat was over 25 years old when he died, and died with surviving parents, but without other dependents. *See* Fla. Stat. Ann. §768.21(6)(2). Additionally, although Pat was over 25 years of age at the time of his death, Pat's parents are nonetheless entitled to recover for their own mental pain and suffering arising out of this wrongful death action due to the fact that Pat died without any other survivors. *See* Fla. Stat. Ann. §768.21(4).

Dr. Herman Miller, an economic consultant testified as an expert that, as a result of Pat's untimely death, he experienced a net economic loss of $1,120,304.00. The Court should therefore award the Estate of Patrick Fennig, by Thaddeus C. Fennig and Catherine Fennig as personal representatives, $1,120,304.00 in economic damages for the benefit of Pat's parents, Thaddeus C. Fennig and Catherine Fennig. As for the intangible economic damages of the wrongful death recovery, the Court will address those awards below, in an individualized discussion of the claims of Thaddeus C. Fennig and Catherine Fennig.

ii. Thaddeus C. Fennig & Catherine Fennig

Catherine Fennig ("Cassie") and Thaddeus C. Fennig ("Ted") are United States citizens and the parents of Patrick Fennig ("Pat"). (Dec. 9, 2003 Tr. at 3, 44.) Cassie was born in Marshfield, Wisconsin on May 13, 1933. *Id.* at 3. Ted was born on October 14, 1931 in Milwaukee, Wisconsin to Charles and Marie Fennig. *Id.* at 44. For the first nine years of their marriage the Fennigs lived in West Alice, Wisconsin and then moved to Greendale, Wisconsin, a southwest suburb of Milwaukee, in August of 1965. *Id.* at 6.

Cassie described the effect of Pat's death on her as follows:

I was devastated. You finally get to sleep; it takes days. You wake up in the morning and it's the first thing you thought of. When you went to bed at night, it's the last thing you thought of...And it was hard. I had many thank yous to write and it took me a couple of weeks, but I tried to do some each day. Music was no longer important to me. I always had music on in the home. It was hard to pick up a book and read. It took quite a while before I could get things together and-but it's always there. There's a pain in your chest that never goes away.

Id. at 42-43.

Ted testified that it was difficult to sleep following Pat's death. Ted thinks of Pat often. He has regular dreams about Pat. *Id.* at 63-64.

According to Dr. Cable, Cassie is

in loss and loneliness. She, too, has done reasonably well. But she still expresses and demonstrates a strong sense of loss and that she is not through the real loneliness yet. She has found things that fill her time, but there is nothing that replaces Pat for her...Her grief will continue. She will experience it...[S]he will recover, but it will be waves of grief that will come back from time to time; special events, family affairs, holidays, and the like.

(Feb. 10, 2004 Tr. at 130.) Additionally, Dr. Cable testified that Ted, too,

is in loss and loneliness. He has done reasonably well. He is the caretaker for the rest of the family, and he has certainly carried through on his sense of responsibility in that. But he still misses his son very much...He will continue in his grief...[and later] be hit by waves of grief that may come back from time to time.

Id. at 127-28.

Based upon the evidence presented at trial, both Thaddeus and Catherine Fennig have experienced severe mental anguish and suffering as a result of their son's untimely death. Therefore, this Court shall award to the estate of Patrick Fennig, by Thaddeus and Catherine Fennig as Personal Representatives, $5 million for the benefit of his mother Catherine Fennig and $5 million for the benefit of his father Thaddeus C. Fennig to compensate both for the mental pain and suffering both have sustained as a result of their son's death.

f. Estate and Surviving Family Members of Christopher Adams [FN38]

FN38. As will be discussed further below, Christopher Adams' siblings, plaintiffs Mary Young, Daniel Adams, Elizabeth Wolf, Patrick Adams, John Adams, William Adams, and Michael Adams, cannot recover under Florida's wrongful death statute because no evidence was put forth that any was dependent upon the decedent. Accordingly, each must demonstrate that he or she may recover under a valid cause of action for intentional infliction of emotional distress under the laws of the state in which each was domiciled at the time of the attack. A more detailed discussion of their claims will be provided later in this opinion. See *infra* Parts VI.I.2, J.2.

i. Estate of Christopher Adams

Christopher Adams, a Captain in the Air Force, was born on April 18, 1966. (Dec. 10, 2003 A.M. Tr. at 10.) There were eight children in the Adams family, six boys and two girls. Christopher Adams was the oldest of the boys. He is the son of Catherine and John Adams. On June 24, 1976, at the age of 36, John Adams died of kidney failure and a massive heart attack, having been on dialysis for six to eight hours every day during the eight months before he died. He died in a car while most the family was traveling to a Bar Mitzvah of good friends. Christopher was 10 years old when his father died. *Id.* at 111, 113.

Ever since he was a little boy, Christopher wanted to become a pilot. (Dec. 10, 2003 A.M. Tr. at 114.) Even when he was in high school, he would go in airplanes with a certified pilot. *Id.* at 3. Christopher attended Daniel Webster College in New Hampshire because of its ROTC program in which he could learn to be a pilot. *Id.* at 28. After his 20 years in the Air Force, Christopher intended to become a commercial airline pilot. (Dec. 10, 2003 A.M. Tr. at 45; Dec. 10, 2003 P.M. Tr. at 60.) He knew that being a pilot of such a large plane would help in his subsequent career. (Dec. 10, 2003 A.M. Tr. at 6.)

Christopher obtained his flight training in Texas around 1989 or 1990 and was commissioned as a First Lieutenant at Lubbock. Mrs. Adams attended the ceremony, along with

two of the other children, her brother, and Christopher's best friend. *Id.* at 31. Christopher mainly flew a C-130, a huge transport plane for troops, cargo, trucks, and other large items. *Id.* at 31. He was involved in many covert operations in foreign countries. *Id.* at 32, 34. Christopher was responsible for airlifting over 1,000 passengers and over 250 tons of cargo to resupply U.S. Forces in Operation Desert Storm in 1991. He was also chosen to fly a sensitive mission filming the oil fires of Kuwait and supported Operation Promise, a humanitarian airlift into Bosnia where he flew 16 missions under combat conditions delivering over 336 tons of food, equipment, and urgently needed medical supplies. *Id.* at 54.

Sadly, Christopher had not originally been scheduled to be in Saudi Arabia in June 1996. The wife of one of his buddies was expecting a baby, and Christopher told his buddy to stay home and that he, Christopher, would take the tour of duty. (Dec. 10, 2003 A.M. Tr. at 44.)

Christopher's estate is represented by his mother, Catherine Adams. Christopher's estate has asserted claims under Florida's wrongful death statute because he was last domiciled in Florida. As the personal representatives of Christopher's estate, Catherine Adams is the proper plaintiff to bring a wrongful death action under Florida law. *See* Fla. Stat. Ann. §768.20-768.21. In light of the fact that Christopher had no spouse or other survivors as defined by Fla. Stat. Ann. §768.18, any recovery under this wrongful death action is for the benefit of Christopher's mother, Catherine Adams. *See* Fla. Stat. Ann. §768.18.

Based upon the pleadings and evidence presented to the Court, the estate of Christopher Adams has made out a valid claim for wrongful death under Florida law. The beneficiaries of this estate are entitled to recover the present value of any "loss of the prospective net accumulations" of the decedent that might reasonably have been expected but for the wrongful death because, at the time of his death, Christopher was over 25 years old, with surviving parents, but without other dependents. *See* Fla. Stat. Ann. §768.21(6). Additionally, although Christopher was over 25 years of age at the time of his death, his mother is nonetheless entitled to recover for her own mental pain and suffering arising out of this wrongful death action due to the fact that Christopher died without any other survivors. *See* Fla. Stat. Ann. §768.21(4).

Dr. Herman Miller, an economic consultant testified as an expert that, as a result of Pat's untimely death, he experienced a net economic loss of $3,153,953.00. The Court should therefore award the Estate of Christopher Adams, by Catherine Adams as personal representative, $3,153,953.00 in economic damages for the benefit of Christopher's mother, Catherine Adams. As for the intangible economic damages of the wrongful death recovery, the Court will address those awards below, in an individualized discussion of the claims Catherine Adams.

ii. Catherine Adams

Catherine Adams is the mother of Christopher Adams. (Dec. 10, 2003 A.M. Tr. at 8.) Catherine Adams was raised in Brooklyn, and went to public schools in Brooklyn, but did not go to college. *Id.* at 8. Between high school and marriage, she worked in the credit and collection department of International Paper Company. She married her husband, John, when she was 20 years old. Her husband was an only child, born in Brooklyn in 1939. The first of the eight children was born when Mrs. Adams was 21 and the last was born when she was 31. *Id.* at 9-10.

While her husband was alive, Catherine Adams stayed at home taking care of the growing family. Just a few months before he died, she went to work for Eastern Airlines in its security department, beginning each day at 2:00 A.M. Id at 17. When he died, his mother moved in to help with the eight children, but she only lived for four more years. *Id.* at 17-18. After her husband died, Catherine Adams had to work two jobs, both for United Artists, beginning at 9:00 A.M. and going until after midnight, working usually 14-16 hours a day. *Id.* at 19. For the last 23 years, Catherine Adams has been a secretary at Hofstra University. *Id.* at 20.

During the first year after Christopher died, Catherine Adams went to the cemetery every week, and after that at least once a month. She still goes to visit once every other month. *Id.* at 65. Catherine Adams and many members of her family have attended virtually every memorial service held in Florida, Virginia, and Washington after 1996. *Id.* at 71-72. There are many memorials in Long Island for him, and the family itself set up a scholarship at Christopher's college. *Id.* at 73.

Catherine Adams was not able to return to work until the late summer 1996. Even then, it was very hard for her. *Id.* at 74-75. She thinks about Christopher every day. During the last years, September 11, the bombing of the USS Cole, and other terrorist attacks are difficult for her. They bring back all of her terrible memories and make her relive Christopher's death. *Id.* at 84.

According to her son, John, Catherine Adams figuratively died on the day Christopher died. John, who has been a mental health counselor, has never seen anyone so sad. John has worked with a lot of hurt people, but Christopher's death changed his mother in a terrible way. "She kept everybody together and Chris' death changed her. She's different, she's not the same". (Dec. 10, 2003 P.M. Tr. at 68.)

According to Dr. Cable, Catherine Adams

is still in the stage of loss and loneliness. She still continues to miss [her son], to miss the support he gave. The daydreaming is significant…because he is continuing to age in her mind. One of the things that implies is the grief is a changing kind of grief…So that makes it very intense with the grief. Difficult for her to realize now he will never be married, there never will be grandchildren…Her grief will continue…her pain will ease with time, but it's never going to go away. She will experience ongoing bouts of grief in the future.

(Feb. 10, 2004 Tr. at 98-99.)

Based upon the evidence presented at trial, Catherine Adams has experienced severe mental anguish and suffering as a result of her son's untimely death. Therefore, this Court shall award to the estate of Christopher Adams, by Catherine Adams as Personal Representative, $5 million for the benefit of his mother Catherine Adams to compensate her for the mental pain and suffering she sustained as a result of her son's death.

g. Estate and Surviving Family Members of Thanh (Gus) Nguyen

i. Estate of Thanh (Gus) Nguyen

Thanh ("Gus") Nguyen was born in South Vietnam in 1959. He had 14 brothers and sisters. (Dec. 11, 2003 A.M. Tr. at 9.) Gus came to the United States when he was approximately 14 years old. He had a sister, Maria, who was already in the United States, and had married an American serviceman. *Id.* at 10-11. When he first arrived, he went to Illinois with a host family, with whom he lived for about a year. He then moved to Panama City, Florida, where his sister Maria and her husband were living. *Id.* at 11. Eventually, he became an American citizen. He lived in Panama City until he went into the military in 1979. *Id.* at 12-13.

In the Air Force, Gus became a jet engine mechanic. He did his boot camp training in Texas and his technical training in Illinois. *Id.* at 15. In 1983, Gus married his wife, Teresa. He and Teresa had one child, Christopher, who was born in 1984. Eventually, Gus and Teresa were divorced in 1988. *Id.* at 8.

After the divorce, Christopher lived with his father for about eight months of the year and with his mother for approximately four months of the year. *Id.* at 21-22. Gus' life revolved around Christopher. His career was harmed by spending all of his time with Christopher when he would be home. Even though he was a jet engine mechanic on the F-15's, there were many engines that he just didn't have time to study because he wanted to spend all of his spare time with his son. *Id.* at 25. Teresa testified that Gus was "father of the year material." *Id.* at 42.

Gus was deployed to Saudi Arabia in April 1996. At that time, Christopher went to Ohio with his mother for Gus' three-month tour of duty. Gus was supposed to return to America on the morning after the bombing. (Dec. 11, 2003 P.M. Tr. at 24, 65.) Gus had planned to spend three more years in the Air Force after 1996, and then he was going to obtain a college degree. He ultimately wanted to build and develop better airplanes. *Id.* at 17.

Gus' estate is represented by his son, Christopher. Gus' estate has asserted claims under Florida's wrongful death statute because he was last domiciled in Florida. As the personal representative of Christopher's estate, Christopher Nguyen is the proper plaintiff to bring a wrongful death action under Florida law. *See* Fla. Stat. Ann. §768.20-768.21. In light of the fact that Gus is only survived by his son, any recovery under this wrongful death action is for the benefit of his son Christopher. *See* Fla. Stat. Ann. §768.18; 768.21.

Based upon the pleadings and evidence presented to the Court, the estate of Thanh "Gus" Nguyen has made out a valid claim for wrongful death under Florida law. The beneficiaries of this estate are entitled to recover the present value of any "loss of the prospective net accumulations" of the decedent that might reasonably have been expected but for the wrongful death because, at the time of his death, Christopher was survived by a lineal descendant: his son Christopher. *See* Fla. Stat. Ann. §768.21(6). Additionally, as Gus' child, Christopher is entitled to recover for "lost parental companionship, instruction, and guidance and for mental pain and suffering from the date of injury" arising out of this wrongful death action. *See* Fla. Stat. Ann. §768.21(3).

Dr. Herman Miller, an economic consultant testified as an expert that, as a result of Pat's untimely death, he experienced a net economic loss of $596,905.00. The Court should therefore award the Estate of Thanh "Gus" Nguyen, by Christopher Nguyen as personal representative, $596,905.00 in economic damages for the benefit of Gus' son, Christopher Nguyen. As for the intangible economic damages of the wrongful death recovery, the Court will address those awards below, in an individualized discussion of the claims Christopher Nguyen.

ii. Christopher Nguyen

Christopher knows in reality that his father is dead but his heart doesn't accept it. He gets a "blissful look in his eyes when he looks at his dad." *Id.* at 30. He cried a lot after returning to Ohio, but eventually he stopped crying in front of other people. He would just go into his bedroom, lock the door, and cry by himself. *Id.* at 36-37.

When he moved back to Ohio, his grades went down because he lacked the motivation. He would often get angry, and break things. Christopher also began to withdraw socially. He became much more shy, and has stayed that way ever since. *Id.* at 61-64. He is much more reserved, and has a harder time making friends and trusting people. *Id.* at 42.

Shortly after Gus died, Teresa tried to get Christopher to see a psychologist, but Christopher refused to talk to the psychologist about his father. Nothing worked in terms of counseling because Christopher wouldn't open up. *Id.* at 40. He thinks about his father all the time. Each year, June 25 is understandably a very sad day for Christopher.

According to Dr. Cable, Christopher

is in loss and loneliness. He has been forced to grow up very quickly. He lost not only his father, but his best friend and his real support system. So there is a deep sense of loss and loneliness for him…He will continue in grief. Those significant markers down the road are going to be real trial times for him. Just as he indicated "Dad wasn't there for my high school graduation," [his Dad] won't be there for college or when Chris gets married or any of those kind of things. So once again you get those waves of grief that come back because the person is missing from those significant events in life that should be shared.

(Feb. 10, 2004 Tr. at 182-83.)

Based upon the evidence presented at trial, Christopher Nguyen has experienced severe mental anguish and suffering as a result of his father's untimely death. Therefore, this Court shall award to the Estate of Thanh "Gus" Nguyen, by Christopher Nguyen as personal representative, $5 million for the benefit of Christopher Nguyen to compensate him for the mental pain and suffering he sustained as a result of his father's untimely death.

h. Estate and Surviving Family Members of Brian McVeigh

i. Estate of Brian McVeigh

In June 1996, Brian McVeigh, was a twenty-one-year-old Assistant-Crew-Chief in the Air Force. Ex. 16. Although regularly stationed at Eglin AFB, in June 1996, Brian was on assignment in Dhahran, Saudi Arabia, where he resided at the Khobar Towers Complex. *Id.* On June 25, 1996, Brian was killed at Khobar Towers. Ex. 9.

Brian McVeigh was born in Sanford, Florida on March 27, 1975. Ex. 168 at 7-8; Depo. Ex. 1. When Brian was three years old, his parents divorced. Ex. 168 at 8. Sandra had custody of Brian, whose father took no interest or part in rearing Brian. *Id.* In fact, Mr. McVeigh only saw Brian three times after the divorce (in 1978) and never after Brian turned ten.

Id. As a result, Sandra, a single parent, was both mother and father to Brian for most of his life. *Id.* at 27.

Brian grew up in Debary, Florida. *Id.* at 9. Brian was the quintessential American boy. He attended middle school in Deltona, Florida. *Id.* at 11. Brian participated in scouting for most of his childhood. He was a tiger cub, a cub scout, and a boy scout. *Id.* According to Sandra, Brian was a good boy who never caused any trouble. *Id.* at 13.

Brian attended his freshman year of high school at Deltona High School, Deltona, Florida. *Id.* at 15. He attended his sophomore year at a private Christian school, which was also located in Deltona. *Id.* Brian returned to Deltona High School for his junior and senior years in order to be on the wrestling and weightlifting teams. *Id.* Brian excelled at wrestling and weightlifting. *Id.* He graduated from Deltona High School in August 1994. *Id.*; Depo. Ex. 8. Unlike many high school teenagers, Brian was unaffected by peer pressure. *Id.* at 17. He did not drink alcohol or smoke cigarettes. *Id.* He was also very respectful of others. *Id.* at 18. After consulting with his parents, Brian decided to join the Air Force to get some life training. *Id.* at 19; Ex. 170 at 16. After completing his military service in the Air Force, Brian planned on earning a college degree. Ex. 168 at 17.

Brian's estate is represented by his mother and stepfather, Sandra M. Wetmore and James V. Wetmore. Brian's estate has asserted claims under Florida's wrongful death statute because he was last domiciled in Florida. As a personal representative of Brian's estate, Sandra M. Wetmore is a proper plaintiff to bring a wrongful death action under Florida law. *See* Fla. Stat. Ann. §768.20-768.21. [FN39] In light of the fact that Brian had no spouse or lineal descendants, any recovery under this wrongful death action is for the benefit of Brian's mother, Sandra M. Wetmore. *See* Fla. Stat. Ann. §768.18; *supra* note 39.

FN39. As the evidence before this Court shows, James Wetmore is a non-adoptive stepparent to Brian. Under Florida law, a non-adoptive stepparent is deemed *in loco parentis* to the child, as distinct from being considered as the child's parent. *K.A.S. v. R.E.T.*, 914 So.2d 1056, 1062-63 (Fla.Dist. Ct.App.2005). This distinction is important because "a stepparent…or other person standing *in loco parentis* to a child does not acquire all of the rights or assume all of the obligations of a natural parent." *Id.* at 1063. This is in large part due to the fact that a person *in loco parentis* is under no binding obligation to care for the child, whereas-absent an adoption order-the bond between a natural parent and child is permanent. *Id.* In light of Florida's stance limiting the rights of non-adoptive stepparents as to their stepchildren, this Court finds that a non-adoptive stepparent under Florida law may

not seek personal recovery under Florida's wrongful death statute. Cf. *Florida East Coast Ry. Co. v. Jackson*, 65 Fla. 393, 62 So. 210, 211 (1913) (holding under a previous version of Florida's wrongful death statute that it was error for the child's stepfather to join the mother as a plaintiff in the wrongful death action because only parents-and not step-parents-had the right to sue for wrongful death on behalf of their children). Accordingly, though both Sandra and James Wetmore are listed as the personal representatives of Brian's estate, only Sandra Wetmore, as Brian's mother, may properly maintain the action on her son's behalf. To the extent that James Wetmore has sought any damages in his personal capacity as Brian's non-adoptive stepfather, his claim must be denied.

Based upon the pleadings and evidence presented to the Court, the estate of Brian McVeigh has made out a valid claim for wrongful death under Florida law. The beneficiaries of this estate, however, are not entitled to recover the present value of any "loss of the prospective net accumulations" of the decedent that might reasonably have been expected but for the wrongful death because Brian was under 25 years old when he died, and did not have either a surviving spouse or any surviving lineal descendants. Fla. Stat. Ann. §768.21(6)(a)(1). Still, Brian's mother is entitled to recover for her own mental pain and suffering arising out of this wrongful death action due to the fact that Brian left no other survivors. *See* Fla. Stat. Ann. §768.21(4). A discussion of these intangible economic damages of the wrongful death recovery, will be addressed below in an individualized discussion of the claim of Sandra M. Wetmore.

ii. Sandra M. Wetmore

In addition, Sandra became clinically depressed following Brian's death. She saw a psychiatrist and took medications to control her depression for six years. *Id.* at 39-40. For about two years, Sandra lost herself in television and refused to entertain guests at her house. To help his wife rediscover life, James got Sandra involved in horse back riding, something she had enjoyed as a child. *Id.* at 41. Sandra blames her failing health on Brian's death. Two years after Brian's death, she was diagnosed with fibromyalgia. *Id.* at 39. In 2000, she was diagnosed with diabetes. Finally, Sandra was diagnosed with cancer in 2003. *Id.* at 40.

Sandra finds it hard to see parents with their children, especially when the parents are complaining about their children. She testified: "I wish mine was here to misbehave, that would be all right." Although the pain of Brian's death has not gone away, Sandra tries to have a "positive attitude" because Brian would want her to embrace the way he lived and not the way he died. *Id.* at 42. It is hard to be positive, however, because Sandra is forced to remember the tragedy with each new terrorist act, especially since the September 11th attacks on the United States. *Id.* at 35.

As Dr. Cable stated, Sandra

is in loss and loneliness. It's complicated or compounded by her own health issues now. The loss and loneliness is very deep because of the extreme closeness of the relationship she had with her son. They were a team for a lot of years in there, and that makes it very difficult…Her grief will continue for the foreseeable future. I don't think she will ever fully recover.

(Feb. 10, 2004 Tr. at 167.)

Based upon the evidence presented at trial, Sandra Wetmore has experienced severe mental anguish and suffering as a result of her son's untimely death. Therefore, this Court shall award to the Estate of Brian McVeigh, by Sandra M. Wetmore as personal representative, $5 million for the benefit of Sandra M. Wetmore to compensate her for the mental pain and suffering she sustained as a result of her son's untimely death.

i. Estate and Surviving Family Members of Joseph Rimkus

i. Estate of Joseph Rimkus
In June 1996, Joseph Edward Rimkus was twenty-two years old. Ex. 19. Although regularly stationed at Eglin AFB in Florida, in June 1996, Joseph was on assignment in Dhahran, Saudi Arabia where he resided at the Khobar Towers Complex. *Id.* On June 25, 1996, Joseph was killed in the terrorist bombing at Khobar Towers. Ex. 9.

Mrs. Brooks married Joseph John Rimkus ("Mr.Rimkus") in October 1973. Mr. Rimkus was in the military when they married. Ex. 19, at 7. Mrs. Brooks and Mr. Rimkus had three children: Joseph Rimkus, born April 13, 1974, James Rimkus, born September 12, 1975, and Anne Rimkus, born December 28, 1976. *Id.* at 4-5, 44, 71; Ex. 183. Joseph was born at Keesler AFB in Mississippi. Ex. 183. James and Anne were born at Scott AFB in Illinois. (Feb. 5, 2004 Tr. at 44, 71.)

With the exception of a brief stay at Scott AFB, Illinois and two years in Turkey, Joseph and his siblings were raised in the family home in Crestview, Florida. All three children attended grammar school in Crestview. Mrs. Brooks was a stay-at-home mother who would work occasionally and only when the children were in school. Accordingly, she spent a great deal of time with all of her children. Ex. 19, at 8-9.

Mrs. Brooks described Joseph as a "wonderful" and "responsible" boy with a passion for learning. Mrs. Brooks testified that she had a special "connection" with Joseph because he almost died at birth. Joseph's importance within

the family unit changed significantly when Mr. Rimkus deployed to Korea when Joseph was a freshman in high school. *Id.* at 11. When the family dropped Mr. Rimkus off at the airport to deploy to Korea, Mr. Rimkus told Joseph that he was the man of the house and charged him with taking care of his mother and siblings. *Id.* at 74. Mr. Rimkus never communicated with his family since the time of his deployment. *Id.* at 11-12. From that point on, Joseph took charge of the family. Mrs. Brooks testified how Joseph would do the laundry, watch after James and Anne, plan the menu and do the grocery shopping, and keep a family budget. James explained how Joseph delegated and did chores and made "sure that there wasn't anything going on behind my parents back." *Id.* at 12. Mrs. Brooks later divorced Mr. Rimkus in 1991. *Id.* at 4.

Anne testified that Joseph was a parental figure to her, advising her not to drink alcohol, to respect herself, and taught her how to play chess and change the oil in her car. *Id.* at 73-74. Indeed, even at such a young age, Joseph took up his responsibilities with ease and without complaint. Joseph's attitude and assistance was invaluable to Mrs. Brooks, who was working full time and taking college courses in the evening. *Id.* at 11-12.

In addition to running the Rimkus home, Joseph worked several part-time jobs in high school. He worked at a local gym and fish restaurant. Joseph, along with James, even found time to volunteer at a camp for disabled children. Mrs. Brooks testified that Joseph was a "good saver" and was "generous" with his money, giving money to his siblings and his paternal grandmother regularly. *Id.* at 13.

Joseph graduated from Crestview High School in June 1992. Ex. 185. In addition to wanting to serve his country, Joseph joined the military to earn money to pay for college. (Feb. 5, 2004 Tr. at 11.) Joseph's entry into the Air Force did not diminish the closeness of the Rimkus family. Joseph regularly wrote, sent care packages, and/or telephoned to Mrs. Brooks, James, and Anne while he was in the Air Force. *Id.* at 23, 52, 80. Joseph left for Saudi Arabia on his twenty-second birthday. *Id.* at 22.

Joseph's estate is represented by his mother, Bridget Brooks. Joseph's estate has asserted claims under Florida's wrongful death statute because he was last domiciled in Florida. As a personal representative of Joseph's estate, Bridget Brooks is a proper plaintiff to bring a wrongful death action under Florida law. *See* Fla. Stat. Ann. §768.20-768.21. In light of the fact that Joseph had no spouse or lineal descendants, any recovery under this wrongful death action is for the benefit of his mother, Bridget Brooks. *See* Fla. Stat. Ann. §768.18.

Based upon the pleadings and evidence presented to the Court, the estate of Joseph Rimkus has made out a valid claim for wrongful death under Florida law. The beneficiaries of this estate, however, are not entitled to recover the present value of any "loss of the prospective net accumulations" of the decedent that might reasonably have been expected but for the wrongful death because Joseph was under 25 years old when he died, and did not have either a surviving spouse or any surviving lineal descendants. Fla. Stat. Ann. §768.21(6)(a)(1). Still, Joseph's mother is entitled to recover for her own mental pain and suffering arising out of this wrongful death action due to the fact that Joseph left no other survivors. *See* Fla. Stat. Ann. §768.21(4). A discussion of these intangible economic damages of the wrongful death recovery, will be addressed below in an individualized discussion of the claim of Bridget Brooks.

ii. *Bridget Brooks*

Mrs. Brooks resides at 432 Barbados Way, Niceville, Florida. (Feb. 5, 2004 Tr. at 3.) She was born on December 6, 1955 in St. Charles, Missouri. Mrs. Brooks is a United States citizen. She is an operations analyst for the United States Air Force at Eglin AFB, where she was worked for 17 years. *Id.* at 3, 26. Mrs. Brooks is married to Donald Brooks, whom she married after divorcing her first husband, Joseph John Rimkus in 1991. *Id.* at 3-4. Mrs. Brooks married Joseph John Rimkus ("Mr.Rimkus") in October 1973. Mr. Rimkus was in the military when they married. *Id.* at 7.

Joseph's death dramatically affected Mrs. Brooks. Mrs. Brooks visits Joseph's grave, which is an hour away from her house, regularly and on special anniversary dates. Mrs. Brooks also visits Joshua Woody's grave on Joshua's birthday. (Feb. 5, 2004 Tr. at 35.) Mrs. Brooks sought help to cope with Joseph's death. She relied heavily on her faith and has consulted with several priests about her grief. She also participated in a grief support group named "Under Pressure," which is comprised of several women who lost loved ones in the Khobar Towers bombing. *Id.* at 37-39. Mrs. Brooks involvement with Under Pressure helped her immensely with Joseph's death. *Id.* at 37.

Even today, Mrs. Brooks misses Joseph terribly around the holidays. *Id.* at 42. She still hangs Joseph's Christmas stocking in his honor. *Id.* at 68. Mrs. Brooks becomes particularly depressed on the anniversary of the bombing. She experiences additional grief each and every time she learns of another terrorist act committed in the United States or abroad. *Id.* at 42.

According to Dr. Cable:

[Mrs. Brooks] is in loss and loneliness. Her son was her real strength. Her emotions are till very raw. It's still hard for her to talk about what happened. Quite a bit of pain there...I believe her grief will continue for a long time into the future. She will go on with life, but the grief will keep coming back if she thinks about what should be or what should have been now. So it's not going away. [FN40]

FN40. (Feb. 10, 2004 Tr. at 186.)

Based upon the evidence presented at trial, Bridget Brooks has experienced severe mental anguish and suffering as a result of her son's untimely death. Therefore, this Court shall award to the Estate of Joseph Rimkus, by Bridget Brooks as personal representative, $5 million for the benefit of Bridget Brooks to compensate her for the mental pain and suffering she sustained as a result of her son's untimely death.

iii. *James Rimkus*

James Rimkus lives in Crestview, Florida. He was born on September 12, 1975, in Illinois and is United States citizen. James is married to Christina Renee Rimkus, with whom he has a daughter and a stepson. (Feb. 5, 2004 Tr. at 44.)

James Rimkus was completely devastated by his brother's death. Joseph was James' best friend. *Id.* at 47. James looked up to Joseph and considered him a role model and father figure. *Id.* at 48-49. Indeed, Joseph was the first person James wrote to when he was at boot camp. *Id.* at 52. James testified how Joseph and he were like twins.

James' grief was intensified because he was in the Navy and was not allowed to remain with his family following Joseph's death. He had to return to his ship and deploy to the Mediterranean. The Navy also did not offer James any counseling. *Id.* at 63.

James testified that he began drinking more and more after his brother's death and became a severe alcoholic. *Id.* at 64. James did take Adavan, an anti-depressant, for a few months to help him cope with Joseph's death. The prescription did not work because of his drinking. Apparently, James was self-medicating with alcohol. James entered into a Christian rehabilitation clinic after leaving the Navy and has been sober for more than four years. *Id.* at 65.

James has only visited his brother's grave once. It is just too painful for him to visit Joseph's grave. Even today, James is terribly saddened because his children and Anne's future children will never know their uncle Joseph. *Id.* at 67. Although James has had good dreams about Joseph since his death, James tries not to dream about Joseph because it causes him too much grief afterwards. He testified that he misses Joseph especially around the holidays, and on Joseph's birthday.

As Dr. Cable testified, James is in loss and loneliness. He has had to grow up very quickly in a very difficult way. He is, I think, much older than his years. He sounds it; he acts it. It's really aged him. Very emotional, very haunted by his brother's death…Grief will always be with him. Family is his strength. That's the thing that will get him through. But the grief process is still very present.

(Feb. 10, 2004 Tr. at 188-89.)

Because plaintiffs offered no evidence that James Rimkus was financially dependent upon Joseph Rimkus prior to his death, and because damages are only available to siblings under Florida's wrongful death statute when there is evidence that the sibling was wholly or partly dependent upon the decedent, James Rimkus cannot recover for his loss under that statute. See Fla. Stat. Ann. §768.18(1). Instead, James Rimkus is proceeding under an intentional infliction of emotional distress claim. Because James Rimkus was domiciled in Florida on the date of his brother's death in the bombing, Florida law will govern his intentional infliction of emotional distress claim.

As the brother of Joseph Rimkus, James Rimkus has brought an intentional infliction of emotional distress claim against the defendants for pain and suffering caused by the death of his brother. Based upon the evidence presented to the Court, the elements of James Rimkus' intentional infliction of emotional distress claim are met. The defendants conduct in facilitating, financing, and providing material support to bring about this attack was intentional, extreme, and outrageous. As the evidence shows, this horrific act precipitated by the defendants' planning and assistance brought immediate emotional distress to James Rimkus. Finally, it is clear that James Rimkus has continued to experience emotional distress since that time due to the fact that his brother was taken away from him in such a tragic and horrific manner. Therefore, this Court shall award to James Rimkus $2.5 million to compensate him for the emotional distress, pain and suffering that he sustained as a result of his brother's untimely death.

iv. Anne Rimkus

Anne Rimkus lives in Gainesville, Florida. She was born on December 28, 1976 in Illinois and is a United States citizen. (Feb. 5, 2004 Tr. at 71.) Anne, like Mrs. Brooks and James, is still grieving over Joseph.

Anne was particularly close to Joseph. She testified how grateful she is for Joseph stepping in when her father left for Korea and never returned to the family unit. *Id.* at 74-75. As an adult, she now realizes just how much Joseph did for her growing up. *Id.* at 75.

Anne noted that Joseph was the emotional rock that mediated the family relationships. *Id.* Anne misses Joseph's great sense of humor and "uplifting spirit." *Id.* at 75, 79. Anne testified that she has only just now begun to cope with Joseph's death. *Id.* at 86. To deal with these wounds, Anne has recently started to see a counselor at the University of Florida, where she studies sociology. *Id.* at 72, 87.

Anne testified that Joseph's death caused James to close off and distance himself from her. *Id.* at 89. In contrast, Joseph's death caused Mr. Rimkus to reach out to both Anne and James. *Id.* at 88. As Dr. Cable stated, Anne

is still in loss and loneliness, but complicated by guilt issues that have not been resolved…She has a lot of regrets, a lot of unfinished business…She will continue in grief… There is not a really good support system for her, and so she is sort of dealing with everything on her own, and I think that's going to be difficult for her in the years ahead.

(Feb. 10, 2004 Tr. at 190-91.)

Because plaintiffs offered no evidence that Anne Rimkus was financially dependent upon Joseph Rimkus prior to his death, and because damages are only available to siblings under Florida's wrongful death statute when there is evidence that the sibling was wholly or partly dependent upon the decedent, Anne Rimkus cannot recover for her loss under that statute. See Fla. Stat. Ann. §768.18(1). Instead, Anne Rimkus is proceeding under an intentional infliction of emotional distress claim. Because Anne Rimkus was domiciled in Florida on the date of her brother's death in the bombing, Florida law will govern her intentional infliction of emotional distress claim.

As the sister of Joseph Rimkus, Anne Rimkus has brought an intentional infliction of emotional distress claim against the defendants for pain and suffering caused by the death of her brother. Based upon the evidence presented to the Court, the elements of Anne Rimkus' intentional infliction of emotional distress claim are met. The defendants conduct in facilitating, financing, and providing material support to bring about this attack was intentional, extreme, and outrageous. As the evidence shows, this horrific act precipitated by the defendants' planning and assistance brought immediate emotional distress to Anne Rimkus. Finally, it is clear that Anne Rimkus has continued to experience emotional distress since that time due to the fact that her brother was taken away from her in such a tragic and horrific manner. Therefore, this Court shall award to Anne Rimkus $2.5 million to compensate her for the emotional distress, pain and suffering that she sustained as a result of her brother's untimely death.

j. Estate and Surviving Family Members of Kendall Kitson [FN41]

FN41. As will be discussed further below, plaintiffs Steve K. Kitson and Nancy A. Kitson, Kendall Kitson, Jr.'s siblings, cannot recover under Florida's wrongful death statute because no evidence was put forth that either was dependent upon the decedent. Accordingly, each must demonstrate that he may recover under a valid cause of action for intentional infliction of emotional distress under the laws of the state in which each was domiciled at the time of the attack, Texas and Oklahoma, respectively. A more detailed discussion of their claims will be provided later in this opinion. See *infra* Parts VI.E.2.b, L.2.a.

i. Estate of Kendall Kitson, Jr.

In June 1996, Kendall Kitson ("Kenny"), deceased, was a 39 year old mechanic for F-15s and F-16s in the United States Air Force. Ex. 292, at 13. Although regularly stationed in Florida, in June 1996, Kenny was on assignment in Dhahran, Saudi Arabia where he resided at the Khobar Towers Complex. *Id.* On June 25, 1996, Kenny was killed at Khobar Towers. Plaintiffs Kendall Kitson, Sr., Nancy R. Kitson, Nancy A. Kitson, and Steve Kitson are Kenny's father, mother, sister, and brother respectively (collectively, the "Kitson family"). The Kitson family, through counsel, offered affidavits of their testimony in this matter, and their affidavits were admitted into evidence by the Court on February 9, 2004. (Feb. 9, 2004 Tr. at 67-68.) Kenny was born in 1956 in Virginia. Ex. 292, at 4. The Kitson children, like their parents, are all United States citizens. *Id.* at 1.

When Kenny was in high school, he went to a vocational and technical school where he learned about aircraft. Ex. 291 at 8. After high school, Kenny went to college for two years, but did not enjoy college, and wanted to use his hands. After two years in college, Mr. Kitson remembers Kenny coming home from school one day and holding up a T-shirt that read "United States Air Force." Mr. Kitson was surprised to learn that Kenny had joined the military, but he knew how interested he was in aviation since taking the classes in high school. *Id.* Kenny's sister, Nancy, was not surprised when Kenny joined the military and felt that he wanted to follow in their father's footsteps. Ex. 292, at 13.

Kenny wanted to be a pilot when he joined the Air Force, but could not work as a pilot because he did not have perfect vision. Instead, Kenny worked as a mechanic for F-15s and F-16s. On military operations, Kenny would be one of the first people to arrive and one of the last people to leave. Kenny enjoyed the Air Force, and kept reenlisting, and was promoted to Technical Sergeant. He was a flight

line expediter, flight chief, and production superintendent. *Id.*

Kenny had been in the Air Force for 17 years when he was killed. He was only three years away from being able to fully retire. Kenny volunteered to stay in Saudi Arabia during his last tour to help one of his friends who was married and had two daughters, one of whom was ill. *Id.* at 10.

Kenny's estate is represented by his parents, Kendall Kitson, Sr., and Nancy R. Kitson. Kenny's estate has asserted claims under Florida's wrongful death statute because he was last domiciled in Florida. As the personal representatives of Kenny's estate, Kendall Kitson, Sr., and Nancy R. Kitson are the proper plaintiffs to bring a wrongful death action under Florida law. *See* Fla. Stat. Ann. §768.20-768.21. In light of the fact that Kenny had no spouse or other survivors as defined by Fla. Stat. Ann. §768.18, any recovery under this wrongful death action is for the benefit of his parents, Kendall Kitson, Sr., and Nancy R. Kitson. *See* Fla. Stat. Ann. §768.18.

Based upon the pleadings and evidence presented to the Court, the estate of Kendall Kitson, Jr., has made out a valid claim for wrongful death under Florida law. The beneficiaries of this estate are entitled to recover the present value of any "loss of the prospective net accumulations" of the decedent that might reasonably have been expected but for the wrongful death because Kenny was over 25 years old when he died, and died with surviving parents, but without other dependents. *See* Fla. Stat. Ann. §768.21(6)(2). Additionally, although Kenny was over 25 years of age at the time of his death, Kenny's parents are nonetheless entitled to recover for their own mental pain and suffering arising out of this wrongful death action due to the fact that Kenny died without any other survivors. *See* Fla. Stat. Ann. §768.21(4).

Dr. Herman Miller, an economic consultant testified as an expert that, as a result of Kenny's untimely death, he experienced a net economic loss of $2,183,460.00. The Court should therefore award the Estate of Kendall Kitson, Jr., by Kendall Kitson, Sr., and Nancy R. Kitson as personal representatives, $2,183,460.00 in economic damages for the benefit of Kenny's parents, Kendall Kitson, Sr., and Nancy R. Kitson. As for the intangible economic damages of the wrongful death recovery, the Court will address those awards below, in an individualized discussion of the claims of Kendall Kitson, Sr., and Nancy R. Kitson.

ii. Kendall Kitson Sr. & Nancy R. Kitson

Kendall Kitson, Sr., met and married his wife, Nancy R. Kitson, in the late 1930s. He then joined the Navy and served his country in the Navy for approximately 22 1/2 years. Ex.

291, at 3. The Kitsons now reside in Yukon, Oklahoma and Ft. Walton Beach, Florida. *Id.*

Kenny's death has dramatically affected Kendall and Nancy R. Kitson and their lives together. As Mr. Kitson testified in his affidavit:

Kenny's death has ruined my entire family…My life has changed dramatically since Kenny's death. If Kenny were alive, he wouldn't let me sit around like I do. He never let me sit down…We miss Kenny all the time, every day. Some days are harder than others. We miss him terribly on his birthday and on certain days because he loved his mother's potato salad…I miss just seeing Kenny and talking to him. He always used to drive by the house. It's hard to laugh now or have any fun. It's difficult when my wife and I run into his classmates on the street or in a store. We hardly eat or sleep. I used to be a lot more outgoing. My wife and I used to be more social before Kenny's death. Now, we don't do anything.

Ex. 291 at 12, 17-19.

Since Kenny's death, Mr. Kitson sometimes flies into rages about Kenny's death and the news on our country's fight against terrorism. Nancy feels as though her parents now hate the world. Ex. 292, at 26. Mr. and Mrs. Kitson do not like to go out or visit with anyone since Kenny's death. In fact, Mr. Kitson will not visit his daughter Nancy's home because she has so many of Kenny's things on display. *Id.* at 30.

Mrs. Kitson is terminally ill with cancer. Mr. Kitson, as well as his children, are convinced that her declining health is related to their loss of Kenny. Exs. 291, at 23; 292, at 31; 293, at 26. Mrs. Kitson used to visit Kenny's grave all the time and put fresh flowers on it.

As Dr. Cable testified, Mrs. Kitson

is in loss and loneliness. That, of course, is complicated by her own physical condition at this point. She misses her son terribly. Her life was gone with his death, and now literally her life is going…She will never recover. She will die still very much enmeshed in the grief that she is in right now.

(Feb. 10, 2004 Tr. at 144.)

Additionally, Dr. Cable stated that Kendall Kitson, Sr.,

is in intense loss and loneliness. He is also in volatile emotions with a tremendous amount of anger over what happened. He is still experiencing a lot of rage over that. He cannot seem to move on with his grief…[H]e is one of these individuals for whom the grief will never end. I don't think he will ever be able to put things forward in his life. With his wife's death, I think he is one of these individuals who probably will see very little reason for even fighting for himself after that.

Id. at 146-147.

Based upon the evidence presented at trial, both Kendall Kitson, Sr., and Nancy R. Kitson have experienced severe mental anguish and suffering as a result of their son's untimely death. Therefore, this Court shall award to the estate of Kendall Kitson, Jr., by Kendall Kitson, Sr., and Nancy R. Kitson as Personal Representatives, $5 million for the benefit of his mother Nancy R. Kitson, and $5 million for the benefit of his father Kendall Kitson, Sr., to compensate both for the mental pain and suffering both have sustained as a result of their son's untimely death.

k. *Estate and Surviving Family Members of Jeremy Taylor [FN42]*

FN42. As will be discussed further below, plaintiff Starlina Taylor, Jeremy Taylor's sister, cannot recover under Florida's wrongful death statute because no evidence was put forth that she was dependent upon the decedent, her brother. Accordingly, she must demonstrate that she may recover under a valid cause of action under the laws of Kansas, the state in which she was domiciled at the time of the attack. A more detailed discussion of her claim will be provided later in this opinion. See *infra* Part VI.M.2.a.

i. *Estate of Jeremy Taylor*

In June 1996, Jeremy Taylor, deceased, was a 23 year old Senior Airman in the United States Air Force. Although regularly stationed in Florida, in June 1996, Jeremy was on assignment in Dhahran, Saudi Arabia where he resided at the Khobar Towers Complex. Ex. 20. On June 25, 1996, Jeremy was killed at Khobar Towers. Ex. 9.

Plaintiffs Lawrence Taylor, Vickie Taylor, and Starlina Taylor are Jeremy's father, mother, and sister, respectively (collectively, the "Taylor family"). The Taylor family, through counsel, offered affidavits of their testimony in this matter, and their affidavits were admitted into evidence by the Court on February 9, 2004. (Feb. 9, 2004 Tr. at 66-67.)

Jeremy was born in 1973 in Tennessee. Jeremy is remembered by his parents as a "fun person; the class clown who had friends from all different social sections of school. He was very athletic and played soccer almost his entire life…Jeremy was also very creative. Everyone who met Jeremy loved him; he was very talkative and open." Ex. 289, at 10, 15-16.

Jeremy's estate is represented by his parents, Lawrence and Vickie Taylor. Jeremy's estate has asserted claims under Florida's wrongful death statute because he was last domiciled in Florida. As a personal representative of Jeremy's estate, Lawrence and Vickie Taylor are proper plaintiffs to bring a wrongful death action under Florida law. *See* Fla. Stat. Ann. §768.20-768.21. In light of the fact that Jeremy had no spouse or lineal descendants, any recovery under this wrongful death action is for the benefit of his parents, Lawrence and Vickie Taylor. *See* Fla. Stat. Ann. §768.18.

Based upon the pleadings and evidence presented to the Court, the estate of Jeremy Taylor has made out a valid claim for wrongful death under Florida law. The beneficiaries of this estate, however, are not entitled to recover the present value of any "loss of the prospective net accumulations" of the decedent that might reasonably have been expected but for the wrongful death because Jeremy was under 25 years old when he died, and did not have either a surviving spouse or any surviving lineal descendants. Fla. Stat. Ann. §768.21(6)(a)(1). Still, Jeremy's parents are entitled to recover for their own mental pain and suffering arising out of this wrongful death action due to the fact that Jeremy left no other survivors. *See* Fla. Stat. Ann. §768.21(4). A discussion of these intangible economic damages of the wrongful death recovery, will be addressed below in an individualized discussion of the claims of Lawrence and Vickie Taylor.

ii. Lawrence and Vickie Taylor

Mr. and Mrs. Taylor were born in 1950 and 1951, respectively, in Tennessee, and are United States' citizens. Exs. 288, at 3; 289, at 3. When they met, the Taylors were still in high school, but, as Mrs. Taylor describes, "it was love at first sight." The Taylors finished high school and married in 1969. Ex. 289, 3. Soon after they married, Mr. Taylor joined the United States Air Force, and served his country as an aircraft mechanic for 20 years.

A couple of years after the Taylors married, Mrs. Taylor gave birth to their daughter, Starlina, in 1971. *Id.* at 9. Twenty-one months later, in 1973, the Taylors' son Jeremy was born. Jeremy was born prematurely and Mrs. Taylor had several complications during her pregnancy. Ex. 289, at 10.

Jeremy's death has dramatically affected Lawrence and Vickie Taylor and their lives together. As Mr. Taylor testified in his affidavit:

I feel like my life has not been worth anything since Jeremy's death. It doesn't matter what you do or how much money you have or how many good jobs you have, there's just a big chunk missing. A part of my life is gone. Jeremy is gone. Half of our world is gone. I'll never see him again, I'll never see his kids, I'll never know who is wife was, nothing. It stopped. But I can't move on, I'm just there. I drive by his grave every morning going to work and I drive by on my way home. Even though we try to go on with our lives and be there for our grandson, until I die, I just feel like it's another day...I realize that my life could be worse and I have

much to be grateful for, like my material possessions, but it doesn't matter if I lived in the White House or if I lived in a trailer in Alabama, my son is gone. This pain is going to be with me forever, regardless.

Ex. 288, at 25, 30.

Mrs. Taylor drives by her son's grave everyday. The Taylor family decorates Jeremy's grave for the holidays such as Christmas, Valentine's Day, Memorial Day, and Halloween, and they plant flowers nearby. On Jeremy's birthday, the family goes to the cemetery and releases balloons in his memory. Ex. 289, 27. Since Jeremy's death, holidays are especially difficult for the Taylor family. Mr. Taylor does not celebrate holidays anymore. Jeremy's death has totally changed Mrs. Taylor's way of thinking. Ex. 289, 29, 36.

Jeremy's death also had a negative impact on the Taylors' health. For example, Mr. Taylor now takes a pill every night to help him sleep, and another pill twice a day to calm his heart. Exs. 288, at 29; 289, at 33. Mrs. Taylor health has suffered greatly since Jeremy's death. She has gained weight and has had to have knee replacement surgery. Mrs. Taylor is now living in constant pain because she has fibromyalgia, and she doesn't sleep unless she takes sleeping pills. Mrs. Taylor also takes an antidepressant and has arthritis. Ex. 288, at 30.

The Taylors visited a counselor for a year or so after Jeremy's death. They also did individual counseling and parents of murdered children and compassionate friends. Both Mr. and Mrs. Taylor have given up on counseling. Jeremy's death has also been very hard on the Taylors' marriage. Mrs. Taylor feels that her husband is much more distant since Jeremy's death, while also being more affectionate at times than he used to be. Many times he goes to his workshop and stays there in his own little world. Exs. 288, at 28; 289, at 34.

According to Dr. Cable, Lawrence

is in loss and loneliness, but he is also back in the guilt, and also volatile emotions [stages]. There is a lot of anger and such there. So he has got a very complicated kind of grief going on right now. Very bitter, a lot of self blame as well as anger toward others...[H]e is one of these who will never really recover from his grief, because he doesn't see anything that can make it better. The only thing that would be better is if his son would come back. Since that's not going to happen, nothing will ever in his mind make it better.

(Feb. 10, 2004 Tr. at 195-96.)

Similarly, Dr. Cable testified that Vickie

is in loss and loneliness, and that's complicated by the fact that she really has a minimal support system because of her husband's difficulties. He is not able to be a support to her, and he is not willing to get support for himself. So her loss and loneliness is very difficult. Then she is bothered by the premonition, and that complicates it, too…She will continue in her grief for a long period of time. I don't know that she can ever really come out of it.

   Id. at 197-98.

   Based upon the evidence presented at trial, both Lawrence and Vickie Taylor have experienced severe mental anguish and suffering as a result of their son's untimely death. Therefore, this Court shall award to the estate of Jeremy Taylor, by Lawrence and Vickie Taylor as Personal Representatives, $5 million for the benefit of his mother Vickie Taylor, and $5 million for the benefit of his father Lawrence Taylor to compensate both for the mental pain and suffering both have sustained as a result of their son's untimely death.

B. California

1. Causes of Action

a. Wrongful Death

Under California law, a wrongful death cause of action arises "for the death of a person caused by the wrongful act or neglect of another." Cal Civ. Proc.Code §377.60(a). Such a cause of action may be asserted by a number of individuals, including the decedent's surviving spouse, children, personal representative, and, when the decedent has no surviving spouse or children, the decedent's parents. *Id.*; *Nelson v. County of Los Angeles*, 113 Cal.App.4th 783, 6 Cal.Rptr.3d 650, 654-56 (2003).

   A plaintiff asserting a wrongful death claim is entitled to such damages that, under the circumstances of the case, may be just. Cal Civ. Proc.Code §377.61. In California, "just" damages that a wrongful death plaintiff may recover include "lost present and future economic support as well as the pecuniary (as opposed to sentimental) value of such factors as lost comfort, society, companionship, care and protection."[FN43] The amount of available damages in claims brought by a decedent's personal representative are limited, however, and do not include damages for pain, suffering or disfigurement. [FN44]

FN43. *Fox v. Pacific Southwest Airlines*, 133 Cal.App.3d 565, 184 Cal.Rptr. 87, 89 (1982), *disavowed on other grounds by*, *Canavin v. Pacific Southwest Airlines*, 148 Cal. App.3d 512, 196 Cal.Rptr. 82 (1983).
FN44. Cal.Civ.Proc.Code §377.34 ("In an action or proceeding by a decedent's personal representative,…the damages recoverable are limited to the loss or damage that the decedent sustained or incurred before death, including any

penalties or punitive or exemplary damages that the decedent would have been entitled to recover had the decedent lived, and do not include damages for pain, suffering, or disfigurement."); Cal.Civ.Proc.Code §377.61 (stating that "just" damages arising out of a wrongful death action *do not include* those damages allowed under Section 377.34)

b. Intentional Infliction of Emotional Distress

In California, the elements of the tort of intentional infliction of emotional distress are: (1) extreme and outrageous conduct by the defendant with the intent to cause, or with reckless disregard of the probability of causing, emotional distress; (2) the plaintiff suffering severe or extreme emotional distress; and (3) the defendant's conduct is the actual and proximate cause of the plaintiff's emotional distress. *Davidson v. City of Westminster*, 32 Cal.3d 197, 185 Cal. Rptr. 252, 649 P.2d 894, 901 (1982). Under California law, in order for a plaintiff to have standing to recover for an intentional infliction of emotional distress claim, there is a requirement that the conduct either is directed at a plaintiff or occur within the plaintiff's presence. See *Christensen v. Superior Court*, 54 Cal.3d 868, 2 Cal.Rptr.2d 79, 820 P.2d 181, 203-204 (1992). The plaintiff's presence is not, however, always required, and is deemed unnecessary in situations where the defendant is aware of the high probability that the defendant's acts will cause a plaintiff severe emotional distress. *Id.*

   As has been noted by this Court and courts of other jurisdictions, "a terrorist attack-by its nature-is directed not only at the victims but also at the victims' families." *Salazar*, 370 F.Supp.2d at 115 n. 12 (citing *Burnett v. Al Baraka Inv. and Dev. Corp.*, 274 F.Supp.2d 86, 107 (D.D.C.2003)). In this case, the evidence demonstrates that the defendants' motives in planning the attack on the Khobar Towers, and indeed their motives in carrying out a systematic plan of funding and organizing terrorist attacks, were intended to harm both the victims of the attack, and to instill terror in their loved ones and others in the United States. Accordingly, in the case of a terrorist attack as this, the Court finds that the presence element does not need to be proven in order to successfully bring a cause of action for intentional infliction of emotional distress under California law.

   In its discussion of the tort of intentional infliction of emotional distress, comment l to Section 46 of the RESTATEMENT (SECOND) OF TORTS notes that recovery for third-parties has typically been granted to members of the victim's "near relatives." RESTATEMENT (SECOND) OF TORTS §46, cmt. l. The Court finds this approach to be a logical one. Accordingly, under California law, a victim's near relatives, as defined by California's probate code, who were not present may nonetheless have standing to seek redress under a claim of intentional infliction of emotional distress.

2. Plaintiffs

a. Estate and Surviving Family Members of Joshua Woody

i. Estate of Joshua Woody

Josh was killed at Khobar Towers in Dharhan, Saudi Arabia, on June 25, 1996. (Feb. 6, 2004 Tr. at 3, 27; Ex. 9.) Josh was a happy child. Josh loved the outdoors and would go hunting and fishing with his father. Josh also loved motorcycles. *Id.* at 7.

During high school, Josh was a good student who made the honor roll. To stay in shape, Josh ran, swam, and lifted weights. Josh wrestled, played football and worked two jobs during high school, at McDonald's and Beekman Electric. Josh graduated in 1994. *Id.* at 10-11, 32-33.

According to his stepfather, Josh was a "very conscientious, very thorough and very proud of everything he did." He was mechanically talented, and could read a manual once and then rebuild an engine or weld a diamond plate in the bed of a truck. *Id.* at 34-35.

As soon as he turned 16, Josh got his driver's license and started working at McDonald's as a cook. Once the owner of McDonald's learned that Josh was handy mechanically Josh was promoted to the maintenance manager for that store and later for three stores. *Id.* at 37.

After high school, Josh decided to join the United State Air Force. Josh wanted to go to college and he knew that his cousin Joseph had gone into the Army to obtain money for college. Josh had the same plan. Josh enlisted in the Air Force in August 1995 and attended basic training at Lackland AFB in Texas. Josh wrote letters to Bernie from Texas. Josh was next assigned to Sheppard AFB for advanced training to load armaments onto F-16 fighter jets. *Id.* at 11-13, 38.

While Josh was stationed at Sheppard he and a friend took a weekend trip to Oklahoma. During this trip, Josh met Dawn. Josh next received his permanent assignment to the 58th Fighter Squadron at Eglin AFB in Florida. Eventually, Josh and Dawn moved to Florida together and on February 22, 1996, Josh and Dawn were married in Oklahoma. Bernie and George attended the wedding. The day after the wedding, Josh and Dawn and Bernie and George spent the day together looking through antique stores. This was the last time that either George or Bernie saw Josh alive. *Id.* at 13-14, 38-40; Ex. 204 at 109-111, 116.

Josh was deployed to Saudi Arabia on April 3, 1996 and was scheduled to return to Eglin at the end of June 1996. Josh was in very good health. He worked out and used to run on the beach. Josh was a weapons loader on F-15s in the 58th Fighter Squadron. After completing his six years in the Air Force, Josh had plans to go to college and to work for American Airlines. (Feb. 6, 2004 Tr. at 63-64.) Josh was buried next to his best friend Joseph Rimkus on July 5, 1996. Josh and Joe were roommates at Khobar Towers.

Josh's estate is represented by his wife, Dawn Woody. Josh's estate has asserted claims under California's wrongful death statute because he was last domiciled in California. As the personal representative of Josh's estate, Dawn Woody is the proper plaintiff to bring a wrongful death action under California law. *See* Cal Civ. Proc.Code §377.60(a). Because Josh was married at the time of his death, any recovery under this wrongful death action is for the benefit of his wife Dawn Woody. *See* Cal Civ. Proc.Code §377.60(a).

Based upon the pleadings and evidence presented to the Court, the estate of Joshua Woody has made out a valid claim for wrongful death under California law, and the beneficiaries of this estate are entitled to recover the present value of any lost present and future economic support of the decedent that might reasonably have been expected but for the wrongful death. See *supra* note 43 and accompanying text. Though, as Josh's widow, Dawn Woody is entitled to recover personally for the loss of Josh's companionship and protection, the California wrongful death statute does not allow for recovery of damages for any mental pain and suffering Dawn Woody sustained as a result of her husband's death. See *supra* note 44. Accordingly, this Court will limit its analysis presently to a discussion of lost present and future economic earnings of Joshua Woody. A discussion of the intangible economic damages resulting from Dawn Woody's mental anguish shall be dealt with in a discussion of Dawn Woody's individual intentional infliction of emotional distress claim, below.

Dr. Herman Miller, an economic consultant testified as an expert that, were it not for Josh's untimely death, he experienced a net economic loss of $1,981,521.00. The Court therefore awards the Estate of Joshua Woody, by Dawn Woody as personal representative, $1,981,521.00 in economic damages for the benefit of Dawn Woody.

ii. Dawn Woody

Dawn Woody, a United States citizen, is the widow of Joshua Woody. Josh was murdered on June 25, 1996 at Khobar Towers in Saudi Arabia. (Feb. 6, 2004 Tr. at 54.) Dawn was born on May 18, 1972 in Dubuque, Iowa. Dawn met Josh at a party in Miami, Oklahoma during the summer of 1995.

Josh was stationed at Sheppard AFB at the time and he and a friend had taken a weekend trip to Oklahoma. *Id.* at 56.

Josh received his orders to transfer to Eglin AFB in Florida. Josh and Dawn "decided [they] didn't want to be apart." Josh and Dawn moved to Ft. Walton Beach, Florida and got an apartment. They were young and broke but they were happy. *Id.* at 58, Ex. 207. Josh proposed to Dawn in the Fall of 1995 while they were in their car driving home after he picked her up from work. Dawn's family was very happy for Dawn and Josh. Josh and Dawn were married in Claremore, Oklahoma on February 21, 1996.

After the attack on the Khobar Towers, Dawn didn't eat or drink for two days. On Friday, June 28, 1996 the military personnel returned to tell Dawn that Josh was dead and his body had been identified. For a long time, Dawn visited Josh's grave every weekend. *Id.* at 73, Ex. 212.

Dawn testified regarding the effect of Josh's death on her life:

I don't have the self-confidence I used to have. I'm not married. I don't have children…It's difficult and it's just hard. There are certain things I can't do…I don't want people in my home. I used to be social…[I'm] just a lot more closed off than I used to be. I'm not the same person that I was.

(Feb. 6, 2004 Tr. at 77.)

Dawn tried to go back to work a couple months after Josh's death but was unable to cope. It took Dawn about two years to return to work. Dawn eventually decided to return to graduate school to work on her master's degree. The first year was about attending the various memorial services which made it very difficult to function. Dawn was proud of Josh, wanted him to be remembered and believed he deserved all the recognition he received but it was hard for Josh's family. Dawn too was in a lot of pain. *Id.* at 78.

After the attack, Dawn did not initially seek professional help. She joined a support group with the other widows and Bridget Brooks. These women bonded together and became friends. In the past year, at the encouragement of her family, Dawn began seeing a therapist. The therapist told Dawn that Dawn hadn't yet dealt with Josh's death. The therapist recommended that Dawn write a letter to Josh to tell him goodbye. Dawn stopped seeing that therapist because she didn't want to do that and she didn't want to be medicated. *Id.* at 79.

Dawn doesn't like the holidays anymore. Josh's birthday, their wedding anniversary, and the anniversary of Josh's death are especially difficult for Dawn. Dawn sometimes dreams about Josh and wakes up crying. *Id.* at 80. Dawn thinks about Josh every day. *Id.* at 82.

As Dr. Cable testified, Dawn

is still in loss and loneliness…She has put her life back together to a degree with her work and so on, but she still

has a lot of sense of missing him, a lot of sense of emptiness, and a lot of the "What ifs?" for her life…She will continue in loss and loneliness for the period ahead; slowly,…move on to where the grief will re-occur from time to time, but be able to reshape a life.

(Feb. 10, 2004 Tr. at 83-84.)

As the wife of Joshua Woody, Dawn Woody has brought an intentional infliction of emotional distress claim against the defendants for pain and suffering caused by the death of her husband. Based upon the evidence presented to the Court, the elements of Dawn Woody's intentional infliction of emotional distress claim are met. The defendants conduct in facilitating, financing, and providing material support to bring about this attack was intentional, extreme, and outrageous. As the evidence shows, this horrific act precipitated by the defendants' planning and assistance brought immediate emotional distress to Dawn Woody. Finally, it is clear that Dawn Woody has continued to experience emotional distress since that time due to the fact that her husband was taken away from her in such a tragic and horrific manner. Therefore, this Court shall award to Dawn Woody $8 million to compensate her for the emotional distress, pain and suffering that she sustained as a result of her husband's untimely death.

iii. Bernadine Beekman

Bernadine Rose Beekman ("Bernie"), a United States citizen, is the mother of Airman First-Class Joshua E. Woody ("Josh"). (Feb. 6, 2004 Tr. at 2-3.) In 1989, Bernie met George Beekman who was born in Los Angeles, California on December 29, 1939, at the anniversary party of a mutual friend. George was an aerospace engineer who retired in December 1989 before he turned 50. On August 22, 1971, Bernie married John Edward Woody. Bernie and John had four children: Tracy in August 1971; Jonica in April 1974; Josh in October 1975; and Timothy in March 1978. Bernie and Edward were divorced in April 1989. *Id.* at 4.

Bernie testified that even though she has other children, she will never get over losing her son, Josh. Bernie had trouble sleeping in the days and weeks after Josh's death. Sometimes Bernie dreams of Josh. Bernie thinks about Josh every day. Additionally, other terrorist attacks like September 11, 2001 devastate her emotional state.

Bernie has been given some assistance through attending grief counseling sessions. *Id.* at 23-24. Still, as Dr. Cable testified, Bernie "is in loss and loneliness. She was very close to her son and is obviously in a lot of pain right now. That's not about to subside…I would see a good many years yet of continued pain, loss and loneliness, and a need for some real counseling." (Feb. 10, 2004 Tr. at 85.)

As the mother of Joshua Woody, Bernadine Beekman has brought an intentional infliction of emotional distress claim against the defendants for pain and suffering caused by the death of her son. Based upon the evidence presented to the Court, the elements of Bernadine Beekman's intentional infliction of emotional distress claim are met. The defendants' conduct in facilitating, financing, and providing material support to bring about this attack was intentional, extreme, and outrageous. As the evidence shows, this horrific act precipitated by the defendants' planning and assistance brought immediate emotional distress to Bernadine Beekman. Finally, it is clear that Bernadine Beekman has continued to experience emotional distress since that time due to the fact that her son was taken away from her in such a tragic and horrific manner. Therefore, this Court shall award to Bernadine Beekman $5 million to compensate her for the emotional distress, pain and suffering that she sustained as a result of her son's untimely death.

iv. George Beekman

In 1989, Bernie met George Beekman who was born in Los Angeles, California on December 29, 1939, at the anniversary party of a mutual friend. George was an aerospace engineer who retired in December 1989 before he turned 50. Bernie and George were married in Carson City, Nevada in April 1990, and they bought a house together in Corning, California. (Feb. 6, 2004 Tr. at 9-10.) Josh was 15 years old. During the remainder of high school, Josh lived with George and Bernie. George was active in Josh's life, attending his football games and other sports activities. *Id.* at 36.

As Josh's stepfather, George Beekman has brought an intentional infliction of emotional distress against the defendants. [FN45] Based on the evidence presented to the Court, however, Mr. Beekman is not entitled to recover under an intentional infliction of emotional distress claim due to the fact that, as a stepparent, Mr. Beekman lacks sufficient standing to recover for Josh's death.

FN45. Because Josh was survived by his wife, Dawn, and because damages are only available to parents under California's wrongful death statute when there is no surviving spouse or children, Mr. Beekman cannot recover for his loss under that statute. *See* Cal Civ. Proc.Code §377.60.

Under California law, standing to bring a claim against a defendant resulting from the death of an individual is conferred on those who are entitled to inherit property of the deceased under the provisions of the California Probate Code. *See* Cal.Civ.Proc.Code §377.60; Cal. Prob.Code §6402. Inheritance is reserved to near relatives of the deceased. Cal. Prob.Code §6402. Accordingly, in order for Mr. Beekman to

have standing to bring an intentional infliction of emotional distress claim arising from the death of his stepson, Mr. Beekman must qualify as a near relative of Joshua Woody as defined by California's Probate Code.

Under California's Probate Code, parents of the deceased are deemed near relatives for the purposes of inheritance. Cal. Ann. Prob.Code §6402. In California, however, a parent-child relationship only exists in certain circumstances: (1) between a child and the child's natural parents; and (2) in the case of an adoption, the parent-child relationship exists between the child and the child's adoptive parents. *See* Cal. Ann. Prob.Code §6450(a), (b). Indeed, as the California Supreme Court has held, "a stepchild...does not automatically become the 'child' of the stepparent...for purposes of inheritance." *Estate of Joseph*, 17 Cal.4th 203, 70 Cal.Rptr.2d 619, 949 P.2d 472, 479 (1998) (quoting *Estate of Cleveland*, 17 Cal.App.4th 1700, 22 Cal.Rptr.2d 590, 599 (1993)). It stands to reason, then, that a person cannot automatically establish a legally binding parent-child relationship for purposes of inheritance merely by becoming a stepparent.

Instead, California courts have determined that stepparents are deemed parents for purposes of inheritance in one of two situations. First, a stepparent is deemed a parent if the stepparent legally adopts the child as his or her own. [FN46] Second, if the stepparent has not legally adopted the child, California law will nonetheless deem a stepparent a parent if the stepparent can show the stepparent-stepchild relationship was created during the stepchild's minority, and show by clear and convincing evidence that the stepparent would have adopted the stepchild but for a legal barrier. Cal. Ann. Prob.Code §6454.

FN46. See, e.g., *Estate of Cleveland*, 22 Cal.Rptr.2d at 595. Such a requirement makes sense because adoption of a child "extinguishes the rights of natural parents [as to that child] forever," whereas mere guardianship by a stepparent "only suspends the rights of parents." *Id.*

In this case, notwithstanding the relationship Mr. Beekman and Josh had while Josh was alive, there is no evidence presented by plaintiffs that Mr. Beekman legally adopted Josh. Moreover, though the relationship between Mr. Beekman and Josh began while Josh was still a minor, there is no evidence presented before this Court that Mr. Beekman would have adopted Josh, but for a legal impediment. As a result, Mr. Beekman cannot be considered a parent under California law, and is therefore precluded from recovering for damages resulting from his stepson's death. Accordingly, Mr. Beekman's claim for intentional infliction of emotional distress fails for lack of standing, and must therefore be denied.

v. Tracy Smith

Tracy M. Smith, a United States citizen, was born on August 27, 1971 in San Jose, California. Ex. 283 at 1. Tracy is married to Todd Smith and has two children: Joshua, born on April 15, 1998, and Nicholas, born on July 30, 1999. Id at 3. Tracy is a sister of Joshua Edward Woody ("Josh"), who died as a result of a terrorist bombing at the Khobar Towers in Dhahran, Saudi Arabia, on June 25, 1996. Tracy graduated from Los Gatos High School in Los Gatos, California, in June 1989, and is presently employed as a deli clerk for Publix in Kennesaw, Georgia. Id. at 4-5.

Josh's death affected Tracy in many ways. Immediately after Josh's death, Tracy experienced trouble sleeping. Even when she did fall sleep, Tracy would wake herself crying. To this day, Tracy constantly thinks of Josh. Each time she does think about him, her heart sinks. Tracy is particularly emotional on Josh's birthday and on the anniversary of his death. Id. at 22. Moreover, celebrating the holidays has also become less fun for Tracy since Josh's death. Even though Tracy now has her own family, she cannot overcome the emptiness caused by Josh's death. Tracy is saddened that Josh is not alive to celebrate the holidays with her and her sons.

According to Dr. Cable, Tracy is "in loss and loneliness. Like her stepfather, a lot of her grief energies have really gone into worrying about her mother. So there are issues in her own grief that she has not yet been able to deal with...Her grief will continue for a considerable period of time." (Feb. 10, 2004 Tr. at 88.)

As the sister of Joshua Woody, Tracy Smith has brought an intentional infliction of emotional distress claim against the defendants for pain and suffering caused by the death of her brother. Based upon the evidence presented to the Court, the elements of Tracy Smith's intentional infliction of emotional distress claim are met. The defendants' conduct in facilitating, financing, and providing material support to bring about this attack was intentional, extreme, and outrageous. As the evidence shows, this horrific act precipitated by the defendants' planning and assistance brought immediate emotional distress to Tracy Smith. Finally, it is clear that Tracy Smith has continued to experience emotional distress since that time due to the fact that her brother was taken away from her in such a tragic and horrific manner. Therefore, this Court shall award to Tracy Smith $2.5 million to compensate her for the emotional distress, pain and suffering that she sustained as a result of her brother's untimely death.

vi. Jonica Woody

Jonica Woody, a United States citizen, was born on April 28, 1974 in San Jose, California. Jonica is a mother of a five-year old son named Brendan, who was born on December 5, 1998. (Dec. 19, 2003 Tr. at 47-48.) Jonica is the sister of Joshua Woody. She is eighteen months older than Josh. Id. at 48, 57.

Since Josh's death, Jonica has had quite a few dreams about Joshua continuously throughout each passing year. Id. at 59. Jonica testified that Josh's death has affected her in dramatic ways. She lost her emotional rock, close friend and brother in Josh.

Jonica has not received any counseling to help her deal with Josh's death. Id. at 59-60. Josh's birthday, October 6th, Christmas, and other holidays when the family gathers together, are still difficult for Jonica. Id. at 60. Jonica testified that Joshua's death spoiled their future plans. She thinks of Josh "[d]aily, more than once a day, all the time." Id. at 61. As Dr. Cable testified, Jonica

is still very much in loss and loneliness. It is helped by the fact that she has a son, and that has been something to occupy her...Her grief will continue for quite a period of time. She is one who really significantly needs grief therapy. When someone is talking about their grief, everything being as it was seven years ago, there is a lot of unresolved grief there to deal with.

(Feb. 10, 2004 Tr. at 90.)

As the sister of Joshua Woody, Jonica Woody has brought an intentional infliction of emotional distress claim against the defendants for pain and suffering caused by the death of her brother. Based upon the evidence presented to the Court, the elements of Jonica Woody's intentional infliction of emotional distress claim are met. The defendants' conduct in facilitating, financing, and providing material support to bring about this attack was intentional, extreme, and outrageous. As the evidence shows, this horrific act precipitated by the defendants' planning and assistance brought immediate emotional distress to Jonica Woody. Finally, it is clear that Jonica Woody has continued to experience emotional distress since that time due to the fact that her brother was taken away from her in such a tragic and horrific manner. Therefore, this Court shall award to Jonica Woody $2.5 million to compensate her for the emotional distress, pain and suffering that she sustained as a result of her brother's untimely death.

vii. Timothy Woody

Timothy Allen Woody ("Tim"), a United States citizen, was born on March 28, 1978 in California. Ex. 278, at 1. Tim is the younger brother of Josh Woody, who died as a result of a terrorist bombing at the Khobar Towers in Dhahran, Saudi Arabia, on June 25, 1996. *Id.* at 3. In June 1996, Tim entered the United States Navy after graduating from Corning Union High School. He spent four years in the Navy. Tim is currently employed as a stock-person at Wal-Mart in Geneva, New York. *Id.* at 4.

Growing up, Tim remembers always looking up to Josh. Josh was his role model. In his childhood years, Tim would always follow Josh around the house and try to involve himself in whatever Josh was doing. Tim was the typical little brother, and Josh was the typical big brother. *Id.* at 5. Tim lived with his father for several years before starting high school, while Josh lived with their mother. Nevertheless, they remained close, and saw each other regularly. Josh and Tim attended the same high school and they saw each other every day. *Id.* at 6.

After learning about Josh's death, Tim needed to be alone in order to control his emotions. Tim had just graduated from high school and was waiting to enter the Navy. Josh's death was a severe blow to Tim's outlook on life. His big brother, his role model, was gone. Tim was also saddened by the fact that he did not get to say goodbye to Josh. The last time Tim saw Josh was before he left for basic training at Lackland AFB, Texas, around August 1995. *Id.* at 13.

Tim thinks about Josh all the time. Tim keeps pictures of Josh in his wallet as well as mementos of his brother. Tim has often dreamed about Josh since his death. Although he thinks about Josh often in a week, there are certain times of the year when Tim's grief is greater. For example, he becomes particularly moody and sad on Josh's birthday and on the anniversary of his death. On the anniversary of his death, Tim always lights a candle for Josh in his house. *Id.* at 16.

Josh's death changed everything in Tim's life. He no longer has a brother. The holidays and special family events are less joyous. There is a marked emptiness at family events and Josh's absence is overwhelming. Because Tim cannot replace his brother, he fears that he will not recover from the sense of emptiness he feels. Josh's death was devastating to Tim and his entire family. *Id.* at 19-20. As Dr. Cable testified, Tim is

still in loss and loneliness…There was a lot of pent up emotion still inside…He had a very difficult time expressing his feelings…[H]e will continue in grief for a long time to come. He would benefit greatly from some grief therapy, and that would be advised for him.

(Feb. 10, 2004 Tr. at 92-93.)

As the brother of Joshua Woody, Timothy Woody has brought an intentional infliction of emotional distress claim against the defendants for pain and suffering caused by the death of his brother. Based upon the evidence presented to

the Court, the elements of Timothy Woody's intentional infliction of emotional distress claim are met. The defendants' conduct in facilitating, financing, and providing material support to bring about this attack was intentional, extreme, and outrageous. As the evidence shows, this horrific act precipitated by the defendants' planning and assistance brought immediate emotional distress to Timothy Woody. Finally, it is clear that Timothy Woody has continued to experience emotional distress since that time due to the fact that his brother was taken away from him in such a tragic and horrific manner. Therefore, this Court shall award to Timothy Woody $2.5 million to compensate him for the emotional distress, pain and suffering that he sustained as a result of his brother's untimely death.

b. Estate and Family Members of Leland ("Tim") Haun

i. Estate of Leland ("Tim") Haun

Leland T. ("Tim") Haun was killed in the Khobar Towers bombing on June 25, 1996. (Dec. 19, 2003 Tr. at 33; Ex. 2.) Tim was born on April 25, 1963 and was 33 years old when he died. Ex. 4. Tim left behind his wife Ibis ("Jenny") Haun and two step-children: Senator Haun and Milagritos ("Milly") Perez-Dalis.

Tim's estate is represented by his wife, Ibis "Jenny" Haun. Tim's estate has asserted claims under California's wrongful death statute because he was last domiciled in California. As the personal representative of Tim's estate, Jenny Haun is the proper plaintiff to bring a wrongful death action under California law. *See* Cal Civ. Proc.Code §377.60(a). Because Tim was married and had children at the time of his death, any recovery under this wrongful death action is for the benefit of his wife, Jenny Haun, and his two step-children Senator Haun and Milly Perez-Dallis. *See* Cal Civ. Proc.Code §377.60(a). [FN47]

FN47. Senator Haun and Milly Perez-Dallis are the decedent's non-adopted stepchildren, and may therefore only recover if plaintiffs show evidence that the stepparent-stepchild relationship between Tim Haun and his stepchildren was created during the time they were minors, and show clear and convincing evidence that Tim Haun would have adopted the Senator and Milly but for a legal barrier. *See* Cal. Ann. Prob.Code §6454. Here, the Court finds there is sufficient evidence that both elements are met. Tim became Senator and Milly's stepfather when both were still minors. (Dec. 19, 2003 Tr. at 13.) And plaintiffs have presented evidence that he wished to adopt his stepchildren, and would have but for the inability to locate their biological father, which this Court finds to be a sufficient legal barrier to prevent the legal adoption. Ex. 286. This Court is also persuaded by the litany of evidence plaintiffs have submitted that shows Tim Haun held Senator and Milly as his own children, and provided sole financial care for them. *See, e.g.,* (Dec. 19, 2003 Tr. at 13-14.) Accordingly, this Court finds that Senator Haun and Milly Perez-Dallis may recover as beneficiaries to the estate of Leland "Tim" Haun. Consequently, they may also recover for own personal claims arising out of Tim Haun's death, provided the elements of their claims are satisfied.

Based upon the pleadings and evidence presented to the Court, the estate of Leland "Tim" Haun has made out a valid claim for wrongful death under California law, and the beneficiaries of this estate are entitled to recover the present value of any lost present and future economic support of the decedent that might reasonably have been expected but for the wrongful death. [FN48] Though, as Tim's widow, Jenny Haun is entitled to recover personally for the loss of Tim's companionship and protection, the California wrongful death statute does not allow for recovery of damages for any mental pain and suffering Jenny Haun sustained as a result of her husband's death. See *supra* note 44. Accordingly, this Court will limit its analysis presently to a discussion of lost present and future economic earnings of Tim Haun. A discussion of the intangible economic damages resulting from Jenny Haun's mental anguish shall be dealt with in a discussion of her individual intentional infliction of emotional distress claim, below.

FN48. See *supra* note 43 and accompanying text.

Dr. Herman Miller, an economic consultant testified as an expert that, were it not for Tim's untimely death, he experienced a net economic loss of $2,822,796.00. The Court therefore awards the Estate of Leland "Tim" Haun, by Jenny Haun as personal representative, $2,822,796.00 in economic damages for the benefit of Jenny Haun, Senator Haun, and Milly Perez-Dallis, to be distributed in accordance with the method of intestate distribution under California law. As for the intangible economic damages of the wrongful death recovery, the Court will address those awards below, in an individualized discussion of the claim of Ibis "Jenny" Haun.

ii. Ibis ("Jenny") Haun

Jenny Haun is the wife of CPT Tim Haun. She was born in Lima, Peru on July 9, 1959. She is an American citizen. (Dec. 19, 2003 Tr. at 3.) Jenny was raised in Peru by her extended family, including her mother, father, grandparents, uncles, and cousins. Jenny's childhood was a happy one. She attended the best of schools in Peru and participated in activities like gymnastics, drama, and acting. At 14 years

of age, Jenny left Peru for the United States to live with her aunt and uncle in New York. Soon after moving in with her aunt and uncle, though, Jenny decided to get a job and live on her own. *Id.* at 3-4, 7.

When Jenny was 15 years old, she married and had her first child, whom she named Jose Perez. Years later, he changed his name to Senator Haun. At age 16, Jenny had a second child, who she named Milagritos ("Milly") Perez. Jenny's husband had a drug problem, which wreaked havoc on her young family. "Every time he came home, he stole things from me and took my money and my paycheck..." Even though she was only 16 years old, Jenny worked hard to support her children, while also dealing with a husband who tried to steal the money she brought home. *Id.* at 5-6.

At age 19, Jenny divorced her husband, obtained custody of her two children, and moved to Chicago, where there was better pay and more opportunities for her kids. The biological father of Jenny's children never had contact with them again. "The kids don't know their father. My kids call him the sperm donor." *Id.* at 5, 7.

Upon arriving in Chicago, Jenny began working a job and attending school at the Central YMCA Community College. It was difficult for Jenny to make money, attend classes, and raise her children, so she decided to quit school to spend more time with her children. After living in Chicago for five years, Jenny and her children moved to Tucson, Arizona. It was here that Jenny met Tim Haun. *Id.* at 8. Jenny met Tim in April 1990 at a nightclub in Tucson. They married on October 6, 1990. *Id.* at 13.

Jenny was crushed by Tim's untimely death. Jenny also suffered by seeing how Tim's death affected her children. Milly was so unstable after Tim's death that she was put in a mental institution for a short period of time.

Since Tim died, Jenny's entire family has fallen apart. "We don't have any family after Tim's death." *Id.* at 38. Holidays are difficult and the family does not even get together for Christmas anymore. "This [year] is the first time we're going to be together." Other holidays are difficult for Jenny as well-Father's Day, Mother's Day, Easter, Halloween, Thanksgiving, the children's birthdays, and her wedding anniversary. *Id.* at 42-43.

The pain of Tim's death has not subsided for Jenny in the six and a half years since the bombing. She "feel[s] a lot of pain...[her] heart never stops hurting." *Id.* at 41. As Dr. Cable testified, Jenny

is in loss and loneliness. Her loss and loneliness includes this issue of future plans, particularly this having a child together, which creates a real sense of emptiness that they were not able to do that and that that can never be fulfilled. And also loss and loneliness not just for herself, but the impact this has had on her children, because it's had a dramatic impact on them. So she has her own pain for her loss, but her pain for her children as well…She will…also experience significant grief into the future. She has not been able to move off of this "What if?" and the issue of having a child.

(Feb. 10, 2004 Tr. at 40-41.)

Based upon the evidence presented to the Court, the elements of Jenny Haun's intentional infliction of emotional distress claim are met. The defendants' conduct in facilitating, financing, and providing material support to bring about this attack was intentional, extreme, and outrageous. As the evidence shows, this horrific act precipitated by the defendants' planning and assistance brought immediate emotional distress to Jenny. Finally, it is clear that Jenny has continued to experience emotional distress since that time due to the fact that her husband was taken away from her in such a tragic and horrific manner. Therefore, this Court shall award to Ibis "Jenny" Haun $8 million to compensate her for the emotional distress, pain and suffering that she sustained as a result of her husband's untimely death.

iii. Senator Haun

Senator Haun is the step-son of Leland "Tim" Haun. He was born in Newark, New Jersey on June 1, 1975. He is an American citizen. Ex. 286 at 1, 3. Senator spent part of his childhood in New Jersey and Chicago, but when Senator was eight years old, he moved with his mother and sister to Tucson, Arizona. Senator spent the remainder of his childhood in Arizona. *Id.* at 4. Senator's birth father has never been a part of his life. He has only seen his birth father in pictures. *Id.* at 3.

After Jenny and Tim married, the whole family moved into a house on base with Tim. Senator's life quickly changed for the better. The family began eating dinner together, had special family brunches, and took family vacations. Senator developed a close relationship with Tim and began calling him "Dad." (*Id.* at 13-17; Dec. 19, 2003 Tr. at 20.) Senator had a great affection for Tim. Ex. 286 at 14, 20. Tim treated Senator as if he was Tim's own son. (Dec. 19, 2003 Tr. at 22.) In fact, Tim wanted to adopt Senator, but was unable to because nobody could locate Senator's birth father. Senator ended up changing his last name to "Haun" when he was old enough to do so. *Id.* at 21.

After Tim's funeral, Senator had a difficult time accepting that he was gone. Senator never saw his Dad's body and part of Senator still wonders whether Tim really died or whether the military had it all wrong. Senator began feeling depressed and lonely. These feelings were compounded by the fact that it was difficult for Senator to talk to his mother because talking with her and hearing the sadness in her voice made him feel worse. Ex. 286 at 29-30.

Months after Tim died, Senator's wife Clavel left him. Senator's relationship with his wife Clavel began to deteriorate soon after Tim died. They began arguing often and as the relationship regressed, the marriage began falling apart. Clavel left Senator in February of 1997, filed for divorce, and moved to Tucson with their son, Tim, Jr. Senator has not seen his son since 1998. Tim junior is now seven years old and Senator does not even know where Clavel and Tim junior live. *Id.* at 31-32.

Soon after Clavel left Senator, his depression and feelings of loneliness worsened. Senator began drinking and smoking marijuana in the hopes that this would take away the pain he was feeling. Senator's condition continued to decline, however, and in 1999, Senator began hearing voices in his head. He had never heard voices before. Senator began thinking that people were planning something against him. When someone spoke to him, Senator would hear what they were saying, but would also hear other voices. On one occasion, Senator smashed his arm into a glass window at an apartment complex because he heard voices telling him to do it. During this period, Senator felt like the whole world was against him. *Id.* at 33-34.

Throughout 2000 and 2001, Senator's problems continued. He lost his job, then lost his apartment and became homeless. Senator felt depressed and lonely and was still hearing voices in his head. *Id.* at 36. In 2001, Senator eventually sought help and was diagnosed with paranoia and schizophrenia. Over the last two years, Senator has worked with doctors at COPE to address his psychological problems and eliminate the voices in his head. Senator has been seeing a psychiatrist regularly and has also been prescribed different combinations of medication in an attempt to eliminate the voices he hears. Senator currently takes, or has recently taken, multiple medications, including Haldol, Cogentin, Abifill, and Ativan. Today, Senator no longer hears voices in his head. *Id.* at 37.

According to Dr. Cable, Senator Haun

"is still clearly in the loss and loneliness [stage]…[H]e even still is back to some degree in the volatile emotions [stage]. There is still an awful lot of anger and sadness…His father's death has had a tremendous impact on him and has really changed him forever…[H]e very definitely needs professional grief therapy because the impact on him has been so severe…[H]is prognosis is guarded…I would be concerned that without good psychological help, he could have major problems in the future."

(Feb. 10, 2004 Tr. at 44-45.)

As a recognized survivor to Leland "Tim" Haun, Senator Haun has brought a claim of intentional infliction of emotional distress against the defendants. Based upon the evidence presented to the Court, the elements of Senator Haun's intentional infliction of emotional distress claim are met. The defendants' conduct in facilitating, financing, and providing material support to bring about this attack was intentional, extreme, and outrageous. As the evidence shows, this horrific act precipitated by the defendants' planning and assistance brought immediate emotional distress to Senator. Finally, it is clear that Senator has continued to experience emotional distress since that time due to the fact that his father was taken away from him in such a tragic and horrific manner. Therefore, this Court shall award to Senator Haun $5 million to compensate him for the emotional distress, pain and suffering that he sustained as a result of his father's untimely death.

iv. Milly Perez-Dallis

Milly Perez-Dalis is the step-daughter of CPT Tim Haun. She was born in Livingston, New Jersey on December 26, 1977. She is an American citizen. Ex. 287, 1, 3. Milly spent portions of her childhood in New Jersey and Chicago. But when she was five or six years old, Milly moved to Tucson, Arizona with her mother and brother. Milly never knew or spoke to her birth father. She has never even seen him in person. Milly's birth father never provided her, her brother, or her mother with money or support of any kind. *Id.* at 3, 5. Milly was 12 or 13 years old when her mother Jenny began dating Tim. *Id.* at 7.

Dealing with Tim's death was especially difficult for Milly because she had only recently moved to Florida and did not have any close friends there to support her or anyone to talk to. *Id.* at 30. Milly started feeling depressed soon after Tim's death. These feelings of depression intensified when Milly's marriage began falling apart. She was overwhelmed trying to handle things with the military for Jenny, taking care of her children, and at the same time coping with the loss of her Dad and the break-up of her marriage. *Id.* at 34.

After Milly's psychological problems got worse, she was placed in a state mental institution. Nearly two months after Tim's death, Milly's husband sought a divorce and petitioned the court for custody of the children. In his petition for divorce, Milly's husband stated that Tim's death had a great impact on Milly and that as a result of Tim's death, Milly had been placed in a state mental institution, was unstable, and was unable to raise her children. *Id.* at 37-38.

Milly fell apart after this incident. She swallowed a bottle of pills, started drinking heavily, and felt like commit-

ting suicide. Milly had never felt this way before. In a short period of time, she went from being perfectly fine to being entirely unstable. *Id.* at 39.

As a result of her declining mental and psychological state, Milly was again institutionalized. When she was released, Milly returned home to find her husband packing up the house. Milly asked what he was doing and he showed her temporary custody papers that a court had just issued. He informed Milly that he was taking the children and leaving town. Milly ultimately moved back to Tucson, Arizona to be close to her children. Milly was ordered that she could not see her children without supervision. To this day, Milly must still be supervised when she spends time with her kids. *Id.* at 40-43. Beginning in 1999, Milly began receiving psychological help from an agency in Arizona that provided her with a psychiatrist to visit every month. This psychiatrist listened to Milly and diagnosed her with major depression, an anxiety disorder, and a compulsive disorder. *Id.* at 44.

Since Tim's death, Milly has experienced difficulties keeping a job. She gets nervous around people and sometimes struggles with doing normal things that she would never have thought twice about before Tim died. *Id.* at 46. Father's Day, Christmas, and the anniversary of Tim's death are particularly difficult days for Milly. *Id.* at 47. September 11, 2001 was also a difficult day for Milly. *Id.* at 49.

According to Dr. Cable, Milly

is still looking to recapture the past, which she can't get, but she wants to be the way it was before. Her life has simply not been the same since Tim's death. She wants everything to be the way it was. So very much loss and loneliness…I believe her grief is going to continue for a long time into the future. She, too,…really needs some intensive grief therapy to help her get through this. She is going to have a difficult time moving on in life, regaining her balance, really being able to get back to a normal kind of life.

(Feb. 10, 2004 Tr. at 48-49.)

As a recognized survivor to Leland "Tim" Haun, Milly Perez-Dallis has brought a claim of intentional infliction of emotional distress against the defendants. Based upon the evidence presented to the Court, the elements of Milly Perez-Dallis' intentional infliction of emotional distress claim are met. The defendants' conduct in facilitating, financing, and providing material support to bring about this attack was intentional, extreme, and outrageous. As the evidence shows, this horrific act precipitated by the defendants' planning and assistance brought immediate emotional distress to Milly. Finally, it is clear that Milly has continued to experience emotional distress since that time due to the fact that her father was taken away from her in such a tragic and horrific manner.

Though the Court typically awards children of terrorist attack victims $5 million to compensate them for the severe emotional distress associated with losing a parent, the Court does have discretion to adjust the amount of the award in cases where the victim's emotional distress is significantly more extreme. Based upon the evidence presented to this Court, Milly's emotional distress is of such an extreme nature as to warrant an increase in the award for her emotional distress. Therefore, this Court shall award to Milly Perez-Dallis $7 million to compensate her for the emotional distress, pain and suffering that she sustained as a result of her father's untimely death.

c. Shawn Wood

Shawn Michael Wood is an older brother of Justin Wood. He was born in Modesto, California on March 27, 1971. He is an American citizen. (Dec. 4, 2003 P.M. Tr. at 50.) Shawn was raised in Modesto, where he attended and graduated from public school. After graduating from high school, Shawn attended junior college for a short period of time, then left junior college to pursue a career in music. During the day, Shawn worked at a local restaurant and during the evenings, he practiced guitar, wrote songs, and played in bands with his friends. After playing in bands for a short period of time, Shawn decided that he wanted to further pursue a career in the music industry and he enrolled in the Art Institute in Seattle, Washington to study audio production. *Id.* at 51-52.

The days following Justin's death are a blur to Shawn. He remembers being with his family and his girlfriend's family, seeing people he had not seen in a long time, and receiving many flowers and cards. *Id.* at 61. He could not stay focused on school after Justin's death, so he took a semester off from the Art Institute. When Shawn returned to school, his grades suffered. *Id.* at 65.

Justin's death deeply affected Shawn's relationships with his family, especially his father. It was difficult for Shawn to interact with his father because they did not communicate well and because they dealt with Justin's death differently. *Id.* at 72-73.

Shawn has created a web site in Justin's honor and he talks to people through email who have lost loved ones in terrorist attacks. He talks to people who cannot sleep at night, who cannot close their eyes. *Id.* at 77-78. Today, Shawn still thinks of Justin every day. Shawn still keeps some of Justin's possessions on display in his home. Shawn still feels hate and rage as a result of Justin's death. *Id.* at 74. As Dr. Cable testified, Shawn

is in loss and loneliness. It's tempered by his wife and children, which really are a help to him, but it's compounded by his parents' issues, particularly the father in the sense of not only losing his brother, but he doesn't count in his father's life any more either. His loss and loneliness is not just for his brother, but he is very much devoted to all of those who died and honoring all of them…His grief will continue. There will always be reminders, things that make it difficult for him.

(Feb. 10, 2004 Tr. at 211-12.)

As Justin Wood's brother, Shawn Wood has brought a claim of intentional infliction of emotional distress against the defendants. Based upon the evidence presented to the Court, the elements of Shawn Wood's intentional infliction of emotional distress claim are met. The defendants' conduct in facilitating, financing, and providing material support to bring about this attack was intentional, extreme, and outrageous. As the evidence shows, this horrific act precipitated by the defendants' planning and assistance brought immediate emotional distress to Shawn. Finally, it is clear that Shawn has continued to experience emotional distress since that time due to the fact that his brother was taken away from him in such a tragic and horrific manner. Therefore, this Court shall award to Shawn Wood $2.5 million to compensate him for the emotional distress, pain and suffering that he sustained as a result of his brother's untimely death.

C. Louisiana

1. Causes of Action

a. Wrongful Death

In Louisiana, the decedent's survivors [FN49] may bring a wrongful death action when the decedent dies "due to the fault of another." La. Civ.Code Ann. Art. 2315.2(A). Such a cause of action is intended to "compensate the victim's beneficiaries for their compensable injuries following the victim's moment of death." *Mathieu v. Louisiana Dep't of Transp. & Dev.*, 598 So.2d 676, 681 (La.Ct.App.1992). Potential beneficiaries entitled to recovery include the surviving spouse, children, parents, siblings, and grandparents of the deceased, but do not include children who were not legally adopted at the time of the decedent's death. La. Civ. Code Ann. Art. 2315.2(A). Recoverable damages for a wrongful death claim include lost wages, "loss of love and affection, loss of services, loss of support, medical expenses, and funeral expenses." *Id. But see* La. Civ.Code Ann. Art. 2315.2(B) (stating that damages do not include costs for future medical treatment). Surviving relatives under Article 2315.2 may also recover for their own individual pain and suffering sustained as a result of the wrongful death to the decedent. *Robertson v. Town of Jennings*, 128 La. 795, 55 So. 375, 379-80 (1911).

FN49. According to Louisiana Civil Code, the decedent's surviving spouse and children may bring such an action. If there are none, however, then the decedent's parents, siblings, or grandparents-in that order-may bring the action for wrongful death. See La. Civ.Code Ann. Art. 2315.2(A).

b. Intentional Infliction of Emotional Distress
Louisiana courts follow Section 46 of the RESTATEMENT (SECOND) OF TORTS in recognizing the tort of intentional infliction of emotional distress. See *White v. Monsanto Co.*, 585 So.2d 1205, 1208-1210 (La.1991). The elements of the tort of intentional infliction of emotional distress in Louisiana are that: (1) the defendant's conduct was extreme and outrageous; (2) the plaintiff suffered severe emotional distress; and (3) the "defendant desired to inflict severe emotional distress or knew that severe emotional distress would be certain or substantially certain to result from his conduct." *Id.* at 1209. Under Louisiana law, however, there is a requirement that, in order for a plaintiff to recover for a damages caused by injury to another, that plaintiff must have either viewed or immediately come upon the scene of the injury. *See* La. Civ.Code Ann. Art. 2315.6. Louisiana courts have interpreted the term "view" to require the plaintiff's actual presence at the event causing the injury. See *Daigrepont v. State Racing Com'n*, 663 So.2d 840, 841 (La.App.1995) (finding that plaintiffs were entitled to no recovery if "viewing" of injury was only by videotape). Moreover, the Louisiana Supreme Court has left little room for interpretation of this provision, stating that such a law is clear and unambiguous, and therefore no further interpretation of the provision may be made with regard to the legislature's intent in enacting it. *Id.* Accordingly, to the extent that any plaintiffs may not recover under the wrongful death statute, they may not recover under Louisiana law if they were not actually present at the site of the attack.

2. Plaintiffs

a. Estate and Surviving Family Members of Kevin Johnson, Sr.

i. Estate of Kevin Johnson, Sr.
Kevin Jerome Johnson, Sr., was killed in the Khobar Towers bombing on June 25, 1996. (Dec. 4, 2003 A.M. Tr. at 64-65; Ex. 2.) Kevin was born on January 25, 1960. He was 35 years old when he died. Ex. 284, ¶ 4; Ex. A. Kevin is survived by his wife, Shyrl, his biological sons, Kevin Johnson, Jr. and Nicholas Johnson, and his stepson, Che Colson. He is also survived by his mother, Laura Johnson, and his brother, Bruce Johnson.

When he was growing up, Kevin was a very good student. In high school, he was always on the Dean's List and he was accepted to attend Grambling State University. *Id.* at ¶ 14. Kevin was also a hard-worker. He got his first job when he was 15 or 16 years old, helping a local man raise worms, which were then sold to fishermen.

After Kevin finished college at Grambling, he entered into the Air Force. He was eventually assigned to Little Rock Air Force Base in Arkansas upon finishing his military training. Kevin planned on making the military his career and wanted to make sure his three little boys and wife were taken care of. *Id.* at ¶ 23.

Kevin's estate is represented by his wife, Shyrl Johnson. Kevin's estate has asserted claims under Louisiana's wrongful death statute because he was last domiciled in Louisiana. As the surviving spouse and children of Kevin's estate, Shyrl Johnson, Kevin Johnson, Jr., and Nicholas Johnson are the proper plaintiffs to bring a wrongful death action under Louisiana law. *See* La. Civ.Code Ann. Art. 2315.2(A). Any recovery under this wrongful death action is for the benefit of Shyrl Johnson, Kevin Johnson, Jr., and Nicholas Johnson as the surviving children and spouse. *See* La. Civ.Code Ann. Art. 2315.2(A). [FN50]

FN50. Under Louisiana's wrongful death code, surviving parents and siblings may not recover if there is a surviving spouse or surviving children. *See* La. Civ.Code Ann. Art. 2315.2(A)(2), (3). Accordingly, neither Kevin's mother, Laura Johnson, nor his brother, Bruce Johnson, may bring a wrongful death action under Louisiana law. Additionally, as will be discussed below, Che Colson is not a proper plaintiff under Louisiana's wrongful death statute due to the fact that non-adopted stepchildren are not considered "children" under Louisiana's wrongful death code. See *infra* Part VI.C.2.a.vii.; La. Civ.Code Ann. Art. 2315.2(D).

Based upon the pleadings and evidence presented to the Court, the estate of Kevin Johnson, Sr., has made out a valid claim for wrongful death under Louisiana law, and the beneficiaries of this estate are entitled to recover the present value of any lost present and future economic support of the decedent that might reasonably have been expected but for the wrongful death. Dr. Herman Miller, an economic consultant testified as an expert that, due to Kevin's untimely death, he experienced a net economic loss of $1,171,477.00. The Court therefore awards the Estate of Kevin Johnson, Sr., by his surviving spouse and children, $1,171,477.00 in economic damages for the benefit of Shyrl Johnson, Kevin Johnson, Jr., and Nicholas Johnson, to be distributed in accordance with the method of intestate distribution under Louisiana law. A discussion of intangible economic damages of the wrongful death recovery, will be addressed below in an individualized discussion of the claims of Shryl Johnson, Kevin Johnson, Jr., and Nicholas Johnson.

ii. Shryl Johnson

Shyrl Johnson is the wife of Kevin Johnson, Sr. She was born in Shreveport, Louisiana on October 22, 1958. She is an American citizen. (Dec. 4, 2003 A.M. Tr. at 4.) Shyrl was raised in Shreveport, Louisiana by her mother, who was a nurse, and her stepfather, who was an electrician. She attended public school and after graduating from high school, attended college at Northwestern State University. *Id.* at 4-5. During Shyrl's first year at college, she met Greg Colson, whom she later married. Ironically, Kevin Johnson, Sr., was the piano player for Shyrl and Greg's wedding ceremony.

In 1982, Shyrl and Greg had a son, who they named Che. *Id.* at 5-7. Soon after Shyrl had Che's birth, her marriage with Greg fell apart due to Greg's drug addiction. Greg had a severe drug problem and Shyrl did not want her young son being around drugs or people caught up in the drug community. Shyrl and Greg were divorced in 1984. *Id.* at 7, 43-44. After Shyrl and Greg divorced, Greg's relationship with Che continued to be a distant one. Greg would come see Che once in a while on the weekends, but did not visit him on a regular basis. Greg and Che never shared a traditional father-son relationship. *Id.* at 7.

Shyrl has always worked since she graduated from college. When Shyrl was married to Greg, she worked at the Southwestern Electric Power Company as a stenographer. She then transferred to the Shreveport Area School District, where she worked for the school superintendent as a stenographer and secretary. At one point, Shyrl joined the Air Force Reserves as a second job, which she worked on the weekends. *Id.* at 7-8.

Shyrl and Kevin did not meet again until 1986, when Shyrl was going through the confirmation process in the Catholic church. Kevin's mother, Laura Johnson was Shyrl's sponsor through the confirmation process. Shyrl, who had recently divorced her husband Greg, was pleased to become reacquainted with Kevin, whom she remembered from her wedding ceremony, and they quickly became friends. *Id.* at 10.

In the weeks and months following their reacquaintance, Shyrl and Kevin talked on the telephone often. Kevin was stationed at Little Rock AFB at the time and Shyrl was still living in Shreveport, so the two could not see each other often, but they frequently talked to each other on the telephone over the course of three or four months before they began dating. During this period, Kevin went on rotation to Mildenhall AFB in England, but even when he was travel-ling, Kevin kept in touch with Shyrl. Their phone bills were quite high during these three to four months. *Id.* at 12-13. Kevin and Shyrl also kept in touch through letters. *Id.* at 13.

About six months after becoming reacquainted, Shyrl and Kevin began dating. Shyrl was taken with Kevin's smile, his honesty, and his easygoing nature. Shyrl and Kevin dated for four years and were married in 1990. *Id.* at 15; Ex. 51. After Shyrl and Kevin married, Kevin transferred to Patrick AFB in Florida. Kevin wanted to spend more time with the children and the Air Force told him that he would not have to travel as much. Kevin and Shyrl were also told that Kevin would not have to travel to Saudi Arabia, which they both viewed as another benefit of transferring. *Id.* at 48-49.

Kevin was a wonderful husband. Kevin would cook, would clean, would fold clothes. He always listened and would help Shyrl make important decisions in her life. Kevin also encouraged Shyrl to do things that she always wanted to do, like go back to school to become a teacher. (Dec. 4, 2003 A.M. Tr. at 36-37, 39.)

Kevin was also a great father. "He treated Che just like he was his biological father." Kevin played sports with Che, took him to church, and was the father figure that Che never had. *Id.* at 20-23, 38. Kevin and Shyrl also had two children of their own: Kevin and Nicholas. Kevin was a great father with these boys as well. Kevin spent a lot of time with all of the children and enjoyed being a father. He arranged family trips that the kids would enjoy to places like Disney World, St. Louis, and Mud Island, Tennessee and spent his free time with the kids. *Id.* at 46-48.

Shyrl and Kevin had great plans for the future. In the days before Kevin died, he and Shyrl were talking about transferring to Mildenhall AFB in England, which they thought would be great for the children. Shyrl had actually gone to pick up information about Mildenhall on the day she learned about the Khobar Towers bombing. Kevin planned on staying in the military for at least 25 years, then eventually going to work for a commercial airline. *Id.* at 50-53.

Shyrl broke down emotionally immediately after finding out that Kevin had been killed. *Id.* at 66. After the funeral, Shyrl held herself together for about six months, before she just "fell apart." Shyrl has experienced breakdowns since this initial episode, but they have not been quite as bad. She especially misses Kevin "[w]hen things start piling up...because he was always there to balance me out and I miss that. I can talk to him but he's not answering back." *Id.* at 77-79.

Certain days are particularly difficult for Shyrl. September 11, 2001 was one of those days. Shyrl's reaction to the September 11 attack was so severe that she had to leave the classroom she was teaching in and have another teacher take over the class. She left work early that day to pick up her children, so they wouldn't be afraid. "I tried to shelter them as much as I could in not seeing so much of it. But [little] Kevin said, 'it's just like Khobar Towers, mommy. They're just never going to catch them.'" (Dec. 4, 2003 A.M. Tr. at 87-89.)

As Dr. Cable stated, Shyrl

is also in loss and loneliness. She is a widow who sees herself under a great deal of pressure with her job, her children…She has really held herself together as best she could, more for the children than for anything else…She will…continue to grieve in the future…[A]s her children get older, she will be more open to letting her grief come out more. A lot of it is still kept behind closed doors, so to speak…[T]here is going to be a lot of recurrence of grief when the children reach milestones. When they graduate from college, when a child marries, that will tend to bring back a lot of grief for her, because those are times that Kevin should be there to support and be a part of all of that.

(Feb. 10, 2004 Tr. at 53-55.)

As Kevin Johnson's wife, Shyrl Johnson has brought a wrongful death claim arising from the death of her husband, Kevin Johnson, Sr. Based on the evidence presented to the Court, Shyrl Johnson has experienced severe mental anguish and suffering as a result of her husband's untimely death. Therefore, this Court shall award to the estate of Kevin Johnson, Sr., by Shyrl Johnson as Personal Representative, $8 million for the benefit of his wife Shyrl Johnson to compensate her for the mental pain and suffering she sustained as a result of her husband's untimely death.

iii. Kevin Johnson, Jr.

Kevin Johnson, Jr., ("Kevin Jr.") is the son and namesake of Kevin Johnson, Sr. Kevin, Jr., was born in July 1991 and was only four years old when his father was killed. *Id.* at 46.

For a while after Kevin died, Kevin Jr. thought that his dad might just be hurt and lost somewhere in Saudi Arabia. Shyrl believes that Kevin's death hit Kevin Jr. the hardest because he was so young. Kevin Jr. would have nightmares, and often thought he saw ghosts. *Id.* at 61.

To this day, Kevin still has issues related to his father's death. Shyrl enrolled him in Big Brothers, Big Sisters with the hope that he could have a male figure in his life. Six months after enrolling, however, Kevin's big brother was transferred to a different military base, and Kevin lost another male role model. *Id.* at 70-71.

Kevin has issues that Shyrl believes are related to the loss of his father. For example, Kevin is overweight, has

low self-esteem, and has other physical issues. As Dr. Cable testified, Kevin is in the loss and loneliness stage but still

[shows] behaviors that go back into some of the earlier stages [of emotional grieving.] There is still a lot of emotional reaction there, so the volatile emotions [stage]. Probably even some of the disorganization; just not being able to kind of get things in focus…He will continue in significant grief reactions in the foreseeable future…[He is] at risk for developing other kinds of problems as a result of the grief experience.

(Feb. 10, 2004 Tr. at 57-58.)

As Kevin Johnson's son, Kevin Johnson, Jr., has brought intentional infliction of emotional distress and wrongful death claims arising from the death of his father, Kevin Johnson, Sr. As the evidence shows, Kevin Johnson, Jr., was not physically present to witness the harm done to his father. In light of this fact, and the strict construction Louisiana courts place on the presence requirement in intentional infliction of emotional distress claims, Kevin Johnson, Jr., may not recover under an intentional infliction of emotional distress claim relating to his father's death. Accordingly, to the extent that Kevin Johnson, Jr., may recover, he must make a valid claim under Louisiana's wrongful death statute.

Based on the evidence presented to the Court, Kevin Johnson, Jr., has experienced severe mental anguish and suffering as a result of his father's untimely death. Therefore, this Court shall award to the estate of Kevin Johnson, Sr., by Shyrl Johnson as Personal Representative, $5 million for the benefit of his son Kevin Johnson, Jr., to compensate him for the mental pain and suffering he sustained as a result of his father's untimely death.

iv. Nicholas Johnson

Nicholas Johnson is the son of Kevin Johnson, Sr. Nicholas was born in April 1996, and was only two months old when his father was killed. (Dec. 4, 2003 A.M. Tr. at 46.) Nicholas never knew his father, but he has learned about him from Shyrl and from Che Colson. *Id.* at 71. As Nicholas has gotten older, Shyrl has given him more information about his father. Nicholas is "proud of his father and who he is even though he didn't know him." *Id.* at 96.

Even though Nicholas never knew his father, his life has been impacted dramatically by Kevin's death. As Shyrl stated,

[T]he thing that broke my heart just this year, we were coming back from school and I think they had this thing where the fathers come in and my poor baby said, we were driving back home, "I wish I had a daddy, too, just like the other kids." That really just broke my heart. What do you say to a seven-year-old that misses something that he didn't even have but for a short period of time? When you go to functions and there's the mother and the father, that's when he gets kind of like he wishes he had both.

Id. at 71.

According to Dr. Cable, Nicholas

is really just beginning the grief process...He was so young when all of this happened, that it's a blur to him, obviously. As future events unfold in his life, then he is going to have more of a sense of loss, just like now with the school events and no father present...[H]e is at a real loss in that sense of not having personal memories as part of his life...He will have good support from his mother and from his brothers, but he will have significant grief along the way...So there is a long-term impact here for him.

(Feb. 10, 2004 Tr. at 59-60.)

As Kevin Johnson's son, Nicholas Johnson has brought intentional infliction of emotional distress and wrongful death claims arising from the death of his father, Kevin Johnson, Sr. As the evidence shows, Nicholas Johnson was not physically present to witness the harm done to his father. In light of this fact, and the strict construction Louisiana courts place on the presence requirement in intentional infliction of emotional distress claims, Nicholas Johnson may not recover under an intentional infliction of emotional distress claim relating to his father's death. Accordingly, to the extent that Nicholas Johnson may recover, he must make a valid claim under Louisiana's wrongful death statute.

Based on the evidence presented to the Court, Nicholas Johnson has experienced severe mental anguish and suffering as a result of his father's untimely death due to the fact that he will never know his father. Therefore, this Court shall award to the estate of Kevin Johnson, Sr., by Shyrl Johnson as Personal Representative, $5 million for the benefit of his son Nicholas Johnson to compensate him for the mental pain and suffering he sustained as a result of his father's untimely death.

v. Laura Johnson

Laura Elizabeth Johnson is the mother of Kevin Johnson. Mrs. Johnson was born in Shreveport, Louisiana in 1933 and was 63 years old when Kevin was killed. She is an American citizen. Ex. 284, ¶¶ 1-2. Mrs. Johnson was raised and attended school in Shreveport, Louisiana. After graduating from high school, she attended a year-long nursing school program and graduated from the program on May 24, 1954. She has been a nurse for 49 years and still practices on a part-time basis. She has lived in Shreveport her entire life. Id. at ¶ 3.

When Mrs. Johnson heard that Kevin had died in the attack, she was devastated. She left work immediately and

headed home, and prayed that Kevin was still alive. Id. at ¶ 29. Mrs. Johnson did not work for a few months after Kevin's funeral. She returned to work in September. It was difficult for Mrs. Johnson to return to work, "but I knew I had to." Id. at 32.

Since Kevin died, Mrs. Johnson has hung a picture of him in the house so she could see him when she walked in the door. Mrs. Johnson is still grieving over Kevin's death, but she can function in a normal life now. Id. at 35. Mrs. Johnson has relied on her faith in coping with Kevin's death. Id. at 36. Before Kevin died, Mrs. Johnson relied on him to take care of things in case she ever became ill or could not take care of herself. Kevin was responsible, so Mrs. Johnson added his name to her bank account and other important accounts. When Kevin died, Mrs. Johnson realized she was on her own. (Id. at 37; Dec. 4, 2003 A.M. Tr. at 12.)

According to Dr. Cable, Mrs. Johnson "is still in loss and loneliness. Nothing will ever replace Kevin in her life... She will continue to grieve for some time to come...[S]he will manage to go on, but [may not] ever fully recover the loss of her son." (Feb. 10, 2004 Tr. at 62.)

As Kevin Johnson's mother, Laura Johnson has brought intentional infliction of emotional distress and wrongful death claims arising from the death of her son, Kevin Johnson, Sr. As the evidence shows, Laura Johnson was not physically present to witness the harm done to her son. In light of this fact, and the strict construction Louisiana courts place on the presence requirement in intentional infliction of emotional distress claims, Laura Johnson may not recover under an intentional infliction of emotional distress claim relating to her son's death. Accordingly, to the extent that Laura Johnson may recover, she must make a valid claim under Louisiana's wrongful death statute.

Laura Johnson, however, may not maintain a valid wrongful death claim due to the fact that her son Kevin Johnson, Sr., died with a surviving spouse and surviving children. Under Louisiana's wrongful death code, surviving parents may not recover for wrongful death if there is a surviving spouse or surviving children. See La. Civ.Code Ann. Art. 2315.2(A)(2). Accordingly, Laura Johnson's wrongful death claim must also be denied.

vi. Bruce Johnson

Bruce Johnson is the brother of Kevin Johnson. Bruce was born in Shreveport, Louisiana in 1961 and was 35 years-old when Kevin was killed. He is an American citizen. Ex. 285, ¶¶ 1, 3. Bruce attended the Blessed Sacrament Elementary School until sixth grade, then went to Lake Shore Middle School and Washington High School. He graduated from high school in 1978. After high school, he attended and graduated from Louisiana Technical School, where he studied automotive education and automotive technologies. *Id.* at ¶ 3.

Bruce currently works as a paraprofessional for Southern University, where he supervises a unit that oversees special education children and helps them prepare for becoming independent. Bruce is married and has a wife named Connie and two children: Bruce Jr., who is 16, and Broderick, who is 14. Bruce also has a step-daughter named Chavondria. *Id.* at ¶ 4.

Growing up, Bruce and Kevin were close brothers. From an early age, Kevin was very protective of Bruce. He would make sure Bruce did not do anything he wasn't supposed to do. This protective relationship continued until the day Kevin died. Bruce would talk to Kevin about work, personal, or even family issues. Kevin would always listen and always give him helpful guidance. *Id.* at ¶ 7.

Soon after Kevin joined the Air Force, he sat down with Bruce and had a talk about plans for the future. Kevin planned on spending 20 years in the service, then going to work for a commercial airline. *Id.* at ¶ 11. The last time Bruce spoke with Kevin, he asked about Bruce's boys' shoe sizes. Kevin wanted to bring the boys some sneakers from Saudi Arabia when he returned to the United States. *Id.* at ¶ 12.

When Kevin died, Bruce took care of making all the funeral arrangements and contacting people from the military and the local police department. Bruce arranged to have the funeral at St. John's Cathedral, which is where Kevin and Bruce were first baptized and where they had their First Communion. Because Bruce was making all of the arrangements, he could not attend the memorial service at Patrick AFB. Bruce did, however, attend the dedication of the memorial at Patrick AFB a few years after the bombing.

Today, Bruce still visits Kevin's grave often. *Id.* at ¶ 17. After Bruce learned of Kevin's death, everything "just went black for about two straight years. I felt lost because I didn't have Kevin to give me direction in life." *Id.* at ¶ 18. After Kevin died, Bruce began drinking every day. This led to some trouble with the law and Bruce received two DUIs in a short period of time. Bruce received the first one on December 22, 1996, and the second that following July. Bruce also got into some financial difficulties. *Id.* at ¶ 19. Bruce stayed home from work for about three or four weeks after Kevin's death. But after returning to work, he had to take a day or two off every week because going back was just something he was not ready for. Bruce continued to take a day or two off a week for about six months. *Id.* at ¶ 20.

Today, Christmas and Thanksgiving are particularly difficult days for Bruce. Kevin's birthday and the days leading up to Kevin's birthday are also tough. In Dr. Cable's expert opinion, Bruce

is in loss and loneliness. He still thinks of Kevin all the time; never far from his mind. Kevin was his role model, his support system, and that's gone and is not going to be recovered…He will continue to be impacted by the death in the future…but that ten-day period [each year when Kevin and Bruce were the same numerical age] is going to be a significant marker the rest of his life. Even if he is able to move on in general, he is going to have a down time every year where the grief is going to be pretty overwhelming for a while.

(Feb. 10, 2004 Tr. at 64-65.)

As Kevin Johnson's brother, Bruce Johnson has brought intentional infliction of emotional distress and wrongful death claims arising from the death of his brother, Kevin Johnson, Sr. As the evidence shows, Bruce Johnson was not physically present to witness the harm done to his brother. In light of this fact, and the strict construction Louisiana courts place on the presence requirement in intentional infliction of emotional distress claims, Bruce Johnson may not recover under an intentional infliction of emotional distress claim relating to his brother's death. Accordingly, to the extent that Bruce Johnson may recover, he must make a valid claim under Louisiana's wrongful death statute.

Bruce Johnson, however, may not maintain a valid wrongful death claim due to the fact that his brother Kevin Johnson, Sr., died with a surviving spouse and surviving children. Under Louisiana's wrongful death code, surviving siblings may not recover for wrongful death if there is a surviving spouse or surviving children. *See* La. Civ.Code Ann. Art. 2315.2(A)(3). Accordingly, Bruce Johnson's wrongful death claim must also be denied.

vii. Che Colson

Che Colson is the step-son of Kevin Johnson, Sr. Che was born in 1982 and was only 13 years old when Kevin was killed. (Dec. 4, 2003 A.M. Tr. at 7.) Che's birth parents are Shyrl Johnson and Greg Colson. Shyrl and Greg divorced in 1984, when Che was two years old, and Che never had a close relationship with his birth father. Greg developed drug problems and was not around to take care of Che when he was a child, so Shyrl was the only parent in his day-to-day life. *Id.* at 6-7. Che was three and a half or four years old when Shyrl began dating Kevin. *Id.* at 12.

Kevin treated Che like he was his biological father. Che and Kevin maintained their close relationship until the day Kevin died. *Id.* at 38, 46. After Shyrl and Kevin married, Kevin was financially responsible for Che. *Id.* at 46.

The year after Kevin died was very difficult for Che and he "kind of shut down that year, where he wasn't talking to anybody." Shyrl noticed that Che "wasn't showing any emotion to anybody and I couldn't read him. But I do know that his grades suffered. I think it's because he missed that male role model that he had in Kevin. [Kevin] brought stability [from] the male perspective, I would say, for Che." *Id.* at 38-39. As Dr. Cable has stated, Che "feels abandoned…and is in loss and loneliness…He will continue in grief for the foreseeable future…[H]e still has got a number of years ahead of him of trying to come to grips with everything that has happened." (Feb. 10, 2004 Tr. at 55-56.)

As Kevin Johnson's stepson, Che Colson has brought intentional infliction of emotional distress and wrongful death claims arising from the death of his stepfather, Kevin Johnson. As the evidence shows, Mr. Colson was not physically present to witness the harm done to his stepfather. In light of this fact, and the strict construction Louisiana courts place on the presence requirement in intentional infliction of emotional distress claims, Mr. Colson may not recover under an intentional infliction of emotional distress claim relating to his stepfather's death. Accordingly, to the extent that Mr. Colson may recover, he must make a valid claim under Louisiana's wrongful death statute.

Based on the evidence presented to the Court, however, Mr. Colson is not entitled to recover under an intentional infliction of emotional distress claim due to the fact that, as a non-adopted stepson, Mr. Colson lacks sufficient standing to recover for damages relating to Kevin Johnson's death. Under Louisiana law, a decedent's child may properly recover for wrongful death. La. Civ.Code Ann. Art. 2315.2(A)(1). Nevertheless, Louisiana's code specifically states that a "child" is limited to biological children and children by adoption. La. Civ.Code Ann. Art. 2315.2(A)(4)(D). Moreover, this Court is hampered from any flexibility in interpreting this provision due to the fact that "the right of action created by Article 2315 may be extended *only to the statutorily designated beneficiaries enumerated in the article and these classes of beneficiaries must be strictly construed.*" *Craig v. Scandia, Inc.*, 634 So.2d 944, 945 (La.Ct.App.1994) (emphasis added). Accordingly, because Mr. Colson does not fall within the statutorily prescribed classes of individuals who may properly recover under a wrongful death action, Mr. Colson's claim must be denied.

D. Claims Under New Hampshire Law

1. Causes of Action

a. Wrongful Death

Under New Hampshire's wrongful death statute, the administrator of the decedent's estate may bring a cause of action when the decedent's death is "caused by the injury complained of in the action." N.H.Rev.Stat. Ann. §556:12. The damages wrongful death plaintiffs may seek include "the mental and physical pain suffered by the decedent in consequence of the injury, the reasonable expenses occasioned to the estate by the injury, the probable duration of life but for the injury, and the capacity to earn money during the deceased party's probable working life." N.H.Rev.Stat. Ann. §556:12. Recoverable damages also include damages for loss of life and loss of enjoyment of life. See *Bennett v. Lembo*, 145 N.H. 276, 761 A.2d 494, 498 (2000); *Marcotte v. Timberlane/Hampstead Sch. Dist.*, 143 N.H. 331, 733 A.2d 394, 405 (1999). Under New Hampshire law, however, the amount of damages recoverable for the benefit of a decedent's sibling is limited to a total of $50,000, [FN51] unless the sibling shows proof of financial dependency upon the decedent.

FN51. This figure constitutes a sum of $50,000 *in toto*, as opposed to $50,000 per surviving non-dependent relative. Such a figure is justified because the New Hampshire legislature "intended wrongful death actions to benefit the estate, rather than the distributees." *In re Estate of Infant Fontaine*, 128 N.H. 695, 519 A.2d 227, 229 (1986).

b. Intentional Infliction of Emotional Distress

New Hampshire recognizes the tort of intentional infliction of emotional distress, following Section 46 of the RESTATEMENT (SECOND) OF TORTS. Under New Hampshire law, the elements of the tort of intentional infliction of emotional distress are: (1) the defendant intentionally or recklessly inflicted severe emotional distress or was certain or substantially certain that his conduct would cause such distress; (2) the conduct was extreme and outrageous; (3) the defendant's conduct caused the plaintiff's emotional distress; and (4) the plaintiff suffered severe emotional distress. See *Orono Karate, Inc. v. Fred Villari Studio of Self Defense, Inc.*, 776 F.Supp. 47, 51 (D.N.H.1991).

In recognizing the tort of intentional infliction of emotional distress, New Hampshire courts have adopted Section 46 of the RESTATEMENT (SECOND) OF TORTS...See *Orono Karate, Inc.* 776 F.Supp. at 51. Though §46(2) of the Restatement specifically states that only present third parties may recover for an IIED claim, the Caveat to the section leaves open the possibility of other possible situations where a defendant could be liable for intentional infliction of emotional distress under this section. Moreover, Comment l. to the section specifically expands on the Caveat's language, stating that the Caveat was intended "to leave open the possibility of situations in which presence at the time may not be required." RESTATEMENT (SECOND) OF TORTS §46, cmt. l. [FN52]

FN52. Though the Court is cognizant that both the Caveat and comments to a section of the Restatement are not law by any means, they are instructive in helping to interpret the issue at hand.

The Court finds that a terrorist attack is precisely the sort of situation in which presence at the time is not required in light of the severity of the act and the obvious range of potential grief and distress that directly results from such a heinous act. This Court and courts of other jurisdictions have found that "a terrorist attack-by its nature-is directed not only at the victims but also at the victims' families." *Salazar*, 370 F.Supp.2d at 115 n. 12 (citing *Burnett v. Al Baraka Inv. and Dev. Corp.*, 274 F.Supp.2d 86, 107 (D.D.C.2003)). In this case, the evidence demonstrates that the defendants' motives in planning the attack on the Khobar Towers, and indeed their motives in carrying out a systematic plan of funding and organizing terrorist attacks, were intended to harm both the victims of the attack, and to instill terror in their loved ones and others in the United States. Accordingly, in the case of a terrorist attack as this, the Court finds that the presence element does not need to be proven in order to successfully bring a cause of action for intentional infliction of emotional distress under New Hampshire law.

Still, it is of paramount concern to this Court that a line be drawn to prevent a potentially unlimited number of plaintiffs who were not present at the site of the attack from seeking redress. See RESTATEMENT (SECOND) OF TORTS §46, cmt. l. The Restatement has noted that recovery for third-party bystanders has typically been granted to members of the victim's "near relatives." *Id.* State courts have also followed this approach, allowing recovery for the victim's spouse, child, sibling or parents. See, e.g., *Williams v. City of Minneola*, 575 So.2d 683, 690 (Fla.App.1991). The Court finds this approach to be a logical one. Accordingly, under New Hampshire law, a victim's near relatives, as de-

fined by the state's intestate succession statute, who were not present may nonetheless have standing to seek redress under a claim of intentional infliction of emotional distress.

2. Plaintiffs

a. Estate and Surviving Family Members of Peter Morgera

i. Estate of Peter Morgera

Peter Morgera was killed on June 25, 1996 at the Khobar Towers. Ex. 9. He is survived by his two brothers, Michael Morgera and Thomas Morgera. Michael is three years older than Peter, who was 11 months older than Thomas. (Dec. 5, 2003 P.M. Tr. at 94-96.)

After high school Peter attended classes at the University of New Hampshire and had a few different jobs before deciding to join the Air Force. Peter also spent time as a volunteer firefighter in Stratham, New Hampshire. After basic training and technical school, Peter was assigned to a duty station in Germany. *Id.* at 109-111, Ex. 93.

After completing his tour of duty in Germany, Peter was assigned to Eglin AFB in Florida. Peter and Michael spoke on the telephone several times during this period. Michael testified that the Air Force changed Peter. According to his brother, the time Peter spent in the Air Force and the time he spent in Germany had given Peter the confidence to "be much more concerned with the way he lived his life, not for others but for himself." (Dec. 5, 2003 P.M. Tr. at 111-14.) Peter volunteered to be temporarily deployed to Saudi Arabia in place of Stan Dworkin, a higher ranking airman who had a wife and children. *Id.* at 114-115. Fittingly, Peter's tombstone reads "Family, community, country." *Id.* at 128.

Peter's estate is represented by his brother, Michael Morgera. Peter's estate has asserted claims under New Hampshire's wrongful death statute because he was last domiciled in New Hampshire. As the administrator of Peter's estate, Michael Morgera is the proper plaintiff to bring a wrongful death action under New Hampshire law. *See* N.H.Rev.Stat. Ann. §556:12. In light of the fact that Peter is survived solely by his brothers, Michael and Thomas Morgera, any recovery under this wrongful death action is for Michael and Thomas Morgera.

Based upon the pleadings and evidence presented to the Court, the estate of Peter Morgera has made out a valid claim for wrongful death under New Hampshire law. The beneficiaries of his estate are entitled to recover compensatory damages arising from the wrongful death, including "capacity to earn money during the deceased party's probable working life." *See* N.H.Rev.Stat. Ann. §556:12(I). Plaintiffs have presented no evidence of any financial dependency upon the decedent in this case. Therefore, to the extent that Peter Morgera's lost wages exceed $50,000, the total amount of recovery for his estate must be reduced to conform to the $50,000 limit imposed by statute under New Hampshire law.

Dr. Herman Miller, an economic consultant testified as an expert that, as a result of Peter's untimely death, he experienced a net economic loss of $1,294,377.00. In light of the statutory limitation on damages for non-dependent siblings, the Court must therefore award the Estate of Peter Morgera, by Michael Morgera as personal representative, $50,000.00 in economic damages for the benefit of his brothers, Michael and Thomas Morgera, to be distributed in accordance with the method of distribution prescribed under New Hampshire law. *See* N.H.Rev.Stat. Ann. §556:14. As for the intangible pain and suffering damages incurred by Peter's surviving brothers, the Court will address those awards below, in an individualized discussion of the claims of Michael and Thomas Morgera.

ii. Michael Morgera

Michael William Morgera is a United States citizen and the brother of Peter Morgera and Thomas Morgera. Michael is three years older than Peter who was 11 months older than Thomas. (Dec. 5, 2003 P.M. Tr. at 94-96.) Michael was born in Dorchester, Massachusetts on June 4, 1969, and graduated from Exeter Area High School in 1988. Michael is currently employed as a chef at First Impressions Catering. Michael was married to his wife, Kristen, on September 15, 1996. *Id.* at 94-96.

Upon learning of his brother's death, Michael said that he "never felt as much joy as [he] felt pain when [he] lost [his] brother Peter." (Feb. 10, 2004 Tr. at 173.) According to Dr. Cable, Michael

> is in loss and loneliness. His grief is compounded by the whole family history of abuse and emotional scars that all three brothers shared. I think it's hard for him to know what they survived early in life, only to have his brother taken away this way with everything else that had happened... [There's] still a lot of emotional upheaval in his life...His grief will continue for a very long time...I am not sure he is strong enough yet that he could handle any other significant loss in his life right now. I think that would be devastating to him.

> *Id.* at 174.

As the brother of Peter Morgera, Michael Morgera has brought an intentional infliction of emotional distress claim against the defendants for pain and suffering caused by the death of his brother. Based upon the evidence presented to the Court, the elements of Michael Morgera's intentional in-

fliction of emotional distress claim are met. The defendants' conduct in facilitating, financing, and providing material support to bring about this attack was intentional, extreme, and outrageous. As the evidence shows, this horrific act precipitated by the defendants' planning and assistance brought immediate emotional distress to Michael Morgera. Finally, it is clear that Michael Morgera has continued to experience emotional distress since that time due to the fact that his brother was taken away from him in such a tragic and horrific manner. Therefore, this Court shall award to Michael Morgera $2.5 million to compensate him for the emotional distress, pain and suffering that he sustained as a result of his brother's untimely death.

iii. Thomas Morgera

Thomas E. Morgera, a United States citizen, is on active duty in the United States Air Force. He is currently assigned to Andrews AFB with the 89th Airway MXG, a special mission unit. The unit maintains aircraft that serve as Air Force 2 and transport the Vice President, the Joint Chiefs of Staff, and Cabinet Members. Thomas Morgera is a flying crew chief with Air Force 2. He has been in the Air Force for 12 years, and has been assigned to bases throughout the United States and the world. He has been deployed to South America, Guam, and Puerto Rico, the Far East, Japan, Thailand, the Philippines and Micronesia as well as England, Europe, Southwest Asia, Somalia and Kenya. He has been deployed twice to Dhahran AFB in Saudi Arabia and has lived in the Khobar Towers complex. (Dec. 5, 2003 P.M. Tr. at 40-43.)

Thomas Morgera grew up in a small house located at 35 Lewis Street in Chelsea, Massachusetts. As children, Peter and Thomas were inseparable. Thomas' earliest memory of Peter was missing him. He remembers that, when Peter started kindergarten, he would sit in the window all day long waiting for his brother to come home because before Peter went to kindergarten, the two boys played together everyday from the time they woke up until they went to sleep. *Id.* at 45-47.

Thomas and Peter Morgera lived in a difficult and sometimes violent environment as they were growing up. Their parents frequently quarreled and there was much screaming and sometimes physical violence. Thomas recalled that his mother would consume large amounts of alcohol and took illegal drugs. Many times she would not come home at night. Peter and Thomas' parents separated in 1972 when Thomas was approximately six years old. *Id.* at 50-51.

After his parents separated, Thomas, Peter, and Michael stayed with their mother. At this point their mother was home even less than previously. The three boys were left to fend for themselves, and Michael, who was four years older, spent more and more time away from the home. Peter and Thomas often cooked their own meals. On some occasions they would go down the street to their grandmother's house, but their mother warned them not to go their grandmother's house too often for dinner. As a result, they often went without dinner. *Id.* at 51-53.

When Thomas returned to Japan, he was suffering from depression. He wanted to sleep all the time and became introverted. He cut himself off from all others, including his wife and step-daughter. Further, he was deployed from Japan and away from his family soon after he returned there. His wife had no family or other support in Japan. As things worsened for Thomas, his wife left and came home to the United States. Thomas and his wife ultimately separated and divorced.

Thomas' chain of command told him that he could either voluntarily go to psychiatric counseling or they would order him to do so. Thomas met with an Air Force psychiatrist who, after hearing Thomas' story, told Thomas that he had been through more in the last six to eight months than most people go through in their entire lifetime. Thomas still has bad days and thinks often of Peter. *Id.* at 89-90.

Thomas has remarried and has a son who he named Peter James Morgera, II. Thomas gave his son this name because he wants people to ask why his son has this name, so that he has an opportunity to explain who Peter was and what he endured and accomplished in life. *Id.* at 92-93. According to Dr. Cable, Thomas

is still in loss and loneliness. He was greatly affected by Peter's death. He is able to move on to a degree because of his family, his new family. But I think that description he uses of a roller coaster is very accurate-that it's still a lot of ups and downs for him. There is not a sense of real stability. There is still a lot of pain, still a lot of emotion there. Again, for him, it's hard to see-it's hard for him to understand how they could come through so much only to have Peter die this way...He will continue with his grief, more in the sense of waves, because his family will help stabilize his grief to a degree. But there will still be those events and those activities and time when he is going to be kind of overcome for a period with ongoing grief.

(Feb. 10, 2004 Tr. at 177.)

As the brother of Peter Morgera, Thomas Morgera has brought an intentional infliction of emotional distress claim against the defendants for pain and suffering caused by the death of his brother. Based upon the evidence presented to the Court, the elements of Thomas Morgera's intentional infliction of emotional distress claim are met. The defendants' conduct in facilitating, financing, and providing material support to bring about this attack was intentional, extreme,

and outrageous. As the evidence shows, this horrific act precipitated by the defendants' planning and assistance brought immediate emotional distress to Thomas Morgera. Finally, it is clear that Thomas Morgera has continued to experience emotional distress since that time due to the fact that his brother was taken away from him in such a tragic and horrific manner. Therefore, this Court shall award to Thomas Morgera $2.5 million to compensate him for the emotional distress, pain and suffering that he sustained as a result of his brother's untimely death.

E. Texas

1. Causes of Action

a. Wrongful Death

Under Texas' wrongful death statute, a wrongful death action may be brought against a person if that person's "wrongful act, neglect, carelessness, unskillfulness, or default" causes an individual's death. Tex. Civ. Prac. & Rem.Code Ann. §71.002. Such an action is brought for the exclusive benefit of the decedent's surviving spouse, children, and parents. Tex. Civ. Prac. & Rem.Code Ann. §71.004(a). Any one of the surviving spouse, children, or parents of the deceased may bring a wrongful death action. Tex. Civ. Prac. & Rem. Code Ann. §71.004(b).

A wrongful death plaintiff may seek those damages that are "proportionate to the injury resulting from the death." Tex. Civ. Prac. & Rem.Code Ann. §71.010(a). These damages include pecuniary loss, medical expenses, funeral expenses, loss of companionship and society, and mental anguish. See *Wellborn v. Sears, Roebuck & Co.*, 970 F.2d 1420, 1427-29 (5th Cir.1992). Any awarded damages are divided among those entitled to recover and who are alive at the time of the award. Tex. Civ. Prac. & Rem.Code Ann. §71.010(b). Though a right of action exists for all persons within the designated class to recover for wrongful death, under the statute only one wrongful death action can exist to recover a single sum that is apportioned among the entire eligible class. *Texas & P. Ry. Co. v. Wood*, 145 Tex. 534, 199 S.W.2d 652, 654 (1947).

b. Intentional Infliction of Emotional Distress

As a general rule, to state a claim for intentional infliction of emotional distress, the outrageous and extreme conduct must be directed at the plaintiff, although a cause of action may be allowed to an immediate family member who was present at the time. *See* RESTATEMENT (SECOND) OF TORTS §46(2). Some states, however, have done away with the plaintiff presence element altogether. In Texas, however, the issue of whether a plaintiff must be present in order to recover for a claim of intentional infliction of emotional distress has not been specifically addressed by the courts. In cases such as these, the Court must assess whether such a claim would be valid under the laws of that state. See, e.g., *Dammarell v. Islamic Republic of Iran*, 2006 WL 2382704, *175-76 (D.D.C. Aug 17, 2006) (Facciola, J.) (interpreting law of Washington State); *Salazar*, 370 F.Supp.2d at 115 (interpreting Illinois law).

In Texas, the issue of whether a plaintiff must be present in order to recover for a claim of intentional infliction of emotional distress has not been specifically addressed by the courts. The fact that Texas courts have adopted Section 46 of the RESTATEMENT (SECOND) OF TORTS in recognizing the tort of intentional infliction of emotional distress allows this Court to follow the same reasoning regarding the presence requirement set forth previously in this opinion. [FN53] Applying this rationale, this Court finds that the presence element does not need to be proven in order to successfully bring a cause of action for intentional infliction of emotional distress under Texas law, and that standing to seek such recovery is limited to the victim's near relatives who were not present at the time of the attack.

FN53. See *supra* Part VI.D. 1.b.

2. Plaintiffs

a. Estate and Surviving Family Members of Millard Campbell

i. Estate of Millard Campbell
Millard D. Campbell ("Dee") was a Sergeant in the Air Force. (Dec. 6, 2003 A.M. Tr. at 83.) He was killed at Khobar Towers on June 25, 1996. Ex. 9. Dee was born in a small town in California on September 20, 1965, where he lived for just a couple of years and then moved with his family to Angleton, Texas. (Dec. 6, 2003 A.M. Tr. at 89.) Dee went to the public schools in Angleton, graduating from high school in 1984. *Id.* During high school, Dee was a baseball player, and received a baseball scholarship to play baseball in junior college. *Id.* at 109.

Dee became engaged to his future wife, Marie, in the fall of 1986, and shortly after the engagement, he enlisted in the Air Force. *Id.* at 90. Dee was supposed to be on a three-year tour in England, but ultimately he received a humanitarian reassignment back to Texas because his father had cancer. His father died in April 1989. When Dee returned to Texas, he was stationed at Bergstrom Air Force Base in Austin, Texas. There, Dee changed his career field, and started working in flight operations and scheduling. *Id.* at 95.

Marie continued to attend college at Sam Houston State University. She was apart from him during the week, but they were with each other on weekends. Being away from him so that she could go to school was not easy because her school was three hours away from his Air Force Base, but Dee was determined that she get her college degree. *Id.* at 96-97.

After Marie received her college degree, she moved to Austin in order to be with Dee. She worked at a couple of different jobs, the most permanent of which was a job in a retail department store. *Id.* at 97. Dee volunteered to go to Iraq as part of Operation Desert Storm in early 1991. Marie was very worried about this. Dee arrived in the Middle East just a few days before the war started and came home at the end of March or the beginning of April 1991. *Id.* at 98.

In October 1992, Dee and Marie moved to Eglin Air Force Base in Florida, where again, he was with a fighter squadron, being the air controller and scheduling arrivals and departures. *Id.* at 101. Dee was very popular with the other men in the Air Force. He also did his job very well. He re-enlisted for another six years because he loved his job so much. Dee planned to be an air traffic controller in private industry after the conclusion of his tour of duty with the Air Force. *Id.* at 102. Dee returned to Saudi Arabia the second (and last time) in April 1996.

Dee's estate is represented by his wife, Marie Campbell. Dee's estate has asserted claims under Texas' wrongful death statute because he was last domiciled in Texas. As the personal representative of Dee's estate, Marie Campbell is the proper plaintiff to bring a wrongful death action under Texas law. *See* Tex. Civ. Prac. & Rem.Code Ann. §71.004(b). Any recovery under this wrongful death action is for the benefit of his wife, Marie Campbell, and his mother, Bessie Campbell, to be distributed in a manner consistent with Texas law governing intestate property distribution. Tex. Civ. Prac. & Rem.Code Ann. §71.010(b); see also *Texas & P. Ry. Co. v. Wood*, 199 S.W.2d at 654.

Based upon the pleadings and evidence presented to the Court, the estate of Millard "Dee" Campbell has made out a valid claim for wrongful death under Texas law, and the beneficiaries of this estate are entitled to recover the present value of any lost wages and compensatory damages that would have been recoverable had Dee lived. Dr. Herman Miller, an economic consultant testified as an expert that, due to Dee's untimely death, he experienced a net economic loss of $1,572,314.00. The Court therefore awards the Estate of Millard "Dee" Campbell, by Marie Campbell as personal representative, $1,572,314.00 in economic damages for the benefit of Marie Campbell and Bessie Campbell, to be distributed in a manner in accordance with the method of intestate distribution under Texas law. A discussion of intangible economic damages of the wrongful death recovery will be addressed below in an individualized discussion of the claims of Marie Campbell and Bessie Campbell.

ii. Marie Campbell

Marie was born on June 13, 1966, and was raised in Houston. Her parents are still alive, and her father works for a credit union. *Id*. at 83. Marie attended public schools as well, graduating from high school in 1984. After high school, she attended Glen Junior College, in Burham, Texas, where she met Dee. *Id*. When Dee first thought about joining the Air Force, Marie was concerned because her two grandfathers had served in World War II and she only knew of the military in terms of war time. Dee told her not to worry about it. *Id*. at 91. On the afternoon Dee learned he passed his test to join the Air Force, he proposed marriage to Marie, and she accepted. *Id*. at 92.

Dee joined the Air Force on April 15, 1987. Dee and Marie had been married one month earlier, while she was on spring break from school. At first, Dee and Marie moved into Marie's grandfather's house, where she had been living while at school. *Id*. at 92-93. In October 1992, Dee and Marie moved to Eglin Air Force Base in Florida, where again, he was with a fighter squadron, being the air controller and scheduling arrivals and departures. *Id*. at 101.

Dee and Marie never had any children. *Id*. at 113. Dee wanted children but Marie wanted to wait until she was about 32 years old. When Dee died, she had just turned 30. *Id*. at 113. For two years Marie tried not to take any medication, but around 1998 she had to start taking medication to help her. She went on Prozac, then went off of it for a while, but has now been taking it for several years continuously. *Id*. at 145.

Marie continued to teach, but only on a sporadic basis. After missing a number of days, Marie took a leave of absence, and ultimately quit her job altogether. Finally, Marie moved back to Dallas, and eventually went back to school to get a master's degree with teaching certification. Id at 147.

In early 1998, Marie started seeing a licensed professional counselor, and still sees a counselor today. Her feelings fluctuate. Sometimes she sleeps well, but at other times, she wakes up in the middle of the night and dreams about Dee. *Id*. at 148.

She is also followed by the fact that she hasn't had any children, that she had wanted to wait until she was 32 to have children, but that now she is 37. This has also made it difficult to have relationships with another man. She cannot think about marriage because she wakes up every day and thinks about Dee. *Id*. at 149.

As Dr. Cable stated, Marie "still needs medication to help her cope with the depression. So it's a very extreme sense of loss and loneliness, a lot of pain…I see her continuing to grieve in the foreseeable future…[S]he is probably going to need to continue with medication for quite some time." (Feb. 10, 2004 Tr. at 36-37.)

Based upon the evidence presented at trial, Marie Campbell has experienced severe mental anguish and suffering as a result of her husband's untimely death. Therefore, this Court shall award to the estate of Millard "Dee" Campbell, by Marie Campbell as Personal Representative, $8 million for the benefit of his wife Marie Campbell to compensate her for the mental pain and suffering she sustained as a result of her husband's death.

iii. Bessie Campbell

Bessie Amaryllis Campbell was the mother of Millard D. Campbell ("Dee"). Telephone Deposition Tr., Ex. 181 at 5. Bessie was born a little town in Texas on January 25, 1928. Her father was initially a farmer for a period and then became a shipper of jars. Her mother was a homemaker. Mrs. Campbell had two brothers, both of whom served in World War II. *Id*. at 6. Bessie graduated from high school but did not go to college. After high school she went to work in a county clerk's office for three years, and then she met her husband. He was a truck driver at that time and became a mechanic. *Id*. at 8-9. She and her husband had seven children. Dee was the youngest. *Id*. at 10.

After Dee died, Mrs. Campbell went to the cemetery several times a week for a very long time and would talk to Dee. Even today, she goes to the cemetery at least once a week. *Id*. at 36-37. She thinks of Dee every day. At times she can't believe that he's gone and she thinks that "he'll probably walk in the door any minute." She dreams about him a lot. She and her family even endowed a scholarship fund in Dee's name. She put some of her own money into the fund. *Id*. at 38.

She often wakes up in the middle of the night thinking about Dee and as a result can't go back to sleep. *Id*. at 39. Bessie finds it very difficult to watch television when she hears about our soldiers being killed in Iraq because it makes her think about Dee. *Id*. at 41. Life has not been easy for her since her son was killed on June 25, 1996.

According to Dr. Cable, Bessie Campbell

is still really in loss and loneliness. She still has a hard time admitting to his death…Her prognosis is she is one who does cope but it's very difficult. I would see her continuing to experience pain, feelings of emptiness for a considerable period of time in the future.

(Feb. 10, 2004 Tr. at 32-33.)

Based upon the evidence presented at trial, Bessie Campbell has experienced severe mental anguish and suffering as a result of her son's untimely death. Therefore, this Court shall award to the estate of Millard "Dee" Campbell, by Marie Campbell as Personal Representative, $5 million for the benefit of his mother Bessie Campbell to compensate her for the mental pain and suffering she sustained as a result of her son's death.

b. Steve Kitson

Steve Kitson is a brother to decedent Kendall Kitson, Jr. ("Kenny"). As Steve explained in his affidavit to the Court, on June 25, 1996, "the rug was pulled out from under [him.]" Ex. 293 at 10. Up until Kenny's death, Steve was doing very well professionally and making a happy life for himself in Dallas, Texas. *Id.* at 9.

After Kenny's death, Steve's father asked him to quit his job and come and live with them in Florida. *Id.* at 14. Steve gave up his job in Dallas to be with his parents and help them through the difficult time. *Id.* at 14. After living with his parents for a year or so in Florida following Kenny's death, Mr. Kitson then asked Steve to move to Oklahoma and assist him with his properties and farms. For several years now, Steve has lived in one of his parent's homes in Oklahoma and helped his father watch over their properties. *Id.* at 16.

The mornings are the hardest time of day for Steve. The most difficult days for Steve include Kenny's birthday, the anniversary of his death, and holidays. It is difficult for Steve because his friends do not understand what he is going through and so it has created some awkward moments. Steve's therapy is working in the yard and lifting weights. *Id.* at 20-22. Steve has dreamed about Kenny. *Id.* at 24.

According to Dr. Cable, Steve

is in loss and loneliness. He has got his own grief issues, but it's complicated by his parent's bitterness, by his mother's health issues. Kenny was the person who accepted [Steve] for who he was. He doesn't feel any of that now...He is going to have significant difficulties, because he keeps so much into himself and he doesn't really have an outlet...So it's not a good prognosis.

(Feb. 10, 2004 Tr. at 149.)

As the brother of Kendall Kitson, Jr., Steve Kitson has brought an intentional infliction of emotional distress claim against the defendants for pain and suffering caused by the death of his brother. Based upon the evidence presented to the Court, the elements of Steve Kitson's intentional infliction of emotional distress claim are met. The defendants' conduct in facilitating, financing, and providing material support to bring about this attack was intentional, extreme, and outrageous. As the evidence shows, this horrific act precipitated by the defendants' planning and assistance brought immediate emotional distress to Steve Kitson. Finally, it is clear that Steve Kitson has continued to experience emotional distress since that time due to the fact that his brother was taken away from him in such a tragic and horrific manner. Therefore, this Court shall award to Steve Kitson $2.5 million to compensate him for the emotional distress, pain and suffering that he sustained as a result of his brother's untimely death.

F. Ohio

1. Causes of Action

a. Wrongful Death

Under Ohio's wrongful death statute, a civil action may be brought "in the name of the personal representative of the decedent for the exclusive benefit of the surviving spouse, the children, and the parents of the decedent,...[as well as] the other next of kin of the decedent." Ohio Rev.Code. Ann. §2125.02(A)(1). [FN54] A decedent's next of kin may include the decedent's siblings. *Karr v. Sixt*, 146 Ohio St. 527, 67 N.E.2d 331, 335 (1946). Available compensatory damages for a wrongful death action include pecuniary damages, loss of support, services, society and prospective inheritance, as well as pain and suffering incurred by the bereaved plaintiff. The surviving spouse, children and parents of the decedent, if any, are "rebuttably presumed to have suffered damages by reason of the wrongful death." Ohio Rev.Code. Ann. §2125.02(A)(1). The decedent's next of kin, however, bear the burden of proving that the alleged damages were suffered. Ohio Rev.Code. Ann. §2125.02(A)(1); *Shoemaker v. Crawford*, 78 Ohio App.3d 53, 603 N.E.2d 1114, 1119-21 (1991).

FN54. Under Ohio law, a personal representative from a foreign state is not precluded from bringing an action under Ohio law on behalf of the decedent's estate and its beneficiaries. *See* Ohio Rev.Code Ann. §2113.75. Therefore, notwithstanding the fact that Cecil Lester-the personal representative of the estate of Christopher Lester-was domiciled in West Virginia at the time of the attack, he may nonetheless maintain this action on behalf of the estate and its beneficiaries.

2. Plaintiffs

a. Estate and Surviving Family Members of Christopher Lester

i. Estate of Christopher Lester

In June 1996, Christopher Lester ("Chris") was nineteen years old. Ex. 14. Although regularly stationed at Wright Patterson AFB in Ohio, in June 1996, Chris was on assignment in Dhahran, Saudi Arabia where he resided at the Khobar Towers Complex. *Id.* On June 25, 1996, Chris was killed at Khobar Towers as a result of the terrorist bombing. Ex. 9. As previously noted, [FN55] Chris was the only decedent of the 17 decedents whose estates are represented in this trial who survived the blast for a discernable amount of time prior to his death.

FN55. See *supra* Part V.D.

Plaintiffs Judy Lester, Cecil Lester, Cecil Lester, Jr., and Jessica Lester are Chris' mother, father, brother, and sister respectively (collectively, the "Lester family"). The Lester family testified at the trial of this matter on December 8, 2003.

Before he entered the Air Force, Chris was an outstanding athlete. He loved football and played on various football teams from the time he was six years old until he graduated from high school. *Id.* at 6. Chris was known as being pleasant, honest, sweet, loving, and generous. *Id.* at 6. Most remarkable about Chris was his ever-present smile. *Id.* at 5. Throughout school, Chris was an outstanding student his whole life. He never received a grade below a "B." *Id.* He was a member of the Honors Society at Pineville High School, where he graduated in 1995. Chris always talked about going to college and he joined the Air Force to pay for college. *Id.* at 7-8. Chris planned on taking college courses when he returned from his deployment in Saudi Arabia. *Id.* at 8.

Christopher's estate is represented by his parents, Cecil Lester, Sr., and Judy Lester. Christopher's estate has asserted claims under Ohio's wrongful death statute because he was last domiciled in Ohio. As a personal representatives of Christopher's estate, Cecil Lester, Sr., and Judy Lester are proper plaintiffs to bring a wrongful death action under Ohio law. *See* Ohio Rev.Code. Ann. §2125.02(A)(1). Under Ohio law, any recovery under this wrongful death action is for the benefit of his parents, Cecil Lester, Sr., and Judy Lester, as well as his siblings, Cecil Lester, Jr., and Jessica Lester, who have proven that they suffered damages resulting from Christopher's death. [FN56]

FN56. See *infra* Parts VI.F.2.a.iii, iv.

Based upon the pleadings and evidence presented to the Court, the estate of Christopher Lester has made out a valid claim for wrongful death under Ohio law. The beneficiaries of this estate are entitled to recover the present value of compensatory damages, including lost wages that the decedent might reasonably have been expected to earn but for the wrongful death. Dr. Herman Miller, an economic consultant testified as an expert that, as a result of Christopher's untimely death, he experienced a net economic loss of $1,960,466.00.

Additionally, Christopher's beneficiaries are entitled to pain and suffering damages suffered by Christopher because he survived in extreme pain for a time following the attack. In cases where victims survive an attack for a period of time, courts typically award a lump sum award. *Haim*, 425 F.Supp.2d at 71-72. In light of Dr. Parson's testimony that Christopher Lester was alive for 15 minutes after the attack, and was conscious for 10 minutes, this Court finds that the estate of Christopher Lester should be awarded an additional $500,000.

Accordingly, the Court should award the Estate of Christopher Lester, by Cecil Lester, Sr., and Judy Lester as personal representatives, $1,960,466.00 in economic damages, plus $500,000 in personal pain and suffering damages for the benefit of Cecil Lester, Sr., Judy Lester, Cecil Lester, Jr., and Jessica Lester, to be distributed in a manner consistent with the statute governing intestate distribution of property under Ohio law. A discussion of intangible economic damages of the wrongful death recovery, will be addressed below in an individualized discussion of the claims of Cecil Lester, Sr., Judy Lester, Cecil Lester, Jr., and Jessica Lester.

ii. Cecil Lester, Sr. & Judy Lester

Judy and Cecil Lester met when Judy was still in high school. *Id.* at 4. They were married on February 4, 1972. *Id.* Judy and Cecil Lester have three children: Cecil Lester, Jr. ("Cecil Jr."), born in 1974; Chris, born in 1977, and Jessica Lester, born in 1987. *Id.* at 3-4. All three children were born in Beckley, West Virginia. *Id.* The Lester children, like their parents, are all United States citizens. *Id.* at 55, 71.

Chris' death has dramatically affected Judy and Cecil and their marriage. Judy was so distraught that for several years after Chris' death, she prayed to God to help her get through each day. She could not sleep. *Id.* at 29. Indeed, Cecil testified that Judy still wakes up at night and cries. *Id.* at 25. Judy feels incomplete since Chris died. *Id.* at 29. In order not to think about Chris, both Judy and Cecil intentionally keep themselves busy. Although Judy questioned her faith in

God when Chris died, she now believes her faith is allowing her to heal. *Id.* at 51.

Similarly, Cecil is not the same man since Chris' death. Mr. Lester testified that things he once took a lot of joy in no longer interest him anymore. Cecil rarely fishes and hunts anymore. He cannot get himself to go motorcycle riding at all. Cecil has lost interest in football. *Id.* at 28.

Cecil also explained that Judy and he deal with Chris' death differently. Judy finds it helpful to talk about Chris. *Id.* at 51. She also has pictures and memorabilia of Chris throughout the house. *Id.* at 32; Ex. 105. Cecil is the opposite. He becomes upset and emotional when discussing Chris. *Id.* at 51. Cecil returned to work six weeks after Chris' funeral. A year later, Cecil's employer asked him to see a counselor because he was not focused at his job. He saw the counselor several times but did not find counseling helpful because it is too painful to talk about Chris. *Id.* at 52-53.

Even though they deal with Chris' death differently, both Judy and Cecil think about Chris every day. *Id.* at 32, 54. For the first five years following Chris' death, Judy visited his grave two or three times a week. Presently, she visits Chris' grave about every other week. *Id.* at 20. Cecil visits Chris' grave three or four times a month. *Id.* at 48. Both Judy and Cecil Lester clean Chris' tombstone when they visit. *Id.*; Ex. 104.

According to Dr. Cable, Judy

is still in loss and loneliness, but she has made conscious efforts to try to move on. She has got a lot of guilt issues, and the guilt is this not being able to protect her son...She will continue with her grief. She was a mother for whom the mother role was very important. Her sense of having failed to protect her son is an issue that's not going to resolve itself quickly.

(Feb. 10, 2004 Tr. at 155-56.)

Additionally, Dr. Cable stated that Cecil

is still in loss and loneliness. He can't seem to let go; holding on to those memories. The dreams are a part of those ongoing memories. He just can't seem to move to the next step along the way...His grief will continue. I think he is one of these individuals who likely will have a very difficult time ever getting his life really back together again.

(Feb. 10, 2004 Tr. at 158.)

Based upon the evidence presented at trial, both Cecil Lester, Sr., and Judy Lester have experienced severe mental anguish and suffering as a result of their son's untimely death. Therefore, this Court shall award to the estate of Christopher Lester, by Cecil Lester, Sr., and Judy Lester as Personal Representatives, $5 million for the benefit of his mother Judy Lester, and $5 million for the benefit of his father Cecil Lester, Sr., to compensate both for the mental pain and suffering both have sustained as a result of their son's untimely death.

iii. Cecil Lester, Jr.

Cecil Jr. was utterly crushed by his brother's death. Chris was Cecil Jr.'s confidant. Cecil Jr. shut down emotionally after Chris died. Cecil Jr. believes that the effect that Chris' death had on him directly affected his own marriage. He wouldn't share his emotions with his wife, and found it difficult to talk with her. (Dec. 8, 2003 Tr. at 67.)

According to Judy, "Cecil Jr. and Chris [were] like twins...there was 2-1/2 years between them, but you would never know that. When they were together, they were like best of friends, playmates and they just loved each other." *Id.* at 30. Because of their close relationship, Chris' death has left an unspeakable void in Cecil Jr.'s life. Cecil, Jr. thinks about Chris every day. Like his father, Cecil Jr. does not enjoy fishing or hunting anymore since Chris' death, and believes that he has become less sociable since Chris died. *Id.* at 68-69.

Cecil Jr. has dreamed often about Chris. He visits Chris' grave on the holidays, and drives by Chris' grave two or three times a day on his way to and from work. *Id.* at 66-67.

As Dr. Cable stated, Cecil

is still in loss and loneliness. He also has some elements of guilt...that [their] last conversation, [their] last time together had an element of an argument to it...[I]n his own mind, it was not the way to end his relationship to his brother...His grief will continue. He will always have a feeling of needing to be the protector for others. His brother's [death] will affect his life in may ways throughout his life.

(Feb. 10, 2004 Tr. at 163-64.)

Based upon the evidence presented at trial, Cecil Lester, Jr., experienced severe mental anguish and suffering as a result of his brother's untimely death. Therefore, this Court shall award to the estate of Christopher Lester, by Cecil Lester, Sr., and Judy Lester as Personal Representatives, $2.5 million for the benefit of his brother Cecil Lester, Jr., to compensate him for the mental pain and suffering he sustained as a result of his brother's untimely death.

iv. Jessica Lester

Jessica Lester is the sister of Christopher Lester. She was nine years old when Chris died. (Dec. 8, 2003 Tr. at 30.) Jessica remembers Chris "as being so friendly and happy all the time." He was a cheerful person who played and watched movies with her. *Id.* at 75-76. He was a great big brother to her.

Since Chris' death, Jessica visits Chris' grave about once or twice a month. *Id.* at 78. Jessica is saddened by the void Chris' death has caused her and her family. She laments the fact that she does not have Chris in her life anymore.

As Dr. Cable stated, Jessica

is in loss and loneliness. Her grief is complicated by the age she was at the time that this happened...She not only lost a brother, but she lost a father figure and she lost a part of her own identity...She will continue in her grief for a long time. I think she will begin to recover, but I think that down the road the issue she may face is that when she marries, when she has children, the regrets that Chris can't be there to be a part of those things. Because of the significant role he played in her life, she is going to miss that he can't be a significant role in the rest of her family's life at that point.

(Feb. 10, 2004 Tr. at 160-61.)

Based upon the evidence presented at trial, Jessica Lester experienced severe mental anguish and suffering as a result of her brother's untimely death. Therefore, this Court shall award to the estate of Christopher Lester, by Cecil Lester, Sr., and Judy Lester as Personal Representatives, $2.5 million for the benefit of his sister Jessica Lester to compensate her for the mental pain and suffering she sustained as a result of her brother's untimely death.

G. Minnesota

1. Causes of Action

a. Wrongful Death

Under Minnesota's wrongful death statute a court-appointed trustee may bring an action "when death is caused by the wrongful act or omission" of another. Minn.Stat. Ann. §573.02. The amount of recovery for a wrongful death action is the amount the judge "deems fair and just in reference to the pecuniary loss resulting from the death." Minn.Stat. Ann. §573.02. Pecuniary loss includes loss of income, as well as "loss of advice, comfort, assistance, and protection." *Rath v. Hamilton Standard Div. of United Tech. Corp.*, 292 N.W.2d 282, 284-85 (Minn.1980) (quoting *Gravley v. Sea Gull Marine, Inc.*, 269 N.W.2d 896, 901 (Minn.1978)).

Any damages awarded in a wrongful death action are "for the exclusive benefit of the surviving spouse and next of kin, proportionate to the pecuniary loss severally suffered by the death." Minn.Stat. Ann. §573.02. "Next of kin" are those blood relatives who may properly recover under Minnesota's intestacy statute, and include the decedent's children, parents, and siblings. *Wynkoop v. Carpenter*, 574 N.W.2d 422, 427 (Minn.1998).

b. Intentional Infliction of Emotional Distress

Minnesota recognizes the tort of intentional infliction of emotional distress, and has adopted Section 46 of the RESTATEMENT (SECOND) OF TORTS. See *Dornfeld v. Oberg*, 503 N.W.2d 115, 117 (Minn.1993). Accordingly, the elements of the tort of intentional infliction of emotional distress under Minnesota law are: (1) extreme and outrageous conduct; (2) the conduct is intentional or reckless; (3) the conduct causes emotional distress; and (4) the emotional distress is severe. *Dornfeld*, 503 N.W.2d at 117. In order for a defendant's conduct to be considered extreme and outrageous, it must be "so atrocious that it passes the boundaries of decency and is utterly intolerable to the civilized community." *Hubbard v. United Press Intl., Inc.*, 330 N.W.2d 428, 438-39 (Minn.1983).

In Minnesota, the issue of whether a plaintiff must be present in order to recover for a claim of intentional infliction of emotional distress has not been specifically addressed by the courts. The fact that Minnesota courts have adopted Section 46 of the RESTATEMENT (SECOND) OF TORTS in recognizing the tort of intentional infliction of emotional distress allows this Court to follow the same reasoning regarding the presence requirement set forth previously in this opinion. [FN57] Applying this rationale, this Court finds that the presence element does not need to be proven in order to successfully bring a cause of action for intentional infliction of emotional distress under Minnesota law, and that standing to seek such recovery is limited to the victim's near relatives who were not present at the time of the attack.

FN57. See *supra* Part VI.D. 1.b.

2. Plaintiffs

a. Additional Surviving Family Members of Brent Marthaler

i. Matthew Marthaler

Matthew Lucas Marthaler ("Matt"), a United States citizen, was Brent Marthaler's brother. Matt was born in St. Paul, Minnesota on February 19, 1975. (Dec. 3, 2003 Tr. at 110.) Matt is one year younger than his brother Kirk, and one year older than his brother Brent.

Matt testified that Brent's funeral service at the church in Minnesota "was a blur." In the days and weeks following Brent's death, Matt "made sure that [his] Mom and Dad were able to go to work the next day and soldier on." Matt then returned to the base in Meridan, Mississippi and told his Chief, "I'll hold on for as long as you tell me but I don't have much left for the Navy. I just got my heart ripped out."

Matt felt isolated following Brent's death. Matt visited Kirk in Alabama every chance he could even though they were stationed about 200 or 300 miles away from each other. *Id.* at 120-22. He still thinks of Brent often. *Id.* at 127.

According to Dr. Cable, Matt

is in loss and loneliness. He has had a very difficult time coping with his brother's death...Following the death and the family estrangement, he was the only member of the family speaking to everybody...He will have continuing grief for a good many years to come. He is one again that...is in need of some real grief therapy. The fact that this is the first time in all these years he has really talked about this would clearly say there is a need to have an opportunity to share and to deal with it. He, too, will have grief that re-emerges with significant life events in the future.

(Feb. 10, 2004 Tr. at 79-80.)

As the brother of Brent Marthaler, Matthew Marthaler has brought an intentional infliction of emotional distress claim against the defendants for pain and suffering caused by the death of his brother. Based upon the evidence presented to the Court, the elements of Matthew Marthaler's intentional infliction of emotional distress claim are met. The defendants' conduct in facilitating, financing, and providing material support to bring about this attack was intentional, extreme, and outrageous. As the evidence shows, this horrific act precipitated by the defendants' planning and assistance brought immediate emotional distress to Matthew Marthaler. Finally, it is clear that Matthew Marthaler has continued to experience emotional distress since that time due to the fact that his brother was taken away from him in such a tragic and horrific manner. Therefore, this Court shall award to Matthew Marthaler $2.5 million to compensate him for the emotional distress, pain and suffering that he sustained as a result of his brother's untimely death.

ii. Kirk Marthaler

Kirk Charles Marthaler, a United States citizen, was Brent Marthaler's brother. Kirk was born in St. Paul, Minnesota on December 8, 1973. (Dec. 3, 2003 Tr. at 82.) Kirk is one year older than his brother Matt and was two years older than Brent. As children, the three brothers were very close.

Kirk attended the memorial service at Eglin AFB in Florida with his parents and brother and Katie and Katie's family. Brent's body was returned to Minnesota after the memorial service. Kirk remembers that the funeral home director called the Marthaler home and told Herm and Sharon that he was not sure if they wanted to do an open casket. The

funeral home was willing to take the wrapping and gauze off of Brent only if they received strict instructions to do so. The funeral home explained that the injuries to Brent were horrific, and the Air Force had done a very clean job of wrapping him. The funeral home explained that if they had undressed the wrapping, they would not be able to make him viewable. The funeral home director asked if Herman would come in first and view the body. Kirk was sent to do this. Kirk recalled that viewing his brother's body in the casket was the most hollow thing he had ever felt in his life. He then had to call his parents and tell them what he had seen. *Id.* at 102-04.

Kirk blames himself for his brother's death because he was the one who convinced Brent to join the Air Force and become a jet airplane mechanic. *Id.* at 105-08. He laments the fact that he and Brent "could've been best friends [but] me and my brother spent too much time competing. We never had an opportunity to become best friends." *Id.* at 108-09.

As Dr. Cable stated, Kirk is

very much in loss and loneliness, but with guilt added in his case. He sees what he will miss the rest of his life in terms of a relationship with his brother, how the family had changed, and how the family and Kirk will never be the same again...The grief will continue, and that with every major event in life, he will be struck by the fact that Brent isn't here to be a part of that. So a very strong sense of yearning...[T]he grief will be re-emerging for many years to come.

(Feb. 10, 2004 Tr. at 77-78.)

As the brother of Brent Marthaler, Kirk Marthaler has brought an intentional infliction of emotional distress claim against the defendants for pain and suffering caused by the death of his brother. Based upon the evidence presented to the Court, the elements of Kirk Marthaler's intentional infliction of emotional distress claim are met. The defendants' conduct in facilitating, financing, and providing material support to bring about this attack was intentional, extreme, and outrageous. As the evidence shows, this horrific act precipitated by the defendants' planning and assistance brought immediate emotional distress to Kirk Marthaler. Finally, it is clear that Kirk Marthaler has continued to experience emotional distress since that time due to the fact that his brother was taken away from him in such a tragic and horrific manner. Therefore, this Court shall award to Kirk Marthaler $2.5 million to compensate him for the emotional distress, pain and suffering that he sustained as a result of his brother's untimely death.

H. Wisconsin

1. Causes of Action

a. Wrongful Death

Under Wisconsin's wrongful death statute, a decedent's personal representative may bring an action when the decedent's death is "caused by a wrongful act, neglect or default" of another. Wis. Stat. Ann. §§895.03, 895.04(1). If the decedent dies without a surviving spouse, any damages inure to the benefit of the decedent's "lineal heirs." Wis. Stat. Ann. §895.04(2). "Lineal heirs" include the decedent's parents. Wis. Stat. Ann. §§852.01(1)(c). Damages recoverable in a wrongful death action include pecuniary damages, nonpecuniary damages limited to $350,000, as well as medical and funeral expenses. Wis. Stat. Ann. §§895.04.

b. Intentional Infliction of Emotional Distress

Under Wisconsin law, a plaintiff must prove the following elements to establish a successful claim of intentional infliction of emotional distress: (1) the defendant's conduct was intended to cause emotional distress; (2) the defendant's conduct was extreme and outrageous; (3) the defendant's conduct caused plaintiff's emotional distress; and (4) the plaintiff "suffered an extreme disabling emotional response to the defendant's conduct." *Rabideau v. City of Racine*, 243 Wis.2d 486, 627 N.W.2d 795, 802-03 (2001). In Wisconsin, the issue of whether a plaintiff must be present in order to recover for a claim of intentional infliction of emotional distress has not been specifically addressed by the courts. The fact that Wisconsin courts have adopted Section 46 of the RESTATEMENT (SECOND) OF TORTS in recognizing the tort of intentional infliction of emotional distress allows this Court to follow the same reasoning regarding the presence requirement set forth previously in this opinion. [FN58] Applying this rationale, this Court finds that the presence element does not need to be proven in order to successfully bring a cause of action for intentional infliction of emotional distress under Wisconsin law, and that standing to seek such recovery is limited to the victim's near relatives who were not present at the time of the attack.

FN58. See *supra* Part VI.D. 1.b.

2. Plaintiffs

a. Paul Fennig

Mark Fennig and Paul D. Fennig are United States citizens and the brothers of Patrick Fennig ("Pat"). Exs. 281, at 1-3; 282, at 1, 3-4. In high school, Pat and Paul had common interests and friends, and were close to each other. Ex. 281, at 7.

Pat's death affected Paul deeply. He has dreams of Pat and him spending time together. Paul thinks about Pat every day. He is sorry that he did not have a chance to say goodbye to Pat. There is a void in Paul's life without Pat. Paul has trouble understanding why Pat was killed. Ex. 281, 21-22. Things are particularly difficult for Paul when his friends bring up Pat out of the blue. Nevertheless, though it hurts him emotionally to think of his dead brother, it means a lot to Paul that his friends remember Pat so fondly. Ex. 281.

According to Dr. Cable, Paul

is in loss and loneliness. He was very close to his brother growing up. That closeness is something that he misses desperately. So the loneliness persists. Even though his life is full, there is an element there that's not be replaced that's not been taken care of...He will continue with this grief in the future. He will move on, but there will always be an element of regret there. There will always be for him something missing, something that's just incomplete in his life.

(Feb. 10, 2004 Tr. at 134-35.)

As the brother of Patrick Fennig, Paul Fennig has brought an intentional infliction of emotional distress claim against the defendants for pain and suffering caused by the death of his brother. Based upon the evidence presented to the Court, the elements of Paul Fennig's intentional infliction of emotional distress claim are met. The defendants' conduct in facilitating, financing, and providing material support to bring about this attack was intentional, extreme, and outrageous. As the evidence shows, this horrific act precipitated by the defendants' planning and assistance brought immediate emotional distress to Paul Fennig. Finally, it is clear that Paul Fennig has continued to experience emotional distress since that time due to the fact that his brother was taken away from him in such a tragic and horrific manner. Therefore, this Court shall award to Paul Fennig $2.5 million to compensate him for the emotional distress, pain and suffering that he sustained as a result of his brother's untimely death.

b. Mark Fennig

Mark Fennig is a brother to Patrick Fennig ("Pat"). Throughout their lives together, Mark and Pat shared many common interests. As children, both Mark and Pat loved building model airplanes with each other. (Ex. 282, 9.) As adults, Pat and Mark developed a common interest in fine cigars.

Mark returned to work about a week after Pat's death hoping that a normal routine would help him deal with everything. Mark was distracted for several months after Pat's death. It was very difficult to concentrate on his work.

Mark's Catholic upbringing, faith, and family provided support for him after Pat's death.

Mark has kept a number of Pat's personal belongings. The one that means the most to him is a cigar humidor. It is displayed in Mark's office and holds the cigars that he received from Pat after his death. Ex. 282, 23.

Holidays, anniversaries, and birthdays are difficult for Paul and Mark. Each involves personal reflection by Mark and his family. Thanksgiving and Memorial Day also have much more meaning for Mark now. Mark and his family attend a Memorial Day procession and service at the cemetery and in their village. Mark's sons are involved in the boy scouts and take part in the procession which affords Mark the opportunity to share his memories of Pat with his sons. The Fennig family has a toast on major holidays in memory of Pat. Ex. 281, 23; 282, 24. Mark has not been able to shake the feeling of being cheated. Mark has been cheated out of a relationship with his brother and having an uncle for his sons. Ex. 282, 25.

According to Dr. Cable, Mark

is in loss and loneliness…He still shows a lot of concern over his mother, worries about how she is doing. Mark, being the oldest, has sort of been the family protector, so he still sees himself as having some responsibility…His grief will certainly continue. He is fortunate in that he does have a good support system. But because he is so concerned about everybody else, he is not necessarily getting some of his own needs met and getting his own grief resolved. So he will have a road yet ahead of him.

(Feb. 10, 2004 Tr. at 132-33.)

As the brother of Patrick Fennig, Mark Fennig has brought an intentional infliction of emotional distress claim against the defendants for pain and suffering caused by the death of his brother. Based upon the evidence presented to the Court, the elements of Mark Fennig's intentional infliction of emotional distress claim are met. The defendants' conduct in facilitating, financing, and providing material support to bring about this attack was intentional, extreme, and outrageous. As the evidence shows, this horrific act precipitated by the defendants' planning and assistance brought immediate emotional distress to Mark Fennig. Finally, it is clear that Mark Fennig has continued to experience emotional distress since that time due to the fact that his brother was taken away from him in such a tragic and horrific manner. Therefore, this Court shall award to Mark Fennig $2.5 million to compensate him for the emotional distress, pain and suffering that he sustained as a result of his brother's untimely death.

I. New York

1. Causes of Action

a. Intentional Infliction of Emotional Distress

New York, adopting the approach taken in Section 46 of the RESTATEMENT (SECOND) OF TORTS, recognizes intentional infliction of emotional distress as a tort. *Howell v. New York Post Co.*, 81 N.Y.2d 115, 596 N.Y.S.2d 350, 612 N.E.2d 699, 702 (1993). The elements of intentional infliction of emotional distress under New York law are: "(i) extreme and outrageous conduct; (ii) intent to cause, or disregard of a substantial probability of causing, severe emotional distress; (iii) a causal connection between the conduct and injury; and (iv) severe emotional distress." *Id.*

In New York, the issue of whether a plaintiff must be present in order to recover for a claim of intentional infliction of emotional distress has not been specifically addressed by the courts. Two factors persuade this Court to find that the presence requirement for intentional infliction of emotional distress is unnecessary in this case. First, New York courts have adopted Section 46 of the RESTATEMENT (SECOND) OF TORTS in recognizing the tort of intentional infliction of emotional distress. Second, the Southern District of New York held in *In re Terrorist Attacks on September 11, 2001*, 349 F.Supp.2d 765, 829-30 (S.D.N.Y.2005) that non-present survivors of victims of the September 11, 2001, attacks on the World Trade Center and Pentagon were able to bring a claim of intentional infliction of emotional distress against the perpetrators of the attacks. [FN59] These two reasons allow this Court to follow the same reasoning regarding the presence requirement set forth previously in this opinion. [FN60] Applying this rationale, this Court finds that the presence element does not need to be proven in order to successfully bring a cause of action for intentional infliction of emotional distress under New York law, and that standing to seek such recovery is limited to the victim's near relatives who were not present at the time of the attack.

FN59. Though the precedent set forth by the federal court in the Southern District of New York is not binding on the state courts in New York, in light of the severity of the attacks involved in both cases, the court's opinion carries a great deal of weight in determining whether a presence requirement is necessary in cases involving intentional infliction of emotional distress claims arising out of terrorist attacks.

FN60. See *supra* Part VI.D. 1.b.

2. Plaintiffs

a. Mary Young

Mary Young is the sister of Christopher Adams. She is the oldest of the Adams' children. Mary is a police communications operator in Manhattan. (Dec. 10, 2003 A.M. Tr. at 87.)

On a personal level, Mary has been emotionally effected by Christopher's death. In addition, Mary is angry that she had to watch her mother go through the seven years of grief in dealing with Christopher's death. *Id.* at 99-100.

Mary thinks about the bombing and about Christopher every day. Due to the brutality of the attack that killed Christopher, Mary is much more emotional today than she was in 1996. *Id.* at 100. Ever since Christopher was killed, Mary has had constant trouble sleeping. Additionally, Mary gained about 60 pounds after Christopher died. She went on medication shortly after he died. *Id.* at 102-103. The medication, the insomnia, and the weight gain are all attributable to the trauma and sadness that occurred when Christopher was killed. *Id.* at 102-104.

Christopher's death and the manner in which he was killed has been one of the most devastating things that have ever happened to Mary and to her whole family. As she testified, "Death is part of life but not that way, not the way it all went. It's just not normal." *Id.* at 106.

According to Dr. Cable, Mary

is still in loss and loneliness. She is still very much affected by Chris' death. And her need for ongoing medication, the sleep difficulties, help verify the situation that she is in…Her grief is going to continue, and she probably will need to continue on medication for quite a period of time. Any future losses are going to complicate all of this for her, and probably provide some setbacks, but I see her grief going on for a number of years.

(Feb. 10, 2004 Tr. at 102.)

As the sister of Christopher Adams, Mary Young has brought an intentional infliction of emotional distress claim against the defendants for pain and suffering caused by the death of her brother. Based upon the evidence presented to the Court, the elements of Mary Young's intentional infliction of emotional distress claim are met. The defendants' conduct in facilitating, financing, and providing material support to bring about this attack was intentional, extreme, and outrageous. As the evidence shows, this horrific act precipitated by the defendants' planning and assistance brought immediate emotional distress to Mary Young. Finally, it is clear that Mary Young has continued to experience emotional distress since that time due to the fact that her brother was taken away from her in such a tragic and horrific man-

ner. Therefore, this Court shall award to Mary Young $2.5 million to compensate her for the emotional distress, pain and suffering that she sustained as a result of her brother's untimely death.

b. Daniel Adams

Daniel Adams is the youngest of the Adams children, eight years younger than Christopher. When Daniel first heard that Christopher had been killed, he didn't believe it. He felt powerless, sad, and angry. Daniel remembered everybody in the family crying for days and days. *Id.* at 43. He went to the service at Patrick AFB and to the other services and did so much crying, he couldn't even see out of his eyes. *Id.* at 44. Whenever he sees the American Flag, he thinks of Christopher. *Id.* at 46.

When Christopher died, Daniel had been working but was unable to return to work because he lost much of his motivation. He was angry at God, at the terrorists, and at the government. He visits the cemetery at least once a month. *Id.* at 47.

Prior to Christopher's death, Daniel had trouble with drugs, but stopped using them completely during the five year period before Christopher died. But when Christopher died, Daniel immediately started drinking alcohol. Up to about the middle of 2002, he had been very active in drugs and alcohol constantly for the six-year period after the murder. *Id.* at 47-48. He has obtained counseling from various places. Most of the counseling centers on his reaction to Christopher's dying. *Id.* at 48.

According to Dr. Cable, Daniel "is in loss and loneliness…also some of those earlier stages, the volatile emotions, some of the guilt is very present. He has got a lot of pain, a lot of emotion over Chris. That's not gone away. He is at some great risk…[H]is prognosis is guarded." (Feb. 10, 2004 Tr. at 115-16.)

As the brother of Christopher Adams, Daniel Adams has brought an intentional infliction of emotional distress claim against the defendants for pain and suffering caused by the death of his brother. Based upon the evidence presented to the Court, the elements of Daniel Adams' intentional infliction of emotional distress claim are met. The defendants' conduct in facilitating, financing, and providing material support to bring about this attack was intentional, extreme, and outrageous. As the evidence shows, this horrific act precipitated by the defendants' planning and assistance brought immediate emotional distress to Daniel Adams. Finally, it is clear that Daniel Adams has continued to experience emotional distress since that time due to the fact that his brother was taken away from him in such a tragic and horrific manner. Therefore, this Court shall award to Daniel Adams $2.5

million to compensate him for the emotional distress, pain and suffering that he sustained as a result of his brother's untimely death.

c. Elizabeth Wolf

Elizabeth Wolf was Christopher's only younger sister. She is now married with two children, ages 1 and 2. When Christopher was killed, she felt that she had been abandoned. When she married in 1997, just a year after Christopher's death, it was a time of sadness instead of joy for Elizabeth because Christopher was going to be the one to walk her down the aisle, and he wasn't there. She also felt a sense of guilt because he was not present. *Id.* at 29-30.

Elizabeth continues to feel pain today. Many things bring back the memory of that terrible day, and family gatherings no longer have the same sense of joy that they had before 1996. *Id.* at 32.

After Christopher died, Elizabeth would go to the cemetery once a month. Even today, seven years later, she goes once every two months. *Id.* It hurts Elizabeth that she was never able to say goodbye to him in person. She is hurt that the family wasn't there to help him when he was killed. *Id.* at 34. Other terrorist attacks make her think about Christopher's death all over again because she thinks it's happening again. She thinks about how other families have to go through the pain, the grief, and the anguish which the Adams family has experienced. *Id.* at 35.

According to Dr. Cable, Elizabeth

is in loss and loneliness, with some real feelings of missing [her brother, plus] some issues of guilt...She chose not to view the body, and...there is a lot of regret over not having had that last connection...Her pain is going to continue into the future. She will put a lot of her effort into ways of helping keep Chris' memory alive. That, to her, will be important, that people don't forget [Chris]. That helps her grief as well as helps his memory in her mind.

(Feb. 10, 2004 Tr. at 107-08.)

As the sister of Christopher Adams, Elizabeth Wolf has brought an intentional infliction of emotional distress claim against the defendants for pain and suffering caused by the death of her brother. Based upon the evidence presented to the Court, the elements of Elizabeth Wolf's intentional infliction of emotional distress claim are met. The defendants' conduct in facilitating, financing, and providing material support to bring about this attack was intentional, extreme, and outrageous. As the evidence shows, this horrific act precipitated by the defendants' planning and assistance brought immediate emotional distress to Elizabeth Wolf. Finally, it is clear that Elizabeth Wolf has continued to experience emotional distress since that time due to the fact that her brother

was taken away from her in such a tragic and horrific manner. Therefore, this Court shall award to Elizabeth Wolf $2.5 million to compensate her for the emotional distress, pain and suffering that she sustained as a result of her brother's untimely death.

J. North Carolina

1. Causes of Action

a. Intentional Infliction of Emotional Distress

North Carolina recognizes the tort of intentional infliction of emotional distress. *Stanback v. Stanback*, 297 N.C. 181, 254 S.E.2d 611 (1979). The tort recognized in *Stanback* is in accord with the version found in Section 46 of the RESTATEMENT (SECOND) OF TORTS. *Dickens v. Puryear*, 302 N.C. 437, 276 S.E.2d 325, 332 (1981). The elements of this tort under North Carolina law are: "(1) extreme and outrageous conduct, (2) which is intended to cause and does cause (3) severe emotional distress to another." *Id.* In North Carolina, the issue of whether a plaintiff must be present in order to recover for a claim of intentional infliction of emotional distress has not been specifically addressed by the courts. The fact that North Carolina courts have found their tort of intentional infliction of emotional distress to be in accord with Section 46 of the RESTATEMENT (SECOND) OF TORTS allows this Court to follow the same reasoning regarding the presence requirement set forth previously in this opinion. [FN61] Applying this rationale, this Court finds that the presence element does not need to be proven in order to successfully bring a cause of action for intentional infliction of emotional distress under North Carolina law, and that standing to seek such recovery is limited to the victim's near relatives who were not present at the time of the attack.

FN61. See *supra* Part VI.D. 1.b.

2. Plaintiffs

a. Patrick Adams

Patrick Adams is a brother to Christopher Adams. Patrick thinks about Christopher every day. *Id.* at 18. He often prays to Christopher for guidance, for support, and for help in making the right decisions about his children. *Id.* at 19. He always thinks about Christopher when he reads about other terrorist killings. He thinks about Christopher a lot on April 18, because that was the birthday of both Christopher and Paul Revere, a great patriot. *Id.* at 21. According to Dr. Cable, Patrick is in loss and loneliness. Grief has altered his world view, in a sense; this attitude of live today, you don't know what's coming. But very much misses his brother and what his brother's role would be in his life now…Patrick sill has feelings, empty feelings, that overwhelm him at times… [G]rief [will continue] to be a pretty significant issue for him for a long time.

(Feb. 10, 2004 Tr. at 105-06.)

As the brother of Christopher Adams, Patrick Adams has brought an intentional infliction of emotional distress claim against the defendants for pain and suffering caused by the death of his brother. Based upon the evidence presented to the Court, the elements of Patrick Adams' intentional infliction of emotional distress claim are met. The defendants' conduct in facilitating, financing, and providing material support to bring about this attack was intentional, extreme, and outrageous. As the evidence shows, this horrific act precipitated by the defendants' planning and assistance brought immediate emotional distress to Patrick Adams. Finally, it is clear that Patrick Adams has continued to experience emotional distress since that time due to the fact that his brother was taken away from him in such a tragic and horrific manner. Therefore, this Court shall award to Patrick Adams $2.5 million to compensate him for the emotional distress, pain and suffering that he sustained as a result of his brother's untimely death.

b. John Adams

John Adams is the twin brother of Patrick Adams, and is the younger brother of Christopher Adams by one year. Christopher's death has had a terrible impact on John because Christopher was his power base and gave him strength. *Id.* at 68. John thinks of him a lot, definitely during the holidays, and whenever he sees the flag, and whenever he hears the National Anthem. *Id.* at 68-69. When September 11 occurred, he thought about the experiences of other families. Every year on June 25, John says a prayer and thanks God that there is an angel up in heaven looking over the family. *Id.* at 69. For John, family occasions are not the same anymore. The biggest difference is their mother. She is not the same. *Id.*

As Dr. Cable stated, John is in loss and loneliness:

Chris was the big brother. He was the one everybody looked up to…John has an inner strength and a faith that helps him get by. There is a wistfulness in his voice for a relationship with his brother that can never be. His grief will continue, but he will work on it. He will work to move on.

(Feb. 10, 2004 Tr. at 104.)

As the brother of Christopher Adams, John Adams has brought an intentional infliction of emotional distress claim against the defendants for pain and suffering caused by the death of his brother. Based upon the evidence presented to the Court, the elements of John Adams' intentional infliction of emotional distress claim are met. The defendants' conduct in facilitating, financing, and providing material support to bring about this attack was intentional, extreme, and outrageous. As the evidence shows, this horrific act precipitated by the defendants' planning and assistance brought immediate emotional distress to John Adams. Finally, it is clear that John Adams has continued to experience emotional distress since that time due to the fact that his brother was taken away from him in such a tragic and horrific manner. Therefore, this Court shall award to John Adams $2.5 million to compensate him for the emotional distress, pain and suffering that he sustained as a result of his brother's untimely death.

c. William Adams

William Adams ("Billy") was a brother of Christopher Adams, who was six years older. Billy was the seventh of the eight children in the family and his oldest brother was six years older than he was. Ex. 277, 3. Billy's testimony was admitted by Affidavit. *Id.*

Christopher's death had a huge impact on Billy. (Dec. 3, 2003 P.M. Tr. at 66-67.) About two months after the Khobar Towers incident, Billy moved away from North Carolina to go back up to Long Island to be with his mother. Billy thinks about Christopher every day, especially on holidays, and on June 25. He keeps pictures of Christopher in his home and has Christopher's Air Force Academy sword that Caren gave to him, a flag and a bracelet that Christopher bought for him on one of his previous trips to Saudi Arabia. Ex. 277, 19 and 20.

According to Dr. Cable, Billy

is in the loss and loneliness stage. He does…have some repressed emotion…He will continue in grief for a significant time. There is a strong identification with his brother, and so the loss of his brother will impact him for a long time into the future. There is a need for some real therapy to help him work through and express some of those repressed emotions.

(Feb. 10, 2004 Tr. at 112-13.)

As the brother of Christopher Adams, William Adams has brought an intentional infliction of emotional distress claim against the defendants for pain and suffering caused by the death of his brother. Based upon the evidence presented to the Court, the elements of William Adams' intentional infliction of emotional distress claim are met. The defendants' conduct in facilitating, financing, and providing material support to bring about this attack was intentional, extreme, and outrageous. As the evidence shows, this horrific act precipitated by the defendants' planning and assistance brought immediate emotional distress to William Adams. Finally, it is clear that William Adams has continued to experience emotional distress since that time due to the fact that his brother was taken away from him in such a tragic and horrific manner. Therefore, this Court shall award to William Adams $2.5 million to compensate him for the emotional distress, pain and suffering that he sustained as a result of his brother's untimely death.

d. Michael Adams

Michael Adams, brother to Christopher Adams, was born in 1971; he was the sixth of the eight children. Christopher was five years older than Michael. Ex. 276, at 3-4. Michael's testimony was admitted by way of Affidavit. Ex. 276.

Christopher's death has greatly affected Michael. Michael has kept all the newspaper accounts of Christopher's death and funeral and his medals in a box at his home. He also keeps his green flight suit and keeps a poster of the Khobar Towers after the bombing on the wall above his desk. *Id.* at 27.

Michael thinks a lot about Christopher during the entire month of June, not just June 25, and many other things remind him of Christopher. *Id.* at 29. He thinks of Christopher every time he turns on the news and hears about military casualties. He thinks about the grief that all the families are going through, not only the families of the dead Iraqi soldiers, but also the families of the people who were killed on September 11. *Id.* at 30. Watching his mother today dealing with Christopher's loss brings as much pain to him as Christopher's own death. *Id.* at 32.

It makes Michael very sad to think that Christopher will not be part of the lives of his children. *Id.* at 34. As Dr. Cable stated, Michael

is in loss and loneliness…He has got a lot of pent up emotion there that he really hasn't allowed himself to express…[T]here is some volatile emotions that are not quite out in the open. There is still a lot of effort to protect his mother…He has a lot of pain ahead and a lot of grief work to do.

(Feb. 10, 2004 Tr. at 110.)

As the brother of Christopher Adams, Michael Adams has brought an intentional infliction of emotional distress claim against the defendants for pain and suffering caused by the death of his brother. Based upon the evidence presented to the Court, the elements of Michael Adams' intentional infliction of emotional distress claim are met. The defendants' conduct in facilitating, financing, and providing material support to bring about this attack was intentional,

extreme, and outrageous. As the evidence shows, this horrific act precipitated by the defendants' planning and assistance brought immediate emotional distress to Michael Adams. Finally, it is clear that Michael Adams has continued to experience emotional distress since that time due to the fact that his brother was taken away from him in such a tragic and horrific manner. Therefore, this Court shall award to Michael Adams $2.5 million to compensate him for the emotional distress, pain and suffering that he sustained as a result of his brother's untimely death.

K. Indiana

1. Claims Under Indiana Law

a. Wrongful Death

Under Indiana's wrongful death statute, the decedent's personal representative may bring an action against the person whose wrongful act or omission caused the death of the decedent. Ind.Code Ann. §34-23-1-1. A successful wrongful death plaintiff may recover damages that include "reasonable medical, hospital, funeral, and burial expenses," in addition to the decedent's lost earnings. Ind.Code. Ann. §34-23-1-1. Any damages awarded for reasonable medical, hospital, funeral, and burial expenses inure to the benefit of the decedent's estate, while all other damages are awarded to the benefit of "the widow or widower,…and to the dependent children, if any, or dependent next of kin, to be distributed in the same manner as the personal property of the deceased." Ind.Code. Ann. §34-23-1-1.

"Dependent next of kin" include those individuals who show that: (1) they need support; and (2) the decedent contributed to their support. *Estate of Sears v. Griffin*, 771 N.E.2d 1136, 1139 (Ind.2002). A plaintiff does not have to be wholly dependent on the decedent to be considered a dependent next of kin. *Id.* Instead, a court must examine "the assistance that the decedent would have provided through money, services or other material benefits." *Id.* (quoting *Luider v. Skaggs*, 693 N.E.2d 593, 596-97 (Ind. Ct.App.1998)).

b. Intentional Infliction of Emotional Distress

Indiana recognizes the tort of intentional infliction of emotional distress, following Section 46 of the RESTATEMENT (SECOND) OF TORTS. Under Indiana law, the elements of an intentional infliction of emotional distress claim are: "(1) 'extreme and outrageous conduct' that (2) intentionally or recklessly (3) causes (4) severe emotional distress to another." *Creel v. I.C.E. & Assocs., Inc.*, 771 N.E.2d 1276, 1282 (Ind.Ct.App.2002). In Indiana, the issue of whether a plaintiff must be present in order to recover for a claim of intentional infliction of emotional distress has not been specifically addressed by the courts. The fact that Indiana courts have adopted Section 46 of the RESTATEMENT (SECOND) OF TORTS in recognizing the tort of intentional infliction of emotional distress allows this Court to follow the same reasoning regarding the presence requirement set forth previously in this opinion. [FN62] Applying this rationale, this Court finds that the presence element does not need to be proven in order to successfully bring a cause of action for intentional infliction of emotional distress under Indiana law, and that standing to seek such recovery is limited to the victim's near relatives who were not present at the time of the attack.

FN62. See *supra* Part VI.D. 1.b.

2. Plaintiffs

a. Lewis Cartrette

Lewis W. Cartrette is a United States citizen, and the brother of Earl "J.R." Cartrette, Jr. Exs. 279, 1-2. Lewis was born in Sellersberg, Indiana on November 1, 1976. His parents are Denise Eichstaedt and the late Earl Frederick Cartrette, Sr. Ex. 279, at 4.

Lewis was unable to shake the misery that he felt as a result of J.R.'s death. Lewis shut everyone out and did not want to go on with his life. Lewis was depressed and did not want to function. Lewis testified, "J.R.'s death is the hardest, most painful thing that I have ever had to deal with because just when everything was good, J.R. was killed and there was nothing I could do about it. My brother, my friend was gone." After J.R.'s death, Lewis began using drugs and alcohol, became physically violent, and contemplated suicide on more than one occasion. Lewis had three encounters with the criminal justice system which involved increasingly serious offenses. Lewis lost his job, his wife, his children, his home, and spent one year in jail. Ex. 279, 16-17.

After J.R.'s death, Lewis began seeing a psychiatrist and was prescribed medication. Lewis is no longer seeing the psychiatrist or taking medication. Ex. 279, at 18. Holidays, anniversaries, and birthdays are still particularly difficult days for Lewis. Lewis is remarried and will soon become a father of twins. Lewis' children will never know their uncle J.R. Lewis always wanted his children to have someone like J.R. in their life.

J.R.'s death is also difficult for Lewis when he is around antique cars which J.R. and Lewis both loved. When Lewis thinks about J.R., the pain and misery today is as strong as

it was when Lewis learned of J.R.'s death on June 27, 1996. Ex. 279, at 19-20.

According to Dr. Cable, Lewis

very clearly is in loss and loneliness. He has had major difficulties with his brother's death. His brother was really a father figure as well as a brother to him, very close, and was not there to keep [Lewis] from kind of sinking in what happened to him. So the death has had a major impact on [Lewis], and continues to do so…His problems, his grief, is going to continue in the future. He is in need of grief therapy. He has got a lot of rebuilding of his life to do, and that's going to take a significant amount of time. It's going to be an ongoing struggle for him to get back where he can function effectively.

(Feb. 10, 2004 Tr. at 123-24.)

As the brother of Earl Cartrette, Jr., Lewis Cartrette has brought an intentional infliction of emotional distress claim against the defendants for pain and suffering caused by the death of his brother. Based on the evidence presented to the Court, Lewis Cartrette has satisfied the elements to establish a valid claim for intentional infliction of emotional distress. First, defendants Iran, MOIS, and the IRGC provided material support to Saudi Hezbollah with the intent that Saudi Hezbollah would carry out attacks that would cause severe emotional distress. Second, the tragic bombing of the Khobar Towers by means of material support and civil conspiracy is an act that is nothing short of extreme, outrageous, and beyond all bounds of civil decency. As is the nature of terrorism, terrorists seek to perform acts that are deliberately outrageous and bring about extreme suffering in order to achieve political ends. Third, the defendants' actions in facilitating and supporting the Khobar Towers bombing proximately caused Lewis emotional distress because the material support and direction given to Saudi Hezbollah ensured the event would occur. Finally, the evidence shows that Lewis suffered emotional distress, and that his emotional distress was severe. Accordingly, the Court finds that Lewis Cartrette is entitled to recover from defendants $2.5 million in compensatory damages for the mental anguish and suffering associated with the loss of his brother.

L. Oklahoma

1. Causes of Action

a. Intentional Infliction of Emotional Distress

Oklahoma also recognizes the tort of intentional infliction of emotional distress, having adopted Section 46 of the RESTATEMENT (SECOND) OF TORTS. *Breeden v. League Servs. Corp.*, 575 P.2d 1374, 1376-78 (Okla.1978). To recover damages for intentional infliction of emotional distress under Oklahoma law, the plaintiff must show: "(1) the defendant acted intentionally or recklessly; (2) the defendant's conduct was extreme and outrageous; (3) the defendant's conduct caused the plaintiff emotional distress; and (4) the resulting emotional distress was severe." *Computer Publ'n, Inc. v. Welton*, 49 P.3d 732, 735 (Okla.2002).

In Oklahoma, the issue of whether a plaintiff must be present in order to recover for a claim of intentional infliction of emotional distress has not been specifically addressed by the courts. The fact that Oklahoma courts have found their tort of intentional infliction of emotional distress to be in accord with Section 46 of the RESTATEMENT (SECOND) OF TORTS allows this Court to follow the same reasoning regarding the presence requirement set forth previously in this opinion. [FN63] Applying this rationale, this Court finds that the presence element does not need to be proven in order to successfully bring a cause of action for intentional infliction of emotional distress under Oklahoma law, and that standing to seek such recovery is limited to the victim's near relatives who were not present at the time of the attack.

FN63. See *supra* Part VI.D. 1.b.

2. Plaintiffs

a. Nancy A. Kitson
Nancy A. Kitson is the oldest sibling to Kendall Kitson, Jr. ("Kenny"). After Kenny's death, Nancy took at least one month off of work. She stayed in Florida with her parents. Nancy was the only one to keep many of Kenny's personal items. Ex. 292, 21.

For the first several years after Kenny's death, Nancy attended the memorial services the military hosted in Washington, D.C. and Quantico, Virginia. *Id.* at 22. Nancy does her best to keep going, in spite of her grief. She breaks down sometimes when people ask her how she is or do not know that Kenny was killed. *Id.* at 23.

The most difficult time of the year for Nancy is around Kenny's birthday in October. For many years, Christmas time was also very difficult for Nancy and she would not celebrate the holiday. *Id.* at 24. In addition to her own loss of Kenny, Nancy's grief has been compounded by the tension Kenny's loss has created between herself and her parents. Nancy's parents will not even visit Nancy's daughter. Nancy is very hurt by her parents' failure to love anyone else since Kenny died. *Id.* at 27.

As Dr. Cable stated, Nancy A. Kitson

is in loss and loneliness. She misses her brother terribly, and in addition has to cope with her parents' bitterness,

her mother's illness. Fells very alone in the family and very lonely without Kenny...She, too, will continue to experience grief into the future. The feelings of loss and loneliness will continue.

(Feb. 10, 2004 Tr. at 151-52.)

As the sister of Kendall Kitson, Jr., Nancy Kitson has brought an intentional infliction of emotional distress claim against the defendants for pain and suffering caused by the death of her brother. Based upon the evidence presented to the Court, the elements of Nancy Kitson's intentional infliction of emotional distress claim are met. The defendants' conduct in facilitating, financing, and providing material support to bring about this attack was intentional, extreme, and outrageous. As the evidence shows, this horrific act precipitated by the defendants' planning and assistance brought immediate emotional distress to Nancy Kitson. Finally, it is clear that Nancy Kitson has continued to experience emotional distress since that time due to the fact that her brother was taken away from her in such a tragic and horrific manner. Therefore, this Court shall award to Nancy Kitson $2.5 million to compensate her for the emotional distress, pain and suffering that she sustained as a result of her brother's untimely death.

M. Kansas

1. Causes of Action

a. Outrage
In Kansas the tort of intentional infliction of emotional distress is recognized, although it is called the tort of Outrage. [FN64] Naturally, the elements of Outrage are the same as those for intentional infliction of emotional distress, namely the plaintiff must prove that: "(1) the conduct of the defendant was intentional or in reckless disregard of the plaintiff; (2) the conduct was extreme and outrageous; (3) there was a causal connection between the defendant's conduct and the plaintiff's mental distress; and (4) the plaintiff's mental distress was extreme and severe." *Smith v. Welch*, 265 Kan. 868, 967 P.2d 727, 733 (1998).

FN64. Though the Kansas courts have offered a different moniker for these two torts, the tort of Outrage stems from the same root as intentional infliction of emotional distress: Section 46 of the RESTATEMENT (SECOND) OF TORTS. See *Dotson v. McLaughlin*, 216 Kan. 201, 531 P.2d 1, 7-9 (1975).

In Kansas, the issue of whether a plaintiff must be present in order to recover for a claim of Outrage has not been specifically addressed by the courts. The fact that Kansas courts have found their tort of Outrage to be in rooted in Section 46 of the RESTATEMENT (SECOND) OF TORTS allows this Court to follow the same reasoning regarding the presence requirement set forth previously in this opinion. [FN65] Applying this rationale, this Court finds that the presence element does not need to be proven in order to successfully bring a cause of action for Outrage under Kansas law, and that standing to seek such recovery is limited to the victim's near relatives who were not present at the time of the attack.

FN65. See *supra* Part VI.D. 1.b.

2. Plaintiffs

a. Starlina Taylor
Starlina Taylor is the sister to Jeremy Taylor. Jeremy's death has been particularly difficult for Starlina due to the closeness of her relationship with Jeremy. When Jeremy died, Starlina lost both a brother and her best friend. Moreover, Starlina is grieving the loss of the her relationship with her parents due to the fact that her parents-in particular, her father-have become emotionally unavailable as a result of Jeremy's death. Ex. 289, 35. Further, since Jeremy's death, Starlina has had difficulty maintaining a fulfilling relationship with a man. She has been divorced twice and has trouble letting anyone get close to her. Exs. 289, 35 and 290, 32.

After Jeremy died, Starlina was upset to her stomach all the time and had menopausal symptoms. She also drank excessively from time to time following Jeremy's death. While she visited a counselor for a short period, she felt like it was a waste of time and only added to her father's bills. Ex. 290, 29-30. Starlina feels as though the grief process is getting worse instead of better for her. She is withdrawing into a smaller and smaller group, and there are only a few people who are her friends. Starlina fantasizes about running away and going somewhere where no one knows her. *Id.* at 35.

According to Dr. Cable, Starlina
is in loss and loneliness, feeling very much the loss of her brother, her support system. Then complicated because there is a loss of her father as well. He is no longer effective or functioning in that father role, and so that just makes it more intense of loss and loneliness...She will continue in her grief for a long period of time.
(Feb. 10, 2004 Tr. at 199-200.)

As the sister of Jeremy Taylor, Starlina Taylor has brought an intentional infliction of emotional distress claim against the defendants for pain and suffering caused by the death of her brother. Based upon the evidence presented to the Court, the elements of Starlina Taylor's intentional inflic-

tion of emotional distress claim are met. The defendants' conduct in facilitating, financing, and providing material support to bring about this attack was intentional, extreme, and outrageous. As the evidence shows, this horrific act precipitated by the defendants' planning and assistance brought immediate emotional distress to Starlina Taylor. Finally, it is clear that Starlina Taylor has continued to experience emotional distress since that time due to the fact that her brother was taken away from her in such a tragic and horrific manner. Therefore, this Court shall award to Starlina Taylor $2.5 million to compensate her for the emotional distress, pain and suffering that she sustained as a result of her brother's untimely death.

CONCLUSION

This Court takes note of plaintiffs' courage and steadfastness in pursuing this litigation and their efforts to take action to deter more tragic suffering of innocent Americans at the hands of terrorists. Their efforts are to be commended.
A separate Order and Judgment consistent with these findings shall issue this date.
SO ORDERED.

ORDER & JUDGMENT

In accord with the Findings of Fact and Conclusions of Law issued this date, it is hereby
ORDERED that Default Judgment be entered in favor of plaintiffs and against defendants, jointly and severally, in the amount of $254,431,903.00, which shall be allocated in the following manner:

Estate and Surviving Family Members of Brent Marthaler
- $1,598,688.00 in economic damages to be allocated to the Estate of Brent Marthaler, by Katie Lee Marthaler as personal representative, for the benefit of Katie Lee Marthaler, Herman C. Marthaler, and Sharon Marthaler, to be distributed in a manner consistent with the statute governing intestate distribution of property under Florida law;
- $8 million to be allocated to Katie Lee Marthaler;
- $5 million to be allocated to Herman Marthaler;
- $5 million to be allocated to Sharon Marthaler;
- $2.5 million to be allocated to Matthew Marthaler;
- $2.5 million to be allocated to Kirk Marthaler

Estate and Surviving Family Members of Justin Wood
- $5 million to be allocated to Richard Wood;
- $5 million to be allocated to Kathleen Wood;
- $2.5 million to be allocated to Shawn Wood;

Estate and Surviving Family Members of Michael Heiser
- $3,720,019.00 in economic damages to be allocated to the Estate of Michael Heiser, by Fran and Gary Heiser as personal representatives, for the benefit of Fran and Gary Heiser;
- $5 million to be allocated to Fran Heiser;
- $5 million to be allocated to Gary Heiser;

Estate and Surviving Family Members of Earl Cartrette, Jr.
- $5 million to be allocated to Denise Eichstaedt
- $2.5 million to be allocated to Anthony Cartrette
- $2.5 million to be allocated to Lewis Cartrette

Estate and Surviving Family Members of Patrick Fennig
- $1,120,304.00 in economic damages to be allocated to the Estate of Patrick Fennig, by Thaddeus C. Fennig and Catherine Fennig as personal representatives, for the benefit of Thaddeus C. Fennig and Catherine Fennig;
- $5 million to be allocated to Thaddeus C. Fennig;
- $5 million to be allocated to Catherine Fennig;
- $2.5 million to be allocated to Paul Fennig;
- $2.5 million to be allocated to Mark Fennig;

Estate and Surviving Family Members of Christopher Adams
- $3,153,953.00 in economic damages to be allocated to the Estate of Christopher Adams, by Catherine Adams as personal representative, for the benefit of Catherine Adams;
- $5 million to be allocated to Catherine Adams;
- $2.5 million to be allocated to Mary Young;
- $2.5 million to be allocated to Daniel Adams;
- $2.5 million to be allocated to Elizabeth Wolf;
- $2.5 million to be allocated to Patrick Adams;
- $2.5 million to be allocated to John Adams;
- $2.5 million to be allocated to William Adams;
- $2.5 million to be allocated to Michael Adams;

Estate and Surviving Family Members of Thanh "Gus" Nguyen
- $596,905.00 in economic damages to be allocated to the Estate of Thanh "Gus" Nguyen, by Christopher Nguyen as personal representative, for the benefit of Christopher Nguyen;
- $5 million to be allocated to Christopher Nguyen;

Estate and Surviving Family Members of Brian McVeigh
- $5 million to be allocated to Sandra M. Wetmore;

Estate and Surviving Family Members of Joseph Rimkus
- $5 million to be allocated to Bridget Brooks;
- $2.5 million to be allocated to James Rimkus;
- $2.5 million to be allocated to Anne Rimkus;

Estate and Surviving Family Members of Kendall Kitson, Jr.
- $2,183,460.00 in economic damages to be allocated to the Estate of Kendall Kitson, Jr., by Kendall Kitson, Sr., and Nancy R. Kitson as personal representatives, for the benefit of Kendall Kitson, Sr., and Nancy R. Kitson;
- $5 million to be allocated to Kendall Kitson, Sr.;
- $5 million to be allocated to Nancy R. Kitson;
- $2.5 million to be allocated to Steve K. Kitson;
- $2.5 million to be allocated to Nancy A. Kitson;

Estate and Surviving Family Members of Jeremy Taylor
- $5 million to be allocated to Lawrence Taylor;
- $5 million to be allocated to Vickie Taylor;
- $2.5 million to be allocated to Starlina Taylor;

Estate and Surviving Family Members of Joshua Woody
- $1,981,521.00 in economic damages to be allocated to the Estate of Joshua Woody, by Dawn Woody as personal representative, for the benefit of Dawn Woody;
- $8 million to be allocated to Dawn Woody;
- $5 million to be allocated to Bernadine Beekman;
- $2.5 million to be allocated to Tracy Smith;
- $2.5 million to be allocated to Jonica Woody;
- $2.5 million to be allocated to Timothy Woody;

Estate and Surviving Family Members of Leland "Tim" Haun
- $2,822,796.00 in economic damages to be allocated to the Estate of Leland "Tim" Haun, by Ibis "Jenny" Haun as personal representative, for the benefit of Ibis "Jenny" Haun, Senator Haun, and Milly Perez-Dallis, to be distributed in a manner in accordance with the method of intestate distribution under California law;
- $8 million to be allocated to Ibis "Jenny" Haun;
- $5 million to be allocated to Senator Haun;
- $7 million to be allocated to Milly Perez-Dallis;

Estate and Surviving Family Members of Christopher Lester
- $1,960,466.00 in economic damages, plus $500,000.00 in pain and suffering damages to be allocated to the Estate of Christopher Lester, by

Cecil Lester, Sr., and Judy Lester as personal representatives, for the benefit of Cecil Lester, Sr., Judy Lester, Cecil Lester, Jr., and Jessica Lester, to be distributed in a manner in accordance with the method of intestate distribution under Ohio law;

- $5 million to be allocated to Cecil Lester, Sr.;
- $5 million to be allocated to Judy Lester;
- $2.5 million to be allocated to Cecil Lester, Jr.;
- $2.5 million to be allocated to Jessica Lester;

Estate and Surviving Family Members of Kevin Johnson, Sr.

- $1,171,477.00 in economic damages to be allocated to the Estate of Kevin Johnson, Sr., by Shyrl Johnson as personal representative, for the benefit of Shyrl Johnson, Kevin Johnson, Jr., and Nicholas Johnson, to be distributed in a manner in accordance with the method of intestate distribution under Louisiana law;
- $8 million to be allocated to Shyrl Johnson;
- $5 million to be allocated to Kevin Johnson, Jr.;
- $5 million to be allocated to Nicholas Johnson;

Estate and Surviving Family Members of Peter Morgera

- $50,000.00 in economic damages to be allocated to the Estate of Peter Morgera, by Michael Morgera as personal representative, for the benefit of Michael Morgera and Thomas Morgera, to be distributed in a manner in accordance with the method of intestate distribution under New Hampshire law;
- $2.5 million to be allocated to Michael Morgera;
- $2.5 million to be allocated to Thomas Morgera;

Estate and Surviving Members of Millard "Dee" Campbell

- $1,572,314.00 in economic damages to be allocated to the Estate of Millard "Dee" Campbell, by Marie Campbell as personal representative, for the benefit of Marie Campbell and Bessie Campbell, to be distributed in a manner in accordance with the method of intestate distribution under Texas law;
- $8 million to be allocated to Marie Campbell;
- $5 million to be allocated to Bessie Campbell;

IT IS FURTHER ORDERED that the claims for compensatory damages in the form of lost wages and future earnings for the estates of the following decedents are hereby DENIED:

- Estate of Justin Wood
- Estate of Earl Cartrette, Jr.
- Estate of Brian McVeigh
- Estate of Joseph Rimkus

- Estate of Jeremy Taylor

IT IS FURTHER ORDERED that the claims brought by the following plaintiffs are hereby DISMISSED WITH PREJUDICE:

- James V. Wetmore
- George Beekman Che Colson
- Laura Johnson
- Bruce Johnson

IT IS FURTHER ORDERED that plaintiffs, at their own cost and consistent with the requirements of 28 U.S.C. §1608(e), send a copy of this Judgment and the Findings of Fact and Conclusions of Law issued this date to defendants.

IT IS FURTHER ORDERED that the Clerk of this Court shall terminate this case from the dockets of this Court.

SO ORDERED.

Notes:

1. This case is an extremely rare example of a district court judge overturning virtually an entire Report and Recommendation of a Magistrate Judge in a civil terrorism suit. Magistrate Judge Robinson's decision was very critical of the nature of the evidence presented:

> Dr. Clawson first appeared on December 12, 2003. The court granted Plaintiffs' request that Dr. Clawson be qualified as an expert "in the areas of the Government of Iran, the support of terrorism by the Government of Iran, and the economy of Iran." December 12, 2003 Tr. at 28. However, many of the opinions Dr. Clawson expressed were predicated upon information about which he could not testify; in other instances, the opinions were based largely on speculation.

Heiser v. Islamic Republic of Iran, 2006 WL 1530243 at 5 (D.D.C. 2006) (footnotes omitted).

> Plaintiffs offered no evidence regarding the action of any official, employee or agent of Defendants Islamic Republic of Iran, MOIS or IRGC.

Id. at 6.

> The undersigned, upon consideration of all of the evidence offered by Plaintiffs with respect to the liability of Defendants, concludes that the findings of fact which Plaintiffs propose with respect to liability are not supported by the evidence which Plaintiffs offered during the course of the evidentiary

hearing. More specifically, the undersigned finds that Plaintiffs failed to establish a nexus between the June 25, 1996 bombing and any action or decision of any of the Defendants in these consolidated actions. Accordingly, the undersigned recommends that the court find that Plaintiffs failed to "[establish] [their] claim or right to relief by evidence that is satisfactory to the Court[.]" *Haim*, 2006 U.S. Dist. LEXIS 12816, at *3 (citation omitted).

Id. at 15.

In sum, the evidence offered regarding the liability of any actor with respect to the planning or execution of the July, 1996 bombing at Khobar Towers is limited to (1) testimony regarding the statements of six unnamed "Saudi nationals[,]" and (2) the opinions of Mr. Freeh and Mr. Watson-as "private citizen[s]"-that Saudi Hizbollah, among other entities, assisted in the planning and execution of the bombing. The undersigned finds that such evidence is not "evidence that is satisfactory to the Court" on which a default judgment can be predicated.

With respect to the testimony regarding the statements of the six unnamed individuals who were in custody in Saudi Arabia at the time of the statements, the undersigned observes that none of the six has been tried in the Eastern District of Virginia, where the indictment was returned. Plaintiffs' intention apparently was to rely on the indictment as evidence of the complicity of the six individuals.

However, no reported opinion holds that a default judgment may be predicated upon allegations set forth in an indictment.

Id. at 17 (footnote omitted).

Finally, Mr. Freeh and Mr. Watson stated unequivocally that the conclusions about which they testified were their personal opinions. While the knowledge, expertise and commitment of these men is not questioned herein, the undersigned notes that neither was offered as an expert witness, and their personal opinions-which they were precluded from explaining-are therefore of little relevance in this context.

Id. at 18.

What accounts for the very different perceptions of the evidence by these two experienced jurists? Whose position is more persuasive?

2. What has been Judge Lamberth's role in the development of the jurisprudence of FSIA and Flatow Amendment law?

3. For Judge Robertson's admittedly different view on the issue of causation and his departure from some colleagues on the District of Columbia District Court see *Ungar v. Islamic Republic of Iran*, 211 F.Supp.2d 91 (D.D.C. 2002).

Chapter 9

Plaintiffs

9.1 Victims

Cicippio v. Islamic Republic of Iran, 18 F.Supp.2d 62 (D. D.C. 1998)

JACKSON, District Judge.

Three male U.S. citizens, joined by the spouses of two of them, bring this action for damages for tortious injuries done to them in the course of their kidnapping, imprisonment and torture by agents of the Islamic Republic of Iran ("Iran") between the years 1985 and 1991 in Beirut, Lebanon. Jurisdiction is predicated upon 28 U.S.C. §§1330(a) and 1605(a)(7).

Iran was served with process on April 28, 1997 (see *infra*, n. 4), but did not respond to the complaint, and default was entered November 13, 1997. The case was therefore tried *ex parte* to this Court, sitting without a jury, on July 20-21, 1998. Upon the evidence adduced at trial, from which the facts set forth below are found pursuant to Fed.R.Civ. P. 52(a), the Court concludes that judgments shall be given for plaintiffs.

I.

In the mid-1980's all five plaintiffs were civilians residing in Beirut, Lebanon. David Jacobsen, 54 years of age in 1985 and unmarried, was the chief executive officer of the American University of Beirut Medical Center. [FN1] In 1986, Joseph Cicippio, 56 years old, was comptroller of the American University of Beirut and its hospital, and had recently married plaintiff Elham Cicippio, then a Lebanese citizen. Frank Reed, aged 51 in 1986, owned and operated two private schools in Beirut with a Lebanese partner. Fifi Dalati-Reed, his wife, was a teacher. None had any connection whatsoever with the U.S. government.

FN1. The American University of Beirut is owned by a private non-profit corporation, incorporated and with headquarters in New York. (Testimony of David Jacobsen, Tr. of July 20, 1998, p. 23)

Beginning in May of 1985, each man was independently assaulted, subdued, and abducted by several armed male assailants while on public thoroughfares in the vicinity of their homes or offices. Each was held prisoner separately, at various locations in Beirut or its environs, under similar abject conditions. Their captors have been identified as members of Hizballah, a politico-paramilitary organization sponsored, financed, and controlled by Iran. Hizballah's mission was to exploit the disorder in Lebanon following the Israeli military incursion of 1982 and to diminish American influence in the region. Hizballah was and is a terrorist organization, and Iran is recognized officially as a state sponsor of acts of terrorism, including kidnapping and hostage-taking. [FN2]

FN2. Testimony of Col. David W. Hurley, USMC, Director of Intelligence for the U.S. Marine Corps (Tr. of July 20, 1998, pp. 9-22) Testimony of Dr. Patrick L. Clawson, Director of Research, Washington Institute for Near East Policy, Tr. of July 20, 1998, pp. 70-92; plaintiffs' exhibits 21-30.

Iranian government officials negotiated directly with U.S. National Security Advisor Robert McFarland and Col. Oliver North, USMC, of the U.S. National Security Council, in Teheran, Iran, in May, 1986, over the release of Jacobsen. Iran demanded an exorbitant ransom which the United States refused to pay, and he remained in captivity.

In November, 1986, Col. North was personally alerted by an Iranian official to Jacobsen's imminent release and was thus able to be present when it occurred. (Testimony of Oliver North, Tr. of July 21, 1998, pp. 3-9).

Jacobsen was held in captivity for 532 days, nearly a year and a half. Reed was held for 1330 days, over three and a half years. Cicippio remained a prisoner the longest, 1908 days, or five years and three months.

At trial, each of the three former hostages testified in detail about his ordeal and the inhumane treatment he received. *See* Tr. July 20, 1998 (hereinafter "July 20 Tr.") at 22-68 (Jacobsen); July 20 Tr. at 93-125 (Reed); Tr. July 21, 1998 (hereinafter "July 21 Tr.") at 11-46 (Cicippio). The following summaries do not do full justice to their accounts.

II.

David Jacobsen

Shortly before 8:00 a.m. on May 28, 1985, Jacobsen was walking with a companion between the American University of Beirut campus and the Medical Center. As they crossed an intersection, a van pulled beside them, and two or three men grabbed Jacobsen from behind while another man with a gun fought with the companion. The assailants forced Jacobsen into the van, pistol-whipped, bound and gagged him, and pushed him into a hidden compartment under the floor of the back of the van.

Jacobsen was held captive with several others, in darkness or blindfolded, for 18 months. During that entire time, he says, he was able to see the sunlight twice and the moon once. His captors kept Jacobsen chained by his ankles or wrists, wearing nothing but undershorts and at-shirt. Meals consisted of pita bread and a bit of dry cheese for breakfast, a bowl of rice with a dehydrated soup sauce for lunch, and a piece of bread for dinner. Sometimes his guards would spit into his food before serving him. [FN3]

FN3. This diet, Jacobsen believes, led to frequent gastrointestinal problems, such as excruciating cramps and diarrhea, and rectal bleeding. Upon returning home, Jacobsen also discovered he had microscopic blood in his urine, which he attributes to the regular beatings he sustained during captivity. *See* July 20 Tr. at 64.

In addition to the physical suffering caused by the conditions of confinement, Jacobsen and his fellow prisoners were subjected to regular beatings on all parts of their bodies. Jacobsen was frequently confronted with the prospect of imminent death; at any time a guard might put a gun to his head and threaten to kill him. His captors interrogated him incessantly, accusing him of working for the C.I.A. (which he did not), in the course of which he would be intermittently beaten as well. Although blindfolded, he could overhear other hostages suffering as he was, including the moments of their deaths, constantly fearing that he might be next. He heard the death throes of fellow hostage William Buckley,

and listened as well as a French hostage died of his infirmities and another was executed by gunshot.

As with all the former hostages, the looming uncertainty of the future was a constant demoralizing force for Jacobsen: unlike sentenced criminals, he observed, a hostage is aware only of how long he has been held; he knows nothing as to when, if ever, he will be released. On four occasions Jacobsen's captors intimated that they would release him shortly, only to continue his imprisonment without explanation.

On November 2, 1986, Jacobsen was finally released. Since his release, Jacobsen has been under continuous treatment for post-traumatic stress disorder resulting from his captivity. *See* Pls.' Ex. 18 (Report of Dr. Calvin Frederick of July 16, 1998).

Frank Reed

Frank Reed was abducted in Beirut while on his way to meet his wife for lunch on September 9, 1986. He was held at gunpoint, then thrown into the back of a car and taken to a hideout where he was beaten for several days as a suspected C.I.A. agent. Reed, too, was subjected daily to torture and threats of death. He was kept in solitary confinement for two years, blindfolded and chained to the wall or floor. He contracted persistent eye infections from the blindfold, and scars remain on his wrist to this day from the manacles. For part of his captivity, Reed was held in a six foot-by-six foot room with only rodents for company. During the entire 44 months of his captivity, Reed says, he was never permitted to stand erect; he was constantly shackled in a stooped position.

Because Reed attempted to escape on two occasions, his captors considered him a hard case and punished him accordingly. They tightened his chains to deter future escape attempts. After one escape attempt, electric shocks were administered to his hands and he was forced to kneel on spikes. His captors battered his feet with iron bars. To this day, Reed says, he has no sensation in his feet. He can stand or walk only for short periods. Following his second escape attempt, his guards struck him in the kidneys with a rifle, and for days afterwards his urine was bloody. One guard struck him multiple times on each side of his head with a hand grenade, permanently damaging his hearing. His captors broke Reed's jaw and nose, turned him upside down and beat the soles of his feet with a belt. On another occasion he was kicked in the ribs so forcefully that the bones pierced his skin. One of Reed's captors placed boiling tea kettles on his shoulders, the scars of which remain today.

Reed calculates he was moved about the city 18 times in the course of his captivity, transported in a narrow secret compartment in the bed of a truck, with his arms taped to his side and his mouth gagged. When he was moved, Reed never knew where his captors were taking him or whether he was about to be executed. His greatest fear throughout his captivity was that he would die in solitude, with none of his loved ones aware of his fate.

Reed was released on April 30, 1990. He was taken to Wiesbaden Hospital in Germany and then returned to the United States, where he remained hospitalized at Andrews Air Force Base for 80 days. His doctors discovered that Reed suffered from arsenic poisoning. *See* Pls.' Exs. 8B, 8E. Apparently his captors had laced his food with arsenic for a long period of time, including a large dose before he was released. Since his release, Reed has been in the hospital eleven times and has been treated for severe depression six times. Mrs. Reed testified that as a result of his captivity, her husband is still being medicated for post-traumatic stress disorder and that he has been impotent ever since. *See* July 20 Tr. at 138-39, 141-42.

Joseph Cicippio

Early in the morning of September 12, 1986, while leaving his faculty apartment on the lower campus of the university, Cicippio was approached by a group of three or four young men who asked who he was, and then proceeded to attack him. The assailants pistol-whipped him about the head until he lost consciousness, and then took him to a dwelling he believes to have been in the vicinity of the airport. He was stripped, then given only a robe to wear, and left bleeding, dizzy, and in severe pain.

Cicippio was held imprisoned for the next 1,908 days. He was subjected to terrifying interrogation. Convinced that Cicippio worked for the C.I.A. because he remained in Lebanon after most other Americans had left, his captors sought to force a confession from him by a grisly game of Russian roulette: a revolver was placed to his head with a single bullet in the cylinder. Each denial of a C.I.A. connection produced a pull of the trigger. He was also threatened with castration.

Cicippio, too, was randomly beaten throughout his captivity and forced to watch fellow captives being beaten. "You

never knew when or where it would happen over the years," he testified. "It could happen almost at any hour, day and night." July 21 Tr. at 42. He lived in a constant state of fear.

The terrorists kept Cicippio completely isolated from the outside world. He was confined in rodent- and scorpion-infested cells, and for virtually his entire time in captivity he was bound by chains. Cicippio lost over sixty pounds during his ordeal. During one entire winter he was chained outdoors on an upper-story apartment balcony, exposed to the elements, from which he developed frostbite to both his hands and feet, the effects of which he retains today.

Cicippio suffered from numerous medical problems while in captivity. At one point he was subjected to a surgical procedure in an unknown hospital for an unidentified abdominal problem, the nature of which, to this day, he does not know, other than that he has a ten-inch scar on his abdomen as a memento. A slight stutter, a speech impediment that antedated his capture, was exacerbated by his captivity.

Fifi Delati-Reed and Elham Cicippio

The wives of the hostages suffered as well. *See* July 20 Tr. at 126-43 (Mrs. Reed), 144-59 (Mrs. Cicippio). Fifi Delati-Reed had no independent financial resources and had to find means of support for herself and their young son during her husband's captivity. She also testified as to her own mental anguish in the total absence of information about her husband's fate. Once Reed had returned, however, the worst of her ordeal began. She was forced to cope with the drastic changes in her husband's personality wrought by his captivity. His behavior became increasingly erratic, and in due course Mrs. Reed was compelled to have him involuntarily committed to a mental hospital for treatment, a measure that caused her yet more distress. Mrs. Reed acknowledged that she and her husband have had no marital relations since his release. July 20 Tr. at 142.

Elham Cicippio also testified as to the difficulty of enduring her husband's captivity with no news of him except such occasional macabre reassurance she took that he was probably still alive from his captors' public threats to execute him. She felt helpless, not knowing what, if anything, she might do to procure her husband's release. Extortionists promised to help free her husband if she paid them money, and she did, exhausting her savings before realizing she had been defrauded. On one occasion she appeared on Lebanese television to plead with the captors not to execute her husband.

III.

This Court concludes that it has *in personam* jurisdiction over defendant Iran pursuant to 28 U.S.C. §1330(b), service of process having been properly made pursuant to 28 U.S.C. §1608. [FN4]

FN4. 28 U.S.C. §1608(a) sets forth the procedure for service of process on a foreign state. Service in this case was effected on April 28, 1997 through the Embassy of Switzerland in Tehran, which delivered the summons, complaint, and notice of suit to the Ministry of Foreign Affairs of Iran. Service was confirmed by the U.S. Department of State in a letter from M. Grace Michaud, Consular Affairs Officer, Office of American Citizen Services, Near East and South Asia Division, to the Clerk of this Court, filed July 9, 1997. Notwithstanding the entry of default against the defendant, however, before this Court may enter a judgment against a foreign state, plaintiffs must "establish[ ] [their] claim or right to relief by evidence satisfactory to the [C]ourt." 28 U.S.C. §1608(e). See also *Flatow v. Islamic Republic of Iran*, 999 F.Supp. 1, 6 (D.D.Cir.1998); *Alejandre v. Republic of Cuba*, 996 F.Supp. 1239, 1242 (S.D.Fla.1997).

As this is an action brought against a sovereign foreign state, the Foreign Sovereign Immunities Act ("FSIA"), 28 U.S.C. §§1602-1611, determines the extent of the defendant's amenability to the judicial process of the United States. See *Flatow*, 999 F.Supp. at 10-11 (citing *Verlinden B.V. v. Central Bank of Nigeria*, 461 U.S. 480, 489, 103 S.Ct. 1962, 76 L.Ed.2d 81 (1983)). Title 28 U.S.C. §1330(a), gives U.S. district courts original subject matter jurisdiction over civil actions with respect to which a defendant foreign state is not entitled to immunity under the FSIA. See *Argentine Republic v. Amerada Hess Shipping Corp.*, 488 U.S. 428, 434, 109 S.Ct. 683, 102 L.Ed.2d 818 (1989).

In general, the FSIA affords foreign states immunity from the jurisdiction of U.S. courts, with exceptions made for claims of a particular nature. *See* 28 U.S.C. §1604. One of these exceptions is found at 28 U.S.C. §1605(a)(7). Enacted as an amendment to the FSIA in 1996, §1605(a)(7) enables U.S. courts to entertain cases brought directly against a sovereign foreign state, once it has been formally designated by the U.S. Department of State as a state sponsor of terrorism, that either commits a terrorist act (including "hostage taking" and "torture") on its own, or provides material support to the perpetrators of such an act, which results in the death of or injury to an American citizen. See also *Flatow*, 999 F.Supp. at 12. [FN5]

FN5. For purposes of §1605(a)(7), "torture" is defined as:

any act, directed against an individual in the offender's custody or physical control, by which severe pain or suffering,…whether physical or mental, is intentionally inflicted on that individual for such purposes as obtaining from that individual or a third person information or a confession, punishing that individual for an act that individual or a third person has committed or is suspected of having committed, intimidating or coercing that individual or a third person, or for any reason based on discrimination of any kind.

Torture Victims Protection Act of 1991, Pub.L. No. 102-256, §3(b)(1), 106 Stat. 73, 73 (reprinted at 28 U.S.C.A. §1350 note (West Supp.1997)).

The statutory definition of "hostage taking" is supplied by treaty:

Any person who seizes or detains and threatens to kill, to injure or to continue to detain another person (hereinafter referred to as the "hostage") in order to compel a third party, namely, a State, an international intergovernmental organization, a natural or juridical person, or a group of persons, to do or abstain from doing any act as an explicit or implicit condition for the release of the hostage commits the offence of taking of hostages ("hostage-taking") within the meaning of this Convention.

International Convention Against the Taking of Hostages, *opened for signature* December 18, 1979, art. 1, T.I.A.S. No. 11081 (entered into force for the United States on January 6, 1985).

IV.

The evidence establishes that the United States Department of State has recognized Iran as a state sponsor of terrorism since January of 1984. *See* 49 Fed.Reg. 2836-02 (Jan. 23, 1984 statement of George P. Shultz, Secretary of State); see also *Flatow*, 999 F.Supp. at 9. United States intelligence publications specifically identify Iran as an avowed sponsor of Hizballah (and Hizballah, incidentally, as the kidnappers of David Jacobsen, Frank Reed, and Joseph Cicippio). *See* Pls.' Ex. 21 ("Terrorist Group Profiles," the Vice President's Task Force on Combatting Terrorism report of November 1988; *see also* Pls.' Exs. 24-30 (U.S. Department of State "Patterns of Global Terrorism" reports, 1986-88, 1990-92, 1997). Expert testimony at trial concurred in that conclusion. *See* July 20 Tr. at 15-16, 18, 74; July 21 Tr. at 4-7 (testimony of Cols. Hurley and North, and Dr. Clawson, *supra*, n. 2).

Whether or not the evidence is sufficient to find that Iran seized these hostages on its own, however, it nevertheless openly provided "material support or resources" to Hizballah, and that is sufficient grounds to impose liability under §1605(a)(7). *See* 18 U.S.C. §2339A(b) (defining "material support or resources"). Dr. Clawson estimated that during the time in which the plaintiffs were held hostage, Iran spent between $100 million and $150 million annually in support of terrorist activities. *See* July 20 Tr. at 81. Colonel Hurley also testified that Iran provides military training for the Hizballah, *see* July 20 Tr. at 19-20, and, in his opinion, remains to this day the most active state sponsor of terrorism, specifically targeting Americans abroad. *See* July 20 Tr. at 17-18; *see also* Pls.' Ex. 30 (U.S. Department of State's "Patterns of Global Terrorism: 1997" report). Dr. Clawson declared that the taking of these hostages could not have happened without approval from the highest levels of the Iranian government. *See* July 20 Tr. at 91; *see also* July 20 Tr. at 20 (testimony of Col. Hurley). [FN6]

FN6. "The law of *respondeat superior* demonstrates that if a foreign state's agent, official or employee provides material support and resources to a terrorist organization, such provision will be considered an act within the scope of his or her agency, office, or employment." *Flatow*, 999 F.Supp. at 18 (citing *Guzel v. Kuwait*, 818 F.Supp. 6, 10 (D.D.C.1993)).

It is unnecessary to prove that the support provided by Iran to Hizballah contributed directly to the seizures of Jacobsen, Cicippio and Reed. See *id.* ("Sponsorship of a terrorist group which causes the personal injury or death of a United States national alone is sufficient to invoke jurisdiction.").

V.

The Court also concludes that the evidence presented establishes *prima facie* the plaintiffs' claims against the Islamic Republic of Iran, and that no colorable defense is apparent from the record as a matter of law.

To summarize, plaintiffs have proved to the Court's satisfaction: (1) that they were injured by acts of torture and hostage-taking; (2) that the acts were perpetrated by a group receiving material support from Iran; (3) that the provision of material support was engaged in by Iranian officials, employees, or agents acting within the scope of their office, employment, or agency; (4) that at the time of the acts,

Iran was designated as a state sponsor of terrorism under 50 U.S.C.App. §2405(j) or 22 U.S.C. §2371; (5) that the claimants or victims were U.S. nationals at the time the acts occurred; [FN7] and (6) that similar acts conducted by officials, employees, or agents of the U.S. while acting within the scope of his or her office, employment, or agency, would also be actionable. [FN8]

FN7. *See* 28 U.S.C. §1605(a)(7)(B)(ii). The victims in this case, Joseph Cicippio, David Jacobsen, and Frank Reed were U.S. citizens at the time they were abducted. Since their husbands were victims, the Court also has jurisdiction over the claims of Elham Cicippio and Fifi Delati-Reed.

FN8. *See* U.S. Const. Amend. 5; *Bivens v. Six Unknown Named Agents of Fed. Bureau of Narcotics*, 403 U.S. 388, 91 S.Ct. 1999, 29 L.Ed.2d 619 (1971); *see also* 18 U.S.C. §§1203, 2339A, 2339B, 2340A.

Although the abductions of Cicippio, Reed, and Jacobsen occurred more than a decade prior to the enactment of 28 U.S.C. §1605(a)(7), Congress expressly directed that the statute be given retroactive application. *See* Antiterrorism and Effective Death Penalty Act of 1996, Pub.L. No. 104-132, §221(c), 110 Stat. 1214, 1243 (reprinted at 28 U.S.C.A. §1605 note (West Supp.1997)). Similarly, to the same effect, the ten-year statute of limitations for actions under §1605(a)(7) does not bar the claims in this case because, once again, Congress has provided that victims of terrorism be given benefit of "all principles of equitable tolling, including the period during which the foreign state was immune from suit..." 28 U.S.C. §1605(f). Iran was immune from suit by these plaintiffs under the FSIA until the enactment of §1605(a)(7) in 1996. [FN9]

FN9. See *Cicippio v. Islamic Republic of Iran*, 30 F.3d 164 (D.C.Cir.1994).

VI.

Joseph Cicippio, Frank Reed, and David Jacobsen were "tortured" and "taken hostage" as those terms are defined by 28 U.S.C. §1605(e). Those acts of torture and hostage-taking, all clearly actionable as tortious conduct under U.S. law, [FN10] thus inflicted legally cognizable, profoundly serious, and largely permanent personal injury upon each of the hostages and their spouses. *See* July 20 Tr. at 22-68; 93-125; July 21 Tr. at 11-46; *see also* Pls.' Exs. 8, 10, 17, 18.

FN10. The complaint is drawn in ten counts: three allege tortious conduct, including assault, battery, false imprisonment, and kidnapping (Counts I, V, and VII); three allege violations of "international human rights" (Counts II, VI, and VIII); two allege loss of consortium (Counts III and XI); and two allege intentional and/or negligent infliction of emotional distress (Counts IV and X).

Under 28 U.S.C. §1606, for any claim against a foreign state as to which the foreign state is not entitled to immunity, the foreign state "shall be liable in the same manner and to the same extent as a private individual under like circumstances…" The statute continues, however to provide that "…a *foreign state*…shall not be liable for punitive damages." (Emphasis supplied). Accordingly, the Court must undertake the difficult task of calculating an award of compensatory damages to make plaintiffs whole, while nevertheless avoiding any punitive component that would surely accompany a compensatory award were the defendant at bar not possessed of statutory immunity. There appear to be no truly analogous domestic precedents to assist the Court in doing so. [FN11]

FN11. In *Langevine v. District of Columbia*, 106 F.3d 1018 (D.C.Cir.1997), the D.C. Circuit upheld a jury verdict of $200,000 for bodily injury, pain and suffering resulting from a false arrest and detention in a D.C. police station that lasted no more than a day.

In the only two reported cases to have been brought under §1605(a)(7) in which damages have been awarded,-- *Flatow* and *Alejandre v. Republic of Cuba*, 996 F.Supp. 1239 (S.D.Fla.1997)-- two district courts awarded compensatory damages of $10 million and $8 million, respectively, for wrongful deaths resulting from acts of terrorism.

Prior to his capture, Jacobsen had a promising career in medical administration. After his release, Jacobsen was unable to find a job; prospective employers were reluctant, he discovered, to hire someone who had undergone such an ordeal. *See* July 20 Tr. at 46. Jacobsen estimated that he lost approximately $2.9 million in earnings as a result of his captivity. *See* Pls.' Ex. 38 (calculating loss of income based on his $125,000 salary plus ten percent increase annually at time of kidnapping plus loss of his retirement plan and loss of savings during captivity).

At the time he was kidnapped, Frank Reed was a partner in the operation of two successful private schools outside Beirut. He earned a salary of $100,000 per year and owned 25% of the property and the business, which he estimates were worth $5 million in the aggregate. Reed testified that as a result of his captivity, he lost everything he owned in Lebanon. *See* July 20 Tr. at 95-97. Due to the severity of the beatings he suffered while held hostage, Reed has been

declared permanently disabled and unable to work because of his severe depression and his permanently injured feet. *See* July 20 Tr. at 123-24. His income has been reduced to a monthly social security disability payment of $625. He calculates that he has lost fifteen years of work, plus his 25% share of the schools and their profits, altogether totaling in excess of $2.7 million. *See* July 20 Tr. at 124.

Elham Cicippio testified that her husband was unable to find a job in the United States until approximately 1994. *See* July 20 Tr. at 148-49. Additionally, Joseph Cicippio testified that his loss in salary during the time he was held hostage totals $850,000. *See* July 21 Tr. at 42-43.

The Court concludes that plaintiffs David Jacobsen, Frank Reed, and Joseph Cicippio are entitled to damages for lost wages and business opportunities in the amounts of $2.9 million, $2.7 million, and $850,000, respectively. In addition, plaintiffs are entitled to compensatory damages for pain and suffering and mental anguish.

The Court will award damages to, and cause judgments to be entered for David Jacobsen in the amount of $9.0 million; for Frank Reed in the amount of $16.0 million; and for Joseph Cicippio in the amount of $20.0 million.

Mrs. Cicippio and Mrs. Reed were denied their husbands' society and companionship for 63 and 44 months, respectively. They endured those months in great distress, never knowing if their husbands were being tortured or were even still alive. Even today they continue to suffer from the changes that prolonged captivity and abuse produced in their husbands. In short, they have already endured many years of mental anguish that may have exceeded the grief normally experienced as a result of the death of a loved one, and will in all likelihood continue to do so into an uncertain future. Accordingly, Elham Cicippio and Fifi Delati-Reed are awarded damages and shall each have judgment for $10 million.

It is, therefore, this 27th day of August, 1998,

ORDERED, that the Court finds in favor of the plaintiffs Joseph J. Cicippio, Elham Cicippio, Frank Reed, Fifi Delati-Reed, and David P. Jacobsen, and against the defendant Islamic Republic of Iran; and it is,

FURTHER ORDERED, that the Clerk of this Court forthwith enter judgments against the Islamic Republic of Iran for plaintiffs in the following amounts:

Joseph J. Cicippio:	$20,000,000.00
Elham Cicippio:	$10,000,000.00
Frank Reed:	$16,000,000.00
Fifi Delati-Reed:	$10,000,000.00
David P. Jacobsen:	$ 9,000,000.00

Notes:

1.   The expansive intent of the Klinghoffer Act is evidenced by its comprehensive legislative history. Testifying before the Senate Subcommittee on Courts and Administrative Practice, Deputy Assistant Attorney General Steven R. Valentine specifically requested,

> ...that this provision be amended to include, in addition to the individual directly affected, such additional parties as the estate of the decedent, survivors, and heirs. This will ensure that the bill is fully protective of the interests of all relevant parties to the civil suit.

Antiterrorism Act of 1990, Hearing Before the Subcommittee on Courts and Administrative Practice of Committee on the Judiciary, United States Senate, 101st Congress, Second Session July 25 1990 at 38. In response to a question posed by Senator Thurmond about whether the suggested modification in the language of the bill would "make certain the ability of family members to file a lawsuit," Valentine responded, "It would make clear that which is already implied in the bill. It would remove any doubt that anyone would have as to whether or not they could bring the litigation." *Id.* at 46.

2.   The plaintiffs had previously attempted to sue Iran in 1992, prior to the enactment of the terrorism amendments to the FSIA. *Cicippio v. Islamic Republic of Iran*, 1993 WL 730748 (D.D.C.)

3.   What was the legal basis for the simple statement in footnote 7 that "Since their husbands were victims, the Court also has jurisdiction over the claims of Elham Cicippio and Fifi Delati-Reed"?

4.   In *Peterson v. Islamic Republic of Iran*, 264 F.Supp.2d 46, 60 (D.D.C. 2003) the court discussed whether members of the military are appropriate plaintiffs under the FSIA,

> [I]f the plaintiffs in these actions proved that the U.S. military service members at issue in these cases were part of a peacekeeping mission and that

they operated under peacetime rules of engagement, they would qualify for recovery. As set forth in the above findings of fact, the plaintiffs have demonstrated that the U.S. military service members at issue were part of a peacekeeping mission, and that they were operating under peacetime rules of engagement. Therefore, the Court concludes that the military service members at issue in these cases qualify for recovery.

5.   In *Morris v. Khadr*, 415 F.Supp.2d 1323 (D.Utah 2006), the court found that wounded U.S. soldiers and estates of deceased soldiers were proper plaintiffs under 18 U.S.C. §2333.

6.   The court noted that there had been "only two reported cases to have been brought under §1605(a)(7)." What clue does this provide as to why the plaintiffs in the *Cicippio-Puleo* case were not parties to the original suit?

7.   On at least one occasion, damages were awarded to a non-party:

> Although Maureen Moroney is not a named plaintiff in this action, plaintiff Beverly Surette nonetheless seeks to recover damages for solatium on behalf of Ms. Moroney. While the Court ordinarily will not award damages to a non-plaintiff, the specific circumstances of this action permit such an award to plaintiff on behalf of Ms. Moroney. In similar cases brought in this district, judges have awarded damages to non-plaintiffs who demonstrated a sufficiently close connection to the victim of a terrorist act. See *Stethem v. Islamic Republic of Iran*, 201 F.Supp.2d at 89, n. 18 (awarding damages to siblings of decedent even though only named plaintiffs were decedent's parents); *Higgins v. Islamic Republic of Iran*, 2000 WL 33674311 at *8 (awarding solatium to victim's daughter though not a named plaintiff); *Flatow v. Islamic Republic of Iran*, 999 F.Supp. at 30 ("The testimony of sisters or brothers is ordinarily sufficient to sustain their claims for solatium."). In conformity with this practice, and in recognition of the unique circumstances of this action, the Court finds that plaintiff Beverly Surette may raise a claim for solatium on behalf of Ms. Moroney. For clarity on this point, plaintiff moved to amend the second sentence of paragraph 47 of the complaint, and the Court granted the motion, so that it now reads: "This action

is brought by plaintiff Beverly Surette, Conservator of the Estate of William Buckley, deceased, on behalf of herself and the decedent's heirs-at-law, including Maureen Moroney."

Surette v. Islamic Republic of Iran, 231 F.Supp.2d 260, 271 fn. 9 (D.D.C. 2002).

8.   In *Hartford Ins. Co. v. Socialist People's Libyan Arab Jamahirya*, 422 F.Supp.2d 203 (D.D.C. 2006) the court found that it had subject matter jurisdiction under the terrorism amendments to the FSIA for an airline's insurer's claim against Libya for indemnification and contribution for its expenditures defending and settling death and personal injury claims arising out of the bombing of Pan Am 103. What if any potential does this case have to broaden the scope of civil antiterrorism cases? Could insurance companies become "private attorneys general"?

9.2 Family Members
Bettis v. Islamic Republic of Iran, 315 F.3d 325 (D.C. Cir. 2003).

HARRY T. EDWARDS, Circuit Judge:
In 1985, Father Lawrence M. Jenco, an ordained Catholic priest who was working as the Director of Catholic Relief Services in Beirut, Lebanon, was abducted by Hizbollah, the Islamic terrorist organization. Hizbollah held Fr. Jenco captive for 564 days, and subjected him to near-constant blindfolding, beatings, and psychological torture. Even after Fr. Jenco's release, he remained underweight and weak for a long period, had a changed disposition, and would suffer "flashbacks" to his kidnapping and torture. After Fr. Jenco's death, his estate and family members sued the Islamic Republic of Iran, which had "provided support, guidance, and resources to Hizbollah" in connection with Fr. Jenco's abduction. *Jenco v. Islamic Republic of Iran*, 154 F.Supp.2d 27, 31 (D.D.C.2001). The District Court upheld the claims of Fr. Jenco's estate and his six siblings, awarding over $314 million in compensatory and punitive damages for battery, assault, false imprisonment, and intentional infliction of emotional distress suffered by Fr. Jenco and for intentional infliction of emotional distress suffered by the siblings. The District Court rejected the claims of Fr. Jenco's 22 nieces and nephews, however. The nieces and nephews now appeal. We affirm the judgment of the District Court, because the nieces and nephews are not members of Fr. Jenco's immediate family. *See* RESTATEMENT (SECOND) OF TORTS §46(2)(a).

I. BACKGROUND

A. Father Jenco's Abduction and Captivity

Shortly before 8:00 a.m. on January 8, 1985, five armed men abducted Fr. Jenco as he was on his way to the office of Catholic Relief Services in West Beirut, Lebanon. Hizbollah carried out the kidnapping as part of a widespread terrorist campaign that it conducted during the 1980s. This campaign targeted journalists, university professors, members of the clergy, and United States servicemen. See, e.g., *Wagner v. Islamic Republic of Iran*, 172 F.Supp.2d 128, 131-32 (D.D.C.2001) (detailing the murder of a Navy officer stationed in Beirut by a Hizbollah suicide bomber); *Sutherland v. Islamic Republic of Iran*, 151 F.Supp.2d 27, 30-38 (D.D.C.2001) (detailing Hizbollah's kidnapping, detention, and torture of an American academic in Beirut); *Polhill v. Islamic Republic of Iran*, No. 00-1798 (TPJ), 2001 U.S. Dist. LEXIS 15322, at *2-*7 (D.D.C. Aug. 23, 2001) (same); *Anderson v. Islamic Republic of Iran*, 90 F.Supp.2d 107, 109-11 (D.D.C.2000) (detailing Hizbollah's kidnapping, detention, and torture of an American journalist in Beirut); *Cicippio v. Islamic Republic of Iran*, 18 F.Supp.2d 62, 63-66 (D.D.C.1998) (detailing Hizbollah's kidnapping, imprisonment, and torture of three male U.S. citizens).

As Hizbollah's prisoner, Fr. Jenco was subjected to inhumane conditions. The District Court described his treatment at some length:

From the moment he was abducted, Father Jenco was treated little better than a caged animal. He was chained, beaten, and almost constantly blindfolded. His access to toilet facilities was extremely limited, if permitted at all. He was routinely required to urinate in a cup and maintain the urine in his cell. His food and clothing were spare, as was even the most basic medical care.

He also withstood repeated psychological torture. Most notably, at one point, his captors held a gun to his head and told him that he was about to die. The captors pulled the trigger and laughed as Father Jenco reacted to the small click of the unloaded gun. At other times, the captors misled Fr. Jenco into thinking he was going home. They told him to dress up in his good clothes, took pictures of him, and then said "ha, ha, we're just kidding."

Jenco, 154 F.Supp.2d at 29.

Fr. Jenco's imprisonment also caused great suffering among his family members:

While Father Jenco was being held prisoner, his many siblings and relatives banded together and fought for his release. The family made a practice of meeting every Monday night to discuss what steps they could take to help secure his release. Family members took on various responsibilities, such as communicating with the public, dealing with the media, maintaining contact with the State Department, and raising money to cover the various costs of such a massive effort.

Andrew Mihelich and John Jenco, both nephews of Fr. Jenco, testified that, because of their massive dedication to free Fr. Jenco, the whole family, in effect, became a hostage in one way or another. As a result, many of the traditional family events, such as birthdays, graduations, or religious holidays were overshadowed - or overlooked altogether - on account of the campaign to free Fr. Jenco. Apart from the campaign, the family felt the very personal loss of not having their beloved relative at many family milestones, such as weddings, births, and baptisms. On the whole, according to John Jenco, the family spent the 19 months of Fr. Jenco's captivity on an emotional roller coaster, never knowing how close or far Fr. Jenco was to being released, not to mention returning home unharmed.

Jenco relatives also testified as to the specific effects that the captivity had o[n] Fr. Jenco's brother, John Jenco. John Jenco Jr. testified that, from the first day of captivity to the last day of his own life, John Jenco Sr. was distraught in a way he had never been before. He was able to celebrate the return of Fr. Jenco, but was never fully able, according to John Jenco Jr., become himself again. Similarly, Joseph Jenco testified that the stress of the captivity on Verna Mae Mihelich likely was a factor in her premature death.

Id. at 31-32. The trial court also found that

there is significant evidence of emotional distress among the siblings. Joseph Jenco, Fr. Jenco's brother testified as to the great strain the captivity imposed on himself as well as his brothers and sisters...As well, other witnesses testified as to the stressful and extensive publicity campaign...; the stress of false alarms that Fr. Jenco had been killed or freed...; and constant fear that the campaign to free Fr. Jenco might also end up hurting him and the other hostages.

Id. at 35.

After Fr. Jenco's release, "he returned to the United States and served as a parish priest until his death on July 19, 1996." *Id.* at 29. The District Court found, however, that even after his return home, Fr. Jenco never fully recovered from the grim experience of his imprisonment:

Fr. Jenco continued to suffer the effects of his captivity. For a long period after his return, Father Jenco remained underweight and quite weak. Father Jenco's nephew, David Mihelich, testified that his uncle's disposition was noticeably milder, and indeed never returned to its pre-captivity state. As well, Christopher Morales, a Special Agent with the United States Secret Service, became a close friend of Jenco's after interviewing him about his experience in Lebanon. Agent Morales testified that he witnessed Father Jenco have three separate "flashbacks", that is, moments where Jenco appeared to be aloof of his surroundings and somewhat possessed and disturbed by different images or experiences...In sum, the last 11 years of Fr. Jenco's life were indelibly marred by his kidnapping and torture.

Id. at 29-30.

Although the District Court's findings are more precise with respect to the effects of Fr. Jenco's ordeal on his siblings than on his nieces and nephews, there is no dispute that the nieces and nephews suffered emotional distress by virtue of the harm done to their uncle.

B. The Statutory Framework

Under the Foreign Sovereign Immunities Act ("FSIA"), foreign states generally enjoy immunity from suit in U.S. courts. 28 U.S.C. §1604 ("Subject to existing international agreements to which the United States is a party at the time of enactment of this Act a foreign state shall be immune from the jurisdiction of the courts of the United States and of the States..."). However, in 1996 Congress enacted the "terrorism exception" to the FSIA under 28 U.S.C. §1605(a)(7):

In 1996, as part of the comprehensive Antiterrorism and Effective Death Penalty Act ("AEDPA"), Pub.L. No. 104-132, §221(a), 110 Stat. 1214 (Apr. 24, 1996), Congress amended the FSIA to add a new class of claims for which certain foreign states would be precluded from asserting sovereign immunity. Specifically, the amendment vitiates immunity in cases

in which money damages are sought against a foreign state for personal injury or death that was caused by an act of torture, extrajudicial killing, aircraft sabotage, hostage taking, or the provision of material support or resources...for such an act if such act or provision of material support is engaged in by an official, employee, or agent of such foreign state while acting within the scope of his or her office, employment, or agency[.]

28 U.S.C. §1605(a)(7). In enacting this provision, Congress sought to create a judicial forum for compensating the victims of terrorism, and in so doing to punish foreign states who have committed or sponsored such acts and deter them from doing so in the future. See *Daliberti v. Republic of Iraq*, 97 F.Supp.2d 38, 50 (D.D.C.2000); Molora Vadnais, *The Terrorism Exception to the Foreign Sovereign Immunities Act*, 5 UCLA J. INT'L L. & FOREIGN AFF. 199, 216 (2000).

...

Section 1605(a)(7) has some notable features which reveal the delicate legislative compromise out of which it was born. First, not all foreign states may be sued. Instead, only a defendant that has been specifically designated by the State Department as a "state sponsor of terrorism" is subject to the loss of its sovereign immunity. §1605(a)(7)(A). Second, even a foreign state listed as a sponsor of terrorism retains its immunity unless (a) it is afforded a reasonable opportunity to arbitrate any claim based on acts that occurred in that state, and (b) either the victim or the claimant was a U.S. national at the time that those acts took place. §1605(a)(7)(B).

Price v. Socialist People's Libyan Arab Jamahiriya, 294 F.3d 82, 88-89 (D.C.Cir.2002).

Less than six months after passage of AEDPA, Congress passed an amendment designed to enhance the penalties available in suits implicating 28 U.S.C. §1605(a)(7). *See* Omnibus Consolidated Appropriations Act, 1997, Pub.L. No. 104-208, §589, 110 Stat. 3009, 3009-172 (1997) (codified at 28 U.S.C. §1605 note); *Flatow v. Islamic Republic of Iran*, 999 F.Supp. 1, 12-13 (D.D.C.1998) (describing amendments to FSIA); *see also* Naomi Roht-Arriaza, *The Foreign Sovereign Immunities Act and Human Rights Violations: One Step Forward, Two Steps Back?*, 16 BERKELEY J. INT'L L., 71, 82-83 (1998) (discussing the amendment). This provision is known as the "Flatow Amendment," because its sponsor referred to the Flatow family - whose daughter, Alisa, was killed by a Palestinian suicide bomber while studying in Israel - when speaking in support of the statute. Joseph W. Dellapenna, *Civil Remedies for International Terrorism*, 12

DEPAUL BUS. L.J. 169, 256 n.439 (1999-2000); see also *Flatow*, 999 F.Supp. at 6-9 (describing Alisa Flatow's murder). The Flatow Amendment allows for non-economic and punitive damages against an official, employee, or agent of a foreign state designated as "terrorist." *Price*, 294 F.3d at 87; *Flatow*, 999 F.Supp. at 12-13.

In *Price*, we noted that "[t]he FSIA is undoubtedly a jurisdictional statute which, in specified cases, eliminates foreign sovereign immunity and opens the door to subject matter jurisdiction in the federal courts...There is a question, however, whether the FSIA creates a federal cause of action for torture and hostage taking against foreign states," or only against their "official[s], employee[s], or agent[s]" as specified in the Amendment. 294 F.3d at 87. Two District Court opinions in this circuit have reached different conclusions on the question of whether the Flatow Amendment furnishes a basis for a cause of action against a defendant state. Compare *Roeder v. Islamic Republic of Iran*, 195 F.Supp.2d 140, 171-73 (D.D.C.2002), with *Cronin v. Islamic Republic of Iran*, 2002 WL 31830571, at *8-*9, 2002 U.S. Dist. LEXIS 24115, at *24-*30 (D.D.C. Dec. 18, 2002). Because this question had not been briefed or argued by the parties, the court in *Price* merely "flag[ged] the issue," leaving it for disposition by the District Court in the first instance on remand. *Id.* We need not reach the issue in this case either, because the District Court did not address the matter, Iran has not appealed the judgments in favor of Fr. Jenco's estate and his siblings, and the instant appeal by the nieces and nephews will be resolved against appellants on different grounds.

C. The Litigation in District Court

In this case, the parties do not appear to doubt that Iran is a proper defendant, at least with respect to the claims brought by Fr. Jenco's estate and his siblings. Iran has been designated a state sponsor of terrorism by the Secretary of State. *See* 22 C.F.R. §126.1(d). There is also weighty evidence in the record confirming the involvement of Iran in connection with Fr. Jenco's kidnapping and brutal imprisonment. *Jenco*, 154 F.Supp.2d at 31. Because of Iran's culpability, Fr. Jenco's family brought suit against Iran and the Iranian Ministry of Information and Security ("MOIS") on March 15, 2000. The District Court found that, because of Iran's material support for Hizbollah's hostage taking and torture, the terrorism exception stripped Iran's immunity from suit. It also found the defendants liable "on most, but not all, counts alleged in the plaintiffs' complaint." *Jenco*, 154 F.Supp.2d at 33. The court ultimately awarded over $314 million in compensatory and punitive damages to Fr. Jenco's estate and his siblings. *Id*. at 40.

The District Court rejected the claims of Fr. Jenco's nieces and nephews, who were seeking damages for intentional infliction of emotional distress. The trial court recognized the "tremendous impact that Fr. Jenco's detention had on his nieces and nephews." *Id.* at 36. The court concluded, however, that these family members could not recover under common law because they were not among Fr. Jenco's immediate family. In reaching this decision,, the District Court was guided by §46 of the RESTATEMENT (SECOND) OF TORTS, which purports to delineate common law claims for "Outrageous Conduct Causing Severe Emotional Distress," as follows:

(1) One who by extreme and outrageous conduct intentionally or recklessly causes severe emotional distress to another is subject to liability for such emotional distress, and if bodily harm to the other results from it, for such bodily harm.

(2) Where such conduct is directed at a third person, the actor is subject to liability if he intentionally or recklessly causes severe emotional distress

(a) to a member of such person's immediate family who is present at the time, whether or not such distress results in bodily harm, or

(b) to any other person who is present at the time, if such distress results in bodily harm.

RESTATEMENT (SECOND) OF TORTS §46 (1986).

The District Court noted that in *Sutherland*, another terrorism exception suit, the court allowed the wife of a man whom Hizbollah held hostage for six and a half years to recover damages from Iran for intentional infliction of emotional distress even though the wife was not actually "present" to witness the outrageous conduct against her husband. 151 F.Supp.2d at 50. The "presence" requirement of §46(2)(a) was construed liberally to include this claim, because the court found that the defendants' intent to cause distress to the wife was quite clear from their conduct. *Id.* In the instant case, however, the District Court held that, although the "presence" requirement could be given a generous reading, the "immediate family" requirement of §46(2)(a) could not:

[S]ome lines must be drawn, if, for example, "millions of people who are not present...watch the torture or murder of the President on television."...In hostage cases, this Court finds that the line is best drawn according to the plaintiff's relationship with the victim of the outrageous conduct. That is, to collect for intentional infliction of emotional distress in cases such as this one, the plaintiff need not be present at the place of outrageous conduct, but must be a member of the victim's immediate family.

The Court draws the line with respect to family relationship (and not presence) for two reasons. First, hostage cases are unique in that they implicitly involve a physical separation of the plaintiff from the victim of the outrageous conduct. As a matter of fact, a plaintiff's lack of presence is the *exact source* of his emotional distress. Thus, if the Court were to limit recovery in hostage cases using a "presence" test, plaintiffs would never recover despite there being extremely strong evidence of significant emotional suffering.

Second, comparing the presence test to the family relationship test, courts have been more willing to stretch the boundaries of presence than family relationship.

Jenco, 154 F.Supp.2d at 36 (quoting DAN B. DOBBS, THE LAW OF TORTS §307, at 834 (2000)). And in applying the "immediate family" requirement of §46(2)(a), the District Court adhered to the traditional definition of that term:

This Court defines one's immediate family as his spouse, parents, siblings, and children. This definition is consistent with the traditional understanding of one's immediate family. *See* Dan B. Dobbs, The Law of Torts, §310 (2000) (addressing the scope of recovery in consortium claims).

Jenco, 154 F.Supp.2d at 36 n. 8. The court then found that the nieces and nephews did not satisfy the requirement. *Id.*

The nieces and nephews now appeal the District Court's decision to deny them recovery for intentional infliction of emotional distress. Because Iran did not enter an appearance, the court appointed the Georgetown University Law Center's Appellate Litigation Program as *Amicus Curiae* to present arguments in support of the District Court's judgment. [FN*]

FN* FSIA §1608 states that "[n]o judgment by default shall be entered by a court of the United States...against a foreign state...unless the claimant establishes his claim or right to relief by evidence satisfactory to the court." 28 U.S.C. §1608. The Law Center's efforts to assist the court in its statutory responsibility to evaluate the appellants' claims - both the brief submitted to the court and the oral argument presented by Ms. Abigail V. Carter - have been truly outstanding, for which the court is grateful.

II. ANALYSIS

The sole issue on appeal is whether the District Court erred in denying Fr. Jenco's nieces and nephews recovery under the Flatow Amendment for intentional infliction of emotional distress caused by outrageous conduct directed at Fr. Jenco, where the requirement for recovery at common law - membership in Fr. Jenco's immediate family - is not met. This question is a matter of law for this court to consider *de novo*. See *Princz v. F.R.G.*, 26 F.3d 1166, 1169 (D.C.Cir.1994).

The parties agree that the District Court correctly applied common law (and not local District of Columbia law) to the nieces' and nephews' claims for intentional infliction of emotional distress. The brief of *Amicus Curiae* usefully explains the common law recognized pursuant to the FSIA:

While there is an argument that state substantive tort law may apply to claims brought under the Flatow Amendment, see, e.g., *First Nat'l City Bank v. Banco Para El Comercio Exterior de Cuba*, 462 U.S. 611, 622 n. 11, 103 S.Ct. 2591 [2598 n. 11], 77 L.Ed.2d 46 (1983) (finding that under the commercial exceptions to the FSIA, "where state law provides a rule of liability governing private individuals, the FSIA requires the application of that rule to foreign states in like circumstances"), district courts performing the traditional choice of law analysis in Flatow Amendment cases have consistently applied federal common law. See *Wagner v. Islamic Republic of Iran*, 172 F.Supp.2d 128, 134-35 (D.D.C.2001) (applying federal common law because other possible choices "would eventually lead in other cases to divergent measures of recovery for essentially identical claims against foreign defendants"); *Flatow v. Islamic Republic of Iran*, 999 F.Supp. 1, 15 (D.D.C.1998) (applying "interstitial federal common law" because Congress intended "that the federal courts create coherent national standards...[i]n the interest of promoting uniformity of determinations with respect to the liability of foreign states for the terrorist acts"). Application of federal common law is particularly appropriate because the District of Columbia, which is the dedicated venue for actions against foreign states, *see* 28 U.S.C. §1391(f)(4), does not recognize solatium damages in wrongful death causes of action while the Flatow Amendment

does. See *Runyon v. District of Columbia*, 463 F.2d 1319, 1322 (D.C.Cir.1972) (holding, in a wrongful death case, that "[t]he parties so recovering may not be compensated for their grief"); 28 U.S.C. §1605 note (specifying that plaintiffs may recover "economic damages, solatium, pain, and suffering, and punitive damages"); see also *Stethem v. Islamic Republic of Iran*, 201 F.Supp.2d 78, 89 (D.D.C.2002) ("Because the District of Columbia does not recognize claims for loss of solatium, this Court has recognized this cause of action under the federal common law by relying upon the Second Restatement of Torts.").

FN9 [I]f District of Columbia law were to govern, neither the nieces nor anyone other than Fr. Jenco himself would recover for intentional infliction of emotional distress. Amicus is aware of no case in the District of Columbia permitting someone other than the direct victim of the outrageous conduct to recover for intentional infliction of emotional distress.

Lacking a developed body of federal common law regarding intentional infliction of emotional distress, courts evaluating such claims under the Flatow Amendment have looked to the Restatements, as well as state decisional law. See, e.g., *Sutherland v. Islamic Republic of Iran*, 151 F.Supp.2d 27, 48-52 (D.C.Cir.2001) (applying the Second Restatement of Torts to plaintiff's intentional infliction of emotional distress claim under the federal common law); *Flatow*, 999 F.Supp. at 30 n. 13 (collecting ALR references on state law recovery for solatium damages)[.]

...

In this case, the district court and nieces both rely on section 46 of the Restatement for the substantive law of intentional infliction of emotional distress.

Br. of *Amicus Curiae* at 18-21.

We recognize that some of the cases addressing these FSIA claims refer to "federal common law." Indeed, *Amicus Curiae* does as well. The term "federal common law" seems to us to be a misnomer. Indeed, it is a mistake, we think, to label actions under the FSIA and Flatow Amendment for solatium damages as "federal common law" cases, for these actions are based on *statutory* rights. Without the statute, the claims could not arise. Of course, because these claims are based on a federal statute, their "extent and nature" are "federal questions." *Burks v. Lasker*, 441 U.S. 471, 476, 99 S.Ct. 1831, 1836, 60 L.Ed.2d 404 (1979). But that does not, in this case, "authorize the federal courts to fashion a complete body of federal law." *Id.* at 477, 99 S.Ct. at 1837. Rather, as we note in section II.B., *infra*, because the FSIA instructs that "the foreign state shall be liable in the same manner and to the same extent as a private individual under like circumstances," 28 U.S.C. §1606, it in effect instructs federal judges to find the relevant law, not to make it. In doing this, federal judges have looked to the common law of the states to determine the meaning of "intentional infliction of emotional distress." And as we explain more fully below, federal courts in FSIA and Flatow Amendment cases have accepted §46 of the RESTATEMENT (SECOND) OF TORTS as a proxy for state common law of intentional infliction of emotional distress - as do both appellants and *amicus.*

We will assume, *arguendo,* that the nieces and nephews may proceed against the State of Iran under the Flatow Amendment. We will also accept that, in a case of this sort, "common law," grounded in §46 of the RESTATEMENT (SECOND) OF TORTS, delineates the controlling substantive law. We hold, however, that Fr. Jenco's nieces and nephews cannot recover damages for intentional infliction of emotional distress, because they are not members of Fr. Jenco's immediate family. In reaching this conclusion, it is unnecessary for us to reach the question left open in *Price, i.e.,* whether the FSIA creates a federal cause of action against foreign states. It is also unnecessary for us to decide whether the nieces and nephews satisfy the "presence" requirements of §46(2).

A. The RESTATEMENT (SECOND) OF TORTS §46(1) - Actions for Direct Harm

As noted above, §46(1) is limited to *direct* (not "third party") actions for outrageous conduct causing severe emotional distress:

One who by extreme and outrageous conduct intentionally or recklessly causes severe emotional distress to another is subject to liability for such emotional distress, and if bodily harm to the other results from it, for such bodily harm.

RESTATEMENT (SECOND) OF TORTS §46(1). Appellants claim that, although they were not abducted and caused to suffer the physical punishment that Fr. Jenco faced, they nonetheless were direct targets of Hizbollah, Iran, and MOIS during the 564 days of Fr. Jenco's captivity, and thus may seek relief for severe emotional distress under §46(1). In support of this contention, appellants argue, first, that the kidnapping of Fr. Jenco was used to manipulate his fam-

ily to put pressure on United States Government officials to advance Iran's political goals, and, second, that disinformation released by Iran during the kidnapping was calculated to distress family members.

The District Court focused solely on §46(2) in rejecting appellants' claims, implicitly rejecting any suggestion that appellants could seek relief under §46(1). The District Court clearly did not err in declining to apply §46(1) to appellants' claims. As *Amicus Curiae* correctly notes,

If any person that Iran hoped to distress by holding and torturing Fr. Jenco could recover under section 46(1) as a direct victim of Iran's conduct, virtually anyone claiming he or she was affected could recover. Assuming the nieces are correct that "[a] terrorist organization does not expose itself to the wrath of the world community simply to cause emotional distress to only the hostage's 'immediate family'" (Appellants' Br. at 40), anyone whom Iran and MOIS intended to affect - and who was severely distressed - could recover, including neighbors, parishioners, and friends, the U.S. government, and even the world community, in addition to the victim and his immediate family. Such a result would contravene the parameters of the FSIA - "the foreign state shall be liable in the same manner and to the same extent as a private individual under like circumstances," 28 U.S.C. §1606 -because it would be contrary to the limits placed on recovery for intentional infliction of emotional distress by the Restatement section 46(2) and the states.

Br. of *Amicus Curiae* at 27-28. We agree.

Moreover, permitting the nieces and nephews to recover under §46(1) would undermine the limitations imposed on recovery under §46(2) - most significantly, the "immediate family" requirement. Under appellants' view, anyone who agitated for the hostages' release out of genuine concern, sympathy or grief could claim to be an intended "target," seek redress under §46(1), and avoid the strictures of §46(2). Appellants argue that this expansive interpretation of §46(1) can be avoided by limiting recovery to "family members." This does not work, however, because it defies the terms of §46, and, also, because there is no good reason to distinguish between aggrieved family members and other equally aggrieved persons under appellants' expansive interpretation of §46(1). *Cf.* RESTATEMENT §46(2), cmt. b ("Because of the fear of fictitious or trivial claims, distrust of the proof offered, and the difficulty of setting up any satisfactory boundaries to liability, the law has been slow to afford independent protection to the interest in freedom from emotional distress standing alone.").

Finally, the position espoused by appellants is at odds with the FSIA and the prevailing case law. The statute states that a "foreign state shall be liable in the same manner and to the same extent as a private individual under like circumstances." 28 U.S.C. §1606. As *Amicus Curiae* demonstrates in its brief, appellants can point to no specific line of cases in any jurisdiction that supports their right to recovery under subsection (1). Indeed, the prevailing case law refutes appellants' claim. See, e.g., *Dornfeld v. Oberg*, 503 N.W.2d 115, 119 (Minn.1993) (declining to find reckless driving to be "directed at" any particular motorist within the meaning of the Restatement, in part because "[a]llowing recovery under the present facts would raise the specter that any surviving family member in a car crash caused by a drunk or reckless driver could maintain an action against the driver for intentional infliction of emotional distress").

In support of their argument that subsection (1) should apply in this case, appellants point to *Gill v. Brown*, 107 Idaho 1137, 695 P.2d 1276 (App.1985), for the proposition that a defendant can directly target a plaintiff by striking someone or something, knowing that this conduct will emotionally distress the plaintiff. In *Gill*, the court permitted a married couple to recover for intentional infliction of emotional distress after the defendant allegedly shot and killed their donkey. Although appellants are correct that the defendant in *Gill* targeted the plaintiffs by striking at something dear to them, the donkey was property and not another person with an independent legal right to be free from outrageous conduct. Thus, killing the donkey directly targeted the plaintiffs. *Gill* is therefore consistent with the general rule that courts do not consider a plaintiff to be a direct victim of the defendant's conduct where that conduct more directly targeted another victim. While appellants also cite to district court opinions in cases brought under the Flatow Amendment, none of the cited opinions purports to hold that family members are direct victims of terrorist conduct who may escape the requirements of subsection (2) by recovering under subsection (1).

It is clear that Fr. Jenco's nieces and nephews are not direct victims under §46(1). Therefore, the nieces and nephews must satisfy the requirements of §46(2) in order to gain recovery for intentional infliction of emotional distress.

B. The RESTATEMENT (SECOND) OF TORTS §46(2) - "Third-Party" Claims

Section 46(2) provides that:

(2) Where [outrageous conduct causing severe emotional distress] is directed at a third person, the actor is subject to liability if he intentionally or recklessly causes severe emotional distress

(a) to a member of such person's immediate family who is present at the time, whether or not such distress results in bodily harm, or

(b) to any other person who is present at the time, if such distress results in bodily harm.

RESTATEMENT (SECOND) OF TORTS §46(2). Subsection (2)(a) sets forth the "immediate family" requirement, and subsections (2)(a) and (b) delineate the "presence" requirements. Because appellants do not suggest that their emotional distress resulted in bodily harm, they seek recovery under §46(2)(a), not §46(2)(b). Because we affirm the District Court's construction of "immediate family" under subsection (2)(a), we offer no view on the substantive scope of the "presence" requirements under §46(2).

Appellants claim that the "immediate family" requirement of §46(2)(a) is satisfied in this case, because "[t]he nieces and nephews were 'near relatives' or 'close associates' of Fr. Jenco." Appellants' Br. at 47. This, of course, is not the test enunciated in the Restatement. Rather, §46(2)(a) is perfectly plain in its reference to "immediate family." It does not refer to "family members," "near relatives," "close associates," or persons with whom the victim has "close emotional ties" - rather, it says, plainly, " immediate family." And there is no doubt whatsoever that, in this case, nieces and nephews are not "immediate family" members. Indeed, appellants do not dispute this point. Rather, they claim that §46(2)(a) should be construed liberally to afford "situational justice." Appellants' Br. at 46. As much as we sympathize with appellants' claims, we have no authority to stretch the law beyond its *clear bounds* to satisfy our sense of justice.

In addressing liability for intentional infliction of emotional distress, the Restatement took a progressive position, seeking to advance the common law of 1965. "Academics, rather than courts, were the prime movers in the development of the tort…" Daniel Givelber, *The Right to Minimum Social Decency and the Limits of Evenhandedness: Intentional Infliction of Emotional Distress by Outrageous Conduct*, 82 COLUM. L.REV. 42, 42 (1982); *see also* Annotation, *Modern Status of Intentional Infliction of Mental Distress as Independent Tort*; "Outrage", 38 A.L.R.4th 998 §2, 1985 WL 287349 (1985) ("Recognition of the tort by the drafters of the Restatement stimulated its recognition by the courts, the elements of the tort as described in the Restatement being widely accepted and quoted."). The caveat to §46 says that "[t]he Institute expresses no opinion as to whether there may not be other circumstances under which [an] actor may be subject to liability for the intentional infliction or reckless infliction of emotional distress." RESTATEMENT (SECOND) OF TORTS §46, caveat. And the Comment to §46 observes that the law of intentional infliction of emotional distress is "still in a stage of development, and the ultimate limits of this tort are not yet determined." RESTATEMENT (SECOND) OF TORTS §46, cmt. c. However, although the common law today has largely caught up with the Restatement, Br. of *Amicus Curiae* at 21, no cases in any federal or state court go *beyond* the Restatement to define "immediate family" as including nieces and nephews.

The brief of *Amicus Curiae* furnishes an extraordinary survey of the common law of intentional infliction of emotional distress, with a chart showing the law in every state in which the tort has been elucidated. On the basis of this survey, *Amicus Curiae* concludes, correctly, that there is *no case* that has permitted nieces or nephews to recover for third-party intentional infliction of emotional distress. Br. of *Amicus Curiae* at 47. *See also* "Amended Survey of State Law Relating to Recovery for Intentional Infliction of Emotional Distress (Sometimes Called 'The Tort of Outrage')," Br. of *Amicus Curiae* at Addendum. Appellants' counsel conceded at oral argument that, so far as he knew, *no cases* include nieces and nephews in the definition of "immediate family" for the purpose of intentional infliction of emotional distress. Indeed, counsel conceded in oral argument that he was unaware of any cases in any context holding that nieces and nephews come within the well-understood concept of "immediate family."

We reject appellants' suggestion that the commentary to §46 alters the common law definition of "immediate family." Restatement §46, cmt. l, in addressing "[c]onduct directed at a third person," says that "the decided cases in which recovery has been allowed have been those in which the plaintiffs have been near relatives, or at least close associates, of the person attacked." Appellants argue that this "makes it clear that the 'immediate family' requirement was not intended to bar recovery of those who fall outside the definition of that term." Appellants' Br. at 47. None of the examples in the commentary support this claim. Rather, as noted by *Amicus Curiae*,

[f]ollowing the reference to "near relatives" or "close associates," the commentary explains that "there appears to be no essential reason why a stranger who is asked for a match on the street should not recover when the man who asks for it is shot down before his eyes, at least where his emotional distress results in bodily harm."…Although no immediate family relationship exists in the example, the stranger is present during the extreme and outrageous conduct and suffers bodily injury from his emotional distress. Because the nieces "do not contend that they suffered bodily harm" (Appellants' Br. at 27 n.1), the commentary to section 46 does not assist them. At most, the commentary suggests that when the plaintiff is present and suffers bodily injury from the severe emotional distress, individuals not within the immediate family may recover damages. Indeed the commentary merely provides a gloss on section 46(2)(b), which permits recovery "to any other person who is present at the time, if such distress results in bodily harm." Restatement §46(2)(b).

Br. of *Amicus Curiae* at 43-44.

Furthermore, and more importantly, appellants concede that they cannot find a single case supporting their interpretation of "immediate family." In a few limited circumstances, some courts have allowed relatives who either *resided in the same household* with the victim or were *legal guardians* to recover for negligent infliction of emotional distress. See, e.g., *Sullivan v. Ford Motor Co.*, No. 97-CIV-0593, 2000 WL 343777 (S.D.N.Y. Mar. 31, 2000); *Garcia v. San Antonio Housing Auth.*, 859 S.W.2d 78, 81 (Tex. Ct.App.1993); *Kriventsov v. San Rafael Taxicabs, Inc.*, 186 Cal.App.3d 1445, 229 Cal.Rptr. 768 (1986). And, recently, the District Court allowed recovery for intentional infliction of emotional distress to a woman who, although not legally married to the victim, had lived with him for over 20 years in a "bond that was the functional equivalent of marriage." See *Surette v. Islamic Republic of Iran*, 231 F.Supp.2d 260 (D.D.C.2002). In these cases, the parties in issue were members of the victim's household, and they were viewed as the functional equivalents of immediate family members. In this case, however, appellants merely claim that the nieces and nephews enjoyed a close relationship with Fr. Jenco, which is far short of what §46(2)(a) requires.

To define "immediate family" to embrace nieces and nephews who do not live in the immediate household or have any legal obligation to the victim would stretch the term too far. There is a commonly understood meaning of the term, as reflected in State and common law. Appellants have not pointed to any other source of guidance to which a federal court could properly look in interpreting the FSIA. In seeking to recover, appellants would transform the apparently settled meaning of the Restatement in a manner that would brook few limits, as the nieces and nephews are 22 in number, live in different States, and while suffering emotionally do not claim any further relationship to the victim. Indeed, such expanded recovery in this case might also reduce the fund of Iranian assets accessible in this country to plaintiffs who are more closely related to victims of other cases of Iranian terrorism.

It is not within our authority to extend liability for intentional infliction of emotional distress beyond what has been allowed by the common law or authorized by the statute. To choose to include nieces and nephews within the definition of "immediate family" over, for example, close friends who may be even more egregiously affected by state-sponsored terrorism, seems to us to be well beyond our appropriate role as judges on the federal bench. First, appellants' claims are, at bottom, *statutory* in nature, founded on the FSIA and the Flatow Amendment. We are obliged, therefore, to apply the statute as written. As noted above, the FSIA provides that a "foreign state shall be liable in the same manner and to the same extent as a private individual under like circumstances." 28 U.S.C. §1606. Therefore, we have no free-wheeling commission to construct common law as we see fit. Rather, we are bound to look to state law in an effort to fathom the "like circumstances" to which 28 U.S.C. §1606 refers. The statute instructs us to find the law, not to make it. And, as we have shown, appellants can find no support for their claims in the established common law. Second, the correct substantive foundation for appellants' claims is §46(2)(a), which, as we have shown, furnishes the basis for much of the state common law. What is most significant here is that §46(2)(a) is clear in its terms, at least insofar as the "immediate family" requirement is concerned.

We are mindful that state-sponsored terrorist groups such as Hizbollah transgress all bounds of human decency through the physical and psychological torture of their hostages. However, this fact is not a license for judges to legislate from the bench. Assuming, *arguendo*, that appropriate parties may pursue a cause of action against a foreign state like Iran under the Flatow Amendment, and assuming further that the prevailing common law continues to mirror the requirements of §46(2)(a), relief in cases of this sort will be limited to "immediate family" members. As the law now stands, the nieces and nephews of a victim have no viable basis for a third-party claim of intentional infliction of emotional distress under the statute.

III. CONCLUSION

The nieces and nephews are not direct victims under §46(1), and they are not "immediate family" members under §46(2). Therefore, we affirm the judgment of the District Court rejecting appellants' claims for recovery based on intentional infliction of emotional distress.

Notes:

1.   Why did the court simply rely on the plaintiffs' *legal* relationship to Father Jenco and not look at the *substance* of their relationship? Wouldn't the objectives of the statute be fulfilled by awarding damages to a niece who was raised by an uncle murdered in a terrorist attack? If Father Jenco's nieces and nephews had been very close to him, weren't they "presumed" to have suffered as a result of his kidnapping and thus the intended targets of the terrorists?

2.   Is the following statement consistent with the purpose of the terrorism amendments to the FSIA, "If any person that Iran hoped to distress by holding and torturing Fr. Jenco could recover under section 46(1) as a direct victim of Iran's' conduct, virtually anyone claiming he or she was affected could recover." Isn't tort law intended to make whole *all* targets of the bad act? What if the intended target was "all Americans" or "all Jews" or "all infidels"? How does this analysis compare to other areas of the law where the courts are confronted with similar issues, i.e. public nuisance cases, widespread consumer fraud, mass tort litigation?

3.   Is the court's "immediate family" analysis consistent with the status and nature of the modern American family? In *Flatow*, the court noted there was a "presumption" in favor of family members, "Spouses and relatives in direct lineal relationships are presumed to suffer damages for mental anguish. The testimony of sisters or brothers is ordinarily sufficient to sustain their claims for solatium." *Flatow v. Islamic Republic of Iran*, 999 F.Supp. 1, 30 (D.D.C. 1998).

What about homosexual couples, cohabitating unmarrieds or absentee parents?

4. Why should there be a legal barrier to considering the true *nature* of the relationship? In *Knox v. Palestinian Authority*, 442 F.Supp.2d 62 (S.D.N.Y. 2006) the court awarded damages to the stepchildren of an American murdered by terrorists. The court noted that decisions involving other federal statutes looked deeper than the legal relationship. It specifically followed a ruling under the federal Death on the High Seas Act, in which

> The court looked at the following factors in making its determination: "the relationship of parent to child, continuous living together, harmonious family relationships, and participation of the deceased in family services and his disposition and habit to tender aid, solace and comfort when required."

Id. at 76. Also in *Smith v. Islamic Emirate of Afghanistan*, 262 F.Supp.2d 217, 236 (S.D.N.Y. 2003) the court upheld the claim of a grandmother,

> On these facts, the Court has no reservation about concluding that George's paternal grandmother Marion Thomas is entitled to loss-of-solatium damages. Although plaintiffs have not cited any precedent where a grandparent has been awarded these damages, it is clear that she was George's surrogate mother since 1973 and that they developed an extremely close bond.

Despite this holding, the *Smith* court excluded siblings while acknowledging "the profound effect of George's death on their lives" because "the evidence does not establish a "close emotional relationship." *Id.* at 237.

5. In light of *Knox* and *Smith*, is the *Jenco* court's "immediate family" analysis convincing? Does a priest have an immediate family? If not, does this analysis provide an incentive to terrorists to target certain classes of potential victims?

6. Why did the court choose not to follow *Surette v. Islamic Republic of Iran*, 231 F.Supp.2d 260 (D.D.C. 2002), in which a companion was found to be a proper plaintiff? There the court noted,

> Although the Court is not aware of any case brought under the FSIA in which a court has awarded so-

latium damages to a victim's partner to whom he or she is not legally married, the Court nonetheless concludes that such an award is appropriate in this case. This result is justified by the nature and closeness of the relationship between Beverly Surette and William Buckley for over twenty years, a bond that was the functional equivalent of a legal marriage. The strength of their "close emotional relationship," *Flatow v. Islamic Republic of Iran*, 999 F.Supp. at 30, was recognized by Buckley's family, his colleagues and his employer, and it merits recognition by this Court. For these reasons, the Court will treat Ms. Surette as if she were the legal spouse of William Buckley.

Id. at 270.

7. One court described the intended targets of terrorism as encompassing a large universe:

> Courts have uniformly held that a terrorist attack-by its nature-is directed not only at the victims but also at the victims' families. See *Burnett v. Al Baraka Inv. and Dev. Corp.*, 274 F.Supp.2d 86, 107 (D.D.C.2003) ("A terrorist attack on civilians is of course intended to cause emotional distress to the victims' families."); *Jenco v. Islamic Republic of Iran*, 154 F.Supp.2d 27, 35 (D.D.C.2001) (" 'If the defendants' conduct is sufficiently outrageous and intended to inflict severe emotional harm upon a person which is not present, no essential reason of logic or policy prevents liability.' "). In this case, the evidence demonstrates that defendant's campaign of attacks against Westerners was intended not only to harm the victims, but to instill terror in their loved ones and others in the United States. See *Dammarell*, 281 F.Supp.2d at 109-113.

Salazar v. Islamic Republic of Iran, 370 F.Supp.2d 105, 115 (D.D.C. 2005). If so, why is the class of plaintiffs limited in terrorism suits? If terrorists always seem to "target" a large distant audience, why is the class of plaintiffs so narrow?

8. Generally, the courts have continued to follow *Bettis* and limit the class of plaintiffs in §1605(a)(7) cases. For instance, in *Oveissi v. Islamic Republic of Iran*, 498 F.Supp.2d 268 (D.D.C. 2007) a grandchild was found not to have a cause of action despite an "exceptionally close relationship" with his murdered grandfather.

9.   On the other hand, in *Anderson v. Islamic Republic of Iran*, 90 F.Supp.2d 107 (D.D.C. 2000) the court awarded damages to a child who was born during her father's captivity.

10.   Why are these issues of paramount concern in terrorism cases? Why have plaintiffs sought so aggressively to expand the class of plaintiffs?

9.3 Non-Americans

Biton v. Palestinian Interim Self-Government Authority, 310 F.Supp.2d 172 (D. D.C. 2004).

COLLYER, District Judge.

Avigail Lewis Biton, individually and on behalf of her husband's estate and her children, and Rachel Asraf bring suit under the Antiterrorism Act of 1991 ("ATA"), 18 U.S.C. §2333, and various tort theories against the Palestinian Interim Self-Government Authority, also known as the Palestinian Authority or the Palestinian National Authority ("PA"); the Palestine Liberation Organization ("PLO"); Yasser Arafat, president of the PA and chairman of the PLO; two senior members of the Palestinian Preventive Security Service ("PPSS"); two members of the Palestinian Police Service ("PPS"); and 99 "John Does" for their alleged involvement in the bombing of a school bus in the Gaza Strip on November 20, 2000, that killed two passengers (including Gabriel Biton, husband to Ms. Biton and the father of her children) and wounded nine others (including Ms. Asraf). Pending before the Court is the defendants' motion to dismiss pursuant to Rules 12(b)(1), (b)(2), and (b)(6) of the Federal Rules of Civil Procedure. The defendants assert a lack of personal jurisdiction over the five named individual defendants and the PA; immunity as a sovereign state and a lack of subject matter jurisdiction under the ATA; a lack of subject matter jurisdiction for the Biton family's claims under the ATA and state law; and non-justiciability. The defendants also remark that the conduct in question might be deemed an "act of war" not subject to the ATA, and that Palestinian resistance and self-defense against Israel do not constitute terrorism. The plaintiffs, not surprisingly, oppose dismissal on these grounds.

After a full consideration of the parties' briefs, the entire record, and applicable law, the Court finds that it lacks personal jurisdiction over the named individual defendants but that it may exercise jurisdiction over the PA and PLO. The named individual defendants therefore will be dismissed. The remainder of the motion to dismiss will be denied.

I. BACKGROUND

For purposes of ruling on the instant motion to dismiss, the underlying facts of this case may be simply stated: at approximately 7:30 a.m. on November 20, 2000, a roadside device exploded near a bus that was transporting elementary school children and their teachers from Kfar Darom, an Israeli settlement in the southern Gaza Strip, towards Gush Katif. [FN1] The plaintiffs contend that the defendants are responsible for this bombing and the resulting deaths and injuries. [FN2] At issue now is the jurisdiction of the Court to hear and decide this case. On this preliminary issue, the plaintiffs' respective causes of action and the parties' relationships to the United States are critical.

FN1. These facts are not in genuine dispute at this stage of the litigation, although the defendants point to a lack of evidence that U.S. citizens were the target of the bombing.

FN2. The roadside bombing of the school bus that took Mr. Biton's life and injured Ms. Asraf is believed by some to have been part of the "al-Aqsa Intifada," a series of violent demonstrations and clashes between Palestinians and Israeli Defense Forces that ensued following (now Israeli Prime Minister) Ariel Sharon's controversial visit to the Temple Mount/Haram al-Sharif in Jerusalem in September 2000. *See* Defs.' Mot. to Dismiss Exh. 1.

Plaintiff Avigail Lewis Biton is an American citizen, the widow of Gabriel Biton, and the mother of the Biton children. She sues in her individual capacity under the ATA, which established a federal cause of action for damages resulting from terrorist attacks in foreign countries. Specifically, that statute provides:

Any national of the United States injured in his or her person, property, or business by reason of an act of international terrorism, or his or her estate, survivors, or heirs, may sue therefor in any appropriate district court of the United States and shall recover threefold the damages he or she sustains and the cost of the suit, including attorney's fees. [FN3]

FN3. The ATA defines "international terrorism" as:

activities that-(A) involve violent acts or acts dangerous to human life that are a violation of the criminal laws of the United States or of any State, or that would be a criminal violation if committed within the jurisdiction of the United States or of any State; (B) appear to be intended-(i) to intimidate or coerce a civilian population; (ii) to influence the policy of a government by intimidation or coercion; or (iii) to affect the conduct of a government by mass destruction, assassination, or kidnapping; and (C) occur primarily outside the territorial jurisdiction of the United States, or transcend national boundaries in terms of the means by which they are accomplished, the persons they appear intended to intimidate or coerce, or the locale in which their perpetrators operate or seek asylum[.]

18 U.S.C. §2331(1).

18 U.S.C. §2333(a). Ms. Biton and her children sue for wrongful death, negligence, intentional and negligent infliction of emotional distress, and battery under federal common law. The amended complaint does not allege that any Biton family member, save for Ms. Biton, is or was an American citizen. Plaintiff Rachel Asraf is an American citizen who sues for herself under the ATA and for negligence, intentional and negligent infliction of emotional distress, battery, and assault.

The defendants are the PA, the PLO, and Yasser Arafat (collectively "the Palestinian leadership"); three senior Palestinian officials, Muhammed Dahlan, allegedly the commander in charge of the PPSS, Rashid Abu Shabak, allegedly the deputy commander of the PPSS, and Ghazi Jabali, allegedly the regional commander in the Gaza Strip of the PPS; Muhammed Eid Abdel Kadar Issa, allegedly a member of the PPS and an agent of the "Fatah" faction of the PLO, as well as the "Tanzim" terrorist unit; and John Does 1-99, who allegedly planned and carried out the bombing with the other defendants. None of the named individual defendants is alleged to have any presence, asset, or activity in the United States, except for President Arafat's occasional visits to the United Nations in New York City. The defendants assert that the PA also "is not present in the U.S." Defs.' Mot. to Dismiss at 7.

II. LEGAL STANDARDS

Under Rule 12(b)(1) of the Federal Rules of Civil Procedure, the plaintiffs bear the burden of proving by a preponderance of the evidence that the Court has subject matter jurisdiction to hear this case. *Jones v. Exec. Office of the President*, 167 F.Supp.2d 10, 13 (D.D.C.2001). In deciding such a motion, the Court must accept as true all of the factual allegations set forth in the amended complaint; however, such allegations " 'will bear closer scrutiny in resolving a 12(b)(1) motion' than in resolving a 12(b)(6) motion for failure to state a claim." *Grand Lodge of the Fraternal Order of Police v. Ashcroft*, 185 F.Supp.2d 9, 13-14 (D.D.C.2001) (quoting

5A CHARLES ALAN WRIGHT & ARTHUR R. MILLER, FEDERAL PRACTICE & PROCEDURE §1350). The Court may consider matters outside the pleadings. *Lipsman v. Sec'y of the Army*, 257 F.Supp.2d 3, 6 (D.D.C.2003).

To thwart dismissal under Rule 12(b)(2) of the Federal Rules of Civil Procedure, the plaintiffs must establish personal jurisdiction over each defendant. To this end, the Court may look outside the allegations of the amended complaint. *Helmer v. Doletskaya*, 290 F.Supp.2d 61, 65 (D.D.C.2003). "[T]he Court must accept Plaintiff[s'] claims as true in ruling on a Rule 12(b)(2) motion, unless they are directly contradicted by an affidavit…" *Novak-Canzeri v. Turki Bin Abdul Aziz Al Saud*, 864 F.Supp. 203, 206 (D.D.C.1994).

A motion to dismiss for failure to state a claim under Rule 12(b)(6) of the Federal Rules of Civil Procedure tests the legal sufficiency of the amended complaint. The Court must accept as true all of the plaintiffs' well-pled factual allegations and draw all reasonable inferences in favor of the plaintiff; however, the Court does not need to accept as true any of the plaintiffs' legal conclusions. *Alexis v. District of Columbia*, 44 F.Supp.2d 331, 336-37 (D.D.C.1999). "[An amended] complaint should not be dismissed for failure to state a claim unless it appears beyond doubt that the plaintiff[s] can prove no set of facts in support of [their] claim which would entitle [them] to relief." *Conley v. Gibson*, 355 U.S. 41, 45-46, 78 S.Ct. 99, 2 L.Ed.2d 80 (1957).

III. ANALYSIS

A. Personal Jurisdiction Over the Named Individual Defendants

The defendants begin their motion to dismiss by arguing that the Court may not exercise personal jurisdiction over the five named individual defendants, President Arafat and Messrs. Dahlan, Abu Shabak, Jabali, and Issa. As far as the record reveals, these defendants have no personal connection with the United States. Indeed, the plaintiffs acknowledge that "none of the individual defendants is a resident of the United States or has any commercial or other activities within the United States." Pls.' Opp. to Mot. to Dismiss at 49. The plaintiffs nonetheless assert that the named individual defendants have sufficient contacts with the United States for purposes of establishing personal jurisdiction, in conjunction with proper service of process, under Rule 4(k)(2) of the Federal Rules of Civil Procedure.

Rule 4(k)(2) states:

If the exercise of jurisdiction is consistent with the Constitution and laws of the United States, serving a summons or filing a waiver of service is also effective, with respect to claims arising under federal law, to establish personal jurisdiction over the person of any defendant who is not subject to the jurisdiction of the courts of general jurisdiction of any state.

FED. R. CIV. P. 4(k)(2). The Rule therefore "allows a district court to acquire jurisdiction over a foreign defendant which has insufficient contacts with any single state but has 'contacts with the United States as a whole...' " *In re Vitamins Antitrust Litig.*, 94 F.Supp.2d 26, 31 (D.D.C.2000) (citing Advisory Comm. Note to 1993 Amendment). In *United States v. Swiss American Bank, Ltd.*, 191 F.3d 30 (1st Cir.1999), the First Circuit discussed the parameters of this procedural device.

The rule's fabric contains three strands: (1) the plaintiff's claim must be one arising under federal law; (2) the putative defendant must be beyond the jurisdictional reach of any state court of general jurisdiction; and (3) the federal courts' exercise of personal jurisdiction over the defendant must not offend the Constitution or other federal law.

Id. at 38. In applying this tripartite test here, the question is whether the named individual defendants have sufficient contacts with the United States to satisfy the Due Process Clause of the Fifth Amendment to the U.S. Constitution. [FN4]

FN4. The plaintiffs state that they "have initiated service of process on the defendants pursuant to Fed.R.Civ.P. 4(f)(1) and 4(h)(2) and the provisions of the Hague Convention, and expect that it will be completed during the pendency of this motion." Pls.' Opp. to Mot. to Dismiss at 47.
The plaintiffs urge the Court to adopt "a due process analysis specifically fitted to the unique circumstances of civil actions against foreign terrorists and their sponsors" that has been applied by a fellow district judge of this Court, as well as a district judge on the United States District Court for the Eastern District of New York. Pl.'s Opp. to Mot. to Dismiss at 49. In a case involving the Antiterrorism and Effective Death Penalty Act of 1996 ("AEDPA"), 28 U.S.C. §1605(a)(7)-which amended the Foreign Sovereign Immunities Act ("FSIA"), 28 U.S.C. §1602, to permit lawsuits against state sponsors of terrorism-Judge Royce C. Lamberth of this Court concluded that "a foreign state that

causes the death of a United States national through an act of state-sponsored terrorism has the requisite 'minimum contacts' with the United States so as not to offend 'traditional notions of fair play and substantial justice.' " *Eisenfeld v. Islamic Republic of Iran*, 172 F.Supp.2d 1, 7 (D.D.C.2000) (quoting *International Shoe Co. v. Washington*, 326 U.S. 310, 326, 66 S.Ct. 154, 90 L.Ed. 95 (1945)); see also *Flatow v. Islamic Republic of Iran*, 999 F.Supp. 1, 22 (D.D.C.1998) (same). Judge Thomas C. Platt made a similar ruling in *Rein v. Socialist People's Libyan Arab Jamahiriya*, 995 F.Supp. 325 (E.D.N.Y.1998), *aff'd in part and appeal dismissed in part*, 162 F.3d 748 (2d Cir.1998), which also dealt with the 1996 amendment to the FSIA. Judge Platt stated that "the relevant inquiry with respect to the minimum contacts analysis is whether the effects of a foreign state's actions upon the United States are sufficient to provide 'fair warning' such that the foreign state may be subject to the jurisdiction of the courts of the United States." *Id.* at 330. In finding that Libya could stand trial for the 1988 bombing of Pan Am Flight 103 in Lockerbie, Scotland, Judge Platt held:

Any foreign state would know that the United States has substantial interests in protecting its flag carriers and its nationals from terrorist activities and should reasonably expect that if these interests were harmed, it would be subject to a variety of potential responses, including civil actions in United States courts.

Id.

There is some merit, in early 2004, to the plaintiffs' argument that no foreign terrorist today can fairly assert a lack of "fair warning" that it could be "haled into court" in the United States, *Burger King Corp. v. Rudzewicz*, 471 U.S. 462, 472, 105 S.Ct. 2174, 85 L.Ed.2d 528 (1985); *World-Wide Volkswagen Corp. v. Woodson*, 444 U.S. 286, 297, 100 S.Ct. 559, 62 L.Ed.2d 490 (1980), particularly given the exhaustive antiterrorism policies and other measures implemented by the United States Government following the terrorist attacks on September 11, 2001. However, the differences between the ATA and the FSIA are too great for their common focus on antiterrorism to allow cross-pollination on this issue. The Court consequently declines to extend the due process analysis set forth in *Eisenfeld/Flatow* and *Rein* to ATA claims filed against individual (non-state) defendants. [FN5]

FN5. This Court is not alone in employing a traditional due process analysis to determine whether it may exercise personal jurisdiction over individual defendants in a lawsuit brought under the ATA. In *Ungar v. Palestinian Author-ity*, 153 F.Supp.2d 76 (D.R.I.2001), a district judge on the United States District Court for the District of Rhode Island considered this same issue-with similar arguments in support and in opposition-and dismissed ATA claims against individual officers of various PA/PLO law enforcement and intelligence agencies.

There is one very simple reason why a district court may exercise personal jurisdiction over a foreign state defendant under the FSIA but not a similarly-situated individual defendant under the ATA. Section 1330(b) of the FSIA provides that "personal jurisdiction over a foreign state shall exist as to every claim for relief over which the district courts have jurisdiction…where service has been made under section 1608 of this title." 28 U.S.C. §1330(b); see also *Practical Concepts, Inc. v. Republic of Bolivia*, 811 F.2d 1543, 1548 n. 11 (D.C.Cir.1987) ("[U]nder the FSIA, 'subject matter jurisdiction plus service of process equals personal jurisdiction.' ") (quoting *Texas Trading & Milling Corp. v. Fed. Republic of Nigeria*, 647 F.2d 300, 308 (2d Cir.1981)). The ATA, in contrast, does not contain such an explicit grant of personal jurisdiction. See *Ungar v. Palestinian Auth.*, 153 F.Supp.2d 76, 95 (D.R.I.2001) (noting that §2334(a) provides for venue and nationwide service of process). Of course, a statute cannot confer personal jurisdiction when the U.S. Constitution forbids it. *Gilson v. Republic of Ireland*, 682 F.2d 1022, 1028 (D.C.Cir.1982). The D.C. Circuit held in *Price v. Socialist People's Libyan Arab Jamahiriya* that "foreign states are not 'persons' protected by the Fifth Amendment[.]" 294 F.3d 82, 96 (D.C.Cir.2002). Therefore, so long as subject matter jurisdiction exists under the FSIA and service was proper, there is no "need to examine whether [a foreign state defendant] has the minimum contacts that would otherwise be a prerequisite for personal jurisdiction under the Due Process Clause of the Fifth Amendment." *I.T. Consultants, Inc. v. Islamic Republic of Pakistan*, 351 F.3d 1184, 1191 (D.C.Cir.2003).

Unless the named individual defendants have minimum contacts with the United States that square with the Due Process Clause, which they admittedly do not, the Court may not exercise personal jurisdiction over them under Rule 4(k)(2) of the Federal Rules of Civil Procedure. Accordingly, the named individual defendants will be dismissed from this case.

B. Personal Jurisdiction Over the Palestinian Authority

The defendants also move to dismiss the amended complaint against the PA for lack of personal jurisdiction. [FN6] Un-like the named individual defendants, the PA appears to have sufficient contacts with the United States to satisfy due process concerns. See *Ungar*, 153 F.Supp.2d at 88 (holding that the plaintiffs in that case had "made a prima facie showing that defendants PA and PLO have minimum contacts with the United States as a whole."). The plaintiffs assert that the PA maintains offices and agents, including Hasan Abdel Rahman, in the United States. [FN7] In support, they submit an article from the National News stating that Mr. Abdel Rahman "has been the Washington representative of the Palestine Liberation Organization and Palestinian National Authority since 1994"; a transcript from an online discussion forum hosted by the Washington Post introducing Mr. Abdel Rahman as "chief representative of the Palestinian National Authority and Palestine Liberation Organization, [*sic*] in the United States"; and a biography purportedly received from the PA/PLO describing Mr. Abdel Rahman as "Chief Representative of the P.L.O. and the P.N.A. in the United States [.]" Pls.' Opp. to Mot. to Dismiss Exhs. 6, 7, 4. The plaintiffs further argue that the PA conducts extensive activities in the United States. For example, the PA has employed the lobbying firm of Bannerman & Associates to provide advocacy training and assistance with developing a public relations campaign in the United States. See *id.* Exhs. 5, 9, 10. The PA (and PLO) also entered into a commercial telecommunications contract with International Technologies Integration, Inc. ("ITI"), a Virginia corporation. See *Int'l Techs. Integration, Inc. v. Palestine Liberation Org.*, 66 F.Supp.2d 3 (D.D.C.1999). A lawsuit brought by ITI to confirm an arbitration award "revealed that the PA and the PLO maintain several bank accounts in New York with deposits totaling approximately $18 million [ ]." *Ungar*, 153 F.Supp.2d at 88; *see also* Pls.' Opp. to Mot. to Dismiss Exh. 11.

FN6. The defendants do not challenge the Court's exercise of personal jurisdiction over the PLO.

FN7. The plaintiffs filed a "return of service" affidavit indicating that Mr. Abdel Rahman was served on March 14, 2001, in Washington, D.C. With no evidence or argument to the contrary-the defendants merely state that "[s]ervice on the PA which is not present in the United States is challenged" without explaining why, Defs.' Mot. to Dismiss at 7-the Court finds that Mr. Abdel Rahman is a "managing or general agent" of the PA for purposes of Rule 4(h) of the Federal Rules of Civil Procedure. See *infra* pp. 179-80.

For these reasons, the Court concludes that it may exercise personal jurisdiction over the PA. The plaintiffs have adequately shown that the PA has minimum contacts with the United States under the Fifth Amendment and, in any event, that Mr. Abdel Rahman was personally served with process in Washington, D.C. The motion to dismiss the PA for lack of personal jurisdiction therefore will be denied.

C. Palestinian Statehood

Citing §2337(2) of the ATA and §1604 of the FSIA, the defendants move to dismiss this action on the grounds that Palestine is a sovereign entity. Section 2337(2) prohibits the maintenance of a civil ATA lawsuit against "a foreign state, an agency of a foreign state, or an officer or employee of a foreign state or an agency thereof acting within his or her official capacity or under color of legal authority." 18 U.S.C. §2337(2). The FSIA directs that, with exceptions, "a foreign state shall be immune from the jurisdiction of the courts of the United States and of the States…" 28 U.S.C. §1604; see also *Argentine Republic v. Amerada Hess Shipping Corp.,* 488 U.S. 428, 443, 109 S.Ct. 683, 102 L.Ed.2d 818 (1989) ("[T]he FSIA provides the sole basis for obtaining jurisdiction over a foreign state in the courts of this country[.]").

The defendants contend that Palestine is a "foreign state" under the definition set forth in the Restatement (Third) of the Foreign Relations Law of the United States ("Restatement"). [FN8] Section 201 of the Restatement provides: "Under international law, a state is an entity that has a defined territory and a permanent population, under the control of its own government, and that engages in, or has the capacity to engage in, formal relations with other such entities." Despite the obvious magnitude and controversial nature of this issue, the defendants do not offer or cite any evidence in support of their bid for recognition of Palestinian statehood. *See* Pls.' Opp. to Mot. to Dismiss at 17-18. They simply argue:

FN8. The Second Circuit employs the Restatement's definition of the term "state" when interpreting the FSIA. See *Klinghoffer v. S.N.C. Achille Lauro,* 937 F.2d 44, 47 (2d Cir.1991) (holding that the PLO is not a "state" with immunity).

The State of Palestine has a defined territory in the West Bank, and the Gaza Strip and East Jerusalem, a permanent population numbering in the millions under the control of its own government and engages in and has the capacity to engage in foreign relations with other states.

Palestine issued a declaration of its independence on November 15, 1988 that has at all times thereafter been extant. November 15 is annually celebrated by Palestinians throughout the state and world as independence day.

Statehood is not dependent on recognition.

The mid-east peace process carried forward by the Oslo Accord and other diplomatic measures and means envisions full recognition of Palestinian statehood…The recently expressed willingness of the United States to recognize Palestinian statehood confirms that the definition's criteria are satisfied. The reasons recently given by President Bush and other U.S. Executive Branch officers for delay in expressing recognition signify no doubt that Palestine meets the definitional criteria for statehood, but rather seek to induce adherence to U.S. foreign policies unrelated to the criteria.

Defs.' Mot. to Dismiss at 9-10.

The long-running conflict between the Israelis and the Palestinians has its very origins in the question of statehood between them. The current record does not permit the Court to overlook this reality or to declare that Palestine is now a sovereign state among nations. As a result, the Court must conclude that neither §2337(2) of the ATA nor §1604 of the FSIA bars this lawsuit. See *Tel-Oren v. Libyan Arab Republic,* 726 F.2d 774, 804 (D.C.Cir.1984) (Bork, C.J., concurring) (expressing the view that neither the PLO, the Palestine Information Office, nor the National Association of Arab Americans "seem[s] to be a state under international law"); *Knox v. Palestine Liberation Org.,* No. 03-4466, 306 F.Supp.2d 424, ----, 2004 WL 385024, *5, 2004 U.S. Dist. LEXIS 3128, at *16 (S.D.N.Y. Mar. 2, 2004) (holding that "there does not exist a state of Palestine which meets the legal criteria for statehood…").

D. Stating a Claim under the ATA and Supplemental Jurisdiction

The defendants assert that Avigail Lewis Biton "has no claim under Sec. 2333(a)…because she was not on the bus and was not injured in her 'person, property or business by an act of international terrorism.'" [FN9] Defs.' Mot. to Dismiss at 14. The plaintiffs respond that Ms. Biton's injury is the death of Gabriel Biton, her spouse. This allegedly has caused her to suffer emotional distress, a loss of consortium, and a loss of solatium.

FN9. As the plaintiffs' note, §2333(a) actually states that "[a]ny national of the United States injured in his or her person, property, or business *by reason of* an act of international terrorism, *or his or her estate, survivors, or heirs,* may sue therefor…" 18 U.S.C. §2333(a) (emphasis added).

It is clear that Ms. Biton cannot recover under the ATA as a representative of Mr. Biton's estate or as his survivor, because he was not a U.S. national. If Ms. Biton sues as the principal victim herself, however, she may be able to state a claim if she can allege a cognizable injury that arose by reason of an act of international terrorism. 18 U.S.C. §2333(a). The amended complaint avers that Ms. Biton is "an American citizen" and that her husband's death resulted from "a bombing attack on an Israeli civilian vehicle traveling in the Gaza Strip." [FN10] 2nd Am. Compl. ¶¶ 4, 22. Accordingly, the pertinent issues here are (1) whether emotional distress, a loss of consortium, and a loss of solatium constitute injuries in Ms. Biton's "person, property, or business" and, if so, (2) whether the bombing reasonably could be considered the "cause" of her injuries. 18 U.S.C. §2333(a).

FN10. The Court accepts these facts as true when deciding this Rule 12(b)(6) motion.

The Court concludes that Ms. Biton has properly alleged an "injur[y] in...her person" for purposes of the ATA. *Id.* The statute does not specifically require that a plaintiff suffer *physical* harm prior to filing suit. Moreover, the term "personal injury" means "[a]ny invasion of a personal right, including mental suffering and false imprisonment." [FN11] BLACK'S LAW DICTIONARY (7th ed.1999). Ms. Biton's alleged injuries fall within this widely-accepted definition. The forced loss of "material services[,]...affection, companionship, sexual relations, and the customary amenities of married life" is ordinarily deleterious. *Curry v. Giant Food Co. of the District of Columbia*, 522 A.2d 1283, 1294 (D.C.1987) (defining consortium). Similarly, "mental anguish, emotional pain and suffering, [and] loss of society, companionship, comfort, protection, marital care, attention, advice or counsel" are harmful. *Brooks v. Bienkowski*, 150 Md.App. 87, 818 A.2d 1198, 1200 (2003) (defining solatium). These injuries are cognizable under the plain language, as well as a common-sense interpretation, of the ATA. Consider the following hypothetical scenario: during a terrorist attack in a foreign country, the perpetrators throw a grenade at a car that is owned by a U.S. national and being driven by her (foreign) husband. The car explodes and the driver is killed. It seems unlikely that Congress would have considered damage to a car to constitute an "injury" for purposes of the ATA but not emotional trauma and a loss of companionship from the death of a spouse occurring in the same attack. [FN12] Which would you rather lose, a car or a spouse?

FN11. The ATA "contains all of the elements of a traditional tort...and we must therefore look to tort law and the legisla-

tive history to determine [its scope]." *Boim v. Quranic Literary Inst.*, 291 F.3d 1000, 1010 (7th Cir.2002).
FN12. Under the defendants' interpretation of §2333(a), "Mrs. Biton could sue for the value of the cash in her husband['s] pockets that was incinerated by the bombing, but not for the harm caused to her by the actual death of her husband." Pls.' Opp. to Mot. to Dismiss at 64 n.54.

Ms. Biton also has properly alleged that the bus bombing was the legal cause of her injuries. The Seventh Circuit has interpreted the clause "by reason of" to require a showing of proximate cause. *Boim v. Quranic Literacy Inst.*, 291 F.3d 1000, 1011-12 (7th Cir.2002). "Foreseeability is the cornerstone of proximate cause, and in tort law, a defendant will be held liable only for those injuries that might have reasonably been anticipated as a natural consequence of the defendant's actions." *Id.* at 1012. In most instances, "the existence of proximate cause is a question of fact for the jury." *District of Columbia v. Freeman*, 477 A.2d 713, 716 (D.C.1984). Based on the allegations of the amended complaint, a reasonable jury could find that Ms. Biton's (non-physical) injuries were the foreseeable and natural result of the bombing that killed her husband.

Therefore, the Court finds that Ms. Biton, suing in her individual capacity, has properly stated a claim against the defendants under the ATA.

The defendants next assert that the Court lacks subject matter jurisdiction to hear the Biton family's tort claims. The Bitons predicate jurisdiction of these claims on "the rules of supplemental jurisdiction." 2nd Am. Compl. ¶ 2. The defendants contend that "[t]he Biton plaintiffs have no colorable claim whatsoever under sec. 2333(a) or any other provision of law within this Court's original jurisdiction that could serve as the basis for this Court's exercise of supplemental jurisdiction over the *Biton* pendent claims and the *Biton* children as pendent parties." Defs.' Mot. to Dismiss at 14. Given the defendants' incorrect assumption that none of the plaintiffs has a "colorable claim" under the ATA, see *supra* pp. 13-15, this argument fails.

Section 1367(a) of Title 28 of the United States Code extends to federal district courts supplemental jurisdiction over "claims that are so related to claims in the action within... original jurisdiction that they form part of the same case or controversy under Article III of the United States Constitution. Such supplemental jurisdiction shall include claims that involve the joinder or intervention of additional parties." 28 U.S.C. §1367(a). This provision embodies "the practice of 'pendent party' jurisdiction, allowing the joinder of a party even though there is no independent federal question jurisdiction over that party's claims." *Burnett v. Al Baraka Inv. & Dev. Corp.*, 274 F.Supp.2d 86, 98 (D.D.C.2003). In this case, Ms. Biton has advanced a federal cause of action under the ATA over which this Court has original jurisdiction. All of the plaintiffs' claims "derive from a common nucleus of operative fact"- *i.e.*, the bus bombing in the Gaza Strip. *United Mine Workers of Am. v. Gibbs*, 383 U.S. 715, 725, 86 S.Ct. 1130, 16 L.Ed.2d 218 (1966). The Court chooses to exercise its discretion to hear these related claims in the interests of "economy, convenience, fairness, and comity[.]" *Carnegie-Mellon Univ. v. Cohill*, 484 U.S. 343, 357, 108 S.Ct. 614, 98 L.Ed.2d 720 (1988). Thus, this portion of the motion to dismiss will be denied.

E. Justiciability

According to the defendants, the allegations in the amended complaint "amount to an all-out political attack upon the PA, the PLO, President Arafat, and senior Palestinian officials of such wide scope as to be nonjusticiable, raising issues that are not appropriate for or capable of judicial resolution." Defs.' Mot. to Dismiss at 15. The Supreme Court in *Baker v. Carr* established a framework for determining whether a lawsuit implicates a political question:

Prominent on the surface of any case held to involve a political question is found a textually demonstrable constitutional commitment of the issue to a coordinate political department; or a lack of judicially discoverable and manageable standards for resolving it; or the impossibility of deciding without an initial policy determination of a kind clearly for nonjudicial discretion; or the impossibility of a court's undertaking independent resolution without expressing lack of the respect due coordinate branches of government; or an unusual need for unquestioning adherence to a political decision already made; or the potentiality of embarrassment from multifarious pronouncements by various departments on one question.

369 U.S. 186, 217, 82 S.Ct. 691, 7 L.Ed.2d 663 (1962).

The defendants cite *Linder v. Portocarrero*, 963 F.2d 332 (11th Cir.1992), in support of their argument that "the high level of violence and antipathy during the months since September 2000 have created a situation" rendering the plaintiffs' claims non-justiciable. Defs.' Mot. to Dismiss at 15. In that case, Benjamin Linder, a mechanical engineer and U.S. citizen, went to Nicaragua to construct dams and hydro-

electric plants. In April 1987, he was allegedly tortured and killed by members of the Nicaraguan Democratic Force. Mr. Linder's family filed suit against the individuals allegedly involved and three anti-government military organizations. The District Court dismissed the case based in part on the political question doctrine. The Eleventh Circuit reversed as to the individual defendants but affirmed the dismissal of the defendant organizations on the grounds of non-justiciability. *Id.* at 337.

The District Court in *Linder* gave three reasons for applying the political question doctrine:

First, and perhaps most important, this court can discern no judicially manageable criteria by which to adjudicate the merits of the claim. Second, the real prospect that the parties would not be able to fully gather the data necessary to adjudicate this claim on the merits also points to a finding of non-justiciability. Finally, adjudication on the merits could readily lead to real interference with the conduct of foreign policy by the political branches of government.

Linder v. Portocarrero, 747 F.Supp. 1452, 1457 (S.D.Fla.1990). However, these reasons do not apply with the same force, if at all, to the case at hand. See *Ungar v. Palestinian Auth.*, 228 F.Supp.2d 40, 45 (D.R.I.2002) (distinguishing *Linder* from a fatal car attack in Israel allegedly committed by the terrorist group HAMAS). Adjudication of the complaint in *Linder* would have required the Florida District Court " 'to measure and carefully assess the use of the tools of violence and warfare in the midst of a *foreign civil war'*, and to inquire into 'the relationship between United States policy and the actions of the contras[.]' " *Linder*, 963 F.2d at 335 (quoting the District Court) (emphasis added). Conversely, there are judicially discoverable and manageable standards for deciding the Bitons' and Ms. Asraf's claims, namely the ATA. The ATA created a federal cause of action for acts of "international terrorism," a precisely-defined term. *See* 18 U.S.C. §2331(1). In conjunction with that statute, the "common law of tort provides clear and well-settled rules on which the district court can easily rely[.]" *Klinghoffer v. S.N.C. Achille Lauro*, 937 F.2d 44, 49 (2d Cir.1991). This lawsuit also does not present separation of powers concerns. But see *Tel-Oren v. Libyan Arab Republic*, 726 F.2d 774, 824-26 (D.C.Cir.1984) (Robb, S.C.J., concurring). By enacting the ATA, both the Executive and Legislature have "expressly endorsed the concept of suing terrorist organizations in federal court[.]" *Klinghoffer*, 937 F.2d at 49; *see also* Flatow Amendment, 28 U.S.C. §1605 note (providing a cause of action against an official, employee, or agent of a "state sponsor of terrorism" for personal injury or death "caused by an act of torture, extrajudicial killing, aircraft sabotage, hostage taking, or the provision of material support or resources…for such an act…") (quoting 28 U.S.C. §1605(a)(7)). In the aftermath of September 11, 2001-and even before that tragedy-President George W. Bush and members of Congress have, on numerous occasions, publicly announced multifaceted policies having the goal of condemning terrorist activities. *See, e.g.*, S.J. Res. 22, 107th Cong. (2001).

The Court disagrees with the defendants' characterization of the amended complaint as an "all-out political attack upon the Palestinian government and its officials[.]" Defs.' Mot. to Dismiss at 22. Although the backdrop for this case- *i.e.*, the Israeli-Palestinian conflict-is extremely politicized, this circumstance alone is insufficient to make the plaintiffs' claims non-justiciable. Indeed, "the fact that the issues… arise in a politically charged context does not convert what is essentially an ordinary tort suit into a non-justiciable political question." *Klinghoffer*, 937 F.2d at 49. The political question doctrine should be construed narrowly. For all of these reasons, the motion to dismiss on the grounds of non-justiciability will be denied.

F. Act of War/Self-Defense

Lastly, the defendants argue that "the explosion near Kfar Darom may well be shown to have been part of a conflict that makes it an act of war for purposes of sec. 2336." Defs.' Mot. to Dismiss at 24. The ATA bars a civil action for "injury or loss by reason of an act of war." 18 U.S.C. §2336(a). "[T]he term 'act of war' means any act occurring in the course of-(A) declared war; (B) armed conflict, whether or not war has been declared, between two or more nations; or (C) armed conflict between military forces of any origin [.]" *Id.* §2331(4). Given that the defendants concede that "[t]he facts cannot be determined on this motion[,]" Defs.' Mot. to Dismiss at 24, the Court takes this issue under advisement.

The defendants similarly assert that "[a]ctions by Palestinians in the occupied territories are not intended to intimidate or coerce Israeli civilians or their government…[but instead] to resist and overcome the oppression and end the occupation." *Id.* at 24-25. Whether the bus bombing "appear[ed] to be intended-(i) to intimidate or coerce a civilian population; (ii) to influence the policy of a government by intimidation or coercion; or (iii) to affect the conduct of a government by mass destruction, assassination, or kidnapping" is a disputed

question of material fact. 18 U.S.C. §2331(1) (part of the definition of the term "international terrorism"). On a motion to dismiss, the Court will not determine the defendants' intent in allegedly committing the bus bombing.

IV. CONCLUSION

The motion to dismiss will be granted in part and denied in part. The Court concludes that it may exercise personal jurisdiction over the PA and the PLO; that Palestine is not a "state" for purposes of the FSIA based on the current record; that Avigail Lewis Biton has properly stated a claim under the ATA; that supplemental jurisdiction exists over the Biton family's tort claims; and that this case does not present a non-justiciable political question. The Court also finds that it may not exercise personal jurisdiction over the named individual defendants; the amended complaint allegations against these defendants will be dismissed. Finally, the Court takes under advisement the defendants' act of war/ self-defense arguments. A separate order accompanies this memorandum opinion.

ORDER

For the reasons set forth in the memorandum opinion that accompanies this order, it is hereby

ORDERED that the motion to dismiss is GRANTED in part and DENIED in part. It is

FURTHER ORDERED that defendants Yasser Arafat, Muhammed Dahlan, Rashid Abu Shabak, Ghazi Jabali, and Muhammed Eid Abdel Kadar Issa are DISMISSED from this action due to a lack of personal jurisdiction.

SO ORDERED.

Notes:

1. *Biton* was the first ruling allowing claims of an American citizen for the loss of her non-American spouse. How does this holding comport with the purpose of the Klinghoffer Act?

2. How was Avigail Biton "injured in [] her person, property, or business?"

3. *Biton* was attacked on this point in *Linde v. Arab Bank, PLC*, 384 F.Supp.2d 571, 589 (E.D.N.Y. 2004):

Defendant argues that the *Biton* holding is inconsistent with the legislative history of the ATA, and cites the minutes from the Senate Anti-Terrorism Act Hearing and the House Committee report on the ATA. Def't's Reply Mem. at 19-20, citing ATA Hearing at 31 ("These tragedies reinforce our belief that it is essential that both the Congress and the Executive Branch take measures, such as the present bill, to deter terrorist attacks against American nationals overseas..."); H.R.REP. NO. 102-1040 at 4 ("Summary and Purpose: The purpose of H.R. 2222, the 'Antiterrorism Act of 1991' is to provide a new civil cause of action for international terrorist attacks against U.S. nationals.").

These general statements of purpose, not addressed to the issue here in dispute, offer little if any guidance. In the absence of any limiting language in the statute, the court will not limit the scope of Section 2333(a) to physical injuries to U.S. nationals. The congressional purpose was to grant a remedy to U.S. nationals and their families who suffered from injury to an individual or property as a result of international terrorism. The claims of the U.S. nationals suing based on their nonphysical injuries resulting from acts of international terrorism will not be dismissed.

4.   In *Morris v. Khadr*, 415 F.Supp.2d 1323, 1338-1339 (D.Utah 2006) the court was willing to follow the holding in *Biton* but found the plaintiffs' pleadings deficient,

Based on this holding, the Morris family could state a claim under the ATA for *their* nonphysical injuries that stem from the attack on Mr. Morris. The problem here, however, is that the complaint does not name any member of the Morris family except plaintiff Layne Morris as an injured individual seeking redress under the ATA. Undoubtedly, members of the Morris family have suffered individual injuries--loss of consortium, marital services, companionship, and affection. But since Mr. Morris survived the attack, his family members cannot recover for those injuries derivatively through him; they must do so as individual plaintiffs who allege personal injury in a complaint.

If Ms. Morris and her children were named plaintiffs; if the complaint contained any allegations that described how the attack affected them individually; or if the causes of action sought redress for their individual injuries, this case would fall neatly within Biton's and *Linde's* rationale as extended here. The complaint as it currently stands does none of those things. As a result, the court may award damages only to Mr. Morris as the injured U.S. national, and-since he is still alive-not to the Morris family as "heirs" or "survivors."

5.   What is the significance of the ruling in *Biton*? What would be the result if the court rejected the plaintiffs' arguments? How does expanding the class of plaintiffs impact terrorism claims? Is this ruling unfair to defendants?

Chapter 10

Damages

10.1 Solatium

Flatow v. Islamic Republic of Iran, 999 F.Supp. 1 (D. D.C. 1998).

* * *

This action has been brought for the benefit of decedent Alisa Michelle Flatow's parents, sisters and brother. Under 28 U.S.C.A. §1605 note, United States nationals or their legal representatives have standing to bring a cause of action for damages including solatium where personal injury or death results from state sponsored terrorism. The statute does not, however, define the range of individuals who may be entitled to solatium. Solatium is traditionally a compensatory damage which belongs to the individual heir personally for injury to the feelings and loss of decedent's comfort and society. It began as a remedy for the loss of a spouse or a parent. It has since expanded to include the loss of a child, including in some states the loss of an emancipated or adult child. *Reiser v. United States*, 786 F.Supp. 1334 (N.D.Ill.1992). [FN13] Where the claim is based upon the loss of a sibling, the claimant must prove a close emotional relationship with the decedent. *Miles v. Apex Marine Corp.*, 498 U.S. 19, 111 S.Ct. 317, 112 L.Ed.2d 275 (1990); *Reiser*, 786 F.Supp. 1334.

FN13. *See also* 77 A.L.R.4th 411 §§6,8, 9; 22A Am Jur2d at §277 n. 13-19; 61 A.L.R.4th 413 at §7 (citing cases):

recovery for solatium resulting from death of adult emancipated child permitted: Arkansas, California, Colorado, Hawaii, Illinois, Kansas, Louisiana, Maine, Maryland, Missouri, Nebraska, Texas, Utah, Virginia, Washington, Wisconsin;

recovery for solatium resulting from death of child limited to period of child's minority: Florida, Kentucky, Indiana, Iowa, Michigan, Oregon, Pennsylvania.

Solatium is defined as "Compensation. Damages allowed for injury to feelings." BLACK'S LAW DICTIONARY 1391 (6th ed.1990). Thus mental anguish, bereavement and grief resulting from the fact of decedent's death constitutes the preponderant element of a claim for solatium. Although most courts have not enumerated the bases for their calculations, some courts have indicated what factors entered into the judgment. As damages for mental anguish are extremely fact-dependent, claims require careful analysis on a case-by-case basis.

It is entirely possible to come to terms with the fact of death, and yet be unable to resolve the sense of anguish regarding the circumstances of death. This is particularly true where the death was sudden and violent. [FN14] See, e.g., *Dugal v. Commercial Standard Ins. Co.*, 456 F.Supp. 290 (W.D.Ark.1978); *St. Louis S.R. Co. v. Pennington*, 261 Ark. 650, 553 S.W.2d 436 (1977); *Scoville v. Missouri Pacific R. Co.*, 458 F.2d 639 (8th Cir.1972). How the claimant learned of decedent's death, and whether there was an opportunity to say good-bye or view the body can be a significant factor contributing to the claimant's anguish. In one case a decedent's father saw the plane crash into the building in which his 15-year-old son was working, as well as the resulting fireball which thwarted rescue attempts. The boy's mother was speaking with him on the telephone at the time of impact and heard him die. *Compania Dominicana de Aviacion v. Knapp*, 251 So.2d 18 (Fla.App. 3Dist.1971). Similarly, when advanced medical technology permits the victim's body to survive the event, but without hope of recovery, the decision whether to continue such extraordinary measures or to terminate life support will to some degree always haunt the decision-makers, particularly where, as here, the decision to terminate life support must be implemented by a claimant.

FN14. 61 A.L.R.4th 413 at §20 (citing cases where the courts have considered the violent manner of death as a factor in calculating damages for mental anguish): Arkansas, Missouri, Florida.

Knapp and similar cases, however, spring almost exclusively from negligence. Even where the death results from the most extreme forms of negligence, the primary visceral reaction is to the tragedy. This is not the case with deaths resulting from terrorist attacks, in which the tragedy itself is amplified by the malice which inspired the event. The malice associated with terrorist attacks transcends even that of premeditated murder. The intended audience of a terrorist attack is not limited to the families of those killed and wounded or even just Israelis, but in this case, the American public, for the purpose of affecting United States government support for Israel and the peace process. The terrorist's intent is to strike fear not only for one's own safety, but also for that of friends and family, and to manipulate that fear in order to achieve political objectives. Thus the character of the wrongful act itself increases the magnitude of the injury. It thus demands a corresponding increase in compensation for increased injury.

Spouses and relatives in direct lineal relationships are presumed to suffer damages for mental anguish. The testimony of sisters or brothers is ordinarily sufficient to sustain their claims for solatium. See *Reiser*, 786 F.Supp. 1334. Proof relies predominantly on the testimony of claimants, their close friends, and treating medical professionals, as appropriate. See *Alejandre* at 1249-50; 61 A.L.R.4th 413 at §13. Obvious distress during testimony, or the claimant's inability to testify due to intense anguish is usually considered in fixing the amount for solatium. See, e.g., *Jeffery v. United States*, 381 F.Supp. 505 (D.Ariz.1974). Testimony which describes a general feeling of permanent loss or change caused by decedent's absence has been considered a factor to be taken into account in awarding damages for solatium. See *Wheat v. United States*, 630 F.Supp. 699 (W.D.Tex.1986); *Brownsville Med. Center v. Gracia*, 704 S.W.2d 68 (Tex. App.Corpus Christi 1985). Medical treatment for depression and related affective disorders is another strong indicator of mental anguish. The body may also react to the stress of anguish with pain or illness, particularly stomach and chest pain, and documentation of such disorders are germane to the calculation of solatium.

Courts have also recognized that in the long term, the sudden death of a loved one may manifest itself as "a deep inner feeling of pain and anguish often borne in silence." *Connell v. Steel Haulers, Inc.*, 455 F.2d 688 (8th Cir.1972). Individuals can react very differently even under similar circumstances; while some sink into clinical depression and bitter-

ness, others attempt to salvage something constructive from their personal tragedy. Such constructive behavior should not be considered as mitigating solatium, but rather as an equally compensable reaction, one in which courage to face their own mental anguish prevails in order to survive, and in some circumstances, to benefit another.

A separate loss which is encompassed within solatium is the loss of decedent's society and comfort. Originally, wrongful death acts provided compensation only for the decedent's lost cash income stream. The next evolutionary stage was to recognize the economic value of decedent's personal services to claimant, such as household maintenance and nursing care. [FN15] See, e.g., *Umphrey v. Deery*, 78 N.D. 211, 48 N.W.2d 897 (1951). Many jurisdictions have now expanded recovery for loss of comfort and society to include all benefits which the claimant would have received had decedent lived. *Schaefer v. American Family Mut. Ins. Co.*, 182 Wis.2d 380, 514 N.W.2d 16 (Wis.App.1994). "Society" has evolved to include "a broad range of mutual benefits which 'each family member' receives from the other's continued existence, including love, affection, care, attention, companionship, comfort and protection." [FN16] *Miles v. Apex Marine Corp.*, 498 U.S. 19, 111 S.Ct. 317, 112 L.Ed.2d 275.

FN15. 22A AmJur2d at §253 n. 48; 77 A.L.R.4th 411 at §5; 61 A.L.R.4th 413 at §4(b) (citing cases): Arkansas, Connecticut, Indiana, Massachusetts, Michigan, Mississippi, Missouri, New Hampshire, New Mexico, North Dakota, Ohio, Oregon, Pennsylvania. The Jones Act and the Death on the High Seas Act also preclude claims for loss of non-economic damages, but general maritime law provides a remedy for the death of a longshoreman within territorial waters. See, e.g., *Miles v. Apex Marine Corp.*, 498 U.S. 19, 111 S.Ct. 317, 112 L.Ed.2d 275 (1990); *Sea-Land Services, Inc. v. Gaudet*, 414 U.S. 573, 94 S.Ct. 806, 39 L.Ed.2d 9, *reh'g denied* 415 U.S. 986, 94 S.Ct. 1582, 39 L.Ed.2d 883 (1974); 77 A.L.R.4th 411 at §7; 22A AmJur2d Supp. at 23.
FN16. 77 A.L.R.4th 411 at §§4-5; 22A AmJur2d at §§252, 253 (citing cases): Alaska, Arizona, California, Idaho, Illinois, Indiana, Iowa, Louisiana, Michigan, Minnesota, Mississippi, Montana, Nebraska, New Jersey, New York, North Dakota, Pennsylvania, Rhode Island, South Carolina, South Dakota, Texas, Utah, Vermont Virginia, Virgin Islands, Washington.
The calculations for mental anguish and loss of society share some common considerations. First, the calculation should be based upon the anticipated duration of the injury. Claims for mental anguish belong to the claimants and should reflect anticipated persistence of mental anguish in excess of

that which would have been experienced following decedent's natural death. When death results from terrorism, the fact of death and the cause of death can become inextricably intertwined, thus interfering with the prospects for anguish to diminish over time. Cf. *Larrumbide v. Doctors Health Facilities*, 734 S.W.2d 685 (Tex.App.Dallas 1987).

The nature of the relationship between the claimant and the decedent is another critical factor in the solatium analysis. If the relationship is strong and close, the likelihood that the claimant will suffer mental anguish and loss of society is substantially increased, particularly for intangibles such as companionship, love, affection, protection, and guidance. Numerous factors enter into this analysis, including: strong emotional ties between the claimant and the decedent; decedent's position in the family birth order relative to the claimant; the relative maturity or immaturity of the claimants; whether decedent habitually provided advice and solace to claimants; whether the claimant shared interests and pursuits with decedent; as well as decedent's achievements and plans for the future which would have affected claimants.

Finally, unlike lost wages, which can be calculated with a fair degree of mathematical certainty, solatium cannot be defined through models and variables. Courts have therefore refused to even attempt to factor in the present value of future mental anguish and loss of society. While economic losses can be reduced to present value with simple equations to establish the amount of an annuity established today which would have matched the decedent's ostensible income stream, the scope and uncertainty of human emotion renders such a calculation wholly inappropriate. *Drews v. Gobel Freight Lines, Inc.* 144 Ill.2d 84, 161 Ill.Dec. 324, 578 N.E.2d 970 (1991); *United States v. Hayashi*, 282 F.2d 599 (9th Cir.1960). This is the paradox of solatium; although no amount of money can alleviate the emotional impact of a child's or sibling's death, dollars are the only means available to do so. See, e.g., *Walker v. St. Paul Ins. Co.*, 343 So.2d 251 (La.App.1977), *cert. denied* 345 So.2d 61 (La.1977).

The testimony before the Court described a closely-knit family in which the decedent, Alisa Michelle Flatow, occupied a special niche. The testimony of family, friends and her professor described a person of unique talents with an unusual sensitivity for other family members. Much of the religious orientation of the family seemed to spring from Alisa. To an extent and in a manner which is unique, the slaughter of Alisa Michelle Flatow inflicted pain upon the surviving members of that family. The magnitude of that

suffering is demonstrated by the actions of the Flatow family in founding, administering and maintaining the Alisa Michelle Flatow Foundation, which has to date raised in excess of $200,000 for scholarships. The resort to this avenue as an expression of their feelings is, in the opinion of the Court, unique, praiseworthy, and of necessity, provides a basis for awards to the surviving family members in substantial amounts in recognition of their profound loss.

This action has been brought by Plaintiff on behalf of Alisa Michelle Flatow's parents, Rosalyn and Stephen M. Flatow, sisters Gail, Francine and Ilana Flatow, and brother Etan Flatow. Based upon all of the testimony referred to above, the Court finds that awards in the following amounts are appropriate in compensation for the loss suffered by each individual member of the Flatow family:

Stephen M. Flatow (father):	$5,000,000.00
Rosalyn Flatow (mother):	$5,000,000.00
Gail Flatow (sister):	$2,500,000.00
Francine Flatow (sister):	$2,500,000.00
Ilana Flatow (sister):	$2,500,000.00
Etan Flatow (brother):	$2,500,000.00

Notes:

1.   It was not necessary for Judge Lamberth to stretch the law to include solatium damages in §1605(a)(7) cases as the Flatow Amendment specifically provides for such awards. Why did he expend so much effort then explaining the nature of solatium damages? How common are awards of solatium in the context of traditional tort claims?

2.   *Flatow* ruled that death caused by terrorism warrants a higher damage award than if caused in another manner. Why is this so? Is it true that death by terrorism causes greater harm to the victim's family than death by accidental fire, domestic abuse, or poisoning? What is unique about terrorism that magnifies the harm it causes to victims, their families, and a wide range of individuals?

3.   Some commentators have questioned whether terrorism damage awards are intended to be taken seriously. For instance, concerning the very first judgment under the terrorism amendments to the FSIA, *Alejandre v. Republic of Cuba*, 996 F.Supp. 1239 (S.D.Fla. 1997), scholars at Yale wrote,

> We do not know whether the Alejandre court awarded such high damages with the expecta-

tion that the plaintiffs actually would recover the amounts awarded. Perhaps the judgment was judicial "funny money," the court intending the award only to be a symbol, just as *Filartiga* was, in essence, a symbol. Certainly, the award validated the victims' cause and reinforced the legitimacy of human rights norms.

Michael Reisman and Monica Hakimim, *Illusion And Reality In The Compensation Of Victims Of International Terrorism*, 54 Ala. L. Rev. 561, 569-570 (2003).

4.   Another commentator has noted,

> However, to the extent that one goal of the Act is to publicly shame foreign state defendants that commit or sponsor acts of terror, and to draw media and public attention to the heinousness of their acts, the statute appears to be effective. The filing of each case under the Act, and the judgments entered, have led to national and international news stories. Similarly, if a goal of the Act is to provide victims of state-sponsored terror with their day in court or an opportunity to publicize the atrocities committed against them, then the Act has been effective.

William P. Hoye, *Fighting Fire With…Mire? Civil Remedies And The New War On State-Sponsored Terrorism*, 12 Duke J. Comp. & Int'l L. 105 (2002).

5.   The circumstances surrounding the death of a terrorism victim normally contribute greatly to the severe mental anguish and suffering of the victim's survivors, thereby mandating an appropriate remedy,

> This type of action deserves a reply in damages that will fully compensate for the truly terrible emotional suffering of the surviving parents and siblings.

Eisenfeld v. Islamic Republic of Iran, 172 F. Supp.2d 1, 8 (D.D.C. 2000). However, consortium and solatium claims are identical to intentional infliction of emotional distress claims, "solatium appears in any event to be indistinguishable from intentional infliction of emotional distress." *Wagner v. Islamic Republic of Iran*, 172 F. Supp.2d 128, 136, f.n. 11 (D.D.C. 2001)(citing *D.C. v. Thompson*, 570 A.2d 277 (D.C. 1990). What accounts then for the greater magnitude of terrorism damages awards?

6.   Some have criticized damage awards in default cases as being too cookie-cutter like. Is this criticism justified? Do the courts "automatically" award damages to victims? Consider *Elahi v. Islamic Republic of Iran*, 124 F.Supp.2d 97, 112 (D.D.C. 2000) where the court found that,

> …there was an absence of specific testimony regarding mental anguish and loss of society and comfort experienced by his sister. In addition, while in his younger years, after the divorce of his parents and 21 years prior to his death, Cyrus was a father figure to all his siblings, there was insufficient evidence about the state of Cyrus Elahi's relationship with his sister at the time of his death. See *Flatow*, 999 F.Supp. at 30 (requiring proof of close emotional relationship before awarding damages to siblings). Therefore, there will be no award of damages for anguish or loss of society and comfort suffered by Cyrus Elahi's sister.

7.   What is the effect of allowing solatium damages in terrorism cases? What is the practical significance of broadening the permissible damages to include solatium claims?

8.   Sometimes defendants describe the damages awarded in terrorism cases as a "terrorism premium." Is this description justified? Is there something unique about terrorism that suggests increased damages are warranted? Is terrorism sufficiently different from other types of intentional torts (i.e. murder, rape, torture, false imprisonment) or acts of horrific negligence? Judge Lamberth recognized that an "increase in compensation" is often warranted in terrorism cases,

> Even where the death results from the most extreme forms of negligence, the primary visceral reaction is to the tragedy. This is not the case with deaths resulting from terrorist attacks, in which the tragedy itself is amplified by the malice which inspired the event. The malice associated with terrorist attacks transcends even that of premeditated murder. The intended audience of a terrorist attack is not limited to the families of those killed and wounded or even just Israelis, but in this case, the American public, for the purpose of affecting United States government support for Israel and the peace process. The terrorist's intent is to strike fear not only for one's own safety, but also for that of friends and family, and to manipulate that fear in order to achieve political objectives. Thus the character of the wrongful act itself increases the magnitude of the injury.

It thus demands a corresponding increase in compensation for increased injury.

Flatow v. Islamic Republic of Iran, 999 F.Supp. 1, 30 (D.D.C.1998). What is the *legal* (as opposed to *policy*) basis for this position?

9. How does a court "place a price tag" on the loss of a family member? How is this different from other wrongful death cases?

10. To what extent does the court scrutinize the relationships of the injured and murdered victims and the surviving family members? See *Smith v. Islamic Emirate of Afghanistan*, 262 F.Supp.2d 217 (S.D.N.Y. 2003) for analysis of the quality of the relationship amongst family members.

11. If large awards are not provided to victims who have neither family nor income, is there an incentive to state sponsors of terrorism to victimize a certain class of victims? How do terrorists choose targets?

12. A leading treatise has noted:

> ...it has almost always seemed unjust to say that a child, or nonworking wife or mother, or an aged person is worth nothing to his survivors, and juries have at times rendered substantial verdicts in such cases.

Prosser & Keeton on Torts §127 (1984). Is this concern heightened in civil terrorism cases?

10.2 Damages under 18 U.S.C. §2333
Ungar v. Palestinian Authority, 304 F.Supp.2d 232 (D. R.I. 2004).

V. Damages
18 U.S.C. §2333(a) allows the estate of a United States national who is killed by an act of international terrorism and his or her survivors or heirs to recover threefold the damages they sustain and the cost of the suit, including attorney's fees. See 18 U.S.C. §2333(a).

A. "Survivors" and "Heirs"
The statute does not define "survivors" or "heirs." *Id.* This lack of definition is somewhat problematic because the terms "survivors" and "heirs" are usually defined (or determined) by state law. See, e.g., *Vildibill v. Johnson*, 802 F.2d 1347, 1350 (11th Cir.1986)(accepting Florida Supreme

Court's determination that under state Wrongful Death Act non-dependent parents of an adult child are not "survivors"); *Mingolla v. Minnesota Mining & Mfg. Co.*, 893 F.Supp. 499, 505 (D.Vi.1995)(noting that under Virgin Islands Wrongful Death Act adult children are not "survivors" unless partially or wholly dependent upon decedent for support); *Allen v. Pacheco*, 71 P.3d 375, 380-81 (Colo.2003)("the term 'heirs' under the [Colorado] Wrongful Death Act refers only to lineal descendants of the deceased"); *DeWitt v. Frenchie's Custom Helmets*, No. 93-2332-JWL, 1994 WL 171571, at *2 (D.Kan. Apr. 1, 1994)(finding under Kansas Wrongful Death Act that parents of decedent are not heirs at law where decedent is survived by a child). Yaron Ungar had not been a resident of any state in this country since he was fourteen years old. *See* 7/12/02 Hearing Tr. at 92, 100. Thus, the meaning of the terms "survivors" and "heirs" as used in §2333(a) cannot be determined by referring to the law of a particular state.

Notwithstanding the lack of a definition for "heirs," the court has no hesitancy in finding that Dvir and Yishai, the sons of Yaron, are his "heirs." First, the Complaint alleges that they are his "heirs-at-law," Complaint ¶ 5, and, default having been entered, the allegations of fact in the Complaint must be taken as true, see *Brockton Sav. Bank v. Peat, Marwick, Mitchell & Co.*, 771 F.2d 5, 13 (1st Cir.1985). Second, as Yaron's immediate and direct lineal descendants, it is virtually inconceivable that his sons would not be his heirs. Third, Israeli law provides that when a decedent dies intestate the "legal heirs entitled to succession [are]: (1) Spouse of deceased; (2) children and their descendants and parents of deceased and their descendants." Martindale-Hubbell International Law Digest, Israel Law Digest, Estates and Trusts, Descent and Distribution at 8.

Yaron's parents, Judith and Meir Ungar, and his siblings, Michal Cohen, Amichai Ungar, and Dafna Ungar, do not allege that they are either "heirs" or "survivors." *See* Complaint ¶¶ 6, 8. Presumably they make their claims as "survivors" and not "heirs" since, as noted above, the Complaint asserts that Dvir and Yishai are Yaron's heirs. Cf. *Bridges v. Phillips Petroleum Co.*, 733 F.2d 1153, 1155 (5th Cir.1984)(noting that under Texas law it is well settled that parents and siblings are not heirs of the body); *Barnes v. Robison*, 712 F.Supp. 873, 875 (D.Kan.1989) (finding surviving parent(s) of decedent who left no children to be his heirs under Kansas law, but not his surviving siblings); *Saunders v. Air Florida, Inc.*, 558 F.Supp. 1233, 1235 (D.D.C.1983)(finding parents are not "heirs" under District of Columbia or California law where decedent left a wife and three children). However, because the term "survivors" is not defined in §2333(a) and Yaron's parents and siblings have not specifically pled that they bring this action as "survivors," the court must determine whether the parents and siblings of a decedent who died leaving children are "survivors" within the meaning of the statute.

Black's Law Dictionary defines "survivor" as "[o]ne who survives another; one who outlives another; one who lives beyond some happening; one of two or more persons who lives after the death of the other or others." Black's Law Dictionary 1446 (6th Ed. 1990). This definition is of little assistance here because, applied literally, it means that everyone who outlives the decedent, even a non-relative, is his survivor. On the other hand, some statutes define "survivors" rather narrowly. *See, e.g.*, 38 U.S.C. §1318(a) (defining survivors as "the surviving spouse and...children of a deceased veteran"); Kan. Stat. Ann. §40-3103 (" 'Survivor' means a decedent's spouse, or child under the age of 18 years, where death of the decedent resulted from an injury."). Between the two poles represented by Black's extremely broad definition and the narrow definitions contained in the veterans and Kansas statutes, there are intermediate classifications. See *Cortes v. American Airlines, Inc.*, No. 96-0727-CIV, 1997 WL 33125722, at *3 (S.D.Fla. Nov. 19, 1997)(noting that the Florida Wrongful Death Act defines "survivors" as "the decedent's spouse, children, parents, and, when partially or wholly dependent on the decedent for support or services, any blood relatives and adoptive brothers and sisters"); *Mingolla v. Minnesota Mining & Mfg. Co.*, 893 F.Supp. 499, 505 (D.Vi.1995)(noting same definition in Virgin Islands Wrongful Death Act); *Arnold v. Logue*, 405 Pa.Super. 422, 592 A.2d 735, 738 (1991)(noting that repealed No-Fault Act had defined "survivor" as meaning "(A) spouse; or (B) child, parent, brother, sister or relative dependent upon the deceased for support").

Given the variability of the meaning of the term "survivors," the court looks to the legislative history of the statute for assistance. In *Boim v. Quranic Literacy Institute & Holy Land Foundation For Relief & Development*, 291 F.3d 1000 (7th Cir.2002), the Third Circuit discussed the legislative history of §§2331 and 2333:

That history, in combination with the language of the statute itself, evidences an intent by Congress to codify general common law tort principles and to extend civil liability for acts of international terrorism to the full reaches of traditional tort law. *See* 137 Cong. Rec. S4511-04 (April 16, 1991) ("The [antiterrorism act] accords victims of terrorism the remedies of American tort law, including treble damages and attorney's fees."); *Antiterrorism Act of 1990*, Hearing Before the Subcommittee on Courts and Administrative Practice of Committee on the Judiciary, United States Senate, 101st Congress, Second Session, July 25, 1990

(hereafter "Senate Hearing"), Testimony of Joseph Morris, at 136 ("[T]he bill as drafted is powerfully broad, and its intention...is to...bring [in] all of the substantive law of the American tort law system."). In particular, the statute itself contains all of the elements of a traditional tort: breach of a duty (i.e., committing an act of international terrorism); injury to the person, property or business of another; and causation (injured "by reason of")...

...

The Senate Report on the bill notes that "[t]he substance of [an action under section 2333] is not defined by the statute, because the fact patterns giving rise to such suits will be as varied and numerous as those found in the law of torts. This bill opens the courthouse door to victims of international terrorism." S. Rep. 102-342, at 45 (1992).

Id. at 1010-11 (alterations in original)(emphasis added). The highlighted language at the very least suggests that Congress did not intend that the class of persons able to bring actions pursuant to §2333(a) should be interpreted narrowly. The parents or siblings of a U.S. national killed by terrorists are undeniably "victims of international terrorism" in the sense that they suffer the loss of a close family member.

More substantial evidence of Congress' intent exists. As originally drafted, §2333 allowed compensation only for "any national of the United States..." *Antiterrorism Act of 1990: Hearing Before the Subcomm. on Courts & Admin. Practice of the Senate Comm. on the Judiciary*, 101st Congress 8 (1990) ("Senate Hearing"). The Justice Department suggested that Congress modify the text of the bill to explicitly allow suits by the family members (as "survivors" and "heirs" of the victim). *See* Senate Hearing at 38 (statement of Steven R. Valentine). In a statement to the Senate Subcommittee, Deputy Assistant Attorney General Steven R. Valentine proposed:

that this provision be amended to include, in addition to the individual directly affected, such additional parties as the estate of the decedent, survivors, and heirs. This will ensure that the bill is fully protective of the interests of all relevant parties to the civil suit.

Id. (emphasis added). [FN28] In response to a question from Senator Thurmond as to whether the modification was necessary "to make certain the ability of family members to file a lawsuit on behalf of a slain or injured relative," Senate Hearing at 46, Mr. Lloyd Green, counselor to the Assistant Attorney General in charge of the Civil Division, see *id.* at 25, responded: "It would make clear that which is already implied in the bill. It would remove any doubt that anyone would have as to whether or not they could bring the litigation," *id.* at 46 (statement of Lloyd Green).

FN28. Mr. Valentine also expressed the general position of the Department of Justice regarding the legislation: "The Department supports legislation to provide a new civil remedy against terrorists and a federal forum *for the families and relatives of victims to pursue claims for compensatory damages." Antiterrorism Act of 1990: Hearing Before the Subcomm. on Courts & Admin. Practice of the Senate Comm. on the Judiciary*, 101st Congress 34 (1990) ("Senate Hearing") (statement of Steven R. Valentine) (emphasis added).

Congress accepted the recommendation of the Justice Department and modified the language of §2333 to create a cause of action for "[a]ny national of the United States injured in his or her person, property, or business by reason of an act of international terrorism, or his or her estate, survivors, or heirs…" 18 U.S.C. §2333(a). By including the term "survivors" in the class of persons eligible to bring an action, Congress evidenced an intention that family members who are not legal heirs (such as the parents and siblings of a decedent who leaves children) may bring an action pursuant to the statute. If this were not the case, there would have been no need to include the term "survivors."

Based on the foregoing legislative history and on the substantial policy consideration that allowing parents and siblings to bring actions in their own right (regardless of whether the decedent is survived by a spouse and/or children) increases the deterrent effect [FN29] of the legislation, this court concludes that the term "survivors" as used in §2333(a) includes the parents and siblings of a U.S. national killed by an act of international terrorism. Accordingly, the court finds that Judith and Meir Ungar, Michal Cohen, Amichai Ungar, and Dafna Ungar are "survivors" of Yaron Ungar and are within the class of plaintiffs who may bring an action under the statute.

FN29. Mr. Valentine also testified that it was the position of the Department of Justice that "it is essential that both the Congress and the Executive Branch take measures, such as the present bill, to deter terrorist attacks against American nationals overseas…" Senate Hearing at 31.

B. Measure of Damages

"The measure of damages for causing the death of another depends upon the wording of the statute creating the right of action and its interpretation." Restatement (Second) of Torts §925 (1979). However, §2333(a) does not specify the nature of the damages which may be recovered by the persons entitled to bring an action. In this respect, the statute differs from §1605(a)(7) of the Foreign Sovereign Immunities Act ("FSIA") which specifically identifies the damages re-

coverable as including "economic damages, solatium, pain, and suffering, and punitive damages…" 28 U.S.C. §1605 note. Plaintiffs seek damages for both pecuniary and non-economic losses. *See* Damages Mem. at 18-24. Therefore, this court must determine whether §2333(a) should be interpreted to allow recovery for both pecuniary damages and non-economic damages, including loss of companionship and society and mental anguish experienced by the victim's surviving family members.

The only reported case which this court could find awarding damages pursuant to 18 U.S.C. §2333(a) is *Smith v. Islamic Emirate of Afghanistan*, 262 F.Supp.2d 217, 238-39 (S.D.N.Y.2003), an action arising out of the September 11, 2001, attack on the World Trade Center. The action was brought against certain non-sovereign defendants pursuant to §2333, see *id*. at 220-21, and against Iraq pursuant to 28 U.S.C. §1605(a)(7), see *id*. at 225-26. The *Smith* court awarded damages for funeral expenses, lost earnings, and pain and suffering pursuant to both statutes, but awarded damages for loss of solatium only pursuant to §1605(7). See *id*. at 232-33, 238-39, 240-41. The opinion does not indicate whether plaintiffs sought solatium damages pursuant to §2333(a), and there is no discussion as to how the court determined the nature of the damages available under §2333(a). The court appears to have assumed that the only damages available pursuant to §2333(a) were those for pecuniary loss and for pain and suffering. See *id*. at 232-34, 238-39. Therefore, the opinion is of limited assistance in answering the present question.

In the absence of other case law, the court again looks to the legislative history of the statute. Sections 2331-2338 were enacted as part of the Antiterrorism Act of 1990 ("ATA")[FN30] and were intended to "create a new federal cause of action…[and] a new civil remedy against terrorists…" Senate Hearing at 34 (statement of Mr. Valentine). As the court has previously determined, the legislative history indicates that the ATA was to be construed broadly. Senator Grassley, the bill's co-sponsor, indicated that "it empowers victims with *all* the weapons available in civil litigation." *Antiterrorism Act of 1990: Hearing before the Subcomm. on Intellectual Prop. & Judicial Admin. of the House Comm. on the Judiciary*, 102nd Congress 10 (1992)(emphasis added). This suggests that Congress intended that the full range of damages should be available to persons entitled to bring actions pursuant to §2333(a).

FN30. Sections 2331-2338 were originally enacted in 1990 as part of the Antiterrorism Act of 1990, Pub. L. No. 101-519, sec. 132, 104 Stat. 2250-2253 (1990). This Public Law, however, has no currently effective sections. Nevertheless, these sections were subsequently re-enacted as part of the Federal Courts Administration Act of 1992, Pub. L. No. 102-572, sec. 1003(a)(1)-(5), 106 Stat. 4521-4524 (1992).

Estates of Ungar v. Palestinian Authority, 228 F.Supp.2d 40, 41 n. 1 (D.R.I.2002); see also *Boim v. Quranic Literacy Inst. & Holy Land Found. for Relief & Dev.*, 291 F.3d 1000, 1009 n. 6 (7th Cir.2002).

Limiting compensable losses under the statute to economic losses would not be in accord with a nationwide legislative tendency in the last few decades.

Though recovery for loss of society and comfort is denied under some statutes, it is an item usually recognized and made the basis for an award, at times apparently substantial...

Even jurisdictions that have rejected the loss of society or consortium claim, as such, have permitted one form of it, namely a loss of guidance and advice that the decedent would have provided.

Prosser & Keeton on Torts §127 (5th ed. 1984)(footnotes omitted).

The Florida Supreme Court has observed that the denial of damages for loss of society is based on an "antiquated perception" of the familial relationship as being one of master and servant. *United States v. Dempsey*, 635 So.2d 961, 963 (Fla.1994). The court explained:

Certainly, in 1973, when this Court set forth the elements of damages that a parent of an injured child is entitled to recover, it was apparent that a child's companionship and society were of far more value to the parent than were the services rendered by the child. Thus, there was an obvious need to recognize this element of damages to fully compensate the parent for the loss suffered because of a negligent injury to the child. The recognition of the loss of companionship element of damages clearly reflects our modern concept of family relationships.

Id. at 964; see also *Masaki v. Gen. Motors Corp.*, 71 Haw. 1, 780 P.2d 566, 577-78 (1989)(holding that a parent may recover for the loss of filial consortium of an injured adult child and observing that "services have become only one element of the consortium action while the intangible elements of love, comfort, companionship, and society have emerged as the predominant focus of consortium actions"). In a similar vein, the Supreme Court of North Dakota condemned as a "barbarous concept" the notion that a parent who brings a wrongful death action may only recover for pecuniary loss. *Hopkins v. McBane*, 427 N.W.2d 85, 90 (N.D.1988)(quoting *Wycko v. Gnodtke*, 361 Mich. 331, 105 N.W.2d 118, 121 (1960)). This court agrees with these observations.

Section 2333(a) grants federal rights, and the Supreme Court has stated that:

[W]here federally protected rights have been invaded, it has been the rule from the beginning that courts will be alert to adjust their remedies so as to grant the necessary relief. And it is also well settled that where legal rights have been invaded, and a federal statute provides for a general right to sue for such invasion, federal courts may use any available remedy to make good the wrong done.

Bell v. Hood, 327 U.S. 678, 684, 66 S.Ct. 773, 777, 90 L.Ed. 939 (1946)(footnote omitted). There is no doubt that in bringing this action pursuant to §2333 plaintiffs are invoking a federally created legal right.

The Seventh Circuit, in considering the federally created rights provided by 42 U.S.C. §1983, found that, although the statute was silent on the nature of the damages recoverable under it, the parents of a twenty-three year old son who was fatally shot by a police officer could recover for the loss of his society and companionship. See *Bell v. City of Milwaukee*, 746 F.2d 1205, 1232, 1244-45 (7th Cir.1984), *overruled on other grounds, DeShaney v. Winnebago County Dep't of Social Servs.*, 489 U.S. 189, 109 S.Ct. 998, 103 L.Ed.2d 249 (1989); cf. *Figueroa-Rodriguez v. Aquino*, 863 F.2d 1037, 1045 (1st Cir.1988)(noting that "the measure of damages in section 1983 actions is a matter of federal common law."). In reaching the conclusion that such damages were recoverable, the Seventh Circuit noted that "Section 1983 was enacted not simply to enforce existing wrongful death remedies but to give force to the newly-conceived constitutional amendments, which are remedial in purpose." *Bell v. City of Milwaukee*, 746 F.2d at 1250. [FN31] Similarly here, the legislative history indicates that §2333 was enacted to provide new and additional remedies to victims of international terrorism. See *Boim v. Quranic Literacy Inst. & Holy Land Found. for Relief & Dev.*, 291 F.3d 1000, 1010 (7th Cir.2002)(noting an intent by Congress to codify general tort law principles and extend civil liability to acts of international terrorism to the full reaches of traditional tort law).

FN31. See also *Smith v. City of Fontana*, 818 F.2d 1411, 1418 (9th Cir.1987)(finding that interest in companionship and society exists between parent and child and may be asserted in §1983 action), *overruled on other grounds, Hodgers-Durgin v. de la Vina*, 199 F.3d 1037 (9th Cir.1999); *Trujillo v. Board of County Comm'rs of County of Santa Fe*, 768 F.2d 1186, 1189-90 (10th Cir.1985)(finding sister had actionable right under §1983 for deprivation of right to intimate association with brother who died while incarcerated provided the deprivation was intentional). But see *Valdivieso Ortiz v.*

Burgos, 807 F.2d 6, 7 (1st Cir.1986)(finding that step-father and siblings do not have a constitutionally protected interest in the companionship of their adult son and brother which is actionable under §1983).

The holding in *Valdivieso Ortiz v. Burgos* does not dissuade this court from the conclusion that the parents and siblings of Yaron Ungar may recover damages for the loss of his society and companionship. The court in *Valdivieso* emphasized that its "conclusion is simply that, in light of the limited nature of the Supreme Court precedent in this area, it would be inappropriate to extend recognition of an individual's liberty interest in his or her family or parental relationship to the facts of this case." *Id.* at 10. Here the legislative history of §2333 provides adequate guidance to conclude that Congress intended that surviving family members, including parents and siblings, be allowed to recover damages for loss of society and companionship.

Additionally, the First Circuit, this court, and the Rhode Island Supreme Court have all recognized circumstances in which the loss of society and companionship is compensable. See *Mitchell v. United States*, 141 F.3d 8, 19 (1st Cir.1998)(finding that there is no requirement under Massachusetts law that adult children be financially dependent upon decedent in order to recover for consortium-like damages); *Fritz v. May Dep't Stores Co.*, 866 F.Supp. 66, 70 (D.R.I.1994)(recognizing that unemancipated minor need not suffer physical injury to recover for loss of her mother's society and companionship); *D'Ambra v. United States*, 481 F.2d 14, 20 (1st Cir.1973)(recognizing that loss of society and companionship of minor child are compensable); *Sindelar v. Leguia*, 750 A.2d 967, 972 (R.I.2000) (noting that §10-7-1.2 of R.I. Wrongful Death Act "allows for the bringing of a claim for loss of consortium, where a preexisting relationship between decedent and survivor is relevant to recovery."). [FN32]

FN32. In addition to allowing a spouse to recover for loss of consortium, R.I. Gen. Laws §10-7-1.2 also allows recovery for an unemancipated minor's loss of parental society and companionship and also for a parent's loss of a minor's society and companionship. *See* R.I. Gen. Laws §10-7-1.2 (1997 Reenactment).

One of the purposes of §2333(a) was the deterrence of terrorist attacks. [FN33] The deterrent effect of the legislation will be maximized if it is interpreted to subject terrorists to the broadest possible range of damages. Accordingly, this court finds that §2333(a) should be interpreted to allow for recovery of both pecuniary damages, *cf.* Kristine Cordier Karnezis, Annotation, *Award of Damages under State-Sponsored Terrorism Exception to Foreign Sovereign Immunities*

Act (28 U.S.C.A. §1605(A)), 182 A.L.R. Fed. 1, 13, 2002 WL 31628515 (2002) (noting that damages for economic loss have been awarded in the overwhelming majority of cases brought [under §1605(a)]..."), and also for non-economic damages, including loss of companionship, society, and mental anguish experienced by the victim's surviving family members, including his siblings, cf. *id.* (noting that solatium damages have been awarded in "most [§1605(a)] cases...")

FN33. *See* n. 24.

C. Estate of Yaron Ungar

1. Lost Earnings

At the hearing on July 12, 2002, plaintiffs presented the testimony of Dr. Adrian Ziderman, a professor of economics at Bar-Ilan University in Israel and the holder of a doctorate from the London School of Economics. *See* 7/12/02 Tr. at 66. He was qualified as an expert in economic matters. See *id.* at 68.

At the time of his death, Yaron Ungar was near his 26th birthday and a qualified teacher in Israel. See *id.* at 69-70, 92. He was about to complete his Bachelor of Education degree and had started towards rabbinical ordination. See *id.* at 70. Dr. Ziderman testified that, assuming Mr. Ungar had pursued "a fairly standard successful career in Jewish religious teaching in Israel," see *id.* at 77, the present value of his lost earnings in U.S. dollars was $1,273,028, see *id.* at 81; *see also* Hearing Ex. 6 (Report on Economic Losses Due to the Death of Yaron Ungar) at 10. Dr. Ziderman indicated that this career path assumption was "conservative," 7/12/02 Tr. at 77, because it did not include the possibility that Yaron would also work as a part time rabbi in Israel, see *id.*, or that he would work during sabbaticals (which teachers in Israel have every seventh year), see *id.* at 79. In his report, Hearing Ex. 6, Dr. Ziderman states that "it is now fairly standard for teacher/rabbis to spend periods of time (usually for a minimum period of three years) employed in one of the Jewish communities abroad, particularly in the United States," Hearing Ex. 6 at 10, and that "[a]s [an] American, this scenario [was] a quite realistic one for Yaron, and would result in considerably enhanced earnings," *id.* If this latter career scenario were assumed, Dr. Ziderman believed that "it would be very easy to justify a considerably higher earnings loss figure, reaching some $1,800,000." *Id.* at 11. However, acknowledging that this scenario was "largely speculative, particularly with regard to the estimation of additional earnings," *id.* at 10, Dr. Ziderman made "a minimal estimate by rounding up the earnings loss estimates to $1,400,000 (representing only about an addition of ten percent to total earnings)…" *id.* at 10-11.

The court finds Dr. Ziderman's reasoning persuasive and sets the present value of Yaron Ungar's lost earnings in U.S. dollars as $1,400,000. However, this figure must be adjusted to account for Yaron's personal consumption. *See* 22A Am.Jur. 2D Death §192 (2003)(noting that generally in determining pecuniary loss to the beneficiaries it must determined what proportion of the decedent's probable future earnings or income actually would have gone to the beneficiaries); *Feldman v. Allegheny Airlines, Inc.*, 524 F.2d 384, 389 (2nd Cir.1975)(finding that trial judge's computation of decedent's living expenses was too low for purpose of determining loss of earnings pursuant to Connecticut law); *Daliberti v. Republic of Iraq*, 146 F.Supp.2d 19, 26 (D.D.C.2001)(stating that determination of loss of earnings included "appropriate assumptions as to inflation, rise in productivity, job advancement, *personal consumption* and net earnings")(emphasis added). Using methodology explained in Hearing Ex. 6 at 9, Dr. Ziderman determined that economic loss due to lost earnings, after deduction of Yaron's consumption, is $477,386. I find Dr. Ziderman's methodology to be reasonable, and I adopt the figure of $477,386 as being the amount which should be awarded to the estate for lost earnings.

2. Pain and Suffering

At the hearing on July 12, 2002, Alan Friedman, M.D., whom the court found to be qualified as an expert in trauma medicine and the treatment of people who have suffered trauma, *see* 7/12/02 Hearing Tr. at 36; *see also* Hearing Ex. 4 (CV of Dr. Friedman), testified regarding the injuries suffered by Yaron Ungar, *see* 7/12/02 Hearing Tr. at 41-64. Dr. Friedman stated that he had reviewed the police report concerning the attack (both the original report which is in Hebrew and an English translation of that report), photographs of the crime scene and of the bodies of Yaron Ungar and Efrat Ungar, and the reports of the examination of the bodies. See *id.* at 36-37; *see also* Hearing Exs. 1 (Israeli police report and photographs), 2 (English translation of Hebrew description of 29 crime scene photographs), 3 (crime scene photographs and photographs of bodies), 5 (forensic examination of Yaron Ungar on 6/10/96). Based on that review, Dr. Friedman testified that it appeared the terrorists approached the Ungar car from behind and that as they started to pass the Ungar car on the left they began shooting. *See* 7/12/02 Hearing Tr. at 38-39. There were six bullet holes in the left rear window on the driver's side. See *id.* at 40. Some of these bullets passed through the driver's headrest and struck Efrat Ungar in the back of the head, see *id.* at 40, killing her

instantly, see *id.* at 63. Sixteen bullet holes were found in the driver's side window, indicating that the terrorists fired more rounds as they pulled along side the Ungar car. See *id.* at 41. One of these rounds caused the first injury to Yaron Ungar, striking his left forearm and elbow region. See *id.* at 41. Based on the bullet holes, the location, and the nature of the injury, Dr. Friedman theorized that Yaron threw his arm up instinctively to protect himself. See *id.* at 43. The shot fractured the radius, pushing it through the skin, and caused a number of large, jagged holes in the arm. See *id.* at 41-42. The pain from this wound would have been "tremendous." *Id.* at 44.

After being shot in the left arm, Yaron turned his body to the driver's side and received an almost direct front to back shot to the upper right side of the chest. See *id.* at 44-45; *see also* Hearing Ex. 3. Dr. Friedman stated that the turning was consistent with a person hearing shots coming from his left side and turning to see what was happening. *See* 7/12/02 Hearing Tr. at 45. There were a total of fourteen shrapnel wounds to the chest. [FN34] See *id.* A large wound to the upper right chest could have caused death in fifteen to thirty minutes if the lung was penetrated, but Yaron would still have remained conscious for most of that time. [FN35] See *id.* at 45-46. If the lung was not penetrated, the wound would not have been fatal. See *id.* at 46. Dr. Friedman described the pain caused by this as similar to being hit in the chest with a baseball bat, see *id.* at 48, accompanied by "searing pain," *id.*

FN34. In response to a question from the court as to the source of the shrapnel, Dr. Friedman testified that presumably it came from the "bullet casing." 7/12/02 Hearing Tr. at 46. He noted that one photograph appeared to show "part of the lower case of a shell embedded in a piece of glass." *Id.* at 47.

FN35. There was no internal examination of the body. *See* 7/12/02 Hearing Tr. at 37-38. Dr. Friedman testified that the practice in Israel is not to perform an internal autopsy unless there is a specific question of a criminal act and the authorities are trying to determine a cause of death. See *id.* at 38.

Dr. Friedman theorized that after being struck in the chest, Yaron was thrown backwards so that he was almost lying down on the passenger's seat. See *id.* at 52. While in this slumped position, Yaron was hit in the face by a bullet which entered through the front windshield. [FN36] See *id.* at 52-53. The bullet struck the left side of the nose, traveled up to the base of the eye, fracturing the left orbit, and continued through the crown or temple of the head. See *id.* at 51. This injury caused Yaron's death, although not immediately because the shot did not hit the respiratory centers in the base of the brain. See *id.* Dr. Friedman was unable to estimate how long Yaron would have remained conscious after receiving this wound, see *id.* at 61, but it is clear to the court from the photographs of this horrific injury that the loss of consciousness would have been almost immediate, *see* Hearing Ex. 3 (body examination photographs # 2, # 3). [FN37]

FN36. The police report states that there were both entry and exit bullet holes in the front windshield. *See* Hearing Ex. 2 ¶ 23. In addition, bullet holes were found in the hood, left front headlight, and bumper of the vehicle. See *id.* ¶¶ 4, 9, 21.

FN37. At one point in the testimony, Dr. Friedman appeared to say that Yaron would have been conscious for thirty seconds after being shot in the face. See *id.* at 57. However, Dr. Friedman later testified that he could not "come up with a figure" for this period of time, *id.* at 61, and he subsequently said that thirty seconds was the amount of time from the beginning of the attack to point at which Yaron became unconscious, see *id.* at 62.

In addition to the above injuries, Yaron sustained an injury to the left side of his neck laterally which would not have been fatal although extremely painful. See *id.* at 54. There was no testimony as to when this wound was inflicted. However, from the photographs it appears that this wound may have been sustained at the same time as the fourteen shrapnel wounds to the chest because it is somewhat similar in appearance and in close proximity to them. *See* Hearing Ex. 3 (photographs # 2 and # 4).

Dr. Friedman estimated the time from the first shots striking the vehicle to the point at which Yaron was rendered unconscious by the bullet wound to his face and head as being approximately thirty seconds. See *id.* at 62. Quantifying this period of time is obviously difficult. Dr. Friedman acknowledged that he had no training in crime scene investigation and that he did not know if the Ungar vehicle had increased its speed prior to the first shot being fired. See *id.* at 63-64. While thirty seconds seems to the court to be at the high end of the possible range of time consumed by the attack (with the low end being ten or fifteen seconds), it is not an unreasonable estimate, and the court therefore accepts it.

The physical injuries suffered by Yaron prior to his losing consciousness were severe and caused great pain. In addition, he experienced the mental pain resulting from observing that his wife had been horribly wounded and probably killed while seated next to him and knowing that his young son, lying in the back seat, was in danger of being killed. While this physical and mental agony was of mercifully brief duration, a substantial award for pain and

suffering is justified. Accordingly, I recommend an award of $500,000 for pain and suffering to the estate. Cf. *Smith v. Islamic Emirate of Afghanistan*, 262 F.Supp.2d 217, 238-39 (S.D.N.Y.2003) (awarding $2.5 million for pain and suffering to estate of plaintiff who realized he was trapped and doomed in the North Tower of World Trade Center and likely experienced a very painful death); *Weinstein v. Islamic Republic of Iran*, 184 F.Supp.2d 13, 18, 23 (D.D.C.2002)(awarding $10 million for pain and suffering to estate of bombing victim who survived with severe burns for forty-nine days and who suffered a higher level of pain throughout his stay at the hospital than a patient with his injuries otherwise would have endured because usual doses of pain medication could have lowered his blood pressure and killed him); *Elahi v. Islamic Republic of Iran*, 124 F.Supp.2d 97, 113 (D.D.C.2000)(finding $1 million appropriate compensation for pain and suffering of decedent who apparently struggled with his assassin for thirty seconds before being shot eight times); *Higgins v. Islamic Republic of Iran*, No. 1:99CV00377, 2000 WL 33674311, at *8 (D.D.C. Sept. 21, 2000)(awarding $30 million for pain and suffering where decedent was held captive for 529 days in primitive conditions and whose body indicated grievous injuries and barbaric mutilations); *Eisenfeld v. Islamic Republic of Iran*, 172 F.Supp.2d 1, 5, 8 (D.D.C.2000)(concluding that $1 million was appropriate to compensate for "several minutes" of pain and suffering of bombing victim who expired on the scene); *Flatow v. Islamic Republic of Iran*, 999 F.Supp. 1, 29 (D.D.C.1998)(finding $1 million appropriate to compensate for three to five hours of pain and suffering of bombing victim).

D. Dvir and Yishai Ungar

1. Loss of Companionship, Society and Guidance, and Mental Anguish

At the time of their father's murder, Dvir Ungar was twenty months old and Yishai was ten months old. *See* 7/12/02 Hearing Tr. at 114, 148. Although they are not American citizens, [FN38] 18 U.S.C. §2333(a) contains no requirement that the survivors or heirs of a United States national killed by an act of international terrorism must themselves be citizens of the United States, and this court will not read such a requirement into the statute. Cf. *Anderson v. Islamic Republic of Iran*, 90 F.Supp.2d 107, 113 (D.D.C.2000)(allowing claim of Lebanese wife of American hostage pursuant to 28 U.S.C. §1605(a)(7)); *Cicippio v. Islamic Republic of Iran*, 18 F.Supp.2d 62, 64, 68 n. 7 (D.D.C.1998)(finding that court had jurisdiction over claims brought pursuant to 28

U.S.C. §§1330(a) and 1605(a)(7) of non-citizen spouses of U.S. citizens who had been kidnapped).

FN38. The general requirement for acquisition of citizenship by a child born outside the United States and its outlying possessions and to parents who are married, one of whom is a citizen and the other of whom is an alien, is set forth in 8 U.S.C. §1401(g). The statute provides that the child is also a citizen if, before the birth, the citizen parent had been physically present in the United States for a total of five years, at least two of which were after the parent turned 14 years of age.

Tuan Anh Nguyen v. Immigration & Naturalization Serv., 533 U.S. 53, 59, 121 S.Ct. 2053, 2058, 150 L.Ed.2d 115 (2001). The record indicates that Yaron Ungar was not physically present in the United States for two years after turning age fourteen. *See* 7/12/02 Hearing Tr. at 92, 100.

In assessing damages for loss of companionship and mental anguish, this court finds guidance in the opinion in *Flatow v. Islamic Republic of Iran*, 999 F.Supp. 1 (D.D.C.1998):

The calculations for mental anguish and loss of society share some common considerations. First, the calculation should be based upon the anticipated duration of the injury. Claims for mental anguish belong to the claimants and should reflect anticipated persistence of mental anguish in excess of that which would have been experienced following decedent's natural death. When death results from terrorism, the fact of death and the cause of death can become inextricably intertwined, thus interfering with the prospects for anguish to diminish over time.

The nature of the relationship between the claimant and the decedent is another critical factor in the solatium analysis. If the relationship is strong and close, the likelihood that the claimant will suffer mental anguish and loss of society is substantially increased, particularly for intangibles such as companionship, love, affection, protection, and guidance. Numerous factors enter into this analysis, including: strong emotional ties between the claimant and the decedent; decedent's position in the family birth order relative to the claimant; the relative maturity or immaturity of the claimants; whether decedent habitually provided advice and solace to claimants; whether the claimant shared interests and pursuits with decedent; as well as decedent's achievements and plans for the future which would have affected claimants.

Finally, unlike lost wages, which can be calculated with a fair degree of mathematical certainty, solatium cannot be defined through models and variables. Courts have therefore refused to even attempt to factor in the present value of future mental anguish and loss of society. While economic losses can be reduced to present value with simple equations to establish the amount of an annuity established today which would have matched the decedent's ostensible income stream, the scope and uncertainty of human emotion renders such a calculation wholly inappropriate. This is the paradox of solatium; although no amount of money can alleviate the emotional impact of a child's or sibling's death, dollars are the only means available to do so.

Flatow v. Islamic Republic of Iran, 999 F.Supp. at 31-32 (citations omitted). [FN39]

FN39. A more concise statement of the factors to be considered in determining the award for loss of consortium and solatium was given by the court in *Kerr v. Islamic Republic of Iran*, 245 F.Supp.2d 59 (D.D.C.2003):

(1) whether the decedent's death was sudden and unexpected; (2) whether the death was attributable to negligence or malice; (3) whether the claimants have sought medical treatment for depression and related disorders resulting from the decedent's death; (4) the nature (*i.e.* closeness) of the relationship between the claimant and the decedent; and (5) the duration of the claimant's mental anguish in excess of that which would have been experienced following the decedent's natural death.

Id. at 64.

Applying the first of the factors described above to the circumstances of the present case, the court finds that the duration of the injury is very long. Yaron Ungar was twenty-six years old at the time of his death, and he could have reasonably been expected to live another fifty years. *See* Hearing Ex. 6 (Ziderman Report) at 5 (stating that the life expectancy for Jewish males in Israel is 76.5 years). If he had not been murdered, his sons likely would have enjoyed his companionship for approximately fifty years. Their mental anguish over the murder of their father, while likely to diminish somewhat over time, will always be with them even into old age.

Plaintiffs presented testimony that the relationship between Yaron and his sons was particularly close and loving. *See* 7/12/02 Hearing Tr. at 107-09, 146. As an example of this fact, Judith Dasberg, Yaron's mother-in-law, testified that Efrat once told her that, although she (Efrat) was with the children all day long, when Yaron came home the children focused their attention on him to such an extent that she almost felt she was being ignored. See *id.* at 147. Mrs. Dasberg also noted that the night they received the news of Yaron and Efrat's deaths, Dvir awoke and cried repeatedly for his "daddy," not mentioning his mother. See *id.* at 147-48. The next morning he asked about the absence of both his parents, but that night he had cried exclusively for his father. See *id.* at 148.

Dvir's special attachment to his father was also noted by Yaron's mother, Mrs. Judith Ungar, who is a psychologist with a master's degree. See *id.* at 101, 107. Mrs. Ungar testified that usually there is a special bond between a mother and a child because the father goes to work and has less time with the child. See *id.* at 107-08. However, in the case of Yaron and Dvir, that type of bond was present. See *id.* at 108. She noted that when Dvir cried at night, he would always cry for his father and not his mother. See *id.* Mrs. Ungar described Yaron as doing "everything with [the children]," *id.* at 109, crawling on the floor with them, and generally being the equal of Efrat in terms of providing care to the children, see *id.* The boys now live with the Dasbergs, and Mrs. Dasberg testified that she and her husband, because of their ages, cannot play on the floor with the boys. See *id.* at 151.

The evidence indicates that Yaron intended to be actively involved in the education of his children as a loving and caring parent. See *id.* at 146. He was an educator himself, and he was very good with children. See *id.* at 104. His ability to relate well to young persons was also reflected by his participation in a program for disadvantaged students similar to the Big Brothers organization in the United States. See *id.* at 107. Yishai and Dvir have been deprived of the benefit of the special educational skills and talents which their father possessed.

Dr. Allan Brenman, a child psychologist, testified after having interviewed the children (in Hebrew) and the grandparents (in English). *See* 7/15/02 Hearing Tr. at 8. From the information gathered during these interviews, it appeared to Dr. Brenman that overall the children were doing quite well. See *id.* at 9. They had attached to their grandparents, see *id.* at 12, and this attachment had been facilitated by the fact that their grandparents were familiar persons to them prior to their parents' deaths, see *id.* at 12-13.

At the same time, Dr. Brenman expressed some concerns about the boys. He noted that Dvir has become overprotective of his brother, Yishai, "almost to the point of a dependency…" *Id.* at 9. As an example of this, Dr. Brenman cited the fact that Dvir prefers to play with Yishai and Yishai's friends rather than with children his own age. See *id.* Dr. Brenman also stated that there had been some instances of aggressive behavior by Dvir at school and that this should be monitored to see if it is a pattern of behavior which needed further exploration. See *id.* at 10.

Dr. Brenman testified that the loss of both of their parents had caused the children "psychic trauma," *id.* at 12, al-

though it was difficult to gauge the magnitude and impact, see *id.* at 12-13, 25. He noted that because the children were being raised by their grandparents, they would be "orphaned a second time by the people who basically raised them [and] at a much younger age." *Id.* at 23. Dr. Brennan stated that in the future the children were susceptible to developing depression, anxiety, and post-traumatic stress disorder. See *id.* at 27. He also offered that he would not be surprised if at some point in their lives they required psychotherapy to cope with feelings which may arise. See *id.* In sum, Dr. Brennan opined that although the children were doing well at present, they were at increased risk for developing problems in the future as a result of the loss of both their parents. See *id.* at 25-28.

The fact that the children lost their mother at the same time as their father makes this loss even more traumatic. Given that Dvir and Yishai have been deprived of the companionship of their father for approximately fifty years, including virtually all of their childhood, and that they will eventually know that their father died a bloody and painful death at the hands of terrorists, a substantial award is warranted. The court also takes into consideration the awards for loss of consortium and mental anguish which have been made in other cases involving the death or abduction of a parent in a terrorist attack: *Smith v. Islamic Emirate of Afghanistan*, 262 F.Supp.2d 217, 239-40 (S.D.N.Y.2003)(awarding $3 million to each of six children of victim who died in the North Tower of World Trade Center); *Kerr v. Islamic Republic of Iran*, 245 F.Supp.2d 59, 64 (D.D.C.2003)(awarding $3 million each for solatium to four adult children whose father was shot in the back of the head by terrorists); *Weinstein v. Islamic Republic of Iran*, 184 F.Supp.2d 13, 23 (D.D.C.2002)(awarding $5 million to each adult child of bombing victim); *Sutherland v. Islamic Republic of Iran*, 151 F.Supp.2d 27, 52 (D.D.C.2001)(finding that daughters of kidnapping victim who was held for 6 1/2 years were each entitled to $6.5 million for solatium damages); *Higgins v. Islamic Republic of Iran,* No. 1:99CV00377, 2000 WL 33674311, at *9 (D.D.C. Sept. 21, 2000)(awarding $12 million to high school student for loss of companionship and mental anguish resulting from father's kidnapping, torture and murder); *Alejandre v. Republic of Cuba*, 996 F.Supp. 1239, 1249 (S.D.Fla.1997) (awarding $7.5 million for mental pain and suffering and $.5 million for loss of parental companionship and guidance to college-aged student for death of her father). Accordingly, I recommend that Dvir Ungar and Yishai Ungar each be awarded $10,000,000 for the loss of parental society, companionship, and guidance and mental anguish caused by their father's death. [FN40]

FN40. The court deems it desirable to treat each child equally notwithstanding the evidence of a special bond between Dvir and his father. *See* 7/12/02 Hearing Tr. at 107-08. It is reasonable to infer that a similar special bond would have also developed between Yishai and his father. Also, Dvir enjoyed his father's companionship for twenty months while Yishai's period of enjoyment was limited to ten months. These considerations cause the court to make an equal award to each child.

2. Loss of Parental Services

In addition to the loss of companionship, Dvir and Yishai were deprived of their father's parental services. These services include such tasks as babysitting, feeding, bathing, doing the laundry, getting them ready for school, and similar assistance normally performed by a parent for a child. *See* 7/12/02 Hearing Tr. at 83. While there is no one occupation which would provide all of these services, Dr. Ziderman looked to what he called the care sector of the Israeli economy-for example, people who work with the elderly, nannies, and au pairs-and the cost of providing such care services as the closest substitute for these parental services in order to determine their value. See *id*. Using this approach, he fixed the value of lost parental services to the children as being between $18,011 and $21,010 per year, depending on the educational level of the workers utilized. See *id*. at 86-87. Dr. Ziderman assumed that these parental services would not be required beyond the age of eighteen. See *id*. at 87. Stating that the youngest child was about one year old at the time of his father's death, Dr. Ziderman determined the cost of providing such services for seventeen years. See *id*. at 87-88. Discounting the amount required over seventeen years, Dr. Ziderman determined that the amount was $325,655. *See* Hearing Ex. 6, Supplement. This figure was based on a cost per year of $21,010 which the court finds to be reasonable. In light of the college level education which both of their parents possessed, employment of child care workers possessing a higher level of education is appropriate and fully justified. Therefore, I recommend that the legal guardians of Dvir Ungar and Yishai Ungar be awarded $325,655 ($162,827.50 for each child) for loss of parental services.

E. Judith and Meir Ungar

Yaron's parents, Judith and Meir Ungar, both testified at the hearing. *See* 7/12/02 Hearing Tr. at 89-119. They both described in poignant detail the devastating impact that Yaron's death has had upon them and their family. See *id*. The relationship which they had with Yaron was close, and that closeness continued even after his marriage to Efrat. Every other weekend Yaron, Efrat, and the boys would stay

with them from Friday night to either Saturday night or Sunday morning. See *id*. at 92. Although Mr. and Mrs. Ungar have tried valiantly to carry on for the sake of their other children, a large measure of joy has gone out of their lives. See *id*. at 96, 111-12. Their family life has suffered. See *id*. at 99. Meir Ungar noted that he and his wife both need to know where their adult children are at all times and that his wife is "very nervous about it..." *Id*.

Meir Ungar testified that it was hard for him to participate in activities such as folk dancing, which he formerly enjoyed, because he felt that he did not "have the right to be happy." *Id*. at 96. An associate professor of business administration, specializing in corporate finance, Professor Ungar's rate of publishing has drastically declined since his son's murder, and his promotion to full professor depends almost entirely upon publication of scholarly articles. See *id*. at 97-98.

Mrs. Ungar described the loss of her son as being like a "terrible weight" in her heart that is always with her and stated that she can never enjoy anything, even happy occasions, because the memory of Yaron is always with her. See *id*. at 112. She noted that even when her daughter gave birth to twin daughters, she was unable to be happy. See *id*. at 112-13. Prior to Yaron's death, she sang in a choir, but she no longer participates in it. See *id*. at 112. Her family life suffered as everyone is "more nervous." *Id*. at 113. Mrs. Ungar testified that for a mother to lose a child is "the most horrible thing that can happen." *Id*. at 110. Her pain was compounded by the knowledge of the "cold, cruel and horrible way" in which Yaron had died. *Id*.

The court has no doubt from the testimony presented that Mr. and Mrs. Ungar have suffered and will continue to suffer severe grief and loneliness from Yaron's death. Bearing in mind their suffering and loss, I recommend that Judith Ungar and Meir Ungar each be awarded damages in the amount of $5,000,000 for the loss of society and companionship and mental anguish caused them by the death of their son. This award is comparable to other awards made to parents whose emancipated children have been murdered. See *Smith v. Islamic Emirate of Afghanistan*, 262 F.Supp.2d 217, 238-39 (S.D.N.Y.2003) (awarding $3 million for solatium to father of victim trapped in the North Tower of World Trade Center); *Eisenfeld v. Islamic Republic of Iran*, 172 F.Supp.2d 1, 9 (D.D.C.2000)(awarding for solatium $5 million each to the surviving parents of two bombing victims); *Flatow v. Islamic Republic of Iran*, 999 F.Supp. 1, 32 (D.D.C.1998)(finding award of $5 million each to parents of bombing victim for solatium appropriate); see also *Alejandre v. Republic of Cuba*, 996 F.Supp. 1239, 1249 (S.D.Fla.1997) (awarding $5.5 million for mental pain and suffering and for loss of society and companionship to each of four parents whose sons were murdered when their unarmed civilian plane was shot down over international airspace).

F. Michal Cohen, Amichai Ungar and Dafna Ungar

Each of Yaron's siblings had a special intimate relationship with him. His sister, Michal, who was three years older than Yaron, described a "bond and trust between [them] so that [they] could talk about everything." 7/12/02 Hearing Tr. at 121. This close relationship which had begun during their childhood continued even after Yaron was married. When Efrat was still in the hospital recovering from the birth of Dvir, Michal and Yaron went shopping together to buy things for the baby. See *id.* at 122. On this occasion Yaron told her how lucky he was to have her for a sister, but Michal testified that it was she who was lucky to have Yaron for a brother. See *id.*

Michal recounted how her brother's death had affected her and her family. See *id.* at 123. She observed that when her twins were born two years earlier it should have been the happiest day of her life, but she could not help thinking how sad it was that Yaron was not there and that her twins "won't be able to see this wonderful lovely crazy uncle who would crawl with them and sing with them and jump with them and just teach them…" *Id.* at 123. Michal related how hearing Yaron's favorite song being played in a mall would "paralyze[ ]" her, *id.* at 124, and that "seeing in the distance a tall blond guy," *id.*, would cause her to think for a split second that it was Yaron even though it was illogical, see *id.* The loss of Yaron was always with her. See *id.*

Amichai Ungar testified that he viewed his older brother as his hero and his protector. See *id.* at 127. He described an incident from his childhood when he was knocked down by a large dog and Yaron came running to his aid, knocking the dog off Amichai. See *id.* Amichai read from a letter which Yaron had written to him when Amichai was thirteen which contained brotherly advice and evidenced a close relationship between them. See *id.* at 128. Since his brother's death, Amichai testified that "things aren't the same." *Id.* at 129. He noted that when Dvir and Yishai come to stay with the family, his job is to look after them. See *id.* While Amichai performs this task lovingly, he observed that the ones who are supposed to care for the children are their parents and that he is only their uncle. See *id.* at 129-30. He recounted being at a wedding after Yaron's death, seeing the groom and the groom's brother dancing together, and having to cry to because he realized when he got married Yaron would not be there to dance with him. See *id.* at 131.

Since Yaron's death, Amichai testified that his family has been "very tense." *Id.* at 130. He related that if some-

thing falls, everyone jumps. See *id.* Voicing frustration at how overprotective his parents have become, Amichai noted that even though he is twenty-five years old, his mother will not go to sleep until he is home. See *id.* He also indicated that he will refrain from participating in activities he formerly enjoyed, such as climbing and running on the hills, if there is an element of risk because "I can't let them lose another son." *Id.* at 130.

Yaron's younger sister, Dafna, [FN41] testified that she remembered him as her "big protecting brother," *id.* at 133, and that he always made them laugh and always had a smile on his face. See *id.* She noted that she was only sixteen when Yaron was murdered and that she was robbed of the chance to know him as an adult. See *id.* at 134. His death deeply affected her. See *id.* at 135. She described how after his death she felt the need to talk with Yaron and that she would have a "conversation" with his photograph every night before she went to sleep. See *id.* She even wrote letters to him and Efrat. See *id.*

FN41. When she testified at the hearing, Yaron's younger sister spelled her name as "Daphne." 7/12/02 Hearing Tr. at 132. For consistency, the court uses "Dafna," the spelling which appears in the Complaint.

Dafna also described the current state of the family: "it's not that we always walk around in deep sorrow but in every act that we do we have this on the background of our mind reminding us all the time what ha[s] happened." *Id.* at 136. This description encapsulates the essence of the testimony of the other family members.

The court finds that there was a deep and strong emotional attachment between Yaron and his siblings. Accordingly, I recommend that they each be awarded $2,500,000 for the loss of society and companionship and mental anguish caused by the death of their brother. This award is within the range which other courts have found reasonable for siblings. See *Smith v. Islamic Emirate of Afghanistan*, 262 F.Supp.2d 217, 239-40 (S.D.N.Y.2003)(awarding $2 million for solatium to each sibling of victim of World Trade Center attack); *Kerr v. Islamic Republic of Iran*, 245 F.Supp.2d 59, 64 (D.D.C.2003)(awarding $1.5 million each for solatium to sisters of victim of terrorist shooting attack); *Elahi v. Islamic Republic of Iran*, 124 F.Supp.2d 97, 112 (D.D.C.2000)(concluding that an award for solatium of $5 million each to brothers of assassination victim was appropriate); *Eisenfeld v. Islamic Republic of Iran*, 172 F.Supp.2d 1, 9 (D.D.C.2000) (awarding $2.5 million each to siblings of two bombing victims); *Flatow v. Islamic Republic of Iran*, 999 F.Supp. 1, 32 (D.D.C.1998)(finding award of $2.5 million for solatium to siblings of bombing victim appropriate).

G. Treble Damages

18 U.S.C. §2333(a) provides that plaintiffs "shall recover threefold damages he or she sustains and the cost of the suit, including attorney's fees." 18 U.S.C. §2333(a). After tripling, the amounts which I recommended be awarded to each plaintiff are shown below:

Estate of Yaron Ungar
for lost earnings: $1,432,158.00
for pain and suffering of decedent: $1,500,000.00

Dvir Ungar (son)
for loss of companionship, society, and guidance and mental anguish:
$30,000,000.00
for loss of parental services:
$488,482.50 [FN42]

Judith Ungar (mother)
for loss of society and companionship and mental anguish:
$15,000,000.00

Meir Ungar (father)
for loss of society and companionship and mental anguish:
$15,000,000.00

Michal Cohen (sister)
for loss of society and companionship and mental anguish:
$7,500,000.00

Amichai Ungar (brother)
for loss of society and companionship and mental anguish:
$7,500,000.00

Dafna Ungar (sister)
for loss of society and companionship and mental anguish:
$7,500,000.00

Total: $116,409,123.00

FN42. The amount designated for loss of parental services shall be paid to the legal guardians of Dvir Ungar.

FN43. The amount designated for loss of parental services shall be paid to the legal guardians of Yishai Ungar.

Notes:

1. What was the legal basis for the court importing the damages analysis used in §1605(a)(7) cases when awarding damages under the Klinghoffer Act? Why is it significant that that the court looked to *Flatow* and other cases brought under the FSIA in awarding damages in this §2333 cases?

2. What other measurement tools were available to the *Unger* court? Why did the court spend so much effort surveying the law of damages? Why did the court find that §2333 required such detailed analysis?

3. The court found that Congress' inclusion of family members ("heirs" and "survivors") as claimants under §2333 conforms with the nation-wide tendency in the last few decades, as noted in the leading treatise on tort law,

> [T]hough recovery for loss of society and comfort is denied under some statutes, it is an item usually recognized and made the basis for an award, at times apparently substantial …

> Even jurisdictions that have rejected the loss of society or consortium claim, as such, have permitted one form of it, namely a loss of guidance and advice that the decedent would have provided, at least in the case of deceased parents.

Prosser & Keeton on Torts §127 (1984). Is this an accurate analysis of the state of the law of damages? Do in fact family members of victims in traditional torts (negligence, various forms of sexual abuse, medical malpractice, intentional torts) commonly have a right to claim emotional damages? Does this hold true for non-dependant family members, i.e. adult siblings and parents?

4. What is the effect of importing the §1605(a)(7) award structure to §2333 claims, which by statute are automatically trebled? Does this create extra large awards? If so, is this inconsistent with the purpose of the statute?

5. How does trebling damages serve to *limit* damages awards? If the trebling provision of §2333 did not exist, what other forms of damages would be available to plaintiffs? Would aggregate awards be greater if trebling were not permitted under §2333?

6. Why did plaintiffs' bother to litigate the issue of pre-judgment interest? How did the court's ruling denying pre-judgment interest comport with the legislative history of the act?

10.3 Punitive Damages

Flatow v. Islamic Republic of Iran, 999 F.Supp. 1 (D. D.C. 1998).

LAMBERTH, District Judge.

For the reasons set forth in the accompanying findings of Fact and Conclusions of Law, it is hereby

* * *

FINDINGS OF FACT AND CONCLUSIONS OF LAW

This is an action for wrongful death resulting from an act of state-sponsored terrorism. Defendants have not entered an appearance in this matter. This Court entered Defendants' default on September 4, 1997, pursuant to 28 U.S.C. §1608(e) and Fed.R.Civ.P. 55(a). Notwithstanding indicia of Defendants' willful default, [FN1] however, this Court is compelled to make further inquiry prior to entering a judgment by default against Defendants. As with actions against the federal government, the Foreign Sovereign Immunities Act ("FSIA") requires that a default judgment against a foreign state be entered only after plaintiff "establishes his claim or right to relief by evidence that is satisfactory to the Court." 28 U.S.C. §1608(e); see *Compania Interamericana Export-Import, S.A. v. Compania Dominicana de Aviacion*, 88 F.3d 948, 951 (11th Cir.1996).

FN1. Service of process was accomplished with the assistance of the Swiss Embassy in Tehran, the United States' protecting power in the Islamic Republic of Iran, on June 8, 1997. This Court has yet to receive any response from Defendants, either through counsel's entry of appearance, or through a diplomatic note. The Islamic Republic of Iran is an experienced litigant in the United States federal court system generally and in this Circuit. See, e.g., *Cicippio v. Islamic Republic of Iran*, 30 F.3d 164 (D.C.Cir.1994), *cert. denied* 513 U.S. 1078, 115 S.Ct. 726, 130 L.Ed.2d 631 (1995); *Foremost-McKesson v. Islamic Republic of Iran*, 905 F.2d 438 (D.C.Cir.1990); *Persinger v. Islamic Republic of Iran*, 729 F.2d 835 (D.C.Cir.1984); *Berkovitz v. Islamic Republic of Iran*, 735 F.2d 329 (9th Cir.1984), *McKeel v. Islamic Republic of Iran*, 722 F.2d 582 (9th Cir.1983). The Islamic Republic of Iran also apparently attempted to evade service of process by international registered mail, pursuant to 28 U.S.C. §1608(a)(3). When the service package was returned

to counsel in June 1997, the package had been opened, the return receipt, which counsel had not received, had been completely removed, and the message "DO NOT USA" was written in English across the back of the envelope. This contumacious conduct bolsters the entry of a default judgment. See *Commercial Bank of Kuwait v. Rafidain Bank*, 15 F.3d 238 (2d Cir.1994).

Plaintiff brings this action pursuant to two recently enacted amendments to the FSIA, which grant jurisdiction over foreign states and their officials, agents and employees, and create federal causes of action related to personal injury or death resulting from state-sponsored terrorist attacks. Given these novel enactments, and this Court's special role in the development of foreign sovereign immunity jurisprudence, *see* 28 U.S.C. §1391(f)(4), this Court has engaged in a systematic review of dispositive legal issues prior to making its determination that Plaintiff has established his claim and right to relief to the satisfaction of this Court. [FN2]

FN2. This Court knows of only one other Court which has interpreted these new provisions, the United States District Court for the Southern District of Florida, in an action brought by the families of the Brothers to the Rescue pilots shot down by the Cuban Air Force over the Straits of Florida on February 24, 1996. *Alejandre, et al. v. The Republic of Cuba, et al.,* 996 F.Supp. 1239 (1997). Cases resulting from the bombing of Pan Am Flight 103 have been re-filed under these provisions, and are currently pending before the United States District Court for the Eastern District of New York. See, e.g., *Rein v. Socialist People's Libyan Arab Jamahiriya*, 995 F.Supp. 325 (E.D.N.Y.1998).

FINDINGS OF FACT

This matter came before the Court for an evidentiary hearing on March 2-3, 1998. The Plaintiff proceeded in the manner of a nonjury trial before the Court and the following findings of fact are based upon the sworn testimony and documents entered into evidence in accordance with the Federal Rules of Evidence. Plaintiff has "establishe[d] his claim or right to relief by evidence that is satisfactory to the Court" as required by 28 U.S.C. §1608(e). This Court finds the following facts to be established by clear and convincing evidence, which would have been sufficient to establish a *prima facie* case in a contested proceeding:

1 Plaintiff Stephen M. Flatow, a domiciliary of the State of New Jersey, is the father of Alisa Michelle Flatow, decedent, and is also the Administrator of the Estate of Alisa Michelle Flatow. He brings this action in his own right, as Adminis-

trator of the Estate of Alisa Michelle Flatow, and on behalf of decedent's heirs-at-law, including Rosalyn Flatow, decedent's mother, and decedent's siblings, Gail, age 21, Francine, age 18, Ilana, age 16, and Etan, age 14, all decedent's siblings. Affidavit (Exhibit 2) (Exhibit 2) and testimony of Stephen M. Flatow.

2 Alisa Michelle Flatow was born on October 5, 1974 in the United States. She maintained her United States citizenship throughout her life, and was a United States citizen at the time of her death. Affidavit (Exhibit 2) and testimony of Stephen M. Flatow; Report of the Death Of An American Citizen Abroad (Exhibit 9).

3 At the time of her death, Alisa Michelle Flatow was a twenty-year-old Brandeis University student. For the 1995 spring semester, her junior year at Brandeis University, Alisa Michelle Flatow arranged for and participated in an independent foreign study program in Israel. Affidavit (Exhibit 2) and testimony of Stephen M. Flatow; testimony of Dr. Jonathan Sarna; testimony of Alan Mitrani; testimony of Lauren Sloane; testimony of Gail Flatow; testimony of Francine Flatow; decedent's academic records from Brandeis University.

4 While in Israel, she communicated with her father, Plaintiff Stephen M. Flatow, to ask whether she could travel to a community on the Mediterranean Sea with friends. He reviewed their itinerary with her, and as he believed that the Israeli government would not provide civilian passenger bus service unless it were safe to do so and he gave her permission to travel in Gaza. Affidavit (Exhibit 2) and testimony of Stephen M. Flatow.

5 On April 9, 1995, decedent Alisa Michelle Flatow was a passenger on the number 36 Egged bus, which was traveling from Ashkelon, Israel to a Mediterranean resort in the Gush Katif community. Testimony of Kesari Rusa.

6 At or about 12:05 p.m. local time, near Kfar Darom in the Gaza Strip, a suicide bomber drove a van loaded with explosives into the number 36 Egged bus, causing an explosion that destroyed the bus. Testimony of Kesari Rusa; testimony of Orit Taft; testimony of Ezra Mordecai testimony of and videotape by David Shaenbaum; U.S. DEP'T OF STATE, PATTERNS OF GLOBAL TERRORISM 1995 (April 1996).

7 As a result of the explosion, a piece of shrapnel pierced Alisa Michelle Flatow's skull casing and lodged in her brain,

causing a severe head injury. Testimony of Dr. Allen Fisher; decedent's medical records from the Soroka Medical Center, with translation from Hebrew (Exhibit 3).

8 Immediately after the explosion, Alisa Michelle Flatow slumped over onto her traveling companion, Kesari Rusa. Her eyes were open and her hands clutched. She received emergency medical treatment on the scene. Because her injuries were so severe, she was among the first of the injured which the Israeli Defense Forces medivac'ed by helicopter to the Soroka Medical Center in B'er Sheva for immediate medical attention. Testimony of Kesari Rusa; testimony of and videotape by David Shaenbaum; testimony of Orit Taft.

9 Upon her arrival at the Soroka Medical Center approximately one hour after the bombing, Alisa Michelle Flatow's pulse and respiration were good without medical assistance. Her pupils reacted to light and she responded to deep pain stimuli. She was assessed as a 5 of a possible 15 on the Glasgow coma scale. She had sustained a depressed skull fracture and intracerebral lacerations. Testimony of Dr. Allen Fisher; decedent's medical records from the Soroka Medical Center, with translation from Hebrew (Exhibit 3).

10 From approximately 3 to 5 pm local time, Alisa Michelle Flatow was in emergency surgery; the entrance wound was debrided and a partial craniotomy was performed in order to alleviate pressure from the intracerebral hemorrhaging and concomitant swelling of brain tissue within the skull. Testimony of Dr. Allen Fisher; decedent's medical records from the Soroka Medical Center, with translation from Hebrew (Exhibit 3).

11 To a reasonable degree of medical certainty, Alisa Michelle Flatow suffered extreme bodily pain and suffering for at least three to five hours as a result of the injuries she sustained in the bombing. Testimony of Dr. Gregory Threatte.

12 Plaintiff Stephen M. Flatow first heard of the attack on the radio on April 9, 1995 at approximately 7:45 am EST; he immediately began attempts to contact his daughter. That decedent had been on the number 36 Egged bus was confirmed when one of her traveling companions telephoned her family in the United States. Plaintiff made extraordinary efforts to locate his daughter; after several hours, the Medical Center confirmed that she was being treated there and that she was in grave condition. Plaintiff immediately flew to Israel to be with his daughter. Affidavit (Exhibit 2) and testimony of Stephen M. Flatow; testimony of Rosalyn Flatow; testimony of Alan Mitrani.

13 Shortly after his arrival at the Soroka Medical Center the morning of April 10, 1995, the hospital director and Dr. Allen Fisher, the attending physician, informed Stephen M. Flatow that Alisa Michelle Flatow showed no brain activity, that all physical functions relied upon artificial life support, and that there was no hope for her recovery. Affidavit (Exhibit 2) and testimony of Stephen M. Flatow; testimony of Dr. Allan Fisher; decedent's medical records from the Soroka Medical Center, with translation from Hebrew (exhibit 3).

14 The Flatow family is Jewish and observes Orthodox Jewish practice. Orthodox doctrine reveres the sanctity of life and of the body; the traditional view is that all means should be exerted to prolong life, and that the body must be buried intact. However, Orthodox doctrine also considers the saving of one life to be the saving of an entire universe. Alisa Michelle Flatow's condition presented an opportunity to save lives through organ donation, which is extremely rare in Israel precisely because it is incompatible with the sanctity of life and of the body. After consulting with several Rabbis, Stephen M. Flatow requested that no further extraordinary efforts be exerted on behalf of his daughter, that life support be terminated, and that his daughter's organs be harvested for transplant. Alisa Michelle Flatow died at approximately 10:00 a.m. local time on April 10, 1995. Her organs saved three lives and significantly improved the quality of life for several other persons. Affidavit (Exhibit 2) and testimony of Stephen M. Flatow, testimony of Dr. Allan Fisher decedent's medical records from the Soroka Medical Center, with translation from Hebrew (Exhibit 3); testimony of Ari Mendelson (organ recipient).

15 Alisa Michelle Flatow had been accompanied on the bus by two companions who were also United States nationals and were injured as a result of the explosion. United States nationals often rode this bus line. The attack on the bus caused seven other deaths and many injuries, all involving non-United States nationals. Testimony of Kesari Rusa; testimony of Orit Taft; U.S. DEP'T OF STATE, PATTERNS OF GLOBAL TERRORISM 1995 (April 1996).

16 The Shaqaqi faction of Palestine Islamic Jihad claimed responsibility for and in fact perpetrated the terrorist act which caused the death of Alisa Michelle Flatow. Palestine Islamic Jihad is series of loosely affiliated factions rather than a cohesive group. The Shaqaqi faction is a terrorist cell with a small core membership. Its sole purpose is to conduct terrorist activities in the Gaza region, and its sole source of funding is the Islamic Republic of Iran. Testimony of Dr.

Reuven Paz; testimony of Dr. Patrick Clawson; testimony of former FBI Deputy Assistant Director for Counterterrorism Harry Brandon; U.S. DEP'T OF STATE, PATTERNS OF GLOBAL TERRORISM 1995 (April 1996).

17 The Israeli government informed Stephen M. Flatow that the Shaqaqi faction of Palestine Islamic Jihad had claimed responsibility for the bombing, and that their investigation had confirmed that claim. Affidavit of Stephen M. Flatow (Exhibit 2).

18 In July 1996, Plaintiff Stephen M. Flatow and his counsel met with Ambassador Philip Wilcox, who then served as the Department of State's Coordinator for Counterterrorism. During that meeting, he informed Mr. Flatow that the Department of State was satisfied that the group which had claimed responsibility for the bombing, the Shaqaqi faction of Palestine Islamic Jihad, had in fact perpetrated the bombing, and that the Islamic Republic of Iran provided approximately two million dollars to Palestine Islamic Jihad annually in support of its terrorist activities. Affidavit of Stephen M. Flatow (Exhibit 2).

19 Defendant the Islamic Republic of Iran is a foreign state and has been designated a state sponsor of terrorism pursuant to section 6(j) of the Export Administration Act of 1979 (50 U.S.C.App. §2405(j)) continuously since January 19, 1984. Defendant provides material support and resources to Palestine Islamic Jihad by supplying funds and training for the Shaqaqi faction's terrorist activities in the Gaza Strip region. Testimony of Dr. Reuven Paz, testimony of Dr. Patrick Clawson, testimony of former FBI Deputy Assistant Director for Counterterrorism Harry Brandon.

20 Defendant the Islamic Republic of Iran sponsors the Shaqaqi faction's terrorist activities within the meaning of 28 U.S.C. §1605(a)(7) and 28 U.S.C. §1605 note by providing it with all of its funding. Testimony of Dr. Reuven Paz; testimony of Dr. Patrick Clawson; testimony of former FBI Deputy Assistant Director for Counterterrorism Harry Brandon.

21 Defendant the Iranian Ministry of Information and Security is the Iranian intelligence service, functioning both within and beyond Iranian territory. Acting as an agent of the Islamic Republic of Iran, the Iranian Ministry of Information and Security performed acts within the scope of its agency, within the meaning of 28 U.S.C. §1605(a)(7) and 28 U.S.C.A. §1605 note, which caused the death of Alisa Michelle Flatow. Specifically, the Iranian Ministry of Informa-

tion and Security acted as a conduit for the Islamic Republic of Iran's provision of funds and training to the Shaqaqi faction for its terrorist activities in the Gaza Strip region. Testimony of Dr. Reuven Paz; testimony of Dr. Patrick Clawson; testimony of former FBI Deputy Assistant Director for Counterterrorism Harry Brandon.

22 Defendant Ayatollah Ali Hoseini Khamenei is the Supreme Leader of the Islamic Republic of Iran. Acting as an official of the Islamic Republic of Iran, Defendant Ayatollah Ali Hoseini Khamenei performed acts within the scope of his office, within the meaning of 28 U.S.C. §1605(a)(7) and 28 U.S.C.A. §1605 note, which caused the death of Alisa Michelle Flatow. Specifically, Defendant Khamenei approved the provision of material support and resources to the Shaqaqi faction of Palestine Islamic Jihad. Testimony of Dr. Reuven Paz; testimony of Dr. Patrick Clawson; testimony of former FBI Deputy Assistant Director for Counterterrorism Harry Brandon.

23 Defendant Ali Akbar Hashemi-Rafsanjani is the former President of the Islamic Republic of Iran. Acting as an official of the Islamic Republic of Iran, Defendant Ali Akbar Hashemi-Rafsanjani performed acts within the scope of his office, within the meaning of 28 U.S.C. §1605(a)(7) and 28 U.S.C.A. §1605 note, which caused the death of Alisa Michelle Flatow. Specifically, Defendant approved the provision of material support and resources to the Shaqaqi faction of Palestine Islamic Jihad. Testimony of Dr. Reuven Paz; testimony of Dr. Patrick Clawson; testimony of former FBI Deputy Assistant Director for Counterterrorism Harry Brandon.

24 Defendant Ali Fallahian-Khuzestani is the former head of the Iranian Ministry of Information and Security. Acting as an official of the Islamic Republic of Iran, Defendant Ali Fallahian-Khuzestani performed acts within the scope of his office, within the meaning of 28 U.S.C. §1605(a)(7) and 28 U.S.C.A. §1605 note, which caused the death of Alisa Michelle Flatow. Specifically, Defendant Fallahian approved the provision of material support and resources by the Islamic Republic of Iran to the Shaqaqi faction. Testimony of Dr. Reuven Paz; testimony of Dr. Patrick Clawson; testimony of former FBI Deputy Assistant Director for Counterterrorism Harry Brandon.

25 Defendants the Islamic Republic of Iran, the Iranian Ministry of Information and Security, while acting as an agent of the Islamic Republic of Iran, and Iranian officials Ayatollah Ali Hoseini Khamenei, former President Ali Akbar Hashemi-Rafsanjani, and former Minister Ali Fallahian-Khuzestani, each acting in his official capacity, conspired to provide material support and resources to the Shaqaqi faction of Palestine Islamic Jihad, a terrorist organization, within the meaning of 28 U.S.C. §1605(a)(7) and 28 U.S.C.A. §1605 note, which caused the death of Alisa Michelle Flatow. Testimony of Dr. Reuven Paz; testimony of Dr. Patrick Clawson; testimony of former FBI Deputy Assistant Director for Counterterrorism Harry Brandon.

26 Alisa Michelle Flatow's death was caused by a willful and deliberate act of extrajudicial killing because the explosion was caused by a bomb that was deliberately driven into the bus by a member of the Shaqaqi faction of the Palestine Islamic Jihad acting under the direction of Defendants the Islamic Republic of Iran, the Iranian Ministry of Information and Security, Ayatollah Ali Hoseini Khamenei, Ali Akbar Hashemi-Rafsanjani and Ali Fallahian-Khuzestani.

27 As a result of Alisa Michelle Flatow's death, her Estate suffered a loss of accretions which could have been expected to occur during the course of her anticipated life expectancy in the amount of $1,508,750.00. Report (Exhibit 6) and testimony of Dr. Jerome S. Paige.

28 As a result of Alisa Michelle Flatow's death, her heirs-at-law have suffered an economic loss for the expenses associated with her funeral and final services in the amount of $4,470.00. Funeral Home Invoice (Exhibit 4).

29 As the result of Alisa Michelle Flatow's death, her parents and her surviving sisters and brother have suffered and will continue to suffer severe mental anguish and the loss of her society. Testimony of Stephen M. Flatow; testimony of Rosalyn Flatow; testimony of Gail Flatow; testimony of Francine Flatow, testimony of Ilana Flatow, testimony of Etan Flatow, testimony of Alan Mitrani, testimony of Lauren Sloane, testimony of Kesari Rusa.

I. CONCLUSIONS OF LAW WITH RESPECT TO JURISDICTION

A. THE FOREIGN SOVEREIGN IMMUNITIES ACT CONTROLS THIS ACTION.

As this action is brought against a foreign state, its intelligence service acting as its agent, and three of its officials, acting in their official capacity, [FN3] the Foreign Sovereign Immunities Act of 1976, 28 U.S.C. §§1602- 1611 *et seq.* ["FSIA"], as amended, controls this action. The FSIA must be applied in every action involving a foreign state defendant. *Verlinden B.V. v. Central Bank of Nigeria*, 461 U.S. 480, 489, 103 S.Ct. 1962, 76 L.Ed.2d 81 (1983); 28 U.S.C. §1330. The sole bases for subject matter jurisdiction in an action against a foreign state defendant are the FSIA's enumerated exceptions to immunity. *Argentine Republic v. Amerada Hess Shipping Corp.*, 488 U.S. 428, 434, 109 S.Ct. 683, 102 L.Ed.2d 818 (1989). This Court lacks jurisdiction over this matter unless it falls within one of the FSIA's enumerated exceptions to foreign sovereign immunity. See *Saudi Arabia v. Nelson*, 507 U.S. 349, 355, 113 S.Ct. 1471, 123 L.Ed.2d 47 (1993).

FN3. This Circuit has previously recognized that although the FSIA neither prohibits nor provides for its application to defendants who are natural persons, maintenance of a coherent practice regarding foreign sovereign immunity weighs heavily in favor of applying the FSIA to individuals. *First American Corp. v. Al Nahyan*, 948 F.Supp. 1107, 1120 (D.D.C.1996) citing *Herbage v. Meese*, 747 F.Supp. 60, 66 (D.D.C.1990). The FSIA has thus been construed to apply to individuals for acts performed in their official capacity on behalf of either a foreign state or its agency or instrumentality. *El-Fadl v. Central Bank of Jordan*, 75 F.3d 668, 671 (D.C.Cir.1996), citing *Chuidian v. Philippine Nat. Bank*, 912 F.2d 1095, 1099-1103 (9 Cir.1990); *In re Estate of Ferdinand E. Marcos Human Rights Litigation*, 978 F.2d 493, 496-97 (9th Cir.1992); *Kline v. Kaneko*, 685 F.Supp. 386 (S.D.N.Y.1988); *Rios v. Marshall*, 530 F.Supp. 351, 371-72 (S.D.N.Y.1981).

Until the beginning of this century, the United States afforded foreign states absolute immunity from suit in courts of the United States as a matter of common law. See, e.g., *The Schooner Exchange v. M'Faddon*, 11 U.S. (7 Cranch) 116, 3 L.Ed. 287 (1812); *Berizzi Bros. Co. v. S.S. Pesaro*, 271 U.S. 562, 46 S.Ct. 611, 70 L.Ed. 1088 (1926). With the rise of Communism and the consequent outgrowth of state trading and shipping companies, however, the United States began to recognize the restrictive theory of foreign sovereign immunity, which permitted suits arising from a foreign state's commercial activities. See S. SUCHARITKUL, STATE IMMUNITIES AND TRADING ACTIVITIES IN INTERNATIONAL LAW (1959); Friedmann, *Changing Social Arrangements in State-Trading States and their Effect on International Law*, 24 LAW & CONTEMP. PROBS. 350 (1959).

The issuance of the Tate Letter, on May 19, 1952, officially marked this transition for United States practice. *See* Letter from Jack B. Tate, Acting Legal Advisor, to Acting Attorney General (May 19, 1952), *reprinted at* 26 DEP'T OF STATE BULL. 984-985 *and reprinted at* Appendix 2 to *Alfred Dunhill of London v. Republic of Cuba*, 425 U.S. 682, 711, 96 S.Ct. 1854, 48 L.Ed.2d 301 (1976) [hereinafter "Tate Letter"]. The Tate Letter announced that the United States would henceforth follow the restrictive theory in making foreign sovereign immunity determinations. In 1976, in order to promote uniform and apolitical determinations, Congress transferred immunity determinations from the Department of State to the judiciary and otherwise essentially codified the Tate Letter's restrictive theory of foreign sovereign immunity in the FSIA. *See* H.R. REP. NO. 1487, 94th CONG., 2D SESS. at 12, *reprinted in* 1976 U.S.C.C.A.N. 6604, 6610-11; GARY B. BORN AND DAVID WESTIN, INTERNATIONAL CIVIL LITIGATION IN UNITED STATES COURTS at 452-453 (2d ed.1992); *see also* M. Sandler, D. Vagts & B. Ristau, eds., *Sovereign Immunity Decisions of the Department of State*, DIGEST OF UNITED STATES PRACTICE IN INTERNATIONAL LAW 1977 at 1017.

Courts steadfastly refused to extend the FSIA as originally enacted beyond commercial activities, *jure gestionis*, to reach public acts, *jure imperii*, outside the United States. This judicial restraint permitted foreign states to use the FSIA as a shield against civil liability for violations of the law of nations committed against United States nationals overseas. See, e.g., *Nelson*, 507 U.S. 349, 113 S.Ct. 1471, 123 L.Ed.2d 47; *Smith v. Socialist People's Libyan Arab Jamahiriya*, 101 F.3d 239 (2d Cir.1996), *cert. denied* 520 U.S. 1204, 117 S.Ct. 1569, 137 L.Ed.2d 714, *reh'g denied* 520 U.S. 1259, 117 S.Ct. 2427, 138 L.Ed.2d 189 (1997) [hereinafter "*Pan Am 103*"]; *Cicippio v. Islamic Republic of Iran*, 30 F.3d 164 (D.C.Cir.1994), *cert. denied* 513 U.S. 1078, 115 S.Ct. 726, 130 L.Ed.2d 631 (1995); *Princz v. Federal Republic of Germany*, 26 F.3d 1166 (D.C.Cir.1994), *cert. denied*, 513 U.S. 1121, 115 S.Ct. 923, 130 L.Ed.2d 803 (1995).

1. RECENT AMENDMENTS TO THE FOREIGN SOVEREIGN IMMUNITIES ACT CREATE SUBJECT MATTER JURISDICTION AND FEDERAL CAUSES OF ACTION FOR CERTAIN ACTS OF STATE SPONSORED TERRORISM.

In 1996 Congress took action which effectuated an even greater change than that represented by the Tate Letter. In the Antiterrorism and Effective Death Penalty Act of 1996, Congress lifted the immunity of foreign states for a certain category of sovereign acts which are repugnant to the United States and the international community-terrorism. Pub.L.

104-132, Title II, §221(a), (April 24, 1996), 110 Stat. 1241 *codified at* 28 U.S.C.A. §1605 (West 1997 Supp.) [hereinafter "state sponsored terrorism exception"]. That Act created an exception to the immunity of those foreign states officially designated by the Department of State as terrorist states [FN4] if the foreign state commits a terrorist act, or provides material support and resources to an individual or entity which commits such an act, which results in the death or personal injury of a United States citizen. *See* 28 U.S.C. §1605(a)(7)[FN5]; *see also* H.R.REP. NO. 383, 104TH CONG., 1ST SESS.1995 at 137-38, *available at* 1995 WL 731698.

FN4. In addition to the Islamic Republic of Iran, the foreign states currently designated as sponsors of terrorism pursuant to 50 U.S.C.App. §2405(j) are: Cuba, Syria, Iraq, Libya, Sudan and North Korea. *See* 22 C.F.R. §126.1(d) (current through October 31, 1997).

FN5. Pub.L. 105-11 (April 25, 1997), 111 Stat. 22, §1 amended 28 U.S . C. §1605(a)(7)(B)(ii) to substitute "neither the claimant nor the victim was" for "the claimant or victim was not"; *see also* H.R.Rep. No. 48, 105TH CONG ., 1ST SESS. (April 10, 1997), *available at* 1997 WL 177368.

Although the Antiterrorism Act created a forum competent to adjudicate claims arising from offenses of this nature, serious issues remained, in particular, the causes of action available to plaintiffs. Congressman Jim Saxton sponsored an amendment to 28 U.S.C. §1605(a)(7) with the intent to clarify this and other issues. In Congressman Saxton's experience as Chairman of the House Task Force on Counterterrorism and Unconventional Warfare and member of the House National Security Committee, in order for the exception for immunity to have the desired deterrent effect, the potential civil liability for foreign states which commit and sponsor acts of terrorism would have to be substantial. *See* Congressman Jim Saxton, News Release: *Saxton to the Flatow Family: "Be Strong, America Is Behind You"* (February 26, 1997); *see also* NORMAN J. SINGER, 2 SUTHERLAND ON STATUTORY CONSTRUCTION t §48.16 (5th ed.1992, 1997 Supp.) citing *Brock v. Pierce County*, 476 U.S. 253, 106 S.Ct. 1834, 90 L.Ed.2d 248 (1986). Therefore, the amendment to 28 U.S.C. §1605(a)(7) expressly provided, *inter alia*, that punitive damages were available in actions brought under the state sponsored terrorism exception to immunity. *See* H.R. CONF. REP. 863, 104TH CONG, 2ND SESS. 1996 *reprinted at* 1996 U.S.C.C.A.N. 924; Senator Frank Lautenberg, News Release: *Flatow Family's Unprecedented Lawsuit Against Iran Will Help Deter Future Acts of Terrorism* (February 26, 1997). The amendment, *Civil Liability for Acts of State Sponsored Terrorism*, was enacted

on September 30, 1996 as part of the 1997 Omnibus Consolidated Appropriations Act, Pub.L. 104-208, Div. A, Title I §101(c) [Title V, §589] (September 30, 1996), 110 Stat. 3009-172 *reprinted at* 28 U.S.C.A. §1605 note (West 1997 Supp.). This provision of law is commonly referred to as the "Flatow Amendment."

The Flatow Amendment is apparently an independent pronouncement of law, yet it has been published as a note to 28 U.S.C. §1605, and requires several references to 28 U.S.C. §1605(a)(7) *et seq.* to reach even a preliminary interpretation. As it also effects a substantial change to 28 U.S.C. §1605(a)(7), it appears to be an implied amendment. *See* 1A SUTHERLAND ON STATUTORY CONSTRUCTION at §22.13 ("An implied amendment is an act which purports to be independent, but which in substance alters, modifies, or adds to a prior act."); see also *id.* at §22.20-21. The brief explanation of the Flatow Amendment's purpose in the House Conference Report explicitly states that it was intended to increase the measure of damages available in suits under 28 U.S.C. §1605(a)(7). *See* H.R. CONF. REP. 863, 104TH CONG, 2ND SESS.1996, *reprinted at* 1996 U.S.C.C.A.N. 924. Both the Flatow Amendment and 28 U.S.C. §1605(a)(7) address the same subject matter, and were enacted during the same session of Congress, only five months apart. Interpretation *in pari materia* is therefore the most appropriate approach to the construction of both provisions, 1A SUTHERLAND ON STATUTORY CONSTRUCTION at §22.32. The amendment should be considered to relate back to the enactment of 28 U.S.C. §1605(a)(7) as if they had been enacted as one provision, *id.* at §§22.29-31, 34-36, and the two provisions should be construed together and in reference to one another. *Id.* at §22.29 n. 16 citing *United States v. Dickerson*, 310 U.S. 554, 60 S.Ct. 1034, 84 L.Ed. 1356 (1940). Interpretation of 28 U.S.C. §1605(a)(7) and the Flatow Amendment *in pari materia* demonstrates the coherent legislative intent behind the two enactments.

2. 28 U.S.C. §1605(a)(7) AND 28 U.S.C.A. §1605 note APPLY RETROACTIVELY FOR THE PURPOSES OF ESTABLISHING SUBJECT MATTER AND PERSONAL JURISDICTION.

Although the events complained of herein occurred more than a year prior to the enactment of the Antiterrorism and Effective Death Penalty Act of 1996, 28 U.S.C. §1605(a)(7) provides a basis for subject matter jurisdiction. Congress has expressly directed the retroactive application of 28 U.S.C. §1605(a)(7) in order to further a comprehensive counterterrorism initiative by the legislative branch of government:

The amendments made by this subtitle shall apply to any cause of action arising before, on or after the date of the enactment of this Act [April 24, 1996].

§221(c) of Pub.L. 104-132. As the Supreme Court has stated with respect to the application of legislation to pre-enactment conduct, "[w]here congressional intent is clear, it governs." *Kaiser Aluminum & Chemical Corp. v. Bonjorno*, 494 U.S. 827, 837, 110 S.Ct. 1570, 108 L.Ed.2d 842 (1990). Although the application of statutes to pre-enactment conduct is traditionally disfavored, see *Bowen v. Georgetown University Hospital*, 488 U.S. 204, 109 S.Ct. 468, 102 L.Ed.2d 493 (1988), where "Congress has expressly prescribed the statute's proper reach[,] there is no need to resort to judicial default rules." *Landgraf v. USI Film Products*, 511 U.S. 244, 271, 114 S.Ct. 1483, 128 L.Ed.2d 229 (1994).

Furthermore, the state sponsored terrorism exception to foreign sovereign immunity is a remedial statute. It creates no new responsibilities or obligations; it only creates a forum for the enforcement of pre-existing universally recognized rights under federal common law and international law. See, e.g., *Alvarez-Machain v. United States*, 107 F.3d 696, 702 (9th Cir.1996), *cert. denied*, 522 U.S. 814, 118 S.Ct. 60, 139 L.Ed.2d 23 (1997) (discussing Torture Victim Protection Act). As with all other civil jurisdiction statutes, 28 U.S.C. §1605(a)(7) " 'speak[s] to the power of the courts rather than to the rights or obligations of the parties.' " *Landgraf*, 511 U.S. at 274 (discussing Civil Rights Act of 1991) (citation omitted). Almost all courts have upheld the retroactive application of long-arm statutes. *See* 2 SUTHERLAND ON STATUTORY CONSTRUCTION at §41.09 citing *McGee v. International Life Ins. Co.*, 355 U.S. 220, 78 S.Ct. 199, 2 L.Ed.2d 223 (1957).

At the time of the act complained of herein, the terrorist acts enumerated in 28 U.S.C. §1605(a)(7) were federal criminal offenses, *see* 18 U.S.C. §2331. Given mounting Congressional frustration at the refusal of the federal courts to find jurisdiction in cases such as *Princz, Pan Am 103, Cicippio*, and *Nelson*, and the progressive development of United States legislation and jurisprudence on the subject of *jus cogens* violations, see, e.g., *Hilao v. Estate of Marcos*, 103 F.3d 767; *Kadic v. Karadzic*, 70 F.3d 232; *Abebe-Jira v. Negewo*, 72 F.3d 844 (11th Cir.1996), *cert. denied*, 519 U.S. 830, 117 S.Ct. 96, 136 L.Ed.2d 51 (1996); *Cabiri v. Assasie-Gyimah*, 921 F.Supp. 1189 (S.D.N.Y.1996); *Filartiga v. Pena-Irala*, 630 F.2d 876 (2d Cir.1980); *Xuncax v. Gramajo*, 886 F.Supp. 162 (D.Mass.1995). See also *Princz*, 26 F.3d at 1176 (D.C.Cir.1994) (Wald, J., dissenting), the creation of an exception to foreign sovereign immunity which provides jurisdiction over foreign state perpetrators of the acts enumerated in 28 U.S.C. §1605(a)(7) should not have been unanticipated. "[A]ny expectation…[to the contrary]…is rightly disturbed." *Cabiri*, 921 F.Supp. at 1195-96 (S.D.N.Y.1996) (discussing Torture Victim Protection Act), citing *Landgraf*, 511 U.S. at 273-275.

The Islamic Republic of Iran in particular has been aware of United States policy condemning international terrorism at least since the 1979-1981 hostage crisis in Tehran. It has been continuously designated a state sponsor of terrorism since January 19, 1984. Its continued support of terrorist groups has prompted the United States to suspend diplomatic relations and participate in the international embargo, including extraordinary enforcement measures such as trade restrictions. *See* U.S. DEP'T OF STATE, PATTERNS OF GLOBAL TERRORISM at 23; Iran and Libya Sanctions Act of 1996, Pub.L. 104-72, 104TH CONG., 2D SESS. (August 5, 1996), 110 Stat. 1541. As international terrorism is subject to universal jurisdiction, Defendants had adequate notice that their actions were wrongful and susceptible to adjudication in the United States. Eric S. Kobrick, *The Ex Post Facto Prohibition and the Exercise of Universal Jurisdiction over International Crimes*, 87 COLUM. L. REVV. 1515, 1528-30 (1987) (concluding that criminal statutes apply retroactively to international terrorist acts).

Therefore, the state sponsored terrorism provision implicates no Constitutionally protected interest which would prohibit the application of 28 U.S.C. §1605(a)(7) to pre-enactment conduct.

3. FEDERAL COMMON LAW PROVIDES THE RULES OF DECISION IN CASE BROUGHT PURSUANT TO 28 U.S.C. §1605(a)(7) AND 28 U.S.C.A. §1605 note.

This action is brought pursuant to a new exception to the FSIA which was created as part of a federal initiative to combat international terrorism, the Antiterrorism and Effective Death Penalty Act of 1996. The state sponsored terrorism provisions represent a sea change in the United States' approach to foreign sovereign immunity. For the first time, Congress has expressly created an exception to immunity designed to influence the sovereign conduct of foreign states and affect the substantive law of liability for non-immune acts. *Cf.* H.R. Rep. 94 1487 at 12, *reprinted at* 1976 U.S.C.C.A.N. at 6610; *First National City Bank v. Banco para el Comercio Exterior de Cuba*, 462 U.S. 611, 619-20, 103 S.Ct. 2591, 77 L.Ed.2d 46 (1983).

Cases under the FSIA have considered choice of law issues almost exclusively within the commercial context, and have applied state rules of decision. See, e.g. *First National City Bank*, 462 U.S. at 620; *Joseph v. Office of the Consulate General of Nigeria*, 830 F.2d 1018, 1025 (9th Cir.1987); *Guzel v. State of Kuwait*, 818 F.Supp. 6, 10 (D.D.C.1993); *Skeen v. Federative Republic of Brazil*, 566 F.Supp. 1414, 1417 (D.D.C.1983); *see also* Joel Mendal Overton, II, *Will the Real FSIA Choice-of-Law Rule Please Stand Up?*, 49 WASH. & LEE L. REV. 1591 (1992). The notable exception is *Liu v. Republic of China*; however in that case, as the political assassination occurred in California, there was no true conflict for choice of law purposes. 892 F.2d 1419, 1425-26 (9th Cir.).

The federal choice of law rule follows that of the RESTATEMENT (SECOND) OF CONFLICTS, which provides that the law of the place of the tort is to apply. See *Liu*, 892 F.2d at 1425 *citing* RESTATEMENT (SECOND) OF CONFLICTS §175 (1969). The Gaza legal code derives from an amalgamation of British mandate law, Egyptian law and Palestinian Authority directives and laws. *See* 1996 COUNTRY REPORTS ON HUMAN RIGHTS: ISRAEL AND THE OCCUPIED TERRITORIES at §1(e); *available at* http://www.state.gov./www/global/-human_rights/1996_hrp_ report/occterr.html; in addition to the administrative difficulties associated with interpreting this unfamiliar foreign law, the United States has a much stronger interest than the Palestinian Authority in Gaza in adjudicating this action arising from a United States citizen's wrongful death. When another jurisdiction has a stronger interest and closer connections to the case, it is appropriate to apply that jurisdiction's law. RESTATEMENT (SECOND) OF CONFLICTS §175 (1969).

The Supreme Court has recognized that the FSIA "codifies the standards governing foreign sovereign immunity as an aspect of substantive federal law" and that its application will "generally require interpretation of numerous points of federal law." *Verlinden*, 461 U.S. at 497. Subsequently, Congress created jurisdiction and federal causes of action for personal injury or death resulting from state-sponsored terrorism, including its own statute of limitations. These actions indicate Congressional intent that the federal courts create coherent national standards to support this initiative of national significance. In the interest of promoting uniformity of determinations with respect to the liability of foreign states for the terrorist acts of its officials, agents, and employees, this Court will employ interstitial federal common law to determine whether the terrorist acts were within the scope of their office, agency, or employment, as well as any other conclusions of law which typically rely upon state law. [FN6] See *United States v. Belmont*, 301 U.S. 324, 57 S.Ct. 758, 81 L.Ed. 1134 (1937); *In re Air Crash Disaster Near Saigon, South Vietnam, on April 4, 1975*, 476 F.Supp. 521, 527 (D.D.C.1979); *see also* Sandra Engle, Note, *Choosing the Law for Attributing Liability Under the Foreign Sovereign Immunities Act; A Proposal for Uniformity*, 15 FORDHAM INT'L L.J. 1060 (1991/1992).

FN6. As the dedicated venue for actions against foreign states, *see* 28 U.S.C. §1391(f)(4), the law of District of Columbia provides an appropriate model in developing a federal standard for this determination. See also *Stanford v. Kuwait Airways Corp.*, 89 F.3d 117 (2d Cir.1996).

4. THE EXTRATERRITORIAL APPLICATION OF THE FSIA'S RECENT AMENDMENTS IS PROPER.

Article I of the Constitution establishes that Congress has "authority to enact laws applicable to conduct beyond the territorial boundaries of the United States." *Aramco*, 499 U.S. at 260-61 (1991). This Court's only duty is to determine "whether Congress chose to attach liability to the conduct outside the United States…[A]s a court of the United States, we cannot look beyond our own law." [FN7] *United States v. Alcoa*, 148 F.2d 416, 443 (2d Cir.1945). Congressional intent and legislative purpose demonstrate that 28 U.S.C. §1605(a)(7) not only applies to extraterritorial conduct, but that one of its express purposes is to affect the conduct of terrorist states outside the United States, in order to promote the safety of United States citizens traveling overseas. *See* 142 C.R. S3454-1 (April 17, 1996) (remarks of Senator Hank Brown on consideration of the conference report); 142 C .R. H2129-05, H2132 (March 13, 1996) (remarks of Representative Ileana Ros-Lehtinen on the proposed Antiterrorism Act); *see* 2A SUTHERLAND ON STATUTORY CONSTRUCTION §45.05, §45.09.

FN7. Nevertheless, the extraterritorial application of the state sponsored terrorism exceptions is consistent with international law; three of the five bases for the exercise of extraterritorial jurisdiction are implicated in actions by United States victims of foreign state sponsored terrorism: passive personality (nationality of victim), protective (national security interests), and universal (subject to jurisdiction wherever the offender may be found). *See* RESTATEMENT (THIRD) FOREIGN RELATIONS LAW OF THE UNITED STATES (1986) at §402(2)-(3), §403, §423.

Indicia of Congressional intent are readily apparent. See, e.g., *EEOC v. Aramco*, 499 U.S. 244, 260, 111 S.Ct. 1227, 113 L.Ed.2d 274 (1991) (superseded by statute) (Marshall, J., dissenting) citing *Foley Brothers*, 336 U.S. at 285 (1949) (extraterritorial application may be discerned from the entire range of conventional sources). As 28 U.S.C. §1605(a)(5) already provides jurisdiction over state-sponsored terrorist acts in the United States, see *Liu*, 892 F.2d 1419; *Letelier v. Republic of Chile*, 488 F.Supp. 665 (D.D.C.1980), the state sponsored terrorism exception would be redundant if it were held to apply only within the United States. The provision's arbitration requirement indicates that Congress intended 28 U.S.C. §1605(a)(7) to create subject matter jurisdiction for claims arising from conduct which occurred within a foreign state. If Congress did not intend for 28 U.S.C. §1605(a)(7) to apply to extraterritorial conduct, the arbitration requirement, which only applies in cases arising from acts which occur within a defendant foreign state's territory, would be superfluous. *See* 28 U.S.C. §1605(a)(7)(B)(i). Therefore Congress inherently expressed its understanding that this provision would necessarily apply to extraterritorial conduct.

The general presumption against extraterritorial application exists to prevent inadvertent interference with foreign relations. See *NLRB v. Catholic Bishop of Chicago*, 440 U.S. 490, 500, 99 S.Ct. 1313, 59 L.Ed.2d 533 (1979); *McCulloch v. Sociedad Nacional de Marineros de Honduras*, 372 U.S. 10, 21-22, 83 S.Ct. 671, 9 L.Ed.2d 547 (1963); *Foley Brothers v. Filardo*, 336 U.S. 281, 69 S.Ct. 575, 93 L.Ed. 680 (1949). In actions pursuant to the state sponsored terrorism provisions, however, there is no danger of inadvertent interference with foreign relations; Congress specifically restricted its application to foreign state defendants which the State Department has determined are foreign state sponsors of terrorism. *See* 28 U.S.C. §1605(a)(7)(A). There is nothing inadvertent about these two new amendments. Indeed, Justice Blackmun has opined that the presumption against extraterritorial application is inherently inapposite to statutes which on their face involve foreign relations, as Congress necessarily considered "distinctively international subject matter." *Sale v. Haitian Centers Council*, 509 U.S. 155, 206-07, 113 S.Ct. 2549, 125 L.Ed.2d 128 (1993) (Blackmun, J., dissenting) (distinguishing *United States v. Curtiss-Wright Export Corp.*, 299 U.S. 304, 57 S.Ct. 216, 81 L.Ed. 255 (1936)).

This Court concludes that the application of the state sponsored terrorism provisions to extraterritorial conduct is proper.

B. SUBJECT MATTER JURISDICTION

In order to establish subject matter jurisdiction pursuant to 28 U.S.C. §1605(a)(7), a claim must contain the following statutory elements:

(1) that personal injury or death resulted from an act of torture, extrajudicial killing, aircraft sabotage, or hostage taking; and

(2) the act was either perpetrated by the foreign state directly or by a non-state actor which receives material support or resources from the foreign state defendant; and

(3) the act or the provision of material support or resources is engaged in by an agent, official or employee of the foreign state while acting within the scope of his or her office, agency or employment; and

(4) that the foreign state be designated as a state sponsor of terrorism either at the time the incident complained of occurred or was later so designated as a result of such act; and

(5) if the incident complained of occurred with the foreign state defendant's territory, plaintiff has offered the defendants a reasonable opportunity to arbitrate the matter; and

(6) either the plaintiff or the victim was a United States national at the time of the incident; and

(7) similar conduct by United States agents, officials, or employees within the United States would be actionable.

28 U.S.C. §1605(a)(7) and 28 U.S.C.A. §1605 note. While elements (4)-(6) are pure questions of fact, elements (1)-(3) and (7) are mixed questions of law and fact, and, in the absence of settled precedent, require interpretation.

1. A SUICIDE BOMBING IS AN ACT OF EXTRAJUDICIAL KILLING.

Plaintiff describes the cause of his daughter's death as an "extrajudicial killing" within the meaning of 28 U.S.C. §1605(a)(7). The state-sponsored terrorism exception to immunity expressly adopts the definition of extrajudicial killing set forth in the Torture Victim Protection Act of 1991. *See* 28 U.S.C. §1605(e)(1). That Act defines an "extrajudicial killing" as a *deliberated killing* not authorized by a previous judgment pronounced by a regularly constituted court affording all judicial guarantees which are recognized as indispensable by civilized peoples. Such term, however, does not include any such killing that, under international law, is lawfully carried out under the authority of a foreign nation.

Pub.L. 102-256 at §3(a), 106 Stat. 73 (March 12, 1992), *reprinted at* 28 U.S.C.A. §1350 note. (emphasis added). Deliberate is defined as:

...Carried on coolly and steadily, especially according to a preconceived design; given to weighing facts and arguments with a view to a choice or decision; careful in considering the consequences of a step;...

BLACK'S LAW DICTIONARY 426-27 (6th ed.1990); *see also* H.REP. 102-367(I), 1992 U.S.C.C.A.N. 84. Other courts have found that summary executions, for example, would be considered "extrajudicial killings" within the meaning of 28 U.S.C.A. §1350 note. See *Lafontant v. Aristide*, 844 F.Supp. 128 (E.D.N.Y.1994) (dicta). In actions brought under the Alien Tort Statute, 28 U.S.C. §1350, and the Torture Victim Protection Act, courts have suggested, in the context of command responsibility, that a course of indiscriminate brutality, known to result in deaths, rises to the level of "extrajudicial killings." See *Hilao*, 103 F.3d at 776-77; *Kadic*, 70 F.3d at 242; *Paul v. Avril*, 901 F.Supp. 330, 335 (S.D.Fla.1994); *Xuncax v. Gramajo*, 886 F.Supp. 162, 170 (D.Mass.1995); *Forti v. Suarez-Mason*, 672 F.Supp. 1531, 1537-38 (N.D.Cal.1987). See also *In re Yamashita*, 327 U.S. 1, 14, 66 S.Ct. 340, 90 L.Ed. 499 (1946) ("...a deliberate plan and purpose to massacre and exterminate...unarmed noncombatant civilians...*without cause or trial*...and without military necessity.") (emphasis added).

The state sponsored terrorism exception to immunity was enacted as part of a comprehensive legislative initiative to squelch international terrorism-the Antiterrorism and Effective Death Penalty Act of 1996. *See* 2A SUTHERLAND ON STATUTORY CONSTRUCTION at §47.03. Previous treatments of international terrorism by Congress therefore appropriately inform the interpretation of "deliberated killing". *Id.* at §22.32. One statute *in pari materia* defines terrorism as

...mean[ing] premeditated, politically motivated violence perpetrated against noncombatant targets by subnational groups or clandestine agents.

22 U.S.C. §2656f(d)(2). As the state sponsored terrorism exception expressly incorporates a definition from the United States criminal code chapter on international terrorism, another definition from that chapter is also apropos:

(1) the term "international terrorism" means activities that-

A. involve violent acts or acts dangerous to human life that are a violation of the criminal laws of the United States or of any State, or that would be a criminal violation if committed within the jurisdiction of the United States or of any State;

B. appear to be intended-

i) to intimidate or coerce a civilian population;

ii) to influence the policy of a government by intimidation or coercion;

iii) to affect the conduct of a government by assassination or kidnapping; and

(C) occur primarily outside the territorial jurisdiction of the United States, or transcend national boundaries in terms of the means by which they are accomplished, the persons they appear intended to intimidate or coerce, or the locale in which their perpetrators operate or seek asylum;...

18 U.S.C. §2331. Attempts to reach a fixed, universally accepted definition of international terrorism have been frustrated both by changes in terrorist methodology and the lack of any precise definition of the term "terrorism." *See, e.g.,* U.S. DEP'T OF STATE, PATTERNS OF GLOBAL TERRORISM at vi, 1, 17; Louis Rene Beres, *The Meaning of Terrorism-Jurisprudential and Definitional Clarifications*, 28 VAND. J. TRANSNAT'L L. 239 (1995). Therefore, the United States characterizes rather than enumerates acts for the purposes of designating foreign state sponsors of terrorism and defining criminal terrorist offenses under federal law. Each of the acts listed in 28 U.S.C. §1605(a)(7) fully conform with the foregoing definitions and provisions.

This Court concludes that a suicide bombing conforms with each of the foregoing provisions and definitions, and therefore is an act of "extrajudicial killing" within the meaning of 28 U.S.C. §1605(a)(7).

2. THE ROUTINE PROVISION OF FINANCIAL ASSISTANCE TO A TERRORIST GROUP IN SUPPORT OF ITS TERRORIST ACTIVITIES CONSTITUTES THE PRO-

VISION OF MATERIAL SUPPORT OR RESOURCES WITHIN THE MEANING OF 28 U.S.C. §1605(a)(7).

The state-sponsored terrorism provision adopts the definition of "provid[ing] material support or resources" set forth in the federal criminal code. 28 U.S.C. §1605(a)(7) incorporates 18 U.S.C. §2339A(a) by reference, which provides that:

..."material support or resources" means currency or other financial securities, financial services, lodging, training, safehouses, false documentation or identification, communications equipment, facilities, weapons, lethal substances, explosives, personnel, transportation, and other physical assets, but does not include humanitarian assistance to persons not directly involved in such violations.

This Court concludes that the routine provision of financial assistance to a terrorist group in support of its terrorist activities constitutes "providing material support or resources" for a terrorist act within the meaning of 28 U.S.C. §1605(a)(7). Furthermore, as nothing in 18 U.S.C. §2339A or 28 U.S.C. §1605(a)(7) indicates otherwise, this Court also concludes that a plaintiff need not establish that the material support or resources provided by a foreign state for a terrorist act contributed directly to the act from which his claim arises in order to satisfy 28 U.S.C. §1605(a)(7)'s statutory requirements for subject matter jurisdiction. Sponsorship of a terrorist group which causes the personal injury or death of a United States national alone is sufficient to invoke jurisdiction.

3. THE PROVISION OF MATERIAL SUPPORT AND RESOURCES TO A TERRORIST GROUP IS AN ACT WITHIN THE SCOPE OF A FOREIGN STATE'S AGENT'S AND HIGH OFFICIALS' AGENCY AND OFFICES.

The law of *respondeat superior* demonstrates that if a foreign state's agent, official or employee provides material support and resources to a terrorist organization, such provision will be considered an act within the scope of his or her agency, office or employment. See, e.g., *Guzel*, 818 F.Supp. at 10; *Skeen*, 566 F.Supp. at 1417.

In the District of Columbia, whether an employer is liable for the torts of its employee depends on whether the tort was at least in part "actuated" by an intent to advance the employer's business, and the tort must be foreseeable given the employee's duties. *Weinberg v. Johnson*, 518 A.2d 985, 990 (D.C.1986); *Guzel*, 818 F.Supp. at 10. The acts of an employee under these circumstances, whether lawful or not, and whether expressly prohibited by the employer or not, can be imputed to the employer.

In order for an agent, official, or employee's unlawful conduct to be imputed to a government, however, the government must share a degree of responsibility for the wrongful conduct. The government must have engaged in the wrongful conduct, either deliberately or permissively, as a matter of policy or custom. See, e.g., *Monell v. N.Y. Dep't of Social Services*, 436 U.S. 658, 694-95, 98 S.Ct. 2018, 56 L.Ed.2d 611 (1978) (discussing municipal liability under 42 U.S.C. §1983). This Court concludes that if a foreign state's heads of state, intelligence service, and minister of intelligence routinely provide material support or resources to a terrorist group, whose activities are consistent with the foreign state's customs or policies, then that agent and those officials have acted squarely within the scope of their agency and offices within the meaning of 28 U.S.C. §1605(a)(7) and 28 U.S.C.A. §1605 note.

4. UNITED STATES OFFICIALS WOULD BE LIABLE FOR PROVIDING MATERIAL SUPPORT OR RESOURCES TO A TERRORIST GROUP WITHIN THE UNITED STATES.

The Flatow Amendment, 28 U.S.C.A. §1605 note, clarifies that the liability of foreign states and their officials must be comparable to that of the United States and its agents, officials, and employees officials. This Court concludes that if officials of the United States, while acting in their official capacities, provide material support and resources to a terrorist group which executed a suicide bombing within the United States, those officials would not be immune from civil suits for wrongful death and personal injury. See U.S. CONST. AMEND. 5; 42 U.S.C. §1983.

C. PERSONAL JURISDICTION

The FSIA provides that personal jurisdiction over defendants will exist where Plaintiff establishes the applicability of an exception to immunity pursuant to 28 U.S.C. §1604, §1605, or §1607 and service of process has been accomplished pursuant to 28 U.S.C. §1608. *See* 28 U.S.C. §1330(b); *Verlinden*, 461 U.S. at 485 n. 5. Although service in accordance with 28 U.S.C. §1608 has been calculated to provide adequate notice to foreign state defendants, *see* H.REP. 94-1487 at 23-26, *reprinted at* 1976 U.S.C.C.A.N. at 6622-25, Courts must make further inquiry; Congress cannot grant jurisdiction where it would be improper under the Constitution. *Verlinden*, 461 U.S. at 491; *Texas Trading & Milling Corp. v. Federal Republic of Nigeria*, 647 F.2d 300, 308 (2d Cir.1981).

1. A FOREIGN STATE IS NOT A "PERSON" FOR THE PURPOSES OF CONSTITUTIONAL DUE PROCESS ANALYSIS.

The Supreme Court has addressed personal jurisdiction in the context of the Foreign Sovereign Immunities Act only twice, and only in dicta. See *Verlinden*, 461 U.S. at 484 n. 5; *Republic of Argentina v. Weltover*, 504 U.S. 607, 619-620, 112 S.Ct. 2160, 119 L.Ed.2d 394 (1992). However, these brief analyses indicate that foreign states may not be entitled to all aspects of Constitutional Due Process guaranteed to individuals. The Court in *Verlinden* did not address whether an analysis beyond the statutory requirements was necessary to establish personal jurisdiction. See *Verlinden*, 461 U.S. at 485 n. 5. The Court in *Weltover* did not find it necessary to decide this issue, given the presence of "minimum contacts" sufficient to satisfy the Due Process Clause under the facts of that case, During its discussion of direct effects and minimum contacts in *Weltover*, however, the Court referred to *South Carolina v. Katzenbach*, in which it had stated that the "States of the Union are not persons for the purpose of the Due Process Clause," 504 U.S. at 619-20 *quoting* 383 U.S. 301, 323-24, 86 S.Ct. 803, 15 L.Ed.2d 769 (1966).

As suggested in *Weltover*, the issue of whether a foreign state is a "person" for the purposes of Constitutional Due Process analysis has rarely, if ever, been squarely presented for consideration, 504 U.S. at 619-20. Most courts have simply assumed that foreign states were entitled to Constitutional Due Process protections, just as courts have assumed that foreign corporations are entitled to Constitutional Due Process protections, at least with respect to the assertion of personal jurisdiction. Once these trends were initiated, on the basis of an assumption, courts have been reluctant to reexamine this issue. See, e.g., *Afram Export Corp. v. Metallurgiki Halyps, S.A.*, 772 F.2d 1358, 1362 (7th Cir.1985) (Posner, J.) ("Countless cases assume that foreign companies have all the rights of U.S. citizens to object to extraterritorial assertions of personal jurisdiction...The assumption has never to our knowledge actually been examined, but it probably is too solidly entrenched to be questioned at this late date"). This Court does not face Judge Posner's disadvantage; 28 U.S.C. §1605(a)(7) provides a clean slate.

The merger of subject matter and personal jurisdictional inquiries under the FSIA has contributed to the confusion in the jurisprudence of personal jurisdiction over foreign states. The majority of cases brought under the FSIA involve commercial activity, which requires an evaluation of the activity's effects in the United States. "Direct effects" language closely resembles that of Constitutional Due Process "minimum contacts." Tandem consideration of these overlapping yet fundamentally discrete analyses as a matter of practice in several Circuits has exacerbated the situation. *See, e.g.,* Hadwin A. Cald, III, *Interpreting the Direct Effects Clause of the Foreign Sovereign Immunities Act's Commercial Activities Exception*, 59 FORDHAM L. REV. 91 (1990). Commentators have noted this reference as a signal that, if the issue were squarely presented, it might decide that a foreign state is not a "person" for the purposes of Constitutional Due Process. *See, e.g.* Sarah K. Schano, Note, *The Scattered Remains of Sovereignty for Foreign States After Republic of Argentina v. Weltover-Due Process Protection or Nothing*, 27 VAND. J. TRANSNAT'L L. 63 (1994). The assumption thus persists that a full Constitutional Due Process analysis is required in all actions against foreign states.

It may seem appropriate to consider the foreign state commercial actor as a "person" for the purposes of Constitutional Due Process analysis, considering that

when a government becomes a partner in any trading company, it divests [sic] itself...of its sovereign character, and takes that of a private citizen. Instead of communicating to the company its privileges and its prerogatives, it descends to a level with those with whom it associates itself, and takes the character which belongs to its associates...

Bank of the United States v. Planters' Bank of Georgia, 22 U.S. (9 Wheat.) 904, 907, 6 L.Ed. 244 (1824). However, the FSIA requires something more substantial than "minimum contacts" with the United States in order to sustain subject matter jurisdiction under the commercial activity exception. *See* 28 U.S.C. §1605(a)(2); *Verlinden*, 461 U.S. at 490 ("Congress protected from this danger...by enacting substantive provisions requiring some form of substantial contact with the United States."). The other exceptions to immunity each have an inherent jurisdictional nexus with the United States, which exceeds "minimum contacts" requirements. See *id.*; H.REP. 94-1487 at 13-14, *reprinted at* 1976 U.S.C.C.A.N. at 6611-12. Therefore, an inquiry into personal jurisdiction over a foreign state need not consider the rubric of "minimum contacts"; the concept of "minimum contacts" is inherently subsumed within the exceptions to immunity defined by the statute. See *Id.*

Citing *South Carolina v. Katzenbach*, 383 U.S. at 323-24 and *Insurance Corp. of Ireland, Inc. v. Compagnie des Bauxites de Guinee*, 456 U.S. 694, 702, 102 S.Ct. 2099, 72 L.Ed.2d 492 (1982), Judge Silberman has noted the inadequacy of personal jurisdiction doctrine in cases involving disputes between governments within federal systems. See *United States v. Ferrara*, 54 F.3d 825, 832-33 (D.C.Cir.1995) (Silberman, J., concurring); *see also* Harold S. Lewis, Jr., *The Three Deaths of "State Sovereignty" and the Curse of Abstraction in the Jurisprudence of Personal Jurisdiction*, 58 NOTRE DAME L. REV. 699 (1983). When extended to the international system, the deficiencies of jurisprudence of personal jurisdiction increase exponentially, particularly in actions against foreign states.

The Supreme Court has already recognized that a State of the United States is not entitled to substantive due process. *South Carolina v. Katzenbach*, 383 U.S. at 323-24. Similarly, several lower courts have held that the federal government, state governments, political subdivisions and municipalities within the United States are not considered "persons" for the purposes of Fifth Amendment due process analysis. See *State of Okl. By and Through Derryberry v. Federal Energy Regulatory Commission*, 494 F.Supp. 636 (D.C.Okl.1980); *City of Sault Ste. Marie, Mich. v. Andrus*, 532 F.Supp. 157 (D.D.C.1980); *El Paso County Water Imp. Dist. No. 1 v. International Boundary and Water Com'n, U.S. Section*, 701 F.Supp. 121 (W.D.Tex.1988). See also *Will v. Michigan Dep't of State Police*, 491 U.S. 58, 64, 109 S.Ct. 2304, 105 L.Ed.2d 45 (1989) ("in common usage, the term 'person' does not include the sovereign, and statutes employing the word are ordinarily construed to exclude it"). While these decisions have been made primarily within the context of federalism, see, e.g., *In re Herndon*, 188 B.R. 562, 565 n. 8 (E.D.Ky.1995) ("a governmental entity is not a 'person' "), in *Weltover*, the Supreme Court hints that this logic should be extended to the interrelationships between states in the international arena. 504 U.S. at 619. The only other court which has touched upon this issue has concluded that foreign states, like States of the Union, are not "persons" subject to liability under various federal statutes. See *Rios v. Marshall*, 530 F.Supp. 351, 372 n. 22 (S.D.N.Y.1981).

One judge of this Court anticipated this step five years prior to *Weltover*. In *Palestine Information Office v. Shultz*, the Court held that "[i]f the States of the Union have no due process rights, then a 'foreign mission' qua 'foreign mission' surely can have none." 674 F.Supp. 910, 919 (D.D.C.1987). Given the parallels in the procedural deference granted to both the United States and foreign states, [FN8] this Court

concludes that foreign states should hold comparable status to States of the Union and the federal government for the purposes of Constitutional Due Process analysis. But cf. *The Export Group v. Reef Industries*, 54 F.3d 1466, 1476 (9th Cir.1995) (discussing substantive law of liability). As the Supreme Court has recognized, personal jurisdiction can be waived because

FN8. The House Report expressly states that the provisions are identical. H.Rep. 94-1487 at 25-26, *reprinted at* 1976 U.S.C.C.A.N. at 6624-25. *Compare* Fed.R.Civ.P. 12(a)(3) *and* 28 U.S.C. §1608(d) (time to answer); Fed.R.Civ.P. 55(e) *and* 28 U.S.C. §1608(e) (requirements for entry of default judgment).

[t]he requirement that a court have personal jurisdiction flows not from Art. III, but from the Due Process Clause. The personal jurisdiction requirement recognizes and protects an individual liberty interest. It represents a restriction on judicial power not as a matter of sovereignty, but as a matter of individual liberty.

Insurance Corp. of Ireland v. Compagnie des Bauxites de Guinee, 456 U.S. at 703. It would be illogical to grant this personal liberty interest to foreign states when it has not been granted to federal, state or local governments of the United States. [FN9]

FN9. This conclusion applies not only to the foreign state, but also to the foreign state's agents officials and employees for acts performed in their official capacity. See, e.g., *Matter of Reserves Development Corp.*, 78 B.R. 951 (W.D.Mo.1986). The argument against Constitutional Due Process protections may in fact be even stronger in the case of foreign state officials; aliens outside the United States are not entitled to Constitutional protection, even in the criminal context. See *Air Line Stewards and Stewardesses Ass'n, Intern. v. Northwest Airlines, Inc.*, 162 F.Supp. 684 (D.Minn.1958).

The House Report's language is unambiguous-it states that *in personam* jurisdiction has been accommodated inherently within the statute; the language does not, whether expressly or by implication, grant a liberty interest for the purposes of substantive due process analysis. *See* H.Rep. 94-1487 at 13-14, *reprinted at* 1976 U.S.C.C.A.N. at 6611-12. Foreign sovereign immunity, both under the common law and now under the FSIA, has always been a matter of grace and comity rather than a matter of right under United States law. *Verlinden*, 461 U.S. at 486, citing *Schooner Exchange v. M'Faddon*, 11 U.S. (7 Cranch) 116, 3 L.Ed. 287 (1812). Where neither the Constitution nor Congress grants a right, it is inappropriate to invent and perpetuate it by judicial fiat.

See, e.g., Jay Conison, *What Does Due Process Have to Do With Jurisdiction?*, 46 RUTGERS L. REV. 1071 (1994).

2. A FOREIGN STATE WHICH CAUSES THE PERSONAL INJURY OR DEATH OF A UNITED STATES NATIONAL THROUGH AN ACT OF STATE-SPONSORED TERRORISM HAS "MINIMUM CONTACTS" WITH THE UNITED STATES.

Even if foreign states are invariably "persons" for the purposes of Constitutional Due Process analysis, Constitutional requirements have been met in this case. In *International Shoe Co. v. Washington*, the Supreme Court expressly rejected a rigid formula for discerning the contacts necessary to satisfy due process. 326 U.S. 310, 316, 66 S.Ct. 154, 90 L.Ed. 95 (1945). The reluctance to establish a minimum threshold of contacts based upon abstractions has persisted; " '[d]ue process,' unlike some legal rules, is not a technical conception with a fixed content unrelated to time, place and circumstances." *Cafeteria and Restaurant Workers Union, Local 473 v. McElroy*, 367 U.S. 886, 895, 81 S.Ct. 1743, 6 L.Ed.2d 1230 (1961). Each case requires evaluation in light of its own unique facts and circumstances, in order to ensure that the exercise of jurisdiction complies with "fair play and substantial justice." *International Shoe*, 326 U.S. at 316.

The Supreme Court has recognized that "reasonableness considerations sometimes serve to establish the reasonableness of jurisdiction upon a lesser showing of minimum contacts than would otherwise be required." *Burger King v. Rudzewicz*, 471 U.S. 462, 483-84, 105 S.Ct. 2174, 85 L.Ed.2d 528 (1985). In a case evaluating a statute designed to implement United States policy to curb terrorism, the Court of Appeals for the District of Columbia Circuit stated that given "the broad discretion granted to the executive branch in foreign policy matters, appellants misstate the degree of [procedural due] process due..." *Palestine Information Office v. Shultz*, 853 F.2d 932, 942 (D.C.Cir.1988) (discussing the Foreign Missions Act). The Court held that while policy interests would never completely supplant the Due Process Clause, some areas were so committed to the political branches, such as foreign policy, that a statute implementing that policy could significantly lower the threshold of constitutional requirements, so long as there existed other processes to protect the defendant's interests.

Prior to the state sponsored terrorism amendments, the lingering effects of personal injury incurred overseas and continuing in the United States did not satisfy the requirements, usually under the commercial activities section, that the ef-

fects of the act be "direct." See *Princz*, 26 F.3d 1166; *Martin v. Republic of South Africa*, 836 F.2d 91 (2nd Cir.1987). See also *Persinger v. Islamic Republic of Iran*, 729 F.2d 835 (D.C.Cir.1984) (U.S. Marine barracks overseas not within the United States for purposes of 28 U.S.C. §1605(a)(5)). The state sponsored terrorism exception, however, provides an express jurisdictional nexus based upon the victim's United States nationality. *See* 28 U.S.C. §1605(a)(7)(B)(ii). The Departments of State and Justice have determined that

the legislation ensures that, where United States courts assume jurisdiction over a foreign sovereign, there is a nexus to the United States. This limitation balances the United States' interest in providing a forum for American victims of specified outrageous conduct against the interest of foreign governments in not being forced to defend actions with no connections to the United States.

Brief of the United States as Amicus Curiae at 27-28, *Pan Am 103*, 101 F.3d 239 (2d Cir.1996). [FN10] This reading is consistent with that of the Supreme Court in *Verlinden*, that Congress "enact[e]d [in the FSIA] substantive provisions requiring some form of substantial contact with the United States." 461 U.S. at 490.

FN10. The main issue on appeal was whether violations of *jus cogens* were an implied waiver of sovereign immunity in United States courts within the meaning of 28 U.S.C. §1605(a)(1); the United States argued as *Amicus Curiae* against a finding of implied waiver. The Brief was filed on June 12, 1996, after the enactment of the Antiterrorism Act, but prior to the enactment of the Flatow Amendment.
When a state has been designated a state sponsor of terrorism and has been subject to economic sanctions, including an international boycott, for almost 14 years, there inherently will be very few contacts with the foreign states and its officials, as typically conceived in the commercial context. However, this case is brought against the Islamic Republic of Iran and its officials for actions in its sovereign capacity. Sovereign contacts, therefore, should be sufficient to sustain general jurisdiction over Defendants, at least for the purposes of 28 U.S.C. §1605(a)(7). Even commercial actions under the FSIA embrace the concept of nationwide contacts. See *Meadows v. Dominican Republic*, 817 F.2d 517 (9th Cir.1987); *Ruiz v. Transportes Aereos Militares Ecuadorianos*, 103 F.R.D. 458 (D.D.C.1984). The contacts between Interpol and the Department of Justice in the course of performing international criminal investigations have been held to generate sufficient contacts to support personal jurisdiction over Interpol for a defamation action in United States

Courts. *Steinberg v. International Criminal Police Organization*, 103 F.R.D. 392 (D.D.C.1984).

Even in the absence of diplomatic relations, states actors, as a matter of necessity, have substantial sovereign contact with each other. They inherently interact as state actors in the international community and as members of the United Nations-the suspension of diplomatic relations has more political than practical ramifications, as the states will maintain unofficial contact through "interest sections" under the auspices of another state's "protecting power."Apolitical functions, such as service of process in this matter, continue to operate, albeit in a more circuitous fashion, through such contacts. This Court concludes that even if a foreign state is accorded the status of a "person" for the purposes of Constitutional Due Process analysis, a foreign state that sponsors terrorist activities which causes the death or personal injury of a United States national will invariably have sufficient contacts with the United States to satisfy Due Process.

3. FAIR PLAY AND SUBSTANTIAL JUSTICE REQUIRE THAT UNITED STATES COURTS EXERCISE JURISDICTION OVER FOREIGN STATE SPONSORS OF TERRORISM WHOSE SPONSORSHIP RESULTS IN THE DEATH OR PERSONAL INJURY OF UNITED STATES NATIONALS.

The emphasis of the Due Process analysis required for jurisdiction pursuant to 28 U.S.C. §1605(a)(7) is most properly focused on the evaluation of fair play and substantial justice. See, e.g., *International Shoe Co. v. Washington*, 326 U.S. 310, 316, 66 S.Ct. 154, 90 L.Ed. 95.

All states are on notice that state sponsorship of terrorism is condemned by the international community. United States policy towards state sponsors of terrorists, has been made abundantly clear since the 1979-1981 hostage crisis in Tehran and the ensuing suspension of diplomatic relations with and establishment of international boycotts against foreign state sponsors of terrorism. Foreign state sponsors of terrorism could not reasonably have expected that the United States would not respond to attack on its citizens, and not undertake measures to prevent similar attacks in the future. In light of the mounting Congressional frustration at the inability of United States victims of foreign state abuses to obtain relief from any forum, it is manifest that Congress enacted 28 U.S.C. §1605(a)(7) to ensure fair play and substantial justice for American victims of state sponsored terrorism.

As terrorism has achieved the status of almost universal condemnation, as have slavery, genocide, and piracy, and the terrorist is the modern era's *hosti humani generis*-an enemy of all mankind, this Court concludes that fair play and substantial justice is well served by the exercise of jurisdiction over foreign state sponsors of terrorism which cause personal injury to or the death of United States nationals.

D. FED. R. CIV. P. 12(b)(6) DEFENSES

Usually Fed.R.Civ.P. 12(b)(6) defenses are considered taking the facts in a light most favorable to the non-moving party. *Campbell-El v. District of Columbia*, 881 F.Supp. 42, 43 (D.D.C.1995). However, because Defendants have defaulted, this Court has already made its findings of fact in Section II, *supra*. On the basis of those findings of fact, this Court concludes as a matter of law that, for the following reasons, Defendants could not sustain a successful Fed.R.Civ.P. 12(b)(6) defense to this action.

* * *

5. PUNITIVE DAMAGES

a. FOREIGN STATE SPONSORS OF TERRORISM ARE SUSCEPTIBLE TO PUNITIVE DAMAGES.

Prior to the state sponsored terrorism amendments, the FSIA absolutely prohibited the award or recovery of punitive damages against the foreign state itself. *See* 28 U.S.C. §1606; *Letelier v. Republic of Chile*, 502 F.Supp. 259 (D.D.C.1980) (judgment). The Flatow Amendment, however, departs from the prior enactment by expressly providing a cause of action for punitive damages for state sponsored terrorism. No other provision of the FSIA expressly states the nature of remedies available, because the FSIA as otherwise enacted is not intended to affect the substantive law of liability so as to affect the primary conduct of foreign states. *See cases pre-dating the Flatow Amendment, e.g., First National City Bank*, 462 U.S. at 619-20; *Liu*, 892 F.2d at 1425.

The state-sponsored terrorism exception, however, was enacted explicitly with the intent to alter the conduct of foreign states, particularly towards United States nationals traveling abroad. Congressman Saxton, the Chairman of the House Task Force on Counterterrorism and Unconventional Warfare, was convinced that the only way to accomplish this goal was to impose massive civil liability on foreign state sponsors of terrorism whose conduct results in the death or personal injury of United States citizens. As compensatory damages for wrongful death cannot approach a measure of damages reasonably required for a foreign state to take notice, Congressman Saxton sponsored the Flatow Amendment in order to make the availability of punitive damages indisputable. *See* Saxton, News Release; *see also* 2 SUTHERLAND ON STATUTORY CONSTRUCTION at §48.16 citing *Brock v. Pierce County*, 476 U.S. 253, 106 S.Ct. 1834, 90 L.Ed.2d 248 (1986).

b. PUNITIVE DAMAGES AWARDED AGAINST A FOREIGN STATE'S OFFICIALS, AGENTS AND EMPLOYEES FOR THE PROVISION OF MATERIAL SUPPORT AND RESOURCES TO A TERRORIST GROUP WHOSE ACTS RESULT IN THE PERSONAL INJURY OR WRONGFUL DEATH OF A UNITED STATES NATIONAL CAN BE IMPUTED TO THE FOREIGN STATE.

The FSIA is not intended to affect the substantive law of liability or the attribution of liability between co-defendants. *See* H.REP. 94-1487 at 12, *reprinted at* 1976 U.S.C.C.A.N. at 6610; *First National City Bank*, 462 U.S. at 619-20 (discussing agencies and instrumentalities); *see also* Note, *When May a Sovereign Be Held Liable for the Acts of Her Instrumentalities Under the Foreign Sovereign Immunities Act? The Effect of the McKesson Decision*, 1 TULSA J. COMP. & INT'L L. 285 (1994). Even if 28 U.S.C. §1606 applies to causes of action brought directly against a foreign state pursuant to the state sponsored terrorism exception to immunity and the Flatow Amendment, a foreign state sponsor of terrorism can still be indirectly liable for punitive damages under the principles of *respondeat superior* and vicarious liability.

Individuals acting in their official capacities are considered subject to the FSIA pursuant to 28 U.S.C. §1603(b), as "agencies or instrumentalities" of the foreign state. *See generally* Joan Fitzpatrick, *The Claim to Foreign Sovereign Immunity by Individuals Sued for International Human Rights Violations*, 15 WHITTIER L. REV. 465 (1994). Not one court has held that a foreign state official acting in an official capacity is a "foreign state" within the meaning of 28 U.S.C. §1603(a). Furthermore, the Flatow Amendment expressly provides that money damages, including punitive damages, are available in actions against a foreign state's agents, officials and employees who perform acts which invoke jurisdiction pursuant to the state sponsored terrorism exception to the FSIA. 28 U.S.C.A. §1605 note. This Court concludes that an individual acting within the scope of his or her agency, office, or employment is therefore susceptible to causes of action for punitive damages.

The Flatow Amendment expressly provides that punitive damages are available against the agents of a foreign state, but does not limit the term "agent" to an individual, nongovernmental actor. A governmental unit of a foreign state can act as an agent of the foreign state, if, for example, it acts with the authority of the government, but not within the scope of its dedicated function. This Court concludes that in order for a cause of action for punitive damages to lie against a governmental unit acting as the state's agent, the cause of action must be based not upon any alleged role as a policymaker, but rather upon its implementation of policy at the operational level. Nevertheless, whether the intelligence service of a foreign state should be considered part of the "foreign state" itself, or its "agency or instrumentality" for the purposes of the FSIA, is an issue of first impression. But see *Trajano v. Marcos*, 978 F.2d 493, 497 (whether Philippine Military Intelligence was an "agency or instrumentality" raised by defense but not addressed by the Court). A foreign state's intelligence service most closely meets 28 U.S.C. §1603(b)'s definition of an "agency or instrumentality" as: a separate legal person which is neither a citizen of a State of the United States nor created under the laws of a third country; an organ of a foreign state; operated by public employees paid by the foreign state; and occupying a unique role defined and granted by the government. See *Corporacion Mexicana De Servicios Maritimos, S.A. v. M/T RESPECT*, 89 F.3d 650, 654-55 (9th Cir.1996); *Intercontinental Dictionary Series v. De Gruyter*, 822 F.Supp. 662, 673 (C.D.Cal.1993). But see *Transaero, Inc. v. La Fuerza Aerea Boliviana*, 30 F.3d 148, 151-53 (D.C.Cir.1994), *cert. denied*, 513 U.S. 1150, 115 S.Ct. 1101, 130 L.Ed.2d 1068 (1995).

The Ninth Circuit has held that the " 'scope of employment' provisions of the tortious activity exception [28 U.S.C. §1605(a)(5)] essentially requires a finding that the doctrine of *respondeat superior* applies to the tortious acts of individuals." *Joseph*, 830 F.2d at 1025, *quoted in Liu*, 892 F.2d at 1425. A variation of *respondeat superior*, command responsibility, has formed the basis of judgments against high-ranking foreign military officers under the Torture Victim Protection Act. See *Hilao*, 103 F.3d at 776-77; *Kadic*, 70 F.3d at 242; *Paul*, 901 F.Supp. at 335; *Xuncax*, 886 F.Supp. at 170. See also *In re Yamashita*, 327 U.S. at 14; *Forti*, 672 F.Supp. at 1537-38.

The state sponsored terrorism exception to immunity and the Flatow Amendment similarly employ the principles of *respondeat superior* and command responsibility to create both subject matter jurisdiction and a federal cause of action.

The operative language of 28 U.S.C. §1605(a)(7) [FN11] parallels the definition of *respondeat superior*: an employer is liable in some cases for damages "proximately resulting from acts of employee done within scope of his employment in the employer's service." BLACK'S LAW DICTIONARY at 1311-1312 (6th ed.1990). The Flatow Amendment employs similar language to identify actionable conduct. If a plaintiff can establish subject matter jurisdiction pursuant to 28 U.S.C. §1605(a)(7), this Court concludes that the principal's vicarious liability will attach pursuant to 28 U.S.C.A. §1605 note.

FN11. 28 U.S.C. §1605(a)(7): "if such act or provision of material resources is engaged in by an official, employee or agent of such foreign state while acting within the scope of his office, employment or agency."

Sponsorship of terrorist activities inherently involves a conspiracy to commit terrorist attacks. As a co-conspirator, both with its own agents, officials and employees, and with others, such as the terrorist organization and the ultimate perpetrators, the foreign state is also a joint tortfeasor. As the FSIA was not intended to affect the substantive law of liability, and in particular the allocation of liability, this Court concludes that a foreign state sponsor of terrorism is jointly and severally liable for all damages assessed against co-defendant officials, agents, and employees.

c. PUNITIVE DAMAGES MAY BE AWARDED IN CASES ARISING FROM PRE-ENACTMENT CONDUCT BY FOREIGN STATE SPONSORS OF TERRORISM.

Because 28 U.S.C. §1605(a)(7) and 28 U.S.C.A. §1605 note are read *in pari materia*, the enumerated bases for money damages, including punitive damages, in the Flatow Amendment are deemed to relate back to the state sponsored terrorism exception to immunity. *See* 1A SUTHERLAND ON STATUTORY CONSTRUCTION §§22.31-36. For substantially the same reasons set forth in the subject matter jurisdiction discussion at part III(A)(2),(4) *supra*, the Flatow Amendment, 28 U.S.C.A. §1605 note, applies to pre-enactment extraterritorial conduct by foreign states. [FN12] The Flatow Amendment, like the state sponsored terrorism exception to immunity, is remedial; both merely "add[ ] to the means of enforcing existing obligations." *Id.* at §41.09. Even statutes which permit recovery in excess of compensatory damages are not automatically penal in nature. The primary purpose of 28 U.S.C. §1605(a)(7) and 28 U.S.C.A. §1605 note, *in pari matiera*, is to create a remedy for United States citizen victims of foreign state sponsored terrorism. The secondary effect of deterring terrorism through the im-

position of punitive damages does not prohibit application of the Flatow Amendment to pre-enactment conduct. *See* 3 SUTHERLAND ON STATUTORY CONSTRUCTION at §60.04-05.

FN12. The same statute of limitations and discovery limitations expressly apply to 28 U.S.CA. §1605 note as to 28 U.S.C. §1605(a)(7); there is no basis to imply that Congressional intent regarding 28 U.S.C.A. §1605 note's application to pre-enactment conduct would be any different. *See* 28 U.S.C.A. §1605 note at §(b)(1).

The only plausible basis for a Constitutional challenge, Due Process, must fail. The state sponsored terrorism exception and the Flatow Amendment represent a valid exercise of police power by the federal government, which cannot lack Due Process. 2 SUTHERLAND ON STATUTORY CONSTRUCTION at §41.06 n. 45 citing *Weaver v. Graham*, 450 U.S. 24, 101 S.Ct. 960, 67 L.Ed.2d 17 (1981) ("the use of such powers by the government is itself a way of exercising and affording due process of law.") Furthermore, a state has "no vested right to nonliability for injuries caused by public officers before the enactment of a statute permitting recovery." *Id.* at §41.06 n. 37 citing *Evans v. Berry*, 262 N.Y. 61, 186 N.E. 203 (1933).

II. CONCLUSIONS OF LAW WITH RESPECT TO LIABILITY AND DAMAGES

A. WRONGFUL DEATH

The recent amendments to the FSIA, 28 U.S.C. §1605(a)(7) and 28 U.S.C.A. §1605 note, establish a cause of action for wrongful death proximately caused by an act of state sponsored terrorism. Although the FSIA does not define the scope of this new federal cause of action, typically, a wrongful death statute is designed to compensate decedent's heirs-at-law for economic losses which result from decedent's premature death. *See, e.g.*, D.C. CODE ANN. §16-2701 (Michie 1981); see also *Alejandre v. Republic of Cuba*, 996 F.Supp. 1239 , 1249-50 (S.D.Fla.1997).

There are two separate items of economic loss resulting from the death of Alisa Michelle Flatow, the funeral expenses and the loss of accretions to her Estate.

The funeral bill in the amount of $4,470.00 was introduced into evidence. The Court notes that various costs associated with the death and final services were undertaken by the United States government and the government of the State of Israel, for which there exist no appraisal or other method to determine an accurate figure. The Court finds that the funeral bill amount set forth above is reasonable and the services detailed are those anticipated for final services.

The Plaintiff also introduced testimony from Dr. Jerome S. Paige with regard to loss of accretions to the Estate. His testimony as to a projected professional profile for Alisa Michelle Flatow, had she lived, was supported in great detail by her professor and mentor at Brandeis University, Dr. Jonathan D. Sarna, and this testimony was in turn corroborated by her classmates Alan Mitrani and Lauren Sloane, as well as by Plaintiff Stephen M. Flatow and the decedent's sister, Francine Flatow. Finally, the Plaintiff introduced into evidence the records for the decedent Alisa Michelle Flatow from Brandeis University, which indicated that she was a Dean's List student throughout her college career. The Court finds absolutely no reason to doubt any particulars of this testimony.

The testimony of Dr. Paige reviewed the methodology of calculation of economic loss, which the Court finds to be appropriate, including the assumptions as to inflation, rise in productivity, job advancement, personal consumption, and net earnings. Further, the discount rate applied by Dr. Paige appears to the Court to be extremely conservative, as it is based upon risk-free securities over an extended period of time, as detailed by official United States Department of the Treasury publications. The discount rate applied varies from 5.53% to 5.89%. Although Dr. Paige computed the net economic loss on the basis of both typical mean earnings with a Master's degree and with a Master's Degree in physical/occupational therapy, the Court finds that given the overwhelming body of testimony indicating that Alisa Michelle Flatow would have become a physical/occupational therapist, a calculation based upon that assumption is more appropriate.

Applying these factors, the Court finds that value of the loss of accretions to the Estate of Alisa Michelle Flatow of $1,207,000.00, given by Dr. Paige, is reasonable. As indicated by Dr. Paige, this figure must be factored by an estimate of Alisa Michelle Flatow's increased earnings potential, given her exceptional academic performance. The Court finds that the minimal adjustment which should be made to the loss of accretions based upon ample evidence of Alisa Michelle Flatow's superior academic performance would be a 25% increase, thereby yielding a total loss of $1,508,750.00.

Accordingly, the total amount of economic damages proven by clear and convincing evidence in this case is $1,513,220.00.

B. SURVIVAL DAMAGES-PAIN AND SUFFERING

Causes of action which could have been brought by the decedent but for decedent's death may be asserted for the benefit of the Estate. *See, e.g.*, D.C. CODE ANN. §12-101 (Michie 1981). Such actions are separate and distinct from any claim of wrongful death by decedent's heirs-at-law, *Hoston v. United States*, 566 F.Supp. 1125 (D.D.C.1983). Redundant recovery may not be had under both wrongful death and survival statutes. *Runyon v. District of Columbia*, 463 F.2d 1319 (D.C.Cir.1972). If Plaintiff presents sufficient evidence of conscious pain and suffering, determination of the compensation has largely been relegated to the discretion of the trier of fact by courts in this jurisdiction based upon factors including the duration and nature of the suffering endured. The United States Court of Appeals for the District of Columbia Circuit has firmly established that the trier of fact has broad discretion in calculating damages for pain and suffering. *Taylor v. Washington Terminal Co.*, 133 U.S.App. D.C. 110, 409 F.2d 145, *cert. denied*, 396 U.S. 835, 90 S.Ct. 93, 24 L.Ed.2d 85 (1969).

The Plaintiff in this action has elicited extensive testimony on the extent of pain and suffering resulting from the acts above described. Testimony by witness Kesari Rusa, who was seated next to Alisa Michelle Flatow on the bus, described clutching of Alisa Michelle Flatow's hands following the explosion, at which time her eyes were open. The videotape taken at the scene depicts witness David Shaenbaum assisting with the administration of fluids as a part of treatment on the scene, at which time no breathing assistance or resuscitation efforts were necessary. The records of the Soroka Medical Center indicate that upon arrival Alisa Michelle Flatow demonstrated a strong pulse and independent respiration. Indeed, breathing assistance was initiated only as a part of the surgical procedures which followed. Alisa Michelle Flatow was responsive to external pain stimuli and her pupils reacted to light until the early evening hours. These facts are demonstrated both by the medical records and by the testimony of Dr. Allen Fisher, the attending physician. Further, the testimony of Dr. Gregory Threatte included his opinion as a pathologist that conscious pain and suffering continued for at least three to five hours.

This Court finds that the above-referenced testimony is credible and convincing. This Court further finds that an appropriate amount of compensatory damages for Alisa Michelle Flatow's pain and suffering is $1,000,000.00.

* * *

D. PUNITIVE DAMAGES

The recent amendments to the FSIA included the right to punitive damages for personal injury or death resulting from an act of state sponsored terrorism. *See* 28 U.S.C. §1605(a)(7); 28 U.S.C.A. §1605 note. Punitive damages are designed "to punish [a defendant] for his outrageous conduct and to deter him and others like him from similar conduct in the future." RESTATEMENT (SECOND) TORTS §908(1) (1977) ; see also *Pacific Mut. Life. Ins. Co. v. Haslip*, 499 U.S. 1, 15, 111 S.Ct. 1032, 113 L.Ed.2d 1 (1991). As only one court has thus far entered an award of punitive damages under these new amendments, see *Alejandre* at 1250-53, Plaintiff looks to traditional principles of tort law and analogous opinions under the Alien Tort Claims Act, 28 U.S.C. §1350, and the Torture Victim Protection Act, 28 U.S.C.A. §1350 note, for guidance.

General principles of tort law identify elements which factor into the analysis of whether to award punitive damages, and the appropriate amount of damages, including the character of the defendant's act; the nature and extent of harm to plaintiff that the defendant caused or intended to cause; the need for deterrence; and the wealth of the defendant. RESTATEMENT (SECOND) TORTS 908(1)-(2) (1977).

In *Filartiga v. Pena-Irala*, 577 F.Supp. 860, 865 (E.D.N.Y.1984), the Court indicated that the character of the act is the paramount consideration in determining whether, and to what extent, punitive damages are warranted. The evidence shows that the Defendants subsidize a group, the Shaqaqi faction of Palestine Islamic Jihad, which has no social agenda other than to undermine the Middle East peace process through terrorist attacks, primarily against Israeli targets.

As it proved impossible to fight terrorism by bringing the terrorists themselves to justice, Congress created jurisdiction over and rights of action against foreign state sponsors of terrorism. By creating these rights of action, Congress intended that the Courts impose a substantial financial cost on states which sponsor terrorist groups whose activities kill American citizens. This cost functions both as a direct deterrent, and also as a disabling mechanism: if several large punitive damage awards issue against a foreign state sponsor of terrorism, the state's financial capacity to provide funding will be curtailed.

In the only precedent under this statute, the District Court for the Southern District of Florida assessed three percent of the value of the Cuban Air Force's MiG fleet, $137.7 million, as punitive damages for the murder of three American private aircraft pilots. *Alejandre* at 1253. Cases under the Alien Tort Claims Act and the Torture Victim Protection Act often result in multimillion dollar punitive damages awards against individual defendants for torture and extrajudicial killings. See id at 1251 n. 10 (citing cases). The Torture Victim Protection Act has become notorious for its pyrrhic victories; although Courts have entered remarkably high punitive damages awards, the defendants are invariably judgment-proof. *See* Christopher W. Haffke, *The Torture Victim Protection Act: More Symbol than Substance*, 43 EMORY L.J. 1467 (1994); Jennifer Correale, *The Torture Victim Protection Act: A Vital Contribution to International Human Rights Enforcement or Just a Nice Gesture?*, 6 PACE INT'L L. REV. 197 (1994); *see also* Jean-Marie Simon, *The Alien Tort Claims Act: Justice or Show Trials?*, 11 B.U. INT'L L.J. 1 (1993).

The attack on the No. 36 Egged bus in the Gaza Strip which inflicted fatal injuries to Alisa Michelle Flatow and seven Israelis has been demonstrated by the testimony to have been part of an extensive campaign of terror carried out to obtain the political ends of the Islamic Republic of Iran. The Court can find no case law in support of the proposition that premeditated violent acts undertaken upon civilian targets are a legitimate part of the actions of any government. Factors which may be considered in determining an appropriate amount of punitive damages may be grouped under a few broad headings, including: (1) the nature of the act itself, and the extent to which any civilized society would find that act repugnant; (2) the circumstances of its planning; (3) Defendants' economic status with regard to the ability of Defendants to pay; and (4) the basis upon which a Court might determine the amount of an award reasonably sufficient to deter like conduct in the future, both by the Defendants and others.

Alisa Michelle Flatow died as a result of an unanticipated attack, from the effects of shrapnel which penetrated her brain. The device used to inflict these injuries consisted of an explosive charge surrounded by an ersatz collection of metal fragments whose intended purpose was to inflict injury in the most severe manner imaginable upon those exposed to the device. While the death of any young person is tragic, a killing under these circumstances extends to the very limits of any human being's capacity to inflict pain and suffering upon another. The evidence has shown that in addition to Alisa Michelle Flatow, this bus was filled with other young people, and therefore Alisa Michelle Flatow, together with the other young persons aboard the bus, rather than being a mere incidental casualty of a violent act, was in fact the target of this malicious activity.

The videotape taken at the scene, together with the testimony of at least four witnesses on the scene, makes clear that the attack was the result of careful planning and was carried out with what might be described as vicious inspiration. This too calls for an appropriate response.

The economic position of the Defendants in this case was detailed in very precise expert testimony by Dr. Patrick Clawson. That testimony set forth precise information, widely published, regarding Iranian economy. Most significantly, Dr. Clawson testified, based upon information obtained from that published, reliable reports, the Islamic Republic of Iran's oil exports generate hard currency income of at least twelve billion dollars per year. Clearly, the Defendants in this case are able to respond in damages to an award in a very significant amount.

Dr. Clawson's testimony detailed an annual expenditure of approximately seventy-five million dollars for terrorist activities. Dr. Clawson testified that the Islamic Republic of Iran is so brazen in its sponsorship of terrorist activities that it carries a line item in its national budget for this purpose.

Based upon his analysis of past interaction between the current Iranian government and the United States, in particular the 1979-81 hostage crisis and the United States' reflagging of Kuwaiti oil tankers, Dr. Clawson testified that in his opinion, the Islamic Republic of Iran, when implementing its national policy, is extremely responsive to the ultimatums made by the United States government. Dr. Clawson stated that in his opinion, a factor of three times its annual expenditure for terrorist activities would be the minimum amount which would affect the conduct of the Islamic Republic of Iran, and that a factor of up to ten times its annual expenditure for terrorism must be considered to constitute a serious deterrent to future terrorist activities aimed at United States nationals.

This Court is cognizant that the purpose of this statute is to deter acts of terrorism which result in the death or personal injury of United States nationals. In this Court's judgment, in order to ensure that the Islamic Republic of Iran will refrain from sponsoring such terrorist acts in the future, an award of punitive damages in the amount of three times the Islamic Republic of Iran's annual expenditure for terrorist activities is appropriate.

CONCLUSION

This Court possess subject matter jurisdiction over this action and personal jurisdiction over Defendants. Plaintiff has established to this Court's satisfaction, pursuant to 28 U.S.C. §1608(e), and by clear and convincing evidence, that Defendants, the Islamic Republic of Iran, the Iranian Ministry of Information and Security, Ayatollah Ali Hoseini Khamenei, former President Ali Akbar Hashemi-Rafsanjani, and former Minister Ali Fallahian-Khuzestani, are jointly and severally liable for all damages awarded by this Court to Plaintiff Stephen M. Flatow, in his own right, as Administrator of the Estate of Alisa Michelle Flatow, and on behalf of decedent's heirs-at-law, for their provision of material support and resources to a terrorist group which caused the extrajudicial killing of Alisa Michelle Flatow.

Notes:

1.   Does including punitive damages in the statute tip the scales in favor of victims? Are punitive damages warranted in terrorism cases? Are they more important in terrorism cases than in other remedial tort actions? What are the forces and considerations under girding the economics of terrorism cases and how does this relate to the award of punitive damages?

2.   Consider the case of an unmarried, unemployed 80 year old woman with no close relatives killed in a suicide bombing by. How would damages be calculated? How would the purpose of antiterrorism statutes be fulfilled in a case brought by her estate? How would the results differ if the suit was brought under the Flatow Act and the Klinghoffer Act? Which statute would be more effective in achieving the purposes behind these statutes? Does this example suggest why punitive damages are necessary?

3.   Initially it was unclear whether punitive damages could be awarded against a state sponsor of terrorism under the terrorism amendments. However, after dozens of terrorism decisions, *Roeder* made its way to the Court of Appeal for the District of Columbia, which followed its own prior precedents in other areas of the law to determine whether the governmental offices of state sponsors of terrorism fit within the "agency and instrumentality" language of the Flatow Amendment,

> One other preliminary issue deals with the legal status of Iran's Ministry of Foreign Affairs. The Flatow amendment to the FSIA, set forth at

28 U.S.C. §1605 note, provides a cause of action against officials, employees, and agents of foreign states. Because it is unclear whether the amendment also provides a cause of action against the foreign state, plaintiffs maintain that the Ministry of Foreign Affairs is merely an agent of Iran, not its alter ego. In *Transaero, Inc. v. La Fuerza Aerea Boliviana*, 30 F.3d 148, 149-50 (D.C.Cir.1994), we concluded that a nation's air force is a "foreign state or political subdivision" rather than an "agency or instrumentality" of the nation for purposes of the service-of-process provisions of the FSIA. "Any government of reasonable complexity must act through men organized into offices and departments." *Id.* at 153. We adopted a categorical approach: if the core functions of the entity are governmental, it is considered the foreign state itself; if commercial, the entity is an agency or instrumentality of the foreign state. A nation's armed forces are clearly on the governmental side. *Id.* For similar reasons, the Ministry of Foreign Affairs must be treated as the state of Iran itself rather than as its agent. The conduct of foreign affairs is an important and "indispensable" governmental function. *Kennedy v. Mendoza-Martinez*, 372 U.S. 144, 160, 83 S.Ct. 554, 563, 9 L.Ed.2d 644 (1963).

Roeder v. Islamic Republic of Iran, 333 F.3d 228, 234-235 (D.C. Cir. 2003). Although this decision did not, strictly speaking, deal with punitive damages, it effectively rewrote the law with respect to awarding punitive damages against Iran's terrorism arm, its Ministry of Information and Security ("MOIS"). Until *Roeder*, virtually all FSIA cases brought against Iran routinely awarded punitive damages against both the state and the MOIS. Subsequently, courts stopped making such awards,

In light of the decision in *Roeder*, plaintiffs are hard-pressed to argue that MOIS is an "agent or instrumentality" of Iran, rather than Iran itself. Although the *Roeder* court was not directly considering the question of punitive damages under §1606, its ruling indicates that the categorical approach to analyzing the §1603 distinction between the foreign state and an "agency or instrumentality" of the foreign state applies to FSIA contexts other than the service-of-process provision at issue in *Transaero*. Applying the categorical approach here leads inexorably to the conclusion that MOIS should be treated as the foreign state itself. The undisputed

evidence is that MOIS, named as an official Iranian ministry in 1983 or 1984, is the "intelligence service of Iran," and was, in fact, merely a continuation of the well-respected intelligence agency that had existed under the pre-revolutionary Iranian regime...Plaintiffs have presented no evidence to suggest that the intelligence activities conducted by MOIS in the early 1980s or, for that matter, the activities conducted by MOIS today, had or have any commercial effect or purpose. Indeed, it is difficult to conceive how intelligence and security activities-in this case, providing training and support for terrorism abroad in order to advance Iran's political agenda-could be considered predominantly "commercial" rather than "governmental."

Dammarell v. Islamic Republic of Iran, 281 F.Supp.2d 105, 200 -201 (D.D.C. 2003).

10.4 "Standard" Terrorism Damages
Jenco v. Islamic Republic of Iran, 154 F.Supp.2d 27 (D.D.C. 2001).

LAMBERTH, District Judge.

On March 15, 2000, the plaintiffs [FN1] filed a multi-count complaint alleging that the defendants were responsible for Lawrence M. Jenco's kidnapping, detention, and torture over a 1 1/2 year period. The defendants, despite being properly served with process, failed to answer this charge in any way. Thus, the Court entered the defendants' default on January 5, 2001.

FN1. When originally filed on March 15, 2000, the only named plaintiff in this case was the Estate of Lawrence M. Jenco. After trial, the plaintiff, pursuant to Federal Rule of Civil Procedure 15(b), amended the complaint to conform with the evidence presented at trial. The complaint was amended to include the brothers, sisters, nephews, and nieces of the decedent Lawrence Jenco. Further, since the trial, the plaintiffs have adduced additional evidence of the pain and suffering of the Fr. Jenco's relatives. The Court has considered this additional evidence in making its decision.

Notwithstanding this entry of default, a default judgment against a foreign state may not be entered until the plaintiffs have "establishe[d] [their] claim or right to relief by evidence that is satisfactory to the Court." 28 U.S.C. §1608(e). Thus, the Court held a bench trial to receive evidence from the plaintiffs. Again, the defendants failed to appear.

Based on the evidence presented to the Court, and the law applicable to this case, the Court finds a default judgment merited. Further, the Court awards appropriate compensatory relief. Finally, the Court finds that the Estate of Fr. Jenco is entitled to punitive damages.

I. FINDINGS OF FACT

A. Father Jenco's Experience [FN2]

FN2. As a co-hostage of, for example, Terry Anderson and Thomas Sutherland, Fr. Jenco's experience was substantially similar to their experiences. Thus, for further description of Fr. Jenco's experience, see *Anderson v. The Islamic Republic of Iran*, 90 F.Supp.2d 107, 113 (D.D.C.2000); *Sutherland v. The Islamic Republic of Iran*, 151 F.Supp.2d 27; *Cicippio v. The Islamic Republic of Iran*, 18 F.Supp.2d 62, 68 (D.D.C.1998). *See also* Fr. Lawrence M. Jenco, Bound to Forgive (1995); Plaintiffs' Exhibit 21 (post-captivity interview with Fr. Jenco); Terry Anderson, Den of Lions (1993); Thomas Sutherland & Jean Sutherland, At Your Own Risk (1996).

In early 1985, Lawrence M. Jenco, an ordained priest in the Catholic church, was working in Beirut, Lebanon as the Director of Catholic Relief Services. On the morning of January 8, he was abducted by five armed men and imprisoned for the next for 564 days. After his release, he returned to the United States and served as a parish priest until his death on July 19, 1996.

From the moment he was abducted, Father Jenco was treated little better than a caged animal. He was chained, beaten, and almost constantly blindfolded. His access to toilet facilities was extremely limited, if permitted at all. He was routinely required to urinate in a cup and maintain the urine in his cell. His food and clothing were spare, as was even the most basic medical care

He also withstood repeated psychological torture. Most notably, at one point, his captors held a gun to his head and told him that he was about to die. The captors pulled the trigger and laughed as Father Jenco reacted to the small click of the unloaded gun. At other times, the captors misled Fr. Jenco into thinking he was going home. They told him to dress up in his good clothes, took pictures of him, and then said "ha, ha, we're just kidding." Fr. Jenco Interview, Plaintiffs' Exhibit 21, at 93.

Even after his release and return to the United States, Fr. Jenco continued to suffer the effects of his captivity. For a long period after his return, Father Jenco remained underweight and quite weak. Father Jenco's nephew, David Mihelich, testified that his uncle's disposition was noticeably milder, and indeed never returned to its pre-captivity state. As well, Christopher Morales, a Special Agent with the United States Secret Service, became a close friend of Jenco's after interviewing him about his experience in Lebanon. Agent Morales testified that he witnessed Father Jenco have three separate "flashbacks", that is, moments where Jenco appeared to be aloof of his surroundings and somewhat possessed and disturbed by different images or experiences. *See* Feb. 15, 2001 Tr. at 10-13.

In sum, the last 11 years of Fr. Jenco's life were indelibly marred by his kidnapping and torture. With that established, the Court turns to the next issue: who were his captors?

B. Father Jenco's Captors and Their Connections to the Iranian Government

The testimony of numerous witnesses at trial convinces the Court that Father Jenco's captors were members of the Islamic group Hizbollah and that Hizbollah was funded and controlled by the Iranian government and the Iranian Ministry of Information and Security.

1. Fr. Jenco's Captors

Based on the evidence presented at trial, it is clear that Fr. Jenco was kidnapped and detained by the Islamic fundamentalist group Hizbollah. This conclusion is supported by the testimony of several witnesses. For example, Jenco's co-hostage, Terry Anderson, testified that their captors were "very, very pro-Iranian," and that Iranian Revolutionary Guards were involved in the kidnapping and detention of the hostages. *See* Tr. at 116. Anderson further testified that he and his co-hostages knew that they were being held in Hizbollah territory, and at one point, were even held at Hizbollah headquarters. *See* Tr. at 116. Moreover, several years after his release, Anderson interviewed the secretary general of Hizbollah who as much as admitted to the kidnappings. *See* Tr. at 118. Thomas Sutherland, another co-hostage of Jenco's, also testified as to the identity of his captors. The captors, according to Sutherland, were clearly part of an Islamic Jihad group, who, when the death of the Ayatollah Khomeini was reported, wept quite openly. *See* Tr. at 238.

Perhaps that most persuasive evidence that Jenco's captors were members of Hizbollah came from Ambassador Robert Oakley and Dr. Patrick Clawson. Oakley, a former advisor to the National Security Council on Middle East affairs, testified bluntly on this subject. Consider the following colloquy from trial:

Q. Is there any doubt in your mind [Ambassador Oakley] that through that period of 1985 through 1991 that the

Hizbollah, backed by Iran, financially and otherwise, was holding Tom Sutherland as a hostage?

A. No, there [is] none.

See Tr. at 21. Dr. Patrick Clawson, an experienced researcher and writer on Iranian politics, testified similarly. When asked by the Court whether Sutherland, Jenco's cohostage, was "initially seized by Hizbollah...and held by them throughout the time?", Clawson responded "Yes, your Honor." Tr. at 58.

Further support for the conclusion that Fr. Jenco was captured and detained by Hizbollah is provided by precedent. For instance, in *Anderson v. The Islamic Republic of Iran*, 90 F.Supp.2d 107, 113 (D.D.C.2000), the Court found that Terry Anderson, Sutherland's co-hostage for almost his entire captivity, was captured by Hizbollah and that "Iran provided Hizbollah [FN3] with funding, direction and training for its terrorist activities in Lebanon, including the kidnapping and torture of Terry Anderson." See also *Cicippio v. The Islamic Republic of Iran*, 18 F.Supp.2d 62, 68 (D.D.C.1998) (finding that Hizbollah was responsible for the kidnapping and detention of David Jacobson, a co-hostage of Sutherland, Anderson, and Jenco).

FN3. There does not appear to be a consensus on the spelling of "Hizbollah", as it is often spelled "Hezbollah" as well.

2. Hizbollah's Connection to the Iranian Government

In addition to finding that Fr. Jenco was seized by Hizbollah, the Court also finds that The Islamic Republic of Iran and the Iranian MOIS provided support, guidance, and resources to Hizbollah. The most persuasive testimony on this issue came from Jenco's experts: Ambassador Oakley, Robert McFarlane, and Dr. Clawson. Ambassador Oakley testified that "radical elements highly placed within the government of Iran are giving operational policy advice to terrorists in Iran, specifically terrorists operating under the name Islamic Jihad or Hizbollah." Tr. at 19. Similarly, Robert McFarlane, former National Security Advisor, testified that Hizbollah was a "terrorist group...formed in the early 1980s under the sponsorship of the government of Iran." Tr. at 29; *see also* Tr. at 31 (opining that Hizbollah was formed with the "volunteering of [Iranian] financial support" as well as "Iranian personnel"). As well, Dr. Clawson testified that the Iranian government and the Iranian MOIS were behind the formation and funding of Hizbollah, and that Hizbollah is very much under the control of the Iranian government. *See* Tr. at 41-42. Finally, Middle East expert Dr. Reuven Paz testified that almost all of Hizbollah's activities-whether social, religious, or terrorist-were funded by the Iranian government.

Dr. Paz added that the Iranian government also provides Hizbollah substantial non-financial support, such as arms and ammunition. *See* Videotape Testimony of Ruven Paz, Feb. 7, 2001.

C. The Pain and Suffering of Father Jenco's Family

While Father Jenco was being held prisoner, his many siblings and relatives banded together and fought for his release. The family made a practice of meeting every Monday night to discuss what steps they could take to help secure his release. Family members took on various responsibilities, such as communicating with the public, dealing with the media, maintaining contact with the State Department, and raising money to cover the various costs of such a massive effort.

Andrew Mihelich and John Jenco, both nephews of Fr. Jenco, testified that, because of their massive dedication to free Fr. Jenco, the whole family, in effect, became a hostage in one way or another. As a result, many of the traditional family events, such as birthdays, graduations, or religious holidays were overshadowed-or overlooked altogether-on account of the campaign to free Fr. Jenco. Apart from the campaign, the family felt the very personal loss of not having their beloved relative at many family milestones, such as weddings, births, and baptisms. On the whole, according to John Jenco, the family spent the 19 months of Fr. Jenco's captivity on an emotional roller coaster, never knowing how close or far Fr. Jenco was to being released, not to mention returning home unharmed.

Jenco relatives also testified as to the specific effects that the captivity had of Fr. Jenco's brother, John Jenco. John Jenco Jr. testified that, from the first day of captivity to the last day of his own life, John Jenco Sr. was distraught in a way he had never been before. He was able to celebrate the return of Fr. Jenco, but was never fully able, according to John Jenco Jr., become himself again. Similarly, Joseph Jenco testified that the stress of the captivity on Verna Mae Mihelich likely was a factor in her premature death.

II. CONCLUSIONS OF LAW

Based on the events described above, the plaintiffs make the following allegations:

(1) The estate of Fr. Jenco alleges battery, assault, and false imprisonment.

(2) All plaintiffs allege the intentional infliction of emotional distress.

Given these claims, the Court is faced with the following three questions, which it answers in the order presented:

(1) Are The Islamic Republic of Iran and the Iranian MOIS, immune under the Foreign Sovereign Immunities Act from the alleged claims?;

(2) Are the Islamic Republic of Iran and the Iranian Ministry of Information and Security (if not immune) liable under the claims alleged?; and

(3) If the defendants are found liable, to what damages are the plaintiffs entitled?

A. Foreign Sovereign Immunity [FN4]

FN4. In cases such as this one, courts have sometimes referred to the immunity issue as a jurisdictional issue. See, e.g., *Elahi v. Islamic Republic of Iran*, 124 F.Supp.2d 97, 105 (D.D.C.2000). In FSIA cases, they are one in the same. As the Supreme Court explained: "Under the [FSIA], a foreign state is presumptively *immune* from the *jurisdiction* of United States courts; unless a specified exception applies, a federal court lacks subject-matter jurisdiction over a claim against a foreign state." *Saudi Arabia v. Nelson*, 507 U.S. 349, 355, 113 S.Ct. 1471, 123 L.Ed.2d 47 (1993) (emphasis added).

The Foreign Sovereign Immunities Act ("FSIA") grants foreign states and their agents immunity from liability in United States courts. *See* 28 U.S.C. §1602 *et seq.* In 1998, however, Congress specifically suspended this immunity for personal injuries "caused by an act of torture, extrajudicial killing, aircraft sabotage, hostage taking, or the provision of material support or resources...for such an act."[FN5] 28 U.S.C. §1605(a)(7). The injurious act (or the provision of resources in support thereof), to give rise to liability, must be committed by "an official, employee, or agent of a foreign state, while acting within the scope of his or her office." 28 U.S.C. 1605(a)(7).

FN5. Although this statute was passed after the events described in this case, Congress explicitly made the statute applicable to pre-enactment conduct. *See* Pub.L. No. 104-132, §221(c) (stating that the statute "shall apply to any cause of action arising before, on or after the date of enactment of this Act"). See also *Flatow*, 999 F.Supp. at 13.

The Court finds that, based on the evidence presented at trial and recounted above, Lawrence M. Jenco was taken hostage and tortured within the meaning of 28 U.S.C. §1605(a)(7). That Fr. Jenco was taken hostage and detained for 19 months is, of course, patently undeniable. With respect to torture, the Court finds that the deprivation of adequate food, light, toilet facilities, and medical care for 564 days amounts to torture within the meaning of section 1605(a)(7). [FN6]

FN6. From a statutory construction perspective, "torture", as used in the context of 28 U.S.C. 1605(a)(7), must have a meaning independent of "hostage taking". See *Babbitt v. Sweet Home Chapter of Communities for a Great Oregon*, 515 U.S. 687, 698, 115 S.Ct. 2407, 132 L.Ed.2d 597 (1995). Thus, the pains normally attendant to being a hostage, most notably the loss of liberty and contact with loved ones, although clearly *tortuous* within the common meaning of the term, cannot qualify as torture under 28 U.S.C. 1605(a)(7).

The Court next finds that, based on the evidence presented at trial and recounted above, Fr. Jenco was kidnapped by the Islamic fundamentalist group Hizbollah and that the Islamic Republic of Iran and the Iranian MOIS provided "material support or resources" to Hizbollah within the meaning of 28 U.S.C. §1605(a)(7). This conclusion is squarely buttressed by precedent. [FN7]

FN7. In a case similar to this one, Judge Kotelly of this Court opined: "it is now the universally held view of the intelligence community that Iran was responsible for the formation, funding, training, and management of Hizbollah." *Higgins v. The Islamic Republic of Iran*, Civ. A. No. 99-377 (D.D.C.2000). As well, Judge Jackson declared in *Anderson* that the defendants "financed, organized, armed, and planned Hizbollah operations in Lebanon and elsewhere." *Anderson*, 90 F.Supp.2d at 112; see also *Flatow v. The Islamic Republic of Iran*, 999 F.Supp. 1, 18 (D.D.C.1998) (Lamberth, J.) (finding that The Islamic Republic of Iran and the Iranian MOIS were liable under the doctrine of *respondeat superior* for the terrorist acts of the Palestine Islamic Jihad, whose source of funding was the government of Iran); *Eisenfeld v. The Islamic Republic of Iran*, 2000 WL 1918779, 2000 U.S. Dist. LEXIS 9545 (D.D.C.2000) (stating that "there is no question that Hamas, [an organization quite similar and related to Hizbollah] received massive material and technical support from the...Islamic Republic of Iran").

In summary, the Court finds that Fr. Lawrence Jenco was taken hostage and tortured by the Islamic fundamentalist group Hizbollah. The Court further finds that the defendants, The Islamic Republic of Iran and the Iranian MOIS, "provi[ded]...material support or resources...for [these] acts." 28 U.S.C. §1605(a)(7). The Court also finds that the provision of resources was an act committed by "an official, employee, or agent of a foreign state, while acting within the scope of his or her office." 28 U.S.C. 1605(a)(7). Based on these findings, the Court therefore concludes that the defendants are not immune from liability in this Court.

B. Liability

Under 28 U.S.C. §1606, a "foreign state...not entitled to immunity...shall be liable in the same manner and to the same extent as a private individual under like circumstances." Applying standard rules of liability, the Court finds the defendants liable on most, but not all, counts alleged in the plaintiffs' complaint. In making this conclusion, the Court applies federal common law. See *Flatow v. The Islamic Republic of Iran*, 999 F.Supp. 1, 14-15 (D.D.C.1998) (choosing federal common law after a federal choice of law analysis).

1. Battery

According to the Restatement (Second) of Torts, a defendant has committed battery if "he acts intending to cause a harmful or offensive contact with [a] person", and a "harmful contact with the person...directly or indirectly results." Restatement (Second) of Torts, §13 (1965); see also *Sphere Drake Ins. P.L.C. v. D'Errico*, 246 F.3d 682, 2001 WL 135670, at *2 (10th Cir.2001); *United Nat. Ins. Co. v. Penuche's, Inc.*, 128 F.3d 28, 32 (1st Cir.1997).

Based upon the evidence presented in open court, the Court finds that Lawrence M. Jenco suffered harmful contact, and that that contact was the result of intentional acts attributable to both the Islamic Republic of Iran and the Iranian MOIS. Thomas Sutherland and Terry Anderson testified as to the typical treatment of hostages, which included beatings and rough treatment. These acts, which were intentionally committed by Jenco's captors, are attributable to the defendants because the defendants substantially funded and controlled Hizbollah. *See* Section I.B.2 and note 7, *supra*. As such, the defendants are liable under the tort doctrines of *respondeat superior* and joint and several liability. See *Flatow*, 999 F.Supp. at 26-27 (finding The Islamic Republic of Iran and the Iranian MOIS liable under the doctrines of *respondeat superior* and joint and several liability).

Thus, finding that Lawrence Jenco did indeed suffer a harmful contact, and that the acts causing such contact were attributable to the defendants, the Court finds the defendants liable for the battery of Jenco.

2. Assault

According to the Restatement (Second) of Torts, a defendant has committed an assault if "he acts intending to cause a harmful or offensive contact with [a] person, or an imminent apprehension of such a contact" and the person is "thereby put in such imminent apprehension." Restatement (Second) of Torts, §21 (1965); see also *Truman v. U.S.*, 26 F.3d 592, 596 (5th Cir.1994); *Manning v. Grimsley*, 643 F.2d 20, 22 (1st Cir.1981).

Based upon the evidence presented in open court, the Court finds that Lawrence Jenco was put in an imminent apprehension of harmful or offensive conduct, and that the apprehension was the result of intentional acts attributable to both the Islamic Republic of Iran and the Iranian MOIS. The most notable instance of such conduct is the mock execution which the Hizbollah captors administered to Jenco. Such behavior has long been regarded as an archetypal assault. *See* Keeton et al., Prosser & Keeton on Torts, §11, at 46 (5th ed.1984).

These acts, which were intentionally committed by Jenco's captors, are attributable to the defendants because the defendants substantially funded and controlled Hizbollah. *See* Section I.B.2 and note 7, *supra*. As such, the defendants are liable under the tort doctrines of *respondeat superior* and joint and several liability. See *Flatow*, 999 F.Supp. at 26-27 (finding The Islamic Republic of Iran and the Iranian MOIS liable under the doctrines of *respondeat superior* and joint and several liability).

3. False Imprisonment

According to the Restatement (Second) of Torts, "[a]n actor is subject to liability to another for false imprisonment if

(a) he acts intending to confine [a person] within boundaries fixed by the actor, and

(b) his act directly or indirectly results in such a confinement of the other, and

(c) the other is conscious of the confinement or is harmed by it.

Restatement (Second) of Torts, §35 (1965); *King v. Crossland Sav. Bank*, 111 F.3d 251, 255 (2nd Cir.1997); *Richardson v. U.S. Dept. of Interior*, 740 F.Supp. 15, 26 (D.D.C.1990).

There is no question in the Court's mind, or anyone else's for that matter, that Lawrence Jenco was falsely imprisoned by Hizbollah for 564 days. Further, as explained above, *see* Section I.B.2 and note 7, *supra.*, these acts are attributable to the defendants because the defendants substantially funded and controlled Hizbollah. As such, the defendants are liable under the tort doctrines of *respondeat superior* and joint and several liability. See *Flatow*, 999 F.Supp. at 26-27 (finding The Islamic Republic of Iran and the Iranian MOIS liable under the doctrines of *respondeat superior* and joint and several liability).

4. Intentional Infliction of Emotional Distress

According to the Restatement (Second) of Torts, "one who by extreme and outrageous conduct intentionally or recklessly causes severe emotional distress to another is subject to liability for such emotional distress." Restatement (Second) of Torts, §46 (1986); see also *Holbrook v. Lobdell-Emery Mfg. Co.*, 219 F.3d 598, 600 (7th Cir.2000); *Ross v. Saint Augustine's College*, 103 F.3d 338, 343 (4th Cir.1996).

With respect to Fr. Jenco himself, the Court has little hesitation concluding that he suffered severe emotional distress at the hands of his captors, Hizbollah. The conduct of Hizbollah, in taking someone hostage for 564 days quite easily qualifies as extreme and outrageous. Further, there was substantial testimony as to the extreme stress of captivity, which even continued once Father Jenco was freed. *See* Feb. 15, 2001, Tr. at 5. Finally, as explained above, *see* Section I.B.2 and note 7, *supra.*, these acts are attributable to the defendants because the defendants substantially funded and controlled Hizbollah. As such, the defendants are liable under the tort doctrines of *respondeat superior* and joint and several liability. See *Flatow*, 999 F.Supp. at 26-27 (finding The Islamic Republic of Iran and the Iranian MOIS liable under the doctrines of *respondeat superior* and joint and several liability).

With respect to the Fr. Jenco's six siblings, the Court finds that the defendants are liable for their emotional distress. First, there is significant evidence of emotional distress among the siblings. Joseph Jenco, Fr. Jenco's brother testified as to the great strain the captivity imposed on himself as well as his brothers and sisters. *See* Feb. 15, 2001, Tr. at 4-5, 19. As well, other witnesses testified as to the stressful and extensive publicity campaign, Tr. at 18-19, 30-32; the stress of false alarms that Fr. Jenco had ben killed or freed, Tr. at 1; and constant fear that the campaign to free Fr. Jenco might also end up hurting him and the other hostages. Tr. at 27.

Second, the Court finds that the defendants either intended such distress to result, or acted in callous disregard of the risk that such distress would result. As the Court reasoned in *Sutherland v. The Islamic Republic of Iran*, 151 F.Supp.2d 27, 50 (D.D.C.2001), "when an organization takes someone hostage, it is implicitly intending to cause emotional distress among the members of that hostage's immediate family." Thus, consistent with the reasoning in *Sutherland*, and the authority cited therein, the Court finds that Fr. Jenco's siblings suffered the tort of intentional infliction of emotional distress.

With regard to the emotional distress claims of Fr. Jenco's 22 nieces and nephews, the Court finds that they may not recover. In deciding emotional distress claims under federal common law, the Court has, for the most part, followed the Restatement (Second) of Torts. Section 46 of the Restatement (Second), entitled "Outrageous Conduct Causing Severe Emotional Distress", states:

Where [extreme and outrageous] conduct is directed at a third person, the actor is subject to liability if he intentionally of recklessly causes severe emotional distress

(a) to a member of such person's immediate family who is present at the time, whether or not such distress results in bodily harm, or

(b) to any other person who is present at the time if such distress results in bodily harm.

Restatement (Second) of Torts §46 (1965). In *Sutherland*, the Court parted somewhat from the Restatement by permitting Thomas Sutherland's wife, Jean Sutherland, to recover for the severe distress she suffered during and after her husband's 6 1/2 years of captivity. Although she was in Beirut for most of the 6 1/2 years, it cannot be said that she was actually "present" at her husband's exposure to extreme and outrageous conduct. Nonetheless, the Court permitted her recovery because the defendants' intent to distress her was quite implicit in the nature of the defendants' conduct. In this respect, the holding was squarely on point with the analysis of the leading and most recent tort treatise:

If the defendants' conduct is sufficiently outrageous and intended to inflict severe emotional harm upon a person which is not present, no essential reason of logic or policy prevents liability.

Dan B. Dobbs, The Law of Torts §307, at 834 (2000).

Nonetheless, that treatise itself admits that some lines must be drawn, if, for example, "millions of people who are not present...watch the torture or murder of the President on television." *Id.* In hostage cases, this Court finds that the line is best drawn according to the plaintiff's relationship with the victim of the outrageous conduct. That is, to collect for intentional infliction of emotional distress in cases such as this one, the plaintiff need not be present at the place of outrageous conduct, but must be a member of the victim's immediate family. [FN8]

FN8. This Court defines one's immediate family as his spouse, parents, siblings, and children. This definition is consistent with the traditional understanding of one's immediate family. *See* Dan B. Dobbs, The Law of Torts, §310 (2000) (addressing the scope of recovery in consortium claims).

The Court draws the line with respect to family relationship (and not presence) for two reasons. First, hostage cases are unique in that they implicitly involve a physical separation of the plaintiff from the victim of the outrageous conduct. As a matter of fact, a plaintiff's lack of presence is the *exact source* of his emotional distress. Thus, if the Court were to limit recovery in hostage cases using a "presence" test, plaintiffs would never recover despite there being extremely strong evidence of significant emotional suffering.

Second, comparing the presence test to the family relationship test, courts have been more willing to stretch the boundaries of presence than family relationship. Thus, while presence has often been found where the plaintiff merely had "substantially contemporaneous knowledge", see *Nancy P. v. D'Amato*, 401 Mass. 516, 517 N.E.2d 824 (1988) (equating presence with "substantial contemporaneous knowledge of the outrageous conduct"), family relationship has been found lacking in unmarried cohabitants and present in married but separated spouses. See *Elden v. Sheldon*, 46 Cal.3d 267, 250 Cal.Rptr. 254, 758 P.2d 582 (1988) (finding family relationship lacking among co-habitants); *Planned Parenthood, Inc. v. Vines*, 543 N.E.2d 654 (Ind.App.1989) (finding family relationship intact despite spousal separation).

Applying the family relationship test to the claims of Fr. Jenco's nieces and nephews, the Court finds that their claims must fail. In deciding as such, the Court bears in mind the tremendous impact that Fr. Jenco's detention had on his nieces and nephews. As mentioned above, Fr. Jenco was sorely missed in his role as friend, uncle, and priest. Moreover, the effort to free Fr. Jenco caused further suffering in the many family events that went un-celebrated, or even unnoticed. But the Court also must bear in mind the realities of tort law and the necessity of limiting recovery to a definable scope of individuals.

* * * * * *

Having found the defendants liable on the counts described above, the Court next proceeds to the calculation of damages.

C. Damages

The Foreign Sovereign Immunities Act specifically permits plaintiffs suing under section 1605(a)(7) to pursue "money damages which may include economic damages, solatium, pain, and suffering." 28 U.S.C. §1605 note. After reviewing the arguments presented by the plaintiffs, and the law applicable thereto, the Court makes the following conclusions regarding damages.

1. Compensatory Damages

(a) Fr. Jenco

The Estate of Lawrence M. Jenco seeks compensatory damages for his battery, false imprisonment, emotional distress, economic loss, and loss of consortium. Based on the testimony presented in open court, the Court finds Fr. Jenco entitled to $5,640,000.

In setting Fr. Jenco's damages at $5,640,000, the Court follows the formula which has evolved as a standard in hostage cases brought under section 1605(a)(7). This formula grants the former hostage roughly $10,000 for each day of his

captivity. Thus, Terry Anderson, a co-hostage of Fr Jenco's who was detained for 2,540 days was awarded $24,540,000. See *Anderson*, 90 F.Supp.2d at 113. Similarly, Joseph Cicippio, who was held hostage by Hizbollah for 1,908 days, received $20,000,000; Frank Reed, who was held hostage by Hizbollah for 1,330 days received $16,000,000; and David Jacobson, who was held hostage by Hizbollah for 532 days received $9,000,000. See *Cicippio*, 18 F.Supp.2d at 64, 70.

Any skepticism about the adequacy of this formula must overcome the steep presumption that Congress has tacitly approved its use. In all of the above cases, the formula was developed and applied *prior* to October 28, 2000. On that day, Congress enacted the Victims of Trafficking and Violence Protection Act of 2000. The Act obligated the United States Treasury to pay terrorist victims-including the hostages described above-the amount awarded them at trial. Congress must be presumed to have been aware of the damages formula, and its failure to alter or amend it in any way amounts to a tacit approval of the scheme. See *Flood v. Kuhn*, 407 U.S. 258, 283-284, 92 S.Ct. 2099, 32 L.Ed.2d 728 (1972) (declining to overturn prior precedent where Congress "by its positive inaction" has allowed prior decisions to stand). Thus, this Court finds $5,640,000 to be an appropriate award for the Estate of Lawrence Jenco.

(b) Fr. Jenco's Siblings [FN9]

FN9. Having denied the emotional distress claims of Fr. Jenco's nieces and nephews, the Court also denies any claim for solatium damages. The Flatow Amendment, 28 U.S.C. §1605 note, clearly contemplates solatium recovery as a measure of *damages*, not as an independent cause of action. Fr. Jenco's four surviving siblings and the estates of his two deceased siblings seek damages for their emotional distress. Based on the testimony presented to the Court, the Court finds all siblings entitled to $1.5 million each. [FN10]

FN10. Although two of the siblings died prior Fr. Jenco, and would therefore be thought to collect less damages than other siblings, a closer analysis reveals this to be incorrect.
Fr. Jenco was returned to his family in July 1986. His brother, John F. Jenco died nearly nine years later, on March 25, 1995. Similarly, Fr. Jenco's sister, Verna Mae Mihelich, died May 5, 1996. Finally, only a couple months later, on July 19, 1996, Fr. Jenco himself died.
The Court finds that the substantial majority of suffering over Fr. Jenco's captivity occurred during his captivity and in the years immediately following his return. Thus, although two siblings are deceased, all of the siblings likely suffered similar amounts. To hold otherwise would be to hold that the

remaining four siblings suffered a particularized grief after 1996 that was directly caused by the captivity and concurrently not related to Fr. Jenco's death. While this, of course, is possible, there has been very little (if any) testimony on this aspect of damages.

Out of the many cases brought by U.S. citizens against Iran for terrorist acts, only four have considered the issue of awarding damages to the victim's siblings. In each of those cases, the Court awarded damages to the siblings. In *Flatow v. The Islamic Republic of Iran*, 999 F.Supp. 1, 32 (D.D.C.1998), a case involving the bombing death of Alisa Flatow in Israel, this Court awarded $2.5 million to each of Alisa's siblings. Similarly, in *Eisenfeld v. The Islamic Republic of Iran*, 2000 WL 1918779 (D.D.C.2000), another bombing case resulting in the deaths of two U.S. citizens, this Court awarded $2.5 million to each of the victims siblings. Finally, in *Elahi v. The Islamic Republic of Iran*, 124 F.Supp.2d 97, 109-12 (D.D.C.2000), a case involving the assassination of a U.S. citizen, Judge Joyce Hens Green awarded each of the victim's siblings $5 million. Particularly compelling to the Court in *Elahi* was the finding that, although only a sibling, the victim in fact fulfilled the role of father for his brothers, resulting in an extraordinarily close relationship.

In the case at hand, there has been extensive testimony as to the grief that Fr. Jenco's siblings suffered during, and to some extent after, his captivity. There has also been repeated testimony as to the family's special pride in having a Roman Catholic priest as a family member, as well as special enjoyment in having him perform sacraments for the family. These factors suggest that the siblings' damages in this case should approach the damages in *Elahi*, where there was demonstrative evidence of a very special relationship between the victim and his siblings.

This case however is distinguishable from *Elahi*, as well as *Flatow* and *Eisenfeld*, in that Fr. Jenco returned alive to be with his family for nearly a decade before his death. Without underestimating the grief suffered while Fr. Jenco was in captivity, or the grief that accompanied the change in his disposition after his return, it was surely a monumental relief to have him back home in Joliet. The Court has little doubt that the siblings in *Flatow*, *Eisenfeld*, and *Elahi* would pay substantial sums just to have a single day spent with their deceased sibling. Thus, the safe return of Fr. Jenco after his captivity cannot be underestimated.

2. Punitive Damages

The Court is finally faced with issue of whether punitive damages should be levied against the defendants. According to the Restatement (Second) of Torts, such damages are merited in cases involving "outrageous conduct." *See* Restatement (Second) of Torts, §908(1) (1965). In the case at hand, the Court has little hesitation finding that the depraved and uncivilized conduct of The Islamic Republic of Iran and the Iranian MOIS qualifies as outrageous conduct. As the Court found in *Sutherland v. The Islamic Republic of Iran*, the defendants' conduct

would seem to be the quintessential embodiment of outrageousness. They stole a human being from his family and-for [over a year]-blindfolded him, chained him, beat him, and deprived him of adequate food, clothing, and medical care. In most places, it is unlawful to treat even a stray dog in such manner.

Sutherland, 151 F.Supp.2d at 51-52.

Thus, finding that punitive damages are merited, the Court proceeds to determine the appropriate amount. In determining the level of punitive damages to impose, a court is to look at four factors: "the character of the defendant's act; the nature and extent of harm to plaintiff that the defendant caused or intended to cause; the need for deterrence; and the wealth of the defendant." *Flatow*, 999 F.Supp. at 32 (citing Restatement (Second) of Torts §908(1)-(2) (1965)). With regard to the first factor, the Court has just noted the exceedingly heinous nature of the Iranian MOIS's acts. With regard to the second factor, the far-reaching and long-lasting damages caused by these acts were explained above in the Court's Finding of Facts.

With regard to deterrence, there is a mixture of opinion whether a monetary penalty from a United States court will have a deterrent effect on the Iranian MOIS's behavior. Some argue that the Iranian MOIS operates in an extrajudicial world, and that judicial penalties will therefore be ineffectual; others argue that the MOIS's extrajudicial behavior is exactly the reason to levy greater and greater penalties on the them. A third view was proffered by Dr. Clawson at trial: the failure to impose substantial punitive damages after several previous impositions might be construed by MOIS as a capitulation by the United States in the debate over the legitimacy of hostage-taking. As such, the failure to impose punitive damages might actually be construed as a condonation of MOIS's rogue behavior. *See* Tr. at 74.

Finally, with regard to the wealth of the defendants, the Court finds the defendants quite wealthy. As explained above, the Iranian MOIS has approximately 3000 employees and is the largest spy organization in the Middle East. As Dr. Clawson testified at trial, the Iranian government funnels most of its terrorist dollars, somewhere near $100 million annually, through the Iranian MOIS. *See* Tr. at 61. This suggests that not only is the Iranian MOIS wealthy, but the Iranian government, its supporter, is at least as large and wealthy.

Thus, at the very minimum, the defendants are undoubtedly in possession of many hundreds of millions dollars.

The Court, guided by Dr. Clawson's expert opinion as well as previous decisions on substantially similar cases, finds $300,000,000 in punitive damages to be merited. That amount is thrice the annual funding provided by the Iranian government to MOIS. Not only is Dr. Clawson's expert opinion persuasive, the Court is not at all convinced that punitive damages are wholly ineffectual. Previous cases awarding punitive damages against MOIS have only been decided in the past three years. Since that time, there have been no reported hostage incidents involving Hizbollah and United States nationals. Further, it is doubtful that the full punitive effect of the prior damage awards have yet taken hold. The process of collecting an international debt is a long and laborious process, and it is therefore quite possible that the deterrent effect of the fines has yet to be fully felt.

Further, $300 million is an amount consistent with the punitive damages levied several times in the past. See *Anderson*, 90 F.Supp.2d at 114 (awarding $300 million in punitive damages against MOIS for the kidnapping and detention of Terry Anderson); *Flatow*, 999 F.Supp. at 34 (awarding $225 million-three times Iran's reported expenditure on terrorist activities-to the estate of a terrorist victim).

III. CONCLUSION

Today, the Court hopes to make whole, as much as legally possible, those hurt by the captivity of Fr. Jenco. Although judicial remedies will greatly support the plaintiffs' recovery, full recovery can only be attained by each plaintiff in his own way. Perhaps the words of Fr. Jenco himself are most appropriate on this issue. In an interview after his release, Fr. Jenco recalled his attempt at keeping a set of clothes clean so that he could wear them on the day of his release. He ultimately failed in this effort, but nonetheless garnered strength from it.

And those are the interesting things, clean things in life, you know, there's symbolism to it. That I was clinging to. After a while, I just gave it up, gave up the whole idea up. I was down to a button at the end. And I just threw it away and I said to God you can have the button, and that was kind of the break for me. To cling to nothing. And I've learned now not to cling to [any]thing.
Jenco Interview, June 24, 1988, at 93-94.
Thus, for the foregoing reasons, the Court finds that defendants shall be jointly and severally liable to the following entities for the following compensatory damages:

The Estate of Fr. Jenco:	$5,640,000
The Estate of John F. Jenco	$1,500,000
The Estate of Verna Mae Mihelich	$1,500,000
Joseph M. Jenco	$1,500,000
Elizabeth J. Blair	$1,500,000
Mary S. Francheschini	$1,500,000
Richard G. Jenco	$1,500,000

Further, the defendants shall be jointly and severally liable to estate of Lawrence M. Jenco for $300,000,000 in punitive damages. A separate order consistent with this Opinion shall issue this date.

Notes:

1.   Awarding damages in terrorism cases is notoriously difficult. As one court stated, "there is no market where pain and suffering are bought and sold, nor any standard by which compensation for it can be definitely ascertained, or the amount actually endured can be determined [.]" *Weinstein v. Islamic Republic of Iran*, 184 F.Supp.2d 13, 22 (D.D.C. 2002) (citation omitted).

2.   Some commentators have noted the fairly formulaic nature of terrorism awards under §1605(a)(7). Courts too have adopted certain postulates about awarding damages, such as, "Parents of victims typically receive smaller awards than spouses, but receive larger awards than siblings." *Blais v. Islamic Republic of Iran*, 459 F.Supp.2d 40, 60 (D.D.C. 2006). Is this different from other areas of the law? Does the fact that virtually all civil terrorism judgments have been rendered by the less than two dozen judges and magistrate judges of the District Court for the District of Columbia account for this standardization? Or that there have been virtually no jury awards under the FSIA or Klinghoffer Act? It is interesting to note that a jury in *Saperstein v. The Palestinian Authority*, 2007 WL 684318 (S.D. Fla. 2007) awarded $16 million to a victim of Palestinian terrorism who lost his remaining arm and was determined to be 90% disabled. While the decision is on appeal, the award clearly comports with the range of damages awarded by the judges of the District of Columbia District Court.

3.   In a series of cases beginning with *Cicippio v. Islamic Republic of Iran*, 18 F.Supp.2d 62 (D.D.C. 1998) courts began to award $10,000 per day to plaintiffs who were taken hostage. This formula has been widely criticized but the courts have continued to defend its use,

Any skepticism about the adequacy of this formula must overcome the steep presumption that Congress has tacitly approved its use. In all of the above cases, the formula was developed and applied *prior* to October 28, 2000. On that day, Congress enacted the Victims of Trafficking and Violence Protection Act of 2000. The Act obligated the United States Treasury to pay terrorist victims-including the hostages described above-the amount awarded them at trial, or in other words, about $10,000 per day of captivity. Congress must be presumed to have been aware of the damages formula, and its failure to amend it in any way amounts to a tacit approval of the scheme.

Sutherland v. Islamic Republic of Iran, 151 F.Supp.2d 27, 51 (D.D.C. 2001).

4.   This formula has continued to be used in the most recent terrorism cases. *Levin v. Islamic Republic of Iran* --- F.Supp.2d ----, 2007 WL 4564399, 18 (D.D.C. 2007). ("In cases involving the compensation of kidnapping victims, courts have awarded damages for pain and suffering based on a per diem calculation of $10,000 per day of captivity.") Nonetheless, the courts have not been straight jacketed by this formula,

> This formula has not been applied in every hostage taking case brought under the FSIA, however. In several cases, the Court has adjusted the amount of the per diem award based on the severity of the maltreatment suffered by the plaintiff, while in other cases the Court has not applied a per diem approach at all because of the brevity of the captivity. See, e.g., *Stethem v. Islamic Republic of Iran*, 201 F.Supp.2d 78, 87-89 (D.D.C. 2002) (awarding plaintiff severely beaten over a fifteen hour period $500,000 for that pain and suffering); *Higgins*, 2000 WL 33674311 at *8 (awarding approximately $57,000 per day of captivity to family of Army colonel held by Hezbollah for 529 days prior to being executed.); *Hill v. Republic of Iraq*, 175 F.Supp.2d 36, 48 (D.D.C. 2001) (awarding Americans held by Iraq prior to Desert Storm between $3,000 and $5,000 per day of captivity and lump sum awards for psychological injuries between $100,000 and $500,000).
>
> In light of the severity of his beatings (which were greatly exacerbated by his bowel obstruction) and the brevity of confinement (four days), the Court finds that the per diem approach is not appropriate in this case. Indeed, it would be a perverse application of the formula to find that Cronin is only entitled to $40,000. Cf. *Langevine v. Dis-*

trict of Columbia, 106 F.3d 1018 (D.C.Cir. 1997) (upholding a jury verdict for $200,000 for pain and suffering resulting from a false arrest and detention in a D.C. police station that lasted no more than a day). Such a small award would not only utterly fail to compensate Cronin for his injuries; it would essentially reward those that committed these heinous acts for beating him so severely over such a short period of time that he either had to be released after just a few days or he would have died. Therefore, using other cases brought under the FSIA as a benchmark, the Court finds that a lump sum award of $1,200,000 is appropriate in this case.

Cronin v. Islamic Republic of Iran, 238 F.Supp.2d 222, 234-234 (D.D.C. 2002).

5.   A unique request for damages was made on behalf of an estate of an individual assassinated by Iran:

> The plaintiff requests damages for the years of fear that Cyrus Elahi endured before his assassination. According to the plaintiff, this "pre-impact emotional distress," which occurred well before the actual incident that resulted in death, is compensable in an action for survival damages…The general rule in survival actions is that damages are limited to those suffered during the period between injury and death. *See* HARPER, JAMES & GRAY, 4 THE LAW OF TORTS §24.6, p. 474 (2d ed.1986). The cases cited by the plaintiff similarly stand for the unremarkable proposition that mental anguish flowing from wrongful conduct of the defendant is compensable. In this case, the wrongful conduct of the defendant was the "extrajudicial killing" of Cyrus Elahi. The "pre-impact emotional distress," while perhaps real, was not a result of the specific incident of wrongful conduct complained of by the plaintiff. The distress felt by Cyrus Elahi was the result of the pre-existing threat to his life, and existed independent of the ultimate act of assassination. Therefore, no damages for such pre-impact distress are available.

Elahi v. Islamic Republic of Iran, 124 F.Supp.2d 97, 112 (D.D.C. 2000). How does this ruling comport with Iran's explicit public pronouncement about its intent to target its enemies? Had Elahi not been killed but merely harassed and threatened, would he have been able to claim "pre-impact" damages? If so, why did the court reject this measure of damages when he was assassinated?

Chapter 11

Impact of the Algiers Accord

Roeder v. Islamic Republic of Iran, 333 F.3d 228 (D.C. Cir. 2003).

RANDOLPH, Circuit Judge:

Americans taken hostage in Iran in 1979 and held for 444 days brought a class action on behalf of themselves, and their spouses and children, against the Islamic Republic of Iran and its Ministry of Foreign Affairs. The district court, Sullivan, J., issued a comprehensive opinion and ordered the action dismissed for failure to state a claim. *Roeder v. Islamic Republic of Iran,* 195 F.Supp.2d 140 (D.D.C.2002). Among the several issues presented on appeal, the principal question is whether legislation specifically directed at this lawsuit, and enacted while the case was pending in the district court, provided a cause of action for the hostages and their families.

I.

The district court ably summarized the case and the reasons for its decision:

"Members of this plaintiff class previously attempted to sue Iran, but their claims were dismissed because Congress had not waived Iran's sovereign immunity. *See Persinger v. Islamic Republic of Iran,* 729 F.2d 835 (D.C.Cir.1984); *McKeel v. Islamic Republic of Iran,* 722 F.2d 582 (9th Cir.1983); *Ledgerwood v. State of Iran,* 617 F.Supp. 311 (D.D.C.1985). In 1996, Congress passed the Federal Anti-Terrorism and Effective Death Penalty Act ("the 1996 Anti-terrorism Act") and the Flatow Amendment, which together waived foreign sovereign immunity and created a cause of action for individuals harmed by state-sponsored acts of terrorism. 28 U.S.C. §1605(a)(7) and note. With the assistance of their counsel, plaintiffs brought this action under those statutes, arguing that this new cause of action applied to the 1979 hostage taking in Tehran, and asking for compensatory and punitive damages of $33 billion.

"Iran chose not to defend its actions in this Court, despite its long history of adjudicating claims in this Circuit. *See, e.g., McKesson HBOC, Inc. v. Islamic Republic of Iran,* 271 F.3d 1101 (D.C.Cir.2001). Plaintiffs therefore proceeded with their claims unopposed, and at plaintiffs' request the Court entered a default judgment on liability on August 13, 2001. The Court scheduled a date for a trial to hear evidence on damages, at which several of the plaintiffs were scheduled to testify about their experiences. The Court did not look lightly upon requiring plaintiffs to relive their terrible ordeal and appreciated the difficulty of both testifying and witnessing such testimony.

"On the eve of trial, however, the State Department, recently made aware of plaintiffs' claims, attempted to intervene, vacate the judgment, and dismiss the suit. Plaintiffs' hopes of recovery were once again placed in jeopardy. The United States argued that the Algiers Accords, the 1980 bilateral agreement between the United States and Iran, by which the hostages' release was secured, and its implementing regulations, contain a prohibition on lawsuits arising out of the hostage-taking at issue here. *See* Govt's Mem. in Supp. of Mot. to Vacate of 10/12/01. Because no act by Congress had specifically abrogated the Accords, the government argued, that agreement precludes plaintiffs' claims and the case should be dismissed. The United States also raised several other arguments interpreting the Foreign Sovereign Immunities Act that this Court lacked jurisdiction to hear plaintiffs' claims, and that plaintiffs' claims should be dismissed on the merits.

"Because of the last-minute nature of the government's [motion] to intervene, rather than deny plaintiffs, many of whom had traveled from distant parts of the country, the opportunity to present their testimony on the record, the Court proceeded with the trial. For two days, the Court heard the harrowing accounts of 444 days spent in captivity from both the former hostages and their family members. The Court scheduled a later date to hear argument on the government's motions and established a briefing schedule to afford the plaintiffs an opportunity to respond to the government's arguments. The Court also directed plaintiffs' counsel to explain why they had not brought the Algiers Accords to the Court's attention earlier.

"On November 28, 2001, the date that the government's reply brief was due, the case took yet another dramatic turn. The government informed the Court that Congress had recently passed, and the President had signed on that very day, an appropriations bill with a provision amending the Foreign Sovereign Immunities Act that specifically referred to this case. *See* Subsection 626(c) of Pub.L. 107-77, 115 Stat. 748 (2001) ("Subsection 626(c)"). After hearing argument from counsel on the impact of the appropriations rider, this Court expressed its serious concern about the lack of clarity in Congress' recent action.

"After the Court took this case under advisement, Congress acted yet again. On December 20, 2001, Congress passed yet another appropriations rider that added a technical amendment to Subsection 626(c) and contained language in its legislative history purporting to explain the legislative intent behind the earlier Subsection 626(c). *See* Section 208 of the Department of Defense and Emergency Supplemental Appropriations Act, Pub.L. 107-117, 115 Stat. 2230 ("Section 208"). However,…while Congress' intent to interfere with this litigation was clear, its intent to abrogate the Algiers Accords was not.

"Were this Court empowered to judge by its sense of justice, the heart-breaking accounts of the emotional and physical toll of those 444 days on plaintiffs would be more than sufficient justification for granting all the relief that they request. However, this Court is bound to apply the law that Congress has created, according to the rules of interpretation that the Supreme Court has determined. There are two branches of government that are empowered to abrogate and rescind the Algiers Accords, and the judiciary is not one of them. The political considerations that must be balanced prior to such a decision are beyond both the expertise and the mandate of this Court. Unless and until either the legislative or executive branch acts clearly and decisively, this Court can not grant plaintiffs the relief they seek." *Roeder,* 195 F.Supp.2d at 144-45.

The Algiers Accords, mentioned in the district court's summary, is an executive agreement of importance to this case. In order to secure the hostages' release, the United States froze Iranian government assets, imposed trade sanctions,

prosecuted a claim before the International Court of Justice, and undertook a military rescue operation. *See Persinger v. Islamic Republic of Iran,* 729 F.2d 835, 837 n. 1 (D.C.Cir.1984). These efforts failed. On January 19, 1980, the United States entered into the Algiers Accords, settling a broad range of disputes between this country and Iran. *See generally* Iran-United States: Settlement of the Hostage Crisis, 20 I.L.M. 223 (1981). As part of the Accords, the United States agreed to "bar and preclude the prosecution against Iran of any…claim of…a United States national arising out of the events…related to (A) the seizure of the 52 United States nationals on November 4, 1979, [and] (B) their subsequent detention." *Id.,* Declaration of the Government of the Democratic and Popular Republic of Algeria, General Principles, ¶ 11, 20 I.L.M. at 227. The hostages were released the next day. President Carter, on his last full day in office, issued an executive order directing the Secretary of the Treasury to issue regulations implementing this provision, and directing and authorizing the Attorney General to take appropriate measures to notify the judiciary of the Order. Non-Prosecution of Claims of Hostages and for Actions at the United States Embassy and Elsewhere, Exec. Order No. 12,283, 46 Fed.Reg. 7927 (Jan. 19, 1981); *see also* Prohibition Against Prosecution of Certain Claims, 31 C.F.R. §535.216(a). After the change in administrations, President Reagan ratified this executive order and related ones. Suspension of Litigation Against Iran, Exec. Order No. 12,294, §8, 46 Fed.Reg. 14,111 (Feb. 24, 1981).

II.

A.

One of the issues plaintiffs raise is whether the district court erred in permitting the United States to intervene as a defendant. We wonder how a reversal of that ruling would assist plaintiffs. The Foreign Sovereign Immunities Act - FSIA - does not automatically entitle a plaintiff to judgment when a foreign state defaults. The court still has an obligation to satisfy itself that plaintiffs have established a right to relief. 28 U.S.C. §1608(e). The district court did not mention the Algiers Accords when the default judgment was entered, but that was because plaintiffs' counsel had not alerted the court to the Accords. [FN1] After the Justice Department informed the court of the Accords, the court performed its duty under §1608(e) and determined that plaintiffs were not entitled to relief. We see no basis for assuming that the court, having become aware of this impediment to plaintiffs' action, would have reached a different result if it had denied the government's motion to intervene. In other words, even if the Justice Department had appeared only in the capacity of *amicus curiae,* the outcome would not have changed.

FN1. The court criticized plaintiffs' counsel for failing to "bring to this Court's attention the Algiers Accords and implementing regulations despite the FSIA's requirement that plaintiffs 'establish[ed] [their] claim or right to relief by evidence that is satisfactory to the Court.' 28 U.S.C. §1608(e)." *Roeder,* 195 F.Supp.2d at 185 (alterations in original).

At all events it is clear to us that the court properly granted the United States leave to intervene as of right. Federal Rule of Civil Procedure 24(a) provides that an applicant for intervention must file a "timely application" and demonstrate that it has "an interest relating to the property or transaction which is the subject matter of the action" and that "the applicant is so situated that the disposition of the action may as a practical matter impair or impede the applicant's ability to protect that interest, unless the applicant's interest is adequately represented by existing parties." *See also Smoke v. Norton,* 252 F.3d 468, 470 (D.C.Cir.2001). The district court correctly analyzed each of these factors. Timeliness is measured from when the prospective intervenor "knew or should have known that any of its rights would be directly affected by the litigation." *Nat'l Wildlife Fed'n v. Burford,* 878 F.2d 422, 433-34 (D.C.Cir.1989), *rev'd on other grounds sub nom. Lujan v. Nat'l Wildlife Fed'n,* 497 U.S. 871, 110 S.Ct. 3177, 111 L.Ed.2d 695 (1990). Here, the government moved to intervene less than thirty days after the State Department received notice of the potential conflict with the executive agreement. As to the government's interest, plaintiffs suppose it is in providing Iran with a defense. That is incorrect. The government's interest is in upholding the Algiers Accords, an interest that would be impaired if plaintiffs obtained a judgment in violation of the Accords. We have already decided that the interest of the United States in meeting "its obligations under the executive agreement with Iran" entitled it to intervene as a defendant. *See Persinger,* 729 F.2d at 837. And because Iran failed to appear before the district court, the interest of the United States was not represented by the existing parties.

Although the government thus satisfied the requirements of Rule 24(a), decisions of this court hold an intervenor must also establish its standing under Article III of the Constitution. *See, e.g., Fund for Animals, Inc. v. Norton,* 322 F.3d 728, 731-32 (D.C.Cir.2003); *Bldg. & Constr. Trades Dep't v. Reich,* 40 F.3d 1275, 1282 (D.C.Cir.1994). The court's opinion in *Rio Grande Pipeline Co. v. FERC,* 178 F.3d 533, 538 (D.C.Cir.1999), identified a split in the circuits on the subject of intervenor standing. We were deal-

ing there with intervention in the court of appeals under 28 U.S.C. §2348. As to intervention in the district court, requiring standing for an applicant wishing to come in on the side of a plaintiff who has standing runs into the doctrine that Article III is satisfied so long as one party has standing. *See, e. g., Watt v. Energy Action Found.,* 454 U.S. 151, 160, 102 S.Ct. 205, 212, 70 L.Ed.2d 309 (1981); *Am. Soc'y for the Prevention of Cruelty to Animals v. Ringling Bros. & Barnum & Bailey Circus,* 317 F.3d 334, 338 (D.C.Cir.2003). Requiring standing of someone who seeks to intervene as a defendant, *see Fund for Animals,* 322 F.3d at 730-32, runs into the doctrine that the standing inquiry is directed at those who invoke the court's jurisdiction. *See Virginia v. Hicks,* 539 U.S. 113, 123 S.Ct. 2191, 2196-98, 156 L.Ed.2d 148 (2003). Still, there is no need to dwell on the issues thus raised. With respect to intervention as of right in the district court, the matter of standing may be purely academic. One court has rightly pointed out that any person who satisfies Rule 24(a) will also meet Article III's standing requirement. *Sokaogon Chippewa Cmty. v. Babbitt,* 214 F.3d 941, 946 (7th Cir.2000). So here. The United States established that it was in imminent danger of suffering injury in fact - a breach of its obligations under the Accords. There was a "causal connection between the injury and the conduct complained of" and the injury was capable of judicial redress. *Bennett v. Spear,* 520 U.S. 154, 167, 117 S.Ct. 1154, 1163, 137 L.Ed.2d 281 (1997). The United States therefore had standing as a defendant-intervenor.

With this much settled, the error of plaintiffs' claim that the United States could not properly move to vacate the default judgment becomes apparent. The United States was not asserting defenses personal to the parties in default - Iran and its Ministry of Foreign Affairs. The government entered the case to assert its own defenses under the Algiers Accords. As an intervenor, the United States "participates on an equal footing with the original parties to a suit." *Bldg. & Constr. Trades Dep't,* 40 F.3d at 1282. The United States therefore had the right to move under Rule 60(b) of the Federal Rules of Civil Procedure to vacate the default judgment against the defendants.

B.

One other preliminary issue deals with the legal status of Iran's Ministry of Foreign Affairs. The Flatow amendment to the FSIA, set forth at 28 U.S.C. §1605 note, [FN2] provides a cause of action against officials, employees, and agents of foreign states. Because it is unclear whether the amendment also provides a cause of action against the foreign state, [FN3] plaintiffs maintain that the Ministry of Foreign Affairs is merely an agent of Iran, not its alter ego. In *Transaero, Inc. v. La Fuerza Aerea Boliviana,* 30 F.3d 148, 149-50 (D.C.Cir.1994), we concluded that a nation's air force is a "foreign state or political subdivision" rather than an "agency or instrumentality" of the nation for purposes of the service-of-process provisions of the FSIA. "Any government of reasonable complexity must act through men organized into offices and departments." *Id.* at 153. We adopted a categorical approach: if the core functions of the entity are governmental, it is considered the foreign state itself; if commercial, the entity is an agency or instrumentality of the foreign state. A nation's armed forces are clearly on the governmental side. *Id.* For similar reasons, the Ministry of Foreign Affairs must be treated as the state of Iran itself rather than as its agent. [FN4] The conduct of foreign affairs is an important and "indispensable" governmental function. *Kennedy v. Mendoza-Martinez,* 372 U.S. 144, 160, 83 S.Ct. 554, 563, 9 L.Ed.2d 644 (1963).

FN2. "An official, employee, or agent of a foreign state designated as a state sponsor of terrorism...while acting within the scope of his or her office, employment, or agency shall be liable to a United States national or the national's legal representative for personal injury or death caused by acts of that official, employee, or agent for which the courts of the United States may maintain jurisdiction under [28 U.S.C. §1605(a)(7)] for money damages which may include economic damages, solatium, pain, and suffering, and punitive damages if the acts were among those described in [§1605(a)(7)]." 28 U.S.C. §1605 note.

FN3. In view of the Flatow amendment's failure to mention the liability of foreign states, it is "far from clear" that a plaintiff has a substantive claim against a foreign state under the Foreign Sovereign Immunities Act. *Price v. Socialist People's Libyan Arab Jamahiriya,* 294 F.3d 82, 87 (D.C.Cir.2002); *see also Bettis v. Islamic Republic of Iran,* 315 F.3d 325, 330 (D.C.Cir.2003). We have yet to decide the question and see no reason to do so here.

FN4. Plaintiffs suggest that the legislative intent expressed in 28 U.S.C. §1606 and the principles of respondeat superior and ratification create liability for Iran based upon the actions of its Ministry of Foreign Affairs. Because the two defendants are not legally distinct, plaintiffs must show an abrogation of the Algiers Accords to subject either defendant to liability.

III.

This brings us to the principal issue. The authority of the President to settle claims of American nationals through

executive agreements is clear. *See Am. Ins. Ass'n v. Garamendi,* 539 U.S. 396, 123 S.Ct. 2374, ----, 156 L.Ed.2d 376, 2003 WL 21433477, at *11 (U.S. June 23, 2003); *id.* at ----, at *23 (Ginsburg, J., dissenting). There is no doubt that laws passed after the President enters into an executive agreement may abrogate the agreement. The question here is whether legislation enacted while the case was pending abrogated the Algiers Accords.

The FSIA provides generally that a foreign state is immune from the jurisdiction of the United States courts unless one of the exceptions listed in 28 U.S.C. §1605(a) applies. *See Argentine Republic v. Amerada Hess Shipping Corp.,* 488 U.S. 428, 434-35, 109 S.Ct. 683, 688-89, 102 L.Ed.2d 818 (1988). At the time plaintiffs filed their complaint and up to entry of the default judgment of liability, none of the exceptions applied to this case. Section 1605(a)(7)(A), added as part of the Antiterrorism and Effective Death Penalty Act of 1996, allowed an exception to the immunity bar if plaintiffs showed that the foreign state had been designated a state sponsor of terrorism when the act occurred or as a result of the act. 28 U.S.C. §1605(a)(7)(A) (2000). Iran had not been so designated.

After the United States moved to intervene and vacate the default judgment, Congress amended the FSIA. A provision in an appropriations act stated that §1605(a)(7)(A) would be satisfied (that is, the immunity of the foreign state would not apply) if "the act is related to Case Number 1:00CV03110(ESG) [sic] in the United States District Court for the District of Columbia." Departments of Commerce, Justice, and State, the Judiciary, and Related Agencies Appropriations Act, 2002, Pub.L. No. 107-77, §626(c), 115 Stat. 748, 803 (2001). Six weeks later, Congress corrected an error in the case number: "Section 626(c) of the Departments of Commerce, Justice, and State, the Judiciary and Related Agencies Appropriations Act, 2002 (Public Law No. 107-77) is amended by striking '1:00CV03110(ESG)' and inserting '1:00CV03110(EGS).' " Department of Defense and Emergency Supplemental Appropriations for Recovery from and Response to the Terrorist Attacks on the United States Act, 2002, Pub.L. No. 107-117, Div. B, §208, 115 Stat. 2230, 2299 (2002) (currently codified at 28 U.S.C.A. §1605(a)(7)(A) (Supp.2003)).

Together, these amendments created an exception, for this case alone, to Iran's sovereign immunity, which would otherwise have barred the action. The evident purpose was to dispose of the government's argument, in its motion to vacate, that plaintiffs' action should be dismissed because Iran had not been designated a state sponsor of terrorism at the time the hostages were captured and held, and that Iran's later designation (in 1984) rested not on the hostage crisis but on its support of terrorism outside its borders. Mem. of P. & A. in Supp. of the United States' Mot. to Vacate the Default J. and Dismiss Pls.' Claims at 12-13 (Oct. 12, 2001) [hereinafter "Mot. to Vacate"]; *see also* Determination Pursuant to Section 6(i) of the Export Administration Act of 1979 - Iran, 49 Fed.Reg. 2836 (Jan. 23, 1984).

The question remained whether the Algiers Accords, on which the United States had relied as a second ground for dismissal, Mot. to Vacate at 18-23, survived the amendments. The Accords required the United States to " bar and preclude the prosecution against Iran of any pending or future claim of…a United States national arising out of the events…related to (A) the seizure of the 52 United States nationals on November 4, 1979, [and] (B) their subsequent detention…" 20 I.L.M. at 227; *cf. Belk v. United States,* 858 F.2d 706, 706 (Fed.Cir.1988) (affirming summary judgment for the United States in action by some of the plaintiffs here asserting that the barring of their actions by the Accords constituted a taking by the government). The amendments do not, on their face, say anything about the Accords. They speak only to the antecedent question of Iran's immunity from suit in United States courts. Plaintiffs therefore urge us to consider statements in the "Conference Report" on the second appropriations act, which made the technical correction to the case number. These statements, plaintiffs say, show that Congress expressly recognized a conflict between their lawsuit and the Accords and passed the amendments to resolve the conflict in plaintiffs' favor.

Some words about conference reports are in order. After the House and the Senate pass different versions of legislation, each body appoints conferees to resolve disagreements between the House and Senate bills. If a majority of the conferees from each body agree, they submit two documents to their respective houses: a conference report presenting the formal legislative language and a joint explanatory statement that explains the legislative language and how the differences between the bills were resolved. Each body must vote on approving the conference report in its entirety and may not approve it only in part or offer any amendments. *See generally* STANLEY BACH & CHRISTOPHER M. DAVIS, CONGRESSIONAL RESEARCH SERVICE, CONFERENCE REPORTS AND JOINT EXPLANATORY STATEMENTS (2003).

Plaintiffs told us at oral argument that both houses voted on the language of the conference report. This is accurate. But it is not the conference report - which consists of the text of the legislation - on which plaintiffs rely. The statements they think important are in the joint explanatory statement, which is in the form of a committee report. While both the conference report and the joint explanatory statement are printed in the same document, Congress votes only on the conference report. Courts, including the Supreme Court, have not always been precise about this, referring sometimes to material in joint explanatory statements as the conference report. *See, e.g., City of Columbus v. Ours Garage & Wrecker Serv., Inc.,* 536 U.S. 424, 440, 122 S.Ct. 2226, 2236, 153 L.Ed.2d 430 (2002) (quoting the "Joint Explanatory Statement of the Committee of Conference" in H.R. CONF. REP. NO. 103-677, at 87 (1994), and referring to it as the "Conference Report"); *INS v. St. Cyr,* 533 U.S. 289, 317, 121 S.Ct. 2271, 2288-89, 150 L.Ed.2d 347 (2001) (quoting the "Joint Explanatory Statement of the Committee of Conference" in H.R. CONF. REP. NO. 104-828, at 222 (1996), and referring to it as the "Conference Report"); *see also* George A. Costello, *Average Voting Members and Other "Benign Fictions": The Relative Reliability of Committee Reports, Floor Debates, and Other Sources of Legislative History,* 1990 DUKE L.J. 39, 48 ("Almost invariably, courts employ the shorthand 'committee report' when referring to the explanatory statement of the managers…"). We do not say material in the joint explanatory statement is of no value in determining Congress' intent. *See Demby v. Schweiker,* 671 F.2d 507, 510 (D.C.Cir.1981) (opinion of MacKinnon, J.); *see also Moore v. District of Columbia,* 907 F.2d 165, 175 (D.C.Cir.1990) (en banc). The point is that contrary to what plaintiffs suggest, the explanatory remarks in the "conference report" do not have the force of law.

The joint explanatory statement relating to Congress' first amendment, §626(c), contains nothing to indicate that any conferee took account of the Algiers Accords. The only relevant remarks are that the amendment "quashes the State Department's motion to vacate the judgment obtained by plaintiffs in [this case]" and that the United States is not required to "make any payments to satisfy the judgment." H.R. CONF. REP. No. 107-278, at 170 (2001). The motion of course was on behalf of the United States, not the State Department, and it is open to question whether Congress may dictate the outcome of a particular judicial proceeding. [FN5] We put these matters to the side. The government's motion to dismiss rested not only on plaintiffs' failure to bring their case within one of the exceptions to the general rule of foreign sovereign immunity, but also on the bar set up in the Algiers Accords. The text of §626(c) is consistent with removing the government's first argument for dismissal. It says nothing about the second.

FN5. We do not decide whether the amendments, relating as they did specifically to a pending action, violated separation-of-powers principles by impermissibly directing the result of pending litigation. *See Plaut v. Spendthrift Farm, Inc.*, 514 U.S. 211, 240, 115 S.Ct. 1447, 1463, 131 L.Ed.2d 328 (1995); *Robertson v. Seattle Audubon Soc'y*, 503 U.S. 429, 441, 112 S.Ct. 1407, 1414-15, 118 L.Ed.2d 73 (1992). The joint explanatory statement relating to §208, which corrected the typographical error in §626(c), declares that the earlier amendment "quashed" the "Department of State's motion to vacate" and mentions that, in the intervening weeks, the "Department of State" continued to argue that the judgment should be vacated. It then explains the meaning of §626(c): "The provision...acknowledges that, *notwithstanding any other authority,* the American citizens who were taken hostage by the Islamic Republic of Iran in 1979 have a claim against Iran under the Antiterrorism Act of 1996 and the provision specifically allows the judgment to stand..." H.R. CONF. REP. NO. 107-350, at 422-23 (2001) (emphasis added). This statement, and the italicized language in particular, is the type of language that might abrogate an executive agreement - if the statement had been enacted. But Congress did not vote on the statement and the President did not sign a bill embodying it. [FN6]

FN6. Upon signing the first appropriations act, President Bush stated: "the Executive Branch will act, and encourage the courts to act, with regard to Subsection 626(c) of the bill in a manner consistent with the obligations of the United States under the Algiers Accords..." Statement by President George W. Bush Upon Signing H.R. 2500, 2002 U.S.C.C.A.N. 886, 887 (Nov. 28, 2001). In signing the bill containing the technical correction, the President issued a similar statement. *See* Statement by President George W. Bush Upon Signing H.R. 3338, 2002 U.S.C.C.A.N. 1776, 1778-79 (Jan. 10, 2002).

There is thus no clear expression in anything Congress enacted abrogating the Algiers Accords. Yet neither a treaty nor an executive agreement will be considered " 'abrogated or modified by a later statute unless such purpose on the part of Congress has been clearly expressed.' " *Trans World Airlines v. Franklin Mint Corp.*, 466 U.S. 243, 252, 104 S.Ct. 1776, 1782, 80 L.Ed.2d 273 (1984) (quoting *Cook v. United States*, 288 U.S. 102, 120, 53 S.Ct. 305, 311-12, 77 L.Ed. 641 (1933)); *see Weinberger v. Rossi*, 456 U.S. 25, 32,

102 S.Ct. 1510, 1515-16, 71 L.Ed.2d 715 (1982); *Comm. of United States Citizens Living in Nicaragua v. Reagan*, 859 F.2d 929, 936-37 (D.C.Cir.1988). The way Congress expresses itself is through legislation. While legislative history may be useful in determining intent, the joint explanatory statements here go well beyond the legislative text of §208, which did nothing more than correct a typographical error. Moreover, the explanatory statements, rather than explain the language of §208, deal with the previously enacted §626(c). Such legislative history alone cannot be sufficient to abrogate a treaty or an executive agreement. *See Gray Panthers Advocacy Comm. v. Sullivan*, 936 F.2d 1284, 1288 (D.C.Cir.1991).

Courts have insisted on clear statements from Congress in other contexts. These include a waiver of federal sovereign immunity, *see United States v. Nordic Village, Inc.*, 503 U.S. 30, 33-34, 112 S.Ct. 1011, 1014-15, 117 L.Ed.2d 181 (1992); retroactivity of statutes, *see Landgraf v. USI Film Products*, 511 U.S. 244, 271-72, 114 S.Ct. 1483, 1500-01, 128 L.Ed.2d 229 (1994); repeal of habeas jurisdiction, *see St. Cyr*, 533 U.S. at 298-99, 121 S.Ct. at 2278-79; waiver of Eleventh Amendment immunity, *Dellmuth v. Muth*, 491 U.S. 223, 230-31, 109 S.Ct. 2397, 2401-02, 105 L.Ed.2d 181 (1989); and a significant alteration in the balance of power between Congress and the President, *see Armstrong v. Bush*, 924 F.2d 282, 289 (D.C.Cir.1991). In *Dellmuth*, a case dealing with a waiver of Eleventh Amendment immunity, the Court held that if "Congress' intention is 'unmistakably clear in the language of the statute,' recourse to legislative history will be unnecessary; if Congress' intention is not unmistakably clear, recourse to legislative history will be futile..." 491 U.S. at 230, 109 S.Ct. at 2401. Executive agreements are essentially contracts between nations, and like contracts between individuals, executive agreements are expected to be honored by the parties. Congress (or the President acting alone) may abrogate an executive agreement, but legislation must be clear to ensure that Congress - and the President - have considered the consequences. The "requirement of clear statement assures that the legislature has in fact faced, and intended to bring into issue, the critical matters involved in the judicial decision." *Gregory v. Ashcroft*, 501 U.S. 452, 461, 111 S.Ct. 2395, 2401, 115 L.Ed.2d 410 (1991). The kind of legislative history offered here cannot repeal an executive agreement when the legislation itself is silent. *See Comm. of United States Citizens*, 859 F.2d at 936-37.

As against this, plaintiffs say that we should not presume that Congress, in passing the amendments, did "a futile thing." *Halverson v. Slater*, 129 F.3d 180, 185 (D.C.Cir.1997). But we are presuming no such thing. The amendments were not futile acts. If constitutional, *see supra* note 5, the amendments had the effect of removing Iran's sovereign immunity, which the United States had raised in its motion to vacate. This enabled plaintiffs to argue that the Accords were not a valid executive agreement. [FN7] Plaintiffs in fact made this argument in the district court (but they do not make it here). *See* Pls.' Supplemental Brief at 9-12 (Jan. 22, 2002); 195 F.Supp.2d at 168. That the district court rejected the argument is of no moment. Plaintiffs' opportunity to have it decided resulted directly from the amendments.

FN7. For example, a member of the panel at oral argument raised the question whether an international agreement is binding if it is not entered into voluntarily but "at the point of a gun" to obtain release of the hostages.
Plaintiffs also cite §2002 of the Victims of Trafficking and Violence Protection Act of 2000, Pub.L. No. 106-386, §2002, 114 Stat. 1464, 1541-42, to show that they have stated a cause of action. Section 2002 states only that if an individual has a judgment against Iran, the United States will pay it if the statutory requirements are satisfied. The question in this case is whether plaintiffs are legally entitled to such a judgment. We agree with the district court that they are not.

We have considered plaintiffs' other arguments but see no need to set forth our reasons for rejecting them.

Notes:

1.   What are the competing interests of the three branches of the government in this case? What are the policy considerations that underlie the administration's position? What pressures are evident on each of the three branches of government in their consideration of the victims' legal claims? What compels the government to take a position in this case? What was the perceived risk to the United States if the government did not prevail? How does this conflict with the policy considerations announced by Congress in enacting the Flatow Amendment? What other options were available to the court in responding to the government's statement of interest?

2.   How might this case be interpreted as a struggle between the three branches of government? What role do citizens have in this dispute?

3.   How can the President "contract away" the right of the victims? What voice did the victims have in the negotiation of the Algiers Accord?

4.   What does the manner and timing of United States' entry into this case say about the role of the government in terrorism cases?

5.   What does the case suggest about defenses available to foreign state defendants in terrorism cases?

6.   What are the long-term implications for terrorism victims after the *Roeder* ruling? What are the risks to victims in pursuing Flatow Amendment claims after *Roeder*? What does the decision suggest about the future role of the United States government in cases against foreign states where there are significant ongoing foreign policy concerns?

7.   How are "core government functions" defined? Is this analysis appropriate and applicable in an age of multinational corporations, outsourcing of military functions, and regional terrorist organizations that are either created by state sponsors of terrorism (i.e. Hezbollah) or that sell their services to state patrons (i.e. HAMAS, Palestinian Islamic Jihad)?

8.   A recurring theme in civil terrorism law has been the role of the government in impeding and blocking victims' claims. This has been a source of great frustration to plaintiffs. Hence, former hostage David Roeder, a U.S. Air Force attaché at the Tehran embassy stated, "[I]t never occurred to me when I was getting the crap beat out of me in a Tehran jail cell that I would one day fight the same government that I was defending…It's just so demoralizing." Neely Tucker, in *Lawsuit Against Iran, Former Hostages Fight U.S, Government Calls Frozen Assets Untouchable*, Wash. Post, Dec. 13, 2001, at A1.

Chapter 12

Financial Support Cases

Burnett v. Al Baraka Investment & Development Corp.,
292 F.Supp.2d 9 (D. D.C. 2003).

ROBERTSON, District Judge.
This memorandum addresses the second group of dispositive motions to be considered in this action brought by victims and representatives of victims of the terrorist attacks
of September 11, 2001. My opinion on the first group of
motions is reported as *Burnett v. Al Baraka Invest. & De-
vel. Corp.,* 274 F.Supp.2d 86 (D.D.C.2003) (*"Burnett I"*).
The motions now before me, filed by Prince Turki Al-Faisal
bin Abdulaziz Al-Saud ("Prince Turki") and Prince Sultan
bin Abdulaziz Al-Saud ("Prince Sultan"), seek dismissal on
grounds, *inter alia,* of lack of subject matter jurisdiction and
lack of personal jurisdiction. The motions have been fully
briefed. Oral argument was presented on October 17, 2003.

It is undisputed that, at all times relevant to this action,
Prince Turki was the Director of Saudi Arabia's Department
of General Intelligence ("DGI" or "Istakhbarat"). [FN1] It
is also undisputed that, at all times relevant to this lawsuit,
Prince Sultan was Saudi Arabia's third-ranking government
official. He was-and is-minister of defense and aviation, inspector general of the armed forces, chairman ex-officio of
Saudi Arabian Airlines, chairman of the Supreme Council
for Islamic Affairs ("Supreme Council"), and head of the
Special Committee of the Council of Ministers ("Special
Committee"). The Supreme Council carries out the foreign
policies of Saudi Arabia as they relate to Islamic Affairs
conducted abroad, including making recommendations to
the Council of Ministers about requests for assistance from
Islamic organizations based outside of Saudi Arabia. The
Special Committee exercises discretion over disbursements,
which have included grants to Islamic charitable organizations, in furtherance of the national and foreign policy of
Saudi Arabia, as determined by the Council of Ministers.

FN1. Prince Turki is now Ambassador of Saudi Arabia to
the United Kingdom.

The Third Amended Complaint ("3AC") makes the following allegations as to Prince Turki:

• that "Osama bin Laden offered [him] the engineering equipment available from his family's construction company and
suggested bolstering Saudi forces with Saudi militants who
he was willing to recruit." Complaint, at ¶¶ 340-41.

• that, as head of DGI, he "was in a position to know the
threat posed by bin Laden, al Qaeda, the Taliban." *Id.,* at ¶
343.

• that he "had an ongoing relationship with Osama bin Lad-
en from the time they first met in Islamabad, Pakistan," and
personally met with bin Laden "at least five times...during
the mid-eighties to mid-nineties." *Id.,* at ¶¶ 341, 344.

• that, in 1995, while under his direction, Istakhbarat "decided to give massive financial and material support to the
Taliban." *Id.,* at ¶ 344.

• that he is "implicate[d]...as the facilitator of [money transfers from wealthy Saudis] in support of the Taliban, al Qaeda, and international terrorism" and that "Istakhbarat served
as a facilitator of Osama bin Laden's network of charities,
foundations, and other funding sources." *Id.,* at ¶¶ 346,
350.

• that, in July 1998, he attended a meeting in Kandahar,
Afghanistan, which led to an agreement that "Osama bin
Laden and his followers would not use the infrastructure in
Afghanistan to subvert the royal families' control of Saudi government and in return, the Saudis would make sure
that no demands for the extradition of terrorist individuals,
such as Osama bin Laden, and/or for the closure of terrorist facilities and camps." And that, "[a]fter the meeting, 400
new pick-up trucks arrived in Kandahar for the Taliban, still
bearing Dubai license plates." *Id.,* at ¶¶ 344, 348.

• that, in 1998 and 1999, he met with the Taliban, and that he "promised to provide oil and generous financial assistance to the Taliban." *Id.*

• that he "was instrumental in arranging a meeting in Kandahar between Iraqi senior intelligence operative [sic], the Ambassador to Turkey Faruq al-Hijazi, and Osama bin Laden, in December of 1998." *Id.,* at ¶ 349.

• that he is "implicated" in the funneling of money "from the Saudi-based company, Mushayt for Trading Establishment...through Spanish corporations to entities and individuals known to be associated with the al Qaeda terrorist organization in Europe." *Id.,* at ¶¶ 345, 376.

As to Prince Sultan, the 3AC alleges:

• that he met with "Osama bin Laden[, who] offered the engineering equipment available from his family's construction company and suggested bolstering Saudi forces with Saudi militants who he was willing to recruit." *Id.,* at ¶ 340.

• that he "took radical stands against western countries and publically supported and funded several Islamic charities that were sponsoring Osama bin Laden and al Qaeda operations," including the International Islamic Relief Organization ("IIRO"), the Muslim World League ("MWL"), the World Assembly of Muslim Youth ("WAMY") and Al-Haramain Islamic Foundation ("Al-Haramain"). *Id.,* at ¶ 353.

• that he "has been involved in the sponsorship of international terrorism through the IIRO and other Saudi-funded charities." *Id.,* at ¶ 354.

• that "[a] Saudi embassy press release announced in April 2001 that 'Prince Sultan affirms [the] Kingdom's Support' for the Palestinian Intifada, to the tune of $40 million already disbursed to 'the families of those martyred' and other 'worthies.' " *Id.,* at ¶ 355.

• that, having knowledge of "the role of Saudi charitable entities...in financing the al Qaeda terrorist organization," he "personally funded [the Islamic charities identified in ¶ 353]" with donations amounting to at least $6,000,000. *Id.,* at ¶¶ 358-59.

• that, "[s]ince the IIRO's creation in 1978, [he] participated by donations and various gifts to the charity. In 1994 alone, he donated $266,652 to the [IIRO]. Since 1994, the amount funneled by [him] into IIRO is reported to be $2,399,868."

[His] role in directly contributing to and in the oversight of IIRO evidences his material sponsorship, aiding and abetting of international terrorism. [He] maintains close relations with the IIRO organization headquarters and knew or should have known these assets were being diverted to al Qaeda." *Id.,* at ¶ 360.

• that "[he] is also a large financial contributor of the [MWL]. [He] donated during a television fundraising campaign for MWL: The total collection made as a result of the television campaign was SR 45,000,000, with the Emir of Riyadh, Prince Sultan, donating a million Saudi Riyals ($533,304)." *Id.,* at ¶ 361.

• that "[he] is also a regular donator to the [WAMY]... WAMY has been officially identified as a 'suspected terrorist organization' by the FBI since 1996 and has been the subject of numerous governmental investigations for terrorist activities." *Id.,* at ¶ 362.

• that, "[a]t best, [he] was grossly negligent in the oversight and administration of charitable funds, knowing they would be used to sponsor international terrorism, but turning a blind eye. At worst, [he] directly aided and abetted and materially sponsored al Qaeda and international terrorism." *Id.,* at ¶ 363.

I. SUBJECT MATTER JURISDICTION

Prince Turki and Prince Sultan assert foreign sovereign immunity and argue in their motions that the Foreign Sovereign Immunities Act of 1976, 28 U.S.C. §1602 *et seq.* ("FSIA"), does not overcome that immunity. The FSIA-in effect a series of exceptions to a general rule of immunity for foreign sovereigns-confers original jurisdiction in district courts over claims for relief "with respect to which the foreign state is not entitled to immunity under [the FSIA] or under any applicable international agreement." 28 U.S.C. §1330(a); *see Argentine Republic v. Amerada Hess Shipping Corp.,* 488 U.S. 428, 439, 109 S.Ct. 683, 102 L.Ed.2d 818 (1989) ("The FSIA provides the sole basis for obtaining jurisdiction over a foreign state in federal court."). "The FSIA 'must be applied by the district courts in every action against a foreign sovereign, since subject-matter jurisdiction in any such action depends on the existence of one of the specified exceptions to foreign sovereign immunity.' " *Id.* at 434-35, 109 S.Ct. 683 (quoting *Verlinden B.V. v. Cent. Bank of Nigeria,* 461 U.S. 480, 493, 103 S.Ct. 1962, 76 L.Ed.2d 81 (1983)). [FN2]

FN2. The FSIA confers jurisdiction over *non-jury* actions, but it is not grounds for dismissal that the claims against Prince Turki and Prince Sultan are joined with jury-triable claims against other defendants. *See generally In re Air Crash Disaster Near Roselawn, Ind. on Oct. 31, 1994,* 96 F.3d 932, 947 (7th Cir.1996); *Engle v. Mecke,* 24 F.3d 133, 135 (10th Cir.1994); *Group Health Inc. v. Blue Cross Ass'n,* 793 F.2d 491, 498 (2d Cir.1986).

Individual office holders can enjoy foreign sovereign immunity, *see El-Fadl v. Cent. Bank of Jordan,* 75 F.3d 668, 671 (D.C.Cir.1996), but "not…for acts that are not committed in an official capacity." *Jungquist v. Sheikh Sultan Bin Khalifa Al Nahyan,* 115 F.3d 1020, 1027 (D.C.Cir.1997). In their separate motions, Prince Turki and Prince Sultan (i) assert that the allegations against them relate only to actions taken in their official capacities, and (ii) argue that the claims against them do not fit within any of the FSIA's exceptions to the general rule of immunity.

"Generally, in entertaining a motion to dismiss, the district court must accept the allegations of the complaint as true, and construe all inferences in the plaintiff's favor." *Id.* at 1027 (citing *Foremost-McKesson, Inc. v. Islamic Republic of Iran,* 905 F.2d 438, 440 n. 3 (D.C.Cir.1990)). However, "[w]here the motion to dismiss is based on a claim of foreign sovereign immunity, which provides protection from suit and not merely a defense to liability,…the court must engage in sufficient pretrial factual and legal determinations to satisfy itself of its authority to hear the case before trial." *Id.* at 1027-28 (citation and internal quotation marks omitted). The district court must "go beyond the pleadings and resolve any disputed issues of fact the resolution of which is necessary to a ruling upon the motion to dismiss." *Phoenix Consulting Inc. v. Republic of Angola,* 216 F.3d 36, 40 (D.C.Cir.2000).

A. OFFICIAL CAPACITY

Where there is a dispute about whether an individual was acting in an official capacity, "the relevant inquiry…focuses on the nature of the individual's alleged actions, rather than the alleged motives underlying them." *Jungquist,* 115 F.3d at 1028. And, if there was a convergence between official duties and personal interest, "[s]uch a circumstance does not serve to make [the] action any less an action of [a] sovereign." *Chuidian v. Philippine Nat. Bank,* 912 F.2d 1095, 1107 (9th Cir.1990).

Prince Turki and Prince Sultan vigorously dispute the accuracy of the allegations against them. For purposes of their motions, however, they assert that, whatever their ac-

tions, they were performed in their official capacities. Prince Turki maintains that any acts he may have done with respect to the Taliban were consistent with his duties as the Director of Istakhbarat. Prince Sultan maintains that his role in providing financial assistance to the International Islamic Relief Organization, the Muslim World League, the World Assembly of Muslim Youth or Al-Haramain Islamic Foundation, was official, in his capacity either as Chairman of the Supreme Council, or as head of the Special Committee.

1. *Prince Turki*

Prince Turki has submitted several documents to support his position. One is his own declaration. In it, he states that "[a]ll of [his] interactions with Osama bin Laden, Al-Qaeda, and the Taliban were in [his] official capacity as Director of the DGI." Prince Turki Decl., at ¶ 5. He states that Saudi Arabia "provided no [direct] aid to the Taliban" and that, in June 1998, he met with Taliban leader Mullah Omar in Kandahar "to convey an official Saudi request to extradite Osama bin Laden to Saudi Arabia for trial." *Id.,* at ¶¶ 8, 11. He states that in September 1998, "when [he] returned to Kandahar for another meeting with Mullah Omar to pursue Osama bin Laden's extradition, Mullah Omar spoke to [him] abusively and declared that the Taliban would not extradite Osama bin Laden, whom Mullah Omar praised," *id.,* at ¶ 12; and that, as a result of Omar's refusal to extradite bin Laden, "[he] recommended that Saudi Arabia withdraw its representative from Kabul and suspend diplomatic relations with the Taliban Government, which Saudi Arabia did in September 1998," *id.,* at ¶ 13.

In response to the allegation that he or Istakhbarat was a "facilitator" of money transfers or provided material resources to al Qaeda, bin Laden, or the Taliban, Prince Turki declares that, "[a]t no time during the period in question did [he] or the DGI knowingly transfer funds or facilitate the transfer of funds, either directly or indirectly, to Osama bin Laden or Al-Qaeda." *Id.,* at ¶ 14. He also states that "[n]either [he] nor, to [his] knowledge, anyone else in the Saudi government ever reached any agreement with any representatives of Osama bin Laden or Al-Qaeda regarding the extradition of terrorists…[or] offered material assistance to representatives of Osama bin Laden or Al-Qaeda in exchange for not attacking Saudi Arabia. Neither [he] nor, to [his] knowledge, anyone else in the Saudi government ever promised to provide oil and financial assistance to the Taliban. Neither [he] nor, to [his] knowledge, anyone else in the Saudi government ever arranged for 400 pick-up trucks to be delivered to Kandahar for the benefit of the Taliban." *Id.,* at ¶ 16.

Prince Turki has also submitted a transcript of an December 10, 2001, interview he conducted with ABC News: Nightline. During the interview, an ABC News tape of Osama bin Laden was played. According to the transcript, upon learning of Prince Turki's mission to Kandahar to secure his extradition, bin Laden stated: "He returned empty-handed. He looked ashamed, as if he had come at the request of the American government. It's none of the business of the Saudi regime to come and ask for handing over Osama bin Laden." Tr., *Nightline* (ABC television broadcast, December 10, 2001).

The plaintiffs contend that "[n]othing in [their] allegation [about Prince] Turki's role as facilitator related in any way to his position in the Saudi government," Response, at 15, but they have made no showing that any of Prince Turki's alleged actions were taken other than in his official capacity. The absence of such a showing compels the conclusion that the allegations against Prince Turki only relate to actions he took in his official capacity. Further, because the plaintiffs' suggestions of individual activity are only conclusory, I will not grant plaintiffs' request for jurisdictional discovery. Under these circumstances, "discovery would 'frustrate the significance and benefit of entitlement to immunity from suit.'" *El-Fadl*, 75 F.3d at 671 (quoting *Foremost-McKesson*, 905 F.2d at 449).

2. Prince Sultan

Prince Sultan has also filed documents in support of his submission, including declarations by financial officers of the IIRO, the MWL, the WAMY, and Al-Haramain to the effect that donations to their organizations were received from Saudi funds on behalf of Saudi Arabia, but not from or on behalf of Prince Sultan personally. *See* Saleh Abdullah Al Saykhan Decl., at ¶¶ 3-4; Ali Muhammad Al-Kamal Decl., at ¶ C; Mutaz Saleh Abu Unuq Decl., at ¶ 4; Khalid Eid Al-Dhahiri Decl., at ¶¶ 3-4. These affidavits have limited probative value, lacking proper foundations to establish that the affiants could have known the actual source of the monies they received, and not having been subjected to cross-examination. The value of the plaintiffs' showing that Prince Sultan did give money to these organizations in his personal capacity, however, is no greater: Saudi press agency releases (the proper translations of which are in dispute) referring to Prince Sultan's contributions as personal; a May 3, 2003 Global News Wire discussing the selection of Prince Sultan for the Sheikh Rashid Humanitarian Personality of the Year Award in honor of his contributions to charity, and a January 21, 1999 Ain-Al-Yaqeen article stating that "Prince Sultan...donated half a million riyals to the [IIRO] in the

Kingdom of Saudi Arabia [and that t]his donation was the second instalment of the generous annual donation of one million riyals which His Royal Highness the Prince gives to the organi[z]ation."

The record does not support a clear resolution of the disputed issue of fact necessary to a ruling on the motion to dismiss the claims plaintiffs have made against Prince Sultan in his personal capacity, *see Phoenix Consulting, supra*. To the extent Prince Sultan was acting in his official capacity when he made or approved donations to the IIRO, the WML, the WAMY and Al-Haramain, however, he is entitled to immunity-unless one or more of the exceptions to the FSIA applies.

B. EXCEPTIONS TO IMMUNITY

When exceptions to the FSIA are invoked-here plaintiffs rely upon the "commercial activities" exception, 28 U.S.C. §1605(a)(2), and the "noncommercial tort" exception, 28 U.S.C. §1605(a)(5) [FN3]-it is the defendants' burden to prove them inapplicable. *Phoenix Consulting, supra*. To sustain that burden, "the defendant may challenge either the legal sufficiency or the factual underpinning of an exception." *Id*. As the Court of Appeals has explained:

FN3. The Princes also say that the 3AC invokes the "state-sponsored terrorism" exception, 28 U.S.C. §1605(a)(7). However, "only a defendant that has been specifically designated by the State Department as a 'state sponsor of terrorism' is subject to the loss of its sovereign immunity" under this exception. *Bettis v. Islamic Republic of Iran*, 315 F.3d 325, 329 (D.C.Cir.2003) (citation omitted). It is undisputed that the Kingdom of Saudi Arabia had not been designated a "state sponsor of terrorism" on September 11, 2001. The state-sponsored terrorism exception is inapplicable.

If the defendant challenges only the legal sufficiency of the plaintiff's jurisdictional allegations, then the district court should take the plaintiff's factual allegations as true and determine whether they bring the case within any of the exceptions to immunity invoked by the plaintiff. In some cases, however, the motion to dismiss will present a dispute over the factual basis of the court's subject matter jurisdiction under the FSIA, that is, either contest a jurisdictional fact alleged by the plaintiff, or raise a mixed question of law and fact. When the defendant has thus challenged the factual basis of the court's jurisdiction, the court may not deny the motion to dismiss merely by assuming the truth of the facts alleged by the plaintiff and disputed by the defendant. Instead, the court must go beyond the pleadings and resolve any disputed issues of fact the resolution of which is necessary to a ruling upon a motion to dismiss.

Id. at 40 (internal citations omitted).

1. *§1605(a)(2) commercial activity exception*

The "commercial activity" exception is invoked only with respect to Prince Sultan and is readily disposed of. Under this exception, foreign states are not immune in any case

in which the action is based upon a commercial activity carried on in the United States by the foreign state; or upon an act performed in the United States in connection with a commercial activity of the foreign state elsewhere; or upon an act outside the territory of the United States in connection with a commercial activity of the foreign state elsewhere and that act causes a direct effect in the United States.

28 U.S.C. §1605(a)(2). "Crucial to each of the three clauses of [§] 1605(a)(2) is the phrase 'commercial activity.'" *Tex. Trading & Milling Corp. v. Fed. Republic of Nigeria,* 647 F.2d 300, 307 (2d Cir.1981). "Commercial activity" is defined by the FSIA as:

either a regular course of commercial conduct or a particular commercial transaction or act. The commercial character of an activity shall be determined by reference to the nature of the course of conduct or particular transaction or act, rather than by reference to its purpose.

28 U.S.C. §1603(d). The issue, then, is "whether the particular actions that the foreign state performs (whatever the motive behind them) are the *type* of actions by which a private party engages in trade and traffic or commerce." *Saudi Arabia v. Nelson,* 507 U.S. 349, 360-61, 113 S.Ct. 1471, 123 L.Ed.2d 47 (1993) (quoting *Republic of Argentina v. Weltover, Inc.,* 504 U.S. 607, 614, 112 S.Ct. 2160, 119 L.Ed.2d 394 (1992) (internal quotation marks omitted; emphasis in original)).

Admittedly, this standard is open to more than one interpretation, depending on how one broadly the court defines the type of action allegedly engaged in by Prince Sultan. *See Segni v. Commercial Office of Spain,* 835 F.2d 160, 166 (7th Cir.1987) (quoting H.R. REP. No. 94-1487, at 16 (1976), *reprinted in* 1976 U.S.C.C.A.N. 6604, 6615 ("It has seemed unwise to attempt an excessively precise definition of [commercial activity], even if that were practicable.")). Here, the plaintiffs have encouraged a very broad definition. They

argue that the IIRO, the WML, the WAMY, and Al-Haramain participated in commercial activity either by "providing charitable services or engaging in terrorist activities." Memorandum of Law in Opposition to Motion of Prince Sultan to Dismiss the Claims Against Him, at 26. They say that these organizations (each of them a defendant in this action), financed al Qaeda's "purchasing [of] equipment, renting [of] property, [and] manufacturing [of] bombs" and that Prince Sultan's contributions were "'in connection' with this commercial activity." *Id.* They also encourage the Court to find that these contributions had the "direct effect" in the United States of causing the September 11 attacks, by finding that the attacks could not have been carried out without Saudi funding and that the very purpose of the funding was to carry out that type of attack. *Id.,* at 27.

The act of contributing to a foundation is not within our ordinary understanding of "trade and traffic or commerce," nor, apparently, was it within the contemplation of the Congress that enacted the FSIA in 1976:

As the definition [of "commercial activity"] indicates, the fact that goods or services to be procured through a contract are to be used for a public purpose is irrelevant; it is the essentially commercial nature of an activity or transaction that is critical. Thus, a contract by a foreign government to buy provisions or equipment for its armed forces or to construct a government building constitutes a commercial activity. The same would be true of a contract to make repairs on an embassy building. Such contracts should be considered to be commercial contracts, even if their ultimate object is to further a public function.

By contrast, a foreign state's mere participation in a foreign assistance program administered by the Agency for International Development (AID) is an activity whose essential nature is public or governmental, and it would not itself constitute a commercial activity…However, a transaction to obtain goods or services from private parties would not lose its otherwise commercial character because it was entered into in connection with an AID program…

H.R. REP. No. 94-1487, at 16, *reprinted in* 1976 U.S.C.C.A.N. at 6615.

Granted that "the primary purpose of the Act is to 'restrict' the immunity of a foreign state to suits involving a foreign state's public acts," *Tex. Trading,* 647 F.2d at 308, it is nevertheless too much of a stretch to find the allegations against Prince Sultan "connect[ed] to" commercial activity.

2. §1605(a)(5) noncommercial tort exception

Plaintiffs' invocation of the "noncommercial tort" exception requires a deeper analysis. Section 1605(a)(5) provides in relevant part that:

(a) A foreign state shall not be immune from the jurisdiction of courts of the United States or of the States in any case-

(5)...in which money damages are sought against a foreign state for personal injury or death, or damage to or loss of property, occurring in the United States and caused by the tortious act or omission of that foreign state or of any official or employee of that foreign state while acting within the scope of his office or employment...

28 U.S.C. §1605(a)(5). Subsection A then provides an exception to this exception:

[Section (a)(5)] shall not apply to...any claim based upon the exercise or performance or the failure to exercise or perform a discretionary function regardless of whether the discretion be abused...

28 U.S.C. §1605(a)(5)(A).

Prince Turki and Prince Sultan argue that plaintiffs cannot possibly establish the causal links that would be necessary to bring the noncommercial tort exception into play. In any event, they argue, the allegations of the 3AC describe the exercise of discretionary functions-decisions by Prince Turki, as Director of DGI, about how to protect the Saudi people from terrorism, and decisions by Prince Sultan, as Chairman of the Supreme Council or head of the Special Committee, as to which organizations should be given government monies in furtherance of Saudi policies.

a. *Noncommercial torts*

The 3AC alleges that Prince Turki "served as a facilitator of Osama bin Laden's network of charities, foundations, and other funding sources," and that he "provide[d] oil and generous financial assistance" to the Taliban. It also alleges that Istakhbarat, while under Prince Turki's direction, "decided to give massive financial and material support to the Taliban." The 3AC alleges that Prince Sultan "publicly supported and funded several Islamic charities that [he knew] were sponsoring Osama bin Laden and al Qaeda operations," including the IIRO, the MWL, the WAMY and Al-Haramain. In simple terms, these allegations amount to claims that Prince

Turki and Prince Sultan, acting in their official capacities, funded or provided material resources to those who funded or provided material resources to the terrorists who perpetrated the September 11th attacks.

The question is whether those claims can be made to fit within the noncommercial tort exception. The answer is, only if it has been properly alleged that the plaintiffs' claims are "for personal injury or death...*caused by* the tortious act or omission of...any official...of [a] foreign state while acting within the scope of his office." [FN4]

FN4. Prince Turki and Prince Sultan also argue that the words "occurring in the United States" of §1605(a)(5) preclude the claims against them under this exception because the *entire* tort must have occurred in the United States, meaning both the tortious conduct and the injury resulting from that conduct, and all of their alleged actions took place in Saudi Arabia or elsewhere. I disagree. "[T]he Foreign Sovereign Immunities Act,...preserves immunity for tort claims unless *injury or death occurs in the United States.*" *Tel-Oren v. Libyan Arab Republic,* 726 F.2d 774, 775 (D.C.Cir.1984) (Edwards, J., concurring; emphasis added); *see also Letelier v. Republic of Chile,* 488 F.Supp. 665, 665 (D.D.C.1980). The deaths and injuries of which the plaintiffs complain "occurr[ed] in the United States."

These motions do not present the occasion for a general disquisition on the subject of causation, however. To repeat an observation I made in deciding the first round of dispositive motions in this case, it is still "too soon to attempt a precise formulation of the level of knowledge and intent or certainty of causation that will be necessary to get plaintiffs' claims to a jury," *Burnett I,* 274 F.Supp.2d at 102. Such a precise formulation is, in any case, not necessary to a decision on the FSIA issue presented here. An attenuated chain of causation may or may not suffice to require persons who cannot claim foreign sovereign immunity to answer for the September 11 attacks, but, in the context of motions to dismiss claims brought under the FSIA, I must "start from the settled proposition that the subject-matter jurisdiction of the lower federal courts is determined by Congress 'in the exact degrees and character which to Congress may seem proper for the public good.' " *Amerada Hess,* 488 U.S. at 433, 109 S.Ct. 683 (quoting *Cary v. Curtis,* 44 U.S. (3 How.) 236, 245, 11 L.Ed. 576 (1845)). And I am bound by Circuit precedent:

It has repeatedly been recognized that, although cast in general terms, the "tortious act" exception was designed primarily to remove immunity for cases arising from traffic accidents. This is scarcely to say that the exception applies *only* to traffic accidents; rather, the point is that *the legislative history counsels that the exception should be narrowly construed so as not to encompass the farthest reaches of common law.*

MacArthur Area Citizens Ass'n v. Republic of Peru, 809 F.2d 918, 921 (D.C.Cir.1987) (internal citations omitted; emphasis added).

In the FSIA context, plaintiffs' allegations that (i) Prince Turki or Prince Sultan funded (ii) those who funded (iii) those who carried out the September 11th attacks would stretch the causation requirement of the noncommercial tort exception not only to "the farthest reaches of the common law," but perhaps beyond, to terra incognita. I find, accordingly, that the noncommercial tort exception afforded by §1605(a)(5) is not applicable. [FN5]

FN5. This conclusion is buttressed by the language of another FSIA exception, §1605(a)(7): "A foreign state shall not be immune from the jurisdiction of courts of the United States…in any case-(7)…in which money damages are sought against a foreign state for personal injury or death that was caused by an act of torture, extrajudicial killing, aircraft sabotage, hostage taking, *or the provision of material support or resources…* for such an act if such act or *provision of material support* is engaged in by an official…of such foreign state while acting within the scope of his or her office…" (emphasis added). The noncommercial tort exception, §1605(a)(5), makes no mention of the "provision of material support." A canon of statutory construction holds that "where Congress includes particular language in one section of a statute but omits it in another section of the same Act, it is generally presumed that Congress acts intentionally and purposefully in the disparate inclusion or exclusion." *Russello v. United States,* 464 U.S. 16, 23, 104 S.Ct. 296, 78 L.Ed.2d 17 (1983) (citations and internal quotation marks omitted); *see also, e.g., AT&T Corp. v. F.C.C.,* 323 F.3d 1081, 1086 (D.C.Cir.2003). This method of statutory construction "announces a presumption, not a hard-and-fast rule," *New England Public Communications Council, Inc. v. F.C.C.,* 334 F.3d 69, 76 (D.C.Cir.2003), but it is a powerful presumption that both the Supreme Court and the D.C. Circuit have applied to the FSIA's exceptions. *See Amerada Hess,* 488 U.S. at 441, 109 S.Ct. 683 ("Congress' decision to use explicit language in §1605(a)(2), and not to do so in §1605(a)(5), indicates that the exception in §1605(a)(5) covers only torts occurring within the territorial jurisdiction of the United States.");

Persinger v. Islamic Republic of Iran, 729 F.2d 835, 843 (D.C.Cir.1984) ("[A] comparison of the noncommercial tort exception-section 1605(a)(5)…-with the commercial activity exception, section 1605(a)(2), demonstrates that Congress intended the former to be narrower than the latter…When Congress uses explicit language in one part of a statute to cover a particular situation and then uses different language in another part of the same statute, a strong inference arises that the two provisions do not mean the same thing."). In this case, the allegations against Prince Turki and Prince Sultan describe the "provision of material support or resources," but the FSIA exception which recognizes such acts, §1605(a)(7), does not apply here, *see, supra,* n. 3, and, by application of the *Russello* presumption, the omission of "provision of material support" from §1605(a)(5) should be treated as intentional.

b. *Discretionary function*

My ruling that the 3AC does not bring the claims against Prince Turki and Prince Sultan within the "noncommercial tort" exception makes it unnecessary to decide whether the "discretionary function" exception (to the exception) also applies. In case a reviewing court should reject that ruling, however, I will briefly state my reasons for concluding that the official acts plaintiffs ascribe to Prince Turki and Prince Sultan are squarely covered by the "discretionary function" language of subsection A. Were it not for the plaintiffs' reliance upon *Letelier v. Republic of Chile,* 488 F.Supp. 665, 673 (D.D.C.1980), and *Liu v. Republic of China,* 892 F.2d 1419 (9th Cir.1989), indeed, this conclusion would be nearly self-evident: Prince Turki, as director of intelligence, taking acts to protect Saudi Arabia from terrorism, and Prince Sultan, as chairman of the Supreme Council, making recommendations to the Council of Ministers about requests for assistance from Islamic organizations outside Saudi Arabia or, as head of the Special Committee, deciding what disbursements should be made to Islamic charitable organizations, were clearly making "decisions grounded in social, economic, and political policy." *United States v. S.A. Empresa de Viacao Aerea Rio Grandense* (" *Varig Airlines* "), 467 U.S. 797, 814, 104 S.Ct. 2755, 81 L.Ed.2d 660 (1984).

Plaintiffs rely upon *Letelier v. Republic of Chile,* 488 F.Supp. 665, 673 (D.D.C.1980), and *Liu v. Republic of China,* 892 F.2d 1419 (9th Cir.1989), for the proposition that there is "no discretion to 'perpetrate conduct designed to result in' terrorist attacks." Plaintiff's Mem. of Law in Opposition to Motion of Prince Sultan to Dismiss, at 22. The two cases do instruct that, in appropriate circumstances, terrorist acts cannot be considered "discretionary," but they are factually distinguishable from this case. *Letelier* and *Liu* involved causal links significantly shorter and more direct than those alleged here: in *Letelier,* the foreign sovereign and sovereign officeholders were alleged to have "caused or aided" in the assassinations; in *Liu,* the foreign state was held vicariously liable for the actions of its employee, criminal acts of a rather different character and order. *See Letelier,* 488 F.Supp. at 673 (holding that "there would be no 'discretion' within the meaning of section 1605(a)(5)(A) to order or to aid in an assassination and were it to be demonstrated that a foreign state has undertaken any such act in this country, that foreign state could not be accorded sovereign immunity under subsection (A) for any tort claims resulting from its conduct"); *Liu,* 892 F.2d at 1430 (excepting from immunity, under §1605(a)(5), a foreign state which benefitted from a government employee's use of governmental authority to silence, by murder, an outspoken critic of the government).

II. PERSONAL JURISDICTION

Prince Sultan does not enjoy foreign sovereign immunity from claims that arise from contributions he allegedly made to the IIRO, the WML, the WAMY, and Al-Haramain in his personal capacity. His motion to dismiss those claims accordingly asserts, not lack of subject matter jurisdiction-which is conferred by the ATA for the claims of United States nationals and by the ATCA for the claims of foreign nationals, [FN6] *see Burnett I*-but lack of personal jurisdiction. "[B]ecause the [ATA] provides for nationwide service of process," [FN7] the relevant Due Process inquiry for personal jurisdiction purposes, assuming that the defendant has been properly served, "is whether the defendant has had minimum contacts with the United States." *Busch v. Buchman, Buchman & O'Brien, Law Firm,* 11 F.3d 1255, 1258 (5th Cir.1994) (citations omitted). That inquiry, in turn, is constrained by the question of whether " 'maintenance of the suit...offend[s] 'traditional notions' of fair play and substantial justice.' " *Int'l Shoe Co. v. Washington,* 326 U.S. 310, 316, 66 S.Ct. 154, 90 L.Ed. 95 (1945) (citation omitted).

FN6. The plaintiffs have also alleged RICO as a basis for this Court's jurisdiction, but, for the reasons explicated in *Burnett I,* 274 F.Supp.2d at 100-02, jurisdiction does not lie against Prince Sultan under this statute.

FN7. The venue provision of the ATA provides that: [a]ny civil action under section 2333 of this title against any person may be instituted in the district court of the United States for any district where any plaintiff resides or

where any defendant resides or is served, or has an agent. Process in such a civil action may be served in any district where the defendant resides, is found, or has an agent. 18 U.S.C. §2334(a).

Plaintiffs have made a desultory effort to sustain their burden of showing that Prince Sultan's visits to the United States (and his presence here years ago as a college undergraduate) would support the assertion of personal jurisdiction over him. They have not indicated, however, how official visits, or speaking engagements, or an American education, might have been connected with their cause of action. *See, e.g., Douglas Battery Mfg. Co. v. Taylor Auto Supply, Inc.,* 537 F.Supp. 1072, 1074 (M.D.N.C.1982) ("The nature and quality of defendant's contacts with North Carolina and their lack of connection with the plaintiff's cause of action convince the Court that asserting personal jurisdiction over the defendant for this cause of action would be unfair."); *Kulko v. Superior Court of California,* 436 U.S. 84, 93-94, 98 S.Ct. 1690, 56 L.Ed.2d 132 (1978) (holding that temporary visits to state insufficient basis for assertion of in personam jurisdiction over unrelated action); *Munchak Corp. v. Riko Enters., Inc.,* 368 F.Supp. 1366, 1374 (M.D.N.C.1973) (holding that unrelated activities of defendant in forum state do not constitute minimum contacts). Nor have they provided even a basic outline of how their showing of minimum contacts might be enhanced by jurisdictional discovery. [FN8]

FN8. My order of July 7, 2003, indicating that discovery would be permitted on the FSIA claim as to Prince Sultan, was not informed by the briefing on the instant motions and is no longer operative.

Plaintiffs' principal argument, instead, is essentially that Prince Sultan brought himself within the jurisdiction of this Court (or any American court that might entertain an ATA action against him) when he "purposefully directed" his allegedly tortious activities at residents of the United States.

This jurisdictional argument invokes the Supreme Court's decisions in *Calder v. Jones,* 465 U.S. 783, 104 S.Ct. 1482, 79 L.Ed.2d 804 (1984), and *Burger King Corp. v. Rudzewicz,* 471 U.S. 462, 105 S.Ct. 2174, 85 L.Ed.2d 528 (1985). *Calder* was brought by California residents in California state court against Florida residents who had published an allegedly libelous article in a national journal. The Supreme Court overruled the defense of lack of personal jurisdiction, holding that "about 600,000 copies of the publication were sold in California, and that jurisdiction was proper based on the 'effects' in California of th[e defendants] Florida-based conduct." *United States v. Ferrara,* 54 F.3d 825, 828 (D.C.Cir.1995) (citing *Calder,* 465 U.S. at 785, 789-90, 104

S.Ct. 1482). The D.C. Circuit's *Ferrara* decision explained that *Calder* was based on the Supreme Court's observations

that the defendants' allegedly tortious actions were 'expressly aimed' at California; that they knew the article 'would have a potentially devastating impact' on its subject in California; and that, under these circumstances, they should have anticipated being 'haled into court' in that State.

Id. (internal citations omitted).

In *Burger King,* the Supreme Court held that due process was not offended when a federal court in Florida asserted personal jurisdiction over a Michigan franchisee in a breach of contract action by a Florida franchisor, rejecting "talismanic jurisdiction formulas," 471 U.S. at 485, 105 S.Ct. 2174, but finding after a detailed factual analysis that the franchisee had established a substantial and continuing relationship with the franchisor's Miami headquarters, had received fair notice from the contract documents and the course of dealing that he might be subject to suit in Florida, and had failed to demonstrate how jurisdiction in that forum would otherwise be fundamentally unfair, *id.* at 487, 105 S.Ct. 2174.

The sum of plaintiffs' allegations against Prince Sultan in his personal capacity is that he personally donated money to the IIRO, the WML, the WAMY and Al-Haramain, knowing that those foundations funded terrorist organizations including Al Qaeda. The 3AC stops well short of alleging that Prince Sultan's actions were "expressly aimed" or "purposefully directed" at the United States, allegations that might have satisfied *Burger King, supra,* and *Keeton v. Hustler Magazine, Inc.,* 465 U.S. 770, 774-75, 104 S.Ct. 1473, 79 L.Ed.2d 790 (1984). Plaintiffs do argue that anyone whose actions have led to terrorist activity in the United States should reasonably anticipate that he might be subject to suit here whether or not he himself has targeted the United States. As Justice Brennan observed in *Burger King,* however:

[T]he Court has consistently held that [foreseeability of causing injury in another State] is not a "sufficient benchmark" for exercising personal jurisdiction. Instead, "the foreseeability that is critical to due process analysis…is that the defendant's conduct and connection with the forum State are such that he should reasonably anticipate being haled into court there." "…[I]t is essential in each case that there be some act by which the defendant purposefully avails itself of the privilege of conducting activities within the forum

State, thus invoking the benefits and protections of its laws." This "purposeful availment" requirement ensures that a defendant will not be haled into a jurisdiction solely as a result of "random," "fortuitous," or "attenuated" contacts, or of the "unilateral activity of another party or third person."

471 U.S. at 474-75, 105 S.Ct. 2174 (internal citations omitted); *see also Wallace v. Herron,* 778 F.2d 391, 394-95 (7th Cir.1985). It was a commercial course of dealing that made it foreseeable that Burger King's Michigan franchisee would be haled into court in Florida. Nothing like that sort of purposeful availment is alleged here.

* * * * * *

It is unnecessary to reach or decide the other arguments advanced by Prince Turki and Prince Sultan in their motions to dismiss. The claims against them for acts allegedly done in their official capacities will be dismissed for lack of subject matter jurisdiction. The claims against Prince Sultan for acts allegedly done in his personal capacity will be dismissed without prejudice for lack of personal jurisdiction. An appropriate order accompanies this memorandum.

ORDER

For the reasons set forth in the accompanying memorandum, the motion to dismiss of defendant Prince Turki Al-Faisal bin Abdulaziz Al-Saud is **granted**, and the claims against him will be **dismissed**; the motion to dismiss of defendant Prince Sultan bin Abdulaziz Al-Saud is **granted**: the claims against him in his official capacity will be **dismissed**, and the claims against him in his personal capacity will be **dismissed without prejudice**.

<u>Notes:</u>

1.   Why have "second generation" statutory terrorism cases targeted banks and other financial sponsors? What are the advantages and disadvantages of suing financial institutions, as opposed to foreign states and terrorist organizations?

2.   Much of the decision turned on evidentiary considerations. What are the unique evidentiary problems confronted by terrorism victims? Why did the plaintiffs rely on news reports and press releases? Why are the plaintiffs forced to argue that a defendant "was implicated in giving money" or "took radical stands"? What do these statements indicate about the "proof problems" confronted by victims?

3. How does this case show potential targets of "material support and assistance" litigation ways to insulate themselves from terrorism law suits?

4. In the past, there was complete identity between rulers and their states. Hence, in France Louis the XIV stated, "l'etate c'est moi." In the last century the law made distinctions between actions committed in an "official capacity" vs. "individual capacity." While sensible with respect to modern western states, does this dichotomy fit the context of this case? Since much of terrorism is sponsored by non-western states and supporters residing in monarchical or dictatorial regimes, is this analysis anachronistic? Is the court guilty of making a category mistake?

5. Evidentiary issues are paramount in terrorism cases for a variety of reasons. Here, the court was unusually concerned about the evidence submitted by *both* sides,

> These affidavits have limited probative value, lacking proper foundations to establish that the affiants could have known the actual source of the monies they received, and not having been subjected to cross-examination. The value of the plaintiffs' showing that Prince Sultan did give money to these organizations in his personal capacity, however, is no greater: Saudi press agency releases (the proper translations of which are in dispute) referring to Prince Sultan's contributions as personal; a May 3, 2003 Global News Wire discussing the selection of Prince Sultan for the Sheikh Rashid Humanitarian Personality of the Year Award in honor of his contributions to charity, and a January 21, 1999 Ain-Al-Yaqeen article stating that "Prince Sultan… donated half a million riyals to the [IIRO] in the Kingdom of Saudi Arabia [and that t]his donation was the second installment of the generous annual donation of one million riyals which His Royal Highness the Prince gives to the organi[z]ation."

Id. at 16.

6. While the plaintiffs' failure to satisfy the court's evidentiary concerns is somewhat understandable in light of their inability to obtain discovery and the inherently secretive nature of terrorists and their supporters, what accounts for the defendants' inability to provide proper affidavits?

7. Why did the plaintiffs look to the "traffic accident" exception to the FSIA 28 U.S.C. §1605(a)(5) as a method of obtaining subject matter jurisdiction? Why did the court play the terrorism exception, §1605(a)(7), against §1605(a)(5)? How did the plaintiffs' pleadings fall into this trap? Could they have characterized the actions of the Saudi princes differently to achieve an alternate result? What options were available to the court in construing §1605(a)(7)?

8. The court felt "bound" by the ruling in *MacArthur Area Citizens Ass'n v. Republic of Peru*, 809 F.2d 918, 921 (D.C.Cir. 1987) and adopted a narrow interpretation of §1605(a)(5),

> It has repeatedly been recognized that, although cast in general terms, the "tortious act" exception was designed primarily to remove immunity for cases arising from traffic accidents. This is scarcely to say that the exception applies *only* to traffic accidents; rather, the point is that *the legislative history counsels that the exception should be narrowly construed so as not to encompass the farthest reaches of common law.*

Had the court distinguished *MacArthur*, would the subject matter jurisdiction of the federal courts, in the context of terrorism litigation, have been significantly enlarged? What counter forces come into play?

Linde v. Arab Bank, 384 F.Supp.2d 571 (E.D.N.Y. 2005).

GERSHON, District Judge.

Plaintiffs in the above captioned suits are United States citizens, or their estates, survivors, and heirs, who have been victims of terrorist attacks in Israel since September 2000. The sole defendant in all three cases, and in four additional suits filed by separate groups of plaintiffs, [FN1] is a financial institution headquartered in Jordan with a federally licensed and regulated branch office in New York. Plaintiffs bring several claims under the civil remedy provision of the Anti-Terrorism Act ("ATA"), 18 U.S.C. §2333, and bring common law claims for intentional infliction of emotional distress. The Linde plaintiffs' motion for a preliminary injunction, which was premised on the fifth claim for relief in the Linde First Amended Complaint, was denied on November 29, 2004. *See Linde v. Arab Bank, PLC*, 353 F.Supp.2d 327 (E.D.N.Y.2004). Defendant now brings motions to dismiss the complaints in these three suits under Rule 12(b)(6) of the Federal Rules of Civil Procedure and on *forum non conveniens* grounds. (The Linde plaintiffs and the Litle plaintiffs have each filed a First Amended Complaint, while the Coulter plaintiffs have filed only a complaint. For purposes of this opinion, all three documents will be referred to simply as "complaints.")

FN1. Additional motions to dismiss, which were filed on July 22, 2005, are now pending in two of these cases, *Almog v. Arab Bank,* 04-CV-5564, and *Afriat-Kurtzer v. Arab Bank,* 05-CV388. In addition to bringing claims under the Anti-Terrorism Act, which are similar to the allegations in the *Linde, Litle,* and *Coulter* suits, plaintiffs in these two related cases also bring claims under the Alien Tort Claims Act. A sixth case, *Bennett v. Arab Bank,* 05-CV-3183, was filed on July 1, 2005, and a seventh, *Roth v. Arab Bank,* 05-CV-3738, was filed on August 5, 2005.

FACTUAL ALLEGATIONS AND CLAIMS

All three complaints contain nearly identical allegations regarding Arab Bank's conduct and each posit the same theories of culpability. The factual allegations concerning each plaintiff's injuries are, of course, unique to each plaintiff. To the extent these factual differences impact the legal analysis, they will be explained separately below. The following is a summary of the allegations common to all three complaints. The alleged facts are assumed to be true for the purposes of defendant's motions to dismiss. [FN2]

FN2. Defendant has submitted affidavits and other matters outside the pleadings in the course of briefing its motions to dismiss. Because motions for summary judgment would be premature, the Rule 12(b)(6) motions will not be converted to Rule 56 motions, and the court will not consider these factual submissions in support of the motions.

Plaintiffs allege that, on September 29, 2000, following the collapse of peace negotiations between the State of Israel and the Palestinian Authority, Palestinian terrorist groups launched what quickly became known in Arab parlance as the Al Aqsa Intifada or Intifada Al Quds-the "Second Intifada" in western parlance. This Second Intifada was marked from the outset by numerous acts of extreme violence, including multiple murders of civilians by Palestinian terrorist groups. These terrorists utilize suicide bombers as their preferred method of carrying out such attacks. The suicide bombers are regarded as martyrs by the terrorist groups and their sympathizers. [FN3] The objectives of the Second Intifada include intimidating and coercing the civilian population of Israel and attempting to influence the policy of the Israeli government to withdraw from territory it presently controls.

FN3. Defendant's attempt to discount this allegation on the basis that the term "martyr" has several different usages is disingenuous. Plaintiffs' allegations clearly concern the use of the term martyr to describe those who are killed or injured while carrying out suicide attacks in support of the Second Intifada.

The complaints identify the Islamic Resistance Movement ("HAMAS"), the Palestinian Islamic Jihad ("PIJ"), and the Al Aqsa Martyrs Brigade ("AAMB") as prominent terrorist organizations operating in Palestinian controlled territory. Each of these organizations has been designated as a Foreign Terrorist Organization ("FTO") by the United States Secretary of State. The complaints also identify several charities that plaintiffs allege operate as front organizations for HAMAS, assisting it in carrying out its terrorist activities. These include Al-Ansar Charity, Ramalla Charitable Committee, Tulkarem Charitable Committee, the Islamic Association (Gaza) a/k/a Al Jamay Al-Islamiya, Al Mujama Al-Islami, Nablus Charitable Committee, Jenin Charitable Committee, and Islamic Charity Society of Hebron. Plaintiffs allege that these charitable organizations are in reality agents of HAMAS. Although these organizations hold themselves out as legitimate charities and collect money in the name of humanitarian purposes, they in fact route large sums of money to support the violent activities of HAMAS and other terrorist organizations. These organizations thus serve as agents of HAMAS and are able both to solicit and to launder money on HAMAS's behalf. They raise money to support all areas of HAMAS's operations. Several of the charities maintain bank accounts at Arab Bank through which the Bank provides them with financial services, such as receiving deposits and processing wire transfers. The complaints allege that the Bank knows that these organizations are fronts which support HAMAS's terrorist activities, and that the Bank's continued provision of banking services to these groups facilitates their illegal activities. The complaints identify one Arab Bank account number that plaintiffs allege belongs to HAMAS itself, and which HAMAS uses to collect funds in support of violent activities. [FN4]

FN4. According to the Declaration of Shukry Bishara, the Chief Banking Officer of Arab Bank, in Support of Defendant's Motion to Dismiss, the Bank "closed this account, froze the balance of its funds and reported it to the appropriate authorities" following the commencement of plaintiffs' suits.

On or about October 16, 2000, the Saudi Committee In Support of the Intifada Al Quds ("Saudi Committee") was established as a private charity registered with the Kingdom of Saudi Arabia. According to the Saudi Committee, its purpose is to support the "Intifada Al Quds" and "all suffering families-the families of the martyrs and the injured Palestinians and the disabled." According to plaintiffs, the Saudi Committee constitutes a professional fundraising apparatus intended to subsidize the Palestinian terror campaign and to bankroll HAMAS and the PIJ.

The Saudi Committee furnishes what plaintiffs variously term a "comprehensive insurance death benefit" or a "universal death and dismemberment plan," consisting of a payment of $5,316.06, to the families of Palestinian terrorists killed in service of the Intifada. (At oral argument, plaintiffs explained that this sum is the U.S. Dollar equivalent of 20,000 Saudi Riyals.) Lesser benefits are provided when the terrorist is either injured or captured by Israeli security forces. Although plaintiffs sometimes refer to these payments as "insurance" benefits, the scheme is not alleged to be a traditional pooled risk insurance plan, where individuals pay premiums against the risk of some future event. Rather, plaintiffs are alleging that the plan is, in effect, a reward for perpetrators of suicide attacks. Families claim this reward by obtaining an official certification of their deceased relative's status as a martyr, which includes an individualized martyr identification number. In order to obtain this certificate, families must provide the Saudi Committee with the martyr's name, personal information, and details concerning the date and manner of death.

Plaintiffs allege that the Bank is the exclusive administrator of the death and dismemberment benefit plan. Once the Saudi Committee prepares a list of eligible martyrs, the list is provided to the Bank. Arab Bank, in consultation with the Saudi Committee and local representatives of HAMAS, finalizes the lists, maintains a database of persons eligible to receive benefits under the death and dismemberment plan, and opens a dollar account for each beneficiary. Families who choose to collect the benefit must present to the Bank an official certification from the Palestinian Authority that includes the individualized identification number of the martyr. If the documentation proves satisfactory, Arab Bank issues a receipt to the designated recipient of the benefit. Plaintiffs allege that these payments create an incentive to engage in terrorist acts by rewarding all Palestinian terrorists, regardless of their affiliation with a particular group.

The complaints detail the numerous terrorist attacks in which plaintiffs themselves or their decedents were injured. For the sake of brevity, only one attack from each complaint will be described. The Linde complaint describes an attack on May 18, 2003. On that day, plaintiff Steven Averbach, a citizen of the United States and of Israel, was seated on a commuter bus heading toward Jerusalem when a man dressed as a religious Jew boarded the bus and then detonated explosives. Seven people were killed and twenty injured in the attack, including plaintiff Averbach, who sustained severe damage to his spinal cord when a ball bearing that had been packed in the explosives lodged between his C3 and C4 vertebrae, rendering him a quadriplegic. HAMAS claimed responsibility for the attack, and the bomber was later identified by his family as Bassem Jamil Tarkrouri.

The Litle complaint describes the bombing of Bus No. 2 in Jerusalem on August 19, 2003, from which a number of plaintiffs derive their injuries. HAMAS claimed responsibility for the bombing, in which plaintiff Mendy Reinitz, a citizen of the United States and of Israel, sustained shrapnel wounds in the shoulder and back and underwent surgery. Although some shrapnel was removed, some will remain in his body for the rest of his life. Mendy's brother, Yissocher Dov Reinitz, and father, Mordechai Reinitz, were also riding the bus that day; both were killed in the attack. Other relatives are also plaintiffs.

The Coulter complaint describes the suicide bombing of a Sbarro pizza restaurant on August 9, 2001, in Jerusalem. Fifteen people were killed and approximately 130 injured in this attack, in which a suicide bomber detonated a bomb packed with nails and metal bolts. The claims of the Nachenberg, Finer, Green, Greenbaum, and Danzig families, brought in the Coulter complaint, stem from this attack. The bomber was identified as Izz Ad-Din Shuhail Ahmad Al-Masri, a terrorist acting on behalf of HAMAS. The Al-Masri family received two payments into an Arab Bank account following this act, one from the Saudi Committee, totaling $5,316.16 (or 20,000 Saudi Riyals), and one from the Al-Ansar charity, totaling $6000.

All three complaints describe a specific benefit transaction for a suicide bomber named Dia A-Tawil. After perpetrating a suicide bombing attack on behalf of HAMAS on March 27, 2001, he was designated Palestinian Authority martyr number 449. His father, Hussien Mohamed Favah Tawil, presented the martyr certification to the Bank and received a confirmatory receipt stating that the benefit was paid to his Arab Bank account in Ramallah.

Plaintiffs also allege that funds raised by the Saudi Committee in Saudi currency, and deposited in the Committee's Arab Bank accounts, are then routed through the Bank's New York branch office, where they are converted to U.S.

dollars, since Saudi currency cannot easily be converted into Israeli currency; the funds are then transferred to Arab Bank branches located in the West Bank in Israel and used to fund terrorist activities.

Based on these allegations, the Linde plaintiffs assert the following claims: Count One alleges that Arab Bank aided and abetted the murder, attempted murder, and serious bodily injury of United States nationals, in violation of 18 U.S.C. §2332(a), (b), and (c), by providing substantial assistance to terrorists through the administration of the universal death and dismemberment plan for families of suicide bombers, and through the provision of other financial services. Count One alleges that Arab Bank "knew or recklessly disregarded" that it was providing material support for acts of international terrorism, that the charities were fronts that played a major role in raising funds for HAMAS, and that the Bank's activities substantially assisted dangerous criminal acts.

Count Two alleges that Arab Bank conspired to commit murder and attempted murder, in violation of 18 U.S.C. §2332(b), by agreeing to "perform extraordinary banking and administrative services for the Saudi Committee, Hamas, the PIJ, and AAMB," including exclusive administration of the death and dismemberment benefit plan, in order to "support terrorist activities pursuant to a common scheme to encourage and incentivize acts of terrorism."

Count Three alleges that Arab Bank provided material support to terrorists, in violation of 18 U.S.C. §2339A, by providing "extraordinary financial and administrative services," including exclusive administration of the death and dismemberment benefit plan to the families of suicide bombers and other terrorists.

Count Four alleges that Arab Bank provided material support to a designated foreign terrorist organization, in violation of 18 U.S.C. §2339B, by knowingly transferring funds from and to agents of HAMAS. [FN5] Plaintiffs further allege that, without the Bank's assistance in this regard, it would have been substantially more difficult to implement the death and dismemberment benefit plan.

FN5. Counts Four and Five contain erroneous statutory citations. However, the actual allegations contained in those counts, as well as subsequent briefing and argument, make clear to which statutory sections plaintiffs are referring.
Count Five alleges that the Bank's failure to comply with regulatory requirements to retain the assets of designated foreign terrorist organizations and report them to the Secre-

tary of State, as required by 18 U.S.C. §2339B(a)(2), itself constitutes the provision of material support to a designated FTO.

Count Six alleges that Arab Bank provided financial services to HAMAS, the PIJ, AAMB, and the Saudi Committee by collecting funds, with the knowledge that such funds have been and will be used to facilitate acts intended to cause death or serious bodily injury to civilians, such as plaintiffs. Plaintiffs contend that these financial services constitute financing of terrorism in violation of 18 U.S.C. §2339C.

Count Seven alleges that Arab Bank's provision of banking and other services to HAMAS, the PIJ, the AAMB and other international terrorists, including administering the death and dismemberment benefit plan, was itself an act of international terrorism as defined by the ATA, in that these actions were "involved" in violent criminal acts that injured plaintiffs and appeared to be intended to coerce or intimidate the people, government policy, or government conduct of Israel. Although the complaint does not cite a specific criminal provision identifying a specific act of international terrorism defendant is alleged to have committed or aided and abetted or conspired to commit, the briefs make clear that the crimes are violations of the material support and financing provisions, Sections 2339A, 2339B, and 2339C.

Finally, Count Eight alleges claims for intentional infliction of emotional distress.

The legal claims of the Litle plaintiffs and the Coulter plaintiffs are identical, except that the Litle plaintiffs omit Count Five of the Linde complaint (which is based on defendant's failure to comply with regulatory requirements), and the Coulter complaint omits Count Eight of the Linde complaint, which asserts claims of intentional infliction of emotional distress. [FN6]

FN6. Thus, both the Litle First Amended Complaint and the Coulter complaint consist of a total of seven counts, compared to the eight counts in the Linde First Amended Complaint.

DISCUSSION

In considering a motion to dismiss made pursuant to Rule 12(b)(6) of the Federal Rules of Civil Procedure, the court must accept the factual allegations in the complaint as true and draw all reasonable inferences in favor of plaintiffs. *Bolt Electric, Inc. v. City of New York*, 53 F.3d 465, 469 (2d

Cir.1995). Dismissal is appropriate only where it appears beyond doubt that plaintiffs can prove no set of facts in support of their claims that would entitle them to relief. *Id.*

Pleading Standard

Defendant, relying heavily on cases from the racketeering and securities fraud contexts, argues that plaintiffs are required to plead specific facts from which its knowledge of the wrongful acts alleged could be inferred. Although the Bank claims that it is not trying to impose a heightened pleading standard, the effect of the Bank's argument would indeed be to impose a higher standard.

Rule 8(a) of the Federal Rules of Civil Procedure requires only that a pleading contain "a short and plain statement of the claim showing that the pleader is entitled to relief." The Supreme Court has recently reiterated that the notice pleading standard is a limited one:

Given the Federal Rules' simplified standard for pleading, '[a] court may dismiss a complaint only if it is clear that no relief could be granted under any set of facts that could be proved consistent with the allegations.' *Hishon v. King & Spalding,* 467 U.S. 69, 73 [104 S.Ct. 2229, 81 L.Ed.2d 59] (1984). If a pleading fails to specify the allegations in a manner that provides sufficient notice, a defendant can move for a more definite statement under Rule 12(e) before responding. Moreover, claims lacking merit may be dealt with through summary judgment under Rule 56. The liberal notice pleading of Rule 8(a) is the starting point of a simplified pleading system, which was adopted to focus litigation on the merits of a claim.

Swierkiewicz v. Sorema N.A., 534 U.S. 506, 514, 122 S.Ct. 992, 152 L.Ed.2d 1 (2002); *see also Leatherman v. Tarrant County Narcotics Intelligence & Coordination Unit,* 507 U.S. 163, 167-69, 113 S.Ct. 1160, 122 L.Ed.2d 517 (1993). The first circuit court of appeals to address a private damages claim brought under the ATA applied the liberal pleading standard of Rule 8(a). *See Boim v. Quranic Literacy Institute,* 291 F.3d 1000, 1008 (7th Cir.2002). I agree that there is no reason to do otherwise.

Statutory Claims Under 18 U.S.C. §2333

Plaintiffs bring their suit pursuant to 18 U.S.C. §2333, enacted as part of the Anti-Terrorism Act ("ATA" or "the Act"), which provides in relevant part:

Any national of the United States injured in his or her person, property, or business by reason of an act of international terrorism, or his or her estate, survivors, or heirs, may sue therefor in any appropriate district court of the United States and shall recover threefold the damages he or she sustains and the cost of the suit, including attorney's fees.

18 U.S.C. §2333(a). The ATA, at Section 2331(1), defines "international terrorism" as "activities that"

(A) involve violent acts or acts dangerous to human life that are a violation of the criminal laws of the United States or of any State, or that would be a criminal violation if committed within the jurisdiction of the United States or of any State;

(B) appear to be intended-

(i) to intimidate or coerce a civilian population;

(ii) to influence the policy of a government by intimidation or coercion; or

(iii) to affect the conduct of a government by mass destruction, assassination or kidnapping; and

(C) occur primarily outside the territorial jurisdiction of the United States, or transcend national boundaries in terms of the means by which they are accomplished, the persons they appear intended to intimidate or coerce, or the locale in which their perpetrators operate or seek asylum.

Thus, in order to state a claim for civil damages under Section 2333(a), plaintiffs must allege that they were injured "by reason of" a crime that constitutes an act of international terrorism, as so defined.

Plaintiffs identify the following crimes as the predicate acts of international terrorism on which they are basing civil liability under Section 2333: murder, attempted murder, and serious bodily injuries to United States citizens, in violation of 18 U.S.C. §2332(a), (b), and (c); conspiracy to commit murder and attempted murder of United States citizens, in violation of 18 U.S.C. §2332(b); provision of material support to terrorists, in violation of 18 U.S.C. §2339A; provision of material support to designated foreign terrorist organizations, in violation of 18 U.S.C. §2339B; and financing of terrorism, in violation of 18 U.S.C. §2339C.

The violent acts alleged by plaintiffs as giving rise to their injuries, *i.e.,* murder, attempt or conspiracy to commit murder, and physical violence that results in serious bodily injury, clearly qualify as "activities that involve violent acts or acts dangerous to human life," and thus fall within Section 2331(1)(A). Defendant does not challenge the sufficiency of plaintiffs' allegations with respect to the apparent purpose and location of these acts, as required by Section 2331(1)(B) and (C). [FN7] Thus, plaintiffs have alleged that they were injured "by reason of an act of international terrorism," as required by Section 2333(a). Defendant's argument that plaintiffs must allege that they were injured by reason of Arab Bank's conduct simply misstates the statutory requirement. As will be explained below, Arab Bank's liability in this case depends on whether the Bank can be held liable, directly or secondarily, for its conduct in allegedly assisting the terrorists, but there can be no dispute that plaintiffs have plead adequately that they were injured by acts of international terrorism.

FN7. In briefing these motions, defendant has not seriously disputed that the majority of the attacks qualify as acts of international terrorism within the meaning of the ATA. With respect to defendant's argument that a few plaintiffs have alleged injuries resulting from drive-by shootings and other street crime, as opposed to acts of international terrorism, there is nothing on the face of the complaints to indicate that these crimes were not intended as acts of international terrorism as required by the statute. None of the facts alleged as to these acts establish that they were ordinary violent crimes, for example, robberies or personal vendettas, and none of the facts alleged remove the possibility that plaintiffs can prove they were acts of terrorism. If, at trial, plaintiffs fail to prove that these acts were terror attacks, rather than "mere" street crime, they will have failed to establish a claim under the ATA. However, at this stage of the litigation, dismissing these claims would be premature.

In addition to murder, plaintiffs identify violations of the material support and terrorist financing laws as predicate crimes. Violations of 18 U.S.C. §§2339A and 2339B, which make it a crime to provide material support to terrorists and to designated foreign terrorist organizations, respectively, are included in Section 2331(1)'s broad definition of "international terrorism," *see Boim,* 291 F.3d at 1014-15, as are violations of 2339C, which prohibits the financing of terrorism. Thus, violations of these provisions can serve as predicate crimes giving rise to civil liability under the ATA.

Section 2339A, entitled "Providing material support to terrorists," provides that "[w]hoever provides material support or resources...knowing or intending that they are to be used in preparation for, or in carrying out, [various federal crimes],...or attempts or conspires to do such an act," shall be guilty of a crime. 18 U.S.C. §2339A(a).

Section 2339B deals with material support for organizations that have been formally designated as foreign terrorist organizations by the Secretary of State under the procedures set out in Section 219 of the Immigration and Nationality Act, codified at 8 U.S.C. §1189. *See* 18 U.S.C. §2339B(g)(6) (defining "terrorist organization" as an organization designated as a terrorist organization under Section 219 of the Immigration and Nationality Act). It provides that "[w]hoever knowingly provides material support or resources to a foreign terrorist organization, or attempts or conspires to do so, shall be" guilty of a crime. 18 U.S.C. §2339B(a)(1).

Both Section 2339A and Section 2339B define "material support or resources" as "any property, tangible or intangible, or service, including currency or monetary instruments or financial securities, *financial services,* lodging, training, expert advice or assistance, safehouses, false documentation or identification, communications equipment, facilities, weapons, lethal substances, explosives, personnel ..., and transportation, except medicine or religious materials." 18 U.S.C. §2339A(b) (emphasis added); *see* 18 U.S.C. §2339B(g)(4) (incorporating the definition of "material support or resources" used in Section 2339A).

Section 2339C addresses the financing of terrorism, and provides that whoever, meeting the jurisdictional requirements set forth in subsection (b),

by any means, directly or indirectly, unlawfully and willfully provides or collects funds with the intention that such funds be used, or with the knowledge that such funds are to be used, in full or in part, in order to carry out-

(A) an act which constitutes an offense within the scope of a treaty specified in subsection (e)(7), as implemented by the United States, or

(B) any other act intended to cause death or serious bodily injury to a civilian, or to any other person not taking an active part in the hostilities in a situation of armed conflict, when the purpose of such act, by its nature or context, is to intimidate a population, or to compel a government or an international organization to do or to abstain from doing any act, shall be [guilty of a crime].

18 U.S.C. §2339C(a)(1). An act may constitute an offense under the statute without a showing that the funds were ac-

tually used to carry out the predicate act of terrorism. 18 U.S.C. §2339C(a)(3).

Plaintiffs' claims under the ATA are based on two factual theories of conduct. The first factual theory is that the Bank's activities in administering the death and dismemberment benefit plan created an incentive for the commission of the terrorist acts by Palestinians in Israel which injured plaintiffs and thus substantially assisted their commission. The second factual theory concerns the banking services the Bank provides to the various organizations which plaintiffs allege are fronts for, or agents of, HAMAS, a designated foreign terrorist organization. Plaintiffs contend that, on the basis of these two factual courses of conduct, the Bank may be held secondarily liable for their injuries under theories of civil aiding and abetting and civil conspiracy. Plaintiffs also maintain that the Bank's actions constituting material support for terrorists and terrorist organizations in violation of 18 U.S.C. §§2339A and 2339B and financing in violation of 18 U.S.C. §2339C create direct bases for liability.

The Availability of Secondary Liability

Defendant contends that plaintiffs have failed to allege facts from which it can be inferred that its own acts, as opposed to those of the terrorists, proximately caused their injuries, and challenges plaintiffs' reliance on secondary liability under theories of civil aiding and abetting and civil conspiracy. However, Section 2333 does not limit the imposition of civil liability only to those who directly engage in terrorist acts. The statute specifies the class of plaintiffs who may sue under the civil remedy provision- *i.e.,* those U.S. nationals who are injured "by reason of an act of international terrorism." As noted above, plaintiffs have alleged that their injuries were caused by suicide bombings or other attacks that, for pleading purposes, meet the definition of "international terrorism." When it comes to determining the proper defendants for claims under Section 2333, however, the statute is silent. *See Boim,* 291 F.3d at 1010 ("Although the statute defines the class of plaintiffs who may sue, it does not limit the class of defendants, and we must therefore look to tort law and the legislative history to determine who may be held liable for injuries covered by the statute.").

Defendant, relying principally on the Supreme Court's decision in *Central Bank of Denver v. First Interstate Bank of Denver,* 511 U.S. 164, 114 S.Ct. 1439, 128 L.Ed.2d 119 (1994), where the Court refused to allow civil aiding and abetting liability under Section 10(b) of the Securities and Exchange Act of 1934, argues that plaintiffs may not pro-

ceed on theories of civil aiding and abetting and civil conspiracy liability. For the reasons set forth comprehensively by the Court of Appeals for the Seventh Circuit in *Boim,* I conclude that aiding and abetting liability is available under the ATA. *See Boim,* 291 F.3d at 1018-21. In *Boim,* the court found *Central Bank* not determinative and summarized its reasons as follows:

First, *Central Bank* addressed extending aiding and abetting liability to an implied right of action, not an express right of action as we have here in section 2333. Second, Congress expressed an intent in the terms and history of section 2333 to import general tort law principles, and those principles include aiding and abetting liability. Third, Congress expressed an intent in section 2333 to render civil liability at least as extensive as criminal liability in the context of the terrorism cases, and criminal liability attaches to aiders and abettors of terrorism. *See* 18 U.S.C. §2. Fourth, failing to extend section 2333 liability to aiders and abettors is contrary to Congress' stated purpose of cutting off the flow of money to terrorists at every point along the chain of causation.

Boim, 291 F.3d at 1019. *Boim* also noted that the government, in an amicus brief, which the Court had solicited on appeal, supported the availability of secondary civil liability under the ATA.

I further find that civil conspiracy liability, not addressed in *Boim,* is also available. The statute expressly includes conspiracy to engage in terrorist acts under its criminal provisions, and there is no reason to treat the civil provisions as excluding this type of liability. *See Boim,* 291 F.3d at 1020 (noting that Congress, in Section 2333, expressed an intent "to make civil liability at least as extensive as criminal liability").

The Scope of Secondary Liability

The scope of civil aiding and abetting liability was set forth in *Halberstam v. Welch,* 705 F.2d 472 (1983), in what the Supreme Court in *Central Bank* described as a "comprehensive opinion on the subject." *Central Bank,* 511 U.S. at 181, 114 S.Ct. 1439. In *Halberstam,* the Court of Appeals for the D.C. Circuit, relying heavily on The Restatement (Second) of Torts, §876 (1979), upheld civil aiding abetting and liability, and also civil conspiracy liability, against a woman who had knowingly and substantially assisted her co-defendant, a murderer, by performing otherwise legal services, such as acting as banker, bookkeeper and secretary, knowing that these activities assisted his illegal activities, even though she had no specific knowledge of, or intent to commit, the particular illegal activity, *i.e.,* murder, with which she and he were civilly charged. As the court stated, "Although her own acts were neutral standing alone, they must be evaluated in the context of the enterprise they aided, *i.e.,* a five-year-long burglary campaign against private homes." *Halberstam,* 705 F.2d at 488. The Court noted that "the implications of tort law in this area [civil remedies for criminal acts] as a supplement to the criminal justice process and possibly as a deterrent to criminal activity cannot be casually dismissed." *Halberstam,* 705 F.2d at 489. Here, Congress has expressly made criminal the providing of financial and other services to terrorist organizations and expressly created a civil tort remedy for American victims of international terrorism.

Section 876 of the Restatement provides,

For harm resulting to a third person from the tortious conduct of another, one is subject to liability if he

(a) does a tortious act in concert with the other or pursuant to a common design with him, or

(b) knows that the other's conduct constitutes a breach of duty and gives substantial assistance or encouragement to the other so to conduct himself, or

(c) gives substantial assistance to the other in accomplishing a tortious result and his own conduct, separately considered, constitutes a breach of duty to the third person.

Plaintiffs rely on all three provisions of Section 876 of the Restatement, paragraph (a) for their conspiracy claim, paragraph (b) for their aiding and abetting claim, and paragraph (c) for their claims under the material support and financing statutes, 18 U.S.C. §§2339A, 2339B and 2339C.

Plaintiffs' allegations are sufficient to establish secondary liability under each one of these theories. As to conspiracy, they adequately allege that Arab Bank knowingly and intentionally agreed to provide services to organizations it knew to be terrorist organizations and that they were injured by an overt act which was done in furtherance of the common scheme. It is not necessary that they allege that Arab Bank either planned, or intended, or even knew about the particular act which injured a plaintiff. *See Halberstam,* 705 F.2d at 487. The factual allegations of the complaints sufficiently support an inference that Arab Bank and the terrorist organizations were participants in a common plan under which Arab Bank would supply necessary financial services to the organizations which would themselves perform the violent acts. Administering the death and dismemberment benefit plan further supports not only the existence of an agreement but Arab Bank's knowing and intentional participation in the agreement's illegal goals. No more is required.

The same allegations support aiding and abetting liability. The complaints allege that the financial services provided by Arab Bank, and the administration of the death and dismemberment benefit plan, provided substantial assistance to international terrorism. They also allege that the Bank's administration of the benefit plan encouraged terrorists to act. These allegations are well within the mainstream of aiding and abetting liability. They describe the wrongful acts performed by the terrorists, the defendant's general awareness of its role as part of an overall illegal activity, and the defendant's knowing and substantial assistance to the principal violation. *See Halberstam,* 705 F.2d at 477. With respect to defendant's administration of the death and dismemberment benefit plan, as the Court in *Halberstam* noted, quoting from Comment d to Clause (b) of Section 876 of the Restatement: "Advice or encouragement to act operates as a moral support to a tortfeasor and if the act encouraged is known to be tortious it has the same effect upon the liability of the adviser as participation or physical assistance."

Defendant's protestations about causation and knowledge are contrary to these principles. Just as there was no requirement for aiding and abetting liability in *Halberstam* that the murderer would not have acted as he did but for his co-defendant's conduct, there is no requirement of a finding that the suicide bomber would not, or could not, have acted but for the assistance of Arab Bank. Plaintiffs readily acknowledge that, in order to prevail on their claims premised on the Bank's alleged administration of the death and dismemberment benefit plan, they must prove that each of the victims was in fact killed by terrorists (as defined in the statute and as opposed, for example, to apolitical criminals) and that each of the killers was within the coverage of the plan. Such proof would be sufficient to hold the Bank secondarily liable, assuming the other elements of liability were established, even though it would not satisfy a "but for" causation requirement. As to plaintiffs' claims premised on their second factual theory- *i.e.,* that the Bank's provision of financial services constitutes material support to, or financing of, foreign terrorist organizations-plaintiffs acknowledge that they will have to prove that the Bank provided these services to the particular group responsible for the attacks giving rise to their injuries.

Defendant also argues that plaintiffs' claims must fail because they do not allege, and cannot prove, that the death and dismemberment benefit payments motivated the attacks which caused their injuries. However, plaintiffs need not prove motive in order to succeed in their claims. Plaintiffs acknowledge that they are unlikely to be able to prove the motive behind any particular attack. Their theory is that the death and dismemberment benefit plan, allegedly administered by Arab Bank, creates an incentive for suicide bombings, whether or not it is also a motive in any particular instance. The Bank's active participation in creating such an incentive is a sufficient basis for liability under the broad scope of the ATA, which imposes secondary liability on those who substantially assist acts of terrorism. *See Humanitarian Law Project v. Reno,* 205 F.3d 1130, 1136 (9th Cir.2000), *cert. denied,* 532 U.S. 904, 121 S.Ct. 1226, 149 L.Ed.2d 136 (2001) (noting that "even contributions earmarked for peaceful purposes can be used to give aid to the families of those killed while carrying out terrorist acts, thus making the decision to engage in terrorism more attractive"). Plaintiffs also argue that the willingness of Arab Bank, a major institution in the Middle East, to perform services for the terrorists helps to legitimize terrorism and, in that way as well, furthers its assistance to them.

Finally, the allegations that Arab Bank breached independent duties, indeed committed criminal acts in violation of the material support and financing statutes, are sufficient to establish secondary liability under Section 876(c) of the Restatement.

Scienter

Arab Bank seeks dismissal of the first seven counts of the Linde complaint, and the corresponding counts of the Litle and Coulter complaints, on the ground that plaintiffs have not sufficiently alleged knowledge and intent. To the extent that defendant is arguing that plaintiffs have not alleged sufficient facts to establish an evidentiary basis for their allegations of knowledge and intent, defendant simply misapprehends the pleading standard. It is not entitled to dismissal based on the argument that plaintiffs must plead more than the requisite knowledge and intent, either as to their substantive claims or their claims of aiding and abetting and conspiracy. [FN8]

FN8. To the extent that plaintiffs have pled reckless conduct, as well as knowledge, the allegations of recklessness do not defeat their allegations of knowledge. There is, however, no statutory basis for plaintiffs' argument that recklessness would be sufficient to meet the statutory requirements. Arab Bank also argues, in effect, that the requisite intent is the specific intent to cause the acts of terrorism which injured the plaintiffs. The Bank is incorrect.

Each of the various statutory provisions upon which plaintiffs rely for the underlying criminal activity alleged to meet the standards of Section 2333 has a different formulation of the required *mens rea. See Humanitarian Law Project v. Gonzales,* 380 F.Supp.2d 1134, 1145-48 (C.D.Cal.2005) (describing the history of the enactment of these statutes). Under Section 2332, murder, as defined in 18 U.S.C. §1111(a), requires "malice aforethought." No one disputes that plaintiffs have sufficiently alleged that the mental state of the persons who performed the acts which injured them meet that standard.

The dispute centers on the mental state required of the Bank. Section 2339A makes it a crime to provide material support or resources "knowing or intending that [the resources] are to be used in preparation for, or in carrying out" terrorist attacks. Section 2339C also requires knowledge or intent that the funds are to be used to carry out terrorist attacks and, in addition, requires that the conduct be willful. To violate Section 2339B, it is required only that one "knowingly provide[ ] material support or resources" to a designated foreign terrorist organization. *See Humanitarian Law Project,* 380 F.Supp.2d at 1144-48. None of these provisions, however, requires specific intent to commit specific acts of terrorism. [FN9]

FN9. The district court in *Humanitarian Law Project v. Gonzales* describes Sections 2339A and 2339C as including a "specific intent requirement," while explaining that Congress dispensed with this requirement in Section 2339B. 380 F.Supp.2d at 1145-47. However, as that court held, Sections 2339A and 2339C only require knowledge or intent that the resources given to terrorists are to be used in the commission of terrorist acts. Neither requires the specific intent to aid or encourage the particular attacks that injured plaintiffs. With respect to Section 2339B, in *Humanitarian Law Project v. Reno,* the Court of Appeals for the Ninth Circuit, addressing a First Amendment challenge to Section 2339B's prohibition against providing material support to designated foreign terrorist organizations, rejected the claim that the prohibition is unconstitutional unless the person providing material support has the specific intent to aid in the organization's unlawful purposes. *Humanitarian Law Project,* 205 F.3d at 1133. The court noted that "[m]aterial support given to a terrorist organization can be used to promote the organization's unlawful activities, regardless of donor intent. Once the support is given, the donor has no control over how it is used." *Id.,* 205 F.3d at 1134. Moreover, "all material support given to such organizations aids their unlawful goals." *Id.,* 205 F.3d at 1136; *see also id.,* 205 F.3d at 1138 n. 5 (explaining that the term "knowingly" in Section 2339B "modifies the verb 'provides,' meaning that the only scienter requirement here is that the accused violator have knowledge of the fact that he has provided something, not knowledge of the fact that what is provided in fact constitutes material support"); *Humanitarian Law Project,* 380 F.Supp.2d at 1148.

That the intent urged by Arab Bank is not required has been confirmed by Congress's December 17, 2004 amendment of Section 2339B to add the language:

To violate this paragraph, a person must have knowledge that the organization is a designated terrorist organization (as defined in subsection (g)(6)), that the organization has engaged or engages in terrorist activity (as defined in section 212(a)(3)(B) of the Immigration and Nationality Act) [8 U.S.C. §1182(a)(3)(B)], or that the organization has engaged or engages in terrorism (as defined in section 140(d)(2) of the Foreign Relations Authorization Act, Fiscal Years 1988 and 1989) [22 U.S.C. §2656f(d)(2)].

See Humanitarian Law Project v. Reno, 205 F.3d at 1133-34. [FN10] Congress thus appears to have expressed its disagreement with decisions, relied upon by Arab Bank, imputing an intent requirement into Section 2339B equivalent to the intent requirement of Section 2339A, *e.g., U.S. v. Al-Arian,* 308 F.Supp.2d 1322, 1337-39 (M.D.Fla.2004). [FN11] *See Humanitarian Law Project,* 380 F.Supp.2d at 1147 (noting that, in adopting the 2004 amendment, Congress incorporated the Ninth Circuit's holding in *Humanitarian Law Project v. Reno* and rejected the holding of *United States v. Al-Arian*).

FN10. Defendant does not argue that the December 2004 amendment to Section 2339B does more than clarify the statute's reach; that is, it does not argue that the amendment changed the statute from one requiring specific intent to one no longer requiring specific intent. *See also Humanitarian Law Project,* 380 F.Supp.2d at 1147 (noting that the 2004 amendment "clarified" the *mens rea* requirement).

FN11. I note that the court in *Al-Arian* considered its conclusion consistent with the Seventh Circuit's decision in *Boim* insofar as *Boim* required, for civil liability, that the defendant intend to help in the terrorist organization's unlawful

activities. *Al-Arian,* 308 F.Supp.2d at 1339 n. 33. Insofar as *Boim* is read as requiring more than knowledge that the organization to which material support is provided is designated or is engaged in terrorist activities, I find that it is not consistent with the language of Section 2339B.

As explained by the district court in *Humanitarian Law Project v. Gonzales,* the legislative history of Section 2339B indicates that it was enacted in order to close a loophole left by Section 2339A, which would have allowed terrorist organizations to raise funds "under the cloak of a humanitarian or charitable exercise" and then divert the funds to terrorist activities. *Humanitarian Law Project,* 380 F.Supp.2d at 1146 (citing H.R. Rep. 104-383, at *43 (1995)). Also, Congress expressly found that "foreign organizations that engage in terrorist activity are so tainted by their criminal conduct that any contribution to such an organization facilitates that conduct." Antiterrorism and Effective Death Penalty Act of 1996, Pub.L. 104-32, §301(a)(7), 110 Stat. 1214, 1247 (1996). Thus, Section 2339B is violated if the Bank provides material support in the form of financial services to a designated foreign terrorist organization and the Bank either knows of the designation or knows that the designated organization has engaged or engages in terrorist activities.

Defendant cites the decision in *In re Terrorist Attacks on September 11, 2001,* 349 F.Supp.2d 765 (S.D.N.Y.2005), in which claims brought against a number of Middle Eastern banks under the ATA were dismissed, as dispositive of the claims in this case. *In re Terrorist Attacks* concerned a group of consolidated actions bringing claims against a range of defendants related to the terrorist attacks of September 11, 2001. Each of the pleadings contained only a few paragraphs of allegations against the defendant banks. The Court held that, absent knowledge of the terrorist activities, the banks could not be liable for injuries caused by money routinely passing through them. Although plaintiffs in those cases did allege that some of the banks had ties to HAMAS, there was no allegation of any connection between HAMAS and Osama Bin Laden, Al Qaeda, or the September 11th attacks, so those allegations were insufficient to state a claim against the banks for injuries arising from the September 11th attacks. *See In re Terrorist Attacks,* 349 F.Supp.2d at 831-35.

By contrast, here, plaintiffs allege both that the Bank plays a central role in a well-publicized plan to reward terrorists killed and injured in Palestinian suicide attacks in Israel and that the Bank knows that the groups to which it provides services are engaged in terrorist activities. The very groups that the Bank is alleged to support are the same groups alleged to be responsible for the terrorist attacks that injured the plaintiffs. Nothing in the complaints suggests that Arab Bank is a mere unknowing conduit for the unlawful acts of others, about whose aims the Bank is ignorant. Although the Bank would like this court to find, as did the court in *In re Terrorist Attacks,* that it is engaged in "routine banking services," *see* 349 F.Supp.2d at 835, here, given plaintiffs' allegations regarding the knowing and intentional nature of the Bank's activities, there is nothing "routine" about the services the Bank is alleged to provide.

Arab Bank also seeks dismissal on the ground that plaintiffs fail to allege the involvement of upper level management employees in the misconduct alleged. Once again, defendant attempts to impose a standard of pleading beyond that required by the rules. It is sufficient, for pleading purposes, for plaintiffs to allege the knowledge and intent of Arab Bank and not spell out their proof. For that reason, it is unnecessary to address whether the allegations made regarding the conduct of certain high level employees, including the Chairman of the Arab Bank, are sufficient as an evidentiary matter.

Claims Based Upon Violations of 18 U.S.C. §2339C

Each of the three complaints asserts a claim that the Bank provided and collected funds "with the knowledge that such funds have been and will be used, in part, to facilitate acts intended to cause death or serious bodily injury to civilians," in violation of 18 U.S.C. §2339C. Arab Bank argues that plaintiffs' allegations are insufficient to plead a violation of this section. As used in Section 2339C, "the term 'provides' includes giving, donating, and transmitting," and "the term 'collects' includes raising and receiving." 18 U.S.C. §2339C(e)(4) & (5). Reading this section together with the material support provisions, the statute thus distinguishes between providing "financial services," which is addressed in Sections 2339A and 2339B (which include "financial services" in their definition of "material support"), and financing, *i.e.*, the providing or collecting of funds, which is addressed in Section 2339C. However, as just noted, the term "provides" includes "transmitting" funds, and the term "collects" includes "receiving" funds. It is these terms upon which plaintiffs rely in pleading a violation of Section 2339C. Plaintiffs seek to reach the banking activities of receiving deposits and transmitting funds between accounts on the basis that the accounts (and funds) belong to groups engaged in terrorist activity, *i.e.*, the charity fronts that operate as agents of HAMAS.

Plaintiffs acknowledge that, under this claim, they will have to prove that Arab Bank knew that the funds it received as deposits and transmitted to various organizations were to be used for conducting acts of international terrorism. Because the complaints allege such knowledge on the part of the Bank, this claim will not be dismissed.

Scope of Injuries Actionable Under the ATA

Defendant argues that the claims of over fifty plaintiffs in the Coulter case and over fifty plaintiffs in the Litle case must be dismissed because they have failed to allege that their claims arise from an injury to a U.S. national. Section 2333(a) states, in relevant part, that "[a]ny national of the United States injured in his or her person, property, or business by reason of an act of international terrorism, or his or her estate, survivors, or heirs, may sue therefor..." Defendant argues that the scope of this language is not sufficiently broad to reach these plaintiffs, who are U.S. citizens suing for various non-physical injuries, such as emotional distress and loss of consortium, after their family members, who were not U.S. nationals, became victims of acts of international terrorism. The specific question raised by defendants' argument is whether Section 2333(a)'s language specifying that a U.S. national may recover for injuries to his or her "person, property, or business" encompasses the injuries alleged by these plaintiffs. Defendant has not sought dismissal of the similar claims brought by other nationals whose decedents were also nationals. In effect then, defendant argues that the claims it seeks to dismiss are derivative, not independent, and must be dismissed for that reason. [FN12]

FN12. Different American jurisdictions have treated spousal claims either as derivative, and therefore requiring the existence of a claim in the physically injured spouse, see, e.g., *Liff v. Schildkrout,* 49 N.Y.2d 622, 632, 427 N.Y.S.2d 746, 404 N.E.2d 1288 (1980), RESTATEMENT (SECOND) OF TORTS §693 cmt. e (1977), or as independent. *See, e.g., Lareau v. Page,* 39 F.3d 384, 390 (1st Cir.1994) (noting that, "[u]nder Massachusetts law, claims for loss of consortium are independent, rather than derivative, of the claim of the injured person").

The parties recognize that only one court has examined this issue. That court concluded that injuries of this type constitute injuries in the plaintiff's "person" under the ATA, stating, "[t]he statute does not specifically require that a plaintiff suffer *physical* harm prior to filing suit" and that "the plain language, as well as a common-sense interpretation, of the ATA" dictate that such plaintiffs should be able to recover. *See Biton v. Palestinian Interim Self-Government Author-*

ity, 310 F.Supp.2d 172, 181-182 (D.D.C.2004) (emphasis in original). The court expressed doubt that Congress could have intended that U.S. nationals could recover for losses of property yet not for losses of family members, simply because those family members were not U.S. nationals. *See id.* Defendant argues that the *Biton* holding is inconsistent with the legislative history of the ATA, and cites the minutes from the Senate Anti-Terrorism Act Hearing and the House Committee report on the ATA. Def't's Reply Mem. at 19-20, citing ATA Hearing at 31 ("These tragedies reinforce our belief that it is essential that both the Congress and the Executive Branch take measures, such as the present bill, to deter terrorist attacks against American nationals overseas..."); H.R.REP. NO. 102-1040 at 4 ("Summary and Purpose: The purpose of H.R. 2222, the 'Antiterrorism Act of 1991' is to provide a new civil cause of action for international terrorist attacks against U.S. nationals.").

These general statements of purpose, not addressed to the issue here in dispute, offer little if any guidance. In the absence of any limiting language in the statute, the court will not limit the scope of Section 2333(a) to physical injuries to U.S. nationals. The congressional purpose was to grant a remedy to U.S. nationals and their families who suffered from injury to an individual or property as a result of international terrorism. The claims of the U.S. nationals suing based on their nonphysical injuries resulting from acts of international terrorism will not be dismissed.

Claims Based Upon Violations of 18 U.S.C. §2339B(a)(2)

The fifth counts of the Linde and Coulter complaints each allege that the Bank, by failing to comply with its obligation under 18 U.S.C. §2339B(a)(2) to retain any funds under its control in which it knows a foreign terrorist organization has an interest and to report the existence of such funds to the Secretary of the Treasury, provides material support to a foreign terrorist organization, in violation of 18 U.S.C. §2339B(a)(1). (The Litle complaint does not assert this claim.) Section 2339B(a)(2) provides that,

Except as authorized by the Secretary [of the Treasury], any financial institution that becomes aware that it has possession of, or control over, any funds in which a foreign terrorist organization, or its agent, has an interest, shall-

(A) retain possession of, or maintain control over, such funds; and

(B) report to the Secretary the existence of such funds in accordance with regulations issued by the Secretary.

Subsection (b) of Section 2339B provides for civil penalties imposed by the government against financial institutions that violate these requirements.

Plaintiffs appear to contend that violations of Section 2339B(a)(2) constitute, in and of themselves, material support for foreign terrorist organizations. As I held in my decision denying a preliminary injunction based on alleged violations of Section 2339B(a)(2), violations of the reporting requirements "are neither criminal violations nor acts of international terrorism, as defined by the statute." *Linde,* 353 F.Supp.2d at 331. Because this claim is an attempt to recast civil violations of the reporting requirements as criminal acts of providing material support, it must be dismissed. Thus, Count Five of the Linde First Amended Complaint and Count Five of the Coulter complaint are each dismissed.

I note, however, that plaintiffs' claim that the Bank provided material support to a designated FTO (found in Count Four of all three complaints), which does constitute an act of international terrorism, may be shown through a variety of evidentiary means, which may include proof of violations of the requirements regarding retention and reporting of FTO funds.

Intentional Infliction of Emotional Distress

Finally, those Linde and Litle plaintiffs who sue as survivors bring common law claims for intentional infliction of emotional distress. Defendant argues that the complaints fail to state a claim for intentional infliction of emotional distress and that the claims of a number of plaintiffs are time barred.

The tort of intentional infliction of emotional distress has four elements: (1) extreme and outrageous conduct; (2) intent to cause, or disregard of a substantial probability of causing, severe emotional distress; (3) a causal connection between the conduct and the injury; and (4) severe emotional distress. *E.g., Howell v. New York Post Co., Inc.,* 81 N.Y.2d 115, 121, 596 N.Y.S.2d 350, 612 N.E.2d 699 (1993).

Violent terrorist attacks, almost by definition, qualify as the type of conduct that is "so outrageous in character, and so extreme in degree, as to go beyond all possible bounds of decency, and to be regarded as atrocious, and utterly intolerable in a civilized community," as to come within the ambit of the tort. *See* Restatement (Second) of Torts, §46 cmt. d (1965). However, plaintiffs' claims of intentional infliction of emotional distress do not seek to reach the conduct of the terrorists who carried out the suicide attacks; rather, they are aimed at the Bank's conduct in supporting those who are responsible for carrying out the attacks. Although plaintiffs' allegations are sufficient to make out statutory claims under the ATA, which is aimed at "cut[ting] off the flow of money to terrorists at every point along the causal chain of violence," *Boim*, 291 F.3d at 1021, the Bank's conduct is too removed to support common law claims for intentional infliction of emotional distress. If plaintiffs succeed in proving their civil claims under the ATA, they will be able to recover for their emotional damages. However, the allegations in the complaints fall short of stating a separate claim for intentional infliction of emotional distress against the Bank under the common law. [FN13]

FN13. Defendant also argues that the complaints should be dismissed on the ground of *forum non conveniens* and that plaintiffs should refile their claims in Jordan. The ATA has a provision that deals expressly with issues concerning convenience of the forum in cases brought under Section 2333. It reads:

The district court shall not dismiss any action brought under section 2333 of this title on the grounds of the inconvenience or inappropriateness of the forum chosen, unless-

(1) the action may be maintained in a foreign court that has jurisdiction over the subject matter and over all the defendants;

(2) that foreign court is significantly more convenient and appropriate; and

(3) that foreign court offers a remedy which is substantially the same as the one available in the courts of the United States. 18 U.S.C. §2334(d).

Defendant has failed to meet its burden of showing that this heightened standard for dismissal under the ATA has been met. Given the deference owed to plaintiffs' choice of forum; that the locations of the activities alleged are Israel and New York; the defendant's failure to establish that a Jordanian court would be significantly more convenient and appropriate; and the absence of "substantially the same" remedy in a Jordanian court, dismissal on *forum non conveniens* grounds is denied.

CONCLUSION

The motions to dismiss are granted in part and denied in part. The following claims are dismissed: Count Five (violation of the reporting requirements in 18 U.S.C. §2339B(a)(2))

and Count Eight (intentional infliction of emotional distress) of the Linde Complaint; Count Seven (intentional infliction of emotional distress) of the Litle Complaint; and Count Five (violation of the reporting requirements in 18 U.S.C. §2339B(a)(2)) of the Coulter Complaint. Defendant's motions to dismiss the remaining claims are denied.

SO ORDERED.

Notes:

1.   Why is the correct interpretation and Arabic translation of "martyr" crucial in this case? What does this concern suggest about the difficulties adjudicating terrorism cases in U.S. courts?

2.   Why is the liberal pleading standard in federal court particularly important in terrorism cases? How does this standard also create a trap for plaintiffs who typically confront motions to dismiss in response to their often vague or conclusory allegations?

3.   Consistent with their nature, most terrorists perform their activities in illegal and clandestine groups and are unlikely to maintain records in the manner of commercial or governmental organizations. How do plaintiffs typically obtain information about the actions of terrorists? Does the fact that Arab Bank appeared in this case help or hinder the plaintiffs?

4.   How is the "death and dismemberment benefit plan," which the bank allegedly administered, particularly important with respect to HAMAS terrorism? According to the plaintiffs, why is this plan important to their case? Why are HAMAS members incentivized by this plan? What is the bank's factual response to this allegation?

5.   If plaintiffs are successful, what impact will a judgment have with respect to extending liability to banking organizations in the non-terrorism context?

6.   What effect will the following holding of the court have on banking institutions generally?

> It is not necessary that they allege that Arab Bank either planned, or intended, or even knew about the particular act which injured a plaintiff. *See Halberstam*, 705 F.2d at 487. The factual allegations of the complaints sufficiently support an inference that Arab Bank and the terrorist organizations

were participants in a common plan under which Arab Bank would supply necessary financial services to the organizations which would themselves perform the violent acts. Administering the death and dismemberment benefit plan further supports not only the existence of an agreement but Arab Bank's knowing and intentional participation in the agreement's illegal goals. No more is required.

7. What is the relationship between the court's finding and the decision in *Boim*? Does the court reject the analysis in *Boim*? A hint is found in footnote 9, which states, "Insofar as *Boim* is read as requiring more than knowledge that the organization to which material support is provided is designated or is engaged in terrorist activities, I find that it is not consistent with the language of Section 2339B."

8. What exactly must the plaintiffs prove under §2339A-C to be successful?

9. How does the court distinguish *In re: Terrorist Attacks on September 11, 2001*, 349 F.Supp.765 (S.D.N.Y. 2005)? What evidence did Arab Bank provide to prove that it performed only routine banking services?

10. What does the dismissal of the plaintiffs' intentional infliction of emotional distress claims suggest about the efficacy of the Klinghoffer Act?

Strauss v. Credit Lyonnais, S.A., No. 06-0702, 2007 WL 2296832 (E.D.N.Y. Aug. 6, 2007).

SIFTON, Senior Judge.

Plaintiffs, United States citizens and the estates, survivors and heirs of deceased United States citizens, who have been or were victims of terrorist attacks in Israel, bring this action against defendant, Crédit Lyonnais, S.A. ("Crédit Lyonnais") alleging that defendant is civilly liable to the plaintiffs for damages, pursuant to 18 U.S.C. §2333(a), [FN1] because it (1) aided and abetted the murder, attempted murder, and serious bodily injury of American nationals located outside the United States in violation of 18 U.S.C. §2332; (2) knowingly provided material support or resources to a foreign terrorist organization ("FTO") [FN2] in violation of 18 U.S.C. §2339B; [FN3] and (3) unlawfully and willfully provided or collected funds with the intention that such funds would be used, or with the knowledge that such funds would be used for terrorist purposes in violation of 18 U.S.C. §2339C. [FN4] Now before this Court is defendant's motion

to dismiss plaintiffs' claims based on the Eleventh, Twelfth and Thirteenth Attacks alleged in the Complaint, pursuant to Federal Rule of Civil Procedure 12(b)(6), on the grounds that these claims are time-barred. For the reasons set forth below, defendant's motion to dismiss claims based on the Eleventh, Twelfth and Thirteenth Attacks is granted.

FN1. The statute reads, in relevant part:
Any national of the United States injured in his or her person, property, or business by reason of an act of international terrorism or his or her estate, survivors, or heirs, may sue therefor in any appropriate district court of the United States and shall recover threefold the damages he or she sustains and the cost of the suit, including attorney's fees.
18 U.S.C. §2333(a).

FN2. Pursuant to Section 209 of the Immigration and Nationality Act, 8 U.S.C. §1189, the Secretary of State, in consultation with the Secretary of Treasury and the Attorney General may designate an organization as a foreign terrorist organization if:
(a) the organization is a foreign organization;
(b) the organization engages in terrorist activity or terrorism, or retains the capability and intent to engage in terrorist activity or terrorism; and
(c) the terrorist activity or terrorism of the organization threatens the security of United States nationals or the national security of the United States.

FN3. The statute reads, in relevant part:
Whoever knowingly provides material support or resources to a foreign terrorist organization, or attempts or conspires to do so, [is guilty of a crime]…To violate this paragraph a person must have knowledge that the organization is a designated terrorist organization…has engaged in terrorist activity…or that the organization has engaged in or engages in terrorism.
18 U.S.C. §2339B.

FN4. The statute reads, in relevant part:
Whoever…by any means, directly or indirectly, unlawfully and willfully provides or collects funds with the intention that such funds be used, or with the knowledge that such funds are to be used in full or in part, in order to carry out… [an] act intended to cause death or serious bodily injury to a civilian, or to any other person not taking an active part in the hostilities in a situation of armed conflict, when the purpose of such act, by its nature or context, is to intimidate a population or to compel a government or an international organization to do or to abstain from doing any act, shall be punished as prescribed in subsection (d)(1).
18 U.S.C. §2339C.

Factual Background

Familiarity with the underlying facts of this case is presumed. They are discussed at length in this Court's prior decision in this action, *Strauss v. Crédit Lyonnais, S.A.,* 2006 WL 2862704 (E.D.N.Y.2006). Only those facts relevant to the present motion are referred to herein. They are drawn from the Amended Complaint and are presumed to be true for the purposes of this motion, as required by applicable case law. *See Chambers v. Time Warner, Inc.,* 282 F.3d 147, 152 (2d Cir.2002).

The Terrorist Attacks

In the Amended Complaint, plaintiffs identify thirteen separate attacks between 2001 and 2003 which caused their injuries. Of relevance to the present motion are three attacks which occurred in 2001.

1. [On] December 1, 2001 Nabil Halabiya and Osama Mohammad Id Bahr, two HAMAS suicide bombers, blew themselves up in a pedestrian mall in Jerusalem as part of a coordinated double suicide bombing…Eleven (11) people were murdered and over one hundred (100) people were injured. Bahr had been recruited by Jamal al-Tawil, the chairman of the Al-Islah Charitable Society since 2000. The Al-Islah Charitable Society is one of HAMAS's key charitable front organizations in the West Bank. Amend. Compl., ¶ 308 (the "Eleventh Attack").

2. On August 9, 2001, a HAMAS suicide bomber detonated a bomb packed with nails and metal bolts at the Sbarro's Pizzeria in Jerusalem. Fifteen (15) people were killed in this attack…and approximately one hundred and thirty (130) people were injured. The suicide bomber was identified as Izz Ad-Din Shahail Ahmad Al-Masri. Amend. Compl., ¶¶ 360-362 (the "Twelfth Attack").

3. On March 28, 2001, Fadi Attallah Yusuf Amer, a HAMAS suicide bomber, blew himself up outside a gas station near Kfar Sava, killing tow teenagers waiting for a bus…Four (4) other people were injured. Amend. Compl., ¶ 439 (the "Thirteenth Attack").

Comité de Bienfaisance et de Secours aux Palestinians a/k/a Comité Bienfaisance pour la Solidarité avec la Palestiene ("CBSP")

CBSP is a non-profit corporation organized in 1990 with its headquarters in France. According to plaintiffs, CBSP is part of HAMAS's fund-raising infrastructure. In 1997 the Government of Israel declared CBSP an "unlawful organization" because of its affiliation with HAMAS and the support it provided to HAMAS front organizations. Between 2001 and 2003, French authorities also investigated CBSP's alleged terrorist connections. In August 2003, President George W. Bush identified CBSP as a HAMAS fund-raising entity and placed it on the Office of Foreign Assets Control ("OFAC") list as a Specially Designated Global Terrorist ("SDGT") organization.

CBSP's Accounts at Crédit Lyonnais

CBSP opened accounts at Crédit Lyonnais in 1990. In 2000 the defendant began to notice unusual transfers of funds as described below occurring in CBSP's main accounts. Crédit Lyonnais did not, however, close CBSP's accounts or freeze any funds at that time. In 2002 Crédit Lyonnais began the process of closing CBSP's accounts. In September 2003 Crédit Lyonnais completed the process of closing CBSP's accounts at the bank.

The plaintiffs allege that between 2000 and 2003 Crédit Lyonnais knowingly transferred funds from CBSP to institutions within HAMAS's financial division, including the Orphan Care Society, Al-Islah, the Ramallah Al-Bireh Charitable Society, the Jenin Charity Committee, the Hebron Islamic Association, the Tulkarem Charity Committee, Al-Mujama al-Islami, the Islamic Charitable Society in the Gaza Strip, Al-Salah Society and the Muslim Youth Association of Hebron (collectively, "HAMAS controlled organizations").

Procedural Background

On October 5, 2006, this Court dismissed the claims arising from the Eleventh, Twelfth and Thirteenth Attacks as barred by the statute of limitations, since those attacks occurred, respectively, on December 1, 2001, August 9, 2001, and March 28, 2001 and the Original Complaint was filed on February 16, 2006, after the expiration of the four year limitations period set forth in 18 U.S.C. §2335(a). However, plaintiffs were granted leave to amend their Complaint. *See Strauss,* 2006 WL 2862704, at *1.

On November 6, 2006, plaintiffs filed an Amended Complaint which is substantively the same as the Original Complaint with the exception of several new paragraphs discussing "Plaintiffs' Knowledge Concerning Defendant's Conduct." These paragraphs state that plaintiffs do not speak or read French or Arabic fluently; that plaintiffs were unaware of the fact that CBSP had a financial relationship with the defendant or that defendant provided material support to HAMAS, nor could such information have been obtained through the exercise of reasonable diligence; that defendant never publicly disclosed that CBSP was its customer or disclosed the nature of the financial services provided to CBSP or the beneficiaries of wire transfers it sent to third parties on behalf of CBSP, preventing plaintiffs from discovering the relationship between defendant and CBSP; that plaintiffs do not possess any expert or technical knowledge concerning the means by which HAMAS, CBSP and other entities receive or transfer funds from persons or entities in Europe to HAMAS and had no access to non-public information as to defendant's relationship with such entities; that plaintiffs could not, through due diligence, have been aware of any suspicious activity reports generated with respect to CBSP due to the confidentiality of such reports, and that plaintiffs did not have access to international banking or wire transfer records or French police or intelligence reports concerning CBSP, HAMAS or banks which provided services to those entities. Amend. Compl., ¶¶ 537-541. According to plaintiffs' Amended Complaint, "plaintiffs could not have discovered, through the exercise of reasonable diligence, that Crédit Lyonnaise provided financial services to either CBSP or HAMAS at any time before the second quarter of 2005, when non-public information regarding defendant's relationship with CBSP first became available to plaintiffs." *Id* . at ¶ 542.

Discussion

Defendant again moves to dismiss claims based on the Eleventh, Twelfth and Thirteenth Attacks on the grounds that they are barred by the four year statute of limitations in 18 U.S.C. §2335(a). [FN5] Plaintiffs argue that the claims are subject to the tolling provisions of 18 U.S.C. §2335(b) as well as the diligence-discovery rule of accrual and equitable tolling.

FN5. 18 U.S.C. §2335(b) provides that, for actions brought under §2333(a),

The time of the absence of the defendant from the United States or from any jurisdiction in which the same or similar action arising from the same facts may be maintained by the plaintiff, or of any concealment of the defendant's whereabouts, shall not be included in the 4-year period set forth in subsection (a).

Plaintiffs, in their brief, concede that this "concealment" provision is not applicable here.

I. Section 2335 Tolling

18 U.S.C. §2335(b) provides for tolling of the four year statute of limitations for actions brought under 18 U.S.C. §2333. Section 2335(b) reads:

The time of the absence of the defendant from the United States or from any jurisdiction in which the same or a similar action arising from the same facts may be maintained by the plaintiff, or of any concealment of the defendant's whereabouts, shall not be included in the 4-year period set forth in subsection (a).

According to plaintiffs, since the nature of Crédit Lyonnais's association with CBSP was "inherently self-concealing" due to the provisions of French banking law which prohibited Crédit Lyonnais from revealing confidential customer information or the fact that CBSP was a customer, this tolling statute should apply. [FN6] Plaintiffs' Memorandum of Law, p.1 n.2. As I noted in my previous Opinion in this action, "[r]esearch by the parties and by this Court has produced no decision interpreting this 'concealment' provision." *Strauss,* 2006 WL 2862704, at *8. [FN7]

FN6. The relevant secrecy law is Article L 511-33 of the French Monetary and Financial Code, which reads:
Any member of a Board of Directors and, if applicable, of a Supervisory Board, and any person who, in whatever capacity, participates in the management or administration of a credit institution or is employed by one, is bound by professional secrecy, under the terms and subject to the penalties provided for in Article L. 571-4.
See http://195.83.177.9/code/liste.phtml?lang=uk & c=25 & r=920/

FN7. In that Opinion, I found that "the parameters of section 2335(b)'s concealment doctrine need not be determined here because the complaint makes no allegation that defendant concealed its identity as CBSP's bank or its transfer of funds for CBSP to various HAMAS controlled organizations." *Strauss,* 2006 WL 2862704, at *8. Plaintiffs now allege Crédit Lyonnais's connection to the CBSP was "self-concealing" due to the nature of French law.

"Whereabouts"

Under the plain language of the statute, the limitations period is tolled for 'concealment' only when a defendant conceals his "whereabouts," which means "[t]he general locale where a person or thing is." BLACK'S LAW DICTIONARY 1626, (8th ed. 2004) ("BLACK'S"). That definition is consistent with the first half of §2335(b), which tolls the limitations period when a defendant is physically absent from a jurisdiction in which the action can be brought. Accordingly, under a plain reading of the statute, the tolling period in §2335(b) was designed to remedy problems related to a court's ability to assert jurisdiction over a defendant. [FN8]

FN8. Plaintiffs make no claim that Crédit Lyonnais ever concealed its location or otherwise put itself outside of the jurisdiction of the courts of this or any other country.

However, plaintiffs cite legislative history of this provision which indicates that a defendant's concealment of "where-abouts" encompasses concealment of his identity and acts. Specifically, plaintiffs cite the Senate Report on the Anti-Terrorism Act of 1992 ("ATA"), [FN9] which states that: "This section provides for a 4-year statute of limitations, but in recognition of the peculiar characteristics of terrorism, it tolls the statute of limitation during any periods when the terrorists have concealed their *acts or identities* or remain outside of the United States." [FN10] S.Rep. 102-342 (Report on P.L. 102-572, Federal Courts Administration Act of 1992, July 27, 1992) (emphasis added).

FN9. Sections 2333 and 2335 were enacted pursuant to the ATA, signed into law on October 29, 1992.
FN10. There is no other legislative history referring to this provision. An earlier version of §2335, with the identical text, was signed into law in 1990 and then repealed in 1991, apparently due to the fact that it was included in the 1990 act by mistake. *See* Pub.L. 101-519, §132(b)(4).

There is no legislative history discussing the issue of "concealment" in the 1990 version.
"The starting point for [the] interpretation of a statute is always its language," *Community for Creative Non-Violence v. Reid,* 490 U.S. 730, 739, 109 S.Ct. 2166, 104 L.Ed.2d 811 (1989) and, as the Supreme Court has "stated time and again...courts must presume that a legislature says in a statute what it means and means in a statute what it says there." *Connecticut Nat. Bank v. Germain.* 503 U.S. 249, 253, 112 S.Ct. 1146, 117 L.Ed.2d 391 (1992). "When the words of a statute are unambiguous, then, this first canon is also the last: 'judicial inquiry is complete.' " *Id.* (quoting *Rubin v. U.S.,* 449 U.S. 424, 430, 101 S.Ct. 698, 66 L.Ed.2d 633 (1981)); *see also Exxon Mobil Corp. v. Allapattah Services, Inc.,* 545 U.S. 546, 568, 125 S.Ct. 2611, 162 L.Ed.2d 502 (2005) ("As we have repeatedly held, the authoritative statement is the statutory text, not the legislative history or any other extrinsic material. Extrinsic materials have a role in statutory interpretation only to the extent they shed a reliable light on the enacting Legislature's understanding of otherwise ambiguous terms."); [FN11] *Aslanidis v. U.S. Lines, Inc.,* 7 F.3d 1067, 1073 (2d Cir.1993) ("If the words of a statute are unambiguous, judicial inquiry should end, and the law interpreted according to the plain meaning of its words."); *but see U.S. v. Skinner,* 946 F.2d 176, 178 (2d Cir.1991) ("Where...the statutory language is unambiguous, absent legislative history that contradicts that language, we will not adopt a different construction of the statute.").

FN11. The Court in *Allapattah Services* noted that one of the problems with relying on legislative history is that judicial reliance on legislative materials like committee reports, which are not themselves subject to the requirements of Article I, may give unrepresentative committee members-or, worse yet, unelected staffers and lobbyists-both the power and the incentive to attempt strategic manipulations of legislative history to secure results they were unable to achieve through the statutory text.
545 U.S. 546 at 568.

In the present situation, the statutory language is clear and precise and unambiguous. Without the single Senate Report cited by plaintiffs, there would no reason whatsoever to doubt that "whereabouts" refers the location of defendants who were concealing their whereabouts so as to avoid the exercise of jurisdiction by courts. Nor is this one of those "rare and exceptional circumstances...when a contrary legislative intent is clearly expressed." *Ardestani v. I.N.S.,* 502 U.S. 129, 136, 112 S.Ct. 515, 116 L.Ed.2d 496 (1991) (internal citations and quotations omitted); *see also Watt v. Alaska,* 451 U.S. 259, 266, 101 S.Ct. 1673, 68 L.Ed.2d 80 (1981) ("[T]he plain-meaning rule is...an axiom of experience than a rule of law, and does not preclude consideration of persuasive evidence if it exists...The circumstances of the enactment of particular legislation may persuade a court that Congress did not intend words of common meaning to have their literal effect.") (internal citations and quotations omitted). Granting plaintiff's argument that the ATA was developed in order to make it easier for U.S. citizens to effectively prosecute civil lawsuits against terrorists, Congress's having limited its tolling rule to only those cases in which a defendant's presence in an appropriate jurisdiction could not be ascertained does not contradict that purpose. Indeed, as cited by plaintiffs, in introducing the original version of the ATA, Senator Charles E. Grassley stated that "[u]nfortunately, victims who turn to the common law of tort or Federal statutes, find it virtually impossible to pursue their claims because of reluctant courts and *numerous jurisdictional hurdles.*" 136 Cong. Rec. 7592 (1990) (emphasis added). Since the plain meaning of the statute resolves "jurisdictional hurdles," such a reading is consistent with the overall legislative intent of the ATA and there is no "reason to believe that strict adherence to the language of the Act would subvert its purpose." *U.S. v. Payden,* 759 F.2d 202, 204 (2d Cir.1985). Accordingly, since plaintiffs make no allegation that Crédit Lyonnais concealed its whereabouts, the tolling provision of §2335(b) is unavailable.

"Concealment"

Assuming, *arguendo,* that the statute tolls the limitations period for those who conceal their acts or identities, and not just their location, §2335(b) is only available if there was "concealment," which plaintiffs have not alleged. According to plaintiffs, information which cannot be discovered due to the impact of French law is properly considered 'concealed' under the tolling statute. Black's Law Dictionary defines concealment as:

1. The act of refraining from disclosure; esp., an act by which one prevents or hinders the discovery of something; a cover-up. 2. The act of removing from sight or notice; hiding. 3. Insurance. The insured's intentional withholding from the insurer material facts that increase the insurer's risk and that in good faith ought to be disclosed...

"Concealment is an affirmative act intended or known to be likely to keep another from learning of a fact of which he would otherwise have learned. Such affirmative action is always equivalent to a misrepresentation and has any effect that a misrepresentation would have..." Restatement (Second) of Contracts §160 cmt. a (1979).

active concealment. The concealment by words or acts of something that one has a duty to reveal...

fraudulent concealment. The affirmative suppression or hiding, with the intent to deceive or defraud, of a material fact or circumstance that one is legally (or, sometimes, morally) bound to reveal...

passive concealment. The act of maintaining silence when one has a duty to speak...

BLACK'S at 306-07; *see also Caputo v. Pfizer, Inc.,* 267 F.3d 181, 190 (2d Cir.2001) (Distinguishing "fraud" from "concealment" and defining concealment to mean "engaged in acts to hinder...discovery."); *In re Shoesmith,* 135 F. 684, 687 (7th Cir.1905) (Concealment in bankruptcy law "implies an act done or procured to be done, which is intended to prevent or hinder. It covers something more, however, than a mere failure to disclose.") (Cited in *Continental Bank & Trust Co. of New York v. Winter,* 153 F.2d 397, 399 (2d Cir.1946)).

In each of these definitions, concealment is an act by one party which prevents another from discovering something, by affirmatively hiding information or by failing to disclose information which one had some obligation to reveal. [FN12] "Concealment" does not refer to a situation in which something simply could not be discovered due to circumstances. In the present case, there is alleged no affirmative act performed to prevent plaintiffs from discovering that CBSP was a client of Crédit Lyonnais, nor is it alleged that Crédit Lyonnais was under an obligation to disclose such information and chose not to. [FN13] What is alleged

is simply that Crédit Lyonnais kept its client information a secret in accordance with French law.

FN12. Even the first definition, "refraining from disclosure" suggests that the one who concealed information had some obligation to disclose and decided not to do so.

FN13. In fact, plaintiffs stated at oral argument that "we're not arguing that [defendant] had any obligation to [disclose the identity of their customers." Transcript of Record at 4, *Strauss, et al v. Crédit Lyonnais,* No. 06-CV-0702 (June 7, 2007).

A review of case law dealing with the term "self-concealing," which is used by plaintiffs, reveals that the term is used in reference to fraud where "the defendant...engaged in some misleading, deceptive or otherwise contrived action or scheme, in the course of committing the wrong, that was designed to mask the cause of action." *S.E.C. v. Jones,* 476 F.Supp.2d 374, 382 (S.D.N.Y.2007) (internal quotations omitted). [FN14] For example, "passing off of a sham article as one that is genuine is an inherently self-concealing fraud, whether what is passed off is a fake vase sold as a real antique...or a collusive bid purporting to reflect genuine competition." *State of N.Y. v. Hendrickson Bros., Inc.,* 840 F.2d 1065, 1083 (2d Cir.1988) (internal citations omitted); *see also* BLACK'S at 307 ("concealment rule" applies where "defendant's conduct...hinders or prevents a plaintiff from discovering the existence of a claim."). Again, this application of the term 'concealment' requires some affirmative act of hiding or deception by defendants. [FN15] Since none has been alleged, the tolling provision of §2335(b) does not apply.

FN14. This term is used in connection with the common law "concealment rule" for fraud which states that

when there has been no negligence or laches on the part of a plaintiff in coming to the knowledge of the fraud which is the foundation of the suit, and when the fraud has been concealed, or is of such character as to conceal itself, the statute does not begin to run until the fraud is discovered by, or becomes known to, the party suing, or those in privity with him.

Bailey v. Glover, 21 Wall. 342, 88 U.S. 342, 349-50, 22 L.Ed. 636 (1874).

FN15. I also note that most circuits which have interpreted the term "conceals" in the misprision of felony statute to require an affirmative act of concealment. *See* 18 U.S.C. §4 ("Whoever, having knowledge of the actual commission of a felony cognizable by a court of the United States, conceals and does not as soon as possible make known the same to some judge..."); *U.S. v. Sampol,* 636 F.2d 621,

653 (D.C.Cir.1980); *U.S. v. Wilkes,* 1992 WL 188133, at *2 (4th Cir.1992); *U.S. v. Hall,* 1995 WL 449627, at *10 (5th Cir.1995); *Burman v. I.N.S.,* 1994 WL 378354, at *3 (6th Cir.1994); *U.S. v. Daddano,* 432 F.2d 1119, 1124 (7th Cir.1970); *U.S. v. Bolden,* 368 F.3d 1032, 1037 (8th Cir.2004); *U.S. v. Rivera,* 1994 WL 497317, at *2 (9th Cir.1994); *U.S. v. Gould,* 1996 WL 108497, at *1 (10th Cir.1996); *Itani v. Ashcroft,* 298 F.3d 1213, 1216 (11th Cir.2002). In *U.S. v. Caraballo-Rodriguez,* 480 F.3d 62 (1st Cir.2007), the First Circuit suggested, without deciding, that the statute may not require an affirmative act. However, even in that case, it is clear that the court believed the statute created a disclosure obligation, which plaintiffs have not alleged here.

II. Diligence-Discovery Rule & Equitable Tolling

To evaluate plaintiffs' arguments regarding the diligence-discovery rule of accrual and equitable tolling, it is first appropriate to distinguish between the doctrines, concepts which often overlap in case law. *See Heins v. Potter,* 271 F.Supp.2d 545, 552 (S.D.N.Y.2003) (noting that statute of limitations law is "less than straightforward").

Normally, a cause of action accrues on the date a party is injured. *See Heins v. Potter,* 271 F.Supp.2d 545, 552 (S.D.N.Y.2003) (citing *Cada v. Baxter Healthcare Corp.,* 920 F.2d 446, 450 (7th Cir.1990)). The so-called 'diligence-discovery rule' cited by plaintiffs acts to delay the date of accrual "where a plaintiff demonstrates that his injury was inherently unknowable at the time he was injured." *Barret v. U.S.,* 689 F.2d 324, 327 (2d Cir.1982); *see also Guccione v. U.S.,* 670 F.Supp. 527, 536 (S.D.N.Y.1987). [FN16]

FN16. "This special rule of accrual may also be applied where it has been shown that the plaintiff was blamelessly ignorant of his claim due to the [defendant's] deliberate concealment of its facts." *Guccione,* 670 F.Supp. at 536. Plaintiffs have not alleged any deliberate concealment.
In contrast, the doctrine of equitable tolling applies after the claim has already accrued, "suspending the statute of limitations to prevent unfairness to a diligent plaintiff." *Haekal v. Refco, Inc.,* 198 F.3d 37, 43 (2d Cir.1999) (quoting *Irwin v. Department of Veterans Affairs,* 498 U.S. 89, 95, 111 S.Ct. 453, 112 L.Ed.2d 435 (1990)) (internal quotation marks omitted); *see also Potter,* 271 F.Supp.2d at 552-54 ("[W]here a defendant's wrongful, affirmative conduct prevents a plaintiff from learning that he has been injured, the plaintiff's cause of action has not accrued…However, when a plaintiff knows or should have known of his injury-i.e., his claim has accrued-but the defendant's wrongful, affirmative acts prevent him from learning about other facts that might support a cause of action, then tolling may apply.") (internal

citations omitted). With this distinction in mind, I evaluate the claims alleged to have arisen from the Eleventh, Twelfth and Thirteenth Attacks.

Diligence-Discovery Rule

As noted, the diligence-discovery rule delays the date of accrual for a cause of action "where a plaintiff demonstrates that his injury was inherently unknowable at the time he was injured." *Barret,* 689 F.2d at 327. To take advantage of this rule, a plaintiff must show that diligence would not have disclosed the relevant facts. *Guccione,* 670 F.Supp. at 536 ("Whether a plaintiff 'should have known' these critical facts, even if he did not actually know them, is decided by reference to whether a reasonable person exercising due and reasonable diligence would have discovered such facts.").

The Second Circuit has made clear that when evaluating the date of accrual under the diligence-discovery rule, the cause of action accrues when a plaintiff is sufficiently aware of the facts so as to have knowledge regarding the existence of a legal claim. In *Kronisch v. U.S.,* 150 F.3d 112, 121 (2d Cir.1998), the Second Circuit stated that the 'diligence-discovery rule' applies "where plaintiff would reasonably have had difficulty discerning the fact or cause of injury at the time it was inflicted." *Kronisch v. U.S.,* 150 F.3d 112, 121 (2d Cir.1998). The court in *Kronisch* went on to note that "[d]iscovery of the 'critical facts' of injury and causation is not an exacting requirement…[requiring knowledge only of] the basic facts of the injury, i.e., knowledge of the injury's existence and knowledge of its cause or of the person or entity that inflicted it." *Id.* (internal citations and quotations omitted). Further, the court noted that the "plaintiff need not know each and every relevant fact of his injury or even that the injury implicates a cognizable legal claim. Rather, a claim will accrue when the plaintiff knows, or should know, enough of the critical facts of injury and causation to protect himself by seeking legal advice." *Id.* (internal citations and quotations omitted). Accordingly, under *Kronisch,* the essential question determining the time of accrual is at what point a plaintiff is sufficiently aware of enough critical facts which would lead a reasonable person to seek the advice of an attorney in evaluating the next steps.

Other circuits have held that the diligence-discovery rule does not apply so long as the plaintiff is aware of the injury and its *immediate* cause, so that plaintiff is put on notice to the fact that his legal rights have been invaded. *See Zeleznik v. U.S.,* 770 F.2d 20, 23 (3d Cir.1985) (Where plaintiffs were aware of injury and immediate cause, plaintiffs' claims were time barred even though they could not, through reasonable diligence, have discovered that the government was responsible for the injury since, although the limitations period does not begin to run "until [the injured party] learns of his injury," once a plaintiff is aware of his injury and its *immediate* cause, the statute of limitations begins to run, even if [plaintiff] is not aware of others who were involved in causing the injury…An injured party with the knowledge of injury and its immediate cause is in no worse position than any other plaintiff who must determine whom to sue in a obscure factual context."); *Dyniewicz v. U.S.*, 742 F.2d 484, 486 (9th Cir.1984) ("Discovery of the cause of one's injury, however, does not mean knowing who is responsible for it. The 'cause' is known when the immediate physical cause of the injury is discovered."); *Richman v. U.S.*, 709 F.2d 122, 123-24 (1st Cir.1983) ("[I]f a pedestrian were struck by a negligent driver, the statute would run in favor of his undisclosed employer, and the barkeeper who allowed him to drink too much, even if the pedestrian were ignorant of their existence. There would be no limit to when the government might be sued if a plaintiff could assert ignorance as an excuse for not pursuing her claim within the statutory period."). [FN17]

FN17. As plaintiffs rightly note, the claims in these cases and in *Kronisch* were made under the Federal Tort Claims Act ("FTCA"), and the "Supreme Court has admonished that the courts should carefully construe the statute of limitations for the FTCA so as not to extend the limited waiver of sovereign immunity beyond that which Congress intended." *Zeleznik*, 770 F.2d at 22. However, the rules elucidated in these cases does not appear to be based on any considerations which are peculiar to FTCA claims, nor is there any other reason to believe that the rule of accrual would differ in that context. Moreover, several courts in this circuit, when dealing with private suits, have cited the *Kronisch* standard. *See Potter*, 271 F.Supp.2d at 555; *Pelman ex rel. Pelman v. McDonald's Corp.*, 2003 WL 22052778, at *6 (S.D.N.Y.2003) (overturned on other grounds); *Bronx Chrysler Plymouth, Inc. v. Chrysler Corp.*, 212 F.Supp.2d 233, 244 (S.D.N.Y.2002).

In this case, plaintiffs clearly had access to information which did or should have made them aware of the existence of a cause of action and should have led them to seek counsel shortly after the attacks, namely the facts of their injuries and the role of HAMAS as the organization responsible for such injuries. [FN18] Thus, the fact that they were not aware of all possible defendants is not determinative of plaintiffs' awareness of their potential cause of action and does not delay the date of accrual, even if identification of other defendants was not immediately knowable. [FN19] Accordingly, the claims relating to the Eleventh, Twelfth and Thirteenth Attacks are not subject to tolling under the diligence-discovery rule of accrual.

FN18. As I noted in my previous opinion, evidence was also available as early as 1997 as to CBSP's funding of HAMAS, when the Israeli government designated the first of these groups as a terrorist organization on the basis of its financial support for HAMAS. To the extent that plaintiffs attempt to distinguish this case on the grounds that plaintiffs in other cases had "a circle…[to] look to for a potential defendant," plaintiffs could have looked to HAMAS as a defendant. Transcript of Record at 8. The fact that other actions against HAMAS have resulted in default judgment and non-payment does not mean that plaintiff had no one to bring the action against, just that the particular defendant was, for all intents and purposes, judgment-proof.

FN19. Plaintiffs cite the decision in *Liuzzo v. U.S.*, 485 F.Supp. 1274 (E.D.Mich.1980), in which the children of a civil rights worker murdered by the Ku Klux Klan were allowed to bring suit against the government after the FBI's role in her murder was disclosed even though the statute of limitations has expired, on the grounds that the plaintiffs were unable to discover who had caused them their injury. As noted by the Second Circuit in *Barret*, an essential element in that case was the government's concealment of the FBI's involvement, accomplished by President Johnson's speech on national television confirming that all of the Ku Klux Klan members involved had been arrested due to the diligence of the FBI agents. 689 F.2d at 330 ("[In *Liuzzo*,] as here, misrepresentations and concealed information had justifiably led the plaintiffs to believe that those responsible for their parent's death had been punished.").

Equitable Tolling/Equitable Estoppel

Equitable tolling is available only in "extraordinary" circumstances." *Pearl v. City of Long Beach*, 296 F.3d 76, 85 (2d Cir.2002) (quoting *Miller v. International Telephone & Telegraph Corp.*, 755 F.2d 20, 24 (2d Cir.1985) (internal quotation marks omitted); *see also Chapman v. ChoiceCare Long Island Term Disability Plan*, 288 F.3d 506, 512 (2d Cir.2002) ("[T]he burden of proving that tolling is appropriate rests on the plaintiff."). "Courts may evaluate whether it would be proper to apply [equitable tolling] doctrines, although they are to be applied sparingly," *National R.R. Passenger Corp. v. Morgan*, 536 U.S. 101, 113-114, 122 S.Ct. 2061, 153 L.Ed.2d 106 (2002), and "[p]rocedural requirements established by Congress for gaining access to the federal courts are not to be disregarded by courts out of a vague sympathy for particular litigants." *Baldwin County Welcome Center v. Brown*, 466 U.S. 147, 152, 104 S.Ct. 1723, 80 L.Ed.2d 196 (1984).

Two different tolling doctrines are discussed in the case law, equitable tolling and equitable estoppel. In the Seventh Circuit, "the difference between equitable tolling and equitable estoppel...is the defendant's wrongful conduct"-equitable estoppel applies where the defendant actively prevented the plaintiff from pleading in time, while equitable tolling applies where the plaintiff, exercising due diligence, is unable to obtain the information necessary for his claim through no fault of the defendant." *Potter,* 271 F.Supp.2d at 552 (citing *Cada,* 920 F.2d at 449-451). However, in the Second Circuit, case law requires some affirmative misconduct by a defendant to invoke either doctrine. In *Cerbone v. International Ladies' Garment Workers' Union,* 768 F.2d 45, 49-50 (2d Cir.1985), the Court of Appeals explained: "Unlike equitable tolling, which is invoked in cases where the plaintiff is ignorant of his cause of action because of the defendant's fraudulent concealment, equitable estoppel is invoked in cases where the plaintiff knew of the existence of his cause of action but the defendant's conduct caused him to delay in bringing his lawsuit." *See also Allstate Ins. Co. v. Valley Physical Medicine & Rehabilitation, P.C.,* 475 F.Supp.2d 213, 232 (E.D.N.Y.2007) ("Plaintiffs urge this Court to adopt the Seventh Circuit's standard for equitable tolling, which does not require an effort by the defendant to prevent the plaintiff from suing...In the Second Circuit, however, equitable tolling requires that a plaintiff establish both that there was 'fraudulent concealment' of the violation and the plaintiff exercised 'due diligence' to discover the claim.") (internal citations and quotations omitted); *Shapiro v. William Douglas McAdams, Inc.,* 1995 WL 313120, at *4 (E.D.N.Y.1995) (Declining to adopt the reasoning of other circuits and "reject the Second Circuit holding that equitable tolling requires the employer's affirmative conduct."); *Angotti v. Kenyon & Kenyon,* 929 F.Supp. 651, 656 (S.D.N.Y.1996) ("[J]ust as equitable estoppel is triggered by the defendant's conduct, in this Circuit, the doctrine of equitable tolling is similarly limited."); *Potter,* 271 F.Supp.2d at 554-55 (noting that the distinction between the tolling doctrines in the Second Circuit is that equitable tolling applies when plaintiff "is unaware of facts supporting a cause of action," while equitable estoppel applies "only when a plaintiff is aware of his cause of action."). [FN20]

FN20. In *Veltri v. Building Serv. 32 B-J Pension Fund,* 393 F.3d 318, 323 (2d Cir.2004), the Second Circuit, citing *Cada,* noted that "[t]he relevant question is not the intention underlying defendants' conduct, but rather whether a reasonable plaintiff in the circumstances would have been aware of the existence of a cause of action." However, the court's decision in that case related to a situation where the defendant concealed from the plaintiff information relating to his cause of action, and cited to *Cerbone,* .

Plaintiffs cite to *Jerry Kubecka, Inc. v. Avellino,* 898 F.Supp. 963, 971 (E.D.N.Y.1995), in which the district court noted that tolling depends on "the inability of the plaintiffs to discover the essential facts." However, that case is distinct from the present one since the Complaint alleged that the defendants, members of an organized crime family, used "fraudulent and violent means to conceal their involvement" in the activities which gave rise to the Complaint. *Id.* at 967. Such active concealment is not alleged here. Moreover, the court in *Avellino* specifically cites *Cada* as legal precedent and, as discussed above, the Seventh Circuit's view of equitable estoppel differs from the Second Circuit's, which is controlling precedent in this court. No research reveals case law in which the statute of limitations has been tolled for a blameless defendant.

In the present case, plaintiffs have alleged no conduct on the part of Crédit Lyonnais which prevented plaintiff from discovering Crédit Lyonnais's relationship with CBSP during the limitations period. Indeed, as discussed above, plaintiffs themselves concede that defendant did not fraudulently conceal its activities, alleging only that the activities were "inherently self-concealing." Since the Second Circuit requires some affirmative act by defendants to invoke either tolling doctrine and plaintiffs have alleged no such act, I conclude that plaintiffs have failed to plead facts which demonstrate that equitable tolling or equitable estoppel should apply to the Eleventh, Twelfth and Thirteenth Attacks. [FN21]

FN21. The result that plaintiffs are thus barred from pursuing their claims is consistent with the purpose of limitations periods, which "protect defendants...from incurring liability on stale claims because of lost evidence,...[and] also from bearing the burden of defending against stale claims regardless of whether liability is eventually established." *Steele v. U.S.,* 599 F.2d 823, 829 (7th Cir.1979); *see also Mohasco Corp. v. Silver,* 447 U.S. 807, 826, 100 S.Ct. 2486, 65 L.Ed.2d 532 (1980) ("[I]n the long run, experience teaches that strict adherence to the procedural requirements specified by the legislature is the best guarantee of evenhanded administration of the law.").

Defendant has also argued that common law tolling doctrines are not available where the statutory text, such as §2335(b), explicitly provides the circumstances under which a limitations period may be tolled. *See U.S. v. Beggerly,* 524 U.S. 38, 48, 118 S.Ct. 1862, 141 L.Ed.2d 32 (1998) ("Equitable tolling is not permissible where it is inconsistent with the text of the relevant statute" and a statute that provides "that the statute of limitations will not begin to run until the plaintiff 'knew or should have known of the claim...'

has already effectively allowed for equitable tolling."); *but see Chung v. U.S. Dept. of Justice,* 333 F.3d 273, 277 (D.C.Cir.2003) ("That there is an express provision in the statute for tolling is, to be sure, a factor that weighs against tolling for any reason not specified in the statute...But neither the Supreme Court nor any other court has deemed that negative implication alone sufficient."); *Hedges v. U.S.,* 404 F.3d 744 (3rd Cir.2005). However, since I find that the common law tolling doctrines do not apply to the facts of this case even if they are available, I need not determine whether the statutory text of §2335(b) limits their availability. I also need not determine whether plaintiffs have sufficiently set forth facts in the Complaint demonstrating that they could not, through the exercise of reasonable diligence, have discovered that Crédit Lyonnais served as CBSP's bank.

Conclusion

For the reasons set forth above, defendant's motion to dismiss claims in the Amended Complaint based on the Eleventh, Twelfth and Thirteenth Attacks is granted. The clerk is directed to transmit a copy of the within to all parties.

Notes:

1. After *Strauss,* what avenues are available to plaintiffs in suits against banks? Will bank secrecy and confidentiality laws undermine all attempts by victims to hold liable financial institutions that are suspected of assisting terrorist organizations? What other options were available to the court in balancing the interests of the parties?

2. If banking activities are "inherently self-concealing" and presumably confidential, how would a plaintiff ever learn about a seemingly innocent financial institution that provides financial services (i.e. "material support and assistance") to a terrorist organization or individual terrorists? Would obtaining such information be illegal and implicate plaintiffs criminally?

3. Other attempts to expand the liability of financial institutions on the basis of providing routine banking services have been rejected. In *Stutts v. De Dietrich Group,* 2006 WL 1867060 (E.D.N.Y. 2006) the court dismissed the §2333 claims of Department of Defense contractors working in the Persian Gulf during the 1991 Gulf War. They sought to hold correspondent banks under letters of credit liable for providing support for the sale of goods and services to Iraq (a state sponsor of terrorism in 1991). Relying on the holding in *Boim,* supra, the court dismissed the claims:

> Plaintiffs' sole allegation of conduct by the Bank Defendants is that they issued letters of credit in favor of the Supplier Defendants. *See* Compl. ¶ 111. The plain language of the ATA compels the conclusion that, by engaging in commercial banking activity, the Bank Defendants were not involved in "violent acts or acts dangerous to human life." Nor were their actions designed to coerce civilians or government entities as required under §2331. Thus, the Bank Defendants' conduct does not constitute international terrorism...Plaintiffs in this case are correct that the statutory history of §2331 *et seq., see Boim,* 291 F.3d at 1009-11, indicates Congress's intent that liability under the statute is far-reaching. Nevertheless, plaintiffs fail to sufficiently allege facts showing the Bank Defendants' knowledge and intent.

Id. at 2-3.

Chapter 13

Role of the U.S. Government

13.1 Right to Block Suits, 18 U.S.C. 2336 (c)

§2336. Other limitations

(a) Acts of War.--No action shall be maintained under section 2333 of this title for injury or loss by reason of an act of war.

(b) Limitation on Discovery.--If a party to an action under section 2333 seeks to discover the investigative files of the Department of Justice, the Assistant Attorney General, Deputy Attorney General, or Attorney General may object on the ground that compliance will interfere with a criminal investigation or prosecution of the incident, or a national security operation related to the incident, which is the subject of the civil litigation. The court shall evaluate any such objections in camera and shall stay the discovery if the court finds that granting the discovery request will substantially interfere with a criminal investigation or prosecution of the incident or a national security operation related to the incident. The court shall consider the likelihood of criminal prosecution by the Government and other factors it deems to be appropriate. A stay of discovery under this subsection shall constitute a bar to the granting of a motion to dismiss under rules 12(b)(6) and 56 of the Federal Rules of Civil Procedure. If the court grants a stay of discovery under this subsection, it may stay the action in the interests of justice.

(c) Stay of Action for Civil Remedies.—

(1) The Attorney General may intervene in any civil action brought under section 2333 for the purpose of seeking a stay of the civil action. A stay shall be granted if the court finds that the continuation of the civil action will substantially interfere with a criminal prosecution which involves the same subject matter and in which an indictment has been returned, or interfere with national security operations related to the terrorist incident that is the subject of the civil action. A stay may be granted for up to 6 months. The Attorney General may petition the court for an extension of the stay for additional 6-month periods until the criminal prosecution is completed or dismissed.

(2) In a proceeding under this subsection, the Attorney General may request that any order issued by the court for release to the parties and the public omit any reference to the basis on which the stay was sought.

Note:

1. The Justice Department has intervened to stay a civil terrorism suit under 18 U.S.C. §2336(c). What, if anything, does this suggest about the government's pursuit of terrorists who kill or harm American citizens in foreign countries? What does this suggest about the importance of civil terrorism suits?

13.2 Statement of Interest, 28 U.S.C. §517

Interests of United States in pending suits

The Solicitor General, or any officer of the Department of Justice, may be sent by the Attorney General to any State or district in the United States to attend to the interests of the United States in a suit pending in a court of the United States, or in a court of a State, or to attend to any other interest of the United States.

Notes:

1. After $300 million in judgments were entered in *Knox* and *Ungar* against the Palestinian Authority and the Palestine Liberation Organization, the plaintiffs-judgment creditors sought to attach various assets of the judgment-debtors. The PA and PLO then made repeated demands of the U.S. government to intervene and rescue them from the plaintiff's collection proceedings. The State Department has so far refused all attempts by the PA and PLO to intervene on their behalf, save for when U.S. treaty obligations have been implicated. For example, when the Ungar orphans attached the PLO office building in Manhattan, implicating the Headquarters Agreement (which governs United Nations accred-

ited organizations and their operations), the State Department intervened to thwart the attachment.

2.   Sometimes the government has taken multiple positions in a single case. For instance, in *Rubin* when plaintiffs attached a house formerly used by the Shah of Iran's son in Lubbock, Texas and blocked by the State Department for 25 years, the court sought the opinion of the U.S. government. The Justice Department responded (after 60 days!) in a single sentence: "In response to the Court's Order of September 24, 2004, the United States of America hereby respectfully informs the Court that, under the current legal framework, the United States is not in a position to interpose any objection to the seizure and sale of the property at issue..." *Rubin v. Islamic Republic of Iran*, 03-MC-014 docket #10. Later in another jurisdiction, the government doggedly opposed the Rubin victims' attempt to attach less than $10,000 in Iranian bank accounts. *Rubin v. Islamic Republic of Iran*, 2005 WL 670770 (D.D.C. 2005). While in a third Rubin collection proceeding in Illinois, the State Department filed four separate statements of interest when the victims sought to attach Iranian antiquities held by the University of Chicago.

3.   Frequently there is dramatic irony in the position taken by the U.S. government when victims try to collect their judgments. A good example is found in *Rubin v. Islamic Republic of Iran*, 484 F.3d 149 (2nd Cir. 2007). In New York, the plaintiffs-judgment creditors sought to attach funds held at the Bank of New York in an account titled to Bank Melli, which the U.S. Department of the Treasury had described as a "wholly owned instrumentality" of the Islamic Republic of Iran. During the proceedings, the Department of Justice filed a statement of interest opposing attachment. The district court denied the attachment based on the Terrorism Risk Insurance Act §201, following the position advanced by both Bank Melli and the Department of Justice. A year later, in April 2007, the Second Circuit upheld the decision and noted that the U.S. took the side of Iran "in support of Bank Melli." Shortly thereafter, Bank Melli removed the funds from the United States. A few months later, the United States government took, in its words, "major actions...to counter Iran's bid for nuclear capabilities and support for terrorism by exposing Iranian banks, companies and individuals that have been involved in these dangerous activities and by cutting them off from the U.S. financial system." According to a Treasury Department press release, Bank Melli is "Iran's largest bank [which] provides banking services to entities involved in Iran's nuclear and ballistic missile programs, including entities listed by the U.N. for their involvement in those programs... Through its role as a financial conduit, Bank Melli has facilitated numerous purchases of sensitive materials for Iran's nuclear and missile programs. In doing so, Bank Melli has provided a range of financial services on behalf of Iran's nuclear and missile industries including opening letters of credit and maintaining accounts." The government further noted that Bank Melli "was used to send at least $100,000,000.00" to Iran's terrorist fronts, including HAMAS, who perpetrated the triple suicide bombing which harmed the *Rubin* plaintiffs. Nonetheless, the government cooperated with Iran's terrorism financing arm in court, helped to shield it from legitimate U.S. judgment creditors, and only when its funds were removed from the U.S. did the government take action to block the funds!

4.   In *Acree*, supra, the government filed a motion to intervene two weeks *after* the District Court entered judgment for plaintiffs. While the trial court denied the motion as untimely, the Court of Appeals reversed and found that, "The United States possesses weighty foreign policy interests that are clearly threatened by the entry of judgment for appellees in this case. Although the United States filed its motion after the District Court had entered its judgment, appellees have asserted no prejudice arising from the intervention." *Id.* at 43. What policy considerations give rise to this level of deference by the courts? Would the United States be afforded similar deference in a case to which it was a party, for instance an appeal from an administrative agency or a criminal prosecution?

13.3 Executive Orders
Smith v. Federal Reserve Bank of New York, 346 F.3d 264 (2nd Cir. 2003).

KATZMANN, Circuit Judge.
This litigation arises from the attacks upon the United States on September 11, 2001, and takes place in the context of ongoing American military and reconstruction activity in Iraq. It involves competing claims to the disposition of certain Iraqi assets held by the Federal Reserve Bank of New York. On the one hand, Plaintiffs, who are relatives of victims who perished in the World Trade Center catastrophe, seek a declaration that they are entitled to execute against those assets to satisfy a judgment they hold. On the other hand, Defendants contend that those assets should return to Iraq, where they are desperately needed for military and rebuilding efforts. In a very real sense, this case implicates questions of national security and foreign affairs, as well as immediate experiences of collective loss, fear, and grief.

As a Court, our task is limited to interpreting the statutes governing the disposition of those assets in a way that is faithful to Congressional meaning. Because we conclude that the plain language of the statutes that govern dictates that the funds Plaintiffs seek to attach are no longer available for that purpose, we affirm the judgment of the district court.

BACKGROUND

Plaintiff Raymond Anthony Smith is the half-brother of George Eric Smith and the executor of his brother's estate. George Smith, who worked in the World Trade Center's South Tower, was killed in the September 11 terrorist attack that caused the collapse of both Trade Center Towers. Plaintiff Katherine Soulas is the wife of Timothy Soulas and executrix of his estate. Mr. Soulas, who worked in the North Tower, also died in the September 11 attacks.

Raymond Smith brought an action in the United States District Court for the Southern District of New York (Baer, *J.*) on behalf of the estate on November 14, 2001, pursuant to 18 U.S.C. §2333(a), which authorizes suits to remedy injuries resulting from international terrorism. Smith named the Islamic Emirate of Afghanistan, the Taliban, al Qaeda, and Osama bin Laden as defendants. Katherine Soulas brought a similar action in the Southern District of New York, both individually and on behalf of the estate and her minor children, against the same defendants on November 15, 2001. The district court consolidated the two cases by Order dated January 23, 2002. On June 10, 2002, Smith and Soulas ("Plaintiffs") amended their Complaint to add Saddam Hussein and the Republic of Iraq as defendants pursuant to the Foreign Sovereign Immunities Act, 28 U.S.C. §§1330, 1602-1611 (2003).

None of the defendants appeared. The district court entered a default judgment against all defendants and held an inquest to address various issues, including damages, on February 28, 2003. *See Smith v. Islamic Emirate of Afghanistan,* 262 F.Supp.2d 217, 220 (S.D.N.Y.2003) (" *Smith I*"). In a detailed opinion dated May 16, 2003 (as amended), the district court noted, with respect to sovereign defendants such as Iraq and Hussein, that some quantum of proof as to liability was required to award damages in the event of a default. *See id.* at 222 (citing 28 U.S.C. §1608(e)). The district court then analyzed the decisions of this Court and of the courts in our sister circuits and concluded that the quantum of proof required to sustain damages against a defaulting sovereign is identical to that required to withstand a motion for judg-

ment as a matter of law pursuant to Federal Rule of Civil Procedure 50: whether sufficient evidence is proffered that a reasonable jury could render a verdict in favor of plaintiff. *Id.* at 223-24 (citing *Ungar v. Islamic Republic of Iran,* 211 F.Supp.2d 91, 98 (D.D.C.2002)). Amidst the debate about whether Iraq was involved in the September 11 attacks, the district court reviewed Plaintiffs' proffered evidence, which largely consisted of the expert testimony of Robert James Woolsey, Jr., the former Director of the Central Intelligence Agency, and of Dr. Laurie Mylroie, an expert on Iraq, and concluded that "plaintiffs have shown, albeit barely, 'by evidence satisfactory to the court' that Iraq provided material support to bin Laden and al Qaeda." *Smith I,* 262 F.Supp.2d at 232 (quoting 28 U.S.C. §1608(e)). The court went on to award Plaintiffs total damages of approximately $104 million, with Iraq deemed responsible for approximately $63.5 million of the total. *Id.* at 240-41. Final judgment was entered on July 14, 2003. The judgment is not at issue in this appeal, and we assume its validity for the present purposes.

Plaintiffs brought the present declaratory judgment action against defendants Federal Reserve Bank of New York and the Honorable John W. Snow, Secretary of the Treasury ("Defendants") in July 2003, seeking to satisfy their judgment against the Republic of Iraq by attaching certain Iraqi assets that are held by the Federal Reserve Bank of New York (the "Assets"). Plaintiffs sought this relief pursuant to the authority of section 201 of the Terrorism Risk Insurance Act, Pub. L. No. 107-297, 116 Stat. 2322 (Nov. 26, 2002) ("TRIA"), which states that "in every case in which a person has obtained a judgment against a terrorist party on a claim based upon an act of terrorism,...the blocked assets of that terrorist party...shall be subject to execution...in order to satisfy such judgment." TRIA §201, 116 Stat. at 2337.

Defendants opposed the attachment, moving for summary judgment on two grounds. First, they noted that President George W. Bush, acting pursuant to the authority granted him by the International Emergency Economic Powers Act, 50 U.S.C. §§1701-1707 (as amended) (2003) ("IEEPA"), had issued an Executive Order confiscating all frozen Iraqi assets held by the government and vesting title to those assets in the United States Department of the Treasury. *See* Exec. Order No. 13,290, 68 Fed. Reg. 14,307 (Mar. 20, 2003) (the "March 20th Order"). Therefore, Defendants argued, the funds at issue were no longer "blocked funds" for purposes of TRIA when Plaintiffs' judgment was entered. Defendants further pointed out that section 1503 of the Emergency Wartime Supplemental Appropriations Act of 2003, Pub. L. No. 108-11, 117 Stat. 559 (Apr. 16, 2003) ("EWSAA"), gave the

President the authority to "make inapplicable with respect to Iraq" any law "that applies to countries that have supported terrorism." EWSAA §1503, 117 Stat. at 579. Defendants argued that the President had exercised this authority and made TRIA inapplicable to Iraq, thereby undermining Plaintiffs' right to execute against the funds. *See* Presidential Determination No. 2003-23, 68 Fed. Reg. 26,259 (May 7, 2003); *see also* Message to the Congress Reporting the Declaration of a National Emergency with Respect to the Development Fund for Iraq, 39 Weekly Comp. Pres. Doc. No. 21, at 647-48, 2003 WL 13973315 (May 26, 2003) (specifically referencing TRIA §201 as among the laws made inapplicable by the May 7 Executive Order).

In a thorough opinion, the district court accepted both of Defendants' arguments and granted summary judgment in Defendants' favor. *See Smith v. Fed. Reserve Bank,* No. 03-Civ.-5658(HB), 2003 WL 22103452, 2003 U.S. Dist. LEXIS 15949 (S.D.N.Y. Sept. 11, 2003) (" *Smith II*"). By Order dated September 19, 2003, the district court denied Plaintiffs' motion for a stay pending appeal. Plaintiffs moved before this Court for a stay, and on September 23, 2003, a two-judge panel of this Court enjoined Defendants from disposing of the assets in question until the case was decided on the merits and set an extremely compressed briefing schedule. [FN1]

FN1. A two-judge panel heard the motion because the third judge was recused. *See* 2d Cir. R. 0.14(2).
The case was argued on September 29, 2003. We affirmed the district court and lifted the stay in an unpublished Order issued the same day, with opinion to follow. This is that opinion.

DISCUSSION

The district court based its decision to grant summary judgment in favor of Defendants on two independent grounds. *Smith II,* 2003 WL 22103452, at *6, *8, 2003 U.S. Dist. LEXIS 15949, at *20, *26. We may affirm the decision below on either theory, or on any other basis that we find in the record. *Prisco v. A & D Carting Corp.,* 168 F.3d 593, 610 (2d Cir.1999). We review a district court's decision to grant summary judgment *de novo. See Sherman v. Mamaroneck Union Free School Dist.,* 340 F.3d 87, 92 (2d Cir.2003).

I. The Statutory Scheme

We begin by reviewing the web of statutory provisions that governs the disposition of the Iraqi Assets. These Assets are designated as "blocked" pursuant to sections 202 and 203 of IEEPA, 50 U.S.C. §§1701-1702. IEEPA §1701 authorizes the President to exercise the powers given to him elsewhere in the act to deal with an "unusual and extraordinary threat, which has its source in whole or substantial part outside the United States, to the national security, foreign policy, or economy of the United States." 50 U.S.C. §1701(a). In order to exercise these powers, the President must declare a national emergency with respect to that threat. *Id.* The specific powers that the President may exercise are set forth in 50 U.S.C. §1702. Only two of these powers are relevant to this appeal. The first is set forth in §1702(a)(1)(B), which states that the President may:

investigate, block during the pendency of an investigation, regulate, direct and compel, nullify, void, prevent or prohibit, any acquisition, holding, withholding, use, transfer, withdrawal, transportation, importation or exportation of, or dealing in, or exercising any right, power, or privilege with respect to, or transactions involving, any property in which any foreign country or a national thereof has any interest by any person, or with respect to any property, subject to the jurisdiction of the United States

Id. §1702(a)(1)(B). [FN2] The statute thus grants the President discretion to "block" assets of hostile nations in a time of national emergency, a power that then-President George H.W. Bush exercised in Executive Order 12,722, which froze all assets of the Iraqi Republic in the United States in response to Iraq's invasion of Kuwait in 1990. *See* 55 Fed. Reg. 31,803 (Aug. 2, 1990) (declaring a national emergency and ordering that "[a]ll property and interests in property of the Government of Iraq…are hereby blocked").

FN2. The phrase "block during the pendency of an investigation" was added to §1702 by the USA Patriot Act. *See* Pub. L. No. 107-56, §106, 116 Stat. at 277. There is no dispute as to the President's power to block the assets under the statute's original formulation. *See Dames & Moore v. Regan,* 453 U.S. 654, 670-74, 101 S.Ct. 2972, 69 L.Ed.2d 918 (1981) (recognizing President's pre-Patriot Act authority to block assets pursuant to IEEPA); *cf. Propper v. Clark,* 337 U.S. 472, 483-84, 69 S.Ct. 1333, 93 L.Ed. 1480 (1949) (discussing President's power to block assets pursuant to the Trading with the Enemy Act).
In 2001, Congress amended 50 U.S.C. §1702 to grant the President additional authority. *See* Uniting and Strengthening America by Providing Appropriate Tools Required to Intercept and Obstruct Terrorism (USA PATRIOT) Act of 2001, Pub. L. No. 107-56, §106, 115 Stat. 272, 277-78 (Oct.

26, 2001). The new subsection empowered the President, "when the United States is engaged in armed hostilities," to:

confiscate any property, subject to the jurisdiction of the United States, of any foreign person, foreign organization, or foreign country that he determines has planned, authorized, aided, or engaged in…hostilities or attacks against the United States; and all right, title, and interest in any property so confiscated shall vest, when, as, and upon the terms directed by the President, in such agency or person as the President may designate from time to time, and upon such terms and conditions as the President may prescribe, such interest or property shall be held, used, administered, liquidated, sold, or otherwise dealt with in the interest of and for the benefit of the United States.

50 U.S.C. §1702(a)(1)(C). This provision is the primary statutory authority upon which the President relied in issuing his March 20th Order, which confiscated the Iraqi funds. *See* 68 Fed. Reg. 14,307 ("All blocked funds held in the United States in accounts in the name of [Iraq and its agents] are hereby confiscated and vested in the Department of the Treasury.").

In 2003, Congress again legislated in the area of frozen assets of terrorist-supporting states when it passed section 201 of TRIA. Section 201 states that:

[n]otwithstanding any other provision of law, and except as provided in subsection (b), in every case in which a person has obtained a judgment against a terrorist party on a claim based upon an act of terrorism,…the blocked assets of that terrorist party (including the blocked assets of any agency or instrumentality of that terrorist party) shall be subject to execution or attachment in aid of execution in order to satisfy such judgment to the extent of any compensatory damages for which such terrorist party has been adjudged liable.

TRIA §201(a), 116 Stat. at 2337. Section 201 goes on to define "blocked assets" as "any asset seized or frozen by the United States under…section [ ] 202…of the International Emergency Economic Powers Act (50 U.S.C. §1702)." *Id.* §201(d), 116 Stat. at 2339. There is no dispute that the Iraqi Assets at issue were "blocked funds" within the meaning of TRIA §201(a) at the time the President issued the confiscation Order.

The final statutory provision relevant to this appeal is EWSAA, Pub.L. No. 108-11, 117 Stat. 559 (Apr. 16, 2003).

EWSAA, the most recent enactment of all the statutes at issue here, authorizes the President to "make inapplicable with respect to Iraq…any…provision of law that applies to countries that have supported terrorism." EWSAA §1503, 117 Stat. at 579. Defendants contend that the President exercised this authority on May 7, 2003, when he issued Presidential Determination No. 2003-23 and made TRIA inapplicable to Iraq. *See* 68 Fed. Reg. 26,259. Presidential Determination 2003-23 invokes the authority of EWSAA and states that it "make[s] inapplicable with respect to Iraq…any…provision of law that applies to countries that have supported terrorism." *Id.* There is no dispute that TRIA is a law that applies to countries that support terrorism. *See* TRIA §201(d)(4), 116 Stat. at 2340.

Because this appeal also concerns an attempt to execute assets in satisfaction of a judgment, we also review briefly the law regarding execution. Federal Rule of Civil Procedure 69 governs the use of execution for money judgments. Rule 69 states that the "[p]rocess to enforce a judgment for the payment of money shall be a writ of execution, unless the court directs otherwise. The procedure on execution…shall be in accordance with the practice and procedure of the state in which the district court is held, existing at the time the remedy is sought, except that any statute of the United States governs to the extent that it is applicable." Fed.R.Civ. P. 69(a). There is no relevant federal statute at issue, so any judgment issued by the Southern District of New York would proceed according to New York law. *Id.; cf.* N.Y. C.P.L.R. §§5221-5227 (McKinney 2003) (setting forth procedures for writ of execution). Although the original document was not provided to the Court, we note that the docket sheet for *Smith I,* which was provided, indicates that a writ of execution was issued by the district court on July 29, 2003. *Cf. Smith II,* 2003 WL 22103452, at *1 n. 1, 2003 U.S. Dist. LEXIS 15949, at *2 n. 1 (noting issuance and service of writ of execution).

II. The TRIA Claim

The district court's first holding is that section 201 of TRIA does not provide a basis for the plaintiffs to attach the Assets. *See Smith II,* 2003 WL 22103452, at *2-*6, 2003 U.S. Dist. LEXIS 15949, at *6-*10. To reiterate, section 201 of the Act states that:

[n]otwithstanding any other provision of law, and except as provided in subsection (b), in every case in which a person has obtained a judgment against a terrorist party on a claim based upon an act of terrorism,…the blocked assets of that

terrorist party (including the blocked assets of any agency or instrumentality of that terrorist party) shall be subject to execution or attachment in aid of execution in order to satisfy such judgment to the extent of any compensatory damages for which such terrorist party has been adjudged liable.

TRIA §201(a), 116 Stat. at 2337.

Plaintiffs' theory of the case is premised upon the idea that section 201 of TRIA represents a Congressional mandate-akin to an appropriation-that the frozen Iraqi Assets be used only to compensate plaintiffs who have judgments against the Iraqi government. According to this theory, the President acted without authority when he confiscated blocked Iraqi assets and directed their use for a purpose other than satisfying victims' judgments.

Plaintiffs' interpretation hinges on the statute's use of the imperative "shall." Thus, throughout their brief, Plaintiffs write that "Congress declared, in section 201 of TRIA, that…these frozen Iraqi funds ' *shall*' be used to satisfy the judgments of victims of State sponsored terror such as the plaintiffs here." Br. for Plaintiff-Appellants at 8; *see also id.* at 4 ("Congress explicitly mandated that the subject funds *shall* be used to compensate victims of terrorism."); *id.* at 5 ("Congress' specific, express intent was for these plaintiffs to be compensated from frozen Iraqi funds.") These assertions are presented in a conclusory fashion, however, bereft of any explanation of why the language of the statute compels such a reading.

Instead of offering a text-based argument, Plaintiffs make much of a passage in the House Conference Report, which states that "[i]t is the intent of the Conferees that Section 201 establish that such judgments [against terrorist states] are to be enforced. Section 201…make[s] clear that all such judgments are enforceable against any assets or property [covered by the statute]." H.R. Conf. Rep. No. 107-779, at 27 (Nov. 13, 2002). They further rely on remarks by Senator Tom Harkin indicating that Congress intended the "blocked assets" referenced in TRIA §201 "to include any asset of a terrorist party that has been seized or frozen by the United States in accordance with law." 148 Cong. Rec. S11528 (daily ed. Nov. 19, 2002).

We disagree with Plaintiffs' interpretation of the statute. First, we do not believe that TRIA §201 is analogous to an appropriation. [FN3] Although Plaintiffs consistently imply that TRIA is an appropriation-most notably through their repeated reference to the President's confiscation as a "reap-

propriation"-nowhere do they argue directly that section 201 operates literally as an appropriation. If they did, they would have to confront the challenge of explaining how these funds constituted "appropriations." *See* 31 U.S.C. §1301(d) ("A law may [only be] an appropriation…if the law specifically states that an appropriation is made."); *see also* U.S. Const. art I, §9, cl.7 ("No Money shall be drawn from the Treasury, but in Consequence of Appropriations made by Law"). [FN4] Second, the language of section 201 cannot reasonably be read to mandate that terrorist assets be blocked in perpetuity. [FN5] It states simply that blocked assets "shall be subject to execution or attachment in aid of execution." 116 Stat. at 2337. We believe that the plain meaning of that language is to give terrorist victims who actually receive favorable judgments a right to execute against assets that would otherwise be blocked. Thus, although the statute applies broadly to "every case in which a person has obtained a judgment," it confers no entitlement on victims who have not yet obtained judgments. Neither does it guarantee that any blocked assets will in fact be available when a particular victim seeks to execute on a judgment. [FN6] Most important, nothing in the statutory language evinces Congressional intent to divest the President of authority to confiscate terrorist assets as provided in IEEPA §1702(a)(1)(C).

FN3. The district court also understood Plaintiffs' reading of section 201 as entailing the view that TRIA was an "appropriations measure." *Smith II,* 2003 WL 22103452, at *5, 2003 U.S. Dist. LEXIS 15949, at *15.

FN4. For this reason, Plaintiffs' discussion of the impoundment cases, which all deal with explicit Congressional appropriation, is unavailing.

FN5. The discretionary nature of the President's authority to block assets pursuant to section 203 of IEEPA, *see* 50 U.S.C. §1702(a)(1)(B), implies a similar discretion to unblock assets. Certainly, Plaintiffs do not argue otherwise. The lack of any constraint on the President's discretionary power to unblock assets-and thereby to remove them from the ambit of TRIA §201-casts further doubt on Plaintiffs' interpretation of §201.

FN6. In addition to the possibility that blocked assets may become unblocked or confiscated, they may also be depleted by the claims of other victims.

To the extent Plaintiffs contend that the first clause of section 201 of TRIA, which reads, "[n]otwithstanding any other provision of law," operates to abrogate the President's IEEPA confiscation authority as it pertains to blocked terrorist assets, we are unconvinced. As the district court noted, the "notwithstanding" clause applies only when some "other provision of law" conflicts with TRIA. *Smith II,* 2003 WL

22103452, at *4, 2003 U.S. Dist. LEXIS 15949, at *13; *cf. Hill v. Republic of Iraq,* No. Civ.A. 1:99-CV-03346TP, 2003 WL 21057173, at *4, 2003 U.S. Dist. LEXIS 3725, at *10-*11 (D.D.C. Mar. 11, 2003) (holding that "notwithstanding" language of TRIA superseded conflicting non-attachment provisions of other statutes). We see no conflict here. As we have already explained, section 201 operates to empower a plaintiff with a "judgment" against a "terrorist party" to execute against any "blocked assets" of that party. TRIA §201(a), 116 Stat. at 2337. It imposes no obligation on the President to maintain such funds for future attachment. Indeed, by defining "blocked assets" in TRIA §201(d)(2)(A) by reference to IEEPA §1702, the very statute that authorizes the President, in his discretion, both to block *and* to confiscate terrorist assets as circumstances warrant, Congress implicitly acknowledged that not all assets procured by the United States from terrorists would be available for execution pursuant to TRIA §201.

Finally, although we ordinarily will not look to legislative history when the language of a statute is clear, *see Conn. Nat'l Bank v. Germain,* 503 U.S. 249, 254, 112 S.Ct. 1146, 117 L.Ed.2d 391 (1992), the history of TRIA §201 is entirely consonant with the interpretation suggested by the statutory language. The Conference Report excerpt cited by Plaintiffs indicates Congress's commitment to making terrorism judgments enforceable against terrorists' blocked assets, [FN7] but it cannot reasonably be stretched, as Plaintiffs would have us do, to divest the President of authority to confiscate blocked assets. There is more than a semantic difference between blocking assets and confiscating them. As Senator Harkin, in the remarks quoted by Plaintiffs, noted, the term "blocked assets" reaches broadly to include any property seized or frozen by the United States. But it does not reach so broadly as to encompass confiscated property. To seize or freeze assets transfers *possessory* interest in the property. *See Dames & Moore,* 453 U.S. at 673-74 & n. 5, 101 S.Ct. 2972. But confiscation, pursuant to IEEPA §203(a)(1)(C), transfers *ownership* of terrorist property by vesting right, title, and interest as the President deems appropriate. *See* 50 U.S.C. §1702(a)(1)(C); *Regan v. Wald,* 468 U.S. 222, 228 n. 8, 104 S.Ct. 3026, 82 L.Ed.2d 171 (1984); *Propper,* 337 U.S. at 482-84, 69 S.Ct. 1333. Indeed, Senator Harkin added an important caveat to his remarks: "[A]ny assets as to which the United States claims ownership are not included in the definition of 'blocked assets' [in TRIA §201] and are not subject to execution or attachment under this provision." 148 Cong. Rec. S11528 (daily ed. Nov. 19, 2002).

FN7. The full text of Senator Harkin's remarks reveals something of the context of this enactment. Senator Harkin notes that the Executive had, in his view, interfered in the attempts of plaintiffs to enforce final judgments against frozen assets, and states that "[section 201] establishes once and for all, that *such judgments are to be enforced* against any assets *available* in the U.S., and that the executive branch has no statutory authority *to defeat such enforcement under standard judicial processes,* except as expressly provided in this act." *Id.* (emphasis added). We believe this further indicates that at least some members of Congress were primarily concerned with securing the right of execution for plaintiffs that had already obtained judgments. The reference to "standard judicial processes" suggests traditional post-judgment remedies such as writs of execution.

In sum, we conclude that on March 20, 2003, well before Plaintiffs had obtained a final judgment against the Republic of Iraq from the district court, the President was within his authority conferred by IEEPA §1702(a)(1)(C) in ordering the confiscation of blocked Iraqi assets. By the time Plaintiffs obtained a final judgment, the President had vested title in the confiscated assets in the United States Department of the Treasury and there simply were no more "blocked assets" in the Federal Reserve Bank's custody against which Plaintiffs could execute. [FN8] Because Plaintiffs cannot establish that section 201 of TRIA segregated the Assets specifically for their use or that the President's confiscation of the Assets was unlawful, their claim must fail. We therefore affirm the district court on this basis.

FN8. Precisely because Plaintiffs did not have a judgment at the time of confiscation, we are not presented with any issues that might arise under the Takings Clause, U.S. Const. amend. V. In any event, the President's March 20th order provides for an exception for amounts sufficient to satisfy judgments subject to execution at the time the President signed the order. *See* Exec. Order No. 13,290, 68 Fed. Reg. 14,307, at §1(b).

III. The EWSAA Claim

The court additionally concluded that Presidential Determination No. 2003-23, 68 Fed. Reg. 26,259 (May 7, 2003), had "made [TRIA] inapplicable with respect to Iraq," pursuant to section 1503 of EWSAA, 117 Stat. at 579. Plaintiffs challenge this conclusion, arguing that Congress did not grant such authority to the President, and that such delegation would be unconstitutional even if it were intended. Because we conclude that the President's confiscation of the Iraqi assets resolves this appeal, we need not reach this issue and express no views on the constitutionality of section 1503.

CONCLUSION

We readily acknowledge the importance of satisfying judgments in all cases. The horrific context of the matter at hand with the loss of life and its tragic consequences only underscores that imperative. Nothing we do here abrogates that judgment. We determine only that Plaintiffs must look elsewhere to satisfy it.

For the foregoing reasons, the judgment of the district court is affirmed. The mandate shall issue forthwith.

13.4 Payment of Judgments
Victims of Trafficking and Violence Protection Act of 2000, Pub. L. No. 106-386 §2002, 114 Stat. 1543 (2000).

PAYMENT OF CERTAIN ANTI-TERRORISM JUDGMENTS.
(a) PAYMENTS.--
(1) IN GENERAL.--Subject to subsections (b) and (c), the Secretary of the Treasury shall pay each person described in paragraph (2), at the person's election--
(A) 110 percent of compensatory damages awarded by judgment of a court on a claim or claims brought by the person under section 1605(a)(7) of title 28, United States Code, plus amounts necessary to pay post-judgment interest under section 1961 of such title, and, in the case of a claim or claims against Cuba, amounts awarded as sanctions by judicial order on April 18, 2000 (as corrected on June 2, 2000), subject to final appellate review of that order; or
(B) 100 percent of the compensatory damages awarded by judgment of a court on a claim or claims brought by the person under section 1605(a)(7) of title 28, United States Code, plus amounts necessary to pay post-judgment interest, as provided in section 1961 of such title, and, in the case of a claim or claims against Cuba, amounts awarded as sanctions by judicial order on April 18, 2000 (as corrected June 2, 2000), subject to final appellate review of that order.

Payments under this subsection shall be made promptly upon request.
(2) PERSONS COVERED.--A person described in this paragraph is a person who--
(A)(i) as of July 20, 2000, held a final judgment for a claim or claims brought under section 1605(a)(7) of title 28, United States Code, against Iran or Cuba, or the right to payment

of an amount awarded as a judicial sanction with respect to such claim or claims; or
(ii) filed a suit under such section 1605(a)(7) on February 17, 1999, December 13, 1999, January 28, 2000, March 15, 2000, or July 27, 2000;
(B) relinquishes all claims and rights to compensatory damages and amounts awarded as judicial sanctions under such judgments;
(C) in the case of payment under paragraph (1)(A), relinquishes all rights and claims to punitive damages awarded in connection with such claim or claims; and
(D) in the case of payment under paragraph (1)(B), relinquishes all rights to execute against or attach property that is at issue in claims against the United States before an international tribunal, that is the subject of awards rendered by such tribunal, or that is subject to section 1610(f)(1)(A) of title 28, United States Code.
(b) FUNDING OF AMOUNTS.--
(1) JUDGMENTS AGAINST CUBA.--For purposes of funding the payments under subsection (a) in the case of judgments and sanctions entered against the Government of Cuba or Cuban entities, the President shall vest and liquidate up to and not exceeding the amount of property of the Government of Cuba and sanctioned entities in the United States or any commonwealth, territory, or possession thereof that has been blocked pursuant to section 5(b) of the Trading with the Enemy Act (50 U.S.C. App. 5(b)), sections 202 and 203 of the International Emergency Economic Powers Act (50 U.S.C. 1701-1702), or any other proclamation, order, or regulation issued thereunder. For the purposes of paying amounts for judicial sanctions, payment shall be made from funds or accounts subject to sanctions as of April 18, 2000, or from blocked assets of the Government of Cuba.
(2) JUDGMENTS AGAINST IRAN.--For purposes of funding payments under subsection (a) in the case of judgments against Iran, the Secretary of the Treasury shall make such payments from amounts paid and liquidated from--
(A) rental proceeds accrued on the date of the enactment of this Act from Iranian diplomatic and consular property located in the United States; and
(B) funds not otherwise made available in an amount not to exceed the total of the amount in the Iran Foreign Military Sales Program account within the Foreign Military Sales Fund on the date of the enactment of this Act.
(c) SUBROGATION.--Upon payment under subsection (a) with respect to payments in connection with a Foreign Military Sales Program account, the United States shall be fully subrogated, to the extent of the payments, to all rights of the person paid under that subsection against the debtor foreign state. The President shall pursue these subrogated rights as

claims or offsets of the United States in appropriate ways, including any negotiation process which precedes the normalization of relations between the foreign state designated as a state sponsor of terrorism and the United States, except that no funds shall be paid to Iran, or released to Iran, from property blocked under the International Emergency Economic Powers Act or from the Foreign Military Sales Fund, until such subrogated claims have been dealt with to the satisfaction of the United States.

(d) SENSE OF THE CONGRESS.--It is the sense of the Congress that the President should not normalize relations between the United States and Iran until the claims subrogated have been dealt with to the satisfaction of the United States.

(e) REAFFIRMATION OF AUTHORITY.--Congress reaffirms the President's statutory authority to manage and, where appropriate and consistent with the national interest, vest foreign assets located in the United States for the purposes, among other things, of assisting and, where appropriate, making payments to victims of terrorism.

Notes:

1.   What are the policy considerations in favor of the government paying the outstanding judgments against state sponsors of terrorism? If the United States pays terrorism judgments, does "terrorism pay"?

2.   Some commentators have sharply criticized legislation that allows the U.S. government to pay terrorism judgment creditors,

> Thus, the United States Treasury is likely to swallow most, if not all, of the payments made under the Justice for Victims of Terrorism Act. In addition, the United States is likely to continue making such payments. A bill currently circulating in Congress would provide for payments to all judgment creditors who filed suit on or before October 28, 2000. While passage of that bill would ensure greater equity as between claims, it would only exacerbate the problem of the United States paying the judgments issued against terrorist states.

If there is a clear national decision to compensate American victims of terrorism abroad as we compensate victims of crime domestically, what Congress and the courts have wrought is quite appropriate, even though one would remark on the vast differences in level of compensation to the different victim groups. We are a wealthy nation and we certainly have the right to spend our money as we wish. But if we are pretending that this is a technique for making rogue governments pay for their terrorism, and that it represents an advance of international human rights law, then we are involved in a charade.

Michael Reisman and Monica Hakimi, *Illusion And Reality In The Compensation Of Victims Of International Terrorism*, 54 Ala. L. Rev. 561, 581-582 (2003).

3.   How does interference with the collection efforts of terrorism judgment creditors impact U.S. foreign policy? What is the likely interpretation of governments such as Iran when the U.S. government pays terrorism judgments? Does this provide an incentive to Iran to commit terrorist acts against Americans?

4.   In *Hegna v. Islamic Republic of Iran*, 402 F.3d 97 (2nd Cir. 2005), plaintiffs who filed claims under the Victims of Trafficking and Violence Protection Act and received payment from the government continued to pursue collection activities and sought to attach Iranian diplomatic property in New York. The court upheld the district court determination that "they had relinquished [their right to collect] as a condition of accepting payment under the VTVPA..." *Id.* at 99. The plaintiffs sought similar attachments in various jurisdictions and each time they were met by similar opposition from the U.S. Department of Justice.

5.   What does this statute suggest about the role of politics in compensating terrorism victims? Why were so few victims included in this act? Does the VTVPA privatize politics and political connections over litigation?

Chapter 14

Proving the Case

14.1 Standard of Proof
28 U.S.C. §1608 (e)

No judgment by default shall be entered by a court of the United States or of a State against a foreign state, a political subdivision thereof, or an agency or instrumentality of a foreign state, unless the claimant establishes his claim or right to relief by evidence satisfactory to the court. A copy of any such default judgment shall be sent to the foreign state or political subdivision in the manner prescribed for service in this section.

Notes:

1.   The relationship between causation and §1608(e) was analyzed in *Sisso v. Islamic Republic of Iran*, 448 F.Supp.2d 76, 86 fn. 13 (D.D.C. 2006),

> Furthermore, because causation is a substantive element of any tort claim and 28 U.S.C. §1608(e) requires that the "claimant establish[ ] his claim or right to relief by evidence satisfactory to the court," there is little risk that a defaulting foreign state will end up being held liable for overly remote consequences. *See Kilburn*, 376 F.3d at 1130 ("Whatever the ultimate source [of plaintiff's cause of action] may be, it will no doubt carry with it–as a matter of substantive law–its own rules of causation.")

2.   In considering the apparent leniency of this section, the Court of Appeals for the District of Columbia has noted,

> Other than protection against procedural default, with the possibility of a relaxed evidentiary burden on the FSIA plaintiff, *see supra* Legislative History, a non-immune foreign state is subject under the FSIA to federal common law for determining the amount of damages a plaintiff can recover, with qualifications not relevant here.

Hill v. Republic of Iraq, 328 F.3d 680, 684 (D.C.Cir. 2003).

3.   Not unexpectedly, the "satisfactory to the court" standard for granting default judgment against a foreign state under the Foreign Sovereign Immunities Act (FSIA) has been interpreted differently by the judges who have heard default judgment hearings. In *Campuzano v. Islamic Republic of Iran*, 281 F.Supp.2d 258 (D.D.C. 2003) Judge Urbina found that the standard is identical to the requirement for entry of default judgment against the United States contained in Fed. R.Civ.P 55(e), which provides, "no default [judgment] shall be entered against the United States or an officer or agency thereof unless the claimant establishes his claim or right to relief by evidence satisfactory to the court." In *Bodoff v. Islamic Republic of Iran*, 424 F.Supp.2d 74, 78 (D.D.C. 2006) Judge Lamberth found the requirements of §1608(e) are "established by clear and convincing evidence, which would have been sufficient to establish a *prima facie* case in a contested proceeding." In *Peterson v. Islamic Republic of Iran*, 264 F.Supp.2d 46, 48 (D.D.C. 2003) Judge Lamberth indicated that the "clear and convincing" standard is appropriate because the statute permits punitive damages and is "required in the District of Columbia to support a claim for punitive damages." In *Hill v. Republic of Iraq*, 175 F.Supp.2d 36, 38 n. 4 (D.D.C. 2001) Judge Jackson described the standard under §1608(e) as "evidence of a nature and quality to support summary judgment."

4.   The court is permitted to accept as true plaintiff's uncontroverted evidence. *Blais v. Islamic Republic of Iran*, 459 F.Supp.2d 40 (D.D.C. 2006). Frequently evidence is presented in the form of sworn affidavits or prior transcripts. *Botvin v. Islamic Republic of Iran*, 510 F.Supp.2d 101 (D.D.C. 2007). Transcripts from prior proceedings involving the same attack are sufficient to establish liability. *Haim v. Islamic Republic of Iran*, 425 F.Supp.2d 56 (D.D.C. 2006). In *McCarthy v. Republic of Cuba*, 354 F.Supp.2d 1347 (S.D.Fla. 2005) plaintiffs were permitted to rely on a Florida state court judgment which found the Republic of

Cuba liable for the extrajudicial torture and killing of plaintiff's husband by offering in evidence a certified copy of state court's judgment and affidavits that the judgment had not been satisfied.

5.   Liability is often proven in untraditional methods in terrorism cases. For instance there is significant reliance on expert witnesses, often because of the very difficult problem of obtaining information from state sponsors of terrorism and terrorist organizations about the inner workings of terrorist organizations and cells. Additionally, judicial notice is utilized frequently in terrorism cases as a method of supporting plaintiffs' claims. *Blais v. Islamic Republic of Iran,* 2006 WL 2827372 (D.D.C. 2006). Often expert testimony is provided in combination with judicial notice of U.S. government publications. *Simpson v. Socialist People's Libyan Arab Jamahiriya,* 470 F.3d 356, 361(D.C. Cir. 2006). Why are these methods of proving elements of terrorism cases used so often? What does this suggest about the type of proof available to victims?

6.   Despite the seemingly relaxed standards, courts are very careful to analyze the evidence submitted and will deny default judgment if the evidence is found to be insufficient,

> Plaintiffs' evidence for the proposition that Iran's support for terrorism caused the murders of Yaron and Efrat Ungar is more attenuated than that presented in any previous §1605(a)(7) case of which I am aware…
>
> Here, plaintiffs have established that Iran provided extensive support to HAMAS, but their proof does not link that support to the Ungar murders specifically. The men who killed Yaron and Efrat Ungar received funding and weapons from other sources as well as HAMAS, they were not in contact with HAMAS for several months spanning the date of the Ungar murders, and their confessions do not support the experts' opinions that the attack was a "perfect example" of what Iranian training could accomplish. Except for the experts' opinions, indeed, there is no record support for the proposition that Ghanimat and his men received any training from HAMAS members in the spring of 1996 or that they ever received specialized training in shooting from moving cars…
>
> The absence of a clear link from the Iran-HAMAS "partnership" to Ghanimat and his group is fatal to plaintiffs' conspiracy theory. There is no proof that the murderers knew of or agreed to

participate in a "common and unlawful plan whose goals [were] known to all members"; or that the Ghanimat group, allegedly at the end of a long "chain" conspiracy, knew of the existence of the larger conspiracy; or that the Ghanimat group knew of the necessity of the other alleged co-conspirators or were in fact dependent upon them. No reasonable juror could find the defendants liable on a conspiracy theory without speculating about matters that have not been established in this record-that Ghanimat and his group had guilty knowledge of the Iran-HAMAS partnership and that they understood and shared its alleged goal of disrupting the Israel-PLO peace process.

Ungar v. Islamic Republic of Iran, 211 F.Supp.2d 91, 98 -100 (D.D.C. 2002).

7.   In *Wagner v. Islamic Republic of Iran*, 172 F.Supp.2d 128, 136 (D.D.C. 2001), a default judgment case, damages were denied because the evidence was found to be not credible,

> With regard to Michael's *ante mortem* pain and suffering, there is minimal evidence to suggest that Michael may have survived the initial bomb explosion, dying from his physical injuries some minutes later, during which he may well have been in agony. Raymond and Steven Wagner both recall that at Michael's funeral at Arlington National Cemetery they were told by someone who had been present at the U.S. Embassy on the day of the bombing that Michael was alive in the rubble shortly after the explosion, although he expired moments later. Unfortunately, neither was able to recall the individual's name, and being without any indicia as to the credibility of the account, the Court is unable to ascribe any probative value to the hearsay assertion of an unidentified eyewitness. The Court has no option but to deny the plaintiffs' claims for Michael's pain and suffering.

See also Elahi v. Islamic Republic of Iran, 124 F.Supp.2d 97, 112 (D.D.C. 2000) where the court denied a sibling recovery because " there was an absence of specific testimony regarding mental anguish and loss of society and comfort experienced by his sister" and thus denied recovery…there was insufficient evidence about the state of Cyrus Elahi's relationship with his sister at the time of his death."

8. Some commentators have tried to distinguish terrorism default judgment litigation from "normal cases" where the defendants typically challenge evidence. What do the discussions in *Ungar*, *Wagner*, and *Elahi* suggest about the nature of the evidence presented and the level of the court's scrutiny in terrorism cases? Are judges in terrorism cases passive jurists or activist fact finders?

14.2 Obtaining Information from the Government

Burnett v. Al Baraka Inv. & Development Corp., 323 F.Supp.2d 82 (D. D.C. 2004).

WALTON, District Judge.

On April 23, 2004, the Emergency Motion of the United States to Quash Deposition of Sibel Edmonds, or for Protective Order ("Gov't Mot.") was filed with the Court in the above-captioned case, [FN1] wherein the government asserted that "information sought by the deposition subpoena is protected by the state secrets privilege, a privilege already asserted and under review in the context of another case[,]" *Edmonds v. United States Department of Justice*, Civil Action No. 02-1448 (D.D.C.). Gov't Mot. at 1. On April 26, 2004, this Court held a hearing on the motion and issued an Order granting the government's emergency motion and provisionally quashed the subpoena for the deposition of Sibel Edmonds until such time as the Court could fully evaluate the government's position. Apr. 26, 2004 Order. Attorney General John Ashcroft subsequently submitted a declaration to the Court on May 14, 2004, formally asserting the "claim of the state secrets privilege in order to protect the foreign policy and national security interests of the United States." May 14, 2004 Notice of Filing, Exhibit ("Ex.") 1 (Declaration of John Ashcroft) ¶ 2. Upon reviewing the Attorney General's Declaration, on June 18, 2004, this Court issued an Order for the plaintiffs to produce a list of questions they propose to ask the deponent and for the United States to respond to this list of questions with an *ex parte* declaration, detailing why the state secrets privilege precludes the deponent from responding to each question. June 18, 2004 Order. Upon consideration of the parties' submissions, the *ex parte in camera* reviews of classified declarations, and for the reasons set forth below and more fully explained in the Memorandum Opinion addressing the government's motion to dismiss filed in the *Edmonds* case that is being issued contemporaneously with this Order, the Court will grant in part and deny in part the government's motion to quash the subpoena. Accordingly, the plaintiffs are prohibited from asking those questions that would reveal information the government has properly asserted falls under the umbrella of the state secrets privilege, but the plaintiffs are permitted to ask the deponent those questions that the government has not raised objections to in its *ex parte* declaration.

FN1. Pursuant to 28 U.S.C. §517, "[t]he Solicitor General, or any officer of the Department of Justice, may be sent by the Attorney General to any State or district in the United States to attend to the interests of the United States in a suit pending in a court of the United States, or in a court of a State, or to attend to any other interest of the United States."

Federal Rule of Civil Procedure 45(c)(3)(A)(iii) states that "[o]n timely motion, the court by which a subpoena was issued shall quash or modify the subpoena if it requires disclosure of privileged or other protected matter and no exception or waiver applies[.]" Fed.R.Civ.P. 45(c)(3)(A)(iii). The government has asserted that "[t]he information over which the state secrets privilege has been asserted is information that would be disclosed by Ms. Edmonds' testimony here, and is information for which the disclosure, or risk of inadvertent disclosure, would cause serious damage to the national security and foreign policy interests of the United States." Gov't Mot., Statement of Interest of the United States of America in Support of Emergency Motion to Quash Deposition of Sibel Edmonds, or for Protective Order ("Gov't Stat.") at 2. As indicated above, this Court has reviewed *ex parte* the classified declaration submitted by the government in response to the Court's June 18, 2004 Order, which details why the state secrets privilege prohibits the plaintiffs from asking the deponent certain proposed questions. For all of the reasons expressed by this Court in its Memorandum Opinion addressing the government's motion to dismiss filed in the *Edmonds* case that is being issued contemporaneously with this Order, the Court concludes that the state secrets privilege has been properly invoked by the Attorney General and, following a review of the classified declarations submitted by the government, finds that if the plaintiffs' proposed questions that have been objected to by the government were propounded to the deponent, there is a "reasonable danger" that "secrets of state" would be revealed. *In re United States*, 872 F.2d 472, 475 (D.C.Cir.1989). The Court notes that while some of these objectionable questions may seem innocuous, one of the many concerns to the Court is that should the defendants desire to cross-examine the deponent on the veracity of her claims, which undoubtedly would occur, the deponent would inevitably have to reveal privileged information in order to establish the basis and source of her knowledge. Moreover, the government accurately asserts that "it is clear that each of the categories of information sought by plaintiffs in this case will require a discussion and description of the nature of Ms. Edmonds' duties with the FBI, information that is protected by the state secrets privilege and that has been classified by the FBI." Gov't Stat. at 12. As the District of Columbia Circuit has stated:

> [i]t requires little reflection to understand that the business of foreign intelligence gathering in this age of computer technology is more akin to the construction of a mosaic than it is to the management of a cloak and dagger affair. Thousands of bits and pieces of seemingly innocuous information can be analyzed and fitted into place to reveal with startling clarity how the unseen whole must operate.

Ellsberg v. Mitchell, 709 F.2d 51, 58 (D.C.Cir.1983) (quoting *Halkin v. Helms,* 598 F.2d 1, 8 (D.C.Cir.1978)). Therefore, because the Court finds that the government has properly invoked the state secrets privilege, and that Rule 45(c)(3)(A)(iii) mandates that the Court prohibit the plaintiffs from asking those questions objected to by the government in its *ex parte* declaration submitted to the Court, it is hereby this 6th day of July, 2004

ORDERED that the Emergency Motion of the United States to Quash Deposition of Sibel Edmonds, or for Protective Order is GRANTED IN PART AND DENIED IN PART. It is

FURTHER ORDERED that the plaintiffs are prohibited from asking the following Proposed Questions: 2, 5, 7, 8, 9, 13, 16-31. Accordingly, the plaintiffs are only permitted to ask the deponent the remaining proposed questions that were not objected to by the government in its *ex parte* classified declaration, specifically, Proposed Questions: 1, 3-4, 6, 10-12, 14-15. [FN2] It is

FN2. Although the government's obligation to preserve the classified declarations that were reviewed by this Court in connection with this case is obvious, the Court reminds the government of its obligation to maintain the classified declarations in their original state until the appellate process has been exhausted.

FURTHER ORDERED that the government shall be permitted to have a representative present at any deposition of Sibel Edmonds to monitor compliance with this Order and to otherwise ensure that state secrets are not revealed. [FN3]

FN3. In the event government counsel interjects an objection to a question posed to or a response being provided

by Ms. Edmonds during the course of the deposition, the proceedings as to that question or response shall cease immediately and shall not proceed further until the matter is brought to the Court and a ruling on the objection is issued by this Court.

SO ORDERED.

Notes:

1. Why would the Attorney General himself submit a declaration (affidavit) in this case?

2. This case involved over 3000 U.S. victims of the 9/11 attacks against, amongst others, Osama Bin Laden, who the U.S. government had been hunting for years in a worldwide search. Nonetheless, the government was punctilious about protecting each privilege available to it and to counter the victims' discovery attempts. What does this suggest about the role of government in civil terrorism cases?

14.3 Jurisdiction Discovery in §1605(a)(7) cases
Wyatt v. Syrian Arab Republic, 362 F.Supp.2d 103 (D. D.C. 2005).

URBINA, District Judge.
DENYING SYRIA'S MOTION TO DISMISS; ORDERING THE PARTIES TO SUBMIT A JOINT JURISDICTIONAL DISCOVERY PLAN; GRANTING THE PLAINTIFFS LEAVE TO AMEND THEIR COMPLAINT WITH A MORE SPECIFIC STATEMENT OF THE LAW ON WHICH THEY WILL BASE THEIR CAUSES OF ACTION

I. INTRODUCTION

This case involves the defendant's alleged support of a terrorist group (the Kurdistan Workers Party or "PKK") that abducted and held certain of the plaintiffs hostage in the early 1990s. The plaintiffs seek damages from the Syrian Arab Republic ("Syria" or the "defendant") and the PKK for injuries resulting from the alleged hostage taking. Syria now moves to dismiss, claiming that the court lacks personal and subject-matter jurisdiction and that the plaintiffs fail to state a claim. For the reasons that follow, the court denies Syria's motion to dismiss on personal jurisdiction grounds; denies without prejudice Syria's motion to dismiss on subject-matter jurisdiction grounds; orders the parties to submit a plan for conducting discovery on Syria's alleged support of the

PKK; denies without prejudice Syria's motion to dismiss for failure to state a claim; and grants the plaintiffs leave to amend their complaint to include a more specific statement of the law on which they will base their causes of action.

II. BACKGROUND

A. Factual Background

The plaintiffs allege as follows. On August 30, 1991, several of the plaintiffs (Ronald E. Wyatt and Marvin T. Wilson) were traveling in a van in Turkey when they "were stopped and surrounded by approximately ten vehicles commanded by the PKK." 2d Am. Compl. ("Compl.") ¶ 20. The PKK entered the van, removed the plaintiffs at gunpoint, and eventually held Wyatt and Wilson for twenty-one days in eastern Turkey. *Id.* ¶¶ 21-22. The PKK forced Wyatt and Wilson to

> march for up to eleven hours at a time and made [them] live outdoors exposed to the elements without food, shelter, or clothing…denied [Wyatt and Wilson] medical care, the ability to communicate with their families or the outside world, subjected [them] to indoctrination and brainwashing attempts and…otherwise mistreated [them].

Id. ¶ 22.

The PKK and Syria "intended" the hostage-taking to (a) harm Turkish tourism; (b) embarrass the Turkish government; and (c) "utilize Wyatt and Wilson (and the other non-party hostages) as human bait to lure Turkish rescue personnel into ambushes in order to kill them." *Id.* ¶ 23. The PKK placed certain demands and conditions on the release of Wyatt and Wilson; the PKK made these demands and conditions to "outside parties," including governments of the United States, Britain, Australia, and Turkey. *Id.* ¶ 23. In particular, the PKK demanded that: (a) the United States terminate its financial and military support of Turkey; (b) the United States, Britain, Australia and Turkey support an independent Kurdish state; (c) the international community recognize the PKK's right to control portions of Turkish territory; and (d) the Turkish government provide increased civil rights to Kurds. *Id.*

The plaintiffs further allege that

> [a]t all times relevant to this complaint and for at least a decade prior to the abduction of plaintiffs, Syria routinely provided financial, technical, logistical and other material support and resources to the PKK for the express purpose of causing and facilitating the commission of terrorist acts, including acts of extrajudicial killing and hostage-taking.

Id. ¶ 28. As examples of this support, the plaintiffs cite Syria's (a) assistance and participation in hostage-taking (including the hostage-taking of Wyatt and Wilson); (b) supply of weapons, ammunition, and false passports to the PKK; (c) establishment and maintenance of the PKK headquarters and offices in Syria; (d) provision of a safe haven and shelter in Syria to senior PKK commanders; (e) establishment and maintenance of various PKK training and military bases; (f) provision of military and terrorist training to PKK members; and (g) establishment and maintenance of PKK's logistical infrastructure in Syria. *Id.* ¶ 29.

B. Procedural History

The plaintiffs filed their initial complaint in July 2001 and an amended complaint in March 2003. In February 2004, in light of *Cicippio-Puleo v. Islamic Republic of Iran,* 353 F.3d 1024 (D.C.Cir.2004), this court *sua sponte* granted the plaintiffs leave to amend their complaint "to clarify the jurisdictional basis for suit, the defendants and the capacity in which each defendant is sued, the cause of action for each claim, the relief requested for each claim, and any other matters affected by the intervening precedent." Mem. Op. (Feb. 23, 2004) at 1-2. The plaintiffs filed their second amended complaint on March 18, 2004. In that complaint, the plaintiffs listed as defendants the Syrian Arab Republic, the Syrian Ministry of Defense, Mustafa Tlass (the Syrian Minister of Defense), Ghazi Kanaan (a Syrian military officer), and the PKK. Compl. ¶¶ 15-19.

The defendants (with the exception of the PKK) filed their motion to dismiss in May 2004. Believing that Syria's motion attacked the factual basis of the court's subject-matter jurisdiction, in September 2004 the plaintiffs moved to compel jurisdictional discovery. The court granted the plaintiffs' motion in November 2004 and ordered the parties to submit a joint jurisdictional discovery plan. Syria moved for reconsideration several days later, arguing that the court should avoid discovery because the complaint could be dismissed on grounds that would not subject a foreign sovereign to burdensome discovery. On December 14, 2004, the court granted Syria's motion for reconsideration, holding that the most appropriate course of action would be for the parties to complete the chain of briefing on Syria's motion to dismiss prior to any discovery. Accordingly, the parties never submitted a discovery plan.

On January 26, 2005, the plaintiffs filed a notice of voluntary dismissal of their claims against the Syrian Ministry of Defense, Mustafa Tlass, and Ghazi Kanaan. Pls.' Notice of Dismissal at 1. Thus, the only defendants remaining in this case are Syria and the PKK. Finally, on February 15, 2005, the plaintiffs (irked by what the plaintiffs label as Syria's "maneuver of breathtakingly blatant bad-faith," "bait-and-switch" tactics, and a "frivolous and pointless claim") submitted a motion to strike certain sections of Syria's reply to the plaintiffs' opposition to Syria's motion to dismiss. Pls.' Mot. to Strike at 2. Rather than wait for the chain of briefing to come to a close on this latest submission, the court moves forward, mindful of the arguments in the plaintiffs' motion, expecting that the parties will work together in a more collegial manner, and quite confident that the court will craft an appropriate response to the mischief or other inappropriate behavior which may surface as this case proceeds.

III. ANALYSIS

A. The Court Denies Syria's Motion to Dismiss for Lack of Subject-Matter Jurisdiction

1. Legal Standard for a Rule 12(b)(1) Motion to Dismiss Under the FSIA

The Foreign Sovereign Immunities Act ("FSIA") is "the sole basis for obtaining jurisdiction over a foreign state in our courts." *Argentine Republic v. Amerada Hess Shipping Corp.,* 488 U.S. 428, 434, 109 S.Ct. 683, 102 L.Ed.2d 818 (1989). The basic premise of the FSIA is that foreign sovereigns are immune from suit in the United States unless the action falls under one of the specific exceptions enumerated in the statute. 28 U.S.C. §1604; *Price v. Socialist People's Libyan Arab Jamahiriya,* 389 F.3d 192, 196 (D.C.Cir.2004) (" *Price II* "). If the foreign sovereign is not immune, the federal district courts have exclusive jurisdiction over the action. 28 U.S.C. §§1330, 1604; *Daliberti v. Republic of Iraq,* 97 F.Supp.2d 38, 42 (D.D.C.2000) (citing *Amerada Hess,* 488 U.S. at 434-35, 109 S.Ct. 683).

Under the FSIA, the foreign sovereign has "immunity from trial and the attendant burdens of litigation, and not just a defense to liability on the merits." *Phoenix Consulting, Inc. v. Republic of Angola,* 216 F.3d 36, 39 (D.C.Cir.2000) (quoting *Foremost-McKesson, Inc. v. Islamic Republic of Iran,* 905 F.2d 438, 443 (D.C.Cir.1990)). The special circumstances of a foreign sovereign require the court to engage in more than the usual pretrial factual and legal determinations. *Foremost-McKesson,* 905 F.2d at 449. The D.C. Circuit has noted that it is particularly important that the court "satisfy itself of its authority to hear the case" before trial. *Id.* (quoting *Prakash v. Am. Univ.,* 727 F.2d 1174, 1179 (D.C.Cir.1984)).

Once a foreign-sovereign defendant asserts immunity, the plaintiff bears the burden of producing evidence to show that there is no immunity and that the court therefore has jurisdiction over the plaintiff's claims. *Daliberti,* 97 F.Supp.2d at 42 (citations omitted). A court may dismiss a complaint brought under the FSIA only if it appears beyond doubt that the plaintiff can prove no set of facts in support of his claims that would entitle him to relief. *Id.* (citations omitted). Once the plaintiff has shown that the foreign defendant is not immune from suit, the defendant bears the burden of proving that the plaintiff's allegations do not bring the case within one of the statutory exceptions to immunity. *Phoenix Consulting,* 216 F.3d at 40.

The exception to foreign sovereign immunity at issue in this case is the state-sponsored terrorism exception, codified at 28 U.S.C. §1605(a)(7), that Congress enacted as part of the comprehensive Antiterrorism and Effective Death Penalty Act ("AEDPA"), Pub.L. No. 104-132, §221(a), 110 Stat. 1214 (Apr. 24, 1996), which provides that foreign sovereigns are not immune when

[m]oney damages are sought against a foreign state for personal injury or death that was caused by an act of torture, extrajudicial killing, aircraft sabotage, hostage taking, or the provision of material support or resources...for such an act if such act or provision of material resources is engaged in by an official, employee, or agent of such foreign state while acting within the scope of his or her office, employment, or agency[.]

28 U.S.C. §1605(a)(7). The statute gives three additional requirements for the exception to apply: (1) the foreign state must be designated as a state sponsor of terrorism at the time the act occurred or was designated as such as a result of such an act; (2) the plaintiff must afford the foreign state a reasonable opportunity to arbitrate the dispute if the act occurred within that state's territory; and (3) either the claimant or the victim must have been a United States national at the time the act occurred. 28 U.S.C. §1605(a)(7)(A)-(B).

On a Rule 12(b)(1) motion to dismiss in an FSIA case, the defendant may challenge either the legal sufficiency or the factual underpinning of an exception. *Phoenix Consulting,* 216 F.3d at 40. Given that a foreign-state actor's entitlement to immunity from suit is a critical preliminary determination, the parties have the responsibility, and must be afforded a fair opportunity, to define issues of fact and law, and to submit evidence necessary to the resolution of the issues. *Foremost-McKesson,* 905 F.2d at 449 (*citing Gould, Inc. v. Pechiney Ugine Kuhlmann & Trefimetaux,* 853 F.2d 445, 451 (6th Cir.1988)). Thus, the court must resolve the substantive immunity-law issues of section 1605 before reaching a decision on subject-matter jurisdiction. *Id.* (citations omitted).

If the defendant challenges the legal sufficiency of the plaintiff's jurisdictional allegations, the court should accept the plaintiff's factual allegations as true and determine whether such facts bring the case within any of the exceptions to foreign-state immunity invoked by the plaintiff. *Id.* This standard is similar to that of Rule 12(b)(6), under which dismissal is warranted if no plausible inferences can be drawn from the facts alleged that, if proven, would provide grounds for relief. *Price v. Socialist People's Libyan Arab Jamahiriya,* 294 F.3d 82, 93 (D.C.Cir.2002) (" *Price I* "). The plaintiff need not set out all of the precise facts on which he bases his claim to survive a motion to dismiss. *Id.*

If the defendant challenges the factual basis of the court's jurisdiction, however, the court may not deny the motion to dismiss merely by assuming the truth of the facts alleged by the plaintiff. *Phoenix Consulting,* 216 F.3d at 40. Instead, the court must resolve any disputed issues of fact, the resolution of which is necessary to a ruling upon the motion to dismiss. *Id.; Price I,* 294 F.3d at 90; *Foremost-McKesson,* 905 F.2d at 449. The court has "considerable latitude in devising the procedures it will follow to ferret out the facts pertinent to jurisdiction," but it must give the plaintiff "ample opportunity to secure and present evidence relevant to the existence of jurisdiction." *Phoenix Consulting,* 216 F.3d at 40 (quoting *Prakash,* 727 F.2d at 1179-80). To avoid burdening a foreign sovereign that proves to be immune from suit, however, the court should carefully control and limit jurisdictional discovery. *Id.; Foremost-McKesson,* 905 F.2d at 449.

2. The Plaintiffs' Do Not Base Their Claims of Hostage Taking and Extrajudicial Killing on the Acts of an Official, Employee, or Agent of Syria

The defendant argues that 28 U.S.C. §1605(a)(7) does not apply to this case and that Syria therefore retains sovereign immunity. Def.'s Mot. to Dismiss ("Def.'s Mot.") at 10. Specifically, the defendant argues that the plaintiffs fail to allege hostage taking, extrajudicial killing, or the provision of material support and resources for such acts. *Id.* at 10-16. Before getting to these arguments, however, the court must resolve an issue that has not quite made an explicit appearance in either side's briefing, but the jurisdictional nature of which cannot escape discussion. As indicated, the plaintiffs attempt to invoke this court's jurisdiction by alleging hostage taking, extrajudicial killing and the material support for such acts. Although the parties dispute each of these allegations, the parties do not address *who,* as far as 28 U.S.C. §1605(a)(7) is concerned, must conduct the hostage taking or killing.

The plaintiffs do not claim that Syria directly conducted the alleged acts or that the PKK is an agent of Syria. Rather, the issue is Syria's provision of support and resources to the PKK. As §1605(a)(7) makes clear, however, "an official,

employee, or agent of [the] foreign state" must commit the alleged torture, extrajudicial killing, provision of resources, etc. "while acting within the scope of his or her office, employment, or agency[.]" 28 U.S.C. §1605(a)(7); *Kilburn v. Socialist People's Libyan Arab Jamahiriya,* 376 F.3d 1123, 1129 (D.C.Cir.2004) (stating that foreign states lose immunity for acts of torture, extrajudicial killing, or hostage taking " *engaged in by an official, employee, or agent' of the state itself*") (quoting 28 U.S.C. §1605(a)(7)) (emphasis added). Because the plaintiffs do not claim that an official or employee of Syria committed terrorist acts or that the PKK is an "agent" of Syria, but only that Syria provided support to a group that committed terrorist acts, the court cannot base its subject-matter jurisdiction on hostage taking or killing. *Kilburn,* 376 F.3d at 1130-31 (differentiating theories of material support and theories of agency). Accordingly, the plaintiffs' only basis for subject-matter jurisdiction over the defendant is a successful demonstration that the defendant provided "material support or resources" to the PKK for such acts. *Cf. id.* (referring to Libyan *agents* in Lebanon who Libya funded and directed to purchase an American hostage so that Libya could kill him).

3. For a Nation to Lose Immunity for Providing Material Support and Resources for a Terrorist Act, at Least One of the Terrorist Acts Enumerated in §1605(a)(7) Must Occur

Another preliminary matter arises with regard to the provision of material support or resources. The plaintiffs argue that the court has jurisdiction pursuant to §1605(a)(7) regardless of whether the provision of material support leads to hostage taking or extrajudicial killing. Pls.' Opp'n at 16 (stating that if the plaintiffs demonstrate that "they were harmed as a result of defendants' provision of material support and resources to the PKK, defendants will be liable *irrespective of whether the abduction itself constitutes an act of hostage taking or extrajudicial killing* ") (emphasis added). The defendant maintains that "[t]he occurrence of at least one of the acts enumerated in §1605(a)(7) is an element necessary for the section's application." Def.'s Mot at 16 (citing *Kilburn v. Republic of Iran,* 277 F.Supp.2d 24, 32 (D.D.C.2003)). The court agrees with the defendant.

Subject matter jurisdiction arises pursuant to the provision of material support and resources component of §1605(a)(7) only when the defendant provides such support for an act of torture, extrajudicial killing, aircraft sabotage, or hostage taking *and* one of those acts occurs. [FN1] The text of §1605(a)(7), although not precise, directs this result: the statute waives immunity when a plaintiff seeks damages "for personal injury or death that was caused by an *act* of torture, extrajudicial killing, aircraft sabotage, hostage taking, *or the provision of material support or resources...for such an act* [.]" 28 U.S.C. §1605(a)(7) (emphasis added). Under the plaintiffs' reading, however, a nation could provide material support and resources to a group of terrorists for the purpose of hostage taking, the group could then use that support for an unrelated purpose (for example, to build a cafeteria), and a plaintiff could bring suit for injury proximately caused by that support (for example, a slip and fall in the cafeteria). Although Congress no doubt sought in §1605(a)(7) to address the fungibility of money, the court rejects the plaintiffs' broad reading of §1605(a)(7). *See* H.R.Rep. No. 104-383, at 62 (1995) (noting that a lawsuit pursuant to §1605(a)(7) "must allege that the terrorist act *was undertaken* ") (emphasis added).

FN1. A nation loses immunity even if the support it provides does not directly fund the particular terrorist act that injured or killed the victim. *Kilburn,* 376 F.3d at 1130 (noting that money is fungible and "terrorists organizations can hardly be counted on to keep careful bookkeeping records"). The only requirement is that the provision of support proximately causes the terrorist act. *Id.* Presumably, then, a nation could lose immunity by providing support to a terrorist group for general torture purposes when the group instead decides to take a hostage or sabotage an aircraft. *Id.* Congress, it seems, recognized that a court's main concern should be a nation's general funding of terrorist activities (those activities listed in §1605(a)(7)), not determining whether a rogue nation's henchman misallocates the hostage taking funds for acts of torture, extrajudicial killing, or aircraft sabotage. *Id.* at 1129 (citing H.R.Rep. No. 104-383, at 62 (1995)).

4. The Plaintiffs' Claim of Extrajudicial Killing Fails

Section 1605(e)(1) adopts the definition of extrajudicial killing contained in the Torture Victim Protection Act of 1991: "the term 'extrajudicial killing' means a deliberated killing not authorized by a previous judgment pronounced by a regularly constituted court affording all the judicial guarantees which are recognized as indispensable by civilized peoples." 28 U.S.C. §1350 note. The plaintiffs allege that "[d]uring the course of the PKK operation in which Wyatt and Wilson were abducted and held hostage, the PKK murdered at least two Turkish security personnel who were attempting to rescue the hostages." Compl. ¶ 35. These murders, the plaintiffs argue, constitute acts of extrajudicial killing (for which Syria provided material support and resources) within the meaning of 28 U.S.C. §1605(a)(7). *Id.* Syria

responds that "the deaths of soldiers presumably unknown and unrelated" to the plaintiffs cannot provide a ground for removing sovereign immunity. Def.'s Mot. at 14 (noting that "[n]o sufficient causal connection is alleged or could be alleged between personal injury to [the plaintiffs] for which plaintiffs might sustain and claim damages and the deaths of the Turkish soldiers as alleged").

The deaths of two Turkish soldiers are events separate from the events that caused the injuries the plaintiffs allegedly suffered. Nevertheless, the plaintiffs attempt to lump together their own injuries and the death of the soldiers into an overall terrorist operation of extrajudicial killing-as if to say, but for the hostage taking, the deaths of the Turkish soldiers would not have occurred. Pls.' Opp'n at 11 (claiming that "[b]ecause the terrorist operation in which plaintiffs were abducted was intended to and did in fact cause the extrajudicial killing of the Turkish rescue personnel, that operation as a whole constitutes 'an act of...extrajudicial killing' ") (quoting 28 U.S.C. §1605(a)(7)). The plaintiffs try to support their argument with this court's decision in *Campuzano v. Islamic Republic of Iran*, which held that a Hamas bombing that injured the plaintiffs was an act of extrajudicial killing. 281 F.Supp.2d 258, 269-70 (D.D.C.2003). But in that case, the extrajudicial killing injured the plaintiffs, *id.;* here, the death of Turkish soldiers caused no injury to the plaintiffs, other than perhaps diminishing their hopes of a rescue. Because the plaintiffs' theory thus takes §1605(a)(7) well beyond its express purpose of compensating American nationals for terrorist acts, and because the plaintiffs provide no case law that supports their position, the court rejects the plaintiffs' claim of extrajudicial killing.

5. The PKK Committed Hostage Taking Within the Meaning of 28 U.S.C. §1605(a)(7), but the Parties Dispute Whether Syria Provided Material Support and Resources to the PKK to Facilitate Hostage Taking

As indicated above, because Syria or its agent did not commit an act of hostage taking, the plaintiff must show that Syria provided material support to the PKK to commit that act. The court therefore faces two separate issues: whether Syria provided such support, and whether the PKK committed hostage taking. The court addresses the latter issue first.

a. The PKK Committed Hostage Taking Within the Meaning of 28 U.S.C. §1605(a)(7)

The FSIA defines "hostage taking" according to how that term is used in Article 1 of the International Convention

Against the Taking of Hostages ("ICATH"). 28 U.S.C. §1605(e)(2). As the D.C. Circuit stated in *Simpson:*

"Hostage taking" occurs under the ICATH (and so under the FSIA) when a person "seizes or detains and threatens to kill, to injure or to continue to detain another person in order to compel a third party...to do or abstain from doing any act as an explicit or implicit condition for the release of a hostage." Article I, ICATH, U.N. GAOR, Supp. No. 39, U.N. Doc. A/34/39 (1979). The essential element of the hostage-taking claim is that the intended purpose of the detention be to accomplish the sort of third-party compulsion described in the convention.

Simpson, 326 F.3d at 234-35; *Price I,* 294 F.3d at 94 (holding that a complaint failed to state hostage taking where the complaint pointed "to no nexus between what happened to [the plaintiffs] in Libya and any concrete concession that Libya may have hoped to extract from the outside world").

The plaintiffs allege that the PKK placed certain demands and conditions on the release of Wyatt and Wilson-specifically, that (a) the United States terminate its financial and military support of Turkey; (b) the United States, Britain, Australia and Turkey support an independent Kurdish state; (c) the international community recognize the PKK's right to control portions of Turkish territory; (d) the Turkish government provide increased civil rights to Kurds. Compl. ¶ 23. The defendant responds that "political, national and ethnic aspirations of the PKK are incapable of serving as the kind of a condition of release required by *Price* [.]" Def.'s Mot at 12. The defendant also claims that seizing tourists was a "continuing activity" that did not have a *quid pro quo* demand as an implicit or explicit condition of release. *Id.* at 13.

The PKK's demands and conditions on the release of Wyatt and Wilson satisfy the definition of hostage taking in §1605(a)(7). The defendant protests that lofty aspirations cannot constitute a condition of release. Def.'s Reply at 4 (arguing that "achievement of these objectives cannot be readily ascertained and it would be difficult to determine whether or not the conditions have been met"). At some point, the defendant's argument might be valid-an act of hostage taking to compel a god to destroy America presumably would go beyond any reasonable understanding of intending to accomplish third-party compulsion, if a god could be considered a "third-party." *Cf. United States v. Lin,* 101 F.3d 760, 766 (D.C.Cir.1996) (holding that the domestic statute that implements the International Convention Against the Taking of Hostages does not "differentiate between the various motivations that might prompt a person to take hostages in order to compel action by a third person"). But unrealistically trying to force nations to abstain from providing

assistance to disliked causes or seeking international recognition of one's own cause is *de rigueur* with terrorists. *E.g., United States v. Hammoud,* 381 F.3d 316, 325 (4th Cir.2004) (discussing Hizballah's goal of destroying Israel). Nothing in the text of §1605(a)(7), the definition of hostage taking to which it refers, or the case law thereon requires immediately achievable concessions. *But see* Def.'s Reply (requiring "quickly and decisively achieved" objectives). On the contrary, the case law speaks of the hostage taker's hope and intent. *Price I,* 294 F.3d at 94-95. [FN2]

FN2. In this regard, the court does not find persuasive Syria's attempt to draw attention to a factual dispute about whether the hostages eventually escaped or were released. *E.g.,* Reply at 5. The PKK could have taken hostages with the intent to compel third party action as a condition of release and, after a period of time, released the hostages for any number of reasons (for example, after a determination that the hostages would not help the PKK achieve its goals). There is no indication in the International Convention Against the Taking of Hostages that such a scenario would not still qualify as hostage taking-indeed, the Convention and the caselaw appear far more focused on the intent of the hostage taker at the time of the initial taking of the hostage. *See* Article I, ICATH, U.N. GAOR, Supp. No. 39, U.N. Doc. A/34/39 (1979); *Simpson II,* 326 F.3d at 234-35 (holding that "[t]he essential element of the hostage-taking claim is that the intended purpose of the detention be to accomplish the sort of third-party compulsion described in the convention").

Moreover, the court is reluctant to follow the defendant's lead and analyze the likelihood of a Kurdish state or a reduction in American support of Turkey, an academic task better suited to political scientists. Instead, the court looks for "any concrete concession" that the PKK "may have hoped to extract from the outside world." *Id.* Termination of financial and military support of Turkey, increased support of Kurdish causes and, ultimately, the creation of a Kurdish state strike the court as these types of concrete concessions. *Cf. id.* (holding that "detention for the goal of expressing support for illegal behavior" does not constitute the taking of hostages). Accordingly, the PKK's demands and conditions on the release of Wyatt and Wilson satisfy the definition of hostage taking in §1605(a)(7).

b. Syria's Alleged Provision of Material Support and Resources to the PKK

Having determined that the PKK committed an act of hostage taking (sufficient to overcome a Rule 12(b)(1) motion to dismiss), the court proceeds to determine whether Syria provided material support and resources to the PKK for that act. As indicated above, the plaintiffs allege that

> [a]t all times relevant to this complaint and for at least a decade prior to the abduction of plaintiffs, Syria routinely provided financial, technical, logistical and other material support and resources to the PKK for the express purpose of causing and facilitating the commission of terrorist acts, including acts of extrajudicial killing and hostage-taking.

Compl. ¶ 28; *see also id.* ¶ 29 (listing examples of this support). At a previous stage of this case when Syria opposed jurisdictional discovery, the court determined that the dispute between the parties regarding Syria's support of the PKK constituted a challenge to the factual basis of the court's jurisdiction. As the court stated,

> [t]he plaintiffs argue that a section of the defendants' motion to dismiss concerning due process presents a challenge to the factual basis of the court's jurisdiction. That section states that a State Department assessment of global terrorism "casts serious doubt on the accuracy of the extravagant claim in the complaint of support furnished to the PKK by Syria in 1991 and reinforces the complaint's fatal deficiency in failing to allege or show any connection between the support that was allegedly furnished by Syria to the PKK and the events in 1991 that are the subject of this action."

Wyatt v. Syrian Arab Republic, 225 F.R.D. 1, 3-4 (D.D.C.2004) (citations omitted). Although the court noted the defendant's argument that its discussion was in the context of personal jurisdiction, the court went on to indicate that

> the defendants also maintain that "the complaint's allegations of support are so extreme and exaggerated as to be implausible on their face and as a matter of common sense." In other words, the defendants believe that the plaintiffs' allegations are so factually deficient as to move the allegations beyond the realm of factual dispute and into implausibility. Although the defendants make clear they have other arguments for dismissing the plaintiffs' complaint, they leave no doubt that the court will be returning to the issue of material support. Because material support will remain an issue, and because the plaintiffs have made at least a colorable claim that the defendants provided this support, the court will not allow the defendants to escape discovery simply by claiming that a disputed fact is so disputed that it is no longer really a fact at all.

Id. (citations omitted).

Although this court initially granted the plaintiffs' motion to compel discovery, on reconsideration the court held that the parties should complete the briefing on the defendant's motion to dismiss to determine if there were a way of resolving the case short of subjecting a foreign sovereign to discovery. Having now determined (after the benefit of full briefing on the motion to dismiss) that an act of hostage taking did indeed occur for jurisdictional purposes, the court arrives at the same place it did on November 2, 2004: the need for jurisdictional discovery on the issue of Syria's alleged provision of material support and resources to the PKK. [FN3] Before ordering the parties to submit a plan regarding how that discovery should proceed, however, the court takes a moment to reject Syria's remaining arguments for dismissing the complaint.

FN3. Syria also disputes whether the PKK communicated its conditions for the release of the plaintiffs to any third parties. *E.g.,* Reply at 3 (stating that "[t]here is no sufficient allegation in the complaint that the PKK communicated [its] 'conditions' to any government or government officials or any other third party as prerequisites for the release"). As indicated above, however, the plaintiffs allege that the PKK placed certain demands and conditions on the release of Wyatt and Wilson to "outside parties," including governments of the United States, Britain, Australia, and Turkey. *Id.* ¶ 23. Moreover, *Simpson II* and other cases make clear that the hostage takers need not communicate with the outside world with a high degree of clarity and precision. *Simpson II,* 326 F.3d at 234 (noting that the sought-after third party action can be "an explicit *or* implicit condition for the release of a hostage") (emphasis added); *see also Price I,* 294 F.3d at 94 (same). Of course, in the absence of any communication to third-parties, it is difficult to image how the defendant could "accomplish the sort of third-party compulsion described in the convention." 326 F.3d at 234. It does not appear that Syria alleges such a total failure of communication. Nevertheless, because the court must be satisfied regarding "its authority to hear the case," *Foremost-McKesson,* 905 F.2d at 449 (quotations omitted), the parties may elect to pursue this matter in jurisdictional discovery.

B. The Court Rejects Syria's Due Process Arguments [FN4]

FN4. Because the plaintiffs have voluntarily withdrawn their claims against the Syrian Ministry of Defense, Mustafa Tlass, and Ghazi Kanaan, the defendant's argument regarding the plaintiffs' failure to serve those individuals, Def.'s Mot at 5-7, is moot.

Syria argues that jurisdiction in this court would violate Syria's due process rights because Syria lacks minimum contacts with the United States and is unable to challenge the Executive Branch's designation of Syria as a terrorist state. Defs.' Mot. at 7. The court need not linger long on these arguments, for as the defendant concedes, binding law in this circuit is not in its favor. *Id.* at 8 (citing *Price I,* 294 F.3d at 99). Indeed, as the court stated in *Price I,* "the Constitution imposes no limitation on the exercise of personal jurisdiction by the federal courts over [foreign sovereigns.]" 294 F.3d at 86.

In addition to their due process claims under American law, the defendant generally claims that this court's exercise of jurisdiction over Syria "is unreasonable and impermissible under applicable principles of international law." Def.'s Mot. at 9 (citing RESTATEMENT (THIRD) FOREIGN RELATIONS LAW OF THE UNITED STATES (1986) at §403). In *Flatow v. Islamic Republic of Iran,* a case involving Iran's provision of material support to a terrorist group that engaged in homicide bombings, Iran raised a similar argument. 999 F.Supp. 1, 15 n. 7 (D.D.C.1998). The court in that case limited its analysis to a determination that Congress intended extraterritorial application of §1605(a)(7), but also noted that jurisdiction over Iran would be consistent with international law. *Id.* As the court stated, "extraterritorial application of the state sponsored terrorism exceptions is consistent with international law; three of the five bases for the exercise of extraterritorial jurisdiction are implicated in actions by United States victims of foreign state sponsored terrorism: passive personality (nationality of victim), protective (national security interests), and universal (subject to jurisdiction wherever the offender may be found)." *Id.* (citing RESTATEMENT (THIRD) FOREIGN RELATIONS LAW OF THE UNITED STATES (1986) at §§402(2)-(3), 403, 423). This court sees no reason to depart from the analysis in *Flatow.* Accordingly, assuming *arguendo* that the defendant may raise principles of international law as a defense to personal jurisdiction, the court determines that it can maintain jurisdiction over Syria consistent with the principles of international law governing extraterritorial jurisdiction. *Id.*

C. The Plaintiffs State a Claim On Which Relief Can Be Granted

1. Legal Standard for Rule 12(b)(6) Motion to Dismiss

A Rule 12(b)(6) motion to dismiss tests the legal sufficiency of a complaint. *Browning v. Clinton,* 292 F.3d 235, 242 (D.C.Cir.2002). The complaint need only set forth a short and plain statement of the claim, giving the defendant fair notice of the claim and the grounds upon which it rests. *Kingman Park Civic Ass'n v. Williams,* 348 F.3d 1033, 1040 (D.C.Cir.2003) (citing FED R. CIV. P. 8(a)(2) and *Conley v.*

Gibson, 355 U.S. 41, 47, 78 S.Ct. 99, 2 L.Ed.2d 80 (1957)). "Such simplified notice pleading is made possible by the liberal opportunity for discovery and the other pre-trial procedures established by the Rules to disclose more precisely the basis of both claim and defense to define more narrowly the disputed facts and issues." *Conley,* 355 U.S. at 47-48, 78 S.Ct. 99 (internal quotation marks omitted). It is not necessary for the plaintiff to plead all elements of his prima facie case in the complaint, *Swierkiewicz v. Sorema N.A.,* 534 U.S. 506, 511-14, 122 S.Ct. 992, 152 L.Ed.2d 1 (2002), or "plead law or match facts to every element of a legal theory." *Krieger v. Fadely,* 211 F.3d 134, 136 (D.C.Cir.2000) (internal quotation marks and citation omitted).

Accordingly, "the accepted rule in every type of case" is that a court should not dismiss a complaint for failure to state a claim unless the defendant can show beyond doubt that the plaintiff can prove no set of facts in support of his claim that would entitle him to relief. *Warren v. District of Columbia,* 353 F.3d 36, 37 (D.C.Cir.2004); *Kingman Park,* 348 F.3d at 1040. Thus, in resolving a Rule 12(b)(6) motion, the court must treat the complaint's factual allegations-including mixed questions of law and fact-as true and draw all reasonable inferences therefrom in the plaintiff's favor. *Macharia v. United States,* 334 F.3d 61, 64, 67 (D.C.Cir.2003); *Holy Land Found. for Relief & Development v. Ashcroft,* 333 F.3d 156, 165 (D.C.Cir.2003); *Browning,* 292 F.3d at 242. While many well-pleaded complaints are conclusory, the court need not accept as true inferences unsupported by facts set out in the complaint or legal conclusions cast as factual allegations. *Warren,* 353 F.3d at 39; *Browning,* 292 F.3d at 242.

2. The Plaintiffs State Valid Claims

The plaintiffs list a variety of tort theories on which they seek to recover from the defendants. Compl. ¶¶ 37-60 (specifying causes of action for false imprisonment, civil conspiracy and aiding and abetting, intentional and/or negligent infliction of emotional distress, assault, battery, loss of consortium and solatium, and economic damages). Syria argues, quite accurately, that the plaintiffs "allege no source, statutory or otherwise," on which to base a cause of action for the above claims. Def.'s Mot. at 17. Syria further argues that such omission merits dismissal pursuant to Rule 12(b)(6). *Id.* But Syria places a greater burden on the plaintiffs than notice pleading requires. *Swierkiewicz,* 534 U.S. at 511-14, 122 S.Ct. 992; *Krieger,* 211 F.3d at 136. [FN5] Accordingly, the court denies Syria's motion to dismiss for failure to state a claim.

FN5. The court does not read *Acree v. Iraq,* 370 F.3d 41 (D.C.Cir.2004), to have modified the threshold for surviving a Rule 12(b)(6) motion to dismiss. In *Acree,* the D.C. Circuit *sua sponte* dismissed a complaint where the plaintiffs, like the plaintiffs in this case, relied on "generic" common law torts but did not specify "any other specific source in state, federal, or foreign law for their cause of action." *Id.* at 59. The D.C. Circuit ordered the parties "to consider this issue in preparation for oral argument," but it would seem that the parties showed up at court without doing their homework. *Id.* (noting that "[w]hen pressed repeatedly at oral argument, appellees offered no coherent alternative"). Thus, as the court stated, "[a]t oral argument, counsel for appellees gestured again toward generic common law torts, but generic common law cannot be the source of a federal cause of action." *Id.* Under those circumstances, and at a juncture in the litigation where the plaintiffs had obtained a "nearly-billion dollar default judgment against a foreign government whose present and future stability has become a central preoccupation of the United States' foreign policy," the court found that "exceptional circumstances" justified dismissal for failure to state a claim. *Id.* at 58-59.

D. The Court Grants the Plaintiffs Leave to Amend Their Complaint

Although the court denies Syria's motion to dismiss for failure to state a claim, the court believes that this litigation will proceed most efficaciously if the parties establish which law will apply. In their opposition to Syria's motion to dismiss, the plaintiffs appear to lean strongly in favor of application of District of Columbia tort law, Pls.' Opp'n at 20, a choice which this court favors as well, *see, e.g., Flatow v. Islamic Republic of Iran,* 999 F.Supp. 1, 14-15 (D.D.C.1998) (noting the "administrative difficulties associated with interpreting...unfamiliar foreign law" and the fact that "the United States has a much stronger interest than [the foreign entity] in adjudicating [an] action arising from a United States citizen's [injury]"). [FN6] Nevertheless, Syria argues that "[t]he law to be applied will most likely be the law of Turkey." Reply at 8.

FN6. Although *Acree* rejected *Flatow's* reliance on "generic" formulations of tort law, 370 F.3d at 59, the statement in *Flatow* of the policy considerations behind imposing a uniform law in §1605(a)(7) cases remains valid.

To resolve this dispute, the court directs the plaintiffs to amend their complaint with a statement of which law they seek to apply. Aside from inserting the relevant law and

making any changes to reflect the dismissed defendants, the plaintiffs may not otherwise modify the complaint. Syria may then determine whether to bring another Rule 12(b)(6) motion. Such motion may only challenge the sources of law on which the plaintiffs base their complaint and should take into account the arguments the plaintiffs raise in their opposition to the section of the defendant's current motion to dismiss regarding application of D.C. law. *See* Pls.' Opp'n at 16-23 (arguing, *inter alia,* that the United States has a stronger interest than the foreign fora, that administrative difficulties would arise in the application of foreign law, that Congress sought for federal courts to create coherent national standards in actions under §1605(a)(7)).

IV. CONCLUSION

For all the foregoing reasons, the court denies Syria's motion to dismiss on personal jurisdiction grounds; denies without prejudice Syria's motion to dismiss on subject matter jurisdiction grounds; orders the parties to submit within 45 days of the issuance of this opinion a joint plan for conducting discovery on the issue of whether Syria provided material support and resources to the PKK; denies without prejudice Syria's motion to dismiss for failure to state a claim; and grants the plaintiffs leave to amend their complaint with a more specific statement of the law on which they will base their causes of action. An order consistent with this Memorandum Opinion is separately and contemporaneously issued this 3rd day of March, 2005.

Notes:

1. Why did the plaintiffs request jurisdictional discovery? What information did they hope to obtain through the discovery process?

2. Why does the defendant resist discovery? What concerns does Syria have about the plaintiffs' discovery demands? Are Syria's fears justified? What are Syria's unstated concerns?

3. Why is the court concerned not to "burden" Syria with unnecessary discovery? Are non-state defendants afforded this type of deference? Why are foreign sovereigns generally protected from discovery?

4. What mechanisms can the court employ to control the scope of jurisdictional discovery? Does the court utilize those mechanisms here?

5. In a subsequent proceeding with respect to enforcing the jurisdictional discovery plan which is the subject of this decision, Syria argued that the plan would,

> compromis[e] Syria's sovereignty and inflict[ ] other harm upon Syria's national interests." The defendant also argues that court ordered jurisdictional discovery "runs the risk of impinging harmfully on the present tensions in the Middle East affecting relations between the U.S. and Syria."

Wyatt v. Syrian Arab Republic, 2006 WL 1328263 at 1 (D.D.C. 2006). Despite these concerns, the court ruled,

> The plaintiffs' depositions of Syrian officials responsible for "liaising and maintaining contact with the PKK" should suffice in ferreting out Syria's alleged support of the PKK, assuming of course that Syria complies with the court's discovery order fully and in good faith.

Id. at 2.

6. On what basis could the court order Syria to produce such a witness? What result would obtain if Syria didn't comply with this order to provide the "liasing" deponent?

7. What is the relationship between jurisdictional discovery and merits-based discovery in the context of terrorism litigation? In *Vine v. Republic of Iraq*, 459 F.Supp.2d 10, 18, fn. 7 (D.D.C. 2006) the interplay between jurisdictional discovery and the merits of a §1605(a)(7) action was described,

> The court disagrees that discovery is needed at this time, for in cases where a jurisdictional determination is "inextricably intertwined with the merits of the case," that determination should be postponed until "the merits are heard." *Herbert v. Nat'l Acad. of Sciences*, 974 F.2d 192, 198 (D.C.Cir. 1992); *see also Lawrence v. Dunbar*, 919 F.2d 1525, 1530 (11th Cir. 1990). This is such a case, given that a showing that plaintiffs were held hostage would resolve the merits of this case. *See Green v. Hill*, 954 F.2d 694, 697 (11th Cir. 1992) ("Jurisdiction and the merits are intertwined if a decision on one would effectively decide the other").

14.4 Collateral Estoppel
Klieman v. Palestinian Authority, 424 F.Supp.2d 153 (D. D.C. 2006).

PAUL L. FRIEDMAN, District Judge.

The estate, survivors and heirs of Esther Klieman, a United States citizen, have brought this action under Section 2333 of the Antiterrorism Act of 1991 ("ATA"), 18 U.S.C. §§2331 *et seq.*, and various tort theories, against the Palestinian Authority (the "PA"), also known as the Palestinian Interim Self-Government Authority and the Palestinian National Authority; the Palestine Liberation Organization (the "PLO"); Al Aqsa Martyrs Brigade; Fatah; Tanzim; Force 17; Yasser Arafat, now deceased; and five other individuals. [FN1] Now pending before the Court are (1) the motion of the Palestinian Authority and the Palestine Liberation Organization (together referred to herein as "defendants") to dismiss the complaint; (2) plaintiffs' motion for partial summary judgment; and (3) defendants' motion for the abatement of all proceedings in this case for three months, until May 1, 2006. The Court heard oral argument on the first two of the three motions on December 15, 2005.

FN1. The ATA claim appears in Count One of the complaint. The common law tort theories, pled pursuant to 28 U.S.C. §1367, are negligence, gross negligence, and intentional and negligent infliction of emotional distress (Counts Two through Five), as well as similar causes of action under Israeli law (Counts Six through Eight). Plaintiffs also assert a claim for punitive damages (Count Nine).

I. BACKGROUND

As alleged in the complaint, on March 24, 2002, a terrorist attack was carried out on a public transport bus traveling "on the Abud bypass road, near the village of Umm Safah, north of Ramallah, in the State of Israel or in territories administered or controlled by the State of Israel." Complaint ¶ 23; *see also id.* ¶¶ 1, 22, 24. The attack, in which one of the named individuals is alleged to have opened fire on the bus with a Kalachnikov Automatic rifle, resulted in the death of Esther Klieman. *Id.* ¶¶ 24, 25. Plaintiffs contend that defendants are responsible for the attack and, accordingly, have brought this action under the ATA, which establishes a federal cause of action for damages resulting from terrorist attacks in foreign countries.

The ATA provides in relevant part:

Any national of the United States injured in his or her person, property, or business by reason of an act of international terrorism, or his or her estate, survivors, or heirs, may sue therefor in any appropriate district court of the United States and shall recover threefold the damages he or she sustains and the cost of the suit, including attorney's fees.

18 U.S.C. §2333(a). The ATA, in turn, defines "international terrorism" as "activities" that:

(A) involve violent acts or acts dangerous to human life that are a violation of the criminal laws of the United States or of any State, or that would be a criminal violation if committed within the jurisdiction of the United States or of any State;

(B) appear to be intended--(i) to intimidate or coerce a civilian population; (ii) to influence the policy of a government by intimidation or coercion; or (iii) to affect the conduct of a government by mass destruction, assassination, or kidnapping; and

(C) occur primarily outside the territorial jurisdiction of the United States, or transcend national boundaries in terms of the means by which they are accomplished, the persons they appear intended to intimidate or coerce, or the locale in which their perpetrators operate or seek asylum.

18 U.S.C. §2331(1).

Defendants, relying on Rules 12(b)(1) and 12(b)(6) of the Federal Rules of Civil Procedure, seek dismissal on four grounds. First, they assert sovereign immunity from suit under both Section 1604 of the Foreign Sovereign Immunities Act ("FSIA"), 28 U.S.C. §§1602 *et seq.,* and Section 2337(2) of the ATA. Defendants PA and PLO Supporting Memorandum of Points and Authorities in Support of Their Rule 12(b) Motion ("Def.Mem.") at 2, 13-31. [FN2] Second, defendants argue that dismissal is warranted because the case presents non-justiciable political questions. *Id.* at 2, 31-33. Third, they argue that Section 2336(a) of the ATA mandates dismissal because the action is for injury caused by an "act of war." *Id.* at 2, 33- 55. Fourth, and finally, defendants contend that the activities alleged in the complaint fail to satisfy the statutory definition of "international terrorism" in Section 2331 of the ATA. *Id.* at 2, 38. [FN3]

FN2. On November 16, 2004, the Court entered a Scheduling Order setting forth a briefing schedule for defendants' dispositive motions. Although not expressly provided for in the Scheduling Order, on December 1, 2004, plaintiffs filed a motion for partial summary judgment on the sole issue of whether defendants are entitled to sovereign immunity. Defendants opposed the motion on the ground that the issue of sovereign immunity would

be before the Court in connection with defendants' motion to dismiss, as contemplated by the Court's Scheduling Order. *See* Defendants Opposition to Plaintiffs Motion for Partial Summary Judgment at 1-2. Subsequently, on March 18, 2005, defendants filed their motion to dismiss, which now has been fully briefed and argued by the parties. Accordingly, the Court will render a decision on both defendants' motion to dismiss and plaintiffs' motion for partial summary judgment, treating defendants' submissions in connection with their motion to dismiss as a formal response on the merits to plaintiffs' motion for partial summary judgment.

FN3. Defendants also assert that improper service of process and lack of personal jurisdiction warrant dismissal and request leave to assert these grounds for dismissal if the Court denies their pending motion. *See* Def. Mem. at 2-3.

Defendants also have moved for the abatement of all proceedings in this case, until May 1, 2006, pending receipt by defense counsel of instructions from the new political leadership that has emerged from the Palestinian parliamentary elections that were held on January 25, 2006. *See* Defendants' Motion for the Abatement of All Proceedings in This Case for Three Months Pending Receipt by Defense Counsel of Instructions From the New Political Leadership in Palestine. ("Def. Mot. for Abatement").

II. DISCUSSION
A. Applicable Legal Standards

Under Rule 12(b)(1) of the Federal Rules of Civil Procedure, plaintiffs bear the burden of establishing by a preponderance of the evidence that the Court has subject matter jurisdiction. *See Rosenboro v. Kim,* 994 F.2d 13, 17 (D.C.Cir.1993); *Shekoyan v. Sibley Int'l Corp.,* 217 F.Supp.2d 59, 63 (D.D.C.2002). Although the Court may dispose of a motion to dismiss on the basis of the complaint alone, it may consider materials beyond the pleadings when evaluating a motion to dismiss for lack of subject matter jurisdiction under Rule 12(b)(1). *Armstrong v. Vance,* 328 F.Supp.2d 50, 53 (D.D.C.2004); *Ass'n of Merger Dealers, LLC v. Tosco Corp.,* 167 F.Supp.2d 65, 69 (D.D.C.2001); *Rann v. Chao,* 154 F.Supp.2d 61, 64 (D.D.C.2001); *Scolaro v. D.C. Bd. of Elections and Ethics,* 104 F.Supp.2d 18, 22 (D.D.C.2000); *see Herbert v. National Academy of Sciences,* 974 F.2d 192, 197 (D.C.Cir.1992) ("[W]here necessary, the court may consider the complaint supplemented by undisputed facts evidenced in the record, or the complaint supplemented by undisputed facts plus the court's resolution of disputed facts.").

A motion to dismiss pursuant to Rule 12(b)(6) challenges the adequacy of the complaint on its face, testing whether the plaintiffs properly have stated a claim. Materials outside of the four corners of the complaint generally may not be considered in evaluating a Rule 12(b)(6) motion. *See United States ex rel. New v. Rumsfeld,* 350 F.Supp.2d 80, 88-89 (D.D.C.2004). "[A] complaint should not be dismissed for failure to state a claim unless it appears beyond doubt that the plaintiff[s] can prove no set of facts in support of [their] claim which would entitle [them] to relief." *Conley v. Gibson,* 355 U.S. 41, 45-46, 78 S.Ct. 99, 2 L.Ed.2d 80 (1957); *see Browning v. Clinton,* 292 F.3d 235, 242 (D.C.Cir.2002); *Sparrow v. United Air Lines, Inc.,* 216 F.3d 1111, 1113 (D.C.Cir.2000). In evaluating a motion to dismiss, the Court must accept the factual allegations in the complaint as true and draw all reasonable inferences in favor of plaintiffs. *See Harris v. Ladner,* 127 F.3d 1121, 1123 (D.C.Cir.1997). While the complaint is to be construed liberally, the Court need not accept factual inferences drawn by plaintiffs if those inferences are not supported by facts alleged in the complaint, nor must the Court accept the plaintiffs' legal conclusions. *See Nat'l Treasury Employees Union v. United States,* 101 F.3d 1423, 1430 (D.C.Cir.1996); *Kowal v. MCI Commc'ns Corp.,* 16 F.3d 1271, 1276 (D.C.Cir.1994).

Summary judgment shall be granted if the pleadings, depositions, answers to interrogatories and admissions on file, together with the affidavits or declarations, if any, demonstrate that there is no genuine issue as to any material fact and that the moving party is entitled to judgment as a matter of law. FED. R. CIV. P. 56(c). Material facts are those that "might affect the outcome of the suit under the governing law." *Anderson v. Liberty Lobby, Inc.,* 477 U.S. 242, 248, 106 S.Ct. 2505, 91 L.Ed.2d 202 (1986). When considering a motion for summary judgment, "the evidence of the non-movant is to be believed, and all justifiable inferences are to be drawn in [their] favor." *Id.* at 255, 106 S.Ct. 2505; *see Washington Post Co. v. U.S. Dep't of Health and Human Servs.,* 865 F.2d 320, 325 (D.C.Cir.1989).

B. Defendants' Motion to Dismiss
1. Sovereign Immunity

* * *

Citing Section 2337(2) of the ATA and Section 1604 of the FSIA, defendants move to dismiss this action on the ground that Palestine is a sovereign entity. *See* Def. Mem. at 13-31. Section 2337(2) prohibits the maintenance of a

civil ATA lawsuit against "a foreign state, an agency of a foreign state, or an officer or employee of a foreign state or an agency thereof acting within his or her official capacity or under color of legal authority." 18 U.S.C. §2337(2). The FSIA similarly directs that, with exceptions not relevant here, "a foreign state shall be immune from the jurisdiction of the courts of the United States and of the States..." 28 U.S.C. §1604; *see also* 28 U.S.C. §1603(a) (indicating that the term "foreign state" under the FSIA includes "a political subdivision of a foreign state or an agency or instrumentality of a foreign state"). [FN5]

FN5. Defendants concede that "[n]either the PA nor the PLO are, of themselves, states." Def. Mem. at 15. Instead, after acknowledging that "[i]t is the statehood of Palestine that must be analyzed in this case," defendants contend that they "are essential elements of Palestine performing core governmental functions" and they therefore are entitled to immunity. *Id.*

Although neither the FSIA nor the ATA define the term "foreign state," two things are apparent from the case law. First, an assertion of sovereign immunity under Section 2337(2) of the ATA is the functional equivalent of an assertion of sovereign immunity under Section 1604 of the FSIA. *Compare Argentine Republic v. Amerada Hess Shipping Corp.,* 488 U.S. 428, 434, 109 S.Ct. 683, 102 L.Ed.2d 818 (1989) ("[T]he text and structure of the FSIA demonstrate Congress' intention that the FSIA be the sole basis for obtaining jurisdiction over a foreign state in our courts.") *with Ungar v. Palestine Liberation Org., 402 F.3d 274, 282-83 (1st Cir.2005)* ("Nothing in either the language or legislative history of the ATA gives any indication that Congress intended the newer statute to supercede, rather than to mirror, the detailed jurisdictional framework described in the FSIA...[W]e regard an assertion of sovereign immunity under the ATA...as being functionally equivalent to an assertion of sovereign immunity under the FSIA."). Second, courts consistently have concluded that the meaning of the term "foreign state," as it relates to a sovereign power, should be derived by application of the standard set forth in the Restatement (Third) of the Foreign Relations Law of the United States (the "Restatement"). *See Ungar v. Palestine Liberation Org., 402 F.3d at 283; Kadic v. Karadzic,* 70 F.3d 232, 244 (2d Cir.1995); *Klinghoffer v. S.N.C. Achille Lauro,* 937 F.2d 44, 47-49 (2d Cir.1991); *Doe v. Islamic Salvation Front,* 993 F.Supp. 3, 9 (D.D.C.1998). [FN6]

FN6. It also may be argued--and not unreasonably--that, for the purposes of the FSIA, a foreign state is an entity that has been recognized as a sovereign by the United States government. *See Ungar v. Palestine Liberation Org., 402 F.3d at 284 n. 6.* As of the date of this Opinion, however, the United States has not recognized Palestine as a sovereign nation.

Defendants contend that Palestine meets the standard set forth in the Restatement, which provides in Section 201: "Under international law, a state is an entity that has a defined territory and a permanent population, under the control of its own government, and that engages in, or has the capacity to engage in, formal relations with other such entities." Restatement (Third) of the Foreign Relations Law of the United States §201 (1986); *see* Def. Mem. at 3, 15-29. [FN7] In support of this argument, defendants have submitted an affidavit by Nasser Al-Kidwa, the Ambassador of Palestine to the United Nations, dated June 13, 2003--originally submitted in *The Estate of Yaron Ungar v. Palestinian Authority,* C.A. No. 00-105L (D.R.I.)--purporting to show that while "Palestine does not have all the rights, privileges and duties of a full member of the United Nations," that fact "does not affect its statehood." Affidavit of Ambassador Nasser Al-Kidwa ¶ 31. Attached to the affidavit as exhibits are the United Nations General Assembly and Security Council Resolutions relating to the issue of Palestinian statehood.

FN7. Defendants also rely on comment d to Section 201 of the Restatement, which provides: "A state need not have any particular form of government, but there must be some authority exercising governmental functions and able to represent the entity in international relations."

Def. Mem. at 24 (quoting Restatement (Third) of the Foreign Relations Law of the United States §201 cmt. d (1986)).

In response, plaintiffs argue that defendants' assertion of sovereign immunity is barred by the doctrine of collateral estoppel. *See* Plaintiffs' Memorandum of Points and Authorities in Opposition to Defendants' Motion to Dismiss ("Pl. Opp'n") at 4-10; Memorandum in Support of Plaintiffs' Motion for Partial Summary Judgment Against Defendants Palestinian Authority and Palestine Liberation Organization at 3-13. Under the doctrine, "a final judgment on the merits in a prior suit precludes subsequent relitigation of issues actually litigated and determined in the prior suit, regardless of whether the subsequent suit is based on the same cause of action." *NextWave Pers. Commc'ns, Inc. v. FCC,* 254 F.3d 130, 147 (D.C.Cir.2001) (citing *I.A.M. Nat'l Pension Fund v. Indus. Gear Mfg. Co.,* 723 F.2d 944, 947 (D.C.Cir.1983)). Collateral estoppel applies when "(i) the issue previously adjudicated is identical with that now presented, (ii) that issue was actually

litigated in the prior case, (iii) the previous determination of that issue was necessary to the end-decision then made, and (iv) the party precluded was fully represented in the prior action." *Thomas v. Gen. Servs. Admin.,* 794 F.2d 661, 664 (Fed. Cir.1986) (internal quotes and citations omitted).

The Court agrees with plaintiffs and concludes that the doctrine of collateral estoppel precludes relitigation of the issues surrounding defendants' assertion of sovereign immunity. This case is one of at least six ATA lawsuits currently pending against defendants; in all six cases the defendants are represented by the same attorneys; and in all six cases they have raised the same issues of fact and law--even relying on the same Al-Kidwa affidavit--with respect to Palestinian statehood. And in every case that has reached the point of decision, the court either has rejected their sovereign immunity argument on the merits, *see Ungar v. Palestine Liberation Org., 402 F.3d at 282-92; Gilmore v. Palestinian Interim Self-Gov't Auth.,* 422 F.Supp.2d 96, 100-102, 2006 WL 711264, at *3-5 (D.D.C.2006); *Estates of Ungar v. Palestinian Auth.,* 315 F.Supp.2d 164, 174-87 (D.R.I.2004); *Biton v. Palestinian Interim Self-Gov't Auth.,* 310 F.Supp.2d 172, 180-81 (D.D.C.2004) ("*Biton I* "); *Knox v. Palestine Liberation Org.,* 306 F.Supp.2d 424, 430-48 (S.D.N.Y.2004), or has done so under the doctrine of collateral estoppel. *See Biton v. Palestinian Interim Self-Gov't Auth.,* 412 F.Supp.2d 1, 4-5 (D.D.C.2005) ("*Biton II* "). [FN8]

FN8. On February 7, 2005, in the matter of *Shatsky v. Syrian Arab Republic,* Civil No. 02-2280 (D.D.C.)--yet another ATA action against defendants currently pending in this District--the court entered a minute order denying a motion to dismiss filed by defendants, which included an assertion of sovereign immunity.

Although the Court can conceive of circumstances under which it would be reluctant to apply the doctrine of collateral estoppel to bar defendants' assertion of sovereign immunity--for example, if the United States government now recognized Palestine as a sovereign nation--defendants have presented no compelling reason why they should be permitted to re-litigate these already decided issues in this case. Defendants' bald assertion that "the issues of statehood and immunity presented by this case are unique and differ in significant respects from the issues as presented" in prior adjudications is plainly inadequate. Reply Memorandum by Defendants Palestinian Authority and Palestine Liberation Organization in Support of Their Rule 12(b) Motion at 8. [FN9] Furthermore, nothing in the recent political developments concerning the Palestinian leadership, which is the subject of defendants' motion for the abatement of proceedings, militates against application of the doctrine of collateral estoppel here. [FN10] Indeed, defendants have presented no meaningful argument otherwise in their motion for the abatement of proceedings.

FN9. After tracing the historical background of Palestine from World War I to the modern day, *Ungar v. Palestine Liberation Org., 402 F.3d at* 284-88, and applying the Restatement's definition of a "state," Judge Selya for the First Circuit in *Ungar* concluded that none of the evidence, including the same documents appended to the Al-Kidwa affidavit here, proffered by defendants separately or together satisfied the requirements for statehood under applicable principles of international law; thus there is no sovereign immunity. *Id. at* 292. Judge Lagueux in *Estates of Ungar* and Judge Marrero in *Knox* traversed much the same historical ground and legal documents and reached the same conclusions. *See Estates of Ungar v. Palestinian Auth., 315 F.Supp.2d at* 174-87; *Knox v. Palestine Liberation Org., 306 F.Supp.2d at* 431-39.

FN10. The Court also finds no support for defendants' attempt to revive their assertion of sovereign immunity emanating from the Statement of Interest of the United States of America ("Statement"), filed on September 12, 2005, in *Estate of Ungar v. Palestinian Authority,* 18 MS 0302 (S.D.N.Y.), in opposition to the *Ungar* plaintiffs' effort to enforce a total of $116 million in judgments obtained in the United States District Court for the District of Rhode Island against the Palestinian Authority and the Palestine Liberation Organization. The Statement, which is silent on the issue of Palestinian statehood, expressly is limited to an argument that the *Ungar* plaintiffs' attempt to enforce the judgments by

seeking the sale and eviction of the Palestinian Permanent Observer Mission to the United Nations, located in New York City, directly implicates the foreign policy interests of the United States, as recognized by the Foreign Missions Act, 22 U.S.C. §§4301, *et seq.,* which confers on the Secretary of State the authority to regulate all transactions regarding mission property. *See* Statement at 2 n. 2 ("This Statement does not address the merits of the underlying litigation," which included a rejection of defendants' assertion of sovereign immunity, "but rather only the particular remedies being sought here.").

For the reasons stated, the Court not only will deny defendants' motion to dismiss on sovereign immunity grounds but also will grant summary judgment to plaintiffs on their claim that sovereign immunity does not divest the Court of jurisdiction to hear this case.

2. Political Question / Non-Justiciability

Defendants next argue that this case should be dismissed because it presents non-justiciable political questions. *See* Def. Mem. at 31-33. As the parties recognize, in *Baker v. Carr,* 369 U.S. 186, 82 S.Ct. 691, 7 L.Ed.2d 663 (1962), the Supreme Court articulated six factors to identify a political question that is non-justiciable:

Prominent on the surface of any case held to involve a political question is found [1] a textually demonstrable constitutional commitment of the issue to a coordinate political department; or [2] a lack of judicially discoverable and manageable standards for resolving it; or [3] the impossibility of deciding without an initial policy determination of a kind clearly for nonjudicial discretion; or [4] the impossibility of a court's undertaking independent resolution without expressing lack of the respect due coordinate branches of government; or [5] an unusual need for unquestioning adherence to a political decision already made; or [6] the potentiality of embarrassment from multifarious pronouncements by various departments on one question.

Id. at 217, 82 S.Ct. 691. Asserting without elaboration that the instant case touches upon every *Baker v. Carr* factor, defendants' basic argument is that the prosecution of this lawsuit will burden "the long running Middle East peace process." Def. Mem. at 31.

The Court finds defendants' argument unconvincing and the authority on which defendants rely inapposite. For example, Judge Robb's concurring opinion in *Tel-Oren v. Libyan Arab Republic,* 726 F.2d 774, 823 (D.C.Cir.1984) (Robb, J., concurring), on which defendants primarily rely, while similarly involving an armed attack on a civilian bus in Israel, does not support defendants' position that this case presents non-justiciable political questions because that decision predated the enactment of the ATA, which expressly provides, in Section 2333(a), a civil remedy in federal court for United States nationals injured by acts of international terrorism. *See Tel-Oren v. Libyan Arab Republic,* 726 F.2d at 822 (Bork, J., concurring) (although the Alien Tort Claims Act, 28 U.S.C. §1350, does not authorize the courts "to enter into sensitive areas of foreign policy," only a statute or treaty expressly creating a cause of action "[c]ould direct courts to entertain cases like this one"). [FN11] Defendants' reliance on Judge Bates' opinion in *Doe v. Israel,* 400 F.Supp.2d 86 (D.D.C.2005), also is misplaced. In that case, the court merely concluded that the political question doctrine constituted an alternative ground to dismiss claims against the State of Israel, Israeli government entities, and Israeli officials--all of which (and whom) the court already had determined to be immune from suit under the FSIA. *See id.* at 111. As demonstrated above, defendants here have no such immunity. Moreover, unlike defendants in the present case, the defendants in *Doe v. Israel* were not being sued under the ATA.

FN11. Although Judge Bork's concurring opinion in *Tel-Oren* suggests that the enactment of a statute like the ATA--a possibility that he thought "improbable" at the time--would not necessarily foreclose political question doctrine challenges to federal court jurisdiction in lawsuits brought under such a statute, *see Tel-Oren v. Libyan Arab Republic,* 726 F.2d at 822 (Bork, J., concurring), the proliferation of terrorism-related statutes, the "Executive Branch's repeated condemnations of international terrorism," *Klinghoffer v. S.N.C. Achille Lauro,* 937 F.2d at 49 n. 3, and the numerous judicial decisions that have been rendered in actions brought under the ATA--all since the time of Judge Robb's and Judge Bork's pronouncements--lead the Court to conclude that this ship already has sailed with defendants left standing on the dock clinging to the language of two concurring opinions that have been overtaken by legislative action.

What is more--similar to their assertion of sovereign immunity-- defendants unsuccessfully have advanced the same political question doctrine argument on numerous prior occasions in which they have been sued under the ATA. *See Ungar v. Palestine Liberation Org., 402 F.3d at 279-82; Klinghoffer v. S.N.C. Achille Lauro,* 937 F.2d at 49-50; *Gilmore v. Palestinian Interim Self-Gov't Auth.,* 422 F.Supp.2d 96, 99-100, 2006 WL 711264, at *2-3; *Biton II,* 412 F.Supp.2d at 5-6; *Biton I,* 310 F.Supp.2d at 180- 81; *Knox v. Palestine Liberation Org.,* 306 F.Supp.2d at 448-49. In *Biton II,* for example, Judge Collyer rejected defendants' position in an ATA action brought by the wife of a man who was killed when a roadside device exploded near a bus that was transporting elementary school children and their teachers in the southern Gaza Strip. Judge Collyer stated, in language with which this Court agrees:

"This is a tort suit brought under a legislative scheme that Congress enacted for the express purpose of providing a legal remedy for injuries or death occasioned by acts of international terrorism." *Ungar, 402 F.3d at 280.* There is no flaw in this Court's ability to address Plaintiff's claims: Congress explicitly committed these issues to the federal courts under the ATA. Similarly, the Court has access to "judicially manageable standards for resolving the issue[s] before it," *id.,* from both existing ATA caselaw and traditional tort caselaw. The "initial policy determination" involved here has already been made by the U.S. Congress: Americans injured by terrorist acts can sue their attackers in U.S. courts and the Court can manage this case to resolution of Defendants' alleged li-

ability without "expressing lack of the respect due coordinate branches of government." *Baker,* 369 U.S. at 217, 82 S.Ct. 691. The fifth and sixth factors from *Baker v. Carr* do not apply because a decision in this individual case will have no consequences concerning "political decision[s] already made" and will raise only the question of Defendants' alleged liability regarding this single bombing of a bus. Thus, nothing in *Baker v. Carr* counsels against having this case proceed.

Biton II, 412 F.Supp.2d at 6. As plaintiffs point out, defendants have made no attempt to distinguish any of these prior decisions in their moving papers. *See* Pl. Opp'n at 13-14. [FN12]

FN12. The Court is unpersuaded by defendants' efforts to renew their political question doctrine argument in their motion for the abatement of proceedings and finds no support for defendants' position in the cases cited in that motion.

Persuaded by the reasoning and holdings of the courts that have rejected the same non-justiciability arguments presented by defendants here, the Court concludes that the political question doctrine does not preclude judicial resolution of this case.

3. Act of War

In perhaps their strongest argument, defendants contend that the acts alleged in the complaint are not subject to litigation in this Court because they constitute "acts of war" over which the ATA does not extend jurisdiction. *See* Def. Mem. at 33-55. Section 2336(a) of the ATA provides that "[n]o action shall be maintained under section 2333 of this title for injury or loss by reason of an act of war." Section 2331(4), in turn, defines "act of war" as "any act occurring in the course of-- (A) declared war; (B) armed conflict, whether or not war has been declared, between two or more nations; or (C) armed conflict between military forces of any origin." Defendants limit their argument to Section 2331(4)(C) by asserting, essentially, that the alleged attack on the public transport bus was an act of war occurring in the course of armed conflict between military forces. *See* Def. Mem. at 35-37.

According to defendants, "[t]he statutory definition of act of war in [Section] 2331(4)(C) is broad. It covers 'any act' without limit or qualification and requires only that the act be one occurring in the course of armed conflict between military forces of any origin." Def. Mem. at 35. "The act itself," their argument continues, "need not consist of or include actual combat. An intent to strengthen or advance or to weaken or harm the interests of one side or the other to the armed conflict by the act is sufficient." *Id.* More to the point, defendants contend that the "ATA encompasses acts of war against civilians" and that as a "general proposition violent acts on civilians and their property are readily considered acts of war." *Id.* at 37 (noting that the events of September 11, 2001 have been treated as an act of war by President Bush, the United Nations and U.S. courts). Defendants further insist that, even if the alleged attack on a civilian bus were found to violate the rules of war and armed conflict, the ATA still would bar this action:

If illegal the attack may well be a war crime and subject to sanctions as such. However, neither the heinousness nor legality of acts of war occurring in the course of armed conflict is germane to the application of sec. 2336(a). Sec. 2336(a) when applicable bars civil actions under ATA sec. 2333 for "any act" without regard to its nature or seriousness, or whether the act if not barred by sec. 2336(a) would constitute international terrorism actionable under the ATA.

Id. at 39.

Regarding Section 2331(4)(C)'s requirement that the act occur "in the course of...armed conflict between military forces of any origin," defendants assert that there was "ongoing and daily armed conflict between Israeli military and Palestinian military forces throughout the West Bank and Gaza" during the relevant period. Def. Mem. at 35; *see also id.* at 35-36 (noting that the complaint, in paragraphs 10-13, alleges the existence of active Palestinian military forces). Defendants also maintain that the Israeli government "consistently [has] characteriz[ed] the fighting as armed conflict." *Id.* at 40; *see also, e.g., id.,* Exhibit 13 at 55 ("Israel is engaged in an armed conflict short of war.") (The First Statement of the Government of Israel to the Sharm El-Sheikh Fact-Finding Committee, Dec. 28, 2000).

Defendants also present policy arguments to explain why the allegations in the complaint should be considered an "act of war." They argue that, whereas the "ATA is intended to deter international terrorism against U.S. nationals," no such deterrent effect results from applying Section 2333 to an act carried out as "part of the ongoing armed conflict between Israelis and Palestinians." Def. Mem. at 38. Specifically, defendants contend that the "violence on which this case is based...like all acts in such an ongoing armed conflict, was not directed at persons targeted as Americans." *Id.* Along similar lines, after stating that "[t]housands of innocent civilians on both sides have been killed or wounded in this conflict," defendants assert that "[f]or the American legal system to make multimillion dollar awards under the ATA for individual deaths occurring in the course of such 'daily bloodshed' would be disruptive of efforts to achieve peace and reconciliation and disserve the overall interests of justice." *Id.* at 39; *see also id.* at 38 ("[T]he incongruity of

allowing the recovery of damages, as the ATA does, only to American nationals, is readily apparent and has the potential to result in disparities of recovery that are offensive to justice and common sense and complicate or embarrass foreign policy interests of the United States."). [FN13]

FN13. While the Court of course must construe the statute written by Congress and, if it is ambiguous, determine what Congress meant by the term "act of war," the policy arguments advanced in defendants' memorandum of law properly are matters for Congress, not the judiciary. *See Pigford v. Veneman,* 355 F.Supp.2d 148, 169-70 (D.D.C.2005).

Plaintiffs' response is simple: "[A]s a matter of law, an attack on a civilian bus which results in the murder of one or more innocent civilians cannot be deemed to have occurred '*in the course of*' war between nations or armed conflict within the meaning of §2331." Pl. Opp'n at 26 (emphasis added). [FN14] Although, at the time plaintiffs submitted their opposition to defendants' motion to dismiss, no court yet had interpreted the meaning of Section 2331(4)'s "in the course of" language, plaintiffs argue that, in numerous other contexts, courts consistently have "interpreted the phrase 'in the course of' as a gatekeeper phrase that is intended to exclude as a matter of law a subset of conduct which--because of its nature and substance--deviates from and/or is insufficiently related to the general set of conduct governed by the provision in question." *Id.* at 19.

FN14. Although plaintiffs expressly do not dispute that an "armed conflict" existed in the West Bank at the time of the events alleged in the complaint, they assert that such a determination "would necessitate significant fact-finding." Pl. Opp'n at 17. According to plaintiffs, however, disposition of the "act of war" question does not require the Court to determine (1) whether an "armed conflict" existed; or (2) whether defendants constitute "military forces of any origin" within the meaning of Section 2331(4)(C). *See id.* at 18. Plaintiffs nevertheless argue

that none of the organizations named as defendants in this case qualify as "military forces of any origin." *See* Plaintiffs' Sur-Reply in Further Opposition to Defendants' Motion to Dismiss at 5.

Plaintiffs note, for example, that the Controlled Substances Act, 21 U.S.C. §§801, *et seq.,* which generally prohibits the distribution of narcotics, exempts a "practitioner" from its criminal provisions. *See* 21 U.S.C. §829. The statutory definition of "practitioner" includes a physician who dispenses and a pharmacist who prescribes "a controlled substance *in the course of* professional practice or research." 21 U.S.C. §802(21) (emphasis added). According to plaintiffs, however, on the basis of the statutory phrase "in the course of," courts "have consistently held that a person who meets the definition of 'practitioner' as a matter of fact...will nevertheless be excluded as a matter of law from the criminal immunity granted to a 'practitioner' if that person distributes a narcotic...in violation of the rules of legitimate medical practice." Pl. Opp'n at 20 (citing *United States v. Collier,* 478 F.2d 268, 272 (5th Cir.1973); and *United States v. Rosenberg,* 515 F.2d 190, 197-198 (9th Cir.1975)). In other words, a physician or pharmacist is immune from criminal prosecution only when acting as a doctor or druggist "in the course of professional practice," not when he or she "step[s] outside the bounds of professional practice" and, for example, prescribes or dispenses large quantities of drugs to drug addicts according to graduated fee scales depending on the amount of drugs prescribed or dispensed; then he or she acts like any other "large-scale 'pusher,' not as a physician [or pharmacist]" and may be prosecuted criminally. *United States v. Moore,* 423 U.S. 122, 132, 143, 96 S.Ct. 335, 46 L.Ed.2d 333 (1975).

Plaintiffs offer numerous other examples where courts, in other contexts, have interpreted the phrase "in the course of" in a similar fashion to exclude from the scope of a statutory provision a subset of conduct that, by its nature and substance, deviates from or is not sufficiently related to the general set of conduct otherwise governed by the provision. Pl. Opp'n at 26, *see id.* at 22-26; *O'Donnell v. Great Lakes Dredge & Dock Co.,* 318 U.S. 36, 42-43, 63 S.Ct. 488, 87 L.Ed. 596 (1943) (construing the Jones Act, 46 App. U.S.C.A. §688); *Colon v. Apex Marine Corp.,* 832 F.Supp. 508, 513-15 (D.R.I.1993), *aff'd,* 35 F.3d 16 (1st Cir.1994) (same); *Vincent v. Harvey Well Serv.,* 441 F.2d 146, 147 (5th Cir.1971) (same); *Kalantar v. Lufthansa German Airlines,* 276 F.Supp.2d 5, 10-14 (D.D.C.2003) (construing Article 17 of the Warsaw Convention, reprinted following 49 U.S.C. §40105); *Abu Hamdeh v. American Airlines, Inc.,* 862 F.Supp. 243, 247-48 (E.D.Mo.1994) (same).

Perhaps most relevant for present purposes, plaintiffs contend that, in the context of applying the "political offense" exception to extradition, courts have held "that any act that violates the rules of warfare and armed conflict--such as a terrorist attack on civilians--is excluded as a matter law from being deemed to have occurred in the course of or incidental to war or armed conflict." Pl. Opp'n at 30; *see Matter of Doherty,* 599 F.Supp. 270, 274-76 (S.D.N.Y.1984) (extradition of IRA member alleged to have participated in ambush against British soldiers); *In re Extradition of Atta,* 706 F.Supp. 1032, 1042 (E.D.N.Y.1989) (extradition of PLO member alleged to have participated in attack against

Israeli bus in West Bank); *Ahmed v. Wigen,* 726 F.Supp. 389, 405-407 (E.D.N.Y.1989), *aff'd,* 910 F.2d 1063 (2d Cir.1990) (same); *Matter of Extradition of Marzook,* 924 F.Supp. 565, 577- 78 (S.D.N.Y.1996) (extradition of Hamas leader alleged to have participated in numerous terrorist attacks against civilians); *Marzook v. Christopher,* 1996 WL 583378, at *2-3 (S.D.N.Y. Oct. 10, 1996) (same). [FN15]

FN15. The "political offense" exception is a subject all its own, which this Court need not discuss at length. Suffice it say that the Court agrees with the analyses of Judges Korman and Weinstein, respectively, in *In re Extradition of Atta,* 706 F.Supp. at 1042-50; and *Ahmad v. Wigen,* 726 F.Supp. at 402-09.

Plaintiffs also assert that other federal statutes governing the identical subject matter--terrorism and violations of international law--support the interpretation of the scope of Section 2336(a) that they urge. *See* Pl. Opp'n at 38-40 (criminal provisions of the ATA, *inter alia,* Sections 2332, 2339A and 2339B); *id.* at 40-42 (War Crimes, 18 U.S.C. §2441); *id.* at 42-46 (Alien Tort Claims Act, 28 U.S.C. §1350). For example, they argue that, with respect to the war crimes statute, defendants' interpretation of the ATA would create an impermissible conflict between the provisions of Section 2331 and Section 2441, "because it would single out and exclude §2441 from the criminality component of the definition of 'international terrorism' in §2331 which applies by its plain terms to any 'violation of the criminal laws of the United States'--including of course §2441." Pl. Opp'n at 41. Such an interpretation, plaintiffs submit, "would create an absurd situation wherein persons guilty of War Crimes in which an American is killed would face the death penalty under §2441, but would not face civil liability under §2333." *Id.* [FN16]

FN16. Like defendants, plaintiffs present policy-based arguments as well, asserting that the rationale behind applying the "political offense" doctrine to exclude terrorist acts that violate the international law of armed conflict--namely, the vital interest of the United States in combating terrorism--"applies with equal or even greater force to the interpretation of the 'in the course of' requirement of §2331." Pl.

Opp'n at 36. According to plaintiffs, because Congress intended the ATA to be construed broadly and because the legislative history of Section 2333 shows an unequivocal congressional intent to deter and punish acts of international terrorism, "Congress clearly did not intend the limitation on actions for 'acts of war' contained in §2336(a) (as defined in §2331) to exclude from civil liability acts of terrorism that are not legitimate 'acts of war' under international law." *Id.* at 36-37.

The Court is persuaded by plaintiffs' arguments and concludes that the statutory phrase "in the course of" necessarily imposes limitations on what "acts" constitute "acts of war" within the meaning of Section 2333(a)--as defined in Section 2331(4). As a matter of law, an act that violates established norms of warfare and armed conflict under international law is not an act occurring in the course of armed conflict. An armed attack on a civilian bus, such as the one plaintiffs have alleged in the complaint, violates these established norms. *See Kadic v. Karadzic,* 70 F.3d 232, 242 (2d Cir.1995) (violent acts against civilians, committed in the course of open hostilities, "long have been recognized in international law as violations of the law of war") (citing *In re Yamashita,* 327 U.S. 1, 14, 66 S.Ct. 340, 90 L.Ed. 499 (1946)); *Ahmad v. Wigen,* 726 F.Supp. at 409 (killing civilian on civilian bus "must be characterized as a random act of murderous terrorism, rather than a protected political offense").

Subsequent to the completion of briefing on defendants' motion to dismiss, Judge Collyer of this Court rejected an "act of war" argument under Section 2331(4)(C), similar to the one advanced by defendants here. *See Biton II,* 412 F.Supp.2d at 7 (characterizing defendants' argument as an assertion "that the bombing of a school bus was an act of war occurring in the course of an armed conflict between military forces of any origin"). [FN17] Although stating in dicta that "[i]t is not immediately obvious that an attack on a settler, who intentionally went into Palestinian territory to claim it for Israel, would automatically and necessarily be a 'terrorist' attack against a 'civilian,'" *id.* at 10, Judge Collyer in *Biton II* concluded that "[t]he circumstances of the alleged attack--on a recognized school bus full of students and teachers--and the status of those noncombatants lead the Court to conclude that the attack did not occur 'during the course of' an armed conflict as a matter of law," *id.* at 10-11. Here, too, the alleged attack was committed on a recognized public transport bus, and it is undisputed that all of the passengers on the bus were non-combatant civilians. Accordingly, without deciding whether there existed "armed conflict between military forces of any origin" within the meaning of Section 2331(4)(C), the Court concludes that the armed attack alleged in the complaint did not occur "in the course of" an armed conflict.

FN17. It appears that *Biton II* is the only decision squarely addressing--after full briefing by opposing parties--the scope of the ATA's prohibition against civil lawsuits for injuries resulting from an "act of war," and in particular Section 2331(4)'s "in the course of" language. The only other deci-

sion the Court could locate that addresses Section 2336(a)'s "act of war" exclusion is Judge Cassell's opinion in *Morris v. Khadr,* 415 F.Supp.2d 1323 (D.Utah 2006), a case involving an attack against United States armed forces in Afghanistan by alleged members of al Qaeda. In the course of granting plaintiffs' motion for default judgment because the defendant had failed to respond to the complaint, Judge Cassell in *Morris v. Khadr* analyzed the "act of war" exclusion *sua sponte* and concluded that it did not apply to divest the court of jurisdiction. 415 F.Supp.2d at 1330. Specifically, he found that al Qaeda could not be considered a "military force[ ] of any origin" under Section 2331(4)(C). *See id.* at 1333 ("A conventional dictionary definition of 'military' is 'armed forces' or the persons serving in them. 'Armed forces,' in turn, are 'the combined military, naval, and air forces *of a nation.*'") (footnotes omitted).

4. International Terrorism

In an argument not unrelated to their "act of war" claim, defendants also assert that dismissal is warranted because "this case fails to satisfy the statutory definition of 'international terrorism'" in Section 2331(1) of the ATA. *See* Def. Mem. at 2. Specifically, defendants contend that "[e]nding an illegal belligerent occupation is an objective that is not within ATA sec. 2331's definition of international terrorism." Def. Mem. at 38; *see also id.* (quoting from a news article in which an Israeli settler states that Palestinian acts of violence committed against Israeli settlers are "specifically designed to make people leave").

Plaintiffs have two straightforward responses to this argument. They first contend that if the attack that killed Ms. Klieman was conducted to "end an illegal belligerent occupation," as defendants have asserted, then the attack plainly meets Section 2331's definition of "international terrorism," as an activity that "'appear[s] to be intended…to intimidate or coerce a civilian population [or] to influence the policy of a government by intimidation.'" Pl. Opp'n at 14 (quoting 18 U.S.C. §2331(1)). Plaintiffs also submit that defendants' intent in carrying out the attack is not properly decided on a motion to dismiss. *See id.* at 15.

Whether defendants' alleged activities "appear[ed] to be intended--(i) to intimidate or coerce a civilian population; (ii) to influence the policy of a government by intimidation or coercion; or (iii) to affect the conduct of a government by mass destruction, assassination, or kidnapping," within the meaning of Section 2331(B), are disputed questions of material fact. The Court cannot determine defendants' intent in allegedly committing the attack in the context of a motion to dismiss; that is a question for trial or, at a minimum, for summary judgment. *See Gilmore v. Palestinian Interim Self-Gov't Auth.,* 422 F.Supp.2d 96, 101-102, 2006 WL 711264, at *5; *Biton I,* 310 F.Supp.2d at 185.

C. Defendants' Motion for the Abatement of Proceedings

In their abatement motion, defendants seek an order holding further proceedings in this case in abeyance until May 1, 2006, pending receipt by defense counsel of instructions from the new political leadership that has emerged from the Palestinian parliamentary elections that were held on January 25, 2006. *See* Def. Mot. for Abatement at 2 ("In view of the election's outcome, its uncertain consequences, and new officials yet to be determined, it is not clear what the instructions will be with respect to positions to be taken by the defendants [in this case]."). Defendants also attempt to resurrect the sovereign immunity and political question doctrine arguments raised in their motion to dismiss. *See id.* at 2 ("There is a real question whether the cases are now non-justiciable as a threshold matter under the political question doctrine."); Reply Memorandum of Defendants Palestinian Authority and Palestine Liberation Organization in Support of Their Motion for Abatement of Proceedings at 3 ("Palestine firmly believes that U.S. courts lack jurisdiction to adjudicate the ATA cases. Palestine is under no obligation to litigate these cases on the merits.").

Having considered defendants' motion, the Court concludes that the requested abatement of proceedings in this case is unnecessary. For the reasons stated above, defendants' sovereign immunity and political question doctrine arguments are without merit. Moreover, during the Court's December 15, 2005 hearing on defendants' motion to dismiss, the Court gave defendants sixty days from the entry of an order denying their motion to dismiss--should the Court so rule--in which to raise additional defenses related to jurisdiction. As a result, defendants are not required to file another pleading in this case until after May 1, 2006.

III. CONCLUSION

For the foregoing reasons, defendants' motion to dismiss is denied; defendants' motion for the abatement of proceedings is denied; and plaintiffs' motion for partial summary judgment is granted. A separate Order to that effect shall issue this same day. Defendants shall have sixty (60) days from the date of that Order to raise additional jurisdictional defenses by motion. Plaintiffs shall file any response thirty (30) days thereafter, and defendants shall file any reply twenty (20) days after plaintiffs file their response.

ORDER

For the reasons stated in the Opinion issued this same day, it is hereby

ORDERED that plaintiff's motion for partial summary judgment [17] is GRANTED; it is

FURTHER ORDERED that defendants' motion to dismiss the complaint [36] is DENIED; it is

FURTHER ORDERED that defendants' motion for the abatement of proceedings [47] is DENIED; and it is

FURTHER ORDERED that defendants shall have sixty (60) days from the date of this Order to raise additional jurisdictional defenses by motion; plaintiffs shall file any response thirty (30) days thereafter; and defendants shall file any reply twenty (20) days after plaintiffs file their response.

Notes:

1.   Why is the doctrine of collateral estoppel particularly significant and applicable in civil terrorism cases? What practical and procedural hurdles does collateral estoppel help plaintiffs overcome?

2.   If the defendants anticipated being confronted with a collateral estoppel argument, why would they submit evidence that they previously offered in prior cases involving the same issue, i.e. the affidavit of Nasser Al-Kidwa? These defendants were found to have previously recycled their evidence and arguments:

> Defendants acknowledge that each of these actions [*Ungar, Knox, Biton, Gilmore, Shatsky*] raises the same issues of fact and law concerning the statehood of Palestine and the immunity of the PLO and PA...In fact, the evidence submitted by Defendants in conjunction with their Supplemental Motion in this litigation consists entirely of the same Affidavit of Nasser Al-Kidway dated June 13, 2003, and attached exhibits, upon which they relied in *Ungar.* Memo for Reconsideration at 3-4. Defendants have not rebutted any of the Plaintiffs' arguments in this regard and the Court deems the matter conceded.

Biton v. Palestinian Interim Self-Government Authority, 412 F.Supp.2d 1, 5 (D.D.C. 2005).

3.   Is there a reason the defendants do not alter or update the evidence they submit to the court in each successive case? What would be the effect of providing new evidence in each case?

Chapter 15

Collection Issues

15.1 Execution

Federal Rules of Civil Procedure

Rule 69. Execution

(a) In General.

(1) Money Judgment; Applicable Procedure.
A money judgment is enforced by a writ of execution, unless the court directs otherwise. The procedure on execution — and in proceedings supplementary to and in aid of judgment or execution — must accord with the procedure of the state where the court is located, but a federal statute governs to the extent it applies.

(2) Obtaining Discovery.

In aid of the judgment or execution, the judgment creditor or a successor in interest whose interest appears of record may obtain discovery from any person — including the judgment debtor — as provided in these rules or by the procedure of the state where the court is located.

Notes:

1. What are the differences between collecting terrorism judgments and typical commercial judgments? What about the nature of the typical terrorism defendant- judgment debtors (rogue state sponsors of terrorism, terrorists, and designated terrorist organizations) creates legal impediments to collecting judgments? Are they likely to conduct regular business activities in the U.S., invest here or have significant assets in the United States that are available for execution?

2. Collection litigation in the United States is conducted almost exclusively in state courts. Why is this so? What practical considerations confront terrorism judgment creditors in federal court?

3. How will this rule affect collection of civil terrorism judgments? Is levying an execution against a foreign state sponsor of terrorism, terrorist or designated terrorist organization ever possible? Or likely? What are the judgment creditors' impediments to execution? What is the interplay between state collection proceedings and federal practice?

4. Is post judgment discovery against terrorist judgment debtors realistic?

5. By definition, virtually all state sponsors of terrorism and designated terrorists and organizations have had their assets blocked in the U.S. On occasion, funds of state sponsors are actually held by the U.S. Treasury. While it would seem that such assets provide a perfect avenue for collection of judgments issued under the terrorism amendments to the FSIA, the efforts of judgment creditors are routinely opposed by the government and generally unsuccessful. See *Flatow v. Islamic Republic of Iran*, 74 F.Supp.2d 18 (D.D.C. 1999).

6. In *Flatow* Judge Lamberth expressed the frustration of the courts in denying collection to the judgment holders. In quashing a writ of attachment against Iranian funds held by the Treasury, he noted,

> The Court concludes by acknowledging the apparent unfairness that attends its grant of the United States' motion to quash. Indeed, the Court regrets that its ruling today forestalls plaintiff's efforts to execute a judgment that was issued by this Court. *Flatow,* 999 F.Supp. at 5. Moreover, the Court appreciates plaintiff's frustration with the White House's present efforts to block his recovery, *see* Stephen M. Flatow, *In This Case, I Can't Be Diplomatic,* The Washington Post, November 7, 1999, at B2, particularly in light its previous pledges of support. Nonetheless, this Court must remain faithful to its proper role within our constitutional system,

which requires courts to follow the rule of law, not their own individual conceptions of what is fair or just.

Id. at 25. In a subsequent attempt by the Flatow family to reach Iranian assets Judge Lamberth stated,

> ...the Court regrets that plaintiff's efforts to satisfy his judgment against Iran have proven futile. Indeed, in light of his lack of success thus far, it appears that plaintiff Flatow's original judgment against Iran has come to epitomize the phrase "Pyrrhic victory." Yet, unless or until Congress decides to enact a law that authorizes the attachments plaintiff seeks, this Court lacks the proper means to assist him with such endeavors.

Flatow v. Islamic Republic of Iran, 76 F.Supp.2d 16, 27-28 (D.D.C. 1999).

15.2 Terrorism Risk Insurance Act §201

§201 of Title II of the Terrorism Risk Insurance Act of 2002 (Public Law 107-297; 116 Stat. 2322) ("TRIA") provides that:

> Notwithstanding any other provision of law, and except as provided in subsection (b), in every case in which a person has obtained a judgment against a terrorist party on a claim based upon an act of terrorism, or for which a terrorist party is not immune under section 1605(a)(7) of title 28, United States Code, the blocked assets of that terrorist party (including the blocked assets of any agency or instrumentality of that terrorist party) shall be subject to, execution or attachment in aid of execution in order to satisfy such judgment to the extent of any compensatory damages for which such terrorist party has been adjudged liable.

Notes:

1. Section 1611 of the FSIA provides that:

> Notwithstanding the provisions of section 1610 of this chapter, the property of a foreign state shall be immune from attachment and from execution, if-
> (1) the property is that of a foreign central bank or monetary authority held for its own account, unless such bank or authority, or its parent foreign government, has explicitly waived its immunity from

attachment in aid of execution, or from execution, notwithstanding any withdrawal of the waiver which the bank, authority or government may purport to effect except in accordance with the terms of the waiver; or
> (2) the property is, or is intended to be, used in connection with a military activity and
> (A) is of a military character, or
> (B) is under the control of a military authority or defense agency.

28 U.S.C. §1611(b). In *Weininger v. Castro*, 462 F.Supp.2d 457, 498-99 (2006), the court analyzed the impact of this provision in light of TRIA §201(a),

> TRIA §201(a) is appended to §1610, which provides the sole bases for exceptions to immunity from execution of property. Section 1611(b) in turn states that a foreign central bank's property is immune "[n]otwithstanding the provisions of 1610." Notably, §1611(b) lists certain exceptions to this immunity--such as waiver--that are found in §1610(a), but it does not list exceptions based on terrorism. Plaintiffs argue that §1611(b) presents no impediment to execution because TRIA §201(a)'s provisions apply "notwithstanding any other provision of law." TRIA §201(a), codified at §1610 note. As previously noted, the intent of the "notwithstanding" language in TRIA is "to target statutory exceptions to immunity," *Holy Land Found.*, 445 F.3d at 787, and "to the extent that a foreign country's sovereign immunity potentially conflicts with Section 201(a), the 'notwithstanding' phrase removes the potential conflict." *Smith*, 280 F.Supp.2d at 319, *judgment *499 aff'd*, 346 F.3d 264 (2d Cir.2003). Accordingly, TRIA, which was enacted later in time than §1611, overrides the immunity conferred in §1611.

Weinstein v. Islamic Republic of Iran, 274 F.Supp.2d 53 (D.D.C. 2003).

LAMBERTH, District Judge.

This matter comes before the Court on the motion of the United States to quash plaintiffs' writs of attachment [40-1], which was filed on January 31, 2003. Upon consideration of the United States's motion, plaintiffs' brief in opposition thereto, the reply brief of the United States, and the applicable law in this case, the Court finds that the United States's motion to quash should be granted in part and denied in part.

I. PROCEDURAL BACKGROUND

On February 25, 1996, Ira Weinstein, an American citizen, was injured in a suicide bombing undertaken by members of Hamas in Jerusalem, and died on April 13 of that year. Plaintiffs initiated the present suit on October 27, 2000 under the Foreign Sovereign Immunities Act ("FSIA"), 28 U.S.C. §1605, as amended.

On February 6, 2002, this Court entered a default judgment against defendants, and awarded plaintiffs $33.2 million in compensatory damages and $150 million in punitive damages. *Weinstein v. Islamic Republic of Iran,* 184 F.Supp.2d 13 (D.D.C.2002). Plaintiffs' counsel later served three writs of attachment, which are dated November 26, 2002, upon the U.S. Departments of State, Defense, and Treasury. The writs notified these agencies that "any money, property or credits other than wages, salary and commissions of the above named defendant(s), are seized...and you are required to hold it and not to pay or surrender it to the defendant(s) or to anyone else without an order from this court." The cover letters transmitted with the writs noted that the writs "appl[y], *inter alia* and *without limitation,* to the Iran Foreign Military Sales Program account within the Foreign Military Sales ('FMS') Fund and to any other assets, credits or funds of the instant judgment debtors and their agencies and instrumentalities within the FMS Fund," as well as to four identified Bank of America accounts "if the funds in any of these accounts are found to be funds of the instant judgment debtors or their agencies and instrumentalities held by the United States."

On January 31, 2003, the United States filed a motion with this Court seeking to quash the three writs of attachment issued against the Departments of State, Treasury, and Defense. [FN1] Plaintiffs submitted a brief in opposition to the United States's motion on May 9, 2003. The reply brief of the United States was filed on June 13, 2003.

FN1. The United States appears pursuant to 28 U.S.C. §517, which authorizes the United States to appear in any court in the United States "to attend to the interests of the United States in a suit pending in a court of the United States, or in a court of a State, or to attend to any other interest of the United States."

II. ANALYSIS

Before analyzing the legal questions at issue, it will be necessary to explain the precise scope of the issues before the Court. In their opposition brief, plaintiffs have clarified that the writs of attachment served upon the Departments of Defense, State, and Treasury were not directed towards any Iranian diplomatic or consular real properties located in the United States. The reply brief of the United States appears to accept this representation of plaintiffs. Therefore, the issue of whether the writs of attachment could reach such properties is not before this Court. Instead, the only assets that plaintiffs are seeking to attach are the four Bank of America accounts identified in the attachment writs ("the Bank of America accounts") and the Iran Foreign Military Sales Program account within the Foreign Military Sales Fund ("the FMS account").

The United States asserts that the writs should be quashed because the doctrine of federal sovereign immunity bars the attachment of the assets sought in the writs. Plaintiffs acknowledge that this doctrine is implicated, but contend that the United States has waived its sovereign immunity with respect to the attachment of these assets. Because the question of whether a valid waiver of sovereign immunity exists constitutes a threshold jurisdictional question, the Court will address this issue first.

A. Federal Sovereign Immunity

The doctrine of federal sovereign immunity provides that the United States may not be sued without its express consent. Therefore, absent an express waiver of sovereign immunity, the federal government and its agencies will be immune from suit. *Dep't of the Army v. Blue Fox, Inc.,* 525 U.S. 255, 260, 119 S.Ct. 687, 142 L.Ed.2d 718 (1999). A waiver of sovereign immunity must be "unequivocally expressed in the statutory text" and "is to be strictly construed, in terms of its scope, in favor of the sovereign." *Id.* at 261, 119 S.Ct. 687. Therefore, any ambiguities within the statutory text must be resolved in favor of the sovereign. *See United States v. Williams,* 514 U.S. 527, 531, 115 S.Ct. 1611, 131 L.Ed.2d 608 (1995) ("Our task is to discern the unequivocally expressed intent of Congress, construing ambiguities in favor of immunity.") (citation and internal quotation marks omitted).

This Court has previously explained that the principles of sovereign immunity "apply with equal force to attachments and garnishments." *Flatow v. Islamic Republic of Iran,* 74

F.Supp.2d 18, 21 (D.D.C.1999) (citations omitted). There-fore, if a litigant seeks to attach funds held in the U.S. Trea-sury, he or she must demonstrate that the United States has waived its sovereign immunity with respect to those funds. *Id.* at 22 (concluding that U.S. Treasury funds constituted the property of the United States and could not be attached in the absence of an express waiver of sovereign immunity).

In the instant case, plaintiffs assert that section 201 of the Terrorism Risk Insurance Act of 2002 ("TRIA"), Pub.L. No. 107-297, 116 Stat. 2322 (2002) functions as an express waiver of sovereign immunity, allowing them to attach funds held by the United States. Whether, in fact, the TRIA con-stitutes a waiver of federal sovereign immunity appears to be an issue of first impression. The Court must therefore ex-amine the statutory language, in order to determine whether it demonstrates a clear, unequivocal expression of intent to waive the sovereign immunity of the United States.

Section 201(a) of the TRIA provides:

IN GENERAL.-Notwithstanding any other provision of law, and except as provided in subsection (b), in every case in which a person has obtained a judgment against a terrorist party on a claim based upon an act of terrorism, or for which a terrorist party is not immune under section 1605(a)(7) of title 28, United States Code, the blocked assets of that ter-rorist party (including the blocked assets of any agency or instrumentality of that terrorist party) shall be subject to ex-ecution or attachment in aid of execution in order to satisfy such judgment to the extent of any compensatory damages for which such terrorist party has been adjudged liable.

The term "blocked assets" is defined in section 201(d)(2) as

any asset seized or frozen by the United States under sec-tion 5(b) of the Trading With the Enemy Act (50 U.S.C.App. 5(b)) or under sections 202 and 203 of the International Emergency Economic Powers Act (50 U.S.C. 1701; 1702); and

(B) does not include property that-

(i) is subject to a license issued by the United States Gov-ernment for final payment, transfer, or disposition by or to a person subject to the jurisdiction of the United States in con-nection with a transaction for which the issuance of such li-cense has been specifically required by statute other than the International Emergency Economic Powers Act (50 U.S.C.

1701 *et seq.*) or the United Nations Participation Act of 1945 (22 U.S.C. 287 *et seq.*); or

(ii) in the case of property subject to the Vienna Conven-tion on Diplomatic Relations or the Vienna Convention on Consular Relations, or that enjoys equivalent privileges and immunities under the law of the United States, is being used exclusively for diplomatic or consular purposes.

Plaintiffs assert that by mandating that "the blocked assets of that terrorist party...shall be subject to execution or attach-ment in aid of execution in order to satisfy such judgment," Congress expressly waived the sovereign immunity of the United States with respect to "any asset seized or frozen by the United States" under the two identified statutes that does not fall under the protection of subsection (B). They con-strue the phrase "any asset...seized by the United States" to refer to assets that have been seized by the United States, and are presently being held by the United States. There-fore, plaintiffs explain, Congress has waived the sovereign immunity of the United States with respect to writs seeking to attach any assets seized by the United States from a "ter-rorist party," as defined in the statute, and that are currently being held by the United States.

However, the phrase in question is by no means susceptible to only one interpretation. As the United States points out, it is a mistake to equate "assets seized by" (which refers to assets of which the United States has taken forcible pos-session) with "assets held by" (which refers to assets pres-ently possessed by the United States by a lawful title). For example, the United States might have seized assets from a foreign state sponsor of terrorism at some point in time, but later decided to relinquish its possession of those assets. In such an instance, although the assets would have been "as-sets seized by" the United States, they are not "assets (pres-ently) held by" the United States. In other words, the intent of Congress may simply have been to authorize successful plaintiffs to attach assets that have previously been seized by the United States from state sponsors of terrorism, and that are no longer being held by the United States. This in-terpretation also makes sense in light of the precise phrase in question: "any asset seized or frozen by the United States." Assets that have been frozen by the United States are not necessarily assets that are held by the United States, because the frozen assets might belong to some other entity.

In short, the language of section 201 is susceptible to two meanings, one providing for a waiver of federal sovereign immunity and one that does not provide a waiver of sovereign immunity. As such, this Court cannot conclude that it constitutes a clear, unequivocal waiver of federal sovereign immunity. *See Galvan v. Fed. Prison Indus.,* 199 F.3d 461, 464 (D.C.Cir.1999) ("So long as a statute supposedly waiving immunity has a 'plausible' non-waiver reading, a finding of waiver must be rejected.") (citing *United States v. Nordic Village, Inc.,* 503 U.S. 30, 37, 112 S.Ct. 1011, 117 L.Ed.2d 181 (1992)).

It follows that if the property sought to be attached by plaintiffs is property that (1) has been seized by the United States from a terrorist party and (2) is presently held by the United States, it cannot be attached by their three writs. The Court must therefore examine the assets sought to be attached in order to determine whether they satisfy these two requirements.

B. The FMS Account

Under the Foreign Military Sales Program, the United States sells military equipment and services to foreign nations and international organizations. The program is governed by the Arms Export Control Act of 1976, which is codified at 22 U.S.C. §§2751 *et seq.* Payments to the United States from the participants in the program are deposited into a single account in the U.S. Treasury known as the FMS Account. Plaintiffs seek to attach the portion of the FMS Account attributable to moneys that are to be disbursed to Iran. It is undisputed that this account represents a fund held by the U.S. Treasury. As this Court has observed, "funds held in the U.S. Treasury-even though set aside or 'earmarked' for a specific purpose-remain the property of the United States until the government elects to pay them to whom they are owed." *Flatow,* 74 F.Supp.2d at 21 (citing *Buchanan v. Alexander,* 45 U.S. (4 How.) 20, 11 L.Ed. 857 (1846)). Therefore, the doctrine of federal sovereign immunity bars the attachment of the FMS Account, or any portion thereof, by plaintiffs.

C. The Bank of America Accounts

Plaintiffs also seek to attach four identified Bank of America accounts "if the funds in any of these accounts are found to be funds of the instant judgment debtors or their agencies and instrumentalities held by the United States." Each of these accounts is related in some way to real property located in the United States that was formerly used by the Iranian government for diplomatic or consular purposes. Because the accounts vary in their nature and purpose, it will be necessary for the Court to analyze them separately. However, the Court will provide a brief description of how these accounts came into being.

On November 14, 1979, pursuant to the International Emergency Economic Powers Act, 50 U.S.C. §1701 *et seq.,* and other authorities, President Carter issued Executive Order 12170, which blocked all Iranian assets subject to the jurisdiction of the United States. However, in accordance with the Vienna Conventions on Diplomatic and Consular Relations, the United States allowed Iran to continue to occupy its embassy and other diplomatic residences within the United States. On April 7, 1980, the president announced that the United States was breaking diplomatic relations with the government of Iran. The Secretary of State informed the Iranian government that its embassy and consulates in the United States were to be closed, and that all Iranian diplomatic and consular officials were to leave the country by the next day.

1. The Rental Proceeds Accounts

Two of the Bank of America accounts (the "First and Second Accounts") relate to real property in the United States that formerly served as sites of embassies or consular offices of the nation of Iran. These former Iranian diplomatic properties are presently being leased by the United States to third parties. The monies generated by these leases are placed in the Second Account for immediate disbursal to be used to pay for maintenance and repair expenses of the properties. Any funds generated from these leases that exceed the expected cost of maintenance and repairs are transferred to the First Account on a yearly basis.

The First Account is entitled "Iranian Diplomatic and Consular Property Renovation Account." In another proceeding, this Court determined that this account constituted "United States property, which is immune from attachment by virtue of the doctrine of sovereign immunity." *Flatow v. Islamic Republic of Iran,* 76 F.Supp.2d 16, 24 (D.D.C.1999). Although the United States suggests in its motion to quash that the property might be more properly characterized as the property of Iran, the doctrine of collateral estoppel prevents reconsideration of this issue. Therefore, because this account represents funds held by the United States, it is barred from attachment by plaintiffs on the grounds of federal sovereign immunity.

The Second Account is entitled "U.S. Department of State, Office of Foreign Missions, Iranian Renovation Account." Although the Second Account was also discussed in *Flatow,* the Court made no determination as to whether it represented the property of the United States. *See id.*

A portion of the funds in the Second Account has been designated under the Victims of Trafficking and Violence Protection Act of 2000 to be paid to certain persons who have obtained judgments under the FSIA against Iran. *See* Victims of Trafficking and Violence Protection Act of 2000 ("the Act"), Pub.L. No. 106-386, §2002(b)(2), 114 Stat. 1464, 1542 (directing the Treasury Secretary to make payments to the designated persons "from amounts paid and liquidated from…rental proceeds accrued on the date of the enactment of this Act from Iranian diplomatic and consular property located in the United States"). Although section 201(b) of the TRIA amended the Act, it made no changes to the language of this subsection. The portion of the funds in the Second Account that are thus designated for payments to prevailing FSIA plaintiffs will therefore be unavailable for attachment by the plaintiffs in the present action. It does not appear that this will result in prejudice to plaintiffs, however, because the United States represents that plaintiffs are eligible to be designated by the Secretary of the Treasury to receive payment from these funds in the Second Account.

However, the United States does not represent that the entirety of the Second Account has been designated to satisfy these judgments against Iran. Therefore, the Court must determine whether plaintiffs may attach the portion of the Second Account that has not been so designated.

The United States asserts that plaintiffs may not attach this portion of the Second Account because the Second Account does not fall under the definition of "blocked assets" under the TRIA. As noted above, the TRIA excludes from its definition of "blocked assets" that may be attached by prevailing FSIA plaintiffs "property that…in the case of property subject to the Vienna Convention on Diplomatic Relations or the Vienna Convention on Consular Relations, or that enjoys equivalent privileges and immunities under the law of the United States, is being used exclusively for diplomatic or consular purposes." In turn, "property subject to the Vienna Convention on Diplomatic Relations or the Vienna Convention on Consular Relations" is defined as "any property,…the attachment in aid of execution or execution of which would result in a violation of an obligation of the United States under the Vienna Convention on Diplomatic Relations or the Vienna Convention on Consular Relations, as the case may be." Article 45 of the Vienna Convention on Diplomatic Relations provides, in relevant part, that "[i]f diplomatic relations are broken off between two States, or if a mission is permanently or temporarily recalled…the receiving State must, even in case of armed conflict, respect and protect the premises of the mission, together with its

property and archives[.]" Vienna Convention on Diplomatic Relations, 23 U.S.T. 3227, T.I.A.S. No. 7502, *available at http:// www.un.org/law/ilc/texts/diplomat.htm*. Article 27 of the Vienna Convention on Consular Relations includes a parallel provision: "In the event of the severance of consular relations between two States…the receiving State shall, even in case of armed conflict, respect and protect the consular premises, together with the property of the consular post and the consular archives[.]" Vienna Convention on Consular Relations, 21 U.S.T. 77, T.I.A.S. No. 6820, *available at http://www.un.org/law/ilc/convents.htm*.

The United States asserts that because the funds in the Second Account are being used only to pay for maintenance and repair expenses of the former Iranian diplomatic properties, they constitute property "being used exclusively for diplomatic and consular purposes." Specifically, it explains that the funds are presently being used to fulfill the obligation of the United States under the two Vienna conventions to protect and maintain the former diplomatic properties. Plaintiffs, on the other hand, insist that the term "being used exclusively for diplomatic or consular purposes" should not be construed to refer to funds that are being used to maintain and repair properties that were *formerly* used for diplomatic purposes.

None of the case law cited by plaintiffs or the United States definitely resolves this issue. It is true that in *Liberian Eastern Timber Corp. v. Government of Republic of Liberia,* 659 F.Supp. 606 (D.D.C.1987), another court in this circuit concluded that bank accounts used by the Liberian Embassy were immune from attachment under the Vienna Convention on Diplomatic Relations. But that case involved a functional embassy, not one that had long since been abandoned. More recently, in *Hill v. Republic of Iraq,* 2003 WL 21057173 (D.D.C. March 11, 2003), another court in this circuit ordered that bank accounts held in the name of the former Iraqi embassy in the United States be attached under the TRIA. But the court concluded that the funds in these accounts "were used primarily (if not exclusively) for commercial, rather than diplomatic, purposes." *Id.* at n. 4.

The Court concludes that the more logical argument is that the funds in question fit within the TRIA's definition of property that is "being used exclusively for diplomatic and consular purposes." The sole purpose of the funds in the Second Account is to maintain and repair the former Iranian diplomatic residences within the United States, in accordance with the United States's obligation under both of the Vienna conventions to "respect and protect" the buildings that once constituted these residences. If the Court permitted plaintiffs to attach these funds, the United States would thereby be deprived of the funds that it utilizes to satisfy this obligation. Therefore, such an attachment would result in a violation of an obligation owed by the United States pursuant to the two conventions. The Court therefore finds that the funds in the Second Account that have not been designated to satisfy judgments pursuant to the Victims of Trafficking and Violence Protection Act are nevertheless not subject to attachment because they do not constitute "blocked assets" under the TRIA.

2. The Third and Fourth Accounts

On November 16, 1979, two days after President Carter issued Executive Order 12170 freezing all Iranian assets in the United States, the Treasury Department issued a directive to the Continental Illinois National Bank & Trust: "You are hereby authorized to permit the [Iranian] Consulate General (Chicago) to operate the following checking account with you…You are authorized to make all payments, transfers and withdrawals from and credits to said account, which is necessary for use by such office for its lawful official operations in the United States." On November 19, 1979, the Treasury Department issued a directive to Bank of America similar to the November 16 directive sent to the Continental Illinois National Bank & Trust. The directive authorized the bank to permit the Iranian Consulate General in San Francisco to operate two checking accounts with the bank. As noted above, however, all Iranian embassies and consulates within the United States were closed on April 8, 1980, and all Iranian diplomatic and consular officials were ordered to leave the country by midnight on that date. Some time afterward, Bank of America acquired the Continental Illinois National Bank & Trust.

The Third Account is the checking account that had been used by the Iranian consulate in Chicago, which is entitled "Consulate General of the Islamic Republic in Chicago." The two checking accounts used by the Iranian consulate in San Francisco were combined to form the Fourth Account, which is entitled "Consulate General Iran." The United States claims that despite the fact that these accounts have "presumably [become] inactive (as the signatories on the accounts [have] left the country," they may not be attached by plaintiffs because they constitute property that the United States is obliged to protect under the Vienna conventions.) The Court disagrees. The United States cites no specific provision of the Vienna conventions indicating that the United States is obliged to protect these funds, and the Court has been unable to locate such a provision. Under the Vienna

Convention on Diplomatic Relations, the United States is only obliged to protect "the premises of the mission," which is defined under Article 1 of the convention as "the buildings or parts of buildings and the land ancillary thereto, irrespective of ownership, used for the purposes of the mission including the residence of the head of the mission." Similarly, under the Vienna Convention on Consular Relations, the United States is only obliged to protect "consular premises," which is defined under Article 1 as "the buildings or parts of buildings and the land ancillary thereto, irrespective of ownership, used exclusively for the purposes of the consular post." Therefore, the only property that the United States is obliged to "respect and protect" under the conventions is "the buildings or parts of buildings and the land ancillary thereto, irrespective of ownership, used exclusively for" diplomatic or consular purposes. The accounts in question manifestly do not fit within this definition. Moreover, unlike the Second Account, the Third and Fourth Accounts are not presently being used for any diplomatic or consular purpose, such as to maintain and repair the former Iranian embassies. Finally, the United States does not allege, and this Court does not find, that the accounts were "subject to a license issued by the United States Government for final payment, transfer, or disposition by or to a person subject to the jurisdiction of the United States in connection with a transaction for which the issuance of such license has been specifically required by statute," pursuant to section 201(d)(2)(B)(i) of the TRIA. Therefore, plaintiffs may attach the Third and Fourth Accounts.

III. CONCLUSION

The Court concludes that section 201 of the Terrorism Risk Insurance Act does not provide an express waiver of federal sovereign immunity. Therefore, the FMS Account and the First Account, which are the property of the United States, cannot be attached by plaintiffs to satisfy their judgment against Iran. Additionally, the Second Account does not constitute "blocked assets" subject to attachment under the TRIA. However, the Third and Fourth Accounts are subject to attachment by plaintiffs. It is therefore

ORDERED that the motion of the United States to quash plaintiffs' writs of attachment [40-1] be, and hereby is, GRANTED in part and DENIED in part. It is further

ORDERED that plaintiffs' writs of attachment be, and hereby are, QUASHED as to the Iran Foreign Military Sales Program account within the Foreign Military Sales Fund, and the two Bank of America accounts entitled "Iranian

Diplomatic and Consular Property Renovation Account" and "U.S. Department of State, Office of Foreign Missions, Iranian Renovation Account," which are referred to herein as the First and Second Accounts. It is further

ORDERED that the motion of the United States to quash plaintiffs' writs of attachment be, and hereby is, DENIED as to the two Bank of America accounts entitled "Consulate General of the Islamic Republic in Chicago" and "Consulate General Iran," which are referred to herein as the Third and Fourth Accounts.

SO ORDERED.

Notes:

1.   One court described the remedial legislative purpose of TRIA:

> The TRIA was...specifically intended "to deal comprehensively with the problem of enforcement of judgments rendered on behalf of victims of terrorism in any court of competent jurisdiction by enabling them to satisfy such judgments through the attachment of blocked assets of terrorist parties." 148 Cong. Rec. H8728 (Nov. 13, 2002).

Hill v. Republic of Iraq, 2003 WL 21057173 at 2 (D.D.C. 2003).

2.   As noted, TRIA §201 permits attachments and executions "Notwithstanding any other provision of law," and its clear remedial purpose is to assist American terrorism victims to enforce judgments against terrorist parties:

> TRIA §201 was passed in order to "deal comprehensively with the problem of enforcement of judgments rendered on behalf of victims of terrorism in any court of competent jurisdiction by enabling them to satisfy such judgments through the attachment of blocked assets of terrorist parties. It is the intent of the Conferees that Section 201 establish that such judgments are to be enforced." H.R. Conf. Rep. 107-779, at 27 (2002), reprinted in 2002 U.S.C.C.A.N. 1430, at 1434-35; *see Hill v. Republic of Iraq*, No. 99 Civ. 03346, 2003 WL 21057173, at *2 (D.D.C. Mar. 11, 2003) (discussing enactment of TRIA). As noted by the Second Circuit, the plain meaning of the phrase that blocked assets "shall be subject to execution or at-

tachment in aid of execution" "is to give terrorist victims who actually receive favorable judgments a right to execute against assets that would otherwise be blocked." *Smith ex rel. Estate of Smith v. Fed. Reserve Bank of New York*, 346 F.3d 264, 271 (2d Cir. 2003).

Weininger v. Castro, 462 F.Supp.2d 457, 463 (S.D.N.Y. 2006).

3.   How does the license issue come in to play in collection actions? Who would typically raise this argument and what effect does it have?

4.   Typically, collection proceedings under TRIA §201 involve (and become bogged down by) the issue of licensing. Virtually every decision discussing the issue has confirmed that, "No license by the Office of Foreign Assets Control of the U.S. Treasury Department is required as a precondition" to an execution under TRIA §201. *Daliberti v. J.P Morgan Chase & Co.*, 2003 WL 340734 at 2 (S.D.N.Y. 2003). Accordingly, the federal courts have authorized executions under TRIA without an OFAC license.

5.   The case law applying and interpreting TRIA §201 establishes that the "notwithstanding" language operates to override all statutory limitations on attachment and execution:

> This matter concerns the efforts of plaintiffs, 180 individuals in whose favor default judgments have been entered against the Republic of Iraq ("Iraq"), to satisfy those judgments [against] accounts...that are held by garnishee Riggs Bank NA in the name of the Embassy of Iraq Commercial Office (the "Iraqi Accounts"). Both of these accounts have been blocked since August 2, 1992 pursuant to Executive Order No. 12722 and the International Emergency Economic Powers Act. 50 U.S.C. §§1701-02. Plaintiffs have moved this Court for issuance of an order directing execution against those accounts. The Court finds that each of these accounts is subject to execution under the Terrorism Risk Insurance Act ("TRIA")...

> Section 201 of the TRIA states that "[n]otwithstanding any other provision of law," the blocked assets of a terrorist party "shall be subject to execution or attachment in aid of execution." As this Court has frequently recognized, "the phrase

'notwithstanding any other provision of law,' or a variation thereof, means exactly that; it is unambiguous and effectively supersedes all previous laws." *Energy Transp. Group, Inc v. Skinner,* 752 F.Supp. 1, 10 (D.D.C. 1990); *see also Crowley Caribbean Transp., Inc. v. United States,* 865 F.2d 1281, 1283 (D.C.Cir. 1989) ("[a] clearer statement [than 'notwithstanding any other provision of law'] is difficult to imagine"). Accordingly, by its plain terms, the TRIA overrides any immunity from execution that blocked Iraqi property might otherwise enjoy under the Vienna Convention [on Diplomatic Relations] or the FSIA.

Hill, 2003 WL 21057173 at 1-2.

6.   Similarly, in *Hegna v. Islamic Republic of Iran,* 376 F.3d 485 (5th Cir. 2004), the Court affirmed that (except when the property is being exclusively used for diplomatic or consular purposes) TRIA overrides the immunity provisions of the Vienna Convention and permits execution against diplomatic property subject to the Convention. Accordingly, TRIA's "notwithstanding" language overrides (1) executive blocking orders issued pursuant to IEEPA (2) the FSIA and (3) the Vienna Conventions. This is significant, because it has been consistently held that IEEPA, the FSIA, and the Vienna Convention are themselves all legal regimes of superior and overriding normative force,

> In *Charles T. Main Intern., Inc. v. Khuzestan Water & Power Authority,* 651 F.2d 800 (1st Cir. 1981), the First Circuit held that, "The language of IEEPA is sweeping and unqualified," and that the IEEPA blocking regime empowers the President to override judicial remedies, such as attachments and injunctions, and to extinguish "interests" in foreign assets held by U.S. citizens. *Id.* at 807.

7.   In *Smith v. Federal Reserve Bank of New York,* 346 F.3d 264 (2nd Cir. 2003) judgment creditors of Iraq sought to execute pursuant to TRIA §201 against funds allegedly held by the Federal Reserve. The court noted that,

> Plaintiffs' theory of the case is premised upon the idea that section 201 of TRIA represents a Congressional mandate-akin to an appropriation-that the frozen Iraqi Assets be used only to compensate plaintiffs who have judgments against the Iraqi government. According to this theory, the Presi-

dent acted without authority when he confiscated blocked Iraqi assets and directed their use for a purpose other than satisfying victims' judgments.

Id. at 270. Is this a plausible interpretation of TRIA §201? The court did not agree and found that,

> We disagree with Plaintiffs' interpretation of the statute. First, we do not believe that TRIA §201 is analogous to an appropriation. Although Plaintiffs consistently imply that TRIA is an appropriation-most notably through their repeated reference to the President's confiscation as a "reappropriation"-nowhere do they argue directly that section 201 operates literally as an appropriation. If they did, they would have to confront the challenge of explaining how these funds constituted "appropriations." *See* 31 U.S.C. §1301(d) ("A law may [only be] an appropriation...if the law specifically states that an appropriation is made."); *see also* U.S. Const. art I, §9, cl.7 ("No Money shall be drawn from the Treasury, but in Consequence of Appropriations made by Law"). Second, the language of section 201 cannot reasonably be read to mandate that terrorist assets be blocked in perpetuity. It states simply that blocked assets "shall be subject to execution or attachment in aid of execution."

Id. at 270.

8.   Why did the U.S. government oppose the victims' attempts to collect these long dormant accounts?

9.   Why would the Congress revoke the immunity of terror sponsoring states with respect to the underlying claim but not provide a mechanism to overcome the immunity with respect to attachment?

10. Does the passage of TRIA §201 suggest that Congress did not express "a clear, unequivocal waiver of sovereign immunity"?

11. As a party to the Vienna Convention, does the U.S. have a direct interest in the proceedings that exceed traditional diplomatic and political concerns?

12. What were the risks to the U.S. in the international diplomatic arena if the plaintiffs' attachments had been granted?

13. Has TRIA §201 lived up to its billing as a panacea for terrorism judgment creditors? What additional provisions or changes to the current law would assist victims to satisfy their judgments?

Ministry of Defense and Support for Armed Forces of Islamic Republic of Iran v. Cubic Defense Systems, 385 F.3d 1206 (9th Cir. 2004).

BETTY B. FLETCHER, Circuit Judge:

These consolidated appeals arise from attempts by Stephen Flatow ("Flatow") and Dariush Elahi ("Elahi") to collect on default judgments they obtained against the Islamic Republic of Iran ("Iran") in the United States District Court for the District of Columbia. That court found Iran liable for the terrorist acts that resulted in the deaths of Flatow's daughter and Elahi's brother. In both cases, the district court assessed substantial compensatory and punitive damages against Iran.

In the underlying case, Iran's Ministry of Defense ("MOD") successfully petitioned the District Court for the Southern District of California to confirm an arbitration award issued in its favor by the International Chamber of Commerce ("ICC"). The $2.8 million award had been issued against a supplier of military equipment, Cubic Defense Systems, Inc. ("Cubic"), and related to a claimed breach of contract by Cubic in providing military hardware to MOD. Shortly after the district court confirmed the arbitration award, Flatow moved to intervene in the case. The district court denied Flatow's motion, and that decision is the subject of the appeal in case No. 99-56498. Later, both Flatow and Elahi moved to attach MOD's judgment against Cubic. In turn, MOD moved the district court for a determination that its judgment against Cubic was immune from attachment. The district court granted MOD's motion with respect to Flatow, but denied it with respect to Elahi. Flatow and MOD appeal those determinations in case Nos. 02-57043 and 03-55015, respectively.

JURISDICTION

The denial of a motion to intervene as of right is an appealable final order. *Leisnoi, Inc. v. United States,* 313 F.3d 1181, 1184 (9th Cir.2002). In addition, district court orders entered after the entry of judgment are generally reviewable by a separate appeal. *See United States v. One 1986 Ford Pickup,* 56 F.3d 1181, 1184-85 (9th Cir.1995). We therefore have jurisdiction over the consolidated appeals pursuant to 28 U.S.C. §1291.

BACKGROUND

The Flatow Default Judgment

On April 10, 1995, Alisa Michelle Flatow, an American college student living in Israel, died of injuries she sustained as a result of a suicide bombing in the Gaza Strip. *See Flatow v. Islamic Republic of Iran,* 999 F.Supp. 1, 7-8 (D.D.C.1998). Her father, Stephen Flatow, later brought suit against Iran, its Ministry of Information and Security ("MOIS"), and various Iranian officials in the District Court for the District of Columbia. [FN1] The Iranian government and its officials did not enter an appearance, and the district court entered a default judgment against them on March 11, 1998. *Id.* at 6. Prior to entering judgment, however, the court conducted an evidentiary hearing and set forth detailed findings of fact and conclusions of law. The court found that Flatow had established his claim to relief in that the Iranian government and the other defendants had sponsored terrorist acts and performed acts which caused the death of Flatow's daughter. [FN2] *Id.* at 9-10. The district court also held that it had subject-matter jurisdiction over the action and personal jurisdiction over the defendants. *Id.* at 34. The judgment against the Iranian defendants was for $20,000,000 in compensatory damages and $250,000,000 in punitive damages. *Id.* at 32, 34.

FN1. Flatow sued under the Antiterrorism and Effective Death Penalty Act ("AEDPA"), Pub.L. No. 104-132, 110 Stat. 1241 (1996), and a separate provision known as the "Flatow Amendment," 1997 Omnibus Consolidated Appropriations Act, Pub.L. 104-208, Div. A, Title I §101(c), 110 Stat. 3009-172, *reprinted at* 28 U.S.C.A. §1605 note (West 2003). These provisions purported to provide both a cause of action and a forum to adjudicate claims arising from state-sponsored terrorist attacks which resulted in the death or injury of a United States citizen. *See generally Flatow,* 999 F.Supp. at 12-13. AEDPA also created an exception to the sovereign immunity of foreign states designated as terrorist states in cases in which the foreign state commits a terrorist act or provides support to others who commit such an act. *See id.;* 28 U.S.C. §1605(a)(7).

FN2. Under 28 U.S.C. §1608(e), the district court cannot enter a default judgment against a foreign state until the claimant "establishes his claim or right to relief by evidence satisfactory to the court."

The Elahi Default Judgment

On October 23, 1990, Dr. Cyrus Elahi was assassinated in Paris, France. *See Elahi v. Islamic Republic of Iran,* 124

F.Supp.2d 97, 103 (D.D.C.2000). Dr. Elahi was a naturalized United States citizen and an important official in an Iranian opposition group working from France. *Id.* at 102-03. French authorities arrested a number of Iranian nationals, and determined that the assassination had been orchestrated by the Iranian government through MOIS. *Id.* at 104. In 2000, Dr. Elahi's brother, Dariush Elahi, filed suit against Iran and MOIS in the District Court for the District of Columbia. As with the Flatow case, the Iranian government did not enter an appearance with that court, and the court therefore entered a default judgment in favor of Elahi in December 20, 2000. *Id.* at 99-100. Before entering judgment, the district court issued findings of fact and conclusions of law. The judgment against Iran was for compensatory damages in the amount of $11,740,035, and punitive damages of $300,000,000. *Id.* at 115.

The Case Against Cubic Defense Systems

In October 1977, MOD's predecessor entered into a pair of contracts with Cubic, a California-based defense firm, relating to the sale and servicing of an Air Combat Maneuvering Range ("ACMR") for use by the Iranian Air Force. *Ministry of Def. v. Cubic Def. Systems, Inc.,* 29 F.Supp.2d 1168, 1170 (S.D.Cal.1998). Following the Iranian revolution of 1979, the delivery of the ACMR did not take place for reasons that the two parties dispute. *See id.* In September 1991, and pursuant to the terms of the contracts, MOD filed a request for arbitration with the ICC in Zurich, Switzerland. *Id.* After submissions from both MOD and Cubic, the ICC ruled in favor of MOD and issued a Final Award requiring Cubic to pay MOD $2.8 million. *Id.* at 1171.

In June 1998, MOD filed a petition in the District Court for the Southern District of California to confirm the award entered by the ICC pursuant to the New York Convention. [FN3] *Id.* at 1170. After reviewing Cubic's arguments in opposition, the district court granted MOD's petition and confirmed the ICC Award on December 7, 1998. *Id.* at 1174. [FN4] Both Cubic and MOD took cross appeals of the district court's decision, and those appeals remain pending.

FN3. "The New York Convention" refers to the United Nations Convention on the Recognition and Enforcement of Foreign Arbitration Awards, *opened for signature* June 10, 1958, 21 U.S.T. 2517, 330 U.N.T.S. 3, *reprinted in* 9 U.S.C.A. §201 note (West 2003).

FN4. Throughout this opinion, we will refer to this $2.8 million judgment entered against Cubic and on behalf of MOD as the "Cubic judgment."

On February 1, 1999, Flatow filed a Motion for Leave to Intervene in the district court. Flatow pointed out that he had obtained a Summons in Garnishment directed at Cubic from the District Court for the Eastern District of Virginia, and that he expected to receive an Order of Condemnation from that court as to MOD's cause of action in the Cubic case. The district court denied Flatow's motion on April 6, 1999, finding that, under Rule 24(a)(2) of the Federal Rules of Civil Procedure, the motion was untimely and Flatow had failed to establish "an interest relating to the property or transaction which is the subject matter of the litigation." On June 10, 1999, Flatow filed a motion for reconsideration of the district court's decision, but the district court denied the motion on August 10, 1999. Flatow filed a notice of appeal from the denial of his motion for reconsideration on September 9, 1999. We heard oral arguments on this appeal (99-56498) on December 6, 2001, but vacated submission of the case pending the resolution of a motion by MOD to dismiss the appeal. MOD claimed that Flatow's acceptance of payments under the Victims of Trafficking and Violence Protection Act of 2000 rendered him unable to collect against the Cubic judgment. We directed that MOD's motion to dismiss be filed in the district court and stayed the intervention appeal pending that court's decision.

At the same time that Flatow's motion to intervene was being rejected, Flatow filed a notice of lien with the district court on April 27, 1999. The notice indicated that Flatow had registered his default judgment against Iran in the Southern District of California, and claimed that any monies to be distributed as part of the Cubic judgment should be directed to him. A similar notice of lien was filed by Elahi on November 1, 2001.

On September 13, 2002, MOD filed motions seeking a judicial determination that its judgment against Cubic Defense Systems was immune from attachment by both Flatow and Elahi. The district court heard oral argument on the motion on October 28, 2002, and rendered its decision on November 26, 2002. The district court granted MOD's motion as to Flatow and ordered the striking of Flatow's notice of lien, but it denied the motion as to Elahi, finding that MOD's judgment was not immune from attachment by Elahi. *Ministry of Def. v. Cubic Def. Systems Inc.,* 236 F.Supp.2d 1140, 1152 (S.D.Cal.2002) (hereinafter "District Court Order"). Both Flatow and MOD filed timely appeals.

DISCUSSION

I. The Denial of Flatow's Motion to Intervene

We examine first the district court's decision to deny Flatow's motion to intervene as of right under Rule 24(a)(2) of the Federal Rules of Civil Procedure in the underlying litigation between MOD and Cubic. Ordinarily, we review the denial of a motion to intervene de novo. *See Arakaki v. Cayetano,* 324 F.3d 1078, 1082 (9th Cir.2003). However, Flatow's appeal is not from the denial of the motion to intervene itself but from the denial of his motion for reconsideration of that decision. We therefore review for an abuse of discretion. *Smith v. Pac. Properties Dev. Corp.,* 358 F.3d 1097, 1100 (9th Cir.2004).

We have previously explained that an applicant for intervention as of right under Rule 24(a)(2) must comply with the following four requirements:

(1) the application for intervention must be timely;

(2) the applicant must have a "significantly protect able" interest relating to the property or transaction that is the subject of the action; (3) the applicant must be so situated that the disposition of the action may, as a practical matter, impair or impede the applicant's ability to protect that interest; and (4) the applicant's interest must not be adequately represented by the existing parties in the lawsuit.

Southwest Ctr. for Biological Diversity v. Berg, 268 F.3d 810, 817 (9th Cir.2001). In this case, the district court denied Flatow's motion for leave to intervene on the grounds that the motion was untimely and that Flatow had failed to establish an interest relating to the property or transaction which is the subject matter of litigation.

We conclude that the district court did not abuse its discretion in refusing to reconsider its determination regarding Flatow's motion to intervene. Flatow claimed to meet the "significantly protectable interest" prong of the Rule 24(a)(2) test because he is a judgment creditor of MOD and therefore has an interest in ensuring he is able to collect on his judgment. Our court has already rejected this line of argument, however, in a decision issued after the briefs were filed in these appeals. *See United States v. Alisal Water Corp.,* 370 F.3d 915, 920-21 (9th Cir.2004). In *Alisal Water,* we explained that the mere interest in the prospective collectability of a debt is insufficient to satisfy the requirements of Rule 24(a)(2), unless that interest is related to the

underlying subject matter of the action. In this case, Flatow asserts no interest related to the underlying dispute between MOD and Cubic. Therefore, under *Alisal Water,* the district court properly rejected Flatow's attempt to intervene as of right in the underlying litigation. [FN5]

FN5. Because we affirm the district court's decision on this ground, we need not consider whether Flatow's motion to intervene was timely, and we decline to do so.

We affirm the district court's denial of Flatow's motion for reconsideration.

II. Flatow's Waiver of Claims Against Iran

MOD argues that Flatow has waived any claim that he may have had on the Cubic judgment through his acceptance of payments under section 2002 of the Victims of Trafficking and Violence Protection Act of 2000, Pub.L. No. 106-386, 114 Stat. 1464 ("Victims Protection Act"). The district court agreed with MOD and ordered the district court clerk to strike the lien that Flatow had placed on the Cubic judgment. District Court Order at 1152. Because the district court's decision presents purely legal questions, we review it de novo. *Ballaris v. Wacker Siltronic Corp.,* 370 F.3d 901, 910 (9th Cir.2004).

In enacting section 2002 of the Victims Protection Act, Congress created a mechanism through which individuals holding judgments against Iran or Cuba, based on those nations' sponsorship of terrorist activity, could collect damages from a special fund established by the United States government. Claimants had to choose between either (a) recovering 110 percent of the compensatory damages awarded in the judgment in return for relinquishing any rights as to compensatory or punitive damages, or (b) recovering 100 percent of the compensatory damages and relinquishing all rights as to compensatory damages but relinquishing only certain rights as to the punitive damages portion of their judgment. Victims Protection Act sections 2002(a)(1) and (a)(2). Claimants choosing option (b) would be required to relinquish "all rights to execute against or attach property that is at issue in claims against the United States before an international tribunal, that is the subject of awards rendered by such tribunal, or that is subject to section 1610(f)(1)(A) of title 28, United States Code." Victims Protection Act section 2002(a)(2)(D).

Neither Flatow nor MOD disputes that Flatow opted for option (b) under the Victims Protection Act and that he therefore received a payment of 100 percent of the compensatory damages he was awarded in the default judgment issued by the District Court for the District of Columbia. What the parties do dispute is the breadth of the relinquishment provision quoted above and whether it covers the judgment MOD obtained against Cubic. MOD does not argue that the Cubic judgment is either at issue in claims before an international tribunal or the subject of awards rendered by such a tribunal. Instead, MOD claims that the Cubic judgment is "property...that is subject to [28 U.S.C. §1610(f)(1)(A)]." Determining the viability of MOD's claim requires us to follow a labyrinthine path through several statutes and regulations.

Title 28 U.S.C. §1610(f)(1)(A) provides that

Notwithstanding any other provision of law, including but not limited to section 208(f) of the Foreign Missions Act (22 U.S.C. 4308(f)), and except as provided in subparagraph (B), any property with respect to which financial transactions are prohibited or regulated pursuant to section 5(b) of the Trading with the Enemy Act (50 U.S.C.App. 5(b)), section 620(a) of the Foreign Assistance Act of 1961 (22 U.S.C. 2370(a)), sections 202 and 203 of the International Emergency Economic Powers Act (50 U.S.C. 1701-1702), or any other proclamation, order, regulation, or license issued pursuant thereto, shall be subject to execution or attachment in aid of execution of any judgment relating to a claim for which a foreign state (including any agency or instrumentality or such state) claiming such property is not immune under section 1605(a)(7).

MOD argues that the Cubic judgment is subject to this provision because it is "property with respect to which financial transactions are prohibited or regulated pursuant to...sections 202 and 203 of the International Emergency Economic Powers Act [("IEEPA")]" or regulations issued pursuant to those sections.

We therefore turn to sections 202 and 203 of the IEEPA, which generally provide authority for the President to regulate financial transactions and other transfers of property involving a foreign country when he declares a national emergency with respect to any "unusual and extraordinary threat" emanating from outside the United States. *See* IEEPA section 202, 50 U.S.C. §1701. As relevant here, section 203 of the IEEPA provides that "the President may, under such regulations as he may prescribe...regulate...any transactions involving[ ] any property in which any foreign country or a national thereof has any interest by any person, or with respect to any property, subject to the jurisdiction of the United States." 50 U.S.C. §1702(a)(1). [FN6] The President

has exercised this authority with respect to Iran since 1979, when President Carter declared a national emergency with respect to that country in response to the taking of hostages in the United States Embassy in Tehran. *See* Exec. Order No. 12,170, 44 Fed.Reg. 65,729 (Nov. 14, 1979). Pursuant to that and subsequent declarations, [FN7] the President-through the Department of the Treasury-has established two regulatory schemes relating to transactions involving Iran: the Iranian Assets Control Regulations ("IACR"), 31 C.F.R. pt. 535 (2003), which regulate transactions involving Iranian property subject to United States jurisdiction, and the Iranian Transactions Regulations ("ITR"), 31 C.F.R. pt. 560, which regulate trade and financial transactions between United States entities and Iran. [FN8] *See Flatow v. Islamic Republic of Iran,* 305 F.3d 1249, 1255 (D.C.Cir.2002). Only the IACR are relevant to our analysis of this aspect of the case.

FN6. The full language of the relevant portion of section 203 is as follows:

At the times and to the extent specified in section 1701 of this title, the President may, under such regulations as he may prescribe, by means of instructions, licenses, or otherwise-

(A) investigate, regulate, or prohibit-

(i) any transactions in foreign exchange,

(ii) transfers of credit or payments between, by, through, or to any banking institution, to the extent that such transfers or payments involve any interest of any foreign country or a national thereof,

(iii) the importing or exporting of currency or securities, by any person, or with respect to any property, subject to the jurisdiction of the United States;

(B) investigate, block during the pendency of an investigation, regulate, direct and compel, nullify, void, prevent or prohibit, any acquisition, holding, withholding, use, transfer, withdrawal, transportation, importation or exportation of, or dealing in, or exercising any right, power, or privilege with respect to, or transactions involving, any property in which any foreign country or a national thereof has any interest by any person, or with respect to any property, subject to the jurisdiction of the United States.

50 U.S.C. §1702(a)(1)(A) and (B).

FN7. Since 1979, the President has issued several declarations continuing the state of emergency with respect to Iran. *See, e.g.,* Continuation of Iran Emergency, 66 Fed.Reg. 56,966 (Nov. 8, 2001); Continuation of Iran Emergency, 62 Fed.Reg. 51,591 (Sept. 30, 1997); Continuation of Iran Emergency, 55 Fed.Reg. 47,453 (Nov. 9, 1990).

FN8. Both regulatory schemes are administered by the Office of Foreign Assets Control (OFAC), an entity within the Department of the Treasury.

Title 31 C.F.R. §535.201 provides that

No property subject to the jurisdiction of the United States or which is in the possession of or control of persons subject to the jurisdiction of the United States in which on or after [November 14, 1979] Iran has any interest of any nature whatsoever may be transferred, paid, exported, withdrawn or otherwise dealt in except as authorized.

Section 535.311 defines "property" for purposes of §535.201 to include "judgments." The combination of these regulations makes clear that the Cubic judgment is property regulated by the IACR and that the IACR have been enacted pursuant to sections 202 and 203 of IEEPA. This means, in turn, that the Cubic judgment is "subject to" 28 U.S.C. §1610(f)(1)(A), as provided for in the Victims Protection Act, and that Flatow therefore relinquished all rights to execute against or attach that judgment when he received payments under the Act.

Flatow's arguments against this conclusion are unavailing. Flatow first claims that reading the relevant statutes and regulations to preclude attachment of the Cubic judgment would create a conflict between the Victims Protection Act and the duties embodied in the New York Convention to enforce foreign arbitral awards. The New York Convention, however, has been fully enforced in this case; the district court has confirmed the ICC award obtained by MOD against Cubic. *See Ministry of Def. v. Cubic Def. Systems, Inc.,* 29 F.Supp.2d 1168 (S.D.Cal.1998). The award has, in essence, been transformed into a judgment of a federal court, and the New York Convention is now irrelevant to whether that judgment can be attached by a third-party. [FN9] *Cf. Victrix S.S. Co. v. Salen Dry Cargo A.B.,* 825 F.2d 709, 713 n. 2 (2d Cir.1987) ("[T]he [New York] Convention does not apply to the enforcement of judgments that confirm foreign arbitration awards.").

FN9. The New York Convention remains relevant, however, to the original dispute between MOD and Cubic, which is still on appeal.

Flatow's second argument is that the Cubic judgment is not currently "regulated" by the IEEPA. Flatow points out that 31 C.F.R. §535.579(a)(2) provides that "[t]ransactions involving property in which Iran or an Iranian entity has an interest are authorized where…[t]he interest in the property of Iran or an Iranian entity…arises after January 19, 1981."

This provision is one of several general licenses which authorize particular categories of transactions involving Iranian property. *See* 31 C.F.R. §§535.504-535.580; *see also* 31 C.F.R. §501.801(a) (defining general licenses). Flatow contends that §535.579(a)(2) is applicable to the Cubic judgment because it is property in which MOD gained an interest after January 19, 1981. With this much we agree. *See* section III. D., *infra.* Flatow further contends, however, that §535.579 "deregulates" the Cubic judgment, so as to render it property not subject to regulation under IEEPA. With this proposition we cannot agree. As noted earlier, 31 C.F.R. §535.201 prohibits any dealings in Iranian property subject to the jurisdiction of the United States "except as authorized." Section 535.579 then "authorize[s]" transactions involving certain property, including the Cubic judgment. The fact that a range of conduct is authorized or permitted does not mean that it is not regulated; to the contrary, the fact that §535.579 purports to *authorize* transactions related to the Cubic judgment reinforces the notion that the judgment is property regulated by the Iranian regulations and IEEPA. *See Flatow,* 305 F.3d at 1255 ("The fact that a transaction is authorized by an OFAC license confirms that it is 'regulated' by IEEPA and by regulations or licenses issued pursuant thereto."). We note, for instance, that any transactions involving the Cubic judgment remain subject to the record-keeping requirements set out at 31 C.F.R. §501.601. [FN10] Moreover, our reading of the relevant statutes and regulations is the one adopted by OFAC, [FN11] which is charged with administering the Iranian regulations, and OFAC's interpretation is entitled to deference. *See Consarc Corp. v. United States Treasury Dep't, Office of Foreign Assets Control,* 71 F.3d 909, 914 (D.C.Cir.1995) (holding that OFAC is entitled to *Chevron* deference in its interpretations of IEEPA). For these reasons, we reject Flatow's contention that §535.579 or any other general or specific licenses render the Cubic judgment not "regulated" by IEEPA.

FN10. 31 C.F.R. §501.601 provides:

Except as otherwise provided, every person engaging in any transaction subject to the provisions of this chapter [which includes both the IACR and ITR] shall keep a full and accurate record of each such transaction engaged in, *regardless of whether such transaction is effected pursuant to license or otherwise,* and such record shall be available for examination for at least 5 years after the date of such transaction. (emphasis added).

FN11. As we explain more fully below, the notice issued by OFAC to implement the payment scheme set up by the Victims Protection Act warned that "virtually all Iranian…property within the jurisdiction of the United States is 'property with respect to which financial transactions are prohibited or regulated pursuant to' IEEPA..." 65 Fed.Reg. 70,382, 70,384 (Nov. 22, 2000).

Flatow's final argument is that our reading of the statutes and regulations would lead to an absurd result. *Cf. United States v. Martinez-Martinez,* 369 F.3d 1076, 1085 (9th Cir.2004) ("[A] statute must not be construed in a way that produces absurd results..."). Because virtually all Iranian property in the United States is regulated under IEEPA, Flatow argues that he may never be able to collect on the punitive portion of his default judgment. Flatow would therefore have given up a payment of 10 percent of his compensatory damages under the Victims Protection Act for a nonexistent possibility. We recognize that Flatow's ability to collect the punitive damages portion of his judgment is severely restricted under the scheme set up by Congress in the Victims Protection Act. We do not believe, however, that our reading of the statutes would lead to an absurd result; Flatow may yet be able to collect against Iranian property not subject to the Iranian regulations. [FN12] Moreover, at the time of Flatow's selection under the Victims Protection Act, Flatow was aware-or should have been aware-that his ability to collect the punitive damages portion of the default judgment would be quite limited. The notice implementing the payment scheme established by the Act warned claimants in Flatow's position of the consequences of retaining a right to pursue punitive damages:

FN12. For instance, Flatow may be able to collect the remainder of his judgment against Iranian property not subject to the jurisdiction of the United States.

Because of the comprehensive sanctions programs in place against Iran pursuant to IEEPA and against Cuba pursuant to TWEA, *see* 31 C.F.R. Parts 515, 535, and 560, virtually every transaction involving Iranian or Cuban property within the jurisdiction of the United States is either "prohibited" or "regulated," i.e., permitted only by a general license in regulations promulgated by the Office of Foreign Assets Control (OFAC), Department of the Treasury, or by a specific license issued by OFAC...Thus, virtually all Iranian or Cuban property within the jurisdiction of the United States is "property with respect to which financial transactions are prohibited or regulated pursuant to" IEEPA or TWEA. *Section 2002(a)(2)(D)* [of the Victims Protection Act] *therefore prohibits an applicant who elects the 100 per cent option from seeking to execute his or her punitive damage award against, or from seeking to attach, virtually all Iranian or Cuban assets within the jurisdiction of the United States.*

Notice: Payments to Persons Who Hold Certain Categories of Judgments Against Cuba or Iran, 65 Fed.Reg. 70,382, 70,384 (Nov. 22, 2000) (emphasis added). The plain meaning of the statute and regulations precludes relief for Flatow.

We hold that Flatow relinquished any claim as to the Cubic judgment when he accepted payments under the Victims Protection Act.

III. Elahi's Ability to Attach the Cubic Judgment

It is undisputed that Elahi did not receive payments under the Victims Protection Act, so that issue does not apply to his case. MOD argues, however, that Elahi may not attach the Cubic judgment because he has not shown that any of the exceptions to foreign sovereign immunity from attachment set out in the Foreign Sovereign Immunities Act of 1976 ("FSIA" or "the Act"), 28 U.S.C. §§1602-1611, are applicable in this case. We review the existence of sovereign immunity de novo. *See Park v. Shin,* 313 F.3d 1138, 1141 (9th Cir.2002).

A. MOD's Purported Waiver of Sovereign Immunity

The district court found that sovereign immunity did not prevent Elahi from attaching the Cubic judgment because MOD had waived its immunity by both submitting to arbitration at the ICC and then seeking to have the ICC award confirmed in a federal court. As we explain below, the district court erred in this portion of its analysis by confounding two different aspects of foreign sovereign immunity.

The FSIA is "a comprehensive statute containing a set of legal standards governing claims of immunity in every civil action against a foreign state or its political subdivisions, agencies, or instrumentalities." *Republic of Austria v. Altmann,* 541 U.S. 677, 124 S.Ct. 2240, 2249, 159 L.Ed.2d 1 (2004) (quoting *Verlinden B.V. v. Central Bank of Nigeria,* 461 U.S. 480, 488, 103 S.Ct. 1962, 76 L.Ed.2d 81 (1983)) (internal quotations omitted). The FSIA codified the "restrictive" theory of foreign sovereign immunity, which held that a foreign sovereign's immunity is "confined to suits involving the foreign sovereign's public acts, and does not extend to cases arising out of a foreign state's strictly commercial acts." *Verlinden,* 461 U.S. at 487, 103 S.Ct. 1962. However, while the FSIA represented a significant development in how claims of foreign sovereign immunity are to be adjudicated in the courts of this country, it did not repeal the conceptual framework of foreign sovereign immunity as it had developed prior to the FSIA's passage. In particular, the FSIA preserved a distinction between two different aspects of foreign sovereign immunity: jurisdictional immunity-that is, a foreign sovereign's immunity from actions brought in United States courts-and immunity from attachment-a foreign sovereign's immunity from having its property attached or executed upon. *See Conn. Bank of Commerce v. Republic of Congo,* 309 F.3d 240, 252 (5th Cir.2002). The FSIA's structure demonstrates that it preserves the distinction between these two types of immunity. On the one hand, §1604 establishes a default rule that a foreign sovereign will be immune from the jurisdiction of United States courts unless one of the exceptions set out in §1605 applies; on the other hand, §1609 provides that the property of foreign states and their instrumentalities will be immune from attachment and execution unless one of the exceptions set out in §1610 applies. A foreign sovereign's waiver of immunity is one of the exceptions to both jurisdictional immunity and immunity from attachment. *See* 28 U.S.C. §§1605(a)(1), 1610(a)(1) and (b)(1).

Elahi contends that MOD's actions in seeking to confirm the ICC award against Cubic resulted in an implicit waiver of its foreign sovereign immunity. [FN13] We agree to the extent that Elahi is referring to MOD's jurisdictional immunity from suit. In other words, we agree that MOD implicitly waived its immunity from being subjected to the jurisdiction of United States courts when it sought to confirm the ICC award; in fact, MOD concedes as much. MOD Brief in no. 03-55015 at 6. The question we must address, however, is whether MOD's waiver of jurisdictional immunity also constituted a waiver of its immunity from attachment of its property under 28 U.S.C. §§1610(a)(1) or (b)(1).

FN13. Elahi appears to concede that MOD is an agency and instrumentality of Iran and is therefore subject to the provisions of the FSIA. *See* 28 U.S.C. §1603(b) (defining an "agency or instrumentality" of a foreign state). Under 28 U.S.C. §1603(a), MOD also qualifies as a "foreign state" for purposes of the FSIA.

Prior to the passage of the FSIA, the courts that had addressed this question had held that a foreign state's waiver of jurisdictional immunity did not constitute a waiver of its immunity from attachment of its property. *See Flota Maritima Browning de Cuba, S.A. v. Motor Vessel Ciudad de la Habana,* 335 F.2d 619, 626 (4th Cir.1964) ("A distinction has been drawn between jurisdictional immunity and immunity from execution of the property of a sovereign, and waiver of

the former is not necessarily a waiver of the latter."); *Dexter & Carpenter v. Kunglig Jarnvagsstyrelsen,* 43 F.2d 705, 708 (2d Cir.1930) (holding that waiver of jurisdictional immunity does not waive immunity from attachment); *Rich v. Naviera Vacuba S.A.,* 197 F.Supp. 710, 722-23 (E.D.Va.1961) (same). The FSIA narrowed the scope of immunity from attachment, [FN14] but as we explained above, the structure of the Act makes clear that it preserved the traditional distinction between the two forms of immunity. The scant post-FSIA authority that speaks on the subject suggests that the statute did not change the earlier rule that waiver of jurisdictional immunity does not constitute a waiver of immunity from attachment. *See* Restatement (Third) of Foreign Relations Law of the United States §456(1)(b) (noting that under international law, "a waiver of immunity from suit does not imply a waiver of immunity from attachment of property, and a waiver of immunity from attachment of property does not imply a waiver of immunity from suit."); *DeLetelier v. Republic of Chile,* 748 F.2d 790, 798-99 (2d Cir.1984) (noting that, in enacting FSIA, Congress did not intend "to reverse completely the historical and international antipathy to executing against a foreign state's property even in cases where a judgment could be had on the merits"). For these reasons, and because we construe the waiver provisions in FSIA narrowly, *see Joseph v. Office of the Consulate Gen. of Nigeria,* 830 F.2d 1018, 1022 (9th Cir.1987), we conclude that MOD's waiver of jurisdictional immunity did not also constitute a waiver of its immunity from having its property attached.

FN14. Prior to the FSIA, foreign states and their instrumentalities enjoyed virtually absolute immunity from having their property attached or executed upon. *See Conn. Bank of Commerce,* 309 F.3d at 251-52. The legislative history of the FSIA makes clear that its drafters intended to "modify this rule by partially lowering the barrier of immunity from execution, so as to make this immunity conform more closely with the provisions on jurisdictional immunity" in FSIA. H.R. Rep. 94-1487, at 27 (1976), *reprinted in* 1976 U.S.C.C.A.N. 6604, 6626 (hereinafter "FSIA House Report").

B. Attachment Under §1610(b)(2) of the FSIA

Even though we reject the district court's finding that MOD had waived its sovereign immunity from attachment, we nonetheless affirm its determination that the Cubic judgment is subject to attachment by Elahi because we conclude that the judgment is subject to the exception in §1610(b)(2) of the FSIA. [FN15] The relevant part of that section provides that

FN15. We may affirm the district court on any ground supported by the record. *City Solutions, Inc. v. Clear Channel Communications,* 365 F.3d 835, 842 (9th Cir.2004) (quoting *Dixon v. Wallowa County,* 336 F.3d 1013, 1018 (9th Cir.2003)).

[A]ny property in the United States of an agency or instrumentality of a foreign state engaged in commercial activity in the United States shall not be immune from attachment in aid of execution, or from execution, upon a judgment entered by a court of the United States or of a State after the effective date of this Act, if-

…

the judgment relates to a claim for which the agency or instrumentality is not immune by virtue of section 1605(a)(2), (3), (5), or (7), or 1605(b) of this chapter, regardless of whether the property is or was involved in the act upon which the claim is based.

28 U.S.C. §1610(b)(2). This provision will apply to the Cubic judgment if: 1) MOD is engaged in commercial activity in the United States; and 2) Elahi's claim is one for which MOD is not immune by virtue of 28 U.S.C. §1605(a)(7).

MOD was "engaged in commercial activity" within the meaning of 28 U.S.C. §1610(b). The phrase "commercial activity" is defined by FSIA as meaning "either a regular course of commercial conduct or a particular commercial transaction or act." 28 U.S.C. §1603(d). The statutory definition further makes clear that "[t]he commercial character of an activity shall be determined by reference to the nature of the course of conduct or particular transaction or act, rather than by reference to its purpose." *Id.; see also Saudi Arabia v. Nelson,* 507 U.S. 349, 356, 113 S.Ct. 1471, 123 L.Ed.2d 47 (1993). MOD's dispute with Cubic arose out of a contract between MOD's predecessor and Cubic for the purchase of military equipment. We have twice recognized that "a contract to purchase military supplies, although clearly undertaken for public use, is commercial in nature…" *Joseph v. Office of the Consulate Gen. of Nigeria,* 830 F.2d 1018, 1023 (9th Cir.1987); *see also Park v. Shin,* 313 F.3d 1138, 1145 (9th Cir.2002) (quoting *Joseph*). Although perhaps not technically bound by these statements, we find them persuasive because they are consistent with the legislative history of the FSIA, *see* FSIA House Report at 16 ("[A] contract by a foreign government to buy provisions or

equipment for its armed forces…constitutes a commercial activity."), and with the holdings of other courts which have considered the question. *See McDonnell Douglas Corp. v. Islamic Republic of Iran,* 758 F.2d 341, 349 (8th Cir.1985) (holding that "the intent of the purchasing sovereign to use the goods for military purposes does not take the transaction outside of the 'commercial' exception to sovereign immunity"); *Virtual Def. & Dev. Int'l, Inc. v. Republic of Moldova,* 133 F.Supp.2d 1, 7-8 (D.D.C.1999) (holding that contract for sale of MiG-29 fighters was commercial activity for purposes of FSIA). We therefore hold that MOD is engaged in commercial activity in the United States within the meaning of the FSIA because of its contractual relationship with Cubic.

We also conclude that Elahi's claim is one for which MOD is not immune by virtue of 28 U.S.C. §1605(a)(7). 28 U.S.C. §1605(a)(7) explains that "a foreign state shall not be immune from the jurisdiction of the courts of the United States" in cases involving state-sponsored terrorist activity. The term "foreign state" in 28 U.S.C. §1605(a)(7) is defined in 28 U.S.C. §1603(a), which states that a "foreign state" as used in the statute "includes a political subdivision of a foreign state or an agency or instrumentality." Thus, under §1605(a)(7), once a foreign state has engaged in state-sponsored terrorist activity, all of its agencies and instrumentalities are likewise not immune from jurisdiction.

In this case, Elahi seeks to attach MOD's property to enforce a judgment brought under §1605(a)(7) against Iran, and under §1603(a), Iran was a "foreign state" that included *all* of the "agencies and instrumentalities" of Iran. One of those agencies was MOD. Thus, the underlying removal of Iran's sovereign immunity under §1605(a)(7) also removed the sovereign immunity of MOD, and for the purpose of determining whether MOD lacks immunity from attachment under §1610(b)(2), the underlying D.C. Circuit judgment was one for which MOD was "not immune by virtue of" §1605(a)(7). [FN16]

FN16. Because we conclude that the Cubic judgment is subject to attachment under 28 U.S.C. §1610(b)(2), we do not consider whether the judgment may be subject to attachment under any other exception to immunity from attachment in the FSIA that might apply.

Although §1610(a) also discusses foreign state immunity from attachment, this reading of §1610(b)(2) is consistent with the structure of §1610 as a whole. In §1610(a), Congress denied sovereign immunity from attachment to a foreign state's property "used for a commercial activity" in the

United States. In §1610(b)(2), Congress denied attachment immunity for property of foreign state agencies "engaged in commercial activity." In both instances, the underlying purpose was to deny sovereign immunity from attachment to satisfy judgments against foreign states in circumstances where the foreign government is engaging in commercial activity in the United States-either directly, through the use of particular property, or indirectly, through the commercial activities of an agency or instrumentality.

While we hold that a foreign state agency is not immune from attachment of its property to satisfy a judgment against a foreign state so long as the conditions of §1610(b)(2) are met, we do not hold that the property of any foreign state agency or instrumentality can be used to satisfy any judgment against a foreign state. Rather, once it has been established that a foreign state agency or instrumentality has no immunity from attachment of its property under §1610(b)(2), it is then necessary also to determine whether the agency or instrumentality is liable so that its property may be attached. We explained that attachment immunity and attachment liability are distinct issues in *Flatow v. Islamic Republic of Iran,* 308 F.3d 1065, 1069 (9th Cir.2003). While "[t]he enumerated exceptions to the FSIA provide the exclusive source of subject-matter jurisdiction over civil actions brought against foreign states,...the FSIA does not resolve questions of [attachment] liability. Questions of liability are addressed by *Bancec,* [FN17] which examines the circumstances under which a foreign entity can be held substantively liable for the foreign government's judgment debt." *Id.* (internal citation omitted).

FN17. The full citation of *Bancec* is *First National City Bank v. Banco Para El Comercio Exterior De Cuba,* 462 U.S. 611, 103 S.Ct. 2591, 77 L.Ed.2d 46 (1983) but is commonly known as the " *Bancec* " case.

In *Bancec,* the Supreme Court held that foreign agencies and instrumentalities, even those wholly owned by a foreign government, are subject to a presumption of separate judicial status. 462 U.S. at 626-27, 103 S.Ct. 2591. Thus, in the ordinary course of business, a foreign instrumentality will *not* have its property subject to attachment to satisfy a judgment against a foreign state, regardless of §1610(b)(2). The Court noted, however, that there are a number of situations in which that presumption of separate status can be overcome. *Id.* at 627-28, 103 S.Ct. 2591. Most significantly for our purposes here, the presumption of separate status can be overcome when it can be shown that the "corporate entity is so extensively controlled by its owner that a relationship of principal and agent is created." *Id.* at 629, 103

S.Ct. 2591. In *Walter Fuller Aircraft Sales Inc. v. Republic of the Philippines,* 965 F.2d 1375, 1380 n. 7 (5th Cir.1992), for example, the Fifth Circuit discussed five " *Bancec* " factors to determine when the presumption of separate judicial status should be overcome in determining attachment liability. *See id.* (describing "(1) the level of economic control by the government; (2) whether the entity's profits go to the government; (3) the degree to which government officials manage the entity or otherwise have a hand in its daily affairs; (4) whether the government is the real beneficiary of the entity's conduct; and (5) whether adherence to separate identities would entitle the foreign state to benefits in United States courts while avoiding its obligations"); *see also Flatow I,* 308 F.3d at 1071 n. 9 (discussing *Walter Fuller*). Here, an analysis of MOD's relationship to Iran with respect to each of these factors makes clear that the *Bancec* presumption of separate judicial status is overcome; MOD is a central organ of the Iranian government under direct control of the government. As a result, MOD not only lacks immunity from attachment but is also liable for attachment of its property to enforce the underlying judgment against Iran.

In sum, to determine whether the property of a foreign state agency or instrumentality can be attached to enforce a judgment against a foreign state, we apply a two-step analysis. First, we look at whether the judgment is one for which the agency is not immune from attachment under FSIA; and second, if so, we determine whether the foreign agency or instrumentality should be held liable for attachment under *Bancec.* Applying this two-step analysis to this case, we find that a) MOD's Cubic judgment falls under the exception to foreign sovereign immunity from attachment set out in 28 U.S.C. §1610(b)(2); and b) MOD is liable for attachment of its property to enforce a judgment against Iran under *Bancec.*

C. Exemptions from Attachment Under §1611 of FSIA

MOD argues that, even if the Cubic judgment is subject to attachment under §1610 of FSIA, Elahi is still precluded from attaching the judgment because it falls under one of the exemptions from attachment set out in 28 U.S.C. §1611(b). We examine each of the arguments advanced by MOD in turn.

1. The Cubic Judgment as Military Property Under §1611(b)(2) of the FSIA

MOD argues that the Cubic judgment is exempted from attachment because it is the type of military property described in §1611(b)(2) of the FSIA. That section provides that

Notwithstanding the provisions of section 1610 of [the FSIA], the property of a foreign state shall be immune from attachment and from execution, if

…

the property is, or is intended to be, used in connection with a military activity and

(A) is of a military character, or

(B) is under the control of a military authority or defense agency.

28 U.S.C. §1611(b)(2). MOD appears to concede that the Cubic judgment is not property of a military character under subparagraph (A), [FN18] instead stressing that the judgment falls under subparagraph (B) as property under the control of a military authority or defense agency. Our inquiry focuses on whether the Cubic judgment is property that is, or is intended to be, used in connection with a military activity.

FN18. The FSIA's legislative history makes clear that the Cubic judgment is not property of a military character for purposes of this provision. *See* FSIA House Report at 31 ("[P]roperty is of a military character if it consists of equipment in the broad sense-such as weapons, ammunition, military transport, warships, tanks, communications equipment.").

We agree with the district court's conclusion that the Cubic judgment is not exempt from attachment under 28 U.S.C. §1611(b)(2). *See* District Court Order at 1149. The plain language of §1611(b)(2) requires MOD to establish that there is some present or future intended use for the property that is connected to military activity. In addition, the FSIA's legislative history emphasizes that "property will be immune only if its present or future use is military (e.g., surplus military equipment withdrawn from military use would not be immune)." FSIA House Report at 31. MOD has made no showing that any proceeds from the Cubic judgment are to be used in any way related to Iran's military activities; [FN19] in fact, MOD's only statements regarding the future of any monies stemming from the judgment is that they are to revert to Iran's Central Bank. *See* section III. C. 2., *infra*. We therefore hold that Elahi is not barred from attaching the Cubic judgment by virtue of the military property exemption set out in 28 U.S.C. §1611(b)(2). [FN20]

FN19. We note, however, that even if MOD had argued that the proceeds from the Cubic judgment were destined to fund military activities, such an indirect relation between the property at issue and military activities may not be sufficient to make the exemption applicable.

FN20. MOD argues that our reading of the statute would run counter to the congressional purpose behind the military property exemption, which was to encourage purchases of military equipment in the United States. While we agree that Congress intended to provide some protection to purchases of military equipment by foreign governments, we reject MOD's contention that Congress meant this protection to be absolute.

2. The Cubic Judgment as Property of a Central Bank under §1611(b)(1) of the FSIA

MOD argues that if the Cubic judgment is not to be treated as military property under §1611(b)(2) of the FSIA, it should then be considered the property of Iran's central bank under §1611(b)(1). The relevant portion of that section provides that

Notwithstanding the provisions of section 1610 of [the FSIA], the property of a foreign state shall be immune from attachment and from execution, if

…

the property is that of a foreign central bank or monetary authority held for its own account…

28 U.S.C. §1611(b)(1). During the district court proceedings, MOD introduced the declaration of Dr. Assadollah Karimi, an alleged specialist in Iranian banking law, who concluded that "all sums relating to the ministries and governmental institutions [of Iran] do belong to the Bank Markazi [Iran's central bank] and that they have to be settled to the Treasury General's account to be expended in due time according to the budget act." Karimi Declaration ¶ 16. MOD claims that, because any proceeds of the Cubic judgment would revert to Iran's central bank, it falls under the scope of §1611(b)(1).

We agree with the district court's conclusion that the Cubic judgment is not exempted from attachment under §1611(b)(1) of the FSIA. The plain language of the statute requires that the property at issue not only belong to a foreign state's central bank, but also be "held for [the central bank's] *own account…*" 28 U.S.C. §1611(b)(1) (emphasis added). The FSIA's legislative history makes clear that the exemption was meant to apply to

funds of a foreign central bank or monetary authority which are deposited in the United States and "held" for the bank's or authority's "own account"-i.e., funds used or held in connection with central banking activities, as distinguished from funds used solely to finance the commercial transactions of other entities or of foreign states.

FSIA House Report at 31. Even if the statements in Dr. Karimi's declaration could be stretched to mean that the Cubic judgment belonged to Iran's central bank, MOD cannot show that the judgment is "used or held in connection with central banking activities." [FN21] Indeed, MOD's position in this case would mean that virtually any funds belonging to any Iranian agency would be subject to the central bank exemption. We reject such a broad reading of §1611(b)(1) and hold that the Cubic judgment is not exempted from attachment by that provision.

FN21. The district courts that have considered the central bank exemption so far have read it narrowly; in some cases, the exemption has been found not to apply even where the funds unquestionably belonged to the foreign state's central bank. *See Banco Central de Reserva del Peru v. Riggs Nat'l Bank of Washington, D.C.,* 919 F.Supp. 13, 17 (D.D.C.1994) (holding that central bank exemption did not apply to an account of Peru's central bank because the funds were being used to guarantee loans to commercial banks and not as part of central banking activities); *Weston Compagnie de Finance et D'Investissement, S.A. v. Republica del Ecuador,* 823 F.Supp. 1106, 1114 (S.D.N.Y.1993) (holding that some of the funds belonging to Ecuador's central bank were not exempted from attachment because they were used for commercial banking purposes).

* * *

We conclude that the Cubic judgment is not exempted from attachment under either prong of §1611(b) of the FSIA.

D. The Impact of the Iranian Regulations on Elahi's Attachment

MOD argues that the Iranian regulations issued pursuant to the IEEPA, 31 C.F.R. pts. 535 and 560, prohibit attachment of the Cubic judgment by Elahi. Elahi points out, correctly, that MOD did not raise this issue before the district court. Although we could decline to reach the issue for that reason,

we exercise our discretion to consider the merits of MOD's arguments. *See Abramson v. Brownstein,* 897 F.2d 389, 391 (9th Cir.1990) ("We may consider an argument not raised in the district court...if it is an issue of law not dependent on a factual record developed by the parties.").

As we explained in section II, *supra,* the Cubic judgment is property regulated by the United States through the IACR, 31 C.F.R. pt. 535. In particular, 31 C.F.R. §535.201 provides that "[n]o property subject to the jurisdiction of the United States...in which on or after [November 14, 1979] Iran has any interest of any nature whatsoever may be transferred, paid, exported, withdrawn or otherwise dealt in except as authorized." If this were all that the regulations provided, MOD would likely be correct that the regulations would prevent Elahi from attaching the Cubic judgment. However, the regulations also provide for general licenses which authorize broad classes of transactions-transactions that would otherwise be prohibited by §535.201. *See* 31 C.F.R. §§535.504-535.580. One of these general licenses provides that "[t]ransactions involving property in which Iran or an Iranian entity has an interest are authorized where...[t]he interest in the property of Iran or an Iranian entity...arises after January 19, 1981." 31 C.F.R. §535.579(a)(2). MOD's interest in the Cubic judgment "arose" on December 7, 1998, when the district court confirmed the ICC award against Cubic. *MOD v. Cubic Def. Systems, Inc.,* 29 F.Supp.2d 1168 (S.D.Cal.1998). Therefore, because any transactions involving the Cubic judgment are authorized under 31 C.F.R. §535.579, Elahi is not barred from attaching the judgment by the IACR. [FN22]

FN22. The Iranian Transactions Regulations, 31 C.F.R. pt. 560, impose separate restrictions on the ability to transfer funds from a United States entity to an Iranian entity. *See* 31 C.F.R. §560.216. However, these regulations would not come into play where Elahi successfully attaches the judgment against Cubic, since the funds would then be transferred from Cubic to Elahi, thereby bypassing any Iranian entities.

E. MOD's Collateral Attacks on Elahi's Default Judgment

In its reply brief and in supplemental filings, MOD has raised new arguments attacking the original default judgment that Elahi is seeking to enforce. MOD contends that we can consider these late-raised arguments because they challenge the subject-matter jurisdiction of the District Court for the District of Columbia when it issued the default judgment. We address briefly MOD's contentions.

The Supreme Court has explained that "[a] defendant is always free to ignore [a] judicial proceeding, risk a default judgment, and then challenge that judgment on jurisdictional grounds in a collateral proceeding." *Ins. Corp. of Ireland, Ltd. v. Compagnie des Bauxites de Guinee,* 456 U.S. 694, 706, 102 S.Ct. 2099, 72 L.Ed.2d 492 (1982); *see also Practical Concepts, Inc. v. Republic of Bolivia,* 811 F.2d 1543, 1547 (D.C.Cir.1987). It is therefore clear that MOD could have mounted a collateral attack on the Elahi default judgment in the proceedings below on the ground that the D.C. district court lacked either personal or subject-matter jurisdiction. MOD did not mount such a challenge below, however, nor did it do so in its opening brief before this court. Because personal jurisdiction-unlike subject-matter jurisdiction-is waivable, *see Ins. Corp. of Ireland,* 456 U.S. at 703, 102 S.Ct. 2099 ("Because the requirement of personal jurisdiction represents first of all an individual right, it can, like other such rights, be waived."), MOD has waived any collateral challenges to the default judgment based on the issuing court's lack of personal jurisdiction. *See Am. Ass'n of Naturopathic Physicians v. Hayhurst,* 227 F.3d 1104, 1107 (9th Cir.2000) ("[A]lthough [Hayhurst] certainly did have the right to object to personal jurisdiction after the default judgment was entered against him, he then squandered that opportunity by failing to raise it.").

The analysis is different regarding collateral attacks challenging the issuing court's subject-matter jurisdiction because that type of jurisdiction "can never be forfeited or waived." *United States v. Cotton,* 535 U.S. 625, 630, 122 S.Ct. 1781, 152 L.Ed.2d 860 (2002). [FN23] We conclude, however, that none of the claims that MOD has raised to attack the default judgment issued by the D.C. district court actually challenge that court's subject-matter jurisdiction-that is, its power to hear the case. *See id.* MOD's arguments regarding the constitutionality of the statutes underlying the default judgment are challenges to the merits of the decision, not to the court's jurisdiction. 28 U.S.C. §1330(a) provides that district courts shall have original jurisdiction of any non-jury civil action against any foreign state or its agency or instrumentality, so long as such action falls under one of the exceptions to foreign sovereign immunity. As we have explained, see section III. B., *supra,* Elahi's action fell under the state-sponsored terrorism exception to sovereign immunity set out in 28 U.S.C. §1605(a)(7). The District Court for the District of Columbia therefore had subject-matter jurisdiction over Elahi's claim.

FN23. We do not hold that the non-waivability of subject-matter jurisdiction means that a party can wait as long as MOD has to raise its collateral attack. However, because MOD's claims fail on the merits, we will assume for purposes of this case that subject-matter jurisdiction is an issue that can be raised at any point, even in proceedings mounting a collateral attack on a default judgment.

MOD relies heavily on a recent decision by the Court of Appeals for the District of Columbia, *Cicippio-Puleo v. Islamic Republic of Iran,* 353 F.3d 1024 (D.C.Cir.2004). In *Cicippio,* the D.C. Circuit held that "neither 28 U.S.C. §1605(a)(7) nor the Flatow Amendment, nor the two considered in tandem, creates a private right of action against a foreign government." *Id.* at 1033. MOD argues that, because the D.C. Circuit's holding in *Cicippio* makes clear that the D.C. district court erred in issuing the default judgment, that judgment is void *ab initio* and should not be enforced. As we have explained, however, "[a] judgment is not void merely because it is erroneous." *United States v. Holtzman,* 762 F.2d 720, 724 (9th Cir.1985) (quoting 11 Charles Alan Wright & Arthur R. Miller, Federal Practice and Procedure §2862 at 198 (1973)). A judgment is void only if the issuing court lacked subject-matter jurisdiction over the action or if the judgment was otherwise entered in violation of due process. *Tomlin v. McDaniel,* 865 F.2d 209, 210 (9th Cir.1989). As we explained above, the district court for the District of Columbia did have subject-matter jurisdiction over Elahi's action. In fact, the D.C. Circuit in *Cicippio* recognized that Congress had conferred subject-matter jurisdiction over the type of action Elahi brought against Iran, even as it concluded that Congress had not created a cause of action upon which a plaintiff like Elahi could proceed. *See Cicippio,* 353 F.3d at 1034 ("[28 U.S.C. §1605(a)(7)] confers subject-matter jurisdiction on federal courts over [lawsuits for damages for certain enumerated acts of terrorism], but does not create a private right of action."). MOD has also not shown that the district court that issued the default judgment in favor of Elahi acted in a manner inconsistent with due process. *Cf. In re Center Wholesale, Inc.,* 759 F.2d 1440, 1448 (9th Cir.1985) (holding judgment void because aggrieved party had not received adequate notice of the proceedings).

For these reasons, we reject MOD's collateral challenges to Elahi's default judgment.

CONCLUSION

We affirm the district court's denial of Flatow's motion for leave to intervene, as well as its determination that Flatow has relinquished any claim to attaching the Cubic judgment by accepting payments pursuant to the Victims Protection Act. We also affirm the district court's decision that the Cubic judgment is subject to attachment by Elahi and reject MOD's collateral attacks on Elahi's default judgment.

AFFIRMED.

Notes:

1.   What is the relationship between "jurisdictional immunity" and "immunity from execution?" Is it possible that the drafters of the 1996 terrorism amendments to the FSIA intended that the attachment sections of the FSIA would thwart collection of judgments entered against state sponsors of terrorism?

2.   What policy concerns and interests underlie the assumption that immunity from suit is weaker than immunity from execution?

3.   What does this case suggest about the availability of assets in the U.S. for judgment creditors of Iran to pursue?

4.   What is the relationship between the Flatow and Elahi judgment creditors? There are dozens of outstanding and unpaid judgments against Iran. Are the victims in competition with each other in the search to locate and attach assets?

5.   This decision was overturned by *Ministry of Defense and Support for the Armed Forces of the Islamic Republic of Iran v. Elahi*, 546 U.S. 450 (2006). Assisting Iran's Ministry of Defense was the U.S. Solicitor General:

> The Ministry filed a petition for certiorari asking us to review that decision. The Solicitor General agrees with the Ministry that we should grant the writ but limited to the Ministry's Question 1, namely whether "the property of a foreign state *stricto sensu,* situated in the United States" is "immune from attachment...as provided in the Foreign Sovereign Immunities Act." Pet. for Cert. i (citing §§1603(a), 1610(a)). The Solicitor General also asks us to vacate the judgment of the Court of Appeals and remand the case for consideration of whether the Ministry is simply a "foreign *state*" (what the Ministry calls "a foreign state *stricto sensu*") or whether the Ministry is an "agency *or instrumentality*" of a foreign state (as the Ninth Circuit held).

Id. 451-451. The parties have continued to litigate this matter with numerous new twists arising at each stage. See *Ministry of Defense and Support for Armed Forces of Islamic Republic of Iran v. Cubic Defense Systems, Inc.*, 495 F.3d 1024 (9th Cir. 2007).

15.3 Immunity from Attachment
§1609. Immunity from attachment and execution of property of a foreign state

Subject to existing international agreements to which the United States is a party at the time of enactment of this Act the property in the United States of a foreign state shall be immune from attachment arrest and execution except as provided in sections 1610 and 1611 of this chapter.

§1610. Exceptions to the immunity from attachment or execution

(a) The property in the United States of a foreign state, as defined in section 1603(a) of this chapter, used for a commercial activity in the United States, shall not be immune from attachment in aid of execution, or from execution, upon a judgment entered by a court of the United States or of a State after the effective date of this Act, if--
(1) the foreign state has waived its immunity from attachment in aid of execution or from execution either explicitly or by implication, notwithstanding any withdrawal of the waiver the foreign state may purport to effect except in accordance with the terms of the waiver, or
(2) the property is or was used for the commercial activity upon which the claim is based, or
(3) the execution relates to a judgment establishing rights in property which has been taken in violation of international law or which has been exchanged for property taken in violation of international law, or
(4) the execution relates to a judgment establishing rights in property--
(A) which is acquired by succession or gift, or
(B) which is immovable and situated in the United States: *Provided,* That such property is not used for purposes of maintaining a diplomatic or consular mission or the residence of the Chief of such mission, or
(5) the property consists of any contractual obligation or any proceeds from such a contractual obligation to indemnify or hold harmless the foreign state or its employees under a policy of automobile or other liability or casualty insurance covering the claim which merged into the judgment, or
(6) the judgment is based on an order confirming an arbitral award rendered against the foreign state, provided that at-

tachment in aid of execution, or execution, would not be inconsistent with any provision in the arbitral agreement, or

(7) the judgment relates to a claim for which the foreign state is not immune under section 1605(a)(7), regardless of whether the property is or was involved with the act upon which the claim is based.

(b) In addition to subsection (a), any property in the United States of an agency or instrumentality of a foreign state engaged in commercial activity in the United States shall not be immune from attachment in aid of execution, or from execution, upon a judgment entered by a court of the United States or of a State after the effective date of this Act, if--

(1) the agency or instrumentality has waived its immunity from attachment in aid of execution or from execution either explicitly or implicitly, notwithstanding any withdrawal of the waiver the agency or instrumentality may purport to effect except in accordance with the terms of the waiver, or

(2) the judgment relates to a claim for which the agency or instrumentality is not immune by virtue of section 1605(a) (2), (3), (5), or (7), or 1605(b) of this chapter, regardless of whether the property is or was involved in the act upon which the claim is based.

(c) No attachment or execution referred to in subsections (a) and (b) of this section shall be permitted until the court has ordered such attachment and execution after having determined that a reasonable period of time has elapsed following the entry of judgment and the giving of any notice required under section 1608(e) of this chapter.

(d) The property of a foreign state, as defined in section 1603(a) of this chapter, used for a commercial activity in the United States, shall not be immune from attachment prior to the entry of judgment in any action brought in a court of the United States or of a State, or prior to the elapse of the period of time provided in subsection (c) of this section, if--

(1) the foreign state has explicitly waived its immunity from attachment prior to judgment, notwithstanding any withdrawal of the waiver the foreign state may purport to effect except in accordance with the terms of the waiver, and

(2) the purpose of the attachment is to secure satisfaction of a judgment that has been or may ultimately be entered against the foreign state, and not to obtain jurisdiction.

(e) The vessels of a foreign state shall not be immune from arrest in rem, interlocutory sale, and execution in actions brought to foreclose a preferred mortgage as provided in section 1605(d).

(f)(1)(A) Notwithstanding any other provision of law, including but not limited to section 208(f) of the Foreign Missions Act (22 U.S.C. 4308(f)), and except as provided

in subparagraph (B), any property with respect to which financial transactions are prohibited or regulated pursuant to section 5(b) of the Trading with the Enemy Act (50 U.S.C. App. 5(b)), section 620(a) of the Foreign Assistance Act of 1961 (22 U.S.C. 2370(a)), sections 202 and 203 of the International Emergency Economic Powers Act (50 U.S.C. 1701-1702), or any other proclamation, order, regulation, or license issued pursuant thereto, shall be subject to execution or attachment in aid of execution of any judgment relating to a claim for which a foreign state (including any agency or instrumentality or such state) claiming such property is not immune under section 1605(a)(7).

(B) Subparagraph (A) shall not apply if, at the time the property is expropriated or seized by the foreign state, the property has been held in title by a natural person or, if held in trust, has been held for the benefit of a natural person or persons.

(2)(A) At the request of any party in whose favor a judgment has been issued with respect to a claim for which the foreign state is not immune under section 1605(a)(7), the Secretary of the Treasury and the Secretary of State should make every effort to fully, promptly, and effectively assist any judgment creditor or any court that has issued any such judgment in identifying, locating, and executing against the property of that foreign state or any agency or instrumentality of such state.

(B) In providing such assistance, the Secretaries--
(i) may provide such information to the court under seal; and
(ii) should make every effort to provide the information in a manner sufficient to allow the court to direct the United States Marshall's office to promptly and effectively execute against that property.

(3) Waiver.--The President may waive any provision of paragraph (1) in the interest of national security.

Notes:

1.   How is immunity from attachment raised? Is an asset itself "immune" or must the foreign state "claim" the immunity? Can a court deny the attachment if the foreign state sponsor of terrorism does not claim the immunity?

2.   Who can raise the immunity? In *Rubin v. Islamic Republic of Iran*, 436 F.Supp.2d 938 (N.D.Ill. 2006) the victims-judgment debtors attached Iranian antiquities held by the University of Chicago which were packed and prepared

for shipment to Iran. Both the United States and the University of Chicago argued that the antiquities were immune from attachment. The court found,

> The [University of Chicago and the Field Museum] argue that the magistrate judge erred by not also taking into account the "negative treatment Iran has received in U.S. courts," which according to the citation respondents "diminishes Iran's 'incentive to set in motion the arduous process needed to vindicate [its] rights.' " [This] brazen accusation that the courts of the United States are hostile to Iran and that, as a result, Iran should be excused from bothering to assert its rights, is wholly unsupported.

The citation respondents also contend that the long list of cases cited above in which Iran defended itself "demonstrates that Iran faces numerous 'practical barriers' to suit in the form of extensive defense costs"...The burdens Iran would have faced in this suit would have been inconsequential compared...Iran only needed to assert its immunity in order to protect its rights...To the extent Iran would have incurred fees and costs to defend itself, the citation respondents have made no effort to establish that Iran's defense costs would have been any more burdensome than the costs any defendant to multiple suits faces. Furthermore, the jurors in *Powers* stood to gain little financially, while Iran stands to retain what appears to be a coveted and irreplaceable collection of artifacts.

Id. at 945.

Appendix A

Statutes

---

1. Alien Tort Claims Act, 28 U.S.C. §1350

The district courts shall have original jurisdiction of any civil action by an alien for a tort only, committed in violation of the law of nations or a treaty of the United States.

2. Foreign Sovereign Immunities Act, 28 U.S.C. §1602 et seq.

§1602. Findings and declaration of purpose

The Congress finds that the determination by United States courts of the claims of foreign states to immunity from the jurisdiction of such courts would serve the interests of justice and would protect the rights of both foreign states and litigants in United States courts. Under international law, states are not immune from the jurisdiction of foreign courts insofar as their commercial activities are concerned, and their commercial property may be levied upon for the satisfaction of judgments rendered against them in connection with their commercial activities. Claims of foreign states to immunity should henceforth be decided by courts of the United States and of the States in conformity with the principles set forth in this chapter.

§1603. Definitions

For purposes of this chapter--
(a) A "foreign state", except as used in section 1608 of this title, includes a political subdivision of a foreign state or an agency or instrumentality of a foreign state as defined in subsection (b).
(b) An "agency or instrumentality of a foreign state" means any entity--
(1) which is a separate legal person, corporate or otherwise, and
(2) which is an organ of a foreign state or political subdivision thereof, or a majority of whose shares or other ownership interest is owned by a foreign state or political subdivision thereof, and
(3) which is neither a citizen of a State of the United States as defined in section 1332(c) and (e) of this title, nor created under the laws of any third country.
(c) The "United States" includes all territory and waters, continental or insular, subject to the jurisdiction of the United States.
(d) A "commercial activity" means either a regular course of commercial conduct or a particular commercial transaction or act. The commercial character of an activity shall be determined by reference to the nature of the course of conduct or particular transaction or act, rather than by reference to its purpose.
(e) A "commercial activity carried on in the United States by a foreign state" means commercial activity carried on by such state and having substantial contact with the United States.

§1604. Immunity of a foreign state from jurisdiction

Subject to existing international agreements to which the United States is a party at the time of enactment of this Act a foreign state shall be immune from the jurisdiction of the courts of the United States and of the States except as provided in sections 1605 to 1607 of this chapter.

§1605. General exceptions to the jurisdictional immunity of a foreign state

(a) A foreign state shall not be immune from the jurisdiction of courts of the United States or of the States in any case--
(1) in which the foreign state has waived its immunity either explicitly or by implication, notwithstanding any withdrawal of the waiver which the foreign state may purport to effect except in accordance with the terms of the waiver;
(2) in which the action is based upon a commercial activity carried on in the United States by the foreign state; or upon an act performed in the United States in connection with a commercial activity of the foreign state elsewhere; or upon an act outside the territory of the United States in connection with a commercial activity of the foreign state elsewhere and that act causes a direct effect in the United States;
(3) in which rights in property taken in violation of international law are in issue and that property or any property exchanged for such property is present in the United States in connection with a commercial activity carried on in the United States by the foreign state; or that property or any property exchanged for such property is owned or operated by an agency or instrumentality of the foreign state and that agency or instrumentality is engaged in a commercial activity in the United States;
(4) in which rights in property in the United States acquired by succession or gift or rights in immovable property situated in the United States are in issue;
(5) not otherwise encompassed in paragraph (2) above, in which money damages are sought against a foreign state for personal injury or death, or damage to or loss of property, occurring in the United States and caused by the tortious act or omission of that foreign state or of any official or employee of that foreign state while acting within the scope of his office or employment; except this paragraph shall not apply to--
(A) any claim based upon the exercise or performance or the failure to exercise or perform a discretionary function regardless of whether the discretion be abused, or
(B) any claim arising out of malicious prosecution, abuse of process, libel, slander, misrepresentation, deceit, or interference with contract rights;

(6) in which the action is brought, either to enforce an agreement made by the foreign state with or for the benefit of a private party to submit to arbitration all or any differences which have arisen or which may arise between the parties with respect to a defined legal relationship, whether contractual or not, concerning a subject matter capable of settlement by arbitration under the laws of the United States, or to confirm an award made pursuant to such an agreement to arbitrate, if (A) the arbitration takes place or is intended to take place in the United States, (B) the agreement or award is or may be governed by a treaty or other international agreement in force for the United States calling for the recognition and enforcement of arbitral awards, (C) the underlying claim, save for the agreement to arbitrate, could have been brought in a United States court under this section or section 1607, or (D) paragraph (1) of this subsection is otherwise applicable; or

(7) not otherwise covered by paragraph (2), in which money damages are sought against a foreign state for personal injury or death that was caused by an act of torture, extrajudicial killing, aircraft sabotage, hostage taking, or the provision of material support or resources (as defined in section 2339A of title 18) for such an act if such act or provision of material support is engaged in by an official, employee, or agent of such foreign state while acting within the scope of his or her office, employment, or agency, except that the court shall decline to hear a claim under this paragraph--

(A) if the foreign state was not designated as a state sponsor of terrorism under section 6(j) of the Export Administration Act of 1979 (50 U.S.C. App. 2405(j)) or section 620A of the Foreign Assistance Act of 1961 (22 U.S.C. 2371) at the time the act occurred, unless later so designated as a result of such act or the act is related to Case Number 1:00CV03110(EGS) in the United States District Court for the District of Columbia; and

(B) even if the foreign state is or was so designated, if--

(i) the act occurred in the foreign state against which the claim has been brought and the claimant has not afforded the foreign state a reasonable opportunity to arbitrate the claim in accordance with accepted international rules of arbitration; or

(ii) neither the claimant nor the victim was a national of the United States (as that term is defined in section 101(a)(22) of the Immigration and Nationality Act) when the act upon which the claim is based occurred.

(b) A foreign state shall not be immune from the jurisdiction of the courts of the United States in any case in which a suit in admiralty is brought to enforce a maritime lien against a vessel or cargo of the foreign state, which maritime lien is based upon a commercial activity of the foreign state: *Provided*, That--

(1) notice of the suit is given by delivery of a copy of the summons and of the complaint to the person, or his agent, having possession of the vessel or cargo against which the maritime lien is asserted; and if the vessel or cargo is arrested pursuant to process obtained on behalf of the party bringing the suit, the service of process of arrest shall be deemed to constitute valid delivery of such notice, but the party bringing the suit shall be liable for any damages sustained by the foreign state as a result of the arrest if the party bringing the suit had actual or constructive knowledge that the vessel or cargo of a foreign state was involved; and

(2) notice to the foreign state of the commencement of suit as provided in section 1608 of this title is initiated within ten days either of the delivery of notice as provided in paragraph (1) of this subsection or, in the case of a party who was unaware that the vessel or cargo of a foreign state was involved, of the date such party determined the existence of the foreign state's interest.

(c) Whenever notice is delivered under subsection (b)(1), the suit to enforce a maritime lien shall thereafter proceed and shall be heard and determined according to the principles of law and rules of practice of suits in rem whenever it appears that, had the vessel been privately owned and possessed, a suit in rem might have been maintained. A decree against the foreign state may include costs of the suit and, if the decree is for a money judgment, interest as ordered by the court, except that the court may not award judgment against the foreign state in an amount greater than the value of the vessel or cargo upon which the maritime lien arose. Such value shall be determined as of the time notice is served under subsection (b)(1). Decrees shall be subject to appeal and revision as provided in other cases of admiralty and maritime jurisdiction. Nothing shall preclude the plaintiff in any proper case from seeking relief in personam in the same action brought to enforce a maritime lien as provided in this section.

(d) A foreign state shall not be immune from the jurisdiction of the courts of the United States in any action brought to foreclose a preferred mortgage, as defined in section 31301 of title 46. Such action shall be brought, heard, and determined in accordance with the provisions of chapter 313 of title 46 and in accordance with the principles of law and rules of practice of suits in rem, whenever it appears that had the vessel been privately owned and possessed a suit in rem might have been maintained.

(e) For purposes of paragraph (7) of subsection (a)--

(1) the terms "torture" and "extrajudicial killing" have the meaning given those terms in section 3 of the Torture Victim Protection Act of 1991;

(2) the term "hostage taking" has the meaning given that term in Article 1 of the International Convention Against the Taking of Hostages; and

(3) the term "aircraft sabotage" has the meaning given that term in Article 1 of the Convention for the Suppression of Unlawful Acts Against the Safety of Civil Aviation.

(f) No action shall be maintained under subsection (a)(7) unless the action is commenced not later than 10 years after the date on which the cause of action arose. All principles of equitable tolling, including the period during which the foreign state was immune from suit, shall apply in calculating this limitation period.

(g) Limitation on discovery.--

(1) In general.--(A) Subject to paragraph (2), if an action is filed that would otherwise be barred by section 1604, but for subsection (a)(7), the court, upon request of the Attorney General, shall stay any request, demand, or order for discovery on the United States that the Attorney General certifies would significantly interfere with a criminal investigation or prosecution, or a national security operation, related to the incident that gave rise to the cause of action, until such time as the Attorney General advises the court that such request, demand, or order will no longer so interfere.

(B) A stay under this paragraph shall be in effect during the 12-month period beginning on the date on which the court issues the order to stay discovery. The court shall renew the order to stay discovery for additional 12-month periods upon motion by the United States if the Attorney General certifies that discovery would significantly interfere with a criminal investigation or prosecution, or a national security operation, related to the incident that gave rise to the cause of action.

(2) Sunset.--(A) Subject to subparagraph (B), no stay shall be granted or continued in effect under paragraph (1) after the date that is 10 years after the date on which the incident that gave rise to the cause of action occurred.

(B) After the period referred to in subparagraph (A), the court, upon request of the Attorney General, may stay any request, demand, or order for discovery on the United States that the court finds a substantial likelihood would--

(i) create a serious threat of death or serious bodily injury to any person;

(ii) adversely affect the ability of the United States to work in cooperation with foreign and international law enforcement agencies in investigating violations of United States law; or

(iii) obstruct the criminal case related to the incident that gave rise to the cause of action or undermine the potential for a conviction in such case.

(3) Evaluation of evidence.--The court's evaluation of any request for a stay under this subsection filed by the Attorney General shall be conducted ex parte and in camera.

(4) Bar on motions to dismiss.--A stay of discovery under this subsection shall constitute a bar to the granting of a motion to dismiss under rules 12(b)(6) and 56 of the Federal Rules of Civil Procedure.

(5) Construction.--Nothing in this subsection shall prevent the United States from seeking protective orders or asserting privileges ordinarily available to the United States.

§1606. Extent of liability

As to any claim for relief with respect to which a foreign state is not entitled to immunity under section 1605 or 1607 of this chapter, the foreign state shall be liable in the same manner and to the same extent as a private individual under like circumstances; but a foreign state except for an agency or instrumentality thereof shall not be liable for punitive damages; if, however, in any case wherein death was caused, the law of the place where the action or omission occurred provides, or has been construed to provide, for damages only punitive in nature, the foreign state shall be liable for actual or compensatory damages measured by the pecuniary injuries resulting from such death which were incurred by the persons for whose benefit the action was brought.

§1607. Counterclaims

In any action brought by a foreign state, or in which a foreign state intervenes, in a court of the United States or of a State, the foreign state shall not be accorded immunity with respect to any counterclaim--

(a) for which a foreign state would not be entitled to immunity under section 1605 of this chapter had such claim been brought in a separate action against the foreign state; or

(b) arising out of the transaction or occurrence that is the subject matter of the claim of the foreign state; or

(c) to the extent that the counterclaim does not seek relief exceeding in amount or differing in kind from that sought by the foreign state.

§1608. Service; time to answer; default

(a) Service in the courts of the United States and of the States shall be made upon a foreign state or political subdivision of a foreign state:

(1) by delivery of a copy of the summons and complaint in accordance with any special arrangement for service between the plaintiff and the foreign state or political subdivision; or

(2) if no special arrangement exists, by delivery of a copy of the summons and complaint in accordance with an applicable international convention on service of judicial documents; or

(3) if service cannot be made under paragraphs (1) or (2), by sending a copy of the summons and complaint and a notice of suit, together with a translation of each into the official language of the foreign state, by any form of mail requiring a signed receipt, to be addressed and dispatched by the clerk of the court to the head of the ministry of foreign affairs of the foreign state concerned, or

(4) if service cannot be made within 30 days under paragraph (3), by sending two copies of the summons and complaint and a notice of suit, together with a translation of each into the official language of the foreign state, by any form of mail requiring a signed receipt, to be addressed and dispatched by the clerk of the court to the Secretary of State in Washington, District of Columbia, to the attention of the Director of Special Consular Services--and the Secretary shall transmit one copy of the papers through diplomatic channels to the foreign state and shall send to the clerk of the court a certified copy of the diplomatic note indicating when the papers were transmitted.

As used in this subsection, a "notice of suit" shall mean a notice addressed to a foreign state and in a form prescribed by the Secretary of State by regulation.

(b) Service in the courts of the United States and of the States shall be made upon an agency or instrumentality of a foreign state:

(1) by delivery of a copy of the summons and complaint in accordance with any special arrangement for service between the plaintiff and the agency or instrumentality; or

(2) if no special arrangement exists, by delivery of a copy of the summons and complaint either to an officer, a managing or general agent, or to any other agent authorized by appointment or by law to receive service of process in the United States; or in accordance with an applicable international convention on service of judicial documents; or

(3) if service cannot be made under paragraphs (1) or (2), and if reasonably calculated to give actual notice, by delivery of a copy of the summons and complaint, together with a translation of each into the official language of the foreign state--

(A) as directed by an authority of the foreign state or political subdivision in response to a letter rogatory or request or

(B) by any form of mail requiring a signed receipt, to be addressed and dispatched by the clerk of the court to the agency or instrumentality to be served, or

(C) as directed by order of the court consistent with the law of the place where service is to be made.

(c) Service shall be deemed to have been made--

(1) in the case of service under subsection (a)(4), as of the date of transmittal indicated in the certified copy of the diplomatic note; and

(2) in any other case under this section, as of the date of receipt indicated in the certification, signed and returned postal receipt, or other proof of service applicable to the method of service employed.

(d) In any action brought in a court of the United States or of a State, a foreign state, a political subdivision thereof, or an agency or instrumentality of a foreign state shall serve an answer or other responsive pleading to the complaint within sixty days after service has been made under this section.

(e) No judgment by default shall be entered by a court of the United States or of a State against a foreign state, a political subdivision thereof, or an agency or instrumentality of a foreign state, unless the claimant establishes his claim or right to relief by evidence satisfactory to the court. A copy of any such default judgment shall be sent to the foreign state or political subdivision in the manner prescribed for service in this section.

§1609. Immunity from attachment and execution of property of a foreign state

Subject to existing international agreements to which the United States is a party at the time of enactment of this Act the property in the United States of a foreign state shall be immune from attachment arrest and execution except as provided in sections 1610 and 1611 of this chapter.

§1610. Exceptions to the immunity from attachment or execution

(a) The property in the United States of a foreign state, as defined in section 1603(a) of this chapter, used for a commercial activity in the United States, shall not be immune from attachment in aid of execution, or from execution, upon a judgment entered by a court of the United States or of a State after the effective date of this Act, if--

(1) the foreign state has waived its immunity from attachment in aid of execution or from execution either explicitly or by implication, notwithstanding any withdrawal of the

waiver the foreign state may purport to effect except in accordance with the terms of the waiver, or

(2) the property is or was used for the commercial activity upon which the claim is based, or

(3) the execution relates to a judgment establishing rights in property which has been taken in violation of international law or which has been exchanged for property taken in violation of international law, or

(4) the execution relates to a judgment establishing rights in property--

(A) which is acquired by succession or gift, or

(B) which is immovable and situated in the United States: *Provided*, That such property is not used for purposes of maintaining a diplomatic or consular mission or the residence of the Chief of such mission, or

(5) the property consists of any contractual obligation or any proceeds from such a contractual obligation to indemnify or hold harmless the foreign state or its employees under a policy of automobile or other liability or casualty insurance covering the claim which merged into the judgment, or

(6) the judgment is based on an order confirming an arbitral award rendered against the foreign state, provided that attachment in aid of execution, or execution, would not be inconsistent with any provision in the arbitral agreement, or

(7) the judgment relates to a claim for which the foreign state is not immune under section 1605(a)(7), regardless of whether the property is or was involved with the act upon which the claim is based.

(b) In addition to subsection (a), any property in the United States of an agency or instrumentality of a foreign state engaged in commercial activity in the United States shall not be immune from attachment in aid of execution, or from execution, upon a judgment entered by a court of the United States or of a State after the effective date of this Act, if--

(1) the agency or instrumentality has waived its immunity from attachment in aid of execution or from execution either explicitly or implicitly, notwithstanding any withdrawal of the waiver the agency or instrumentality may purport to effect except in accordance with the terms of the waiver, or

(2) the judgment relates to a claim for which the agency or instrumentality is not immune by virtue of section 1605(a) (2), (3), (5), or (7), or 1605(b) of this chapter, regardless of whether the property is or was involved in the act upon which the claim is based.

(c) No attachment or execution referred to in subsections (a) and (b) of this section shall be permitted until the court has ordered such attachment and execution after having determined that a reasonable period of time has elapsed following the entry of judgment and the giving of any notice required under section 1608(e) of this chapter.

(d) The property of a foreign state, as defined in section 1603(a) of this chapter, used for a commercial activity in the United States, shall not be immune from attachment prior to the entry of judgment in any action brought in a court of the United States or of a State, or prior to the elapse of the period of time provided in subsection (c) of this section, if--

(1) the foreign state has explicitly waived its immunity from attachment prior to judgment, notwithstanding any withdrawal of the waiver the foreign state may purport to effect except in accordance with the terms of the waiver, and

(2) the purpose of the attachment is to secure satisfaction of a judgment that has been or may ultimately be entered against the foreign state, and not to obtain jurisdiction.

(e) The vessels of a foreign state shall not be immune from arrest in rem, interlocutory sale, and execution in actions brought to foreclose a preferred mortgage as provided in section 1605(d).

(f)(1)(A) Notwithstanding any other provision of law, including but not limited to section 208(f) of the Foreign Missions Act (22 U.S.C. 4308(f)), and except as provided in subparagraph (B), any property with respect to which financial transactions are prohibited or regulated pursuant to section 5(b) of the Trading with the Enemy Act (50 U.S.C. App. 5(b)), section 620(a) of the Foreign Assistance Act of 1961 (22 U.S.C. 2370(a)), sections 202 and 203 of the International Emergency Economic Powers Act (50 U.S.C. 1701-1702), or any other proclamation, order, regulation, or license issued pursuant thereto, shall be subject to execution or attachment in aid of execution of any judgment relating to a claim for which a foreign state (including any agency or instrumentality or such state) claiming such property is not immune under section 1605(a)(7).

(B) Subparagraph (A) shall not apply if, at the time the property is expropriated or seized by the foreign state, the property has been held in title by a natural person or, if held in trust, has been held for the benefit of a natural person or persons.

(2)(A) At the request of any party in whose favor a judgment has been issued with respect to a claim for which the foreign state is not immune under section 1605(a)(7), the Secretary of the Treasury and the Secretary of State should make every effort to fully, promptly, and effectively assist any judgment creditor or any court that has issued any such judgment in identifying, locating, and executing against the property of that foreign state or any agency or instrumentality of such state.

(B) In providing such assistance, the Secretaries--

(i) may provide such information to the court under seal; and

(ii) should make every effort to provide the information in a manner sufficient to allow the court to direct the United States Marshall's office to promptly and effectively execute against that property.

(3) Waiver.--The President may waive any provision of paragraph (1) in the interest of national security.

§1611. Certain types of property immune from execution

(a) Notwithstanding the provisions of section 1610 of this chapter, the property of those organizations designated by the President as being entitled to enjoy the privileges, exemptions, and immunities provided by the International Organizations Immunities Act shall not be subject to attachment or any other judicial process impeding the disbursement of funds to, or on the order of, a foreign state as the result of an action brought in the courts of the United States or of the States.

(b) Notwithstanding the provisions of section 1610 of this chapter, the property of a foreign state shall be immune from attachment and from execution, if--

(1) the property is that of a foreign central bank or monetary authority held for its own account, unless such bank or authority, or its parent foreign government, has explicitly waived its immunity from attachment in aid of execution, or from execution, notwithstanding any withdrawal of the waiver which the bank, authority or government may purport to effect except in accordance with the terms of the waiver; or

(2) the property is, or is intended to be, used in connection with a military activity and

(A) is of a military character, or

(B) is under the control of a military authority or defense agency.

(c) Notwithstanding the provisions of section 1610 of this chapter, the property of a foreign state shall be immune from attachment and from execution in an action brought under section 302 of the Cuban Liberty and Democratic Solidarity (LIBERTAD) Act of 1996 to the extent that the property is a facility or installation used by an accredited diplomatic mission for official purposes.

3. Flatow Amendment 28 U.S.C. §1605 note

Civil Liability for Acts of State Sponsored Terrorism

(a) An official, employee, or agent of a foreign state designated as a state sponsor of terrorism designated under section 6(j) of the Export Administration Act of 1979 [section 2405(j) of the Appendix to Title 50, War and National Defense] while acting within the scope of his or her office, employment, or agency shall be liable to a United States national or the national's legal representative for personal injury or death caused by acts of that official, employee, or agent for which the courts of the United States may maintain jurisdiction under section 1605(a)(7) of title 28, United States Code [subsec. (a)(7) of this section] for money damages which may include economic damages, solatium, pain, and suffering, and punitive damages if the acts were among those described in section 1605(a)(7) [subsec. (a)(7) of this section].

(b) Provisions related to statute of limitations and limitations on discovery that would apply to an action brought under 28 U.S.C. 1605(f) and (g) [subsecs. (f) and (g) of this section] shall also apply to actions brought under this section.

No action shall be maintained under this action [SIC] if an official, employee, or agent of the United States, while acting within the scope of his or her office, employment, or agency would not be liable for such acts if carried out within the United States.

4. Klinghoffer Act, 18 U.S.C. §2331 et seq.

§2331. Definitions

As used in this chapter--

(1) the term "international terrorism" means activities that--

(A) involve violent acts or acts dangerous to human life that are a violation of the criminal laws of the United States or of any State, or that would be a criminal violation if committed within the jurisdiction of the United States or of any State;

(B) appear to be intended--

(i) to intimidate or coerce a civilian population;

(ii) to influence the policy of a government by intimidation or coercion; or

(iii) to affect the conduct of a government by mass destruction, assassination, or kidnapping; and

(C) occur primarily outside the territorial jurisdiction of the United States, or transcend national boundaries in terms of the means by which they are accomplished, the persons they appear intended to intimidate or coerce, or the locale in which their perpetrators operate or seek asylum;

(2) the term "national of the United States" has the meaning given such term in section 101(a)(22) of the Immigration and Nationality Act;

(3) the term "person" means any individual or entity capable of holding a legal or beneficial interest in property;

(4) the term "act of war" means any act occurring in the course of--

(A) declared war;

(B) armed conflict, whether or not war has been declared, between two or more nations; or

(C) armed conflict between military forces of any origin; and

(5) the term "domestic terrorism" means activities that--

(A) involve acts dangerous to human life that are a violation of the criminal laws of the United States or of any State;

(B) appear to be intended--

(i) to intimidate or coerce a civilian population;

(ii) to influence the policy of a government by intimidation or coercion; or

(iii) to affect the conduct of a government by mass destruction, assassination, or kidnapping; and

(C) occur primarily within the territorial jurisdiction of the United States.

§2332. Criminal penalties

(a) **Homicide.**--Whoever kills a national of the United States, while such national is outside the United States, shall--

(1) if the killing is murder (as defined in section 1111(a)), be fined under this title, punished by death or imprisonment for any term of years or for life, or both;

(2) if the killing is a voluntary manslaughter as defined in section 1112(a) of this title, be fined under this title or imprisoned not more than ten years, or both; and

(3) if the killing is an involuntary manslaughter as defined in section 1112(a) of this title, be fined under this title or imprisoned not more than three years, or both.

(b) **Attempt or conspiracy with respect to homicide.**--Whoever outside the United States attempts to kill, or engages in a conspiracy to kill, a national of the United States shall—

(1) in the case of an attempt to commit a killing that is a murder as defined in this chapter, be fined under this title or imprisoned not more than 20 years, or both; and

(2) in the case of a conspiracy by two or more persons to commit a killing that is a murder as defined in section 1111(a) of this title, if one or more of such persons do any overt act to effect the object of the conspiracy, be fined under this title or imprisoned for any term of years or for life, or both so fined and so imprisoned.

(c) **Other conduct.**--Whoever outside the United States engages in physical violence--

(1) with intent to cause serious bodily injury to a national of the United States; or

(2) with the result that serious bodily injury is caused to a national of the United States;

shall be fined under this title or imprisoned not more than ten years, or both.

(d) **Limitation on prosecution.**--No prosecution for any offense described in this section shall be undertaken by the United States except on written certification of the Attorney General or the highest ranking subordinate of the Attorney General with responsibility for criminal prosecutions that, in the judgment of the certifying official, such offense was intended to coerce, intimidate, or retaliate against a government or a civilian population.

18 U.S.C.A. §2332a

(a) Offense against a national of the United States or within the United States.--A person who, without lawful authority, uses, threatens, or attempts or conspires to use, a weapon of mass destruction--

(1) against a national of the United States while such national is outside of the United States;

(2) against any person or property within the United States, and

    (A) the mail or any facility of interstate or foreign commerce is used in furtherance of the offense;

    (B) such property is used in interstate or foreign commerce or in an activity that affects interstate or foreign commerce;

    (C) any perpetrator travels in or causes another to travel in interstate or foreign commerce in furtherance of the offense; or

    (D) the offense, or the results of the offense, affect interstate or foreign commerce, or, in the case of a threat, attempt, or conspiracy, would have affected interstate or foreign commerce;

(3) against any property that is owned, leased or used by the United States or by any department or agency of the United States, whether the property is within or outside of the United States; or

(4) against any property within the United States that is owned, leased, or used by a foreign government,

shall be imprisoned for any term of years or for life, and if death results, shall be punished by death or imprisoned for any term of years or for life.

(b) Offense by national of the United States outside of the United States.--Any national of the United States who, without lawful authority, uses, or threatens, attempts, or conspires to use, a weapon of mass destruction outside of the United States shall be imprisoned for any term of years or for life, and if death results, shall be punished by death, or by imprisonment for any term of years or for life.

(c) Definitions.--For purposes of this section--

(1) the term "national of the United States" has the meaning given in section 101(a)(22) of the Immigration and Nationality Act (8 U.S.C. 1101(a)(22));

(2) the term "weapon of mass destruction" means--

    (A) any destructive device as defined in section 921 of this title;

    (B) any weapon that is designed or intended to cause death or serious bodily injury through the re-

lease, dissemination, or impact of toxic or poisonous chemicals, or their precursors;

    (C) any weapon involving a biological agent, toxin, or vector (as those terms are defined in section 178 of this title); or

    (D) any weapon that is designed to release radiation or radioactivity at a level dangerous to human life; and

(3) the term "property" includes all real and personal property.

§2332b. Acts of terrorism transcending national boundaries

(a) Prohibited acts.--

(1) **Offenses.**--Whoever, involving conduct transcending national boundaries and in a circumstance described in subsection (b)--

    (A) kills, kidnaps, maims, commits an assault resulting in serious bodily injury, or assaults with a dangerous weapon any person within the United States; or

    (B) creates a substantial risk of serious bodily injury to any other person by destroying or damaging any structure, conveyance, or other real or personal property within the United States or by attempting or conspiring to destroy or damage any structure, conveyance, or other real or personal property within the United States;

in violation of the laws of any State, or the United States, shall be punished as prescribed in subsection (c).

(2) **Treatment of threats, attempts and conspiracies.**--Whoever threatens to commit an offense under paragraph (1), or attempts or conspires to do so, shall be punished under subsection (c).

(b) Jurisdictional bases.--

(1) **Circumstances.**--The circumstances referred to in subsection (a) are--

    (A) the mail or any facility of interstate or foreign commerce is used in furtherance of the offense;

    (B) the offense obstructs, delays, or affects interstate or foreign commerce, or would have so obstructed, delayed, or affected interstate or foreign commerce if the offense had been consummated;

    (C) the victim, or intended victim, is the United States Government, a member of the uniformed services, or any official, officer, employee, or agent of the legislative, executive, or judicial branches, or of any department or agency, of the United States;

(D) the structure, conveyance, or other real or personal property is, in whole or in part, owned, possessed, or leased to the United States, or any department or agency of the United States;

(E) the offense is committed in the territorial sea (including the airspace above and the seabed and subsoil below, and artificial islands and fixed structures erected thereon) of the United States; or

(F) the offense is committed within the special maritime and territorial jurisdiction of the United States.

(2) **Co-conspirators and accessories after the fact.**-- Jurisdiction shall exist over all principals and co-conspirators of an offense under this section, and accessories after the fact to any offense under this section, if at least one of the circumstances described in subparagraphs (A) through (F) of paragraph (1) is applicable to at least one offender.

(c) **Penalties.**--

(1) **Penalties.**--Whoever violates this section shall be punished--

(A) for a killing, or if death results to any person from any other conduct prohibited by this section, by death, or by imprisonment for any term of years or for life;

(B) for kidnapping, by imprisonment for any term of years or for life;

(C) for maiming, by imprisonment for not more than 35 years;

(D) for assault with a dangerous weapon or assault resulting in serious bodily injury, by imprisonment for not more than 30 years;

(E) for destroying or damaging any structure, conveyance, or other real or personal property, by imprisonment for not more than 25 years;

(F) for attempting or conspiring to commit an offense, for any term of years up to the maximum punishment that would have applied had the offense been completed; and

(G) for threatening to commit an offense under this section, by imprisonment for not more than 10 years.

(2) **Consecutive sentence.**--Notwithstanding any other provision of law, the court shall not place on probation any person convicted of a violation of this section; nor shall the term of imprisonment imposed under this section run concurrently with any other term of imprisonment.

(d) **Proof requirements.**--The following shall apply to prosecutions under this section:

(1) **Knowledge.**--The prosecution is not required to prove knowledge by any defendant of a jurisdictional base alleged in the indictment.

(2) **State law.**--In a prosecution under this section that is based upon the adoption of State law, only the elements of the offense under State law, and not any provisions pertaining to criminal procedure or evidence, are adopted.

(e) **Extraterritorial jurisdiction.**--There is extraterritorial Federal jurisdiction--

(1) over any offense under subsection (a), including any threat, attempt, or conspiracy to commit such offense; and

(2) over conduct which, under section 3, renders any person an accessory after the fact to an offense under subsection (a).

(f) **Investigative authority.**--In addition to any other investigative authority with respect to violations of this title, the Attorney General shall have primary investigative responsibility for all Federal crimes of terrorism, and any violation of section 351(e), 844(e), 844(f)(1), 956(b), 1361, 1366(b), 1366(c), 1751(e), 2152, or 2156 of this title, and the Secretary of the Treasury shall assist the Attorney General at the request of the Attorney General. Nothing in this section shall be construed to interfere with the authority of the United States Secret Service under section 3056.

(g) **Definitions.**--As used in this section--

(1) the term "conduct transcending national boundaries" means conduct occurring outside of the United States in addition to the conduct occurring in the United States;

(2) the term "facility of interstate or foreign commerce" has the meaning given that term in section 1958(b)(2);

(3) the term "serious bodily injury" has the meaning given that term in section 1365(g)(3);

(4) the term "territorial sea of the United States" means all waters extending seaward to 12 nautical miles from the baselines of the United States, determined in accordance with international law; and

(5) the term "Federal crime of terrorism" means an offense that--

(A) is calculated to influence or affect the conduct of government by intimidation or coercion, or to retaliate against government conduct; and

(B) is a violation of--

(i) section 32 (relating to destruction of aircraft or aircraft facilities), 37 (relating to violence at international airports), 81 (relating to arson within special maritime and territorial jurisdiction), 175 or 175b (relating to biological weapons), 175c (relating to variola virus), 229 (relating to chemical weapons), subsection (a), (b), (c), or (d) of section 351 (relating to congressional, cabinet, and Supreme Court assassination and kidnaping), 831 (relating to nuclear materials), 832 (relating to participation in nuclear and weapons of mass destruction threats to the United States) [FN1] 842(m) or (n) (relating to plastic explosives), 844(f)(2) or (3) (relating to arson and bombing of Government property risking or causing death), 844(i) (relating to arson and bombing of property used in interstate commerce), 930(c) (relating to killing or attempted killing during an attack on a Federal facility with a dangerous weapon), 956(a)(1) (relating to conspiracy to murder, kidnap, or maim persons abroad), 1030(a)(1) (relating to protection of computers), 1030(a)(5)(A)(i) resulting in damage as defined in 1030(a)(5)(B)(ii) through (v) (relating to protection of computers), 1114 (relating to killing or attempted killing of officers and employees of the United States), 1116 (relating to murder or manslaughter of foreign officials, official guests, or internationally protected persons), 1203 (relating to hostage taking), 1361 (relating to government property or contracts), 1362 (relating to destruction of communication lines, stations, or systems), 1363 (relating to injury to buildings or property within special maritime and territorial jurisdiction of the United States), 1366(a) (relating to destruction of an energy facility), 1751(a), (b), (c), or (d) (relating to Presidential and Presidential staff assassination and kidnaping), 1992 (relating to terrorist attacks and other acts of violence against railroad carriers and against mass transportation systems on land, on water, or through the air), 2155 (relating to destruction of national defense materials, premises, or utilities), 2156 (relating to national defense material, premises,

or utilities), 2280 (relating to violence against maritime navigation), 2281 (relating to violence against maritime fixed platforms), 2332 (relating to certain homicides and other violence against United States nationals occurring outside of the United States), 2332a (relating to use of weapons of mass destruction), 2332b (relating to acts of terrorism transcending national boundaries), 2332f (relating to bombing of public places and facilities), 2332g (relating to missile systems designed to destroy aircraft), 2332h (relating to radiological dispersal devices), 2339 (relating to harboring terrorists), 2339A (relating to providing material support to terrorists), 2339B (relating to providing material support to terrorist organizations), 2339C (relating to financing of terrorism), 2339D (relating to military-type training from a foreign terrorist organization), or 2340A (relating to torture) of this title;

(ii) sections 92 (relating to prohibitions governing atomic weapons) or 236 (relating to sabotage of nuclear facilities or fuel) of the Atomic Energy Act of 1954 (42 U.S.C. 2122 or 2284);

(iii) section 46502 (relating to aircraft piracy), the second sentence of section 46504 (relating to assault on a flight crew with a dangerous weapon), section 46505(b)(3) or (c) (relating to explosive or incendiary devices, or endangerment of human life by means of weapons, on aircraft), section 46506 if homicide or attempted homicide is involved (relating to application of certain criminal laws to acts on aircraft), or section 60123(b) (relating to destruction of interstate gas or hazardous liquid pipeline facility) of title 49; or

(iv) section 1010A of the Controlled Substances Import and Export Act (relating to narco-terrorism).

§2332d. Financial transactions

(a) **Offense.**--Except as provided in regulations issued by the Secretary of the Treasury, in consultation with the Secretary of State, whoever, being a United States person, knowing or having reasonable cause to know that a country is designated under section 6(j) of the Export Administration Act of 1979 (50 U.S.C. App. 2405) as a country supporting international terrorism, engages in a financial transaction with the government of that country, shall be fined under this title, imprisoned for not more than 10 years, or both.

(b) Definitions.--As used in this section--
(1) the term "financial transaction" has the same meaning as in section 1956(c)(4); and
(2) the term "United States person" means any--
(A) United States citizen or national;
(B) permanent resident alien;
(C) juridical person organized under the laws of the United States; or
(D) any person in the United States.

§2332e. Requests for military assistance to enforce prohibition in certain emergencies

The Attorney General may request the Secretary of Defense to provide assistance under section 382 of title 10 in support of Department of Justice activities relating to the enforcement of section 2332a of this title during an emergency situation involving a weapon of mass destruction. The authority to make such a request may be exercised by another official of the Department of Justice in accordance with section 382(f)(2) of title 10.

§2332f. Bombings of places of public use, government facilities, public transportation systems and infrastructure facilities

(a) Offenses.--
(1) In general.--Whoever unlawfully delivers, places, discharges, or detonates an explosive or other lethal device in, into, or against a place of public use, a state or government facility, a public transportation system, or an infrastructure facility--
(A) with the intent to cause death or serious bodily injury, or
(B) with the intent to cause extensive destruction of such a place, facility, or system, where such destruction results in or is likely to result in major economic loss,

shall be punished as prescribed in subsection (c).
(2) Attempts and conspiracies.--Whoever attempts or conspires to commit an offense under paragraph (1) shall be punished as prescribed in subsection (c).

(b) Jurisdiction.--There is jurisdiction over the offenses in subsection (a) if--
(1) the offense takes place in the United States and--

(A) the offense is committed against another state or a government facility of such state, including its embassy or other diplomatic or consular premises of that state;
(B) the offense is committed in an attempt to compel another state or the United States to do or abstain from doing any act;
(C) at the time the offense is committed, it is committed--
(i) on board a vessel flying the flag of another state;
(ii) on board an aircraft which is registered under the laws of another state; or
(iii) on board an aircraft which is operated by the government of another state;
(D) a perpetrator is found outside the United States;
(E) a perpetrator is a national of another state or a stateless person; or
(F) a victim is a national of another state or a stateless person;
(2) the offense takes place outside the United States and--
(A) a perpetrator is a national of the United States or is a stateless person whose habitual residence is in the United States;
(B) a victim is a national of the United States;
(C) a perpetrator is found in the United States;
(D) the offense is committed in an attempt to compel the United States to do or abstain from doing any act;
(E) the offense is committed against a state or government facility of the United States, including an embassy or other diplomatic or consular premises of the United States;
(F) the offense is committed on board a vessel flying the flag of the United States or an aircraft which is registered under the laws of the United States at the time the offense is committed; or
(G) the offense is committed on board an aircraft which is operated by the United States.

(c) Penalties.--Whoever violates this section shall be punished as provided under section 2332a(a) of this title.

(d) Exemptions to jurisdiction.--This section does not apply to--
(1) the activities of armed forces during an armed conflict, as those terms are understood under the law of war, which are governed by that law,

(2) activities undertaken by military forces of a state in the exercise of their official duties; or

(3) offenses committed within the United States, where the alleged offender and the victims are United States citizens and the alleged offender is found in the United States, or where jurisdiction is predicated solely on the nationality of the victims or the alleged offender and the offense has no substantial effect on interstate or foreign commerce.

(e) **Definitions.**--As used in this section, the term--

(1) "serious bodily injury" has the meaning given that term in section 1365(g)(3) of this title;

(2) "national of the United States" has the meaning given that term in section 101(a)(22) of the Immigration and Nationality Act (8 U.S.C. 1101(a)(22));

(3) "state or government facility" includes any permanent or temporary facility or conveyance that is used or occupied by representatives of a state, members of Government, the legislature or the judiciary or by officials or employees of a state or any other public authority or entity or by employees or officials of an intergovernmental organization in connection with their official duties;

(4) "intergovernmental organization" includes international organization (as defined in section 1116(b)(5) of this title);

(5) "infrastructure facility" means any publicly or privately owned facility providing or distributing services for the benefit of the public, such as water, sewage, energy, fuel, or communications;

(6) "place of public use" means those parts of any building, land, street, waterway, or other location that are accessible or open to members of the public, whether continuously, periodically, or occasionally, and encompasses any commercial, business, cultural, historical, educational, religious, governmental, entertainment, recreational, or similar place that is so accessible or open to the public;

(7) "public transportation system" means all facilities, conveyances, and instrumentalities, whether publicly or privately owned, that are used in or for publicly available services for the transportation of persons or cargo;

(8) "explosive" has the meaning given in section 844(j) of this title insofar that it is designed, or has the capability, to cause death, serious bodily injury, or substantial material damage;

(9) "other lethal device" means any weapon or device that is designed or has the capability to cause death, se-rious bodily injury, or substantial damage to property through the release, dissemination, or impact of toxic chemicals, biological agents, or toxins (as those terms are defined in section 178 of this title) or radiation or radioactive material;

(10) "military forces of a state" means the armed forces of a state which are organized, trained, and equipped under its internal law for the primary purpose of national defense or security, and persons acting in support of those armed forces who are under their formal command, control, and responsibility;

(11) "armed conflict" does not include internal disturbances and tensions, such as riots, isolated and sporadic acts of violence, and other acts of a similar nature; and

(12) "state" has the same meaning as that term has under international law, and includes all political subdivisions thereof.

§2332g. Missile systems designed to destroy aircraft

(a) **Unlawful conduct.**--

(1) **In general.**--Except as provided in paragraph (3), it shall be unlawful for any person to knowingly produce, construct, otherwise acquire, transfer directly or indirectly, receive, possess, import, export, or use, or possess and threaten to use--

(A) an explosive or incendiary rocket or missile that is guided by any system designed to enable the rocket or missile to--

(i) seek or proceed toward energy radiated or reflected from an aircraft or toward an image locating an aircraft; or

(ii) otherwise direct or guide the rocket or missile to an aircraft;

(B) any device designed or intended to launch or guide a rocket or missile described in subparagraph (A); or

(C) any part or combination of parts designed or redesigned for use in assembling or fabricating a rocket, missile, or device described in subparagraph (A) or (B).

(2) **Nonweapon.**--Paragraph (1)(A) does not apply to any device that is neither designed nor redesigned for use as a weapon.

(3) **Excluded conduct.**--This subsection does not apply with respect to--

(A) conduct by or under the authority of the United States or any department or agency thereof or of a State or any department or agency thereof; or

(B) conduct pursuant to the terms of a contract with the United States or any department or agency thereof or with a State or any department or agency thereof.

(b) Jurisdiction.--Conduct prohibited by subsection (a) is within the jurisdiction of the United States if--

    (1) the offense occurs in or affects interstate or foreign commerce;

    (2) the offense occurs outside of the United States and is committed by a national of the United States;

    (3) the offense is committed against a national of the United States while the national is outside the United States;

    (4) the offense is committed against any property that is owned, leased, or used by the United States or by any department or agency of the United States, whether the property is within or outside the United States; or

    (5) an offender aids or abets any person over whom jurisdiction exists under this subsection in committing an offense under this section or conspires with any person over whom jurisdiction exists under this subsection to commit an offense under this section.

(c) Criminal penalties.--

    (1) In general.--Any person who violates, or attempts or conspires to violate, subsection (a) shall be fined not more than $2,000,000 and shall be sentenced to a term of imprisonment not less than 25 years or to imprisonment for life.

    (2) Other circumstances.--Any person who, in the course of a violation of subsection (a), uses, attempts or conspires to use, or possesses and threatens to use, any item or items described in subsection (a), shall be fined not more than $2,000,000 and imprisoned for not less than 30 years or imprisoned for life.

    (3) Special circumstances.--If the death of another results from a person's violation of subsection (a), the person shall be fined not more than $2,000,000 and punished by imprisonment for life.

(d) Definition.--As used in this section, the term "aircraft" has the definition set forth in section 40102(a)(6) of title 49, United States Code.

§2332h. Radiological dispersal devices

(a) Unlawful conduct.--

    (1) In general.--Except as provided in paragraph (2), it shall be unlawful for any person to knowingly pro-duce, construct, otherwise acquire, transfer directly or indirectly, receive, possess, import, export, or use, or possess and threaten to use--

        (A) any weapon that is designed or intended to re-lease radiation or radioactivity at a level dangerous to human life; or

        (B) any device or other object that is capable of and designed or intended to endanger human life through the release of radiation or radioactivity.

    (2) Exception.--This subsection does not apply with respect to--

        (A) conduct by or under the authority of the United States or any department or agency thereof; or

        (B) conduct pursuant to the terms of a contract with the United States or any department or agency thereof.

(b) Jurisdiction.--Conduct prohibited by subsection (a) is within the jurisdiction of the United States if--

    (1) the offense occurs in or affects interstate or foreign commerce;

    (2) the offense occurs outside of the United States and is committed by a national of the United States;

    (3) the offense is committed against a national of the United States while the national is outside the United States;

    (4) the offense is committed against any property that is owned, leased, or used by the United States or by any department or agency of the United States, whether the property is within or outside the United States; or

    (5) an offender aids or abets any person over whom jurisdiction exists under this subsection in committing an offense under this section or conspires with any person over whom jurisdiction exists under this subsection to commit an offense under this section.

(c) Criminal penalties.--

    (1) In general.--Any person who violates, or attempts or conspires to violate, subsection (a) shall be fined not more than $2,000,000 and shall be sentenced to a term of imprisonment not less than 25 years or to imprisonment for life.

    (2) Other circumstances.--Any person who, in the course of a violation of subsection (a), uses, attempts or conspires to use, or possesses and threatens to use, any item or items described in subsection (a), shall be fined not more than $2,000,000 and imprisoned for not less than 30 years or imprisoned for life.

    (3) Special circumstances.--If the death of another results from a person's violation of subsection (a), the person shall be fined not more than $2,000,000 and punished by imprisonment for life.

§2333. Civil remedies

(a) Action and jurisdiction.--Any national of the United States injured in his or her person, property, or business by reason of an act of international terrorism, or his or her estate, survivors, or heirs, may sue therefor in any appropriate district court of the United States and shall recover threefold the damages he or she sustains and the cost of the suit, including attorney's fees.

(b) Estoppel under United States law.--A final judgment or decree rendered in favor of the United States in any criminal proceeding under section 1116, 1201, 1203, or 2332 of this title or section 46314, 46502, 46505, or 46506 of title 49 shall estop the defendant from denying the essential allegations of the criminal offense in any subsequent civil proceeding under this section.

(c) Estoppel under foreign law.--A final judgment or decree rendered in favor of any foreign state in any criminal proceeding shall, to the extent that such judgment or decree may be accorded full faith and credit under the law of the United States, estop the defendant from denying the essential allegations of the criminal offense in any subsequent civil proceeding under this section.

§2334. Jurisdiction and venue

(a) General venue.--Any civil action under section 2333 of this title against any person may be instituted in the district court of the United States for any district where any plaintiff resides or where any defendant resides or is served, or has an agent. Process in such a civil action may be served in any district where the defendant resides, is found, or has an agent.

(b) Special maritime or territorial jurisdiction.--If the actions giving rise to the claim occurred within the special maritime and territorial jurisdiction of the United States, as defined in section 7 of this title, then any civil action under section 2333 of this title against any person may be instituted in the district court of the United States for any district in which any plaintiff resides or the defendant resides, is served, or has an agent.

(c) Service on witnesses.--A witness in a civil action brought under section 2333 of this title may be served in any other district where the defendant resides, is found, or has an agent.

(d) Convenience of the forum.--The district court shall not dismiss any action brought under section 2333 of this title on the grounds of the inconvenience or inappropriateness of the forum chosen, unless--

> **(1)** the action may be maintained in a foreign court that has jurisdiction over the subject matter and over all the defendants;
>
> **(2)** that foreign court is significantly more convenient and appropriate; and
>
> **(3)** that foreign court offers a remedy which is substantially the same as the one available in the courts of the United States.

§2335. Limitation of actions

(a) In general.--Subject to subsection (b), a suit for recovery of damages under section 2333 of this title shall not be maintained unless commenced within 4 years after the date the cause of action accrued.

(b) Calculation of period.--The time of the absence of the defendant from the United States or from any jurisdiction in which the same or a similar action arising from the same facts may be maintained by the plaintiff, or of any concealment of the defendant's whereabouts, shall not be included in the 4-year period set forth in subsection (a).

§2336. Other limitations

(a) Acts of war.--No action shall be maintained under section 2333 of this title for injury or loss by reason of an act of war.

(b) Limitation on discovery.--If a party to an action under section 2333 seeks to discover the investigative files of the Department of Justice, the Assistant Attorney General, Deputy Attorney General, or Attorney General may object on the ground that compliance will interfere with a criminal investigation or prosecution of the incident, or a national security operation related to the incident, which is the subject of the civil litigation. The court shall evaluate any such objections in camera and shall stay the discovery if the court finds that granting the discovery request will substantially interfere with a criminal investigation or prosecution of the incident or a national security operation related to the incident. The court shall consider the likelihood of criminal prosecution by the Government and other factors it deems to be appropriate. A stay of discovery under this subsection shall constitute a bar to the granting of a motion to dismiss under rules 12(b)(6) and 56 of the Federal Rules of Civil Procedure. If the court grants a stay of discovery under this subsection, it may stay the action in the interests of justice.

(c) Stay of action for civil remedies.—

(1) The Attorney General may intervene in any civil action brought under section 2333 for the purpose of seeking a stay of the civil action. A stay shall be granted if the court finds that the continuation of the civil action will substantially interfere with a criminal prosecution which involves the same subject matter and in which an indictment has been returned, or interfere with national security operations related to the terrorist incident that is the subject of the civil action. A stay may be granted for up to 6 months. The Attorney General may petition the court for an extension of the stay for additional 6-month periods until the criminal prosecution is completed or dismissed.

(2) In a proceeding under this subsection, the Attorney General may request that any order issued by the court for release to the parties and the public omit any reference to the basis on which the stay was sought.

§2337. Suits against Government officials

No action shall be maintained under section 2333 of this title against--
(1) the United States, an agency of the United States, or an officer or employee of the United States or any agency thereof acting within his or her official capacity or under color of legal authority; or
(2) a foreign state, an agency of a foreign state, or an officer or employee of a foreign state or an agency thereof acting within his or her official capacity or under color of legal authority.

§2338. Exclusive Federal jurisdiction

The district courts of the United States shall have exclusive jurisdiction over an action brought under this chapter.

§2339. Harboring or concealing terrorists

(a) Whoever harbors or conceals any person who he knows, or has reasonable grounds to believe, has committed, or is about to commit, an offense under section 32 (relating to destruction of aircraft or aircraft facilities), section 175 (relating to biological weapons), section 229 (relating to chemical weapons), section 831 (relating to nuclear materials), paragraph (2) or (3) of section 844(f) (relating to arson and bombing of government property risking or causing injury or death), section 1366(a) (relating to the destruction of an energy facility), section 2280 (relating to violence against maritime navigation), section 2332a (relating to weapons of mass destruction), or section 2332b (relating to acts of terrorism transcending national boundaries) of this title, section 236(a) (relating to sabotage of nuclear facilities or fuel) of the Atomic Energy Act of 1954 (42 U.S.C. 2284(a)), or section 46502 (relating to aircraft piracy) of title 49, shall be fined under this title or imprisoned not more than ten years, or both.

(b) A violation of this section may be prosecuted in any Federal judicial district in which the underlying offense was committed, or in any other Federal judicial district as provided by law.

§2339A. Providing material support to terrorists

(a) Offense.--Whoever provides material support or resources or conceals or disguises the nature, location, source, or ownership of material support or resources, knowing or intending that they are to be used in preparation for, or in carrying out, a violation of section 32, 37, 81, 175, 229, 351, 831, 842(m) or (n), 844(f) or (i), 930(c), 956, 1114, 1116, 1203, 1361, 1362, 1363, 1366, 1751, 1992, 2155, 2156, 2280, 2281, 2332, 2332a, 2332b, 2332f, or 2340A of this title, section 236 of the Atomic Energy Act of 1954 (42 U.S.C. 2284), section 46502 or 60123(b) of title 49, or any offense listed in section 2332b(g)(5)(B) (except for sections 2339A and 2339B) or in preparation for, or in carrying out, the concealment of an escape from the commission of any such violation, or attempts or conspires to do such an act, shall be fined under this title, imprisoned not more than 15 years, or both, and, if the death of any person results, shall be imprisoned for any term of years or for life. A violation of this section may be prosecuted in any Federal judicial district in which the underlying offense was committed, or in any other Federal judicial district as provided by law.

(b) Definitions.--As used in this section--
(1) the term "material support or resources" means any property, tangible or intangible, or service, including currency or monetary instruments or financial securities, financial services, lodging, training, expert ad-

vice or assistance, safehouses, false documentation or identification, communications equipment, facilities, weapons, lethal substances, explosives, personnel (1 or more individuals who may be or include oneself), and transportation, except medicine or religious materials;

(2) the term "training" means instruction or teaching designed to impart a specific skill, as opposed to general knowledge; and

(3) the term "expert advice or assistance" means advice or assistance derived from scientific, technical or other specialized knowledge.

§2339B. Providing material support or resources to designated foreign terrorist organizations

(a) Prohibited activities.--

(1) Unlawful conduct.--Whoever knowingly provides material support or resources to a foreign terrorist organization, or attempts or conspires to do so, shall be fined under this title or imprisoned not more than 15 years, or both, and, if the death of any person results, shall be imprisoned for any term of years or for life. To violate this paragraph, a person must have knowledge that the organization is a designated terrorist organization (as defined in subsection (g)(6)), that the organization has engaged or engages in terrorist activity (as defined in section 212(a)(3)(B) of the Immigration and Nationality Act), or that the organization has engaged or engages in terrorism (as defined in section 140(d)(2) of the Foreign Relations Authorization Act, Fiscal Years 1988 and 1989).

(2) Financial institutions.--Except as authorized by the Secretary, any financial institution that becomes aware that it has possession of, or control over, any funds in which a foreign terrorist organization, or its agent, has an interest, shall--

(A) retain possession of, or maintain control over, such funds; and

(B) report to the Secretary the existence of such funds in accordance with regulations issued by the Secretary.

(b) Civil penalty.--Any financial institution that knowingly fails to comply with subsection (a)(2) shall be subject to a civil penalty in an amount that is the greater of--

(A) $50,000 per violation; or

(B) twice the amount of which the financial institution was required under subsection (a)(2) to retain possession or control.

(c) Injunction.--Whenever it appears to the Secretary or the Attorney General that any person is engaged in, or is about to engage in, any act that constitutes, or would constitute, a violation of this section, the Attorney General may initiate civil action in a district court of the United States to enjoin such violation.

(d) Extraterritorial jurisdiction.--

(1) In general.--There is jurisdiction over an offense under subsection (a) if--

(A) an offender is a national of the United States (as defined in section 101(a)(22) of the Immigration and Nationality Act (8 U.S.C. 1101(a)(22))) or an alien lawfully admitted for permanent residence in the United States (as defined in section 101(a)(20) of the Immigration and Nationality Act (8 U.S.C. 1101(a)(20)));

(B) an offender is a stateless person whose habitual residence is in the United States;

(C) after the conduct required for the offense occurs an offender is brought into or found in the United States, even if the conduct required for the offense occurs outside the United States;

(D) the offense occurs in whole or in part within the United States;

(E) the offense occurs in or affects interstate or foreign commerce; or

(F) an offender aids or abets any person over whom jurisdiction exists under this paragraph in committing an offense under subsection (a) or conspires with any person over whom jurisdiction exists under this paragraph to commit an offense under subsection (a).

(2) Extraterritorial jurisdiction.--There is extraterritorial Federal jurisdiction over an offense under this section.

(e) Investigations.--

(1) In general.--The Attorney General shall conduct any investigation of a possible violation of this section, or of any license, order, or regulation issued pursuant to this section.

(2) Coordination with the Department of the Treasury.--The Attorney General shall work in coordination with the Secretary in investigations relating to--

(A) the compliance or noncompliance by a financial institution with the requirements of subsection (a)(2); and

(B) civil penalty proceedings authorized under subsection (b).

(3) Referral.--Any evidence of a criminal violation of this section arising in the course of an investigation by the Secretary or any other Federal agency shall be referred immediately to the Attorney General for further investigation. The Attorney General shall timely notify the Secretary of any action taken on referrals from the Secretary, and may refer investigations to the Secretary for remedial licensing or civil penalty action.

(f) Classified information in civil proceedings brought by the United States.--

(1) Discovery of classified information by defendants.--

(A) Request by United States.--In any civil proceeding under this section, upon request made ex parte and in writing by the United States, a court, upon a sufficient showing, may authorize the United States to--

(i) redact specified items of classified information from documents to be introduced into evidence or made available to the defendant through discovery under the Federal Rules of Civil Procedure;

(ii) substitute a summary of the information for such classified documents; or

(iii) substitute a statement admitting relevant facts that the classified information would tend to prove.

(B) Order granting request.--If the court enters an order granting a request under this paragraph, the entire text of the documents to which the request relates shall be sealed and preserved in the records of the court to be made available to the appellate court in the event of an appeal.

(C) Denial of request.--If the court enters an order denying a request of the United States under this paragraph, the United States may take an immediate, interlocutory appeal in accordance with paragraph (5). For purposes of such an appeal, the entire text of the documents to which the request relates, together with any transcripts of arguments made ex parte to the court in connection therewith, shall be maintained under seal and delivered to the appellate court.

(2) Introduction of classified information; precautions by court.--

(A) Exhibits.--To prevent unnecessary or inadvertent disclosure of classified information in a civil proceeding brought by the United States under this section, the United States may petition the court ex parte to admit, in lieu of classified writings, recordings, or photographs, one or more of the following:

(i) Copies of items from which classified information has been redacted.

(ii) Stipulations admitting relevant facts that specific classified information would tend to prove.

(iii) A declassified summary of the specific classified information.

(B) Determination by court.--The court shall grant a request under this paragraph if the court finds that the redacted item, stipulation, or summary is sufficient to allow the defendant to prepare a defense.

(3) Taking of trial testimony.--

(A) Objection.--During the examination of a witness in any civil proceeding brought by the United States under this subsection, the United States may object to any question or line of inquiry that may require the witness to disclose classified information not previously found to be admissible.

(B) Action by court.--In determining whether a response is admissible, the court shall take precautions to guard against the compromise of any classified information, including--

(i) permitting the United States to provide the court, ex parte, with a proffer of the witness's response to the question or line of inquiry; and

(ii) requiring the defendant to provide the court with a proffer of the nature of the information that the defendant seeks to elicit.

(C) Obligation of defendant.--In any civil proceeding under this section, it shall be the defendant's obligation to establish the relevance and materiality of any classified information sought to be introduced.

(4) Appeal.--If the court enters an order denying a request of the United States under this subsection, the United States may take an immediate interlocutory appeal in accordance with paragraph (5).

(5) Interlocutory appeal.--

(A) Subject of appeal.--An interlocutory appeal by the United States shall lie to a court of appeals from a decision or order of a district court--

(i) authorizing the disclosure of classified information;

(ii) imposing sanctions for nondisclosure of classified information; or

(iii) refusing a protective order sought by the United States to prevent the disclosure of classified information.

(B) Expedited consideration.--

(i) In general.--An appeal taken pursuant to this paragraph, either before or during trial, shall be expedited by the court of appeals.

(ii) Appeals prior to trial.--If an appeal is of an order made prior to trial, an appeal shall be taken not later than 10 days after the decision or order appealed from, and the trial shall not commence until the appeal is resolved.

(iii) Appeals during trial.--If an appeal is taken during trial, the trial court shall adjourn the trial until the appeal is resolved, and the court of appeals--

(I) shall hear argument on such appeal not later than 4 days after the adjournment of the trial;

(II) may dispense with written briefs other than the supporting materials previously submitted to the trial court;

(III) shall render its decision not later than 4 days after argument on appeal; and

(IV) may dispense with the issuance of a written opinion in rendering its decision.

(C) Effect of ruling.--An interlocutory appeal and decision shall not affect the right of the defendant, in a subsequent appeal from a final judgment, to claim as error reversal by the trial court on remand of a ruling appealed from during trial.

(6) Construction.--Nothing in this subsection shall prevent the United States from seeking protective orders or asserting privileges ordinarily available to the United States to protect against the disclosure of classified information, including the invocation of the military and State secrets privilege.

(g) Definitions.--As used in this section--

(1) the term "classified information" has the meaning given that term in section 1(a) of the Classified Information Procedures Act (18 U.S.C. App.);

(2) the term "financial institution" has the same meaning as in section 5312(a)(2) of title 31, United States Code;

(3) the term "funds" includes coin or currency of the United States or any other country, traveler's checks, personal checks, bank checks, money orders, stocks, bonds, debentures, drafts, letters of credit, any other

negotiable instrument, and any electronic representation of any of the foregoing;

(4) the term "material support or resources" has the same meaning given that term in section 2339A (including the definitions of "training" and "expert advice or assistance" in that section);

(5) the term "Secretary" means the Secretary of the Treasury; and

(6) the term "terrorist organization" means an organization designated as a terrorist organization under section 219 of the Immigration and Nationality Act.

(h) Provision of personnel.--No person may be prosecuted under this section in connection with the term "personnel" unless that person has knowingly provided, attempted to provide, or conspired to provide a foreign terrorist organization with 1 or more individuals (who may be or include himself) to work under that terrorist organization's direction or control or to organize, manage, supervise, or otherwise direct the operation of that organization. Individuals who act entirely independently of the foreign terrorist organization to advance its goals or objectives shall not be considered to be working under the foreign terrorist organization's direction and control.

(i) Rule of construction.--Nothing in this section shall be construed or applied so as to abridge the exercise of rights guaranteed under the First Amendment to the Constitution of the United States.

(j) Exception.--No person may be prosecuted under this section in connection with the term "personnel", "training", or "expert advice or assistance" if the provision of that material support or resources to a foreign terrorist organization was approved by the Secretary of State with the concurrence of the Attorney General. The Secretary of State may not approve the provision of any material support that may be used to carry out terrorist activity (as defined in section 212(a)(3)(B)(iii) of the Immigration and Nationality Act).

§2339C. Prohibitions against the financing of terrorism

(a) Offenses.--

(1) In general.--Whoever, in a circumstance described in subsection (b), by any means, directly or indirectly, unlawfully and willfully provides or collects funds with the intention that such funds be used, or with the knowledge that such funds are to be used, in full or in part, in order to carry out--

(A) an act which constitutes an offense within the scope of a treaty specified in subsection (e)(7), as implemented by the United States, or

(B) any other act intended to cause death or serious bodily injury to a civilian, or to any other person not taking an active part in the hostilities in a situation of armed conflict, when the purpose of such act, by its nature or context, is to intimidate a population, or to compel a government or an international organization to do or to abstain from doing any act, shall be punished as prescribed in subsection (d)(1).

(2) Attempts and conspiracies.--Whoever attempts or conspires to commit an offense under paragraph (1) shall be punished as prescribed in subsection (d)(1).

(3) Relationship to predicate act.--For an act to constitute an offense set forth in this subsection, it shall not be necessary that the funds were actually used to carry out a predicate act.

(b) Jurisdiction.--There is jurisdiction over the offenses in subsection (a) in the following circumstances--

(1) the offense takes place in the United States and--

(A) a perpetrator was a national of another state or a stateless person;

(B) on board a vessel flying the flag of another state or an aircraft which is registered under the laws of another state at the time the offense is committed;

(C) on board an aircraft which is operated by the government of another state;

(D) a perpetrator is found outside the United States;

(E) was directed toward or resulted in the carrying out of a predicate act against--

(i) a national of another state; or

(ii) another state or a government facility of such state, including its embassy or other diplomatic or consular premises of that state;

(F) was directed toward or resulted in the carrying out of a predicate act committed in an attempt to compel another state or international organization to do or abstain from doing any act; or

(G) was directed toward or resulted in the carrying out of a predicate act--

(i) outside the United States; or

(ii) within the United States, and either the offense or the predicate act was conducted in, or the results thereof affected, interstate or foreign commerce;

(2) the offense takes place outside the United States and--

(A) a perpetrator is a national of the United States or is a stateless person whose habitual residence is in the United States;

(B) a perpetrator is found in the United States; or

(C) was directed toward or resulted in the carrying out of a predicate act against--

(i) any property that is owned, leased, or used by the United States or by any department or agency of the United States, including an embassy or other diplomatic or consular premises of the United States;

(ii) any person or property within the United States;

(iii) any national of the United States or the property of such national; or

(iv) any property of any legal entity organized under the laws of the United States, including any of its States, districts, commonwealths, territories, or possessions;

(3) the offense is committed on board a vessel flying the flag of the United States or an aircraft which is registered under the laws of the United States at the time the offense is committed;

(4) the offense is committed on board an aircraft which is operated by the United States; or

(5) the offense was directed toward or resulted in the carrying out of a predicate act committed in an attempt to compel the United States to do or abstain from doing any act.

(c) Concealment.--Whoever--

(1)

(A) is in the United States; or

(B) is outside the United States and is a national of the United States or a legal entity organized under the laws of the United States (including any of its States, districts, commonwealths, territories, or possessions); and

(2) knowingly conceals or disguises the nature, location, source, ownership, or control of any material support or resources, or any funds or proceeds of such funds--

(A) knowing or intending that the support or resources are to be provided, or knowing that the support or resources were provided, in violation of section 2339B of this title; or

(B) knowing or intending that any such funds are to be provided or collected, or knowing that the funds were provided or collected, in violation of subsection (a), shall be punished as prescribed in subsection (d)(2).

(d) Penalties.--

(1) Subsection (a)--Whoever violates subsection (a) shall be fined under this title, imprisoned for not more than 20 years, or both.

(2) Subsection (c)--Whoever violates subsection (c) shall be fined under this title, imprisoned for not more than 10 years, or both.

(e) Definitions.--In this section--

(1) the term "funds" means assets of every kind, whether tangible or intangible, movable or immovable, however acquired, and legal documents or instruments in any form, including electronic or digital, evidencing title to, or interest in, such assets, including coin, currency, bank credits, travelers checks, bank checks, money orders, shares, securities, bonds, drafts, and letters of credit;

(2) the term "government facility" means any permanent or temporary facility or conveyance that is used or occupied by representatives of a state, members of a government, the legislature, or the judiciary, or by officials or employees of a state or any other public authority or entity or by employees or officials of an intergovernmental organization in connection with their official duties;

(3) the term "proceeds" means any funds derived from or obtained, directly or indirectly, through the commission of an offense set forth in subsection (a);

(4) the term "provides" includes giving, donating, and transmitting;

(5) the term "collects" includes raising and receiving;

(6) the term "predicate act" means any act referred to in subparagraph (A) or (B) of subsection (a)(1);

(7) the term "treaty" means--

(A) the Convention for the Suppression of Unlawful Seizure of Aircraft, done at The Hague on December 16, 1970;

(B) the Convention for the Suppression of Unlawful Acts against the Safety of Civil Aviation, done at Montreal on September 23, 1971;

(C) the Convention on the Prevention and Punishment of Crimes against Internationally Protected Persons, including Diplomatic Agents, adopted by the General Assembly of the United Nations on December 14, 1973;

(D) the International Convention against the Taking of Hostages, adopted by the General Assembly of the United Nations on December 17, 1979;

(E) the Convention on the Physical Protection of Nuclear Material, adopted at Vienna on March 3, 1980;

(F) the Protocol for the Suppression of Unlawful Acts of Violence at Airports Serving International Civil Aviation, supplementary to the Convention for the Suppression of Unlawful Acts against the Safety of Civil Aviation, done at Montreal on February 24, 1988;

(G) the Convention for the Suppression of Unlawful Acts against the Safety of Maritime Navigation, done at Rome on March 10, 1988;

(H) the Protocol for the Suppression of Unlawful Acts against the Safety of Fixed Platforms located on the Continental Shelf, done at Rome on March 10, 1988; or

(I) the International Convention for the Suppression of Terrorist Bombings, adopted by the General Assembly of the United Nations on December 15, 1997;

(8) the term "intergovernmental organization" includes international organizations;

(9) the term "international organization" has the same meaning as in section 1116(b)(5) of this title;

(10) the term "armed conflict" does not include internal disturbances and tensions, such as riots, isolated and sporadic acts of violence, and other acts of a similar nature;

(11) the term "serious bodily injury" has the same meaning as in section 1365(g)(3) of this title;

(12) the term "national of the United States" has the meaning given that term in section 101(a)(22) of the Immigration and Nationality Act (8 U.S.C. 1101(a)(22));

(13) the term "material support or resources" has the same meaning given that term in section 2339B(g)(4) of this title; and

(14) the term "state" has the same meaning as that term has under international law, and includes all political subdivisions thereof.

(f) Civil penalty.--In addition to any other criminal, civil, or administrative liability or penalty, any legal entity located within the United States or organized under the laws of the United States, including any of the laws of its States, districts, commonwealths, territories, or possessions, shall be liable to the United States for the sum of at least $10,000, if a person responsible for the management or control of that legal entity has, in that capacity, committed an offense set forth in subsection (a).

§2339D. Receiving military-type training from a foreign terrorist organization [FN1]

(a) Offense.--Whoever knowingly receives military-type training from or on behalf of any organization designated at the time of the training by the Secretary of State under section 219(a)(1) of the Immigration and Nationality Act as a foreign terrorist organization shall be fined under this title or imprisoned for ten years, or both. To violate this subsection, a person must have knowledge that the organization is a designated terrorist organization (as defined in subsection (c)(4)), that the organization has engaged or engages in terrorist activity (as defined in section 212 of the Immigration and Nationality Act), or that the organization has engaged or engages in terrorism (as defined in section 140(d)(2) of the Foreign Relations Authorization Act, Fiscal Years 1988 and 1989).

(b) Extraterritorial jurisdiction.--There is extraterritorial Federal jurisdiction over an offense under this section. There is jurisdiction over an offense under subsection (a) if--

(1) an offender is a national of the United States (as defined in 101(a)(22) [FN2] of the Immigration and Nationality Act) or an alien lawfully admitted for permanent residence in the United States (as defined in section 101(a)(20) of the Immigration and Nationality Act);

(2) an offender is a stateless person whose habitual residence is in the United States;

(3) after the conduct required for the offense occurs an offender is brought into or found in the United States, even if the conduct required for the offense occurs outside the United States;

(4) the offense occurs in whole or in part within the United States;

(5) the offense occurs in or affects interstate or foreign commerce; or

(6) an offender aids or abets any person over whom jurisdiction exists under this paragraph in committing an offense under subsection (a) or conspires with any person over whom jurisdiction exists under this paragraph to commit an offense under subsection (a).

(c) Definitions.--As used in this section--

(1) the term "military-type training" includes training in means or methods that can cause death or serious bodily injury, destroy or damage property, or disrupt services to critical infrastructure, or training on the use, storage, production, or assembly of any explosive, firearm or other weapon, including any weapon of mass destruction (as defined in section 2232a(c)(2) [FN3]);

(2) the term "serious bodily injury" has the meaning given that term in section 1365(h)(3);

(3) the term "critical infrastructure" means systems and assets vital to national defense, national security, economic security, public health or safety including both regional and national infrastructure. Critical infrastructure may be publicly or privately owned; examples of critical infrastructure include gas and oil production, storage, or delivery systems, water supply systems, telecommunications networks, electrical power generation or delivery systems, financing and banking systems, emergency services (including medical, police, fire, and rescue services), and transportation systems and services (including highways, mass transit, airlines, and airports); and

(4) the term "foreign terrorist organization" means an organization designated as a terrorist organization under section 219(a)(1) of the Immigration and Nationality Act.

5. Torture Victim Protection Act, 28 U.S.C. §1350 note

Section 1. Short Title.

This Act may be cited as the 'Torture Victim Protection Act of 1991'.

Sec. 2. Establishment of civil action.

(a) Liability.--An individual who, under actual or apparent authority, or color of law, of any foreign nation--
(1) subjects an individual to torture shall, in a civil action, be liable for damages to that individual; or
(2) subjects an individual to extrajudicial killing shall, in a civil action, be liable for damages to the individual's legal representative, or to any person who may be a claimant in an action for wrongful death.

(b) Exhaustion of remedies.--A court shall decline to hear a claim under this section if the claimant has not exhausted adequate and available remedies in the place in which the conduct giving rise to the claim occurred.

(c) Statute of limitations.--No action shall be maintained under this section unless it is commenced within 10 years after the cause of action arose.

Sec. 3. Definitions.

(a) Extrajudicial killing.--For the purposes of this Act, the term 'extrajudicial killing' means a deliberated killing not authorized by a previous judgment pronounced by a regularly constituted court affording all the judicial guarantees which are recognized as indispensable by civilized peoples. Such term, however, does not include any such killing that, under international law, is lawfully carried out under the authority of a foreign nation.

(b) Torture.--For the purposes of this Act--

(1) the term 'torture' means any act, directed against an individual in the offender's custody or physical control, by which severe pain or suffering (other than pain or suffering arising only from or inherent in, or incidental to, lawful sanctions), whether physical or mental, is intentionally inflicted on that individual for such purposes as obtaining from that individual or a third person information or a confession, punishing that individual for an act that individual or a third person has committed or is suspected of having committed, intimidating or coercing that individual or a third person, or for any reason based on discrimination of any kind; and
(2) mental pain or suffering refers to prolonged mental harm caused by or resulting from--
(A) the intentional infliction or threatened infliction of severe physical pain or suffering;
(B) the administration or application, or threatened administration or application, of mind altering substances or other procedures calculated to disrupt profoundly the senses or the personality;
(C) the threat of imminent death; or
(D) the threat that another individual will imminently be subjected to death, severe physical pain or suffering, or the administration or application of mind altering substances or other procedures calculated to disrupt profoundly the senses or personality.

6. State Sponsors of Terrorism

http://www.state.gov/s/ct/c14151.htm

Countries determined by the Secretary of State to have repeatedly provided support for acts of international terrorism are designated pursuant to three laws: section 6(j) of the Export Administration Act, section 40 of the Arms Export Control Act, and section 620A of the Foreign Assistance Act. Taken together, the four main categories of sanctions resulting from designation under these authorities include restrictions on U.S. foreign assistance; a ban on defense exports and sales; certain controls over exports of dual use items; and miscellaneous financial and other restrictions.

Designation under the above-referenced authorities also implicates other sanctions laws that penalize persons and countries engaging in certain trade with state sponsors. Currently there are five countries designated under these authorities: Cuba, Iran, North Korea, Sudan and Syria.

Country	Designation Date
Cuba	March 1, 1982
Iran	January 19, 1984
North Korea	January 20, 1988
Sudan	August 12, 1993
Syria	December 29, 1979

7. Export Administration Act, 50 App. U.S.C. §2405(j)

(a) Authority

(1) In order to carry out the policy set forth in paragraph (2)(B), (7), (8), or (13) of section 3 of this Act [section 2402(2)(B), (7), (8), or (13) of this Appendix], the President may prohibit or curtail the exportation of any goods, technology, or other information subject to the jurisdiction of the United States or exported by any person subject to the jurisdiction of the United States, to the extent necessary to further significantly the foreign policy of the United States or to fulfill its declared international obligations. The authority granted by this subsection shall be exercised by the Secretary, in consultation with the Secretary of State, the Secretary of Defense, the Secretary of Agriculture, the Secretary of the Treasury, the United States Trade Representative, and such other departments and agencies as the Secretary considers appropriate, and shall be implemented by means of export licenses issued by the Secretary.

(2) Any export control imposed under this section shall apply to any transaction or activity undertaken with the intent to evade that export control, even if that export control would not otherwise apply to that transaction or activity.

(3) Export controls maintained for foreign policy purposes shall expire on December 31, 1979, or one year after imposition, whichever is later, unless extended by the President in accordance with subsections (b) and (f). Any such extension and any subsequent extension shall not be for a period of more than one year.

(4) Whenever the Secretary denies any export license under this subsection, the Secretary shall specify in the notice to the applicant of the denial of such license that the license was denied under the authority contained in this subsection, and the reasons for such denial, with reference to the criteria set forth in subsection (b) of this section. The Secretary shall also include in such notice what, if any, modifications in or restrictions on the goods or technology for which the license was sought would allow such export to be compatible with controls implemented under this section, or the Secretary shall indicate in such notice which officers and employees of the Department of Commerce who are familiar with the application will be made reasonably available to the applicant for consultation with regard to such modifications or restrictions, if appropriate.

(5) In accordance with the provisions of section 10 of this Act [section 2409 of this Appendix], the Secretary of State shall have the right to review any export license application under this section which the Secretary of State requests to review.

(6) Before imposing, expanding, or extending export controls under this section on exports to a country which can use goods, technology, or information available from foreign sources and so incur little or no economic costs as a result of the controls, the President should, through diplomatic means, employ alternatives to export controls which offer opportunities of distinguishing the United States from, and expressing the displeasure of the United States with, the specific actions of that country in response to which the controls are proposed. Such alternatives include private discussions with foreign leaders, public statements in situations where private diplomacy is unavailable or not effective, withdrawal of ambassadors, and reduction of the size of the diplomatic staff that the country involved is permitted to have in the United States.

(b) Criteria

(1) Subject to paragraph (2) of this subsection, the President may impose, extend, or expand export controls under this section only if the President determines that--
(A) such controls are likely to achieve the intended foreign policy purpose, in light of other factors, including the availability from other countries of the goods or technology proposed for such controls, and that foreign policy purpose cannot be achieved through negotiations or other alternative means;
(B) the proposed controls are compatible with the foreign policy objectives of the United States and with overall United States policy toward the country to which exports are to be subject to the proposed controls;
(C) the reaction of other countries to the imposition, extension, or expansion of such export controls by the United States is not likely to render the controls ineffective in achieving the intended foreign policy purpose or to be counterproductive to United States foreign policy interests;
(D) the effect of the proposed controls on the export performance of the United States, the competitive position of the United States in the international economy, the international reputation of the United States as a supplier of goods and technology, or on the economic well-being of individual United States companies and their employees and communities does not exceed the benefit to United States foreign policy objectives; and

(E) the United States has the ability to enforce the proposed controls effectively.

(2) With respect to those export controls in effect under this section on the date of the enactment of the Export Administration Amendments Act of 1985 [July 12, 1985], the President, in determining whether to extend those controls, as required by subsection (a)(3) of this section, shall consider the criteria set forth in paragraph (1) of this subsection and shall consider the foreign policy consequences of modifying the export controls.

(c) Consultation with industry

The Secretary in every possible instance shall consult with and seek advice from affected United States industries and appropriate advisory committees established under section 135 of the Trade Act of 1974 [19 U.S.C.A. §2155] before imposing any export control under this section. Such consultation and advice shall be with respect to the criteria set forth in subsection (b)(1) and such other matters as the Secretary considers appropriate.

(d) Consultation with other countries

When imposing export controls under this section, the President shall, at the earliest appropriate opportunity, consult with the countries with which the United States maintains export controls cooperatively, and with such other countries as the President considers appropriate, with respect to the criteria set forth in subsection (b)(1) and such other matters as the President considers appropriate.

(e) Alternative means

Before resorting to the imposition of export controls under this section, the President shall determine that reasonable efforts have been made to achieve the purposes of the controls through negotiations or other alternative means.

(f) Consultation with Congress

(1) The President may impose or expand export controls under this section, or extend such controls as required by subsection (a)(3) of this section, only after consultation with the Congress, including the Committee on Foreign Affairs of the House of Representatives and the Committee on Banking, Housing, and Urban Affairs of the Senate.

(2) The President may not impose, expand, or extend export controls under this section until the President has submitted to the Congress a report--

(A) specifying the purpose of the controls;

(B) specifying the determinations of the President (or, in the case of those export controls described in subsection (b)(2), the considerations of the President) with respect to each of the criteria set forth in subsection (b)(1), the bases for such determinations (or considerations), and any possible adverse foreign policy consequences of the controls;

(C) describing the nature, the subjects, and the results of, or the plans for, the consultation with industry pursuant to subsection (c) and with other countries pursuant to subsection (d);

(D) specifying the nature and results of any alternative means attempted under subsection (e), or the reasons for imposing, expanding, or extending the controls without attempting any such alternative means; and

(E) describing the availability from other countries of goods or technology comparable to the goods or technology subject to the proposed export controls, and describing the nature and results of the efforts made pursuant to subsection (h) to secure the cooperation of foreign governments in controlling the foreign availability of such comparable goods or technology.

Such report shall also indicate how such controls will further significantly the foreign policy of the United States or will further its declared international obligations.

(3) To the extent necessary to further the effectiveness of the export controls, portions of a report required by paragraph (2) may be submitted to the Congress on a classified basis, and shall be subject to the provisions of section 12(c) of this Act [section 2411(c) of this Appendix].

(4) In the case of export controls under this section which prohibit or curtail the export of any agricultural commodity, a report submitted pursuant to paragraph (2) shall be deemed to be the report required by section 7(g)(3)(A) of this Act [section 2406(g)(3)(A) of this Appendix].

(5) In addition to any written report required under this section, the Secretary, not less frequently than annually, shall present in oral testimony before the Committee on Banking, Housing, and Urban Affairs of the Senate and the Committee on Foreign Affairs of the House of Representatives a report on policies and actions taken by the Government to carry out the provisions of this section.

(g) Exclusion for medicine and medical supplies and for certain food exports

This section does not authorize export controls on medicine or medical supplies. This section also does not authorize export controls on donations of goods (including, but not limited to, food, educational materials, seeds and hand tools, medicines and medical supplies, water resources equipment, clothing and shelter materials, and basic household supplies) that are intended to meet basic human needs. Before export controls on food are imposed, expanded, or extended under this section, the Secretary shall notify the Secretary of State in the case of export controls applicable with respect to any developed country and shall notify the Administrator of the Agency for International Development in the case of export controls applicable with respect to any developing country. The Secretary of State with respect to developed countries, and the Administrator with respect to developing countries, shall determine whether the proposed export controls on food would cause measurable malnutrition and shall inform the Secretary of that determination. If the Secretary is informed that the proposed export controls on food would cause measurable malnutrition, then those controls may not be imposed, expanded, or extended, as the case may be, unless the President determines that those controls are necessary to protect the national security interests of the United States, or unless the President determines that arrangements are insufficient to ensure that the food will reach those most in need. Each such determination by the Secretary of State or Administrator of the Agency for International Development , and any such determination by the President, shall be reported to the Congress, together with a statement of the reasons for that determination. It is the intent of Congress that the President not impose export controls under this section on any goods or technology if he determines that the principal effect of the export of such goods or technology would be to help meet basic human needs. This subsection shall not be construed to prohibit the President from imposing restrictions on the export of medicine or medical supplies or of food under the International Emergency Economic Powers Act [50 U.S.C.A. §1701 et seq.]. This subsection shall not apply to any export control on medicine, medical supplies, or food, except for donations, which is in effect on the date of the enactment of the Export Administration Amendments Act of 1985 [July 12, 1985]. Notwithstanding the preceding provisions of this subsection, the President may impose export controls under this section on medicine, medical supplies, food, and donations of goods in order to carry out the policy set forth in paragraph (13) of section 3 of this Act [section 2402(13) of this Appendix].

(h) Foreign availability

(1) In applying export controls under this section, the President shall take all feasible steps to initiate and conclude negotiations with appropriate foreign governments for the purpose of securing the cooperation of such foreign governments in controlling the export to countries and consignees to which the United States export controls apply of any goods or technology comparable to goods or technology controlled under this section.

(2) Before extending any export control pursuant to subsection (a)(3) of this section, the President shall evaluate the results of his actions under paragraph (1) of this subsection and shall include the results of that evaluation in his report to the Congress pursuant to subsection (f) of this section.

(3) If, within 6 months after the date on which export controls under this section are imposed or expanded, or within 6 months after the date of the enactment of the Export Administration Amendments Act of 1985 [July 12, 1985] in the case of export controls in effect on such date of enactment, the President's efforts under paragraph (1) are not successful in securing the cooperation of foreign governments described in paragraph (1) with respect to those export controls, the Secretary shall thereafter take into account the foreign availability of the goods or technology subject to the export controls. If the Secretary affirmatively determines that a good or technology subject to the export controls is available in sufficient quantity and comparable quality from sources outside the United States to countries subject to the export controls so that denial of an export license would be ineffective in achieving the purposes of the controls, then the Secretary shall, during the period of such foreign availability, approve any license application which is required for the export of the good or technology and which meets all requirements for such a license. The Secretary shall remove the good or technology from the list established pursuant to subsection (l) of this section if the Secretary determines that such action is appropriate.

(4) In making a determination of foreign availability under paragraph (3) of this subsection, the Secretary shall follow the procedures set forth in section 5(f)(3) of this Act [section 2404(f)(3) of this Appendix].

(i) International obligations

The provisions of subsections (b), (c), (d), (e), (g), and (h) shall not apply in any case in which the President exercises the authority contained in this section to impose export controls, or to approve or deny export license applications, in order to fulfill obligations of the United States pursuant to treaties to which the United States is a party or pursuant to other international agreements.

(j) Countries supporting international terrorism

(1) A validated license shall be required for the export of goods or technology to a country if the Secretary of State has made the following determinations:
(A) The government of such country has repeatedly provided support for acts of international terrorism.
(B) The export of such goods or technology could make a significant contribution to the military potential of such country, including its military logistics capability, or could enhance the ability of such country to support acts of international terrorism.
(2) The Secretary and the Secretary of State shall notify the Committee on Foreign Affairs of the House of Representatives and the Committee on Banking, Housing, and Urban Affairs and the Committee on Foreign Relations of the Senate at least 30 days before issuing any validated license required by paragraph (1).

(3) Each determination of the Secretary of State under paragraph (1)(A), including each determination in effect on December 12, 1989, shall be published in the Federal Register.

(4) A determination made by the Secretary of State under paragraph (1)(A) may not be rescinded unless the President submits to the Speaker of the House of Representatives and the chairman of the Committee on Banking, Housing, and Urban Affairs and the chairman of the Committee on Foreign Relations of the Senate--
(A) before the proposed rescission would take effect, a report certifying that--
(i) there has been a fundamental change in the leadership and policies of the government of the country concerned;
(ii) that government is not supporting acts of international terrorism; and
(iii) that government has provided assurances that it will not support acts of international terrorism in the future; or
(B) at least 45 days before the proposed rescission would take effect, a report justifying the rescission and certifying that--
(i) the government concerned has not provided any support for international terrorism during the preceding 6-month period; and

(ii) the government concerned has provided assurances that it will not support acts of international terrorism in the future.
(5)(A) As used in paragraph (1), the term "repeatedly provided support for acts of international terrorism" shall include the recurring use of any part of the territory of the country as a sanctuary for terrorists or terrorist organizations.

(B) In this paragraph--
(i) the term "territory of a country" means the land, waters, and airspace of the country; and
(ii) the term "sanctuary" means an area in the territory of a country--
(I) that is used by a terrorist or terrorist organization--
(aa) to carry out terrorist activities, including training, financing, and recruitment; or
(bb) as a transit point; and
(II) the government of which expressly consents to, or with knowledge, allows, tolerates, or disregards such use of its territory.
(6) The Secretary and the Secretary of State shall include in the notification required by paragraph (2)--
(A) a detailed description of the goods or services to be offered, including a brief description of the capabilities of any article for which a license to export is sought;
(B) the reasons why the foreign country or international organization to which the export or transfer is proposed to be made needs the goods or services which are the subject of such export or transfer and a description of the manner in which such country or organization intends to use such articles, services, or design and construction services;
(C) the reasons why the proposed export or transfer is in the national interest of the United States;
(D) an analysis of the impact of the proposed export or transfer on the military capabilities of the foreign country or international organization to which such export or transfer would be made;
(E) an analysis of the manner in which the proposed export would affect the relative military strengths of countries in the region to which the goods or services which are the subject of such export would be delivered and whether other countries in the region have comparable kinds and amounts of articles, services, or design and construction services; and
(F) an analysis of the impact of the proposed export or transfer on the United States relations with the countries in the region to which the goods or services which are the subject of such export would be delivered.
(k) Negotiations with other countries
(1) Countries participating in certain agreements

The Secretary of State, in consultation with the Secretary, the Secretary of Defense, and the heads of other appropriate departments and agencies, shall be responsible for conducting negotiations with those countries participating in the groups known as the Coordinating Committee, the Missile Technology Control Regime, the Australia Group, and the Nuclear Suppliers' Group, regarding their cooperation in restricting the export of goods and technology in order to carry out--

(A) the policy set forth in section 3(2)(B) of this Act [section 2402(2)(B) of this Appendix], and

(B) United States policy opposing the proliferation of chemical, biological, nuclear, and other weapons and their delivery systems, and effectively restricting the export of dual use components of such weapons and their delivery systems, in accordance with this subsection and subsections (a) and (l) of this section.

Such negotiations shall cover, among other issues, which goods and technology should be subject to multilaterally agreed export restrictions, and the implementation of the restrictions consistent with the principles identified in section 5(b)(2)(C) of this Act [section 2404(b)(2)(C) of this Appendix].

(2) Other countries

The Secretary of State, in consultation with the Secretary, the Secretary of Defense, and the heads of other appropriate departments and agencies, shall be responsible for conducting negotiations with countries and groups of countries not referred to in paragraph (1) regarding their cooperation in restricting the export of goods and technology consistent with purposes set forth in paragraph (1). In cases where such negotiations produce agreements on export restrictions that the Secretary, in consultation with the Secretary of State and the Secretary of Defense, determines to be consistent with the principles identified in section 5(b)(2)(C) of this Act [section 2404(b)(2)(C) of this Appendix], the Secretary may treat exports, whether by individual or multiple licenses, to countries party to such agreements in the same manner as exports are treated to countries that are MTCR adherents.

(3) Review of determinations

The Secretary shall annually review any determination under paragraph (2) with respect to a country. For each such country which the Secretary determines is not meeting the requirements of an effective export control system in accordance with section 5(b)(2)(C) [section 2404(b)(2)(C) of this Appendix] the Secretary shall restrict or eliminate any preferential licensing treatment for exports to that country provided under this subsection.

(l) Missile technology

(1) Determination of controlled items

The Secretary, in consultation with the Secretary of State, the Secretary of Defense, and the heads of other appropriate departments and agencies--

(A) shall establish and maintain, as part of the control list established under this section, a list of all dual use goods and technology on the MTCR Annex; and

(B) may include, as part of the control list established under this section, goods and technology that would provide a direct and immediate impact on the development of missile delivery systems and are not included in the MTCR Annex but which the United States is proposing to the other MTCR adherents to have included in the MTCR Annex.

(2) Requirement of individual validated licenses

The Secretary shall require an individual validated license for--

(A) any export of goods or technology on the list established under paragraph (1) to any country; and

(B) any export of goods or technology that the exporter knows is destined for a project or facility for the design, development, or manufacture of a missile in a country that is not an MTCR adherent.

(3) Policy of denial of licenses

(A) Licenses under paragraph (2) should in general be denied if the ultimate consignee of the goods or technology is a facility in a country that is not an adherent to the Missile Technology Control Regime and the facility is designed to develop or build missiles.

(B) Licenses under paragraph (2) shall be denied if the ultimate consignee of the goods or technology is a facility in a country the government of which has been determined under subsection (j) of this section to have repeatedly provided support for acts of international terrorism.

(4) Consultation with other departments

(A) A determination of the Secretary to approve an export license under paragraph (2) for the export of goods or technology to a country of concern regarding missile proliferation may be made only after consultation with the Secretary of Defense and the Secretary of State for a period of 20 days. The countries of concern referred to in the preceding sentence shall be maintained on a classified list by the Secretary of State, in consultation with the Secretary and the Secretary of Defense.

(B) Should the Secretary of Defense disagree with the determination of the Secretary to approve an export license to which subparagraph (A) applies, the Secretary of Defense shall so notify the Secretary within the 20 days provided for consultation on the determination. The Secretary of Defense shall at the same time submit the matter to the President for resolution of the dispute. The Secretary shall also submit the

Secretary's recommendation to the President on the license application.

(C) The President shall approve or disapprove the export license application within 20 days after receiving the submission of the Secretary of Defense under subparagraph (B).

(D) Should the Secretary of Defense fail to notify the Secretary within the time period prescribed in subparagraph (B), the Secretary may approve the license application without awaiting the notification by the Secretary of Defense. Should the President fail to notify the Secretary of his decision on the export license application within the time period prescribed in subparagraph (C), the Secretary may approve the license application without awaiting the President's decision on the license application.

(E) Within 10 days after an export license is issued under this subsection, the Secretary shall provide to the Secretary of Defense and the Secretary of State the license application and accompanying documents issued to the applicant, to the extent that the relevant Secretary indicates the need to receive such application and documents.

(5) Information sharing

The Secretary shall establish a procedure for information sharing with appropriate officials of the intelligence community, as determined by the Director of Central Intelligence, and other appropriate Government agencies, that will ensure effective monitoring of transfers of MTCR equipment or technology and other missile technology.

(m) Chemical and biological weapons

(1) Establishment of list

The Secretary, in consultation with the Secretary of State, the Secretary of Defense, and the heads of other appropriate departments and agencies, shall establish and maintain, as part of the list maintained under this section, a list of goods and technology that would directly and substantially assist a foreign government or group in acquiring the capability to develop, produce, stockpile, or deliver chemical or biological weapons, the licensing of which would be effective in barring acquisition or enhancement of such capability.

(2) Requirement for validated licenses

The Secretary shall require a validated license for any export of goods or technology on the list established under paragraph (1) to any country of concern.

(3) Countries of concern

For purposes of paragraph (2), the term "country of concern" means any country other than--

(A) a country with whose government the United States has entered into a bilateral or multilateral arrangement for the control of goods or technology on the list established under paragraph (1); and

(B) such other countries as the Secretary of State, in consultation with the Secretary and the Secretary of Defense, shall designate consistent with the purposes of the Chemical and Biological Weapons Control and Warfare Elimination Act of 1991 [22 U.S.C.A. §5601 et seq.].

(n) Crime control instruments

(1) Crime control and detection instruments and equipment shall be approved for export by the Secretary only pursuant to a validated export license. Notwithstanding any other provision of this Act [sections 2401 to 2420 of this Appendix]--

(A) any determination of the Secretary of what goods or technology shall be included on the list established pursuant to subsection (l) of this section as a result of the export restrictions imposed by this subsection shall be made with the concurrence of the Secretary of State, and

(B) any determination of the Secretary to approve or deny an export license application to export crime control or detection instruments or equipment shall be made in concurrence with the recommendations of the Secretary of State submitted to the Secretary with respect to the application pursuant to section 10(c) of this Act [section 2409(c) of this Appendix],

except that, if the Secretary does not agree with the Secretary of State with respect to any determination under subparagraph (A) or (B), the matter shall be referred to the President for resolution.

(2) The provisions of this subsection shall not apply with respect to exports to countries which are members of the North Atlantic Treaty Organization or to Japan, Australia, or New Zealand, or to such other countries as the President shall designate consistent with the purposes of this subsection and section 502B of the Foreign Assistance Act of 1961 [22 U.S.C.A. §2304].

(o) Control list

The Secretary shall establish and maintain, as part of the control list, a list of any goods or technology subject to export controls under this section, and the countries to which such controls apply. The Secretary shall clearly identify on the control list which goods or technology, and which countries or destinations, are subject to which types of controls under this section. Such list shall consist of goods and technology identified by the Secretary of State, with the concurrence of the Secretary. If the Secretary and the Secretary of State are unable to agree on the list, the matter shall be referred to the President. Such list shall be reviewed not less frequently than every three years in the case of controls maintained co-operatively with other countries, and annually in the case of all other controls, for the purpose of making such revisions as are necessary in order to carry out this section. During the course of such review, an assessment shall be made periodically of the availability from sources outside the United States, or any of its territories or possessions, of goods and technology comparable to those controlled for export from the United States under this section.

(p) Effect on existing contracts and licenses

The President may not, under this section, prohibit or curtail the export or reexport of goods, technology, or other information--
(1) in performance of a contract or agreement entered into before the date on which the President reports to the Congress, pursuant to subsection (f) of this section, his intention to impose controls on the export or reexport of such goods, technology, or other information, or
(2) under a validated license or other authorization issued under this Act [sections 2401 to 2420 of this Appendix], unless and until the President determines and certifies to the Congress that--
(A) a breach of the peace poses a serious and direct threat to the strategic interest of the United States,
(B) the prohibition or curtailment of such contracts, agreements, licenses, or authorizations will be instrumental in remedying the situation posing the direct threat, and
(C) the export controls will continue only so long as the direct threat persists.
(q) Extension of certain controls

Those export controls imposed under this section with respect to South Africa which were in effect on February 28, 1982, and ceased to be effective on March 1, 1982, September 15, 1982, or January 20, 1983, shall become effective on the date of the enactment of this subsection [July 12, 1985], and shall remain in effect until 1 year after such date of enactment. At the end of that 1-year period, any of those controls made effective by this subsection may be extended by the President in accordance with subsections (b) and (f) of this section.

(r) Expanded authority to impose controls

(1) In any case in which the President determines that it is necessary to impose controls under this section without any limitation contained in subsection (c), (d), (e), (g), (h), or

(m) of this section, the President may impose those controls only if the President submits that determination to the Congress, together with a report pursuant to subsection (f) of this section with respect to the proposed controls, and only if a law is enacted authorizing the imposition of those controls. If a joint resolution authorizing the imposition of those controls is introduced in either House of Congress within 30 days after the Congress receives the determination and report of the President, that joint resolution shall be referred to the Committee on Banking, Housing, and Urban Affairs of the Senate and to the appropriate committee of the House of Representatives. If either such committee has not reported the joint resolution at the end of 30 days after its referral, the committee shall be discharged from further consideration of the joint resolution.

(2) For purposes of this subsection, the term "joint resolution" means a joint resolution of the matter after the resolving clause which is as follows: "That the Congress, having received on a determination of the President under section 6(o)(1) of the Export Administration Act of 1979 with respect to the export controls which are set forth in the report submitted to the Congress with that determination, authorizes the President to impose those export controls.", with the date of the receipt of the determination and report inserted in the blank.

(3) In the computation of the periods of 30 days referred to in paragraph (1), there shall be excluded the days on which either House of Congress is not in session because of an adjournment of more than 3 days to a day certain or because of an adjournment of the Congress sine die.

(s) Spare parts

(1) At the same time as the President imposes or expands export controls under this section, the President shall determine whether such export controls will apply to replacement parts for parts in goods subject to such export controls.

(2) With respect to export controls imposed under this section before the date of the enactment of this subsection [Aug. 23, 1988], an individual validated export license shall not be required for replacement parts which are exported to replace on a one-for-one basis parts that were in a good that was lawfully exported from the United States, unless the President determines that such a license should be required for such parts.

8. Foreign Assistance Act of 1961, 22 U.S.C. §2371

(a) Prohibition

The United States shall not provide any assistance under this chapter, the Agricultural Trade Development and Assistance Act of 1954 [U.S.C.A. §1691 et seq.], the Peace Corps Act [22 U.S.C.A. §2501 et seq.], or the Export-Import Bank Act of 1945 [12 U.S.C.A. §635 et seq.] to any country if the Secretary of State determines that the government of that country has repeatedly provided support for acts of international terrorism.

(b) Publication of determinations

Each determination of the Secretary of State under subsection (a) of this section, including each determination in effect on December 12, 1989, shall be published in the Federal Register.

(c) Rescission

A determination made by the Secretary of State under subsection (a) of this section may not be rescinded unless the President submits to the Speaker of the House of Representatives and the chairman of the Committee on Foreign Relations of the Senate--
(1) before the proposed rescission would take effect, a report certifying that--
(A) there has been a fundamental change in the leadership and policies of the government of the country concerned;
(B) that government is not supporting acts of international terrorism; and
(C) that government has provided assurances that it will not support acts of international terrorism in the future; or
(2) at least 45 days before the proposed rescission would take effect, a report justifying the rescission and certifying that--
(A) the government concerned has not provided any support for international terrorism during the preceding 6-month period; and
(B) the government concerned has provided assurances that it will not support acts of international terrorism in the future.
(d) Waiver

Assistance prohibited by subsection (a) of this section may be provided to a country described in that subsection if--
(1) the President determines that national security interests or humanitarian reasons justify a waiver of subsection (a) of this section, except that humanitarian reasons may not be used to justify assistance under subchapter II of this chapter (including part IV, part VI, and part VIII), or the Export-Import Bank Act of 1945 [12 U.S.C.A. §635 et seq.]; and
(2) at least 15 days before the waiver takes effect, the President consults with the Committee on Foreign Affairs of the House of Representatives and the Committee on Foreign Relations of the Senate regarding the proposed waiver and submits a report to the Speaker of the House of Representatives and the chairman of the Committee on Foreign Relations of the Senate containing--
(A) the name of the recipient country;
(B) a description of the national security interests or humanitarian reasons which require the waiver;
(C) the type and amount of and the justification for the assistance to be provided pursuant to the waiver; and
(D) the period of time during which such waiver will be effective.
The waiver authority granted in this subsection may not be used to provide any assistance under this chapter which is also prohibited by section 2780 of this title.

9. Designation of Foreign Terrorist Organizations, 8 U.S.C. §1189

(a) Designation

(1) In general

The Secretary is authorized to designate an organization as a foreign terrorist organization in accordance with this subsection if the Secretary finds that--

(A) the organization is a foreign organization;

(B) the organization engages in terrorist activity (as defined in section 1182(a)(3)(B) of this title or terrorism (as defined in section 2656f(d)(2) of Title 22), or retains the capability and intent to engage in terrorist activity or terrorism) [FN1]; and

(C) the terrorist activity or terrorism of the organization threatens the security of United States nationals or the national security of the United States.

(2) Procedure

(A) Notice

(i) To Congressional leaders

Seven days before making a designation under this subsection, the Secretary shall, by classified communication, notify the Speaker and Minority Leader of the House of Representatives, the President pro tempore, Majority Leader, and Minority Leader of the Senate, and the members of the relevant committees of the House of Representatives and the Senate, in writing, of the intent to designate an organization under this subsection, together with the findings made under paragraph (1) with respect to that organization, and the factual basis therefor.

(ii) Publication in Federal Register

The Secretary shall publish the designation in the Federal Register seven days after providing the notification under clause (i).

(B) Effect of designation

(i) For purposes of section 2339B of Title 18, a designation under this subsection shall take effect upon publication under subparagraph (A)(ii).

(ii) Any designation under this subsection shall cease to have effect upon an Act of Congress disapproving such designation.

(C) Freezing of assets

Upon notification under paragraph (2)(A)(i), the Secretary of the Treasury may require United States financial institutions possessing or controlling any assets of any foreign organization included in the notification to block all financial transactions involving those assets until further directive from either the Secretary of the Treasury, Act of Congress, or order of court.

(3) Record

(A) In general

In making a designation under this subsection, the Secretary shall create an administrative record.

(B) Classified information

The Secretary may consider classified information in making a designation under this subsection. Classified information shall not be subject to disclosure for such time as it remains classified, except that such information may be disclosed to a court ex parte and in camera for purposes of judicial review under subsection (c) of this section.

(4) Period of designation

(A) In general

A designation under this subsection shall be effective for all purposes until revoked under paragraph (5) or (6) or set aside pursuant to subsection (c).

(B) Review of designation upon petition

(i) In general

The Secretary shall review the designation of a foreign terrorist organization under the procedures set forth in clauses (iii) and (iv) if the designated organization files a petition for revocation within the petition period described in clause (ii).

(ii) Petition period

For purposes of clause (i)--

(I) if the designated organization has not previously filed a petition for revocation under this subparagraph, the petition period begins 2 years after the date on which the designation was made; or

(II) if the designated organization has previously filed a petition for revocation under this subparagraph, the petition period begins 2 years after the date of the determination made under clause (iv) on that petition.

(iii) Procedures

Any foreign terrorist organization that submits a petition for revocation under this subparagraph must provide evidence in that petition that the relevant circumstances described in paragraph (1) are sufficiently different from the circumstances that were the basis for the designation such that a revocation with respect to the organization is warranted.

(iv) Determination

(I) In general

Not later than 180 days after receiving a petition for revocation submitted under this subparagraph, the Secretary shall make a determination as to such revocation.

(II) Classified information

The Secretary may consider classified information in making a determination in response to a petition for revocation. Classified information shall not be subject to disclosure for such time as it remains classified, except that such information may be disclosed to a court ex parte and in camera for purposes of judicial review under subsection (c) of this section.

(III) Publication of determination

A determination made by the Secretary under this clause shall be published in the Federal Register.

(IV) Procedures

Any revocation by the Secretary shall be made in accordance with paragraph (6).

(C) Other review of designation

(i) In general

If in a 5-year period no review has taken place under subparagraph (B), the Secretary shall review the designation of the foreign terrorist organization in order to determine whether such designation should be revoked pursuant to paragraph (6).

(ii) Procedures

If a review does not take place pursuant to subparagraph (B) in response to a petition for revocation that is filed in accordance with that subparagraph, then the review shall be conducted pursuant to procedures established by the Secretary. The results of such review and the applicable procedures shall not be reviewable in any court.

(iii) Publication of results of review

The Secretary shall publish any determination made pursuant to this subparagraph in the Federal Register.

(5) Revocation by Act of Congress

The Congress, by an Act of Congress, may block or revoke a designation made under paragraph (1).

(6) Revocation based on change in circumstances

(A) In general

The Secretary may revoke a designation made under paragraph (1) at any time, and shall revoke a designation upon completion of a review conducted pursuant to subparagraphs (B) and (C) of paragraph (4) if the Secretary finds that--

(i) the circumstances that were the basis for the designation have changed in such a manner as to warrant revocation; or

(ii) the national security of the United States warrants a revocation.

(B) Procedure

The procedural requirements of paragraphs (2) and (3) shall apply to a revocation under this paragraph. Any revocation shall take effect on the date specified in the revocation or upon publication in the Federal Register if no effective date is specified.

(7) Effect of revocation

The revocation of a designation under paragraph (5) or (6) shall not affect any action or proceeding based on conduct committed prior to the effective date of such revocation.

(8) Use of designation in trial or hearing

If a designation under this subsection has become effective under paragraph (2)(B) a defendant in a criminal action or an alien in a removal proceeding shall not be permitted to raise any question concerning the validity of the issuance of such designation as a defense or an objection at any trial or hearing.

(b) Amendments to a designation

(1) In general

The Secretary may amend a designation under this subsection if the Secretary finds that the organization has changed its name, adopted a new alias, dissolved and then reconstituted itself under a different name or names, or merged with another organization.

(2) Procedure

Amendments made to a designation in accordance with paragraph (1) shall be effective upon publication in the Federal Register. Subparagraphs (B) and (C) of subsection (a)(2) of this section shall apply to an amended designation upon such publication. Paragraphs (2)(A)(i), (4), (5), (6), (7), and (8) of subsection (a) of this section shall also apply to an amended designation.

(3) Administrative record

The administrative record shall be corrected to include the amendments as well as any additional relevant information that supports those amendments.

(4) Classified information

The Secretary may consider classified information in amending a designation in accordance with this subsection. Classified information shall not be subject to disclosure for such time as it remains classified, except that such information may be disclosed to a court ex parte and in camera for purposes of judicial review under subsection (c).

(c) Judicial review of designation

(1) In general

Not later than 30 days after publication in the Federal Register of a designation, an amended designation, or a determination in response to a petition for revocation, the designated organization may seek judicial review in the United States Court of Appeals for the District of Columbia Circuit.

(2) Basis of review

Review under this subsection shall be based solely upon the administrative record, except that the Government may submit, for ex parte and in camera review, classified information used in making the designation, amended designation, or determination in response to a petition for revocation.

(3) Scope of review

The Court shall hold unlawful and set aside a designation, amended designation, or determination in response to a petition for revocation the court finds to be--

(A) arbitrary, capricious, an abuse of discretion, or otherwise not in accordance with law;

(B) contrary to constitutional right, power, privilege, or immunity;

(C) in excess of statutory jurisdiction, authority, or limitation, or short of statutory right;

(D) lacking substantial support in the administrative record taken as a whole or in classified information submitted to the court under paragraph (2), [FN2] or

(E) not in accord with the procedures required by law.

(4) Judicial review invoked

The pendency of an action for judicial review of a designation, amended designation, or determination in response to a petition for revocation shall not affect the application of this section, unless the court issues a final order setting aside the designation, amended designation, or determination in response to a petition for revocation.

(d) Definitions

As used in this section--

(1) the term "classified information" has the meaning given that term in section 1(a) of the Classified Information Procedures Act (18 U.S.C. App.);

(2) the term "national security" means the national defense, foreign relations, or economic interests of the United States;

(3) the term "relevant committees" means the Committees on the Judiciary, Intelligence, Foreign Relations of the Senate and the Committees on the Judiciary, Intelligence, and International Relations of the House of Representatives; and

(4) the term "Secretary" means the Secretary of State, in consultation with the Secretary of the Treasury and the Attorney General.

10. Victims of Trafficking and Violence Protection Act of 2000, Pub. L. No. 106-386, §2002, 114 Stat. 1464 (2000).

SEC. 2002. PAYMENT OF CERTAIN ANTI-TERRORISM JUDGMENTS.

(a) PAYMENTS.--

(1) IN GENERAL.--Subject to subsections (b) and (c), the Secretary of the Treasury shall pay each person described in paragraph (2), at the person's election--

(A) 110 percent of compensatory damages awarded by judgment of a court on a claim or claims brought by the person under section 1605(a)(7) of title 28, United States Code, plus amounts necessary to pay post-judgment interest under section 1961 of such title, and, in the case of a claim or claims against Cuba, amounts awarded as sanctions by judicial order on April 18, 2000 (as corrected on June 2, 2000), subject to final appellate review of that order; or

(B) 100 percent of the compensatory damages awarded by judgment of a court on a claim or claims brought by the person under section 1605(a)(7) of title 28, United States Code, plus amounts necessary to pay post-judgment interest, as provided in section 1961 of such title, and, in the case of a claim or claims against Cuba, amounts awarded as sanctions by judicial order on April 18, 2000 (as corrected June 2, 2000), subject to final appellate review of that order.

Payments under this subsection shall be made promptly upon request.

(2) PERSONS COVERED.--A person described in this paragraph is a person who--

(A)(i) as of July 20, 2000, held a final judgment for a claim or claims brought under section 1605(a)(7) of title 28, United States Code, against Iran or Cuba, or the right to payment of an amount awarded as a judicial sanction with respect to such claim or claims; or

(ii) filed a suit under such section 1605(a)(7) on February 17, 1999, December 13, 1999, January 28, 2000, March 15, 2000, or July 27, 2000;

(B) relinquishes all claims and rights to compensatory damages and amounts awarded as judicial sanctions under such judgments;

(C) in the case of payment under paragraph (1)(A), relinquishes all rights and claims to punitive damages awarded in connection with such claim or claims; and

(D) in the case of payment under paragraph (1)(B), relinquishes all rights to execute against or attach property that is at issue in claims against the United States before an international tribunal, that is the subject of awards rendered by such tribunal, or that is subject to section 1610(f)(1)(A) of title 28, United States Code.

(b) FUNDING OF AMOUNTS.--

(1) JUDGMENTS AGAINST CUBA.--For purposes of funding the payments under subsection (a) in the case of judgments and sanctions entered against the Government of Cuba or Cuban entities, the President shall vest and liquidate up to and not exceeding the amount of property of the Government of Cuba and sanctioned entities in the United States or any commonwealth, territory, or possession thereof that has been blocked pursuant to section 5(b) of the Trading with the Enemy Act (50 U.S.C. App. 5(b)), sections 202 and 203 of the International Emergency Economic Powers Act (50 U.S.C. 1701-1702), or any other proclamation, order, or regulation issued thereunder. For the purposes of paying amounts for judicial sanctions, payment shall be made from funds or accounts subject to sanctions as of April 18, 2000, or from blocked assets of the Government of Cuba.

(2) JUDGMENTS AGAINST IRAN.--For purposes of funding payments under subsection (a) in the case of judgments against Iran, the Secretary of the Treasury shall make such payments from amounts paid and liquidated from--

(A) rental proceeds accrued on the date of the enactment of this Act from Iranian diplomatic and consular property located in the United States; and

(B) funds not otherwise made available in an amount not to exceed the total of the amount in the Iran Foreign Military Sales Program account within the Foreign Military Sales Fund on the date of the enactment of this Act.

(c) SUBROGATION.--Upon payment under subsection (a) with respect to payments in connection with a Foreign Military Sales Program account, the United States shall be fully subrogated, to the extent of the payments, to all rights of the person paid under that subsection against the debtor foreign state. The President shall pursue these subrogated rights as claims or offsets of the United States in appropriate ways, including any negotiation process which precedes the normalization of relations between the foreign state designated as a state sponsor of terrorism and the United States, except that no funds shall be paid to Iran, or released to Iran, from property blocked under the International Emergency Economic Powers Act or from the Foreign Military Sales Fund, until such subrogated claims have been dealt with to the satisfaction of the United States.

(d) SENSE OF THE CONGRESS.--It is the sense of the Congress that the President should not normalize relations between the United States and Iran until the claims subrogated have been dealt with to the satisfaction of the United States.

(e) REAFFIRMATION OF AUTHORITY.--Congress reaffirms the President's statutory authority to manage and, where appropriate and consistent with the national interest, vest foreign assets located in the United States for the purposes, among other things, of assisting and, where appropriate, making payments to victims of terrorism.

11. Hague Convention on Service Overseas

The States signatory to the present Convention,
Desiring to create appropriate means to ensure that judicial and extrajudicial documents to be served abroad shall be brought to the notice of the addressee in sufficient time,
Desiring to improve the organisation of mutual judicial assistance for that purpose by simplifying and expediting the procedure,
Have resolved to conclude a Convention to this effect and have agreed upon the following provisions:

Article 1
The present Convention shall apply in all cases, in civil or commercial matters, where there is occasion to transmit a judicial or extrajudicial document for service abroad.
This Convention shall not apply where the address of the person to be served with the document is not known.

CHAPTER I – JUDICIAL DOCUMENTS
Article 2
Each Contracting State shall designate a Central Authority which will undertake to receive requests for service coming from other Contracting States and to proceed in conformity with the provisions of Articles 3 to 6.
Each State shall organise the Central Authority in conformity with its own law.

Article 3
The authority or judicial officer competent under the law of the State in which the documents originate shall forward to the Central Authority of the State addressed a request conforming to the model annexed to the present Convention, without any requirement of legalisation or other equivalent formality.
The document to be served or a copy thereof shall be annexed to the request. The request and the document shall both be furnished in duplicate.

Article 4
If the Central Authority considers that the request does not comply with the provisions of the present Convention it shall promptly inform the applicant and specify its objections to the request.

Article 5
The Central Authority of the State addressed shall itself serve the document or shall arrange to have it served by an appropriate agency, either –

a) by a method prescribed by its internal law for the service of documents in domestic actions upon persons who are within its territory, or
b) by a particular method requested by the applicant, unless such a method is incompatible with the law of the State addressed.

Subject to sub-paragraph *(b)* of the first paragraph of this Article, the document may always be served by delivery to an addressee who accepts it voluntarily.
If the document is to be served under the first paragraph above, the Central Authority may require the document to be written in, or translated into, the official language or one of the official languages of the State addressed.
That part of the request, in the form attached to the present Convention, which contains a summary of the document to be served, shall be served with the document.

Article 6
The Central Authority of the State addressed or any authority which it may have designated for that purpose, shall complete a certificate in the form of the model annexed to the present Convention.
The certificate shall state that the document has been served and shall include the method, the place and the date of service and the person to whom the document was delivered. If the document has not been served, the certificate shall set out the reasons which have prevented service.
The applicant may require that a certificate not completed by a Central Authority or by a judicial authority shall be countersigned by one of these authorities.
The certificate shall be forwarded directly to the applicant.

Article 7
The standard terms in the model annexed to the present Convention shall in all cases be written either in French or in English. They may also be written in the official language, or in one of the official languages, of the State in which the documents originate.
The corresponding blanks shall be completed either in the language of the State addressed or in French or in English.

Article 8
Each Contracting State shall be free to effect service of judicial documents upon persons abroad, without application of any compulsion, directly through its diplomatic or consular agents.
Any State may declare that it is opposed to such service within its territory, unless the document is to be served upon a national of the State in which the documents originate.

Article 9

Each Contracting State shall be free, in addition, to use consular channels to forward documents, for the purpose of service, to those authorities of another Contracting State which are designated by the latter for this purpose.

Each Contracting State may, if exceptional circumstances so require, use diplomatic channels for the same purpose.

Article 10

Provided the State of destination does not object, the present Convention shall not interfere with –

a) the freedom to send judicial documents, by postal channels, directly to persons abroad,

b) the freedom of judicial officers, officials or other competent persons of the State of origin to effect service of judicial documents directly through the judicial officers, officials or other competent persons of the State of destination,

c) the freedom of any person interested in a judicial proceeding to effect service of judicial documents directly through the judicial officers, officials or other competent persons of the State of destination.

Article 11

The present Convention shall not prevent two or more Contracting States from agreeing to permit, for the purpose of service of judicial documents, channels of transmission other than those provided for in the preceding Articles and, in particular, direct communication between their respective authorities.

Article 12

The service of judicial documents coming from a Contracting State shall not give rise to any payment or reimbursement of taxes or costs for the services rendered by the State addressed.

The applicant shall pay or reimburse the costs occasioned by-

a) the employment of a judicial officer or of a person competent under the law of the State of destination,

b) the use of a particular method of service.

Article 13

Where a request for service complies with the terms of the present Convention, the State addressed may refuse to comply therewith only if it deems that compliance would infringe its sovereignty or security.

It may not refuse to comply solely on the ground that, under its internal law, it claims exclusive jurisdiction over the subject-matter of the action or that its internal law would not permit the action upon which the application is based.

The Central Authority shall, in case of refusal, promptly inform the applicant and state the reasons for the refusal.

Article 14

Difficulties which may arise in connection with the transmission of judicial documents for service shall be settled through diplomatic channels.

Article 15

Where a writ of summons or an equivalent document had to be transmitted abroad for the purpose of service, under the provisions of the present Convention, and the defendant has not appeared, judgment shall not be given until it is established that –

a) the document was served by a method prescribed by the internal law of the State addressed for the service of documents in domestic actions upon persons who are within its territory, or

b) the document was actually delivered to the defendant or to his residence by another method provided for by this Convention,

and that in either of these cases the service or the delivery was effected in sufficient time to enable the defendant to defend.

Each Contracting State shall be free to declare that the judge, notwithstanding the provisions of the first paragraph of this Article, may give judgment even if no certificate of service or delivery has been received, if all the following conditions are fulfilled-

a) the document was transmitted by one of the methods provided for in this Convention,

b) a period of time of not less than six months, considered adequate by the judge in the particular case, has elapsed since the date of the transmission of the document,

c) no certificate of any kind has been received, even though every reasonable effort has been made to obtain it through the competent authorities of the State addressed.

Notwithstanding the provisions of the preceding paragraphs the judge may order, in case of urgency, any provisional or protective measures.

Article 16

When a writ of summons or an equivalent document had to be transmitted abroad for the purpose of service, under the provisions of the present Convention, and a judgment has been entered against a defendant who has not appeared, the judge shall have the power to relieve the defendant from the effects of the expiration of the time for appeal from the judgment if the following conditions are fulfilled –

a) the defendant, without any fault on his part, did not have knowledge of the document in sufficient time to defend, or knowledge of the judgment in sufficient time to appeal, and *b)* the defendant has disclosed a *prima facie* defence to the action on the merits.

An application for relief may be filed only within a reasonable time after the defendant has knowledge of the judgment.

Each Contracting State may declare that the application will not be entertained if it is filed after the expiration of a time to be stated in the declaration, but which shall in no case be less than one year following the date of the judgment.

This Article shall not apply to judgments concerning status or capacity of persons.

CHAPTER II – EXTRAJUDICIAL DOCUMENTS

Article 17

Extrajudicial documents emanating from authorities and judicial officers of a Contracting State may be transmitted for the purpose of service in another Contracting State by the methods and under the provisions of the present Convention.

CHAPTER III – GENERAL CLAUSES

Article 18

Each Contracting State may designate other authorities in addition to the Central Authority and shall determine the extent of their competence.

The applicant shall, however, in all cases, have the right to address a request directly to the Central Authority.

Federal States shall be free to designate more than one Central Authority.

Article 19

To the extent that the internal law of a Contracting State permits methods of transmission, other than those provided for in the preceding Articles, of documents coming from abroad, for service within its territory, the present Convention shall not affect such provisions.

Article 20

The present Convention shall not prevent an agreement between any two or more Contracting States to dispense with –

a) the necessity for duplicate copies of transmitted documents as required by the second paragraph of Article 3,
b) the language requirements of the third paragraph of Article 5 and Article 7,
c) the provisions of the fourth paragraph of Article 5,
d) the provisions of the second paragraph of Article 12.

Article 21

Each Contracting State shall, at the time of the deposit of its instrument of ratification or accession, or at a later date, inform the Ministry of Foreign Affairs of the Netherlands of the following –

a) the designation of authorities, pursuant to Articles 2 and 18,
b) the designation of the authority competent to complete the certificate pursuant to Article 6,
c) the designation of the authority competent to receive documents transmitted by consular channels, pursuant to Article 9.

Each Contracting State shall similarly inform the Ministry, where appropriate, of –
a) opposition to the use of methods of transmission pursuant to Articles 8 and 10,
b) declarations pursuant to the second paragraph of Article 15 and the third paragraph of Article 16,
c) all modifications of the above designations, oppositions and declarations.

Article 22

Where Parties to the present Convention are also Parties to one or both of the Conventions on civil procedure signed at The Hague on 17th July 1905, and on 1st March 1954, this Convention shall replace as between them Articles 1 to 7 of the earlier Conventions.

Article 23

The present Convention shall not affect the application of Article 23 of the Convention on civil procedure signed at The Hague on 17th July 1905, or of Article 24 of the Convention on civil procedure signed at The Hague on 1st March 1954.

These Articles shall, however, apply only if methods of communication, identical to those provided for in these Conventions, are used.

Article 24

Supplementary agreements between Parties to the Conventions of 1905 and 1954 shall be considered as equally applicable to the present Convention, unless the Parties have otherwise agreed.

Article 25

Without prejudice to the provisions of Articles 22 and 24, the present Convention shall not derogate from Conventions containing provisions on the matters governed by this Convention to which the Contracting States are, or shall become, Parties.

Article 26

The present Convention shall be open for signature by the States represented at the Tenth Session of the Hague Conference on Private International Law.

It shall be ratified, and the instruments of ratification shall be deposited with the Ministry of Foreign Affairs of the Netherlands.

Article 27

The present Convention shall enter into force on the sixtieth day after the deposit of the third instrument of ratification referred to in the second paragraph of Article 26.

The Convention shall enter into force for each signatory State which ratifies subsequently on the sixtieth day after the deposit of its instrument of ratification.

Article 28

Any State not represented at the Tenth Session of the Hague Conference on Private International Law may accede to the present Convention after it has entered into force in accordance with the first paragraph of Article 27. The instrument of accession shall be deposited with the Ministry of Foreign Affairs of the Netherlands.

The Convention shall enter into force for such a State in the absence of any objection from a State, which has ratified the Convention before such deposit, notified to the Ministry of Foreign Affairs of the Netherlands within a period of six months after the date on which the said Ministry has notified it of such accession.

In the absence of any such objection, the Convention shall enter into force for the acceding State on the first day of the month following the expiration of the last of the periods referred to in the preceding paragraph.

Article 29

Any State may, at the time of signature, ratification or accession, declare that the present Convention shall extend to all the territories for the international relations of which it is responsible, or to one or more of them. Such a declaration shall take effect on the date of entry into force of the Convention for the State concerned.

At any time thereafter, such extensions shall be notified to the Ministry of Foreign Affairs of the Netherlands.

The Convention shall enter into force for the territories mentioned in such an extension on the sixtieth day after the notification referred to in the preceding paragraph.

Article 30

The present Convention shall remain in force for five years from the date of its entry into force in accordance with the first paragraph of Article 27, even for States which have ratified it or acceded to it subsequently.

If there has been no denunciation, it shall be renewed tacitly every five years.

Any denunciation shall be notified to the Ministry of Foreign Affairs of the Netherlands at least six months before the end of the five year period.

It may be limited to certain of the territories to which the Convention applies.

The denunciation shall have effect only as regards the State which has notified it. The Convention shall remain in force for the other Contracting States.

Article 31

The Ministry of Foreign Affairs of the Netherlands shall give notice to the States referred to in Article 26, and to the States which have acceded in accordance with Article 28, of the following –

a) the signatures and ratifications referred to in Article 26;

b) the date on which the present Convention enters into force in accordance with the first paragraph of Article 27;

c) the accessions referred to in Article 28 and the dates on which they take effect;

d) the extensions referred to in Article 29 and the dates on which they take effect;

e) the designations, oppositions and declarations referred to in Article 21;

f) the denunciations referred to in the third paragraph of Article 30.

In witness whereof the undersigned, being duly authorised thereto, have signed the present Convention.

Done at The Hague, on the 15th day of November, 1965, in the English and French languages, both texts being equally authentic, in a single copy which shall be deposited in the archives of the Government of the Netherlands, and of which a certified copy shall be sent, through the diplomatic channel, to each of the States represented at the Tenth Session of the Hague Conference on Private International Law.

12. Interests of United States in Pending Suits, 28 U.S.C. §517

The Solicitor General, or any officer of the Department of Justice, may be sent by the Attorney General to any State or district in the United States to attend to the interests of the United States in a suit pending in a court of the United States, or in a court of a State, or to attend to any other interest of the United States.

Resources

Statutes

Alien Tort Claims Act, 28 U.S.C. §1350

Antiterrorism and Effective Death Penalty Act of 1996, 28 U.S.C. §1605(a)(7)

Designation of Foreign Terrorist Organizations, 8 U.S.C. §1189

Export Administration Act, 50 U.S.C. §2405(j)

Flatow Amendment, 28 U.S.C. §1605 note

Foreign Assistance Act of 1961, 22 U.S.C. §2371

Foreign Sovereign Immunities Act, 28 U.S.C. §1602 et seq.

Hague Convention on Service Overseas

Interests of United States in Pending Suits, 28 U.S.C. §517

Klinghoffer Act, 18 U.S.C. §2331 et seq

Right to Block Suits, 18 U.S.C. 2336 (c)

Statement of Interest, 28 U.S.C. §517

Terrorism Risk Insurance Act §201

Torture Victim Protection Act, 28 U.S.C. §1350 note

Victims of Trafficking and Violence Protection Act of 2000, Pub. L. No. 106-386 §2002, 114 Stat. 1543 (2000).

Cases

Acree v. Republic of Iraq, 370 F.3d 41 (D.C.Cir. 2004).

Alejandre v. The Republic of Cuba, 996 F.Supp. 1239 (S.D. Fla. 1997).

Almog v. Arab Bank, PLC, 471 F.Supp.2d 257 (E.D.N.Y. 2007).

Anderson v. Islamic Republic of Iran, 90 F.Supp.2d 107 (D.D.C. 2000).

Argentine Republic v. Amerada Hess Shipping Corp., 488 U.S. 428 (1989).

Baker v. Carr, 369 U.S. 186 (1962).

Barcelona Traction (Belg. v. Spain), 1970 I.C.J. 2 (Feb. 5).

Bettis v. Islamic Republic of Iran, 315 F.3d 325 (D.C. Cir. 2003).

Biton v. Palestinian Interim Self-Government Authority, 412 F.Supp.2d 1 (D.D.C. 2005).

Biton v. Palestinian Authority, 310 F.Supp.2d 172 (D.D.C. 2004).

Blais v. Islamic Republic of Iran, 459 F.Supp.2d 40 (D.D.C. 2006).

Blais v. Islamic Republic of Iran, 2006 WL 2827372 (D.D.C. 2006).

Bodoff v. Islamic Republic of Iran, 424 F.Supp.2d 74 (D.D.C. 2006).

Boim v. Quranic Literacy Institute, 291 F.3d 1000 (7th Cir. 2002).

Botvin v. Islamic Republic of Iran, 510 F.Supp.2d 101 (D.D.C. 2007).

Burnett v. Al Baraka Investment & Development Corp., 323 F.Supp.2d 82 (D.D.C. 2004).

Burnett v. Al Baraka Investment & Development Corp., 292 F.Supp.2d 9 (D.D.C. 2003).

Campuzano v. Islamic Republic of Iran, 281 F.Supp.2d 258 (D.D.C. 2003).

Cicippio v. Islamic Republic of Iran, 18 F.Supp.2d 62 (D.D.C. 1998).

Cicippio v. Islamic Republic of Iran, 30 F.3d 164 (D.C. Cir. 1994).

Cicippio v. Islamic Republic of Iran, 1993 WL 730748 (D.D.C. 1993).

Cicippio-Puleo v. Islamic Republic of Iran, 353 F.3d 1024 (D.C. Cir. 2004).

Collette v. Socialist Peoples' Libyan Arab Jamahiriya, 362 F.Supp.2d 230 (D.D.C. 2005).

Cronin v. Islamic Republic of Iran, 238 F.Supp.2d 222 (D.D.C. 2002).

Daliberti v. J.P Morgan Chase & Co., 2003 WL 340734 (S.D.N.Y. 2003).

Daliberti v. Republic of Iraq, 97 F.Supp.2d 38 (D.D.C. 2000).

Dammarell v. Islamic Republic of Iran, 281 F.Supp.2d 105 (D.D.C. 2003).

Eisenfeld v. Islamic Republic of Iran, 172 F. Supp.2d 1 (D.D.C. 2000).

Elahi v. Islamic Republic of Iran, 124 F.Supp.2d 97 (D.D.C. 2000).

Filartiga v. Pena-Irala, 630 F.2d 876 (2d Cir. 1980).

Flatow v. Islamic Republic of Iran, 74 F.Supp.2d 18 (D.D.C. 1999).

Flatow v. Islamic Republic of Iran, 76 F.Supp.2d 16 (D.D.C. 1999).

Flatow v. Islamic Republic of Iran, 999 F.Supp. 1 (D.D.C. 1998).

Haim v. Islamic Republic of Iran, 425 F.Supp.2d 56 (D.D.C. 2006).

Hartford Ins. Co. v. Socialist People's Libyan Arab Jamahiriya, 422 F.Supp.2d 203 (D.D.C. 2006).

Hegna v. Islamic Republic of Iran, 402 F.3d 97 (2d Cir. 2005).

Hegna v. Islamic Republic of Iran, 376 F.3d 485 (5th Cir. 2004).

Heiser v. Islamic Republic of Iran, 466 F.Supp.2d 229 (D.D.C. 2006).

Heiser v. Islamic Republic of Iran, 2006 WL 1530243 (D.D.C. 2006).

Higgins v. Islamic Republic of Iran, 2000 WL 33674311 (D.D.C. 2000).

Hill v. Republic of Iraq, 328 F.3d 680 (D.C. Cir. 2003).

Hill v. Republic of Iraq, 2003 WL 21057173 (D.D.C. 2003).

Hill v. Republic of Iraq, 175 F.Supp.2d 36 (D.D.C. 2001)

Holy Land Foundation for Relief and Development v. Ashcroft, 219 F.Supp.2d 57 (D.D.C. 2002).

IIT v. Vencap, Ltd., 519 F.2d 1001 (2d Cir. 1975).

In re: Terrorist Attacks on September 11, 2001, 349 F.Supp. 765 (S.D.N.Y. 2005)

Jenco v. Islamic Republic of Iran, 154 F.Supp.2d 27 (D.D.C. 2001).

Kadic v. Karadzic, 70 F.3d 232 (2d Cir. 1995).

Kilburn v. Republic of Iran, 277 F.Supp.2d 24 (D.D.C. 2003).

Kilburn v. Socialist People's Libyan Arab Jamahiriya, 376 F.3d 1123 (D.C. Cir. 2004).

Klieman v. Palestinian Authority, 424 F.Supp.2d 153 (D.C. 2006).

Klinghoffer v. SNC Achille Lauro, 937 F.2D 44 (2d Cir. 1991).

Knox v. Palestinian Authority, 442 F.Supp.2d 62 (S.D.N.Y. 2006).

Knox v. Palestine Liberation Organization, 306 F.Supp.2d 424 (S.D.N.Y. 2004).

Levin v. Islamic Republic of Iran, 2007 WL 4564399 (D.D.C. 2007).

Linde v. Arab Bank, PLC, 384 F.Supp.2d 571 (E.D.N.Y. 2004).

MacArthur Area Citizens Ass'n v. Republic of Peru, 809 F.2d 918 (D.C.Cir. 1987)

Matter of Extradition of Marzook, 924 F.Supp. 565 (S.D.N.Y. 1996).

McCarthy v. Republic of Cuba, 354 F.Supp.2d 1347 (S.D.Fla. 2005).

Ministry of Defense and Support for Armed Forces of Islamic Republic of Iran v. Cubic Defense Systems, Inc., 495 F.3d 1024 (9th Cir. 2007).

Ministry of Defense and Support for the Armed Forces of the Islamic Republic of Iran v. Cubic Defense Systems, 385 F.3d 1206 (9th Cir. 2004).

Ministry of Defense and Support for the Armed Forces of the Islamic Republic of Iran v. Elahi, 546 U.S. 450 (2006).

Morris v. Khadr, 415 F.Supp.2d 1323 (D.Utah 2006).

Mwani v. bin Laden, 417 F.3d 1 (D.C. Cir. 2005).

Oveissi v. Islamic Republic of Iran, 498 F.Supp.2d 268 (D.D.C. 2007).

Peterson v. Islamic Republic of Iran, 264 F.Supp.2d 46 (D.D.C. 2003).

Price v. Socialist People's Libyan Arab Jamahiriya, 274 F.Supp.2d 20 (D.D.C. 2003).

Price v. Socialist People's Libyan Arab Jamahiriya, 294 F.3d 82 (D.C. 2002).

Rein v. Socialist People's Libyan Arab Jamahiriya, 995 F.Supp. 325 (E.D.N.Y. 1998).

Republic of Argentina v. Weltover, Inc., 504 U.S. 607 (1992).

Roeder v. Islamic Republic of Iran, 333 F.3d 228 (D.C. Cir. 2003).

Roeder v. Islamic Republic of Iran, 195 F.Supp.2d 140 (D.D.C. 2002).

Rubin v. Islamic Republic of Iran, 484 F.3d 149 (2d Cir. 2007).

Rubin v. Islamic Republic of Iran, 436 F.Supp.2d 938 (N.D.Ill. 2006).

Rubin v. Islamic Republic of Iran, 2005 WL 670770 (D.D.C. 2005)

Rux v. Republic of Sudan, 461 F.3d 461 (4th Cir. 2006).

Salazar v. Islamic Republic of Iran, 370 F.Supp.2d 105 (D.D.C. 2005).

Saperstein v. The Palestinian Authority, 2007 WL 684318 (S.D. Fla. 2007).

Sarei v. Rio Tinto, PLC, 487 F.3d 1193 (9th Cir. 2007).

Saudi Arabia v. Nelson, 507 U.S. 349 (1993).

Simpson v. Socialist People's Libyan Arab Jamahiriya, 470 F.3d 356 (D.C. Cir. 2006).

Sisso v. Islamic Republic of Iran, 448 F.Supp.2d 76 (D.D.C. 2006).

Smith v. Federal Reserve Bank of New York, 346 F.3d 264 (2d Cir. 2003).

Smith v. Islamic Emirate of Afghanistan, 262 F.Supp.2d 217 (S.D.N.Y. 2003).

Smith v. Socialist People's Libyan Arab Jamahiriya, 886 F.Supp. 306 (E.D.N.Y. 1995).

Sosa v. Alvarez-Machain, 542 U.S. 692 (2004).

Stethem v. Islamic Republic of Iran, 201 F.Supp.2d 78 (D.D.C. 2002).

Strauss v. Credit Lyonnais, S.A., 2007 WL 2296832 (E.D.N.Y. Aug. 6, 2007).

Stutts v. De Dietrich Group, 2006 WL 1867060 (E.D.N.Y. 2006).

Surette v. Islamic Republic of Iran, 231 F.Supp.2d 260 (D.D.C. 2002).

Sutherland v. Islamic Republic of Iran, 151 F.Supp.2d 27 (D.D.C. 2001).

Tel-Oren v. Libyan Arab Republic, 726 F.2d 774 (D.C. Cir. 1984).

Ungar v. Islamic Republic of Iran, 211 F.Supp.2d 91 (D. D.C. 2002).

Ungar v. Palestinian Authority, 304 F.Supp.2d 232 (D. R.I. 2004).

Ungar v. Palestinian Authority, 228 F.Supp.2d 40 (D.R.I. 2002).

Ungar v. Palestinian Authority, 153 F.Supp.2d 76 (D. R.I. 2001).

U.S. v. Holy Land Foundation for Relief and Development, 493 F.3d 469 (5th Cir. 2007).

U.S. v. One 1997 E35 Ford Van, VIN 1FBJS31L3VHB70844, 50 F.Supp.2d 789 (N.D.Ill. 1999).

Verlinden B.V. v. Central Bank of Nigeria, 461 U.S. 480 (1983).

Vine v. Republic of Iraq, 459 F.Supp.2d 10 (D.D.C. 2006).

Wagner v. Islamic Republic of Iran, 172 F. Supp.2d 128 (D.D.C. 2001).

Weininger v. Castro, 462 F.Supp.2d 457 (2006).

Weinstein v. Islamic Republic of Iran, 184 F.Supp.2d 13 (D.D.C. 2002).

Weinstein v. Islamic Republic of Iran, 274 F.Supp.2d 53 (D.D.C. 2003).

Weiss v. Nat'l Westminster Bank, PLC, 242 F.R.D. 33 (E.D.N.Y. 2007).

Wyatt v. Syrian Arab Republic, 2006 WL 1328263 (D.D.C. 2006).

Wyatt v. Syrian Arab Republic, 362 F.Supp.2d 103 (D.D.C. 2005).

Law Reviews

Aceves, William J., *Affirming the Law of the Nations in U.S. Courts*, 49-JUN Fed. Law. 33 (2002).

Dellapenna, Joseph W., *Civil Remedies for International Terrorism*, 12 DePaul Bus. L.J. 169 (1999/2000)

Glannon, Joseph W. and Atik, Jeffery, *Politics And Personal Jurisdiction: Suing State Sponsors Of Terrorism Under The 1996 Amendments To The Foreign Sovereign Immunities Act*, 87 Geo. L.J. 675 (1999)

Hoye, William P., *Fighting Fire With . . . Mire? Civil Remedies And The New War On State-Sponsored Terrorism*, 12 Duke J. Comp. & Int'l L. 105 (2002)

Kim, Jeewon, *Making State Sponsors Of Terrorism Pay: A Separation Of Power discourse Under the Foreign Sovereign Immunities Act*, 22 Berkeley J. Int'l L. 513 (2004)

Koh, Harold Hongju, *Transnational Public Law Litigation*, 100 Yale L.J. 2347 (1991)

Lucas, Helen C., *The Adjudication of Violations of International Law Under the Alien Tort Claims Act: Allowing Alient Plaintiffs Their Day in Court*, 36 DePaul L. Rev. 231, 236 (1987)

Reisman, W. Michael and Hakimim, Monica, *Illusion And Reality In The Compensation Of Victims Of International Terrorism*, 54 Ala. L. Rev. 561 (2003).

Rosenfeld, Jennifer A., *The Antiterrorism Act of 1990: Bringing Terrorists to Justice the American Way*, 15 Suffolk Transnat'l L.J., 726 (1992)

Sealing, Keith, *"State Sponsors Of Terrorism" Is A Question, Not An Answer: The Terrorism Amendment To The FSIA Makes Less Sense Now Than It Did Before 9/11*, 38 Tex. Int'l L.J. 119 (2003)

Vairo, Georgene, *Remedies for Victims of Terrorism*, 35 Loy. L.A. L. Rev. 1265 (2002)

Whidden, Michael J., *Unequal Justice: Arabs In America And United States Antiterrorism Legislation*, 69 Fordham L. Rev. 2825 (May 2001)

Books

Allan Gerson and Jerry Adler, *The Price of Terror* (HarperCollins Publishers, 2001).

Dan B. Prosser and Robert E. Keeton, *Torts, Fifth Edition* (Publisher*, 1984).

Jeffrey F. Addicott, *Terrorism Law: the Rule of Law and the War on Terror, Second Edition* (Lawyers & Judges Publishing, 2004).

Jeffrey F. Addicott, *Terrorism Law: Cases, Materials, Comments, Fourth Edition* (Lawyers & Judges Publishing, 2007).

Tal Becker, *Terrorism and the State: Rethinking the Rules of State Responsibility* (Hart Publishing, 2006).

Wayne McCormack, *Understanding the Law of Terrorism* (LexisNexis Matthew Bender, 2007).

Other

Antiterrorism Act of 1990, Hearing Before the Subcommittee on Courts and Administrative Practice of Committee on the Judiciary, United States Senate, 101st Congress, Second Session July 25 1990.

Message to the Congress Reporting the Declaration of a National Emergency With Respect to the Development Fund for Iraq, 39 WEEKLY COMP. PRES. DOC. 647, 647-48 (May 22, 2003).

Neely Tucker, in *Lawsuit Against Iran, Former Hostages Fight U.S, Government Calls Frozen Assets Untouchable*, Wash. Post, Dec. 13, 2001.

State Department Designation of State Sponsors of Terrorism, http://www.state.gov/s/ct/c14151.htm

Tate Letter, 24 Dep't of State Bull. 984-985 (1952).

Wyatt v. Syrian Arab Republic, 2007 WL 552111 (Appellate Brief) (D.C.Cir. Feb 16, 2007).

About the Authors

James P. Steck is a Connecticut attorney, currently serving as a Law Clerk for the Connecticut Superior Court. A graduate of Bloomsburg University of Pennsylvania and Roger Williams University School of Law, he lives in Connecticut with his wife, Michelle, and their dog.

David J. Strachman is a partner at McIntyre, Tate & Lynch in Providence, Rhode Island, and concentrates in representing victims of international terrorism and other litigation matters. He is an adjunct professor at Southern New England School of Law and has taught civil terrorism law at Roger Williams University. A graduate of Brandeis University and Boston University School of Law, he served as legal counsel to the Rhode Island House Minority Leader and is a frequent lecturer on terrorism law and CLE instructor on domestic relations/family court matters and probate law. He is the co-author of numerous CLE publications.

Index

Terrorism Law: Materials, Cases, Comments, Fourth Edition
by Jeffrey F. Addicott

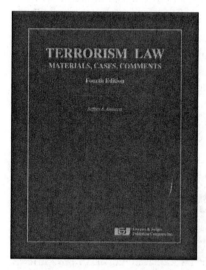

As the first edition of Terrorism Law suggests, terrorism, like crime, can never be completely eradicated. Over the past few years, as previous editions were released, the United States has faced many changes and challenges pertaining to the War on Terror, and continues to do so today. Although it was realized at the time the war started that legal and policy challenges would exist, no one could have predicted exactly what events would occur. Much has changed since September 11, 2001 in both the law and policy areas. The biggest challenges have become realistically fighting and winning the War on Terror under a democratically based rule of law, and protecting human rights and civil liberties in an ongoing wartime situation. It has been determined that the United States of America must accomplish three things: identify and appreciate the threat of militant Islamic global terrorism; do a better job of bringing the battle to the terrorists and the nations that harbor them; and promote and sustain a dedicated democracy building campaign in new governments such as those Afghanistan and Iraq.

The fourth edition of Terrorism Law has been updated to include new developments in this war as well as some of our nation's and the world's biggest challenges while fighting it. You'll find information on cyberterrorism, bioterrorism, effects of the War on Terror on civil liberties, understanding the necessity for the Law of War and the Rule of Law, a new paradigm for war and terrorism avoidance, the role of the military in promoting human rights, interrogation techniques and what defines torture, use of civil litigation in the War on Terror, a history of the War on Terror and why America must stay the course and abide by the Rule of Law when fighting this war. This new edition is designed to be used as a reference and text in this emerging area of law. It includes many appendices containing important American and international documents pertaining to the War on Terror as well as discussion questions, citations of legal cases pertaining to terrorism, and bibliographic information for further reference.

Topics Include

- What is terrorism?
- The War on Terror
- Expanding the War on Terror
- Civil liberties and civil litigation and the War on Terror
- Necessity and rationale for the Law of War—lessons from My Lai
- Interrogation techniques and what is torture
- Contractors on the battlefield
- Cyberterrorism
- Bioterrorism
- A new paradigm for war and avoiding terrorism
- The role of the military and Army Special Forces in promoting human rights

Product Code: 6028 • 8.5x11 • 557 pages • Casebound

Forensic Aspects of Chemical and Biological Terrorism
by Cyril H. Wecht

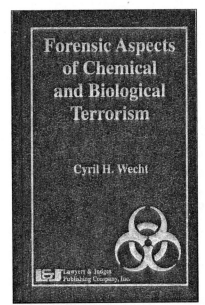

Since the attacks of September 11, 2001, the US has become more aware of its vulnerability to terrorist attacks. Every day our media reports on the possibility of an attack on our soil or an attack on our overseas citizens or military personnel. As terrorist become more determined to cause chaos, the possibility of them using chemical or biological weapons increases. An attack of this nature in any county would pose a great danger to the entire world.

History shows us how easily deadly viruses spread through populations because of travel, unrecognized symptoms, and unorganized healthcare. In today's world, people are able to travel greater distances in a short time. In only a few hours a disease could be spread to multiple continents. In addition, technological advancements have made it easier for terrorist to produce and release biological weapons that could be used in public areas. Therefore, in order to prevent attacks, or contain the spread of disease or chemical exposure if an attack happens, the response must be quick, organized and thorough.

Forensic Aspects of Biological and Chemical Terrorism is an eye-opening resource for healthcare professionals, 911 operators, emergency response personnel, medical examiners, coroners, hospital administrators and public health officials. It provides valuable insight into what areas need improvement, what roles each of the responders should have, and how this all can be accomplished. It also extensively covers the investigation of an attack from the signs and symptoms of various diseases and chemical exposure to how the crime scene should be handled. This timely resource is a must have for anyone involved in public health and public safety. Foreword written by Senator Arlen Specter of Pennsylvania.

Topics Include

- Identification of biological and chemical terrorism
- Smallpox
- Injury characteristics and treatment
- Forensic toxicology
- Public health aspects and protective measures
- Criminal investigation
- Airport security
- Psychological aspects of biological and chemical terrorism
- Legal considerations relating to terrorism

Product Code: 6672 • 6x9 • 450 pages • Casebound

State Open Government Law & Practice in a Post 9/11 World
Edited by Jeffrey Addicott, Loren Cochran,
Lucy Dalglish, and Nathan Winegar

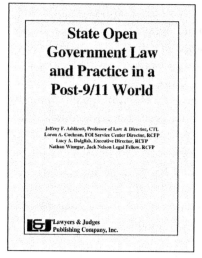

State Open Government Law and Practice in a Post-9/11 World is your guide to changes in U.S. state public information laws in the wake of the 9/11 terrorist attacks, and changes in national public information laws in countries with elevated terrorist threats and activity.

Part One, prepared by the Reporters Committee for Freedom of the Press, gives you access to six important topics in state government law: Critical Infrastructure, Cyber Security, First Response, Political Structure, Public Health, and Terror Investigation. Each section is alphabetized by state and provides you with information on legal limits on public access to government information as related to the War on Terror.

Part Two, compiled by the Center for Terrorism Law, informs you of national public information laws in countries at high risk for terrorist threats: Colombia, France, Israel, and the United Kingdom. This section explores how other countries handle the issue of public access to information and allows for comparison and contrast with U.S. policies.

Topics Include

- Critical Infrastructure
- Cyber Security
- First Response
- Political Structure
- Public Health
- Terror Investigations
- State public information law
- Public information law in countries with high terrorist activity

Product Code: 4438 • 8.5x11 • 385 pages • Softbound

Biological and Chemical Warfare Agents Slide Chart

This unique slide chart provides quick information about biological and chemical agents. On side one you will find three categories of biological agents. For each agent listed you will be able to discover whether the agent is a bacteria, toxin or virus, the historical use of the agent, treatments available and more. Side two of the chart contains information on chemical weapons.

To learn about a specific chemical or biological agent, all you have to do is slide the arrow next to the agent you are interested in. Next, read across to learn about the method of contamination and historical use, then look at the window below to find out about signs and symptoms, vaccinations and treatments. An ideal quick reference tool when learning the key points about these dangerous and deadly weapons.

Topics Include

- Anthrax
- Brucellosis and Cholera
- Glanders
- Plague and Q fever
- Tularemia
- Typhoid Fever and Typhus
- Hemorrhagic Feber/Ebola
- Smallpox and Yellow Fever
- Botulinus Toxin
- Ricin Toxin and Saxitoxin
- Sarin Nerve Gas and VX and Mustard Gas
- Tabun
- Hydrogen Cyanide
- Phosgene

Product Code: 0635 • 8.5x11 • Slide Chart

These and many more products available through our catalog.

Download a free catalog at www.lawyersandjudges.com

Lawyers & Judges Publishing Company, Inc.
PO Box 30040 • Tucson, AZ 85711
800-209-7109 • FAX 800-330-8795
e-mail: sales@lawyersandjudges.com

www.lawyersandjudges.com

www.lawyersandjudges.com